MOTHERMYSTERIES

MOTHERMYSTERIES

Maren Tonder Hansen

SHAMBHALA
Boston & London
1997

SHAMBHALA PUBLICATIONS, INC.
HORTICULTURAL HALL
300 MASSACHUSETTS AVENUE
BOSTON, MASSACHUSETTS 02115
http://www.shambhala.com

9 8 7 6 5 4 3 2 1

First Edition

Printed in the United States of America

⊗ This edition is printed on acid-free paper that meets the
American National Standards Institute Z39.48 Standard.

Distributed in the United States by Random House, Inc.,
and in Canada by Random House of Canada Ltd.

Library of Congress Cataloging-in-Publication Data
Hansen, Maren Tonder.
MotherMysteries / Maren Tonder Hansen.
p. cm.
ISBN 1-57062-252-3 (pbk. : alk. paper)
1. Motherhood.   2. Childbirth.   3. Hansen, Maren Tonder.
4. Mothers—California—Biography.   I. Title.
HQ759.H245   1997   97-13517
306.874'3—dc21   CIP

Dedicated to the Mother
in her many manifestations

and to

Steve, Jesse, Alia, and Elijah

Contents

—◦❦◦—

Contents

Acknowledgments

I am grateful to my family for their myriad roles in the genesis of this book. Family members generously read, edited, and offered encouraging feedback. These are the specific people with whom I explore the mysteries of love, death, and regeneration: Stephen, Jesse, Alia, and Elijah, Alan and Lois, John, Topher and Kristi, Andy and Maurice, Maddie and Andie, Margaret, Lisa and Wayne. I especially appreciate my mother for her deep understanding of the mysteries.

My husband, Steve, offered enduring support: always believing in the importance of this book, loving the writer in me, willing to have extended conversations on psyche and nature, and graciously shouldering the financial burden of our family during my two years of writing. The love and support of Steve and our children—Jesse, Alia, and Elijah—is the food of life.

I want to thank particular teachers who guided me in ways that were crucial in the development of this book. I am grateful to Bob Kimball, who over the years insisted on honoring my soul, through patient example teaching me how, and for our year of dialog during my writing. Chris Downing offered encouragement and advice from the beginning stages of this book all the way through final editing. Her finest gift to me is her steadfast example of valuing personal experience as a source of wisdom. I am grateful to Joseph Campbell, a great gentleman who opened many doors for me, and who, with such grace, integrated the depth of his knowledge into his daily being. For seventeen years, Jean Houston has been an important teacher to me, inspiring in the depth and complexity of her being, always challenging me to be more. I am grateful to Jean for the ways she led me into the intellectual infrastructure and the openness of heart and soul so that I could understand the mysteries. Norman Cousins extended himself in many ways to encourage me in the writing of this book, a gift graciously given and most gratefully received. I thank Ginette Paris and David Miller, who each generously offered their time and expertise in personal consultations.

It has always been true for me that I learn as much from my friends as I do from books and formal teachers. I am profoundly grateful to my friends who are willing to enter into deep and open conversations about our lives. I thank my friends from the grove for sustaining me through times of doubt and for their abilities to enter the depths: Shira Musicant, Kate Smith-Hansen, Hendrika DeVries, Kathee Miller, and Benita Darshana-Reid. I have been appreciative of many friends for their interest in this writing project and their love. Particular thanks to Meg Whitaker Greene, Susan Ferrant, Jaquelin Pearson, Mie Collins, Roberta O'Leary, and Kathy Cowell.

I want to acknowledge the contributions of three young women, who, in turn, over the years helped with baby-sitting, housekeeping, laundry, and errands. My thanks to Suzy, Ingrid, and Lorilee for the loving ways they entered our lives.

My agent, Loretta Barrett, was wise and steady in finding a suitable home for this book and expert in navigating the business mysteries. I am grateful to her and to my friend Wayne Muller for directing me to Loretta. I have an abiding respect for my editor, Emily Hilburn Sell, and for the other folks at Shambhala Publications, who understood from the beginning the importance of this book's being written in the feminine, personal voice. Emily supported me in ways that I had never imagined possible from an editor, always leading me back into trusting myself. I also thank my in-house editor, Kendra Crossen, and my copyeditor, Susan Cohan, for their good work.

During the final month of editing this book, I had the distinct pleasure of an afternoon of cross-country skiing by myself. Far into a mountain trail in the Sierras, I lay down on my back in the soft snow. No other people were around. No sound of machines. In the quiet peace, snow fell from the branch of a pine tree. A small bird flew to a different branch. The weave of spirit and matter on this lovely earth fills me with love, beauty, and gratitude.

OPENING

I RECEIVED NO WARNING that I would be stolen away from my normal life, abducted into a realm I never knew existed. Although it came as a shock to lose control over my own life, and indeed, there were plenty of trials along the way, the treasures that were revealed are greater to me than gold and rubies and sapphires.

How many women before me have walked this path, stumbled over the semiburied rock, fallen down into the hole that didn't seem to have been there before, down into the belly of the earth, landing before the temple of the MotherMysteries? How many women have crossed the threshold, wandered the labyrinthian halls, entered this chamber or that one, to receive the mysteries of the Mother?

During the last three thousand years of human history, these mysteries have mostly remained unspoken on the face of the earth. There have been, and still are, reasons for this silence. But now, as we approach the demands of a new millennium, there are reasons to risk speaking the mysteries aloud. Contained within the MotherMysteries are the essential laws of living, dying, and regeneration. If we will open to these teachings, take them deep inside us so that our daily activity dances in rhythm with these mysteries, we will cocreate a new millennium worth living for, worthy of our children's children.

A woman becomes pregnant, and suddenly she is carried far

beyond the self she previously knew, carried into alignment with forces much larger than the individual. She is a vessel through which Life proceeds, the inexorable march. In the eye of creation, the woman-becoming-a-mother knows something, feels the forces that ignite all of life.

When a woman mingles with creation, grows a new life in her body, tends that new being into the world, what does she come to know? What life mysteries does she witness, feel, absorb in her soul? What does it mean to be initiated into the temple of the MotherMysteries? I will tell as much of this story as I know.

My story stays within a hormonally defined period of time: pregnancy, birth, and mothering a newborn baby. In this biologically driven stage, a woman is, first and foremost, an instrument of nature. The modern human boundaries between conscious and unconscious, mind and body, human and nature, become liquidated in a new mother, making this an ideal time to get an uncensored peek into the archetypal Mother.

In conversation with other mothers—friends, colleagues, or clients—I am moved by how deeply motherhood touches each woman. It is both the hardest work and the most beautiful work of our lives. We certainly all have many things to say about becoming a mother, on both the upside and the downside, but overriding all is a nearly universal sense of motherhood as one of the most meaningful, sacred experiences of a woman's lifetime. Becoming a mother is a journey of the soul, a journey into the heart of life, into rhythms of nature that unite us all.

I have noticed how much we like to talk about our pregnancies, our births, and our babies. It seems that these stories need to be spoken into the light of day, heard by another person, somehow turned and re-turned in the mind. We struggle to bring the watery depths of motherhood into more conscious understandings, to harvest the meanings of this soul journey.

Throughout my life as a maiden, I simply assumed I knew what it meant to be a mother. After all, I studied under my own mother my whole life. I can't imagine an education that runs deeper than that. I felt sure that I would do what my mother did, that someday I would have my own children.

Although I did have a reasonable grasp of the external behaviors of mothering, for thirty-two years I did not have a clue about the *interior process* of becoming a mother. It never occurred to me to wonder how being a mother would transform who I am and what I touch in the universe. I never suspected the ways that being a mother would work my soul.

The onset of pregnancy catalyzed a series of physical, psychological, and spiritual processes. A baby began to grow in my body. I began the transformation from maiden into mother. And the doors to the MotherMysteries magically opened. I stepped through.

I began to explore a museum buried within me, filled with thousands upon thousands of years of archetypal images of the feminine psyche—the mother lode. I meandered the many chambers, receiving the collective wisdom of our foremothers, the images filling me, initiating me into the mysteries of the Great Mother. To my astonishment, I discovered that even though the feminine mysteries are no longer ritually enacted in an ancient temple in Eleusis, they live forevermore in an inner world to which we all have access.

The journey into the MotherMysteries is always a personal story, running deep in the heart and soul of the mother. Each woman brings the particularity of her life to the journey: her personal psychology and life circumstances, her relationship with a specific mate, and her relationship with a particular developing child.

Yet within this profoundly personal journey of mothering are elemental forms that unite all mothers. There is a dimension in the mother story that goes beyond the personal, into cultural and archetypal realms that are relevant not only to the mother but also to our global village.

For twenty thousand years, the Great Mother Goddess reigned supreme in the human imagination. For twenty thousand years, human existence was oriented around the image of a divine Mother who was the source of all creation and whose earth body we all returned to in death.

During the last several thousand years, Western culture has been cut off from a living relationship with the Mother and other archetypal aspects of the feminine. It seems important to ask what effect this might have on the human condition and on the condition of the planet as a whole.

The MotherMysteries do not live as objective truths, amputated from personal life. Isolating them from personal relationships violates their essence. It is far more fertile to see the MotherMysteries play in a life, a particular life, mine or someone else's, to see how the divine mixes with the mundane, how the eternal joins the temporal, how the archetypal mingles with the personal. The spiritual forces of the Mother do not live in the sky. The Mother lives on earth, in matter, in human relationships and daily life.

Of all the MotherMysteries revealed to me, this is the one of which I am surest: the deepest mysteries of existence are woven into the fabric of the mundane; the mysteries are always here to be seen and known, in the simplest of acts, in every manifestation of being. The mysteries are immanent in each moment; what is elusive is our presence.

The moment a sperm enters an egg is a very small event in terms of space, and a brief event in terms of time, but the ripples, the reverberations that grow and echo throughout time and space are of enormous consequence for all involved. Who can know in that moment what will come forth?

A woman does not automatically become a mother the minute she is handed a baby. Becoming a mother is an ongoing process: transformations worked over time. To what extent will we give ourselves to these transformations? Nature abducts us on the journey, drawing us into the essential pulse of creation: we go, sometimes kicking and struggling against these forces, sometimes content to float along, at times stunned into stillness in our meetings with the great mysteries.

FIRST CHILD

Nowhere are we closer to the sublime secret of all origination than in the recognition of our own selves, whom we always think we know already. Yet we know the immensities of space better than we know our own depths, where—even though we do not understand it—we can listen directly to the throb of creation itself.

—C. G. Jung
Collected Works 8:380

ABDUCTION

LOOKING BACK, now that all has been said and done, I realize I did not go gently into that good night. I was not beckoned by a kindly finger toward the temple of the MotherMysteries. I did not hear a call from the depths to which I yearned to respond. No. I was abducted.

My life as a single, professional woman was going just fine. I was an ordained Unitarian Universalist minister and a psychotherapist with a private practice. I was studying with some fine teachers of mythology and Jungian psychology. I was in love with a man who also loved me. We traveled. We lived by the beach. Life was good.

This innocent state of mind is a classic beginning for a mythic journey. Some woman (she could be any one of us) is going about her life, involved in the ordinary human activities of work, love, and play. But there is a certain sense of blindness about how she is moving through the world. There is a sense in which she is a fool. She thinks she is in charge of her life. Little does she know. Does she sense who is sneaking up from behind? No!

In my thirtieth year, completely out of the blue, my DNA bounded onto center stage, boisterously demanding, "Honey, let's get pregnant!" It was as if a separate creature who had long been slumbering suddenly awakened. Somewhat startled and amused, I turned my head to see who this insistent creature was. Not Sleeping Beauty! She was not subtle, demure. She talked loud, required a lot of attention. My ego didn't stand a chance against her. It wasn't long before all I could think about was wanting a baby. Within a year, I was married and trying to get pregnant.

First phase of abduction complete. Ego is no longer in control. The Goddess of Fecundity rules! The individual will has been snuffed by the forces of fertility. Another woman—captured.

At the time, I did not realize I had been captured. My pitiful little ego scrambled to get on its feet, to claim that all was under control. My ego said ridiculous things like, "Wow, I sure am obsessing about being pregnant," or, "I really think I'd like to start a family now." As if "I" were in charge. The conscious part of my psyche had suddenly been relegated to a minor role in a major drama that "I" was not authoring. Unbeknownst to me, forces ancient and powerful lurched forward, grabbed me from behind, abducted me for their own purposes. I was merely a vessel through which to accomplish their goal: perpetuation of the human species.

Why did I have to be abducted? I would have had a baby someday. I didn't need to be abducted to do that. Or did I? I have given this matter much thought.

On a purely biological level, it would be folly to rely on individual free will to perpetuate life on earth; that's too risky a proposition. The individual must be subsumed into the will of nature.

It is the biological destiny of a woman to become obsessed with wanting a baby. Nature wants a woman to have babies. Not that this is necessarily in the best interests of the woman herself.

The needs of the individual may conflict with the needs of nature.

It appears that nature offers women a lot of latitude about when to have a baby. But in most cases, if we do not mate before a certain imminent biological deadline, nature intervenes, sucking us into the gravitational field of the Great Mother Goddess; we become one with her, we do what she does.

The ego, particularly when it has developed for thirty-two years, does not surrender easily to the authority of the Mother Goddess—or anyone else, for that matter. The ego, especially in the first few decades of a life, thinks that it is the center of existence, that it controls things, is the one and only God. The ego rebels against the idea that other figures exist within the psyche, that they, too, come and go as they please, with intentions and purposes all their own, quite apart from the intentions of ego. For the most part, ego pretends that these other psychic beings do not exist. The other figures within the human psyche—for instance, the archetype of the Great Mother—tend to remain in the unconscious, orchestrating things from behind, through dreams, fantasies, and obsessions.

Perhaps here we begin to see the need for the abduction. Does ego ever consent to take a journey into the depths? Isn't the whole point of the soul journey that it takes you places beyond the control of ego, beyond the domain of conscious daily life? It takes you into the vast world of the unconscious, which extends beyond the personal, beyond the human species into the psyche of nature.

The ego can hear whispers from promised lands, can be intrigued hearing the request of the soul to learn the deeper ways, but in the end, ego must be abducted by the larger and more powerful forces of the unconscious. Ego gets forcefully taken away from where it planned to be, loses control, and it hates that.

Let us acknowledge that being abducted into the depths is inevitable in every human life. We each will be spirited away, perhaps many times within one lifetime. A divorce may tumble a person into the underworld. Often the death of a parent or mate leads one into that dark night. The journey into the realm of soul making can be painful, difficult, and dark as well as beautiful and meaningful. But we all go, at one time or another.

Why must ego be abducted to the underworld? Because a life lived only on the surface of things, only on the conscious earthly plane, leaves us incomplete. A fertile life on earth must be seeded with the wisdom of the underworld. Each of us must journey into the unconscious depths, wander the ways of the soul, so that our days on earth are pregnant with the divine.

Because the archetype fascinates consciousness and is dynamically very much superior to it, the ego consciousness . . . is not only attracted by it but easily overwhelmed. The outcome is seizure by the archetype, disintegration of consciousness, and loss of the ego.

—Erich Neumann
The Great Mother, p. 75

I'M NOT PREGNANT

I AM SITTING OUTSIDE at a sunny café table with two hours free for lunch waiting for my friend Kathee. Like me, she is a psychotherapist, and she wants to be pregnant. Waiting, alone, I begin to sink into the darkness I feel. For six months, I have been trying to get pregnant. I am one of the few women I know who in her thirties has never been pregnant before. I've always been careful about birth control, but so have some of my friends who did get pregnant. I've heard that it is more difficult for older women to get pregnant: the eggs don't fertilize as easily, and there is increased likelihood that the fallopian tubes have been scarred by infection.

What if I can't get pregnant? It's almost intolerable for me to think I might not be able to give birth to my own children, and yet my body is telling me it's a real possibility. I have always imagined that I would bear my own biological children. Even when I wasn't sure I would find a husband I wanted, I knew I would bear children. Luckily for me, I found a husband I want, and he wants to have children too, but he's not quite so obsessed by it as I am. I want a baby more than I've ever wanted anything. So I sit with this pain, facing the possibility that I might not be able to conceive a child.

Every month, my ultimate concern is getting pregnant. I mark on the calendar when I will ovulate, and we make love every day during that time. Then I wait a week, which I consider a complete waste of time; I wish it to hurry up and be over so that I can notice my breasts getting tender, feel a bit of nausea: waiting for the day when I won't start menstruating. I've enacted this dramatic cycle six times now, except it always ends with blood.

The thing I want most in the world right now I can't have. This is hard. I'm used to getting what I want. I figure out what I want and work really hard for it. Make it happen. But in trying to get pregnant, I have to wait—days, weeks, months—and still I can't make it happen. My heroic ego is of no use here. There is some anonymous body power in charge that I can't seem to control. All I can think about is what is *not* happening. A dark veil covers everything.

Some people say stupid New Age stuff to me: "Maybe the soul of the baby you're supposed to get isn't ready to come back to earth yet." Or worse: "Maybe you're not ready to be pregnant yet." Why is it that fourteen-year-old girls having sex for the first time in the backseat of a borrowed car get pregnant while I have to go through all these psycho-spiritual-physiological permutations and still get nowhere?

Other friends are also trying to get pregnant. There is something humiliating about this phrase "trying to get pregnant." "We're trying to get pregnant." There's a pretty simple thing to do to get pregnant, so to have to try really hard at it somehow implies that one doesn't do it very well. A male friend is seeing an infertility specialist. His disappointment and humiliation are endless. He said that last week he successfully impregnated a frog. Another friend has also been trying to get pregnant for months, and she, too, is in pain about it. She calls me every week with tips on getting pregnant: no more hot tubs because it raises the body temperature too much for sperm and eggs; don't eat raw fish because it could have worms; and so on. We follow all her tips, but we aren't pregnant.

My friend Kathee arrives. She asks the question everyone else asks me, "Are you pregnant yet?" I ask her the same. We aren't. At least she isn't worried that she can't get pregnant. For three months, a baby grew in her body, but then she had a miscarriage. She holds the fear that she will get pregnant, begin to love and hope for the baby inside her, and then the baby will be carried away again. It doesn't help that four of our friends are newly pregnant. All of a sudden everyone is pregnant—except us.

We have a glum lunch, depressing ourselves about what we aren't. At least it's good to talk with a friend who can allow the darkness of it and who shares the ache.

We finish our lunch and return to our respective psychotherapy practices; unbeknownst to us at that time, each of us is pregnant.

Thus, my pregnancy began with a cosmic joke. Very funny. I stressed myself out for six months trying to get pregnant, desolate about being barren, and in my time of least hope, the one period I was convinced I wasn't pregnant, the Great Mother bestowed her magic.

It's as if, in the beginning of our time together, the Mother Goddess wanted to establish that I am not in charge of fecundity. I consider this to be the first MotherMystery revealed to me: creation is the domain of the Mother Goddess; she bestows fertility. I might want to be pregnant, might feel that desire, but the powers of creation dwell not in the human ego.

My ego had been so worn down from months of hoping and crashing that I finally began to surrender. It was only then that I understood what my friend Shira had said. One time when I was depressed about not getting pregnant, she told me, "Maren, not getting pregnant is part of the process of getting pregnant. You're already in the process of being pregnant." I thought to myself, "Wow. This woman is really reaching to find something to say to comfort me," and I accepted her kindness but discarded her ridiculous message. But her message began to echo in my mind like a Zen koan: not getting pregnant is part of the process of getting pregnant. Having borne two children herself, Shira had been initiated into the MotherMysteries. She knew that the controlling ego cannot be in charge of pregnancy; in some cases, it must be exhausted into submission. My ego had to run head-on into a brick wall for six months in order to realize the limits of its powers. Then came the gift: the Great Mother granted life in my womb.

In the structure of the mythic journey that Joseph Campbell delineated, this is a crucial point: crossing the threshold out of the land of ordinary human affairs into the spirit world. My ego did not choose to cross that threshold. The Mother Goddess pulled me across, sucking me into her gravitational field so that I could learn the ways of growing a new life, learn the mysteries of the Mother.

The bearing of children is a biological task. The roots of the maternal instinct reach back into the deepest layers of a woman's nature, touching forces of which she may be profoundly unconscious. When a woman becomes pregnant these ancient powers stir within her, whether she knows it or not, and she disregards them only at her peril.

—M. Esther Harding
The Way of All Women, p. 167

Initiation

eighteen days pregnant

I AM SO GRATEFUL to be pregnant, to be given the gift of a life growing in my womb. The joy of this gift fills me, fills our marriage. Thank you, powers in the universe—whoever and whatever you may be—for letting me conceive.

Being pregnant feels as though I've received a shot of cosmic adrenaline. It's so much more than a fertilized egg growing in a womb. I feel pregnant in a multitude of ways. My feelings, daily events, dreams, my marriage all seem to be impregnated by— what? What is it? It's like being in an energy field, a pregnant field, pregnant with meaning, where each ordinary event is revealed in its profundity. It's like suddenly finding myself inside a Greek drama or a Shakespearean play.

During coffee hour at the Unitarian church, my friend Ellen asked me to step aside so that she could speak to me alone. Intense and passionate, she confided to me that becoming a mother was the most profound spiritual and psychological experience in her life. I could feel her feelings as she spoke; tears that

I could not explain spilled from my eyes. The whole scene felt surreal. Why did she tell me this? Was she a harbinger, a messenger, preparing me for matters to come?

My inner life has become so fertile, all else pales beside it. I think something really important is happening. But it's so dreamy and elusive that I can't remember it unless I take notes—about my dreams, about what I am feeling and thinking, about what is happening in my body.

For most of my adult life, I have loved dreams, both my own and other people's. What I love about dreams is that they offer windows into the depths of the unconscious. I have made a practice of remembering my dreams, recording them in detail, and listening to what they might have to say. For me, dreams are as real and valid as any waking experience.

Many a time I have heard someone say, "I don't have dreams," or, "I can't ever remember my dreams." Science has shown us that indeed we all do dream for four or five periods per night. I, too, have experienced that these messages from the unconscious can be difficult to pull into consciousness. It takes desire and practice (and pen and paper!) to catch them before they slip away.

The other comment I often hear is, "My dreams are just about boring, ordinary stuff, and they don't even make sense." In all my years of working with dreams, I have never met a dream that was boring. They may appear simple at first glance, or even silly, but when carefully opened, dreams speak eloquently with depth and complexity. Dreams don't always seem to make sense to our daily waking consciousness. The unconscious has its own way of talking: it loves riddle, rhyme, metaphor, puns, symbols, images. It can be a joy and pleasure to learn to speak the language of the unconscious.

Each dream carries its own teachings, gifts from the deeper dimensions. It takes some detailed work to harvest these gifts. But the rewards offer a window into the soul, both the individual soul and the soul of the whole.

Recently, a dream came to me with some big news. In the

dream, I felt drawn into a spell, a numinous otherworld. I feel that this dream not only speaks to me personally but is also a portal into a collective feminine soul.

> My husband and I arrive in a car at a small town of ruins in Iowa that my friend Thomas told us about. These are Greek ruins. Piles of stone ruins, surrounded by walls of stacked rocks about eight feet high. Now, I am walking around with a woman whom I do not know. She picks up a stone. It is half gold. She keeps it. I realize there is much gold to be found here.
>
> Still outdoors, I go over to a worship area. On one side is a church pulpit, and on the opposite side is an altar. On a round table in front of the altar sits a full-bodied Mother Goddess statue. She is beautiful. I stand before her and contemplate her. Suddenly, I realize that what I am experiencing is from the ancient holy feminine mysteries. I am stunned.

The beauty and awe I felt in the dream stay with me through my waking hours. Through this dream, I am being carried somewhere, somewhere I yearn to be.

The dream seems to be introducing me to a particular "landscape." I feel I am being asked to see this place, to know it. What is this place I've been taken to? Where are we?

The dream suggests that this is a very old place—a place of worship, a holy place. In the dream, we are located in Iowa, earthy, quiet, with gently rolling mound-shaped hills—a feminine landscape. This is a place I know and love. I roamed these hills as a maiden, throughout my undergraduate years. Now, with guidance from my friend and religious mentor Thomas, I return to this land with my husband and a new life growing within me. The normal, daily time-space of my life has changed because of this event called pregnancy, and my psyche is exploring this new place. I arrive at this sacred place in the company of men, Thomas and my husband, Steve. Yet the actual exploration of the place occurs with a woman, not a personal friend but an anonymous representative of womanhood.

Perhaps this dream is introducing me into the Mother phase

of my life. The ancient Greeks imagined three basic stages of a woman's life—maiden, mother, and crone—and each goddess of the pantheon primarily represented one of these stages. No longer am I the young maiden. Is my pregnancy an onset of maturation into my self as a woman? I realize I have little idea what it means to mature as a woman or as a mother. What is this process? What are the characteristics of a mature woman? What will I come to know in myself?

Yet the powerful, luminous feeling of the dream suggests more. Could it be that, as the dream suggests, this is an initiation into the mysteries of the Holy Mother? Even though my rational mind is confused by this, my feelings answer yes. What does this really mean? How could it be?

In the dream, this sacred place, which once was tended, is now in ruins. The image of ruins suggests that the forms and institutions that once honored the feminine mysteries have been abandoned by the collective culture, neglected across millennia, left for dead.

Indeed, in my waking life, I have visited such ruins in Greece and Turkey. I have walked the ruined temples of Artemis in Ephesus, of Hera in Kos, of Demeter and Persephone in Eleusis, of Athena at Delphi. I have studied others, even more ancient, in Europe and the Middle East. The grandeur of these ancient goddess temples has been reduced to mostly rubble, a pillar standing here or there, scattered stones carved with symbols, hidden by overgrown weeds. The sites of the ancient feminine mysteries were destroyed, in ruins, either forgotten or rendered little-understood tourist attractions. I grieved for these abandoned temples, grieved for the collective feminine wisdom that was lost when they were destroyed. It broke my heart that I would never be initiated into the mysteries of my female ancestors.

In my dream, the ruins are in Iowa. What could the psyche be trying to say by placing them in Iowa? I don't know of any goddess temples that existed in Iowa. Is the psyche implying that the remains of the goddess temples are not confined to literal places? Am I inexplicably in a different time-space dimension where I do have access to the goddess ruins?

How could I have been so blind? How could I have made such a mistake? All these years, I only understood the goddess religions as cultural forms, housed in stone temples or forest cathedrals, tended by women and men who passed the gnosis down through sacred art, myth, and ritual, generation after generation. With the cultural forms killed off by the patriarchal invaders—the temples smashed, the symbols and rituals forbidden—I mistakenly thought that the mysteries were irretrievably lost, that they existed only in time and place.

I did not think carefully. I now realize that the mysteries of the Great Mother are archetypal. These fundamental forms continue to live in the collective unconscious of all individual human beings, regardless of cultural institutions. The essence of the Mother Goddess lives in the human psyche because it is part of the psyche of nature. She is the psyche of fecundity of which all life partakes.

It is true that I will never experience the fullness of the Eleusinian Mysteries of Demeter and Persephone, nor many of the other ritualized feminine mysteries. But now I see, to my utter amazement, that the wellspring of those ancient goddess religions, the essential MotherMysteries, are being passed on to me in my pregnancy. What I've wanted for so long, what I fervently wished for but never thought I could get, is happening. I am drinking from the same well that sourced my foremothers, waters deep and clear, the waters of the Great Mother. These waters are available to us all.

Now that I think about it, it makes sense. The Swiss psychologist Carl Jung said that the archetypes are inherently intertwined with instinct.[1] When the Great Mother archetype awakened in me, I began to feel deep urges to get pregnant and have a baby. In this process of pregnancy, the archetypal images that are woven into the maternal instinct are revealing themselves before my very eyes, in living, breathing experience. I am stunned.

In the dream, the woman who accompanies me through the ruins picks up a stone, sees that it is half gold, and keeps it. In this simple image, the psyche shows several things. In the ruins of this sacred place, there are still things of value to be found, including the greatest value—gold. I am also shown that, although the gold is here, I must look for it, as my companion did. What a woman experiences in this place of the MotherMysteries must be picked up, carefully examined, kept.

I am intrigued that the stone is half gold and half ordinary mineral. Already in my daily life I am seeing this to be true. Some of my pregnancy is so precious, but some of it, like nausea and the hormonal roller coaster, are ordinary minerals that I would rather throw away. However, this dream image of the stone shows that the two are bound together: the gold is united with ordinary mineral. This feels like a teaching of the Mother-Mysteries: the ordinary is wedded to the sacred. They are not separate. The spirituality that dwells here is bound to daily, common life.

In the dream, the walls of stone are eight feet high. Eight feet is high enough that a human being cannot see over these walls. If you are standing outside these walls, you cannot see what lives on the inside. If you step inside these walls, you cannot see what lives on the outside.

What a simple and beautiful way for the psyche to state what is true. During the thirty-one years I lived outside these walls, never did I imagine what I now see standing inside—even though I studied ancient goddess religions for nearly ten years, even though I researched ancient initiations into the feminine mysteries, even though as a psychotherapist I specialized in the psychological and spiritual journeys of women. I am astonished that I focused so much on the experience of women but never even glimpsed the MotherMysteries until I became pregnant.

I was never able to see what is on the inside of these walls until, by becoming pregnant, I magically entered the inner chamber. These are mysteries, in part, because even if you hear the secrets, even if someone tells you all about them, it is only through living experience that you can understand the truth beneath the words. Initiation into the mysteries is not a process of telling but rather a process of experiencing. When a person stands outside the walls of the mystery chamber, she cannot see what lives on the inside.

Similarly, once a woman is on the inside of the walls, external reality all but disappears. I can barely focus on the outside world anymore. I am not interested in the *Los Angeles Times,* the *CBS Evening News.* That's no longer news to me. My inner reality is the compelling news for me now.

In the dream, the Mother Goddess statue sits on a round table in front of the altar. She is opposite to the rectangular, upright pulpit: the place of opinions, words, sermons, traditionally the place of the masculine. As a former parish minister, I occupied this pulpit of Logos. Ironically, it was difficult for me to maintain intimate contact with my soul while I was working as a parish minister.

In the dream, across from the pulpit, in the round space sits a statue of the Goddess. She seems to be a more inward place, eros, body. She is who I am turning toward now. I begin to contemplate her. Gazing upon her, I realize yet another of the MotherMysteries: her knowledge is contained within her body; if you really notice her body, you will know her wisdom. Her breasts are generous, abundant, heavy with nourishment for another. Her belly is round, full. With what? What grows inside of her? A spiral on the belly draws the destiny of what lives inside her: from the center evolves a narrow path, cycling round and round, finally opening out into the world. Her body weight ensures that she is earthbound, impossible to blow away, unlikely to swim off in watery currents. She is joined with the earth, steady, slow-moving. She is the Mother. I am her daughter. She is beginning to teach me her mysteries. I must witness her body; these mysteries are beginning to blossom in my pregnant body as well.

I can't believe all this is happening. I wanted to get pregnant because I wanted to have a baby. I had no idea I would be carried into the depths of creation. Creation is occurring in my body. It is dawning upon me that creation is not simply a physical event; a psyche, ideas, even feelings interact with physical matter in the process of creation. Spirit and matter. Before this, I imagined myself external to creation. Now I am inside, inside the walls of the MotherMysteries, ineffably beautiful.

[A] pregnant woman is no longer what she has been—the embodiment of the personal—she is one of "the Mothers."
—M. Esther Harding
The Way of All Women, p. 171

RAGING HORMONES

two months pregnant

OH, AM I NAUSEATED! I wake up in the morning, stand up out of bed, and feel as if I'm going to throw up. This feeling continues throughout the day. Certain smells are intolerable: cigarette smoke and especially broccoli. Why did nature invent broccoli? My mother, who also threw up during pregnancy, told me to eat dry crackers before I get out of bed and keep eating them throughout the day. Wherever I go, my Saltines go. I even sleep with them next to me. My sheets crunch with cracker crumbs.

Some days I am so miserable I just cry. I hate people who tell me, "Well, at least it's only three months." Only three months? Are these people crazy? Three months of feeling nauseated almost every moment of every day is not "only three months."

What happened to the MotherMysteries? I want more sacred dreams, more teachings of feminine wisdom. Gagging? Vomiting? This can't be part of the sacred teachings.

I was in a psychotherapy session with a client yesterday, and while she was talking, I was pretty sure I was going to throw up soon. I wondered if I should just run out of the room when the time came. Or should I delicately pull out my crackers and nibble on one, hoping to stave off the inevitable? I may need to quit working for awhile, because I can't pay proper attention to another person right now.

I have a constant yeast infection, little impetigo bumps all over my skin, gigantic breasts, and gigantic rage. Bigger rage than I've ever known before. Goddess rage. Over the least little things. Up to eight episodes a day. One day, as I was driving down Patterson Road, a car turned right in front of me. I became enraged! I had a vision of stomping on my accelerator and ramming his car. Some vestige of my former self pulled me back to my senses and said a prayer, "Oh, please, God, don't let me kill anybody today."

I went to see my obstetrician. I told him either my hormones are going wild or else I've had a psychotic break. At least, he laughed. I guess he's seen women like me a few thousand times before. He said I am producing high levels of progesterone as well as other hormones, which is both good news and bad news. The good news is that, with high progesterone, I am less likely to have a miscarriage, which is my constant fear. The bad news is nausea and rage. And all these little bumps.

So I think the way to handle this ordeal is to act as if I were watching a movie called *Maren with Raging Hormones*. I don't need to adopt this as my permanent identity, like "I'm crazy" or "I'm a raging lunatic." No, that isn't me. That's hormones.

But who is "me" anymore? The me I used to know has been so thoroughly challenged, turned upside down, reorganized, permeated by other forces, that perhaps I am finally seeing how ludicrous it is to be attached to one solitary idea of who I am. *Either* I am a raging lunatic *or* I am not? Can't both be true at the same time? I am a raging lunatic *and* I am not? Clearly, there are moments where the raging lunatic has the starring role, but other characters are also present within me: an overwhelmed young woman who is being carried far beyond her previous self, a professional therapist, a wife and a friend who longs to be loved. I'm beginning to feel like social event of various characters, coming to know the entire party as "me."

Teachers of depth psychology and Eastern religions tell us

that an individual's being is much greater than the narrow little ego with whom most of us identify. Jean Houston enjoys exhorting, "You're not just a sack of skin and bones dragging around a dreary little ego!" Anybody who is having a difficult time understanding this lesson could get a crash course in it by getting pregnant.

When I told my brother John, who is a doctor, that I am pregnant, he warned, "Be prepared. You're no longer in control. Now your hormones are in the saddle."

That is absolutely to the point. I am no longer in control of my body or my mind. The woman I used to refer to when I said "I" barely exists anymore. "I" am being drowned out by—what? What is it? Is it hormones? Is it DNA? Is it the Mother Goddess? "I" have been abducted, not just once, but again and again, pulled into this overwhelming process of pregnancy—abducted physically, psychologically, spiritually. I can barely find the woman I used to be.

Why is nature doing this? How does my current state of being serve the purposes of nature? I assume nature would not make me a sick, enraged, weepy, pathetic, and miserable person for no reason at all. So why? To wear me down? To temporarily erase me as a woman with a will of my own, a personality of my own? Is that the point of this? Is this what the Mother Goddess wants? For me to surrender all ideas I cherish about who I am, what I want, so that her will is mine? I believe so.

The Mother Goddess does not want a pregnant woman with ideas of her own. She wants to control pregnant women, to make us sick when we smell cigarettes so that we will stay away from them, to make us so nauseated and miserable that we withdraw from a busy life into a quieter pace. She knows how to create new life successfully, and she doesn't want us to bungle it with fancy ideas of our own. Let's face it: how often has human consciousness served the cause of life on the planet? OK, there you have it.

My ego has been pulled under. Everything in me feels pulled down under, into murky spaces where I cannot see clearly, into realms where I am controlled by forces far greater than I could ever fight. It is remarkable how my ego struggles to surface, tries to regain control. And yet the truth is that I am descending. I am not sure into what. The most I can ascertain is that I am descending into the primal world of nature, where the psyche of nature rules.

I am reminded of the ancient Sumerian earth and sky Goddess, Inanna. The story of Inanna's descent into the underworld dates back to a period between 1900 BCE and 3500 BCE.[1]

Like me, Inanna was accustomed to living on the earth, where she had her particular control over things. But there came a time when she needed to descend into the underworld. She felt she had to attend the funeral rites of the man who had been her dark sister's husband. As was decreed by Ereshkigal, the Queen of the Underworld, Inanna had to enter the realm of the dead "naked and bowed low," "crouched and stripped bare." There were seven gates on the way into the underworld. At each of these gates, Inanna was stripped of some of her regalia, only then to crouch before the seven judges. Ereshkigal completed Inanna's journey to the realm of the dead: she killed Inanna, hung her corpse from a wooden peg where for three days her flesh rotted, until finally, through a series of upper world interventions, Inanna was brought back to life on earth.

Inanna shows us that an Earth Goddess must be in relationship to the Land of the Dead. The Greek myth of Demeter and Persephone bears a similar message. The rhythmic interplay of life and death is the way of nature, the way of all life. Life, death, rebirth. This archetypal pattern does not refer only to physical life; it is also reflective of the life of the soul, which is more the emphasis in the story of the death and rebirth of Jesus Christ. The story of Jesus bears many similarities to the Inanna story, such as hanging on a wooden peg for three days until the resurrection. This pattern—of a three-day death preceeding the renewed life—may be common in myths because it follows the moon's cycle, and the moon was a primary referent for ancient peoples. For three days, the moon is "dead" before the new moon appears.

The intimation of these death and rebirth stories is that, in order to know our true nature, in order to grow into wholeness, we must die in certain ways. Death is an inherent part of the spiral into new life. A forest fire rages through the land, burning off the old wood and grasses, ravaging life as it was. Following the fire, the death, is an amazing regeneration of life: the soil is enriched; grasses, trees, plants sprout, grow, and sustain new life.

That may be well and good in nature or mythology, but it is quite a different matter to witness death in one's own life. This pattern of life-death-regeneration is not simply a story about the Gods and Goddesses, or nature; these are also stories about us. Each of us, in our lifetime, will be stripped bare, abducted by forces larger than ourselves, and descend to the underworld, where we experience the death of something in ourselves. These stories show us that only when we surrender to the necessity of death is it possible for new life to emerge, a new life richer and deeper than before.

I certainly did not intend a journey to the underworld. No one asked me if I wanted to go. I just said I wanted a baby. And now, I am headed down. Like Inanna, at each of the seven gates, I am progressively stripped of my regalia: stripped of my physical vanity through nausea and a rash of bumps, stripped of my will, stripped of my ability to formulate coherent ideas. Increasingly, I am rendered "naked and bowed low." I fear what else is to come. I fear meeting the Queen of the Underworld.

Yet I know that something in me needs to die in order to become a mother. My heroic ego needs to die. I need to quit having so many ideas, to quit galloping around the world. How else could I learn the ways of patient receptivity? How else could I surrender into being a piece of meat as nature wants me to be? How else could I comprehend the wisdom inherent in being a piece of meat?

I am headed for surrender—a death of sorts. Yet I must trust that new life will emerge, not only in the form of a baby but in the form of an enriched soul, a deepened way of being in myself.

This story of Inanna's descent speaks to me in many ways. I am perplexed that she consciously and courageously marched into her descent: she knew what she needed. I didn't know. I had to be abducted. But now I find myself being stripped at the seven gates, heading for a death that I cannot fully grasp, heading for mysteries that my dark sister will teach me: witnessing and participating in death so that I can integrate this knowledge into my life on earth, so that I can be truly fertile.

I see women all around me who are mothers. They lived through pregnancy and birth and a baby. If they did it, I guess I can, too. They are reaching out to me, welcoming me, and I find this greatly reassuring.

Now that I am pregnant, mothers talk to me in a way that's different from how they talked to me before. There is an intimacy between mothers that I had never perceived before, and now mothers are including me in that. I feel as if I've been admitted to a secret club. What is this club? What are the secrets?

The one thing that almost all my mother-friends talk about is the joy of bearing a child, saying it is the central religious experience of their lives. As the MotherMysteries begin to unfold in my personal experience, mysteries both light and dark, I am beginning to see what they mean.

> Nothing changes or grows without the food of some other sacrifice. This is the basis of women's experience of child-bearing and of all blood mysteries that create and maintain life. It is known to matriarchal consciousness and to modern physics. It is the basis of psychology and transformation of any kind. . . .
>
> —Sylvia Brinton Perera
> *Descent to the Goddess*, pp. 54–55

THE ONE LIFE EATS ITSELF

three months pregnant

ONE COULD MAKE a case that a woman does not need to be a genius to be pregnant. It requires practically nothing. She really doesn't have to do much, think much. A male ejaculates sperm into her vagina, nine months pass, and *voilà*, she has a baby! Cows do it. Dogs do it. Except for the sex, even vegetables do it.

However, one can also make a case that pregnancy demands everything of a woman. Pregnancy asks that she sacrifice her ego, her sense of individuality, her self-determination, her body, her mind, her feelings. In turn, a pregnant woman becomes infused with the genius of nature. A pregnant woman has the unique opportunity to be inside the process of creation and to be conscious in the genesis.

Perhaps we all have that opportunity every day. The genius of nature is always at work in us, in the beating of the heart, the inhalation and exhalation of the lungs, the vital exchange among the cells. We each could bring our conscious attention to these brilliant acts of nature within us. But how many of us do? What makes pregnancy such a good opportunity to join the mind of nature is that it eclipses almost everything else; nature wants the pregnant woman to focus on the pregnancy above all else, and a crucial part of this focus is the most peculiar stirring of feelings for a tiny fetus.

I am intensely passionate about this possible-baby growing in my belly. I can't justify it. Really, how big is this fetus? Maybe three inches long. It probably weighs about as much as a letter.[1] I feel oceanic waves of love for this tiny creature. My body and mind and feelings are all nestled around this possible-baby, myself as a possible-mother, and my husband as a possible-father, in this miracle of life involving the three of us. I find it absolutely compelling; it's all I want to think and talk about.

Almost every day, I stare at Lennart Nilsson's book of intrauterine photographs of fetuses so that I may know what my baby looks like. Even though I'm sure that nature could do this job perfectly well without my mind, I want to participate consciously. I want to know what is going on. I want to help. What can I do? I sleep a lot. Eat well. Exercise. Don't smoke cigarettes or inhale toxic fumes. Take vitamins with folic acid. Read dozens of books on pregnancy. Contemplate the miracle of life. Be happy.

Today I made a cardiovascular system. Well, not all in one day, but I worked on it today. Somewhere inside of me is the know-how to build a human body. How do I relate to the part of myself that "knows" how to create a cardiovascular system? Do "I" know that? Not consciously. But this wisdom is in my body, dwells in me, is right now doing the job right here in my swelling belly.

Isn't it funny? I look as if I am doing nothing. I am quiet and sit still. No action. The most complex, sophisticated work of my life is occurring while I am holding still, allowing the life force to work through me. I want to be in this partnership in a full way, respecting and learning from the genius of nature and also bringing my human gifts of consciousness and feeling into relationship with the forces of creation.

One of the qualities I treasure about women is that most of us tend to take things personally. I remember the story Joseph Campbell told, crediting his women students at Sarah Lawrence College with pushing him to apply myth to personal life experience. In his charming manner, willing to acknowledge his human foibles, Campbell told of being a young professor who had just completed a brilliant lecture on cross-cultural mythology, feeling more than a bit impressed with himself. As is likely to happen to an inflated ego, a young woman's hand shot up right after the lecture's grand finale, with the piercing question, "Yes, Dr. Campbell, but what does that have to do with life?"

That story mirrors for me what I often wondered throughout my own school years but never had the audacity to ask. So many teachers imparted knowledge but failed to anchor the knowledge in the relevance of life experience. I am restless with abstract knowledge; I need it to be connected to something: tell me what it means to a life, tell me why it matters to you and to me. Facts and theories only come alive for me when I can feel their personal and interpersonal meaning.

The majority of women I have known, either as friends or through my professional work, conduct their lives from a home base that is personal, an internal home built upon feelings and relationships. We venture out into the world in myriad ways—into a full range of careers and activities. But always we are in a conversation with home base, with the personal.

Most of what I know I have learned through personal mediums: through relationships, through reading biographies and novels, through carefully noticing other people in my work as a minister and a psychotherapist, and by going deeply inside myself. I do like to think, yet my thinking is interlaced with feeling, with daily experience, with the felt sense of being a person. For me, first comes feeling and experience, then emerges thinking.

I am always stunned when I hear a man exclaim in frustration, "Why must women take things so personally!" If I don't experience my life personally, then what is the point of being a person? I cannot imagine going through life *not* taking things personally.

Joseph Campbell taught me something that I am learning to take personally through my experience of pregnancy. He said that, in the Hindu tradition, there are five basic sheaths that enclose the life mystery. He detailed each of them. In my mind, numbers two, three, four, and five seem to have floated away. However, the first sheath caught my attention and now stands in the center of my daily life. Each day I see this sheath from a slightly different angle. As I come to understand the mystery more, I realize I could contemplate it my entire life; the meanings and nuances are infinite. The mystery is "The One Life Eats Itself."

Like all mysteries, it must be pondered for some time before it means anything. Even more than pondering, actual experience of the mystery best reveals its meaning. Conveniently, all of us have many experiences of the One Life Eating Itself.

In our earthly arrangement, we are interdependent with other life-forms. A big fish survives by eating smaller fish. A termite survives by eating wood. A tree survives by eating nutrients from the soil, eating water and sun. My body keeps living because I consume elements of the One Life: air, cow's milk, a tomato, a chicken.

Countless diverse individuals form the life community. We are Many. And also, at the same time, we are One. We form one life organism, a Life Body, of which we are temporary parts. How does the One Life survive? By eating itself. The One Life goes on, individual forms evolving and dissolving, eating and being eaten.

This is an intriguing thought on an abstract level, but it may take on some discomforting dimensions when we take it personally. How do we feel about eating other life to sustain ourselves? And more to the disquieting heart of the matter, how do we feel about being eaten by other life creatures?

Most of my life, I have been squeamish about eating and being eaten within the animal kingdom. I have a hard time consciously eating other animals: it's not an ethical problem for me; I just feel repulsed when I think I am eating pig flesh. Many a mealtime I have averted eyes and mind to distance myself from the source of the food on my plate. I don't want a trout's head sitting in front of me. I don't want cow's blood on my plate.

I live far away from the eating habits of the lioness. She personally runs down her dinner and kills it, tears its flesh apart with her canines, laps its blood. I have grown accustomed to the distance afforded by grocery stores and cooks. I don't want to touch a raw turkey or pull its innards out, much less chop its head off. Once I move beyond the category of animal flesh, I am able to be more contentedly mindful of the source of my food. I feel fine, and grateful, thinking about the source of my food while eating bread, bananas, corn, zucchini, tomatoes.

I must confess that the role of "the eater" is far more palatable to me than the role of "the eaten." I don't want other creatures eating me. I really don't like it that dust mites are constantly eating me. I feel angry when a mosquito drinks my blood. The thought of parasitic worms and a long tapeworm in my intestines horrifies me. And please, God, don't let a large animal eat me.

Whether we like it or not, whether we allow ourselves to know it or not, always we live within these conditions of existence, of eating and being eaten. I often have not liked it and have usually declined awareness of it. But now it has become personal and compelling. As I stare at my swelling belly, I want to know: where did my baby come from?

I remember when I grew a vegetable garden in Berkeley during my second year of graduate theological education. I just couldn't get over the fact that I put a seed in the ground, watered it, and a few months later out came a carrot. When I pulled out that carrot, I thought to myself, "It's just like the real ones in the grocery store!" I was so alienated from the processes of nature that my criterion for "real" food was what I knew from the grocery store. Even though intellectually I knew that food was grown with seeds, soil, and water, I had little experience with that end of things. My daily experience over the years was that food came from the grocery store.

The compelling reality now is that a potential human being is developing within my body and may someday even come out, drink milk, and become an adult. How could this happen?

I know the standard line about the sperm and the egg, the multiplying cells, DNA, and so on. I know the explanation about life being sparked by God. Yet to me, these are external answers, delivered in textbooks or by biology professors or ministers. I memorized the lines, but I don't know what they mean.

It matters to me now. Where does life come from? This life in my belly came from a joining of my husband's life and my own. A new life is born out of pre-existing life. As I think about the various forms of life, I see that this is true across the board. Each form of life has the capacity to produce a new life similar to itself. Some require a mate; some can do it on their own.

The One Life Gives Birth to Itself and The One Life Eats Itself. Surely this is the central mystery of the Great Mother Goddess. She "knows" how to transform her body to create new life. She knows how to transform the life-body into death and the death-body into life.

I realize how separated I have been from nature. I don't really know—deep in my bones—that life is born out of other life. I don't have a full relationship with what I eat. I don't know where it came from, how it was treated, who its mother was. I have never watched a baby being born. I have never held a person who is dying.

What have we lost by becoming so separated from nature's cycles? Birth and death are hidden in hospitals. We are cut off from knowing how people come into the world and how people leave the world. Where can we learn about how to give birth and how to die? How can we know the fullness of life when we are deprived of the beginnings and endings? How can we know that The One Life Gives Birth to Itself and The One Life Eats Itself?

Never before in my life has such a large creature eaten me.

This fetus is growing in my body because he or she is eating me. That's how this little baby gets nourishment: by eating my body. To my amazement, I find that I want to give myself to this baby. For the first time in my life, I want to be sacrificed, to have something taken from me to feed The One Life. I want to be aware that The One Life Eats Itself, to know who and what I am eating, and who and what is eating me. I want to participate. For the first time, I find participating in The One Life Eating Itself meaningful and joyous.

Perhaps this is the idea of religious communion. In Christianity, Roman Catholic and Episcopal believers enact a sacred ritual of being fed by a priest a wafer and a drink of wine or grape juice, said to symbolize the body and the blood of Jesus Christ. The communicant is asked to take the blood and the body of Jesus within her so that she is fed the essence of him, so that her body contains his body.

A similar tradition of ingesting the essence of a deity occurred in ancient Greece through the Eleusinian Mysteries of Demeter and Persephone. For a period of two thousand years, beginning about 1400 BCE, each autumn multitudes journeyed to Eleusis for the highly secretive rites. After a period of fasting, participants drank a brew of fermented barley, which some scholars believe had hallucinogenic effects. The initiates ingested the body of the grain mother and the grain maiden, Demeter and Persephone, in the drinking of the barley. Taking barley within one's own body, uniting with barley, meant to join with the grain Goddesses. Only then could the initiates experience the mysteries of the Goddesses.

We become, in part, what we eat. What we take into our bodies literally fills our cells, bones, blood, heart, brain. Perhaps, too, there is a consciousness inherent in a particular food that we also inherit upon eating that food. Certainly this is the idea suggested by Christian holy communion. A communicant takes in the blood and body of Christ so that she can receive his spirit.

We could also say, "We are what eats us." If this fetus continues to eat me and eventually gets born, then my body will be in the very cells of his or her body. I will continue to feed this baby's body with milk from my breasts and love. Someday, if the natural order of things goes well, I will die, and this baby will be all that remains of me.

Indeed, we partake of The One Body: wine, bread, pomegranates, milk, eggs, potatoes. The energies of the individual bodies mingle throughout the One Body in a holy communion of eating and being eaten. The One Life Eats Itself. This is the mystery embodied by the Earth Mother.

In my alienated modern circumstance, I walked to the refrigerator to get an egg. It would have been so much more congruent if I had walked to a chicken roost to receive one of the hen's eggs. Alas. On that grocery store egg, around the midsection, I wrote, "The One Life Eats Itself." Then I turned the egg upside down and wrote, back to back with the first saying, "The One Life Gives Birth to Itself." I laid the egg in a nest of real grass that I pulled from the lawn, all nestled in a woven wicker basket, placed in the exact center of our dining table. And there it sat: all that I hungered to know.

Mary . . . became the sole inheritor of all the names and forms . . . of the goddess-mother in the Western World.

—Joseph Campbell
The Masks of God: Occidental Mythology, p. 45

THE VIRGIN MARY AND ME

five months pregnant

IS IT POSSIBLE that a born and bred Unitarian Universalist, a devout Berkeley feminist, and a student of the hedonist pleasures of youth could wake up one morning to discover that she is the Virgin Mary?

It's preposterous. It's inexplicable. But it's true: I feel I am the Virgin Mary. I know her. I feel her deep within me. I feel sacred. Holy. I know I am carrying the Divine Child inside my body. Other people perceive me through the eyes of this world—walking, talking, eating, working—and they call me "Maren," assuming I am the same person they used to know. But I am deep inside the dreamy land of pregnancy, so far into inner spaces that my primary companion throughout these days, my soul mate, is the Virgin Mary.

Perhaps I should have seen this coming. These past weeks I have been increasingly aware of myself as a vessel through which Life is marching. I am a container that is being used by the creative life force—not a treasured individual, just some woman's body. The driving force of life cares not a whit for some little ego named Maren Hansen. It doesn't care about what I feel or want, what degrees I have, to whom I am married. "Does she have good eggs?" That matters. "Can we create a new life within her?" That's what matters.

Should I be insulted that nature is "just using me"? I am a little bit. But mostly I am honored to be used by the life force, to participate in creation. Life is using me to perpetuate itself. I am yet another vessel in which the miracle of life is manifesting for the zillionth time.

Oh, but it feels like the first time. I feel I am the first woman ever to be pregnant. I feel special. Chosen. I know that the life stirring within me is sacred. I feel sure that this growing baby is a boy, and he is part God. He is the baby Jesus. And I am the Virgin Mary.

This is not an easy piece of reality for me. Rationally, I am aware that I am not literally the Virgin Mary, nor am I carrying the baby Jesus, nor am I the first woman ever to be pregnant. My analytic mind has it figured this way: the idea of a Virgin Mother is archetypal—that is, a form within the human imagination; it lives in the collective unconscious of all human beings. For thousands of years in civilizations such as the Egyptians, the Aztecs, and the Greeks, Virgin Mother Goddesses have been worshiped. When a particular image appears in varied cultures throughout the ages, such repetition indicates it is archetypal.

We can study archetypes objectively, through such collective mediums as mythology, art, and religion. But each of us also has subjective experiences of these archetypes throughout our lives. Carl Jung observed that an archetype experienced subjectively "takes hold of the individual in a startling way, creating a condition of 'being deeply moved.' . . . The archetype presents itself as numinous, that is, it appears as an experience of fundamental importance."[1]

My pregnant body is filled with the archetype of the Virgin Mother, and as with any activated archetype, it easily overpowers the ego. My ego has become flooded and identified with the Virgin Mother archetype in the particularized form of the Virgin

Mary. From a Jungian psychological perspective, this makes perfect sense. However, it does not alter the disquieting fact that I am in deep and sacred love with the Virgin Mary, that I feel she is living within me. Sometimes, as I walk down the street, a person looks directly at me, smiles gently and knowingly, and my first thought is, "He sees that I am the Virgin Mary." And I experience that immensely satisfying sense of feeling known, being seen for my true self.

I give profound thanks to Carl Jung and his followers for building the conceptual framework of archetypes and the collective unconscious. Now I can place these inner experiences without worrying that I've gone off the deep end—which leaves me free to move to the next problem on my list: humiliation. How can I tell my family and friends? We don't even believe in the Virgin Mary.

I am searching my mind to see who the Virgin Mary is and what she has meant to me. Perhaps these associations will offer clues about why she is so luminous to me now.

My introduction to Mary was offered by my eight-year-old best friend and playmate, Loretta. As a Catholic attending parochial school, Loretta had more information on Mary than did I. Once I went to confession with Loretta. I watched my friend walk through an open doorway into a wooden closet, about the size of two telephone booths stuck together. She closed her door. She had told me that behind the other door sat the priest. Waiting for her, I tried to imagine what happened behind these closed doors. After a few minutes, Loretta came back out, went to a pew, where she knelt, crossed herself, and prayed. Later that day, I asked Loretta a million questions. Midway through her explanations, we came up with a plan: she would teach me the sequence of confession, and I could pretend I was Catholic and do it with the priest! I rehearsed going into the confessional; saying, "Forgive me, Father, for I have sinned"; and telling the priest (role-played by Loretta) all the nasty thoughts and acts I had committed the past week. Then he would forgive me, assign me penance. I would go to the pew to kneel and say the prescribed number of Our Fathers and Hail Marys. Loretta helped me memorize these prayers.

Hail Mary, full of grace,
The Lord is with thee.
Blessed art thou among women,
And blessed is the fruit of thy womb, Jesus.

Holy Mary, Mother of God,
Pray for us sinners now
And at the hour of our death.

By Friday, we chickened out. We were afraid the priest would catch us in our game, and then there would be a lot to confess— and not only to the priest. Plus, Loretta was being such a stickler for details, insisting that I had to eat fish for Friday dinner if I was going to confession on Saturday, and the taste of fish made me gag.

For the next fifteen years, I didn't think too much about the Virgin Mary. However, in retrospect, I believe she was a reigning influence within junior high and high school, wherein almost all the students believed in an unwritten code of sexual morality dictating that a girl was either—and these were the terms used—a *prude* or a *whore*. A whore was a girl who allowed boys to touch her breasts or genitals or had sexual intercourse. It was a compliment to be called a prude. A girl could only be popular if she was a prude. This judgmental, simplistic either/or categorization of female sexuality, which wounded so many of us, is rooted in the Christian good woman–bad woman, Virgin Mary– Mary Magdalene split. But who thought about that in high school?

However, I did think about it during my three years as a student in the Graduate Theological Union. Although I was in a Unitarian Universalist seminary, I was required to learn Christian church history. Naive and astonished, I wandered the stacks of the GTU library, discovering volume after tome of argument and defense about the Immaculate Conception, the Assumption of Mary into heaven with Christ, whether Mary was a virgin before, during, and after she gave birth to Jesus. For two thousand years, people had poured their lifework into justifying what I considered to be irrelevant, nit-picking details of religion.

In one apocryphal text of the Bible, I discovered an incredible scene in which Mary had just given birth to Jesus. Mary's midwife tells a friend that yes, miraculously, following birth, Mary's hymen was still intact. Filled with doubt and desiring proof, the midwife's friend inserted her finger into Mary's vagina to "test her condition." The intruder's hand was "consumed by fire" for distrusting the word of God as spoken through Mary. Miraculously, when the midwife's friend touched the baby Jesus, her hand was healed.[2] About 649 years later, it was declared official: the Lateran Council determined Mary's postpartum virginity to be Church dogma.

Mary is held to be the role model for Christian women, the ideal woman to emulate. Mary's mother conceived Mary immaculately; Mary in turn conceived Jesus without sexual intercourse, gave birth to the savior of the human race, and emerged with an intact hymen! You try it! What kind of a role model is that?

In seventeen years of formal education, plus countless sessions of Sunday school, no one had ever mentioned to me that, throughout the majority of human civilization, Goddesses were worshiped. One courageous teacher at my seminary taught a class on the ancient Goddess religions. I learned that for twenty-five thousand years, Goddesses were worshiped throughout the earth.[3] Most of what we know about these Goddesses comes through archeological excavations. Scholars have uncovered evidence of Goddess-worshiping cultures in Anatolia (Turkey), Egypt, Palestine, Asia, Mesopotamia, Eastern and Western Europe, among American Indians, and in South America.[4] In the beginning, God was a woman.[5]

The Goddess was worshiped as the source of all being. Somehow, out of her moist, dark, mysterious self, she bore life. The Goddess also claimed life, bringing the dead back into her great body, ever transforming the living into the dead into the living.

Unlike the later Judeo-Christian God, she was not dualistic: she held life and death as a unity. As she shows us through the cycle of the moon, she bears new life, wields death, only to return again with new life.

It is understandable that feminine deities were worshiped during the development of agriculture. A woman "knew" how to grow a baby human being within her body, how to nourish that baby with milk from her breasts. All persons were born from the body of a woman. All animals were born from the body of a female. The mysteries of creating life dwelled within the feminine. The perception of this prodigious feminine power carried over into agriculture as well: women tended the gardens; they understood fertility and could make things grow.

While studying the Goddesses, I repeatedly came across the theme of the Virgin Mother. The Greek Goddess Artemis, the Aztec Goddess Chimalman, the Egyptian Goddess Nut (pronounced "Newt") were all Virgin Mothers. But so were the love Goddesses Aphrodite, Ishtar, and Anath.[6] The concept of a "Virgin Mother" didn't make much sense to me. I read explanations that the ancient meaning of the term *virgin* wasn't about a hymen, broken or intact. *Virgin* was a term for a woman who was not married, not the property of a husband. *Virgin* referred to a quality of being: a woman sufficient and whole unto herself.[7]

As was apparent in the examples of the love Goddesses, *virgin* did not necessarily mean absence of sexual activity. Many of the Virgin Goddesses were paired with lovers, consorts, or sons. The primary feature of this pairing was that annually the Virgin Mother would either kill her young male consort or lose him to death, only then to reconceive him or be reunited with him in the season of spring. This mythic motif of life, death, and regeneration reflects the fundamental reality of the life drama as it is enacted upon earth. This ancient religious theme is the ground from which Christianity grew, repeating in yet a new way the theme of life, death, and resurrection.

I can't say this explanation made complete sense to me while

I was a single woman in graduate school, but I accepted it. I felt no burning desires to know more about Virgin Mothers.

But lo and behold, at five months pregnant, possessed by the Virgin Mary, the desires are burning. I have to know more. On an emotional level, I am so in love with her that I am driven to know her better. One yearns to know one's beloved. On an intellectual level, I am stupefied that this is happening inside me; I have to try to figure it out. I am reading everything I can find about the Virgin Mary and Virgin Mothers.

Theologian Joan Engelsman has observed that Mary was an unusually autonomous woman in New Testament accounts. She came and went remarkably freely and did not appear to be under the control of any man, including Joseph, even though she was married to him.[8] Mary seems to be a virgin in the ancient sense of the word—a woman who owned herself—and yet she is also a virgin in the later Christian sense of the term, which emphasizes an intact hymen and no sexual intercourse.

I resent the twist of meaning that Christianity added to the ancient sense of *virgin*. The Christian notion is that Eve burdened us all by leading us into original sin, which got us expelled from the Garden of Eden. The Christian theologian Augustine established that sexual intercourse was the way people transferred original sin,[9] so it was only through Mary, who was herself conceived immaculately and who conceived Jesus without transferring the original sin through intercourse, that we could have a "pure" person who would save us all.[10] These ideas—of woman tempting man into sin, and sex as the way we transfer sin to our children—revile the dignity of women and men and sexuality.

What galls me further is the insistence of the Catholic Church that Mary is the one ideal female for all women and girls to emulate. Mary does not represent the whole story of womanhood. She is, or can be, one facet in a female's lifetime. However, to expect her to be the reigning archetype for all women in all our myriad developmental phases is simply wrong.

In the Greek pantheon, Goddesses were often differentiated

with respect to life stage. For example, Persephone was a maiden goddess, pure and innocent as the new moon. Demeter was the full, bountiful Earth Mother. And Hecate was the crone, the essence of the dying moon, the wise old woman who knows the ways of spirit and divination. Acknowledging this diversity within the female life span feels supportive of wholeness and truth.

Quite literally, the worship of Mary was superimposed on the worship of the Great Goddesses. In Ephesus, where the temple of Artemis was one of the Seven Wonders of the World, and Artemis was devoutly worshiped, it was declared that this indeed was the place where the Virgin Mary had spent her final days. Now Christians flock to see her sacred site, which includes a house in which she supposedly lived. Later in history, many Gothic cathedrals were built on the exact grounds where Goddesses had been worshiped.[11] Christianity has wrestled with the power of the Virgin Mary for two thousand years, trying to satisfy the popular devotion to her while at the same time also maintaining the supremacy of Jesus and God. In many Catholic cultures, Mary still threatens to become more a focus of worship than Jesus himself.[12]

Why all my haggling about the Virgin Mary compared to the more ancient Virgin Mother Goddesses? Isn't this simply the history of all religions: one specific form of an archetype replaces another, the meaning of the symbols shifts, the old religion is syncretized into the new religion? Why do I keep feeling anger and resentment toward the Virgin Mary when I began with spontaneous love and identification with her?

Perhaps if Mary held the wholeness of the Virgin Mother Goddess, I could more fully accept her. But I agree with other feminist theologians that Mary is a distorted form of the archetype,[13] incapable of revealing the full mysteries of the Virgin Mother. Through Mary, the archetype was repressed, deformed like a tender shoot that has been prevented by a heavy rock from growing upright in the way it internally desires, in the way that nature intended. Mary became a distorted form of the Mother Goddess.

What disturbs me about the Virgin Mary is that her body is denied and separated from the essence of childbearing. So much of the ineffable magic of motherhood is grounded in matter. Mater. Sex. Semen. A swelling belly. The body heaving in rhythmic contractions. Blood. Breast milk. The ancient Goddess figurines often have huge, pendulous breasts, a rounded full belly, abundant hips and thighs. The ancient Mother Goddess's power was one with her body. Mary's birthing did not honor the mysteries of the body in childbirth, the magnificent inner knowings of baby and mother that culminate in one human being's emerging out of another human being's body. The story of Mary's birthing denies the mysteries of the body, of nature, the mysteries of the feminine.

The fundamental life mystery is addressed by all religions. In the ancient Goddess religion, it is explained by a Great Goddess who is parthenogenetic: she conceives and gives birth out of the Oneness that is herself. She does not need a partner to create new life. She is the One from whom all being arises—the Source. She is the One Life that gives birth to itself. She is the Virgin Mother. The origin, the original, untouched by anything external to herself, she gives birth from her essence. This is the Virgin Mother.

Finally, I feel I have reached bedrock: the One Life Gives Birth to Itself. The Virgin Mother is the dark mystery out of which all existence is pushed. This feels to me to be the fundamental meaning of *Virgin Mother*—the One from Whom All Becoming Emerges. And I, part of the One Life Giving Birth to Itself, am participating in her mysteries.

It would be simpler for me if I were saying to myself, "I feel like the Virgin Mother." I could easily live with that. In fact, I feel deep contentment in my identification with the Virgin Mother. But the difficult fact is that I am saying, "I feel like the Virgin *Mary*." Why is my psyche identifying with Mary and not the more generic Virgin Mother or even a specific Virgin

Mother? Is it because the only Virgin Mother we have really held in our Christian cultural awareness for the past two thousand years is Mary?

Even though I have such basic problems with Mary, is there also something about her that I am being asked to know? Is there something more for me to understand about the Virgin Mary?

Mary was a human woman. She was engaged to a human man, Joseph. But the seed of God was planted in Mary's womb. The ordinary ways of nature, of man and woman, were suspended. Something special, out of the ordinary was occurring. The baby growing in Mary's womb was half-human and half-God. Within her body, Mary mediated the division between God and human, between heaven and earth. She received, nourished, and delivered the Divine Child who could heal us all.

By her example, it occurs to me now that Mary challenges us to do the same. Are we willing to receive the seed of the Divine? In what ways can we contain the divine seeds planted within us, nurturing their budding life? And can we, like Mary, in humble surroundings with scant social support, deliver our divine gifts into the world?

Mary, perhaps more than anyone on earth, understands how a pregnant woman feels: she, too, is a Holy Mother, impregnated by the Divine, carrying the Holy Child within her, knowing that her child brings the possibility of healing us all.

As Campbell wisely observed, in her pregnancy and mothering, Mary challenges us to an inner knowing: I am deity, and I am human; I am infinite, and I am limited; I am virgin, and I am mother; I am of the earth, and I am of the heavens.[14]

> Hail Mary, full of grace,
> The Lord is with thee.
> Blessed art thou among women,
> And blessed is the fruit of thy womb, Jesus.
>
> Holy Mary, Mother of God,
> Pray for us . . . now
> And at the hour of our death.

Although Nature has provided a strong mechanism, which might almost be called a *physiological initiation* for mothers, . . . under civilized conditions more and more obstacles have been put in its path, therefore the natural (and relatively unconscious) transition from girlhood to motherhood no longer always functions smoothly.

—Carol Baumann
"Psychological Experiences Connected with
Childbirth," p. 336

MAKING A NEST

six and one-half months pregnant

I AM BEGINNING to wonder whether part of nature's logic behind a nine-month gestation period for human beings is that a woman needs that much time to metamorphose into a mother. There is no doubt in my mind: I am being gestated, too. I have never experienced such a concentrated period of change as during pregnancy.

The physical changes inspire awe. Sometimes, when I look at my body, I feel so proud of its wisdom, how easily it knows how to grow a baby, as if this were not our first time. But other times, when I look at my body, I think, "That couldn't possibly be my body. Is this big-breasted, round-bellied, waddling duck me???"

So many physical challenges and adjustments are required of pregnant women! It seems to go in phases: for a few weeks, my incarnation is unmanageable, my body is a foreign country; then I grow accustomed to this new form, learning to live and move in it with some measure of comfort, only a few weeks later to return to the awkward phase of new and still stranger bodily contortions.

There are weeks when I need to pee every thirteen minutes. One day, while in line at the grocery store, I discover that when I sneeze, urine leaks out, not just a little bit. One day my belly button, which in the old days was perfectly rounded and gracefully tucked into my flat stomach about one-third of an inch, this treasured belly button is pushed out! Horrified, I protest, "I'm not a person with a poked-out belly button!" For all the world to see through my dresses, my T-shirts, this protuberance is my farthest point east. Any thing or person that brushes against my front side grates against my highly sensitive poked-out belly button, a sensation that makes me cringe worse than fingernails on a chalkboard. Complete strangers seem to feel permission to fondly rub my big belly, as if it were communal property, which I find intrusive in and of itself but want to scream when they mindlessly rub back and forth over my poked-out belly button. Yet these bodily changes must be adjusted to, worked around, including the ultimate athletic feat: getting out of the bathtub.

I have come to understand that nature gestates psychological qualities in the mother to increase the odds of success for a new life. What might these psychological characteristics be? Patience? In-the-moment presence? Blinding love for the Little One? Certainly, these qualities are growing in me.

I am disturbed by how little the field of psychology understands a woman's maturation from maiden into mother. This is a fundamental psychological development in most women's lives, and yet very little has been written about it. What are the psychological changes that must occur for a maiden to turn into a mother? What happens to a woman's psyche as she moves from being a solitary body to living as two together in pregnancy? What happens to the ego as a woman's life focus moves off her own self onto the care of another?

It's curious to me how much the psychological changes during pregnancy are biologically driven. We tend to think of human maturity, particularly beyond adolescence, as mostly a matter of resolving personal psychological issues, based upon personal choice. But in this pregnancy, I see how I am a perfectly programmed creature of nature. I am like the bear who goes into a cave to hibernate when the air grows chill. I am like the monarch butterfly, who flies many hundred miles to avoid the harsh winter and, with perfect navigation, lands at a site she has never visited before, the wintering grounds of her ancestors. I am flying by the automatic pilot of nature. I am enacting what nature has so ingeniously programmed me to do. Seeing myself in this state causes me to seriously question the fantasy of human free will. It is obvious to me that the biological imperatives rule supreme and can conquer the human ego whenever they feel the need.

When I think back over my pregnancy thus far, I am startled by my striking resemblance to a kidnapping victim. My mind and body really were kidnapped out of an ego-tailored existence, abducted into the deep rhythms of nature, drugged by hormones that at first made me so horribly nauseated and then so blissfully passive that I had no will to escape. I fell in love with my captor. I am smitten with the Mother Goddess, feel privileged to be her slave. Locked within the temple of the MotherMysteries, I have been exploring the many rooms, beginning to learn the age-old secrets, the mysteries of the Mother.

But paradoxically, a dream came to me, issuing a wake-up call. A certain alarm was sounded by my psyche, saying, "Wake up! Enough of the meaningful musings. It's time to get practical." Jolted awake, I am disoriented.

> In the dream, I am trying to figure out the best things to buy for the baby. I see that a Volvo baby car seat costs $16,000! That seems too expensive, but I do need a baby car seat. Next, I become aware that I need to get a nest egg. The nest egg is a weave shade that hangs under a round lightbulb on the kitchen ceiling.

I am examining these two suggestions from the unconscious. Number one: I need a baby car seat. This is obviously true. I wouldn't consider allowing a baby to be in a car without a car seat. I lost a close friend to an automobile crash, and I will do everything in my power to prevent that from happening again. My psyche considered a Volvo car seat. As far as I know, Volvo doesn't make a baby car seat.

Currently, Steve and I own two sports cars, which each seat two. At the very least, I would say we need a car that seats three people. Should I get a station wagon? Isn't that what parents drive—station wagons? I would like to get a Volvo station wagon because it is one of the safest cars on the road, but they are expensive. Actually, what I really want is an armored tank to transport my baby on these lunatic freeways of Southern California.

I feel I would do just about anything to keep this baby safe. I acutely feel the dangers in the world. Cigarette smoke, automobile accidents, murderers. Ant and roach spray, nuclear energy facilities, electromagnetic fields. My life has become dominated by fierce protective urges about our baby. I never used to be obsessed with safety before I got pregnant, but now I worry about every little thing that could harm my baby.

Because nature seems to be almost entirely controlling this process of pregnancy, I must conclude that nature wants me to worry. Why? How is it in nature's interest for me to worry about every little this and that that could hurt my baby? Is a mother's worry biologically useful? Does this anticipatory maternal worry help me make choices that increase the odds of the baby's survival? I think so. Could anticipatory worry be another psychological quality that nature gestates in a mother?

The dream also suggested that I need to get a nest egg. What is a nest egg? Isn't it extra money set aside, a financial cushion for security? I don't have to worry about that. I am blessed with a husband who takes fiscal responsibilities very seriously. In fact, Steve is so concerned about this baby's financial security that he practically has the kid's college fund completed, not to mention two other savings plans, and I haven't even given birth yet. His behavior seems a bit extreme, but surely men have their own versions of preparing for a baby, and let it be noted that I am hardly in a position to criticize irrational parental urges.

In the dream, the nest egg looked like a bird's nest, holding a round lightbulb, like a big egg. It was in the kitchen, the place of preparations and nourishment. Maybe my psyche is suggesting that it is time to weave a nest into which I can lay my "egg."

OK. How do you make a nest for a baby? What does a baby need? Practically everything! Babies come completely unfurnished. Oh my God, this is serious. I have to make a nest. Well, how hard could it be? We need a crib and a diaper-changing area. We need to buy clothes for the baby. Several of the five hundred pregnancy books I've been reading contain lists of what you need to buy for the baby.

Birds do not need to turn to page 317 to find a list that explains how to make a nest. Their instinct tells them what to do. They know how to select a place protected from the hazards of weather and predatory animals for a secure nest, which materials to collect, and how to weave them together. Well, I don't. I don't seem to have any instinct that tells me how to do that. The only instinct I have thus far came in a dream, suggesting, "Get a car seat and make a nest." I'll bet my anxiety now about making a nest is instinctive also, nature's way of making sure I get the job done. Armed with these seemingly meager instincts of "nest anxiety" and "anticipatory maternal worry" and the layette list on page 317, I must forge ahead with the task of making a nest.

Certain experiences are common to all human beings. One of these is the sense of feeling overwhelmed, lost, not knowing what is the right way:

> What if I'm doing it the wrong way?
> Will something bad happen if I do it the wrong way?
> I know this isn't the right way.
> No, hang on, maybe it *is* the right way.
> Jeez I don't know.
> I'm lost in this maze.
> How do I get out of this mess?

To varying degrees, we all go through these insecure feelings of being lost and scared, anxious, be it while navigating a love relationship, composing a life or a career, or parenting children. It is a real deficit of our culture that we don't have archetypal teachings about how to move through these feelings of being lost and anxious.

Ancient people built labyrinths. I think it would be very helpful to concretize, to externalize the dark experiences of fear and doubt. We could get a different perspective on these feelings if they were living out in the world rather than only in a dark corner of the mind. What did the ancient labyrinths teach?

Perhaps the labyrinth we all know best is from the Palace of Knossos on Crete. The confounding maze from which no one could extricate himself or herself was built in response to an equally confounding human drama. The labyrinth turned out to be a physical representation of a personally and culturally tangled existential dilemma.

In answer to the prayers of King Minos, the sea God Poseidon gave him a fine white bull born of the sea. This bull was a divine sign confirming King Minos's leadership and was intended to be sacrificed immediately. But King Minos fancied his bull, imagining the value this prized specimen might bring to him. He betrayed his promise to Poseidon by not killing it, foolishly substituting a different bull from his herd in its place for sacrifice.

The miffed Poseidon worked in mysterious ways. He made sure the queen also fancied the bull, so much so that she asked the master carpenter Daedalus to build a wooden life-size simulacrum of a cow, in which she situated herself and thus made love with the coveted bull. Many moons passed, and the queen gave birth to a monster, the Minotaur, with the head of a bull attached to the body of a human. Ashamed and afraid, King Minos ordered Daedalus to build a maze, so complex and confusing that no one could escape, and deep within its bowels, King Minos hid the Minotaur. But monsters must be fed. Every eight years, seven young Athenian men and seven young Athenian women were forced to enter the labyrinth, condemned to take one path or another, never sure which turn might confront them with the devouring bull-man monster but knowing that all roads led to the same ultimate fate.[1]

A young Athenian hero, Theseus, determined to end the sacrifice of his people once and for all, volunteered to be one of the seven men sent into the labyrinth. When King Minos's daughter Ariadne laid eyes on young Theseus as he stepped off the boat, she was immediately enamored with him. In a quick conversation, Ariadne agreed to help Theseus find a way out of the labyrinth, and in exchange, Theseus agreed to marry Ariadne and take her away from Crete. Ariadne consulted the carpenter Daedalus, who offered simple advice: give Theseus a skein of red linen thread to attach to the entrance and then unravel as he journeyed into the labyrinth. Brave Theseus eventually faced the bull-man monster, slew him with a knife, and followed the red linen thread back to the entrance, emerging into the light of day.[2]

As fate would have it, the young hero Theseus emerged from the labyrinth only to face the confounding maze of his life. He went on to betray his love with Ariadne and carelessly cause the death of his beloved father, ending up in the underworld, ruled by Hades and Persephone, where he was turned to stone.

All throughout this myth, there exists the tension between the ways of the Gods and Goddesses and the mortal heroic ego, the tension between the ways of immortals and the ways of human civilization, the increasing split between animal and human. The heroic ego of Theseus did not triumph. The depths of Poseidon's sea world and the underworld persevered.[3] If there is one overarching lesson of this myth of Theseus and the labyrinth, surely it is that the labyrinth and the underworld must be experienced; the confounding depths cannot be circumvented or denied.

Only two persons ever escaped the labyrinth at Knossos. First was Theseus, by way of following the unraveled thread that showed him where he had been. As the audience of Theseus's fate, we must view his escape as only temporary, since he concluded his life in the underworld. Nonetheless, Theseus did escape the labyrinth with the help of a material reminder of where he had come from.

How important and useful it can be to have external reminders of the past, to remember where we have been. As we navigate the confounding mazes of life, perhaps it is necessary to remember where we have been in the past: as individuals, as a family lineage, as a species, as expressions of nature. Where did we come from? Are we asked to remember the intimacy between the animal and the human? Are we asked to know that we, too, are the Minotaur, part animal and part human? Does the knife of the heroic ego, attempting to slay the beast, ever triumph, or do the deep patterns of nature ultimately claim us all?

The second person who lived to tell of his escape from the labyrinth was the man who built it: Daedalus. When King Minos discovered that Daedalus had helped Theseus escape, he sentenced Daedalus and his son Icarus to be imprisoned in the labyrinth. Though Daedalus had constructed the labyrinth, even he could not find his way out. With characteristic ingenuity, he crafted two pairs of wings made of feathers and wax. Daedalus and Icarus attached the wings to their bodies and, like birds, ascended out of the labyrinth. Daedalus warned his son of the dangers of flying too high, but young Icarus was so exhilarated by flying that he did not heed his father's warning: Icarus's wings melted from the heat of the sun, and he fell into the sea, never to be seen again. Daedalus made a safe landing in Sicily, living testimony that when caught in a hopeless conundrum, sometimes one must find a way to rise above the situation, to elevate one's consciousness above the entanglements—although, of course, not too high above.[4]

I would like a full-size labyrinth so that I could rehearse for my life. I would practice entering a complex maze, knowing that it would be extremely difficult to find my way through and once again out. Is it too New Age of me to want a labyrinth that does not contain a devouring monster in the center? Is facing threats, fear, and death integral in the archetypal experience of the labyrinth? I would practice walking in faith, wandering in the not-knowing, again and again addressing my fear, my doubt, my anxiety. I would take a path, not knowing where it would lead, not sure that this path would ever reach the center or an exit, and nonetheless, over time, I would learn to walk with presence of mind, open eyes, and trust.

Perhaps more difficult yet, I am forced to wander the labyrinthine paths of modern America, wondering whether any path leads to the center or whether all march circuitously nowhere. The bull will devour us, death will triumph, the One Life Will Eat Itself, even if we try to cover nature with cement, even when we proclaim ourselves superior to nature.

Armed only with a hand-copied layette list from page 317, I walk the endless aisles of Thrifty Drug Store, anxious in my not-knowing, wondering whether I can ever extricate myself from this overwhelming maze of products. Four aisles jam-packed with the essentials for a baby. My list says I need six receiving blankets, but I don't know what a receiving blanket is. My bowels clench with anxiety, and I waddle to the bathroom hidden in the inner recesses of the stockroom. In the respite of the toilet stall, I counsel myself that it is not necessary to furnish the entire nest now; for today, it would be OK to take the manageable step of educating myself by studying the contents of these aisles at Thrifty Drug.

Buoyed, I approach the aisles again. Cotton baby T-shirts? Yes. The snap kind or the pull-over-the-head kind? How would I know? Cream for stretch marks? Absolutely. Small cotton blankets in which you wrap a newborn—hey, also known as "receiving blankets"! A blanket in which to receive the baby. OK, I like that. How do you figure out which nipples to buy among this dizzying array? Silicone or brown rubber? Orthodontic or that stiff little straight nipple? Forget it, I'm just going to use my own. In the diaper section, I need a computer to factor in all the variables: boy, girl; newborn, 10–18 pounds, 13–24 pounds; Huggies, Pampers, or Luvs; thin, ultrathin, thick, or stretchy.

And does a baby really need powder, Desitin, and all that other stuff? I hate American consumerism. I hate doing this.

My mother is coming to visit soon. Surely, she will know what to buy. She raised four children. Together we can go to a baby store and figure out what I need. Some friends want to give us a baby shower, which I'm very pleased about, except that I have to register for it. I pray that my mom will help me register for the baby shower.

I still go to work every day, but since I'm not accepting new clients, my work schedule has become light. On one hand, I'm glad to have more free time. But on the other hand, work is so reassuring and safe because I am doing something that I was educated to do and that I have done for a long time.

In my newfound free time, I seem to be doing things that I don't really know how to do: work a computer, look for a house to buy, shop for a used Volvo, try to get the VCR to quit blinking "12:00," prepare a nest, prepare for labor. I'm struggling to figure it all out. Mostly, it just makes me feel anxious—anxious and empty.

I buy things. I feel empty inside. I look so full, and yet I feel so empty.

All the Great Mothers are born from the primeval ocean or the watery abyss, the primordial womb of life from which all created forms emerge: the ideogram for the Sumerian goddess Nammu was the sea; Isis was "born from the all-wetness"; Hathor is "the watery abyss of heaven"; Nut, the sky goddess, lets fall her milk as rain; Aphrodite is born from the foam of the sea.

—Anne Baring and Jules Cashford
The Myth of the Goddess, p. 557

The Fatal Sea

seven months pregnant

I FEEL PERILOUSLY close to the climax of pregnancy. It is disturbing to see my belly get so big, and then bigger with each passing week. Increasingly, I am getting trapped into childbirth. This creature is growing so large inside me, and the only way to get it out is to push it out through my vagina! This horrifies me, it seems impossible, yet with each passing day, I take a step closer to my fate.

When I sense the panic creeping up, I steadfastly counsel myself: "Yes, you are feeling frightened as you approach your first birth. It is a profound life passage for you. Soon, you will do what millions of women before you have done: push a baby human being out of your body. Look around you at the women who have children. They did it, and you can, too. In your birthing, you will need to surrender to your body. Your body knows exactly what to do. You must trust your body. I know you can do that."

Perhaps I go on a bit more, but at some point, it is futile. The panic is so strong it cannot be held at bay by calm counsel. The panic seizes me from behind, I feel terror, terrorized moments of eternity, and then, mercifully, somehow, the terror and the panic are spent. Gone for the moment.

This panic has just begun recently and has happened only a few times, which is quite enough. What is scaring the wits out of me? Am I afraid of the pain of childbirth? Am I afraid I am going to die?

I am afraid of being overpowered by forces unspeakably large. I feel like a novice surfer preparing to go out into the forty-foot waves of the North Shore, entering a force so much larger than myself, so far beyond my control.

I am approaching an event of magnitude unprecedented in my life, except for my own birth into the world, an event I do not consciously remember. I have made a decision: for this birth, I want to be fully awake, present, conscious, my mind working together with my body. I want to participate in what nature does. I want to know childbirth physically, emotionally, spiritually. For these reasons, and for the protection of the baby, I have decided to give birth without the use of any pain medication. Many of my friends have had drug-free births and are encouraging me in this. In fact, in my circles, it is politically incorrect to use drugs during birth. There is a real social pressure for drug-free birthing.

I am inexorably drifting toward childbirth. It scares me that I can't back out—say, "Sorry, I changed my mind, I'm not really ready for this now, it's a little too frightening for me, maybe later." What is this fear that seizes me? The best clues I have are wrapped in a recent dream:

I am riding in a car with two men, one driving and the other in the backseat. They are my friends and my instructors. We talk about what movies there are to see. There are three movies I haven't seen. Maybe I should spend all day Saturday seeing these three movies.

Suddenly, my mind becomes clear: I quit thinking about what

I *should* do and realize what I *want* to do. I tell the driver, "The truth is I'm not motivated to do anything. That just isn't where my energy is. I don't want to write papers or go to movies."

I think about how judgmental I used to be of girls who spent an entire year in preparation for their wedding. Now I realize that I am doing the same ʼ ɪg, only spending a year preparing for a baby.

We gc   ɪburger place. The two male in-
sʰ   ɪlish an article with them. I say,
              sted in now," but I worry that
              ɪofessional opportunity.
              ɪnd walk down many steps
              ɪ man are standing on the
              l, sheltered under a lava
              ɪh the lava cave ceiling,
              ʼ not experiencing the
              ʼery buffered version
              ʼp washing over us,
              ʼn has some intel-
              ʼn there. Not me.
              ɪirs back to sea

              three flights
              are people
              ɪg.
              ʼe a male
teac   ʼe refer-
ence   ɪnswer
flashes   and
what ca   ɪ no
end. It is

It's hard tc   ɪs overpowering with
The beginninɪ   ɪs that I am not driving
the car. I am noɪ   ɪining where I go. I have no
driving ambitions.   ɪs excursion, I am a passenger. This
point seems to make itself repeatedly throughout my pregnancy:

I am not in the driver's seat. Apparently, I must be a person who needs to be reminded often.

The number three appears so many times throughout this dream that it cannot be ignored: two men friends plus me, three movies, three stories down below sea level, a man plus a woman plus me being overpowered by ocean waves. The dream came on March 31, or 3-31, the eve of our one-year wedding anniversary, an auspicious and appropriate time to imagine three. On a personal level, my husband, myself, and a growing baby; on a more universal level, the masculine, the feminine, and the evolving life that emerges from the two.

The dream calls into question my image of myself, particularly with regard to femininity. In the past, I scorned girls who devoted a whole year of their lives to planning their wedding. (As if getting married was the pinnacle of a girl's life. Didn't they have anything else to do? It seemed so Barbie Doll-esque.) Now I find myself caught with my own shadow, forced to acknowledge that that shadow I am criticizing is mine, seeing that I am a woman who is devoting nearly a whole year of her life preparing for a baby.

Perhaps I misjudged the girls who spend a year of their lives planning a wedding. Maybe I did not understand that there was an internal process interwoven with their external preparations. In the past, I would have been critical of a woman who spent nearly a year dwelling on her pregnancy, thinking, "Get a life." Now I am inside this process of pregnancy, thinking, "Why go anywhere else? Everything I ever wanted is right here."

I realize I am losing interest in the more traditionally masculine realm of publishing papers and career, even reading newspapers and watching movies. This level of news and drama in the human collective is no longer compelling for me. However, I am reluctant to let go of my career development, fearing I will miss an opportunity. This is also part of my waking awareness. As I am pulling away from reading the professional literature, no longer teaching, reducing my clinical work, I feel anxious about being left behind by my colleagues. Might I become "just a mother"?

Who would I be if I had no professional identity? My generation of women vowed we would never be "just" mothers and housewives. We would be career women, financially independent, powerful in a man's world. We became psychologically defended against motherhood as an identity. This defense was helpful, and perhaps necessary, to get us out of the constrictions of the past. But this defense is causing me anxiety as I greet my swelling belly. If I relax my guard, will I slip back into the socially prescribed grooves worn deep by thousands of years?

I like the way the dream juxtaposes the fast-food restaurant with the awareness that I am taking a year to prepare for a baby. In this lengthy preparation of pregnancy, I feel fed and nourished in deeper ways than I have ever experienced. This is slow food. I feel so close to the pulse of life, the fundamental powers in the universe. I am learning so much about my ego in relationship to the larger forces. I am learning about Being and Becoming. And I am in love. I am immersed in a feminine quality of being that I never dared touch before; I am shocked to be here, to find the deep ways it is moving me.

In my waking life, I think of myself as being intimate with the ocean. I have lived on the Pacific Coast for ten years. I walk along the beach almost daily and swim. Like a manic child, I endlessly ride waves on a Boogie board. I love to paddle our inflatable yellow boat out to the kelp beds to look at sea lions. Snorkeling is one of my favorite activities in the whole world. Until quite recently, I would have said I love the ocean.

Certainly, I have felt fear about the ocean before. I have been scared while bodysurfing in big waves. I am fearful of sharks, and once a huge black bat ray scared me half to death. But most of the ocean places I have related to throughout the world have been gentle, hospitable.

It is becoming clear to me that I have known only a tiny, little bit of the ocean. I have not seen the whole ocean.

In the dream, I descend three stories below sea level—no

longer on the surface of the ocean but far down beneath the surface. I am grateful for the safety my psyche offered by placing me in a protected lava cave. I am given an opportunity to view the depths of the ocean without actually experiencing its full force.

The lava cave has a small opening in the ceiling, where the ocean waves pour through. As if I am in a womb, looking up at a vulva with a vaginal opening, where oceanic waters pour through. I recall that the Mother Goddess is often associated with caves and that, in ancient times, childbirth often occurred in caves. In the presence of another woman and a man, I glimpse the oceanic depths. The waves wash over us, knock us down. I know there is no way to fight the ocean, that the ocean is infinitely more powerful than I could ever be. I am overwhelmed with awe and fear in the midst of this power.

In the dream, when I was three stories below sea level, I experienced awe, terror, and the sense of being overwhelmed by a superior power. I glimpsed the "mysterium fascinans" (the fascinating mystery) and the "mysterium tremendum"[1] (the awesome mystery).

I feel deep fear and anxiety as I approach the most major event of my life since my own birth. Not since then have I been pulled so deeply by the forces of nature, beyond my control, drawn into the threshold of creation, where life and death stand back to back. Those moments of bringing a new life into the world comprise a doorway—possibly an entrance, possibly an exit. I feel the fear of being in that doorway, seeing what lives on either side—the terrifying great mystery, and knowing that I cannot control which side of the doorway I, or my baby, will end up on.

Soon the ebb and flow of powerful waves will conquer my body. In two months, I will be pulled into those overpowering waves, tossed about, knocked down, submitted to rhythmic forces that I know I cannot possibly fight. When I think about that, I feel terrified. I am afraid to be drawn into the oceanic waves.

In the dream, I am convinced the ocean depths are no place to stand to prove an intellectual point, as the male figure was doing. Those depths are filled with raw, primitive power. I peeked into that oceanic power, got scared, and wanted to get out of there, to scurry back up to the human surface, sea level. I feel awe and fear in the face of the power of the ocean, the power of giving birth, and the power of my unconscious.

The fatal sea. *Fatal.* Rhymes with *natal.* Bearing a child certainly dictates the direction of a woman's fate. In this fate—the deep feminine and childbirth—I must surrender my will to the forces of nature, knowing they will overpower me, and yet within that context, I must trust—trust my body and nature. What a bunch of nonsense! Death is part of nature, and I don't want to die.

OK, realistically, what are my odds of dying in childbirth? I have read that for every one hundred thousand births in America, eight result in the death of the mother. That is not a negligible statistic, particularly for a pregnant woman. However, it certainly beats the odds of surviving childbirth in Africa, India, or China.[2] Because I live in affluent white America, and have been conscientious about prenatal care, it's unlikely that I will die while giving birth. But it's possible.

From the origin of our species, childbirth has been the great killer of women. For scores of millennia, women have been staring down death during childbirth, many losing the battle. Surely this ancestral memory is imprinted in the female psyche. Fifty years of modern medicine cannot erase the instinctive fear of death while approaching birth.

Physical death is not the only threat. Psychological threats run rampant. In a woman's psyche, the first birth inevitably brings a death. The era of the young, free, solitary woman dies. This cannot be undone. Who will I be as a mother? Will I survive only as "the mother of ——"?

At least among Jungians, there is general agreement that when a woman gets married, this brings to an end the life stage of the Virgin-Maiden. I think that was true for me in certain ways. I cried practically every day for two months before my wedding. It was as if the crying cleared open space in my body and soul so there was room to say "Yes" to my husband. I was keenly aware that the act of marrying a specific person would alter the direction of my fate, whereas marrying any other person would dictate a different direction. That loss of control over my future scared me. But I have to say that I have felt remarkably myself in our relationship. I don't feel as if I lost myself in marriage. I don't feel that the independent, solitary woman in me died when I married.

For me, the death that marriage brought about is small change next to the death that childbearing heralds. I feel grief about losing my old self. I feel afraid of the death and the physical ordeal and the magnitude of the life powers that will soon draw me in. Yet curiously, I am drawn to know more about the fatal sea.

Jung referred to the ocean as "the great primordial image of the mother, who was once our only world."[3] The ocean is the vast and great One. Within that undifferentiated chaos of ocean was born a one-cell amoeba, which multiplied, differentiated; one fine day, some creatures crawled out of the ocean onto land.

In creation myths, the ocean is perceived as the primal source out of which Being emerges. In Sumeria, the Goddess of the primeval sea, Nammu, was worshiped for thousands of years. In Babylonia, the Goddess of the Great Deep, the primordial ocean, was Tiamat.[4] The Canaanite Goddess Asherah was called "The Lady of the Sea," even though she was also an earth Goddess. The Egyptian Goddess Isis was also associated with the generative powers of the ocean, "born in the all-wetness."[5]

I am fascinated to see this ancient symbol of the ocean as the primordial creator of life, the One essence that can transform itself and reproduce life. I had not consciously considered this symbol before now, and yet it surfaced in my unconscious through this dream, through my pregnancy. What is occurring in my personal mind and body is in alignment with an age-old dimension of human experience; mysteriously, the images of the collective unconscious are available in my psyche in a more active way now than I have ever experienced.

The vast chaos of the sea seems to have scared other people besides me. The bottom line is that humans don't really belong in the ocean anymore. We might swim in it, sail on it. But we crawled out of that place a long time ago. The ocean is not where humans live. The ocean hosts the most ancient, primal forces of nature. In the beginnings of our planet, there was the ocean. In its ebb and flow stir the endless possibilities of life and death and regeneration.

As my fate is drawing me nearer to swimming within those primal forces of nature, as I feel the pull of the riptides and glimpse where I am destined, I feel terror. The ocean knows no morals. The ocean will not look upon me with mercy, noting, "She has been a good person, so we will be kind to her in child-birth." The sea is no place of rewards and punishments: it is more primitive than that.

The theme of crawling out of the primal ocean, of conquering the chaotic depths of the sea, is basic in the human psyche. It speaks to our origin as a species, and it speaks to the struggle each individual makes out of the watery darkness of the womb into the light of the external world, out of the watery uncon-scious toward consciousness. There is something touching about this human quest to defy the fatal sea, to conquer the chaotic waters. And yet, developmentally, as valuable and neces-sary as our defiance may be, ultimately the waters of the fatal sea claim victory over each and every one of us.

I am now beginning to understand that a woman is destined not only to get out of the primordial sea but then, later in her life, to go back in, to merge again with the tumbling sea of cre-ation. As Campbell observed, "the power of the tides of life both in the sea and in the womb, is the principle personified in the queen."[6]

I have noticed that my pregnant psyche is now in a different location than it was in earlier pregnancy. The images I had in the first few months of pregnancy centered around being ab-ducted to the underworld. My ego was dragged into death, kick-ing and screaming.

The underworld strikes me as the proper place to be in early pregnancy. It is the place of the dead, and surely the ego of a pregnant woman must die, must be conquered by the forces of nature. The underworld is the place of the ancestors, of the human lineage. As a woman grows a new life in her womb, she must go to the underworld because she is assuming her place in her lineage of ancestors, both past and future. This is a big responsibility. By claiming her place within the family lineage, she fully receives her inheritance and passes it on to the next generation: the family physical traits and the family psychological complexes—all that still sleeps in the family unconscious. She inherits and passes on the familial and the cultural history.

Near the beginning of the second trimester, my psyche moved to the realm of the ocean. Most of my pregnant dreams have been located in the ocean. Often, in these dreams, I am just floating or swimming in warm waters. In waking life, I crave warm waters: heated swimming pools, Palm Springs, especially the gentle beaches of Hawaii. My psyche is close to the sea. Am I floating in the amniotic fluids in identification with my baby? Are these memories of my own beginnings in my mother's womb? Am I being rocked in the warm waters of creation as I become a mother?

Like the ocean, I have watery boundaries, permeable walls of water vaguely separating me from other people and forces. I am liquid, fluid. The fluid in my body is oceanic, salty water like the ocean. Amniotic fluids cushion my baby. The baby and I are floating bodies, sensually moving in water, carried by powerful tides.

I am learning that there are forces in this universe that pull us into them—forces far beyond our control. They draw us in, and we exist within their rhythms, their laws. Perhaps this is always true. We always exist within the forces, but we do not always know it. Maybe we only know it when we are caught off guard by a crashing wave while swimming in the sea, tumbled in a wave so big that it is difficult to determine which direction is up and which is down, and whether our lungs have enough air to make it to the surface. Maybe we only know it when the waves of pleasure sweep us away in love. Maybe we only know it when the waves of labor draw us into their rhythms. But I am beginning to suspect that always we exist within fields of forces that govern us, and any free will that we imagine we possess exists only in the context of these larger force fields.

This dream of the fatal sea is a preview, a trailer of the movie soon to be in my local theater—an introduction, a contemplation. It is not yet time for the birth. At seven months pregnant, it is enough for me to notice that my energy is pulling away from the affairs of the culture, away from newspapers, career, publishing papers—to observe that I am being drawn into the depths of nature. It is enough to begin learning how to surrender.

The final segment of the dream shows me that I had an experience in the depths of the ocean but did not put words to it until the masculine teacher prodded me. With his help, I was able to become conscious of my experience and articulate my knowings. In this pregnancy, my mind and body are openings through which the cosmic energies are pouring. In this time, it is important for me to stay in touch with my male teachers, the ones who ask me what I know, who prod me to pull my knowings into conscious reflection and words.

The male teacher in the dream poses an interesting question, "In the histories of religion, what is the reference to this?"—*this* meaning the descent into the overpowering ocean and the flight back up. Upon waking reflection, it occurs to me that the question in the dream is, How is this referent to the *histories* of religion? Historically, do entire religions do what I did: descend into the deep feminine; peek and get scared, overwhelmed; and retreat back up to the affairs of the culture as presented in newspapers and fast-food hamburger joints?

Ultimately, the answer is "the fatal sea"—to see into our fate, to know that we belong with the mysterious and fascinating powers of birth, death, and regeneration and that, together, we are infinite.

The baby has virtually filled all the available space in the uterus. Most babies turn upside down at some point during the seventh month and then seem to fit more comfortably. By now you may be able to distinguish the baby's bottom from a foot or a knee. When you lie in the bath you can enjoy watching the baby swivel from one side of your abdomen to the other. Foot and knee movements are more jerky than whole-body movements and hands produce soft flutters like sea anemones moving. Other people may now be able to feel the baby kicking when they place a hand on your abdomen.

—Sheila Kitzinger
The Complete Book of Pregnancy and Childbirth,
pp. 68–69

FEELING THIS BABY MOVE INSIDE ME

seven and one-half months pregnant

I WOULD BE HAPPY if I never did another thing in my whole life but lie on my bed, head propped up by pillows, hands on my belly, seeing and feeling this baby move inside me. My baby stretches—slow, sensuous movements, rolling hills across my vast belly. All other reality becomes mute; all I know is the beauty of this creature stirring within me. My baby is alive, is moving. He significantly alters my landscape. I dare to say "he" because, since the third month of pregnancy, I have felt sure this baby is a boy.

I am helpless in the face of his movements, couldn't control them if I wanted to, can only sense him, admire him, love him. I am holding still, yet there is enormous action inside me. A creature who is probably fifteen inches long is moving independently within my body. I've never felt anything that could be compared to this.

I get quiet. And I wait. Like a tourist anticipating Old Faithful: when will the next eruption be? Sometimes, the baby is inert for hours. Sometimes, he just gently stretches and rearranges his position to get a bit more comfortable. Sometimes—usually, when I lie down to sleep—he starts his aerobics class! I can see and feel his body in remarkable detail. Elbow out. Knee up. Kick, kick, kick. During this vigorous exercise, the skin on my belly resembles a wet sheet thrown over a person struggling to get out.

It's quite a peculiar sensation to have something vigorously move from within my body, an autonomous force, not me. I can be completely unprepared for a sudden jolt or a huge rearrangement where my body distends visibly. It's a shock. I think, "Whoa! I didn't do that. Someone else is in here, too." I am learning how to be in my body while another creature also lives here. I am hosting this baby, not yet an independent creature, but one with certain autonomy. Kick, kick, kick.

My body is a theater in the round. I can feel the baby move from the depths of my innards: my bladder, my uterus, my intestines all feel the baby move. I can also sense the baby's movements from outside my skin. Already my hands seem to want to stay close to him; I discover them resting on my belly and caressing him. Suddenly, he pushes up against my hand. I see a series of movements erupt across my belly, the way a trail of earth bulges up while a gopher tunnels below.

This is absolutely marvelous. I don't want to go anywhere or do anything else—just lie still for hours into eternity and feel my baby move.

No one else is quite as captivated by this as I am. Friends may rest their hand on my belly for thirty seconds to feel a movement. My husband will place his hands on my bowling ball belly while we read in bed or watch TV, occasionally shouting, "It moved!" engendering further movements. He doesn't have these sensations in his body thirty times a day, so it probably hasn't sunk into his mind as much as it has mine: we have a live baby in here.

For seven and a half months, my relationship with our baby has been mostly a one-way street. I am the one who thinks of him. I massage him, talk to him, feed him. Mostly, he just lies around in my uterus and grows. But increasingly, he is beginning to relate back to me. He jumps when I scare him. He stirs when he hears my voice. He shows me his elbows and knees. It's wonderful. I yearn to relate to him more. I think of the day when I will hold him in my arms, guide him to my breast. The day when he will look up at me with complete trust and faith, and smile.

The flowing breast is the essential image of trust in the universe. Even the faintest pattern of stars was once seen as iridescent drops of milk streaming from the breast of the Mother Goddess: the galaxy that came to be called the Milky Way.

—Anne Baring and Jules Cashford
The Myth of the Goddess, p. 10

PRACTICING BREAST-FEEDING

eight and one-quarter months pregnant

THREE MORE WEEKS before the baby is due! I am trying to get ready in all the different ways that seem to be required: baby supplies, instructional classes on how to take care of a newborn, mentally rehearsing for a calm and drug-free labor. The spiritual and psychological preparations seem to have taken a backseat to logistical realities. Very soon we're going to have a baby in this house.

In a recent dream, I was practicing breast-feeding. The dream is causing me to reflect on the value of my breasts, and for the first time, I am understanding my breasts as a feminine mystery.

In the dream, I am nursing a baby on my right breast. Finally, it seems as if it is time to switch to the left breast, which I do. But then I remember I should have burped the baby after the first breast. I hold her up against my shoulder, pat her back, and then I remember that gently rubbing the baby's back is enough, you don't need to pat it. As I return to nursing from my left breast, I remember that I'm supposed to position the baby with her tummy and face directly facing my tummy and breast, so that her neck is not twisted as she swallows.

Mother of God! How am I ever going to nurse a baby when I have to remember all these things?

I am troubled that I don't instinctively seem to know how to breast-feed a baby. What have we come to? Why do I have to take a class to learn how to breast-feed? Isn't breast-feeding an instinct, something I should just naturally know how to do? My dog didn't go to La Leche classes, and she nursed her puppies just fine. Are human beings so far away from our instincts that we must cognitively learn these things, rehearsing them in the neocortex until they become second nature? Why don't I just naturally know how to nurse a baby? Will the knowing come to me when I hold a baby in my arms? Am I this dumb because I live in a culture in which nursing is hidden?

I never got to really stare at a woman nursing a baby. I wanted to. I wish somebody would have let me watch up close for a long time and shown me where the milk squirts out, because I still can't see where the holes are in my nipples. I don't have colostrum coming out yet. I'm living on blind faith that my nipples really do have holes and there really will be milk squirting out of them for my baby when he sucks.

I have seen mothers nursing in public or friends nursing in their homes. Almost all of the moms I know breast-feed. Breast-feeding is medically and socially acknowledged as the preferable option for mother and baby because of both the nutritional quality of the breast milk and the beneficial bonding that comes with nursing. This was not true in my mother's generation. My mother defied American social convention to breast-feed her children and had the good fortune to find a pediatrician who supported her. As I think back upon it, I must have seen my mother nurse my two younger brothers, but I can't recall the memory. Even with my close friends, I have been reluctant to ask if I could get close and look at them nursing for a long time. I am drawn toward the nursing couple in fascination yet feel an equally strong compunction to look away.

I have told myself the reason I look away from the nursing couple is to give them privacy. Perhaps that is true, but I also think I look away because I am embarrassed to stare at another woman's breasts, afraid that my curiosity would be interpreted as sexual interest.

God knows we've all noticed each other's breasts, but the facts must be ascertained from quick glances. Small, perky breasts. Cone-shaped breasts. A slight mound with a raisin nipple. Big, pendulous breasts with large nipples that announce themselves through all blouses. A woman's breasts are important—to her and, it seems, to everyone else.

I remember back to my puberty years when my breasts began to develop. I was fascinated and pleased with this change in my body but felt intensely private about it. I was shy and couldn't handle too much attention in general, but I couldn't bear the thought of some boy at school noticing my new breasts. I sheltered my breasts from public view by rounding my shoulders forward, sinking my chest in.

That year, in sixth grade, some special event occurred during which we watched television in our school classroom. Was it the World Series? A commercial came on, advertising the "Cross Your Heart" bra, "lifting and separating." I was mortified at the mention of breasts in school. I wanted to run out of the classroom. All the boys giggled.

My mother and I went shopping to buy a "training bra." That's what everyone called a girl's first bra. I don't know what it's supposed to train the breasts to do. Sit up? I think the training bra is meant to provide cover for the breast, to hide it more than a mere cotton blouse, to disguise the definition of the nipple. I was pleased with my training bra, but that, too, felt very private to me.

Throughout my adult life, I have been astonished at the extent to which most men feel entitled to women's breasts. Many men seem to feel perfectly free to stare at a woman's breasts during conversation. Complete strangers drive by in anonymous cars yelling comments to women walking down the street about their breasts. I have never considered this a compliment. I feel it is an invasion of my privacy. I do not feel free or comfortable in the public domain when men act as if my body is their business. What's wrong with these guys? Don't they have any respect for privacy? I don't stare at a man's penis while I talk to him. I don't drive down the street yelling out my car window, "Nice cock," to strange men.

When I feel my bodily privacy violated, Artemis surges forth in me—Artemis, "Lady of the Wild Mountains." Artemis is the Greek Goddess of untamed nature. She lives in the wilderness, accompanied by deer, birds, and sometimes bears. Self-contained, she lives the wild ways, quite apart from human civilization. Artemis is intensely private, feels violated when she is seen but does not wish to be seen. One day, Acteon, a mere mortal hunting in the wilderness, happened across Artemis while she was bathing naked in a pond. Taken by surprise, seen when she did not intend to be seen, Artemis was enraged. She immediately turned Acteon into a stag. His own hunting dogs did not recognize him and tore him to shreds. This is what Artemis does to those who intrude upon her privacy. Although I lack her magical powers, this is my impulse as well.

In modern America, breasts are celebrated as a sex stimulant for men. Maybe that is part of nature's purpose for breasts, to sexually attract a mate.

There is some fantasy of a perfect breast that Americans pursue. Women buy bras to make their breasts look sexier: black lace, underwire to push up the breasts and make cleavage, padding to make them look bigger, firmer. The quest for the perfect breast—the idealized breast. What are we really wanting?

Women get breast lifts and get surgically implanted silicone pads so they can have large and shapely breasts like twenty-year-old *Playboy* models. This is not an honoring of the reality of breasts, the diversity of breast shapes and sizes, the changing nature of breasts over time. This is some kind of mental fantasy that women are trying to force their bodies to conform to—a fantasy that defies nature and the true nature of breasts. Ironically, all the effort in the quest for the perfect breast does not seem to have led us toward a genuine love or reverence for the breast. Think about the various nicknames people use for breasts: knockers? boobs? titties? These are not names for a revered body part.

On the verge of giving birth to a child, I am entering a new sense about my breasts. Nature's purpose for my breasts is to nourish a new life on earth. My breasts will soon do what breasts are meant to do: fill with milk to be sucked by a baby. In a mystery of transformation, my body will take the best nourishment from the food I eat and convert it into breast milk that is nutritiously perfect for a newborn. As my baby grows older, my body will know how and when to change the fat content of the milk, all perfectly suited to my baby's needs. My mammary glands will work on the law of supply and demand: the more the baby sucks, the more milk they will produce. My breasts are brilliant! I admire them more than ever before. I will be able to feed and comfort my baby from my own body! The flesh of my body will feed the flesh of his body. This is holy communion. This is the One Life Eating Itself. This nourishing, life-giving aspect of breasts feels so right to me. I have never been prouder of my breasts.

How I wish that, as a young teenager, when my breasts began to bud, a group of mothers, including my own mother, in a religious community had marked this event in my life. I wish they had designed a ritual for me and other pubescent girls in which they said:

> Now you are becoming a woman. No longer is your chest flat like a boy's or a young girl's. You are growing breasts, growing into a woman. We welcome you as a woman. Your breasts are the gift of life itself flowing through you. Someday, if you bear a child, your body will transform some of its life into breast milk, feeding the life of your baby. You will nourish another being through your breasts. Your body is joining the body of the life-giving Goddess, the Goddess of Regeneration. This is a sacred

mystery of the female. Its meanings will unfold to you over time. Above all, remember this: your breasts belong to your feminine nature; they contain the magic and the mystery of life itself.

As far back as twenty-seven thousand years ago, breasts were venerated as a central aspect of the Great Mother Goddess.[1] The One Who Gives Life had breasts, and her breasts were numinous, filled with the sacred magic of life and transformation.

Thousands of these Goddess figurines have been excavated in the geographic area between southern France and central Siberia. The parts of the body that are emphasized are the breasts, the vulva, and the buttocks, and with the pregnant figurines, the belly. The breasts are often huge. Many figurines feature the rounded twosome of breasts, counterbalanced by the rounded twosome of buttocks. These are not sexually titillating figurines; they are sacred icons of the creative powers of the feminine, of the Great Mother.[2]

There are beautiful images of the Goddess holding her full breasts, offering her nourishment. There are figurines of Goddesses who are also part animal, such as the Bird Goddess or the Sow Goddess, nursing a baby. Ancient pottery vases shaped as the Goddess—again, often part animal—were designed with holes in the nipples so that milk or other libations could flow out for nourishment.[3] This is an honoring of the reality of breasts. This is an awareness of breasts, particularly the milk-filled breast, as a great and fascinating mystery.

In Ephesus, near the western coast of Turkey, there remains today the ruins of the great temple of Artemis. In this temple was a huge statue of Artemis, blackened like the earth, the ancient color of fertility. Animal heads adorn this figure of the Goddess. All across her torso are multiple rows of breasts. Scholars have debated whether this is Artemis or Cybele[4] and whether these are breasts or beehives, since there are no discernible nipples.[5] To me, these arguments do not alter the fundamental meaning of the statue. These breasts are part of our animal nature, something we female mammals all share. It is through our

Diana of Ephesus (Many-Breasted Artemis). Rome, second
century CE. Museo Archeologico Nazionale, Naples.
Courtesy Alinari/Art Resource, N.Y.

animal instinct that we nurse our young. Through these breasts
comes the honey of life itself, offering abundant nourishment.
This capacity to nourish other life is a divine aspect of the feminine.

My mammalian breasts are living tributes: to the animal nature that dwells in my core, to the body wisdom that is preparing colostrum and milk, to the maternal urge to suckle a baby.

In my dream, the baby I am nursing is a girl. For five months, I have felt so sure that I am carrying a boy baby, and now, at this late date, I am dreaming of a girl! Could I have been wrong for all these months? Is my baby a "she"?

But I must remember that the dream is a statement of the psyche and not necessarily a literal statement of external reality. It is a symbolically crafted story intended to convey a certain meaning. Perhaps it is symbolically necessary for the dream baby to be a girl. The breast is something in and of itself, an aspect of the feminine: to convey this meaning, the psyche shows a girl baby as the recipient of the wonders and pleasures of the breast. The girl baby places breast-feeding in the interior of the feminine psyche, quite separate from the meaning a breast has acquired in the masculine psyche or in male-female relations.

I love the girl in the dream, love the meaning of the breast she helped me find. But I still think I'm carrying a boy.

> [O]urs is the age above all others that has desacralized Nature: generally speaking, the Earth is no longer instinctively experienced as a living being as in earlier times, or so it would seem from the evidence of pollution (itself a term that originally meant the profaning of what was sacred). And now is also the time when the whole body of the Earth is threatened in a way unique to the history of the planet.
>
> —Anne Baring and Jules Cashford
> *The Myth of the Goddess,* pp. xi–xii

This Nest Is Not Safe

nine months pregnant

NATURE HAS COMMANDED ME to make a nest. Instinct has absolutely taken me over. Every cell in my body is oriented toward making a safe nest for my baby. I feel very little choice in this matter. This is nature's version of totalitarian mind control. I can't recall any other time in my life in which I have been so subject to a biological imperative. I must make a safe place for this new life.

I paint the walls fresh white. I wash everything in sight. Tack new lining inside the family bassinet, the same bassinet I lay in thirty-two years ago. I put a cotton flannel sheet on the mattress and arrange blankets. On the wall above the bassinet, I hang a curved ribbon of five small rainbow-colored teddy bears holding hands. This is for the visual stimulation of my baby.

I am attuned to a level of cleanliness and sanitation that exceeds anything I have ever known before. Have I ever in my life scrubbed a floor baseboard? Never. The thought never occurred to me before now. I can see myself, see how ridiculous I am scouring this little house, but I am an automaton, programmed to clean.

I am acutely aware, practically obsessed with preventing potential dangers to my baby. I've bought smoke alarms, a fire extinguisher, a used Volvo. I am helpless in the face of my urges. Nature wants a safe nest so this baby can survive.

I feel so much love, such deep desire to protect this vulnerable new being. I want to straighten up the world, to welcome my baby proudly to the beauty of life on earth. I want everything to be right, to be clean, to be pretty so that I can welcome my beloved to a world that I love. But I see danger everywhere. This is not a safe nest. I know it. I am stricken by this knowledge. I lie across my bed weeping with grief.

Nature is commanding me to do something that I cannot do. My whole body is driven to make a safe nest, but I am cursed with the realization that our little family nest exists within the larger context of our collective nest. Deep in my mother-body, I feel the dangers of our world: the polluted air, toxic oceans, nuclear power plants on earthquake fault lines, guns everywhere, pesticides in the earth, water, and food. These are not intellectual concerns to me now; these are felt threats to my baby. Day after day, I am raw with grief—a grief I can only compare to mourning the loss of a loved one.

I cannot make a safe nest for my baby, and it is torturing me.

How could we have created such a hazardous world for mothers to bring babies into? I hate human beings for messing up this earth. Damn the companies that make the environment toxic because all they care about is profit. Damn testosterone and paranoia and war machines. Damn all of us and our cars for polluting our air and eating away the ozone layer.

I am enraged that my nest is compromised. Do only mothers care about life? Are the mothers supposed to love their babies and grieve sending their grown babies off to war so the rest of the world can go about its manic, greedy, self-serving heroics?

I am working hard to grow a good, healthy baby and to prepare a safe, loving home. I can't go out and clean up the whole world, too. As a mother, I feel abandoned by the human community. Why isn't everybody trying to make the nest safe for babies? Where are the people who will protect the nest? My husband can't do it alone. Where are the other men? Where are the elders? Why isn't everybody guarding the nest, encircling the nest for the babies?

I feel crazed. I want to run down the street, a wild woman in panic, screaming to summon allies, "Please help me! Help me clean up the world for my baby!"

But I just sit in my living room and sob. Nature is commanding me to make a safe nest, and I don't know where to begin. It's too big for me. But I can't go on rearranging furniture and hanging rainbow teddy bears on the wall, pretending that is enough.

I know there are other people who treasure life. I know there are many people working hard to make our planet a safer place for life, now and into the future. I don't know whether the world is a more dangerous place now than it used to be. Certainly, we have the capacity to damage life in large-scale, irreparable ways. Yes, I think the hazards are worse now, the consequences more long-term. It does seem that we live in a world where so very few people consider the consequences of their actions for the life community over time. How many of us practice the seven generation rule: considering the effect our actions will have on the next seven generations?

I fiercely love this life stirring in my belly. In much the same way, I have fallen in love with the life force. The archetype of Mother Earth is intimately connected with my personal feelings as a mother, to the point where I can barely separate them. The harm that comes to any life I feel as though it were harm done to my baby. The human threat to the very foundations of life on this little planet I feel as personal violations of my beloved.

Nature's life insurance policy is motherly love. When it becomes impossible for a mother to protect her young, the maternal instinct gets perverted. When the desire to create a new life, to nourish and love a baby, cannot grow in its natural way, then this instinctual urge gets twisted, ingrown, sick, so that a woman will either choose not to bear a child at all or, in extreme cases, kill her children to protect them.

The instinct to bear new life is already being perverted because of the threats the human community poses to life. I know that many women are choosing not to bear new life because the nest is not safe. I have heard women say, "I will not bring a child into this world because I don't think anybody will want to be here two decades from now." The prospects for a healthy and full life on our planet look so dim to them that they prefer not to bring a child into it. I find this heartbreaking.

For mothers, this is an unbearable double bind. The most basic instinct within us is to create, nurture, and protect new life, and yet humans are creating a planet on which that is increasingly difficult to do. Mother condor lays her eggs. But because of the pesticides she has ingested, her body can no longer make the eggshell strong. Her eggs cannot mature into life, are drawn back into death. What does this do to mother condor? What is it doing to the rest of us?

It came to the attention of the media that those shiny apples most of us eat—one a day keeps the doctor away—are usually large, shiny, and red because they are sprayed with growth-regulating chemicals and coated with wax mixed with fungicides. Certainly, there are thousands of examples of such human stupidity, but what I like best about this one is that it perfectly demonstrates the archetypal double bind of the mother: in offering her child an apple, the Good Nurturing Mother *against her will* becomes the Big Bad Witch: "Here, darling. Eat this apple. (Ha ha ha.)"

Species become extinct almost every day. The human species is not immune. It sounds so dramatic to say. But when you add up radioactive waste, the arms race, ozone depletion, toxic chemicals in groundwater, it is hard to see how the planet can get out of this alive without kicking off human beings.

This bears a particular grief for mothers. For a time, our bodies are aligned with creation. In becoming mothers, we join with the Mother of us all. Her creation is sacred to us. If people want life to continue on this planet, everyone better encircle the nest, stand guard for the work of the mothers, protect the babies, make this a nest that is safe for life.

She is in need of the nurse's presence, and of her power to help in the right way and at the right moment, should something go wrong. But all the same she is in the grip of natural forces and of a process that is as automatic as ingestion, digestion, and elimination, and the more it can be left to nature to get on with it the better it is for the woman and the baby.

—D. W. Winnicott
Babies and Their Mothers, p. 74

BIRTH

ON TUESDAY EVENING, Steve and I went to a Thai restaurant. I felt strange. My consciousness was deep and slow. My senses were so acute that I seemed to be hallucinating: visually, everything looked new and fresh; I perceived intricate detail and movement. When all the senses are this awake, time proceeds slowly, almost hangs still in the air. I was not hungry, but mindful that I needed to keep my body nourished in preparation for labor, I nibbled at a salad with a delicious spicy peanut dressing. The world was alive in each moment, each moment graced in calming beauty.

I warned Steve, "I'm being carried away. I know I will go into labor soon." We finished eating. I drifted out of the restaurant and into our car (which fortunately, Steve was driving), floated home and into bed.

At 4:30 the next morning, I awoke feeling warm fluid running between my legs. Sleepily perplexed, I wondered, am I wetting the bed? Then a bolt of lightning hit my mind: my bag of waters broke! I dashed to the bathroom and sat on the toilet gushing amniotic fluid. The rush of waters and the rush of my psyche reminded me of river rafting when you hit a channel where the rapids propel you into inexorable movement; nothing is possible but to whoosh forward. I felt exhilarated and nervous. I thought to myself, "This is it. This is the moment the last nine months have been leading up to. The time has finally arrived. It is now. Now I will begin the birth process."

For months, this had been my fantasy of how I wanted to begin labor: the breaking of the bag of waters. I wanted this for two reasons. First, I knew it would probably lead to a quick labor. Second, I love the poetic image of rushing waters carrying forth new life. The possibilities of existence have long been swimming in the ocean depths. The first life on earth was borne from the waters. Elements of the oceans still live within our bodies; more than three-fourths of the human body is composed of water. For nine months, my baby lay on a little pillow of cosmic fluids. Now, a surge in the waters is propelling us into birth.

My childbirth books advise a woman to let the husband sleep as long as possible so he will have plenty of energy for a long labor. That always struck me as ridiculous. Still, I decided I'd wait awhile to wake Steve. I needed some time alone to get oriented, to gather my forces toward courage and a steady presence. I began to breathe deeply, to repeatedly open myself to each advancing moment.

Now what? What should I do now that this time has arrived? I stuck a bath towel between my legs like an enormous diaper and waddled into the kitchen to make a cup of peppermint tea with honey so that I, too, would have energy for a long labor. I found my obstetrician's instruction sheet: "What to Do When Labor Begins." It said to call him anytime day or night if the membranes ruptured, so I phoned him at 5:00 AM. He must have had a lot of practice sounding awake and cheerful in the middle of the night. He asked if I was having contractions yet. Not really, just moderate menstrual-type cramps. He said that I would probably enter early labor soon, that I should go to the hospital when the contractions last about a minute and are three to five minutes apart, and congratulations.

From bed, Steve sleepily called to me, "Is everything OK, honey?" I waddled into the bedroom and, barely able to control the surging excitement in my voice, announced, "My bag of waters broke." Steve yelled, "Oh God!" and ducked under the covers. I laughed. I knew a minute later he would be dressed and organizing everything.

At a quarter before six, I had my first contraction. I was standing at the back of the blue and green flowered couch when something grabbed my uterus hard. In turn, I grabbed the back of the couch, staring blankly at a blue and green flower. After about thirty seconds, we both let go. So that's a contraction! Well, if these were going to get more painful, I had better get dressed right away. It didn't really matter what I put on because soon I was going to take it off. I planned to be naked except for a hospital gown while I was in labor. The important part of my ensemble was a pair of earrings. The earrings were brass, with an embossed image of the Greek Goddess Artemis walking in tandem with her totem animal, the deer.

Artemis was the Goddess who helped women during childbirth. The first woman she helped was her own mother, who suffered in labor for nine days: miraculously, as soon as Leto pushed Artemis out of her body, Artemis turned around and aided her mother in the difficult birth of her twin, Apollo.

Artemis lives in the realm of the wilderness, moving freely among the wild animals. She is at home with animal instinct, preferring it to the tamed ways of human civilization. Artemis guides a woman into her instinctive animal body, helps her submit to the knowledge of the body. She does not fear blood, vomit, amniotic fluid, diarrhea. She trusts the ways of the body.

I knew I needed Artemis to help lure me out of my civilized, polite ways into my animal body. I prayed to her for a quick and easy labor and a healthy baby.

One contraction followed another. I was resisting the pain,

trying to brace against it. Just as the books said, the contractions came as waves, building up to a crest of pain and then subsiding. As each new wave came, my attitude was, "Oh no, here comes another one." The pain surprised me. I was astonished by how much energy was shooting through my body.

At 8:20 AM, we headed for Goleta Valley Hospital, less than a mile away. As if we were headed to put out a fire, we got in Steve's Porsche, sped out of the driveway, raced down our lane, and found ourselves square behind a wide-load tractor going two miles per hour!

We checked in at the nursing station, and they showed us to our birthing room. It had pretty wallpaper, a stuffed comfortable chair, one birthing bed, a private shower, and a bathroom. When the nurse examined me, I was 100 percent effaced and three centimeters dilated. Yes! Moving right along! The contractions grew stronger and hurt more, but I felt OK. With each building wave of pain, I opened my throat to make loud primal sounds like someone chanting or perhaps like a cow giving birth. Some-one in my childbirth education class recommended this; it was fun and lessened the pain. Then the fun stopped. It was just pain. "Oh God no," I protested each time a wave came to claim me.

I was doing the Lamaze breathing, trying to remember the different breathing for the different stages of labor. Frankly, when I hit a certain level of pain, exhaling while saying "hee, hee, hee, who" was so ridiculously inadequate that I gave up on that and just did my own deep breathing. I liked the cleansing breaths, exhaling forcefully to clear the tension out of my body. My friend Kate, our labor coach, was with us. I wasn't using any pain-killing drugs. I declined several hospital procedures: I did not want my pubic hair shaved, I did not want an enema, nor did I want an episiotomy. The thought of someone cutting the skin between my vagina and my anus was abhorrent to me.

Throughout the labor, I was conscious and aware, able to say what I needed. I had a focal object: a special object to stare at for concentration during a contraction. I hadn't understood how important the focal object was until I was in labor. Throughout much of the labor, I felt the imminent possibility of exploding into wild chaos. It didn't really matter what the object was; just having one object that I blankly stared at for each contraction kept my mind harnessed to the task. Unfortunately, my object was placed on a metal table that was mounted on wheels. In the middle of one contraction, a nurse unknowingly wheeled my focal object out of the room. I panicked and yelled at her and almost fell into the abyss. She didn't understand what I meant, so I quickly settled on a new, more stable focal item: the corner where the two walls met by the ceiling. That's what I stared at while I bellowed.

Steve was very loving and right beside me the whole time. At about 10:20 AM, Steve comforted me, saying I was doing great. Pathetically, I said, "I feel I can't go on." I heard those words with an eerie detachment: the woman who said those words was different from the woman who heard those words. I didn't really feel that way. Then I realized, "Oh, that sounds like something a woman in transition would say." I guess the head nurse thought the same thing because she said, "I think we better check her." Sure enough, in two hours, I had dilated from three to nine centimeters! Yes! It was a fast labor and very intense. The urge to push was beginning. My obstetrician was not on duty that morning, a real disappointment to me. His stand-in showed up in my labor and delivery room wearing street clothes, chirpily inquiring, "How are we doing?" The last thing I needed in the room was a Boy Scout. Coldly, I commanded him, "Suit up."

There were two nurses with me, plus Kate and Steve. The nurses were friendly and introduced themselves by their first names; this in contrast to the obstetrician, who announced himself as Dr. Smith. He examined me, looked at the nurses' report, and then went out into the hall to read a book. That annoyed me. Why were all the people who had first names in the room doing the hard work, when the person who was doing the least claimed the most esteemed title? I noticed the nurses also resented him. What the hell, I mused, I'm the only person in this room in a position to do something about this inequity. The next time the obstetrician came in to check on me, I said with authority, "Ralph, can you load the camera? We need someone to load the camera." He obliged, and we all felt better.

For two hours, I pushed. I wasted one whole hour pushing as if I was windsurfing, holding onto a bar and squatting. I went nowhere, and it hurt like hell. Then I lay on my side to push. I needed someone to push against my foot as hard as I was pushing, a counterforce so my foot wouldn't cramp. Maybe it would have been better for my foot to push against a wall or something solid. I was afraid to push as hard as I needed to. I was afraid my insides would push out.

I felt so discouraged. My mind landed on a memory of a photograph of me at about age seven sitting on concrete steps, bare knees together, feet apart, elbows planted on my knees, hands supporting my face, which was set in cloudy, pouting anger. I was mad. I wasn't going to be cooperative and nice anymore. I wanted to quit—to get up off that bed and say, "Look, I tried. I can't get this damned baby out, and I'm sick of this pain so I'm leaving. Somebody else can do it."

Even though I didn't say a word, my labor coach saw it in me. She tried to encourage me, saying, "No one else can get that baby out. You have to do it." The head nurse also saw my emotional reality. She brought her face about two inches from my face, eyeball to eyeball, and said sternly, "Push!"

I heard that head nurse, but I did not acknowledge her. I wasn't going to be nice to her after she said that to me. She was right, and I knew it, but I hated her right then. Also, I suddenly understood that I had to pull all my energy and focus inside myself, that I couldn't afford at this point to give anything to anyone else in the room. I realized I had been pushing the same way that I try to open a stubborn lid on a jar while someone else is in the kitchen: try a little bit, but if it's too hard, just look inept and the other person will take over. I realized how much of my life I look as if I'm trying but I'm not really trying as hard as I can.

So there I was with a big baby stuck in my uterus or vaginal canal or wherever he was, and there was no way out but to go into the pain and the terror and push. I had to do it myself. I closed my eyes to summon everything inside me, to bring it all down into my dark belly, all forces pushing the baby out. The pressure in my vaginal canal was almost intolerable. I could feel my labia tearing one place and then another as the baby was coming down, but I only noticed it. I no longer considered the pain as an excuse to quit.

My labor coach coaxed, "Help this baby out. Come on now, pretty soon you're going to have a baby in your arms." Huh! I didn't care about any baby. I was in pain, and I wanted out. I accepted my fate that pushing was the only way for me to get out of pain. My pubic bone was under such pressure I feared it would shatter. I thought, "So be it. Let it shatter. I need to get this over. I don't even care if I die. I just need it to be over."

Kate cried, "You can see the baby's head!" Steve moved near my hips to watch the baby being born. Someone held a mirror up for me to see. I looked briefly, but I couldn't do what I needed to do if any of my energy was externalized. I needed my eyes closed, bringing all my focus and strength inside me, pushing the baby out. Besides, I felt in a flash of annoyance, *Why do I need to look? I know exactly where the baby is.* The head came out. I moaned softly, "Oh, thank God thank God thank God." I took another breath and pushed the body out. Someone exclaimed, "It's a boy."

The two more important things to me right then were: (1) it's a baby, and (2) it's out! He gasped for air and cried. In that brief, crucial moment of his evolution, he ceased being an ocean creature, wiggled onto land, and sucked air into his lungs for the first time.

Time suspended, hanging in midair. I gazed upon this creature lying skin to skin across my belly and breast. Just inches away from where he had lived for nine months, yet for him, I imagined it might as well have been a different planet. My arms cradled a pink, scrunched-up, fat worm with frog legs and big

The Aztec Goddess Tlazolteotl giving birth to the Sun God.
Pre-Columbian. Courtesy of Dumbarton Oaks Research Library
and Collections, Washington, D.C.

eyes gazing at me with faith and trust, infinitely open in that moment. Our beautiful baby Jesse! I was in deep peace and joy. My hands gently massaged his soft skin, rubbing the white vernix in like lotion. I kissed and nuzzled his soft head where it wasn't covered by the funny hat to keep his head warm. I cooed love talk to him. I held his little foot in the palm of my hand.

Steve was awestruck. His face looked beautiful. He sat beside me, looking both radiant and stunned. He said a lot of nice things to me about what a good job I did and about our baby. I became extremely overwhelmed. I wanted a sip of juice, but so much was happening in my internal experience that it seemed hours before I actually reached for the cup and drank.

Then someone told me I had to push out my placenta. Oh no, I was in no mood to push any other things out of me. To my surprise I felt a wonderful sensual pleasure and relief as my placenta easily slid out of me. I asked to see the placenta. It was so big! It looked like a huge steak. I asked the nurses to save it for me in the refrigerator. That big organ grew for the sole purpose of nourishing Jesse. Now that its lifework was finished, I wanted to give it a respectful burial.

The doctor began to sew up my very torn perineum. Steve held our baby while I was being sewn up. I could barely tolerate anyone touching my vagina or any more pain. I hissed loudly to Steve, "Tell that doctor to get out of my vagina." The doctor seemed happy when he was able to leave, but he couldn't have been as happy as I was. Even though I already had blankets over me, my legs began trembling, and soon my entire body was trembling and cold. The nurses laid more warm blankets over Jesse and me. It was important to me that my skin be in contact with his skin, so that my body could fully communicate with his body. He nursed for a few minutes on each breast. I even had colostrum flowing from my breasts. We did it!

I examined every centimeter of my baby. His hands were huge, his toes long. He was twenty-one inches in length and weighed eight pounds twelve and a half ounces! So that's why it hurt so much to push him out. He had a big squished-down nose. Most striking of all was how old he looked. He looked like a little seventy-year-old Jewish mystic. More precisely, it wasn't so much that he looked that way, it was simply apparent that that's who he was. Prior to seeing Jesse, I never thought about a soul as being young or old, but it was immediately obvious that Jesse was an old soul. His eyes were wide open, open to seeing me. In my life, I don't think I've ever looked into eyes so without prejudgment, so open to what existed in the moment. We looked into each other for a long time.

Steve began making telephone calls to announce the birth. Steve called my mother and father first. I wanted to talk with them, but mostly I just cried into the phone. I cried because my mom and dad comforted me after my painful ordeal. I got to become a baby while they comforted me. I cried because of the poignance of this primal life event: a new life came upon earth, and it came out of my body. I became a mother. My parents became grandparents. The first member of the next generation in our family was born. I felt more than I've ever felt in my whole life.

The essence of birth overpowers an individual. In the Bible, there are stories warning that a human being cannot look directly at God: the light is too bright for human eyes to witness; the person will be blinded. A human being cannot look directly into the face of the Divine. My brain waves went flat. I had seen too much, felt too deeply into the mystery, been singed by the fire of creation. I needed to lie in bed alone and not speak.

Sometime later (was it an hour or two hours?), I discovered I could barely walk. I felt as if I'd been hit by a Mack truck. My whole body was sore, but especially my pelvis and crotch were traumatized from the birth, the tearing, and the stitches. When I urinated for the first time, I nearly fainted from the burning and stinging from urine in the lacerations of my labia.

Jesse had been in the nursery, where they bathed him, put in eyedrops, gave him a shot of vitamin K, and I'm not even sure what else. I think he slept in the nursery while I slept in my room. When the nurses brought Jesse back to me, he did not seem familiar. To tell the truth, I might not have known him from any other baby. It's confusing to have all those babies in the hospital. The nurses could have brought in anyone. He seemed like a stranger to me. How could this be? I felt so close to him during our pregnancy. Who had I been close to all that time? I felt shocked and embarrassed that I didn't feel immediate recognition and familiarity with him. I remembered having read that many women feel some sense of strangeness or distance, especially with their first baby, lasting into the first few weeks of life.[1] That was reassuring. I intensely wanted to know him. I held him and cooed to him and experimented with different ways of holding and comforting him—playing mother. But it wasn't all that natural. I didn't just immediately feel intimate with him and didn't immediately know how to be with him.

I had learned how to be with my baby when he lived on the inside of me. I had become very comfortable and confident with that arrangement. But I didn't really know how to be with him now that he was living outside of me.

More important to me than anything else, I wanted him to feel welcomed to life on earth. I wanted to receive him here on this blue planet, with gentle and open love to help ease this vast transition for him. I wanted to be his safe harbor, his comfort. I wanted to be his mother. But it was about as new for me as it was for him. Together, we were going to have to learn to be mother and baby.

AND FURTHERMORE, I TOLD SUSAN

one-day-old baby

THE DAY AFTER Jesse was born, my friend Susan brought flowers to me in the hospital. Stylishly dressed with a silk blouse tucked into a tailored skirt, nylons and heels, her hair coiffed, lipstick and mascara applied, physically prepared for her professional day at the office, Susan was a far sight from me. In her no-nonsense manner, she plunked herself down on the chair next to my bed and said, "Well, how was it? I know I can count on you to tell me the truth about childbirth."

I gingerly crept out of bed for my opening statement. I parted my robe to reveal a giant saggy slump of a stomach, bearing an uncanny resemblance to a basketball, half out of air. No one ever mentioned that I would look six months pregnant *after* childbirth. Susan looked, looked horrified, then quickly buried her eyes in both hands, shaking her head, protesting, "Oh God." This is why I love Susan. She's willing to acknowledge how truly bad things are.

I had a few things to say about childbirth. I was glad she asked. I was mad as a hornet. "Women don't tell the whole truth," I told Susan. "We lie to ourselves, and we lie to each other."

No woman, personally or in the dozens of books I had read, adequately conveyed the terror, excruciating pain, and trauma of childbirth. They called it nice names like "hard work." They pretended that that stupid little breathing exercise saying "hee, hee, hee, who" addresses the reality of a contraction. They assured us that, the minute the baby is born, all pain is forgotten in the bliss of being united as mother and child. And they live happily ever after.

Did anybody say that I would feel traumatized in ways so deep that I had no idea how to begin dealing with it? Did anybody say that my body would be so torn and ravaged that I could barely walk? Did anybody say that my nipples would be so sore from being sucked on that I would wince in pain each time my baby latched on? Did anybody say that I would have contractions *again* while the baby nursed? Well, gee, they forgot to say that.

That afternoon in the hospital, I told Susan that, for the first time in my life, I felt betrayed by women. I was angry, and I did need to talk, but I had a complication. Because of the third-degree tear in my vagina and perineum, the mere possibility of a bowel movement terrified me. To assuage my fears, I took the maximum dosage of stool softeners prescribed by my doctor. In between several urgent trips to the toilet, I told Susan about the conspiracy of silence among women. The only woman I could think of who was forthright about childbirth was the ancient Greek Medea, "They say that we have a safe life at home, whereas men must go to war. Nonsense! I had rather fight three battles than bear one child."[1]

Isn't it eerie that virtually all women act as if childbirth isn't all that bad? Why is that? It's as if all mothers got together and formed a pact: "OK, it's so traumatic that we'd better not tell anybody else, or else women will be too afraid to get pregnant. Our party line will be that it hurts at the time, but you can manage it and it's well worth the rewards." Have they figured it's better for new mothers just to face the reality when they come to it? Why worry them ahead of time? Or is it like so many other aspects of women's lives that are painful and traumatic: we pretend for the world that everything is OK. I told Susan something she already knew: that women are disgustingly, pathologically nice and cheerful, not to mention liars.

No. Wait a minute. This conspiracy idea is off the deep end. New mothers are too isolated and too exhausted to organize a conspiracy. The silence must be ordered from the depths of the unconscious. This must be a conspiracy masterminded by the Great Mother Goddess. Yes, that is much more likely. The Great Mother knows full well that if women knew of the pain ahead of time, or remembered the full truth about childbirth from their past experience, babies would be in short supply. In the interest of perpetuating the human race, she determined that a code of silence must be kept: no woman can utter the truth about child-birth. It must be kept a mystery that you can only perceive when you are in the throes of contractions. With her magical powers, the Great Mother forces women into silence after birth. Postpartum women are speechless from the mystery, so exhausted they can't talk or think, overwhelmed with the task of taking care of a baby, and flooded with love for the baby. The Great Mother creates amnesia, probably administered through the hormones, so that women forget the pain of childbirth.

Weren't all the mystery religions based upon essential life truths that we glimpse into momentarily but forget most of the time? A mystery is by definition shrouded—at best only partly perceived, half revealed and half concealed. In the ancient secret cults, hidden from daily life and public view, initiates were shown the mysteries.

These spiritual mysteries were secrets for several reasons. First, initiates were bound to strict secrecy by their cults. They were assured that the Gods and Goddesses would punish those who spoke the mysteries out loud. Through a Homeric hymn, we learn that, in the ancient Greek Eleusinian Mysteries, if one dared to tell of the mysteries, her tongue "was checked by death." This is analogous to the biblical mandate that you could not utter the name of God out loud.

On a different level, it seems to me that the secrets are mysteries because, if you don't directly experience them, you can't understand them. If you don't have the actual direct experience that "God is love," for example, how can you know what it means? If you don't personally experience the great and terrifying mystery of being in the eye of creation, then how could anybody possibly explain it to you? Are women silent because there are spiritual realities permeating childbirth that simply cannot be conveyed through words, cannot possibly be known unless you experience them firsthand?

But perhaps our forgetting is a just a paltry fact of biological life. Amnesia is nature's way of getting women to get up and do it again. All I know is that I don't want to forget the pain. I want to remember what is true. I might be nature's slave, but I don't want to be nature's stupid slave. I know nature wants me to forget the pain so that I will have more children. But I want to remember the pain, and in light of it, I may or may not choose to have more children. I will fight nature for the right to remember the pain and the right to choose whether I do this again.

Maybe I'm a wimp. Maybe childbirth isn't this hard for most women. Maybe they feel more joyous afterward. Maybe their pain is erased by the pleasure of their baby. But why should I try to shame myself out of my own feelings? I need to deal with what was and is true for me.

Why was this birth so traumatic to me? It was my first birth. I didn't really know what I was doing, and my body had never stretched like that before. My labor was brief compared to most first labors, a total of only seven hours. The contractions came so close together, I barely had enough time to get my mind centered again. I read somewhere that, when the contractions come one on top of another, the uterus doesn't have enough time to get fully oxygenated again, which increases the pain.[2] Also, I bore a big baby. And I was afraid. I know I resisted my animal body. I know my muscles in my pelvis were tense, fighting against the contractions, making them more painful. The part of the labor when I was pushing was the most difficult for me. I was afraid to let my body fully push, afraid my body would push itself inside out.

Perhaps I was wrong to try to be heroic by refusing pain-relieving medication. My mother had advocated a shot of Demerol, saying that that had worked well for her in childbirth. But thirty-two years later, we know that Demerol can depress the newborn's respiration and can slow the infant's responses for weeks.[3] Many of my friends have used the epidural block, the pain reliever of choice for my generation. The good news about the epidural is that the mother is awake and alert, but the bad news is that she loses sensation in the lower part of her body, making it difficult for her to help push or to adjust her pushing. Consequently, there is increased use of forceps deliveries with the epidural block. Also, when the anesthesia enters the baby's bloodstream, it can alter the heart rate and central nervous system and slow bodily functions.[4] Studies have shown that, for a short while after birth, these "epidural block" babies have less muscle tone and strength than nonmedicated babies.[5] The bottom line is that every possible kind of pain reliever presents some risk to the health of the baby. I have been quite clear that if my baby was harmed by my choice for pain relief, I couldn't forgive myself.

But I was harmed by the pain, and it's difficult to live with that, too. I feel traumatized. I'm in no mood to go to the romantic candlelight champagne dinner for new parents that the hospital puts on. I don't know who thought of that idea. Nursing mothers shouldn't be drinking champagne. This fantasy of a romantic dinner eludes me. Anyway, the dining area is far down at the other end of the hall, and I'm not convinced I could get there without a wheelchair.

I know that plenty of other women throughout the world give birth without pain medication. In Holland, only about 5 percent of all mothers use pain-relieving drugs, whereas across the channel in England, nearly 80 percent are medicated.[6] It must be that cultural attitudes are a factor: how a society feels about a woman's body, about birth, and about pain certainly would affect a woman's subjective experience of her birthing.

There was a popular theory after World War II that birth pain exists because we are alienated from our instincts, because modern women fight the animal body while giving birth.[7] Subscribers to this fantasy believe that, in primitive cultures, women give birth without pain. This is a complex issue to sort out. I do believe that fighting the animal body adds to the pain of birth. It seems that the more a woman can assent to her body's wisdom, the more she can agree to ride the waves of contractions, the less pain she will have. On the other side of the argument, the distinguished English pediatrician Aidan Macfarlane declares that ". . . observation of people still living in primitive societies around the world appears to show that there is no culture in which childbirth is painless, and in many cultures women have a much worse time than in our own."[8]

From accounts in the Hebrew scriptures, we are assured that women experienced pain in birth several thousand years ago. In the book of Genesis, because Eve ate fruit from the forbidden tree of knowledge of good and evil, God punished all women: "I will greatly multiply your pain in childbearing; in pain you shall bring forth children."[9] At first glance, this story seems reflective of the kind of spiteful God that one might not want to know. But when the story is heard as a myth, as a metaphor, it carries a different message. *It is because of Eve's consciousness, her knowledge of good and evil, that she is condemned to suffer during childbirth.* This ancient assertion is remarkably similar to the modern argument that human women suffer during birth because we no longer dwell solely in the unconscious field of instinct.

Among the Hebrew people, a woman was deemed unclean after childbirth for forty days in the birth of a boy and eighty days in the birth of a girl. This idea that women were unclean after birth was shared by the ancient Greeks, Zoroastrians, and Arabs.[10] Some people have no gratitude at all. To think of all that women go through to conceive, carry, bear, and nourish a new member of the human race, only to be judged as carriers of original sin and ritually unclean. Talk about sour grapes. What an insidious way to turn the table on the power of the feminine.

If we think about evolution, and the natural selection of successful qualities in species, then why would pain associated with childbirth have survived if it were not somehow biologically useful? In other words, what is nature's purpose in having pain during birth?

The only research I know that sheds light on this was conducted by a South African natural scientist named Eugene Marais. He observed that, for animals lower on the evolutionary chain, reproduction is simple and painless, whereas in more highly evolved, complex animals, birth is accompanied by pain. More highly evolved animals have two other accompanying biological factors: fewer births and newborns who are more dependent on the mother.[11]

To explore a hypothesis he had, Marais conducted an experiment with a herd of deer. In fifteen years of observation of this herd, it was established that, following normal births, the mothers always cared for their newborns. Marais medicated ten of the pregnant deer during their labor and delivery, making them either partly or fully unconscious. Soon after birth, they recovered consciousness, but every single deer mother refused to care for her baby. A different group of deer were not drugged during labor and delivery, but Marais rendered them unconscious for a half hour after the birth: once these deer regained consciousness, they tended their young.[12]

From his research, Marais surmised that the experience of

pain in the process of birth is biologically important. He concluded that, among higher animals, "birth pain is the key which unlocks the doors to mother love. Where pain is negligible, mother love and care are feeble. Where pain is absent, there is absolutely no mother love."[13]

That research and his conclusions have some awesome implications. For starters, it would be wise to wonder how similar human women are to female deer. Is it possible that the practice of using pain relievers during labor and delivery hinders the instinctive bonding of mother and baby? I don't know. I personally have known many women who used pain medication during birth and who have loved their babies passionately from day one. And through my own experience of feeling traumatized by the pain of birth, I have to wonder whether my trauma hindered my flood of love for my baby. A fair amount of my libido is caught up in licking my own wounds, leaving less available to love my baby.

Is pain a necessary part of the initiation into motherhood? In all initiations, there is some level of ordeal, some depth of fear or pain that must be confronted before the treasure is earned. Is the pain one of the ways that nature creates a mother? I don't know whether I love my baby more because I went through such an ordeal to get him.

Social psychologists would talk about this as "effort justification": that we invest more value in anything that we work hard to get. We have to justify the effort of nine months of discomforts, bodily contortions, and worry, so therefore, we adore our babies.

There are other possible reasons that pain could be useful biologically. No woman ever went to sleep during labor and delivery; the pain keeps us mentally alert and sustains our energy during an exhausting physical process.

It all gets even more complex when we hear that difficult-to-believe fact: not all women experience pain in childbirth. Estimates vary that between 3 percent and 14 percent of all women have "totally painless births."[14]

Certainly, different individuals experience pain in different ways. People have different thresholds of pain. Part one of pain is the physical sensation of the nerves sending messages to the brain, and that varies from person to person. Part two of pain is how the brain interprets the messages.[15] What mental sets does an individual bring to the experience: is a mother anxious, fearful that she will die in labor as her grandmother did?

I know that my childbirth preparation classes helped me immensely in dealing with my pain. Knowing the physiology of childbirth, the order of early labor, active labor, transition, and pushing was very helpful in terms of feeling in control, keeping track of where I was in the process. Like a road map. "Oh, we're here now." Reassuring. Understanding the physical aspects of labor gave me a sense of active participation rather than just a passive feeling that "Oh, my God, this horrific thing is happening to me."

I wonder, what do we expect of childbirth? What did I expect? It used to be that one's highest expectation was to emerge with a living baby and a living mother. Now that affluent societies have mostly moved beyond that issue, we want designer births: pretty wallpaper, the right music, the husband cutting the umbilical cord. I don't want to be too flip about designer births, because it was important to me to be specific about how I wanted to give birth and how I wanted my baby treated. Many women are now able to have expectations regarding childbirth that far exceed the survival issues of our ancestors and our less affluent sisters in today's world. Perhaps expecting a birth without pain, without trauma, may be too entitled, too yuppie-ish.

Birth is an enormous transformation for mother and child. The mother's cervix expands from an opening the size of a Cheerio to practically the circumference of a CD-ROM. The cervix softens, thins. The uterus has to squeeze repeatedly to push the baby down through the open cervix, down the vagina, which is three times larger than it's ever been before. The labia bulges open from the pressure. And we expect this isn't going to hurt?

On a psychological and spiritual level, isn't there always some pain to work through, some old karma that needs to be burned off in order for a woman to open her consciousness to larger vistas, to open wide and channel the forces of life? As I think about being in labor, I see how the barrier blocking my progress was the way I hold back from making a full effort. I had to burn through my pouting anger, my reluctance to completely engage my power, evolving to a place where I could summon my full forces to push the baby out. That psychological karma had to be pushed through before I could give birth. I had to give birth to something new in myself before I could give birth to my baby.

What an amazing, mind-boggling, torturous experience it is to push out a baby. How many times will I need to review the birth and tell other people about it before it is able to settle in my mind and body? I'm not so angry after my talk with Susan. She was willing to hear everything.

But don't get me wrong: I still think the Great Mother Goddess tricks women. She tricks us into forgetting the trauma or at least minimizing it as time passes—"Gee, it wasn't really so bad . . ."—so she can continue using women's bodies to bear the next generation. I have vowed never to forget the truth about childbirth, and furthermore, I broke the conspiracy of silence: I told Susan.

In traditional cultures, "home" is a sacred symbol capable of transforming chaos into cosmos and engendering personal wholeness.

—Kathryn Allen Rabuzzi
Encyclopedia of Religion, p. 441

Coming Home

three-day-old baby

EVEN THOUGH I do not at all feel I have the energy, confidence, or expertise to go home, my insurance company has declared this hospital stay over. Today, they sent me home. My grandmother's generation stayed in the hospital for two weeks after childbirth. Strictly from the standpoint of the mother's needs, having two weeks of institutionalized support seems like a good idea to me. I can barely take care of my own needs: getting up to go to the toilet, changing my sanitary pads, eating, showering. Now my milk has come in and my hormones are surging, so that I cry about twelve times a day. And if all that weren't enough, I also have a baby! I nurse him, burp him, change his diaper. I am getting to know him. I clean his umbilical stump and tend his circumcision wound. All these tasks seem enormous but possible under the supervision of the nurses at the hospital. How will I ever manage at home?

This morning, for the first time ever, I dressed Jesse, preparing him for our journey home. Our friends had given us a soft blue baby sweater with matching booties and hat prior to the birth, and this was the outfit I packed for the baby to wear home from the hospital. I've never dressed a baby before. As a child, I rarely spent time dressing dolls. I don't even do all that well dressing myself. Some women have a natural talent for what clothes go with each other, how to accessorize an outfit, but this is not a talent with which I am blessed.

It seemed like hours that I was trying to stuff amorphous baby arms into amorphous baby sleeves. It's not that easy to put on a baby's booties when his feet are kicking all around. Finally, I completed the job. I assessed my creation from head to toe: a blue knit hat covered the head of a wrinkled seventy-year-old Jewish-mystic baby; a blue sweater was laced closed only at the neck, exposing a bare chest and tummy; a scabby stump hung from his belly button; white disposable diapers segued into bare legs and feet covered by blue knit booties. The nurses kindly suggested that we put his hospital gown underneath the sweater. Of course, this meant that I had to take off the sweater, put on the gown, and then put on the sweater all over again.

About forty-five minutes later, the baby and I were dressed. Then we had to pack all our supplies: three bags of diapers; menstrual pads the size of bed mattresses; my hospital barf bowl, which fortunately was unused; a blue striped cotton hat for Jesse; a blue rubber syringe bulb to clear mucous from his nose; and other essentials. I walked out of the hospital door twenty-five feet toward our car, ever so slowly and carefully, trying to avoid the pain of my stitches, trying to make sure I did not drop the baby.

Steve unlocked the doors of our new used Volvo station wagon. In the center of the backseat was the baby car seat. I placed Jesse in the car seat and buckled it. Jesse cried and fussed because he didn't like that. Something was wrong. The belts on the car seat were way too big for him. While Jesse was crying and slumping in the car seat, Steve and I tried to figure out how to make the belts shorter. We finally realized that the belts were set for a toddler, not a newborn, but neither of us had any idea how to fix them. Exhausted, finally I just stuffed some receiving blankets between Jesse and the baby car seat belts, seat-belted myself next to him, and asked Steve to drive the half mile home.

We pulled into our driveway. The mere sight of our home made me cry. Home. The place I go in the world where I can be exactly who I am. The place I rely on for being loved and accepted. The place I go for getting away from a world that sometimes asks more of me than I want to give or that criticizes me. The place of refuge, comfort, ease. The place that has my smells, my pillow, the kind of food I like.

The many meanings of home washed over me as I sat in the car, overwhelmed. Not only was I coming home, but I was coming home in a way that would permanently alter my sense of home. Our home would never be the same again. For the first time, we were welcoming our baby into our home, into what would become his home. The certain smells would soon provide deep comfort to him. The colorful ribbon of teddy bears hanging above his bassinet, over time, would warm his heart each time he saw them. The self that he would grow would become rooted in this weave called home: emotional tones, ways of touching, smells, sounds, psychological complexes. I sat immobilized in the backseat, tears streaming down my face, profoundly touched by this occasion of bringing our baby into our home.

Steve got Jesse and me out of our seat belts. Again, ever so carefully, I carried Jesse, navigating the uneven sidewalk leading up to our front door. We crossed the threshold, and once inside, I collapsed in an overstuffed chair, exhausted, weeping, but Jesse securely in my arms. I did it. I brought a baby home!

Steve tentatively took a seat on the edge of the flowered couch, witnessing my state with concerned equilibrium. I looked at him. I looked at the print flowers on the couch next to him, flowers that I had stared at just three days ago when I was gripped by contractions. I looked at Jesse. I cried harder. Then it happened. The unmistakable sounds of a big, loose bowel movement. We froze. Steve's eyes widened and met mine.

We both giggled nervously, then Steve took charge, getting up to find the diaper-changing area, reassuring himself and me with his monologue, "It's OK, we can take care of this. How hard can it be? Where are the diapers? We have cloth diapers?

They're huge! They're not even folded! It's just like a towel. How do you put them on? Do you know how to fold them? You have to use pins? Where are the pins? Oh, my God, what if we poke the baby?"

"Oh, my God," he exclaimed, collapsing back onto the flowered couch, "we don't even know what we're doing!"

We started laughing, a little bit hysterically. Laughing, crying—it was all the same to me. I was leaking feelings everywhere. Then came divine intervention. The Gods and Goddesses looked upon us and had mercy. There was a knock at the front door. There stood our friend Shira, a seasoned mother of two, holding a dish of baked lasagna. "Shira," we each yelled, our desperate voices tripping over each other to reach her first, "Shira, come in!"

Many women in our society have no experience of babies and some have never had a newborn baby in their arms before. They are anxious that they will not know when the baby is hungry, that they will drop or drown it in the bath, that they will never be able to stop it crying or that the baby who is not crying has stopped breathing. New mothers are often too ashamed to talk about such feelings and may even repress recognition of them.

—Sheila Kitzinger
The Complete Book of Pregnancy and Childbirth, p. 371

What If He Dies

four-day-old baby

What a disastrous first night at home. I can't sleep. What if I'm not watching him and he dies? This is not just a game or some assignment where it doesn't make that much difference if we fail. This is a real, live, brand-new, baby human being who could die if we do something wrong. I feel a heavy responsibility, but I don't feel competent to meet it. What if I don't feed the baby often enough? What if the baby has some terrible pain or illness and I don't know why he's crying? People say babies need to cry, but shouldn't we be wondering why they are crying? That's one of their few means of communicating with us.

I can barely believe that people receive so little education for such a profound life responsibility. I studied for three years after college to prepare to be a minister. To become licensed as a Marriage, Family, and Child Therapist, I had to have a master's degree and three thousand hours of clinical experience, plus pass a written and oral exam. But no education was required for me to become a parent. Out of my own desire, I read a lot of books and took classes: an exercise class for pregnant women, a class in preparation for labor and birth, a breast-feeding class, a "how to care for your baby" class during which I put a disposable diaper on a doll and did other things that seemed absurd at the time but turned out to be helpful. All told, this would be roughly equal to one semester of college-level education. Now I am entrusted with a very new human life, a baby who is almost completely dependent on my ability to care for him. I'm scared to death. I have ample room to make a fatal mistake.

I would have known a lot more about caring for a baby if I lived in a village community. I would have a lifetime of experience to draw upon, living closely with pregnant women, holding other women's newborn babies, helping to dress and care for their babies. But in modern America, we live isolated in single-family homes. We have privacy. Consequently, I am now forced to rely only on my experience from when I was five years old helping my mother with her youngest baby, coupled with a few informational classes. This is crazy. This isn't adequate preparation. Maybe each pregnant woman should be in a mentor relationship with a new mother. The pregnant woman could get a feel for what is to come, and the new mother could have some help. I would feel much more assured now if I had more hands-on experience with a baby.

I can't possibly sleep. What if he suddenly dies in his sleep? Some babies do that. This tiny creature lies in the bassinet that I lay in when I was a baby and that my three brothers lay in when they were babies. We all lived. But last night, as I lay in bed, Jesse's bassinet an arm's length away, every fifteen minutes I got anxious about whether he was still alive, so I had to sit up to see whether he was still breathing. I laid my hand on his back to make sure it was moving. I stuck my finger in front of his nostrils to feel the air coming out. He made it through our first night at home, but how can I keep this up? I'm delusional from lack of sleep.

The problem is this: nine months ago, he didn't exist. Now,

abracadabra, here he is—a baby. Those nine months he was alive only because my body kept him alive. Even though this belief is not entirely rational, I think that if I don't keep him alive, he will die. It's hard to cut that mental umbilical cord. I'm not confident that he's really alive yet. I am afraid that, if I relax, he will die. Actually, it is true that his aliveness is deeply dependent on my awareness of him, breast-feeding, holding, and loving him. But I can't find the right balance in my mind for paying intricate attention to him and yet being able to forget him in my sleep.

I'm not used to having a baby. There have been a few moments when I completely forgot about him. What if I forget about him for very long? What if I got in my car to go grocery shopping and forgot him?

I don't know how to do this mother and baby thing with our bodies separated. Over the last nine months, I learned to trust that, when our bodies are connected, they know what to do and it works fine. During my nap time today, I brought Jesse into bed with me. He slept next to me, occasionally connected at the nipple. This way, I figure, he will not die. My heart beats and my lungs inhale and exhale, reminding his body to do the same in case his body forgets for a moment. He can nurse whenever he wants. I can always hear him cry. I can rest when I feel his body. It is a huge step for both of us that he is living on the outside of my body now. I'm not ready yet to have him be three feet away. Just being on the outside of my skin is about all the separation I'm ready for now.

Why should a baby all of a sudden become so separate from his mother? This strikes me as a peculiar custom. Not all cultures do this. In many other cultures, women "wear" their babies for months, in a sling or strapped to their backs, and they sleep with their babies. I suspect that my agitation about being separate from my baby is not only neurotic fear but that there is some instinctive base to it. I suspect that nature wants me to feel agitated when I am not with my baby, wants me to still be touching, holding, body to body with my baby.

The conscious experience of these ties produces the feeling that her life is spread out over generations—the first step towards the immediate experience and conviction of being outside time, which brings with it a feeling of *immortality*. . . . This leads to a restoration . . . of the lives of her ancestors, who now, through the bridge of the momentary individual, pass down into the generations of the future. An experience of this kind gives the individual a place and a meaning in the life of the generations, so that all unnecessary obstacles are cleared out of the way of the life-stream that is to flow through her. At the same time the individual is rescued from her isolation and restored to wholeness. All ritual preoccupation with archetypes ultimately has this aim and this result.

—C. G. Jung
Aspects of the Feminine, p. 149

THE PARADE OF GENERATIONS

ten-day-old baby

MY MOM AND DAD flew here for a week to help us and to meet their first grandchild. I am deeply touched to see them holding our beloved baby. My dad nestles Jesse's little baby-body into his big Danish man-body; Jesse's little pink fingers curl tightly around my dad's huge gnarled finger. My mom coos familiar little love talk to my baby, love talk she once confided in me, love talk that now I find myself saying to my baby, words and tones that I only realize are hers after they hang in the air, echoing in my mind.

My mother did well loving babies and children, luckily for me; now that same mothering naturally pours out of me. I have inherited the ways of my mother and begun passing them on to my baby. My personal mother now mingles with the archetypal mother, both flowing forth from me with barely a conscious thought.

Life proceeds. Parents bear children, and their children in turn bear children. The old generation dies, and the new generation is born. My grandfather is ninety years old, my father is sixty, my brother is thirty, and my baby is newborn. What force has orchestrated this symmetry of the male lineage in our family?

To regard the ongoingness of life intellectually is one thing; to intimately know and love the individuals in the parade of generations is quite another event. To witness the new life of Jesse coming in, to witness the older life of Steve's father going out. I see what life is, but more important, I feel it, my heart is woven into it all. I am overflowing with these meanings; tears spill many times every day.

My feelings are so strong and unpredictable that I have lost most self-expectation of normalcy. I am leaking the juices of life. My breasts drip milk when I nurse, when I think of Jesse, when I cry, or whenever they feel like it (they seem to have a mind of their own now). Fluids still flow from my uterus. My eyes spill tears.

Two days ago, Steve mistakenly concluded I was well-adjusted and had adequate help, so he went to work. I was stunned that he thought it was OK to leave us and go back to work, especially without even consulting me. I wasn't ready for that. Then, my mom and dad borrowed my car for a few hours to go out to breakfast. What about me? They all left me home with the baby—without a car. I wasn't one of those independent people who could come and go, who could do fun things on a whim, or could even get dressed and go to work. I couldn't go anywhere. I'm stuck at home. All I do is nurse all day, get spit up on, and change diapers. I have no freedom. I used to have a life. I used to come and go. It was really fun when we were all here together, changing diapers, holding and cherishing the baby. But now they all are going on with their lives, and I'm stuck here with a crying baby. Even though my baby is the reason I am grounded at home, my resentment was not directed at him. I guess my maternal love was stronger and deflected my anger elsewhere. The targets of my resentment were Steve and my mom and dad. They left our party, and now it's not a party anymore. They left me, the mother, with the baby. For hours. Alone. The weight of my responsibility is sinking in.

When my parents returned, I told my mom how I felt and cried mightily. Even though I am overjoyed with our baby, I also feel a certain grief at becoming a mother. I keenly feel the loss of my freedom. It's not just me in the world anymore. I had remarkable freedom in my college years, in my various jobs, moving from the Midwest to the West Coast for graduate school, embarking on adventures at a moment's notice. I lived where I pleased and traveled often. My financial needs were minimal, and I was single. I did pretty much what I wanted to do, and it was a lot of fun.

When I got a responsible job as a minister, I still had a lot of choice about how I structured my life. When I got married, I still had a lot of room to come and go and do what I liked. But now I have a baby, and I can't leave him for more than two hours without my breasts' demanding that I return to nurse him. I can't jump in my car anymore and go out to eat. Just stepping out of the house requires that I spend forty-five minutes packing a diaper bag with all that he will need. It's really hitting me that I have lost the solitary quality in my life and lost a great deal of my personal freedom. I am much more dependent on Steve now, too. I am home here with Jesse, dependent on the money Steve makes. That is not a financial hardship, but it is a loss of self-sufficiency and personal freedom.

I wonder whether it's harder for a woman who has been independent and had years of feeling in charge of her own life to surrender when she has a baby. Many of us born during the baby boom following World War II waited until our thirties or even forties to marry and bear children. Many women of my generation are educated and professionally accomplished. Psychologically, we have had the time and space to develop a conscious, differentiated ego. We are used to knowing what we want and directing our lives to achieve our goals. When a woman who has lived this way becomes pregnant, she gets dragged back into the unconscious depths of nature, into a dreamy and passive field of energy, where she is a vessel for the creative forces of life. This is a hard fall for the ego, a difficult psychological death. Presumably, as the baby grows older, and particularly when a woman is no longer under the spell of the mother hormones, the ego is able to surface again. For now, I must accept that on faith.

There is a children's arcade game that has six big holes on the game board. When the player inserts a quarter, a gopher head pops up through one of the holes. The player's job is to whack the gopher over the head with the provided rubber hammer, cramming it back down under again. The arcade gopher is clever—it pops up one hole and then another but almost always gets smacked down under again. In many respects, this is an apt analogy of the mother's ego during the process of pregnancy, birth, and being with a baby. This hormonally defined period of time is governed by the unconscious forces of nature. Nature is not stupid, would not allow a woman's ego to be in charge of the process. The ego, whenever it gains enough desire or strength to pop its head up above the surface, will almost surely be smacked over the head, pushed back down again. It seems wise to wonder how the ego feels about being hammered down time and again. The natural energies that rise through the ego become frustrated that they can't express themselves. How does a woman live with this? Where does she channel the frustration? Toward her baby? Her husband? Does she turn the anger toward herself? Does she assuage the frustration by eating a lot?

Although it's only an academic question for me, I do wonder whether pregnancy is easier for the ego of a younger woman who has not yet embarked on an autonomous adult life. Her ego has not had a chance to gather strength and demand its ways in the world. She smoothly slides from psychological dependency on her parents into dependency upon on a husband. Is it easier for her to live in the spacey, unconscious rhythms of mother and baby because she has not yet functioned independently in her life, has not yet developed a strong ego? However, I can also imagine that it could be more frustrating for the ego to postpone a self-directed life for so long.

I guess the real questions here are about the developmental psychology of women: when is a female's ego naturally most ready to develop, and what happens to the life of the ego during the era of childbearing? Does nature intend that ego development in women be delayed beyond the childbearing years?

In addition to my ego's feeling like the gopher repeatedly whacked over the head with a rubber hammer, the other problem in my life now is figuring out how to work all our yuppie baby equipment. I have put focused energy into trying to set up the stroller with the bassinet attachment in order to take Jesse for a walk. I can't figure it out. Then there's putting together the baby swing or the baby canvas seat so he can be propped up to see what's going on in the room, or how to adjust the Snugli for carrying the baby like a mother kangaroo. It takes hours to figure out how to set up, adjust, and use all this stuff. I don't really know why I am bothering. Jesse doesn't like any of the yuppie baby equipment; he just wants to be held in warm human arms. And walked.

A person practically needs a Ph.D. in engineering to put the baby car seat together and in the car properly. My mom and dad, with a combined thirty-four years of formal education, and having raised four children of their own, struggled for more than an hour to readjust the straps of the car seat to fit a newborn and then to strap it in the car properly. I am overwhelmed and have little free time; I can't figure this stuff out on my own, and Steve is not the mechanical type. If it weren't for my parents' being here to help me, I probably would not have left the house until Jesse started kindergarten.

Mom, Dad, Jesse, and I went on our first outing—to the botanical garden. Dad wore the Snugli strapped against his chest. Jesse slept happily through the walk. At one point, a tiny gnat landed on an exposed part of Jesse's face. My dad immediately transformed into a protective Father Bear: he swiftly pinched the gnat to a quick and sure death between his thumb and forefinger. It was funny to watch his overreaction to a little gnat but sweet to see his fierce instinct to protect his grandson. Inexplicably, I felt guarded and protected as well.

I have written a lot about this under the heading: "primary maternal preoccupation." In this state mothers become able to put themselves into the infant's shoes, so to speak. That is to say, they develop an amazing capacity for identification with the baby, and this makes them able to meet the basic needs of the infant in a way that no machine can imitate, and no teaching can reach.

—D. W. Winnicott
Babies and Their Mothers, pp. 36–37

THE BABY WITHIN

three-month-old baby

ON FRIDAY, September 13, I turn thirty-three years old. Thirty-three, a three-month-old baby, now three in our little family. All threes. As my friend Debra pointed out, on my last birthday, Jesse was only a hope and a dream. Now he is a pervasive reality.

In pregnancy, I had long, dreamy periods of time to muse about life and write. Now I write little snippets, bits of something until the baby wakes up. Everything is susceptible to being interrupted by the baby's needs: a shower, phone conversations, cooking. Any project is subject to suddenly being shelved, left half-finished for weeks. So many things are left half-done now. A shower becomes laced with tension—will he wake up and cry before I wash out the cream rinse? At any moment, I could be pulled away by the baby's needs. Almost everything is secondary to the baby's needs. Never before in my life have I been so subject to interruption. It makes me feel nervous in my activities because I want to complete a job, but the meter could run out at any time without advance notice. I feel most centered and happy when I am with Jesse, holding him and caring for him. Nothing interrupts that.

I have become immersed in Jesse. While I was pregnant and had time to think, I thought about a baby's being in a symbiotic relationship with the mother. An infant does not experience an existence separate from the mother. The baby lives inside the psychic field of the mother. The baby lives through the mother and in identification with the mother. If a mother is tense and anxious, the baby will feel tense and anxious. If a mother drinks caffeine, the nursing baby later drinks caffeine. The boundaries are blurred, and the baby does not separate himself from his mother. I understood this.

What did not occur to me is that I, too, would be part of this symbiosis—that the symbiosis is in many ways a mutual dependence. I am so deeply immersed in Jesse that I get confused about whether a particular event happened to him or to me. For example, yesterday when I sat in the beauty parlor and the attendant was preparing to streak my hair, she asked me whether I had any open cuts on my head. I became confused: was it me or was it Jesse? One of us had a scratch on the scalp that had bled a bit. I remembered being aware of the scratch and a bit concerned about it, but I could not differentiate whether it was my head that was scratched or Jesse's. Finally, I remembered what the scratch looked like and decided it must have been on Jesse's head for me to have seen it.

I am deeply inside him, as he is deeply inside me. We're not really two separate beings yet. He is physically attached to me now only through our breast-feeding. But psychically, emotionally, spiritually, we are intertwined in a way I have never consciously known before. I need to be with him maybe as much as he needs to be with me. I need to nurse him as much as he needs to drink my milk, and at about the same time. At night, I often awaken slightly before he does. I lie still in bed, and soon he stirs, wanting to nurse. I am symbiotically attached, too. It makes sense to me that this is true. Why would nature take a chance that a mother would be responsible enough to want to hold, be with, and nurse her baby? That's too risky. Nature, through the power of hormones and who knows what else, keys the mother into a deep symbiosis with the baby, in most cases guaranteeing her presence and nurturance.

It's a good system. I admire it. But it is such a surprise to find myself an equal partner in the symbiosis. I find it almost intolerable to be separated from Jesse for more than three hours. I am deeply in love with him and need him in order to feel right. We are a couple, two, and yet one.

We are ruled by one body. It is not mine, not his. Together, we dwell within the body of the Great Mother. The depths and nuances of the Mother archetype are staggering. Each person has experienced the Mother from the vantage point of the child. Each child has a personal mother or primary caregiver, associating a whole host of feelings, smells, moods, attitudes with that personal mother. In addition, we each have unconscious experiences of the Mother archetype, in our dreams, through fairy tale and myth, through a relationship with the earth, and through female divinities. Beyond that, many adult women go on to experience the Mother archetype from the vantage point of the personal mother. Far too little psychological research has been conducted on the individual mother's subjective experience. I had no idea I would be possessed as I am, no premonition of the depth of feeling or the beauty of living in this Mother archetype.

I am intricately tuned in to Jesse as a baby. I can sense what he needs, what he is communicating, how he feels. I talk to him, and I know what he is saying back to me in his own little baby way. It's remarkable how well we communicate. I don't think I could explain how I know what he is "saying," but I just do.

Being this tuned in to a baby has affected the way I perceive and relate to other people. When I am talking to a grown-up person, often I see the baby inside of him or her, and because I am so accustomed to speaking directly to the baby, I speak right to the baby in that grown-up, the vulnerable, dependent, innocent one inside. Almost my entire being now is keyed toward loving the baby, and this love for the baby is not restricted to my personal baby.

I am able to reach the baby in my husband. I am able to touch the baby in my friends. I see strangers on the street, and I feel how precious they are; I know that that person is some mother's baby. I want to protect that mother's baby, don't want him to be homeless or malnourished or harmed in the myriad ways that so many people are harmed in the world. My heart holds each person I encounter as a treasured baby. I wonder about how the world could be if we all acknowledged, and felt, that each one of us is a treasured baby.

I have often thought that the true meaning of one's age lies in the sum of all the ages preceeding the current one. I am thirty-three years old. Contained in that thirty-three years is myself as a baby, myself as a two-year-old, a six-year-old, a teenager, and so on. Each of those ages is still alive in me; I can still slip and slide between them. With luck, we outgrow certain characteristics of certain ages. But lurking not far below the surface is still a two-year-old who cries "mine" when someone takes my toy.

Being a mother is a paradox for the baby within me. Curiously, in nurturing Jesse, I often feel I am simultaneously nurturing the baby within me. However, it has become painfully clear to me that a major psychological shift in becoming a parent is that I must regularly sacrifice the needs and desires of the child within *me* for this external child named Jesse. What I want and need is secondary to Jesse's needs and wants. Sometimes, like the many nights when I have had broken, interrupted sleep, my inner baby gets frustrated and angry. Sometimes, my inner child throws a temper tantrum, refusing to sacrifice any more. But then I see Jesse's needs, and somehow, something in me rises to meet the occasion.

The truth is, there are three children in our household: Jesse, Steve, and Maren. Jesse crowds the child in Steve and me. Jesse almost always needs a mother. I can accept that. But if that's not difficult enough, my husband wants a mother sometimes, too!

No way! I'm exhausted as a mother. I want him to be the big person so I can be the child.

How can we find enough energy to tend a baby and still attend to our relationship as husband and wife? How will we possibly find enough time and energy to nurture ourselves and each other?

The Mother Goddess, wherever she is found, is an image that inspires and focuses a perception of the universe as an organic, alive and sacred whole, in which humanity, the Earth and all life on Earth participate as "her children." Everything is woven together in one cosmic web, where all orders of manifest and unmanifest life are related, because all share in the sanctity of the original source.

—Anne Baring and Jules Cashford
The Myth of the Goddess, p. xi

KNOWING THE MOTHER

five-month-old baby

TODAY I RODE my bicycle (all by myself!) on the bike path through the bird sanctuary, past the beach, up to the university, all simply for fun. The campus was empty for the holidays. My junket may not sound like much to most people, but for a mother of an infant, this was a luxurious vacation.

As if in a dream, I came upon a landscape I had never seen before. Centered in a lush grassy area was a blue stone pyramid, perhaps two feet high. Five feet out from the pyramid was a circle of boulders arranged in clusters of three, each cast in the four directions—north, south, east, west. No other people were around. How had I suddenly landed in this magical garden? I stood looking at it, reflecting. The ancient form of the pyramid stood at the center. A person could look at the center but not sit in the center. In my life, I do not occupy the center of attention anymore. It is amazing to me how easily I have moved off center stage, how utterly willing I am to grant my baby the starring role while I support him from the wings. The pyramid shows us a way to be: broad contact with the ground, the earth, and yet aspiring, extending up and outward, toward the vast spaces beyond us.

In the circle of stones surrounding the pyramid, I wondered where I belong. If I was to place myself within this landscape, where would my proper place be? East? South? I sat on each of the rocks to find which one I liked and which one liked me. I found a rock that felt the most comfortable and settled into my place within the mandala.

I began to reflect on my life as a mother. I carried a baby for nine months in my body, gave birth to him, and now he is five months old. Now that I am several miles away from him, and alone, removed from the unconscious field of responding to endless immediate needs and demands, I am able to see our lives more clearly. This place offers me a view of my life as a mother.

I feel so much love for Jesse: my whole being is oriented around taking care of him, protecting him, cherishing him. And curiously, that feeling extends outward: I feel that way toward all of life. More than ever before, I cherish the life on earth, want to protect life on our planet, and keenly feel that responsibility as a mother. Part of my responsibility as a mother is to make sure there is a planet worth living on as my baby and other babies grow up.

In becoming a personal mother, a channel has opened in my relationship with Mother Earth. The image that comes to my mind is round dials, concentric circles overlapping each other, beginning with a small one in the center, becoming larger as they extend out further. I feel as if the openings in these dials have all become aligned with each other, creating an open channel of energy flowing between the different layers. My personal mothering is connected to that of other human mothers, which is connected to that of mothers of other species. We open into the essential energies of fertility and fecundity and nurturing that permeate the earth, the ecosystem, life itself. In these alignments, the knowings are able to mingle, inform one another.

More than ever before, I am convinced that by deepening into one's own experience, a person can access the soul of all Being.

I keep circling around what it means to be a mother, uncovering layer under layer until I believe I come to the center: to be a mother is to enter into a sacred agreement with nature to host a new life, to grow that new life within you, loving that life with all your heart and soul, protecting the new being, while slowly, over time, with tender hands guiding it toward independence.

Once a female is inside this covenant, she is one with all mothers, regardless of nation, race, or socioeconomic divisions, and even regardless of species. Mother deer entered into the same contract that I did. So did mother quail and mother cats. I cherish their babies in a new way now, similar to the way that I cherish my own baby.

My experiences within the Mother archetype have carried a sacred quality. Because an archetype permeates so many layers of reality, it does facilitate the religious experience: carrying the individual beyond the narrow confines of the pedestrian self into the multiple layers of existence and meaning contained within the soul of the whole.

The Mother archetype is an essential idea of the universe, a Platonic form permeating all levels of existence. This archetype is not only a structure within the human imagination but rather a fundamental idea, an implicit form undergirding the explicit forms of the material world. When an archetype becomes activated within a person's psyche, the images and meanings of implicit reality that mostly remain invisible become apparent in the material realm. That which was always there, but could not be seen before, can now be seen.

What are some of the visible forms through which human beings have perceived the mysteries embodied in the Mother archetype? Certainly, the pregnant woman and the nursing mother. We have ample archeological evidence that these visibles were symbols, carrying the invisible essence of the Mother. The full moon was also an ancient and common symbol of the

Mother. The Tree of Life. The sea. The Earth Mother. The snake or serpent. The cow.

I think of the apple tree in my yard. That tree works all year, in ways both visible and invisible, to bear apples in the spring. Her roots push deep inside the earth, intertwining with a soil whose body is an ever-changing conversation between dead and living plants, microorganisms, and minerals. The earth body continually converts death to life and life to death, cycling, re-cycling within her body, the life body.

The mother has grown in me, and that enables me to more intimately know Mother Earth. I feel the processes of the earth mentored the mother in me, that Mother Earth is the archetypal Mother and that all other mothers emanate from her, emulate her, are her representatives. In Mother Earth's body is revealed the essence of regeneration, fertility, nurturing, food, transfor-mation. The earth is the womb from which all life comes and to which all return in death, only to be worked, over and over, minutely, transformed into new life.

Often I have seen the Earth Mother from afar. Through bear-ing a child, I became her daughter in a new way; she became my mother in a new way. We are one. I have done what she does. My body transformed various life energies into a new life. The mystery of the generation of life channeled through my body; for brief times, I felt that mystery, knew that mystery.

In spite of all that I have learned from the Great Mother, there is still a crucial gap in my knowledge. I do not really know the Mother in her darkness, in her ability to welcome death. I do not welcome death. The earth seems to hold life and death side by side with perfect ease. I can't. I don't want to. There are fundamental ways in which I am still outraged that we all must die.

Now that I am a mother, my outrage has only increased. I am alert day and night so that my baby will not die. One hundred times every day, I make choices to help keep him alive: pick up the thumbtack that fell from the wall so it won't accidentally poke him, feed him organic baby food, strap him in his car seat even when he screams about it. My "anticipatory mother worry" is in full gear. I scout his immediate reality and his near future for potential dangers and make sure he avoids them. My job is to keep him alive and well. How can I also hold the possibility of his death? I don't know how I could continue living if he died. I love him so much, am vulnerable in my deep love for him. I can't bear to let him cry in his crib for ten minutes; his pain is intolerable for me. Isn't this what nature wants of me as his mother?

How can the Earth Mother hold both life and death? Isn't she asking us to protect the babies given to us at all costs, even the cost of our own lives? Doesn't she demand that we love our babies so ferociously that we will move mountains to save them? How can I not live in fear of his suffering, evading death at each turn? I do not understand this yet. I do not want to understand it. This is an unbearable double bind of motherhood: loving one particular life so intimately, so intricately every day, all toward the end of letting go, letting him be independent, eventually letting him die.

This is an age-old dilemma for mothers. This dilemma is poignantly displayed in the Greek myth in which the Goddess Demeter loses her daughter Persephone.

Demeter was the great Goddess of Grain, the Earth Mother. Persephone was a happy young maiden, the apple of her mother's eye. One lovely day, Persephone was skipping through the hills of Greece with her young friends, admiring wildflowers. One flower off in the distance, a narcissus flower, intoxicated Persephone with its scent and beauty, lured her away from her friends. Suddenly, the earth roared, quaked, cracked open, and out flew Hades, King of the Underworld, his black chariot pulled by black horses. Racing by, he grabbed Persephone firmly around the waist, despite her kicking and screaming, and quickly vanished back down through the crevice.

A dark grief enveloped Demeter. How barren the earth was without her beloved Persephone! Who had abducted her sweet Persephone? For nine days and nights, Demeter wandered this earth, weeping and wailing, searching for her daughter. In her grief, Demeter could no longer be fertile. It was as if she herself had been carried into the underworld. The inner barrenness she experienced through her loss was reflected in the outer condition of the land and animals: no life could grow.

After nine days, Demeter found out who had taken her daughter and where. Furious at Zeus and all the divinities for allowing her daughter's abduction, Demeter refused to be associated with Olympus. She disguised herself as an old woman, wandering to the town of Eleusis, just outside of Athens. She sat by a well looking into its depths, yearning for her daughter. Four pretty maidens came by to draw water for their household. Demeter asked them where she could acquire work in a household. So it came to pass that Demeter was hired to be the nanny for the household of the King of Eleusis, her charge being the baby Demophoon. The grieving mother, Demeter, needed to hold and love a baby.

Both Demophoon's mother and Demeter feared the potential harm that could come to the precious baby. Demophoon's mother told Demeter that the baby was born to her late in life, her only boy, and he was much prayed for. She told Demeter that if she could nurse this baby to adolescence, she would greatly reward her. The mother's phrase, "*If you would nurse him and he would reach adolescence,*"[1] revealed her awareness that not all babies survive until adolescence. The mother lives with the awareness of the possibility of the child's death.

We see that Demeter was also grieved by the mortality of baby Demophoon. She knew that, as a human, he must suffer, and eventually he must die. This aspect of the Mother archetype that Demeter is representing—the mother who tends the baby—cannot bear to see the beloved baby suffer and die. To defy the intolerable, Demeter set about to make baby Demophoon immortal, that he might live forever as a God. Each day, Demeter rubbed special ambrosia on his baby skin, she breathed her sweet breath onto his body, and each night, she held him in a special fire,[2] the alchemy necessary for creating immortality.

One evening, Demophoon's mother peeked into the room while Demeter was holding him in the fire; she screamed and wailed for her baby. Demeter's plan was ruined. Enraged, Demeter screamed, "Humans are short-sighted, stupid, ignorant of the share of good or evil which is coming to them. You by your foolishness have hurt him beyond curing. . . . I would have made your son deathless and ageless all his days and given him imperishable honor. But now it is not possible to ward off death and destruction."[3] Demeter expresses the angst of all mothers about their children: it is not possible to ward off death and destruction.

Demeter, upon losing her daughter Persephone, shows us that the loss of a child brings an inner death to the mother, an internal winter, barren and desolate. The myth elaborates on this theme by going on to show us that both Demeter and baby Demophoon's mother grieved that the baby would inevitably suffer and die. Both of the mothers did what they possibly could to ward off the suffering and death. We see the perspective of the mothers, and we feel it in our hearts.

The value of a myth largely lies in seeing the multiple perspectives within the story, together composing a complex truth. Greek mythologist Carl Kerényi wisely directed our attention toward the complicity of the Earth Mother Goddess, Gaia, in the abduction of Persephone.[4]

Gaia was a much less differentiated, more ancient, and therefore less dualistic Earth Goddess than was Demeter. Gaia herself planted the tempting narcissus flower that lured Persephone away from her girlfriends, allowing Hades to abduct her. Gaia, in her wisdom, cooperated in Persephone's journey to the underworld. Why? In her earth wisdom, Gaia knew that Demeter, as a Goddess of the fertility of the earth, must be intimate with the ways of death. Death and life are inherent partners. This is the wisdom and wholeness embodied by the ancient Great Goddesses: life evolves into death, which evolves into regeneration of new life. Each year, Persephone must spend one-third of the year as Queen of the Underworld, reigning over the dead.

The remainder of the year, she joins Demeter on earth. Life and death are woven together in the body of Persephone and in the pairing of Demeter and Persephone.

Even though Demeter and Persephone are in many ways one Goddess, their functions have been differentiated into two Goddesses. Demeter holds the role of the nurturing mother and the grieving mother, as well as the fertility of the earth. Persephone, in her immature stage, is the prototypical maiden, frolicking with her friends amid the flowers. In her maturity, Persephone embodies integrated knowledge of life and death, which is ultimately the mystery of fertility.

As for myself, I am saturated with the energies of Demeter. When I read about Demeter and what she experienced, I feel deeply understood. I know that Demeter understands what I feel. And because a myth is a story that grows through many generations of telling, I trust that multitudes of other women throughout human history have felt vulnerable in their love for their babies, have worked day and night to fend off harm to their babies, have agonized over the suffering and death that will come, that must come to their babies. To live in the psychic company of mothers brings me comfort. To contain and work with the love and the anguish is the path of the mother; millions of women before me have negotiated this path, and I will, too.

I find myself unable to hold the awareness of the mature Persephone. If I identify with Persephone at all in my life now, it is while she is still a maiden, in that brief moment when Hades has his arm clasped about her waist, poised to whisk her off to the underworld, while Persephone is screaming, "no!" I am still on earth struggling against Hades, fighting an abduction into the darkness of death. Like Demeter, I rub oils on my baby, breathe my sweet breath onto him, and do a million other things to prevent his pain and suffering and death.

In spite of the anguish that mothering can bring, motherhood also brings a profound healing. The Mother archetype offers human women an opportunity to reunite with nature, to find again our original nature.

As a twentieth-century woman, I was distant from nature, felt I had a fair amount of control over my instincts. I liked nature, thought I even loved nature, but what did I really mean? That watching the sunset over the ocean evoked deep feelings of beauty and peace within me? That hiking on trails in the mountains fed me in ways I could not articulate?

Wilderness carries a reflection, a reminder of one's own original self. The soul drinks deeply from nature, nourishing elusive memories—memories of wholeness and belonging. But in my mind, although I cherished experiences of natural beauty, I never really considered myself an equal animal within that ecology. I felt that nature was Other, was different and separate from me—until I became pregnant.

My rational mind was a featherweight fighter matched against the hormonal powers of the Mother Goddess. Like it or not, agree to it or not, I became one with nature. Forced to surrender my ego, I was drawn deep into the ways of nature, cast in alignment with nature, aligned with my original nature. I instinctively walked the ways of the Great Earth Mother.

Whether we are conscious of it or not, women still emulate the Great Earth Mother. Through childbirth, a woman can heal the split between human and nature. Through childbirth, a woman can become one with life; she is a representative of nature, aligned with nature. The healing in becoming a mother is that, through the process of bearing a new life, we are intimately united with life again, one with the rhythms of nature; we are constitutent members of the life community; we belong to life. Life no longer belongs to us. We belong to life.

The English word *religion* is derived from the Latin *religare,* meaning "to bind back to the source." Indeed, the process of pregnancy, birth, and tending a baby has returned me to sources so deep within that I never knew they existed. I have tapped into my essential woman nature—earthy, wise, passionate—and yet I have also chosen to witness this journey consciously, to see what it is, to reflect, to speak about what it is. While tapping back into my deepest roots, I have grown immeasurably. My

soul and spirit have been fed as never before. I stand with humility and joy before the body of the Great Mother, offering gratitude for her blessings. I hope that I can conduct my life, day by day, in a way that honors what the Great Mother has taught me. I want to stand true in the world as one of her representatives.

SECOND CHILD

> There are holy things that are not communicated all at once: Eleusis always keeps something back to show those who come again.
>
> —Seneca
> *Quaestiones Naturales* VII 30 6

I WANT A BABY

twenty-month-old son

THERE IS NO LONGER a baby in my arms. Jesse is growing up. He doesn't drink milk from my breast anymore. He walks and talks and is a substantial force in the world. He goes to a toddler play group on the three mornings when I work, and he even has a best friend. He says things like "No" and "Mine!" He doesn't want to be my little baby anymore. Where did my baby go? I miss the way I felt when I held my baby. I love this budding boy. I love watching his body and spirit grow. But this boy is not a baby.

I have become well acclimated to parenthood. I love being a mother and have settled into a daily life of part-time work; mundane chores of grocery shopping, meal preparation, and housework; and the delights of discovering the world through a toddler's eyes.

My ego has been cruising at the helm, comfortably steering this ship. Even before my son's first birthday, my ego had regained a sense of control. I've felt in charge of myself and my life once again. Yet while I have been holding the steering wheel, forces were stirring in the watery depths, creating currents, pushing the boat straight into the vortex of the Great Mother. I WANT A BABY!

Isn't this experience a *déjà vu*? Haven't I been here before? Of course! This is just what happened to me the first time the Great Mother abducted me. I feel so stupid. My ego didn't learn a thing. It went right back into thinking it was in charge of my life.

Once again, I feel shocked to be taken over by the Great Mother. She has such intense energy that I feel scared by her. The desire she creates in me to get pregnant is so powerful; I feel I will bowl over everyone and everything to get what I want. I will get pregnant, defying rational plans, good sense, or any other obstacles.

My ego concocted this dumb, little rational story about our plan to conceive a second child. I reasoned that it had taken six months to get pregnant the first time, so it would be a good idea to allow a leisurely amount of time to conceive. This would take the stress out of trying to get pregnant. Also, I wanted to space our children three years apart, as the developmental psychologist Burton White begs parents to do, in order to give each one an abundant babyhood, flush with parental attention.

My rational plan to arrange this perfectly spaced procession of children ultimately amounted to a pathetic attempt of my ego to reassure itself that "I" am in charge. However, the Mother Goddess in me was champing at the bit, raring to go. She moved swiftly and surely.

I regret that I don't own stock in a home pregnancy test company. I purchased a lot of those tests while we were trying to get pregnant with our first child. Every month, I went through ups and downs, of wondering whether I was pregnant, noticing every little possible sign—tender breasts, frequent urination, feeling queasy—then I would confide in Steve that I was pretty sure I was pregnant. I would buy a home pregnancy test, and we would wait breathlessly to see whether the doughnut would remain colorless or turn the magical blue. After about the fourth test, Steve said it was all making him too neurotic and he needed some distance from this testing phase of things.

After mutually agreeing on our rational plan for conceiving a second child, I noticed that my menstrual period was several days late. So of course, I went to the drugstore to buy a pregnancy test. I collected my morning urine, a bit skeptical myself. With the eyedropper, I filled the vial with urine and put the diagnostic stick in the vial. I waited the required fifteen minutes, pulled out the stick, when what appeared before my very eyes? A blue doughnut!

"Steve!" I yelled. "Steve, the donut turned blue." He called back absentmindedly, "Oh." "Steve," I yelled again. "I'm pregnant. We got pregnant on our practice run!"

The best I can figure out, this baby was conceived near the spring equinox. This is a wonderful omen. The equinox, be it spring or fall, is the time of year when there is a perfect balance of light and dark. The hours of sunlight last as long as the hours of darkness. The spring equinox is a central holy day of the Goddess, marking the time of year when the fertility of the darkness is ready to manifest into the light of earth, the rebirth of life. Baby bunnies are born, eggs hatch, tulips poke above the ground. The life force pushes through.

The due date for my baby is December 19. It is possible that this baby could be a few days late and be born on the winter solstice, also a holy day of the Great Mother. I am so thoroughly thrilled to be pregnant that all I can think about are these wonderful omens. I am surprised by the reaction of other people when I reveal my due date. They seem disappointed, suggest that this is not a good thing, that the child will have an immediate disadvantage because his or her birthday is so close to Christmas. I am so giddy about being pregnant that I simply reply, "If Mary can do it, so can I."

I am propelled into the future. Now we *have* to buy a house. For more than a year now, I have gone out once a week with our real estate agent to look for a house to buy. Even when I find a house that I like and that we can afford (rarely an easy combination), often Steve doesn't like it. The truth is that Steve won't like any house because he can't bear to leave where we are. He has lived in this little rental cottage on a cliff above the ocean for fifteen years. Every day he swims in the ocean and meanders the beach. He loves the ocean. He doesn't mind a bit that our house is so little and decrepit and permeable to lizards and frogs and twice a snake because, in his mind, the beach is where he lives. But I will be firm now. There is no way two adults and two kids can live in this tiny space. Our landlady is helping my cause because she has informed us that our rental agreement is effectively over.

The mother in me is thrilled. I want a house. Everything in me is talking about babies, children, home, family, house. Now we will get serious and actually buy a house instead of pretending that we're going to buy a house.

Inanna is, above all, a lunar goddess who gives life as the waxing moon and then withdraws it as the waning moon. . . . Inanna as the moon is the life principle that seeks its own sacrifice and is reborn from its own darkness.
—Anne Baring and Jules Cashford
The Myth of the Goddess, pp. 191–93

It Looks Like Mitosis

five weeks pregnant
twenty-one-month-old son

WHOOSH! I'm being swept away again, sucked back into the watery currents of creation. It's absolutely remarkable how I get taken over by these forces when I become pregnant. My body is not my own anymore. I no longer own my self. The waters I drink from are magically alchemical; I can barely comprehend what grows within me: in my body, my feelings, my thoughts. I am in this experience, and at the same time I am watching, trying to bring these watery depths into my consciousness.

As in my first pregnancy, dreams are coming to me, calling me to their places, so fascinating and compelling that nothing else really matters. I live in these deep inner spaces, which my mind can barely discern. Perhaps the only thing that is really clear is how much this experience means to me.

I am in awe of my dream from last night. I dreamed about the moon, what the moon means. Before this dream, I never really thought about the moon's meaning anything. It was just there in the sky, and sometimes it was bright, and often it looked pretty at night. But last night, I discovered inner meanings of the moon, meanings that probably always could be seen, but I had not previously been available as one who could see.

Dad, my brother Topher, and I are going down a rural Nebraska road in a car. It is night. My dad is driving. Through the front windshield, we look up into the sky, seeing a new crescent moon. Then, to the left of that, we see a dying crescent moon that is black, moving toward the new moon. The dark crescent meets the light crescent and then overlays it, so that all is dark. This eclipse is stunning and beautiful.

My dad tells my brother to take a photograph of it, which he does, but at the same time, an airplane flies by in front of the moon. I think that the headlights of the airplane will mess up the photograph.

I look closely at the moon-meeting. With a sudden burst of realization, I say, "It looks like mitosis! The biggest process in the universe looks exactly like the smallest process!"

I awake from the dream very excited by what I have seen and my realization. Are the biggest processes in the universe akin to the smallest processes?

As the cells are rapidly dividing, growing, and dividing again to form a baby human body, is part of my psyche aware of this process? Is a person capable of consciously knowing mitosis in her own body?

Since much of college biology is vague in my mind, I go to the dictionary to clarify *mitosis*. I am amazed at the similarity between the description of mitosis and the image of the lunar eclipse in the dream. Mitosis is a biological process of cell division. "The nuclear chromatin is formed into a long thread which in turn breaks into segments (chromosomes) that are *split lengthwise: the halves come together in two sets* each forming the nucleus for a new cell" (italics mine).[1]

We are accustomed to looking outside ourselves for real knowledge. We turn to science books to learn about mitosis and creation. Some people turn to religious books to learn about creation. But creation can also be known by turning inside to look. Known in a different way perhaps. We've been conditioned to think that the real things, the important things, are objective and happen out there somewhere. It is difficult to fully appreciate that the actual process of creation occurs in the body of a pregnant woman. Creation is more than an external story or a scientific process or a theological doctrine. It also is a deeply personal, felt, experienced event. This real thing, this revered act—creation—is occurring in my body, now, and I am experiencing it.

In the dream, I felt a visceral connection with the moon. I felt a sense of "me" as I watched the moon. I felt that what happens in the moon's life also happens in my life. The life process in which I participate is the life process in which all Being participates. I can see these life processes in the sky, in the earth, in me. We belong together. We are a family.

On a microscopic level, the cells divide, and soon a baby will have grown large enough to divide from the mother. Similarly, on a macroscopic level—for example, in the big bang theory—gases, rock, and other matter had a *big* division, spinning off all sorts of relatively autonomous bodies, among them the earth.

Are the biggest processes in the universe similar to the smallest processes?

In the dream, I am located in Nebraska, where I spent most of my childhood, and I am with two members of my family, my dad and my middle brother, probably the two most rational members of our family. Dad is driving, in control. I'm along for the ride and free to look around. We are in nature, on a rural road. It is night, the time when we can see the moon—lunar time—far from the rational light of day. Symbolically, the rational aspects are going for a ride, asked to witness the lunar realities of the night.

The masculine figures in the dream want to capture, to record the lunar eclipse with a photograph. This contrasts with my more feminine inclination to simply experience, witness, and feel in each fleeting moment. A human-made invention, the airplane, a machine that is different from an organic life process, perhaps interferes with photographing the event of the lunar eclipse. This could be a symbolic way of saying that the forces of modern technology cancel out the ability to capture the miracles of nature. Is the essence of the dark moon such that it cannot be captured? Does part of the moon wish not to be seen?

Psyche has paired the masculine and the feminine in this dream. Perhaps the suggestion is that it's not enough merely to experience this life event, that it is important also to attempt to bring conscious awareness to these experiences of the life mysteries, to make a record of them. My father has often urged me in that direction.

We look at the moon. It is there for us to see and know each night. But until now, I have completely missed the inner meaning of the moon. Now I am glimpsing it, feeling the depths of possibility within the moon image, but I am struggling to articulate even to myself what meanings I sense.

I know the rhythmic lunar cycle has oriented people on earth from the beginning of human time. The moon showed us our first calendar, the marking of twenty-eight-day cycles from one new moon to the next, thirteen cycles composing a year.

When the light is a sliver on the right side, we say that this is a new moon. When the sun's light shows us a full circle on the moon face, we say that this is a full moon. And when the sliver of light is on the left side of the moon, we say that this is the waning, old moon. It is a curious thing: we speak of the moon, but we are probably not saying much about the moon itself at all. Mostly we are speaking of our perspective, what we imagine, what we know in ourselves as we look at the moon.

A new crescent moon has an ancient symbolic association with the maiden Goddess, the aspect of the feminine that is young and virginal. The new moon contains the possibilities of new life, most of which have yet to be revealed.

The dying crescent moon tends to be associated with the wise old crone, who knows the ways of divination and death. The waning moon shows us the withdrawal of life. The old moon dies into a period of emptiness, only then to be reborn into a new moon.

As is true in the body of a woman, the changing light reflected on the moon embodies the mysteries of transformation, cycling every twenty-eight days into the possibilities of new life. In many languages, the words for *moon* and *menstruation* are either the same or similar.[2]

In the human imagination, the moon is associated with fertility. Many ancient peoples believed that the moon causes pregnancy and that the moon presides over the birth of the child.[3]

In the dawn of the agricultural age, about 7000 BCE, planting and harvesting were the domain of women because of women's close association with the fertile powers of the moon. Ancient agricultural practices, and some modern ones such as biodynamic farming, are linked with lunar cycles in the timing of planting and harvesting. We still speak of a "harvest moon."

Jungian analyst M. Esther Harding wrote about the dark moon and the light moon, and her words carry me closer to my own dream images. Harding sees the dark moon as representative of our instinctive animal selves, that which is primal and without the light of consciousness or civilization. Harding believes it is important for a woman to consciously come into relationship with her instinctive self, to acknowledge the power of instinct as it lives within her and yet to know that the instinctive power is not hers but belongs to a much larger force, binding the woman to this larger force.[4] Consciously coming to terms with her instinct is an important developmental achievement in a woman's life.

This idea of a woman's coming to terms with the instinct that dwells within her seems to me to be right at the heart of the MotherMysteries. In my first pregnancy, and now in this one, it has been fascinating to watch instinct take me over, to so effectively orchestrate this complex process of growing a baby and a mother. Much of the meaning I feel in pregnancy and mothering is tied to my awareness that this instinct belongs to nature, to all life-forms, and that I am one with life.

Perhaps the dream image of the eclipse refers to an eclipse of my conscious, individual self. When the forces of nature take over in pregnancy, they do tend to eclipse the self a woman previously cherished. The ego identity is eclipsed by instinct, by nature. The self becomes sacrificed, disappears, while creation takes over to make new life.

It is peculiar to watch how passive I get when I become pregnant. Normally—that is, when I am not pregnant—I have an active, functional neocortex, engaged in long-range thinking, strategic planning, and abstract ideas. But it seems that, as soon as these mother hormones kick in, I lose my sense of drive, my will, my ability to think conceptually and into the future. I become passive and present. I am body and feelings. A big, soft, slow container for Being and Becoming.

It makes sense to me that the dark moon symbolizes instinct. But it is more than that. The dark crescent moon is also death in the human imagination and not just a symbolic death of the ego. Death is a partner in life—the dying moon.

Is the image of my dream about a dark, dying energy wiping out the light of new life? That scares me. I'm afraid that means I'm going to lose this baby. Does my dream mean I'm going to miscarry? Perhaps not, because in the dream, when I see this eclipse in the sky, I feel awe and beauty and excitement. But perhaps in the mind of nature, death evokes awe, beauty, and excitement.

There is something important to know in the dark moon, but it's so hard for me to find. I am acculturated into thinking that what is dark is bad, evil, scary, that what is light is good. It's this troubling, dualistic, Judeo-Christian thinking: good and bad, light and dark, mother and whore; never the two shall meet.

What lives in our imagination of the dark side of the moon? The dark side of the moon is hidden from the light of day, the sun, consciousness. Passion could live there, creativity, instinct, madness, lunacy. Here's a riddle: what is moist, dark and cold, difficult to see? A cave, a well, the ocean depths, a forest at night, death, the mysteries of life.

The dark moon is something in and of itself, regardless of human symbolism and imagination. The dark moon is. It is a piece of reality that simply is. Most pieces of life are like that. Being. Without enlightened reflection. Without being seen. This dark moon, life simply being itself without consciousness, also lives in me—particularly when I am pregnant. I get into a mode of Being, of being life. A dark, lunar state of being.

Mircea Eliade talks about the full cycle of the moon as birth, life, death, and resurrection, understanding that early humans came to see their own essential destiny reflected in the stages of the moon. In the moon, people can see that "death is indissolubly linked with life . . . and above all, that death is not final, that it is always followed by a new birth."[5]

The ancient Sumerian Goddess Inanna was a lunar goddess, holding within her one body both the possibilities of the new moon and the dying moon. She brought new life into the world, and she took life away, but both life and death occurred within her body. This unification of life and death is difficult for me to really know; I want to keep them separate. And yet, as a creature who is currently involved in the mysteries of fertility, this knowledge is filtering through to me.

The sunlight reflected on the orbiting moon shows earthlings that something gets born out of nothing, that it grows to fullness, declines, goes back into nothingness, only to be born yet again. We can see this cycle in the sky. When we bring our eyes down, where else do we see this same process? Do we see it in ourselves? In our gardens? Do we see this archetypal pattern of birth, death, and resurrection in the great religious stories: Jesus of Nazareth, Demeter and Persephone of Greece, Isis and Osiris of Egypt?

A woman experiences something while she is pregnant and brings forth a new life into the world. She knows something in this process. She knows something about what life is. I found this with my last pregnancy, and again now, but I also found that it requires real effort to clarify what I know, to form my knowing into thoughts and words.

[T]he snake is the representative of the world of instinct, especially of those vital processes which are psychologically the least accessible of all. Snake dreams always indicate a discrepancy between the attitude of the conscious mind and instinct, the snake being a personification of the threatening aspect of that conflict.

—C. G. Jung
Collected Works, 5:396

AD NAUSEAM

two months pregnant
twenty-two-month-old son

THE PAST THREE WEEKS have been difficult. I constantly battle low-level nausea. Two or three times a day, I have intense surges of feeling as if I am going to throw up. Rarely do I actually vomit. I don't really care whether I do or I don't vomit; it's the nausea that debilitates every moment, warping all other reality.

Morning sickness is not an adequate descriptor. I have all-day-and-night sickness. I'm not happy talking about the way I feel as "nausea" either. This pregnancy sickness is not just an event in my stomach. It's not an isolated upset organ. There is a psyche to nausea, a mind-set that permeates every little bit of life. I am queasy as I encounter the world. With each task, each person I meet during the day, I try to find something in myself that isn't queasy that can relate. That may work for a short time. But ignoring my fundamental feeling for too long makes it worse. Like a jealous child, my nausea draws attention back to itself by announcing that we are going to throw up.

Last weekend, Steve and Jesse and I went to a dinosaur exhibit at the Natural History Museum. Three of my close women friends were there with their young families. The women were gathered talking, and when they saw me, they opened their circle, taking me in. They asked me how I am. I burst into tears. I told them how terrible I am. It was some relief to quit trying to act like a non-nauseated woman. Crying gave me relief also. My friends cooed and loved and comforted me. Our little scene seemed straight out of the Natural History Museum of Women. How many times over the ages has a community of women comforted one of their own who is sick in pregnancy?

Meanwhile, back at the ranch, I have resigned from my jobs of cooking dinner and cleaning the house. I can't do those things anymore. Preparing food, particularly raw meat, is intolerable. Even the smell of vegetables sickens me. And cleaning? Who cares? So what. Let the dust mites and the ants take care of it.

My predominant daily reality centers on nausea, food, headaches, and figuring out how to cope with what must be done. This does not exactly make for fascinating conversation. I feel bad for being such a drain on Steve and my friends. Alternately, I'm so miserable I care only about myself.

It's hard to be a good mother to Jesse now. I don't feel like following him around the neighborhood or "making muffins" in the sandbox. I get angry at him easily and dread long hours when I'm with him alone. It's just that I am so miserable all I want to focus on is me. When I am responding to Jesse's desires and needs, I feel impatient, even panicky, because I really have to get back to myself. The one compromise activity I have found—what works for me and for him—is to lie down on the brown fuzzy pad, reading books and singing songs. I can do that. He likes being close to me, and I love "reading" him books with my eyes closed, feeling his warm body and smelling him. After a while, he needs more action. Thank goodness Steve comes home from work to play with Jesse. I hope Jesse doesn't notice how much I'm not really present. What a ridiculous thing to say. Of course, he notices that his mother isn't really present. I guess I just hope it isn't hurting him too much.

My best comfort is to be alone in a darkened room, curled up on the couch with a warm blanket and my pillow, watching family shows on TV, the ones that nurture children, like *The Donna Reed Show* and *Little House on the Prairie*. I softly moan and whimper, an animal licking my wounds—wounds from a reality that took me over and made me sick, eclipsing a person I can vaguely remember.

Several weeks ago, I had a dream that I can now see marked the onset of this pregnancy sickness.

> I am in an amusement park. I buy a ticket to a ride that is a roller coaster shaped like a serpent, with a serpent's head painted on the front car and a tail at the end car. I realize that the ride imitates a serpent. It goes fast and twists around like a roller coaster but stays flat on the ground and makes use of centrifugal force. I walk around toward the back of the ride but decide not to sit there because you get whipped around too much at the tail end. So I get in one of the front seats, and a woman I know gets in beside me. With one hand, I hold onto the seat, and with the other arm, I brace myself against the front. The ride begins. I close my eyes the entire way. I make the excuse to myself that I am closing my eyes because I like the way the wind feels on my face, but really it is because, if I opened my eyes, I would get vertigo.

I awoke from that dream feeling nauseated, foggy, and very sluggish. And I have felt that way ever since. Basically, I still am in a front-row seat on this serpent roller coaster, bracing myself against the vertigo.

The serpent is taking me for a ride. Who is this serpent? Who is taking me for the ride of my life, a ride so intense that I can't even open my eyes?

One would be hard-pressed to come up with a symbol more ubiquitous throughout human history than the serpent. The serpent first appeared as the Mother Goddess during the Neolithic era,[1] the one life energy containing all possibilities and giving birth to these possibilities.

The snake was the embodiment of regenerative powers, for the snake had the ability to slough off its old skin, giving birth to itself in a new skin. This mystery of transformation is an essential feature of the Mother archetype. Because of the ability to live, die, and give birth to a new self, the serpent represents the secrets of immortal life.

The serpent is energy, libido, the life force. In various myths, we see serpents who can fly, or coil up around a tree or other ascending objects, but most often the serpent is in intimate contact with the earth. Its body slithers along the earth. This intimacy with the earth makes the snake evocative of instinct, of the animal body, the nature body, in full contact with the *prima materia*.

As was true of the ancient Mother Goddesses, the snake holds both the life-giving and the death-wielding functions of life. With blinding swiftness, the snake can strike, kill with poisonous venom. The snake can wound, and the snake can heal.[2] In the ancient Greek healing sanctuaries of Asklepios, in a ritual ceremony, it was the snake who whispered the source of the disease to the ill person: to know the wound was to know the healing.

It seems clear to me that I am riding on the Great Mother Serpent, being whirled around on the earth, gathering the *prima materia* for a new human being. This process is so powerful, creates such centrifugal force, that all I can do is hold on, brace myself, and try not to throw up.

I do believe that part of the difficulty of the ride lies in the split between animal instinct and the consciousness of the ego. Perhaps the spinning and whirring are necessary to shake off the ego, to dizzy the neocortex, so that the pregnant woman's libido can descend into the realm of animal instinct. The pregnant woman is asked to move belly to belly with the earth.

It is difficult to fully surrender into the realm of instinct. I feel threatened by the profundity of the maternal demand to

Terracotta figurine from Piskokephalo. The female's serpentine arms surround her body. Minoan, Late Old Palace period, ca. 1800 BCE. Archaeological Museum, Heraklion, Crete.

Courtesy Nimatallah/Art Resource, N.Y.

surrender into nature, into instinct. I want to resist. It is a humiliating thing to notice about myself, but after a few weeks of pregnancy nausea, I pathetically raise my arm, waving the white flag. I give up. Fine, the Mother Goddess won. She's in charge. I don't care who rules me anymore, just please let me quit feeling nauseated.

The power of creation is too strong for a human ego, an individual body. It whips her far beyond her normal boundaries. Who could stand in the eye of creation and not feel dizzy? Of course, a woman has vertigo when creation occurs in her body. My dream about riding the serpent makes more sense to me as an explanation of the way I feel than the medical story that a pregnant woman is nauseated because she has high levels of progesterone.

The Rites are gone—yet the mystery remains. The unconscious has an autonomous way of making itself known; if
people do not gather anymore on a sacred road to search
for their lost souls, the gathering together and the search
will be translated into the movement and language of our
interiors. Rites of passage have turned inward where they
are lived out as stages of psychic transformation.

—Nor Hall
Mothers and Daughters, pp. 35–36

THERE IS SOMETHING TERRIFYING

three and one-half months pregnant
twenty-three-month-old son

THERE IS SOMETHING TERRIFYING about being pregnant.
Hardly anybody talks about it. We prefer to speak about pregnancy as a meaningful and fulfilling time in a woman's life. We
seem to agree that it's OK to mention the myriad physical discomforts (and let's face it, there are plenty of those). A woman
may discreetly mention to a close friend her anxiety about the
possibility of giving birth to a baby who is not healthy and
whole. Or in a light, jocular way, we may confide occasional
nightmares about giving birth to a deformed monster.

Yes, there is something terrifying about being pregnant. Most
of the time, the terror seems securely buried, but then without
warning, suddenly a crevice opens, and the terror pushes up,
revealing its monstrous face again. I stifle a scream of horror,

jump into action trying to stuff the terror back down into the depths, where I can once again mostly forget about it and go on living as though it does not exist—until it rears its head again.

After several recent occasions of running from this terror, my curiosity got the better of me. I forced myself to stop and look at the terror. What I saw resembles a science fiction horror novel. Chapter 1 introduces us to the main character, a nice, ordinary, *unsuspecting* woman. She gets pregnant. She and her nice, ordinary husband rejoice, thinking they have been blessed with what will become a baby.

The next chapter opens inside her uterus. Dwelling inside her womb is an organism that looks pretty weird. It looks sort of like a tiny sea horse. The organism is rapidly multiplying, dividing cell after cell at a rate that boggles the imagination. It attaches itself to this nice woman's uterus, creating a tube between itself and her body, feeding off her blood and flesh.

The next few chapters tell a bittersweet story. Although this nice couple feels blessed with the gift of life, it is true that the woman is suffering. The organism is reminiscent of a walk-in—a spirit from outer space who descends to inhabit a person—taking over the person's mind and feelings and soul, so that even though it looks like the person-who-used-to-be, in fact the old person is a mere shell of her former self, a disguise for the walk-in. The woman appears disoriented, doesn't seem to feel or be herself. She vomits. She yells at her dear husband with a rage that leaves him astonished and speechless. Yet through it all, she tenderly rubs her rounding belly, falling in love with her fantasy of the little baby who grows inside her.

Chapters 7 and 8 show us that this parasite grows bigger and bigger. It becomes so large that it distends the woman's body, pushing it out here and there to make space for its insatiable appetite. This creature takes over so much space that the woman's belly distorts out as if a basketball were inside her. Naively, stupidly, she gently strokes her belly, cooing love talk to it, having never seen it, *imagining* it is a baby.

By Chapter 9, the creature has gotten all it wanted from her, sucked enough of her blood and flesh, and now wants out. How will this giant soon-to-be ex-parasite get out of her? What??? It will push its way out through her vagina? But it is too big! It will blow her body apart. It's impossible. She won't live through it. She will writhe in pain, screaming, her body will heave uncontrollably. Wave after wave of contortions rack her body. She begs for drugs. She pleads with the doctors to cut her belly open, to take it out that way. Her vaginal opening stretches wide, wider, opened big as a basketball hoop while a hairy ball pushes its way out. Another push. Now it is all the way out. The doctors and nurses gasp. The mother issues a bloodcurdling scream. It's not human. It's not a baby. It's THE ALIEN!!!

My terror fantasy exhausts itself, disintegrates, percolates down through the ground. It will surface again in time. But for now, it is over. I get a grip on myself. For the time being, I resemble a measured, even woman.

It is terrifying to host the unknown. To graciously open one's innermost sanctuaries, to offer the food and drink of one's own body, to feed a new life that we have never seen. That we cannot see for nine months.

Who's in there? Is it human? Is life so competent that it can really produce a standard model of a human being the majority of the time? What if one of the aberrations is growing within me? I am sacrificing so much to host this new life: my body, my soul, my heart. I am sacrificing for someone whom I do not know and have never seen. For someone I am increasingly falling in love with. But will this someone be a vampire? An alien?

Yesterday, another weird fantasy sped through my brain: I was in the hospital, giving birth to twins who were grossly deformed. I cried and asked for Jesse so that I could hold him to be comforted.

Perhaps the fantasy of giving birth to grossly deformed twins is merely a metaphor for my daily life. Some alien, weirdo, grossly deformed, double-dosed reality has taken over my body and mind. I am grieving about how this separates me from my beloved child, Jesse—yearning to be the mother who can hold him again, the way I used to.

I remember that, in my first pregnancy, also in the early months, I went through a period of fantasizing about twins. The strange thing about this twin fantasy is that, in my sane moments (which do seem to be few and far between these days), I would not want to have twins: one baby is plenty for me. But in both of these pregnancies, I have had a desire for twins in the first trimester. This desire shows itself mainly in fleeting daydreams that follow this story line: I am carrying twins, but the doctors don't yet know it. When they find out that I am carrying twins, I act appalled, but really, secretly, deep down I am thrilled.

There is something inherent in the reality of twins that ignites the imagination and, at least in my case, that ignites the imagination of a pregnant woman. I decide to go on a mythological search to explore the ways twins have lived in other people's imaginations. I find the archetype of twins springing up in mythologies everywhere: the Iroquois of North America, the Dogon of West Africa, ancient Greece and Rome, biblical stories, Zoroastrians from ancient times, and the modern Near East and India.[1]

There are divine twins, often associated with creation myths. Clearly, a pregnant woman qualifies as being inside a creation myth. The theme that runs through the myriad examples of divine twins is that they represent two principles within a unity: good and bad, order and chaos, female and male,[2] suggesting a belief that, in the created world, there are differences and these differences emerge out of one essence. Some cultures view these differences as opposing principles, whereas some cultures, such as the Dogon of West Africa, view them as complementary qualities necessary for wholeness.[3]

In the Dogon mythology, the primordial couple were born twins. Each one had both male and female characteristics, but one was slightly more endowed with female, whereas the other was slightly more male. Each was human from the waist up, the

lower half shaped as a serpent. Their bodies were green and
sleek, covered with delicate green hairs, suggestive of the growth
of vegetation.[4] In an intimation of wholeness, the twins embodied the pairing of different qualities: female and male, and
human and amphibian.

Separate and together. One and two. This feels to be the essence of twins. They emerge from the one source, finding themselves differentiated. They are different, and they are the same.
They are one, and they are two. This stirs me in more ways than
I can explain. I am one person, one woman, and yet two persons
are now housed in my body. One woman on her way to becoming two persons: mother and baby.

Two ovaries. Two breasts. Two buttocks. Two is one doubled.
There is a sacred power of multiplication. There is a force in life
that creates two out of one. One cell divides into two. There is a
strength and stability in two, in the doubling power.

Also, in the archetype of twins, there is something reminiscent of the soul. In the mythology of human twins (as opposed
to divine twins), there is a consistent theme of a spiritual coun-
terpart, suggesting that each mortal human has a spiritual twin,
a soul or higher self. Throughout human history, many human
beings have sensed that the conscious ego is not an only child;
there is a deeper sense of Self, a spiritual twin who continually
beckons the ego toward the true home.

A beautiful illustration of this sense of a spiritual twin is the
Gnostic myth in the apocryphal Acts of Thomas, a story called
the Hymn of the Pearl. A young prince must go into the foreign
land of Egypt to recover the lost pearl. Once in Egypt, he falls
under the spell of magic, and he forgets who he is. He can no
longer recall his true nature or his destiny. Lost, in a foreign
country, alone, he begins to receive messages sent to him by his
twin (who remains home in the land of Israel), messages designed to awaken him, to help him remember who he is and
where he comes from. The story concludes with the prince remembering his way, returning to his true home, greeted by, and
finally to be reunited with, his twin.[5]

In my first pregnancy, and now in this one, I have also had a recurring fantasy that the baby I am carrying is deformed. What is this about? Is it fear that one's baby will not be healthy? Is it the lingering knowledge that not all life is born healthy and normal? Could it be a desire for that which is not normal?

Some of the twin mythologies throughout the world address this fantasy of a deformed baby. The mere notion of two of anything almost exactly alike invites comparison. We search out the differences. Most comparisons result in one's being judged superior to the other. The biblical Cain and Abel. The Egyptian Seth and Osiris. One brother is inferior, represents the darkness, barrenness, perhaps evil.

In the West African Dogon story, the bad brother, Yurugu, tries to create life but simply ends up with monsters. Something in the human psyche is aware of forces within the world that create monsters, deformed versions of life. Angry that he could only create monsters, Yurugu decides to force all people to suffer, injecting pain into the lives of good people.[6] The Dogon teach us that, in the human world, we all live with deficiencies, with suffering, with the monstrous.

In most of these good twin/bad twin mythologies, it is interesting to notice that the bad twin or sibling is subdued but never destroyed. People have long known that forces of light and darkness exist in this world and it is folly to think that one could be eradicated. Light and dark are complementary qualities, both necessary in life on earth. Somehow, in our daily lives, we must find a way to balance a dynamic existence with each of the twins.

Standing in the midst of the endless possibilities of creation, some dark and some light, I must somehow agree to house the life that has been given to me before I know who or what it is. To deeply open and host a new life requires a magnitude of faith and trust that I have never known before.

Thousands of years ago, well before the advent of Christianity, human beings began decorating eggs, particularly during the time of the spring equinox.[7] The egg. A newly developing life encased in a shell. What lives inside that eggshell? What creature will peck its way out of the shell, emerging into our world?

The egg symbolizes the mystery of new life. Part of the mystery is that the developing life is unknown. Would this new life bring good or ill? Petitioning the forces of creation, hoping to influence the divine creative spirit, people painted eggs, carefully drawing symbols with positive connotations, often using the color red, a color imagined to bring good luck. In the Ukraine and Russia, people painted small, intricate geometric designs on eggs. Each Ukrainian family had its own secret formula to make dye and particular familial designs that they painted. The painted eggs were prominently featured within the home, imagined to offer protection from destructive forces of nature such as fire and lightning.[8]

The egg was a religious symbol of new life in ancient Egypt, China, Greece, and Persia. The egg also became a symbol within Christianity, evoking the possibilities and celebration of new life. In the early days of the Church, Christians brought eggs to the priests to be blessed during the Easter season.[9]

I, too, feel the insecurity about what is inside my egg. I, too, feel the need for my fertilized egg to be blessed. I want to petition the forces of nature, painting symbols and colors summoning good luck for this egg growing within me. Please let the life hidden inside, the life that we cannot see—please let it be balanced on the side of health and goodness.

Artemis forbids the hunter to wound an animal instead of killing it, leaving it to go its way limping and suffering. In the same way, if one values the integrity of life, one must sacrifice the fetus already marked by the rejection . . . of those who should receive it with love.

—Ginette Paris
Pagan Meditations, p.141

SORTING THROUGH THE EXPERIENCE OF AMNIOCENTESIS

four months pregnant
two-year-old son

PREGNANT AND THIRTY-FIVE years old. When I asked my obstetrician about the risks of bearing a Down's syndrome baby, he said I was entering the gray area: statistically, a woman's odds of bearing a baby with genetic defects rise significantly beginning at age thirty-five.

Females are born with their full supply of eggs. There is such an interesting feel of infinity to this: I was born with the eggs that created my babies. For thirty-five years, my eggs have lain in waiting. For twenty years now, one egg a month has been coaxed into one fallopian tube or the other. Does the egg hope to be met by a sperm? Does the egg die disappointed? How much does the egg want life? In approximately twenty years of ovulating—that's approximately two hundred and forty eggs, or a clean twenty dozen—only two have met a sperm and been able to unfold their possibilities.

One of those eggs is now two years old, and his name is Jesse. The other egg is multiplying madly in my womb. But the sobering fact is that this egg is thirty-five years old, as old as I am. When eggs get this old, their genetic material begins to break down, mutate. I have never imagined myself to be a person who has old eggs, and the mere suggestion has forced me to look at myself again. I would never know whether this particular multiplying egg is too old until the baby is born, unless I have an amniocentesis, which is the course my doctor recommends.

Amniocentesis is a common procedure, routine among my peers—educated, white, professional, health-conscious women, thirty-five years and older. I've read arguments against amniocentesis. Some women are opposed to amniocentesis because they feel it is a medical-technological invasion into a personal, natural human process. Some couples are not willing to take the minimal risk of accidentally inducing a spontaneous miscarriage, which indeed is a possibility that accompanies amniocentesis. Some people won't consider amniocentesis because they are unwilling to abort a fetus, even if genetic defects are present.

My husband had his own feelings against amniocentesis. "There are just some things that are beyond human control. You can't control the baby you get," he said.

Even though there is truth in what Steve said, I find it rather shocking the extent to which we *are* able to make choices about the baby we get, through prenatal genetic testing and abortion. My husband prefers less human intervention in the natural order.

In our family arrangement, I am the primary parent. Day after day, I would live with a Down's syndrome child much more than would my husband. When I assessed my personal future, and our family's future with a child who had genetic defects, I knew that I would vastly prefer to avoid bearing a baby with genetic defects. I wanted to have an amniocentesis. Steve agreed to support me in my decision.

I hopped on the "amnio" bandwagon. "Amnio." That's what everybody calls it. We feel so friendly and casual with this procedure, we call it by its nickname—a nickname that denies its murky depths, that belies the anxiety and anguish it brings for the mother.

I called my friend Joanne, so I could learn more about what I was soon to experience. She had been through two amnios. Joanne told me, "The needle they use to go from your belly into the uterus is really long, and that's the part I was scared about. So I told the doctor ahead of time not to let me see the needle. But even though you can't see it, you can *feel* it going through the layers of tissue." She reassured me, "Afterward it's no big deal. I felt a little queasy, but that may have been because I was so nervous. Don't worry, you'll be fine."

I wasn't fine. During the week before the scheduled amnio, a fear began to grow in me. I felt anxious and nervous. When I tried to get specific about what frightened me, all I could think of was the long needle piercing through my growing belly. I think my psyche dimly perceived the profundity of this upcoming event and how utterly unprepared I was to meet it.

There was a living image in my mind that spontaneously appeared when I felt apprehensive: a small group of wild horses in an open field of wild grasses. Sometimes this image of the horses was as clear and real to me as if I looked out a window and saw them. Sometimes, when I saw the wild horses, they were grazing quietly. Sometimes they would be agitated. Sometimes I saw chaos break loose, their powerful bodies stampeding in panic. Always the horses lived in a place that was far beyond my control. The place where the wild horses roamed was different from the land of reason. They lived in wild and natural places, places of instinct, survival. The reassuring stories I told myself ("Thousands of women do this," and "It only takes a few minutes") never entered the land of the wild horses.

On some level of my psyche, far below the realm of reason

and statistics, even below the realm of the reassurance of friends, I felt terrified of amniocentesis. The terror seemed to dwell in the realm of my instinctive animal body. The wild horse did not want to be captured, laid out on a table, pierced by a five-inch needle that sucked amniotic fluid from the womb. The wild horse just wanted to be left in the field, to move and graze and run as she pleased, to swell and birth in her own way. If her baby horse had genetic defects, nature would determine its course.

The morning of the amniocentesis, I was beside myself. I wonder whether literally I had exited my body and was "beside myself." The wild horses were stampeding. I had followed doctor's orders: don't urinate in the morning and drink a quart of water because the sonogram requires a full bladder. Having a very full bladder but denying the body's urge to urinate is in itself a violation of the instinctive body and is deeply uncomfortable.

The nurse who greeted us was so friendly that I asked Steve whether we knew her. She was beautifully sensitive to our emotional needs. Her job was to do the sonogram, the first part of the procedure. I lay on my back on a table while the nurse gently rubbed a handheld instrument around my belly, painlessly bouncing sound waves off my innards. The purpose of the sonogram, she explained, was to examine the fetus visually, to determine his or her position and the position of the umbilical cord. She turned on the screen monitor, and abracadabra, to our complete astonishment—right there on TV was our baby!

In a high cooing voice, like a mother examining her newborn, I gasped, "Oh, my little baby! Isn't it beautiful? Look! Ten fingers! My God! Honey, look, there's its leg!" The nurse guided us through the images on the screen: the four chambers of the heart, a forming spine, the eyes. A sixteen-week-old human fetus.

My husband and I were in awe before the miracle of seeing a very new human life. We felt the early stirrings of love for a baby that was created from our bodies—our baby. We were equally stunned by the miracle of human technology, enabling us to see on television a detailed image of the fetus growing inside my belly. We gasped and exclaimed, suddenly in the midst of wonders far beyond what we had been prepared for.

In this state of beauteous awe, I crashed headfirst into the larger context of the amniocentesis. This viewing of our baby on the miracle machine was to ascertain whether it had genetic defects and, if so, to abort it. I fell down, way down into a moral abyss.

In sixteen weeks of being pregnant, I already had so many feelings about this growing baby and myself. I had hopes and dreams invested in us already. Our family and friends had already begun to weave their love and anticipation around us. We were deep into the process, both physically and emotionally, of gestating a new human being. What I saw on the sonogram TV screen bore remarkable resemblance to a newborn baby. Seeing this baby evoked my maternal love even more. How could I possibly get an abortion at this point?

What if our baby did have Down's syndrome or a different genetic defect? I knew I would choose to abort, but it would set off an avalanche of sorrow. The woman inside me who loves babies would be brokenhearted.

If I had an abortion, everywhere I went in the world, I would have to explain to friends and colleagues and clients why I was not pregnant anymore. My grief would not only be my own, it would also be public. In imagining my choice for an abortion, do I feel shame, too? Shame that I would kill what I once loved? Shame that I love conditionally? Shame that I choose my happiness over the possibility of another life?

Part of what's confusing to me is that I vacillate between thinking about the creature in my womb as "my baby" and thinking about it as "a fetus." Medically, it is considered a fetus. It does not have a neocortex, couldn't breathe or eat or have a beating heart on its own.

However, in five more months, it could be my newborn baby. A mother's love does not just spring forth full-blown at birth; it grows over the nine-month pregnancy and deepens throughout a lifetime. So in my emotional reality, this is a baby, my baby, the beginnings of my baby.

When the rational woman inside me speaks, she refers to what lies in my womb as "a fetus." The emotional woman inside me calls it "my baby." I am aware of each of these women inside me, but they do not know each other. They would have no idea how to speak to each other, could not communicate. In the middle of the amniocentesis procedure, I found myself in the awkward position of understanding both sides of the abortion debate within myself.

The nurse told us that, based on the visual check on the sonogram, the fetus looked normal and whole. Steve was anxious, too, and suggested that that was adequate information and we should stop there. I insisted that we proceed with the genetic testing of the amniotic fluid. I hadn't come this far to go halfway. The nurse said I could urinate, which brought immense relief.

We were taken to a different room, where another sonogram machine lived. A doctor we had never met before came in saying hello. Within a minute, he located the fetus on the television screen, gave me a shot of local anesthetic, and inserted a long needle into my belly. I didn't look. But just as Joanne said, I could feel the needle entering my uterus, and my uterus spoke unequivocally, "Get out!" After a few minutes, the needle was out. I got dressed, and we walked out of his office with a bill that totaled nearly a thousand dollars, including lab fees.

All that day, and the next day, too, I felt cramping in my uterus. I was afraid I would have a spontaneous miscarriage. The place where the needle had entered my uterus was sore. Alone, I placed my hand on my belly, breathed gently into my womb to relax, and tried to reassure my baby, "It's OK. It's over now. I won't ever let anyone poke a needle into your house again. I promise. You can relax. You'll be fine now. I love you, and I'm going to take care of you." Then another voice intruded, blurting out, "Unless I decide to kill you."

All day, I struggled with how to reassure this baby inside me. I couldn't find a statement that was both honest and comforting.

The fact remained: if something was genetically wrong with this fetus, I would end his or her life.

I could not reconcile the two women within me. The Nurturing Mother wants to protect all life, to love each baby unconditionally. She will fight until death protecting her baby from harm. The Rational Woman imagines the future, evaluates difficult options, makes choices about quality of life for herself and her family, including saying no to a developing new life.

I began to wonder. What if the baby was genetically fine, but on the sonogram we had seen a deformed hand? Or what if the heart was not properly formed? Would we abort? What if a woman wants a baby girl and discovers she is carrying a boy? When do we think it is OK to abort? Are only perfect babies OK? Who offers women guidance through these murky questions? We received so-called excellent medical care, and no one spoke to us about anything but medical risks and statistics.

There is precedence in nature for ending the life of deformed babies. Nature aborts one out of every five fertilized and attached eggs in a human woman because something isn't quite right.[1] Various animal species, including some human cultures, leave weak or abnormal young to die or even kill those newborns. It is not only the law but the perhaps inscrutable wisdom of nature that only the strongest survive. Nature's interest is in sustaining life but only when it is realistic given the larger ecology. When the presence of an individual life—a sapling tree, for instance—is not sustainable given its proximity to other trees, nature snuffs the little sapling.

Esther Harding notes that "primitive people are as a rule entirely cold-blooded about disposing of unwanted infants and usually have some quite efficient, if not altogether harmless, method of procuring abortion."[2] Abortion, and the selective killing of newborn babies, have been commonly practiced throughout human history.[3]

Nature, in its particular wisdom, creates life and destroys life. This is the essence of the Great Mother Goddess. She understands the necessity of death, the desirability of death in the cycle of life. The Instinctive Mother does not only nurture new life; when the conditions for survival are poor, she has the wisdom to wield death.

My friend who had a miscarriage in her third month of pregnancy said that, in some ways, it was as profound for her as giving birth to her son. In her grief, she said she was forced to comprehend that her mother-body was a vessel for death as well as life. She channeled the creatrix and the destructress.

I now have the luxury of knowing that I will not be forced to know my mother-body as a vessel for death, at least not for now. I will not have to become intimate with my ability to create death, not yet. I have been reassured by medical science that I am carrying a healthy baby. I have also been told that I am carrying a baby girl. I feel fortunate. I can now fully weave my love around this baby. I can also begin to love and imagine a baby girl, how it will be to mother a daughter.

Safely out of the ambiguous trenches of amniocentesis, I think more about the issue of abortion. We say that life is sacred. Both sides of the abortion debate hinge on this value. Those who favor a woman's right to choose abortion believe that life is sacred—that the needs of already existing sacred lives must be honored and that we must be able to adequately care for a sacred new life. Those who oppose abortion believe that every potential life is a gift from God and must be accepted on earth—that to abort a fetus is murder of a human being. For me, the question becomes this: is all life sacred at all costs? Perhaps life is so sacred that *quality* of life becomes a moral imperative; sometimes potential life must be sacrificed to adequately honor existing life.

We say that life is sacred. As if we can separate ourselves from death. As if life and death do not belong together. Is every egg sacred? Every sperm? Every cell must die and does. We say that the gift of life is sacred, and we are right. We must create sacred contexts wherein sacred life can dwell. Sacred families. Sacred health care. Sacred education. Sacred birth control.

As a society, we are in the midst of gigantic dilemmas about what we are able to know and how we can shape creation and destruction. We can play God, but we are not morally prepared for the role.

We live with the conditions of existence, and they are ambiguous. It takes a certain strength to touch into these ambiguities, and as Bertrand Russell encouraged, to develop a tolerance for ambiguity. Herein may lie some wisdom on the moral issue of abortion. The conception of a life, sacred as that is, is so profoundly defined by context that it defies any prescribed set of moral rules. Life is ambiguous. We cannot and should not expect pat answers or simple feelings around issues of life and death.

There are many lifetimes of work to be done in service of the belief that life is sacred. We can work to make a world that is respectful of the gift of life in all its wondrous shapes and forms. We can learn to take more seriously the human events of love, intimacy, birth control, and conception. We can deepen the conversation about abortion, in authentic and loving ways. Perhaps when persons with opposing points of view are willing to know the truth of the "other," a new and deeper truth will emerge. But always we will return to our basic ground: life sometimes presents us with painful choices between imperfect realities. On a good day, we choose with wisdom and love—and a tolerance for ambiguity.

[I]f I were asked to name the chief benefit of the house, I should say: the house shelters daydreaming, the house protects the dreamer, the house allows one to dream in peace.

—Gaston Bachelard
The Poetics of Space, p. 6

Moving

four and one-half months pregnant
two-year-old son

WE BOUGHT A HOUSE. Whoo-eee, that's a big step. It's a lot of papers to sign with a lot of words that I have only recently come to understand, accompanied by a lot of big consequences. The financial obligation scares me half to death.

When what I really wanted to do was lie on the couch curled up with a blanket and book, instead I have to bend over in a dirty garage filled with spiders and their webs, sorting out boxes of old junk. After sorting through dozens of such sagging cardboard boxes, patterns emerge; differences in how Steve and I order the world become apparent. All the boxes labeled "Maren" have one category of item filling each box. All books in one box. All photographs in one box. All miscellaneous junk in one box. In contrast, every single box labeled "Steve" contains a remarkably similar pastiche: abandoned pens and pencils; lists scrawled on yellow legal pads of things to do at work and notes from workshops; cassette tapes (some in cases, some not); pennies, nickels, dimes, and quarters; plus some additional surprises. This is OK, I tell myself: home ought to be a place where a person gets to order the world in his or her own way. However, this ideal becomes more complicated when two different people create a home together. This mildly amusing line of contemplation sustains me through sorting a few more boxes of junk. More than once, I consider simply torching the garage.

We are moving: dismantling the old order, not yet mantling the new order. The odd thing is how important it seems to move our old junk to a new house. We don't have much of value: a good bed mattress, a crib and a box full of baby toys, two bicycles and a toddler push car, a set of dishes crafted by a potter we know, four matching bath towels. Photographs and old journals. Books. Almost everything else would probably be best thrown away. Most of what we have in our little apartment is junk. But it is *our* junk. It is the junk that we see every day, the old stuffed chair that we sit in and the blue flowered couch that has held so much. In a peculiar way that is hard to justify, our junk helps to make our place "home."

We are leaving our little cottage on a cliff above the beach. For sixteen years, Steve has lived here. For five years, I have lived here. We know this beach in all its seasons, the daily dramas of tides and storms and migrating whales. At night, rhythmic waves crash against the shore, obliterating the other noise of the world, reassuring us into sleep. We bodysurf these waves. Once, we accidentally sank a boat in this ocean, and postmortem christened it *Underwater.* We buried our pet cat here, named (while living) Underfoot. We cultivated a vegetable garden here by the sea and an herb garden. I planted a lawn for Jesse. We watched the sun sink down into the ocean almost every night.

I pack boxes. I lift boxes. I try not to lift boxes that are too heavy. I am working every moment, as a psychotherapist, mother, and packer. We hired a moving company to pack the kitchen and do the moving on the big day. They are a cut-rate outfit, so we have to help pack, lift, and move, too. The moving company assesses how many movers are needed by the amount of space the client lives in. I told them we have a three-room apartment, plus a bathroom and single garage.

On the big day, they send two movers. After seven hours of work, Steve and I and the movers are still knee-deep in stuff from the kitchen. One of the movers looks overwhelmed and says, "This is taking much longer than I thought." I freeze. I thought that line was reserved for Steve and me. If the movers are saying that to us, we are in deep trouble. When will we get to our new house, and how will it ever become a home, and where will we sleep, and how can I ever get comfortable on a couch again?

The new house is an empty, depressing cavern. The walls and curtains bear stains from years of cigarette smoke. The kitchen has neon lime green linoleum covering practically everything: the counters, the telephone desk, and all the places where the white paint has scraped off the cabinets and doors.

For most of our adult lives, we have lived like students: old used couches, bookshelves made of boards and bricks, art posters tacked to the walls. Our blue flowered couch sits lonely and dwarfed in a huge, empty living room. Our used-to-be waterbed frame with a mattress lies in the master bedroom across from the dresser and mirror that belonged to my maternal grandmother. Jesse's crib is finally set up in his room. An ironing board is set up in the other bedroom. Boxes are stacked everywhere. The only reassuring feeling of home is that Jesse's toys are already scattered everywhere.

Jesse is manic, partly from being repressed all day during the hard work of moving and partly because he is liberated from a cramped apartment with a postage-stamp-sized yard into a full acre of land and a real house. He races from room to room, memorizing the entrances and exits, the layout of the house. He rides his push toy car up and down the wood floor of the long, narrow bedroom hallway, which frankly only reminds me of a bowling alley.

I fear that, if I don't stop working and lie down, I might miscarry. It's been way too much work and stress, lifting, and carrying, for me. We are bone-tired. We go to bed. But we are miserable in bed. There is no noise. It is so quiet here we can't go to sleep. For years, day and night, the tumble of ocean waves was the constant sound in our home. Here it is so quiet we can distinguish the smallest sounds of animals outside. We must have drifted off to sleep, because when I next awake, it is dark. I am alarmed. Steve bolts upright in bed. I jump up, race to see whether Jesse is OK. Outside, someone or something is screaming as if it is being murdered. Loud. Maaahw. Maaahw. Could it be a cat fight? Raccoons? Opossum? We don't know who or what lives around here. Steve thinks it's peacocks. I can't relax in this place. It's not home. We just spent a fortune buying a house, but we have no home. I want to be cozy in my internal spaces. Instead, I'm in a cavernous house with a million boxes of junk everywhere, and worse yet, I am the person who is supposed to do something about it.

I'm not equipped to transform this depressing cavern into a home. I sense the magnitude of the job, but I can't imagine where to begin, what to do. A friend who looked at this house with us told me that it has no moldings anywhere. What's a molding?

There is the task of unpacking all the boxes of stuff, rearranging that reassuring junk in this new space. Then, there is the category of painting walls, washing curtains or throwing them away, and getting moldings. But more daunting than all of that work is the feat of making a home. How does one make a home?

I feel I am living in someone else's house. What do we need to do to get the energy of the past occupants out of here? This place smells like somebody else. The walls are foreign; they do not contain any memories of us, any crayon marks from an angry toddler, any splattered paint jobs that we did. The carpet is pearly white, obviously not claimed by us yet. None of it is ours. Nothing in the house speaks back to us, reminds us of who we are, reminds us of all that we have imagined and done here and before here.

The French philosopher Gaston Bachelard said that the essence of home is "inhabited space," a weave of daydreams, hopes, memories. Home is invested with all that we hope to keep close to us and all that we hope to keep out. It is protection and comfort—refuge from a threatening world. Home is a fantasy and a concrete reality through which we imagine ourselves and order our cosmos. Home contains us, orders the chaos of our lives.

How much time and experience will it take for us to inhabit all the spaces of this house and yard? It is hard to face the fact that it will take years to invest our souls and psyches into this land and house. I am homesick now. Sick for lack of a home. I want a home, and I do not have one anymore, and I can't get one soon, not the deep, comforting home that I want.

Never before have I owned a home. How can I reconcile the person I feel I am with the person who owns a house and is coresponsible for a big monthly mortgage payment? The word *monthlies* has acquired a new meaning. Who is this person who suddenly owns a Maytag washer and dryer? And drives a Volvo station wagon? And is married, with a two-year-old boy and a bun in the oven? Who is this establishment, middle-class grown-up?

For the first time in my life, I am asked to be a person who tends home, who makes home for a family—a real home—and I have no idea how to do it. I don't know the first thing about interior decorating, and what's more, I'm not sure that's what I want to spend my time doing.

I never really imagined myself as a homemaker. I have been clear about my desire to work professionally and also clear about my desire to be a mother. But when I bought into the mother business, I did not understand to what a large extent the cooking and food business and the housecleaning business and the homemaking business were included, like a package deal. I don't like spending hours picking things up and putting them away, or doing laundry. I'm just learning the distinction between a molding and a floorboard. I certainly don't know why this house has such a depressing look, nor do I know how to correct that. However, it is clear that if we are to have a home, I will be the one who will orchestrate that process. My husband has even less interest and ability in homemaking than I, not to mention that he has had little time at home these recent months.

Is homemaking the work of the mother? I know that historically it has been relegated to women. I know some men who are good homemakers, so I don't think it's only a women's thing. Personally, I never accepted the mantle until I became a mother. The biological imperative to make a nest for one's baby stirs a deep desire, not simply to make a functional shelter but to make a home, a space worthy of its occupants both present and future, a safe haven.

I am now a homemaker. Ten years ago, no one could have convinced me I would be here. I wonder, do I want to be a homemaker? Do I think it is important work to make a home? How does one do it? If my life becomes so focused on homemaking and mothering, absorbed in these realms of the personal, what will become of my relationship to the larger world? What about careers and politics and the affairs of the culture? What do I really want to tend with my life energy?

At some point, it's all irrelevant philosophizing. My most pressing need is to establish a home because my soul craves it. I need to feel a sense of home—where I can be comfortable and feel good. I need to be in a cozy nest with the baby girl who is growing in my belly, a place where we can lie on the couch together, with blankets and pillows that smell right, where we can watch *Little House on the Prairie*.

. . . Goddess religion was earth-centered, not heaven-centered, of this world not otherworldly, body-affirming not body-denying, holistic not dualistic. The Goddess was immanent, within every human being, not transcendent, and humanity was viewed as part of nature, death as a part of life. Her worship was sensual, celebrating the erotic, embracing all that was alive. The religious quest was above all for renewal, for the regeneration of life, and the Goddess was the life force.

—Elinor Gadon
The Once and Future Goddess, p. xii

WOMEN AND RELIGION

six months pregnant
two-year-old son

I WAS WATCHING TELEVISION last night. Pope John Paul II, the spiritual leader of the Roman Catholic Church, was speaking to the masses, surrounded by the chosen upper echelon of persons who had devoted their lives to the religious institution, all of whom were men. This visual image of only men in robes emphasized that the Catholic Church is a patriarchal kingdom, ruled by men.

How different I am from those priests on television. Unadorned by fancy robes or titles, I am almost irretrievably sunken into a couch with my swollen feet propped up on a footstool. I wear baggy T-shirts. I am called the name that innumerable women are called: Mom. However, like the high priests, I, too, have been chosen: I am filling with the miracle of life. Millions of women have been chosen for this sacred duty before me. With some luck, millions of women will be chosen for this sacred duty after me. Obviously, men cannot join our club, but beyond that, we are not too exclusive an outfit. We accept members regardless of race, socioeconomic class, religious preference, and even sexual preference. There are many of us who, in quiet ways, fill with the mysteries of life, tend the spirits of others, and deepen the life of the soul in our daily acts of mothering. I believe there are very few priests who know this about us.

Particularly because I am a woman who went to seminary and am an ordained minister, I have been aware of the male dominance in organized religion for quite some time. Even though many women are in theological schools today, we still confront a severe masculine bias in theology and religious institutions. I was the first woman minister in the Unitarian Universalist church I served, having to mediate all sorts of issues for the first time. One blunt person framed one problem this way, "When I look at you while you are giving a sermon, I have a hard time taking you seriously because you are a pretty woman." Navigating the treacherous crosscurrents between female authority and female sexuality within a church made this swimmer tired.

Although I can get worked up about the preponderance of masculine energy in religious institutions, most of the time I am not, and the reason for my calm is simple: I don't want what they have. If I were a devout Catholic and wanted to become a priest serving a congregation, I'm sure my nerve endings would be closer to the surface.

But the human psyche is a miracle unto itself, always alert for daily images and situations that could be of use in nudging a person toward wholeness. Knowing that the male Catholic gathering on television was not enough to push my buttons fully, my psyche embellished the story in a dream that same night, escorting me directly to my cutting edge.

I am at a gathering of the Graduate Theological Union held at the Pacific School of Religion. I am with other women who are also on the periphery of established religion because we are adamant that theology and religious practice should fully respect women. Several women speak briefly about what they believe. I raise my hand to speak. Right before I get to my final and most important statement about the feminine, a male cleric interrupts me. Pretending that he thought I was finished, but knowing full well that he was cutting me off, he says in a pompous intellectual manner, "I, too, was moved by the words of Ms. Hansen. However, even if I were inclined toward her religion, I could not accept it because it has no ethics."

I am furious that he interrupted me and tried to squash what I was saying with such a closed-minded judgment. I insistently raise my hand to speak again, now to make two points. The first point is that he has insulted my religiousness. I do have an ethical base, and I would hope that religious people could be open to hearing each other rather than issuing blanket judgments about their differences. I was going to frame my second point as a question, but now I decide to state it more forcefully. I ask us all to imagine what would emerge if women gathered in religious community to explore and take seriously women's experience. I wonder aloud about all the different ways that religion would change if women were genuinely included, not only in leadership positions but also if the depths of the female experience were addressed in ritual and theology.

The curse of it all is that I still am participating in dialog with male theologians who refuse to see the value of including females in theology. Why can't I simply decide that male-based theologies and chauvinist ministers/priests are of no interest to me, that in fact they are mostly irrelevant to what I experience and find important in the world? Why can't I go about my own religious business in life, accepting that I cannot change the mainstream? For some reason, I still feel compelled to bring more female influence into established religion.

There are many fine feminist theologians who insist that women be included in Judaism and Christianity. Many are pushing for "inclusive language" in the Bible and in worship services. Although these are good women fighting the hard fight, my friend Meg disagrees with this approach. She thinks "inclusive language" only confuses people, obscuring the reality that Judaism and Christianity are primarily theologies emerging from a male perspective in the world.

Surely, some of my desire to interface with organized religion is a deep desire to have a religious community. I yearn for an organized religion that meets my deepest needs. I want to be with a group of people who hold the mysteries of birth and death, of male and female, of inner spiritual development and ethical action. I want a religious community that teaches me, challenges my depths, evokes my soul.

The fact of the matter is that I am a deeply religious woman who does not fit in any of the prevailing organized religious systems. I love studying world religions and mythology. I admire much about the practice of Jewish religion. The Christian stories point to truths that I find meaningful. I have enjoyed learning about Buddhism, Sufism, Hinduism, Taoism, and Islam. But I have always been an outsider to these traditions.

When I hear the stories of Judaism and Christianity or Buddhism, I have to make several translations to get from the stories to what is true in my own experience. The guiding stories of these religions are not my primary stories. I can understand the stories, but they do not work for me unconsciously. They don't teach me what I am yearning to know about my feminine nature, about the natural world, about the soul of the whole. There doesn't seem to be any existing religious system that adequately contains and reflects what I sense about the depths of existence. I feel separated, caught in an awkward crevice in history where the new collective religious stories and images are only now beginning to be whispered through individuals.

There is some advantage to not having cultural forms that reflect my religious sense. I am forced to rely on myself, to know what is true for me by looking to my authentic experience, claiming my internal authority. No pope or priest mediates my religion. No dogma dictates how I commune with the Divine or what I know to be holy.

The disadvantage is that I have to figure out so much by myself and that I do not have an established religious community. I do gather with my women friends each full moon and for the solstices, equinoxes, and other special occasions. We create rituals in nature, based on what is stirring us in our lives. We are exploring that which is speaking through us. These friends are my religious community to the extent that I have one.

I know many persons who are spiritual but do not participate in organized religion. Yet we still live with the essential religious desires. We want to know where we came from. Where will we go and what will happen after we die? What is the meaning in suffering? How can we join our personal consciousness with the cosmic consciousness? Some find the divine in nature. Some are guided toward the holy through dream work and Jungian psychology. Some are drawn to the old religions of the Goddesses and the Gods. Some worship science.

The more I enter into my own femininity, the more I see how very little organized religion knows about the female experience. I felt this way before I started having babies, but becoming a mother has multiplied my feeling tenfold. I have been profoundly taken by the religious insights, feelings, and communions that I have experienced becoming a mother. More than any other era of my life, this has been a deeply religious time.

There is no doubt in my mind that becoming a mother is a spiritual journey and that most women who are becoming mothers experience similar images and feelings. Pregnancy is one spiritual teaching after another. Among other things, pregnancy grows the soul of the mother. Spontaneously, some larger force in life speaks through the mother in dreams, images, fantasies, daily bodily experiences. I have been listening carefully. I have eagerly received these religious teachings, reveling in the beauty and meaning they bring to my life.

Being something of a theologian, I have tried to make sense of what I have experienced, tried to find reflections of this depth in the stories of the world religions. I have consistently noticed that the ancient stories of the Goddess religions resonate most with my experience. Perhaps this should not be surprising: the Goddess religions come from a period of history in which the female was understood and valued and, more particularly, a time when the mother was understood and valued.

I don't have any complete religious system worked out around what I am experiencing. It's not that I've written the mother's version of Thomas Aquinas's *Summa theologiae*. But it is quite clear that my religious journey is deeply involved with my life experience as a woman, with echoes of the ancient Goddesses woven through it all, with the feminine dimension of the Divine.

In response to the criticism of the male theologian in my dream, I don't know whether the Goddess religions have an ethical basis, although I think it's an interesting idea to explore. It would take more expertise than I have to adequately answer the question about whether the MotherMysteries or Goddess religions have an ethical base.

I can, however, speak about what I have come to know in my own life. In my personal experience, motherhood has deepened my ethical sensibilities. Loving one human being so intricately has expanded my capacity to love others. Like the loaves and the fishes, my love has multiplied. I love mothers and babies everywhere. I want to protect them from harm, to help them grow healthy bodies and lives. My love has extended to other species and to the earth as a bio-organism.

It is correct to recognize that the ethics of nature differ from the human ethics of modern religion. In nature, each being eats and is eaten, often brutally. In nature, the weak die; life that cannot be sustained is quickly extinguished.

To what extent can the Goddess religions or the MotherMysteries be equated with nature? Are they one and the same? To a large extent, the Great Mother Goddess and nature are the same. A mother is drawn into the forces of nature; her willingness to be a vessel of nature is the source of her genius.

In the process of subsuming her will into nature's will, a woman becomes intimate with the deepest mysteries. A woman witnesses the essential forces of life, she joins these forces, becomes one with them. She acquires the wisdom of nature.

But a human woman also brings love to the equation. She brings consciousness to the equation. As human mothers, we bring a unique combination of qualities into the world: nature, love, consciousness. Has this combination ever before been widely represented on the planet? I think this is nature's unique gift to modern women. Why might the living biosphere evolve this combination of traits at this particular point in evolution? Is there something about the unification of nature, love, and consciousness that is important, perhaps even necessary, for the continuation of life on the planet? What happens inside a human being who unites nature's deepest patterns with consciousness and love? What do we come to know?

Perhaps consciousness is the most difficult gift for mothers to open. The work of the mother mostly drifts in unconscious waters: instinct, body wisdom, the moment-to-moment existence of responding to the needs of the child. To find time alone, reflective time, may be the most difficult trial for a woman who seeks to garner the wisdom of her mother journey.

In the deepest psychological and spiritual ways, a woman is transformed as she becomes a mother. This wisdom, this love, all that she comes to know in her transformation, is the treasure that she wins in the spiritual journey into motherhood.

I have wondered about how theology and religious institutions would be different if they were open to the wisdom of the mother. Now, I am seeing that the life wisdom mothers are acquiring must be brought into the cultural conversation, not just in religion but in all spheres: personal relationships, education, business, environmental matters, foreign policy, and education. What would happen if we spoke our truth as mothers, on behalf of our own babies, on behalf of the babies of all mothers throughout the world, human and animal alike, and on behalf of the life force that blessed us in our creations?

Ultimately, the only choice is whether to listen carefully and with respect to what is wanting to speak through us, to tend to the life of the soul and the requests of the soul, and to bring our voices to the larger community. As Jesus said, "He who has ears to hear, let him hear."[1] She, too.

It is a special thesis of mine that mothers, unless they are psychiatrically ill, do orientate to their very specialised task [primary maternal preoccupation] during the last months of pregnancy, and that they gradually recover from this in the course of weeks and months after the birth process.

—D. W. Winnicott
Babies and Their Mothers, p. 36

OH, NO NOT THAT AGAIN

seven months pregnant
two-year-old son

MY FRIEND KATHY had her baby last night—a ten-pound girl. Kathy called me about 9:00 pm, less than two hours after the birth. She sounded like her normal self: balanced, calm, pleasant. How could that possibly be? My mind reeled: she just came out of the nightmare I have been dreading, yet she sounded like a relaxed, normal woman who was drinking a cup of tea.

I have been panicking about entering labor and childbirth again. In what might be acts of masochism, I pore through my childbirth books, challenging myself *not* to avert my eyes from photographs of a vaginal opening bulged wide open by a hairy, round head that's pushing through, and my voice blurts out, "Oh, no! Not that again!" I am terrified to enter that pain again. I do not want to surrender to that process. I can barely face all the fear I feel about going into labor and pushing a baby out of my body again. And yet, at this stage of the game, with eight weeks to go, what choice do I have?

The trauma from my first birth is not fresh anymore. I don't sit around dwelling on it. It doesn't creep up on me when I'm not looking. But as I inexorably drift toward labor, the old wounds are restimulated. Worse than the mere future is the prospect of the future informed by the past. In two months, I will go into labor again, and this time, I know what I'm getting into. I know how much pain it is. How awful the pushing is. How intolerable the pressure is.

My friend Kathy credited her unruffled state to her epidural anesthetic. She said she felt no pain in the lower half of her body, yet she was awake and alert. I am reevaluating my attitude toward painkilling medication in childbirth. Maybe I'll be less dogmatic this time. I want to allow myself the freedom to ask for a shot of Demerol if the birth is too traumatic for me. It's not that I'm planning to use pain medication, but I want to allow myself the option. Actually, I doubt that I will ask for Demerol since I am concerned about sharing so much of the narcotic with my baby, and I would be unforgiving of myself if my baby's breathing was depressed because of it. The epidural doesn't appeal to me because of the loss of sensation in the lower body. I want to know where the baby is, to be able to open my pelvis more if need be, to push the baby out. It would bother me to not have any bodily information about what is happening in the birth and how I could help.

A few persons have commented to me that my second labor will not necessarily be as difficult as my first. I have heard that the second labor is often easier because a woman's body has stretched before in that way and she knows more of what she is doing the second time around. Maybe what they say is true. But maybe it isn't. None of us knows what my second labor and delivery will be like. No one can predict or control what will happen, when or how I will emerge from birth, and with whom.

For seven months, I have been floating on a raft, gently down the stream. Merrily, merrily, merrily, merrily . . . oh, my God, the current is pulling me. Landmarks are ringing like alarm bells: the rapids are nearing. I can't swim back. I can't get to the shore. Soon, I will be swept into the terrifying mystery, and I know it. I will be caught in powerful currents, pummeled by the rushing waters, shoved into rocks, pushed over the edge where the water falls. Finally, I will be dumped into the pool beneath the waterfall, dead or alive, dumped into a pool that is remarkable in its quiet.

Childbirth is a rite of passage so intense physically, psychologically, emotionally, spiritually, that most other events in a woman's life pale next to it. In our modern lives, there are few remaining rituals of initiation, few events that challenge a person's mettle down to the very core. Childbirth remains a primary initiatory event for a woman.

Birth is an ordeal. So is pregnancy, for that matter. Physical transformations in a fascinating partnership with psyche and spirit. In the last trimester of pregnancy, a woman's psyche is drawn toward preparation for childbirth. She must begin to prepare mentally and physically for her immense task. But how? How does she prepare herself for such an enormous event?

Eat well, sleep a lot, take childbirth education classes, and rehearse with your labor partner. That's easy. The more pressing issue is how to prepare emotionally, psychologically, spiritually for facing the ordeal. Is there any possible way I could approach this second birth without fear and dread?

Like an athlete preparing for the Olympics, I must gather my forces. Nourish my body for optimal performance. Steady my mind, so that the fear from the past does not dictate the present or the future. I must find a way to work through the trauma from my first birth. I don't really know how to clear the fear. I understand intellectually that I want to be open to whatever realities present themselves with this birth, that I don't want to enter labor with expectations of pain and torment based on past experience that may not be applicable to my current situation. But the practical matter of shifting from these leftover feelings of the past into openness to the present—ah, that is a tricky feat.

I want someone else to take care of this for me. I'm noticing that, during my first labor, and right now, when I feel mired in the ordeal, my first impulse is to resign, let someone else deal with it. There is some courage and perseverance that I lack. I'm not one of those heroes who look danger and pain in the face, vowing to conquer it and emerge victorious. I look danger in the face and say, "Forget it. I didn't really want to do that anyway."

Why couldn't I be married to one of those men who take on the labor pains of the woman? My younger brother is sort of like that. During the early months of pregnancy with his first child, he was extremely tired, only to go on to gain quite a bit of weight before the baby was born. During the labor and birth of his second child, he had excruciating lower back pain, unrelenting until the baby was born. We all laughed about it. But it is true that there is a tradition of men who absorb the birthing pains of women.

Scholars talk about this phenomenon using the French term *couvade,* differentiating between "couvade syndrome" and "ritual couvade."

Couvade syndrome includes any bodily symptoms of pregnancy and birth that a father experiences in his own body. The father may or may not be conscious of these symptoms in himself.

Ritual couvade involves elaborate cultural rituals in which the father "takes on" the physical experiences of the mother in pregnancy, birth, and postpartum recovery. Ritual couvade customs are most often found in "small-scale societies," especially among the aboriginal Ainu of Japan, other Pacific Island cultures, and Caribbean and South American societies.[1]

Couvade rituals may include the husband's observing food taboos for several months surrounding the birth, the husband's restricting his normal activities before and after the birth, perhaps staying closer to home and working less. In some couvade rituals, the husband is secluded, either with the wife or sometimes in a men's house or alone, during pregnancy and postpartum recovery. Sexual abstinence is an aspect of some couvade rituals.

The couvade practice that interests me most is when the man writhes in pain during childbirth, with various attendants assisting him, while in the next room, alone, the mother painlessly pushes a baby out of her body. In the Hawaiian tradition, the *kahuna pale keiki,* the shaman attending the labor and birth, often transfers the pains of labor from the birthing woman to someone else. The pains could be transferred to any person or even to family animals, such as dogs and horses.

A modern Hawaiian woman tells a couvade story that makes me happy every time I read it. "The last painless birth in our family was when my older sister was born. In the next room slept a lazy relative. My uncle, who was the kahuna, prayed to Haumea (the goddess of birth), and directed that the pain be given to that lazy brother-in-law of his. This poor fellow, who had been enjoying his sleep, began to moan and groan until after my sister was born."[2]

Why bother with a theoretical discussion of couvade when, in several months, we could try the real thing? How hard could it be to find a shaman who practices couvade in Southern California? Or for that matter, surely there are still kahunas on the Big Island of Hawaii who transfer the birthing pains. I wouldn't want to inflict this suffering upon my husband. God knows, he has been empathetic and supportive in so many other ways in this act of creation. No, I want him there with me, focusing on me, taking care of me. Perhaps we could transfer the pain to our neighbor's dog, the big, white, fluffy one who barks day and night.

Oh, it all boils down to this: I want someone to take my suffering away, to take the pain and the difficulty upon themselves. I don't want to bear this burden by myself. My mind seeks one hundred and one ways to escape facing my fate alone. I am guessing that other women have felt this way also, that part of the function of couvade is that a woman feels other people are helping her carry out her heroic task.

What are the other functions of couvade? It obviously serves some deep need for men and women. Not only is it an established ritual in many cultures, but even in societies that do not observe ritual couvade, this phenomenon arises spontaneously in the psyche of certain men.

From a cultural perspective, particularly in ancient times, couvade makes sense as a way to establish paternity. Prehistoric people did not recognize the role of the male in reproduction. The couvade ritual might well have been a symbolic and public way for the man to announce that he will be the father of the child, stay close to home, protect the mother and child from physical and spiritual danger.[3]

Many religious traditions have evolved, in part, because they provide sound community health practices. The couvade practice of sexual abstinence prior to and after the birth is indeed in the best health interests of the mother.

With regard to the eternal struggle for power, some social scientists see couvade as an attempt by men to usurp the power of women.[4] Most ancient human civilizations worshiped the Great Goddess, the divine power who gave life and took it away. The magical power to become full with life and to give birth bestowed a reverence upon the female that is difficult for the modern psyche to fathom.

Several thousand years before the birth of Christ, gradually the Goddess-worshiping cultures were taken over by more male-dominant cultures, which worshiped a male God. Barbara Walker writes, "Since birth-giving was the only true mark of divinity in primitive belief, the first gods to claim any sort of supremacy had to claim also the ability to give birth. In fact, usurpation of the feminine power of birth-giving seems to have been the distinguishing mark of the earliest gods."[5]

An example of this religious revisionism begins with the ancient Sumerian Goddess Nin-ti, who was often referred to as "Lady of the Rib." *Ti* in her name translates into two meanings: "rib" and "life." In Sumerian myths, it was said that while the baby was in the womb, the Goddess Nin-ti used the ribs of the human mother to fashion the bones of the baby.

This association between ribs and the powers of creation surfaced later in the Old Testament story of the creation of humankind. "So the Lord God caused a deep sleep to fall upon the man, and while he slept took one of his ribs and closed up its place with flesh; and the rib which the Lord God had taken from the man he made into a woman and brought her to the man. Then the man said, 'This at last is bone of my bones and flesh of my flesh; she shall be called Woman, because she was taken out of Man.' "[6]

The attempt of human males and the male Gods to claim the role of birth-giver smacks of womb envy and power grabbing. I particularly object to the physiological disfigurations that the male gods went through in order to give birth: giving birth through their mouths or the head of the penis or the head or the thigh.[7] The natural physiology of birth is not honored in modern religion; as a woman and a mother, this offends me.

In some couvade practices, all the birth attendants are in the room with the agonizing man, fussing over him, while the woman labors alone unattended. The man then spends weeks in bed recovering from the birth, while the mother gets up and tends the baby, the house, and the bedridden husband.

I prefer honoring the male powers of creation in a gender-appropriate way. I love the Egyptian story of Osiris, wherein his erect phallus annually floods the Nile River Valley with semen, fertilizing the land, planting the wet seeds of life.

In couvade experiences, I see a deep human impulse to participate in the great feminine mystery. We can call that womb envy or womb fascination, but more than that, I understand it as the desire to participate in the mystery of the Other.

I can only imagine the perspective of the father-to-be. I imagine that his role feels nebulous. Yes, he planted the sperm nine months ago; genetically, the baby is half his. But he has had little, if any, relationship to the baby during the nine months the mother has lived with it in the most intimate ways. Does his unconscious pull him into identification with his birthing wife, so that he, too, experiences the *mysterium tremendum*? Does he merge into her psyche and body so that he, too, experiences the pangs of creation and pushes forth a new life?

Participation mystique is commonly accepted in psychological discussions about the mother and child. The baby "participates" in the mother's body, moods, psychological atmosphere. The baby and the mother have fluid boundaries, identifying with each other to the extent that they are, in many ways, one. Why do we not recognize that the father, too, may dissolve into this unconscious creative field? The creative forces of nature take over the body of the woman. The baby, too, is commanded to participate in these forces of creation. Why shouldn't this also be true, to at least some extent, for the father?

Many fathers now join childbirth education classes, are active labor coaches, in meaningful ways supporting the birthing mother. They orient themselves around the needs and feelings of the mother. They witness and assist as the baby is pushed out of her body. They cut the umbilical cord. They hold the baby, skin to skin. In this profound intimacy, it is only natural that the father's empathy leads him into some identification with the woman's experience. For some men, that empathy extends into the physiological experience of pregnancy and labor.

As a woman who has given birth once, and is soon to enter the fire again, I know something about what I want. I want my husband to be fully present for me again. I want him to tend me, comfort me, encourage me, take care of whatever details the world presents in those hours, so I don't have to think about them. I want my husband to suffer with me, but not too much. I don't want him to suffer so that I need to worry about him or that other people need to worry about him. I want to be the focus of attention. I want to keep this primarily as an event of my body, as an initiation of my psyche. But I also want a partner to help me hold the magnitude of it all. I want to feel a sense of oneness, that the two of us joined forces into one creative act. I want to know that he will help me bear the pain, the terrifying mystery, and the joy of giving birth. After the birth, I want my man to stay close to me, to nurture me, even baby me. During the first few weeks of our baby's life, I want my husband to tend to our older child and to the ongoing details of running a household.

It is the facing of great challenges that transforms the ordinary person into a hero. The aspiring hero must meet and conquer her fear, gather the mental and spiritual and physical forces necessary to accomplish the task successfully. Although there will always be allies and guides available to the hero along the way, ultimately each hero must face the challenge alone. Sensing the magnitude of the birth event, the fear and trepidation a woman feels while facing it, knowing that finally she must summon the fullness of herself to labor and birth—it is precisely this that makes childbearing a profound initiation in a woman's life. Out of the stuff of an ordinary self, a woman must pull together the courage and the skill to dance in writhing ecstasy with the forces of creation.

Because of this identification with his mother's unconscious the child is in a condition of *participation mystique* with her. Whatever lives unrecognized in her unconscious exists also in the psyche of the child, albeit in nebulous form. A recognition of this link is a most powerful incentive to a woman to grapple more seriously than ever before with the problems of her own psychological development. If [her children] are not to be harmed, she must keep her problems in consciousness and really struggle with them—then the children will not suffer. But if she remains unaware of something of which she should be conscious the child will be affected unfavorably.

—M. Esther Harding
The Way of All Women, p. 190

EATING LEFTOVERS FROM CHILDHOOD

eight months pregnant
two-year-old son

THE GESTATION AND BIRTH of a child activate innumerable physiological processes within a woman. I am convinced there are psychological processes that become activated in tandem with the physical. I have noticed that each stage of pregnancy brings with it its own psychological issues. It is clear that, in early pregnancy, a woman must contend with a lost sense of ego and self-determination as she surrenders herself to nature. In the final trimester of pregnancy, a woman must come to terms with the enormous task of birth that she is soon to face. Not only are there psychological issues common to particular stages of pregnancy, birth, and the mother-baby couple; I will go further to say that accompanying each of these psychological/physical stages are specific archetypal images, such as the Ocean, an Egg, Twins, the Tree of Life, the Moon.

Psychological literature is rife with theories about the mother—all from the vantage point of the child. How the mother was too much of this or too little of that, and therefore, the child has problems. That may be true. But what concerns me is that a primary, perhaps *the* primary, event in most women's lives—bearing a child—is largely ignored in the field of psychology. We have little grasp of the complexity of the psychological development from maiden into mother and the woman's subjective experience of motherhood.

Early in his work, Jung spoke about the mother and child relationship as "participation mystique,"[1] in reference to the deep unconscious identification in which a baby lives with his or her mother. This idea was carried forward by Erich Neumann in his works *The Child* and *The Great Mother*. Neumann recognized that there are archetypal differences in the development of males and females, especially in relationship to the mother, and although he intended to write about that in his book *The Child*, he died before he was able to do so.[2]

Among Jungian psychologists, it is accepted that the unconscious material of parents is passed on to their children through participation mystique and identification. Jungians believe that the unresolved personal unconscious issues of the parents will be absorbed by the children, on down through the generations until an individual is willing and able to take on the task of bringing some of these unresolved unconscious issues into conscious awareness.

This might sound too theoretical, but there are ample examples that therapists can offer of how this psychodynamic plays out in individual lives. A mother who feels that sexuality is something to be hidden, something of which to be ashamed, will pass on to her children *unconsciously* the message that sex is bad and the body is bad. She will never have to state this attitude overtly to her children. Her hiding of her own body will teach her children. The way she holds and touches her children's bodies will pass on her beliefs. The way she touches her babies' genitals while changing diapers will pass on an unconscious message.

It's not as though the mother should try to hide her unconscious stuff from her children, as if that would even be possible. The point is that the care a woman takes to provide a healthy physical environment in pregnancy and for her newborn baby should also be accompanied by an equal amount of care for the psychological atmosphere that she provides for the child.

A pregnant woman is afforded the opportunity—through participation mystique with her baby—to revisit her own infancy, only this time from a more conscious vantage point. Her own experiences as a baby, which have long lain dormant in her unconscious, perhaps surprisingly surface through dreams, memories, images, moods, feelings projected onto her baby. Like the musical themes in a symphony, the themes originating in her childhood come back around again, in somewhat different form, but unmistakably the same themes. Pregnancy and giving birth recapitulate the mother's unfinished issues from her own childhood. The mother's early psychological material comes back around, now able to be seen in the light of differentiated consciousness.

New mothers who were not well nurtured as children may have particular difficulty devoting their full love to the external baby. It is as if the inner baby becomes jealous and cannot stand to watch the mother give love to another child when the inner child has not had her own fill. I have been touched by this psychological process in other women, and now yet again, I am stumbling upon it myself. In a dream last night, my psyche informed me that there is some old food sitting around, leftovers from the place of my childhood, that need to be eaten and digested before the birth of my daughter.

In the dream, I am with a man and a woman in Omaha, Nebraska. We are walking around in the neighborhood where I lived as a child. We cut through the backyard of Jan's parents' house. We see Jan and speak, hoping it's OK that we are there. We go into their kitchen. I am hungry, so I open the refrigerator. There is leftover sushi. And leftover deviled eggs with green peas stuck all around them. I eat an egg but am not sure it is really OK that I eat their food.

Jan's younger brother, who is nice but is sort of an inferior masculine figure, comes into the kitchen. We walk with him into the living room. Just as we are getting ready to leave, the doorbell rings. It is a group of men, maybe ten of them, and they have come from outer space. They are the Birth Squad. We are a little afraid of them. They force us back into the living room, where there are many large floor pillows, and they enter the house. I realize that we will not be allowed to leave, that we are stuck there with them.

The dream is located in the place of my childhood home from when I was in fifth grade to eighth grade. That time in my life was filled with disturbing events, not the least of which was the onset of adolescence. Jan, the woman whose family's house we are inside in the dream, was disturbed psychologically. The dream portrays her brother as having psychological weaknesses also.

My psyche seems to be wanting to revisit this old scene of psychological disturbance. The issues of my past seem still to be left over; they need to be eaten again, digested before something can be born.

The house where I eat leftover food from childhood is the same house that contains the possibility of healing. It strikes me as funny that the living room resembles a setting for group therapy, a large room with generous pillows for sitting on the floor. Am I being asked to participate in group therapy with ten alien men from outer space and a slightly mentally disturbed man who used to be my neighbor?

I am confronted with a massive masculine intrusion from

outer space (as opposed to internally directed inner space) and a weak male figure. My feminine ego must find a way to be in relation to these men. Yet at the same time, I sense that these men also have something to teach me.

Because of the hunger inside me, I eat leftover food—sushi, which is rarely good the next day, and deviled eggs with round green peas stuck all over them. The fish and the eggs are both fertility symbols. My psyche did not present newly laid eggs. Nor fried eggs sunny-side up. Not poached eggs, not scrambled, not soft-boiled. My psyche presented deviled eggs, eggs that have been worked over several times and have a dark side to them, a devil side. This food is a metaphor for the psychological material I must digest again: it is not fresh, new; it has been worked over several times and has a shadow side to it.

Because of my amniocentesis, I know that I am giving birth to a daughter. I wonder whether there is something I am needing to digest with regard to being a daughter, something that must be processed from my daughterhood in order that I may evolve into being the mother of a daughter.

As I review my childhood, I think that the primary unfinished issue for me is that I abandoned my authentic feminine nature. As a young child, I was very sensitive, emotional, and mystical. I can remember going outside after breakfast one morning, lying down beneath our enormous oak tree, and looking at it. The next thing I knew, my mother called me in for lunch. Where had I been for those hours? I couldn't have said in words, but I had a feeling of the place, a feeling of quiet beauty. Time and again, as a child, I would merge with nature or a person; that was my way of knowing things in the world.

But this mode didn't work with linear time. I wasn't where I was "supposed" to be at the "right" time. To keep up with school and our family schedule, I had to pay attention and hurry up. So I buried my authentic nature with a facade of a good girl who was on time, answered succinctly, and was oriented around the demands of others. But in order to do this, I had to be anxious, could not permit relaxing into myself. Only when I was alone would I sink into my feminine nature and allow my own pace.

In the dream, as my time of birth was near, ten alien creatures who say they are the Birth Squad come into the house. It is overwhelmingly masculine energy. They seem to think that they are in charge of my birth, that I must submit to them, that the birth will be in this house, in the living room, on the pillows. But the dream stops there; there is no actual birthing scene.

On a conscious level, these are very much issues in my life: getting centered in my own self (home), honoring my own experience of reality, and fending off masculine intrusions (my own and others) into my feminine way of being. I am working to reclaim my own natural pacing, validating the importance of my authentic feminine nature, my feeling and merging ways of knowing.

As I near the time of giving birth to a daughter, I am being asked to eat these leftover issues of mine as a girl. It remains to be seen how I will digest this food. It remains to be seen how I will relate to the masculine Birth Squad that wants to control my birth.

I can feel my waking-life resistance to eating this leftover food. I can feel the ickiness of being pulled into the old unconscious material. And yet I want to resolve it. I feel a deep tenderness about having a daughter. I have many feelings about what I want to pass on to her as a female and what I do not want her to have to bear as a female. I must take on the work that is mine, so that my daughter will not have to eat this leftover food. I want to participate not only in physical evolution; I want to do my job in the evolution of consciousness. I hope that, in this recapitulation, I can do the necessary work so that my daughter will not have to inherit this unfinished material.

> It is an essential characteristic of psychic figures that they
> are duplex or at least capable of duplication; at all events
> they are bipolar and oscillate between their positive and
> negative meanings. . . . The figure corresponding to the
> Kore in a woman is generally a double one, i.e., a mother
> and a maiden, which is to say that she appears now as the
> one, now as the other.
>
> —C. G. Jung
> *Aspects of the Feminine*, pp. 144–45

BETRAYED BY THE MAIDEN

eight and one-fourth months pregnant
two-year-old son

I HAVE BEEN increasingly concerned about the prospect of a
newborn baby and a toddler and a house to manage while my
husband is working fifteen hours a day in his job, so we decided
to hire an *au pair*. I interviewed maybe a dozen young women
who have landed in Southern California from Germany or Swit-
zerland or Sweden. Many of them have never lived apart from
their family before. They are around nineteen years of age,
mostly inexperienced in the world, and in the transition between dependence and independence.

Last month, I hired Helen from Germany. Helen is quiet,
sweet, polite yet reserved. She did not appear to have eating
disorders or alcohol/drug problems, which elevated her above
most other candidates. The deal is that we give her a room in
our house, she eats meals with us, has some use of my car, is
paid one hundred and twenty-five dollars a week, while in ex-

change, she gives roughly thirty-five hours of childcare and help with housework.

Even though I had begun to fantasize about how I would decorate the baby's room, I willingly gave up that room to Helen. I would gladly have the baby live in our bedroom in exchange for help with housekeeping and children. Although I must say it bothers me that her clothes and things are strewn all over the room I liked so much. It's something of an intrusion to have a virtual stranger living in our house. I do not feel as free in our house, nor do I feel the privacy I once did. Helen has shown some of the adolescent resentment toward me that a teenager does when her mother asks her to do something. The thought occurs to me that I have just inherited someone else's teenager, and this might be lunacy, given the complexity of my life already. Still, I decide the downsides can be transcended, or at least ignored, in light of the advantages an *au pair* can bring.

In my well-crafted plan, Helen from Germany started to work for us while I was seven months pregnant, to give Jesse, me, and Steve plenty of prenatal time to develop a relationship with her. I imagined that by the time the baby is born, Helen will know where the grocery store is, what gas station we use, how to load the dishwasher. I also hoped that she could help me get the house in better order before the baby is born.

Today, three weeks before my baby is due, the day before Thanksgiving, when I will be hosting the extended family dinner, Helen says she needs to speak with me. Visibly uncomfortable and nervous, she tells me she wants to quit. I am shocked. I try to talk with her, to see what the problem is and whether we can work something out. She tells me she did not realize how much work it would be. She says she does not want to do so much housework. She says she will pack her things and leave today. Now.

My mind reels. All my careful planning just blew out the window. In three weeks, I am going to have a baby—and no help. I am scared. I am enraged. I am carrying more responsibility than I ever have in my whole life. I am stretched to the max, physically, emotionally, putting in long hours every day trying to finish moving into this house and preparing for this enormous event in Jesse's life and our lives, and this maiden quits on me because she didn't realize it would be so much work?

Gee. Was I interfering with her life? Was I supposed to be the generous mother to her, providing her with a home and a car and food and money, asking almost nothing in return? In her mind, was I simply a convenient home base, a mother to be used so that she could date boys in California? That was a far cry from my idea about our arrangement. My scenario was that she would be a mother's helper, a younger sister, helping with the intimate daily realities of house and children. I trusted her with my son. I allowed her to enter our home and join the dinner table of our family. I let her drive my car. On top of all that, I paid her money every week. And now, when I need her most, she is deserting me—because she wants to have more fun, more freedom. I feel betrayed by her. I hate her for ruining my carefully organized plan for our family with a new baby. All these volcanic feelings hurl through my mind while I stare blankly at Helen of Germany. I want to yell all this at her, and more, while my hands squeeze around her throat. Instead, I swallow my feelings and politely ask her, would she be willing to postpone her leaving for two hours, baby-sitting Jesse while I grocery shop for Thanksgiving? Helen says yes, I think relieved by the opportunity to appear generous and receive my gratitude.

It takes a half hour to drive to the natural foods store, but I want an organic turkey and organic produce. During the drive, I begin to process my rage.

I feel weighted down with sober, large responsibilities. A house mortgage. Mountains of laundry. Trying to attend fully to Jesse while my mind and body are being pulled toward this new baby. Grocery shopping. Remodeling a kitchen. (What kind of cupboard pulls do I want? How would I know? It turns out that there are about a hundred and fifty styles.) How can I possibly be a good mother to two children? Already the quality of time and love that I give Jesse are diminished. I have an overworked and stressed husband who needs me also. It's not exactly as though I am an infinite source of love and support. I'm not the huge breast with milk always flowing, ready for all who need to come suck off me. I feel stressed. I am working harder than I have ever worked in my whole life, and I still can't catch up with all that needs to be done. I need to be supported, too. I need help.

But with resentment, it is dawning on me that the mother cannot turn to the maiden for help. The life agenda of the mother is at odds with the life agenda of the maiden. What are the developmental concerns of the older maiden? Boys. Getting distance from the mother. Getting a tan. Experimenting with alcohol and/or other drugs and sex. Freedom. Self-definition.

It might be psychologically impossible for the maiden to be in service to the mother. The libido of the older maiden is oriented toward separating from the mother, toward not joining the agenda of the mother, toward establishing her own agenda. It might be that the life task of the nineteen-year-old maiden is to leave the mother, to betray the mother.

Yes, I decide, those little bitch-maidens will always betray the mothers. They only know how to take from the mother. If they do happen to know how to give to the mother, they rarely want to. They imagine that mothers are people to use, annoying older women who must be tolerated for purposes of food and shelter, and occasionally for emotional shelter.

The bottom line for me is that I am outraged that she gets to quit—and I don't. She gets the role of *puella,* the eternal girl, in this drama, wherein her pouting line is, "I don't want to do so much housework." Then she packs her bags and leaves.

I am cast, or have cast myself, in the role of the downtrodden mother. I'm in a life position now where I can't pack my bags and quit. I am deep into the mother-wife-housekeeper. There's no turning back. I don't love feeling so stressed, so weighted by responsibility. But I am stepping up to the hard work of home ownership, marriage, parenting. Frankly, I don't want to do so much housework all the time either. It taxes the maiden within me.

There is still a maiden in me who wants someone else to be the mother, to do the hard work, to bear the ultimate responsibility. It is scary to fully inherit the role of the mother. To have a maiden quitting on me threatens my stability as a mother.

Sometimes, like a rebellious horse, I want to rear on my hind legs, kicking my servitude away, fighting the harness and saddle. If I have to be harnessed—and God knows that much of the time I *want* to be harnessed as a wife and a mother—I want someone to help me. Intermittently to walk by my side, also wearing the metal bit, also allowing her hairs to be matted down by the strapped-on saddle.

Alone, I walk the aisles of the natural foods store, numbly loading my cart with yams, lettuce, carrots, celery, tomatoes. I am in the twilight zone, spaced out. I suddenly feel very uncomfortable in my bowels. I stand immobilized in front of the beets, trying to discern what is happening. I realize that my bowels are cramping. I waddle-run for the stockroom to use the toilet. I realize how upset I am, even though I had that helpful half-hour talk with myself on the way here. When I think I'm fine, I return to my shopping cart. I move on to the broccoli and the cauliflower, but I am uneasy. I have to leave my cart and waddle-run to the toilet again. When I return to the produce section, I begin to feel a cramp in my uterus. Mother of God! I'm having a contraction. My mind panics. I am going into labor in a grocery store with my cart a quarter full, the day before Thanksgiving, and my *au pair* has just quit. This baby isn't supposed to come for three more weeks. I am so emotionally flooded that I edge toward catatonia; I just stand like a mannequin, holding onto the handle of my cart.

Barclay, one of the owners of the store, who reminds me of a large, friendly dog—say, a golden retriever—spots me and bounds over to give me a hug. Surrounded by the bigness of his body and spirit, I break down in his arms. He gives me what I needed more than anything in this moment—someone to hold me so that I don't have to be the all-competent mother. My tears and words spill out: I think I'm in labor, but it's three weeks early; I'm having diarrhea; my cart is not full for Thanksgiving; and my *au pair* just quit.

Barclay springs into action. He is my hero. With his arm securely around me, he takes me into the back office, helps me lie down on a couch, and asks whether I need to go to the hospital. I don't know yet. We decide to phone Steve. Steve, too, surrounds me with love and care. Barclay finishes my Thanksgiving shopping while Steve and I talk. My body calms down. I decide that I can drive home. Barclay puts my groceries in the car for me, and once again, I take the steering wheel.

I want to go home. I want to lie in bed so that this baby girl can get closer to her due date before she comes out. My extended family can make Thanksgiving dinner. Helen from Germany can get out of my sight. I don't ever want to see a maiden again, much less allow one in my house again. They can't be trusted. They are perfectly willing to betray the mother. I still would like to have help with the house and children, but I can't imagine ever trusting a maiden again. Maybe an older woman, who is accustomed to shouldering responsibility, who no longer cares about a tan.

I have to wonder: now that I am a mother, what has become of the maiden in me? Did she just die when I became a wife and mother? Or does she continue to live somewhere, a mere survival existence, buried under mountains of maternal obligation? Does she feel that, because she can no longer act out the maiden, no one else should either? Does she resent the carefree maiden girls in her midst? The maiden in me will not see the light of day for many moons now. There will be a baby to care for. A toddler to care for. A husband to care for. A house to care for. There will be no room for a maiden to care only for herself. I lie in my bed, filling with this awareness, trying not to have a baby yet.

One general idea goes right through what I have to say:
that is, that there are natural processes which underlie all
that is taking place; and we do good work as doctors and
nurses only if we respect and facilitate these natural processes.

—D. W. Winnicott
Babies and Their Mothers, p. 71

BIRTH

eight and one-half months pregnant
two-and-one-half-year-old son

AFTER LUNCH TODAY, Jesse wanted to take a walk to the
creek. That seemed like an easy request to satisfy. I am aware
that soon I will not be able to indulge him so conveniently.
Already I feel guilty about abandoning him as my only child;
soon I will be bringing home another beloved with whom he
must learn to share his mother. The ground he stands upon will
shake, change shape. This marks the first real crisis in his little
life. At age two and a half, he will become the older child, imagined to be competent enough to fend for himself in certain ways,
when viewed in the same frame with a newborn baby. Of course,
I will walk with him to the creek.

The past week I have been lying down, trying not to give
birth to this baby yet. It's a peculiar action: trying not to go into
labor. Yesterday, my obstetrician declared that I am "ripe."
"Ripe" means that my cervix is thin as paper, soft, and opened
as wide as my wedding ring. Now I am within two weeks of my
due date, which is considered a "full-term" pregnancy, meaning

there is no cause for alarm because my doctor predicted I will give birth today or tomorrow.

Being "ripe" amuses me. With sympathy, I caress the tippy-top branches of the Valencia orange tree in our orchard, bowed low toward the ground, weighted by full-term fruit. I take the fruit between my two hands, palpating it: is it juicy, is it soft enough so that it will be sweet? I smell the navel of the orange, where it attaches to the tree. Is the scent fragrant? Is the orange ready to separate from the tree?

I feel excited to be ripe. Oh, there are several dozen tasks on my list that will not get done before the baby arrives, but I have moved beyond caring about my list. A current of joyful anticipation carries me through the day. When will the baby be ready to be born? When will I go into labor? Does my body decide when to go into labor, or does the baby's body decide? Or is this a consensual decision, a conversation of chemistry that determines the onset of the transformation from one to two?

Jesse and I happily walk a quarter mile down the hill to Cold Spring Creek. He is buoyant with energy, independent, too big a boy to hold mommy's hand. We throw stones into the creek, hoping to make a big splash. We restructure the mud banks with our sticks. After a while, I am feeling drained and it is time for Jesse's nap, so we head for home. But Jesse is tired now, and walking up the hill proves too much for him. He stalls out, whining, "Carry me." "Carry me"? I can barely get myself up the hill! I play little coaxing games, advancing us maybe a hundred yards before he stalls out again. It is too hot for me. I feel irritated by the heat, the resistance of my son, and the too-much-ness of the task of getting me and Jesse up the hill to our home. What delusion caused me not to bring the stroller? I carry Jesse for a little bit, but his weight causes a bulging feeling against my cervix. I coax and carry, coax and carry, "I think I can, I think I can," and finally, the little blue train makes it up over the top of the hill.

I waste no time settling Jesse for his nap. Thankfully, he does not protest. In search of a cure for "hot and tired and irritable,"

I prepare a bath for myself. I have the sensation of light little menstrual cramps in my uterus. Could this be the very beginning of labor? It's so mild. However, my previous two days read like the "Possible Signs of Labor" section from a pregnancy book: effacement and dilation of the cervix, losing the mucus plug, bloody show, diarrhea, irritability, altered consciousness.

I decide to phone Steve. I really don't think I've started labor, but since he is a half hour away from me, and the hospital is a half hour away from our home, I would feel better if he came home now.

By the time Steve arrives home, I know I am beginning labor, but still the pain is very mild. I call the young couple who will come stay with Jesse while we are at the hospital. Because my cervix is so ripe, and my first labor was only seven hours, we decide to go to the hospital even though the contractions are ever so manageable. We take one last nude photograph of me, pick up my hospital bag, kiss Jesse's sweet sleeping face, and leave.

I am giddy. I feel excited, as though I were going to my birthday party. Of all things, Steve and I discuss finances on the way to the hospital. My words are grounded in reality, but my affect is flighty. Never before have I conducted a vivacious conversation about money.

We arrive at the nurses' station for the birthing center only to find out that my doctor failed to send my carefully prepared file to the hospital. About the third time the nurse asks me a question that I had already answered, my temper flares. My anger moves the process along more quickly. They ask me to stand on the scale and then show us to our room. I undress, put on the hospital gown, and lie down to be examined. The nurse puts her gloved hand inside me, whisks her hand out, and quickly excuses herself. Another nurse comes in and performs the same examination. She exclaims, "My God. You're seven centimeters dilated!"

They race to call my doctor. It turns out that he is getting his hair cut. I don't know whether the haircut never started, got finished, or was half-finished. All I know is he shows up soon. He is a very comfortable presence in the room. He does not feel like an intruder or a stranger.

I am elated. This isn't bad. I am managing the pain easily. Letting my body lead me, I pace and move throughout the room, stretching my back, bending my knees in a balletlike *plié*. My slow motions remind me of the Chinese martial art of T'ai Chi. Deep primal "ahhs" and "ooohs" beginning in my belly open a channel up through my throat and out my mouth. Sometimes I am an agitated mountain lion, pacing, growling. Sometimes I race for the toilet. My bowels are cleansing themselves. All unnecessary things in my body need to clear out. Everything is clearing and opening and moving: my body moves, my throat opens for the big, deep sounds. There is a strange, primitive beauty to this dance that is dancing through me. I move far beyond the borders of human civilization. Mostly naked, prowling, howling, forced to allow my diarrhea to be seen on the floor. Someone inside of me is mortified, remembering the age-old injunction against pooping on the floor in front of strangers, but I am beyond the point of possible return. I am in the body of nature, engrossed with the physical demands of the moment, keeping the energy channeled, moving, clearing all resistance to stay present in the moment. No one in the room tries to pull me back into human civilization, not my husband, my doctor, nor the nurses. They encourage me a bit, praise me, but mostly, they keep a respectful distance, allowing this primal dance.

The contractions become more intense. I no longer have the strength to stand and pace. I sit upright in the birthing bed. Finally, it is time to push. I can't explain why, but part of me comes out of the submersion into my animal body. I come into focused relationship not only with myself but also with Steve and the obstetrician. I become conversational. Perhaps it is because I feel afraid. The pushing had been the most traumatic part of my first birth. And now it is time to push. I am mentally clear, feel in control of myself and my birthing. After one painful pushing contraction, I sit up straight and tersely announce to

Steve and my doctor, "This is not the crowning glory of woman-hood." Then I collapse back onto the bed.

Several contractions later, I am in the thick of childbirth, deep in feelings and pain. During one contraction, I hear myself cry softly, "I want my mommy." I want to cry "mommy" over and over, but the feeling is so intimate and private that I cannot allow the words out loud in front of anyone else. I repress the words, only crying while my husband holds me and comforts me.

Changing faster than stormy weather, that mood passes and new clouds blow in. Mightily, I push and scream. I get mad. I sit up and tell the doctor, "I'm not having fun anymore. This hurts too much. Give me drugs." A shocked expression comes over his face, "Oh, no! It would hurt the baby now. You're two pushes away from having her out. Here, put your hand inside your vagina," he urges, guiding my hand. "You can feel her head." I reach inside myself. My fingers touch a soft, velvety wet, furry head. The indescribable beauty transforms me. All feelings are stilled into reverence, the deep, calm beauty of the moment. Dovelike coos squeeze out my throat. I come into immediate relationship with my baby. I want to push her out, to bring her forth to me. Three more pushes. The last push too hard, not controlled enough. At ten minutes before six, she shoots out, really fast.

Steve lays her across my stomach. She lies still, eyes wide open, looking at me. She is so quiet inside, exquisitely beautiful. That still, breathless moment between us suspends time. Is it Steve or the doctor who interrupts us? She is too still. She is not crying or moving, and her skin is turning blue. I become alarmed. The doctor jumps into action, rubbing her vigorously, taking her out of the room to give her oxygen. Alarmed, Steve follows him. I am stunned. What is happening? Where did my baby go? In about one minute, they all come back. Steve is shaken by what he has seen. But all I know is that my baby is back in my arms and she is fine. She knows exactly what to do when I bring her to my breast. I caress her small body, caked with whitish vernix and a bit of blood. She is absolutely beautiful. Her head is small and round, her features vivid, her energy open. Someone places a hat on her head to keep her warm and blankets on the two of us. We nurse and nurse, feeling so happy and good.

The Mother Goddess herself could not have convinced me that childbirth could be this manageable. Beginning from the moment I wondered whether the little cramps I felt were contractions, ending when my daughter's body came out of mine, the entire event lasted two and a half hours. I did not feel I would blow apart as she came out. I do not feel traumatized. I feel happy and energetic.

She is a small baby, and I am sure that was a factor in this easy birth. Just eighteen and a half inches long and only six pounds eleven ounces. As I have talked with family and friends on the phone, I notice that I feel some shame about her being small, that somehow, as her mother, I failed to make her a big baby. I took care of my health, ate a lot, exercised, slept well. But she was two weeks early. Jesse had been such a large baby that I had expected she would be, too. I come from Danish-Irish stock. We are big-boned, tall, substantial bodies. She is petite, and I am not. It never occurred to me that I could give birth to a petite daughter. She came from me, is a female like me, is me, and yet is not me.

We call our baby-sitters, asking them to bring Jesse over to the hospital that evening. I want to bring him to me and to bring him to his new sister. I need to gather the circle of our family. I feel strong emotion anticipating his arrival. In my fantasy, over and over, he opens the door to my room and I burst into tears, sobbing as I open my arms to embrace him. I try to steady my emotions so that, when he actually does arrive, I will not overwhelm him. He opens the door to my room just a peek, adorable in his little hospital gown, tentatively looking at me, Steve, the bassinet holding the unknown. I control myself, a mask of warm calm in my voice, beckoning him to come over to us. I introduce him to Alia, lift her from the bassinet, and hold her while also holding Jesse. I help Jesse "hold" his baby sister. He seems a bit dazed by it all, but it is wonderful to see him and to bring our new family together for the first time.

That night after the birth, to my complete surprise, I begin to have contractions—stronger and more painful contractions than I had during labor! My uterus, which had gradually stretched wide to contain a baby, now is beginning the arduous journey back to its normal size. In nature's grand design, the nursing of the baby stimulates the uterine contractions: the uterus must get small again. The nurse massages my uterus, actually digging her hands into it and rubbing hard. My doctor prescribes pain medication. The pain pills barely touch the pain. I do not sleep that night. I hold my breath, bracing myself each time my baby nurses.

The pain continues throughout the next day. I worry about going home from the hospital feeling exhausted. Alia and I stay in the hospital a second night so that I can get more rested and physically stabilized. Again, I have severe cramps throughout the night, but at least Alia is healthy, beautiful, and doing fine.

> We could therefore say that every mother contains her daughter in herself and every daughter her mother, and that every woman extends backwards into her mother and forwards into her daughter.
>
> —C. G. Jung
> *Aspects of the Feminine*, p. 149

THE WOMAN SITTING ON THE FLOOR CRYING

two-day-old daughter
two-and-one-half-year-old son

I'M IN TERRIBLE SHAPE. All morning, I have been crying. My hormones are rampaging. My breasts are full and sore. I'm exhausted from the pain of postpartum uterine contractions. Various doctors and nurses come into my room, offering consolation and advice, and I just keep crying.

I am afraid to go home with our baby. Our kitchen is still being painted. The fumes from the paint are not healthy to breathe. Jesse has a terrible cold and cough, and surely Alia will catch his virus. How can I bring a newborn baby into this flawed nest?

I have forgotten how to be with a newborn baby. It's only been two and a half years, yet I can barely remember what to do. She is so small, and I don't know her yet.

I have no idea how to be a mother to two children. It seems impossible. I know how to love and attend to one child. But two? Does attending to one mean ignoring the other? How can

I love and be present for two children? My love is monogamous. One husband. One child. I learned that I can only love one at a time. Now, suddenly, I must learn polygamous mother love. I must learn to love two different children with all my heart and soul, at the same time. I think I can't, so I won't go home from the hospital.

Worse than any fears about taking care of my baby and having two children is this oppressive dream I awoke from this morning. The raw grief from the dream clings to my skin like unbearably humid heat. I can't shake the dream. I've cried, accepted advice that shores up the ego, talked with a friend on the phone. The feeling from the dream is of such raw pain, of being too far gone emotionally to climb back out. In desperation, I decide to return to the unconscious terrain of the dream. Perhaps by going into the dream again, I will be able to get out. I enter the dream again, this time buffered by paper and pen.

I am leaving our house to take Jesse to his school. I am not organized at all. I didn't have time to make his lunch, so I will have to go home later to do it and then take it to his school. Also, I forgot to help him practice opening his mouth like a hippopotamus. And he needs a haircut.

I drop Jesse off at school and go to a place to get my own hair cut. A group of adults are sitting around a conference table in a seminar room. Bob, my mentor and theological professor, is standing, talking to a woman who is sitting on the floor crying, hiding behind my cotton skirts. Bob addresses a logical exposition to her. She can't find any response. I am her translator. I angrily say to Bob, "So what? What does that mean to her? What does that have to do with her reality?" The woman keeps hiding her face behind my cotton floral print skirt.

Then, at the seminar table, my minister friend Robbie is at one end of the table, Bob at other end. Bob is lecturing about something and interjects a statement, a personal statement directed to me, but it is couched in language that only I understand. He is commenting on something he knows about me. I am pleased and surprised, saying, "How did you know?" Bob

warmly replies, "Congratulations." Then Robbie says he thinks
Bob made a brilliant logical exposition a while back, to which I
replied, "So what?" Robbie says he would like to explore the
exposition further.

I see in the early part of my dream that I am concerned about
neglecting Jesse. As the birth interrupted the haircut of my obstetrician, so, too, it is interrupting my ability to fully tend to
Jesse. In the dream, I think he needs a haircut, and I didn't have
time to make his lunch or to help him practice opening his
mouth wide like a hippopotamus. None of these are serious or
life-threatening neglects, but they weigh on me.

My ego, the one who calls herself "I" in the dream, goes to a
seminar to get her hair cut. Is this a place for trimming my
vanity? Or similar to the situation with my obstetrician, is this a
civilized ego place that must be interrupted in order to attend to
the primitive demands of birth?

There is a dialectic present in the seminar room. Two men/
two women. Logical expositions/sobbing. The men at the heads
of the table/the women standing and sitting on the floor. The
theoretical/the personal. But to ensure that I don't simply de-
nounce the masculine/theoretical/logical, my psyche has anchored this energy in two men whom I love and respect.

My dream ego is the translator. She is bilingual. She is able to
speak both the language of the men in a theological seminar and
the language of the woman sitting on the floor crying.

Who is this woman sitting on the floor crying, hiding behind
my cotton flowered skirt? Clearly, she needs my protection,
needs me to be her advocate. In the dream, she never speaks. I
must speak for her. I must find some way to protect her way of
being, particularly in the face of these bright, logical, kind men.

When my pediatrician knocked on the door of my hospital
room this morning, I think he was astonished to find me sobbing in bed. He asked me what was wrong. I told him the unabridged truth, "There's a woman who is sitting on the floor
crying, and she's hiding behind a cotton flowered skirt, and no

one has really addressed her." At first, he was (understandably) bewildered. Then his mind protested, unwilling to accept that I could be this person. "Oh, no," he said, with such kindness in his voice. "You have so many resources to draw from. You're a wonderful mother. You can do this." As I continued to cry, he mentioned the possibility of a postpartum-depression support group.

I know he meant well. Good intentions came from his heart. But the way he related to the woman sitting on the floor crying is absolutely central to this problem. She can't understand logical things; that's not her language. She can't be bucked up by remembering her personal strengths. She needs to be addressed in her own reality. She needs someone who can protect her space so that she can express her feelings in her own way on her own terms. She needs people who are willing to enter *her* reality, something that none of the men or logical women have done. Why isn't anyone on the floor communicating with her on her level?

The woman in me who's sitting on the floor scared, hiding, and crying hasn't been addressed by anyone since she gave birth. Lots of masculine voices—and wonderful ones, too—in my dreams and in waking life, all with good-sense tips, advice, encouragement, information. But no one, including me, has addressed the woman inside who is sitting on the floor, feeling overwhelmed about her life now. This morning, I found her. She wants to cry and hide and be taken care of by another woman.

The woman sitting on the floor crying is scared and overwhelmed. She quite recently pushed a newly created human being out from her body. She is still overwhelmed by the power and mystery of this event.

Throughout my birth experience, I coped very well, was conscious of all that was going on, and was in charge of myself and how the hospital staff treated me. I was lucid, conversational, in many ways in control.

On the more unconscious side of things, my body knew to move and stretch during labor. My voice knew the deep, primordial sounds. I intuitively knew that to open my throat is to open my cervix and birth canal. This knowing feels connected to the part of the dream that speaks of opening the mouth wide like a hippo.

While I was pushing my baby out, the most painful and intense part of my labor, I discovered myself saying, "I want my mommy." When I heard these words, I began to cry. This yearning is complex and deep. In part, I think I wanted the presence of an older woman, a mother who had been through this experience of giving birth—to give me guidance, to understand me without any words, and to give me hope in the fear/despair that usually comes at some point during a birth. In part, I wanted *my* mother, the woman who pushed me out of her body, who loves me as her baby. I was in such pain that I needed my mommy. I needed a mother as I was becoming a mother again.

In many traditional cultures, mothers are with their daughters during childbirth, intimating the infinity of women. My mother is a daughter. I am her daughter. I drew a daughter from my body who may one day draw a daughter from her body who may one day . . . The presiding mother is a guardian of the gate; she is guide and protector of the feminine mysteries. The woman giving birth cannot and should not try to hold all the roles. She needs a protector. Her husband can be a male protector. But she also needs a female protector.

Particularly in the hospital setting, I think I needed a woman who could protect my need for feminine rhythms. I wish I had had ritually protected space after the birth to allow my molecules to rearrange undisturbed, to feel and be with this profound life experience.

In the dream, the crying woman was sitting on the floor, her realm, while everyone else was standing. After birth, a woman needs to be addressed in her own realm. She needs time to sense herself as a woman, as a mother. Perhaps a woman needs time where she can hide behind the floral skirts of another woman who will be her translator to the rest of the world. Perhaps she needs to crouch behind the shelter of her mother's skirts. Her psyche and body need time to lie fallow. This is the rhythm of nature. After the harvest of crops, the land must rest, lie fallow, rejuvenate its essential being. This organic life process takes time.

This dream about the neglect of the vulnerable feminine is the psychological atmosphere into which my daughter was born. Her mother was conscious, competent, in control, handling things well. A tidal wave of a dream had to wipe out that mother in order to gain attention for the sobbing young woman who does not speak the language of the competent ego.

Ironically, in the quintessential feminine act—childbirth—the deep, vulnerable feminine was ignored. There was a woman sitting on the floor crying, and no one, including me, addressed her in her own language. This is my personal psychological context and the collective cultural context into which my daughter has been born. As mother and daughter, we are challenged with the task of learning to respect the deep feminine. In ways that I cannot now predict, I feel sure that, throughout our lives, she will help me with this task, and that I will help her.

Maternity is a serious and arduous undertaking and those who are not prepared to make personal sacrifices for it are in no position to attempt it.

—M. Esther Harding
The Way of All Women, p. 177

Colic

two-month-old daughter
two-and-one-half-year-old son

ON ALIA'S FOURTH DAY of life, our pediatrician diagnosed colic. For two months now, we've survived—barely. Colic is a foreign country, impossible to understand unless one has lived there. For example, consider the quality of time while cleaning the kitchen with a noncolicky baby who lies on blankets on the floor, gurgling and batting at hanging toys with his hands and feet. Every few minutes, the mother might go over to the baby, tickle his fat chin, talk love talk to him, and rearrange the toys. Now consider the exact same amount of time, cleaning the exact same kitchen with a colicky baby who is screaming in pain the entire time, needing to be held constantly. Bending to put the dishes into the dishwasher while holding a baby. Wiping off the table while holding a baby who is crying in your ear. Sweeping the floor while holding a baby is a complicated physical act, to say nothing of the emotional and psychological hurdles. I have never been so stressed in my entire life.

Steve is under enormous demands at work and has to focus almost all of his energy there. Jesse goes to a preschool three mornings a week and is home the rest of the time. I am not able to give much to Jesse. I almost always need to be holding Alia; frequently, she is crying, sometimes just fussing, sometimes frantically screaming.

The other day, Jesse came to me to say something—I saw his mouth move while he was looking directly at me. But I was holding our baby and could only hear crying in my ear. "What?" I yelled. He moved his lips again, but still I heard no words. I yelled at him, "Honey, talk loud, I can't hear you." But his lips didn't move anymore. He gave up. He just turned around and walked away. I know this is substandard mothering, but what can I do? When Alia sleeps, which is only twenty minutes twice a day, I must choose: do I make a beeline for Jesse to give him something, or do I sit still, listening to silence, trying to repair myself? None of us are happy. We are all just trying to hang on.

Medical science has not been able to move beyond the broad definition of colic as severe abdominal pain that affects as much as 20 percent of all infants and can last up to four months of age.[1] Nobody really knows what causes it or how to treat it. Is it air trapped in the tummy after feeding? Is it stress? An allergic reaction? An inherited predisposition?

To some extent, it helps to busy our minds with attempts to solve the problem of colic. First, we tried altering my diet, in hopes of eliminating offending foods from my breast milk. No caffeine, no chocolate, no alcohol, no orange juice or other citrus, no dairy products. As my youngest brother so aptly inquired, "What does that leave?" Not only do I feel deprived of these pleasures; it doesn't seem to make any difference in the colic. We've tried massage, polarity therapy, chiropractic, a baby swing, a hammock. None of it makes any difference, except that time passes while we chase the latest cure.

The one thing we have done that seems to help ease Alia's abdominal pain is an exercise the pediatrician taught me, dubbed the "J" motion. An adult holds Alia, one hand securely encircling her upper thigh, the other hand cradling her neck, gently sweeping her through the air, high above the head then down low, drawing with her body a large imaginary letter "J."

Back and forth, back and forth, this motion calms her. The downside to this technique is that, within five minutes, my shoulder and arm muscles are screaming for mercy. Consequently, we have taken to inviting a large supply of adults over to our house. Especially big strong men are popular now. On Superbowl Sunday, we exhausted eight adults, taking turns doing the "J" motion with Alia.

When I was a baby, I had colic. In my baby book, my mother noted that I was troubled with colic during my first four months of life. She wrote, "First month I held her every night from six to ten o'clock." Unfortunately, in 1952, my pediatrician saw fit to prescribe phenobarbital for my colic. I am shocked by this. Even though I imagine it was standard practice forty years ago, I don't think any doctor today would consider exposing the fragile and developing central nervous system of a newborn to a narcotic in order to treat colic.

Alia's cries of pain stir deep feelings in me. I am devastated that my beautiful little baby is in such pain. It is almost intolerable to see such a little one suffer, my baby, the beloved I am here to protect. I grieve for her. I grieve for myself: the ways that I am suffering as her mother, all the while remembering that I cried like this when I was an infant. This is not the beginning that I want for my daughter, was not the beginning that I wanted for myself.

I have made a commitment that feels very important to me. I have vowed to hold Alia while she is in pain. Holding her does not stop her pain, but at least, she has the larger context of being held in the midst of the pain. I have worried that, in confronting such pain in the first few months of her life, she might conclude that it is not a good idea to live in a body. I feel that, by holding her, loving her, she may have an experience of life beyond the pain, that she may desire to continue living. When I hold Alia while she cries, everything gets mixed up: am I holding her or myself as a crying baby? I grieve for my past pain, which is oddly present now in Alia's pain. Somehow, madly, there is healing for me in this trauma she and I are living through together.

So I hold her, many hours each day—until my arms and back ache. Then Steve holds her. Then I hold her more. And I hold in my mind what the British pediatrician and psychoanalyst D. W. Winnicott said: "An infant who is held well enough is quite a different thing from one who has not been held well enough."[2]

Alia cries for at least several hours during the day, although not always at the same time. And then, usually, she begins crying again around 10:30 PM. Sometimes, I walk with her, patting her back. Sometimes, when my back is tired, I lie propped up in bed with her body on top of my chest, patting her. An hour of baby crying is an inordinately long time. Sometimes, I feel I can't stand it any longer, and I go wake up Steve. Steve has a magical touch, which I can't exactly figure out. He hoists her high on his shoulder, pounding her back with a vehemence that concerns me, but I notice it is calming to Alia. He paces back and forth, singing "Summertime" in a loud, deep voice that is not always in tune. The entire scene makes me laugh, but not too loudly, because assistance is so welcome.

Steve has taken to sleeping in a different bedroom so that he can actually sleep and therefore function the next day at work. As for me, each night is a quilt: pieces of sleep patched together with nursing and crying. Sometimes, I cry, too. It helps to release my sadness and stress. Because it has been so long that I have been functioning on broken sleep, my mind is a gray fog bank. I move through each day in a daze, fulfilling my duties, a mentally ill automatron.

I am barely making it through this colic. I have never been so raw from stress in my life. I am a mere mortal. I'm not built to be around a crying baby so much, to manage on such little sleep, to work so hard in the salt mines. All over my skin are exposed raw nerve endings, which are set off by the smallest provocation. I feel that something has permanently altered in my central nervous system, that parts of my electrical wiring are fried.

Several nights ago, Steve saw how desperate I was when he came home from work. He offered to take care of Jesse and Alia and told me to go soak in the hot tub. Sitting outside, in the dark, the warm water began to melt me. I cried for myself. Staring through tears at the high hedge in our yard that separates us from our neighbors, I realized that I am in a psychological position now where I can peer over the hedge into the land of postpartum psychosis. How very close I am, and yet only by good luck am I here, on this side of the hedge, not on the other side of the hedge—at least, not yet.

It's peculiar to be clinically observing myself, knowing what deep trouble I'm in and completely unable to do anything about it. I think I am in a postpartum depression. Quite likely my hormones are going wacko, complicated by sleep deprivation and the situational stress of colic. I just can't seem to control my feelings and thoughts. I can't think clearly about what to do or how to make this situation better. I can't summon the part of my brain that organizes for the future—the part that could call a baby-sitter for tomorrow or, more difficult, hire a regular baby-sitter. I am overwhelmed in the present.

I dare not allow myself to enter the vast swamps of sadness, despair, and rage that I feel. With judgment that I'm sure must be dubious, but is the best I can do at the time, I resolve to be a functional workhorse. I will put on blinders to avoid overstimulation, and I will stay focused on whatever task is in front of me, one foot in front of the other, day after day. I won't talk about my feelings much. I won't grant them too much importance. I will do what works. I will do what must be done.

I must find a baby-sitter so that I can have some relief. I know I need to have some breaks, to get out of this chaotic household, to be alone and take a walk. But I worry about Alia: who else in the world besides Steve and me would hold and love her through all that screaming? I don't think I could do it for anyone else's baby. It's just that nature helps me do it for my own baby. What if the baby-sitter tried to comfort her for twenty minutes and then just put her in her crib to "cry it out"? That's not acceptable to me.

And then there is the problem of finding a baby-sitter. I can't bear the thought of having to interview a maiden, trusting some young woman again who might betray me. I'm so overwhelmed, unconscious, overloaded I can't seem to do anything about it. I handle only immediate needs that are right in front of me. Make lunch. Put a Band-Aid on a bleeding owie. Fold clothes. Change diapers. I move from one absorbing moment to the next, with almost no consciousness of past or future. I have taken to plastering pink stick-'em notes on the walls I pass most frequently, especially the wall by the phone, each piece a reminder of something urgent to do, which would otherwise completely escape my mind.

Dare I go on? Dare I go beyond speaking of stress, sadness, feeling overwhelmed in the midst of colic? As difficult as it has been for me to accept, I shall remember this as the year rage grew in me. When too much noise or too many demands get heaped together, a pressure grows inside me, building, intensifying, until, like Mount Vesuvius, I blow. Red-hot lava and rocks blow sky-high, erupting into the air before my very eyes, landing wherever they will.

One of the hallmarks of nature is that seeds are always lying dormant, waiting for the proper environmental conditions so that the particular life can begin to develop. In fact, worm eggs can remain dormant in the soil for up to one hundred years— nature's ingenious insurance policy against drought. When the rains eventually come, saturating the soil to its depths, the worms swell to life.[3]

The psyche cannot be separated from matter. Clearly, within the human psyche lie seeds with their own particular timetable and environmental requirements. What comes to life has very much to do with the ecosystem surrounding it.

Inside of me, peacefully sleeping for thirty-five years, lay the seed of rage. I used to be a nice person. I almost never yelled at anyone. Marital arguments were usually reasonable—though pained—conversations, attempts to reach mutual understanding. When I was annoyed with my child, I was almost always able to reach inside, finding a patient maternal response. I was a good mother. My relationship with my child was marked by love, presence, and respect.

But too much stress rained on me. Without my knowledge, and especially without my permission, volatile rage began to grow in me.

I find myself short-tempered and impatient in ways that are reminiscent of my father when I was a child, yet my father always managed to keep the lid on his feelings.

In my family of origin, it was not acceptable to display anger on its own terms. The general rule was that anger must be funneled through the rational filter, mentally processed to the point where it could be aired in polite company. This year, the year rage grew in me, I have decided differently. I think I would hurt myself if I kept this rage unexpressed. I have made a commitment to express the anger, in its own language. This has meant hitting pillows, going into my car to scream and rant and rave. I am absolutely clear that it is not OK to hit the children ever or to hurt my husband or myself physically. But I spew anger in words and expressions, choosing verbal violence over physical violence.

One day, after a volcanic eruption, crushed by guilt, I went to find Jesse. "Honey, did Mommy roar like a lion? Sometimes, I feel too stressed, and I get mad and roar like a lion. It's not your fault, and I'm sorry I get angry like that, but I need to let my feelings out." I know this is terrible. I know it is hurting Jesse and Alia, I know it is hard for Steve that I am so angry, and God knows this is hurting me. After I explode, my nerves are raw for hours. I ache and feel awful. I just don't seem to have the personal resources to meet all the demands in my moment-to-moment existence. I'm trying so hard, but I simply can't do all that is asked.

Words fly out of my mouth—words from my childhood. I hear myself yell at Jesse the same words the mother who lived up the street from us used to yell thirty years ago in exasperation at the most devilish of her six children, "Judas Priest, Richard!!!!!!!!!!" At first, I heard myself yell, "Judas Priest, Jesse," or,

"Judas Priest, Alia," but now, to humor myself, I say, "Judas Priest, Richard."

Will my children be haunted all their lives by this raging, mad woman, this dark, devouring mother who takes me over? I wanted to be the ever-kind and bountiful Earth Mother. But in twists of fate and time, I become the raging Kali.

Kali Ma. The Dark Mother. She who devours her own children. The bloody one.

Kali has become known in the Western world primarily in her violent, destructive aspect. We think of her as the ancient Hindu Goddess who engages in hideous acts of destruction. This is correct as far as it goes. What is also true, and our omission says volumes about our modern Western psyche, is that Kali was every bit as much the creatrix as the destructress.

Kali was one of the ancient Mother Goddesses—she who was called by many names and worshiped throughout the earth. She was the One Source, who gave birth, sustained life, and wielded death. She was life and death and rebirth. The bloodiness of Kali was both the fertile blood of the womb and the blood of savage killing—equal forces within existence. Kali was nourishing, compassionate, loving. She was violent, heartless, cold as ice, hot as fire. Kali was the Source of All Being. Form. Formlessness.

Our Western dualistic minds have repressed knowledge of the life-giving aspect of Kali, choosing only to know her terrifying rampages. Kali has become the feminine shadow. She embodies all that we refuse to acknowledge, fear to know in the feminine experience. Isolated into one demonic Goddess, we can all fear Kali, distance ourselves from her, proclaim her evil.

My conscious self was able to pull off a convincing masquerade of the kind, sweet feminine (disturbed only by minor episodes of bitchiness) for more than three decades. And then, the environmental conditions became ripe for a psychic push toward wholeness. The repressed negative feminine erupted. Mount Vesuvius belched hot fire, singeing all who stood near.

I am too stressed-out to be nice and polite anymore. Kali has laid claim to me. She is asking me to know the wholeness of myself as woman and mother. Kali Ma—she who bears life, who sustains, and she who destroys life. This is not an easy request. I'm not sure how to place this within my actual daily maternal behavior. Perhaps I can come into psychological relationship with Kali, within myself, separate from my actual behavior, especially with my children. No, the truth of the matter is I can't. I don't have free time to do that inner work. I don't have time to think about how I act. I'm just surviving moment to moment.

I am in a life circumstance where Kali possesses me at a moment's notice, wreaking havoc in our lives. But it is not as if I choose to channel this hurricane-force rage. When Kali storms through me, I am just as destroyed as anyone else in my path. As if struck by lightning, my nerves are fried after the Kali energy subsides. I feel flat, exhausted, guilty, ashamed. It takes hours to recover.

Last week, I ventured into a store that sells blue jeans and assorted tops. I'd never been in the store before but had seen it when I drove by. Alia seemed to be having a good morning so I thought we could go shopping, just like other moms and babies do, before we had to pick up Jesse from Toddler Time. I needed a pair of jeans. I have no jeans to wear because I am still too fat to fit into any of my prepregnant jeans. I can't stand to think of how fat I really am.

We go into the store, and Alia is awake in her carriage but, miraculously, not crying. This skinny punk salesgirl helps me. I have no idea what size I wear. Assuredly, I am in the category of "large," but unfortunately, with jeans, one must claim a specific number size. Unsure what my number size is, and afraid to make any kind of commitment, especially in front of a skinny salesgirl, I collect about a hundred pairs of different-sized black and blue ice-washed jeans and try to cram me, Alia in her carriage, and all those jeans into this little box of a dressing room about the size of a phone booth. The store is so cheap the walls are just rough slabs of wood. Or maybe the rough wood slabs are part of the decor, creating an outdoorsy image. I don't know. What I do know is that I get splinters in my knuckles trying to squish Alia's carriage next to the wall so I can make enough room to get in and out of my pants.

I start with a pants size I can live with psychologically. I can't even begin to get those zipped! One pair after the next don't fit me right, look weird for one reason or another. Then I notice the tag on one pair: "DEFECTIVE." In disbelief and shock, I grab all my other pairs to see what their tags say. They are all defective! I think, what the hell am I doing in a store buying defective jeans?—but by this time, it is too overwhelming and too late to go to another store.

Something altered each one of these pairs of jeans from the master pattern. Something didn't go the way it was supposed to. Something bad happened, some twist of fate, and they became defective. I am in a store that sells the jeans that other stores reject because they aren't normal, aren't formed the way they are supposed to be. This is the most unbelievable nightmare: if I want to end up with a pair of jeans, I have to try to make something work even though the entire context is defective.

Alia starts to get fussy, and soon we must leave to go pick up Jesse. As fast as I can, I struggle to get in and out of the remainder of the defective jeans. I lose my balance and fall against the wood slab wall, and my underpants get stuck on a staple on the wall where a poster used to be, and I can't get myself unstuck, and Alia starts to cry hard so I just rip my underpants off the staple.

"How are you doing?" asks the punk salesgirl standing outside my slab door. "OK," I lie.

I try to hold Alia at the same time as I try on pants, but she cries even when I hold her. I am getting enraged trying to do the impossible, so I put her back into the carriage and let her cry while I try on jeans. I know that what I am doing is wrong, but I cannot stand the thought of walking out of this store empty-handed. However, I am afraid someone might report me for child neglect, so while I try on jeans behind the privacy of the slab, I talk in case someone is listening out there, faking it as if

I am holding her: "It's OK, honey. Hmmmmmm. There you go, baby. Let Mama hold you close. It's OK."

Alia's stomach is cramping, and she is screaming with pain. I am so angry and tense and freaked-out that I throw on my own clothes, pick her up, holding her with one arm, and with the other arm bulldoze the empty carriage out of the dressing room, ramming it through innumerable round racks of defective jeans, straight out to my car. I unlock the door, collapse into the driver's seat, and stuff my breast in her mouth.

It is quiet in my car. I blow out air, like some people blow out cigarette smoke. Again. Thank God it is quiet. I am raw. I look at this little baby earnestly sucking on me. Her whole existence depends on me. I am her food. She drinks me. Nobody else needs me the way she does. When she screams in pain, everything inside me organizes around protecting her, trying to make it better, trying to make it stop hurting. I love her so much. When she cries, hour after hour, I suffer seeing that my baby is in pain, but after a while, something shifts, and then I'm enraged. I feel I have to *make* her stop crying. I feel like shaking her; yelling "Shut up"; throwing her against the wall, out the window, anything to make her stop crying. Then, suddenly I become aware of how violent I am feeling. In horror, I think, how could I hurt a baby? A baby! All that rage collapses away from her and onto me. I hate myself.

After a while, something, out of somewhere, remembers to breathe. Inhale. Exhale. Inhale. Piece by raw piece, I begin to breathe together a self again. I begin to breathe together a mother and daughter again. I breathe together some love again.

First and foremost the woman experiences her transformative character naturally and unreflectingly in pregnancy, in her relation to the growth of her child, and in childbearing. Here woman is the organ and instrument of the transformation of both her own structure and that of the child within her and outside her. . . . After childbirth the woman's third blood mystery occurs: the transformation of blood into milk, which is the foundation for the primordial mysteries of food transformation.

—Erich Neumann
The Great Mother, pp. 31–32

ALCHEMICAL VESSEL

five-month-old daughter
three-year-old son

PRAISE THE GODS AND GODDESSES, Alia got over colic after four months! She smiles, coos, has her own charming language.

Oh, it is so good to be a normal family, no longer disfigured by colic. Even though the work of having small children is staggering, we now also are equally steeped in joy and love. I found a baby-sitter who does happen to be a maiden but is also accustomed to working for a living. She comes for several hours each day, helping with household tasks and taking care of my children while I go for a walk. I feel some balance in myself once again.

Jesse relates to Alia now. Intuitively, he knows to come down to her level. He crawls circles around Alia while she reaches out to him, smiling and "talking." Jesse includes her in his dramas: sometimes, she's Dumbo, often simply the baby. I am sorry to say that I am cast as Mrs. Jumbo. The three of us do things together during the day. I sometimes load pillows in our big wagon, propping Alia against Jesse and the pillows while we go for a walk up the street. Jesse is proud of Alia, telling passersby that she's his baby.

I realize how central my body is in my mothering. I grant my children access to my body. I share my breasts while nursing. I share my lap with them. My hands, lips. For me, mothering is comprised of so many bodily events. Mothering comes from places of instinct, body, the unconscious. A woman does not mother from her neocortex. Paradoxically, the more I bring conscious awareness to this process, the more I make choices to surrender to my instincts. The more I learn by consciously participating in this fantastic process of nature, the more fulfilled I feel.

When I lay Alia belly-down on the floor, she works herself into a bridge, hands and feet pushing against the floor, body arched high in the air. She reminds me of the Egyptian Sky Goddess, Nut (pronounced "Newt"), arching over the earth.

In the very early days, Nut used to lie face-down, flat on top of her younger brother Geb—enmeshed, undifferentiated. The Sun God, Ra, demanded that the two be separated. Following orders, the God of Air, Shu, hoisted Nut up by her waist, holding her up, arched high above her brother earth.[1] Nut's underbelly was a wonder of shining stars, twinkling over the earth.

All that cycles through the earth cycles through the body of Nut. She is the vessel for all of life. Through the container of her body, all of life is born and dies, cycling and recycling. Each morning, Nut gives birth to the sun. The sky is reddened by the blood at the birth. Each evening, she opens her mouth, swallowing the sun, taking it within her so that there may be darkness over the earth. Light and dark, life and death are balanced in the body of Nut.

Nut is the Egyptian Great Mother of the Cosmos, "She Who Bore the Gods."[2] She carries a jug of water, offering moisture for a parched earth. Liquid droplets fall from her breasts through the air to the ground, moistening the earth, nourishing life.

Like Nut, Alia remains stationary over the earth. But unlike Nut, Alia is not content. Alia has become even more differentiated, has desires of her own, wants to go somewhere. With intense concentration, she sways back and forth, trying to gain momentum, knowing the idea is to move forward, but how? After a while, her strength spent, she collapses back onto *terra firma*. She rests. Then her desire stirs again. Like a curious lizard, she arches her back and, head up, looks around. Looking down, Alia can see her reflection in the wax shine on the wide plank floorboards. She is temporarily mesmerized with her mirror image but then, with focused determination, returns to her task of ambulation.

She wants things. Her wanting is a powerful force. I see her strong spirit and realize that, every day, I must strengthen myself so that I can be her mother. Already I know that she is stronger than I am in particular ways, and yet the order of the cosmos is such that I have been placed as her mother. To be her mother, to contain and guide her spirit, I feel that I need to become stronger within myself.

Alia loves nursing, and so do I. Actually, the first month or two of nursing were not greatly pleasurable for me with either child. It took time to get past breast infections, toughening up the nipples, and stabilizing milk demand. Beyond those initial difficulties, it is my firm conviction that there are few pleasures in life that exceed breast-feeding.

I am touched by all that I am able to give her through breast-feeding. By some complex alchemical process, my body selects the best of the nutrition I ingest, transforming that material into breast milk that is perfectly suited for a baby. The fat content of my milk is adjusted by the reigning wisdom of my body to be perfectly suited for the age of my baby and, furthermore, is even adjusted during each nursing session, beginning with more watery milk, getting thicker, creamier as the baby sucks more. I

Isis nursing Horus. Copper, Egyptian, 12th dynasty, ca.
2040—1700 BCE. Aegyptisches Museum, Berlin. Courtesy Foto
Marburg/Art Resource, N.Y.

have read that this is nature's way of ensuring that the baby is
properly hydrated before she fills up on the thicker milk.[3]

I feed my baby from my body. She drinks from me. While
she drinks, she lounges in the luxury of my body: cradled in
one arm, my other hand caressing her chunky thigh or encasing
her little foot within the palm of my hand. Her one hand cups

and guides the breast she is drinking from, while her other hand guards the territory of my other breast, claiming that one, too, as hers, sometimes holding the nipple or leisurely twiddling it between her thumb and forefinger.

Probably more than any other person in my children's lives, I am their formative experience with touching, comfort, and love. The ways I love and touch them will pattern their abilities to give and receive love for the rest of their lives. Already I see that they touch me in the same ways that I touch them, that their touching is coupled with love, that love is an embodied experience for them. I feel certain that this will carry on into their adult love relationships.

It is absolutely clear to me that the mother, or whoever is the primary caregiver, is the baby's first lover. And what a fine love relationship it is! Nature wants a mother and a baby to merge bodies and minds, to touch, to caress, to feel incomplete without the other. Nature has set up an intimacy so fulfilling that neither party will want to leave for a long time.

Since I began having babies, I have paid increasing attention to what I put in my body. When a woman agrees to serve as a transformative vessel in life, certain obligations fall upon her. Nature can only go so far in this transformation business. Nature cannot turn Chee-tos and french fries and diet soda into a healthy baby or healthy breast milk. A woman must supply high-quality raw materials for nature to do its magic in the best way possible.

Our family eats almost solely organic food. We do not use household pesticides or garden pesticides or chemical fertilizers. This is our contribution to nature's alchemical process of reproduction.

From my experience as a mother, I feel keenly attuned to the ways in which all life is intimately related. Chief Seattle's statement, "Whatever we do to the web, we do to ourselves," is not only a spiritual assertion. Literally, when a chemical-manufacturing plant in Los Angeles chooses to dump millions of gallons of DDT into the rivers flowing into the Pacific Ocean, it is dumping the DDT into the fish we eat, the water in which we swim. This toxic material has been dumped into the ecosystem, the one Body of which we all partake. I take that personally. That is an affront to me as a mother and a life citizen.

When automobiles and manufacturing plants exhale toxic fumes into the sky, the Egyptian Sky Goddess, Nut, inhales them, takes them into her body, and returns them back to earth. The milk dripping from her breasts onto the sweet earth is polluted, hurts the plants and trees. I guess most people think that it is acceptable for Nut to be lactating acid rain. Or else they don't know what to do about it. Perhaps she is too far away to care about.

We can adjust the focus on this lens not only to the distant sky but also to the most up close and immediate subject. The milk in the breasts of virtually all nursing mothers contains a variety of toxic pesticides that individual women have accumulated from a lifetime of exposure.[4] The breast milk of 99 percent of all American mothers contains DDE, a dangerous breakdown product of DDT. DDT was banned for use in the United States in 1972,[5] but it is still present in our ecosystem. The abundant stockpiles of DDT that American manufacturers were stuck with after the United States ban were sold for use in agriculture to Third World countries, many of which still manufacture and use DDT. The DDT circles back around to us in the produce we import and eat, migratory animals, and dust particles carried by global winds.[6]

DDT, instead of biodegrading, bioconcentrates and is stored in the fatty tissues of mammals[7] (for example, women's breasts). Not only do almost all of us have DDT breakdown products in our breasts, we also commonly have several other pesticides. Dieldrin, which is also used to kill insects, has been found in the breast milk of 83 percent of mothers. Dieldrin has been shown to cause cancer, birth defects, and reproductive toxicity.[8] Heptachlor (still used for termite extermination), dioxins (used as a pesticide and in paper mills), and chlordane (use has been suspended) are all commonly found in the breast milk of nursing American women.[9]

I have no idea what to do with all the rage I feel about this. My alchemical mother vessel has been used to transform, within my body, the dirty business of modern human beings and feed that poison back into the life community. I feel violated. The most intimate and personal and sacred territory of my life has been violated. My breasts are mine. My breast milk belongs to me and to my baby. The milk-filled breast should be sacrosanct, inviolable. To defile the holy communion between mother and baby is a sin beyond forgiveness.

Against my will, and without my knowledge, I have lovingly fed both of my babies milk that is tainted with chemicals that are known to cause cancer and mutate genes, that are toxic to the central nervous system and may damage the immune system.[10] Also against my will, through a lifetime of exposure, my breasts have become toxic waste dumps, which recent studies have shown increase my odds for getting breast cancer.[11]

A rage burns through me like wildfire. Kill them. Kill the people responsible for mothers' feeding DDT and Dieldrin to our babies. Remove them from the earth; they have proved themselves unworthy of the graces of life.

And yet who might that be that I would kill? Probably I should start with the military-industrial complex—whoever that is. The military began developing these toxic pesticides for use in warfare, beginning in World War I. By 1944, DDT was in domestic production as a war tool. When World War II was over, an aggressive door-to-door marketing campaign sold the military stockpiles of DDT to American farmers, hailing the agricultural revolution. An entire generation of farmers have been boondoggled into thinking that food can best be grown by using synthetic fertilizers and pesticides.

When I think about the work of farming, of working in a partnership with soil and water and seeds and sun to grow new life, I can imagine that a farmer would arrive at a similar set of insights and commitments that a mother comes to from her work. This is true only for a minority of farmers in our country today. Most farmers no longer understand the depths of the transformation mysteries that are contained within the body of nature. They do not know the soil as a living entity. The do not know how to participate within nature to grow food. Most commercial farmers no longer respect or even understand the ingenious model of nature in growing new life.

But why should farmers be criticized more than anyone else? Commercial farming is merely one reflection of a cultural psyche that believes that nature must be conquered, controlled—that nature exists only to serve human beings, that we are isolated and separated from the body of life. Human beings have grown so far away from nature that we do not even comprehend the basic ground rules of the system that our egos are trying to control.

I found a 1954 women's magazine with an advice column for homemakers. The helpful tip was that homemakers could solve the nasty problem of moths' and insects' eating holes in wool blankets in storage by spraying them with DDT, which, the magazine advised, was readily available in small spray canisters in any grocery store. Many of our mothers, doing their best to take care of family and home, were spraying DDT on the blankets under which their children slept. DDT is a tragedy that touched us all.

I have wept bitter tears about the tainting of my breast milk. I have spread the word among my mother friends. I have strengthened my commitment to eat organic food, for myself, my children, and as a way of increasing organic agriculture in order to protect the ecosystem. I give money to several environmental organizations.

What else can I do? I must figure out how to transform my rage and sorrow into other life energy. To keep recycling rage and sorrow is not healthy food for me or the ecosystem. How might I, as a mother, work my feelings of violation over, and over in the alchemical vessel, so that they might change into something else, something that could be good food for life? I do not know yet; I simply know that this is my challenge.

Mothers know something that humanity desperately needs to know: We are nature. We are intimately connected with other life-forms. We can't put toxic chemicals into the Life body without poisoning ourselves. Mothers must find ways of bringing what we know to the cultural conversation. It is not enough to speak these truths only to other mothers. We must bring the fullness of what we know into public conversations about education, health services, business, and foreign policy. We have been gifted with the perspective of Nut, and it has become necessary to speak out loud from our vantage point.

Humanity at large has moved . . . toward a greater consciousness, chiefly through the emergence of a conscious and personal ego whose aims have conflicted with the simple urges which Mother Nature first implanted in our breasts. Thus, as woman has evolved and become more aware of herself as a separate entity—an ego—a conflict has arisen within her psyche between the individual values which she has attained and the ancient, collective, feminine trends. . . .

—M. Esther Harding
The Way of All Women, p. 5

PLEASE, LET ME GO BACK TO WORK

six-month-old daughter
three-year-old son

PLEASE, COULD I GO back to work? Staying home with a baby and a three-year-old is killing me. It never ends. There is never any downtime. There's always another dirty dish in the kitchen, always more dirty clothes to wash or clean clothes to fold, always more clutter to pick up from one room and move to a different room, almost always a need to cuddle or comfort or feed.

Exhausted at the end of a day, I wonder, What did I do today? What does a mother do? One could list all the minute specific tasks, which could be almost as tedious as doing them. However, these tasks share a common theme: a mother conducts the changing forms of matter. A mother begins with a microscopic sperm and egg, which, contained for nine months, change form, again and again, until abracadabra—out comes a baby! Then the mother eats food and drinks water while, within her vessel, a brilliant process occurs, changing that food into milk, which gathers in her breasts to be sucked by the baby. Mother as alchemist. She who contains the changing forms. These are her mysteries. The mysteries of transformation. The changing forms of matter. The mother is always transforming the new into the old, the dirty into the clean, the clean into the dirty. The mother goes to the grocery store, gathers raw materials, brings them into her home: some materials are passed through fire, some mixed with ice, some sprinkled with minerals or oils. Voilà! Dinner! Dinner changing form into nourished bodies. Changing form into dirty dishes. Changing form into poopie diapers. This is the work of the Mother: presiding over, orchestrating, containing the changing forms of matter.

I still vividly recall the moment when, one week after the birth of our first child, I watched my husband dress in a pressed shirt, a necktie, and slacks. He came to me, bent to kiss me and our very fussy baby good-bye, and said regretfully, "I have to go to work." Then he walked out the door. I was sitting in the middle of an unmade bed, dressed in a big T-shirt with spit-up dripping down my shoulders, holding a crying baby, trying to come up with some ingenious thing to do to make him happy. I wanted to run out the door after that escaping man, grab him by that neatly pressed shirt, pull him back, insisting, "Oh, no you don't. *I'm* going to work. You stay here and play with the baby."

It was one of those fascinating moments when insight penetrates the cultural trance: the person dressed in a work costume walking out the door, going to work, is actually escaping the harder work of staying home taking care of a house and a baby and often several other young children. What a scam. And we all so readily protect that scam, calling employment outside the home "work." We ask each other, "Do you work, or do you stay home with your children?"

I've been out there. I've worked a lot of different jobs. I wore the costume of a waitress, a secretary, a church minister, a psychotherapist, and more, and I'm here to report that none of it is as hard as staying home with a baby.

I adore babies. I love being a mother. It is a joy beyond measure to be saturated in love with a baby. There are countless sensual pleasures, nursing, holding, smelling their little head-smell, communicating in smiles and touches and cooing. It is a privilege to be present with a new human being: to watch the individual unfolding; to receive the first smile; to admire the hard work of trying to turn over, learning to sit up; to witness the intense drive to locomote, beginning with creeping forward and climaxing in the miracle of becoming a biped. I get enormous pleasure and satisfaction and fulfillment out of being a mother to a baby.

That said, let's look at what else is true. These little people are a lot of work. The hours are long. The pay is bad. There is an infinite quality to being a mother that can be demoralizing. The tasks are never really finished. There is always more to do. There is no time when you can dust off your hands, exclaiming, "Well, that's done," and go sit on the couch, propping your feet up, congratulating yourself on a job well done. There's little social approval or adulation in this job.

For the mother, one day leaks into the next. There isn't much definition about the beginning of a workday and the end of a workday. When the baby cries at 3:00 A.M., the mother does what must be done. She never gets to go home from work. The mother exists in a subliminally conscious world, an endless process of immediate needs and response. There is little self-definition to her work. Her reality is defined by the needs of others.

At some point within this self-sacrifice, a being inside the mother starts poking its head up, saying, "I want." "I want to think my own thoughts without being interrupted." "I want to choose what I am going to do and actually finish that task." "I want to get dressed without spit-up on my shoulders and without someone messing up my hair."

How do mothers meet the pressing desires of the one who wants something for herself? A privileged few may be able to hire a full-time nanny so that they have leisure time with autonomy. In our current economy, many women must return to work soon after the birth of a baby; the well-being of the family is dependent on their financial contribution. Returning to work outside the home provides a certain kind of independence for a woman, autonomy that is a by-product of economic necessity rather than something consciously chosen.

I am in the nebulous middle ground. My family could survive well without a financial contribution from me. Obviously, we would have more money to spend or save if I were bringing home a paycheck. Economic necessity does not define my choice. Emotional and psychological necessity define my choice. I need to get out of this unconscious endless field for some hours each day, and the only way I can justify and afford that is to work outside the home.

I need to get up in the morning, take a shower, and get dressed. I need to go somewhere where I can think, where I do something, where I accomplish something, and at a certain time it is over, and someone pays me money for it. I need that for about four hours a day. And then I need to come home to hold my baby girl, to cuddle my little boy, to love them, and to submerge myself in laundry and cooking and Band-Aids and owies, in poopie and pee-pee, in tickle games and stories and songs.

Even though I know that what I really want now at this stage in our lives is to leave the house in the morning to go to work part-time, I'm still not sure that it is OK. Why do I need to leave? Is there something deficient about me that I can't be a full-time mother? Is there something in myself that I am running away from? Buried deep down is still the expectation that a mother should be satisfied being a twenty-four-hour-a-day mother and homemaker.

It is tricky to sort through all the layers of issues around re-turning to work a job outside the home. My individual decision is textured not only by my culture but also by my generation. As fate would have it, the second wave of feminism coincided with my adolescence. I grew up in a new wave of women who wanted to break out of the traditional women's roles of wife, mother, and homemaker. We wanted to be the bankers, the law-yers, the doctors, the engineers. We wanted to blow open the rigid definitions of woman, of feminine, of girl, and through our experiments with ourselves, we would create a social order that had enough space for diverse individual human beings.

Throughout my childhood, I simply assumed that I would be a mother, and I simply assumed that I would work outside the home and earn money. I never stopped to think about the inter-faces of those two assumptions.

When Jesse was two and a half months old, I returned to my psychotherapy practice, working three mornings a week. A young woman I knew well came to our home to care for him while I went "to work." I don't think this was a bad arrangement for Jesse. But I have to wonder why I went back to work that soon. It wasn't financially necessary. In terms of the continuity of my clients and the success of my practice, of course, it was better to go back to work at two and a half months rather than six months. But I think the primary energy that got me back to work in two and a half months' time was a psychological de-fense. I was afraid to become "just a mother." The ego I had worked so hard to define, the sense of identity and power and purpose I felt in the world, was threatened by the unconscious waters of motherhood.

On a bodily level, I wasn't ready to return to work. I felt anxious leaving my baby. I was breast-feeding full-time and wanted to continue, so I had to pump breast milk for my baby to drink from bottles while I was gone. First, I tried a manual pump. Imagine a city girl milking a cow for the first time. After twenty minutes, all I had was a sore nipple, muscle cramps in my wrist, and only two ounces of a fluid that suddenly had become more precious than gold. A friend suggested renting a motorized breast pump. I practically mooed through the entire pumping session. I milked myself so that I could "go back to work." The baby was able to drink his milk bottle whenever he wanted. But my breasts didn't realize that I was at the office; they still filled with milk, one therapy session after the next, until sometimes toward the end of the third session, small wet spots surfaced on my blouse. At the end of a morning, I would race home, praying the baby was awake to relieve me.

With my second baby, I have challenged myself to completely immerse in being a mother. For six months now, I have stayed home with an infant and a three-year-old. I feel fully baptized. I am so exhausted that I am dying to "get back to work." Work outside the home would be a vacation. Work would be a respite as long as I could talk to adults, sitting, being present, without interruptions.

Something inside me needs to be worked. Something or someone inside me has ideas, likes to think and communicate in adult ways. There are parts of me, alive and active, that simply are not addressed in being a mother. It's not merely the desire to escape the infinite wheel of mothering. There are genuine energies that rise in me that want to be heard, exercised, evolved. The woman inside me who is driven, has ambitions and ideas, gets frustrated being a mother.

The genuine energies that rise in me and ask to be lived out— what happens to them when they get neglected? What happens to them when no one sees them or talks to them or gives them free rein? Do they just wither on the vine? So many mutually exclusive energies rise from within me that each day becomes a planned massacre: what desires will I kill in myself today? Will it be my desire to watch my daughter crawl over to the couch and pull herself up? Will it be my desire to have a clean kitchen? Will it be my desire to write about what is beckoning my mind?

I believe it works for some women to be in the work of children and home full-time, but for me, it doesn't. I can't operate off some mental construct of what should or shouldn't be. I need to make decisions based on what is true for me.

I struggle with the question of value. Do I value my work as a mother? Do I really believe, deep down, that this work is important? Can I remember that mothering is important when I live in a culture that does not think mothers or children are important? My husband works outside the home, and he gets money and applause and recognition in the world. Thus far in my career as a mother, not one person has stood up to clap when I have changed a poopie diaper or heroically negotiated a day of a crying baby.

I know that, on this issue of valuing the mother, my inner work is incomplete. When someone asks me, "What do you do?" I feel a sense of social embarrassment. When the simple words "I am a mom" come out of my mouth, overwhelming urges stampede each other in a rush to tag onto that statement a list of fifteen things that I used to do professionally, including my future professional plans, all obfuscating the simple truth that doesn't seem important enough.

When a man and a woman choose to bring children into the world, they must also choose how to divide the labor necessary to support this enterprise: earning money, homemaking, and caring for the children. How this labor is divided has considerable consequences for the life of the man, the woman, and the children.

My husband and I have chosen that he be the primary moneymaker and that I be the primary parent. We both feel strongly that we do not want our children in full-time day care, for ourselves or our children.

In one respect, I am so enamored with being a mother that I just ignore career men and women, reveling in my mothering, living in the satisfactions and meanings of that. But a different part of me has a competitive eye open, seeing my husband and friends accumulating more degrees, more licenses, more expertise, and I am jealous. I want that, too. I feel left behind. I'm not witty, urbane, and delivering papers at conferences. I don't have a reputation. Part of me feels that what they do is more important than what I do.

I become marginal professionally by not putting in the necessary time for continuing education, by opening and closing my private practice every time I have a baby, and by being part-time. How sharp can you be at work when you've been up half the night with a child crying from the pain of a middle-ear infection?

Because of my commitment to mothering our children, it has become obvious that I will forge a different career. My career will be interspersed with my children. I know that my experience as a mother will fertilize whatever work I do. In my saner moments, I believe that participating in this extraordinary maternal act of creation will guide, inform, and perhaps even dictate my work for the rest of my life.

Recently, Steve and the kids and I went to an informal dinner party for a visiting professor. I admire this man's breadth of knowledge; he is learned in mathematics, ecology, literature, history. In our conversation, he asked me what I do. I went completely blank. What do I do? I frantically scanned my mind. I used to be a Unitarian Universalist minister. I used to be a psychotherapist with a private practice. I am the mother of two children. As I began to recite this litany, a flush washed up my body, until, red and flustered, I blurted, "I don't know what I do. I'm a dilettante. I've done a lot of things but not for long. I guess I'm a mother." Steadfast, he paused, then quietly replied, "Some people aren't meant to *do* anything; they're meant to *be* something."

Grace. Those words help me find my way. "Being" is my focus. I can do, do, do, one day after the next, but if my actions are not grounded in a deep relation to wise, compassionate being, then I am just creating more noise in the world. We are all meant to be something. Every day we are meant to be something in a slightly more refined way. A man reminded me of one of the teachings of the Great Mother. Be. Be present. Now.

THIRD CHILD

You have ovulated and an egg is traveling along one of the two fallopian tubes toward your uterus. During intercourse one of the millions of sperm your partner has ejaculated has fertilized the egg while still in the fallopian tube. Your baby is a cluster of cells which multiply rapidly as they continue the journey along the fallopian tube.

—Sheila Kitzinger
The Complete Book of Pregnancy and Childbirth, p. 372

CONCEPTION

four-year-old daughter
six-year-old son

FOR MORE THAN A YEAR, we have been planning for Steve's sabbatical leave. Our plan was to live in Bali for five months, then spend our last month in Taiwan and Hawaii, where we have work commitments. We would take Jesse out of first grade for half of the school year, home-schooling him in Bali. We have been reading about Bali and looking at fabulous picture books featuring this magical island in Indonesia. Two things feel primary to us about Bali. First, the people of Bali are intimately related to earth and sea, living simply in a nature-based culture. Second, Bali is a place where religion and art are intertwined and of utmost value. We want to live this way ourselves, to share with our children daily rituals centered on soul and nature, and it's difficult to know where or how to do that in the United States.

This past year, we have also been inching toward the possibility of a third child. From the beginning of our marriage, Steve has been clear that he wants three children. For years, we have referred to this imaginary third child as Elijah, as in the Jewish custom at the Passover seder of setting an extra cup at the table, anticipating the arrival of the prophet.

I have been ambivalent about a third child. As adorable as babies are, they are also stress-filled, hard work. After years of pregnancies, babies, and toddlers, my life is finally beginning to get easier. I have worked to recover a body that somewhat resembles my premotherhood body. A four-year-old and a six-year-old don't require constant attention; I can read a newspaper, have a conversation, do my own work, steal away with my husband for a romantic weekend—all of which is quite pleasurable. So the question for me is, Why ruin that? I fear that having a third child would, like a riptide, pull me out into watery depths again, places of stress, oceanic places where I have so little control. My ego has been reluctant to go under again in the ways that seem to be required in pregnancy and with a baby.

I don't know whether I got caught in the momentum of Steve's excitement or whether the desire for a baby began to stir more strongly in me, but the end result was that we decided on a plan: try to get pregnant at the end of our stay in Bali. That way, I wouldn't have "morning sickness" dimming the sabbatical, and we could possibly have the magic of conceiving this final child of ours in Bali.

Once we agreed on this plan, I began to get very excited about it. It's like offering the Mother Goddess the tiniest bit of food: that morsel only serves to awaken her ravenous appetite.

The carefully crafted plan to conceive during the fourth month of our stay in Bali existed on the ground floor of my psyche. When I got in the elevator, descending several stories down into the recesses of instinct and desire, I couldn't wait to get pregnant. My unconscious flirted with pregnancy: daydreaming, imagining I already was pregnant, seducing my husband, insisting there was no need for birth control at this time of my cycle and believing myself each time I said it.

It is ridiculous how my little ego makes these plans in the

world, so convinced that it is the ruling force, only to be squashed like a tiny ant under the foot of the Great Mother Goddess when she strides with a purpose of her own. This is the third time in less than a decade when I have made the same stupid mistake. My ego doesn't seem to retain the lesson that it is not in charge, particularly when it comes to this matter of babies.

Getting ready to leave for a sabbatical takes about as long as the sabbatical itself. I had to rent out our house, finish a book I had been writing, and close out my psychotherapy practice. Steve labored for months preparing for his six-month absence.

Of course, the people who rented our house wanted it one month earlier than our scheduled departure date. They seemed like desirable tenants, so our family agreed to move out one month early. We put a positive spin on this major inconvenience by renting a beach house in Santa Barbara for a month, imagining it as a warm-up lap for the sabbatical.

I packed three sets of stuff for three different destinations: (1) the contents of all closets, dressers, and bathroom drawers, which had to be stored in cardboard boxes in the garage to make room for the tenants; (2) clothes, toiletries, computers, and other living supplies for one month of work and school at the beach house; (3) a grand total of two suitcases that carried everything we would need for six months of Bali, Taiwan, and Hawaii. The logistics were daunting. We set up our computers on a funky electrical system at the beach house, and our children's car pools were suddenly defunct, but we rhetorically reassured ourselves, "How bad can life be three steps from the beach?"

We had one idyllic week at the beach house—swimming daily, Boogie boarding on the waves, having friends over for barbecues, reexperiencing the familiar lull of the crashing waves as the background for everything.

It was a Sunday morning when I complained to Steve that I was late for my menstrual period and it was making me nervous because I was supposed to get my immunizations for Bali the next day. Having been through these conversations with me so many times over the years, Steve no longer showed interest in my drama of thinking I was pregnant. He blandly replied, "Go buy one of those home pregnancy tests, and then you won't have to worry about it."

I felt a little insulted by his blasé attitude. I went to the drugstore. I bought the pregnancy test. I came home. I peed in the jar. Standing in the bathroom, I put the determining stick into the urine, and it turned blue. Blue? It's blue???

A virtual stampede of energy charged this way, then that way, throughout my mind and body. I was thrilled. Horrified. Disbelieving. Ecstatic. Shocked. Victorious. Self-righteous. How could I get Steve down here immediately, without also bringing our two children? I modulated my voice to normal tones and casually called, "Honey, can you come down here for a moment?" When I saw that he arrived alone, I yanked him through the doorway, closed the door, and locked it. I handed him the test instructions and the blue stick, "Here, read this and tell me what *you* think."

I went into shock. That whole day, I could not formulate complete thoughts in my brain, nor could I speak much. The part of my mind that likes to be in control was blown away. The woman who has her own thoughts and speaks them was silenced, overwhelmed. I had become pregnant, without the final consent of my conscious mind.

Some elemental woman inside so desired to be pregnant that she took over—indeed, *arranged* a pregnancy. Fat and smug, she crossed her arms, leaned back with the satisfaction of a job well done, steeping in the joy of a growing baby. But my conscious voice remained hesitant, still forming rational discourses about stress and time for work and time for pleasure. I knew eventually I would get pregnant, but my ego wanted more time to feel in charge of the deliberations. Once again, abducted by the Great Mother Goddess. Once again, sucked into her gravitational field. Once again, shocked and amazed to be here.

We decided not to tell our kids yet. Steve and I needed to adjust to this matter on our own first. The next day, I took the kids to the travel doctor, to receive the recommended immunizations. I discreetly took him aside and told him that I was newly pregnant. He replied, "Well, then you're not going to Bali." I said, "What? Why not?" He said, "I can give you a number of good reasons: dengue fever, malaria, typhoid fever, smallpox, cholera, yellow fever, hepatitis, traveler's diarrhea.[1] You can't receive any of the immunizations while you're pregnant. Do you really want to risk getting seriously sick in Bali and ending up in a hospital there? Immunizations, antibiotics, and illness would all endanger your pregnancy." At this point I was inside a surreal movie. In my mind, I stumbled backward, far away from this scene. I could observe myself functioning in the room with the doctor, but only as you would see something through binoculars. I simply could not absorb my present reality. Polite to the end, I said something socially appropriate, gathered my kids, and left, offering a feeble excuse to the children, who were jubilant by this reprieve from the dreaded needle.

I drove directly to my gynecologist's office to get an official test. It didn't make sense to cancel four sets of international plane tickets based on a home pregnancy test, and at that moment, it was very important to do something that made sense. I gave the nurse my urine, and several minutes later, she said, "Congratulations."

I was apprehensive about breaking the most recent news flash to Steve. He still was stunned that I was actually pregnant. We had been looking forward to this trip to Bali for so long. It was to be his time away from the heavy demands of his job, relaxed time to focus on research and writing. I knew this was not going to be easy. After the kids were in bed, I invited him to our little bedroom and told him. He became quite agitated, pacing the small floor, his winged desires suddenly clipped. He ranted and raved, "It's ridiculous not to go to Bali. What kind of medical advice are we paying for?" etcetera, and with renewed vigor, he reached his definitive solution, "Fire that travel doctor!" I understood. It would be better to wait a few days before trying to have a rational conversation.

Two days later, we rallied, "Hey, we're adults, we can adjust to a change of plans. There's no tragedy here. No one died. Not even anything bad. Just a big change of plans." I called the travel doctor to ask where we could go. His rule of thumb was to stay away from Third World countries close to the equator: heat, poor sanitation, and poor health care is the combination to avoid. After much ado, two weeks before we were supposed to leave on our trip, we acquired a new set of plane tickets with a new destination, this time circling the Pacific Rim: Tahiti, New Zealand, Australia, Singapore, Taiwan, and Hawaii.

Steve and I were ready to tell Jesse and Alia about my pregnancy. It was officially confirmed, and we felt more balanced about it, so we wanted to share it with them. We all walked out to the beach, the four of us sat in a circle, and we told them. Immediately, Jesse jumped up, high into the air with raised fists, triumphantly exclaiming, "yes! yes! yes! You mated!" He raced to the ocean, ran back to us (sitting dumbfounded), he ran back to the ocean and back to us. Suddenly, disappointment fell across his face, "Why didn't you tell me you were going to mate? Why didn't you ask me to be there?" From Jesse's perspective, mating to create a new baby was a special event in our family, and he couldn't understand being excluded from it. "OK," he said, trying to organize it in his six-year-old mind, "where did you do it?" I was able to speak, "In our bedroom at our house." Impatiently, he replied, "I know. But *where* in the bedroom?"

Alia sat close to me, sucking her pacifier, her eyebrows knitted in concern. Even though she was four years old, she still had a strong streak of wanting to be my baby, even still wanting to nurse, although I had weaned her at fifteen months of age. Alia cherished her position as the baby of the family.

I cautioned the children not to get their hopes up too high about a baby yet, that sometimes in the first three months of a woman's pregnancy, it is possible for her to have a miscarriage. Jesse refused to integrate this information. But in the following weeks, Alia told anyone who would listen, "My mom is pregnant, but we wouldn't really mind if the baby died."

Several days later, Marion, a friend and teacher, and her husband came over to our beach house for dinner. Marion knew what a crisis I was in, and she had become like a mother to me. I so needed an older woman to hold me in all the ways that an older woman can hold a younger woman.

Even though a light rain was falling, we all donned raincoats and umbrellas to walk along the beach before dinner. The mood cast by the dark gray storm comforted me; I could not have tolerated cheerful weather. My life was falling apart. My lack of control over the events of my life disturbed me. It is a shocking experience to make large plans, only to have a larger force wipe those plans off the board. My disorientation was deep. Moving to the beach house was disorienting. Being pregnant was disorienting. Changing our coveted travel plans was disorienting. And because of all that upheaval, I lost my grip on every other detail of our lives.

That very day, I had missed the Chinese New Year's luncheon that Jesse's first-grade class had prepared for the parents. Every other child sat with his or her parents, celebrating the meal the children had cooked. Jesse was the orphan. Even though other families included him, he cried through the entire luncheon. Happy Year of the Monkey. It wasn't that I forgot the Chinese New Year's luncheon; it was that I never even knew about it. I had been in too much turmoil to bother reading the weekly class newsletter that invited the parents. I felt terrible that I missed it, and so did Jesse.

That evening, as Marion and I were walking on the beach, Jesse began crying again. I knew he was disappointed and I was sorry, but the crying seemed excessive to me. Dutifully, I bent down to wipe his tears. Inches from his face, I noticed a red bump on his cheek. My eyes darted around his face: another bump and another and more. I gasped, reeling from yet another blow. I stood up, looked Marion in the eye, and told her, "Jesse has chicken pox." Marion began laughing. She laughed so hard she doubled over. That wise woman laughed and laughed.

Obviously, any conceptions I had about my life were null and void. The cosmos had a few plans of its own, abducting me on some trip, purpose and destination unknown to me. My ego had taken a beating, been humbled to the extent that I could only sit back with my mouth hanging open, passively watching to see what might happen next.

When Marion recovered, she told me about a time in her life years ago when she, too, had been abducted far beyond her conscious intentions, when everything that she had planned for herself was systematically wiped out, contrary to some larger plan that was unfolding, a plan that she was not authoring. She talked about her anger, how she fought and resisted, struggled to make things go the way she wanted them to go. Finally, she was humbled to the point of surrender. She said that then it occurred to her to stop still and ask, "What story am I in? What do God and Goddess want of me?"

This submission of the ego always represents the turning point in myth. The hero or heroine finally is confronted with the fallacy of the omnipotent ego, and a whole wide world opens up. The heroine sees that to successfully navigate the trials in the journey, she must agree to be permeable to the great powers in the universe, and by channeling these powers through her being, she comes to realize her true nature.

I could not contain the absurdity of our life circumstance: I told Steve. As I was telling him, I came across a sobering realization. The bad news was that Jesse had the chicken pox. The really bad news was that Alia did not have the chicken pox (yet). If Alia were exposed immediately, she would still have an eleven- to nineteen-day incubation period and then a week of the pox themselves.[2] We weren't going to leave town for a long time.

Winter storms blew in. All the windows and all but one door of our two-room beach house had to be boarded up because of high surf. The mildew smells were horrific. My sense of smell is heightened in pregnancy, particularly the first few months, and I could smell innuendos of odors that were a curse to behold. I began three months' worth of throwing up. Jesse stayed home and built spaceships out of Legos. Alia went to preschool until she developed the pox. Then she stayed home and played Uno and Barbies. Steve worked and cooked and took care of the kids and tried to cheer me up, which was a big job.

It's not that easy to cancel nonrefundable international plane tickets, especially when it's the second time you've canceled, but faced with the possibility of a pox-ridden child stepping onto an enclosed plane, the airline was cordial about making the change. A relentless optimist, Steve purchased our third set of plane tickets.

> Spiritual life is the bouquet of natural life, not a supernatural thing imposed upon it. The impulses of nature are what give authenticity to life, not obeying rules that come from a supernatural authority.
>
> —Joseph Campbell
> *The Power of Myth,* Program 5

PREGNANT ON THE PACIFIC RIM

two to five months pregnant
four-year-old daughter
six-year-old son

THERE IS GOOD NEWS about this long, pregnant family travel, and there is bad news. For four months now, we have been a nomadic tribe. One day after the next, I meander with my husband and two children through various land- and seascapes, enjoying the view of life from different cultural lenses.

It has been strange to be pregnant and not be home. Instinct calls me to a nest, a constant place with familiar smells. I must regularly converse with my instinct about this unanswered call, reassuring the animal mother that my lack of response is only temporary, that we will be home two months before the baby is born. For now, our family dwells in a movable nest.

I have seen many doctors during this pregnancy thus far, but never the same one twice. I keep a file of my medical records, which provides some continuity in my prenatal health care. My first doctor on this trip was a beautiful, tall, black woman pediatrician from Morocco. She, too, was on an atoll in Tahiti, a narrow strip of a dead coral island called Rangiroa. The heat in Tahiti laid me flat. I wasn't there long before I developed traveler's diarrhea, which was further complicated by the nausea and vomiting of early pregnancy. One day, while buying bottled water, I met her; she promised she would ride her bicycle over to the little hut where I was staying to check on me. The next day, she stood at my door, her small black bag in hand. She took my blood pressure, examined me, and was so kind in caring for me.

The primary work required of me in this journey around the Pacific Rim is a kind of radical "letting go." I don't have any real commitments, other than being in relationship with my immediate family. Almost all of the myriad daily tasks of home life are absent in these travels.

It occurs to me that, on this sabbatical, I have many of the advantages of being dead but few of the disadvantages. There are no phone calls to return. No appointments to keep. No frenetic schedule. No car to repair. But best of all, there is no mail. The daily mail is a modern curse: junk advertising pages mixed with seductive Visa card offers mixed with legal documents and bills, randomly intermingled in piles that are too overwhelming to maintain. The absence of mail is an exhilarating liberation. Furthermore, I have no house to clean. I can't cook meals because the smell of food makes me throw up. I have even surrendered into throwing up. I vomited on three islands in Tahiti, the north and south islands of New Zealand, but only once in Australia. I can now vomit without resistance, allowing the body its way, even feeling a certain intimacy with the land upon which I have contributed something of myself.

I feel suspended in time. In the physical absence of extended family and friends, I have been surprised to notice that certain people are alive in me; they live and talk to me even when they are not here in the flesh. Spontaneously, I hear their comments on various events, and sometimes they counsel me or amuse me with their observations. I am intrigued to notice who lives in me, who the people are on the planet who have entered my spirit, who infuse me, quite regardless of physical presence. The joy is that I get to have this distant perspective on my life, like a dead person reviewing her life, *and,* barring any unseasonable endings, I get to return in the flesh to my beloved places and people.

Traveling brings certain physical inconveniences. Especially in my first trimester, it was hard not to have my preferred foods. My body isn't quite as comfortable in beds other than my own. The places we have been where the weather is hot are tricky for me; I don't take the heat well, especially when I'm pregnant.

We had one adventure that was awful for me. On the northeastern coast of Australia, we rented a four-wheel-drive tin-can jeep to drive up to the remote rain forests that Captain Cook correctly named Cape Tribulation.[1] I couldn't agree more. The road was rutted and potholed in the extreme; we bump-bump-bounced for more than two hours getting there. Sweet Jesse gave me his stuffed dog to cushion my precious belly.

Although, in Australia, there is astonishing beauty and diversity of life species, there are also about a million different things that can kill you. We have been cautioned about the extremely dangerous saltwater crocodiles who will eat you in a snap. These "salties," who can grow up to twenty-one feet long, defy their name by swimming from the ocean up the estuaries into rivers and other fresh waters more than one hundred and fifty miles inland. These salties are distinct from their mellower relatives, the freshwater crocodiles, who, although up to twelve feet long, are generally not aggressive.[2]

In the Northern Territories, we see other people happily swimming in the rivers and gorges. The heat is so oppressive, the cool waters so alluring, that, reluctantly, the children and I have joined them. Steve was never reluctant. The Australians we have met seem to enjoy flaunting the uncertainty of the wild. More than one person has "assured" us, "No worries, mate, there's no salties in here . . . I don't think."

We have seen snakes bigger than fire hoses, laid out in the

road sunning themselves. Once, we were chased around a wilderness park by a primitive four-foot lizard called a goanna. We have seen a frilled-neck lizard and wallabies in the wild and long-necked turtles and other surreal animals.

The rock paintings of the Aborigines captivate me—rock walls, covered by layer upon layer of sacred paintings, depicting the animals and the dreaming spirits. One painting in Kakadu especially speaks to me: in colors of blue and cream and brown is a woman with a child, floating side by side in air or perhaps water. Similar to many of the ancient Mother Goddess depictions throughout the world, their heads are not individualized with detail; the detail is comprised of many dots on the breasts of the mother, representing milk, and a dotted belly section on the mother, showing the sacred site of human creation.[3]

On the northeastern coast of Australia, we could not swim off the exquisitely beautiful beaches because, for seven months out of each year, the box jellyfish swim those waters. Several jocular folks have informed us, "It's not so bad. You only get stung by a box jellyfish once in a lifetime (ha, ha, ha)." This is because the poison of the jellyfish sends a person into anaphylactic shock, paralyzing the circulatory system, causing death within several minutes.

To swim in the ocean, one must take a long boat ride out to the Great Barrier Reef. I have been most content lying in these warm waters, face down with my snorkel and mask, watching whatever happens to swim by. The reef is a magnificent world unto itself; for hours, I float and observe. I have seen more than a few fish that are bigger than I am. I have also seen forests of soft coral, some with long, flexible tendrils like spaghetti, sensually swaying in the waves. I caress this soft coral; the slime it leaves on my hands is nature's sunscreen, effective but smelly. Mostly, I resemble a basking shark, passively floating, open to what drifts near me.

It is heavenly to relax so much, to allow a floaty consciousness, to be with beauty so often, and to have so much time in wilderness land and ocean. We hike and snorkel and swim.

Every day, we have an adventure. How pleasant it is to be with our children with my husband as another full-time parent. How tender it is for our family to bond this way before our new baby arrives.

Jesse has been especially dear toward me. He is protective and nurturing of me in my pregnancy. He is thoroughly invested in this baby; sometimes, I get the feeling he thinks we're having this baby just for him. He offers to rub my back, get me a blanket. I had not anticipated how it would be to bring forth a baby in the presence of conscious older children. Both Jesse's and Alia's feelings about receiving a baby into our family have enriched this pregnancy for me. The baby will not be just mine, or mine and Steve's; this baby will also belong to Jesse and Alia.

From the onset of this trip, I knew I would need to have an amniocentesis abroad. The timing was such that it would be in Australia's northern Queensland. In a town served by three obstetricians, one doctor turned his schedule upside down to help me. He was concerned because I was already sixteen weeks pregnant, and it takes about three weeks to receive the results of the test, and in Australia, it is illegal to receive an abortion after the twentieth week. Not to mention that I would be in Singapore by that time, and neither of us had any idea whether abortion is legal in Singapore. Obviously, I had not thought all of this through carefully enough. In the worst-case scenario, I might have to return to the United States for an abortion.

In the initial exam, I invited Steve and Jesse and Alia to be in the room so they could hear the heartbeat of the baby. Everyone was thrilled. Then the doctor said, "Now, your husband should take the children to the waiting room so I can examine you down there," pointing at my crotch. Down there? Down under? My children are more comfortable saying "vagina" than that obstetrician was, which caused me to be a little disoriented as to what decade we were in.

The actual amniocentesis was several days later. As much as I was grateful to that doctor for helping me, I still have to say the experience was a nightmare. Per his instructions, my bladder was uncomfortably filled with two quarts of water. I was tense, in a foreign country with a doctor whom I normally would not have chosen. He would not permit Steve to be in the room with me because it was a small room and too crowded. I was alone with strangers. He did not use anesthetic. It hurt as the long needle pushed through my belly. He was not as adept as was the doctor performing the amniocentesis during my second pregnancy. My body was rigid with tension. I was trying to breathe to relax, but the fear was too strong for me to manage. After almost five torturous minutes of his moving the needle around inside my uterus, he said he was not getting any amniotic fluid and had to pull the needle out and try all over again. Despair! I could barely stand the tension and pain. He inserted the needle into my belly again, and at least this time he was getting fluid, but it took a long time. I was on that table for nearly forty minutes. I was trying to be cooperative and polite, but inside, I was horrified and shattered. I felt as though I were having a back-alley abortion. The doctor made a comment to me during the procedure that was so appalling that I immediately decided to put it in a distant corner of my mind. I cannot remember exactly what he said, but I do remember that his crude joke revealed that he had no understanding of the way I felt toward the fetus in my womb, that I already cherished it.

When the procedure was over, I dressed and went out to the waiting room. I took Steve aside, so that our children would not know how emotionally devastated I was. My uterus was cramping. I was afraid I would have a spontaneous miscarriage. Trying not to break down right there in the waiting room, I only relayed essential information to Steve: "I'm traumatized. I need you to find me a bed that is comfortable within one and a half blocks of this place, and I need it soon." I sat down with the children, holding very still, and waited.

As usual, Steve came through. Within twenty minutes, he had registered in a hotel and tucked me into bed, where I lay still for eighteen hours tending my wounds. He brought me food, took the children out for adventures, and gave me peace and love. I can't remember too much about those hours in the hotel room. Mostly I slept, handing it all over to my unconscious to sort out. It was too much for me to process consciously. I do recall one scene where I got up to use the bathroom and I remembered that *Roe* v. *Wade* was being legally challenged in the Supreme Court of the United States. I realized how strange, and how desperate, I would feel if I wanted an abortion and could not get a safe one in my own country. I knew then how very important it is to protect a woman's legal right to choose about her pregnancy.

I recovered, sort of, tried to bury the trauma and go on with life. Of course, a certain tension existed over the next three weeks while we were waiting to find out whether the fetus was healthy and whole.

For months, I have been convinced I am carrying a girl. In both previous pregnancies, I intuitively knew the gender of the baby by the third month and was correct both times, so I felt confident. I even knew what I wanted her name to be. I was thrilled to have another girl. My relationship to my four-year-old daughter already has taught me much about the many faces of femininity; she has carried me down pathways of the feminine that I never had explored on my own. I was looking forward to mothering yet another incarnation of the possibilities of the feminine.

We were in a hotel in Singapore when I called in for the amniocentesis results. The doctor told me on the phone that the baby was genetically healthy. I was so relieved to be free from an anguishing decision that all I could focus on was the joy of continuing this pregnancy. "Do you want to know whether it is a boy or a girl?" the doctor asked. "Oh, sure," I replied. "It's a boy," he said. I was stunned, disbelieving. "It's a boy? You're kidding! Are you sure?" He was sure. Steve and Jesse and Alia overheard my end of the conversation. While I was still on the phone, Jesse began jumping up and down on the hotel bed, which is probably against the law in Singapore, yelling, "Yes. Yes, it's a boy. I'm going to have a baby brother. Yes!"

That evening, Alia and I took a bath together. I asked her how she was feeling about the baby now. She continues to be honest about her feelings, and it is interesting to watch her process this developmental milestone in her life. She said that she doesn't want the baby dead anymore, but she still isn't happy about it because she wants to be the baby of the family. When I asked why, she told me that the baby in the family gets the most attention, and she wants to be that person. For four years, she has occupied that position, and she will not relinquish it easily. Even if I wanted to, I don't feel it would be possible to manipulate the way she feels about my pregnancy. I certainly don't want to force her to repress her authentic feelings, adopting a surface happy face while feeling vengeful underneath. I can only trust the organic life process, trust that her psyche knows it has more months to evolve into her new life stage, and that if we talk openly and lovingly, she will come to some positive resolution. I realize how deep my faith is in the intelligence and healing powers of the psyche.

Now, we are released into enjoying Singapore, with its fantastic mix of cultures. I look at endless bolts of fabric from all around the world, wander Little India and Chinatown, eat lunch at a French café, and eat dinner with my bare hands in an Indian restaurant that uses banana leaves as plates. I feel exhilarated by the different energies from all around the world mingling and coexisting in Singapore.

Our next destination is Taiwan, to see our friends and to lead workshops. I will be doing a four-day women's therapy group, working with a translator. Our final leg of the trip is Hawaii, where Steve will do several workshops, and we will meet my family for vacation. Then, like a bird weary of circling the sky, I will swoop down to that familiar nest: home.

The religious meaning of the custom [of giving birth on the ground] is easy to see: generation and childbirth are microcosmic versions of a paradigmatic act performed by the earth; every human mother only imitates and repeats this primordial act of the appearance of life in the womb of the earth. Hence every mother must put herself in contact with the Great Genetrix, that she may be guided by her in accomplishing the mystery that is the birth of a life, may receive her beneficent energies and secure her maternal protection.

—Mircea Eliade
The Sacred and the Profane, pp. 141–42

PLANNING MY LAST BIRTH

seven months pregnant
four-year-old daughter
seven-year-old son

I CALLED THE INSURANCE COMPANY to "precertify" a maternity stay at the hospital. If one does not precertify, this insurance company pays only 80 percent of the cost (if it agrees that the cost qualifies), whereas if one does precertify, it pays 100 percent, after a hefty copayment. The insurance company says it will permit me to be in the hospital for two days to have a baby. However, if I have any complications that necessitate staying in the hospital longer, or if my baby has any complications, I must call the insurance company because I was informed that complications also need to be precertified.

One problem in all of this nonsense is that I can barely remember my own name after I give birth. If I do have any complications, there is not a remote chance that it would occur to me to call my insurance company. Is the company gambling on this? Is part of the company's racket based on women's being too spaced-out to precertify their birthing complications, and so the company gets to pay either none of the cost or 80 percent of the cost? I hope that's not true. That would be really cold-blooded; however, I am suspicious of the ethics of insurance companies.

Anyway, in this absurd bureaucratic preparation for childbirth, I found out that it will cost eight thousand dollars for me to have a baby in the hospital, *not including* the obstetrician's fee or any complications. Eight thousand dollars? For what?? My last birth was a normal vaginal delivery that took two and a half hours from beginning to end. To get my money's worth, I would need the hospital to hire a full orchestra to accompany me. Of course, the insurance company would pay a major share of the cost, but still, the whole thing rubs me the wrong way. It offends me that I have to precertify my birth and that it costs eight thousand dollars plus the obstetrician's fee. It seems appropriate to wonder who this establishment is serving. Thus far, it does not seem particularly relevant to me or my baby.

I am keenly aware that this will be my last birth, my final foray into these mysteries. I want to know birth in a full way, to be in it fully, awake. Birth is a revelation; the doors and windows of the universe are wide open, flashing the bare realities of existence. Much of what is worth knowing is revealed in the birth event. To push a human being out of one's body, to see that life is born from life, to be one with the creative powers. To be overtaken by one's own body, to be led by the wisdom of one's own body. To be led by instinct, the instinct that governs mothers and babies throughout the animal realm. This is a privilege. In my final journey into this wondrous place, I want to know it as fully as I can.

In my first birth, I was afraid and in pain, resisting the contractions and the pushing urges. I was trying to adhere to the dogma of the alternative childbirth community that it is better to have a drug-free birth. The trauma of that birth did not heal until my second birth was completed.

In my second birth, I had resolved to use drugs if I needed them for pain control, but I did not need them. I was remarkably lucid, not afraid. The pain in my second birth was more a psychological pain, in that I tried to be so competent and heroic that I did not make any room for the vulnerable, overwhelmed woman inside. I did not notice her until, two mornings later, a dream ambushed my ego, demanding attention.

Two themes have come clear to me about this third birth. First, I want a diverse feminine presence both within myself and among the persons attending the birth. I want space for a vulnerable scared girl, space for the competent woman, a place for the nurturing earth mother, plenty of room for the roaring wild woman, and more. I want an honoring of the true multiplicity of the feminine.

The second theme is that I want this birth to be a personal event, centered around me and my baby and our family. I don't want an institution to own my birth experience, nor a doctor or a nurse. I don't want anyone intruding on my knowing, my rhythms, my instincts, my desires. I want people involved in my birth who can support the wisdom of the mother-and-baby-body, who are sensitive and generous enough to facilitate our intense journey of body, heart, and soul.

As I increasingly take responsibility for my own birth experience, I feel the palpability of life and of death. In a hospital, where there are doctors and nurses and technologically advanced machines, I relax into a fantasy that everything will be OK, that they would never let my baby die or be born deformed. They are the authorities, responsible for my life, able to control forces of nature such as bacteria, able to fix imperfections of the human body. Doctors are the postmodern gods, healing the sick, granting extended life in return for sacrificial offerings (like money) and worship. I don't blame doctors for this any more than I blame myself; many of us have woven this illusion together. As I peer through the illusion, I see how frightened I am that I cannot control nature, that some birthing mothers die, and some babies die. I feel the danger of this passage through creation, the profound vulnerability inherent in birth.

In my town, there is one team of three licensed midwives. I met each of them individually and asked a million questions. "What if something goes wrong in the birth?" If it is beyond the scope of their ability, they call 911 and we go to hospital. "What are the most common problems in a home birth?" Postpartum hemorrhaging for the mother; respiratory difficulties for the baby. "Will there be oxygen on hand?" Yes. The most reassuring information is that there are usually advance signs for a complicated birth. During regular prenatal care, health professionals monitor the mother's weight, blood pressure, and pulse; check her urine for glucose, protein, and signs of infection; measure the growth of the fetus; check the fetus's heart rate and movements; and determine the position of the baby. This information offers excellent predictors about the birth. After examining me, the midwives are satisfied that I am a "low-risk" pregnant woman and a good candidate for home birth. I have never had a medical emergency. I am healthy, my pregnancy has been healthy, and my previous two births have been uncomplicated vaginal deliveries.

The midwives are three very impressive women. What I notice most about them is the quality of their presence. Perhaps it is because they attend to themselves, psychologically and spiritually, but perhaps also what they do for a living transforms them. For instance, Mary. Mary is clear and quiet inside. She is involved, engaged, but also a spacious step back, so that all reality slows and each intricacy is noticed. She has keen powers of observation: seeing and hearing a level of detail that is extraordinary. She is gentle and loving. But she can also be stern and strict, confronting when necessary. I feel that if a time came when I did not know what to do, Mary would take wise action.

Each midwife asks me questions that I want to answer. How am I feeling in the pregnancy? How is my husband feeling? How are we imagining the home birth? They address my pregnancy as more than a physical event, knowing that feelings, intuitions, soul, and family are also intimately related to the pregnancy. In my appointments with them, I feel cared for as a woman in the full variety of ways in which I experience my pregnancy.

In reading about home birth, I learn that, in Holland, approximately half of all babies are born in the home. The infant mortality rate in Holland is lower than in the United States or England. The Dutch view childbirth as a natural event, believing that the mother should be supported in the revelations of her natural body wisdom. There is some evidence that a woman's labor and delivery go more quickly and happily when she is in an environment where she feels confident and in control. This makes perfect sense to me. If we notice mother animals, we see that they choose a calm, secluded, and secure environment for birthing. One study showed that postpartum depression was experienced by 60 percent of women in hospital deliveries, whereas only 16 percent of women who gave birth in their homes went into a depression.[1]

There are sound reasons for hospital birth, and there are good reasons for home birth. It is up to Steve and me to decide what we feel is best for us. The haunting question for both of us is, What if something did go wrong in a home birth? Could we ever forgive ourselves if our baby was harmed because we were not in a hospital where we could have emergency care immediately?

In our heart of hearts, we want a home birth. Because I am low-risk, and our baby shows all signs of health, we choose the midwives. This is a huge decision, followed by many more decisions, because suddenly we aren't part of someone else's predesigned program; the program is pretty much ours to create.

When a person walks on a path that has been created by someone else, the journey and the destination are fairly clear. One walks the predetermined path, which brings quite a bit of certainty and security, even though some of that sense of security is false. Just because four million other people also walked that path does not necessarily mean it is satisfying, worthwhile, or even safe. Nonetheless, one has company and need not be burdened with so many choices.

Alternatively, one can choose the road "less traveled by," walking in a way that is directed by inner feeling, intuition, smell, beauty, desire. The senses must be fully open; each moment requires decisions about how to move.

Where would I give birth? In a warm bathtub? In the yard under a tree? In the bed where this baby was conceived? What if I am in the animalistic depths of labor and the UPS delivery man rings the doorbell? What if the gardeners show up that day? Or the electric meter reader? Will our neighbors be alarmed by my (shall I use the euphemism) "vocalizing"?

What sheets would we put on the bed? What towels will we sacrifice to the birth? How can we protect the new carpet from blood, amniotic fluid, and all the other bodily fluids that come out during childbirth? What container will we use to save the placenta? In a hospital, all these details are taken care of by someone else. As are the supplies. I ordered a home birth kit that included many of the necessary supplies, but I have to go shopping for additional items.

Then there is the question of who will attend the birth. Would we include Jesse and Alia? One day, I am waxing about how isolated birth and death have become in our culture, how frighteningly unnatural and mysterious they become when people do not participate in these processes with their loved ones. I want Jesse and Alia to be involved in life processes. The next day, I wane: would I feel free to fully enter my labor process—the vocalizing, the diarrhea, the vomiting—with my kids present? Would my children feel traumatized seeing their mother in pain? No matter what the children's emotional state, in any event, I know they would pull Steve's focus away from me when I need him. It doesn't sound that great to have the children present for the birth. We ask the kids how they feel about it. Jesse says he doesn't want to see me in pain, but be sure to call him when it's over. Alia says she would rather be at school.

Who else will we invite? Not that it's a party—but indeed, an honored invitation. We need people on hand: to take the kids, to boil water or whatever you do during a birth, to help me when Steve needs to do something else, to make food or tea. I don't exactly even know what we need people for, but it seems a good idea to have plenty of help. We finalize the invitations: the midwives, my mother, and my friend Susan, and of course, Steve and me.

I want to design a home birth that matches the true nature of birth: physically, emotionally, and spiritually. Many women in the past several decades have refused to define birth as an institutional event, where the authority is handed over to medical professionals. Many women and men have worked to restore the birth experience as a personal event, centered primarily on the mother, baby, and father. Great strides have been taken toward making birth a more personal experience. Women can choose home birth. Women can choose a birthing center, designed to feel homelike, with pastel walls, a couch, and a rocking chair, yet also medically equipped. The father can be present with the mother and hold the newborn, even cut the umbilical cord. One can have a friendly working relationship with the obstetrician. There are many ways in which we have moved beyond a solely medical and institutional interpretation of the birth event.

As I am designing my birth-day, I bump up against the incompleteness of a personal emphasis on birth. The creation of a new human being, delivered to live and breathe on this earth, is much more than a personal event. The birth of a baby is an event of the human species, of nature, of the Holy Spirit. Birth is every bit as much a *collective* event as it is personal. How can we honor the ways in which a woman pushing a new life out of her body is profoundly connected to the human community— all the anonymous living women and men, all our ancestors? How can we honor that the energies moving through the birthing woman make her one with her sisters, the sows and bitches, mares and does? How can we pay homage to the Great Mother Goddess who presides over this creation? How can we celebrate the inseminating and protective Gods? These are questions that move beyond a personal understanding of the birth event.

There is an Aztec Goddess made of clay that Steve bought me years ago. She sits more than two feet tall, face stern with a fixed mouth. She conveys her mysteries through the revelation of her body: enormous breasts upright and proud with large erect nipples, legs parted for all to witness the dark, mysterious cave from which life emerges. She is ferociously feminine. Embodied. Sexual in a way that is not seductive but rather openly proud of her sexual wonders. On several occasions, carpet installers, plumbers, and electricians have walked past her in our house, and I have heard them gasp. I arrange this mighty Aztec goddess on a table across from my bed so that she might guide me in the birth.

I am planning to save the placenta from this birth, to plant in our yard under a tree. Beyond these small steps, I don't know what else to do to acknowledge this birth as belonging to the collective. One individual can't forge collective pathways; by definition, the steps of many persons are required in the collective domain.

There are examples throughout the world in which cultural rituals link an expectant woman to the collective dimensions of her creation. Pregnant women of ancient Crete used to enter the cave of Eileithyia, the Goddess of Childbirth. Near the town of Herakleion, this cave, which Homer mentioned in the *Odyssey* and which still exists, was used for childbirthing rituals dating back to at least 3000 BCE up until the Roman conquest in 67 BCE.[2]

We can only begin to imagine the possibilities of the cult rituals surrounding labor and delivery in this cave of Eileithyia. Throughout the cave are stalagmites, many in humanlike shapes. One rocky protuberance resembles a pregnant woman's belly with a small hollow like a navel in its center. For thousands of years, the pregnant women of Crete rubbed their bellies against this rock, hoping it would bring a safe birth. In a different area of the cave of Eileithyia are stalagmites that look like a mother with children. These rock formations were believed to be earthy embodiments of the Great Mother Goddess. Many fragments of pottery vessels have been found in a circle around these mother and child rock formations, confirming that it was a site of worship and ritual. Also in the cave are clear pools of water, which were believed to have healing properties.[3] In my imagination, I can hear the echoes of the thousands of women over time who entered this cave bringing their deepest fears and hopes to the womb of the earth and to the Goddess. I have heard those sounds in myself, but I had no literal place, and no community, no rituals to contain the sounds, echoing them back to me.

On one of the Hawaiian islands, in a large lava cave where a community lived many years ago, there is a birthing rock. The locals feel strongly that the spirits of the ancestors still live there, so it is imperative to take an offering to them upon entering the cave. The cave is by a river, the twenty-five-foot lava walls and small entry camouflaged by tropical vegetation. I must crouch to enter, finding myself in a dark common living space, two naturally formed cave rooms. As I walk through the two caves, I am able to see out across a large inner courtyard, open to the skies. I see a banyan tree, the same kind of tree that the Buddha sat beneath in his journey toward enlightenment. The banyan tree says it all: a large trunk growing up from the earth, spreading into branches, which curiously grow roots that drop back down to the earth, reaching down into the ground, drawing nutrients and water, a visual form of the circular relationship of above and below. Beyond this tree sits the birthing rock: shorter than I am, a conical shape that my arms fit around. This rock is solid: it will endure any amount of pulling, scratching, leaning that a laboring mother doles out. Maybe ten feet beyond the birthing rock is the entrance to the cave of the dead, where I believe the ancestors are buried. Standing in this sacred place, I fantasize giving birth with the help of this rock. Would I face the community of the living as the forces of nature took over my body in rhythmic contractions? Would I focus on the banyan tree, seeing how it draws from the depths of nature to sustain its living? Or would I prefer to face the dark empty cave of the dead? All these possibilities surround the birthing rock.

I imagine feeling reassured in many ways. Like every other mother in my community, I would have my turn with the rock. The rock and the earth and the banyan tree, by virtue of being themselves, would be my labor coaches, patiently showing me the ways of nature. I can imagine the comfort of holding the same rock that my peers and ancestresses held while they squatted and pushed and groaned. As I stood on the threshold of creation, channeling possibilities of life and death, my friends and family would be on either side of me, in the cave of the living and the cave of the dead. I would hold the cool rock, pulling on it as I squat to open my pelvis; I would clutch the rock hard through my pains, pull against its strength as I push my baby out. There is solace and comfort in belonging to a lineage of women who also endured this pain, entered these mysteries. This collective experience supports the individual in ways more subtle, more essential than can be named.

As I plan my final journey into childbirth, I feel the lack of cultural rituals to support this rite of passage. I am pleased to have the freedom of choices to design my birth experience in ways that are meaningful and appropriate to me personally, but I also feel the absence of ways to connect the birth to the collective realm. Perhaps this is the next evolution of the childbirth movement: to forge birthing practices that link a mother to the collective realities that indeed support each birth—the human community, the community of nature, and the *anima mundi*, the soul of the world.

These might be the Braxton Hicks "rehearsal" contractions, which some women experience as quite painful at times in the last three weeks or so of pregnancy. These then tend to be called "false" labor. All this means is that you thought you were in labor, with good reason, but were not.

—Sheila Kitzinger

The Complete Book of Pregnancy and Childbirth, p. 229

FALSE LABOR

nine months pregnant
four-year-old daughter
seven-year-old son

WHEN OUR FAMILY RETURNED home from the sabbatical, I had a mind-boggling list of things to accomplish. Big basic things to do. Unpack suitcases. Haul all the cardboard storage boxes from the garage to the house and put the contents back in our drawers and closets. Find a kindergarten for Alia. Buy two cars. (We had sold both of our cars before we left on our trip.) Plan a fortieth birthday party for myself. Plan my home birth. Find a person to help me with housekeeping and children.

These jobs had to be completed within two months, before the baby's birth. Finally, by this third pregnancy, I have become realistic: during the first year with a new baby, I can't accomplish anything other than immediate basic care of the family. All less central tasks must either be done before the baby arrives or postponed for at least one year.

The first month of our return home, I was living in a state of grace. Perhaps it was because I was so relaxed. Perhaps I had more perspective on my life because of the distance afforded by traveling. Whatever the reason, my alignment with the universe was so harmonious that life was like a dream, in which all events calmly unfolded in perfect order and time. One day, when I stopped for gas at the neighborhood Shell station, the friendly young woman at the counter who had accepted my payments for years, noticed my large belly and asked, "Oh, please, could I be your nanny?" Manna was falling from heaven. With similar ease and grace, I enrolled Alia in the Waldorf kindergarten, bought a new used Volvo station wagon, and a few other things. But then I got caught in the busy swirl, and I fell from grace. During one prenatal appointment, Mary the midwife discovered that my blood pressure was sky-high. This was shocking to me because, all of my life, I have had enviably low blood pressure.

Mary said, "It's important that you bring your blood pressure down. You need to lie down every morning and every afternoon for two hours each. That's a total of four hours a day." I said, "That's impossible. I have two other children and a lot of things to do." Mary said, "If you want to have your baby at home, you have to lower your blood pressure. If you don't, you will have to deliver in the hospital. You need to take care of yourself and your baby, even though that means making some adjustments."

Mary is so direct and no-nonsense that she magically cuts through other people's neurotic dramas. I learned how to conduct life from the couch. The key to success was that our newly found house-helper came every day for several hours. It would have been impossible without someone to help me. I surrendered into obeying the requests of my body, being in quiet rest some of the time instead of compulsive task orientation all of the time.

One day, while on the couch, I heard a deep, open-throated groaning outside: "Aaaaaauuuuugggggghhhhhhhhhhhh." Did Jesse crash off his skateboard and lie dying in the driveway? Was a wounded bear in my yard moaning its pain? I heard it again. "Aaaaaauuuuugggggghhhhhhhhhhhh." Alarmed, I got up off the couch and raced outside. There was Jesse, happily playing in the dirt pile. "Honey, were you making that sound?" I asked with restrained concern. "Oh, yeah, Mom," he offhandedly replied. "These kids at the Waldorf School told me that's what a woman sounds like when she's giving birth."

Is there no dignity? I am mortified by the thought of second-grade boys hanging out discussing what we mothers do in labor and birth, and imitating us. Do they make fun of us? Jesse wasn't. It was more curiosity for him, a way of understanding what his mother might experience. What a woman does or says in labor definitely belongs in the inner chambers of the Mother-Mysteries; it can be honored and respected within that context. But to have the sounds of labor imitated by curious boys on the playground gave me the same feeling as if a Peeping Tom had watched me making love. I felt as if my privacy had been invaded. It's not that I mind Jesse's knowing, in the context of our relationship; I mind that second-grade boys talk about us on the playground.

As for Jesse and the other second-grade boys, it's probably wonderful for them to glimpse into the feminine mysteries, to be aware of the realities of women, and for them to talk about it with each other. This is healthy and will help shape them as men who are able to be in genuine relationship with women.

During my couch time, twice each day, I drank the tea Mary the midwife prescribed: a blend of hops, chamomile, and skullcap that I swear could put Valium out of business. I also received acupuncture to lower my blood pressure. After one week of the tea and the couch and the needles, I told my Chinese doctor that I was afraid that if my blood pressure went down any further, I was going to be dead. The program worked: my blood pressure dropped to normal. I jumped right back up to work on my fortieth birthday party and a dozen other things I wanted accomplished. Some people never learn.

I thought I was sage; on my third pregnancy, I felt like something of an expert. Certainly, I knew what a contraction was and knew the signs of the onset of labor. I was so experienced that I was focusing on the finer points of how to fully expand my pelvis when the time came, how to facilitate and allow the opening of the birth channel. I did not feel afraid. I knew what I was doing, and I was developing clear ideas of how to do it.

Three and a half weeks before my due date, we discovered that my cervix was mostly effaced and had begun dilating. I was ordered back to the couch. It was tempting to place the midwives in the position of authority, projecting responsibility for my well-being onto them, so that I could be the disobedient one, cheating against their orders. I've seen other mothers do this, too: "My doctor tells me to lie down. I know I should, but I don't." It is interesting to watch how skilled the midwives are at refusing to play this game. They confront me, quietly forcing me to own responsibility for my health and the baby's health.

I lie down for four hours a day and more. I did get up for my fortieth birthday party—forty years old and hugely pregnant.

Three weeks before my due date, I had a contraction. Once a woman has experienced the feeling of a contraction, it is unmistakable. One contraction, medium in intensity. About ten minutes later, another contraction. Then another one. I panicked. This is too early for the baby to come. I called Steve at work. He came home. I called the midwives. The contractions stopped.

About a week later, I began having contractions again—every five minutes. My second labor was only a grand total of two and a half hours. This one might be equally fast, or faster, so I didn't think it was a particularly good idea to sit around timing contractions for an hour. I told Steve I was having regular contractions. I told the kids. I called the midwives, who told me to continue timing the contractions and call them back in a half hour. The contractions were painful. My bowels were clearing. I was needing to breathe through each pain. It was difficult for Jesse to watch me in pain. He was agitated and somewhat anguished. Then the contractions stopped. No more. I phoned my mother. She understood completely. She had a false labor, too, with her fourth baby and was sent home from the hospital, embarrassed.

One evening, contractions came one after the other, strong

ones, about ten minutes apart. By this time, I was fully effaced, and my cervix was two centimeters dilated. I called Steve. I called Susan, my friend who was going to help with the birth, and she came right over. She and I walked arm in arm, up and down the dark street, pausing to breathe through the pain when it came. Then those contractions stopped.

These intermittent false labors were making me and everybody else crazy. I felt humiliated that I kept thinking I was in labor when it wasn't the real thing. Wouldn't you think that, after having two children, I would know when I was in labor? Time and again, my body had rhythmic contractions, sometimes only five minutes apart at regular intervals for an hour, and then nothing; it just stopped.

Steve said he was emotionally exhausted already, just by all this false labor. Both of us had geared our adrenaline for the birth so many times, only then to deflate back to ordinary reality. I was worrying my mother about the timing of when she should come, because I really wanted her here for the birth. My friend Susan didn't seem bothered by all these false starts, and the midwives had seen it all a hundred times before and were perfectly accepting, kindly relaying stories of other experienced mothers' false labors. Defiantly, I announced that I wasn't going to be fooled anymore: this baby was going to have to show his head before I took him seriously.

Nevertheless, with reference to the natural process of childbirth one thing can seldom be forgotten, the fact that the human infant has an absurdly big head.

—D. W. Winnicott
Babies and Their Mothers, p. 75

Home Birth

nine months pregnant
four-year-old daughter
seven-year-old son

Steve and I went to a small gathering in our friend Kate's home to meet a woman shaman from Nepal and to watch her work. Mieli, the shaman, spoke very little English, mostly communicating to an anthropologist friend who translated. About twenty-five men and women filled the living room, sitting on pillows and leaning up against the walls. The flames of candles lit the room, and incense wafted through the air.

In Mieli's shamanistic tradition, the healer takes upon herself the problem of the troubled person. Having heard the disturbance of the first person who requested her help, Mieli proceeded to chant, rocking herself into a deep trance, in which she began shaking wildly, an ecstatic dance of energy enlivening her body and voice. In that place of the depths, she felt able to access the Gods or Goddesses who were causing the trouble, trying to intervene, forging a compromise to benefit the sufferer.

I had never watched a shaman work like this before, and it was quite a wonderful experience, especially to share with friends. When the formal part of the work was completed, my friend Kate introduced me to Mieli, requesting on my behalf a blessing for my birth, an event we have been expecting any day now for the last three weeks. Mieli smiled wide, revealing her joyous spirit and a mouthful of teeth that had not received the dental or orthodontic care that most of us take for granted. She generously agreed. She motioned to me to sit on the pillow while she stood behind me, chanting, appealing to the Gods and Goddesses for a safe birth, a healthy mother and baby, tossing grains of uncooked rice over her shoulder now and then, throwing rice over me sometimes, concluding by handing me three grains of rice, which, through pantomime, she instructed me to eat. My teeth worked that hard rice until it was as broken down as it was going to get, and then I swallowed. Within the hour, I had some contractions, five of them, but this was nothing new.

At 3:30 in the morning, I woke up and went to the bathroom. In my groggy state, it took a minute to realize why I had awakened. Fluid was slightly trickling out of me; my membranes had sprung a leak! This was a welcome sign indeed. Enough of the embarrassing false starts. The breaking of the bag of waters is an almost surefire sign of the onset of labor.

After a few minutes of only mild drizzling, I grabbed a towel and went back to bed. In a hazy state between sleep and consciousness, I rested. About 4:30 A.M., the first contraction seized me. I awakened Steve. Then nothing more for twenty minutes. Another contraction, and then nothing more for a half hour. At 5:25 A.M., the amniotic sac burst, sending forth a gush of waters. The contractions became regular, about every six minutes. Steve awakened my mother. I phoned the midwives and my friend Susan, then stepped into the shower.

The midwives had suggested that we time the contractions. My mom sat calmly in the white wicker chair in my bedroom, looking at her wristwatch at the beginning and end of every contraction I had, neatly writing the times down and also classifying each one as mild, medium, or strong. There is an aspect of my mom's personality that will be tidy and conscientious and organized to the end. She is one of those responsible people you can count on to get the job done well, without needing to show-boat herself. She edited the high school yearbook. She was a Theta in college. She raised four children and taught Sunday school. She became a high school teacher of English and psychology. She is the president of Planned Parenthood in her town. Ten feet away from my circumspect mother was me, sprawled over the bed, bellowing like a sports announcer, giving a blow-by-blow report on my contractions: "Oh, oh, OK, one's coming. OK, it's getting really strong. Ut-oh, ut-oh, it really hurts, oh God (pant, pant, pant). OK, OK, it's getting better. OK, it's almost over. Oh, thank god, it's almost over, it's almost over." The contrast between the two of us in that little snapshot registered in my mind and amused me, filling me with love for us both. She was able to give me what I needed: calm containment, a capable and quiet presence while I wigged out.

Steve called our friends to come pick up Jesse and Alia, to take them to their house for breakfast and then to school. The kids were curious, coming in to check on me, respectfully and with some concern. I tried to be reassuring and normal, but the contractions were getting painful, and I really wanted to be yelling and moaning.

My friend arrived to pick up my kids at 7:00 AM. When I saw her, she opened her arms to hug me, and I burst into tears. As she held me, my belly tightened in a contraction, which blew her away, and she began to cry herself. Only a year ago, she had contractions in her own uterus, birthing her first child. She took Jesse and Alia, which was a great relief for me because now I could enter my labor more fully, turning the volume up.

Over the telephone, my midwife Mary said she would take a shower and then come over to check me. She suggested I walk around the yard to help strengthen the contractions and move the labor along. Within minutes of when she made this suggestion, it became impossible. My bowels were clearing, so I was alternating between bed and toilet. I got stuck on the toilet with a series of contractions that were coming on top of each other so quickly I barely had time to recover in between. The pain was excruciating. I had a grim realization in which I felt a flash of contempt for myself: "I've blown it. There are no drugs here. What kind of dumbo am I to design a situation in which it's impossible to get drugs for pain relief?" I had presumed that this birth would be as easy as my second birth, but it wasn't.

There was no time to wallow in self-contempt. I proceeded to cope with the next contraction. The labor was so intense at this point that I could not dwell on anything of the past. I had to clear my mind and body and feelings continually to meet the next moment. It is amazing how quickly moods, attitudes, feelings flash up and then are cleared during labor. It is like living life on fast-forward. The demands of labor are such that vast amounts of energy must be channeled and moved out. This is true physically, and it is true psychologically.

My midwives Mary and Alice arrived, which I only knew because, at one point, while I was still stuck on the toilet, I became aware of a firm, cool hand pressing against my forehead, her other hand holding the back of my head. Mary knew exactly what I needed. In between contractions, I told her I needed to get to my bed, but I wasn't sure I could make it. Each moment centered only on surviving the pain. Nothing else existed. At the end of a contraction, Mary helped me walk from the toilet ten steps to my bed.

Without thinking about it, I crouched on my bed like a lioness, with Steve sitting beside me, my head pushed into his leg and side. With each contraction, I roared the depths of my pain, my fingers clenching Steve's arm. One time, I began biting hard on Steve's arm and then realized I couldn't do that and switched to biting my pillow instead. Between contractions, which was only two or sometimes three minutes, I didn't talk or move. I just breathed, centered myself, and waited for the next one. I was all business. Nothing extraneous was possible. I only had energy for what was essential.

My legs were beginning to cramp in that crouched position, but it seemed impossible to change anything so major as my body position. Any interruption in my intense concentration threw me into chaotic pain. As long as I was fully focused and loudly roaring, I was one with the pain and could stand it, but not to be fully centered with the pain was intolerable. I gasped out loud, "I need a new position." Mary and Alice rolled me onto my side.

I quickly spoke during a contraction, "Mary, I'm ready to push!" "OK," she said, "go for it." I actually knew what I was doing as I pushed. I could feel the muscles I wanted to use and where to push the baby. I did not feel afraid as I pushed—I felt effective. Steve began to move from being by my head down toward the bottom of the bed so that he could watch the baby come out of my vagina. I panicked, "No, I need you up here." I could feel that Steve was disappointed not to see the baby's head crown, but he stayed by my face, rubbing my head and shoulder. My mom was on the back side of me, massaging my back, pressing firmly where Mary showed her to, against my sacrum. It occurred to me that my mom was pressing the place on my back where she had such pain when, in the birthing of me, I had become stuck on her tailbone.

Susan was holding my top leg up. At one point, she started to let my leg down, thinking I didn't need that, and again I panicked: "No, hold my leg!" I could only talk in staccato words on gasps of air, quickly conveying information so I could return to concentration. Each time I had to talk threatened me with falling into chaos. Any change in my physical environment also threatened to bring chaos.

No changes. Environment and body hold still, concentrate, allow inner movements.

I pushed and pushed. Elated, I gasped, "I'm pushing him out!" I reached inside my vagina to feel his head. Mary coached me to slow down, to push gently so my perineum could stretch slowly and not tear, to push out his head slowly. Suddenly, my vulva was on fire. I screamed. The legendary "rim of fire"! Then the baby's head was out of my body.

"Don't push, just breathe now," instructed Mary. "Wait for the next contraction, then *slowly* push his body out." She was cradling the baby's head and gently supporting both his head and my perineum. The rim of fire had subsided, but the pressure was still intense. I was stretched to the maximum, and I needed relief. I repeatedly said, "I need you to get this baby out of me. I need him out of me." "OK, here you go. Push slowly, gently," coached Mary. I pushed him out. He was crying, and I was crying. Mary received his body from my body, passed him to Steve, who laid him across my belly and breast. Elijah Kai.

He was purplish, marbled with white vernix, especially on his eyes, and streaked with red blood. I know of no greater beauty than looking into the eyes of my newborn baby while he looks into me. His eyes were so open to see.

The midwives arranged blankets and towels around us and put a knit hat on Elijah to keep his head warm. They quietly went about their business, cleaning up the blood and other bodily fluids, leaving Steve, Elijah, me, and my mom to be together quietly. I don't remember anybody saying anything. All I remember is peace.

A bit later, when my placenta decided it was time, it started to work its way out, and I helped by pushing. The midwives kneaded the placenta like bread dough, making sure that it was whole, that no parts had torn off, left inside my uterus. I joined in this kneading activity, palpating my placenta, examining it. It was beefy and huge, like a pound and a half of liver. I was intrigued to examine a body organ so carefully, specifically one of *my* body parts. This was an organ that grew for one purpose: to nourish Elijah's body. Once the placenta completes its mission, it dies. It separates from the uterus, which contracts and expels it.

Mary said it was time to sew up the tear in my perineum. I hate this part more than anything else. While she sewed, she told me that, many years ago, Mark, a close friend to Steve and me, who is a physician, had taught her to administer the local anesthesia and stitch up a woman's tear. That lovely connection helped diminish the pain. While Mary was sewing, Alice weighed Elijah: nine pounds five ounces! No wonder it hurt to push him out. Still, I take pride in growing a big baby. It was 8:20 in the morning. He was born right before Jesse and Alia started school.

I became very hungry. My mother offered to make everyone breakfast: scrambled eggs (appropriate homage to the Great Mother) and toast and orange juice. While my husband, my mother, my friend, my two midwives, and I ate, Elijah slept.

His body was wrapped up tight in a blanket, like a baby burrito. Babies like this containment; it helps them to feel secure. His round fat face, still a bit purplish, was framed by the soft cotton flannel blanket. His face was the picture of perfect peace as he slept. Sunbeams streamed through our bedroom window, softly warming the bed. The fresh morning air was heavenly. I arranged pillows so that I could lie next to Elijah, sleep with him in this dreamy, soft, sunny place. Snuggling him up to my side, with my arm around him, I dozed and drifted for hours, basking in the most delicious bliss I have ever known in my life.

Memories from the birth wandered back in my mind, wanting to be seen again. There was a vivid image of myself channeling the labor pains, crouched like a lioness, roaring and biting and clawing. The raw animal power of this scene fascinates and embarrasses me—did I really do that?

This brings to mind photographs I have seen of a sculpture from Turkey that is eight thousand years old: the birthing Goddess is seated on a throne, her arms supported on the backs of two lionesses, standing on each side of her.[1] Indeed, the wild creatures do join the birthing woman, they roar with her, they guard and protect her, they suffuse her with their ferocious instinctive power. The lion was a primary companion to the Mother Goddess for thousands of years, in Anatolia, Mesopotamia, Egypt, Minoan Crete, and Rome.[2]

Elijah looked like a little doll, like one of my daughter's dolls, bundled up, placed on the bed. "He is real," I told myself. We lay together in the same bed in which he was conceived, the same bed in which he was born. What a lovely beginning for us in our journey together. Tears came to my eyes, washing me with the beauty, the intimacy, the love of this sweet life.

I dozed again and then returned to the experience of the rim of fire. What a shock: the sudden sensation of a circle of fire in my vulva. *Fire* is the right word for it, burning. Several of my friends have told me they felt the rim of fire when the baby crowned, but I never had before. I began to make some connections.

I know what the Ring of Fire is: it's a gigantic circle of fiery volcanoes along the Pacific Rim, running down the west coast of North America and South America, rounding across the ocean to New Zealand up through Indonesia, all along the eastern coast of Asia up to the top of what used to be the Soviet Union, across the sea back to Alaska. On this crack in the earth's plate, along with the volcanoes, occur more than three-quarters of all earthquakes.[3] The Ring of Fire. Rupture. Seismic waves. Matter that once was buried inside dramatically transforming to life on the outside. The nine months in which Elijah grew in my womb geographically took place along the Ring of Fire; he then proceeded to pass through the fire as he was born.

Elijah's beginnings were not only with the Ring of Fire but also very much in the warm waters of the Pacific Ocean. I immersed my pregnant body in this ocean in Southern California, Tahiti, Australia, and Hawaii. In Hawaii, the word *Kai* means Pacific Ocean. Elijah Kai.

On this line of thought about the rim of fire, it occurred to me how very crucial is the circumference of a newborn's head. A small or even a medium-sized head is much easier to pass through one's pelvis and vaginal canal than is a large head. It's better to think about this ahead of time than to realize it the hard way. This is an underdiscussed topic. Why is it that, in those tedious high school health education classes, they don't forewarn women about some of these things that matter in real-life experience? Why is it that no one ever advises younger women that, when assessing the qualities one desires in a future mate, "Look for a man with a small head." There comes a time in one's existence when it really matters.

Alia came home from school first. Her kindergarten class at the Waldorf School had created a gift for me and Elijah. In a wicker basket lay handfuls of freshly plucked green grass, arranged into a nest, two red roses resting within it, thorns carefully removed. Alia shyly approached my bed to give it to me and allowed me to hug her. She looked at our baby and touched his head. This was a profound and far-reaching event in her life; she was stunned and overwhelmed.

Two hours later, Jesse came home from school. At the door of my room, he peeked in, respectfully, excitedly, as though it were Christmas morning and he wondered whether it was permissible yet to come see what Saint Nick had left for him. I welcomed him to my bedside, and he tenderly hugged me. He bent over us, gazing at our bundled newborn, ever so softly stroking the baby's head, and with tears in his eyes, said, "Mom, Elijah means so much to me."

Our society often has a very romanticized stereotype of the new mother in a frothy pink negligée, a cherubic baby in her arms. The violent mood swings of the post-partum period can come as a shock because they are so different from the way you think you *ought* to feel.

—Sheila Kitzinger
The Complete Book of Pregnancy and Childbirth,
pp. 347–48

DEATH OF THE OLD FAMILY

four-day-old son
four-year-old daughter
seven-year-old son

YESTERDAY, MY HORMONES ARRIVED like a herd of elephants, stampeding throughout my body and mind. I hate it when that happens. This hormonal takeover can happen to some extent in menstruation but occurs big-time about the third or fourth day after birth. I seem to feel hurt by the least little thing and could easily cry half the day. My body feels awful: sore, aching, overly full. My breasts could be classified as the eighth wonder of the world—absolutely giant and engorged with milk. When my mother came in the bathroom yesterday morning as I was emerging from my shower, she looked at me in amazement and cried, "Oh, my goodness, you look just like your statue!" The Aztec Goddess statue, with turgid, huge breasts.

It seems that the Great Mother Goddess pushed the mute button on my neocortex. My only available channels are body and feelings—the weeping channel, the leaking channel, the unconditional love channel. But it is too much: I am raw from too much instinct, feeling, and hormones.

I awoke this morning with a dream that was so emotionally painful that I hurried out of bed, hoping to leave it behind. But it came with me as I went into the TV room, where I saw my mom sitting on the couch. I lay down on the couch, my feet curled behind her back, and surrendered into what was psychologically inevitable, telling her the dream.

Our family—which consists only of Maren, Steve, Jesse, and Alia—is hiking together on a dirt trail that runs all along the upper ridge of the Riviera in Santa Barbara. The whole Riviera is wilderness hills—no houses or signs of civilization. We are walking toward the Waldorf School, which Jesse and Alia attend. We pause to look at the view north. Far away, we see a graded slope of small, loose rock upon which dozens of people are working, perhaps on a construction project. We can see that one man has been hurt; someone has put him in a wheelbarrow and is wheeling him down to the bottom of the hill.

The ground across the entire Riviera begins to shake. It is an earthquake, and it's big. We see the people on the hill north of us panic as the gravel begins to slide down the hill in an avalanche. Our family is standing at the highest point on the dirt path along the Riviera, with a large boulder between us and a steep cliff. At first, I hope that we can crouch beside the boulder and be safe. It becomes obvious that the earthquake is of great magnitude and we will be thrown off the mountain. As we are thrown into midair, I realize we will certainly fall to our deaths because it is so far down. In the long moments that we are suspended in air, falling, I am overcome with pain and anguish because I cannot reach Alia. I want so much to be holding her as we fall to death. She seems to be the most vulnerable one of us, the one who needs me most right now. I desperately want to be there for her. I try to extend my arm or leg to her, but she is too far away. I am able to reach my leg toward Jesse so that he can almost touch my toe, and that is enough for him.

I told my mother the dream, crying and sobbing, raw with pain. The grief from the dream was as powerful as if it had been a waking experience.

In a flash of insight, I exclaimed to my mother, "Guess who the earthquake is? Elijah!" My mother understood immediately. We talked about these earthquakes that she and I had experienced. My mother, the one who brought on the earthquake jolting me out of my position as baby of the family when I was not yet three years old, held my foot, listening and recalling her own pain during the earthquakes of her births.

I had not anticipated how thoroughly our family ground would shake when our baby was born. I had been aware for the entire pregnancy that Alia faced some large adjustments, as did the rest of us. My life certainly would change in becoming mother to a newborn, making me also a mother of three children. I had thought about the changes that a new baby would bring to us as individuals, but I had completely missed the reality that our old family system would die.

Our felt identity as a family of four interwoven individuals must necessarily die. Yes, a new family will be born, but it will be a family that we cannot possibly know yet, that can only be known in days and months and years of experience together. We will never again be that old family that we all loved and cherished. I had no idea how much I would grieve the loss of that old family, even in the midst of profound joy with our new baby.

The dream portrays my dilemma succinctly: I cannot hold Alia in this dying. In the past four days, my arms have been filled with a baby most of the time. I am aware how important it is to make time to hold my other children. But it is obvious to us all that my body is geared toward the baby. When I hold Alia, I cannot hold her too close to my chest; my breasts are tender, overflowing with milk for someone else. These breasts, which she cherished for years, are now the private property of someone else. I had anticipated that this would be a major psychological transition for Alia, that she would struggle and grieve her loss.

But I had not considered that I, too, would grieve. She is no longer my baby. Still my beloved daughter, but now the middle child, not my baby.

I cannot protect her from this death. She can no longer be the baby merged with the mother. Her four years, and her status as an older sister, require a separation from the mother, which, by definition, must be negotiated alone. I can love her, support her, but she must find a self that is more separate from me now. There is grief in that separation, perhaps fear also, yet she must find the strength and courage to face the reality of her life now as a more individuated child.

We do not know who we are as a family now. A bit shell-shocked, we each wander through the house, trying to find some familiar routines, some old paths that still work, tentatively testing new ways of being together. I feel different in our family. I no longer have as much time and energy for Jesse or Alia or Steve. I don't know when we will feel settled as a family again, when a new identity will take shape and set.

In each birth, there also lies death. Death of the mother's freedom and independence. Death of libido in the marital relationship. Death of the old patterns within the family. There are tears to be shed, losses to be grieved.

I adore our little earthquake Elijah. Love for him consumes me. His beatific presence awakens love and wonder in each of us, and we are more because of him. He is the one for whom we have been patiently waiting. Peacefully cradled in our arms, opening his eyes to see who we are, he brings fresh promise to us all.

> The mystery of the inexhaustible appearance of life is bound up with the rhythmical renewal of the cosmos. This is why the cosmos was imagined in the form of a gigantic tree; the mode of being of the cosmos, and first of all its capacity for endless regeneration, are symbolically expressed by the life of the tree.
>
> —Mircea Eliade
> *The Sacred and the Profane*, p. 148

THE PLACENTA AND THE TREE OF LIFE

five-day-old son
four-year-old daughter
seven-year-old son

MUCH TO THE DISMAY of my husband, there have been several periods of our married life when a frozen placenta has lived in our refrigerator freezer. When pressed to articulate his concern, he concretizes it through the fear that a helpful houseguest might unknowingly defrost it for dinner one night: midway through the feast, the source of the meat would be revealed.

I saved Jesse's placenta in the freezer for two and a half years because I wanted to plant a fruit tree in his honor, with the placenta buried underneath, but I had no intention of doing this on the land of our rental apartment. No, we had to wait until we bought the house where he would spend his childhood, planting the tree in that land, so that he and the tree could grow together over the years. When we finally bought a house, I was four months pregnant with Alia. I simply transferred Jesse's placenta to the freezer in the new house. I reasoned that, in five short months, our baby would be born, and we could plant the two children's trees at the same time. After thirty cold months, I hauled that placenta out of the freezer, thawing it and planting it under an apricot tree for Jesse in our yard. The placenta for Alia had only been frozen for one week when we planted it under a plum tree for her.

Now, for the third time in my life, I remove Tupperware containing a placenta from our freezer, the placenta that Elijah and I shared, hoping it will defrost overnight.

The processes of pregnancy, birth, and caring for a baby are earthy. The mother is essentially involved with matter. The pregnant woman is absorbed with vomiting or not vomiting, with peeing, with lugging a cumbersome body around, with the bizarre sensation of her belly's squiggling this way and that. The birthing woman is steeped in amniotic fluids, in blood, in diarrhea, in howling with her contracting uterus, pushing a body out of her body, yearning to hold that small body that is covered with blood and vernix and God knows what else, adoring that body, wanting to touch it and feed it from her breast. The mother of a baby learns to accept milk leaking from her breasts, spit-up adorning her shoulders, becomes casual about wiping poop from the baby's bottom, sometimes in unguarded moments with a boy baby gets squirted in the face with urine, casually catches throw-up in the cup of her hand. Motherhood is a very organic matter. The divinities of motherhood cannot possibly live far away in the sky, cool, detached from the material realm, cannot be cerebral. The deities that inform mothering must be up to their elbows in matter.

Steve and Jesse and Alia and I prepare for the tree-planting ceremony, gathering candles, incense, poems, shovels, and of course, the cherished guest of honor. Our beloved gardener gave us an apricot tree for Elijah, to be planted in our yard next to Jesse's apricot tree and Alia's plum tree.

I remove the placenta from the Tupperware. It is still a bit icy, so I lay it on the grass in the sun, checking it occasionally. I pick it up, tentatively at first, hesitant to get blood on my hands, queasy about handling a raw organ, even if it is my own. Is the placenta mine? Or is it Elijah's?

This hunk of meat, vividly colored in reds and blues, did not exist ten months ago. A mysterious authority within nature ordered it to grow so that the fertilized egg in my womb could be fed from my body. The two sides of the placenta look quite different. The side that faced the wall of my uterus looks meaty, like a boneless beef round steak. The side that faced the baby is smooth, except for an embossed image made by veins: the exact image of a tree. The Tree of Life.

The placenta is the intermediary between mother and fetus. Its sole purpose is to transport oxygen and nourishment from the mother's body to the fetus and to transport waste products from the fetal body to the mother for delivery to her kidneys. One of the fascinating aspects of this selfless organ is that a membrane separates the traffic flow between the mother's and fetus's bodies. The mother's blood flows through the placenta on the maternal side of the membrane, while the baby's blood flows through on his or her side. Even though the mother and fetus may have different blood types, the placenta can transpose easily. The placenta is a workhorse; by the ninth month, it filters one hundred gallons of blood each day.[1]

The placenta is a third body, facilitating the biological conversation between mother and baby. Because the placenta gradually takes control of the hormonal levels during pregnancy, it is responsible for sending a message to the milk glands in the breasts to gear up for production. Although the cause of the onset of labor isn't completely understood, it appears that the placenta carries the enormous responsibility for finding just the right time to reduce progesterone levels, thereby inducing labor and delivery.[2]

This organ deserves an honorable burial. Our placenta served Elijah and me beautifully, working hard, willing to die when its task was completed. Holding my placenta, touching it, I am moved to tears by my love and appreciation for it.

We begin our ritual by gathering our family in a circle around the three-foot hole dug in the earth. Elijah lies on a blanket within our circle. On Alia's Fisher-Price red-and-white tape recorder, we play a song by Chrissie Hynde of the Pretenders. Because Chrissie portrays herself as at least as cynical and tough as any of the guys in the rock world, this tender song she sings to her baby is particularly moving.

I sob uncontrollably through the entire song. Alia asks why I am sad. How can I explain my state? In this first week of new-mother hormones, I feel the deep meaning in everything; many times each day, I cry for the beauty and suffering in life. I am in a liminal place, where the juices of the universe flow through me unimpeded. Surrounding the birth experience, the vessel of a woman is opened wide, channeling forces of life and death. Everything is revealed. The world appears as a revelation. The opened woman witnesses the forces of creation and destruction, and even more than that, she feels these events emotionally and in her body. She loves and mourns and is devastated by the beauty of it all. And if she, like me, is attached to life, she feels the fear and the vulnerability, the dangers present at every turn.

I try to explain to my children and husband that I feel so much love and vulnerability that I cannot contain it all. I am so far beyond normal consciousness that I have no idea what they understand of what I say. I gently lay the placenta in the bottom of the three-foot-deep hole dug in the earth. I feel as if I am burying a family member. It seems that I will be sobbing throughout the ceremony. Through tears, I talk to my family about our placenta and how I feel about it. Steve lifts the heavy tree out of its pot and places it over the placenta in the hole. Each of us use our hands to push dirt into the spaces around the tree, so that it is snug in the earth. We hold Elijah so that his hand touches the tree, presses some earth around its roots.

Each member of the family says something, a wish or a blessing for Elijah in his life or something else that moves them. I recite the words from a meditation by the theologian Howard Thurman, "All my life I have eaten fruit from trees that I did not plant, why should I not plant trees to bear fruit for those who may enjoy them long after I am gone? Besides, the man who plants because he will reap the harvest has no faith in life."[3]

All that has nourished me in life has been a gift, freely and generously given. Steve, and Jesse and Alia, and now Elijah, too, have been given to me and give themselves to me. I keenly feel my responsibility but, even more, my *desire* to give back, to plant trees in the world that will nourish others. My children are trees that I tend—in some ways, my gifts to the world. This apricot tree will be nourished by the rich vitamins still saturating the placenta, and in turn, the tree will bear fruit to nourish our family and friends. Once again, our family encircles this tree, closing the ceremony.

I am exhausted from all this emotion. I take my sleeping baby and retire to bed. I need to be where no one is talking, where there is no external stimulation. I need empty space. I need time to unravel what I have seen and felt. My bed, with its soft flannel sheets, and my special pillow and my sleeping baby comfort me.

In my mind's eye, I see the image of a tree—the sturdy, thick trunk rising out of the earth, strong, graduating into smaller branches, which reach out and up and into yet more refined twigs. Each spring, miraculously, soft little buds emerge from these twigs and branches, growing, opening into green leaves. The shelter of these towering trees is a welcome refuge in the heat of summer. What visits will this tree host from bees and birds and spiders and squirrels? Some trees flower; some go on to produce the sweet life of apples or peaches or oranges or figs. But as days pass, there comes for all the season of *denouement*— autumn. The leaves begin to wither, some displaying the fiery beauty of dying in reds, yellows, oranges, and browns. As the winds blow, the leaves release from that which has sustained them. The barren trunk and branches are all that remain. It is the time of quiet, of dark. It is the time of lying fallow, of quietly resting in the forces of death.

The dead leaves at the base of the tree break down, slowly crumbling back into the earth from whence they came. They mingle with the dead and broken bodies of animals, other plants, and rocks, in their intermingling death alchemically transforming into the nourishment of life itself. The roots of the tree reach down into this earth, spreading out to drink the waters of the depths; the food of the dead returns as food for the living.

The tree shows us what it is to be alive. The mysterious cycle of life and death and regeneration are incarnate in the tree. The tree is the revelation of life itself. Is it any wonder that, for all of human history, the tree has been a central religious symbol?

Thousands of years before the birth of Christ, we find evidence of an intimate connection between the Great Goddess and the Tree of Life. In the land of Palestine, Asherah, the Mother of the Gods, was worshiped in sacred groves of trees and in temples. Her body is the Tree of Life. Carvings intertwining the life-filled female body with the body of a tree were placed in her temples and sacred groves. Like the kings of Sumeria and Egypt, the kings of Palestine drank the milky fluid of figs and black mulberries, symbolically drinking from the breast of the Goddess, believing that their power and authority grew from this nectar of life.[4]

When the Hebrews took over the land of Palestine, they asserted the dominance of their single male God, ordering that all the "Asherim" be smashed and destroyed. None of the large wood carvings of Asherah exist anymore. However, archeological excavations throughout Palestine have unearthed small clay figurines of Asherah, dating from between 2000 BCE and 600 BCE. Where we might expect to find legs on these figurines, instead there is a smooth column like a tree trunk. It seems likely that women clasped these clay images in their hands, praying for fertility or a favorable birth.[5]

There are many stories of birth associated with the Tree of Life. The earliest story we know of the birth of Buddha tells of his mother, Queen Maya, journeying toward her mother's home,

Isis and Thutmosis III (Isis as the Tree of Life offering milk), ca.
1479–1425 BCE. West Thebes, Thebes, Egypt.
Courtesy Giraudon/Art Resource, N.Y.

where she hoped to deliver. But along the way, she found a
glorious grove of sal trees, with fragrant flowers, swarming bees,
and flocks of birds. Pausing to enjoy this heavenly scene, Queen
Maya was seized by a labor pain. She gasped and reached up,
just as a limb of the tree reached down to her. She grasped the

limb, and at that moment, the Buddha was born out of her right side.[6]

Adam and Eve were born in the presence of two trees in the Garden of Eden: the tree of immortal life and the tree of knowledge of good and evil. As in other Tree of Life myths, the serpent was present in this Genesis story. The serpent embodies the same mysteries of regeneration as do the tree and the Goddess—shedding the old skin and growing into a new skin.

The Greek God Adonis was born from a tree.[7] The Babylonian God Tammuz lived inside a tree. The Buddha achieved enlightenment under the Bodhi tree.

The Tree of Life also embodies the mysteries of death. The Egyptian God Osiris was encased in a casket within a tamarisk tree. Jesus of Nazareth was hung from a wooden cross. The Sumerian Goddess Inanna hung on a wooden peg rotting for three days in the underworld. In Norse mythology, the God Othin hung on an ash tree for nine days before he acquired the wisdom of the runes.[8] In each of these cases where death was wrought on a tree, the death was transformative, leading to a new life, a life informed by the divine essences.

We have an unconscious need to remember and glorify the wholeness of existence, and the image of the tree has helped human beings across many cultures and differing periods in history fulfill that need.

Joseph Campbell interpreted the tree as "axis mundi," the axis of the world, reaching up to the heavens, down into the depths of the earth, while the branches and roots reach out horizontally. The tree, particularly when viewed as a vertical and horizontal axis, can easily be understood to be a cross.[9]

Campbell reminds us of our ritual of the Christmas tree. Sacrificing a Tree of Life is not unique to Christian culture; it also occurred in ancient Sumeria, Egypt, and Minoan Crete.[10] Each year in the dead of winter, we sacrifice a healthy tree, bringing it into our home to adorn with lights and small objects of beauty. Campbell observed that, in our practice of decorating the Christmas tree, we place a star at the top, while the gifts lie at the ground, joined by the ultimate gift, a crèche with the baby Jesus lying in the cradle.[11] The human psyche needs to be assured that within this season of darkness lies the seed of potential new life and greater life: in the cold, stark winter, this belief is an act of faith.

Our family has just planted a tree in honor of our new baby. What will nurture that tree? All the dead and decomposing bodies of the natural world. The dead and decomposing body of the placenta that joined me to give life to our baby. Some year, this baby will run outside to his tree and pluck off an apricot, slurping its sweet nectar, juices running down his fat chin. And perhaps some year, he will come to know, with humility and gratitude, that "all my life I have eaten fruit from trees that I did not plant."

> All of the references of religious and mythological images
> are to planes of consciousness or fields of experience po-
> tential in the human spirit and these are to evoke attitudes
> and experiences that are appropriate to a meditation on
> the mystery of the sources of your own being.
>
> —Joseph Campbell
> *The Power of Myth*, Program 5

CIRCUMCISION

seven-day-old son
four-year-old daughter
seven-year-old son

TO CIRCUMCISE OR NOT to circumcise, that is the question.
Whether 'tis nobler to cut off that tiny tip of baby penis foreskin
or leave it alone looms large in the psyche. Thousands of years
of religious, cultural, and medical customs inform our opinions.

Male circumcision is customary in my culture. Almost all the
men of my generation are circumcised. Why? It used to be that
circumcision was recommended to keep the penis clean, to help
prevent sexually transmitted disease or urinary tract infection.
In 1971, the American Academy of Pediatrics declared, "There
are no valid medical indications for routine circumcision in the
neonatal period." Since then, its position has become less certain, with evidence emerging that circumcision may decrease
the incidence of urinary tract infections, sexually transmitted
diseases, and penile cancer.[1]

Increasingly, American parents have been choosing not to circumcise, so that now only about 60 percent of American boys

are circumcised. For perspective on our cultural bias, only about 20 percent of boys throughout the world are circumcised, most of whom are Jewish or Muslim. The United States is the only country on earth where male circumcision is widely practiced for nonreligious reasons.[2] The removal of foreskin from a newborn boy's penis is our culturally sanctioned form of genital mutilation.

Various forms of genital mutilation have been practiced throughout human history. Egyptian tombs bear testimony of male castration dating back to 4500 BCE.[3] Penises and/or testicles were cut off for purposes of revenge in war, enslavement, and even to preserve the sweetness of a boyish voice for opera. The much less extreme removal of the penile foreskin has been practiced for thousands of years as religious ritual and for purposes of cleanliness.

There are plenty of countries, particularly in Africa and Asia, in which female circumcision is currently practiced. The Council on Scientific Affairs estimates that some one hundred and ten million girls and women in forty countries are subjected to genital mutilation, ranging from the mild form of removing the foreskin of the clitoris to the extreme of cutting off all labia and the clitoris and sewing the vaginal opening almost entirely closed.[4] I am utterly horrified by accounts of this female genital mutilation. I cannot justify these practices in any possible way. My religion and culture and family are all distant from these practices.

However, male circumcision is commonplace in my culture and family. For us, there is little rational basis for choosing circumcision; it is not our family's religious practice, and certainly, a boy can be taught how to wash his penis. Whatever inclinations we have toward circumcision are primarily irrational.

It seems to me that the quickest way to approach this irrational tangle is to acknowledge that at the center of male circumcision stands the penis, and the penis is a God.

In some ways, paradoxically, the mysteries of the penis resemble the mysteries of the Goddess: life changes form into death, which changes form into the resurrection of life. The penis is the alchemical vessel of transformation: resting in a dormant, soft phase; then suddenly charged with surging forces that render it hard, stiff, masterfully large and tall; climaxing in the shooting of milky fluid carrying forth the seeds of life. Upon completion of its inseminating mission, the penis dies—*la petite mort*—curling back to the warm nest of skin and hair, snuggling into the mysteries of dark and quiet and soft.

The ancient Egyptians understood that the penis is a God. For three thousand years, Egyptian religion revolved around the story of Isis and Osiris.[5] The myth of Isis and Osiris can be understood in a variety of ways: as a creation story, as a tale about the seasons, or as an explanation of the cycles of life. Let us acknowledge that the story of Osiris also reflects the mysteries of the penis.

Osiris, who was the first king of Egypt, guided his people toward civilization. He taught the ways of justice, of respecting the deities, and cultivating the fertility of the earth for grain and fruit. Osiris and Isis ruled this great land in harmony but for their jealous brother Seth. In a carefully plotted scheme, Seth tricked Osiris into lying in a coffin, then quickly nailed it shut, sealed it with lead, and heaved it into the Nile to be carried out to sea.

Distraught with grief, Isis searched far and wide for the casket containing her beloved. When she finally found Osiris's dead body, she gently placed him in her boat to take him back to Egypt. Looking upon her dear husband, overcome with emotion, Isis lay upon Osiris, weeping and kissing him. Suddenly, she was transformed into a large bird, beating her wings over his body, for a few moments able to breathe life back into him. She lowered herself onto the enlivened Osiris and conceived their son Horus. Still fearful of Seth, Isis hid herself and the body of Osiris (once again dead) in the reeds of the riverbank.

One night when the moon was full, Seth discovered the sequestered body of Osiris and, in rage, carved the body into fourteen pieces, scattering the pieces throughout the land of Egypt.

Fourteen nights passed as the Egyptians watched the moon gradually disappear from wholeness into nothing.

At the time of year when the waters of the Nile River begin to swell, it was said that Isis was weeping for the loss of Osiris, searching for his pieces to unite him again in wholeness. The flow of her tears, her suffering in the quest to restore wholeness to her beloved, moistened the parched earth. Isis was able to find all the parts of Osiris except one—the phallus—which had been eaten by a fish. From memory, Isis made a replica of the sacred missing part and reassembled Osiris. Once again, he who had been dead was now given new life. Osiris, who embodied the mysteries of life and death and resurrection, went to the underworld to rule as king.

Each year, during the height of summer, when the Nile River shrinks to a narrow trickle, the land is dry and shriveled, unable to produce life. The Egyptian people said this was the time of year when Osiris was killed by the jealous brother Seth. A time of death.

Each year, when the Nile begins to flood its banks, the Egyptian people know that, in the annually reenacted drama, Isis is reunited with Osiris. Yet again, he fertilizes the moist earth with his seed. New green shoots of life sprout up throughout the Nile Valley, confirming that Osiris lives. At this season, the Egyptian people used to gather near the Nile in the town of Abydos to honor the mysteries of Osiris. They marked the beginning of the Egyptian New Year with a ceremony: the erection of a Djed, a wooden pole with four branches, also known as the pillar of Osiris. When the people laid green garlands upon its branches, the pillar of Osiris looked like a tree. The erection of this phallic pole signaled to all that Osiris was reborn, resurrected, that even after death, life flowed through him again. Embodied in the penis is the mystery cycle of life, death, and regeneration.

Given the central place of the penis in the psyche, circumcision is revealed as much more than a medical decision. Is a circumcised penis better looking than an uncircumcised one? How do they compare as instruments of lovemaking? Do women prefer an uncircumcised man as a lover? It is important to take into account what the majority of boys in one's culture will look like in the junior high or high school locker room: a parent does not want his child to be the one different penis in the group shower. Is the father circumcised? Does the father want his son to have a penis similar to his? Is that bond important to the father? Should parents make the same choice for all of their sons?

Around the time of the birth of our first boy, approximately half of the baby boys in our community were being circumcised. There was a genuine social choice, without risk of being ostracized. After going back and forth on this decision, my husband became clear that it was important to him that his son be circumcised. I did not feel that circumcision would bring harm to our baby more than fleeting pain, so I agreed to the circumcision. But it was important to me that my husband stay with our son during his circumcision, to comfort him and oversee the procedure.

I set about to research the most humane method of circumcision. I interviewed pediatricians who use anesthetic and ones who don't. I talked with a *mohel,* who performs the Jewish religious ceremony of circumcising boy babies on the eighth day of life. Because the nerves in the penis are not on the surface of the skin, a topical anesthetic is useless, and almost everyone agreed that a shot of anesthetic into the penis is as painful as the circumcision itself. Most professionals believe that a good, quick circumcision by an experienced practitioner is the least painful way to go. Depending on the technique used, under good circumstances, a circumcision can be done in about forty-five seconds. Because our pediatrician is skilled and experienced, we asked him to perform the procedure.

Seven years later, we wrestled with this decision again, finally deciding to circumcise our second son also.

I knew I would not be helpful with Elijah while he was being circumcised. My hormones were flowing strongly, and it was intolerable for me to see him crying in pain. It is amazing to watch how nature organizes the mother to do everything possible to protect her baby from pain, making her agitated when she hears the baby cry so that she will protect the baby. It would wipe me out emotionally to watch his circumcision. I would not be comforting to our baby, and I would make the doctor tense. My mother stepped forward, saying she would be glad to stay with Elijah, to cradle his head and love him during the circumcision. Raising her own four children had made her very steady.

Once in our pediatrician's office, I upheld my brave facade for thirty seconds before I broke down crying, explaining to him that I was going to wait in the car during the circumcision, but my mother would stay with my baby. Our normally reserved pediatrician gave me a hug, reassured me, and said he would come get me when it was over.

I fled to the parking lot, locked myself in my Volvo, and cried. After about fifteen minutes, my tears subsided, and I became quizzical: Why had no one come to get me? Where were they? Did something go wrong? No, I decided not to make myself worried. Even if something had gone wrong, I would not be any help. Twenty-five minutes passed. Just as I was about to go inside the office anyway, a young female assistant to the doctor approached my car door. "It's all done," she said. She looked at my puffy red eyes and said sympathetically, "I know just how you feel. When my puppy had shots last week, I cried all morning." I burst out laughing. The absurdity of her comment bumped me out of my pain. From my point of view, my baby was not analogous to her puppy, but she didn't know that. She was a young woman, and her feelings about her puppy were her only referent for how a mother would feel about her baby.

In the examining room, I held my baby. It was obvious that he had cried a lot but was now settled asleep. I asked the doctor what took so long. He reluctantly told me it had been a complicated circumcision and why. He apologized for taking so long, complimented me on my great mother, and sent us on our way. We headed home—my mother, Elijah and I—exhausted by our brief venture into the world.

Elijah and I took a nap together. I nestled his body close to mine. I could tell he had been traumatized. Periodically, his little body would shudder, making little feeble sounds of discomfort. I petted him and reassured him. I was exhausted. At one week postpartum, the world of getting dressed, driving in cars on freeways, and functioning within the social system was too much for me. I was still far too physically and emotionally vulnerable for the world.

When Steve came home from work, he asked about the circumcision. My mom revealed that it had been kind of complicated and bloody. We talked some more, and then Steve and my mom began to make dinner. I heard Elijah cry, so I went to comfort him. Once he quieted, I decided to change his diapers. Unsnapping his sleeper, I pulled off the plastic pants and mused in a spaced-out way as I was unpinning the diapers, "Gee, I never knew the diaper service gave us red diapers, I've only seen white ones." The diaper was an even dark red color. Then the alarm bells rang. "Mom," I called, trying to control my rising panic. "Come in here, please. Mom, was this diaper red when you put it on?"

We saw blood, drip, drip, dripping out of Elijah's bandage over his penis. We yelled for Steve to come in. I immediately phoned the pediatrician, who had closed shop for the day, so I got a woman from the answering service, who said she would give the message to the on-call pediatrician. I told her that it was urgent, that I had a seven-day-old baby who had saturated a diaper with blood. Ten minutes passed. No callback. How much blood can a ten-pound baby lose before his life is threatened? Everything felt surreal. I couldn't get a grip on how to evaluate the situation: was I being overly dramatic? Or worse, was I being underly dramatic? What if we did not take action quickly enough and our baby died?

I called the emergency room and found out that if we showed up there, we would have to wait in line with everyone else, and still a pediatrician would have to be called in. Our best bet was to reach the on-call pediatrician, who, for all we knew, had not yet even picked up his messages. Steve phoned a physician friend, who talked him through how to stop the bleeding. Steve was clear-headed and calm. He carefully removed the bandage and applied pressure to stop the bleeding. I phoned the on-call pediatrician every ten minutes, badgering the answering service to call the doctor immediately. After fifty minutes, he finally called and told us to meet him at the emergency room of the hospital.

I phoned our neighbors at the top of the street to see whether they could take Jesse and Alia for a few hours. I dialed their number and Art answered the phone. I completely lost it, sobbing hysterically, "Art, can you help us? Our baby's bleeding to death, and we have to take him to the hospital." Steve took the phone from me, told Art who was calling, and made the arrangements. We all got in the car, and Steve drove. I sat in the backseat next to Elijah, sobbing. I fell apart. I became possessed by the archetype of the Grieving Mother. I couldn't believe this was happening. Some babies die. Could I be a person whose baby died? This was a nightmare, and I was in it.

When we arrived at the emergency room, because a doctor was waiting there for us, they sent us in right away to an examining room ahead of all the other people in the waiting room. I could observe myself, but I was way beyond myself. I sat on the examining table openly sobbing, holding my baby in my arms, rocking him back and forth. Steve came in, and my mother came in. Various technicians came and went, but I was in a daze of love and grief, rocking and sobbing.

Then the on-call pediatrician came in. He said there were too many people in the room, and so my mom went to the waiting room. Something in me coalesced, took charge, and I magically became a centered person who was able to give the doctor a concise, detailed story of the circumcision and its complications. Even while I was talking, part of me was outside myself observing, amazed that suddenly I had become so precise and controlled and effective. The on-call pediatrician examined Elijah, saying things in too cheerful a voice, like, "Well, no problem.

We can take care of this." The way he said it, we knew he was scared and it was a problem. From there on in, I cried no more. I stayed fully alert and conscious, as did Steve.

The pediatrician called in a urologist, who, coincidentally, knew Steve. The urologist was so calm and competent and reassuring, I knew we were going to be OK. It turned out there was an artery in our baby's penis where usually there is not an artery. That artery was nicked in the circumcision and burst open later that day—hence, all the blood. The urologist said he needed to put in three stitches to close the artery. I braced myself. Not only had my little baby endured the circumcision itself, but now, several hours and a lot of trauma later, for the second time in a day, he had to be strapped to a hard board, this time with a needle repeatedly going through his penis. But brushing close to the possibility of his death relativized the stitches: three minutes of pain was not the worst thing in the world. This time, I stood steadfastly beside Elijah, holding his head and whispering love things to him while he was screaming pain as hard as his little body could. The urologist finished and unstrapped Elijah. I picked up his baby body and held him close to me, and felt as if I was going to faint. I lowered myself to the floor, which alarmed all the medical personnel in the room because of germs, but it was the only steady place I could find to sit down with my baby. Steve was ashen, leaning across the end of the operating table.

The urologist told us that our baby's penis would be fine and that we wouldn't have any further problems with the circumcision. The experience of needing a doctor immediately and not being able to reach one had so traumatized me that I asked the urologist if he would give me his home phone number in case Elijah had an emergency that night. Graciously, the urologist gave me his card, writing down his home phone number.

I held that baby in my arms all night, not once letting him go. I held him to my heart and my breast and loved him all night long. Spent by this rude brush with life, he slept peacefully.

We had been instructed to return the next day to the pediatrician who had performed the circumcision so that he could check the stitches, making sure they were holding well. I have known this man for eight years, and in the last twenty-four hours, I spent a lot of time thinking about how I felt about him. Our pediatrician is a rational man who relates professionally but rarely personally. He came into the examining room a man haunted by a torturous night. He said the emergency room doctor had called him the previous night to inform him about the situation. He said that he was awake much of the night, reviewing the circumcision in his mind and feeling terrible about what had happened.

I said, "I spent quite a bit of time thinking about this, too. It was a nightmare. But I want you to know that I don't blame you. You're a professional. You're good, and you're experienced. Sometimes things go wrong, even when you do your best. I've experienced that in my professional work. I suggest you do what I'm doing: forgive and move on." Tears welled in his eyes. Emotionally flooded, he excused himself from the room.

Mom and Steve and I reviewed the events of the previous day, alone and with each other, again and again. There was so much that needed to be digested. I remembered little things—for instance, that my mom wanted to change her shoes because she didn't want to wear her slippers to the emergency room. I remembered that when we dropped Jesse and Alia off, our neighbors were dressed formally. We found out they were all set to go to a dinner party when we took our children to their house. They chose to help us rather than go to their party.

I kept circling around remembered images of myself from the previous night. I was fascinated and a bit awed to recall that woman I became when my baby's life was in danger. Although I freely run a gamut of emotions in the privacy of my home, I rarely am demonstrative in public. But the woman who was sobbing openly in the emergency room, holding and rocking her precious baby, did not even think about other people—what they thought or saw. She was fully and solidly in herself: the primal, grieving mother. The love a mother has for her baby, and her quintessential desire to protect that baby, carry her far beyond the reaches of neurotic concerns about other people's liking her, approving of her, social reputation, manners, persona.

I was also intrigued by the woman in the emergency room who snapped out of primal grief to give a lucid, succinct, and detailed medical update to the on-call doctor and then the urologist. Who was that woman? Where did she come from? It was as if a new archetype took over, related to the Grieving Mother, yet different. This was the Protective Mother, who astonishingly rises above her personal feeling, transcending all that is unnecessary so that she can do what must be done to help her baby. Some mothers lift up automobiles to save their children. In this case, it was necessary to communicate detailed information to a physician in a calm, rational manner.

How can we comprehend the love and the grief of a mother? It is so much for the Goddess to ask us to love these little beings with all our heart and soul *in the midst* of the vulnerability and transience of life. One of the great tasks in becoming a mother is to learn to hold the depth of love for a child in the face of the vulnerability.

The Great Mother Goddess Demeter agonized over this as does every mother I know. When Demeter's dear daughter Persephone was abducted to the underworld, Demeter wandered the earth, barren, empty in her grief. There was no life in her without her beloved child. The mother is not a mother without a child. Yet Demeter was by her very nature a goddess who brought new life and tended it. She became a nanny for a baby in the town of Eleusis. Demeter could not bear the vulnerability of this new and treasured baby. She could not stand to think that harm or death could come to the baby. So she set about to defy the laws of life: she would make this baby immortal. By day, she held to her disguise as a human nanny. By night, she held the baby in a special fire that would make him like a God, and she rubbed divine oils on his skin. But one night, the baby's human mother peeked into the room, cried out in horror, ruin-ing Demeter's plan and thus restoring the humanity of her baby.

I understand the feelings Demeter had that drove her to try to make that baby immortal. Each day, I anoint my children's bodies with oils in hopes of giving them at least prolonged life. I fasten seat belts, put on sunscreen, lock doors, keep medicines out of reach, turn down the hot-water heater, and a million other ritual acts to keep the forces of harm at bay.

Demeter is the Mother. We all are Demeter. She comforts us in our angst, showing us that she, too, suffers in the depth of her love for her child, that she, too, can barely tolerate the knowledge that harm will come and death will come to the life she loves. She weeps for this truth, rages within this truth, and yet, finally, like all of us, is forced to accept the ever-changing ways of life and death and regeneration.

The mystery of the female body is the mystery of birth, which is also the mystery of the unmanifest becoming manifest in the whole of nature. This far transcends the female body and woman as carrier of this image, for the body of the female of any species leads through the mystery of birth to the mystery of life itself.

—Anne Baring and Jules Cashford
The Myth of the Goddess, p. 8

THE GODDESS OF
WILLENDORF AND ME

five-month-old son
five-year-old daughter
seven-year-old son

LONG, LONG AGO, in a land that had been frozen over with ice, there lived a Great Mother Goddess. We, who sit in our heated houses reading by the lamp, do not know her name; we call her the name of the place where our people discovered her: the Goddess of Willendorf, the Goddess of Laussel, and so on.

In this time of long ago, the lands that we call Europe and Asia were a huge frozen glacier. Few creatures could survive that inhospitable cold: woolly mammoth, woolly rhinoceros, bear, reindeer, and our distant cousins the Neanderthals.

Few of us live to see one hundred years. Jesus of Nazareth was born two thousand years ago. Fifty thousand years ago, that gigantic glacier began to melt. After twenty thousand years of melting, grassy steppe lands were born, nourishing the life possibilities of horses, bison, and cows.[1] Forests began to grow, and the herds of animals, which had heretofore clustered in south-western Europe, began to migrate east. By this time, the Neanderthals had evolved into our closer relatives the modern *Homo sapiens* Cro-Magnon man and woman.[2] Some of these people followed the food east.

Only in the last one hundred years have we learned of the existence of these ancient ancestors. Many caves housing Paleolithic peoples have been discovered and studied, ranging from northern Spain and southwestern France through Germany, Austria, Czechoslovakia, all the way to Lake Baikal in Siberia. Scattered throughout this vast expanse of land was a remarkably uniform worship of the Mother Goddess.

More than one hundred and thirty statues of the Goddess dating back to the late Paleolithic era, from 22,000 BCE to 10,000 BCE, have been discovered. There are no parallel findings of male statues or figurines from this era. Many additional Goddess figurines have been unearthed throughout the world dating from 10,000 BCE until the era of the birth of Jesus, but here I wish to focus on the most ancient figurines.

All of the Paleolithic female figurines are naked, and many are pregnant. Almost always, the breasts, the belly, and the pubic area are emphasized, showing the focus on the generative principle of the Mother. Sometimes, the figurines were painted with red clay, reminiscent of the life-giving and death-bringing blood. Most of these goddess figurines were small enough to hold in one's hand. They were carved of ivory tusk, of bone, and of stone.[3]

Imagine our ancestors holding the tusk of woolly mammoth in their hands. How did they get that tusk? Did they kill that mammoth for their food and warmth? How? Which mates and sons and daughters were wounded or killed in that hunt? Imagine our ancient ancestors carving out of the numinous tusk of woolly mammoth an image that represented the sacrificed life of the animal and the life it nourished for the cave dwellers. For twenty thousand years, our ancestors carved the sacred image of the Great Mother.

The Paleolithic Goddess was the Mother of Life. She gave birth to all that lived, and she brought death to all that died. Within her body, she transformed the stuff of life into death and the stuff of death into regenerated life. She was the earth, the waters, the ice, the woolly mammoth, the man and woman. The Mother Goddess was the one organic unity out of which all life emerged and back into which all forms died.

There are many profoundly moving and beautiful Paleolithic Goddess figurines. One of my personal favorites is what we used to call the "Venus of Willendorf," although I've been informed that it is more correct to refer to her as the "Goddess of Willendorf" so as not to confuse her essence with the later, more differentiated and sexualized Venus figures. The Goddess of Willendorf was found in Austria and is thought to be about twenty thousand years old. She is carved of limestone, four and one-third inches high, a size comfortable to hold in a human hand.[4]

Beginning a physical description of the Goddess of Willendorf from head to toe, we notice that she has a large, round head. The only markings on her head are seven circles made of numerous small diagonal lines, beginning at the crown and ending where one might imagine a mouth to be. She has no facial features, only seven circles adorning her head. Why?

The lack of facial features is easier for me to understand than the seven circles. She bears no facial features because she is not an individual. She is not a specific woman; she is Everywoman. The circles surrounding her head show us something about her nature: she is circular, round like the moon and the pregnant belly. Life that is given comes back round again—infinite cycling and recycling.

The Goddess of Willendorf has relatively delicate shoulders and thin arms, which rest contentedly above enormous, pendulous breasts, each with a generous nipple. These awesome breasts lie against a very full and rounded belly with a large

Goddess of Willendorf. 20,000–18,000 BCE. Naturhistorisches
Museum, Vienna. Courtesy Giraudon/Art Resource, N.Y.

indented navel. The area between her belly and legs is carefully
carved to demarcate the pubic triangle, pointing to the mysterious cave from which life comes. All around this pubic triangle,
her hips and belly spill over into thighs so large they join together all the way down below her knees, finally distinguished
into two separated leg stumps at the bottom. This is a Goddess

who contains life. She channels new life through her body and pushes it forward into the world. Her breasts are filled with milk to nourish new life. She has a serene quality about her that is inward, contained. She both conceals and reveals the mysteries of existence.

When I look at photographs of the Goddess of Willendorf, she reminds me of the depth and power of Mother. I feel proud to be a woman and a mother. I feel touched and comforted by her presence.

Then why am I so horrified that I look like her? Except for my individual facial features, I resemble the Goddess of Willendorf. Why do I find *her* luminous, yet myself a nightmare from hell?

I do tend to gain a lot of weight during pregnancy. I have some reasonable excuses for this. My best excuse is that, when I felt nauseated in the first few months, keeping food in my stomach seemed to provide a helpful buffer from the hormones. But if I am really going to tell the full truth, I also found it fascinating to permit my body to balloon. Growing full was a giddy liberation from the cultural quest for the flat stomach.

I had never been on a diet in my entire life. That is, if we exclude the lunatic afternoon when my friend in high school decided that our stomachs were too fat and prescribed Ex-Lax for us to lose weight. I was a skinny child, fairly athletic. I ate what I wanted to, and my body looked fine—until I started having babies.

The big news for me postpartum—besides the baby—was that those forty pounds did not just melt right off because I was breast-feeding. I was ravenously hungry, and I did what I had always done when I was hungry: eat. When my weight stabilized at twenty pounds above my prepregnancy physique, I gripped myself by the neck and marched straight to an aerobics class. It was humiliating. I was the heaviest woman in the room, and I couldn't follow all those complicated steps. For months, I hid in the back row, occasionally pausing to perform artificial resuscitation on my ego, which was gasping on the floor.

Based now on my track record of three babies, the fact is that no matter what I do, my body looks like the Goddess of Willendorf for almost two years after the birth of a child. I can lower my caloric intake, jump around a bunch on the aerobics classroom floor, and nurse myself dry—none of it changes the fact of my mother-body. The body and the psyche of the Great Mother inhabit me. I look like who I am.

Then a tangled net of arguments and counterarguments ensnares me. Fat is not healthy. (But you shouldn't diet while you are breast-feeding because it will release toxins into the breast milk.) Just accept your body as your mother-body; this is the natural stage for your life now. (Have some respect for yourself and get back in shape.) And on I go, duking it out with myself, trapped within the net.

I feel ashamed of looking this way. When I look in the mirror, I say something to myself about how I don't really look this way—it's the angle of the mirror or my posture. But face it, I do look this way. I am a new mother. My body reads "mother" all over. I look like the ancient archetypal Mother. But I don't want to. I want to be a mother, but I don't want to look like one.

Now this is a confusing double bind: I want to be a mother, but I want to look like a maiden. I want to look sexually attractive, be thin, have a flat stomach and cheekbones.

This is sick. I know it. I never really considered myself part of the pathological American mind-set about women's bodies, until I got fat and middle-aged. It was easy to say that women should just be natural when I was thin, muscular, did not have gray hair. Now I find myself wanting to deny my aging body, to prove that this old gray mare at least looks like what she used to be. Something is terribly wrong with this. This mind-set denies the truth of the female body except in its youth. Where is acceptance for the truth of the mother-body? Where is acceptance for the truth of the middle-aged and the older woman's body?

I saw an image of Aphrodite recently, and as I looked at the Greek Goddess of erotic beauty, I mused that even Aphrodite would not pass muster in modern American judgments. Her thighs are too heavy; they touch too much at the top; her tummy and hips are a bit fatty, as are her arms; and her triceps are not well defined. Would even Aphrodite feel she needed to go on a diet or starve herself or throw up after meals to chase the current American feminine aesthetic? Houston, we've got a problem. It's with inner space: the inner space we have imagined for the feminine—a half-starved girl-woman.

Can we dream together images of healthy and whole women? We need enough room for a variety of women: young, old, natural, primped, mothers, crones, maidens—all of whom have a valued aesthetic. How can we stand up to the forces of misogyny and fashion and marketing who are dictating this life-denying narrow little range of what is acceptable within the feminine?

That challenge seems even bigger than I am. What I do know is that I want to be healthy in my body, which means exercise and losing some of my fat. I also know that I want to look attractive. I also know how very important it feels to me to value the reality of the Mother.

As both a personal and cultural healing, I want to feed this archetypal Mother. I want to know her, to value her, to honor her in my daily living. I want to be one of her honorable representatives in the world. What she has given to me—the beauty and depth of being a vessel for creation, and the earth-shattering love I feel for my babies—is more important to me than anything else in the world. I do not want to be ashamed of her or deny her in any way. There is so much work to do.

The woman of today is faced with a tremendous cultural
task—perhaps it will be the dawn of a new era.

—C. G. Jung
Collected Works, 10:275

THREE CHILDREN

nine-month-old son
five-year-old daughter
seven-year-old son

I HAVE HEARD PEOPLE SAY, "It's not that much harder to have
a third child. Once you have two, it's not much more work to
have a third." Do the people who say this actually have children?

We have three whole, individual children. Each has his or her
own personal needs. Frequently, two or more need something
at the same time. I am mortified when I hear Alia "playing,"
saying to her dolls, "I am so stressed-out. I have all these children, and the baby's crying, and you know it's really hard being
a mom." I wish I were showing her something else, some relaxed
mom who always feels unconditional love for each child and
speaks only in calm, kind tones. Who I am is not really who I
would ideally choose to be as a mom; it simply is the best I am
able to pull together in the thick of multifarious demands.

It is really hard being a mom. My friend Susan came to visit
me one day after work, still dressed in her professional purple
silk suit. She is a clinical psychologist, married, no children.
After one hour of an often-interrupted conversation with me in
the living room, peppered by my three children's playing and
fighting and needing in their normal ways, Susan leaned for-

ward, confiding to me in a whisper, "I couldn't do this. They'd have to lock me up in the psych ward after one day. I'd go stark raving mad. They always want something from you."

It is satisfying to be seen and appreciated in the complexity of the task of mothering. Few people, other than mothers, really grasp the level of competence, intelligence, love, patience, and sheer hard work that is required in the raising of young children. Susan said what I feel sometimes: that I will go crazy from all these constant demands and that I can't do it anymore.

What happens after a mother hits this wall is truly one of the great MotherMysteries. When a woman feels she is at the end of her limits, has no more love or patience or energy left to respond to one more need, suddenly, she is sourced. Where does it come from? Perhaps she takes a deep breath and draws from somewhere inside herself, a place that she never knew existed until the intensity of this demand, and she finds she is able to give more. Perhaps, as she looks upon the face of her child, some flicker in the expression of that beautiful face floods her with love and joy, replenishing her desire to give more. When she was sure she was dead, mysteriously the mother finds herself regenerated. She treasures her children as much as life itself. She would do anything for them, to help them, protect them. She, again, gives herself into relationship with her children.

I think the job "mother of three" would be easier if I raised the children in a more institutionalized sort of way: buy them all the same clothes but in different sizes, take them all to the doctor at the same time, play only with kids who live in the neighborhood.

But what I love about having children is attending to them as individuals, with feelings, interior realities, souls. I want to attend to their individuality, their particular talents. I want to listen deeply to each one of them, to know them well. In this way of raising children, three children isn't the same as two children. We are talking about one whole additional individual. We are talking about soccer games, baseball games, homework, piano lessons, ballet, creative movement class, chiropractic appointments, play dates. There are five individuals in this family, and that's a lot of people to track intricately.

In fact, it's all spilled out of my control. I can't contain this entire family all the time, and that is fascinating to watch. Each of us has our own relationships, and the kids relate to each other. I'm no longer the central axis out of which everything happens. Our family is more like a field of autonomous relationships.

Jesse, at age seven, often counsels me on parenthood. I was out in the yard with Elijah, Jesse, and Steve when Alia walked up to me saying, "Mom, you need to come inside right now. There's a match on the carpet, and I think it's lit." Indeed, a small hole was burned into the new carpet in the living room. Inexplicably, I was calm. I talked to Alia about not playing with matches, and I told her to take some time-out in her room to think about what had happened. I could hear her crying her heart out in her room. After about ten minutes, I wondered aloud whether I should go in to comfort her. Jesse stopped me: "No, Mom, take it from me. I know. She needs to be alone. She needs to work this out inside herself, and if you go into her room, you'll just take that away from her." I'd pay for that advice.

Alia seems to have successfully resolved her dilemma about not being the baby of the family anymore. It has been intriguing and touching to watch her process. As I look back, I see that the only way Alia knew how to be close to me was to be my "baby." Throughout my pregnancy and after Elijah was born, I assured Alia that I still love her and will always love her as my baby and my child, even with a new baby in the family. During Elijah's first year, Alia seems to have made a decision that the way she can be closest to me now is to join me in being a mother. She is close to me because she says what I say, caresses the way I caress. Her identity now is that she is a mother, like me. She will be close to me by *being* me.

The mother and the baby exist as opposite poles on the same axis. When we speak of a mother, a baby is implicitly in the picture—and vice versa. Alia stayed within the mother-baby dialectic, but she switched positions. In some ways, the roles of mother and baby are interchangeable in her psyche; either role will do. She and her friends play mother and baby, preferring the role of mother but agreeable to being the baby. She mothers her dolls in the way I mother her.

In the Waldorf kindergarten that Alia attends, the girls have been fighting all year over who gets to be the Virgin Mary in their daily dramatic play. All the girls want to be the Virgin Mary. The second most desirable role, albeit a distant second for them, is the role of the baby Jesus. Every other role in the nativity scene is completely irrelevant in their minds: Joseph, the donkey, the wise men, the sheep, the cows.

Alia taught me something very important about the religious education of children. It first came up in the nine o'clock questions. My older children like to save the big questions until nine at night or later, when they are snuggled in bed with the lights out: "Mom, what is earth's history?" or "Mom, what is God?"

One late night, I told Alia that we would talk about God the next day. The next day, she reasserted her question. I had a strong beginning, I thought, explaining that this question needs to be talked about in two parts: (1) What or who do we think God is? And (2) what are the practices that help us *experience* God? Alia said, "OK, tell me what you think about God and how you experience God." I did. Then Alia asked, "How does Daddy experience God?" I told her what I imagined and suggested she directly ask him. Then it only seemed right to ask her the same question, "Alia, how do you experience God?" Alia paused in deep thought, then pensively replied, "I don't. Mom, I experience the Virgin Mary."

Tears came to my eyes. Of course, this is where the sacred lives for her in her life experience: in the mother-baby conversation. The divine energy that she has access to in her life experience is rooted in the Mother-Child archetypes, through the only incarnations that she knows: her personal mother and the Virgin Mary. A transcendent God in the sky is too abstract for her, too distant from her daily experience. She relates to that which is imminent.

The era in my life of pregnancies, births, and newborn babies is completed. We are growing up as a family, together, and it is sweet. It is surely the hardest work I've ever done, day and night, day after day after day. Steve and I feel like workhorses. But I can't really think of anything else I'd rather be doing. The intimacy is so wonderful with little children. It is a joy to be with a baby who delights in playing "Here comes the mousy mousy mousy into the housey housey housey" (tickle, tickle). I adore having a young girl in my life who asks me, "What is your favorite color?" And I cherish the boy who summons me every day to play baseball catch in the side yard. I love sharing all this with a man I love, who asks our youngest on the way to the diaper-changing table, "Do you want powder, honey?" So even though we are exhausted, stressed-out, have little social life, don't have time to read books anymore, barely have time to be a married couple, and are mere shells of our former selves, these are the greatest years of our lives.

God knows it has not been simple to transform from a maiden into a mother. Thankfully, nature and daily experience take care of most of the job. However, in thinking about myself as a mother, I have realized that there are several ways in which my personality is not easily suited to motherhood.

Problem number one: I am an introvert in an extroverted job. I naturally seek solitude and contemplative time, which, of course, is impossible in the midst of three children. As a mother, I am continually pulled outside of my own thoughts and feelings into a child's questions or activities or needs. Everything is subject to interruption in this three-ring circus. What happens to a woman who goes for years without a completed thought, completed feelings, or a completed task?

Jean Houston gave me some excellent advice on this matter. She insisted that, above all else, it is essential to take an hour each day to sit quietly, listening deeply to whatever is stirring in the psyche. Mindful attention is necessary in order to harvest the fullness of a life. This is so at odds with the flow of family life, but as impossible as it seems, it also is crucial. Many of the essential dynamics of the cosmos flow through a woman in her mothering. Mothers have much to contribute when we pause to listen deeply, bringing our unconscious knowings into consciousness.

Problem number two: I am essentially a queen, currently masquerading as a servant. This is a kind of reverse permutation of the Cinderella story. As a maiden, I used to wear lovely gowns to go out at night, stepping out of my coach to meet a fine prince with whom to dance and fall in love. When the Fairy Godmother granted my wish, this maiden was transformed into a servant, married with children. I am on my knees mopping spilled milk off the floors. Little people wipe peanut-butter-and-grape-jelly mouths on the ragged, oversized T-shirts that I wear. "Cinderella, do this, do that, get me this, take care of that." Frankly, this endless servitude offends my queen nature.

The work of caring for children is significant and has an immediacy of relationship that is sustaining and meaningful. I cannot say the same for housework. I never imagined that I would spend hours of each day washing dirty clothes, wiping counters, moving clutter from one room to a different room, trying to consolidate all the little pieces of Mr. Potato Head that are scattered throughout the house. The slavish housework that comes as part of the mothering package is not a welcome addition to my life.

Problem number three: The tasks of being a mother are so consuming that I have little time for other aspects of myself, yet these other aspects continue to live and make demands on their own behalf. There are genuine energies that rise in me and ask to be lived out. What happens to them when they get precluded because the Mother requires everything? The woman inside me who has ideas gets frustrated. Ideas, which long ago bubbled up in excitement, stay on the list of "things to do when I have time" for so long that they become stale, a burden rather than a joy. What happens to these energies when I don't see them or talk to them or give them free rein? Do they wither on the vine? Each day, so much wants to live in me, and each day, out of sheer time and energy constraints, I must decide what to neglect.

So I have a few problems with being a mother. And even though these sometimes seem like indulgent complaints, it is important to acknowledge the shadow sides of mothering as well as the glories. I love my children beyond any love I had ever imagined. The beauty I see in their faces takes my breath away. I treasure these three children, each with his or her own teachings and paths.

I have felt it to be a profound privilege that three times I channeled a new creation on earth. Each time a new life grew within me and then came to live on the outside, I was filled with the great and fascinating mystery. On every level—physically, psychologically, spiritually—the processes of pregnancy, birth, and caring for a newborn have been the most compelling and meaningful experiences of my life. The religious impulses in me awakened as never before.

It has been of utmost importance to me to reflect upon these experiences, to explore the meaning of this mother-journey that has touched me so deeply. These meetings with the Great Mother have very much defined me as a human being and as a woman.

I know there are MotherMysteries yet to unfold in the raising of my children and in my relationship to the earth and in the wheel of life. However, unless it is the time of my death, I can't imagine that there will again be a time when the Great Mother takes me over quite as completely as she did in pregnancy, birth, and with a baby. For this privilege, I shall always be grateful. I can only respond by attempting to be faithful to the gifts that the Great Mother revealed.

CLOSING

WHEN A WOMAN LIVES within the hormonally driven era of pregnancy, birth, and a new baby, a window opens wide, giving her unimpeded access to particular mysteries in life—MotherMysteries.

From my three initiations with the Great Mother, I have noticed common patterns in these journeys and want to offer some closing observations.

The journey into the MotherMysteries begins with a call or, for some of us who are hard-of-hearing, an abduction.

Perhaps this call is newsworthy in and of itself. It has long been assumed that women live close to nature, that the call into maternity and instinct is as natural for us as breathing.

In his work on the hero's journey, Joseph Campbell often maintained that women do not need to go on the heroic journey, that women already embody the treasure: "Woman, in the picture language of mythology, represents the totality of what can be known. The hero is the one who comes to know."[1]

A crucial step in sorting out this matter is to distinguish between a woman's experience of herself and that of a man's experience of a woman, an anima figure or a Goddess.

Individual human women must not be confused with the Great Goddess. Both men and women are limited creatures, needing journeys to explore the mysteries of self and world.

I do believe that, in general, women are more intimately connected with nature and matter than are men. Our bodies—in menstruation, pregnancy, birthing, breast-feeding, and menopause—draw us into the rhythms of nature. Yet it is also true that, in the process of evolution, women have developed consciousness, giving us the ability to shape our lives through mindful choices. Some women choose to journey out into the world of careers. Some women choose to delay, or to forego, childbearing.

Many of us who do choose to be mothers have a sense of destiny in our lives in addition to motherhood. Increasingly, women do not simply slide into motherhood unconsciously and easily. It is a choice. And because it is a choice, we must be called into that journey.

Since we have climbed out of nature to some extent, we, too, must be called back in, to learn the ways of fertility, of death, of renewal. We must again become intimate with instinct and matter. Why? Is there some wisdom in the psyche of nature that insists on calling us back into at-oneness with nature?

We pregnant women ventured out of the ordinary world of human affairs, crossed the threshold into the spirit world, met the Divine at every turn. In our labyrinthine journeys, there were trials all right. Challenges. Somehow, time and again, we found resources within ourselves to rise to those challenges, adjusting our bodies to new demands, releasing old ideas about ourselves that didn't apply anymore, opening to the essential laws of nature. These challenges worked us over and over, gradually transforming what used to be a maiden into a mother.

The climax of every mythic journey is the discovery of the sought treasure. It is precisely the treasure that lured the ordinary citizen out of her world in the first place. This is the bounty that one worked so hard to find, sacrificed so much to reach. What lies inside this treasure chest? What pearls, what diamonds?

Repeatedly, in the many stories of the hero's journey, when the hero finally reaches the spot where the treasure lies half buried, what does he find? The ultimate challenge. There is a serpent guarding the treasure, coiled around it. In some myths, the hero surrenders to the serpent or is even killed by the serpent.[2] But in the majority of myths, we see the hero in his greatest act of courage, slaying the serpent in order to win the treasure.[3] The hero emerges with consciousness won out of the unconscious, light won out of the dark, order won out of devouring chaos. The heroic myths primarily speak of conquering instinct, triumphantly resisting the pull into unconsciousness, dependency, the undifferentiated life.

This courageous move of the hero is to be honored. Consciousness and light and order must be won. The winning of these treasures is a necessary stage in individual development and certainly has been important in human evolution.

But when we listen to the journey of the mother, we find that the story takes some curiously different turns. In the mythic journey into the MotherMysteries, a woman is repeatedly asked to *surrender* rather than conquer. *Submit* to the forces of nature. *Be guided* by the teachings of instinct. *Allow* the alchemical transformations. *Open* her body to house a new being.

When the mother finally arrives at the site of the treasure, she, like the hero, finds a serpent coiled around the precious bounty. This, too, is her ultimate challenge. But the mother does not slay the serpent. The mother is challenged to *know* the serpent within herself. The mother must embody the serpent's mysteries of transformation, of life, death, and regeneration.

What lies in the treasure chest? The mother wins the fortune of a baby. It is this baby who is of the greatest value, who must be kept safe, treasured. And there is even more. In the process of changing from a maiden into a mother, in the journey of trials through the labyrinthine temple of the Great Mother, the woman has been initiated into the MotherMysteries. She has embodied the ways of instinct. She has learned about the renewal of life on earth. She knows body and feeling. She has hosted alchemical transformation. She is intimate with nature. All this is the wisdom of the serpent. The mysteries of the serpent coil around every treasured new life. In myths, we consistently see the serpent paired with both the Tree of Life and the Mother Goddess. Integrating the wisdom of the serpent is indeed part of the discovered treasure.

The final challenge in every mythic journey is to find ways to bring the treasure back home, back to ordinary life, back to the community in which we live. Each mother knows the joy and pride of bringing her baby into the family and into the larger community. Each day spent nourishing the life of her baby, loving and tending this new being, is a gift to the world.

The mother has also been given the gift of wisdom—mother wisdom. This is the time when the mother needs a sword. To cut away from the infinity of moment-to-moment demands. To carve out contemplative time to bring the mysteries into conscious awareness, shining light upon the dreamy voyage through the temple of the MotherMysteries. Perhaps this is the most difficult challenge in the mother journey: bringing the MotherMysteries into awareness so that we can bring the wisdom we have been given back into our communities.

Where are the modern stories that teach us about an organic life process of which we are part? Where are the myths that help us to understand the value and necessity of darkness? Where are we to go to learn the ways of life and death and regeneration?

We no longer know the rhythms of the moon, of the sun, of the seasons. We insist on a manic pace of grow-grow-grow, in spite of the natural laws of life, death, and regeneration. We have lost the wisdom of the dark, the fallow, quiet waiting, feeling. These qualities lie in the shadows of Western culture, and it shows. We have lost the regenerative mysteries of the feminine.

As a species, we are meeting our limits in serious ways. The ramifications of nuclear weapons, genetic engineering, pollution that is altering the planetary organism—to name but a few—are life-threatening problems chasing us into the next millennium. The heroic human ego will not meet these challenges successfully.

Through the body of the Mother, the inexhaustible energies of the universe flow.[4] Will we open ourselves to receive the mysteries of the Great Mother? In what ways can we honor and feed the Great Mother? Will we allow her to work through us? The Great Mother is beckoning us, asking us to come closer, wanting to whisper sacred teachings in our ears. She knows something that we need to know.

NOTES

INITIATION
1. Carl Gustav Jung, *The Collected Works of C. G. Jung,* vol. 8, edited by Herbert Read et al., translated by R. F. C. Hull (Princeton, N.J.: Princeton University Press, 1966), pp. 138, 180, 201, 212.

RAGING HORMONES
1. Diane Wolkstein and Samuel Noah Kramer, *Inanna, Queen of Heaven and Earth: Her Stories and Hymns from Sumer* (New York: Harper & Row, 1983), p. 136.

THE ONE LIFE EATS ITSELF
1. Lennart Nilsson, Axel Ingelman-Sundberg, and Claes Wirsen, *A Child Is Born: The Drama of Life before Birth* (New York: Dell Publishing Company, 1966), p. 91.

THE VIRGIN MARY AND ME
1. M. Esther Harding, *Woman's Mysteries: Ancient and Modern* (New York: Pantheon Books, 1955), pp. ix, x.
2. Edgar Hennecke, "The Protevangelium of James," *New Testament Apocrypha,* vol. 1, edited by W. Schneemelcher (Philadelphia: Westminster Press, 1963), p. 385.
3. Marija Gimbutas, *The Language of the Goddess* (San Francisco: HarperSanFrancisco, 1989), p. xix.
4. Ibid., p. xvi.
5. Merlin Stone, *When God Was a Woman* (San Diego: Harcourt Brace Jovanovich, 1978).

6. Elinor W. Gadon, *The Once and Future Goddess* (San Francisco: Harper and Row, 1989), p. 191.
7. Harding, *Woman's Mysteries*, p. 102.
8. Joan Chamberlain Engelsman, *The Feminine Dimension of the Divine* (Philadelphia: Westminster Press, 1979), p. 129.
9. Elizabeth Clark and Herbert Richardson, eds., *Women and Religion: A Feminist Sourcebook of Christian Thought* (New York: Harper & Row, 1977), p. 35.
10. Gadon, *Once and Future Goddess*, p. 189.
11. Ibid., p. 195.
12. Anne Baring and Jules Cashford, *The Myth of the Goddess: Evolution of an Image* (London: Arkana, Penguin Books, 1993), p. 553; Gimbutas, *Language of the Goddess*, p. 319.
13. Engelsman, *Feminine Dimension of the Divine*, p. 121.
14. Joseph Campbell, *The Mythic Image* (Princeton, N.J.: Princeton University Press, 1974), p. 62.

MAKING A NEST

1. Lima De Freitas, "Labyrinth," *Encyclopedia of Religion*, vol. 8, editor in chief, Mircea Eliade (New York: Macmillan, 1986), p. 411; Joseph Campbell, *The Hero with a Thousand Faces* (Princeton, N.J.: Princeton University Press, 1973), pp. 13–15, 23–24.
2. Ibid.
3. De Freitas, "Labyrinth," p. 411.
4. Ibid.

THE FATAL SEA

1. Rudolf Otto, *The Idea of the Holy* (London: Oxford University Press, 1958), pp. 12–40.
2. Stephanie Simon, "Column One: Childbirth in Russia Is Miserable," *Los Angeles Times,* February 22, 1996, pp. A1, A14.
3. Carl Gustav Jung, *The Collected Works of C. G. Jung,* vol. 5, edited by Herbert Read et al., translated by R. F. C. Hull (Princeton, N.J.: Princeton University Press, 1966), p. 251.
4. Anne Baring and Jules Cashford, *The Myth of the Goddess: Evolution of an Image* (London: Arkana, Penguin Books, 1993), p. 185.
5. Ibid., p. 454.
6. Joseph Campbell, *The Mythic Image* (Princeton, N.J.: Princeton University Press, 1974), p. 257.

PRACTICING BREAST-FEEDING

1. Marija Gimbutas, *The Civilization of the Goddess: The World of Old Europe* (San Francisco: HarperSanFrancisco, 1991), p. 222.
2. Ibid.
3. Ibid., p. 234.
4. Anne Baring and Jules Cashford, *The Myth of the Goddess: Evolution of an Image* (London: Arkana, Penguin Books, 1993), p. 329.
5. Ginette Paris, interview by author, Santa Barbara, Calif., February 1996.

BIRTH

1. Aidan Macfarlane, *The Psychology of Childbirth* (Cambridge, Mass.: Harvard University Press, 1977), pp. 55, 56.

AND FURTHERMORE, I TOLD SUSAN

1. Euripides, "Medea," *Euripides Ten Plays,* translated by Moses Hadas and John McLean (New York: Bantam Books, 1960), p. 38.
2. Penny Simkin, Janet Whalley, and Ann Keppler, *Pregnancy, Childbirth and the Newborn: A Complete Guide for Expectant Parents* (Deephaven, Minn.: Meadowbrook Books, 1979), p. 189.
3. Ibid., p. 193.
4. Ibid.
5. Aidan Macfarlane, *The Psychology of Childbirth* (Cambridge, Mass.: Harvard University Press, 1977), pp. 37–38.
6. Ibid., p. 40.
7. Ibid., p. 33.
8. Ibid.
9. *The New Oxford Annotated Bible,* Revised Standard Version, Genesis 3:16 (Oxford, U.K.: Oxford University Press, 1962), p. 5.
10. T. K. Cheyne and J. Sutherland Black, eds., *Encyclopaedia Biblica* (New York: Macmillan, 1901), p. 1503; and *New Oxford Annotated Bible*, Lev. 12:1–5, p. 135.
11. Macfarlane, *Psychology of Childbirth*, p. 34.
12. Ibid.
13. Carol Baumann, "Psychological Experiences Connected with Childbirth: A Preliminary Research," *Studien Zur Analytischen Psychologie C. G. Jungs* (Rascher Verlag, 1955), pp. 339–40.
14. Macfarlane, *Psychology of Childbirth*, p. 35.
15. Ibid.

KNOWING THE MOTHER

1. Homeric "Hymn to Demeter," translated by David G. Rice and John E. Stambaugh, in *The Long Journey Home: Re-visioning the Myth of Demeter and Persephone for Our Time*, edited by Christine Downing (Boston and London: Shambhala Publications, 1994), p. 31.
2. Ibid.
3. Ibid., p. 32.
4. Carl Kerényi, *Essays on a Science of Mythology*, C. G. Jung and C. Kerényi, translated by R. F. C. Hull (Princeton, N.J.: Princeton University Press, 1978), p. 136.

IT LOOKS LIKE MITOSIS

1. *Webster's New Twentieth Century Dictionary Unabridged* (USA: William Collins World Publishing Company, 1978), p. 1152.
2. M. Esther Harding, *Woman's Mysteries: Ancient and Modern* (New York: G. P. Putnam's Sons, 1935), pp. 24, 55.
3. Ibid., p. 23.
4. Ibid., p. 151.
5. Mircea Eliade, *The Sacred and the Profane: The Nature of Religion* (New York and London: Harcourt Brace Jovanovich, 1959), pp. 156–57.

AD NAUSEAM

1. Anne Baring and Jules Cashford, *The Myth of the Goddess: Evolution of an Image* (London: Arkana, Penguin Books, 1993), p. 499.
2. Carl Gustav Jung, *The Collected Works of C. G. Jung*, vol. 5, edited by Herbert Read et al., translated by R. F. C. Hull (Princeton, N.J.: Princeton University Press, 1976), p. 374.

THERE IS SOMETHING TERRIFYING

1. Archive for Research in Archetypal Symbolism, *An Encyclopedia of Archetypal Symbolism: The Archive for Research in Archetypal Symbolism*, edited by Beverly Moon (Boston and London: Shambhala Publications, 1991), p. 376.
2. Ibid.
3. Ibid., p. 363.
4. Ibid.
5. Ibid., p. 376.

6. Ugo Bianchi, "Twins," *The Encyclopedia of Religion*, vol. 15, editor in chief, Mircea Eliade (New York: Macmillan, 1986), p. 102.
7. Lorna J. Sass, "The Incredible, Edible Symbol," *Los Angeles Times,* March 26, 1995, p. H2.
8. Ibid.
9. Ibid.

SORTING THROUGH THE EXPERIENCE OF AMNIOCENTESIS
1. Sheila Kitzinger, *The Complete Book of Pregnancy and Childbirth* (New York: Knopf, 1994), p. 339.
2. M. Esther Harding, *Woman's Mysteries: Ancient and Modern* (New York: Pantheon Books, 1955), p. 22.
3. M. Esther Harding, *The Way of All Women* (New York: Harper & Row, Publishers, Harper Colophon Books, 1975), p. 163.

WOMEN AND RELIGION
1. *The New Oxford Annotated Bible,* Revised Standard Version, Luke 14:35 (New York: Oxford University Press, 1973), p. 1268.

OH, NO! NOT THAT AGAIN!
1. Rita M. Gross, "Couvade," *The Encyclopedia of Religion,* vol. 4, editor in chief, Mircea Eliade (New York: Macmillan, 1986), pp. 132–33.
2. David Meltzer, ed., *Birth: An Anthology of Ancient Texts, Songs, Prayers, and Stories* (San Francisco: North Point Press, 1981), p. 132.
3. Normand Adrien Gilbert, "A Comparative Analysis of Expectant Fathers on Couvade Symptomatology and Associated Personality Traits" (Ph.D. diss., Michigan State University, 1987), p. 8.
4. Gross, "Couvade," p. 133.
5. Barbara Walker, *Women's Encyclopedia of Myths and Secrets* (San Francisco: Harper & Row, 1983), p. 106.
6. *The New Oxford Annotated Bible,* Revised Standard Version, Genesis 2:21–23 (New York: Oxford University Press, 1973), p. 4.
7. Walker, *Women's Encyclopedia of Myths and Secrets,* pp. 106–7.

EATING LEFTOVERS FROM CHILDHOOD
1. Louis H. Stewart, foreword to *The Child,* by Erich Neumann (Boston and London: Shambhala Publications, 1990), p. vii.
2. Ibid., p. 1.

Colic

1. *Personal Health Advisor,* Blue Cross of California ([800] 913-6286), 1996.
2. D. W. Winnicott, *Babies and Their Mothers* (Reading, Mass.: Addison-Wesley Publishing Company, 1987), p. 37.
3. Henry Chaney, Department of Invertebrate Zoology, Santa Barbara Museum of Natural History, interview by author, January 15, 1997.

Alchemical Vessel

1. Anne Baring and Jules Cashford, *The Myth of the Goddess: Evolution of an Image* (London: Arkana, Penguin Books, 1993), p. 153.
2. Ibid., p. 256.
3. Aidan Macfarlane, *The Psychology of Childbirth* (Cambridge, Mass.: Harvard University Press, 1977), p. 85.
4. Ruth M. Heifitz and Sharon S. Taylor, "Mother's Milk or Mother's Poison? Pesticides in Breast Milk," *Journal of Pesticide Reform* 9, no. 3 (fall 1989): p. 16.
5. E. J. Calabrese, "Human Breast Milk Contamination in the United States and Canada by Chlorinated Hydrocarbon Insecticides and Industrial Pollutants: Current Status," *Journal of the American College of Toxicology* 1, no. 3 (1982): pp. 91–98.
6. Caroline Cox, "Pesticides and Breast Cancer: Prevention Is Crucial," *Journal of Pesticide Reform* 16, no. 1 (spring 1996): p. 5.
7. Heifitz and Taylor, "Mother's Milk or Mother's Poison?" p. 15.
8. Ibid.
9. Ibid.
10. Ibid., p. 17.
11. Cox, "Pesticides and Breast Cancer," p. 2.

Conception

1. Star Black and Willard A. Hanna, *Insight Guides: Bali* (Singapore: APA Publications, 1989), p. 296.
2. Benjamin Spock and Michael B. Rothenberg, *Dr. Spock's Baby and Child Care* (New York: Pocket Books, 1985), p. 591.

Pregnant on the Pacific Rim

1. Adrienne Ralph and Lyn McGaurr, eds., *Australia: A Travel Survival Kit* (Hawthorn, Victoria, Australia: Lonely Planet Publications, 1989), p. 474.

2. Ibid., pp. 24–25.
3. Ibid., p. 289.

PLANNING MY LAST BIRTH
1. Aidan Macfarlane, *The Psychology of Childbirth* (Cambridge, Mass.: Harvard University Press, 1977), pp. 29–30.
2. Stuart Rossiter, *Blue Guide Crete* (London and Tonbridge, U.K.: Ernest Benn Ltd., 1974), p. 76.
3. Anna Kofou, *Crete: All the Museums and Archeological Sites* (Athens: Ekdotike Athenon, 1990), pp. 170–71.

HOME BIRTH
1. Anne Baring and Jules Cashford, *The Myth of the Goddess: Evolution of an Image* (London: Arkana, Penguin Books, 1993), p. 83.
2. Ibid., p. 82.
3. *Oh, California,* Houghton Mifflin Social Studies (Boston: Houghton Mifflin Company, 1990), pp. 21, 313.

THE PLACENTA AND THE TREE OF LIFE
1. Sheila Kitzinger, *The Complete Book of Pregnancy and Childbirth* (New York: Knopf, 1994), p. 66.
2. Ibid.
3. Howard Thurman, *Deep Is the Hunger: Meditations for Apostles of Sensitiveness* (Richmond, Ind.: Friends United Press, 1973), p. 48.
4. Anne Baring and Jules Cashford, *The Myth of the Goddess: Evolution of an Image* (London: Arkana, Penguin Books, 1993), pp. 454–56, 498.
5. Ibid., p. 456.
6. Joseph Campbell, *The Mythic Image* (Princeton, N.J.: Princeton University Press, 1974), p. 262.
7. Baring and Cashford, *Myth of the Goddess,* p. 497.
8. Campbell, *Mythic Image,* p. 192.
9. Ibid., p. 190.
10. Baring and Cashford, *Myth of the Goddess,* p. 135.
11. Campbell, *Mythic Image,* p. 190.

CIRCUMCISION
1. "Policy Statement: Report of the Task Force on Circumcision," *Pediatrics,* Journal of the American Academy of Pediatrics, Burlington, Vt. (August 1989).

2. Cathy Joseph, "Compassionate Accountability: An Embodied Consideration of Female Genital Mutilation," *Journal of Psychohistory* 24, no. 1 (summer 1996): p. 11.
3. Ibid.
4. Ibid., p. 5.
5. Jules Cashford, *The Myth of Isis and Osiris,* Barefoot Books (Boston: Shambhala Publications, 1993), p. v.

THE GODDESS OF WILLENDORF AND ME

1. Anne Baring and Jules Cashford, *The Myth of the Goddess: Evolution of an Image* (London: Arkana, Penguin Books, 1993), p. 6.
2. Ibid., p. 683.
3. Ibid., p. 10.
4. Ibid.
5. Ibid.

CLOSING

1. Joseph Campbell, *The Hero with a Thousand Faces* (Princeton, N.J.: Bollingen Foundation, Princeton University Press, 1973), p. 116.
2. Ibid., pp. 109–20, 126–48, 187.
3. Carl Gustav Jung, *The Collected Works of C. G. Jung,* vol. 5, edited by Herbert Read et al., translated by R. F. C. Hull (Princeton, N.J.: Princeton University Press, 1966), pp. 372–73.
4. This is a paraphrase of Joseph Campbell's statement that "myth is the secret opening through which the inexhaustible energies of the cosmos pour into human cultural manifestation," from *The Hero with a Thousand Faces,* p. 13.

A Note to Mothers

I am gathering written accounts of other women's experiences of the MotherMysteries, in hope of gaining an understanding of the range and diversity within the mother-journey.

I invite you to write about the MotherMysteries you encountered, be they similar to or different from mine. The mysteries need not be limited to the beginning stage of pregnancy, birth, and infancy, but can be from any phase in the life of the mother. It would be helpful to name the specific mystery and to tell about the life situation in which you discovered it.

I can only accept stories in written form. Please include your name, address, and phone number, and a stamped, self-addressed envelope if you want your written copy returned. With your permission, I might use your story in a future book or lecture, however, all requests for confidentiality will be honored.

MotherMysteries may be sent to:

Maren Hansen
c/o Shambhala Publications
P.O. Box 308
Boston, MA 02117

John Connolly was born in Dublin in 1968 and is a regular contributor to the *Irish Times*.

Critical acclaim for John Connolly and BAD MEN:

'Connolly creates those rarest of books – literate and beautifully written page-turners.' Mark Billingham, *Daily Mail*

'Will the film version be directed by John Carpenter or Quentin Tarantino? . . . Connolly spins his gruesome yarn with relish.' *Mail on Sunday*

'John Connolly is the new Stephen King. The man can really write . . . he's a master of that brand of deliciously suspenseful horror that thrills with every turn of the page.' *Melbourne Age*

'Connolly writes beautifully, evoking the rugged landscape of Maine and its equally craggy and independent people with a deft pen . . . As a straightforward thriller *Bad Men* works brilliantly, a violent noir novel in the Richard Stark or Lee Child mould.' *Irish Independent*

'His novels are dark; bleak, even. His characters are startlingly nasty and the violence unapologetic, though never gratuitous. Yet he writes with a compassion that's ___ in the genre.' *Sunday Business Post*

'With *Bad Men*, there's ___ ___ nce. This . . . will knock your s___

'John Con___ ___il men and their diabo___ ___ John Connolly's best novel ye___ ___ough menace to keep the pages turn___ ___e small hours.' *Irish Times*

JOHN CONNOLLY
BAD MEN

CORONET BOOKS
Hodder & Stoughton

Copyright © 2003 by John Connolly

First published in Great Britain in 2003 by Hodder & Stoughton
A division of Hodder Headline
First published in paperback in 2004 by Hodder and Stoughton
A Coronet paperback

The right of John Connolly to be identified as the Author of the
Work has been asserted by him in accordance with the Copyright,
Designs and Patents Act 1988.

1 3 5 7 9 10 8 6 4 2

A CIP catalogue record for this title is available
from the British Library

ISBN 0 340 82619 3

Typeset in Sabon by Palimpsest Book Production Limited
Polmont, Stirlingshire

Printed and bound by
Clays Ltd, St Ives plc

Hodder & Stoughton
A division of Hodder Headline
338 Euston Road
London NW1 3BH

For my brother, Brian

Also by John Connolly

EVERY DEAD THING
DARK HOLLOW
THE KILLING KIND
THE WHITE ROAD

Grateful acknowledgement is made for permission to reprint from the following copyrighted works:

Pinetop Seven: lines from "The Fear Of Being Found" (lyrics: Darren Richard) from *Rigging the Toplights* (Self-Help/ Truckstop Records, 1998), © Darren Richard, reprinted by permission of Darren Richard. *www.pinetopseven.com*

Prologue

. . . they are not towers but giants. They stand in the well
from the navel down; and stationed round its bank
they mount guard on the final pit of Hell.

Dante Alighieri, *Inferno*, Canto XXXI

M oloch dreams.

In the darkness of a Virginia prison cell, he stirs like an old demon goaded by memories of its lost humanity. The dream presses upon him once more, the First Dream, for in it lies his beginning, and his end.

In the dream, he is standing on the verge of a dense forest and a smell clings to his clothing, the scent of animal fat and salt water. There is a weight at his right hand: a musket, its rough leather strap hanging almost to the ground. On his belt there is a knife, and a powder horn and a bag of shot. The crossing has been difficult, for the sea was wild and the waves broke upon them with the force of a great hand. They have lost a man on the journey to the island, drowned when one of the bark canoes capsized, and a pair of muskets and a leather bag filled with powder and shot have descended with him beneath the waves. They cannot afford to lose weapons. They are hunted men, even as they are become hunters themselves this night. It is the year of our Lord 1693.

3

Moloch, twisting on his bunk three centuries after the time of his dream, drifts between sleeping and wakefulness for an instant before he is drawn back into this world of images once again, slowly submerging, sinking deeper and deeper like a man drowning in recollection; for the dream is not new, and its coming is by now expected when he lays his head upon the pillow and at last surrenders himself to its hold, his heartbeat loud in his ears, blood pumping.

And blood flowing.

He is aware, as he briefly breaks the surface of his uneasy rest, that he has taken lives before, and will take them again. A conflation of reverie and reality occurs, for Moloch has killed in both dream and wakefulness, although now the distinction between the two realms has grown indistinct.

This is a dream.

This is not a dream.

This is. This was.

There is sand beneath his feet. Behind him, the canoes have been drawn up onto the shore and there are men around him, awaiting his command to move. They are twelve in total. He raises a hand to them and the whites follow him into the woods, the Indians breaking off and sprinting ahead of them. One of them glances back at him, and he sees that the native's face is pitted and scarred, one ear missing, a consequence of mutilation at the hands of his own people.

Wabanaki. A Wabanaki mercenary, an outcast.

The Indian wears his skins with the hair turned inward, in accordance with the demands of the winter season.

'Tanto,' says the native, speaking the name of the god of ill will. The foul weather, the drowning, perhaps even the fact that he is here in this place, surrounded by hated white men, all are ascribable to the actions of the bad god. The Wabanaki is called Crow by the other men. They do not know his tribal name, although it is said that he was once a great man among his people – the son of a chief, a sagamore – and that he would have become chief himself had he not been exiled by them. Moloch does not reply, and the native follows his fellow scouts into the woods without another word.

Later, when he awakes, Moloch will wonder once more at how he knows these things (for the dream has been coming more frequently in recent months, and in ever greater detail). He knows that he does not trust the Indians. There are three of them, two Wabanaki and a Mi'kmaq with a price on his head back at Fort-Anne, vicious men who have pledged themselves to him in return for alcohol and weapons and the promise of rape. They are useful for now, but he feels uneasy around them. They are despised by their own people, and they are intelligent enough to realize that the men to whom they have attached themselves despise them too.

In his dream, Moloch decides that they will have to be killed after their work here is done.

From the trees ahead comes the sound of a brief

scuffle, and moments later the Mi'kmaq killer emerges. There is a boy in his arms, no more than fifteen years of age. He is struggling against his captor's grasp, his cries stifled by the Indian's large hand. His feet kick impotently at the air. One of the Wabanaki follows, holding the boy's musket. He has been apprehended before he can fire off a warning shot.

Moloch approaches, and the boy stops kicking as he recognizes the face before him. He shakes his head, and tries to utter words. The Indian releases his hand from the boy's mouth but keeps a knife pressed to his throat so that he does not cry out. His tongue freed, the boy finds that he has nothing to say, for there is nothing that can be said. No words can prevent what is about to occur. Instead, his breath plumes whitely in the cold night air, as if his essence were already departing his body, his soul fleeing the pain of what his physical being is about to endure.

Moloch reaches out and grips the boy's face in his hands.

'Robert Littlejohn,' he says. 'Did they tell you to keep watch for me?'

Robert Littlejohn does not respond. Moloch can feel him trembling beneath his hand. He is surprised that they have maintained even this level of vigilance for so long. After all, it has been many months since his enforced departure.

It strikes him that they must fear him a great deal.

'Still, they must think themselves safe if they leave only a child to watch the eastern approaches to Sanctuary.' He eases his grip on the boy's skin, and caresses it gently with his fingertips.

'You are a brave boy, Robert.'

He stands and nods at the Indian, and the Mi'kmaq draws the knife across the boy's throat, gripping him by the hair to pull his head back so that the blade will have easier passage. Moloch steps back to avoid the arterial spray, but continues to stare into the boy's eyes as the life leaves them. In his dream, Moloch is disappointed at the nature of the boy's passing. There is no fear in his eyes, although the boy must surely have been terrified during his last seconds on this earth. Instead, Moloch sees only a promise, unspoken and yet to be fulfilled.

When the boy is dead, the Mi'kmaq carries him to the rocks above the beach and casts him into the sea. His body sinks from view.

'We move on,' says Moloch. They ascend to the forest, their footfalls carefully placed, avoiding fallen branches that might snap loudly and alert the dogs. It is bitterly cold, and snow begins to fall, driven into their faces by the harsh wind, but Moloch knows this place, even without the scouts to guide him.

Ahead of them, the Mi'kmaq raises his hand and the party halts. Of the other natives, there is no sign. Silently, Moloch creeps up to the guide's side. He points straight ahead. Moloch can see nothing for a time, until the tobacco glows briefly red as the sentry takes a long draw. A shadow grows behind him, and the man's body arcs against the hilt of the knife. The pipe falls to the ground, shedding red ash on the dirt and dying with a hiss upon the newly fallen snow.

Suddenly the barking begins and one of the settlers' beasts, more wolf than hound, breaks through a patch of scrub and bears down upon a figure to Moloch's left. It leaps, and then there is a gunshot and the dog bucks and twists in midair, dying with a yelp and falling on a patch of stony ground. Now the men are emerging from the cover of the woods and there are voices calling and women shouting and children crying. Moloch raises his musket at a settler who appears as a silhouette in the doorway of one of the cabins, the dying embers of the fire within making him an easy target. It is Alden Stanley, a fisherman like the savior he so adores. Moloch pulls the trigger and Alden Stanley is quickly lost in a cloud of sparks and smoke. When it clears, Moloch glimpses Stanley's feet twitching in the open doorway until finally they grow still. He sees more knives appear, and short-handled axes are drawn as his men move in for close-quarters combat, but there is little fight in these people. They have been caught unawares, convinced of their safety in this remote place, content with only a single sleepy guard and a boy on a rock, and the men are upon them before they even have a chance to load their weapons. The settlers outnumber their attackers by three to one, but that will make no difference to the outcome. Already, they are beaten. Soon, his men will pick their victims from among the surviving women and young girls, before they too are dispatched. Moloch sees one man, Barone, already betrayed by his appetites. There is a child in his embrace, a little girl of five or six, with pretty blond hair. She is wearing a loose ivory gown. Its folds hang like wings from her raised arms. Moloch knows her name. As he watches, Barone throws her to the ground, and the girl is lost to his sight.

Even in his dream, Moloch feels no urge to intervene.

Instead a woman is running, making for the interior, and he moves off in pursuit of her. She is easy to track, her progress noisy until the stones and roots begin to take their toll on her bare feet, tearing at her soles and heels and slowing her down. He moves ahead of her and cuts into her path, so that she is still looking back toward the slaughter when he emerges from his cover, the pale light filtering through the branches casting his shadow across her features.

And when she sees him her fear increases, but he sees the anger there too, and the hatred.

'You,' she says. 'You brought them here.'

His right hand lashes out, catching her across the face and sending her sprawling on the ground. There is blood on her mouth as she tries to rise. Then he is on top of her, pushing her nightdress up over her thighs and belly. She strikes at him with her fists, but he throws aside his gun and holds her arms over her head with his left hand. His right hand fumbles at his belt, and she hears the sound of steel upon leather as the knife is unsheathed.

'I told you I'd return,' he whispers. 'I told you I'd be back.'

Then he leans in closer to her, his mouth almost touching her lips.

'Know me, wife.'

In the moonlight the blade flashes, and in his dream Moloch begins his work.

So Moloch sleeps, believing that he dreams; and far to the north, on the island of which he dreams, Sylvie Lauter opens her eyes.

It is January, in the year of our Lord 2003. The world is skewed. It rests at an angle, as if the physical world has somehow come to resemble her own perception of it. It has always appeared canted to her, in a way, always off-kilter. She has never quite fitted into it. At school, she has found a place with the other outcasts, the ones with the dyed hair and downcast eyes. They give her some sense of belonging, even as they reject the concept of belonging as somehow unsound. None of them belong. The world will not have them.

But now that world is altered. Trees grow diagonally, and a doorway has opened to reveal the night sky. She reaches out to touch it, but her view is obscured by a spider's web. She tries to focus and sees the starburst shatter in the glass. She blinks.

There is blood on her fingers, and blood on her face.

And then the pain comes. There is a great pressure on her legs, and a terrible ache in her chest. To breathe is to be constricted by nails. She attempts to swallow and tastes copper on her tongue. With her right hand she wipes the blood from her eyes and clears her vision.

The hood of the car is crumpled inward, wrapped around the trunk of the oak tree in a twisted embrace. Her legs are lost amid the wreckage of the dashboard and the workings of the engine. She remembers the moment when the car veered out of control upon the slope. The night rewinds for her. The crash itself is a jumble of sights and noises. She recalls feeling strangely calm as the car struck a great shard of sloping concrete, the front lifting as the passenger side of the vehicle left the ground. She remembers branches and green leaves filling the windshield; the dull sound of the impact; a grunt from Wayne that reminded her of the sound he makes when he is puzzled, which is often, or when he climaxes, which is often too. Now rewind again, and she and Wayne are on the edge of the man-made slope, the former site of the old gun emplacements and army bunkers, ready to freewheel down the incline. Now she is breaking into the garage, and watching Wayne steal the car. Now she is on her back upon a mattress, and Wayne is making love to her. He makes love badly, but still he is her Wayne.

Wayne.

She turns to her left and calls his name, but no sound comes. She again forms the word with her lips, and manages a whisper.

'Wayne.'

But Wayne is dead. His eyes are half open, staring lazily at her. There is blood around his mouth, and the steering column is lost in his chest.

'Wayne.'

She begins to cry.

When she opens her eyes, there are lights before her. Help, she thinks. Help is coming. The lights hover around the windshield and the damaged hood. The interior of the car glows with diffused illumination as one of them passes overhead and she wonders at how they can move in that way.

'Help me,' she says.

One of the lights draws closer, nearing the open window to her right, and she can finally see the form behind it. The shape is hunched, and cloaked with leaves and wood and mud and darkness. It smells of damp earth. It lifts its head to her, and in the strange half-light that filters from the lamp in its hand, Sylvie registers gray skin, and dark eyes like oil bubbles, and torn, bloodless lips, and knows that she is soon to join Wayne, that they will travel together into the world beyond this one, and that at last she will find a place where she fits into the great pattern that has remained hidden from her for so long. She is not yet frightened. She simply wants the pain to end.

'Please,' she says to the dead woman at the windshield, but the woman retreats and Sylvie has a sense that she is afraid, that there is something here that even the dead fear. The other lights begin to recede and Sylvie extends an imploring hand.

'Don't go,' she says. 'Don't leave me alone.'

But she is not alone.

A hissing sound comes from close by, and a figure floats beside her at the other side of the glass. It is smaller than the woman, and it holds no light in its hands. Its hair is white in the moonlight, and is so long and bedraggled that it almost entirely covers its face. It moves nearer as Sylvie feels a wave of tiredness wash over her. She hears herself moan. Her mouth opens as she makes another effort to speak, and she no longer has the strength to close it again.

The figure at the window presses itself against the car. Its hands, with their small, gray fingers, clutch the top of the glass, trying to force it further down. Sylvie's vision is dimmed once again, obscured by blood and tears, but she can see that it is a little girl that is trying to enter the car, to join her in her agony.

'Honey,' Sylvie whispers.

Sylvie tries to move and the pain surges through her with the force of a jolt of electricity. It hurts her to turn her head to the right, so that she can see the girl only from the corner of her eye. Momentarily, Sylvie's mind clears. If she can feel pain, then she is still alive. If she is alive, then there is hope. All else is just the imaginings of a mind driven to the edge by trauma and distress.

The woman with the light was not dead.

The child is not floating in the air.

Sylvie feels something brush against her cheek. It hovers before her eyes and its wings make a dull clicking noise as it strikes the windows and roof of the car. It is a gray moth. There are others nearby. She senses them on her skin and in her hair.

'Honey,' she says, haltingly, her hand striking feebly at the insects. 'Get help. Go get your mommy or your daddy. Tell them the lady needs help.' Her eyes flutter closed. Sylvie is fading now. She is dying. She was mistaken. There is no hope.

But the child does not leave. Instead, it leans into the car, forcing its body through the narrow gap between the window and the door; head first, then shoulders. The hissing grows louder. Sylvie feels a coldness at her brow, brushing across her cheeks, coming to rest at last upon her lips. There are more moths now, the sound of them louder and louder in her ears like a scattering of applause. The child is bringing them. They are somehow a part of her. The coldness against her mouth grows in intensity. Sylvie opens her eyes and the child's face is near her own, its hand stroking her forehead.

'No—'

And then fingers begin to probe at her lips, pushing against her teeth, and she can feel old skin crumbling like dust against her tongue. Sylvie thinks instinctively of the moths, of how one of the insects might feel in her mouth. The fingers are deep inside her, touching, probing, gripping, trying desperately to get at the warmth of her, the life within. She struggles against them and tries to scream, but the thin hand muffles her voice. The child's face is close to her own now, but there is still no detail. It is a blur, a watercolor painting left out in the rain, the shades running, blending into one another. Only the eyes remain clear: black and hungry, jealous of life.

The hand withdraws, and now the child's mouth is against her own, forcing it open with her tongue and teeth, and Sylvie tastes earth and rotting leaves and dark, filthy water. She tries to push the child away and feels the old bones beneath the cloak of vegetation and rough, rotted clothing.

Now it is as if her last energies are being drawn from her by the phantom child; a dying girl being preyed upon by a dead girl.

A Gray Girl.

The child is hungry, so very hungry. Sylvie digs her hands into the child's scalp, and her nails rake across her hair and skin. She tries to force her away, but the child is gripping her neck, holding her mouth against her own. She sees other vague shapes crowding behind, their lights gathering, drawn by the intensity of the Gray Girl's hunger, although they do not share her appetites and are still repelled by their fear of her.

Then, suddenly, the child's mouth is no longer against hers, and the feel of the bones is gone. The lights are departing, and other lights are replacing them, these harsher than before, shedding true illumination. A man approaches her, and she thinks that she recognizes him from somewhere. He speaks her name.

'Sylvie? Sylvie?'

She hears sirens drawing closer.

'Stay,' she whispers. She takes hold of his arm and draws him to her.

'Stay,' she repeats. 'They'll come back.'

'Who?' he says.

'The dead ones,' she says. 'The little girl.'

She tries to spit the taste of the child from her mouth, and dust and blood dribble onto her chin. She begins to shake, and the man tries to hold her and comfort her, but she will not be comforted.

'They were dead,' she says, 'but they had lights. Why do the dead need light?'

And the world finally turns to darkness, and she is given the answer that she seeks.

The waves break on the shores of the island. Most of the houses are dark. No cars move on Island Avenue, the little community's main street. Later, when morning comes, the postmaster, Larry Amerling, will be at his desk, waiting for the mail boat to bring the first delivery of the day. Sam Tucker will open the Casco Bay Market and lay out the day's bake of doughnuts and croissants and pastries. He will fill the coffee urns and greet by name those who drop in to fill up their travel cups before they take the first ferry of the day into Portland. Later, Nancy and Linda Tooker will open up the Dutch Diner for its traditional seven hours of business – seven until two, seven days a week – and those who can afford a more leisurely approach to life will wander down for breakfast and a little gossip, eating scrambled eggs and bacon as they look out of the windows and onto the little landing where Archie Thorson's ferry arrives and departs with reasonable regularity and slightly less reasonable punctuality. As midday comes, Jeb Burris will transfer his attentions from the Black Duck Motel to the Rudder Bar, although in winter neither business places great demands upon his time. Thursday to Saturday, Good Eats, the island's sole restaurant, opens for dinner, and Dale Zinner, the chef and owner, will be down at the landing negotiating prices for lobster and crab. Trucks will leave Jaffe Construction, the island's biggest employer (with a total of twenty employees) to deal with Covey Jaffe's current slate of jobs, ranging from house construction to boat repair, Covey being a man who prides himself on the flexibility of his workforce. This being early January, school is still out, so Dutch Island Elementary remains closed, and the older kids will not be taking up space on the ferry to the mainland schools. Instead, some of them will be thinking up new ways to make mischief, new places in which to smoke pot and screw, preferably far from the eyes of their parents or the police. Most will not yet know of the deaths of Wayne Cady and Sylvie

Lauter, and when they learn of the accident the next morning, and its impact sinks in, there may be fears of reprisals from the adult community in the form of parental constraints and increased police vigilance. But in the first moments there will be only shock and tears; boys will remember how they lusted after Sylvie Lauter, and girls will recall with something like affection Wayne Cady's adolescent fumblings. Bottles will be raised in secret, and young men and women will make their pilgrimages to the Cady and Lauter houses, standing in embarrassed silence as their elders hug one another in open grief.

But for now, the only light that burns on Island Avenue, with the exception of the island's twelve (count 'em) streetlamps, can be found in the Dutch Island Municipal Building, home to the fire department, the library, and the police department. A man sits slumped in a chair in the small office that constitutes the home of Dutch Island's police force. His name is Sherman Lockwood, and he is one of the policemen from Portland on permanent rotation for island duty. He still has Sylvie Lauter's blood on his hands and his uniform, and glass from the shattered windshield of the car is caught in the treads of his boots. A cup of coffee lies cold before him. He wants to cry, but he will hold it inside until he returns to the mainland, where he will awaken his still-sleeping wife by pressing his face to her skin and holding her tightly as the sobs shudder through him. He has a daughter Sylvie Lauter's age, and his greatest nightmare is that someday he may be forced to look upon her as he looked upon Sylvie this night, the promise that her life held now given the lie by her death. He holds out his hand, and the light from the desk lamp shows up the dark blood caught beneath his nails and in the wrinkles of his knuckles. He could go back to the bathroom and try to remove the last traces of her, but the porcelain sink is speckled with red and he thinks that if he looks upon those marks he will lose control of himself. And so Sherman balls his hands into fists, eases them into the pockets of his jacket, and tries to stop his body from trembling.

Through the window, Sherman can see a great shape silhouetted against the stars. It is the figure of a man, a man perhaps eighteen inches taller than he is, a man immeasurably stronger, and immeasurably sadder, than Sherman. Sherman is not a native of Dutch Island. He was born and raised in Biddeford, a little south of Portland, and he and his wife still live there, along with their two children. The loss of Sylvie Lauter and her boyfriend, Wayne, is terrible and painful to him, but he has not watched them grow as the man beyond the window has. Sherman is not a part of this tightly knit community. He is an outsider, and it will always be this way.

And yet the giant too is an outsider. His great bulk, his awkwardness, the memories of too many taunts delivered, too many whispers endured, have made him one. He was born here and he will die here without ever truly believing that he belongs.

Sherman decides that he will join the giant in a moment. Not just yet, though.

Not just yet.

The giant's head is slightly raised, as if he can still hear the sound of the Portland Fire Department boat departing, taking the bodies of Sylvie and Wayne back to the mainland for autopsy. In a couple of days' time, the islanders will gather at the main cemetery to watch the coffins as they are lowered silently into the ground. Sylvie and Wayne will be buried close by each other after a joint service out of the island's little Baptist church. Much of the entire winter population will gather, along with media and relatives and friends from the mainland. Five hundred people will walk from the church to the cemetery, and afterward there will be coffee and sandwiches at the American Legion post, with maybe something a little stronger for those who need it most.

And the giant will be among the mourners, and he will grieve with them, and he will wonder.

For he has been told the girl's last words, and he feels unaccountably afraid.

The dead ones.

They were dead, but they had lights.

Why do the dead need light?

But for now the island is quiet once again. It is Dutch Island on the maps, a tiny oval one and a half hour's ferry ride from Portland, far out in Casco Bay on the margin of the outer ring of islands. It is Dutch Island to those who have only recently come here to live, for the island has attracted its share of new residents who no longer wish to stay, or can no longer afford to stay, on the mainland. It is Dutch Island to the reporters who will cover the funeral; Dutch Island to the legislators who will determine its future; Dutch Island to the real estate salesmen driving up property prices; and Dutch Island to the summer visitors who come to its shores each year for a day, a week, a month, without ever really understanding its true nature.

But others still speak of it by its old name, the name the first settlers, the people of Moloch's dream, gave to it before they were slaughtered. They called it Sanctuary, and the island is still Sanctuary to Larry Amerling, and Sam Tucker, and old Thorson, and a handful of others, but usually only when they speak of it among themselves; and they say its name with a kind of reverence, and perhaps just a hint of fear.

It is Sanctuary to the giant too, for his father told him of its history, just as his father told it to him, and similarly back and back again, far into the lost generations of the giant's family. Few outsiders know this, but the giant owns whole sections of the island, bought by his family when nobody wanted to own this land, when even the state was turning down the opportunity to buy islands on Casco Bay. Their stewardship of the land is one of the reasons why the island remains unspoiled, and why its heritage is so diligently protected, its memories so carefully stored. The giant knows that the island is special and so he calls it Sanctuary, like all those who recognize their duty toward this place.

And perhaps it is still Sanctuary also to the young boy who stands amid the breaking waves at Pine Cove, staring out to sea. He does not appear to heed the cold, and the force of the waves does not make him rock back on his heels when they break, nor threaten to suck his feet from their anchorage beneath the surface. His clothes are rough cotton, apart from the heavy cowhide jacket that his mother made for him, hand-stitching it by the fire while he watched patiently, day after day.

The boy's face is very pale, and his eyes are dark and empty. He feels as though he has awakened from a long sleep. He brushes his fingers gently against the bruises on his face, where the grip of the man left its imprint upon him, then touches the memory of the wound on his throat left by the passage of the knife. His fingertips are heavily grooved, as if by time spent in the water.

For the boy, as for the island, there is no past; there is only the eternal present. He looks behind him and sees the movement in the forest, the shapes drifting among the trees. Their wait is almost over, just as his unspoken promise is about to be fulfilled.

He turns back to the sea and resumes his unblinking vigil upon the waiting world beyond.

The First Day

They asked again what was my name,
They asked again what was my name.
And two were dead before they could move,
Two were dead before they could move.
I said, 'That's my name. That's my name,
If you please . . .'

'Outlaw Song' (Traditional)

1

The giant knelt down and watched the gull's beak open and close. The bird's neck was twisted at an unnatural angle and in its single visible eye he saw himself reflected and distorted: his brow shrunken, his nose huge and bulging, his mouth tiny and lost in the folds of his chin. He hung suspended in the blackness of the bird's pupil, a pale moon pendent in a dark, starless sky, and his pain and that of the gull were one. A dry beech leaf fell from a branch above and performed joyful cartwheels across the grass, tumbling tip over stem as the wind carried it away, almost touching the gull's feathers as it passed. The bird, lost in its agony, paid it no heed. Above its head the giant's hand hovered, the promise of mortality and mercy in its grasp.

'What's wrong with it?' said the boy. He had just turned six, and had been living on the island for almost a year. In all that time he had yet to see a dying animal, until now.

'Its neck is broken,' said the giant.

The wind rolling in off the Atlantic tousled his hair and flattened his jacket against his back. Within sight of where he squatted, the eastern shore of the island began its steep descent to the ocean. There were rocks down there, but no beach. The old painter, Giacomelli, kept a boat in the shelter of a glade close by the shore, although he used it only occasionally. In the summer, when the sea was calmer, he could sometimes be seen out on the waters, a line trailing from the boat. The giant wasn't sure if Giacomelli, or Jack as most islanders called him, ever caught anything, but then he guessed that catching things wasn't the point for Jack. The painter rarely even bothered to bait the hooks, and if a fish was foolish enough to impale itself upon a barb, Jack would usually unhook it and cast it back into the sea, assuming he even noticed the tug on the line. Fishing was merely his alibi, an excuse to take the boat out on the waves. The old man was always making sketches while the line dangled unthreateningly, his hand working quickly with charcoals as he added another perspective to his seemingly endless series of representations of the island.

There weren't too many people living over on this side of the island. It was too exposed for some. Sheep sorrel, horseweed, and highbush blackberry colonized patches of waste or open ground, but mostly it was just trees, the island's forest petering out as it drew closer to the cliffs. In fact, this was maybe the closest thing to a concentration of houses over on the eastern shore: the boy and his mother in one; Jack in another; Bonnie Claessen just over the rise to the north; and a sprinkling of others within reasonable walking distance. The view was good, though, as long as one didn't mind looking at empty sea.

The boy's voice called him back.

'Can you help it? Can you make it better?'

'No,' said the giant. He wondered how the bird had ended up here, lying in the middle of a patch of lawn with its neck broken. He thought he saw its open beak move feebly, and its tiny tongue flick at the grass. It might have been attacked by an animal or another bird, although there were no marks upon it. The giant looked around but could see no other signs of life. No gulls glided. There were no starlings, no chickadees. There was only this single, dying gull, alone of its kind.

The boy knelt down and stretched out a finger to prod the bird, but the giant's hand caught it before it could make contact, engulfing it in his palm.

'Don't do that,' he said.

The boy looked at him. There was no pity in his face, thought the giant. There was only curiosity. But if there was not pity, then neither was there understanding. The boy was just too young to understand, and that was why the giant loved him.

'Why?' said the boy. 'Why can't I touch it?'

'Because it is in pain, and you will only increase that pain by touching it.'

The boy considered this.

'Can you make the pain go away?'

'Yes,' said the giant.

'Then do it.'

The giant reached down with both hands, placing his left hand like a shell above the body of the gull, and the thumb and forefinger of his right hand at either side of its neck.

'I think maybe you should look away,' he told the boy.

The boy shook his head. Instead, his eyes were focused on the giant's hands and the soft, warm body of the bird enclosed within their ambit.

'I have to do this,' said the giant. His thumb and forefinger moved in unison, gripping the bird's neck and simultaneously pulling and twisting. The gull's head was wrenched one hundred and eighty degrees, and its pain was brought to an end.

Instantly, the boy began to cry.

'What did you do?' he wailed. 'What did you do?'

The giant rose and made as if to grip the boy's shoulder, but he backed away from him, fearful now of the power in those great hands.

'I put it out of its misery,' said the giant. He was already realizing his mistake in euthanizing the bird while the boy was watching, but he had no experience of dealing with one so young. 'It was the only thing that I could do.'

'No, you killed it. You killed it!'

The giant's hand retreated.

'Yes,' he said. 'I did. It was in pain and it could not be saved. Sometimes, all that you can do is take away the pain.'

But the boy was already running back to the house, back to his mother, and the wind carried his cries to the giant as he stood on their neatly-trimmed lawn. Gently, he cupped the dead gull in his right hand and carried it away to the treeline, where he dug a small hole with the edge of a stone and covered the little thing in earth and leaves, placing the stone at last upon the mound. When he rose again, the boy's mother was walking toward him across the lawn, the boy clinging to her, shielded by her body.

'I didn't know you were out here,' she said. She was trying to smile, both embarrassed and alarmed at the boy's distress.

'I was passing,' said the giant. 'I thought I'd call in, see how you were. Then I saw Danny crouching on the grass, and went over to see what was the matter. There was a gull, a dying gull. I—'

The boy interrupted.

'What did you do with it?'

His cheeks were streaked with the marks of his tears and his grubby-fingered efforts to wipe them away.

The giant looked down upon him. 'I buried it,' he said. 'Over there. I marked the place with a stone.'

The boy released his hold upon his mother and walked toward the trees, his eyes grave with suspicion, as if certain that the giant had somehow spirited the bird away for his own dark ends. When his eyes found the stone he stood before the gull's resting place, his hands hanging loosely by his sides. With the tip of his right foot he tested the earth, half hoping to reveal a small swath of feathers, darkened with dirt now like a discarded wedding gown, but the giant had buried the bird deep and no trace of it was made visible to him.

'It couldn't be saved?' asked his mother.

'No,' said the giant. 'Its neck was broken.'

She spotted the boy and saw what he was doing. 'Danny, come away from there.'

He walked back to her, still refusing to look the giant in the eye, until he was once again by his mother's side. Her arm gripped the shoulder of the boy, and she pulled him closer to her.

'There was nothing anybody could do, Danny. The bird was sick. Joe did the only thing that he could.'

Then, in a whisper to the giant, she added: 'I wish he hadn't seen you kill it. I wish you'd waited until he was gone.'

The giant reddened at the chastisement. 'I'm sorry,' he said.

The woman smiled to herself as she tried to comfort both boy and man simultaneously. He is so big, so strong, she thought, and yet he is made awkward and small by the sorrow of a little boy and his feelings for the boy's mother. This is a strange position in which to find myself, circling this huge man as he circles me, almost – but not quite – touching. It took him so long, so long . . .

'He's still young,' she said reassuringly. 'He'll learn, in time.'

'Yes,' said the giant. 'I guess he will.'

He grinned ruefully, briefly exposing the gaps between his teeth. Then, suddenly conscious that he was revealing them, he allowed the smile to die. He squatted down so that his face was level with that of the boy.

'Good-bye, Danny,' he said.

The boy was still looking at the grave of the gull and did not respond.

The giant turned to the woman. 'Good-bye, Marianne. Are we still okay for dinner?'

'Sure,' she said. 'Bonnie's going to look after Danny for the evening.'

He almost smiled again.

'Say good-bye to Officer Dupree, Danny,' said the woman as the giant prepared to leave. 'Say good-bye to Joe.'

But the boy only turned his face away, burying himself in the folds of her skirt.

'I don't want you to go with him,' he said. 'And I don't want to stay with Bonnie.'

'Hush,' was all his mother could say.

And the giant named Joe Dupree strode toward his Explorer, dirt beneath his nails and the warmth of the bird still palpable on the palm of his hand. Had there been any strangers around to see his face, the sadness upon it would have given them pause. But to the natives on the island, the look upon the huge policeman's face would have seemed as familiar as the sound of breaking waves or the sight of dead fish upon the shore.

After all, he was not called Melancholy Joe for nothing.

He was born huge. His mother would often joke that, had Joe Dupree been a girl, he could almost have given birth to her. They had been forced to cut him out of her, and, well, that was that as far as Eloise Dupree having more children was concerned. She was almost forty by the time her son was born, and both she and her husband were content to remain a one-child family.

The boy grew and grew. For a time, they feared that he was suffering from acromegaly, the ailment of giants, and that their beloved son would be taken from them at an early age, his life span halved or even quartered by the disease. Old Doc Bruder, who was then not so old, sent them to a specialist, who conducted tests before reassuring them that their boy was not acromegalous. True, there were risks associated with his size later in life: cardiovascular disease, arthritis, respiratory problems. Some form of chemical intervention could be considered at a later stage, but he advised them to wait and see.

Joe Dupree continued to grow. He towered over his classmates in elementary school and in high school. Desks were too small, chairs too uncomfortable. He stood out from his peers like the seed of a great tree dropped in the wrong part of the forest, forced to survive amid alder and holly, its strangeness apparent to even the most casual of glances. Older boys baited him, treating him like a handicapped oddity. When he tried to strike back at them, they overwhelmed him with numbers and guile. Even the sporting arena offered him no comfort. He had bulk to go with his size, but he was without grace or skill. His was not an immensity and strength that could be put to use in competition. He lacked the instincts necessary as much as the abilities. His great size was a burden upon the football field and a liability in the wrestling circle. He seemed destined to spend his life either falling over or getting up again.

By the time he was eighteen, Joe Dupree topped out at over seven feet two inches and weighed over 340 pounds. His mass was a millstone in every way. He was intelligent, yet it was assumed by his peers that he was stupid because of how he looked. Instead of proving them wrong, he became what they perceived. He was the freak, the freak from the island (for it was his upbringing on the island that doomed him, as much as anything else; he was already an outsider to the kids from Portland, who thought little of the islanders to begin with, even those of normal size). He retreated into himself, and after high school took a job on the island driving for Covey Jaffe. It was only when the time of his father's retirement drew near that Dupree joined the Portland PD, his size almost an impediment to his acceptance until his family's history in the department was taken into account. When his father at last retired, it seemed natural that Joe Dupree should take over his role as the island's resident policeman, assisted by the existing rotation of cops from the mainland.

Dupree's father had died three years earlier, six months after Eloise had passed away. His father had simply proved unable to live without her. There was no other possible reason for the sudden decline in his health, despite the opinions of doctors and specialists. They had been together for forty-seven years, living in a modest house on this most remote of the inhabited islands, a profoundly enamored couple secure in the center of a close community. Dupree missed them both deeply, his father in particular, for he was forced to travel the same paths, to drive the same roads, to greet the same people, to wear the same uniform as his old man once had. There was a link between the two generations that could not be sundered, and he strengthened it with every day that he worked.

In his darkest moments, Dupree would recall his childhood, and the old man telling him tales from legend and from the Bible: of Goliath, who stood over six cubits; of King Og of Bashan's bed, which was nine cubits long; of the giants of Greek myth, the sons of heaven and earth, who were slain by the Olympians and buried under the earth, their remains creating the mountains of the world; of the Titans, parents of the gods; of Agrius the Untamable, born fully mature and clad in the armor of battle, who waged war on the gods of Olympus after the Titans' defeat; and of Aurgelmir of Norse myth, who was the first being, the father of the giants that followed, and whose body was used to make the very earth itself. Neither deities nor lesser spirits, the giants were beings out of time, and gods and men decreed that they should be destroyed.

Dupree understood the old man's purpose: to make him feel special, part of some great heritage, a gift from the gods, maybe even from God himself. He told his son stories of Pecos Bill, of Paul Bunyan, of the army of giants raised by Frederick the Great. It was all part of his great effort to give his son some comfort. It had not worked, for the Bible contained no stories of laughing girls and mocking boys, and the giants of myth were felled by weapons and wars, not words and enforced isolation – yet he loved the old man for trying.

Dupree looked back at Marianne Elliot's house. Danny had already gone inside, but his mother was standing on the doorstep, watching the dark sea and the white plumes upon it like shards of sunlight glimpsed through stormy skies. He tried to recall how often he had encountered her in this fashion. At first he had thought her hypnotized by the sea, as those who came to the island from away sometimes became, unfamiliar as they were with its rhythms. But once or twice he had caught her unawares and had been struck by the absence of peace in her face. Instead, her expression was one of concern, even fear. He wondered if she had lost someone to the sea yet still found herself somehow bound to it, like the widows of drowned fishermen unwilling to leave the side of the great grave that will not relinquish their loved ones to them. Then she seemed to realize that he was watching her, for she turned to him, raised her hand in farewell, and followed her son indoors.

Dupree started the Explorer's engine and drove toward the coast road, heading east along it. The road did not make a full circuit of the island. There were areas to the northwest, at Stepping Stone Hill, and southwest down by Hunger Cove that were virtually inaccessible by car, but since nobody lived in those areas the absence of roads was no great burden. Still, each spring Dupree would lead a group of volunteers over to Stepping Stone and Hunger and they would cut back the trees and brush that had begun to colonize the dirt trails leading down to the sea, just in case access was ever needed from the main road. It was a tiresome job, but far less irksome than having to build a new trail in a few years' time, or being forced to hack a way through in the event of an emergency.

About a thousand people lived on the island year-round, a figure that at least tripled in summer. The island was large, five miles long and almost two miles wide, one of over 750 islands, islets, and exposed ridges scattered throughout the two-hundred-square-mile vastness of Casco Bay. It was bigger and more populous than its nearest rival, Great Chebeague, but its size meant that most people still lived in relative seclusion, apart from the community that had built up around the main ferry landing, known only as the Cove. The population increased during the summer, but not to the same extent as on the other Casco Bay islands nearer the mainland, like Peaks or Chebeague or Long Island, for Dutch lay much farther to the east, and was more exposed than most. In winter, only the old families remained. Their history was entwined with that of the island, and their names had echoed around its woods for hundreds of years: Amerling and Tooker, Houghton and Hall, Doughty and Dupree.

The heating was turned up high in the Explorer, for it was fiercely cold, even for January. There was talk of storms coming and Thorson, the ferry captain, had posted a warning of possible suspension of the ferry services over the coming week. Already, Dupree had been forced to break up some heated arguments that had arisen at the ferry landing over accusations of excessive timidity on Thorson's part. It was hard for occasional visitors to the island to understand the importance of the ferry link to year-round residents. Casco Bay Ferries, which ran regular ferries to a number of the islands, did not service Dutch Island, due to the distances involved and the relative paucity of passengers, although its mail boat did make daily stops. Thorson's family had been providers of the island's ferry service for over seventy years, taking kids over to high school, students to university, grandparents to visit grandchildren, workers to their offices, patients to the hospital, boyfriends to their girlfriends (and in Dale Zinner's case, boyfriend to his boyfriend, although most folk chose not to comment on Dale's orientation, even if there were some on the island who would never eat in his restaurant on account of Dale being, well, 'not right'), children to aged parents who had been consigned to homes . . . the list was endless. If you needed to buy a new TV, you parked down in the lot by the ferry, climbed on board with a hand trolley, headed over to Circuit City, then used a bus or a cab to get your new TV back to the docks in time for Thorson to help you bring it home again. That also counted for stoves, machine parts, new tires, medicines, ammunition, new clothes for the kids, toys for Christmas, and just about any other item that you cared to mention, apart from the general foodstuffs available in the Casco Bay Market. Thorson's ferry was mainly a people carrier. For larger purchases, like a new car or a piece of serious farm equipment, Covey Jaffe had a construction ferry that could be hired out, but without Thorson's ferry to take care of all the little day-to-day things, life on the island would go from occasionally difficult to damn near impossible. Whether or not to run the ferry in the face of a storm warning was Thorson's call, but Dupree figured he'd talk to the old man over the next day or two and maybe remind him that being overcautious was nearly as bad as being reckless where the ferry was concerned.

Dupree made some casual calls along the way, checking on older residents, following up on complaints, handing out gentle warnings to errant

teenagers, and examining the summer residences of
the wealthy to make sure that the doors and windows remained intact and that nobody had taken
it into his mind to redistribute some of their wealth
to more deserving causes. It was the usual island
routine, and he loved it. Despite the rotation
schedule – twenty-four hours on, twenty-four hours
off, twenty-four hours on, followed by five days off
– Dupree worked almost as much unpaid overtime
as he did scheduled hours. It was unavoidable when
he lived on the island and could be approached after
church or in the store, or even while he was tending
his garden or fixing his roof. It was the way things
ran on the island. Formalities were for funerals.

On his way back to town, Dupree paused by an
old lookout tower, one of a chain of towers across
the islands of Casco Bay built during World War II.
The utility companies had taken to using some of
them as storage facilities or as sites for their equipment, but not this one. Now the door to the tower
was open, the chain that held it closed lying in a
coil upon its topmost step. The towers attracted the
local kids like sugar drawing flies, since they offered
sheltered and relatively remote sites in which to
experiment with booze, drugs, and frequently one
another. Dupree was convinced that a number of
local unwanted pregnancies had their origins in the
shady corners of these towers.

He parked the Explorer and took his big Maglite
from beneath the seat, then headed through the short
grass toward the steps to the tower. It was one of

the smaller constructs built close to the shore, barely three stories high, and its usefulness as a lookout post was virtually negated by the growth of the surrounding trees. Still, Joe was curious to see that some of those trees had been crudely cut back, their branches broken at the ends.

The policeman paused at the base of the steps and listened. No noise came from within, but he felt uneasy. It was, he thought, becoming his natural state. Over these last few weeks, he had become increasingly uncomfortable as he conducted his patrols of the island that had been his home for almost forty years. It seemed to him that it was different, but when he had tried to explain it to Lockwood the older cop had simply laughed it off.

'You been spending too long out here, Joe. You need to take a trip back to civilization once in a while. You're getting spooked.'

Lockwood might have been right in advising Joe to spend more time away from the island, but he was wrong about the nature of his partner's unease. Others, like Larry Amerling, the postmaster, had expressed to Joe a sense that all was not well on Dutch Island – though when they spoke about such things, they used the old name.

They called it Sanctuary.

There had been . . . *incidents*: repeated break-ins at the central lookout tower, involving the destruction of even the strongest lock and chain Dupree could find, and the surge in plant growth on the pathways leading to the Site (and in winter, mind, when all that usually grew was darkness and icicles). Nobody visited the old massacre site during the winter anyway, but if the paths became overgrown, then it would be a hell of a job revealing them again when spring came.

And then there was the accident one week before, the one that had killed Wayne Cady instantly and Sylvie Lauter a little more slowly. The accident bothered Dupree more than anything else. He had been behind Lockwood as the girl spoke her last words about lights and the dead, and Dupree recalled words once spoken by his own father:

'Sometimes there's no grave deep enough to bury a bad death.'

He looked to the south and thought that he could distinguish gaps in the trees: the circle of marsh and bog that marked the approach to the Site. He had not visited it in many months. Perhaps it was now time to return.

From inside the tower came a low scraping noise. Dupree undid the clasp on his holster and laid his hand upon the butt of his Smith & Wesson. He stood to one side of the doorway and called out a warning.

'Police. You want to come out of there right now, y'hear.'

The sound came again, louder now. There were footsteps, and a voice, low and nasal, said: 'It's okay, Joe Dupree. It's okay, Joe Dupree. It's me, Joe Dupree. Me, Richie.'

Joe stepped back as Richie Claessen appeared at

the top of the tower's main staircase, sunlight through the single filthy window on that level casting a soft glow over his features.

'Richie, come on out now,' said Joe. He felt the tension release from his shoulders.

What was I scared of? Why did I have my hand on my gun?

Richie appeared in the doorway, grinning. Twenty-five, and with a mental age of maybe eight. He liked to roam the island, driving his mother to distraction, but nothing had ever happened to him, and, Joe suspected, nothing ever would. Richie probably knew the island better than almost anybody, and it held no terrors for him. During the warm summer months, he even occasionally slept out beneath the stars. Nobody bothered him much, except maybe the local smart-asses when they'd had a drink or two and were trying to impress their girls.

'Hello, Joe Dupree,' said Richie. 'How are you?'

'I'm good, thanks. Richie, I told you before about keeping out of these towers.'

The grin on the face of the boy-man never faded.

'I know, Joe Dupree. Stay out of the towers. I know, Joe Dupree.'

'Yeah, well if you know, then what are you doing in there?'

'It was open, Joe Dupree. The tower was open. I went in to take a look. I like looking.'

Dupree knelt down and examined the chain. The padlock was open, but when he tested the lock by trying to close it, it wouldn't catch, instead sliding in and out of the hole with a soft click.

'And you didn't do this?'

'No, Joe Dupree. It was open. I went in to take a look.'

He would have to come back out here with a new lock, Dupree figured. The kids would probably just break it again, but he had to make the effort. He closed the tower door, then wrapped the chain around the handle to give the impression that it was locked. It would have to do, for now.

'Come on, Richie. I'll give you a ride home.'

He handed the Maglite to the handicapped man and watched with a smile as he shined the light upon the trees and the top of the tower.

'Light,' said Ritchie. 'I'm making lights, like the others.'

Dupree stopped.

'What others, Ritchie?'

Richie looked at him, and grinned.

'The others, in the woods.'

Danny grabbed a can of soda from the refrigerator and wandered down to his mother's bedroom. Pieces of paper lay spread out on the bed before her, as she kneeled on the carpet and tried to sort through them. She had that expression on her face, the one she got when they went over to Portland on the ferry and she had to go into the bank or the car place.

'You okay, honey?' she asked when she noticed him standing beside her.

He nodded.

She sat back on her heels and looked at him seriously.

'Joe had to do what he did, you know? It was the kindest thing for that gull.'

Danny didn't respond, but his face darkened slightly.

'I'm heading over to Jack's house,' he said.

He saw the scowl start to form, and his face grew darker still.

'What?' he said.

'That old man—,' she began, but he cut her off.

'He's my friend.'

'Danny, I know that, but he . . .'

She trailed off as she tried to find the right words.

'He drinks,' she finished lamely. 'You know, too much, sometimes.'

'Not around me.'

They had argued about this before, ever since Jack had fallen down and cut his head on the edge of the table and Danny had come running for her, the old man's blood on his hands and shirt. His mother had thought that he had injured himself, and her relief when she discovered the truth quickly transformed into anger at the old man for putting her through such a shock, however briefly. Joe had come along and administered a little first aid, then spent a long time talking to Jack out on the old man's porch, and since then Jack had been a lot more careful. If he drank now, he drank in the evenings. He was also turning out paintings with a vengeance, though Marianne didn't think much of his art.

'He just paints the same view, over and over,' she said to her son shortly after she and Danny had visited the old man for the first time, paying a neighborly call with cookies.

'It's not the same view,' the boy protested. 'It's different every time.'

But she had merely glanced at the small watercolor that the old man had presented to the boy on their departure, the rocks on either side of the inlet a bluish gray, the sea a dark, threatening green. It was an ugly picture, she thought. All of the old man's pictures were ugly. It was as if he were unable to perceive anything but the most mundane, dreary aspects of the landscape before him. There were no people. Hell, he couldn't even paint birds or clouds, or if he could, he sure never bothered to place them in his pictures. Grays and greens and washed-out blues, that seemed to be the sum total of shades on his palette.

But the boy had placed the painting above his bed and was prouder of it than any of the dozens of other posters and cards and notes that obscured the walls, even prouder of it than he was of his own work, which his mother thought was far better than anything the old drunk was ever likely to produce. Marianne was never going to say that to Jack's face, though. The old painter might have his flaws, but an absence of generosity was not one of them. The house in which they now lived was rented from him, and even by island standards he had asked little for it. She had that much for which to be grateful to him.

'Please, Mom,' said Danny.

If she did not relent there would a tantrum and she would be distracted from the task in hand, and she could not afford to be distracted from it. She gave up and dismissed him with a wave.

'Go, go. But if you think that there's even the slightest thing wrong with Jack, you come straight back home, you hear me?'

He nodded solemnly, then broke for the door. His mother stood and walked to the window, her bedroom looking down onto the path that wound between their property and Jack's house. In the beginning, she had led him along the way herself, either holding his hand or watching anxiously as he bounded ahead. After a while, she had started to let him make the short walk between the two houses alone. It wasn't far, and she could follow his progress every step of the way. She felt that it was important to allow him a little independence, a little room in which to grow. She wanted him to be tougher while simultaneously fearing the consequences of releasing him from her protection. It was the dilemma of every parent, she knew, but a mother without a man to share the raising of a male child felt it more acutely. Sometimes she thought that she was being forced to make choices that were against her nature in order to compensate for someone who wasn't there.

The boy trailed his way down, the soda can still clutched in his hand, like a small, bright fragment of canvas set adrift from the whole, his red windbreaker startlingly bright against the trees. Her eyes remained upon him until he reached the old man's door. She saw him knock and wait patiently, and then the door opened and he was gone.

Vincent 'Jack' Giacomelli had come to Dutch Island in the spring of '67, after he had lost his job teaching at some fancy college on the East Coast. He was a walking history of art, even if his knowledge and appreciation had never enabled him to paint with even one iota of the talent and imagination of those of whom he spoke to others. Things had started to turn black in the summer of '65, when his wife left him for a professor of physics who drove the kind of fancy sports car that physicists (who were, in Jack's experience, so boring they made even mathematicians seem kind of entertaining) were not supposed to know existed. After she went away, Jack's life began to fall apart, or maybe it had been falling apart anyway and that was why she left. Jack was never too sure, and most of that period of his life remained a blur. Truth be told, the blur extended up to a couple of months back, when he had fallen and bumped his head, and Joe Dupree had sat him down on the chair and spoken to him in that way of his, that quiet way that told you that if you didn't shape up and take his advice, then you might as well pack your bags, lock your doors, and head for the mainland, because Joe Dupree wasn't going to have any nonsense on his island.

What Jack couldn't figure was why he didn't feel any resentment toward the policeman. After all, people had been telling him to shape up for the best part of forty years and he'd hadn't given a red cent for their advice. But Joe Dupree was different. There was no other way to put it. When Joe Dupree looked at you in that strange, sad way of his, it was like being an onion beneath a skilled knife, as layer after layer was exposed and discarded until only the very core remained.

Or until nothing at all remained, depending upon how far he went, or the kind of onion you were. Jack had been kind of worried that if Joe Dupree kept peeling he would find out some terrible truth about Jack that the old man himself had never even suspected existed or that he had somehow refused to face. It was the fear that he had nothing left to offer, nothing but bad art and broken promises, and that Joe Dupree was capable of revealing that truth. Once exposed, it could never be hidden again.

After that talk, Jack went on the wagon for a while. It didn't last, of course. It never had before, and even Joe Dupree wasn't likely to have that much of an impact on a hardened booze hound like Jack, but the old man was more careful now, drinking only in the evenings and never, ever taking a bottle to bed with him as he used to do in the good old days. Instead, he began to paint at a faster pace than ever before.

He'd been dabbling with painting for a long time, of course. Jack made some money selling bad oil paintings and worse watercolors to tourists, sometimes from a little stand that he set up down by the waterfront in Portland on sunny weekends, laying on the old salt act as thickly as he could, inventing the kind of family history that a lot of folks around here could claim for real but that in Jack's case was as false as the bottom of a magician's hat. But he earned enough to keep himself in reasonable comfort in a house long since paid for, which was now his to pass on to whomever he chose – a couple of cousins, a handful of nieces and nephews, or his sister Kate, who, if Jack's will was anything to go by, was likely to be one disappointed lady once he was cold in the ground.

The doorbell rang. He wandered down the hallway, his old sneakers making a slapping sound on the bare boards. He was now seventy-one, and while he still – sometimes – felt like a young man, his body generally insisted on reminding him that he was not. His six-foot frame was slightly stooped, his belly rounded and the hair of his head and beard wispy and slightly yellowed. Through the frosted glass of the door he could make out the shape of the boy, disintegrating into black and red shards like watercolors dropped on oil. He opened the door and stepped back in mock surprise.

'Hey, it's the Danmonster.'

The boy stomped past him, not even waiting to be invited in. He walked quickly to the door of

Jack's studio and then looked back at the old man for the first time.

'Is it okay?'

'Sure, sure. You go right ahead. I'll follow you in soon as I get my coffee.'

Outside, daylight was already beginning to fade, igniting lights in the windows of distant houses. Jack retrieved his coffee cup from the kitchen, adding a little hot water to it to heat it up, then followed the boy into his studio. It was a small space, formerly a spare room, but Jack had transformed it by replacing one wall with sliding glass doors, so that the floor became grass that rolled slowly down until it eventually reached the trees that bordered the low cliff edge, the water beyond a dark, threatening blue. The boy was standing before the easel, looking at Jack's latest work in progress. It was another oil, and another attempt to capture the view over the water. Another *unsuccessful* attempt, Jack thought. It was the uncertainty principle in action: the damn thing kept on changing, developing, and the instant he attempted to capture it he became complicit in a lie. Still, there was something calming about the exercise, even as it moved closer and closer to failure with every movement of his hand, every stroke of his brush.

'This isn't like the others,' said the boy.

'Hmm?' said Jack, momentarily distracted by his own failings. 'What did you say?'

'I said this isn't like the others. It's different.'

'Different how?'

Jack joined the boy, then frowned and leaned closer to the canvas. There were marks upon it, like black streaks on the waves. He looked up at the ceiling and tried to determine if dirty water had somehow leaked down through a previously undiscovered crack, but there was nothing. The ceiling was white and unblemished.

Carefully, he reached out with a finger and touched the canvas, then drew his hand back slowly. The marks looked like paint, yet he couldn't feel the texture of the brush strokes beneath his touch. He looked closer and saw that the black marks were under some of his own strokes, the horizontals that he sometimes used in an effort to capture the movement of the sea. Somehow, it seemed that he had managed to paint over the blemishes without noticing.

But that was impossible. There was no way that he could have failed to notice the flaws in the painting.

He took a step back and tried to understand what the marks represented, tilting his head as he went, then paused as he reached the threshold of the hallway. Before him, the shapes became distinguishable as form, and he knew what they represented. He knew also that there was no way that Jack Giacomelli had been responsible for the marks on the canvas, for Jack Giacomelli never added anything to the natural landscape that was his sole inspiration.

'They're people,' said the boy. 'You've put people in your painting.'

The boy was right.

There were two bodies floating in the oiled waters of his painting.

The bodies of men.

The island had been quiet for so very long.

Its past slumbered gently beneath the surface, its exhalations causing the trees to sway, the waters to ripple, the dead leaves to chase one another across the grass like small brown birds in flight. It slept the way one who has endured great pain might sleep, its rest both escape and recuperation. The memory of those who had suffered and died upon it in years gone by drifted through its consciousness, so bound up with the land and the trees and the sea that it was impossible to tell if they had ever truly existed as separate entities.

But there were places upon the island that were a testament to those who had once lived in its gift, and the manner of their passing had ingrained itself upon the very stones themselves. At the heart of the island, barely a mile distant from the Cove, was a small huddle of stones surrounding patches of sunken ground. Seen from the ground, their pattern was indistinct, the placement of the stones seemingly, but not quite, random. Viewed from above, the nature of the monument became clear. Here were corners and fireplaces and chimneys; here were yards and outhouses and pens.

Here, once, were people.

Their end, when it came, scarred the island, and the foundations of the dwellings ran far deeper than those who had built them had ever intended or imagined, stone fusing with stone until the divisions were no longer apparent, the constructions of man and nature becoming one. Only the patterns visible from above, and the half-buried gravestones surrounding a single raised cross, marked this place for what it was.

This was the Site.

For a time – fifty years in the memory of men, but barely a second in the life of the island – there had been no more killing here and the island had remained uninhabited once again, but then more men came, men who were fleeing the consequences of their actions, for places with a history of pain and violence will sometimes draw further pain and violence to themselves. And the island tolerated their presence for a time, until at last it could take it no longer, the soil being incapable of soaking up any more blood, the stones resisting the blackening of fires set in anger.

The men who came to the island brought with them a woman, taken against her will. The men were being hunted for their crimes, and all had a bounty on their heads. Soldiers were searching for them on the mainland, so they took to the sea, hoping to find a place in which they would be safe for a time.

They came at last to the island.

There were four men. They were armed and battle-hardened. They had fought the Indians, the British, the French. They feared no one.

It was fishermen, blown off course by a storm and seeking shelter in the coves of the island, who eventually found the woman. She had built herself a little shelter in the ruins of the old village, feeding on wild fruit and birds and fish to keep herself alive, and had lit a fire in the hope of drawing help.

She had been there for two weeks, and was almost insane when they found her.

Of the men, there was no sign.

They brought her back to the mainland and she was questioned about all that had occurred. She could tell them little. On the first day, they had taken turns with her. On the second day, the men's boat had disappeared, although they had drawn it up on the shore and tied it to a fallen tree.

On the third day, the whispering had started.

It sounded at first like the wind in the trees, yet there was no wind blowing. The voices seemed to come from all around, and the men grew uneasy. Indistinct shapes flitted through the margins of the forest. Knowing that she could not flee, they left her tied to a tree and headed into the woods on the morning of the fourth day. After a little time had gone by, she heard gunshots.

The men did not return.

Soldiers scoured the island, for these were vicious, dangerous individuals, but only one of them was ever found. The soldier who discovered him thought at first that he was looking at the carcass of a small animal, until he touched it with his rifle and felt the skull beneath the hair. They began to dig, uncovering first his scalp, then his face, until finally his arms were revealed, outstretched in a crucifixion pose, and they were able, with difficulty, to pull him from the earth.

His name was Gabriel Moser, and he had been buried alive.

Except perhaps 'buried' was not the right word, for there had been no signs of disturbance at his resting place and already there was grass growing around the crown of his head.

Gabe Moser had not been buried, it seemed. Gabe Moser had been pulled down beneath the earth, and had suffocated in the darkness.

The man named Joe Dupree knew all these things. He knew the history of the island, just as his father and grandfather before him had known it, and they had bequeathed that knowledge to him.

The first one that came was named Thomas Lunt, and he brought with him his wife, Katie, and their children, Erik and Johann. That was in the spring of sixteen ninety-one. With them came the Leggits, Robert and Marie. Marie was pregnant at the time, and would later give birth to a boy, William. Others joined them in the weeks that followed. These are their names. You must remember them. It's important that you remember . . .

At the time, Joe Dupree had not understood, for he was very young. Later, as he grew older, he learned more and more about the island, about what had taken place there. He understood the importance of maintaining peace on the island and of allowing nothing to disturb its calm. Inevitably, people sometimes did foolish things, for where there are people there will be faults, but there had been no wrongful deaths on the island for many years.

Dupree drove to Liberty Avenue and killed the Explorer's engine. Liberty ran southwest to northeast across the island in what was almost a straight line, except where it took a dip to avoid the Site. It had been renamed Liberty Avenue (instead of the rather more mundane Central Avenue) in the aftermath of Pearl Harbor, when Casco Bay became the northern base of the Atlantic fleet. A big fueling depot was established on Long Island, and every kind of ship imaginable, from little cruisers to aircraft carriers, threaded a way through the channels of the bay to take on fuel. A cable capable of detecting the passage of metal objects was stretched across the ocean floor from Bailey Island to Two Lights, and two boats stood vigil over the submarine nets at Hussey Sound, waiting to open the nets in order to allow passage to military shipping.

The two largest coastal defense batteries were situated on Peaks Island, guarding the main approach to Portland, and Dutch Island, the largest of the outlying islands. Both were similarly equipped. The Dutch Island battery had two sixteen-inch guns, as big as any along the Atlantic coast, cast and fabricated at the Watervliet Arsenal in Albany. Each was sixty feet long, weighed fifty tons, and had to be transported to the island on a specially constructed barge. They were fired only once, during target practice, and promptly shattered every window on the island. They were never fired again, and when the war came to an end, they were removed and destroyed.

But the emplacements built to house them remained, great man-made mountains along the island's southeastern shore, and gradually they were reclaimed by grass and bushes and shrubs. A network of tunnels ran beneath them, their great iron doors now hanging from broken hinges, but even the bravest island youths stayed away from the tunnels. Doors that stood open one day would be inexplicably locked by the next. There were echoes where there should not have been echoes, and lights where there should have been only darkness. The island's teenagers were content to use the remains of the emplacements for biking or, if they were of a more adventurous cast, for driving cars diagonally down at the maximum possible speed, their occupants wrenching the wheel to the right or left at the last possible moment and coming to rest facing the road, sweat streaming down their faces, still shrieking in exhilaration.

That was how Sylvie Lauter and Wayne Cady came to be out here. They had boosted an old Dodge from the garage of one of the summer houses, since even if the car was damaged during their activities it would be many months before the damage was discovered, assuming, of course, that they did not harm it so extensively that it had to be abandoned at the emplacement, as had happened on more than one occasion.

The couple had been drinking, for there were cans found strewn across the backseat of the car. Judging by the number of fresh tracks along the emplacement, they had managed two or three runs before Cady lost control of the car, sending it careening at top speed into the oak tree. There were still heavy tire treads marking the car's final path, and fragments of glass and metal lay strewn around the tree, its bark now heavily pitted and speckled with the sap that had bled from within it. Flowers had been placed around its base, along with a couple of beer cans and a pack of Marlboros with two unsmoked cigarettes left inside.

Joe Dupree ran his fingers along the great gouge in the tree, then rubbed them together, crushing grains of bark beneath his fingers. Wayne Cady had hit the steering column with so much force that it entered his chest, killing him within seconds. His girlfriend struck the windshield hard, but her death was caused by the crushing of her lower body. Old Buck Tennier, whose house lay about a quarter of a mile from the emplacement, had heard the sound of the crash and called the cops. By the time Dupree and Lockwood reached the scene, Buck was kneeling by the car, talking to Sylvie. It was then that she had spoken her last. The two cops cut Sylvie and Wayne from the car using the jaws of life after Doc

Bruder, who was still registered as an assistant M.E., declared them dead at the scene. The bodies were transported to the station house in the back of the island's sole ambulance prior to being moved to the mainland. Dupree had taken on the task of telling Sylvie's father and mother, and Wayne Cady's layabout dad. They had all cried in front of him, even Ben Cady, although Ben had been pretty liquored up when Dupree got to his door.

The huge policeman shivered. He kicked at the glass with the toe of his boot and stared into the darkness of the forest as Richie Claessen's words returned to him.

The others, in the woods.

The island had been quiet for so very long.

Now, something was awake.

2

Harry Rylance spread the map over the hood of the rental Mazda and watched as a bead of sweat engulfed Galveston. He had a vague recollection that Galveston had once been pretty much washed away and subsequently rebuilt. Harry had been to Galveston, and why they had bothered to rebuild the place was beyond him. Maybe he was just bitter. He'd been ripped off once by a Galveston hooker who stole his wallet while he was taking a postcoital leak, and ever since then he had been unable even to hear the word 'Galveston' spoken without tensing inside. Thankfully, the opportunities to hear anyone talking about Galveston were comparatively few, which suited Harry just fine.

Now here he was looking at a dark patch of sweat slowly seeping into the map around that self-same thieving hooker hole in the ground. It could be a sign, he thought. Maybe if he hung his head over the map and let another bead of sweat drop, it might just hit the page and tell him where he was, because unless it did Harry Rylance was likely to remain abso-fucking-lutely lost. That would have been okay with Harry if he had been alone on this godforsaken stretch of dirt road. Well, not okay, exactly, but at least he would have been able to figure out where he was in relative silence. Instead—

'Do you know where we're at yet?' said Veronica, and there was that bored, whining tone to her voice that just seemed to burrow into Harry's skull from somewhere right above the bridge of his nose and then keep going until it hit the center of his brain and began picking idly at whatever it found there.

Well, there it was. Harry wasn't alone. He had Veronica Berg with him, and while Veronica was pretty much all that a man could wish for in the sack, and a whole lot more (Harry was not an unimaginative man, but the things that Veronica was prepared to do once her back hit the sheets came close to frightening him at times), she could be a righteous pain in the ass outside the bedroom. She sat in the passenger seat, her shades on, an elbow propped upon the open window, a cigarette dangling from her fingers sending hopeless smoke signals up into the winter sky.

And that was another thing: it was unseasonably warm here. Hell, it was January, and January had no business being hot. Harry Rylance was from Burlington, Vermont, and in Burlington, Vermont, January meant skiing and freezing your ass off and shoveling out the driveway. If you were sweating in January in Vermont, then you were indoors and the heating was up too high. The South was no place for a man to be in January, or any other time, if you asked Harry. Harry didn't do Dixie. He gave up looking at the blue-veined map of the United States in his Rand McNally road atlas, resigned to the fact that his attempt to exchange the trees for the forest had left him no wiser than before, and returned his attentions to the local map. Harry wasn't a great reader of maps, a fact that he tended to keep to himself. A man who admitted publicly that he couldn't read a map might as well start riding sidesaddle and listening to show tunes. Harry wondered if it was some kind of condition that he had, like dyslexia. He just couldn't connect the map, with its tracery of blues and reds and its smears of green, and the natural landscape that he saw around him. It was like showing him the interior of a body, all veins and arteries and bloody meat, and asking him if he could tell who it was yet.

'I said—,' Veronica began, again.

Harry felt the pressure building in the center of his forehead. Her voice was drilling away nicely now. If she kept this up, his head would cave in.

'I heard you. If I knew where we were, we'd be someplace else.'

'The hell is that supposed to mean?'

'It means that if you'd give me a damn minute's peace, then maybe I could figure out where we are and get us where we're meant to be instead.'

'You should have stayed on the highway.'

'I came off the highway because you said you were bored. You wanted to see some scenery.'

'There is no scenery.'

'Well, welcome to the South. The Civil War was

the best thing that ever happened to this place. At least it brought in some visitors.'

'You shouldn't have listened to me.'

'You didn't give me much choice.'

'Don't take that tone with me.'

'Hey, I already got a wife back home. I don't need another one.'

'Fuck you, Harry.'

And he could hear the hurt in her voice and knew that he'd have to worm his way back into her affections if he had any hope of expanding his sexual horizons in the company of Veronica Berg. The annual convention of the Insurance Providers of America wasn't likely to be so riveting that Harry would want to spend the entire weekend sitting in the middle of a bunch of seersuckers nursing a hard-on. He reached in through the car window and touched her moist skin lightly with the palm of his hand. She pulled her face away from him, sending him a clear signal: if she wasn't going to let him touch her face with his hand, then there was a pretty good chance that the rest of her skin would remain a covered mystery to him as well unless he started making up some lost ground.

'Baby, I'm sorry. I didn't mean that.'

She dabbed at a make-believe tear with the tip of a finger. 'Yeah, well, you ought to be more careful about what you say. You can be very hurtful sometimes, Harry Rylance.'

'Sorry,' he repeated. He leaned over and kissed her on the mouth, trying to ignore the taste of nicotine on her breath. That was another thing: her damn smoking. If there was one thing—

'Harry, there's someone coming!'

He looked up, and sure enough, there was a cloud of dust and fumes heading their way. He skipped away from Veronica, took the map in his hand, and waved it at the oncoming vehicle. As it drew closer and the dust cleared some, Harry could see that it was a blue Packard, twenty years old at least. Behind the wheel was a young man with blond hair parted on the right and hanging down over one eye. He stopped and brushed the hair back onto his head with his fingers as he looked at the older man.

Behind him, he heard Veronica purr in approval. The kid *was* good-looking, Harry noticed, maybe a little on the pretty side because of that blond hair, but still a fine-looking young man. Harry wondered if he was turning queer, then decided that the mere fact that he was worried about turning queer probably meant that he wasn't. Still, thought Harry, that kid better not do anything that might offend the law, because if he went to jail his cell mate would never have to buy cigarettes again.

'You lost?' asked the kid. His voice was a little high, almost eerily so. Harry walked over to him and realized that the young man was older than he had first appeared: early twenties at most, but he had the voice of a thirteen-year-old boy waiting for something to happen below his navel.

Fucking backwoods freak, thought Harry.

'Took a wrong turn somewhere back down the

road,' said Harry, which wasn't actually an admission that he was lost but wasn't saying that he knew where he was either. It was a man thing.

'Where you bound?'

What the fuck? *Where you bound?* Who talked like that?

'We're headed for Augusta.'

'You're a long ways from Augusta. That's a whole 'nother state away.'

'I know that. We were planning on taking our time.'

'You on vacation?'

'Business.'

'What d'you do?'

'I sell insūrance.'

'Why?'

'Why what?'

'Why do you sell insurance?'

Harry's brow furrowed. This was all he needed. The kid was obviously some kind of redneck retard driving a clapped-out old Packard up and down backroads, looking for folks to bother. They hadn't been off the plane more than two hours and already the weekend was turning to shit.

'People need insurance.'

'Why?'

'Well, suppose something happens to them. Suppose you crashed your truck, what would you do?'

'It ain't my truck.'

Jesus.

'Okay, well suppose you crashed it anyway, and the guy whose truck it is wanted something done about it.'

'I'd fix it.'

'Suppose it was so badly damaged that it couldn't be fixed?'

'There ain't nothing I can't fix.'

Harry wiped his hand across his face in frustration.

'You get hurricanes down here, right?'

'Sure.'

'What if your house blew away?'

The young man considered this, then nodded.

'If I had a house,' he said, then started the Packard up again. 'Follow me,' he told Harry. 'I'll take you where you need to go.'

Harry smiled in relief and trotted back to the car.

'We're going to follow him,' he told Veronica.

'Okay with me,' she said.

'And put your tongue back in your mouth,' said Harry. 'You're getting drool on your chin.'

They followed the Packard for five miles before Harry started to worry.

'The hell is he taking us?' he said.

'He probably knows a shortcut.'

'A shortcut to where? Louisiana?'

'Harry, it's his country. He knows it better than we do. Calm down.'

'I think the kid's retarded. He was asking me about insurance.'

'You sell insurance. People ask you about it all the time.'

'Yeah, but not like that. The kid acted like he didn't know what insurance was.'

'Maybe he had a bad experience once.'

'Like what?'

'Like trying to make a claim on your firm.'

'Very funny. And it's *our* firm.'

'I just answer the phones. I don't sell bum policies.'

'They're not bum policies. Jesus, you talk like that to other people about what we do?'

'If they're not bum policies, how come they don't pay out like they should?'

'It's complicated.'

'Explain it to me.'

'You wouldn't understand.'

'Fuck you, Harry.'

'Now where is he going?'

Ahead of them, the Packard had made a right and was pulling up in front of an old farmhouse. The kid got out of the car and walked up the steps to the door, then opened it and disappeared inside.

'I don't believe this,' said Harry.

He followed the driveway until he reached the Packard. The place looked like it had seen better days and could now hardly remember them. Trees sheltered the yard, but it wasn't clear why they were needed, because Harry couldn't see another house anywhere nearby. Once this might have been a working farm. There was a barn off to the right, and Harry saw a rusting John Deere standing in the open door, but its tires were flat and its exhaust was severed. He glimpsed overgrown fields through the trees, but nothing had been harvested from them in a very long time. The only thing being farmed here was dirt and weeds. It was quiet, too: no dogs, no people, hell, not even a couple of scrawny chickens trying to survive on dust and stray seeds. A porch ran along the front of the house, great teardrops of white paint flaking from it. Paint was falling too from the façade, and from the window frames and the door. The whole house seemed to be weeping.

Harry opened the car door and called after their guide.

'Hey, kid! What's the deal?'

There was no reply, and suddenly Harry, who considered himself a calm man, all things considered, lost it.

'Fuck!' he shouted. 'Fuck! Fuck! FUCK!'

He climbed out of the car and stomped up to the house. Behind him, he heard Veronica telling him to wait up. He ignored her. All he wanted to do now was get back on the highway, find a hotel, and hit the bar. Hell, maybe they might just drive into the night until they got to Augusta, and screw the idea of taking their time and kicking back along the way. Veronica could just kiss his ass.

He reached the door and peered into the house. The entrance led straight into a living room. All the drapes were drawn and the room was shrouded in darkness. He could see the shapes of chairs and a TV in the corner. Facing him was a kitchen and, beside that, a bedroom that had been converted to storage. To his left, a flight of stairs led up to the second story.

Despite the heat, all of the windows were closed. There was no sign of the kid.

Harry stepped inside, and his nose wrinkled. Something smelled bad in here, he thought. He heard flies buzzing.

'What's happening?' said Veronica, and there was that whining tone to her voice again, except this time Harry barely noticed it.

'Stay there,' he called back. 'And lock the car doors.'

'What—'

'For Christ's sake, just do it!'

She was quiet then, but he heard a snapping sound as the doors locked. Beyond him, the darkness remained untroubled by sound or movement, but for the noise of the insects, still invisible to him.

Harry stepped into the house.

Many miles to the north, two police officers sat at a table in the Sebago Brewing Company in Portland's Old Port. It was shortly after four o'clock and already growing dark. There were few tourists around at this time of year, and the streets, like the bar, were quiet. There was talk of a storm brewing, and the coming of snow.

'I like it better without the tourists,' said the first

cop. She was small and dark, with short hair that barely troubled the nape of her neck. Her limbs were slim, and she appeared almost delicate out of uniform, but Sharon Macy was strong and fast. Cute too, thought Eric Barron. In fact, very cute. She'd joined up only six months before, and in that time it was all that Barron could do to stop himself hitting on her. Barron was smart, and he'd watched as the other cops had made moves on her in bars and clubs, hiding wedding bands in some cases, as if Macy would be dumb enough to fall for that. But Barron had held back, and now he believed that he was one of the few cops who could safely suggest to Macy that they head out for a beer or two after a tour, y'know, to unwind. He could feel her starting to trust him, to relax in his presence, and she didn't seem to mind any when he patted her arm or let his leg rest against hers. Baby steps. Barron was a great believer in baby steps. It might actually have made him a decent cop, if he had cared to be: not flashy or glory-seeking, but con-scientious and careful. Unfortunately, Barron wasn't a decent cop. He had a lot of people fooled, maybe, but even the ones that considered him adequate at worst wouldn't have used the word 'decent' of Barron. He gave off a bad vibe. Nobody was ever going to ask Barron to baby-sit a kid, or pick up a daughter after cheerleading practice. It wasn't any-thing that could be put into words, exactly, but if you were a parent, then Barron was the kind of guy who put you on your guard. Local kids, even the real troublemakers, knew better than to mess with him. Barron liked to pretend that it was because they respected him, but secretly he knew better. He could see it in their faces, those of the boys in particular.

Barron didn't usually go for women like Macy – hell, he didn't usually care much for grown women, period – but Macy was thin, with kind of a boyish ass, and Barron was all for experimentation. Plus he'd been out of the loop for a time, keeping his head down. He'd let his appetites get the better of him a little while back, and had almost brought a ton of trouble down on his head. He needed an outlet for his frustrations.

'It'll be cold out there on the island,' he said. He rubbed his hands over hers, as if trying to increase the circulation to frozen limbs. She smiled at him, then drew her hands away and hid them beneath the table.

Damn, thought Barron. Not a good sign.

'I don't mind,' she said. 'I'm kind of looking forward to it. I've never been out there before.'

Barron took a long pull on his beer. 'There's nothing "out there",' he said. 'Just a bunch of yokels living out some damn island fantasy. Inbreds, mostly. Banjo players.'

She shook her head. 'You know that's not true.'

'You haven't seen it. Believe me, just twenty-four hours of island life and this place will seem like New York and Vegas combined.'

Barron had that tone when he spoke, the know-all one that really grated on Macy. Then again, Macy was just a probationary patrol officer, while Barron was her field training officer. She'd put in her eighteen weeks' basic training, and now was at the end of her six weeks under an FTO. She had almost another two years of probation to go, with transfers to new duties every six months, but she didn't mind that so much. She would just be happy to get away from Barron. He creeped her out, and his attitude toward her wasn't simply that of a senior patrolman to one fifteen years his junior. Barron was just plain bad news. He was one of a handful of cops facing brutality charges, bringing – if you asked Macy – the Portland PD into disrepute at a time when it didn't need it. The force was already under federal review, and morale was suffering. A lot of good cops were simply working toward their twenty-five so they could retire and open a bar somewhere. Cops like Barron only made things worse.

Still, he'd offered to buy her a beer to celebrate the end of their time together and she hadn't been able to refuse. There were one or two other cops in the Sebago, although it wasn't a regular haunt. Barron didn't go to the cop bars. Macy figured that she wasn't the only one who felt uneasy around him.

Macy sipped her beer and watched the cars pass on Middle Street. She was still getting used to Portland, but it reminded her a little of Providence, where her parents lived. There were a lot of young people, although Portland's university wasn't quite as grand as the one back home, and it still had kind of a small-town feel. She liked the fact that there were good bars and decent places to eat in the center of the city. She didn't miss Providence too much, and was happy to leave the bulk of her bad memories behind. If things had worked out there, then Macy would have been married by now, might even have been talking about having a child. Things hadn't worked out, of course, which was why she was sitting in a bar 150 miles away with tired legs and an aching back.

It was strange, but one of the things that she had liked about Max was the feeling he gave her that, even half a century down the line, she would still be discovering new things about him. In the end, it had taken barely eighteen months for her to discover a new thing about Max that blew any hopes of marriage out of the water. Max couldn't remain faithful. Max would screw a keyhole if there wasn't already a key in it. When he couldn't pick up a desperate student on Thayer Street, or a bored secretary during the five-to-eight happy hour (which was how Macy, a bored secretary in a law office, had met him, come to think of it), he'd screw hookers. He even seemed to prefer hookers, she discovered, when he was released on bail and they met for that last time, after she had packed her bags and returned in humiliation to her parents. He confessed everything, spewing poison and bile out onto the table of the diner, so that it seemed that the Formica would corrode beneath it. He would tell the hookers that he was single and would get a kick when they asked how a good-looking guy like him could be single. Even as he spoke about it, his career in tatters around him (associating with hookers was the least of his professional problems, for he had been under surveillance for some time, a consequence of the investigation into the mayor's operation in Providence, and was now facing charges of graft and corruption), she sensed that he still found it flattering. Max was sick, but the sickness was moral as much as psychological. She was just grateful that she had found out the truth before the wedding and not after it.

That was two years ago, and Macy had begun toying with the idea of becoming a cop shortly after. She had been helping out at a voluntary center for women who were victims of domestic abuse, and had heard horror stories from some of them about their dealings with the police. There were good stories too, hopeful stories, but it was the bad ones that stayed with Macy. She wanted to make a difference. It was as simple as that. She had visited Portland in the aftermath of the breakup, while she was still trying to come to terms with what had happened, and had decided that it suited her. It was close enough to her parents to enable her to drive home when she chose, yet far enough away that she would be in no danger of meeting any of Max's old associates (or, God forbid, Max himself). The cost of living was reasonable, and the force was recruiting. Her modicum of legal knowledge and her experience in the battered women's shelter had made her a shoo-in as a recruit. She had no regrets, although working with Barron had been her most trying ordeal yet.

She noticed that Barron had gone quiet. She saw him looking across the bar, and the expression on his face was so hostile that she immediately wanted to leave him there, to get as far away from him as possible, even though his eyes were not on her. Instead, he was watching a man of slightly more than medium height talking to the bartender. He was kind of cute, thought Macy, in a brooding way. He flashed some form of ID, asked a couple of questions, then prepared to move on. He barely paused when he spotted Barron, but it was enough. He held the cop's eyes until Barron looked away, then left the bar. Macy watched him climb into an old Mustang and drive toward the Franklin Arterial.

'Who was that?' she asked.

'Nobody. A fuckup.'

He excused himself to go to the john and told the bartender to rack up two more beers. Macy was barely halfway through her first and she wasn't planning on having another. She looked around the bar and saw Odell from Property. He stepped up beside her and touched his glass to hers.

'End of your six,' he said. 'Congratulations.'

She shrugged and smiled. 'Hey, you know who that guy was, the one who was talking to the bartender a couple of minutes ago? Drives a Mustang.'

Odell nodded. 'Charlie Parker.'

'The P.I.?' As an investigator, she knew, Parker had managed to track down some bad guys. He had quite a reputation, even if it was a mixed one. She had heard talk that Parker was nosing about in the department. She was curious to know why.

'The very same.'

'I got the impression that Barron doesn't like him.'

'There aren't a whole lot of people that Eric Barron does like, and Parker isn't the kind of guy to be top of that list. They had a run-in a couple of years back. Parker was looking into the death of a woman, Rita Ferris. She'd been hooking on the side. After the case was closed, Barron saw Parker at Old Port Billiards and made some comments about the woman.'

'And?'

'Barron went to the men's room. Couple of minutes later Parker followed him in. Only Parker came out. Barron never spoke about what happened in there, but he's got a scar at the right side of his mouth' – Odell pointed with his finger to his own mouth – 'that maybe I wouldn't mention to him, you see what I mean?'

'People who mess with cops don't usually walk away from it so easily.'

'You see anyone rushing to defend Barron's honor?'

'I guess not. I hear Parker's been asking about cops.'

'Cops, rent-a-cops, private security. He's pissing off all the wrong people.'

'You know why?'

'Case a couple of months back. Someone tried to pull a boy from the street over in Gorham. Kid was huffing lighter fuel and was pretty much off his head to begin with, so he couldn't recall much, but he claimed the guy was wearing a uniform under his jacket, and he thought he could see a gun. His parents have money and they've hired Parker to ask some questions. They're afraid the guy might make a play again, either on their kid or someone else's.'

Barron returned from the men's room, and nodded a curt greeting to Odell.

'See you round, I guess,' Odell said to Macy. He nodded at Barron – 'Eric' – then went back to his buddies

'What did he want?' asked Barron.

'Nothing, just wanted to congratulate me on finishing my six.' She could sense Barron simmering beside her. He had a short fuse, and it seemed a good idea to try to stamp it out before the powder keg ignited.

'Tell me more about the island,' she said.

Barron told her that Dutch Island, or Sanctuary as it was sometimes known, was within the jurisdiction of the Portland Police Department, despite its status as the most remote of the inhabited islands on Casco Bay. Dutch wasn't the only island that required a police presence of this kind, but it was the least hospitable. Most Portland cops never had to spend time there. It had one resident policeman, and a couple of others who traveled out on a rotation system. On the other island policed by the Portland PD, Peaks Island, two officers headed out on a boat every day. But when the boat left for Dutch, there was often only one cop on board.

'Why has it got two names?'

'To make it sound interesting,' said Barron. 'But believe me, it isn't. What more do you want to know?'

'What's he like?' asked Macy.

'Who?'

'You know, Dupree. What's he like?'

Barron clicked his tongue in disgust. 'Melancholy Joe? He's a freak.'

'They say he's a giant. I mean, a real giant. Like in the circus, or like that wrestler guy, the one that died.'

'Andre the Giant. No, Joe ain't as big as Andre. Still a big son of a bitch, though. Strong, too. Nobody fucks with Melancholy Joe.'

'Why do they call him that?'

'Because he's a miserable bastard, that's why. Doesn't say much, keeps to himself. You better bring some books out to Dutch Island, because you sure ain't going to be kept up nights talking to Joe.'

'You spend time out there?'

'Just once, when flu took out half of the regular guys. Didn't care much for it. Didn't care much for Joe Dupree, either.'

I bet it was mutual, thought Macy.

'I suppose nothing much happens out there.'

'Not a whole lot. Bored kids stealing cars, breaking into summer houses. The occasional DUI. It's community policing, mainly.'

'But not always?'

'What do you know?' asked Barron.

'Someone said—'

'Who?'

'Just someone. He said Joe Dupree once killed a man out on the island.'

Barron made that clicking sound again. 'Yeah, he killed one of the Lubey brothers. Ronnie Lubey. If he'd been a little faster, then maybe his partner might not have taken a load of buckshot in the leg. Lubey was all liquored up, Dupree and Snowman arrived—'

'Snowman?'

'Yeah, dumb fucking name for a dumb guy. If he'd taken the buckshot in the head, it probably would have done him less damage. Anyway, Dupree and him arrive, Snowman gets shot, and Dupree kills Ronnie Lubey. He was taken off duty for a while, but the investigation cleared him. That's it. Nobody shed too many tears for old Ronnie. He was a bad one. His brother still lives out on Dutch. He hates Joe Dupree like wood hates fire.'

Barron paused. He felt dumb saying what he was about to say, as if Macy was going to laugh at him or call him a liar, but when he'd joined the force, his first partner, Tom Huyler, had sat him down over a beer and told him pretty much what he was

79

about to tell Macy, and old Huyler wasn't the type to joke around. He was Dutch Protestant, and when those people cracked a smile, it was like watching Arctic ice break, but Huyler knew his history. After all, they were some of his people who went out there in the beginning.

His people who were slaughtered.

Because, sure, Dutch Island was quiet, most of the time. There was the odd domestic dispute, the occasional drunk who tried to drive up a tree. But he recalled Huyler telling him the story of the first settlers on the island, how they'd retreated out there after skirmishes with the local Indians in the late 1600s.

Then, according to the history books, there was some internal dispute among the islanders, and somebody was banished. He came back, though, and he brought others with him. The entire population – ten, twelve families, all with children – was slaughtered. It was only in the last hundred, hundred and fifty years that people had started returning to Dutch in numbers, and now the community was large enough to need full-time cops out there.

And sometimes, people went missing. They were the bad ones, mostly. That was the odd thing about it. They were the ones who were no use to anybody, not even to their own families. They were the drunks, the abusers, the wife beaters. True, not all of them went that way, and Dutch still had its share of bad sorts, but they tended to be pretty careful about where they walked and what they did. They didn't stray too far from their homes and they stayed away from the woods at the center of the island, and far away from what was known as the Site, the burial place of the original settlers.

Huyler was dead now, died of a heart attack two years before, but Barron could still see him sitting there, a glass of beer in his hand, talking in those soft tones of his, the occasional strange intonation creeping into his speech, a relic of his family's heritage. Barron had never doubted a word that he had said, not even when he told him about his final tour on Dutch Island, and the death of George Sherrin. Because George Sherrin was the reason why Dutch's less salubrious residents didn't go walking in the woods at night anymore. Nobody wanted to go the way old George did, no sir.

There had always been talk about the Sherrins. Their kids were rebellious and educationally subnormal: real difficult types. Old Frank Dupree, Melancholy Joe's father, had been forced on more than one occasion to haul one or another of the Sherrin kids back to his old man and tell him how the kid had been caught breaking windows or tormenting some poor dumb animal, and the kid would be quiet as he was led back to the house, and old Frank would always feel a tug at his belly as the kid was led inside by George and the door closed silently behind them. Frank suspected that there was something going on there, something vile and rotten, but he could never convince Sherrin's mousy wife, Enid, to talk, and any social workers who ever went near the Sherrins risked getting a gun waved at them or had to run to escape the dogs barking at their heels.

And then, one day, George Sherrin went missing. He didn't come home from a trip out into the woods, his truck loaded up with a saw and chains so he could do a little illegal cutting and collect some cheap fuel for the winter. It was two days before his wife bothered to report it, and Frank Dupree figured that if she hadn't killed him herself, then maybe she was just relieved to have two days without his presence in the house, because if George Sherrin was doing bad things to his children, Frank didn't doubt that his wife knew about it, and that maybe she tried to get him to do bad things to her instead on occasion, just to give the kids a break.

So Frank Dupree and Tom Huyler had made their way into the woods, and after a few hours they'd found George Sherrin's truck, and beside it George's saw. There was a gash in a big pine tree nearby, where George had just started cutting, but then something seemed to have interrupted him, because he never got to finish his task. They had a good look around for George, but there was no trace of him. Later they came back with twenty islanders and they formed a chain through the forest and scoured the bushes and the trees, but George was gone. After a few days, they stopped looking. After a few weeks, they stopped caring. George's kids started getting on better in school and a social worker began calling to the house, and then a couple of times a month Enid Sherrin and the kids took the little ferry over to the mainland and got to talk things through with a doctor who had Crayolas in her drawer and a box of Kleenex on her desk.

One year later, a bad storm hit the coast, and Dutch, being right out there, took the brunt of it. There was thunder, and two trees were felled by lightning bolts, and under one of those trees they found George Sherrin. The pine had been torn partway out of the ground, but its fall was arrested by the surrounding trees so that its broad root structure gaped like a toothed mouth. In the hollow that it left in the ground George Sherrin's remains were discovered, and a murder investigation was initiated. There was no visible damage to his bones – no breaks, no fractures, no holes – but somebody must have put George Sherrin under that tree because he sure hadn't dug himself a hole beneath it and then covered himself up. They took Enid Sherrin in and quizzed her some, but she had her kids to back her up and they all told the same story. Their momma had been with them the whole time after their daddy disappeared. Who else was going to look after them?

There were more puzzles for the investigators to mull over. When the tree and the bones were analyzed, the results made no sense. The way the experts figured it, George Sherrin would have to have been buried under there for thirty years for the roots to grow through his bones the way they had, for they had curled around and through him as if holding him in place. But George Sherrin had been missing for only one year, and there was just no way to account for that degree of growth. No, there had to be some other explanation for the nature of the root spread.

Except nobody had ever come up with one.

'That's the story,' said Barron.

Macy looked at him closely to see if he was joking. He wasn't.

'You say other people have disappeared?'

'*I* don't say. The only one I've heard about is George Sherrin. I think the others are just attempts to add to the legend. You know, people leave the island for their own reasons and don't come back, and suddenly there's another name in the pot. But what I just told you about George Sherrin, well, that's real. You can put that in the bank and watch it draw interest.'

He knocked back his beer and raised his hand for another round. Instead, Macy pushed her untouched second beer in front of him.

'Take mine, I'm all done.'

'You're going? Hey, don't go. Stay a little longer.'

His hand reached for hers, but she went for her jacket instead, narrowly avoiding contact. She put it on and saw Barron's eyes following the zipper as she pulled it over her breasts.

'No, I got to go. I have things to do.'

'What things?' he said, and she could hear something in his tone, something that made her real glad that there were other people around them in the

bar, that they weren't sitting alone in a car somewhere or, worse, back at Barron's place. He'd asked
her back there that afternoon, suggesting they watch
a movie on cable, maybe get some Thai food. She'd
declined and they'd ended up here instead. Suddenly
it seemed to her like the wisest decision she'd made
in a very long time.

'Just things,' she said. 'Thanks for the beer and,
y'know, looking out for me during training.'

But Barron had left her and was now walking
toward the bar. He raised her untouched beer,
leaned over the counter, and poured it into the sink.
She shook her head, picked up her knapsack, and
left the bar.

Macy thought about all that she had been told
as she drove home, about Dupree and the island
and George Sherrin. She thought, too, about Barron,
and shuddered instinctively at the memory of his
touch. The weeks of training under Barron had been
difficult. At first it hadn't been so bad. Barron had
kept his distance and played everything by the book.
But gradually she became increasingly uneasy
around him, conscious always of how close he
would stand to her; of the relish with which he told
self-glorifying stories of inflicting violence on 'smart-
mouths' and 'punks'; and of the looks some of the
street kids would shoot him when he approached
them, like dogs that had been kicked once too often.
It was only in the final weeks that Barron had started
to put some tentative moves on her. He was careful,
aware of the potential for harassment complaints,

or of action by his superiors if they found out that he was even attempting to form a relationship with a probation cop in his charge, but the desire was there. Macy had felt it like a bad rash.

Macy knew that she was pretty, and that she possessed, superficially at least, a kind of vulnerability that drew a certain type of man to her. Scratch that: it drew a whole lot of different types to her, and she had learned to sidestep their attentions with a grace that would have befitted a ballerina. Barron was subtler than most, but it was perhaps that subtlety that was most off-putting. While most men made a frontal assault, Barron was the kind who crept up, like a sneak thief. They were the worst types and had to be watched most closely.

She thought too of an incident that had occurred the night before, one that still troubled her. Macy and Barron had been heading down Congress, doing their standard loop, when they saw him. The lights picked out a figure in a black Alpha Industries aviator's jacket, the hood of his gray jogging top hanging over the back of the jacket and a watch cap on his head. He took one look at the cruiser and started to walk briskly in the opposite direction.

'Will you look at this joker?' said Barron. He depressed the accelerator slightly, causing the patrol car to increase its speed to match the guy. Watch Cap looked over his shoulder, then ran.

'I mean, seriously,' Barron continued. He could have been talking about the return of flared pants or the revival of progressive rock for all the concern in his voice. 'Here's conclusive evidence that a whole lot of criminals are just plain dumb. If this guy could just have kept his head for ten seconds' – he swung the wheel to the right as the suspect made a turn onto Pine – 'then he would have been free and clear. Instead, he decides to outrun Miss Crown Vic here, and I'm telling you now, I don't think this is a healthy man. Look at the vapor trail he's leaving. It's like chasing a crop duster. Okay, screw this. Let's light him.'

Barron hit the gumballs and the siren, and put his foot down hard to the floor. Already, the guy was visibly wilting. When they swung into the parking lot behind him, he seemed almost grateful to be forced to stop. Barron stepped out from behind the wheel seconds later, and the two cops came at him in a narrowing V. The runner had his hands raised and was breathing like he was about to bust a gut. Barron seemed to do a double take when he got close enough to identify the man. It was hardly noticeable, but it was there.

'Hey,' said Barron. 'Terry Scarfe. Look, Macy, it's Terry Scarfe. How you doin', Terry? They let you out? The fuck were they thinking?'

'Maybe they took a vote,' said Macy. Scarfe's name had been on a circulated list of new parolees. According to the other cops, he was a well-known local lowlife. He was just over five feet tall and desperately thin. His face was heavily lined, despite his comparative youth, as though it still bore the imprint of the last foot that had stepped on it.

'Yeah, like a straw poll. You, Terry, are the weakest link. Now get the fuck out of our nice prison. You carrying, Terry?'

Scarfe shook his head.

'You sure now? Because I better not frisk you and find something that draws blood. I gotta say that if you think the airlines are kind of strict, then wait until you get a load of me. I find even a sharp fingernail clipping and I'm going to have you charged with carrying an offensive weapon. And that's in addition to you just being offensive, period. So let me ask you again, Terry? Anything in there we should know about? Sharps? Needles?'

Scarfe found his voice.

'I told you, I got nothing.'

'On the ground,' said Barron.

'Aw, come on, it's cold. I'm telling you—'

Barron moved in fast and shoved him to the ground. Scarfe landed hard on his knees and seemed about to protest, until Barron pushed him down fully and his chin impacted on the ground.

'You didn't have to do that,' Scarfe whined, while Barron patted him down.

'Get up,' Barron said when he was done.

Scarfe got to his feet and rubbed the dirt from his hands.

'Why did you run away from us?' asked Barron.

'I wasn't running away from you. I was running *to* someplace.'

'Someplace where?'

'Someplace else.'

'You want us to take you in? How long you been out on parole?'

'Since Monday.'

'*Monday?*' said Barron loudly. 'You mean you been out just a couple of days and already we've got you for fleeing and for failing to cooperate with your local friendly police department?'

'I told you, I wasn't fleeing. I'm a busy man. I got shit to do.'

'Is it the kind of shit you can do in jail?'

Scarfe looked at him in puzzlement. 'No.'

'Well, you seem in kind of a hurry to get back there. I just figured that maybe it was kind of non-specific shit. You know, independent of geography.'

Scarfe kept his mouth shut.

'You're an asshole, Terry,' said Barron, and his tone was more serious now. 'You're an asshole and you're going to get in some serious trouble again if you don't watch your step. Now get out of here.'

Macy looked at Barron incredulously. 'You're letting him walk?'

'What are we going to arrest him on? Dressing too young for his age?'

'He ran.'

'Yeah, but— Hey, are you still here?'

Scarfe had stopped, seemingly uncertain of what to do now that the two cops were arguing about him. 'I told you to go, so go, before I change my mind.'

Scarfe took one final look at Macy, shrugged, then walked briskly from the parking lot and faded into the night. The two cops faced each other.

'Come on, Macy,' said Barron. 'Don't do that shit.'

'What shit?'

'Criticizing me in front of a cockroach like Terry Scarfe.'

'He wasn't running for nothing. He's got something going on.'

'So, what were we supposed to do? Haul his ass in, then watch him sit on his hands for twelve hours until we get him to court? Maybe we get the right judge and his parole is revoked, and then what? So he serves another six months. Big fucking deal. Terry's more use to us out on the street now. He hears things, and maybe we can lean on him in the future. He owes us now. We got him over a barrel.'

Macy said nothing. They got back in the car and made their way back onto Congress.

'Come on, Macy,' Barron repeated. 'Let it go.'

But Macy remained uneasy for the rest of the shift, and she spoke little to Barron until they were on the steps of headquarters. There, Barron had reached out a hand and grasped her arm.

'Are we okay?' he asked, and Macy looked into his eyes and knew better than to disagree.

'Sure. I just don't have a good feeling about Scarfe. We should have brought him in.'

'He's dumb. If he is up to something, we'll spot it soon enough. At least if he goes down again, it will be for something more than time remaining.'

He gave Macy his best shit-eating grin, then headed toward the lockers. Macy watched him go, and wondered if she'd seen what she thought she'd seen: Barron frisking Scarfe, then palming the small bags of white powder that he'd found in the man's pocket. She said nothing about it to anybody. She didn't figure Barron for a user, and maybe he was holding on to the bags for future use, possibly as payment to snitch junkies, but that didn't sound right either. It simply wasn't worth the risk for Barron to carry drugs, no matter what the excuse.

Which left the possibility that Barron wanted to protect Scarfe. Once again, as she headed for home, Macy was glad that her time with Barron was now over, and despite his stories, she was curious about her upcoming island detail. Macy was not a credulous person, and while police work tended to encourage a certain amount of superstition – lucky shoes, lucky routes, lucky bullets – she was still a little surprised by what Barron had said, and more particularly by the sincerity with which he'd said it. Barron really believed everything he had told her about George Sherrin and Dutch Island, or at least had fewer doubts about it than he might otherwise have been expected to entertain. Still, he had pricked her curiosity, although that would be as close as Barron ever came to pricking anything of Sharon Macy's.

She was curious too about the policeman, the one Barron and the others called Melancholy Joe. His story was pretty well known in Portland: his father and grandfather had both served as police officers, doing the bulk of their time out on Dutch

Island. It was a peculiar arrangement, but it suited the department. They knew the island and its ways, and when police officers from outside the community had been tried on the island in the absence of a member of the Dupree family, the experiment had foundered. Crime – mundane crime, but crime nonetheless – had increased, and the nerves of the cops on temporary duty had become steadily more frayed. In the end, given that nobody particularly wanted to spend time out on Dutch anyway, the Dupree family had become the de facto first family of police work as far as Dutch Island was concerned.

But old Frank Dupree's marriage had produced only one son, and that son was big enough to have even other cops label him a freak. She heard that the cost of altering a police vehicle to suit his size had been met by the department. He carried the standard-issue Portland PD sidearm, the .45 Smith & Wesson, but he had adjusted the trigger guard in his own workshop so that one of his huge fingers could pass through it more easily. Occasionally, one of the local papers would do a story on 'The Giant of Dutch Island,' and during the summer, tourists would sometimes travel out there to catch a glimpse of him or to have their photographs taken alongside him. Joe didn't seem to mind; or if he did, it made no difference to his permanent expression of worried bafflement.

Melancholy Joe. Macy smiled and said the name aloud.

'Melancholy Joe.'

Her headlights caught the sign for the interstate, the wipers striking out at the first drops of rain, and she took the north ramp.

'Sanctuary,' she said, testing the name out. She decided she liked that name better than Dutch.

'Well, it's better than being on traffic duty.'

Moloch lay in silence upon his bunk. From a nearby television came the sound of a news bulletin. There was talk of war, the Middle East going up in flames. His fellow prisoners were filled with blood lust masquerading as patriotic fervor, despite the fact that most of them couldn't even find Nebraska on a map, let alone anywhere further afield. Moloch tuned out the background noise. It wasn't his concern. He had more pressing matters to consider.

His lawyer hadn't been able to tell him much about the grand jury hearing when they'd met ten days before across a bare steel table in the prison's visiting area. 'All I know is that they have a guy named Verso.'

Moloch's mouth twitched, but otherwise he gave no sign of his irritation. 'Is Verso the target of this grand jury?'

'I don't know.'

Moloch leaned in closer to the little man. 'Mr. Braden, why am I paying you if you know nothing?'

Braden didn't back off. He knew Moloch was merely venting steam. 'You finished?' he asked.

Moloch leaned back, then nodded.

'I'm guessing that Verso has spoken to them and offered them something in return for immunity from prosecution. Verso's a nasty piece of work, and you're already locked up for the foreseeable future, so it could be that the county prosecutor might like to see what you can offer them to put Verso away.'

'What do I get in return if I testify? A cell with a view?'

'You'll be due for parole in eight to ten. Testifying will help your case.'

'I don't plan to spend another decade in jail, Mr. Braden.'

Braden shrugged and leaned back. 'Your call. I'll be in the hallway during the proceedings. You can ask for time out as soon as you discover where their questions are leading. If in doubt, take the Fifth.'

Moloch looked down at the table before he spoke again. 'They have something,' he said. 'They don't want Verso, they want me. I'm the target.'

'You don't know that for sure,' said Braden.

'Yes,' said Moloch. 'I do.' He placed his hands together, palm against palm. 'I pay you well, Mr. Braden. You were engaged because you were smart, but don't believe for one moment that you're smarter than I am. I know where you live. I know your family's movements. I know the name of the boy that your daughter—'

'You better stop—'

'—that your daughter *fucks* in your basement while you're watching *The West Wing*. I know these things, Mr. Braden, and you, in turn, know me. I suspect that the commonwealth of Virginia has no intention of ever seeing me released. In fact, I believe that the commonwealth of Virginia has high hopes of executing me and freeing up my cell for someone else. They want capital charges. This grand jury hearing is a trap, nothing more.'

'I have no evidence—'

'I don't care about evidence. Tell me your instincts, your gut instincts. Tell me I'm wrong.'

But Braden said nothing.

'So there's been talk.'

'Rumors, suspicions,' Braden said. 'Nothing more.'

'That Verso is not the target.'

'That Verso is not the target,' Braden echoed.

'Have you spoken to the prosecutor?'

'He wouldn't agree to a meeting.'

'If Verso was the target, he would have met with you. You could have negotiated immunity from prosecution for me. You better believe that any true bill that comes out of this will have my name on it.'

Braden spread his hands. 'I'm doing what I can.'

Moloch wondered if Braden might be secretly happy were he to be found guilty of capital crimes. He shouldn't have threatened the lawyer. The man was frightened enough of him already.

Moloch leaned in closer to his counsel. 'Listen to me, Mr. Braden. I want you to remember a telephone number. Don't write it down, just remember it.'

Carefully and clearly, Moloch whispered the seven digits to the younger man.

'When the details of the hearing are confirmed, I want you to call that number and pass them on. Do not call from your office. Do not call from your home. Do not use your cell phone. If you're wise, you'll take a day trip, maybe into Maryland, and you will make the call from there. Am I clear?'

'Yes.'

'You do this right and you'll be free of me.'

Braden rose and knocked on the door of the meeting room.

'Guard,' he called, 'we're all done here.'

He left without looking back at his client.

Now the preparations were in place. Moloch had received a message, passed in code during an apparently innocuous telephone conversation. They were moving. Progress was being made. All would be in place when the time came.

He closed his eyes and thought of war.

The gray-haired man sat in the Rue de la Course on North Peter, sipping coffee and reading the local throwaway. Groups of young men passed by the windows of the coffeehouse, heading for the depths of the French Quarter. He could hear a thumping bass beat coming from the Coyote Ugly bar next door, battling against the light jazz being played on the sound system behind his head. He liked the Rue de la Course, preferring it to the Café du Monde, where, earlier, he had eaten beignets and listened to the street musicians trying to hustle a buck. At the Café du Monde, coffee came either black or au lait, and the gray-haired man didn't care much for it either way. He liked it black, but with a little cold milk on the side. The Asian waitress at the Café du Monde wasn't prepared to accommodate him, so he had been forced to take his business elsewhere. The Rue de la Course had been a fortuitous discovery. In a way, it had been recommended to him by somebody else.

The Rue de la Course had ceiling fans and walls of what looked like beaten tin, and the tables were lit by green-shaded banker's lamps. He was surprised that it was still a coffeehouse, what with the money that could be made by turning it into a bar. Maybe it had been a bar once, as white lettering on the door still indicated that it sold beer and wine, although the blackboard behind the counter listed only about forty different types of coffee and tea, all iced this and mocha that. The gray-haired man, whose name was Shepherd, preferred his coffee the old way, with the minimum of milk and fuss. It didn't bother him that he couldn't get a drink here. Shepherd wasn't much of a drinker. He hated the way that it made fools out of men and women. In fact, Shepherd had few, if any, vices. He didn't smoke, didn't use drugs, and his sex drive was virtually nil. He wasn't interested in women or men, although he'd tried both just to be sure that he wasn't missing something. Like his aversion toward alcohol, it helped to keep his mind clear.

And so he sat sipping coffee from a mug decorated with the image of a man in a raincoat reading a newspaper at a table, which was very apt, for Shepherd too was wearing a raincoat and sitting at a table reading a newspaper. Circles within circles. Two tables away from him, a young woman wearing green hospital scrubs sat taking notes from a textbook. She seemed to feel his eyes upon her, for she looked up. He smiled casually at her, then went back to the newspaper.

Shepherd didn't like New Orleans. It was a third-world city in a first-world country, so in thrall to graft that it had come to regard corruption as the norm rather than as an aberration. When he walked its streets, all he saw was ugliness, the baseness of the human condition unashamedly revealed. From a seat in the Magnolia Café, he had watched a hard-faced man stand at the doorway of a glorified titty bar, a huge woman with an even harder face standing behind him, rolls of fat dripping over dirty white lingerie. Why would anyone go into such a place, Shepherd wondered: to be ripped off, maybe to be threatened, to smell the cheap scent on a woman one step above whoredom? Such corruption of the spirit and of the soul repelled him, but at least it was obvious, unhidden. There were other forms of corruption that were far more insidious.

The woman in the green scrubs stood, placed her textbook and notebook in a satchel, and left the coffeehouse. After a minute or two had passed, Shepherd also left. He stayed some way behind her, shadowing her from across the street as she headed up Decatur. He did not panic when he lost sight of her among the crowds, for he knew where she was going. To his left, starlings moved in great shrieking circles, hovering above an old chimney stack on Chartres. Above them, the January sky was gray and cheerless. Tourists watched the birds in momentary curiosity, then moved on, somehow unnerved by the sight. Slowly, the birds' numbers depleted as they found their roosts inside the chimney, black shapes descending into a deeper darkness.

By the time he reached the top of Decatur, the woman was nowhere to be seen. He waited ten minutes, then walked to the security gates of a renovated condo and pressed the number nine, followed by the pound key. There was a click, and then a female voice said, 'Who is it?'

'My name is Jeff. I called earlier to make an appointment.' He'd found her ad offering a 'sensual massage' the day before, and had called to arrange a visit.

'Come on up,' she said. The gate buzzed and he entered the yard, following the interior lights to a stairway. He climbed three flights and stopped before the door to number nine. He was about to knock when the door opened.

She had changed out of her scrubs and now wore a satin robe. The ends of her hair were still wet from the shower. She looked a little puzzled as she struggled to remember his face.

'You were in—,' she began, then found

Shepherd's gloved hand clasped firmly around her throat as she was forced into the apartment. Shepherd closed the door silently behind him. He pushed her against the wall and removed his right hand from the pocket of his raincoat so that she could see the knife.

'If you scream, I will hurt you,' he said. 'I don't want to hurt you. If you answer my questions, I promise you that you will not be hurt. Do you understand me?'

She nodded and he released his grip.

'Sit down.'

He followed her into her living room. The drapes were drawn and a single lamp, overhung with a red scarf, was the sole illumination in the room. A door to his right stood open. Inside he could see a massage table covered with a clean white towel.

'I'm sorry to have misled you,' said Shepherd. He stood slightly to one side of her, his left leg slightly forward to protect his groin. He had encountered trouble with women before.

She seemed on the verge of tears. He could hear them in her voice as she asked: 'What do you want?'

Shepherd nodded in satisfaction. 'Good. I don't want to take up any more of your time than I have to. I'd like to know where your boyfriend is.'

She didn't reply.

'Your boyfriend,' he repeated. 'Verso. Or have you forgotten him already?'

'I haven't heard from him.'

Shepherd sighed. His hand moved in a blur of

flesh and metal, drawing a red line from her left shoulder to the top of her right breast. She started to yelp and he covered her mouth with his hand.

'I told you,' he said. 'I don't want to hurt you, but I will if you make me. I will ask you again: where is he?'

'The police have him.'

'The police *where*?'

'In Virginia.'

'Where in Virginia?'

'I don't know.'

Shepherd raised the blade again and she said, louder this time: '*I don't know*. They keep moving him. He's not my boyfriend anymore. I haven't seen him since he turned himself in. All I know is that he's going to be in Norfolk soon. There's a grand jury hearing. He's going to testify.'

'When was the last time that he called?'

She was silent for a time.

'There's a limit to my patience,' he warned her.

'This morning,' she said at last.

'Before or after I called?'

'After. I was just on my way out the door when the phone rang.'

The phone lay on a table to Shepherd's left. There was an answering machine hooked up to it, but it was turned off.

'Why is your machine off?'

'I was going to go out tonight, catch a movie. You were my only appointment.'

'Stand up,' said Shepherd.

She did as she was told. He walked her to the phone table, then told her to kneel, facing away from him.

'Please!' she said.

'Just kneel. I want to star sixty-nine your phone, and I don't want you doing anything stupid while I dial.'

Reluctantly, she knelt. Shepherd pressed the buttons, then listened.

'Chesapeake Inn and Suites,' said a male voice. Shepherd hung up.

Asshole, he thought.

He stepped back from the kneeling woman. She didn't turn around.

'Please,' she said. 'Don't hurt me anymore.'

'I won't,' said Shepherd.

He was a man of his word. She didn't feel a thing.

Harry Rylance had never thought of himself as the nervous type. Nobody ever made a good living out of the insurance business by being nervous. Nervousness was for the suckers who bought the policies. The whole business was predicated on fear. Without it, the insurance industry would sink like a stone and Harry would sink along with it, but Harry had to admit that he was feeling pretty damn nervous now. The creepy retard kid had disappeared and Harry's instinct was to get the hell out of the house and hope that he and Veronica could find their own route back to the highway.

Except the house smelled of dead meat, and there were flies buzzing.

And curiosity was a terrible thing.

Harry padded softly across the floor of the living room, wincing every time a board creaked. In the kitchen, he found a pile of take-out chicken buckets littered with the stripped bones of those midget chickens that the fast food companies raised on some irradiated Pacific atoll; no other way, thought Harry, that you got legs and wings that small. A frying pan stood on the range, pieces of burnt fat adhering to its base, and bugs floated on the surface of the foul-smelling stew that sat in a pot beside it. There was an ancient refrigerator beside the stove, humming and rattling like a crazy old man in a tin cage. Harry reached out to open it, then paused. He could see himself reflected in the metal, his features distorted. Something white was behind him.

Harry spun around and lashed out at the drapes that hung unmoving over the window in the still air. A plate fell from the draining board and shattered on the floor, sending ants scurrying in confusion. Somewhere, a roach clicked.

'Shit,' said Harry, and opened the fridge door.

Apart from a carton of week-old milk, it was empty.

In the freezer compartment, Harry found meat packed in bags. There was a lot of it.

He closed the fridge doors, then went back into the living room. No sounds came from upstairs.

'Hello?' called Harry. 'Kid, you okay up there?'

He began to climb and, for the first time, he heard it: two words of a song, repeated over and over again, the needle caught in the groove of the record.

—*don't care*

—*don't care*

—*don't care*

Elvis, thought Harry. The King don't care.

He reached the top of the steps. There was a bedroom before him, but it was empty, the sheets on the bed thrown back where its occupant had departed from it, leaving it unmade. Beside it was a bathroom, judging by the tiles on the floor, but it stank so bad that Harry's eyes began to water. The door was almost closed. Harry nudged it with his foot, and it opened slowly.

There was a man sitting on the toilet. His pants were around his ankles, and a newspaper dangled from his hand. Instinctively, Harry started to apologize.

'Shit, so—'

Harry stepped back and covered his mouth with his hand, but it was too late. He felt the fluid on his fingers, then bent down to finish puking.

The guy on the john had been shot where he sat, a bloody cloud behind what remained of his head. There wasn't much of his face left either, but Harry figured from his stringy legs, his gray hair and sagging flesh, that the guy was well into his seventies. His white T-shirt was sweat-stained yellow in places, and blood had soaked into the shoulders, leaving stains like epaulettes. His skin was split by gas blisters.

Harry wanted to run, but there was still the sound of Elvis coming from what was probably a bedroom at the end of the hall. He walked slowly to the door and looked inside.

The couple in the bedroom were younger than the old man in the can, much younger. Harry figured them for their late twenties at most. The man had been shot on the floor and lay naked by an open drawer, its contents littering the floor. A box of ammunition had fallen and scattered around him, but there was no gun. There was a bullet hole in his back, barely recognizable amid the damage that had been done to his body. Harry retched, but he had nothing left inside and so he just belched acidic gas.

The woman had dark hair and sat slumped sideways against the pillows and the headboard. She too was naked. The sheets had been pulled away from her body and she'd been cut up pretty bad as well. Despite himself, Harry stepped closer, and something registered in his head. This wasn't a frenzy, thought Harry. No, there was purpose to these wounds. There was—

'Jesus,' whispered Harry.

She had chunks of flesh missing from her thighs and buttocks, where someone had hacked them out. There was flesh missing from the man as well: less flesh, admittedly, but then he was scrawny and muscular, a little like the old man in the john.

A mental image flashed in Harry's mind: the refrigerator, empty but for a carton of sour milk.

And meat. Fresh meat.

Harry ran.

He hit the stairs at speed, taking the steps two at a time. The front door was still open and he could see Veronica sitting behind the wheel, her fingers tapping an impatient cadence on the dashboard. Her eyes widened as she saw him emerge.

'Open the door,' shouted Harry. 'Quickly!'

She reached for the driver's door, still staring at him while her fingers fumbled for the handle. Then she was no longer looking at him but beyond and behind him. Harry heard her scream his name before the world spun around in a circle, and Harry found himself looking first at the car from a sideways angle, then at the ground, then the sky and the house and the grass, all tumbling in a crazy mixture of images that seemed to go on forever but in fact lasted barely a second.

And Harry couldn't understand why, even as he died and his severed head bounced to a halt by the porch steps.

And out on Dutch Island, the man known to some as Melancholy Joe Dupree lay on his bed and watched the rain fall, harder and harder, until at last his view through the window was entirely obscured. His bones, his teeth, his joints, they all ached, as if the effort of supporting his great bulk were slowly becoming too much for them. Joe moaned and buried his face in his pillow, tears forcing themselves from the corners of his eyes.

Make it stop, he begged. Please make it stop.

A face appeared in the darkness beyond his window: a boy's face, the skin blue-gray, the eyes dark. The boy reached out as if to touch the glass, but made no contact. Instead, he watched the man in uniform curl in upon himself on the huge bed, until at last the pain began to ease and Joe Dupree fell into a troubled sleep, tormented by the sound of whispering, by gray figures and tunnels beneath the earth, and by a boy with tainted skin who gazed upon him as he slept.

The Second Day

Not a shred in the papers,
Becoming all too clear
Not a one cares that she got away.

Now the fear of being found
A little less profound
On a face that's never been
Fit to laugh.

Pinetop Seven, 'The Fear of Being Found'

3

Know me, wife.

The dream ended, and now Moloch's features fell before him like rain. It was as though a great many photographs had been taken and shredded, the figures caught in the different frames intermingled, smiling familiarly while glancing against strangers; yet in this downpour of images, this torrent of memories, he was ever the same. There he sat, beside parents unknown, amid siblings now lost and gone. He ran as a boy across sand and through sea; he held a fish on the end of a hook; he cried beside an open fire. This was his history, his past, yet it seemed to encompass not one life but many lives. Some images were sharper than others, some recollections more acute, but they were all linked to him, all part of the great chain of his existence. He was color, and he was sepia. He was black, and he was white. He was of this time, and he was of no time.

Moloch awoke, aware that he was being watched. His ear felt raw where it had been touching the rough, cheap material, the pillow once again drenched with his sweat. He thought that he could smell the woman against his face, could touch her skin, could feel the blade tearing through her flesh. He stirred on his bunk but did not rise. Instead, he tried to identify the man watching him through his smell, his breathing, the soft jangle of the equipment on his belt. Images from the dream still ran through his mind, and he was suddenly aware of how aroused he had become, but he forced himself to concentrate on the figure at the other side of the bars. It was good practice. His incarceration had taken the edge off his abilities in so many ways that he welcomed any opportunity to hone them once more. That was the worst of his imprisonment: the monotony, the terrible similarity of each day to the next, so that every man became a seer, a fortune-teller, capable of predicting the wheres and whens of each hour to come, his precise location at any given time, the irrevocable nature of it all threatened only by the occasional outbreaks of sickness and violence.

Every day the wake-up call came at 6 A.M., heralded by horns and coughing and the flushing of toilets. Two hours later the doors opened and each man stepped outside onto the cold concrete to await the first count of the day. No words were permitted to be exchanged during any of the day's six counts. The shower followed (for Moloch took every opportunity offered to clean himself, viewing any lapse in hygiene as the precursor to a greater collapse), and then breakfast, always taken seated in the same plastic chair, the food seemingly designed solely to provide energy without nutrition.

Then Moloch would take himself to the laundry for his day's work, socializing little with the other men. The noon count came next, then lunch, then more work, followed by an hour in the yard, then dinner, another count, and a retreat to his cell to read, to think. Eight count, then lights out at ten. In the first weeks, Moloch would wake for the late counts, at midnight and four, but no longer. He had received no visitors, apart from his lawyer, for over three years. He made few phone calls and fewer friends. A waiting game was under way and he was prepared to play his part.

Now the game was coming to an end.

Moloch shifted on his mattress, his body once again under his control. Eyes closed, he concentrated on smell and hearing.

Aftershave. Hints of sandalwood.

A small rattle in the throat as the man breathed out. Congestion.

Digestive noises. Coffee on an empty stomach.

Reid.

'Wake up, now,' Reid's voice said. 'It's your big day.'

Moloch lifted his head and saw the thin man standing at the bars, the brim of his hat perfectly level against his forehead, the creases on his uniform like blades set beneath the cloth. Reid looked away and called for 713 to be opened. Moloch remained where he was for a moment or two more, breathing deeply, then rose from his bunk and ran his hands through his hair.

Moloch knew the date. Some inmates lost track of the days while in jail. Many did so deliberately, for there was nothing guaranteed to break the spirit of a man facing twenty years faster than an urge to count the days until his release. Days in prison passed slowly: they were beads on a long thread, an endless rosary of unanswered prayers.

Moloch was different. He counted the days, kept track of hours, minutes, even seconds when the urge took him. Every moment spent inside was an injury inflicted upon him, and when the time came to return those insults to his person he wanted to be sure that he did not miss a single one. His count had reached 1245 days, seven hours and – he glanced at his watch – three minutes spent in the Dismal Creek State Penitentiary, Virginia. His only regret was that the one on whom he desired to revenge himself would not live long enough to enable him to vent his rage to its ultimate degree.

'Stand straight, arms out.'

He did as he was told. Two guards entered, chains dangling from the arms of one. They secured his arms and his feet, the restraints attached in turn to a chain around his chest.

'Don't I even get to brush my teeth?' he asked.

The guard's face was expressionless.

'Why? You ain't going on no date.'

'You don't know that. I might get lucky.'

Reid seemed almost amused.

'I don't think so. You ain't got lucky by now, you ain't never gonna get lucky.'

'Man's luck can always change.'

'I never took you for no optimist.'

'You don't know me.'

'I know enough about you to say that you're gonna die wearing them prison weeds.'

'Are you my judge and jury?'

'No, but come the time, I'll be your executioner.'

He stood aside as the guards brought Moloch out.

'Be seeing you, Mr Reid.'

The older man nodded.

'That's right. Fact is, I aim to be the last thing you see.'

There was a black Toyota Land Cruiser waiting for him in the prison yard. Standing beside it were two armed investigators from the district attorney's office. Moloch nodded a good morning to them, but they didn't respond. Instead, they watched as he was chained to the D ring on the floor of the SUV, then tested the chains and the restraints until they were satisfied that he was fully secured. A wire mesh screen separated the backseat passenger from those in the front. There were no handles on the inside of the rear doors, and a second wire screen ran from the roof of the Cruiser to the floor of the trunk behind Moloch.

The door slammed shut noisily.

'You take good care of him now,' said one of the guards. 'Wouldn't want him getting bruised or nothing.'

'We'll look after him,' said one of the investigators, a tall black man named Misters. His partner, Torres, closed the door on Moloch, then climbed into the driver's seat.

'Settle back,' he said to Moloch. 'You got a long ride ahead of you.'

But Moloch was silent now, content, it seemed, to enjoy a brief taste of life outside the prison walls.

Dupree was sipping coffee in the station house. It was technically his day off, but he was passing and . . .

Well, that was just an excuse. He couldn't stay away from the place. Most of the other cops knew that, and they didn't mind.

'Doug Newton,' he said. He was sipping coffee from the market and eating one of the doughnuts that he had bought for the two cops on duty.

Across from him, Ron Berman was tapping a pencil on the desk, alternating each tap between the tip and the eraser end. Dupree found it mildly annoying but decided to say nothing. He liked Berman, and given that some of the other cops had far more irritating habits than tapping a pencil on the desk (for example, Dupree wondered if Phil Tuttle, Berman's partner on this roster, had ever washed his hands after taking a leak), he was happy enough to let Berman and his pencil be, for the present.

'Doug Newton,' echoed Berman. 'I took the call and put it in the log, but frankly, we both had other things to do, and it's not like it's the first time he's made that kind of claim.'

Dupree reached over and took the log from Berman. There it was, in Berman's neat hand. At 7.30 A.M., just as soon as Berman and Tuttle had settled in, and while it was still dark on the streets, Doug Newton had called in a report of a little girl in a gray dress tormenting his dying mother.

Again.

'You went out there last time, right?' asked Berman.

'Yeah, I went out. We organized a search. I even checked with Portland and with the state police to see if they'd had any reports of missing girls matching the description Newton gave me. There was nothing.'

The first time, Tuttle had answered the call from the Newton place and, having kind of a short fuse, had warned Doug about wasting police time. Now, just this morning, Doug Newton had called in a third report, except this one was different.

This time, he claimed the little girl had tried to climb through the window of his mother's bedroom. Doug had heard the old woman's screams, and had come running just in time to see the little girl disappearing into the trees.

Or so he said.

'You think he's going crazy?' asked Berman.

'He lives with his mother and has never married,' replied Dupree.

'Maybe he just needs to get laid.'

'I never took you for a therapist.'

'I'm multiskilled.'

'You think you could multiskill that pencil back into your drawer? It's like listening to the world's worst drummer.'

'Sorry,' said Berman. He put the pencil into the drawer, then closed it just in case the temptation to retrieve it proved too great.

'I guess Doug's maybe a little odd, but I've never taken him for crazy,' said Dupree. 'He doesn't have the imagination to make stuff up. He's only ever been to two states in his life, and I reckon he's not sure the other forty-eight exist, seeing as how he's never visited them himself. So either he's going crazy or a little girl in a gray dress really did try to get into his mother's bedroom last night.'

Berman thought about this.

'So he's crazy, then?'

Dupree tossed the log back at him.

'Apparently he's mad as a coot. I'll go have a talk with him today. Last thing we need is Doug taking potshots at Girl Scouts selling cookies. Anything else on your mind?'

Berman looked troubled.

'I think Nancy Tooker, down at the diner, may have a thing for me. She gave me extra bacon yesterday. For free.'

'There's a shortage of eligible men on the island. She's a desperate woman.'

'She's a *big* woman.'

'And she's kind of old.'

'She's *seriously* old, and she's got those, y'know, folds of skin hanging from her upper arms.'

'Bingo wings.'

'What?'

'That's what they call them: bingo wings.'

'Jesus, they have a name for things like that? That's scary. You think it would make a difference if I told her I was married?'

'You're not married.'

'I know, but I could get married. It would be worth it to keep her away.'

'My advice is, don't take anything else from her for free. Tell her it's against department policy. Otherwise, you're going to end up paying for that bacon in kind.'

Berman looked like he was about to upchuck his breakfast. 'Stop, don't even say things like that.' Nevertheless, it struck him that Dupree was in surprisingly good humor this morning. Berman guessed that it might not be unconnected to Dupree's slow courtship of the Elliot woman, but he said nothing.

Dupree made a wobbling gesture at his triceps. 'Bingo wings,' he said. 'Great big bingo wings enfolding you as you lie in Nancy Tooker's arms, her naked—'

Berman unclipped his holster.

'Don't make me shoot you,' he said.

'Save the last bullet for yourself,' said Dupree as he headed out. 'It may be your only hope of escape.'

Far to the south, close to the town of Great Bridge,

Virginia, a man named Braun walked back to his car, carrying two cups of coffee on a cardboard tray, packets of sugar poking out of his breast pocket. He crossed the street, slipped into the passenger seat, and handed one of the coffee cups to his companion, whose name was Dexter. Dexter was black, and kind of ugly. Braun was redheaded, but handsome despite it. He had heard all the redhead jokes. In fact, he'd heard most of them from Dexter.

'Careful,' he said, 'it's hot.'

Dexter looked at the plain white cup in distaste.

'You couldn't find a Starbucks?'

'They don't have a Starbucks here.'

'You're kidding me. There's a Starbucks everywhere.'

'Not here.'

'Shit.'

Dexter sipped the coffee.

'It's not bad, but it's no Starbucks.'

'It's better than Starbucks, you ask me. Least it tastes like coffee.'

'Yeah, but that's the thing about Starbucks. It's coffee, but it doesn't taste like coffee. It's not *supposed* to taste like coffee. It's supposed to taste like Starbucks.'

'But not coffee?'

'No, not coffee. Coffee you can get anywhere. Starbucks you can only get in Starbucks.'

Braun's cell phone buzzed. He picked it up and hit the green button.

'Yeah,' he said. He listened for a time, said, 'Okay,' then hung up.

'We're all set,' he told Dexter, but Dexter wasn't paying attention to him.

'Look at that,' said Dexter, indicating with his chin.

Braun followed the direction of the other man's gaze. On a corner, a small black kid who might have been in his early teens but looked younger had just exchanged a dime spot with an older kid.

'He looks young,' said Braun.

'You get up close to him, see his eyes, he won't seem so young. Street's already worn him down. It's eating him up from the inside.'

Braun nodded, but said nothing.

'That could have been me,' said Dexter. 'Maybe.'

'You sell that shit?'

'Something like it.'

'How'd you get out?'

Dexter shook his head, his eyes losing their glare just momentarily. He saw himself in his brand-new Levi's – Levi's then, not those saggy-ass, no-rep jeans that the younger kids wore now, all straps and white stitching – walking across the basketball court, glass crunching beneath the soles of his sneakers. Ex was sitting on a bench, alone, his feet on the seat, his back against the wire of the court, a newspaper in his hands.

'Hey, little man.'

Ex, short for Exorcist, because he loved that movie. Twenty-one, and so secure in himself that he could sit alone on a fall day, reading a newspaper as if he didn't have a care in the world.

'What you want?'

He was smiling, pretending that he was Dexter's best buddy, that he hadn't crippled a twelve-year-old the week before for coming up short, the kid wailing and crying as Ex knelt on his chest and put the gun barrel against the kid's ankle, that same smile on his face as he pulled the trigger.

The kid's street name was Blade, on account of his father being called Gillette. It was a good name. Dexter liked it, liked Blade too. They used to look out for each other. Now there was nobody to look out for Dexter, but he would continue to look out for Blade, as best he could.

Ex's smile was still in place, but any residual warmth it might once have contained had begun to die from the eyes down.

'I said, "Hey, little man." You got nothing to say back to me?'

Dexter, thirteen years old, looked up at Ex and removed his gloved hands from the pockets of his Lakers jacket. He was unused to the weight of the gun, and he needed both hands to raise it.

Ex stared down the stubby barrel of the Bryco. He opened his mouth to say something, but it was lost in the roar of the gun. Ex toppled backward, his head striking the wire fence of the court as he fell and landed in a heap on the ground, his legs splayed against the back of the bench. Dexter looked down on him. The bullet had hit Ex in the chest, and he was bleeding from the mouth.

'Hey,' he whispered. He looked hurt, as if the

young boy had just called him a bad name. 'Hey, little man.'

Dexter tossed the Bryco over the fence and walked away.

'Dexter? You okay?'

Braun nudged Dexter's arm with an elbow.

'Yeah, I'm here. I'm here, man.'

'We got to go.'

'Yeah, we got to go.'

He took one last look at the kid on the corner – *Hey, little man* – then started the car and pulled away.

By coincidence, some twenty miles to the north, two men with a similar racial profile were also drinking coffee, except they had found a Starbucks and were drinking Grande Americanos from big Starbucks mugs. One of them was Shepherd, the gray-haired man of few vices. His companion was named Tell. He wore his hair in cornrows, like the basketball player Allen Iverson used to, and probably for the same reason: because it made white folks uneasy. Tell was reading a newspaper. Tell was very conscientious about reading the newspaper every day. Unfortunately, that newspaper happened to be a day-old tabloid, and in Shepherd's opinion, Tell could have been reading the back of a cornflakes box and been better informed. Tabloids weren't big on analysis, and Shepherd liked to think of himself as an analytical kind of guy.

Two seats down from them, in the otherwise

deserted coffee shop, an Arab was talking loudly on his cell phone, tapping his finger on the table before him to emphasize his points. In fact, he was talking so loudly that Shepherd wasn't even certain that his phone was turned on. The guy behaved like he was trying to *shout* his message all the way to the Middle East, and was holding the cell phone only out of habit. He'd been talking like this for the best part of ten minutes, and Shepherd could see that Tell was getting pissed. He'd watched him start the same story about sex and the music business three times already, which was once more than Tell usually needed to take in what he was reading. Truth be told, Shepherd was kind of unhappy about it himself. He didn't like cell phones. People were rude enough as it was without having another excuse to be bad-mannered.

Tell looked up. 'Hey, man,' he said to the Arab. 'Can you keep it down?'

The Arab ignored him. This led Shepherd to suspect that the Arab was either very arrogant or very dumb, because Tell didn't look even remotely like the kind of person you ignored. Tell looked like the kind of person who would remove your spine if you ignored him.

Tell's face wore a puzzled expression as he leaned in closer to the Arab.

'I said, can you talk a little quieter, please? I'm trying to read my newspaper.'

Shepherd thought Tell was being very polite. It made him nervous.

'Go fuck yourself,' said the Arab.

Tell blinked, then folded his newspaper. Shepherd reached an arm across, holding his friend back.

'Don't,' he said. Over at the counter, one of the staff was watching them with interest.

'You hear what that raghead motherfucker said?'

'I heard. Forget it.'

The Arab continued talking, even after he finished his coffee with a slurp. Tell stood, and Shepherd followed, blocking his partner's access to the Arab. Tell bobbed on the balls of his feet for a second or two, then turned and walked out.

'Show's over,' said Shepherd to the barista.

'I guess.' He sounded a little disappointed.

Tell was already waiting in the van across the street, his fingers tapping a rhythm on the steering wheel. Shepherd got in beside him.

'We going? You know, we got a schedule to keep.'

'No, we ain't going yet.'

'Fine.'

They waited. Ten minutes later, the Arab emerged. He was still talking on his phone. He climbed into a black SUV, did a U-turn, and headed north.

'I hate SUVs,' said Tell. 'They're a top-heavy cab on a pickup's chassis, they drive like shit, they're dangerous, and they're ecologically unsound.'

Shepherd just sighed.

Tell started the van and began following the SUV. They stayed with the Arab until he turned into an alleyway at the side of a trendy Middle Eastern restaurant. Tell parked, then opened the driver's door and headed toward the alleyway. Shepherd followed.

'Hey, Saddam.'

The Arab turned to see Tell bearing down on him. He tried to hit the alarm button on his car keys, but Tell wrenched them from his hands before he got the chance. He hurled the keys to the ground, tore the Arab's cell phone from his left hand, and threw it after the keys. Finally, he dragged the Arab around the back of the building, so that they were hidden from the pedestrians on the sidewalk.

'You remember me?' he said. He pushed the Arab against the wall. 'I'm Mr. Go-Fuck-Myself. The fuck do you get off talking to me like that? I was polite to you, you fuck. I asked you nice, and what do you do? You disrespect me, you SUV-driving motherfucker.'

He slapped the Arab hard across the face. The Arab's face contorted with fear. He was fat, with chubby fingers overloaded with gold rings. He was no match for Tell.

'I'm sorry.'

'No, you ain't sorry,' said Tell. 'You're scared, and that ain't the same thing. I didn't come down here after you, you wouldn't have given me a second thought, and next time you was in Starbucks you'd have shouted your damn head off all over again, disturbing people and giving them a pain in the ass.'

He punched the Arab in the nose and felt it break beneath his fist. The Arab curled up, cupping his damaged nose in his hands.

'So don't tell me you're sorry. Look at you. My people came over here in chains. I bet you flew your ass over here business class.'

He hit the Arab hard across the head with the palm of his hand.

'Don't ever let me see you talking on that phone again, motherfucker. You get one warning, and this is it.'

He began to walk away. Behind him, the Arab leaned against the wall, examined the blood on his fingers, then bent down to retrieve his possessions: his car keys first, then his cell phone. The cell phone made a scraping noise against the concrete as he gathered it up.

Tell stopped. He looked back at the Arab.

'You dumb fuck,' he said.

He walked back, drawing his gun from beneath his jacket. The Arab's eyes widened. Tell kicked him hard in the belly and he fell to the ground. While Shepherd watched, he placed the gun against the Arab's head and pulled the trigger. The Arab spasmed, and then his fingers slowly released their grip on the phone.

'I warned you,' said Tell. 'I did warn you.'

He put the gun back in his belt and rejoined Shepherd. Shepherd cast a last glance back at the dead Arab, then fell into step beside Tell. He looked at his partner in puzzlement.

'I thought your people were from Albany,' he said.

Leonie and Powell sat in silence outside the courthouse, watching as Moloch was led in by the two investigators from the D.A.'s office. Leonie wore her hair in an Afro and looked, to Powell, a little like one of those kick-ass niggers from the seventies, Cleopatra Jones and Foxy Brown. Not that Powell would ever have called Leonie a nigger to her face, or even a dyke, although as far as Powell was concerned, she was both. He didn't doubt for one moment that Leonie would kill him if he uttered either of those words in her presence, and if, by some miracle, he did manage to avoid being killed (and the only way that he could see that happening was if he managed to kill her first), then Dexter would come after him and finish the job. Dexter and Leonie were like brother and sister. Braun seemed to get on okay with her too. Powell wasn't going to screw around with Dexter and Braun, didn't matter how many funny stories Braun told, or how much high-fiving and smiling Dexter fitted into a day.

Powell leaned back in his seat and ran his fingers through his long hair, losing them in the curls at the back. Powell was the kind of guy who would say 'nice mullet' and mean it. His hairstyle was trailer trash crossed with eighties glam metal, and he loved it. His face was unnaturally tanned, and his teeth were bleached so white that they glowed at night. Powell had B-movie star looks, the artificial kind that oozed insincerity. He had even gotten some professional shots taken five or six years back. A couple of newspapers had used them during coverage of his trial. Powell had been secretly pleased, although no offers of acting work had followed his eventual release.

'It's hot,' said Powell.

Leonie said nothing.

He looked over at her, but her eyes were fixed on the courthouse. He knew Leonie hated his guts, but that was kind of why he was with her. He was with Leonie and Tell was with Shepherd because he and Tell were the new guys and they had to be watched closely. It was good practice, nothing more, and Powell didn't resent it. Powell would rather have been with Shepherd, but Tell was such a prickly motherfucker that there was no way of knowing what he might have said to Leonie if he was stuck with her for a day. Shit, they'd be cleaning what was left of him off the inside of the van for the next month. Compared to Tell, Powell was a regular diplomat.

So Powell kept his mouth closed and waited, amusing himself by imagining Leonie in a variety of poses with white girls, Chinese, Latinos, and Powell himself slap bang in the middle. Man, he thought, if she only knew what I was thinking . . .

Sharon Macy spent the morning doing laundry, collecting her dry cleaning, and generally catching up on all of the stuff she had let pile up while she was working. She then drove out to Gold's Gym over at the Maine Mall and did her regular cardiovascular workout, spending so long on the StairMaster that her legs felt like marshmallow when she stepped off, and the machine itself was drenched with her sweat. Afterward, she headed over to the Big Sky Bread Company and was tempted to undo all her good work with a Danish, but instead settled for the soup-and-sandwich deal.

She ate in one of the booths while looking over the southern edition of the *Forecaster*, the free newspaper that dealt with local news in South Portland, Scarborough, and Cape Elizabeth. A cop in the Cape Elizabeth PD was seeking donations of mannequin heads to display his collection of hats from police departments around the world; the South Portland Red Riots golf team had donated a new bus to the school system; and a pair of men's gloves had been found on Mountain Road, Falmouth. Macy was still amazed at the fact that someone would take the time to place an ad in the *Forecaster* in order to return a pair of lost gloves. They were strange people up here: they kept to themselves, preferring to mind their own business and let other folks mind their business in turn, but they were capable of acts of touching generosity when circumstances called for it. She recalled last year's first snowstorm, a blizzard that swept up the coast from just above Boston and blanketed the state as far north as Calais. She had heard sounds in the early morning coming from the parking lot of her apartment, and had looked out to see two complete strangers digging her car out. Not just her car, either, but every car in the lot. They had then shouldered their spades and, identities still unrevealed, had moved on to the car in the next driveway. There was something hugely admirable about such anonymous kindness to strangers.

She skipped to the Police Beat page, scanning the names in the list of arrests and summonses: the usual OUIs, thefts by unauthorized taking or transfer, a couple of marijuana collars. She recognized one or two of the names, but there was nothing worth noting. If there had been, she figured that they would have heard about it on the grapevine by now.

She turned her attentions to the *Casco Bay Weekly*, the Portland free paper. The *CBW* didn't have a police beat column as such, an omission that was the subject of a degree of tension between the newspaper and the Portland PD. The *CBW* had sought details of arrests from the department on a number of occasions and had been presented instead with log sheets from which the names of suspects and the reasons for callouts had been excised, making them virtually useless. The *CBW* was yelling like a cat with its tail caught in a door, the department was growing more belligerent, and the old cycle of hostility between the newspaper and the Portland PD continued to spiral upward. Life, Macy figured, just wouldn't be the same without somebody criticizing the department.

Her meal finished, she drove downtown and parked in the public market's parking garage. She bought some fresh produce from one of the stalls in order to get her parking validated for two hours, then headed up Congress to the library of the Center for Maine History. She walked down the little pathway by the side of the Wadsworth-Longfellow House and entered the reading room, ignoring the sign that invited her to register her name and the reason for her visit in the library's logbook. The librarian behind the desk was in his late seventies, she figured, but judging from the gleam in his eye as he smiled at her, he was a long way from dead.

'Hi, I'd like to see whatever you have on Dutch Island,' she said.

'Sure,' said the man. 'May I ask what your interest is in Dutch?'

'I'm a police officer. I'm heading out there soon. I'm just curious to find out a little about it.'

'You'll be working with Joe Dupree, then.'

'Yes, so I understand.'

'He's a good man. I knew his father, and he was a good man too.'

He disappeared among the stacks behind the counter, and returned with a manila file. It looked disappointingly thin. The librarian registered her expression.

'I know, but there hasn't been too much written on Dutch. Fact is, we need a good history of the islands of Casco Bay, period. All we got here are cuttings, and this.' He removed a thin sheaf of typescript pages from the folder, stapled crudely along the spine.

'This was written maybe ten years ago by Larry Amerling. He's the postmaster out on the island. It's about the most detailed thing we have, although like as not you'll find something too in Caldwell's *Islands of Maine* and Miller's *Kayaking the Maine Coast*.'

He retrieved the books in question for her, then settled back into his chair as she found a space at one of the study tables. There were one or two other people researching in the library, although Macy was the youngest person in the room by almost half a century. Macy opened the folder, took out Amerling's *A Short History of Dutch Island*, and began to read.

Torres and Misters led Moloch back to the Land Cruiser, deliberately keeping up a fast pace, the restraints on Moloch's legs causing the prisoner to stumble slightly on the final steps.

'You asshole, Moloch,' said Torres.

Moloch tried to maintain his concentration. The grand jury hearing had been a bore for him. So they had found the body of a woman, and Verso – small, foolish Verso – was prepared to testify that he had helped Willard and Moloch dispose of her in the woods after Moloch had killed her.

SFW: So fucking what?

As soon as the direction of the prosecutor's questions had become apparent, Moloch had begun to speak like a handicapped man, talking through his nose, the words barely intelligible.

'Is there something wrong with him?' the judge had asked, but it had been Moloch who provided the answer.

'Sorry, Your Honor,' he said, modifying his speech sufficiently for his words to be understood. 'But I was kissing your wife goodnight, and the bitch closed her legs.'

That had been the end of proceedings.

'You hear me?' repeated Torres. 'You're an asshole.'

'Why am I an asshole?' said Moloch. He didn't look at the men at either side of him. Neither did he look at the chains on his hands or his feet, so used was he to the shuffling gait their presence necessitated. He would not fall. The investigators would not allow him to fall, not with people watching, but still they kept him moving quickly, depriving him of even the small dignity of walking like a man.

'You know why.'

'Maybe I just felt the urge to jerk that old judge's chain some.'

'You sure jerked it,' said Torres. 'You surely did. And don't you think it won't come back on you, because it will. You mark my words. They'll take your books away, leave you nothing to do but shit, sleep, and jerk off.'

'Then I'll be thinking of you, except maybe not when I sleep.'

'You fucking asshole, you're a dead man. You'll get the juice for this, doesn't matter how much you mouth off to the judge.'

'Sticks and stones, Mr. Torres, sticks and stones.'

They reached the car, Moloch smiling at last for the cameras, then put him in back and locked his chains once again to the D ring.

'It's been fun spending time with you both,' Moloch said. 'I appreciated the company.'

'Well,' said Torres, 'I can't say I'm looking forward to the pleasure again.'

'And you, Mr. Misters?' said Moloch, but Misters didn't respond. 'Mr. Misters,' repeated Moloch, savoring the words on his tongue, extending the *s* sounds into long washes of sibilance like water evaporating from the surface of a hot stove. 'Wasn't that kind of the name of some suck-ass, white-bread band in the eighties? "Broken Wings," that was them, right?'

Misters remained silent.

'Your partner doesn't say very much, does he?' said Moloch to Torres.

'He's kind of fussy about who he talks to.'

'Well, maybe he'll find it in him to say a few words before the journey's end.'

'You think so?'

'I'm certain. I can be a very interesting conversationalist.'

'I doubt that.'

'We'll see,' said Moloch. 'We'll see.'

And for the next five miles he hummed the chorus

135

of 'Broken Wings', over and over and over again, until Torres broke down and threatened to gag him. Only then, when the young investigator was sufficiently rattled, did Moloch stop.

The surroundings of the library had faded around Macy. She was no longer conscious of the old librarian, the other researchers, the occasional rattle as the main door opened, the cold air accompanying it. Instead, she was lost in the history of Dutch Island, the history of Sanctuary.

The Native Americans had fought hard to maintain their hold on the islands of Casco Bay. Like modern-day tourists, they summered on the islands, fishing and hunting porpoises and seals, even the occasional whale. Chebeague was their main base, but they used others too, and were resentful of the gradual encroachments of white settlers. The islands were the centers of population in the new colonies: they were easy to defend, safer than the mainland, and offered an abundant source of food from the ocean. Macy noticed that a lot of them, like Dutch Island, had multiple names: Great Chebeague was once Merry Island, then Recompense; Peaks Island was formerly Munjoy's, Milton's and Michael's, the name changing as the owners changed.

Despite their relative safety, the islands were still frequently attacked in the late seventeenth century. Settlers who were fleeing the atrocities on Harpswell Neck and other islands nearer the coast built a fort on Jewell, on the Outer Ring. In September 1676, a bloody year with attacks on whites at Casco Neck and Back Cove, the families on Jewell were attacked by eight canoes of warriors and were so disturbed by the experience that they retreated to Richmond Island. For the remainder of the year, the natives rampaged along the coast, annihilating every settlement between the Piscataqua and Kennebec Rivers. The settlers dug in, although some gave up and found safer places to live inland. In 1689, the natives raided Peaks Island, the most accessible island from the mainland, and slaughtered many of its inhabitants. One year later, they returned and forced the remaining settlers from the island.

Dutch Island, named for a Dutch sailor named Chris Herschdorfer, who was briefly shipwrecked there in the seventeenth century, was a different matter. It was farther from the mainland, and the distance made the crossing difficult for the Indians, who had only birch-bark canoes in which to travel. Furthermore, they regarded the island with suspicion, and seemed content to leave it unexplored.

In 1689, shortly after the Indian raid on Peaks, Major Benjamin Church, whose soldiers had been present on Peaks during the course of the Indian raid, led an expedition to the island and found it to be heavily forested, with only a handful of suitable landings for boats. Yet it was to Dutch that a man named Thomas Lunt led a group of settlers in 1691, weary of the running battles he was forced to fight with the natives. In total, thirty settlers joined him in the first two weeks on the island that he renamed Sanctuary, among them survivors of the attacks on Jewell and Peaks, and their numbers continued to increase over the following months. They opted to settle away from the shore, hoping that the higher ground might make them less vulnerable to a surprise attack.

At this point, Amerling's history of the island became less detailed and more speculative, but it seemed that the behavior of one of the settlers, a man named Buer, grew increasingly unpredictable. He became estranged from his family, spending more and more time alone in the thick forest at the center of the island. He was accused of attempted rape by the wife of one of his fellow settlers, and when her husband and three other men attempted to hunt him down as he tried to flee, he killed one of them with a musket shot and then sought shelter from his wife, begging her to hide him, claiming that he had done nothing wrong. But she, fearful for her own life (for she was as disturbed as anyone by the change in her husband), betrayed him to his accusers. He was chained to a post in a barn, but somehow he escaped from the island, stealing a boat and disappearing to the mainland.

He returned some months later, in the winter of 1693, at the head of a party of armed men and renegade Indians, and led the slaughter of the settlers on Sanctuary, including his own wife. One of the settlers, a woman, survived her wounds long enough to tell of what had occurred. Even now, three hundred years later, Macy found herself wincing at the details. There was rape and torture. Many of the women were assaulted, then bound and thrown alive into a patch of bog, where they drowned. No distinction was made between adults and children.

Most of those involved were later hunted down and killed themselves, but Buer and his lieutenant, an Italian rumored to be named Barone, evaded capture. There were those who said that Buer was not his real name, and that a man fitting his description but with the name of Seera was wanted in Massachusetts in connection with the deaths of two women there. In any event, he disappeared after the events on Sanctuary, and was never seen again. Barone, too, vanished. The search for the killers was led by three hunters from the island who had traveled to the mainland to trade on behalf of the settlement and were therefore absent when the massacre occurred. It was said that they tracked down a number of those involved in the attack and dispensed swift justice upon them. Many years later, the grandson of one of those hunters would be among those who resettled Sanctuary. His name was Jerome Dupree.

Amerling also covered the abduction of a woman in 1762, the disappearance of the men who had taken her to Dutch, and the subsequent discovery of one of them buried in the forest. The Dupree name cropped up again and again, and it was one of Joe Dupree's ancestors who made the stone cross that still stood amid the sunken remains of the old settlement and the graves of those who had died there. There was no mention of George Sherrin, who was found entangled in tree roots.

It was Amerling's final paragraph that most intrigued Macy. It read:

> To those looking in upon the island from outside, its history may appear bloody and strange. Yet those of us who have lived here for many years, and whose fathers and grandfathers and great-grandfathers lie buried in the island's cemetery, have grown used to the strangeness of Dutch Island. Here, paths through the forest disappear in the space of a single week, and new paths take their place, so that a man may one day walk a trail familiar to him, yet find himself directed toward new surroundings by the end of it. We are used to the silences and we are used to the sounds that are native only to this small patch of land. We live in the shadow of its history, and walk by the gift of those who have gone before us.

Macy closed the slim volume and returned to the desk, the names encountered in Amerling's history still rattling around in her head. Church. Lunt. Buer. Barone.

Barone. Barron.

It was probably just a coincidence, she thought, although it would explain why Barron was such a creep if his unpleasantness was part of a proud family tradition.

'You find what you were looking for?' asked the librarian.

'No,' said Macy. 'I was hoping for answers.'

'Maybe you'll have better luck on the island.'

'Maybe,' she said.

Out on Sanctuary, Joe Dupree was also finding himself short on answers. He had taken a ride out to Doug Newton's house, as he had promised Berman. Newton and his mother lived near Seal Cove, close to the southernmost tip of the island. Their house was one of the oldest on Sanctuary, and one of the most carefully maintained. Doug had given it a fresh coat of paint the previous spring, so that it seemed to shine amid the trees that surrounded it.

The old woman wasn't long for this earth. Dupree could see it in her face, could smell it in her room. When she died the doctors would find some complicated way to explain her demise, but for Joe and Doug, and perhaps for the old woman herself, there was nothing complicated about it. She was just old. She was in her late eighties and her body was losing its final struggle to keep her alive. Her breathing was shallow and rasping, and the skin on her face and hands was almost translucent in its pallor. She was in no pain but there was nothing that a hospital could do for her now, and so her son had taken her home to die. Debra Legere, who had some nursing experience, dropped by for four or five hours each day, sometimes a little longer if Doug had some work to do, although he was pretty much retired by now. Dupree figured that there was an arrangement between Debra, who was a widow, and Doug, who had never married, but he wasn't about to pry into it. In any case, they were both strict Baptists, so there appeared to be a limit to the amount of arranging that they could do.

Dupree stood at the window of the old woman's room and looked down to the yard below. It was a sheer drop. This side of the house was flat. There was a kitchen under it, but as Doug had never found the need to extend it farther, it remained flush with the main wall. The way Dupree saw it, there was just no way that a little girl could reach the top-most window in the house.

'Did she have a stepladder, Doug?' he asked softly.

Doug's mother had woken briefly when they entered the room but had now slipped back into her troubled sleep.

Doug seemed to think about bristling, then decided that it wasn't worth the trouble.

'I know what you're thinking,' he said. 'It's nothing that I haven't asked myself: how did she get up here? The answer is that I don't know. I'm just telling you what I saw.'

'The window was locked?' Dupree tested the sash with his hand. It seemed solid enough.

'As far as I remember. It could be that I didn't

close it properly and the wind might have blown it open, except that there was no wind that night and, anyway, who ever heard of a wind that could blow a heavy sash window upward?'

Dupree stared into the forest. The window faced northeast. He could see the island's central watchtower from where he stood, and part of the border of sunken trees that marked the boundary of the Site.

'You think I'm crazy?' asked Doug.

Dupree shook his head. He didn't know what to think, except that it still seemed unlikely that a little girl could magic her way twenty feet off the ground in order to attack an old woman in her bedroom. 'You always seemed pretty level-headed to me,' he said at last. 'What can I say? Keep the windows locked, the doors too. You got a gun?'

Doug nodded. 'More than one.'

'Well, for crying out loud don't use any of them. The last thing I want to do is to have to haul you in for shooting someone.'

Doug said that he would bear it in mind. It wasn't exactly a promise that he wouldn't shoot anybody, but it was better than nothing.

Dupree was about to leave the room when a piece of paper, seemingly caught by a draft, rose from a corner by the drapes and then settled again. The policeman leaned down to examine it more closely, and found himself looking at a moth. It was ugly and gray, with yellow markings along its body. Its wings fluttered feebly.

'Doug, can you get me an empty mayo jar, or something with a lid on it?'

The older man found a jelly jar. Dupree scooped the moth from the floor, then refitted the lid carefully. He used his pocketknife to bore a hole in the top, in order to allow the insect some air, although he guessed that it didn't have long to live.

Holding the jar up to the light from the window, he examined the moth, turning the bottle slowly to look at its wings and its markings. Doug Newton squinted at it, then shook his head.

'I've never seen a moth like that before,' he said.

Beside him, Dupree felt an uncomfortable ache spreading across his belly. Suddenly, Doug Newton's tale of a levitating girl didn't seem so far-fetched. He swallowed hard.

'I have,' he said.

They were four miles from the prison, following the banks of the river, when they saw the body. The Dismal Creek Penitentiary lay at the end of an isolated road, with little traffic apart from prison vehicles. Anyone who found himself in trouble on that road was likely to be waiting a long time for help.

'Hell is that?' asked Misters.

'Looks like a woman,' said Torres. 'Pull over.'

The woman lay by the side of the road, her legs splayed, her shoulders and head hidden in the long grass that grew by the hard shoulder. Her legs and buttocks were exposed where her skirt had ridden up over them. They pulled up a few feet away from her and Torres got out, Misters about to follow until Torres told him to stay back.

'Keep an eye on him,' said Torres.

'He's going nowhere,' said Misters, but he still remained close to the car and aware of Moloch, who was watching the proceedings with interest.

The woman was not moving, and Torres could see blood on her back. He leaned down and spread the grass that obscured her head.

'Oh sweet—'

He saw the red exposed flesh where her head should have been, then turned his face away in time to catch the slug on the bridge of his nose. He crumpled to the ground as Misters went for his own weapon, but a shadow fell across him and he looked up to see one of his own, a brother, holding a shotgun on him. From the grass at the other side of the road another man emerged, this one younger, with blond hair and a pretty, almost feminine face. Behind him was a muscular man with short red hair, wearing tight faded jeans and a T-shirt decorated with the Stars and Stripes. The red man took Misters's gun, then used plastic restraints to tie the investigator's hands behind his back. Meanwhile, the blond kid knelt by Torres and removed the keys from his belt and the gun from his holster. Then he walked over to the Land Cruiser, opened the door, and released Moloch from his chains.

Moloch stretched as he emerged from the car, then took Torres's gun from the kid and walked over to where Misters squatted. He raised the gun and pointed at the investigator's head.

'Now, *Mr.* Misters, do you have anything to say to me?'

Misters didn't open his mouth. He looked up at Moloch with mingled fear and disgust.

'I could shoot you,' said Moloch, 'shoot you like the boorish dog that you are.'

He aimed the gun.

'Bang,' he said. He tipped the muzzle to his mouth and blew a stream of imaginary smoke from the barrel.

'But I'm not going to shoot you,' he said.

'We taking him with us?' asked Dexter.

'No.'

'If we leave him, he'll identify us.'

'Really?' asked Moloch.

He stared hard at Misters.

'Oh that my eyes might see and my tongue might speak,' he said. 'Of what wonders might I tell.'

He turned to the young white boy.

'Blind him, then cut his tongue out. He never had much use for it anyway.'

They worked quickly, pushing the SUV into the river, the body of Torres and the woman inside it. Misters they left, bleeding and in shock, by the river-bank. The whole operation had taken less than three minutes.

Braun made a call on his cell phone, and seconds later, they were joined by Powell and Leonie, who had been driving the lookout vans positioned two hundred yards at either side of the ambush area, their sides decorated with the removable logo of a nonexistent forestry company so that, if any other car had taken that road before their work was done, they could be held back with a story about a fallen tree. In the event, no other vehicle had troubled them. Then the little convoy, five men and one woman in two vans, headed at speed toward the highway, and the north.

Dexter, Leonie, and Moloch drove in silence for a time, Dexter glancing occasionally in his side mirror. Three cars behind were Braun, Powell, and the boy, and that suited Dexter just fine. The boy Willard gave him the creeps, the beauty and seeming innocence of him all the more unsettling for what lay beneath. Still, Moloch liked him, and he had proved useful in the end. He had found the woman, trawling the side roads, the bars, and cheap motels for almost a week before he came across 'a suitable candidate', as he'd described her. Then he had killed her and brought her remains to the meeting place on time.

Dexter was a clever guy; maybe not as clever as he thought he was, but still pretty smart, all things considered. He'd done some reading, and liked books on psychology. Dexter figured that if you were going to be dealing with people, then you should try to find out as much as possible about the general principles behind them. He particularly liked the abnormal stuff because, in his line of work, abnormal was what he dealt with on a day-to-day basis. He knew all about sociopaths and psychopaths and assorted other deviants, and had begun to categorize the freaks he had met according to his diagnosis of their particular abnormality.

But Willard . . . Dexter hadn't found a book that dealt with anything quite like Willard before. Willard was off the scale. In fact, Dexter wasn't even sure that Willard was entirely human, although that wasn't the kind of thing that he was about to say out loud in the company of Moloch or anybody else. But sometimes he found Willard staring at him, and when he looked into the kid's eyes it was like falling into a void. Dexter figured that dying in space might feel something like seeing oneself reflected in Willard's eyes: there was only nothingness masquerading as blackness. It wasn't even hostile. It was just blank.

'What are you thinking about?' asked Moloch.

'Stuff.'

'Don't you go giving too much away now.'

'Like I said, just stuff.'

Beside him, Leonie just stared silently at the passing cars.

'Willard stuff?' said Moloch.

'How'd you know that?'

'I was watching you. I saw you look in the mirror. Your face changed. I can read you like a book, Dex.'

'I don't like him. I've never been anything but straight up with you, and I'm telling you the truth of it now. He's out there.'

'He's been useful.'

'Yeah.'

'And loyal.'

'To you.'

'That's all that matters.'

'With respect, man, you been in jail these past few years. Difficult to work with someone who don't answer to anyone but a man in a prison suit.'

'But you managed it.'

'I got a lot of patience, and the Verso thing was a piece of luck.'

'Yes,' said Moloch. 'I take it something is being done about him.'

'As we speak.'

'You should have got Willard to do it. He never liked Verso.'

'I never liked him either, but I didn't dislike the man enough to sic Willard on him. You see what he did to the woman? He cut on her pretty bad.'

'Before or after?'

'I didn't ask.'

'Then I'm not planning on asking either.'

'Me, I figure before.'

'Is this conversation leading somewhere, Dexter?'

'Take a look at the newspaper. It's somewhere back there.'

Moloch, seated in the semidarkness at the back of the van, checked among the boxes and drapes until he found a copy of the *Post-Register*. Its front-page story detailed the discovery of four bodies in a house south of Broughton.

Four bodies and two heads, one male, one female, in the refrigerator.

'It's all over the TV too. Way I figure it, Willard was probably holed up there for a time. You can bet your last nickel that somebody saw him around there and pretty soon his face is going to be plastered right up there beside yours. He's getting worse.'

In the darkness of the van, Dexter heard Moloch sigh regretfully.

'You're saying he's a liability.'

'Damn straight.'

'Then I must be a liability too.'

Dexter glanced back at him.

'You're the reason we're here. Willard ain't.'

It was some minutes before Moloch spoke again from behind Dexter.

'Keep a close eye on him, but do nothing for now.'

Man, thought Dexter, I been keeping a close eye on him since the first time I met him.

Powell was dozing, and there was no conversation between Braun and Willard in the van behind. That suited Braun just fine. Unlike Dexter, the redheaded man didn't have too much against Willard. He just figured him for another one of Moloch's crazies, but that didn't mean he wanted to talk to him more than was absolutely necessary. Of the five people who now accompanied Moloch north, Braun was probably the closest to being a regular guy. Although

a killer, he, like Shepherd, did not favor unnecessary violence, and had willingly acceded to their
request to watch the road while they disposed of
the investigators. Braun was in it for the money: he
was a good wheel man, a reliable operator. He
stayed calm, even in the worst situations. Every
group needed its Braun.

Braun just wanted his share of the cash. He figured that some people were going to get hurt in the
process, but that was nothing to do with him. That
was down to Moloch. Braun would quite happily
have walked away without hurting anyone as long
as the money was in his hand, but Leonie and Dexter
and Willard and the others needed more than that.
They liked a little action. He looked over at Willard,
but the boy's attention was elsewhere, his gaze fixed
on the road. Braun didn't mind the silence, just as
he didn't mind Willard.

Still, he patted the hilt of the knife that lay along
the edge of his thigh, and felt a small surge of reassurance.

Braun didn't *mind* Willard, but he sure as hell
didn't trust him either.

Braun was smarter than any of them.

Willard stared at the blacktop passing beneath them,
and thought of the woman. It had taken her a long
time to stop screaming after the man had died. She
had tried to start the car, and had almost succeeded
before Willard got to the window and broke it with
the blade of the machete. When he took the car

keys in his fingers and yanked them from the ignition, something faded in the woman's eyes. It was the death of hope, and though she started pleading then, she knew it was all over.

Willard had shushed her.

'I ain't going to hurt you,' he had told her. 'I promise. Just you calm down now. I ain't going to hurt you at all.'

The woman was crying, snot and tears dribbling down her chin. She was begging him, the words almost indistinguishable. Willard had shown her the machete then, had allowed her to see him tossing it away.

'Come on now,' he said. 'See, you got nothing to be scared about.'

And she had wanted to believe him. She had wanted to believe him so badly that she allowed herself to do so, and she had permitted him to take her hand and help her from the car. He had turned her away from the remains of the man – 'You don't have to see that' – as he led her toward the house, but something about that gaping doorway, and the blackness within, had set her off again. She tried to run and Willard had to tackle her and take her down by holding on to her legs. He let her scream as he hauled her toward the house by the legs, her nails breaking as she tried to get a grip on the dirt. There was nobody to hear her. Willard cast a longing glance over at the machete lying in the grass. It was his favorite. He could always go back and get it later, he thought.

And he had lots of other toys inside.

Shepherd saw the pizza delivery car first. The Saturn had a big plastic slice strapped to the roof, like a shark fin. Shepherd hoped the guy was making a lot in tips, because the job didn't come with a whole heap of dignity. He started the van and pulled in alongside the kid as he retrieved the pizza boxes from the insulated bag on the backseat. He heard the back of the van open and pulled his ski mask down over his head. Seconds later, Tell, his face also concealed by a mask, forced the kid into the back of the van at gunpoint. There were no other people in the parking lot of the motel.

'Look, man,' said the kid, 'I don't carry more than ten bucks in change.'

'Take off your jacket,' said Tell.

The kid did as he was told, handing it over to Tell. Shepherd leaned across the bench seats at the front of the van and tapped the kid on the shoulder with his gun.

'You stay there and you keep quiet. My friend is going to deliver your pizza for you. After that, we're gonna drive away from here. We'll drop you off along the way. It's up to you whether or not you walk out, or we dump what's left of you. Understand?'

The kid nodded.

'You go to college?' asked Shepherd.

The kid nodded again.

'Figures. You're smart.'

The van door closed, leaving them alone together. Tell, now wearing the kid's red Pizza Heaven jacket, climbed the stairs to the second floor of the motel and knocked on the door. He pulled the ski mask from his face and waited.

'Who is it?' said a voice.

'Pizza,' said Tell.

He saw a face at the window as the curtain moved, then the door opened. There was a guy in a white shirt and red tie standing before him. Behind him was a tall white man with receding hair and a beer gut.

'What do we owe you?' said the D.A.'s investigator as Tell reached a hand into the insulated bag.

'For Mr. Verso,' said Tell, 'it's on the house.'

The bottom of the bag exploded and the investigator staggered backward. Tell's second shot sent him sprawling across the bed. Verso tried to run for the bathroom, but Tell shot him in the back before he got to the door, then stood over him and fired two shots into the back of his head. He fired one more into the man on the bed, then walked swiftly back down to the van. Shepherd started it as soon as Tell reached the door.

'Your mask,' he said.

'Shit.' Tell pulled it back down before he climbed in. Behind him, the pizza delivery guy sat with his knees drawn up to his chin.

'You okay?' asked Tell.

'Yeah,' said the kid.

'You did good,' said Tell. 'You got nothing to worry about. Put this on your head.'

He handed the insulated bag to the kid, who did as he was told. They drove back onto the highway, then pulled over at a deserted rest stop. Tell opened the back door and helped the kid over to one of the wooden picnic benches.

'There's a phone to your right. I was you, I wouldn't use it for about another twenty minutes, okay?'

'Okay.'

'You breathing all right under that thing?'

'I'm fine.'

'Good.'

'Mister?' said the kid.

'Yeah.'

'Please don't kill me.'

As Shepherd had noted, the kid was smart. Tell raised the silenced pistol and pointed it at the insulated bag.

'I won't,' he said, as he pulled the trigger.

They bought coffee and hamburgers at a fast food joint off exit 122 and ate them seated in the back of the van while they waited for Shepherd and Tell to join them. They were avoiding toll booths and were sticking to the speed limits. In the back of the van, Moloch had clipped his hair, shaved his beard, and now wore a pair of black-rimmed glasses. His driver's license claimed that he was John R. Oster of Lancaster, Ohio.

'How much longer?' Moloch asked.

'Hour, maybe,' said Dexter. 'We can rest up then.'

Moloch shook his head. 'We move on. They're already looking for me, and pretty soon my picture will be on every TV station from here to Canada. We need to find her, and find her fast.'

Despite what he said, he wasn't too concerned yet. He had sometimes spoken of Mexico as his preferred final destination in the event of an escape from custody, because Mexico would not extradite Americans facing life sentences, following a decision by the Mexican Supreme Court that life sentences breached a constitutional article that stated all men were capable of being rehabilitated. Moloch didn't believe that for one moment, but he figured that there would be those in the prison population who would recall his comments and who would pass them on. It would not be enough to prevent checks to the north and west as well as to the south, but he hoped that it might force the police to concentrate their efforts on monitoring the southern routes.

He sat back in the van and closed his eyes. He was strong, and he had a purpose. He allowed himself to drift into sleep, and dreamed of a woman.

A woman dying.

4

Danny was pleading.

'Mom, just ten more minutes. *Five* more minutes. Please!'

Marianne peered at him from over the rim of her glasses. Danny was in his pajamas, which was something, but it had taken her an hour to convince him to do even that. He seemed to have grown up so much in the last year, and she was beginning to find him more and more difficult to handle. He was always questioning, always doubting, testing the limits of her authority in every little thing. But that incident with the bird had thrown him, exposing his vulnerability and drawing him back to her for a time, his head pressed against her breasts as he cried over—

Over what? Over the fact that Joe Dupree had been forced to kill the dying bird with his bare hands to put it out of its misery, or because Danny hadn't been allowed to touch it, to play with it first? Danny sometimes hurt creatures: she had watched him do it, had caught him burning ants with a piece of broken bottle or tormenting cats by flinging stones at them. She supposed that a lot of boys behaved that way, not fully understanding the pain that they were causing. In that, maybe Danny was just being a typical six-year-old. She hoped so. She didn't like to think that it might be something deeper, something that he had picked up from his father, some faulty gene transmitted from generation to generation that would manifest itself in increasingly vicious ways as he grew older. She did not like to think of her Danny – because he was *her* Danny, make no mistake about that – becoming such a man.

And he was asking questions now, questions about *him*, and it bothered her that the lies she was forced to tell Danny caused him pain. Danny seemed to have vague memories of his father, and he cried when she told him that he was dead. Not the first time, curiously, but rather on the second occasion, as if it had taken him the intervening days to absorb the information and to come to terms with what it meant to him and for him.

How did he die?

A car accident.

Where?

In Florida.

Why was he in Florida?

He was working there.

What did he work at?

He sold things.

What things?

Misery. Pain. Fear.

He sold cars.

Is he buried, like the people in the graveyard?
Yes, he's buried.
Can we visit him?
Someday.

Someday. Just as someday she would be forced to tell him the truth, but not now. There would be time enough for anger and hurt and blame in the years to come. For now, he was her Danny and she would protect him from the past and from the mistakes that his mother had made. She reached out to him and ruffled his hair, but he seemed to take her gesture for one of acquiescence and bounced back to his perch on the couch.

'No, Danny, no more. You go to bed.'

'*Mom.*'

'No! You go to bed now, Danny Elliot. Don't make me get up from this seat.'

Danny gave her his most poisonous look, then stomped away. She could hear him all the way up the stairs, and then his bedroom door slammed and his bed protested as he threw the full weight of his tantrum upon it.

She let out a deep breath and removed her glasses. Her hands were trembling. Perhaps it was surprising that Danny was as well adjusted as he was, given the lifestyle that he had been forced to lead. For the first two-and-a-half years they had stayed on the road, never remaining long in any place, crisscrossing the country in an effort to stay ahead of any pursuers. Those years had been hellish. They seemed to coalesce into a constant blur of small towns and unfamiliar cities, like a movie screened slightly out of focus. The early months were the hardest. She would wake to every floorboard squeak, every rustle of trash on the street, every tapping of branches upon the window. Even the sound of the AC clicking on in cheap motel rooms would cause her to wake in a panic.

But the worst times came when car headlights swept across the room in the dead of night and she heard the sound of male voices. Sometimes they would laugh and she would relax a little. It was the quiet ones she feared because she knew that when they came for her, they would do so silently, giving her no time to react, no time to flee.

Finally she and Danny had arrived here, settling in the last place that *they* would look, for she had spoken so often about the West Coast, about a place with year-round sunshine and beaches for Danny. She had meant it too. It had long been her dream that they would settle at last out there, but it was not to be. She feared the ones who were looking for her (for they were surely looking, even after all this time) so much that the entire West Coast was not big enough to hide her. Instead, she had retreated to cold and to winter darkness, and to a community that would act as an early warning system for her if they came.

She looked to the refrigerator, where she still had a bottle of unopened wine in case one of her new friends called and offered to curl up in front of the TV for an evening of comedies and talk shows. She so wanted to open it now, to take a single glass, but she needed to keep her head clear. On the kitchen table before her were spread the household accounts, abandoned since the previous night in the hope that a little sleep might make them less forbidding. She wasn't earning enough from her job at the Casco Bay Market to cover her expenses, and Sam Tucker had already asked her to stay home for the rest of the week, promising to make up the hours within the month. That meant that she would either have to look for another job, possibly in Portland – and that was assuming that she could find a job and someone to hold on to Danny after school or in the evenings – or she could take from the 'special fund.' That would necessitate a trip to the mainland, and the mainland always made her nervous. Even the larger banks were a risk: she had already dispersed the funds into accounts in five different banks over three counties – no more than $7,000 in each account – but she was always worried about the IRS or some strange bank regulator of whom nobody had ever heard spotting the connections. Then she would be in real trouble.

And there was the fact that she didn't like using the money. It was tainted. Wherever possible, she tried to get by on what she earned. Increasingly, that was becoming harder and harder to do. True, there was always the knapsack itself, hidden among boxes and spare suitcases in the attic, but she had vowed not to touch that. There was always the chance of succumbing to temptation, of taking out too much and giving Danny and herself some treats, thereby drawing attention to herself. This was a small community, and even though Mainers didn't go interfering in one another's business, that didn't mean that they weren't curious about that business to begin with. It was the downside of living in such a comparatively isolated community, but a sacrifice worth making.

There was also the fact that the money was their escape fund, should she and Danny ever need to move on again quickly. If she began dipping into it for little things, there was the danger that she would come to take its contents for granted, and the little dips would become big dips, and pretty soon the fund would be gone.

And yet there was so much money in it, so much: nearly $800,000. How bad could it hurt to take a little, to buy a decent television, some new clothes, maybe even the game console that Danny wanted? Such small things from so much . . .

She forced the temptation away. No, a bank trip was the only option. She folded her glasses and put them back in their case, then began to gather the papers together.

She was almost done when the knock came on the door.

It had been decided that Leonie would knock. Anyone looking out would see an attractive black woman, smiling brightly. She could pose no threat.

Leonie heard footsteps coming toward the door,

and a curtain moved aside in the semidarkness. She smiled embarrassedly, and raised the map that she held in her hands. Hey, I'm lost, and it's a cold night. Help me out here. Tell me where I went wrong, huh? She didn't even glance to her left, where Dexter stood holding a gun by his thigh, Braun behind him, or to her right, where the boy-man Willard waited, unblinking, his left hand shielding the blade of the knife in case a porch light caught it and drew attention to them. Moloch had remained apart, for the time being, with Shepherd, Powell, and Tell.

Seconds passed, followed by the sound of a chain being undone, and a lock being turned.

The door opened.

Joe Dupree stood on Marianne's doorstep, out of uniform. She had to look up slightly to see his face, his eyes shining brightly amidst the shadows that congregated around them.

'Joe? Is there some problem?'

But Dupree merely shook his head. 'I was just passing. I brought this for Danny.' From behind his back he produced a small wooden gull and handed it to her. She took it carefully in her hands and held it up to the light. It seemed almost crudely carved in places, but it was clear that it was not from lack of craft or care. Rather, the primitivism of the carving was designed to capture something of the bird, a reflection of its nature. He had taken great pains with the head in particular, depicting the beak as slightly open. She could even see a tiny carved tongue in its mouth. The paint was newly dry. She could still smell it on the bird.

'It's beautiful,' she said, and she marveled at how the big man's hands could have created something so small and wondrous, for she had difficulty imagining him even holding the knife in his fist. It must have taken him hours to do it, she thought. He killed the bird, then spent hours re-creating it in wood.

'Would you like to come in?'

'I don't want to disturb you.'

'I've finished what I was doing. I was about to open a bottle of wine,' she lied.

He hesitated, and she pressed home her advantage.

'You're not on duty, right?'

He didn't need much persuasion; just a little. She recalled again all those months that he had spent circling her, like a small male spider working toward a female, unsure of the safety of approaching, in fear of his life. In this case the physical proportions were reversed, but she still had the power. She had wondered why it was taking him so long to approach her, for she had seen the way that he looked at her when she began working in the market, the bashfulness with which he spoke in response to her polite remarks. She had the answer almost as soon as she asked herself the question. She knew it was because of how he looked, his consciousness of his own difference, and so it was she who had broken the ice between them, taking the opportunities to talk with him when they arose, walking with him along Island Avenue when their paths crossed, attracting nudges and smiles from the locals. She wasn't sure, even then, that she was interested in the man himself. Instead, it was his timidity that drew her, the fragility of his self-esteem strangely enticing in such a huge figure.

She stepped aside to let him enter and caught the scent of him as he brushed by her: he smelled of wood and sap and salt water. She breathed it in as discreetly as she could and felt something tug inside her. He was not a conventionally handsome man. His teeth were gapped in places, seemingly too small to create a single wall of enamel in his great mouth. His face was long, but widened at the cheeks and chin. She could see wrinkles around his eyes and mouth, and knew at once that they were the consequence of some pain, perhaps physical, perhaps psychological, and that this man was frequently in distress. She was a little surprised when she began to find him attractive and guessed that it was, at least in part, a combination of his power and size, along with the capacity for gentleness and subtlety that had enabled him to carve the bird out of a piece of driftwood; to deal sensitively with Jack the painter and his problems; in fact, to interact with most of the islanders in such a way that they both liked and respected him, even when he was forced to come down on them for some minor infraction. Marianne Elliot had spent so long among the kind of men who used their power to hurt and intimidate that Joe Dupree's graciousness and humanity naturally appealed to her. She wondered what it might be like to make love to him, and was surprised and embarrassed at the surge of warmth that the fantasy brought. She had not considered her own desires for so long, subsuming them all in order to concentrate on Danny and his wants, and on their combined need for constant vigilance.

Now, as she watched the big policeman sit gingerly down at the kitchen table, the chair too low for him so that his own legs remained at an acute angle, she was conscious of the muscularity of his shoulders, the shape of his chest beneath his shirt, the width of his arms. His hands, twice as large as hers, hovered in the air before him. He cupped them and placed them on the table, then unclasped them and moved them to his thighs. Finally, he folded his arms, jolting the table as he did so and causing a china bowl to tremble gently. He seemed even larger in the confines of the little kitchen, making it appear cluttered even though it was not. She had not seen the inside of his house but was certain that it contained the minimum of furniture, with the barest sprinkling of personal possessions. Anything fragile or valuable would be stored safely away. She felt a great tenderness for the big man, and almost reached out to touch him before she stopped herself and turned instead to the business of the wine. There was a bottle of Two Roads Chardonnay in the fridge, a gift to herself purchased in Boston. She had been saving it for a special occasion, until she realized that she had no special occasions.

Marianne was about to open the bottle, by now instinctively used to doing everything for herself, when he asked her if she would like him to take care of it. She handed over the bottle and the corkscrew. The wine looked like a beer bottle in his hand.

He read the label. 'Flagstone. I don't know it.'

'It's South African.'

'Robert Frost,' he said.

'Sorry?'

'The wine. It's named after a Robert Frost poem. You know, the one about the two roads diverging in a forest.'

She hadn't noticed, and felt vaguely embarrassed by her failure to make the connection.

'It's hard to forget a poem like that on an island covered by trees,' he said, inserting the corkscrew.

'At least you can't get too lost if you take the wrong road,' she replied. 'You just keep going until your feet get wet.'

The plastic cork popped from the bottle. She hadn't even seen him tense as he drew it out. She placed two glasses on the table and watched him pour.

'People still get lost here,' he said. 'Have you been out to the Site?'

'Jack took Danny and me out there, shortly after we arrived. I didn't like it. It felt . . . sad.'

'The memory of what happened still lingers there,

I think. A couple of times each summer, we get tourists in to the station house complaining that the trails out to it should be more clearly marked because they went astray and had trouble finding the road again. They're usually the worst ones, the loudmouths in expensive shirts.'

'Maybe they deserve to get lost, then. So why don't you signpost it better?'

'It was decided, a long time ago, that the people who needed to find it knew how to get to it. It's not a place for those who don't respect the dead. It's not a place for anyone who *doesn't* find it sad.'

He handed her a glass and touched his own gently to its lip.

'Happiness,' he said.

'Happiness,' she said, and he saw hope and sadness in her eyes.

If Marianne was curious about the giant, then he was no less interested in her. He knew little about the woman, except for her name and the fact that she had brought with her enough money to rent her small but comfortable house, yet he had recognized an attraction toward her and thought, however unlikely it might at first appear, that she might feel something for him too. It had taken all of his courage to propose a dinner date, after months of gentle probing, and it had taken a moment or two after she replied for him to realize that she had accepted.

Yet something about her troubled him. No, that wasn't true. It was not about *her*, precisely, but to do with some undisclosed element of her life. Joe

Dupree had learned to read people well. His father had taught him the importance of doing so, and life on the island, with its exposure to the same faces, the same problems day after day, had enabled him to hone his skills, weighing his first perceptions against the reality of individuals as their characters were inevitably revealed to him. He glanced at the woman's fingers as she put the cork back in the bottle and replaced it in the fridge. She sat down opposite him, and smiled a little nervously. Her right hand toyed with her ring finger, yet there was no ring upon it.

It was something that he had seen her do a lot, usually when a stranger came into the store or a loud noise startled her. Instinctively, she would touch her ring finger.

It's the husband, thought Joe.

The husband is the element.

Bill Gaddis was not a happy man. There were a lot of reasons why Bill was unhappy even at the best of times, but now he had a specific reason. He was leaving a fine woman in the sack to answer an insistent knocking at his door, and that made him very unhappy indeed. He might even have been tempted to ignore the knocking, under other circumstances, but around here people had a habit of being good neighbors and the good neighbor at the door might take it into his or her head that, what with the lights being on and no reply coming from the Gaddis house, maybe somebody had had an accident, taken a tumble down some steps or slipped on some water in the kitchen, and nobody wanted to be the one that had to say, 'Hell, I was out there just last night, knocking and knocking. If only I'd checked through the windows, or tried the back door, they'd still be alive today.' And Bill didn't want old Art Bassett or Rene Watterson coming in the back way, hollering and nosing about, expecting to see someone lying on the floor with blood pooling, only to find Bill with his ass in the air and his mind on other things.

He wondered now why they had even decided to settle here. It was Pennsylvania, goddamnit. *Pennsylvania.* As far as Bill was concerned, the only people who settled here willingly were religious zealots who regarded buttons as sinful, and folks that regarded buttons as sinful were likely to cast a harsh eye on Bill Gaddis's activities. Compared to those people, Billy Gaddis was virtually the Antichrist. Camp Hill, Pennsylvania didn't even figure on most maps, but Bill knew that was why they were here, precisely because you had to look hard to find it.

It had its good points, though. His wife had picked up a job at the Holiday Inn in New Cumberland, just off the turnpike, working the desk a couple of evenings each week. On weekends, she took a few hours at the Zany Brainy over at the Camp Hill Mall, spending time with kids to make up for the fact that she was never going to have any of her own. Bill got himself a job driving trucks for a paper company, and they saw just enough of each other to remind themselves why they preferred to see only that much. In the first weeks, Bill would drive over to the Holiday Inn and take a seat in the Elephant & Castle, the English pub attached to the hotel. When she finished her shift, he and his wife would eat there, largely in silence, then return home and sleep at the two farthest extremes of their bed. Eventually, she got herself her own little car, but Bill kept going back to the Elephant & Castle. He'd met a woman there named Jenna, a little older than he was but still good-looking, and pretty soon Bill had even more reason to be grateful for the time his wife spent working, and the regularity of her hours. Now someone was knocking on the door, depriving him of some much-needed R&R.

Bill shrugged on a robe, rearranging it to conceal his dying hard-on, and shuffled to the door, swearing as he went. He left the lights out in the hallway and pulled back the curtain at the side window. He didn't recognize the woman on the step, but she looked fine, maybe even finer than the woman he'd just left, and that was saying something. She had a map in her hands.

Bill swore louder. How hard could it be to get lost with a mall slap-bang in front of you? Christ, if Bill stood on his lawn he could see the mall clear at the top of Yale Avenue. He took his time looking the woman over, lingering upon her breasts. Bill swore once again, this time under his breath and more in admiration than in anger, then opened the door.

He barely had time to register the gun in the woman's hand before she jammed it into the soft flesh under his chin and forced him against the wall. Behind her came a redheaded man, and after him two others: a real pretty boy and a Richard-Roundtree-after-a-beating motherfucker with a big 'stache, who brushed past Bill and headed straight into the house.

'The f—'

'Shut up,' said the woman. She ran her left hand over Bill's body, stopping briefly at his groin.

'We disturb something?'

From the bedroom Bill heard a scream, followed by the sound of Jenna being dragged from the bed.

'Just the two of you?' asked the black woman.

Bill nodded hard, then stopped suddenly as he considered the possibility that the action might get his head blown off. The pretty boy stayed by the half-open door while Bill was forced back into the living room. Jenna was already there, a sheet wrapped around herself. She was sobbing. Bill made as if to go to her, but the woman stopped him and gestured toward the wall. Bill could only shoot Jenna a look of utter helplessness.

And then he heard the front door closing, and footsteps coming along the hallway. Two people, thought Bill. The pretty boy and—

Moloch entered the living room.

'Billy boy!' he said. His eyes flicked toward the

woman, then back again. 'I see you haven't changed a bit.'

'Aw, Jesus, no', said Bill. 'Not you.'

Moloch moved closer to him, reached up to Bill's face, and grasped his hollow cheeks in the fingers of his right hand.

'Now, Billy boy,' said Moloch. 'Is that any way to greet your brother-in-law?'

Dupree nodded approvingly.

'The house looks good,' said Joe. 'You've done a lot with it in the last year.'

He was holding the glass as delicately as he could while she showed him around her home. To Marianne, the glass still looked lost in his grip, with barely enough capacity to offer the policeman a single mouthful. They had paused briefly at her bedroom door and she had felt the tension. It wasn't a bad feeling. After looking in on Danny, who was fast asleep, they went back downstairs.

'I wanted to put our own stamp on it, and Jack didn't object. He helped us out some, when he could.'

'He's a good man. There's been no more trouble, has there? Like before.'

'You mean drinking? No, none that I've seen. Danny likes him a lot.'

'And you?'

'He's okay, I guess. Lousy painter, though.'

Joe laughed. 'He has a distinctive style, I'll give him that.'

'But he was friendly, right from the start, and I'm grateful to him. It was kind of hard when we got here. People seem a little . . . *suspicious* of strangers, I guess.'

'It's an island community. People here tend to stick pretty close together. You can't force your way in. You have to wait for them to loosen up, get to know you. Plus, the island's changed some recently. It's not quite a suburb of Portland, but it's getting there, with people commuting to the mainland for work. Then you have rich folk coming in, buying waterfront properties, forcing up prices so that families that have lived here for generations can't afford to help their kids set up home. The assessments for waterfront properties out here are based on one sale made last year, and the assessor in that case only went back three months to make his valuation. Lot prices increased one hundred per cent because of it, almost overnight. It was all legal, but that didn't make it right. Island communities are dying. You know, a hundred years ago there were three hundred island communities in Maine. Now there are sixteen, including this one. Islanders feel under siege and that makes them draw closer together in order to survive, so outsiders find it harder to gain a foothold. Each group is wary of the other, and never the twain shall meet.'

He drew a breath. 'Sorry, I'm ranting now. The island matters to me. The people here matter to me. All of them,' he added.

She felt the tension again, and luxuriated in it for a moment.

'But working in the store, that's a good way to start,' he continued. 'Folks get to know you, to trust you. After that, it's just plain sailing.'

Marianne wasn't sure about that. Some of those who came into the store still limited their conversations with her to 'Please' and 'Thank you,' and sometimes not even that. The older ones were the worst. They seemed to regard her very presence in their store as a kind of trespass. The younger ones were better. They were happy to see some new blood arriving on the island, and already she'd been hit on a couple of times. She hadn't responded, though. She didn't want to be seen as a threat by any of the younger women. She had thought that she could do without the company of a man for a time. To be honest, she'd had her fill of men, and then some, but Joe Dupree was different.

Joe wasn't like her husband, not by a long shot.

Moloch sat in one of the overstuffed armchairs and sipped a beer.

'Fooling around, Billy boy?' he said. 'Out with the old, in with the new?'

Bill had stopped weeping. He'd had to. Moloch had threatened to shoot him if he didn't.

Bill didn't reply.

'Where is she?' asked Moloch.

Bill still said nothing.

Moloch swallowed, then winced, as if he had just swallowed a tack.

'Queer beer,' he said. 'I haven't had a beer in more

than three years, and this stuff still tastes like shit. I'll ask you one more time, Bill. Where is your wife?'

'I don't know,' said Bill.

Moloch looked at Dexter and nodded.

Dexter grinned, then grabbed Jenna's arm. She was a big woman, verging on plump, with naturally red hair that she had dyed a couple of shades darker. The mascara on her face had run, drawing black smears down her cheeks. As she struggled in Dexter's grasp her sheet fell away, and she tried to pick it up again even as Dexter pulled her back toward the bedroom. She hung back, using her fingers to try to release his grip upon her.

'No-o-o,' she said. 'Please don't.'

She looked to Bill for help, but the only help Bill could offer was to sell out his own wife.

'She works late tonight.' The words came out in a rush. 'Down at the mall.' He finished speaking and looked like he was about ready to retch at what he had just done.

Moloch nodded. 'What time does she finish?'

Bill looked at the clock on the mantel.

'About another hour.'

Moloch looked at Dexter, who had paused by the doorway of the bedroom.

'Well?' Moloch said. 'What are you waiting for? You have an hour.'

Dexter's grin widened. He drew Jenna into the bedroom and closed the door softly behind him. Bill tried to move away from the wall, but the black woman's gun was instantly buried in his cheek.

'I told you,' said Bill. 'I told you where she was.'

'And I appreciate that, Billy boy,' said Moloch. 'Now you just sit tight.'

'Please,' said Bill. 'Don't let him do anything to her.'

Moloch looked puzzled.

'Why?' he asked. 'It's not as if she's your wife.'

Joe helped her to put the glasses away.

'I have to ask you something,' he said.

She dried her hands.

'Sure.'

'It's just—' He stopped, seemingly struggling to find the right words. 'I have to know about the folks that come to the island. Like I said, it's a small, close-knit community. Anything happens, then I need to know why it's happening. You understand?'

'Not really. Do you mean you want to know something about me?'

'Yes.'

'Such as?'

'Danny's father.'

'Danny's father is dead. We split up when Danny was little, then his daddy died down in Florida someplace.'

'What was his name?'

She had prepared for this very moment. 'His name was Server, Lee Server.'

'You were married?'

'No.'

'When did he die?'

'Fall of ninety-nine. There was a car accident outside of Tampa.'

That was true. A man named Lee Server had been killed when his pickup was hit by a delivery truck on the interstate. The newspaper reports had said that he had no surviving relatives. Server had been drinking, and the reports indicated that he had a string of previous DUIs. There weren't too many people fighting for space by Lee Server's graveside when they laid him down.

'I had to ask,' said Joe.

'Did you?'

He didn't reply, but the lines around his eyes and mouth appeared to deepen.

'Look, if you want to back out of tomorrow night, I'll understand.'

She reached out and touched his arm.

'Just tell me: were you asking with your cop's hat on, or your prospective date's hat on?'

He blushed. 'A little of both, I guess.'

'Well, now you know. I still want to see you tomorrow. I've even taken my best dress out of mothballs.'

He smiled, and she watched him walk to his car before she closed the door behind him. She let out a sigh and leaned back against the door.

Dead.

Her husband was dead.

Maybe if she said it often enough, it might come true.

* * *

Bill had curled himself into a ball against the wall, his hands over his ears to block out the noises coming from the bedroom. His eyes were squeezed tightly closed. Only the feel of the gun muzzle against his forehead forced him to open them again. Slowly, he took his hands away from his ears. There was now silence.

It was a small mercy.

'You're a pitiful man,' said Moloch. 'You let another man take your woman, and you don't even put up a fight. How can you live with yourself?'

Bill spoke. His voice was cracked, and he had to cough before he could complete a coherent sentence.

'You'd have killed me.'

'I'd have respected you. I might even have let you live.' He dangled the prospect of life before Bill, like a bad dog being taunted with the treat destined to be denied him.

'How did you find me?'

'If you're going to run away, Bill, then you keep your head down and try not to fall into your old ways. But once a bad gambler, always a bad gambler. You took some hits, Bill, and then you found that you couldn't pay back what you owed. That kind of mistake gets around.'

Bill's eyes closed again, briefly.

'What are you going to do with me?' he asked.

'Us,' corrected Moloch. 'You know, Bill, I'm starting to think that you don't really care about your wife, or that woman in the bedroom. What is her name, by the way?'

'Jenna,' said Bill.

Moloch seemed puzzled. 'She doesn't look like a Jenna. She's kind of dirty for a Jenna. Still, if you say so, Bill. I'm not about to doubt your word on it. Now that we've rephrased the question to include your lady friend and your wife, we can proceed. I think you know what I want. You give it to me, and maybe we can work something out, you and I.'

'I don't know where your wife is.'

'Where *they* are,' said Moloch. 'Jesus, Bill, you only think in the singular. It's a very irritating habit which you may not live long enough to break. She has my son, and my money.'

'She hasn't been in touch.'

'Willard,' said Moloch.

Willard's bleak, lazy eyes floated toward the older man.

'Break one of his fingers.'

And Willard did.

Joe Dupree checked in briefly with the station house. All was quiet, according to Tuttle. As soon as Berman returned, he'd turn in for an hour or two, he said, try to get some sleep.

Dupree drove down unmarked roads, for most of the streets on the island were still without names. It took the cops who came over from the mainland a few years to really get to know the island, which was why those who took on island duty tended to stick with it for some time. You had to learn to always get a phone number when anyone called, because people still referred to houses by reference to their neighbors – even if those neigbors no longer lived there, or had died. You figured out landmarks, turnings, forks in the road, and used them as guides.

Dupree returned again to thoughts of Marianne and her past. He had seen something in her eyes as she spoke of Danny's father. She wasn't telling him the truth, at least not the full truth. She had told him that she had not been married to Danny's father, but he had watched as her hand seemed to drift unconsciously toward her ring finger. She had caught herself in time and tugged at one of her earrings instead, and Dupree had given no indication that he had noticed the gesture. So she didn't want to talk about her husband with a policeman, even one with whom she had a date the following evening. Big deal. After all, she hardly knew him, and he had sensed her fear: fear both of her husband and of the implications of any disclosure that she might make about him. He was tempted to run a check on this Server guy, but decided against it. He wanted their date tomorrow to be untainted by his professional instincts. Perhaps, if they made this thing between them work, she would tell him everything in her own time.

Dexter came out of the room just as Bill stopped screaming.

'I'm glad you did that now, and not earlier,' he told Moloch. 'You might have put me off my game.'

Bill was crying again. His face was pale with shock.

'You okay, Bill?' asked Moloch. He sounded genuinely concerned. 'Nod if you're okay, because when you've recovered Willard can move on to the next finger. Unless, of course, you think you might have something more to tell us?'

Bill was trembling. He looked up and saw the clock on the mantel over Moloch's left shoulder.

'Aw, shit,' he said. His eyes flicked toward the half-open bedroom door. He could see Jenna's shadow moving against the wall as she tried to dress herself. Moloch watched him with amusement.

'You worried about her coming back, maybe finding out about your little piece on the side? Answer me, Bill. I want to hear your voice. It's impolite to nod. You nod at me again, or make me wait longer than two seconds for an answer, and I'll have Willard here break something you have only one of.'

'Yes,' croaked Bill. 'I'm worried about her finding out.'

'A more self-aware man might have realized by now that he had bigger problems to face than his wife discovering his affair. You are a remarkable man, Bill, in your capacity to blind yourself to the obvious. Now, where is my family?'

'I told you, she hasn't been in touch, not with me.'

'Ah, now we're making progress. If she hasn't been talking to you – and I got to be honest here,

Bill, I'd prefer not to be talking to you either, so I can understand her point of view – then she has been talking to her sister, right?'

'Yes.'

'But you're such a piece of shit, Bill, that even your own wife won't tell you where her sister is at.'

'She doesn't tell me anything.'

'But you must know how they communicate?'

'Phone, I guess.'

'Where are your phone records?'

'In the cabinet by the TV. There's a file. But she never uses the house phone. I've looked.'

'Does she receive mail?'

'Yes.'

'Where does she keep it?'

'In a locked box in the bottom drawer of her nightstand.'

Moloch nodded at Willard, and the boy went into the bedroom to search for the box.

As he left the room, car headlights brightened the hallway, dousing their faces and casting fleeting shadows across the room. Leonie pressed the gun against Bill's teeth, forcing him to open his mouth, then shoved the barrel inside.

'Suck it,' she whispered. 'I see your lips move from it and I'll pull the trigger.'

From the bedroom came the sound of sudden movement: Jenna was trying to make for the window to raise the alarm, Moloch guessed. Willard was too quick for her, and the movement ceased. Moloch heard the car door closing; footsteps on the path; the placing of the key in the lock; the door opening, then shutting again; the approach of the woman.

She stepped into the living room. She was older than he remembered her, but then, it had been more than four years since they had last met. In the interim, Moloch had been betrayed and they had run, scattering themselves to the four winds, inventing new lives for themselves. Even with Moloch behind bars, they remained fearful of reprisals.

Patricia had long, lush hair like her younger sister's, but there was more gray in it. She wasn't as pretty, either, and had always looked kind of worn down, but that was probably a consequence of being married to an asshole like Bill. Moloch, who didn't care much either way, still wondered why she had stayed with him. Maybe, after all the fear, she needed someone even semi-reliable to stand beside her.

Patricia took in her husband, huddled on the floor, the woman's gun in his mouth; Dexter, his shirt still untucked; Braun, an open magazine on his lap.

And Moloch, smiling at her from an armchair, a bottle of beer raised in welcome.

'Hi, honey,' he said. 'I'm home.'

All was quiet. Even Bill had stopped sobbing and now simply cradled his damaged hand as he watched his wife. She stood before Moloch, her head cast down. Her left cheek was red from the first slap, and her upper lip was split.

'Look at me,' he said.

She did not move and he struck her again. It was a light slap, but the humiliation of it was greater than if he had propelled her across the room with the force of the blow. She felt the tears roll down her cheeks and hated herself for showing weakness before him.

'I'll let you live,' said Moloch. 'If you help me, I'll let you and Bill live. Someone will stay here with you, just to make sure you don't do anything stupid, but you will be allowed to live. I won't kill her. I just want my money. I don't even want the boy. Do you understand?'

Her mouth turned down at the edges as she tried to keep herself from sobbing aloud. She found herself looking at her husband. She wanted him to stand by her, to be strong for her, stronger than he had ever been. She wanted him to defy Moloch, to defy the woman with the gun, to follow her even unto death. Yet he had never shown that strength before. He had always failed her, and she believed that even now, when she needed him most, he would fail her again.

Moloch knew that too. He was watching what passed between them, taking it in. There might be something there he could use, if only—

Willard came out of the bedroom. There was blood on his hands and shirt. A spray of red had drawn a line across his features, bisecting his face.

Life was gradually seeping back into his eyes. He was like a man waking from a dream, a dream in which he had torn apart a woman whose name he had barely registered, and whose face he could no longer remember.

Bill screamed the name of the dead woman in the bedroom, and his wife knew at last that all that she had suspected and feared was true.

'No, Bill,' was all that she said.

And something happened then. They looked at each other and there was a moment of understanding between them, this betrayed woman and her pathetic husband, whose weaknesses had led these men to their door.

'I'm sorry,' he said. 'I'm sorry for it all. Tell him nothing.'

Bill smiled, and although there was a touch of madness to it, it was, in its way, an extraordinary thing, like a bloom in a wasteland, and in the midst of her hurt and fear, she found it in her to smile back at him with more love and warmth than she thought she would ever again feel for him. Everything was about to be taken from them, or what little they had left, but for these final moments they would stand at last together.

She turned and stared Moloch in the eye.

'How could I live if I sold my sister and my nephew out to you?' she whispered.

Moloch's shoulders sagged. 'Dexter,' he said, 'make her tell us what she knows.'

Dexter's face brightened. He started to walk

across the room, and for an instant, Leonie glanced at him. It was Bill's opportunity, and he took it. He struck out with his uninjured hand and caught Leonie on the right cheekbone, close to the eye. She stumbled back and he reached for the gun, striking her again with his elbow. The gun came free.

Across the room, Braun was already reaching for his weapon. Willard still looked dazed, but was trying to remove his own gun from his belt. The gun in Bill's hand panned across the room, making for Moloch. Moloch grabbed Patricia and pulled her in front of him, using her as a shield.

From the corner of his eye, Bill registered the guns in the hands of the two men, Willard frozen in place, Leonie rising to her knees, still swaying from the impact of the blows, the voices shouting at him.

He looked to his wife, and there came that smile again, and Bill loved her.

He fired the gun, and a red wound opened at his wife's breast. For an instant, all was noise.

Then silence.

They said nothing. Bill lay dead against the wall. Shepherd and Tell were at the door, drawn by the commotion. Patricia Gaddis was still alive. Moloch leaned over her where she lay.

'Tell me,' he said. 'Tell me.'

He touched his finger to the wound in her breast, and she jerked like a fish on a line.

'Tell me and I'll make it stop.'

She spit blood at him and started to tremble. He gripped her shoulders as she began to die.

'I'll find her,' he promised. 'I'll find them both.'

But she was already gone.

Moloch stood, walked over to Willard, and punched him hard in the face. He stumbled back and Moloch hit him again, driving him to his knees.

'Don't you ever do that again,' said Moloch. 'I will tell you what I want from you, and you will do it. From now on, you breathe because I allow you to breathe. You kill only when I say.'

Willard mumbled something.

'What did you say?'

Willard took his hands away from his ruined nose.

'I found it,' said Willard. 'I found the box.'

The letters were postmarked Portland, Maine. Patricia should not have held on to them – her sister had warned her against it – but it was all that she had of her, and she treasured every word. Sometimes she would sit alone in the bedroom and try to catch a hint of her little sister, some trace of her perfume. Even when the scent of her had faded entirely, Patricia believed that she could still detect some faint remnant, for the memory of her sister would never leave her.

'It's not a big city, but she still won't be easy to find,' said Dexter. They were already leaving the scene, departing Camp Hill. Initially, Moloch wasn't sure if the gunshots had been registered by the neighbors, for nobody was on a step or in a yard when they left the house, but minutes later they heard sirens. They had already ditched the van that had been parked at the back of the house as a precaution, but the risk had been worth it.

'And she won't be using her own name,' Dexter continued.

Moloch raised a hand to silence him.

She won't be using her own name.

If she was using an alias, she would need identification, and she could not have assembled that material for herself. She must have approached someone, someone who she believed would not betray her. Moloch went through the names in his head, exploring all of the possibilities, until at last he came to the one he sought.

Meyer.

Karen Meyer.

She would have asked a woman.

They headed for Philly, where they took rooms at a pair of motels off the interstate. Dexter and Braun ate at a Denny's, then brought back food for the others. Both Willard and Leonie had injuries that might have attracted attention, and Moloch could not risk having his face seen. Shepherd and Tell watched TV in their room, the analysts speculating on the order of battle.

'Man, we're gonna bomb those bastards back to the Stone Age,' said Tell.

From what Shepherd could see of their houses,

these people weren't far from the Stone Age to begin with. All things considered, it was likely to be a short but eventful trip for most of them. Still, Shepherd figured that they'd asked for it.

'Eye for an eye,' said Tell.

'It's the way of the world,' Shepherd agreed.

As usual, Dexter and Braun also shared a room. Braun read a book while Dexter watched a DVD on his portable player.

'What are you watching?' asked Braun.

'*Wild Bunch.*'

'Uh-huh. What else you got?'

'*Butch Cassidy and the Sundance Kid. The Thing. The Shootist.*'

Braun put his book down for a moment.

'You always watch movies where the leading men are doomed to die at the end?'

Dexter looked over at Braun.

'They seemed . . . *appropriate.*'

Braun held his gaze.

'Yeah,' he said. 'Whatever.'

He returned to his book. He was reading Thucydides' *History of the Peloponnesian War.* Braun believed in knowing about the past, particularly the past as it pertained to the military, having been an army man himself at one point. The Athenians were about to send out their great fleet, loaded with archers, slingers, and cavalry, to take Sicily, against the advice of the more prudent voices among them. Braun didn't know the intricacies of what was to occur, which was why he had taken up the book to begin with, but he remembered enough of his military history to know that the Athenian empire was sailing toward its ruin.

Moloch lay on the bed in his room and channel surfed until he came to a news bulletin and saw the Land Cruiser being pulled from the river and the shrouded bodies being carried to the waiting ambulance. A picture of Misters appeared on the screen. He still had his eyes and his tongue when the photograph was taken. The cops were looking for eyewitnesses to the incident. They were also taking casts of the tire tracks from the vans. It would not take them long to make the connection between the killings in Pennsylvania and the escape. Moloch calculated they had twenty-four, maybe forty-eight hours to do what needed to be done before the net began to spread farther north.

5

Strange now, or so it seemed, but Marianne had once liked his name. He called himself Edward; not Ted or Ed or Eddie. Edward. It had a kind of patrician ring to it. It was formal, no nonsense.

But she had never liked his second name and had not understood its provenance until it was too late. It was only when she learned more about his ways and began to pick away at his façade that she began to realize the nature of the man with whom she was involved. She had once read a newspaper article about a sculptress who worked with stone and who claimed that the piece she was creating was already present within the medium, so that her task was simply to remove the excess material that was obscuring what lay beneath. Later, Marianne would liken herself to that sculptress, gradually coming to see that what lay concealed under her husband's exterior was something infinitely more complex and more frightening than she had ever imagined; and so it was that she began to fear his name when at last she commenced her search for clues about the man she had married and the secret things that he did.

It had so many forms, so many derivations: Moloch, Malik, Melech, Molech. It could be found in Ammonite traditions, Canaanite, Semite. Moloch: the ancient sun god; the bringer of plagues; god of wealth to the Canaanites. Moloch: the prince of the Land of Tears; Milton's Molech, besmeared with the blood of human sacrifice. The Israelites surrendered their firstborn to him, burning them in fire. Solomon was reputed to have built a temple to him near the entrance to Gehenna, the gates of hell.

Moloch. What kind of man was called by such a name?

And yet, in the beginning, he had been sweet to her. When you lived in Biloxi, Mississippi, where the permanently moored casinos drew the worst kinds, the ones who couldn't afford to go to Florida or Vegas, or who didn't care what their surroundings looked like as long as there was a table, a card shoe, and maybe a cocktail waitress who might be persuaded to offer comfort for a fifty-dollar chip, then any man who didn't try to grab your ass was practically an ambassador for his sex.

And Moloch *was* different. She was working on the *Biloxi Black Beauty*, an imitation showboat painted – despite its name – so many shades of pink that it made one's teeth hurt just to look at it. The cocktail waitresses were forced to wear white corsets like nineteenth-century hookers cleaning up after a john and bunched skirts that, one hundred years before, would have revealed no more than a flash of shin but were now so high that the lower curves of their buttocks were on permanent display, the ruffles of the skirts like stage curtains that had been raised to reveal the main act. In theory, the men weren't supposed to touch them anywhere other than on the back or the arm. In reality, the tips were better if you didn't stick too closely to the letter of the law and allowed them to indulge themselves just a little. If they got too frisky, it was enough to nod at the security guards who dotted the casino in their green blazers, as omnipresent as the artificial potted palms, although the palms were probably more likely to develop as individuals than the *Beauty*'s Deputy Dawgs. They would lean over, one at either side of the drunk (because they were always drunks, the ones who behaved in that way), scooping up his chips and his drink even as he was quickly hustled away from the table, talking to him all the time, calm and quiet, but keeping him moving for, being a drunk, he would find it hard to argue, walk and keep an eye on his remaining chips all at the same time.

Then he would be gone, his departure ignored by the dealer, and eventually someone else would move to take his place at the table. It didn't pay to complain too often, though. There were a lot of girls ready and willing to take your place if you got a reputation as a troublemaker or as a woman who couldn't handle a little attention from the men happily throwing away their savings for a couple of complimentary, watered-down bourbons.

Marianne had been born into a family in the town of Tunica in the cotton country of northwestern Mississippi, close to the Arkansas border. She was raised almost within sight of Sugar Ditch, where slave descendants had lived beside open sewers a couple of blocks from Main Street. Her father ran a little diner on Magnolia Street, but Tunica was so poor it could barely support this meager enterprise. The bank took over the diner and covered its windows with wooden boards. Her father fell apart, and his family fell apart along with him. He grew depressed, then violent. On the day after he struck Marianne so hard across the head that she was deaf in one ear for a week, her mother packed up their things and moved her two daughters to Biloxi, where her own sister lived, and never returned to Tunica again. They existed close to penury, but Marianne's mother could squeeze a nickel until the buffalo shat, and her daughters received schooling and, eventually, found places of their own. Later, she and her husband were reconciled, and he came to live with his wife and her sister for the last three years of his life, a pathetic man destroyed by bad luck, poor judgment, and an inability to stop drinking until the bottle ran dry. He was buried back in Tunica, and two years later his wife was buried alongside him, but by then Tunica had changed. Casinos had brought wealth to what had once been merely a staging post on the way to better things. There was now a carillon clock in a little park downtown that played hymns on the hour, free garbage pickup, even street signs (for in Marianne's youth Tunica could not afford to extend to visitors the luxury of a formal indicator of their whereabouts, a situation of which the late Harry Rylance would undoubtedly have disapproved). Marianne had been considering moving back there to escape Biloxi, for there would be work in Tunica's casinos and the quality of life was considerably better there than on Marianne's stretch of the Gulf Coast, until she met Edward Moloch.

The nature of her father's disintegration, and the sights that greeted her each evening in the casinos, had made her wary and intolerant of those who drank even moderately, but Moloch didn't drink liquor. She asked him for an order as soon as he sat down and placed his chips carefully upon the table, but he refused the offer of a cocktail and instead tipped her a ten for every soda that she brought him. He played seven-card high-low stud quietly, declaring high and low more frequently than any other player, and at least tying each way three times out of five. His clean white shirt was open at the neck beneath a black linen jacket without a single crease. He was a big man for his height, with broad shoulders tapering to a slim waist, and strong thighs. His hair was dark, with no trace of gray, and his face was very thin, with vertical creases running down from each cheekbone and ending on the same level as his mouth, like old wounds that had healed. His eyes were blue-green, with long, dark lashes. Marianne wouldn't have called him handsome, exactly, but he had a charisma about him. He smelled good too. He wore the kind of after-shave that made women pause as they passed him, so that it slipped in under their defenses. And he came out ahead: not so far as to draw attention to himself, but sufficiently above the average for the house to breathe a light sigh of relief when he surrendered his chair. Due in no small part to his generosity, Marianne finished her shift that night with $200 in bills tucked into her purse. It almost made up for the drunks and the maulers.

When her shift finished she decided to walk home in order to stretch her legs and allow a little time to herself. Marianne was an attractive woman, and had learned to play it up on the casino floor but to tone it down for the streets, so she drew few glances as she headed toward Lameuse Boulevard and Old Biloxi.

The guy came at her from an alleyway beside a boarded-up diner. Even in the brief time that she had to see his face before his left hand closed around her mouth and his right around her throat, she knew him. He'd been thrown out earlier for slipping his hand between her legs, working at her painfully with his fingers, and she hadn't been able to get away from him, so firm was his grip. Even the dumb-ass security guys had seen how shaken she was, with her mouth pressed so tightly closed that her lips were almost white. She was asked by the pit boss if she wanted to press charges, but she shook her head. That would be the end of her time at the

Biloxi Black Beauty, and she would have trouble getting work anywhere else too once it came out that she'd asked for the cops to be called and the casino's name appeared in the police blotter, maybe in the local rags too. No, there would be no charges. When she returned to the tables, the man in the black linen jacket with the soda in front of him said nothing to her, but she was certain that he had witnessed all that had occurred.

Now here was the mauler again, some bruising to his cheek where maybe his mouth had got him into a little more trouble than he'd anticipated with casino security, his blond hair matted with sweat, his tan suit wrinkled and torn at the left shoulder. He shifted his grip, pulling her backward into the darkness, whispering in her ear as he did.

'Huh, bitch? Huh, remember me, you fucking bitch?' Over and over. Bitch. Bitch. Bitch.

The alley was L-shaped, an alcove to the right hidden entirely from the street ahead. He spun her round almost gracefully when they reached it and sent her sprawling over a pile of black garbage sacks. Something sharp bit into her thigh. She opened her mouth to scream and he showed her the knife.

'Scream, bitch, and I'll cut you bad. I'll cut you so fucking bad. Take them jeans down, now, y'hear?'

He was fumbling at his own trousers as he spoke, trying to release himself from his pants. His fly was open, his hand inside. He moved forward and made a pass at her with the knife, the blade whistling by the tip of her nose.

'You hear me, bitch?' He leaned toward her and she could see the spittle on his chin. 'You take them off!'

Now she was crying and she hated herself for crying, even as she worked at the button on her jeans, hating the way it parted from the hole so easily, hating that this thing was going to happen to her at the hands of this man.

Hating, hating, hating.

There was a click, and the guy stopped moving. His eyes moved slowly to his right, his head remaining still, as though he hoped that his eyeballs would continue their passage, rotating through his hair and coming to rest so that he could see the man behind him, the man with a gun now pressed into the back of his head.

The man in the white shirt and the creaseless linen jacket.

'Drop the knife,' he said.

The knife fell to the ground, bouncing once on the tip of its blade before coming to rest in the trash.

'Walk to the wall.'

Her attacker did as he was told, and she caught the sharp whiff of ammonia as he passed close to her, and knew that he had wet himself with fear.

And she was pleased.

'Kneel,' said the man with the gun.

The guy didn't move, so the gunman stepped back and raked the barrel of the gun across the

back of his head. He stumbled forward, then fell
to his knees.

'Keep your hands pressed against the wall.'

The man with the gun turned to her.

'You okay?' he asked.

She nodded. She could feel something sour bub-
bling at the back of her throat. She swallowed it
down. He helped her to rise to her feet.

'Go to the end of the alley. Wait for me there.'

She went without question. The would-be rapist
remained facing the wall, but she could hear him
sobbing. At the end of the alleyway she leaned
against the wall, put her palms on her knees, and
leaned down. She sucked great breaths of stale air
into her lungs, tasting polluted water and grease.
Her whole body was shaking and her legs felt weak.
Without the wall to support her, she felt certain
that she would have collapsed. Passersby glanced
at her but no one expressed any concern. This was
a fun town, and people didn't want their fun spoiled
by a sick woman.

Her rescuer – for that was how she already
thought of him – followed her a minute or two
later. In the interim she heard sounds, like a wet
towel slapping against a wall. As he walked toward
her, he was adjusting the leg of his pants.

'Come on.'

'What did you do to him?'

'Hit him some.'

'We should call the police.'

'Why?' He seemed genuinely curious.

'He may try to do it again.'

'He won't do it again. You call the cops, you do it only because you need to, because it makes you feel happier. Believe me, he won't try anything like that again. Now, you want to call them?'

He paused beside her. She thought of the interview she would have to endure, the questions asked at the casino, the face of her boss as he told her that she wouldn't have to come in Monday, wouldn't have to come back ever, sorry, you know how it is.

'No,' she said. 'Let's go.'

He walked with her for a block or two, then hailed a cab. He dropped her off at the door of her apartment, but declined her invitation to come up.

'Maybe I'll see you again?' he said.

She wrote her number on the back of a store receipt and handed it to him.

'Sure, I'd like that. I didn't get your name?'

'My name is Edward.'

'Thank you, Edward.'

Once she was safely inside, the cab pulled away from the curb. She closed the door, leaned against it, and at last allowed herself to cry.

The guy's name was Otis Barger. Moloch read it out from his driver's license. Otis was from Anniston, Alabama.

'You're a long way from home, Otis.'

Barger didn't answer. He couldn't answer. His hands and feet were bound with wire taken from the trunk of Moloch's car, and there was tape over his mouth. One eye was swollen shut, and there was blood on his cheek. His right foot was curled inward at an unnatural angle, broken by the heel of Moloch's boot to ensure that he didn't try to crawl away while Moloch took the woman back to her apartment. He was lying on the garbage bags where, only twenty minutes earlier, Marianne had lain as he prepared to rape her.

Moloch drew a photograph from Barger's wallet. It showed a dark-haired woman – not pretty, not ugly – and a smiling, dark-haired boy.

'Your wife and child?'

Barger nodded.

'You still together?'

Again, Barger nodded.

'She deserves better. I've never met her, but that woman would have to be hell's own whore to deserve you. You think she'll miss you when you're gone?'

This time Barger didn't nod, but his eyes grew wide.

Moloch kicked at the wounded ankle and Barger screamed behind his gag.

'I asked you a question. You think she'll miss you?'

Barger nodded for the third time. Moloch raised the leg of his pants and drew the pistol from the ankle holster. He looked around, kicking at the garbage until he found a discarded chair cushion. He walked to where Barger lay, then kneeled down beside him.

'I don't believe you,' he said. 'What was it you called that lady you tried to rape? Bitch? That was what you called her, wasn't it?'

He slapped Barger hard across the head.

'*Wasn't it?*'

Barger nodded for the fourth, and final, time.

'Well,' said Moloch. 'She's my bitch now.'

Then he placed the cushion against Barger's head, pushed the muzzle of the gun into the fabric, and pulled the trigger.

Marianne knew nothing of this, although, as the years went by, she thought often of that night and wondered what had become of the man in the alley. Moloch would say only that he had beaten him and told him to get out of town. Since he was never seen in Biloxi again, she assumed that was the truth.

Except—

Except that during almost four years together – six months dating, then forty months married in a little house in Danville, Virginia – she had grown increasingly fearful of this man: of his mood swings, of his intelligence, of his capacity for cruelty to her. He knew where to hit her so that it hurt most and bruised least. He knew places on her body where the mere pressure of his fingers was enough to make her scream. There was money, for he always had money, but he gave her only enough to feed their little family of three, for a son had been born to them during that terrible second year. She was required to produce receipts for everything, and every penny had to be accounted for, just as every moment of her day had to be described and justified.

It had begun almost as soon as they were married. It seemed to her that the marriage license was all that he wanted. He had wooed her, made promises to her, provided them with a house to live in. She had given up the job in Biloxi two weeks before the wedding, and he had told her not to take on anything else for a time, that they would travel, try to see a little of this great country. They had a short honeymoon in Mexico, blighted by bad weather and Moloch's moods, but the proposed road trip never materialized. She quickly learned not to mention it, for at best he would mutter and tell her that he was too busy, while at other times he would hold her face, beginning with a caress but gradually increasing his grip until his thumb and forefinger forced her mouth open, and just when the pain began to bring tears to her eyes he would kiss her and release her.

'Another time,' he would say. 'Another time.' And she did not know if he was referring to the trip, or to some promised treat for himself.

The first time he hurt her badly was when he came home from a 'business trip' in Tennessee, about five months into their marriage. She told him that she had found a job for herself in a bookstore. It was only two afternoons each week, and all day Saturday, but it would get her out of the house. You see—

'I don't want you working,' he said.

'But I need to work,' she replied. 'I'm kind of bored.'

'With me?'

The lines in his face deepened, so that she almost expected to glimpse his teeth working through the holes in his cheeks.

'No, not with you. That's not what I meant.'

'So what did you mean? You say you're bored, a man's going to take that to mean something. I don't do it for you anymore? You want somebody else? Maybe you've found somebody else already, is why you want a job, so you'll have an excuse to leave the house.'

'No, it's not that. It's not that at all.'

He was talking as if he were jealous, but there was no real hurt in his words. He was playing a role, and even in her fear she could see that, but it made it harder for her to argue with him when she didn't understand why he was so annoyed. She reached for him and said, 'Come on, honey, it's not like that. You're being—'

She didn't even see him move. One moment they were talking and she was extending her hand toward him, the next her face was pressed against the wall and her arm was being wrenched behind her back. She felt his breath close to her ear.

'I'm being *what*? Tell me. You think you know me? You don't. Maybe I should teach you a little about me.'

His left hand and the weight of his body held

her in place while his right hand slipped beneath her sweater and found her skin. His fingers began moving upon her, exploring.

And then the pain began: in her stomach, in her kidneys, in her groin. Her mouth opened in a silent cry, the agony increasing, turning from yellow to red to black, and the last words she heard were: 'Are you learning now?'

She regained consciousness with him moving on top of her as she lay on the kitchen floor. One month later, she was pregnant. Even now, years later, it still hurt her to think that Danny, her wonderful, beautiful Danny, could have resulted from that night. Perhaps it was the price she had to pay to be given him. If so, then she had continued to pay the price for a long time after, and sometimes, when their infant son cried just a little too much, she would see the light appear in Moloch's eyes and she would run to the boy and quiet him, nearly suffocating him against her.

The child had been a mistake. Moloch wanted no children, and had talked of an abortion, but in the end he had relented. She felt that he did so because he believed it would tie her more closely to him, even as he told her that they were now a family, and would always be a family.

He did not hate her. He loved her. He would tell her that, even as he was hurting her.

I love you.

But if you ever try to leave me, I'll kill you.

* * *

His mistake was to underestimate her. Men had always underestimated her: her father, her uncle (drunk at Thanksgiving, stealing kisses from his niece in the quiet of the kitchen, his mouth open, his hands reaching and touching while she maneuvered herself away, trying to placate him without offending him so that she would not put her family's tenuous status in his house at risk), the men for whom she worked or with whom she slept. It suited her. Where she grew up, men feared and hated women who they suspected were smarter or stronger than they were. It was better to keep your head down, to smile dumbly. It gave you more room to move, when you needed it.

And so she began listening to snatches of telephone conversations, and using her little car, with its small allowance of gas, to track her husband. She picked up receipts for non-existent purchases, just a few here and there, for Moloch had become distracted and no longer checked every item in the kitchen and bathroom. She looked for three-for-two offers, for buy-one, get-one-frees, then squirreled away the freebies for use later. It took her the best part of a year but, slowly, she began to accumulate a little money.

There were areas that were out of bounds to her – the shed, the attic – but now she began to take chances even in those places. In a fit of daring that left her sleepless for days, she called in a locksmith, explaining to him that she'd lost the keys to the garden shed and the attic and that her husband would be furious when he found out.

Then she began to explore.

First, she marked the location of everything in the shed on a piece of paper and made sure always to return each item to its spot on the plan. The attic was more difficult, seemingly littered with trash and old clothes, but still she made a drawing there too.

In the shed she found nothing at first but a gun wrapped in oilcloth and hidden in a box of nails and screws. It took her two more searches – including one in the course of which Moloch had returned home and she had been forced to keep her hands thrust firmly in her pockets for fear that he would see the dirt and rust upon them – to find the hole in one of the boards on the floor. It looked like a flaw in the wood, an absent knot, but when she lifted it she discovered the bag.

She did not have time to count all of the money that it contained, but she reckoned it was close to $900,000, all in twenties and fifties. She put the board back, then returned to the shed twice more to check that she had left no sign of her presence.

In the attic there were items of jewelry, some old, others quite new. She found a small stack of bearer bonds, worth maybe $50,000 in total. She discovered bank account details in the names of unknown men and women, and credit card records carefully noted, even down to the three-digit security number to be found on the backs of the cards.

And she came across a woman's driver's license in the name of Carol-Anne Brenner, a name that caused a buried memory to resonate softly. The next day, while shopping, she stopped at the internet café at the mall and entered the name Carol-Anne Brenner on a search engine. She came up with a doctor, an athlete, a candidate for beatification.

And a murder victim.

Carol-Anne Brenner, a widow, fifty-three. Killed in her home in Pensacola, Alabama, three months earlier. The motive, according to police, was robbery. They were searching for a man in connection with the crime. There was a photofit picture with the report. It showed a young man with blond hair, very pretty rather than handsome, she thought. Police believed that Carol-Anne Brenner might have been having an affair with the young man and that he had wheedled his way into her affections in order to rob her. They had no name for him. Brenner's accounts had been emptied in the days prior to the discovery of her body, and all of her jewelry was missing.

The next day, during her attic search, she found more items of jewelry, and purses, empty, and photographs of women, sometimes alone, sometimes with their families. She also found four driver's licenses and two passports, each with her husband's photograph upon it but each in a different name. The drivers' licenses were tied together with an elastic band, while the passports were in a separate brown envelope. There was a telephone number written on the outside flap.

Marianne remembered the envelope being delivered. A woman had brought it, a woman with short, dark hair and a vaguely mannish stride. She had looked at Marianne with pity and, perhaps, a little interest. The envelope had been sealed then, and Moloch had been furious at the fact that Marianne had been entrusted with it until he confirmed that the seal was intact.

Marianne memorized the number.

Two days later, she called it.

The woman's name was Karen Meyer, and she met Marianne at the mall, Danny sleeping beside them in his stroller. Marianne didn't know why she was trusting her, but she had felt something that day when the woman called with the envelope. And for what she needed, Marianne had nowhere else to turn.

'Why did you call me?' asked Meyer.

'I need your help.'

'I can't help you.'

'Please.'

Meyer looked around, checking faces. 'I mean it. I can't. Your husband will hurt me. He'll hurt all of us. You, of all people, must know what he's like.'

'I know. I mean, I don't know. I don't know what he is anymore.'

Karen shrugged.

'Well, I know what he is. That's why I can't help you.'

Marianne felt the tears begin to roll down her cheeks. She was desperate.

'I have money.'

'Not enough.'

Karen got up to leave.

'No, please.'

Marianne stretched out her hand to restrain her. It locked on her wrist. Karen stopped and looked down at the younger woman's hand.

Marianne swallowed, but kept her eyes on Karen's face. She released her grip, then slipped her hand into the other woman's palm. Tentatively, she touched her gently with her fingers. For a moment, she thought that she felt Karen's hand tremble, until it was suddenly pulled away.

'Don't call me again,' said Karen. 'You do and I swear I'll tell him.'

Marianne didn't watch her leave. Instead, fearful and humiliated, she hid her face in her hands until Karen was gone.

Karen called to the house three days later. Marianne answered the door to find her there, ten minutes after Moloch had left for the day.

'You said you had money.'

'Yes, I can pay you.'

'What do you need?'

'New identities for Danny and me, and maybe for my sister and her husband as well.'

'It'll cost you twenty-five thousand dollars, and I'm nailing you to the wall.'

Marianne smiled despite herself, and after a second's pause, Karen smiled back.

'Yeah, well,' she said. 'I'm being up-front about

it. You're being charged well above the going rate, but I need to cover myself. If he finds out, I'm going to have to run. You understand that?'

Marianne nodded.

'I'll want half now, half later.'

Marianne shook her head. 'I can't do that.'

'What do you mean? You said you had money.'

'I do, but I can't touch it until just before I leave.'

Karen stared at her.

'It's his money, isn't it?'

Marianne nodded.

'Shit.'

'There's more than enough to cover what you ask. I promise you, you'll have it as soon as I'm ready to leave.'

'I need something now.'

'I don't have half, or anything close to it.'

'What can you give me?'

'Two hundred.'

'*Two hundred?*'

Karen slumped against the wall and said nothing for at least a minute.

'Give it to me,' she said at last.

Marianne went upstairs and retrieved the roll of bills from the only safe place she could find in which to keep it: the very center of a carton of tampons. It was a peculiarity of Moloch's. He would not even sleep beside her when she had her period. She handed the roll of ones and fives to Karen.

'Do you want to count it?'

Karen weighed the roll of bills in her hand.

'I figure this is everything that you've hidden away, right?'

Marianne nodded, then said: 'Well, I kept fifty back. That's all.'

'Then that'll be enough, for now.'

She moved to go.

'How long will it take?'

'They'll be ready in two weeks. You can pick them up when you're leaving, and I'll take the rest of my money then.'

'Okay.'

Marianne opened the door. As she did so, the older woman reached out and brushed her cheek. Marianne didn't flinch.

'You'd have done it too, wouldn't you?' said Karen softly.

'Yes.'

Karen smiled.

'You need to work on your seduction technique,' she said.

'I've never had to use it before – under those circumstances.'

'I guess your heart just wasn't in it.'

'I guess not.'

Karen shook her head sadly, walked to her car, and drove away.

Marianne never understood why Moloch had kept the licenses, the purses, the little personal items from the women. She suspected that they were souvenirs, or a means of recalling the women from whom they came, a kind of *aide-mémoire*. Or perhaps it was simply vanity.

Moloch had never told her what he did for a living, exactly. He was, when she asked in those first days, a 'businessman,' an 'independent consultant,' a 'salesman,' a 'facilitator.' Marianne believed that the women, and what had happened to them, was only part of what he was. Now, when she read of raids on stores or on banks, and saw her husband's cash reserve increase; when she heard of a businessman being killed in his car for his briefcase, the contents later revealed to be $150,000 in under-the-counter earnings, and an amount just under that was briefly added to the bag in the shed; when a young woman disappeared in Altoona, the daughter of a moderately wealthy businessman, and her body was found in a ditch after the ransom was paid, she thought of Moloch. She thought of Moloch as she fingered the money; she thought of Moloch as she smelled the burnt powder in the gun among the nails; and she thought of Moloch as she spied the hardened dirt in the treads of his boots, carefully picking it away and placing it in a Ziploc bag, which she bound tightly and squeezed into a tampon inserter.

In those last days, she became aware of an increase in the pitch of his activities. There were more calls to the phone, the phone that she was not allowed to answer. There were more frequent, and longer, absences. The mileage on his car climbed steadily in increments of two hundred miles. He grew yet more distracted, now barely glancing at the receipts from the market and failing even to check the total spent against her allowance for the week.

There were three things that Marianne had learned about Moloch's final operation, through careful listening and the maps and notes that he had locked away in the attic. The first was that it would take place in Cumberland, far to the north of the state and close to the borders of both Maryland and Pennsylvania. The second was that it would involve a bank.

The third was that it would take place on the last Thursday of the month.

She made her plans carefully. She called Karen from a pay-phone and told her the exact time at which she would arrive to pick up the material. She contacted her sister, who lived only a few miles away, yet from whom she had become virtually estranged because of Moloch's paranoia, and told her of her plan, and of the possibility that she and her sorry-ass husband might have to leave the state at some point in the future, but with money in their pockets. Surprisingly, Patricia seemed unconcerned at the prospect of uprooting herself. Bill had recently been let go from a plant job and she saw it as a chance for them both to start over again.

Marianne prepared three changes of clothing for Danny and herself, using what little cash she had left to buy them a new set of clothes cheaply at Marshalls: no-name jeans, plain T-shirts, cotton sweaters from the beneath the yellow, black, and red 'Reduced' sign. These she placed at the bottom of their respective piles of clothing, although she need not have worried, Moloch becoming ever more withdrawn as the day of the operation approached. This was to be his big score, she sensed.

What she could not have known was that Moloch's recent actions were merely one of a number of scams and crimes that he had put into operation over the years, and that there were other men involved, committing insurance frauds, drug rip-offs, minor bank raids in small dusty towns.

Murders.

And these were only the enterprises that produced a profit, for Moloch had his hobbies too. He had more in common with the would-be rapist Otis Barger than might once have seemed possible, except he picked his targets more carefully, from the ranks of whores and addicts and lost souls, and there was never a risk of them talking, because when he was finished with them he disposed of their remains in forests and mountain bogs. Moloch's peculiarity – one, if the truth be known, of many – was his disinclination to have vaginal sex with his victims.

After all, he did not wish to be unfaithful to his wife.

Yet even if she had known all of this at the time, had recognized the unsuspected depths of her husband's degeneracy, Marianne would still have acted as she did. She would still have contacted Karen. She would still have set in motion her escape.

She would still have informed the police of the details of the bank job.

She called them shortly after she had retrieved the cash from the hollow beneath the shed floor and placed it in the trunk of her car, alongside the two small bags that represented all of the possessions she was prepared to take with her. She planned to drive to the rendezvous point, meet Karen, then head on to the bus station and abandon her car there. From there, she would pay cash for two tickets to three different destinations, each bought at a separate window. She would travel on to only one of them, New York, and there she would buy tickets to three different cities, and again head to only one of them. It seemed like a good plan.

She strapped her son into the child seat, then drove to the mall and parked by the pay phone. She lifted the boy out and carried him, still sleeping, to the phone. From there she dialed the dispatcher at the Cumberland PD and asked to be put through to Detective Cesar Aponte. She had read his name in a newspaper one week earlier, when he was quoted during an investigation into a domestic assault case that had left a woman fighting for her life in intensive care. If he was not on duty, she had three other names, all taken from the newspapers.

There was a pause, then a man's voice came on the line. 'Detective Aponte speaking.'

She took a breath, and began:

'There will be a bank robbery today at four

P.M. at a First United in Cumberland. The man leading the robbery is named Edward Moloch. He lives at . . .'

Using Racal, the call was traced back to the pay phone at the mall. By the time the local cruiser arrived, Marianne was gone, and nobody could recall what the woman who had made the call looked like. The only detail that the old woman behind the counter at the Beanie Baby Boutique could remember was that she had an infant boy asleep on her shoulder. Stuck behind the pay phone was an envelope, just as Marianne had told them there would be. It contained Moloch's various false IDs and some, but not all, of the material from the attic relating to what she believed were his past crimes. Most of it remained in the house.

By then, Marianne had arrived at the meeting place, a disused gas station half a mile outside town. She was five minutes late. There was no sign of Karen's car, and for a moment she panicked, fearing that she had been abandoned. Then Karen appeared from the back of the lot, waving her around. She drove, and parked beside a beat-up Oldsmobile.

She got out of the car and saw that Karen had a manila envelope in her hand.

'You've got it? You've got it all?'

'You've got my money?'

Marianne popped the trunk. The black knapsack she had taken was zippered closed. When she opened it, dead presidents blinked in the bright sunlight. Five of the sealed bundles had been opened, then rebound. Marianne handed them to Karen.

'Twenty-five thousand. I counted it this morning.'

'I trust you.'

She handed over the envelope. Marianne slit it with her thumbnail.

'Don't *you* trust *me*?'

'If I didn't trust you, do you think I'd be opening the trunk in front of you?'

'I guess not.'

She examined the passport, the driver's license, the card bearing her social security number. She was now Marianne Elliot instead of Marian Moloch. Her son's name, according to his new birth certificate, was Daniel. Where his father's name should have been, the word 'Unknown' had been written.

'You've left me with my own first name, almost.'

'You've never done this before. The first thing that will give you away is your failure to answer to your new name. It will arouse suspicions and attract attention to you. Marianne is close enough to your given name for you to avoid that problem.'

'And Danny's father?' She had asked Karen to give her son the name Daniel. It was the name that she had always wanted for him, but Moloch had given him his own name, Edward. Now he was Daniel. In her mind, he had always been Daniel.

'You get asked, his name was Lee Server, and he's dead. In there is an obituary for Server. It will tell you all you need to know about him.'

Marianne nodded. She found a set of documents

and IDs for both Patricia and Bill, the photos a little old because they were the only ones she had at hand when Karen had agreed to help her. Once again, they had been left with their own first names.

'I should ask you for more money,' said Karen. 'I had to pay off some people. The paper trail goes right back, even down to death certificates for your father and mother. There's a typewritten sheet of paper in that envelope. Memorize the details on it, then burn it. It's your new family, except you'll never get to know them now. You're an only child. Your parents are dead. It's all very sad.'

Marianne stuffed the material back into the envelope.

'Thank you.'

'How the hell did you ever get involved with this guy?' asked Karen suddenly.

'A man tried to rape me,' she replied. 'He saved me.'

There was a pause.

'Did he?' she asked sadly.

'I trusted him. He was . . . strong.'

She started back toward her car.

'I gave him those names, the ones on the papers that you found in the attic,' said Karen.

Marianne stopped.

'What do you mean?'

'I created them, all but one. He came to me and I did it.'

'Who is he? Who is he really?'

'I don't know. The only name that I didn't give

him is the one he used with you. Moloch was how
I knew him, right from the beginning. I guess he
likes that name a lot.'

She tossed a set of car keys to Marianne.

'This is your car now. Registration is in the glove
compartment. It's clean.'

'I'll give you more money.'

'Didn't cost me much. I'd kept it hidden away
in case I ever had to run. I guess your need's greater
than mine right now.'

Karen helped her move the bags into the trunk
of the new car, then shifted the baby seat to the
Oldsmobile while Marianne carried Danny. He was
awake now, and had begun to cry.

'You'd better get going,' said Karen.

Marianne strapped the still-howling child in, then
stood at the driver's door.

'I—'

'I know.'

Then, without even knowing why, Marianne
walked quickly up to the older woman and kissed
her tenderly on the mouth, then hugged her. After
a moment, Karen responded, hugging her tightly in
return.

'Good luck,' she whispered.

'And to you.'

Then Marianne got in the car and drove away.

There were three First Uniteds in Cumberland, and
each was monitored after Marianne's warning. It
was not her fault that the information she had given

was wrong. Cumberland was merely the base: the bank itself was in Fort Ashby, ten miles south. It was taken just as the doors were being locked for the day. Nobody was killed, although the security guard was pistol-whipped and would never fully recover from his injuries. The silent alarm was not set off until the robbers – five of them – had left the bank. By the time the police could react, the thieves were gone.

Moloch got back to his house shortly before daybreak. The street was quiet. He made one full circuit of the block, then parked at the end of the driveway and entered the house. He walked straight to the back door, passed through the garden in darkness, and unlocked the shed door.

He saw the space where the board should have been, and the empty hollow where his money once lay, and then there were flashlight beams, and shouted orders, and dogs barking.

And as he emerged blinking into the phalanx of armed men, he thought:

Bitch. I'll kill you for this.

The Third Day

Widow'd wife and wedded maid,
Betrothed, betrayer, and betray'd!

Sir Walter Scott, 'The Betrothed'

The Third Day

6

It was close to dawn when they neared their destination. Already there was a faint glow visible in the east, as of a fire distantly glimpsed. They had agreed on a rotation for sleeping and driving, as Moloch was reluctant to pause for any reason. He had the scent of her now, of that he was certain. It had proved easier than expected, for elements outside his control had fallen into place for him: foolish Verso, who had hoped to trade Moloch's life for his own; his idiot brother-in-law, risking his anonymity in order to gamble on meaningless outcomes; and Dexter's casual remark that his wife would not be using her own name, causing tumblers to fall in Moloch's mind.

For most of the journey he remained silent and awake, watching the red lights of the cars on the road streaming toward the void, fading into the distance until they were swallowed up by the blackness. Moloch had been incarcerated for so long that he found himself fascinated by the small details of the lives being lived around him, although there was a distance, perhaps even a coldness, to his interest: it was the curiosity of a small boy marveling at the industry of termites or ants in the moment before he annihilates their mound or torches their nest. He watched the cars go by, their occupants only occasionally visible in the brief flare of a match or the comforting illumination of the dashboard lights, and wondered at how so many could be on the roads and highways at this time, for what mission could be so urgent, what destination so compelling, that it caused them to give themselves up to a journey through the night, forsaking sleep. Moloch suspected that, for some, there was no destination. There was no home waiting, no husband drowsing, no wife sleeping or children dreaming. There was only the illusion of progress and momentum offered by the cocoon of the automobile in the surrounding night. These people were not traveling; they were fleeing, taunted by a false belief that if they ran fast and hard enough they might somehow escape their past or their present, that they might even somehow escape themselves. Moloch closed his eyes and recalled those that had crossed his path and faded from the view of the world as a consequence. For some, he thought, it might almost have been a relief. He licked his lips and waited for the coming of the dream.

Braun, weary now of Willard's unsmiling company, had joined Dexter and Moloch in the lead van, while Leonie had taken the wheel of the second. Farther back along the road, Tell and Powell were engaged in a lengthy discussion of their various sexual conquests, both real and imagined, while Shepherd sat in silent judgment upon them. As the trip had worn on, Shepherd had begun to draw away a little not only from the younger men in the car but from the group as a whole. There had been no opportunity for him to talk with Dexter and Braun since Moloch's escape, and the need to do so was now pressing. They knew one another well, these three men, for they had worked together before under Moloch's aegis. Leonie, too, shared a history with Dexter, although she largely kept her own counsel, choosing to discuss her thoughts only with Dexter and trusting him to relay them, if necessary, to the rest of the group.

Shepherd was concerned about recent developments, including the killing of the investigator down at Dismal Creek and the mutilation of his companion, and the deaths of Moloch's sister-in-law and her husband. He also had real worries about the sanity of at least one of their group.

Of Powell he knew little and, in truth, cared to know even less. He had come highly recommended, and had state time behind him in Maryland and Tennessee. Shepherd found him boorish and ignorant, and the snatches of conversation that were coming from his right did nothing to alter that perception. Tell he liked, but while he understood the possible justification for taking the life of the young pizza delivery man (he was smart, argued Tell after the fact, and might have noticed more than he pretended), he was not convinced that it was necessary, and Tell's inability to make that distinction troubled him. The incident with the cell phone also indicated that Tell's temper was somewhere between short and nonexistent. Shepherd, as previously noted, wasn't a big fan of cell phones. He believed they were contributing to the creation of a ruder, less caring society. There was a time, and it wasn't so very long ago, when people kept their voices down in public, not only because they wished to enjoy a little privacy in their conversations but also because talking too loudly disturbed the people around them. Now, all that was going out the window, along with leaving your car unlocked or your front door open. The fact that people now locked their doors and secured their houses to protect them from criminals like Shepherd was beside the point. Still, Shepherd had never really considered solving the cell phone problem by killing anyone who used one in a discourteous manner. It was a pity that nobody would ever know that excessive conversational volume was the reason behind the Arab's murder. Otherwise, he might have made a nice example to others, convincing them to change their ways. Shepherd figured that Tell would be okay if he could just calm down some, maybe take a deep breath once in a while instead of pulling a trigger. Shepherd would work on him.

But the principal source of Shepherd's unease was Willard, and he knew that Dexter shared that disquiet. Shepherd was a man who believed himself to be in control of his own appetites. He also knew, from past experience, that discipline and restraint in any operation increased the odds of its success, and that once those qualities began to dissipate, a breakdown of some kind inevitably followed. Willard, quite clearly, was incapable of exercising self-control, making Tell look like a Buddhist by comparison. He was an immature man defined by his appetites. Shepherd did not know what ties bound Willard to Moloch, or what made the older man show such indulgence toward the younger. Sometimes, Moloch seemed to demonstrate toward Willard the tenderness of a lover. At other times, he appeared almost paternal, protecting the younger man while reluctantly disciplining him. Whatever Moloch's feelings about him, Willard was becoming more and more unpredictable. As a consequence they were leaving a trail for others to follow, and there would be a reckoning because of it. Shepherd had no intention of sitting on death row, waiting to see if the chair or natural causes would take him first. His share of the money would buy him a comfortable life, if he was careful, and he had every intention of living long enough to spend it. He needed to talk with Dexter and Braun, for something had to be done about Willard.

If Leonie felt unease at the prospect of spending time in Willard's company, she did not show it when Braun asked her to switch vehicles. Braun, for one, suspected that Leonie felt little of anything at all, and that she and Willard might well be blood relatives under the skin. Dexter had used her for jobs a couple of times, with Moloch's agreeement, but Braun still knew nothing about her other than a story Dexter had told him once. Leonie was heading out of some dyke bar in South Carolina – Braun was less surprised to hear that Leonie ate at home than that she'd managed to find a pickup bar in South Carolina – when a pair of guys jumped her in the parking lot. Braun knew their kind, had grown up alongside them: they hated women, particularly independent women, and there was nothing more independent than a woman who didn't need a man for sex. They bundled her into the trunk of their car and drove her to a shack out in the woods. Braun didn't need to know anything more about what happened to Leonie after that, and Dexter didn't tell him much anyway, but he could guess. Afterward, when they saw that she hadn't buckled, they beat on her some, then dumped her out back of the dyke bar, her clothes torn and bloody. She didn't go back inside, though. Instead, she walked to her car, where her gun lay taped beneath the dashboard – she hadn't bothered to carry it into the bar, a mistake that she would never again repeat – and returned to her apartment, where she washed and douched and treated her cuts, then took a couple of sleeping pills and went to bed.

The next morning, she called Dexter. She told him all that had occurred, and he drove down to be with her. It was Dexter who pulled the two guys from the street and brought them back to the shack, where Leonie was waiting. Then he sat outside in his truck, smoking and listening to R. L. Burnside while he watched the road. He heard that hunters found the two men a couple of days later. One of them was still alive, although he died as soon as the medics tried to move him. Dexter figured that Leonie would be kind of unhappy to hear that only one of them had survived for so long. Usually, she was precise about these things, but then she'd been pretty upset at what had been done to her, so it might have clouded her judgment some.

It wasn't that part of the story that had stuck with Braun, though. The guys had got what they deserved, make no mistake about that, and Braun wasn't about to shed any tears for them. No, what gave Braun an insight into Leonie was what those guys saw before they died. One had been married, while the other was dating a woman who worked nights providing technical support for her local ISP. Leonie had visited them both while she was waiting for Dexter to pick up the two men, and just as they'd had fun with her, well, she'd had fun with their women. She'd even taken some pictures before she left.

Dexter said they'd come out pretty good, considering the amount of red in them.

No, Willard wouldn't be screwing with Leonie, not if he had any sense in that pretty-boy head of his.

Tell and Shepherd, meanwhile, appeared to have bonded. Shepherd had told Braun that he was reasonably impressed with how Tell had handled the Verso thing. Like Shepherd, Braun wasn't so sure that Tell had really needed to kill the pizza guy, but there was no way of knowing how much he had taken in, so Tell had probably erred on the side of caution.

Whatever occurred, at least there was Dexter. Braun had known Dexter longer than any other human being, longer even than his own parents. They were like brothers, bound by blood. They shared cars, rooms, even women, although if Braun ever met a woman whom he liked as much as Dexter, then he planned to marry her and not share her with anyone, not even Dexter.

This did not strike Braun as at all odd.

'You ever wonder about names?' asked Dexter, out of nowhere.

'Wonder how?' said Braun.

'About how only some colors become names, and not others.'

'Like?'

'Like black. You know, Mr. Black. Or Mr. White. You got Mr. Green, too, and your Mr. Brown, but that's about it. You ever meet anybody called Blue, or Yellow, or Red. Doesn't happen, except in movies. You think that's strange?'

'You know, it never struck me before.'

'You think it's interesting?'

'No. You got too much time on your hands, is what I think. You need to be doing something useful to keep your mind off shit like that. Just drive.'

'There was a time,' said Dexter, 'when you thought I had a lot of interesting shit to say.'

'I thought you were deep. Then I got to know you.'

'You saying I'm not deep?'

'If you were a pool, little kids could paddle in you.'

'If you were a pool, little kids would piss in you.'

'Just drive, will you? The sooner we get to where we're going, the sooner I can get away from your shallow black ass.'

But both men were smiling as Dexter tapped the gas, Moloch momentarily forgotten in the darkness behind them.

It was the absence of lights that alerted Karen Meyer. She heard the van pulling up outside her house, but no headlights matched its progress. Her first thought was that it was the cops coming, and she ran through a mental checklist as she climbed out of bed and pulled on a pair of jeans over her panties. The dummy passports and driving licenses were hidden in a panel behind her gas stove, accessible only by taking apart the oven from the inside, and she deliberately kept it thick with grease and food waste to discourage any possible search, even if it meant that the oven was rendered practically unusable as a result. Her inks, pens, and dyes were all in her studio, and were indistinguishable from the materials she used in her regular design work. Her cameras were an expensive Nikon, a cheaper Minolta, and a Canon digital. Again, she could argue that these were an essential part of her job, since she often had to take photos as part of her initial preparations. The last batch of material had gone out a few days before, and there was nothing on the slate. She figured that she was clean.

She had moved up to Norwich, Connecticut, to be close to her mother. Her mother had suffered a bad stroke that left her with impaired mobility, and Karen, as the only daughter in the family, had felt responsible for her. Karen's brothers lived over on the West Coast, one in San Diego, the other in Tacoma, but they each sent money to boost the coverage offered by their mom's insurance and to help Karen out, although, unofficially, Karen didn't need their help, because her sidelines were quite lucrative. Still, she wasn't one to turn down free money, and the cash had helped her to rent the pretty house on Perry Avenue in which she now lived. Much as she loved her mom, she couldn't live with the old woman, and her mom wanted to retain some degree of independence anyway. She had a panic button and a day nurse, and Karen was three minutes away from her. It was the perfect arrangement for all of them.

She looked out of the window and saw the van. It was black and comparatively clean – not so beatup that it might attract attention, and not so fresh as to stand out.

There was no other vehicle in sight.

Not cops, she thought.

Her doorbell rang.

Not cops.

She went to her dresser and removed the gun from the drawer. It was a Smith & Wesson LadySmith auto, its grip designed for a smaller, woman's hand. She had never fired it anywhere except on the range, but its presence in the house reassured her. Although Meyer made a point of no longer dealing with violent criminals, there was no telling what some people might do if they were desperate enough.

Barefoot, she padded down the stairs, the gun held close to her thigh. She did not turn on any of the house lights. The streetlamps cast the shadow of a woman against her door.

'Who is it?' she said.

She glanced to her right, where the display panel for the alarm system was mounted, and began checking the sensors in each zone. Front door: OK.

'Karen?' said a woman's voice. 'Karen Meyer?'

'I said, "Who is it?"'

Living room: OK.

'My name is Leonie. I'm in trouble. I was told you could help me.'

'Who told you?'

Dining room: OK.

'His name is Edward.'

Garage: OK.

'Edward what?'

Kitchen: DISARMED.

Her stomach lurched. She felt metal at the nape of her neck. A hand closed over her gun.

'You should know my name,' said a voice. 'After all, it's the only one that you didn't give me.'

Dupree awoke to pain.

His joints and muscles, even his gums, still ached, although he'd taken some painkillers the night before. He felt too weak to lift his own weight from his bed, so he lay still, watching shadows rise and fade like smoke upon the ceiling. He wondered sometimes if the symptoms he felt were phantoms too, shadows cast by the knowledge of his impending mortality. The pain had been coming more frequently in recent months. He had been warned by old Doc Bruder that his size and build left him open to a variety of ailments, and the pain he was experiencing could be the onset of any one of those.

'You're not frail by any means,' the retired physician had said while Joe sat on a couch in the old man's den, Gary Cooper striding down a dusty street on the TV screen, forsaken by his darling, 'but you're not as strong as you look, or as people seem to think you are. Your job puts stresses on you. You're complaining to me of pains in your chest, aches in your joints. I'm telling you that you need to get yourself checked out.'

But Dupree had not taken Bruder's advice, just as Bruder had known that he would not. Dupree was afraid. If he was told that he could no longer do his job, then that job would be taken away from him. His work on the island was more important to him than anything else. Without it, he would be lost. He would die.

Dupree was thirty-eight now, and would be thirty-nine in May. He recalled a picture he had once seen of Robert Pershing Wadlow, the so-called 'Alton Giant', the largest man on record, Wadlow towering over the two men at either side of him, their heads barely reaching his elbows. At eight feet eleven inches tall, he was taller than the enormous bookcase behind him. His hands were buried in the pockets of his dark suit, and he appeared to be teetering to his left, as if on the verge of toppling over, his thin frame buffeted by an unseen wind. Dupree guessed that Wadlow was twenty when the photograph was taken. Two years later he was dead, felled by the great curse that was his condition.

Lying on his bed in the house in which he had grown up, Dupree remembered his father's stories, his tales of old giants, told to reassure a boy who felt himself alienated from his peers by his size. His father had lied to him. They were lies of omission, but lies nonetheless, for his father had tailored his stories to the boy's problems, cutting, distorting, softening.

For his stories were not truly about giants.

They were about the death of giants.

Outside it was still dark. Ordinarily he would have been on his way to the station house by now, but he had juggled the roster so that he could spend the evening with Marianne. He lay back on his bed and tried to rest.

* * *

Sharon Macy sat in the tiny kitchen of her apartment, sipping a mug of hot milk. She had a lot on her mind. Her father was due to enter hospital the following week for a series of tests after he had complained of pains in his back and chest. He was laughing off the concerns of his wife and daughter, but there was a history of cancer in the family and Macy knew that the fear of it was with each of them. Under other circumstances she might have returned home immediately, but the department was already buckling under the combined weight of illness and leave – which was why Macy, although still on probation, had found herself on the island's roster – and she suspected that only a real emergency would enable her to absent herself from duty. Anyway, her father had told her in no uncertain terms that he did not want her hanging around the house fussing over him. Her tour on Sanctuary would leave her with five days off at the end of it. She would drive down to Providence as soon as she was back on the mainland, and would examine her options in the light of what, if anything, her father's tests revealed.

Macy thought too of Barron and the drugs that she had seen him take from Terry Scarfe. Maybe she was mistaken in what she believed had occurred, but she didn't think so. She wished that she had someone with whom she could talk about these things, and for the first time since the break-up of their relationship she felt herself missing Max, or at least missing what he had once represented for her.

To hell with him, she thought. To hell with all of them.

She placed the empty mug in the sink, returned to bed, and at last fell asleep to the sound of a ship in the bay, its horn rising like the cry of a sea creature lost in the darkness, seeking only to return to the safety of its kind.

The call woke Terry Scarfe from a deep, alcohol-induced sleep, and so it took him a couple of seconds to recognize the voice and the distinctive Eastern European accent.

'We have a job for you. Someone has purchased your expertise.'

Even in his dazed state, Terry knew that whatever expertise he might have was worth next to nothing, unless you were dealing in pesetas and were happy just to count the zeros.

'Sure,' he said. Terry wasn't going to argue. He needed some cash. Even if he hadn't needed it, these people weren't the kind that you refused. They owned Terry Scarfe, and he knew it.

'You'll get a call, usual place, fifteen minutes,' the man said, then hung up.

Terry rose, swayed a little, pulled on a pair of sweatpants, sneakers and an old T-shirt over his scrawny body, found his heaviest overcoat, then walked two blocks to the pay phone, picking up a coffee at the Dunkin Donuts along the way. He stood there, shivering despite the warmth of the cup in his hands.

Life had not been particularly kind to Terry Scarfe. Most of the time it seemed to treat him like he had screwed its sister. Other times, it went after him like he had screwed its mother as well. He had one failed marriage behind him, a failure that was due, Terry felt, to a combination of factors, including excessive alcohol intake on the night that he had proposed, his arrest and incarceration shortly after the wedding itself, and the unforgiving (and, in fact, downright unpleasant) nature of the woman to whom he had attached himself. His wife had divorced him while he was in jail on burglary charges, then married someone else while Terry was banged up for possession of a controlled substance. Her significant life events, Terry concluded, seemed to coincide with his government vacations. Maybe if he stayed out of jail for a while, her life wouldn't be quite so good, while the quality of his own existence would improve considerably.

A smarter man than Terry might have concluded that his criminal ambitions for himself far exceeded the talents available to him to achieve them, but like most criminals Terry wasn't particularly smart. Unfortunately, his career options were now even more limited than they were to begin with, and few of them were likely to meet with the approval of the forces of law and order, which was why he was standing beside a telephone in the darkness waiting to talk to someone he had never met and who was unlikely to offer Terry a job tasting beer or testing feather beds for softness. Just as Terry was starting to notice that he could no longer feel his feet, the call came through.

'Terry Scarfe? My name is Dexter.'

Terry thought the guy sounded black. It didn't bother him, except that black people tended to stand out some in Portland, and if the guy was planning on coming up, it could present problems.

'What can I do for you?'

'There's an island, somewhere off the coast there. It's called Dutch Island.'

'Yeah, Dutch. Sanctuary.'

'What?'

'Some folks still call it Sanctuary, that's all, but Dutch, yeah, Dutch is good.'

He heard the black guy sigh.

'You done?'

'Yeah. Sorry.'

'We need you to find out as much as you can about it.'

'Like?'

'Cop stuff. Ferries. Points of access.'

'I'll need to bring in someone else. I know a guy lives out there. He's got no love for the big cop on the island.'

'Big cop?'

'Yeah, fuckin' giant.'

'You're shitting me.'

'Nope, for real.'

'Well, find out all you can. And get your friend to track down a woman. She's using the name Marianne Elliot. She'll have a little boy with her, six years old. I want to know where she lives, who she's friendly with, boyfriends, shit like that.'

'When do you need this by?'

'Tonight.'

'I'll do my best.'

Terry thought that he heard, in the background, a soft pop. Terry knew that sound. Somebody had just taken a bullet.

'No,' said Dexter, 'you'll do better than that.'

Dexter stared down at the body of Karen Meyer. She had never been a pretty woman, but Leonie and Willard had removed what little superficial attractiveness she might have had. They worked well together. It was kind of worrying. Dexter would have to talk to her. He didn't want her getting too close to Willard. He and Shepherd had talked, and the way things were going, Willard wasn't going to be around much longer.

Meyer had been easy to find. She'd transferred her business north, but had left word with the kind of people who might need her services in the future. It had taken Dexter just one phone call to find out where she was.

He'd always thought Meyer was smart, and relatively unsentimental. It was all money with her, and he guessed that the woman had given her a big share of Moloch's stash in return for her help. It must have been a lot to make her risk crossing Moloch. He hoped that she'd had a good time with it because, in those final minutes in her basement, she had paid in spades for what she'd done.

'Did you find someone?' asked Moloch.

'Yeah. He'll cost us five G's to Boston, plus a straight ten percent of whatever is on the island and some favors in the future.'

'He'd better be worth it.'

'They threw in a bonus, as a sign of goodwill.'

Moloch waited, and Dexter smiled.

'They gave us a cop.'

The changeover went smoothly. Lockwood and Barker came out on the first ferry and started the weekly check of the medical and fire equipment at the station house. At 11 A.M., Dupree checked in with them, then drove down Main Street to the post office, parking his old jeep in the lot on the right-hand side of the white clapboard building. He had called Larry Amerling that morning to tell him that there was something that he wanted to talk to him about. It struck him that Amerling might have been expecting the call.

Amerling knew more about the island than anyone else, maybe even more than Dupree himself. His home was filled with books and papers on the history of Casco Bay, including copies of his own book, printed privately and sold at the market and at the bookstores over in Portland. Amerling was a widower, and had been for ten years. His children lived on the mainland, but they visited regularly, little trains of grandchildren in tow. Dupree usually spent Thanksgiving with Amerling, as it was his family's tradition to return to the island and celebrate the feast together. They were good people, even if it was Larry Amerling who had first christened the policeman 'Melancholy Joe'. Only a handful of people used that name, and few of them used it to his face, although the name had stuck among the cops assigned to the island.

Dupree thought that Amerling would be alone when he called, as the old man usually took a half hour's time-out at 11 A.M. to get some paperwork done and drink his green tea, but the postmaster had company that morning. The painter, Giacomelli, was standing against the wall, drinking take-out coffee from the market. He looked troubled. So did Amerling. Dupree nodded a greeting to them both.

'I interrupt something?' he asked.

'No,' said Amerling. 'We've been waiting for you. You want some tea?'

Dupree poured some of the green tea into one of Amerling's delicate little Chinese cups. He held the cup gently in the palm of his hand. The three men exchanged pleasantries and island gossip for a time before lapsing into an uneasy silence. Dupree had spent the morning trying to put his concerns into words, to explain them in a way that did not make him sound like a superstitious fool. In the end, Amerling saved his blushes.

'Jack's here for the same reason you're here, I think,' Amerling began.

'Which would be?'

'There's something wrong on the island.'

Dupree didn't respond. It was Jack who spoke next.

'I thought it was just me, but it isn't. The woods feel different, and . . .'

'Go on,' said Amerling.

Jack looked at the policeman.

'I haven't been drinking, if that's what you're thinking, least of all not enough for this.'

'I didn't think that at all,' said Dupree. There was no way to tell if he was lying or not.

'Well, you may reconsider when you hear this. My paintings are changing.'

Dupree waited a heartbeat.

'You mean they're getting better?'

There was a burst of laughter that eased the tension a little and seemed to relax the painter slightly.

'No, smart-ass. They're as good as they're gonna get. There are marks appearing on the canvases. They look like men, but I didn't put them there. They're in the sea paintings and now they're in some of the landscapes as well.'

'You think someone is sneaking into your house and painting in figures on your work?'

He tried to keep the disbelief from his voice. He almost succeeded, but Jack spotted it.

'I know it sounds weird. The thing of it is, these figures aren't painted on.'

He reached down to the floor and lifted up a board wrapped in an old cloth. He removed the cloth, revealing one of his seascapes. Dupree stepped closer and saw what looked like two men in the shallows. They were little more than stick figures, but they were there. He reached out a finger.

'Can I touch it?'

'Sure.'

Dupree ran his finger over the board, feeling the traces of the brush strokes against his skin. When he came to the figures, he paused, then raised the tips of his fingers to his nose and sniffed.

'That's right,' said Jack. 'They've been burned into the board.'

He picked up a second painting and handed it to Dupree.

'You know what this is?'

Dupree felt uncomfortable even looking at the painting. It was certainly one of Jack's better efforts. He sucked at sea and hills, but he did good trees. They were mostly bare and in the background of the picture, almost hidden by mist, Dupree could make out a stone cross. It was definitely a departure for the painter.

'It's the approach to the Site,' he said. 'I have to tell you, Jack, you're never going to sell this painting. Just looking at it gives me the creeps.'

'It's not for sale. I do some of these for, well, I guess out of my own curiosity. Tell me what you see.'

Dupree held the painting at arm's length and tried to concentrate on it.

'I see trees, grass, marsh. I see the cross. I see—'

He stopped and peered more closely at the detail on the canvas.

'What is that?'

Something gray hung in the dark place between two trees, close by the cross. He almost touched it with his finger, then thought better of it.

'I don't know,' said Jack. 'I didn't paint it. There are others, if you look hard enough.'

And there were. The closer he looked, the more apparent they became. Some were barely blurs, the kind of smears that appeared on photographs when someone moved and the shutter speed was kind of slow. Others were clearer. Dupree thought he could distinguish faces among them: dark sockets, black mouths.

'Are these painted on?'

Jack shrugged his shoulders. 'They look painted to you?'

'No, they look like photographs.'

'You still afraid I might be drinking too much?'

Dupree shook his head. 'I'd say you're not drinking enough.'

Amerling spoke.

'You going to tell me you came here because you're worried about racoons, or have you felt something too?'

Dupree sighed. 'Nothing specific, just an unease. I can't describe it, except to say that it's a sensation in the air, like the prelude to an electrical storm.'

'That's about as good a description as I've heard. Other people have felt it too; the older folk, mostly. This isn't the first time something like this has occurred. It happened before, in your daddy's time.'

'When?'

'Just before George Sherrin disappeared, but it wasn't quite like this. That buildup came quickly, maybe over a day or two, then was gone just as quickly again. This one is different. It's been going on for longer.'

'How long?'

'Months, I'd say, but it's been so gradual most people haven't even noticed it until now, if they've noticed it at all.'

'But you did?'

'I've been feeling it for a while. It was the accident that confirmed it; the accident, and what the Lauter girl said before she died.'

'She was in pain. She didn't know what she was saying.'

'I don't believe that. I don't think you do either.'

'She was talking about the dead.'

'I know.'

Dupree walked to the window of the little office and looked out on Island Avenue. It was quiet, but it wasn't peaceful. Instead, it was like a community awaiting the outbreak of some long-anticipated conflict, or perhaps that was just a tormented policeman, a drunk, and an old romantic trying to impose their own interpretation on an innocent world.

'People have died on the island before now, some of them pretty violently,' Dupree said. 'We've had car crashes, fires, even a homicide or two. You think they all saw ghosts before they died?'

'Maybe.'

Amerling paused.

'But I'd guess not.'

'So why the Lauter girl, and why now?'

'Your father, he told you about the island?'

Once again, Dupree glanced at Jack. He remembered taking the old man out onto his porch, after Danny Elliot had found him with blood pumping from a deep scalp wound. He had been furious with the painter, maybe because he saw in him some of his own flaws, but mostly because he had scared the boy. Now he was about to reveal a part of himself that he had kept hidden from everyone. Jack, however long he might have spent on the island, was still an outsider.

Amerling guessed his thoughts.

'If you're worried about Jack, then I'd lay those worries to rest. He's more sensitive to this place than some who have grandparents buried in the cemetery. I think you can speak safely in front of him.'

Dupree raised his hands helplessly before the painter.

'I understand,' said Jack. 'No hard feelings.'

'He told me,' began Dupree. 'He went through the histories of the families, right from day one. He made me memorize them all. He told me about the slaughter and the new settlement that followed later. He told me about George Sherrin and why he thought Sherrin had been taken. He told me all of it. I never fully understood. I don't think I even believed some of it.'

'But he tried to explain it to you?'

'Yes. He told me what he himself believed. He believed that this place was always different. The Indians didn't come out here, and they used most of these islands before the whites arrived, but for some reason they wouldn't come out to this one.'

Amerling interrupted. 'They had pretty good reasons for not coming here. This island is kind of an anomaly. It's big, but it's way out on the Outer Ring. They only had bark canoes to get them out here. I think it was just too far away for them to worry about it.'

'Well, anyhow, then the settlers came,' continued Dupree, 'and they were killed. My father thought like his father: what happened to them tainted the island, and some remnant, some memory of those events, clung to this place. The violence of the past never went away. Something of it stayed here, like a mark in stone. Now there's a balance on the island, and anything that endangers that balance has to be dealt with. If it isn't . . .'

He swallowed the last of the tea.

'If it isn't dealt with, then something else on the island will deal with it in its own way. My father thought that it had found a way to purge itself of anything that might threaten it, the way a person's system will flush out toxins. That's what happened to Sherrin. He was toxic, and the island dealt with him. That's what my father believed.'

He finished and stared at the leaves in the bottom of his cup. It sounded absurd, but he remembered the look on his father's face as he told him the history of the island. His father was not a superstitious man. In fact, he was the most realistic, no-bullshit man that Dupree had ever met. Frank Dupree was the kind of man who would carry his own ladder around with him just so he could walk under it to show more credulous folks up.

Amerling poured himself some more tea, then offered the pot to Dupree. The policeman declined.

'Why do you drink this stuff, anyway?'

'It keeps me calm,' said Amerling.

After a pause, Dupree reconsidered and extended his cup. 'Any port in a storm,' he said, as the postmaster poured some more of the tea into his cup and Jack's.

'Your father knew that this place was different,' said Amerling. 'We talked about it some, and we both came to more or less the same conclusion. Sometimes, bad things happen in a place and it never truly recovers. The memory of it lingers. Some people are sensitive to it, some aren't. I read once that Tommy Lee Jones, you know, that actor fella, he lived in the cottage where Marilyn Monroe committed suicide, or was murdered, or whatever you believe took her from this earth. Didn't bother Tommy Lee Jones none. He's not that kind of fella, from what I've read. But me, I don't think I could have lived in a place like that, knowing what happened there. I believe, and I may be a fool, that something of its past must remain there, like damp trapped in its walls.

'What happened on Sanctuary was so much worse than a single murder. Like you say, it tainted this island, marked it forever. Then a bunch of rapists took a woman here a long time after, and they disappeared. Flash forward to George Sherrin, and he winds up under the roots of a tree. I was there when they dug him up, and I saw what the roots had done to him.'

Amerling leaned forward, grasping the teacup in both hands.

'He was an evil son of a bitch. There were stories about him, after he died. He tormented and abused his own children and they say he might have hurt children on the mainland.'

'I heard that too,' said Dupree. 'My father believed it was so.'

'Well, if your daddy believed it, then it was true. I got no doubt in my mind now. The island, or whatever dwells here, wouldn't tolerate him, and it got rid of him. There's no better way of putting it than that.'

'But where does that leave the Lauter girl, and Wayne Cady? You're saying they deserved what happened to them?'

'No, I don't think the island played any part in that. They died because they'd been drinking and decided to boost a car. But I think something was drawn to that place as they died, because there's an awareness now. This tension that we've all felt, it's there for a purpose. I think when the crash happened, the nature of the tragedy – sudden, frightening – drew something. It came to see what was happening.'

'Something? Something like what?'

'I don't know. Have you been out to the Site lately?'

'Not for a while.'

'It's almost impossible to get to. The path's become overgrown. There are fallen trees, briers. Even the marshes seem to be getting bigger.'

'You said "almost impossible". Does that mean you've been out there?'

Amerling paused. 'Yesterday. Jack came with me. We didn't stay too long.'

'Why?'

'It's stronger out there. It's like getting too close to the bars of the lion's cage. You can feel the threat.'

'And there are no birds,' said Jack.

'Not out there, not anywhere,' said Amerling. 'Haven't you noticed?'

To tell the truth, Dupree hadn't, but now that he thought about it, there was a silence to the island that he had never experienced before. The only bird that he had seen was the dying gull on Marianne's lawn.

'That's where your daddy and I differed about the island. He believed it was something unconscious, like a force of nature. A tree doesn't think about repairing breaches in its bark, it just does it. He thought the island operated on that level.'

'But you don't?'

'No, and the Lauter girl's last words just confirm

what I believe. Whatever is out there is conscious. It thinks, and reasons. It's *curious*. And it's getting stronger.'

Jesus, thought Dupree, I can't believe I'm having this conversation. If anyone from the department heard me, they'd have me jacketed and locked up in a padded room. But the brass don't come out here, so they don't know what it's like. They don't understand it. Most of them don't understand much about any of the islands, but this one in particular is beyond them. All I can do is hope that nothing happens that would force me to try to explain it to them.

Well, Chief, I guess you could say that the island is haunted, and I think some dead people came to take a look at Sylvie Lauter. Oh, they had lights, did I mention that? They must go through a hell of a lot of batteries, so that's our main lead. We're scouring the island for batteries . . .

'So, why now? Why should it be so strong now?'

'A convergence of circumstances, maybe. A new factor on the island that we don't recognize, or haven't noticed.'

'You think it's dangerous?'

'Maybe.'

'Do you think it's—' Dupree paused, uncertain that he wanted to use the word that came to mind, then relented.

'Do you think it's evil?'

'Evil, that's a moral concept, a human concept,' said Amerling. 'It could be that whatever is on this

island has got no concept of morality and no need
for it. It just wants what it wants.'

'Which is?'

'I don't know that. If I knew it, we wouldn't be
having this conversation.'

'I'm not sure I even want to be having this conversation, as it is.'

The postmaster grinned.

'Anyone else apart from us three was here, they'd
say we were two foolish old men and a giant driven
simple by what was ailing him.' Larry Amerling was
never one to sugar his words, but Dupree felt like
the older man had been reading his thoughts.

Jack interrupted.

'I heard from her father that there was some question about the Lauter girl's death,' he said.

'Yeah, I heard that too,' said Amerling, 'although
I heard it from you.' He cocked an eyebrow at the
painter.

'I just thought you might like to know,' said Jack.
'Hell, you know just about everything else. I figure
a gap in your knowledge would bug you more than
most folks.'

Dupree didn't answer immediately. He wasn't
sure that he should, but then both men already
seemed to know as much as he did, or more.

'They found insect matter in her mouth, and
beneath her fingernails,' he said. 'It came from a
moth, a tomato hornworm. They're big and ugly and
they're all dead by September, and I'm not sure that
I've ever even seen one on this island until recently.'

'I saw one on a tree in the cemetery, when they were laying Sylvie Lauter down,' said Jack. 'I took it home, looked it up in a book, then pinned it to a board. Thought I might paint it sometime.'

'Paint it badly,' said Amerling. 'You'd have to stick a note on it so folks would know what it was.'

'I'm not that bad,' said Jack.

'Yes, you are.'

'You came to my exhibition at the Lions Club.'

'There was free food.'

'I hope it poisoned you.'

'Nope, it was pretty good, unlike what was on the walls.'

Dupree interrupted them.

'Gentlemen! You're like two old dogs fighting. It's embarrassing.'

He picked up his cap and picked at some dust.

'I was out at Doug Newton's place. There was a moth there too, same type. I saw it on the curtains in his mother's bedroom.'

But he wasn't talking to the two older men as much as to himself. He ran his hands through his hair, then placed his cap carefully on his head. Moths. Why moths? Moths were attracted to flames, to light. Was that what it was, some form of attraction toward Sylvie Lauter and the old Newton woman? What did they have in common?

The answer came to him immediately.

Dying, that was what they had in common. Their light was dying.

'How long have we got?' asked Dupree.

'Not long,' said Amerling. 'I go outside, it's like I can hear the island humming. The birds were the last sign. It's bad news when even the birds fear to fly.'

'So what do we do?' asked Dupree.

'We wait, I guess. We lock our doors. We don't go wandering near the Site at night. It's coming soon, whatever it is. Then we'll know. For good or bad, then we'll know for sure.'

7

Moloch allowed them to rest for the remainder of the day, choosing to travel north under cover of darkness. Later that morning, Powell and Shepherd headed down to Marie's Home Cooking and bought enough take-out to keep them going for the day. On the way back to Perry Avenue, they stopped off at Big Gary's Liquor Store and picked up two bottles of Wild Turkey to keep the cold out. Dexter and Braun took an opportunity to rest, once they had finished conversing softly with Shepherd in Karen Meyer's kitchen.

Moloch knew enough about Meyer from their past dealings to suspect that she was the kind of woman who would have few visitors. Her house was the last on the street, sheltered by trees and not overlooked by any of her neighbors. He didn't know if she had a lover, but there were no photographs on the refrigerator, no little tokens of love on the shelf by the cookbooks. He went through her studio, heedless of the fingerprints that he left behind. If they found him, they already had more than enough evidence to justify the taking of his life. It mattered little to him if they added Karen Meyer's name to the final tally.

The studio was neat and her computer was password protected. Moloch guessed that anyone trying to gain access to it without the password would probably have just two or three chances before the computer automatically commenced erasing its memory. He searched her bedroom and found a shoe box on the top shelf of her closet. It contained a collection of letters from a woman named Jessica, most of them expressions of love except for the most recent, dated October 1997, which detailed her reasons for ending the relationship. Jessica had met someone else, apparently. Moloch found it curious that Karen Meyer had retained the breakup letter. It seemed to suggest to him an element of emotional masochism in the forger's personality. Perhaps some part of her might even have enjoyed what Willard and Leonie had done to her in the basement, although he somehow doubted it.

Her body still lay on the basement floor. She had resisted for longer than he expected, which surprised him. He had always thought of Meyer as a pragmatist. She must have known that she would have to tell him what she knew eventually, but something had made her hold out for so long that he feared she would die before she revealed the location of his wife and son. She had feelings for them. Moloch wondered if Meyer and his wife had been lovers. The possibility angered, and aroused, him.

Marianne Elliot. She had kept her first name almost intact, simply expanding it from the original Marian. It was a smart move, typical of Meyer.

Moloch knew that those who assumed new identities sometimes gave themselves away in the first few months by failing to hear their new name when they were addressed by it, or by signing checks, rental agreements, or bank documents with their old name. The easiest way to avoid it was to give them a new name that began with the same letter, preferably even the same two letters, as their old name. So James became Jason, Linda became Lindsay.

Marian became Marianne.

His son was now named Danny, not Edward as they had agreed. Well, perhaps 'agreed' wasn't the right word. His wife had wanted something simple and boyish, but Moloch liked formal names. Trust the bitch to give his son a name like Danny as soon as she was out of his sight.

Moloch didn't much care what happened to the boy. He might take him with him when he left the island, or he might leave him. He hadn't decided yet. All he knew was that he felt no paternal instincts whatever toward him, but his wife would know before she died that it was within his power to do whatever he chose with his son. He would happily pimp him to deviant men if he thought the knowledge of it would increase his wife's agony before her death. In fact, he had just the deviant in mind if it came to that. After all, they would have to pay the cop somehow. It would help him to keep his mouth closed and would give them something to use against him later if his conscience began to trouble him.

He overturned the shoe box and watched as a jumble of photographs fell on Karen Meyer's unmade bed. He went through them with his fingertips, turning over those that had landed face-down, until he found the one that he had guessed – even hoped – might be among them. She was a little different now: her hair was darker and she seemed to be downplaying her natural good looks. When he had met her first in Biloxi, she had used makeup with a delicacy that had impressed him, his experience of casino waitresses having led him to expect all of them to resemble the brides of Mary Kay. Now her face was completely unadorned, her hair lank. Her face was very pale and the photograph, taken in a photo booth, suggested that she had not slept well in a very long time. A perceptive man might look twice at her and begin to see something of the beauty that she was trying to disguise, and a very unusual man might suspect something of the history of pain and abuse that had led her to take such steps. The boy was on her lap, his finger raised to the camera, a birthday crown upon his head.

He had underestimated her, and that was what troubled him more than anything else, even more than the betrayal itself. He had thought that he knew her, knew her as intimately as only one who had explored both pleasure and pain through her could know her. He believed that he had broken her, for what was she but a thing to be used, part of a front to fool those who might come after him;

the loving family man with the neat house, the pretty wife, the little boy who must surely have represented the first step on the road to a home filled with children and grandchildren?

Moloch's was not the routine abuse of drunks and petty sadists, the kind that might at last force the object of their hatred to turn upon them with a gun or a knife out of an instinctive desire for survival. No, Moloch's capacity to hurt – emotionally, physically, psychologically – was more refined than that. The pain, the stress could never be allowed to become unbearable, and needed to be interspersed at times with moments of kindness, even tenderness; reminders of love, need, dependence. Yet somehow, despite it all, she had managed to keep something hidden from him, some vital part of herself that he was unable to touch, and it was that which had enabled her to escape him. He was impressed by what she had achieved. Perhaps they were closer in spirit than he had ever imagined.

He placed the photograph in his jacket pocket, then went back downstairs and turned on the television. Already, the TV news bulletins were describing how the search for the escaped man was expanding, extending the net to take in not only those states along the border but also the southern states as far north as Maryland. Worse, they had trawled for known accomplices and now, in addition to Willard, he had to worry about Dexter and Shepherd. Their pictures had appeared on every news show, along with all known aliases. Their continued involvement was a risk, but a calculated one. Once they got to Maine, they could complete their work in a matter of hours, then head for Canada. Most of the routes across the border were unpatrolled, and those who chose to make the journey could easily slip across. Dexter would make sure of it.

Dexter was clever. That was why he had been entrusted with so much of the organization once it became apparent that Moloch would be forced to face the grand jury. Where Dexter went, Braun and Leonie would follow. As for Shepherd, he was a curious beast. He seemed to drift through his existence, never allowing himself to experience the extremes of pleasure or hatred. He appeared to take little from life, apart, occasionally, from the lives of others. There was no sentimentality to him, and while he was loyal, it was the loyalty of one who has signed a contract and proposes to remain strictly within its bounds. Any breach of its clauses by another would render the contract null and void and Shepherd would do whatever was necessary to extricate himself from its requirements.

As for the redneck, Powell, and Tell, with his cornrows knitted tightly against his skull, taut as his pent-up rage at the world, Moloch knew little of them, except that Dexter vouched for them. They were men who would work for the promise of money, and that was enough. Moloch was not sure how much of his cash the bitch had spent, but there would be enough, he felt certain, to divide the best part of $500,000 between them, maybe even $600,000. The hardest parts – the escape, the associated killings, and the pinpointing of her location – were already behind them. With luck, their work would be done quickly and they would be scattered within two days. If there was less money than they had expected, then Powell and Tell were expendable. The others could take whatever was left. Moloch needed only enough to get him out of the country. After that, he would find ways to make some more. Perhaps he would ask Dexter to join him, once the time was right.

Except there was now a fatalism to Dexter that Moloch had not noticed before, although Moloch had seen it develop often in men like him. After years of violence, the odds in favor of meeting a violent end increased with every passing week. They had stayed too long in the life to imagine that they could enjoy an easy escape at this late stage. Dexter had not become reckless, as some of his kind did, and neither did he appear to have become overly cautious. Instead, that fatalism, that resignation, was written across his face. He looked like a man who wanted to sleep, to sleep and forget.

Moloch had seen him talking with Braun and Shepherd. He had not intervened. He knew the subject of their conversation: Willard, who now lay sleeping in the room across the hall. Moloch loved Willard, and knew that the love was reciprocated. There was a purity to Willard that was almost as beautiful as the boy himself, and unlike

Shepherd, he would be loyal unto death. Moloch could only guess at what went on inside Willard's head, and sometimes wondered what it would be like to probe the younger man's mind. He feared that it would be similar to briefly inhabiting the consciousness of a vaguely self-aware spider: there would be blackness, patience, and a ceaseless, driving appetite that could never be sated, but there would also be inquisitiveness and rage and sensuality. Moloch had no idea where Willard had come from. He had not sought Willard out; rather, Willard had found him, and attached himself to him. He had approached Moloch for the first time in a bar on the outskirts of Saranac Lake, but the older man had been aware of him for some time, for Willard had been hovering at the periphery of his vision all through the previous week. Moloch had made no move against him, although he took to sleeping with his gun at close hand and the locks in his hotel rooms carefully secured. The boy interested him, without Moloch really knowing why.

Then, exactly seven days after Moloch had first sighted him, the boy had entered the bar and taken a seat in the booth across from him. Moloch had seen him coming, and in the time it had taken the boy to walk from the door to the booth Moloch had unholstered his pistol, secured to it a suppressor beneath the table, and wrapped the gun in a pair of napkins. It now lay between his legs, Moloch's right index finger resting lightly upon the trigger.

The boy sat down carefully and placed his hands flat upon the table.

'My name is Willard,' he said.

'Hello, Willard.'

'I've been watching you.'

'I know. I was beginning to wonder why that might be.'

'I have something for you.'

'I'm straight,' said Moloch. 'I don't want what you have to sell.'

The boy showed no offense at the deliberate insult. Instead, his brow simply furrowed slightly, as though he didn't fully understand the import of Moloch's remark.

'I think you'll like it,' he continued. 'It's not far from here.'

'I'm eating.'

'I'll wait until you're done.'

'You want something?'

'I've eaten.'

Moloch finished his plate of chicken and rice, eating with his left hand, his right remaining beneath the table. When he was finished, he laid down a ten and two ones to cover the food and his beer, then told Willard to lead the way. He picked up his coat, wrapped it around the gun, then stayed behind the boy until they left the bar and found themselves in the parking lot. It was a midweek night and only a handful of cars remained. Willard began walking toward a red Pontiac, but Moloch called him back.

'We'll take mine,' he said.

He tossed Willard the keys.

'And you can drive.'

As the boy caught the keys, Moloch struck him hard with the butt of his gun and forced him against the Pontiac. He pushed the gun into the boy's head, then frisked him. He found nothing, not even coins. When he stepped back, there was blood on Willard's face from the wound in his scalp. His face was completely calm.

'You can trust me,' said Willard.

'We get to where we're going, I'll help you clean up that cut.'

'I been cut before,' said Willard. 'It heals.'

They got in the car and Willard drove, unspeaking, for about ten miles, until they were close to High Falls Gorge. He turned left off 86 up a secluded driveway, then pulled up outside a two-story summer house built from maple logs.

'It's in here,' he said.

He opened the door and moved toward the front of the house. Moloch stayed about five feet back from him.

'Anything happens, anything at all, I'll kill you,' said Moloch.

'I told you: you can trust me.'

Willard knelt down and took a key from the flowerpot by the door, then entered the house. He hit the hall lights so Moloch could see that they were alone. Despite his assurances, Moloch searched the house, using the boy as a shield as they entered each room. The house was empty.

'Who owns this place?'

Willard shrugged. 'I don't know their names.'

'Where are they?'

'They left on Sunday. They come up here for weekends, sometimes. You want to see what I have for you? It's in the basement.'

They reached the basement door. Willard opened it and turned on the light. There was a flight of stairs leading down. Willard led, Moloch following.

Near the back wall was a chair, and in the chair was a girl. She was seventeen or eighteen. Her mouth was gagged and her arms and legs had been secured. Her hair was very dark and her face was very pale. She wore a black T-shirt and a short black skirt. Her fishnet stockings were torn. Even in the poor basement light, Moloch could see track marks on her arms.

'No one will miss her,' said Willard. 'No one.'

The girl began to cry. Willard looked at her one last time, then said: 'I'll leave you two alone. I'll be upstairs if you need anything.'

And seconds later, Moloch heard the basement door close.

Now, years later, Moloch thought back to that first night, and to the bound girl. Willard knew him, understood his appetites, his desires, for they existed in a similar, though deeper, form within himself. The girl was a courtship gift to him and he had accepted it gladly.

Moloch loved Willard, but Willard was no longer in control of his hunger, if he had ever truly been able to rein it in. The death of the woman Jenna and the damage inflicted on the bait for the escape indicated that Willard was spiraling down into some dark place from which he would not be able to return. Moloch loved Willard, and Willard loved Moloch, and love brought with it its own duties.

But then, as Moloch knew only too well, and as his wife was about to find out, each man kills the thing he loves.

Danny was kicking up a fuss, as he always did when his mother tried to leave him for an evening. It came from not having a father around, she believed. It had made him dependent, maybe even a little soft, and that worried her. She wanted him to be strong, because at some point he was going to have to learn about the world that they had left behind, and the man who had contributed to his creation. But she also wanted him to be strong for her own selfish reasons. She was tired; tired of the constant fear, tired of looking over her shoulder, tired of having nobody on whom she could depend. She wanted Danny to grow up to be big and tough, to protect her as she had protected him. But that day, it seemed, was a long way off.

'Where are you going?' he asked again, in that whining voice that he adopted when he felt that the world was being unfair to him.

'I told you already. I'm going out to dinner.'

'With Joe?'

'Yes.'

'I don't like Joe.'

'Don't say that, Danny. You know it's not true.'

'It is true. I hate him. He killed a bird.'

'We went through this before, Danny. He had to kill it. It was hurt. It was in so much pain that the kindest thing Joe could have done was to put it out of that pain.'

She had given him the gull carved for him by Dupree. He had looked at it for a moment, then had cast it aside. Later, when she went to retrieve it from the floor, it was gone, but she had glimpsed it on the shelf in Danny's room before they left the house. Her son was a complex little boy.

The car jogged as it hit a dip in the road, the headlights skewing crazily across the trees for a moment. She wondered if she should bring up what had been troubling her since earlier in the evening, or if she should just let it rest until the morning.

She had gone outside to put some water in the car and her attention had been drawn to the little grave that Joe had created for the dead gull. The stone that marked the spot had been moved aside, and the earth was scattered around what was now a shallow hole. The bird was gone, but she had found blood and some feathers scattered around nearby. It could have been an animal that had dug the bird up, she supposed, except that Danny had dirt beneath his nails when he ate earlier that evening, and when she questioned him about it, he simply clammed up. It was only later, when she examined the grave, that she had begun to suspect what had happened.

She decided to leave matters as they were. She hoped to enjoy the night and didn't want to leave her son after an argument.

'Will Richie be at Bonnie's?'

'I'm sure he will,' said Marianne. Richie's mental age wasn't much more than Danny's, but he seemed to care a lot about Danny, and Danny liked the fact that the bigger boy deferred to him. That didn't happen a lot for Danny, who had found it hard to make friends and to settle into school.

She hung a left into Bonnie's driveway and killed the engine. Danny undid his seat belt and waited for her to come around and open the door. Light shone upon them as Bonnie appeared on the steps, her hair loose around her shoulders, a cigarette dangling from the fingers that cupped her elbow. Bonnie Claessen had endured a hard life: a husband who beat her, then ran off with a line dance teacher; a son who would always be dependent upon her; and a succession of men who were at best unsuitable and at worst unstable. Sometimes, Marianne thought, Bonnie Claessen appeared to live her life as if she were being paid by the tear. Then there was the accident, the one in which her nephew Wayne Cady had been killed. Marianne had attended the funeral, along with much of the island, watching as the coffin was lowered into the ground at the small cemetery beside the island's Baptist church, Bonnie's sister so distraught with grief that when the time came to drop dirt upon the coffin she had fallen to her knees and buried her face in the damp earth, as if by doing so she might somehow burrow beneath the ground and join the dead boy.

Bonnie had been strong for her sister that day, but then she was strong in so many ways: it wasn't easy for her raising a disabled son alone, and the state's overburdened mental health system had been of little help to her during her son's life. Much of the funding had traditionally gone to placing mentally ill children in psychiatric hospitals or residential programs, but Bonnie had resisted that from the start. For a time the state had provided at-home help to her after her husband left, but cuts in funding and the prohibitive cost of sending someone out to the island on a regular basis meant that the service was withdrawn after less than a year. Marianne was suddenly terribly grateful that Danny would not be so dependent upon her, and that at some time in the future she might be able to lean on him for support.

Bonnie had been good to her from the beginning and she had returned that goodwill as much as she could, taking Richie for a night to give Bonnie a break, or bringing him on movie trips with Danny on weekends. She had never discussed her past with Bonnie, but Marianne knew that the older woman suspected more than she ever said. Bonnie had been a victim of enough bad men to recognize a fellow sufferer when she met her.

'Thanks for doing this,' Marianne said as she approached the step, her hand on Danny's shoulder.

'It's no problem, hon. How you doing, Danny?'

'Okay,' mumbled Danny.

'Just okay? Well, we'll see if we can change that. There's popcorn and soda inside, and Richie has got some new computer game that I'm sure he's just dying to show you. How does that sound?'

'Okay,' repeated Danny in that same monotone.

Marianne raised her eyes to heaven, and Bonnie gave her an 'I know' shrug in return. 'If I'm not late, I'll drop by to pick him up. Otherwise, I'll be by first thing in the morning.'

'Don't sweat it, hon. You just have a good time.'

Marianne kissed Danny on the cheek, hugged him, and told him to be good, then went back to her car. She waved good-bye as she drove, but Danny was already heading inside and his thoughts of her, and his anger with her, would soon be forgotten with the promise of new games to play. She picked up speed once she was back on the main road, which became Island Avenue. She parked across the street from Good Eats, the sound of bluegrass music coming to her from inside, and checked her makeup in the mirror. She touched up her lipstick, tugged at her hair, then sighed.

She was thirty-two years old and she was going on her first date in years.

With a giant.

Joe Dupree was waiting for her, a beer in front of

him. He was seated at a table by the back of the restaurant, turned slightly sideways so that his legs didn't hit the underside. Once again, she was struck by how out of place he must often feel.

Nothing ever sits right for him. Things are always too small, too tight, too narrow. He lives his life in a constant state of displacement. Even the island itself doesn't seem big enough to hold him. He should be out in open spaces, somewhere like Montana, where he would be dwarfed by the scale of the natural world.

He rose as he saw her approach, and the table shuddered as he struck it with his thigh. He reached down to save a water glass from falling, liquid splashing the table and the single red rose in the vase at its center shedding a leaf as his hand made the clumsy catch. The restaurant was half full, mainly with local people, although she saw a young couple stealing curious glances at the big man. Visitors. Funny how, even after only a year here, she resented the presence of outsiders.

'Hi,' he said. 'I was starting to worry.'

'Danny was kicking up some. He still doesn't like it when I head out without him. If he had his way, he'd be sitting here now demanding french fries and soda.'

'Nothing wrong with that.'

She raised a quizzical eyebrow. 'You want me to go back and get him?'

He lifted his hands in surrender. 'No, you're just fine.'

He reddened, thought briefly about trying to explain what he meant, then decided that it would only get him into further trouble.

In truth, it had been a long time since Joe Dupree had found himself in a social situation with a woman, and he figured that his skills in that area, limited as they were to begin with, were probably pretty rusty by now. Women occasionally came on to him, or they used to when Joe Dupree would take time out from the island to frequent the bars of the Old Port, the island's little diesel ferry taking him over on its last scheduled run. He would drink in the city's bars until one or two in the morning, then call Thorson and have him come pick him up. The old ferry captain didn't usually mind. He didn't sleep much anyway. On those rare occasions when Thorson couldn't make it, Dupree would either hire a water taxi or take a small single room at a cheap hotel, where he would remove the mattress from the bed and place it on the floor, using cushions to support his legs where they overhung the end.

And in those bars, particularly the ones off the tourist trail, he would sometimes attract the attentions of women. He would hear them, two or three of them, laughing in that way that women with alcohol on their breath and sex on their minds will sometimes laugh, a hoarse, unlovely thing from deep inside them, their eyelids heavy, their eyes narrowing, their lips slightly pursed. Their comments would crawl across the dusty floor

I wonder if he's big all over.

The hands and the feet. You always look at the hands and the feet.

or seep like smoke between the tables

I could make room for him.

Hon, they'd have to take something out of you to make room for what he's got.

until at last they reached him and he would acknowledge them with a thin smile, and they would giggle more and look away, or perhaps hold his gaze for a time with a look that spoke of tainted promises.

On some occasions he had taken up the offer made, and had usually regretted it. The last time it happened, he accompanied the woman back to her little house in Saco, so neat and feminine that he instantly felt even more out of place than usual, afraid to move for fear that he might dislodge a china doll from the congregation of pale faces that seemed to gaze at him from every shelf, every ledge. She undressed in her bathroom and entered the bedroom wearing only a too-tight bra and black panties, a little fat spilling out over the straps at her back and the elastic at her waist. She was holding a cigarette, and she placed it in her mouth as she pulled back the sheets on the bed, undid the clasp of the bra, and slid it down her arms before hooking her thumbs into the waistband of her underwear and stepping out of them without once glancing at him. She climbed into the bed, pulled the sheets up to her waist, then smoked her cigarette as he removed his own clothing, his face burning with shame and self-loathing.

He saw in her eyes not lust or need, not even curiosity, but merely the prospect of the temporary alleviation of her boredom with herself and her own desires. She took a last drag on the cigarette before she stubbed it out in the ashtray on the nightstand and pushed back the sheet, inviting him to join her. As he climbed into bed beside her, he heard the springs creaking beneath his weight, smelled the stale odor of smoke upon the pillows, felt her nails already raking five white trails along his thigh as her hand moved toward his sex.

He left her snoring, the china dolls watching him impassively as he slipped through the house, his shoes in his hands. He tugged them on as he sat on her porch steps, then called a cab from a pay phone and returned to the Old Port. On a bench by the Casco Bay Ferry Terminal he waited until light dawned, then walked down to the Miss Portland Diner on Marginal Way and ate breakfast with the fishermen, working his way methodically through a plate of eggs and bacon, keeping his head down so that he would not catch the eye of any other diner. And when Thorson's ferry drew toward the dock, carrying those who had jobs in the city, Joe Dupree was waiting for it, barely nodding at those who disembarked, until at last the boat was empty. He took a seat at the back of the ferry and when no further passengers appeared, Thorson started the engine and carried Joe Dupree away from Portland, the wind wiping the smell of perfume and booze and cigarettes from his clothes and hair, cleansing him of the proof of his sins.

Since then, he had not returned to the bars of the Old Port, and now drank little. He could see the surprise in the faces of the wait staff and in the smile of Dale Zinner when he rose to greet the woman who now sat across from him. He didn't care. It had taken him the best part of a year to work up the courage to ask her out. He liked her son. He liked her. Now she was saying something, but he was so lost in himself that he had to ask her to repeat it.

'I said, it's hard to do anything in secret here. Seems like everyone knows your business before you do.'

He smiled. 'I remember Dave Mahoney – he was heading on for seventy years of age, the old goat – got himself all worked up over a widow woman named Annie Jabar, who lived about half a mile down the road from him. Nothing had happened between them, nothing more than glances over the bingo table at the American Legion, I guess, or hands almost touching across the shelves at the market, but she was giving him the come-on, without a doubt. So one day Dave takes it into his head to do something about it. He puts on his best jacket and pants under his slicker, and heads out in the rain to walk down to Annie Jabar's house. When he got there, she was waiting for him.'

He shook his head in amusement.

'Who?' asked Marianne. 'The widow woman?'

'Nope. Dave's wife. Don't know how she did it, but she got there before he did. I figure she must have sprinted through the woods so that she'd be waiting for him, and she wasn't much younger than Dave. She had a gun, too, Dave's varmint rifle. Dave took one look at her, turned around on his heel, and headed straight back home. Never again looked at the widow woman, or any other woman except his wife. She died a couple of years ago, and I heard tell that Annie Jabar might have hoped that she and Dave could get together now that his wife was gone, but far as I know he's never gone next to near her since that day his wife confronted him and made him look down the barrel of his own rifle.'

'He loved her, then.'

'Loved her and was scared half to death of her. Maybe he figures she might still find a way to get back at him if he steps out of line, or maybe he just misses her more than he ever thought he would. I talk to him sometimes and I think he's just waiting to join her. I think he realized how much she loved him when he saw that she was prepared to shoot him rather than let another woman take him, even at seventy years of age. Sometimes maybe you have to love someone an awful lot to be prepared to kill them.'

His attention was distracted momentarily by movement close to the door, so Dupree did not see the look that passed across Marianne's face. Had he done so, their evening together might have come to an abrupt end, for he would have felt compelled to question her about it. Instead, he was watching a bulky man in a red check shirt, accompanied by his equally bulky wife, approaching the exit. As they left, the man gave Dupree a nod that was part acknowledgment, part dismissal. Marianne glanced over her shoulder, grateful for the distraction, and the man smiled at her before his wife gave him a sharp nudge in the ribs with her elbow that nearly propelled him through the door.

'Tom Jaffe,' said Dupree.

'His father runs the construction business, right?'

'That's right. He's near seventy himself now, but still won't hand over the running of the business to his son. Doesn't trust him. Tom still believes he's the Great White Hope. He was valedictorian the year I graduated high school. Liked to think of himself as an orator.'

'How was his speech?'

'Terrible. It was basically an extended "Screw you" to everybody he'd ever known. Somebody tried to run him over in the parking lot afterward.'

'Maybe it was just a misunderstanding.'

'Nope. I came around for a second try after I missed him the first time. He could run, I'll give him that.'

She laughed then, and for the first time Dupree began to relax. The little restaurant filled up as the evening progressed, but there was never anybody left standing to wait for a table. They talked about music and movies, and each spoke a little of the past, but not too much. In Joe's case, his reticence was a result of embarrassment, shyness, and a feeling that his life on the island would seem somehow parochial and isolated to this woman with a soft Southern accent, a young son, and a firsthand knowledge of places far from this one.

But the woman? Well, her reason for silence was different.

She spoke little of her past, because all that she could give him in return was lies.

They were on dessert when the restaurant door opened and Sally Owen entered. She was one of the bartenders at the Rudder, and had been for as long as Dupree could remember. Rumor was that, when she was younger, she once dragged a guy across the bar for not saying 'please' after he ordered his drink. She was older now, and a little calmer, and contented herself with shooting dark looks at the ruder customers. Now she walked quickly up to their table and spoke to Joe.

'Joe, I'm real sorry to be disturbing you, but Lockwood is dealing with a possible burglary over on Kemps Road, and Barker is out with one of the fire trucks tending to a car fire.'

Dupree couldn't hide his displeasure. He'd asked the cops on duty to try to give him a little space tonight, even if they were snowed under, which seemed unlikely at the start of the day. Still, it wasn't their fault that cars were burning and houses were being burgled, although if they found the people responsible for either event, Joe Dupree was going to have some harsh words to say to the culprits.

'What is it, Sally?'

'Terry Scarfe is in the Rudder, and he's not alone. He's got Carl Lubey in there with him and they're thick as thieves. Just thought you should know.'

Marianne watched Dupree's expression darken. There was sorrow there too, she thought, a reminder of events that he had tried to forget. She knew the story of Carl Lubey's brother. Everybody on the island knew it.

Ronnie Lubey was a minor-league criminal, with convictions for possession with intent and aggravated burglary. On the night that he died, he had a cocktail of uppers and alcohol in his belly and was spoiling for a fight. He'd started shooting out the windows of his neighbor's house, yelling about tree trunks and boundaries, and by the time Joe and Daniel Snowman, who had since retired, arrived out at the house, Ronnie was slumped against a tree trunk, mumbling to himself, puke on his shirt and pants and shoes.

When the two policemen pulled up, Ronnie looked at them, raised the shotgun, and shot wildly from the hip. Snowman went down, his left leg peppered with shot, and after an unheeded warning, Dupree opened fire. He aimed low, hitting Ronnie in the thigh, but the shot busted Ronnie's femoral artery. Dupree had done his best for him, but his priority had been his partner. Snowman survived, Ronnie Lubey died, and his little brother Carl, who also lived on the island, had never forgiven the big policeman.

Marianne didn't know who Terry Scarfe was, but if he was keeping company with Carl Lubey, then he wasn't anyone she wanted to know. During her first month on the island, Carl had tried to come on to her as she sat with Bonnie at the bar of the Rudder. When she turned down his offer of a drink, Carl called her every name he could think of, then tried to reach for her breast in the hope of copping a consolatory feel. She had pushed him away, and then Jeb Burris had climbed over the bar and hauled Carl outside. The young policeman Berman had been on duty that night. Marianne remembered that he had been kind to her and had warned Carl to stay away from her. Since then, she had endured only occasional contact with him when he came into the market. When she passed him on the street or saw him on the ferry, he contented himself with looking at her, his eyes fixed on her breasts or her crotch.

'I'd better go take a look,' Dupree said, as Sally nodded a good-bye and returned to the bar. 'You excuse me for a couple of minutes? I'll be back as soon as I can.'

He rose and laid his hand gently on her shoulder as he passed her by. She brushed his fingers with her hand, and felt his grip linger for a moment before he left her.

Dupree walked down Island Avenue and made a right. Straight downhill on the left was the island's little ferry terminal and across from it was the Rudder Bar. It had an open deck at its rear, which filled up with tourists during the summer but was empty now that winter had come. Inside, he could see lights and a half dozen people drinking and playing pool.

He entered the bar and saw Scarfe and Lubey immediately. They were sitting at the bar, leaning into each other. Lubey raised his glass as Sally came out from the small kitchen behind the bar.

'Hey, Sal, you got any shots that taste like pussy?'

'I wouldn't know what pussy tastes like,' said Sally, glancing at Dupree as he drew closer.

Lubey lifted a finger and extended it to her.

'Then lick here,' he said, and the two men collapsed into laughter.

'How you doing, boys?' said Dupree.

The two men turned in unison to look at him.

'We're not your boys,' said Lubey. His eyes were dull. He swayed slightly as he tried to keep Dupree in focus.

'It's the Jolly Green Giant,' said Scarfe. 'What's wrong, Mr. Giant? You don't look so jolly no more.'

'We don't usually see you over here, Terry. Last I heard, you were doing one to three.'

'I got paroled. Good behavior.'

'I don't think your behavior is so good tonight.'

'What's your problem, *Off – fis – sur*?' said Lubey. 'I'm having a drink with my buddy. We ain't bothering nobody.'

'I think you've had enough.'

'What are you going to do?' asked Lubey. 'Shoot me?'

Dupree looked at him. Lubey held the gaze for as long as he could, then glanced away, a dumb smile playing on his lips. Dupree returned his attention to Scarfe.

'I want you off the island, Terry. Thorson has a crossing in ten minutes. You be on that ferry.'

Scarfe looked at Lubey, shrugged, then slid from his stool and picked up his jacket.

'The Green Giant wants me off the island, Carl, so I got to go. I'll be seeing you.'

'Yeah, be seeing you, Terry. Fight the power.'

Dupree stepped back and watched as Scarfe headed unsteadily for the door, then turned back to Lubey.

'You drive here?' he asked.

Lubey didn't reply.

'I asked you a question, Carl.'

'Yeah, I drove,' said Lubey at last.

'Give me your keys.'

The other man dug into his pockets and found his car keys. As Dupree reached out for them, Lubey dropped them to the floor.

'Whoops,' he said.

'Pick them up.'

He climbed from the stool, bent down gingerly, then toppled over. Dupree helped him to his feet, picking up the keys as he did so. Once he was upright again, Lubey shrugged off the policeman's hand.

'Get your hands off me.'

'You want me to put you in cuffs, I will. We can get a boat over here and you can spend the night in a cell.'

Lubey reached for his coat.

'I'm going,' he said.

'You can pick up your keys from the station house in the morning.'

Lubey waved a hand in dismissal and headed for the door. Behind the bar, Jeb Burris shrugged off an apron and said: 'I'll give him a ride back.'

Dupree nodded.

'Yeah, do that.'

Back outside, he watched as Terry Scarfe and two other people, tourists who'd been eating at the restaurant, climbed on board Thorson's ferry and headed back to Portland.

Scarfe kept looking back at the island, and Dupree, until the ferry faded from view.

Marianne had taken a couple of glasses of wine at dinner, Dupree a single beer. He offered to drive her back to her house and said he would arrange to have her car dropped to her door before eight the next morning. She sat in the passenger seat of Dupree's jeep and stared in silence through the side window. Dupree wanted to believe that it was a comfortable silence, but he sensed her sadness as he drove.

'You okay?'

She nodded, but her mouth wrinkled and he could see that she was near tears.

'It's been a long time, you know?'

He didn't, and he felt foolish for not knowing.

'Since what?'

'Since I had a nice evening with a man. I'd kind of forgotten what it was like.'

He coughed to hide his embarrassment and his secret pleasure.

'You always cry at the end of a nice evening?'

She smiled and wiped at the tears with the tips of her fingers.

'Hell, I must have snail trails running down my face.'

'No, you look good.'

'Liar.'

He hung a right into the driveway of her small house and pulled up outside her door. He looked at her. She looked at him.

'Would you like to come in? I can make you coffee.'

'Sure. Coffee would be good.'

He followed her inside, and sat on the edge of the living room couch as she went to the bathroom to fix her make up. When she came out she went straight to the kitchen and put the kettle on the stove. She swore.

'I'm sorry,' she called. 'I've only got instant.'

'It'll be just like home.'

She peered around the corner of the doorway, unsure if he was being sarcastic.

He caught the look.

'No, honest, it will be just like home. All I ever make is instant.'

'Well, if you say so. Put some music on, if you like.'

He rose and walked to the pile of CDs that lay stacked against the wall. A JVC system stood on the third shelf of the Home Depot bookcase. He tried squatting and looking sideways at the CDs, then kneeling. Finally, he lay flat on the floor and ran his finger down the spines.

'I don't recognize any of this stuff,' he said, as she came into the room carrying two mugs of coffee on a tray.

'You're out of touch,' she said.

'Radio reception sucks this far out, and I don't go over to the mainland as much as I used to. Hey, are the Doobie Brothers still together?'

'I hear Michael McDonald left,' she said, as she entered the room. 'Things aren't looking so good for Simon and Garfunkel either.'

He smelled her perfume as she knelt down beside him, and her arm brushed his hair gently as she reached across and carefully removed a disc from the pile. He placed his hand against the discs beneath, steadying them so that they would not fall. She put a bright blue CD into the player, then skipped through the tracks until she got to number six. Slow funk emerged from the speakers.

'Sounds like Prince,' he said.

She cocked an eyebrow at him. 'Maybe you're not so out of touch after all. You're close. It's Maxwell. This track's called "Til the Cops Come Knockin'." I thought you might appreciate the humor.'

'It's good,' he said. 'The song, I mean. The humor I'm not so sure about.'

She swiped at him playfully, then rose and sipped at her coffee, her body swaying slightly to the music. Dupree watched her from the floor, then turned awkwardly and stood from the knees up. He lifted his coffee mug, instinctively grasping it in his hand instead of trying unsuccessfully to fit his finger through the handle. Little things, he thought. It's the little things you have to remember.

Marianne walked to the window and looked out on the dark woods beyond. Her body grew still. He waited for her to speak.

'The bird—' she began, and he felt his back stiffen in response. Had she also noticed their absence? Instantly, his conversation with Amerling and Jack returned to him, and the pleasure of the evening began to dissipate like smoke.

'The gull that you put out of its misery?'

He felt relieved for a moment, until he thought about Danny and the look on his face after he had killed the bird.

'Like I said, I'm sorry about that,' he interrupted. 'I should have made him walk away.'

'No, it's not that. I think Danny dug it up, after you'd left. I think he dug it up and . . . did something to it.'

'Like what?'

'I found blood and feathers.' She left her fear unspoken, hoping the policeman would pick up on it.

Dupree put his cup down and stood beside her.

'He's a boy. They can be curious about things like that. If you want, I can talk to him.'

'I guess I'm just worried.'

'Has he ever hurt any living animals?'

'I've told him off for throwing stones at cats, and he's mischievous about bugs and stuff, but I don't think he's ever really hurt anything.'

'Well, then. I'd maybe leave him be this time.'

She nodded, but he sensed once again that she was far away from him, walking in the country of her past. He finished his coffee and placed the mug carefully on the tray.

'I'd better be going,' he said.

She didn't reply, but as he moved to get his coat her hand reached for him and laid itself softly upon his arm. He could feel the heat of her through the fabric of his shirt. She looked up at him, and the expression on her face was unreadable.

'I'm sorry,' she said. 'Like I said, it's been a long time. I've forgotten how this should go.'

Then he inclined his head and body toward her, bending almost double to reach her. He kissed her, and her mouth opened beneath his, and her body moved against him. Later, she led him into her bedroom and they undressed in darkness, and he found her by the light of her eyes and the paleness of her skin and the fading scent of her perfume. And for a time, all of their pain was forgotten, and the night gathered them to itself and wrapped them, briefly, in peace.

* * *

And while they made love, the painter Giacomelli sat in his studio, the lamp on the table casting its harsh light across brushes and paints and leaning canvases. Jack wanted a drink. He wanted a drink very badly, but he was too afraid to drink. He wanted to be alert and ready. After his conversation with Dupree and Larry Amerling, he had gone for a late afternoon walk along the wooded trails that crisscrossed the center of the island, but he had not gone as far as the Site. Instead, he had stood at a forest of dead trees, the roots drowned by bog, and looked toward the dark interior in which the ruins lay. There was a stillness there, it seemed, the kind of quiescence that comes on late summer days when the sky is overcast, the heat oppressive and unyielding, and the world waits for the weather to break and the skies to explode violently into rain. He stood on the trail, looking out over the patch of dead beech trees, their trunks gray and skewed as their decaying root structures failed to hold them upright. A mist seemed to hang about them – no, not a mist, exactly, but rather it appeared as if their slow decay had now become visible, the tiny fragments combining to cast a veil over the trees and the ground. He dragged his fingers across the front of his coat and raised his hand before him, expecting to see it coated in gray, but it was clean.

He walked no farther that day.

Now he sat and stared at one of the flawed paintings, which were, in their way, better than anything that he had ever done before, for the waves seemed to move over the bodies, causing them to bob slightly in the tide, and there was a silver light on the waters and the rocks that he had never previously managed to capture, for it had never been apparent to him until now. In fact, he admitted, he couldn't recall adding the sheen of light to the picture either, and no moon hung in the dusk sky of his work.

Or what used to be his work.

Moloch woke.

For a moment he felt himself in the semidarkness of the prison, for in the cell block a dull light hung over all things, even at night. He could hear men snoring, and footsteps. He raised himself from the sweat of his pillow and ran his hands through his hair, then saw Willard, now also awake, watching him from his post beneath the window, the curtains drawn to discourage snoopers.

He had been dreaming again, but this time there was no girl and no killing. Instead, he was alone among the trees, walking through wooded trails, dead leaves crunching beneath his feet, moonlight gilding the branches. Yet when he looked up there was no moon visible, and the skies were black with clouds. Ahead of him lay a darkness, marked only by the thin shapes of dead beech trees, impaled upon the earth like the spears of giants.

And something waited for him in the darkness.

I could map this place, he thought, this landscape of my dreams. I know it well, for I have seen it every night for the last year, and each time it becomes more familiar to me. I know its paths, its rocks, the landings along its coastline. Only that darkness, and what lies within it, is hidden from me.

But in time, I will know that too.

He got to his feet. Willard remained seated, his eyes fixed upon him.

'You okay?' asked Moloch.

'Dexter doesn't like me,' said Willard. 'Shepherd neither.'

'They don't have to like you.'

'I think they want to hurt me.'

Moloch was grateful for the cover of darkness.

'They won't do that. They'll do what I say.'

'What you say,' echoed Willard. He spoke in a monotone.

'That's right. Now let's go downstairs, get something to eat.'

He waited until Willard rose. For a moment they stood together at the doorway, each seemingly unwilling to turn his back on the other. At last, Willard stepped through, and Moloch followed him, just as Moloch had followed him from the bar years before.

I trust you.

Followed him to a house.

They'll do what I say.

Followed him to a woman.

What you say.

And joined him in damnation.

The Last Day

And how can man die better
Than facing fearful odds . . .

Macaulay, 'Horatius'

8

The giant was gone. He left her before the clock read five, for he would soon have to relieve the patrolmen on duty and allow them to catch the ferry back to the mainland. A new cop was coming over on the return leg; a rookie, he said, one who had never been given island duty before. He stroked her hair as he spoke, his arm holding her to him as they lay close together in the false intimacy resulting from their lovemaking.

For it was false. Dupree wanted to be close to her, but how could he draw near when she would tell him so little and when he suspected the veracity of even those small details that she chose to reveal? In the restaurant, he had been startled by how beautiful she looked. During her time on the island, it had seemed to him that she did all that she could not to attract attention, to downplay and even to camouflage her looks. But when she entered Good Eats that night, heads had turned, and Dupree had tried hard not to look smug as she walked to his table. It made him determined that the night should be special for her, for them both. Without being asked, Dale Zinner had taken personal responsibility for their meal, moving between the kitchen and the dining room, solicitous without being overbearing. From their window table overlooking the water they could see the lights of the neighboring islands shining brightly, like small night suns hoping to dazzle the stars. In the candlelight, he had found himself occasionally overawed by her and had concentrated so hard on trying not to break or spill anything that his head hurt by the end of the meal. The only taints upon the evening were the encounter with Lubey and Scarfe at the Rudder, and Dupree's niggling concern at the fact that his companion was still keeping things from him.

Marianne was aware of his unease. Her years spent moving and hiding had heightened her perceptions, making her acutely sensitive to how others were regarding her. Now, alone, she replayed the events of the previous night in her mind, recalling his reactions, his hesitations, the fleeting changes in expression as he listened to her speak. She had not intended the night to end as it had, or if she did, then she had not admitted it to herself. But as the evening went on, and the wine began to have its effect, she wondered what it would be like to make love to him, to take him inside her. She had been a little afraid; afraid of the weight of him, his bulk, and the awkwardness that came with it, for there was little that was graceful about him. He was a man constantly waiting for the sound of falling objects, a man always out of step with the world. But then he came to her bed, and he was gentle, and his touch was surprisingly tender.

She felt guilty for lying to him about her past, but she had no choice in the matter. To tell him the truth could lead to her losing Danny. Worse, it would expose her, and then *he* would find out.

And his people would come.

Lost amid birdsong, the warmth of him still upon the pillow, Marianne began to cry.

Dupree drove first to his own house, where he showered and changed into his uniform. In his bathroom, as he listened to the water running in the shower, he smelled Marianne upon him and felt a twinge of regret that her scent would soon be washed from his body. Later, after he had changed, he picked up his shirt from the night before and brought it to his face. There was a small stain on the material where her face had pressed against him and he touched the traces of makeup with his fingertip. Then he carefully placed the shirt in the bathroom closet, above the laundry basket.

Barker was sitting in the office when he arrived, reading a novel. The sound of running water came from the open bathroom door, where Lockwood was brushing his teeth.

'Sleep well?' asked Barker. He was grinning.

'Pretty good,' said Dupree, maintaining a poker face.

'Dinner good?'

'That was pretty good too.'

'Breakfast?'

'I haven't eaten breakfast yet.'

'You should eat breakfast. You need to keep your strength up. I like a woman to make me breakfast the morning after.'

Dupree scowled at him. 'Is this in the real world, or the fantasy one?'

Now it was Barker's turn to frown. 'Hey, my wife makes breakfast every morning, now that I come to think of it. Sometimes we even have sex the night before. Not often, but sometimes.'

'More than I need to know,' said Dupree. '*So* much more than I need to know.'

Lockwood came out of the bathroom. He walked like a dancer on the balls of his feet. He and the overweight Barker were an unlikely pairing, but Dupree liked them both in their way.

'I borrow you for a few minutes?' Dupree said to Lockwood. He wanted someone to help him bring Marianne's car back to her house, but he wasn't about to ask Barker to do it. Lockwood was less likely to use his suspicions about Dupree's nocturnal activities as a source of humor.

'Sure.'

Lockwood grabbed his jacket and followed Dupree outside.

'I have to take a car back to its owner. I'd like you to follow me in the Explorer, you got nothing else to do, and give me a ride back here afterward.'

'No problem.'

'I appreciate it.'

They drove out to Marianne Elliot's house. Dupree parked outside her front door, leaving the keys in the ignition. He looked up at the window of her bedroom, but the drapes were closed. He wondered what she was doing, until he saw the drapes move slightly and then Marianne was standing at the window, looking down on him. She smiled nervously and gave him a little wave. He waved back, then walked over and got into the Explorer next to Lockwood.

Lockwood looked at him.

'So, did she make you breakfast?'

Dupree reddened.

'I asked you to come along because I didn't think you were as big a horse's ass as Barker.'

Lockwood shrugged.

'Not smaller, just quieter.'

They drove along in silence for a time, until Lockwood asked Dupree if Sally Owen had found him last night.

'Yeah, I took care of it.'

'Lubey give you any trouble?'

'Nope, just shot his mouth off some.'

'You think he and Terry Scarfe were just catching up?'

'I don't know. Maybe they're thinking of forming a book club.'

'A picture book club. Those guys are dumb.'

'Lubey is, but Scarfe is a little smarter. He's like a rat. He'd sell his mother's corpse for cash, if he could bother his ass to dig her up.'

'You think he was dealing on the island?'

Dupree winced. He'd been so distracted by Marianne that he hadn't bothered to search either Scarfe or Lubey, yet he didn't believe Scarfe would be stupid enough to bring drugs over with him. But he hadn't known that Scarfe and Lubey were friendly, and while they had been laughing together the night before, he still got the feeling that they weren't particularly close. Scarfe wanted something from Carl Lubey and that couldn't be good because Carl Lubey had nothing positive to offer anyone.

'I'll keep an eye on Lubey,' he said at last. 'You hear anything about Scarfe over in Portland, maybe you'd give me a call.'

'Will do,' said Lockwood. They turned on to Island Avenue. It was still dark, but the sky was brightening slightly.

'Anything else I should know?' asked Dupree.

'Well, we're still having trouble with the radios. Phones too.'

The problems with the radios were a recent development. The radio system in the Explorer was a dual arrangement. When the Portland PD had updated the island's equipment, the old radio had been left in the Explorer and a second, portable system had been plugged into it. The new radio allowed the patrol cop to stay in touch with both the island base and dispatch over in Portland. The old system, meanwhile, enabled the island police to contact outside agencies such as the state police or the fire department. Over the last week, there had been gaps in transmission. Each of the island cops, Dupree included, had experienced some difficulties in raising either Portland or the station house, while on other occasions there had been the equivalent of a crossed line, faint voices audible in the background of regular transmissions. The radios had been checked and judged to be in perfect working order. 'Ghosts in the machine,' as Lockwood had put it. Now the problem seemed to have spread to the phone lines.

'What about the phones?' asked Dupree.

'Same as the radio. Line was dead at least four times last night, just for a couple of seconds. You know, I picked up, there was nothing, then the dial tone kicked in. Other times there was light static. Could be the storm. Weathermen are saying that it's going to hit the coast sometime tonight, although I've never heard of an approaching snowstorm affecting communications in that way before.'

Dupree didn't reply. He was reminded of his conversation with Amerling and Jack – *It's like the build-up before an electrical storm* – and the task that he had been putting off until after his dinner with Marianne: the visit to the Site.

'You know anything about this rookie cop Macy?' asked Dupree.

'I know she's cute.'

'That'll be a big help.'

'With respect, Joe, it's not like she's entering a war zone.'

'No,' said Dupree. 'I guess not.'

While the two men drove together, Sharon Macy stood in line for the small ferry. She'd heard tales about Thorson and his ferry, most of them (she hoped) gross exaggerations. One of the other field training officers, Christine McCalmon, had jokingly offered her the use of a life jacket for the trip. Macy had gone down to the dock the day before to take a look at the ferry as it left for its early evening sailing. It looked a little rickety, but Macy figured it was better than rowing across Casco Bay in a teapot.

There were three other people beside her at the dock on Commercial Street, all with their eyes fixed on the little diesel boat, which was currently occupied by Thorson and his crewman. Thorson didn't appear to be in too much of a hurry to get along. Macy thought he looked kind of hungover and figured that she could probably arrest him for some form of seagoing violation if she chose, but she guessed that nobody would thank her for it. Maybe if she took out her gun and forced him at gunpoint to get his ass in gear, then she might get their support and admiration. It was cold on the dock and the wind nipped painfully at her nose and ears.

'Cap'n,' said the man beside her, 'what the hell are we waiting for?'

'Supplies,' said Thorson. 'I promised Huddie Harris that I'd bring over some machine parts. His sister said she'd bring them along before five.'

'It's five-fifteen now.'

'Ayuh.'

That was it, thought Macy. Thorson's 'ayuh' was the equivalent of a shoulder shrug, a complete abdication of responsibility. He had promised Huddie his parts, Huddie had probably promised him a couple of six-packs and some cash in return, and nobody was going to be allowed to get in the way of their arrangement. She kicked at a stone and pushed her hands deeper into her pockets as a woman wearing a quilted jacket shuffled along the dock pulling a beaten-up metal box on wheels. Erin Harris: she lived in Portland but spent weekends out on Dutch with her brother. Macy recalled her face from an altercation outside the Eastland Hotel a month or two back, when the wife of one of Erin's sometime boyfriends had decided that enough was enough and that Erin should quit messing with her man. Macy found it kind of difficult to figure out what the man in question saw in either of the women because Erin Harris was ugly on the outside and uglier still on the inside, but she was a bargain compared to the woman with whom she had been slugging it out that night. Barron had tried to intervene but Erin Harris had taken a swing at him and Macy had been forced to spray her. Maced by Macy, as Barron had put it later. It had all been kind of ugly. Macy kept her head down and watched quietly as the box was passed down to Thorson. Erin shot a glance at Macy as she passed. There was no disguising the hostility on her face. Macy didn't look away.

'Okay,' said Thorson. 'All aboard. We're good to go.'

The four passengers climbed aboard the little ferry, each occupying one of the wooden benches beneath the tarp, and minutes later they were heading out to sea, the gulls crying above them and gray waves breaking at the bow. Macy was already in uniform. An L. L. Bean backpack lay at her feet. She had taken Barron's advice and brought a couple of books with her, as well as a Discman and a bunch of CDs. She slipped a CD into the player as Portland grew smaller behind her, the first bars of the Scud Mountain Boys' 'Freight of Fire' filling her ears as the spray splashed her face, Joe Pernice advising her to bring her guns and all her ammunition; and she felt the weight of the pistol beneath her jacket and smiled as she recalled Barron's tales of giants and the bones of men buried beneath pine trees.

Dupree was dealing with another reporter, one who was clearly trying to kill time during the early shift. This one was calling from Florida, so at least the interview didn't have to be conducted face-to-face, which was something. Like most beat cops, Dupree had a natural distrust of reporters. There had been an accident down in the Keys a couple of days earlier, in which three teenagers had drowned after a stolen car went off a bridge. The reporter was trying to pull together a feature about the danger of wayward teens and the accident on Dutch was a good tie-in.

'Yeah, the boy was dead when we got there,' said Dupree. 'There was nothing we could do for him. The girl was badly injured. She died at the scene.' He grimaced even as he said the words, then listened to the next inevitable question.

'We're doing everything we can to ensure that a tragedy like this never happens again. We're looking at ring-fencing the entire area, maybe sowing the slopes with scrap metal to stop anyone taking a car up there again.'

It should have been done years before, thought Dupree. I should have forced them to do it, but they wanted to leave the emplacement as it was, and anyway, kids will be kids. There had never been an accident on the slope before the deaths of Wayne Cady and Sylvie Lauter. It was just one of those things.

The reporter thanked him, then hung up. The clock on the wall read 6:25 A.M. The ferry would be due in soon, bringing with it his partner for the next twenty-four hours. Barker was already down at the little jetty, smoking a cigarette and kicking his heels impatiently, Lockwood sitting quietly beside him.

Dupree wondered again about Sharon Macy. The arrival of a new face was always difficult. The older cops were used to Joe by now, but the younger ones could never hide their feelings toward him when they encountered him for the first time: usually it was just surprise, sometimes amusement, and very occasionally a kind of uneasiness. He knew that there were those who referred to him as a freak. In addition, rookies and trainees rarely got sent out to the islands, but the roster had been hit by illness, family obligations, and amassed vacation time. The department was filling in the gaps with whatever it had.

He climbed into the Explorer and drove down to the dock, trying to pick out the ferry in the semidarkness. It was subsidized by a small tax levied on the island's residents each year. Nobody ever complained about the tax: they valued their independence, but the islanders still needed the safety net that Portland provided, with its stores and hospitals and movie theaters and restaurants. In the event of a medical emergency, like that time Sarah Froness fell off her roof and broke her back while stringing up Christmas lights, the cops on duty could radio for a helicopter pickup from the baseball diamond north of Liberty. It had taken the chopper crew just thirty minutes to get to Dutch on that occasion, and Sarah Froness could still be seen rambling into the market to buy her weekly supply of trash magazines and six-for-five beers, although she didn't go climbing ladders on December 1 anymore and she walked a little more gingerly than before. Sylvie Lauter hadn't been so lucky, and Dupree blamed himself for what had occurred. He replayed the events of that night over and over again, wondering what might have happened if they had gotten to the crash site a little earlier, if old Buck Tennier had made the call as soon as he noticed the revving of the car's engine instead of waiting until he heard the crash. But it wasn't his fault. Dupree and the other cops should have patrolled the area more often, making it too risky for the wilder kids to use it. But Sanctuary was still a big island for a pair of cops to cover. They couldn't be everywhere, and now two young people were dead.

Sanctuary: he had found himself using that name more often in recent days, not only when he was talking to older islanders like Amerling or Giacomelli, but also to visitors and new residents. He had even caught himself using the name when he was speaking with the reporter earlier that morning. He always thought of it as Sanctuary in his own mind, but over the years he had managed to make a distinction between that name and its official name in his day-to-day work. Sanctuary was its past, Dutch was its present. The fact that he was increasingly slipping into the old usage indicated a leaching of the past into his perception of the island, an acknowledgment of its grip upon him, upon all of them.

He thought of Sylvie Lauter's final moments, of her pain and of the blood that had stained his clothing. He thought too of the autopsy and the peculiarities it had uncovered: there had been damage to the back of Sylvie Lauter's tongue and throat, as if something had been forced into her mouth. Maybe she and Cady had been arguing or fooling around before the crash, and somehow she had managed to wound herself. As he had told Jack and Amerling, gray matter had been found in one of the cuts, and had subsequently been identified as wing material from a moth: *Manduca quinquemaculata*, the tomato hornworm moth, a member of the sphinx moth family. Dupree had never seen one, and didn't even know what the insect looked like until a specimen was sent to him from a sympathetic university researcher up in Orono. It had a four-inch wingspan and a large body that tapered almost to a point. Five or six pairs of yellow spots ran down its abdomen. There was a kind of beauty to its wings, which, even on this dead specimen, seemed to shimmer, but overall Dupree thought the insect ugly, the markings on its body and its strange pointed tail making it seem like some peculiar hybrid of moth and reptile.

He had no idea how fragments, however small, of that kind of insect could have found their way into Sylvie Lauter's mouth. Most moths were dead by July or August. This moth's season was June to September, but it was now January and no moth could survive the temperatures on the island. He had asked around, but nobody on the island bred moths. Killed plenty of them, sure, but didn't breed them. Yet somehow Sylvie Lauter had come into contact with a tomato hornworm, the same species of moth that Dupree had found in the Newton woman's bedroom and that now lay dead in its jelly jar beside the original specimen from Orono. It was peculiar, he told himself, but nothing more. For a second, he almost believed it.

Now the ferry could be clearly seen, a finger trail of diesel fumes rising behind it. Joe took his binoculars from the floor and trained them on the boat. It was still too far away to distinguish faces, but he counted six people on board. He experienced a tingling in his fingers. His feet felt too big for his shoes, and despite the cold, the Explorer felt stuffy and warm. He rolled down the window and as the icy breeze hit his face, he realized that he was sweating.

The ferry passed Fort Gorges, rust seeping in tear trails from the bars on its windows, then followed the mail boat route between the Diamonds and Peaks, passing Pumpkin Knob on the right, then Long Island, before leaving Great Chebeague on its left and moving into Luckse Sound, skirting Chebeague once again as it headed into Broad Sound, slaloming between Bangs and Stave, Bates and Ministerial, the tiny islands that dotted Casco Bay, so many of them that they had been christened the Calendar Islands because it was once believed that there were 365 in all.

Slowly, a larger island began to emerge, rising slightly at its wooded center, the white finger of an observation tower visible at its highest point, a small, unmanned lighthouse at its northeastern extreme: Dutch Island, although Macy preferred the old nomenclature of Sanctuary. Macy had been curious about why Sanctuary should have remained in the jurisdiction of Portland. After all, Long Island, which was closer to the shore, was the responsibility of the Cumberland County Sheriff's Department. Sanctuary, meanwhile, was farther out, beyond even Jewell Island.

Barron had shrugged when she'd asked. 'It goes way back,' he said. 'It's tied up with the first settlers and with the ones that came after. It's to do with the Duprees as well. They used to be pretty wealthy, and they funded a lot of development in Portland, particularly after the fire of eighteen-sixty-six. That money's gone now, but the ties remain. The folks out on Dutch voted to remain under Portland's jurisdiction, they pay taxes, and with Melancholy Joe out there being a martyr and doing more than his fair share, it doesn't cost the city too much.'

Macy could see a black-and-white Explorer parked above the passenger shelter. The slowly rising sun shone on the windshield.

The giant was waiting.

The ferry docked and Macy shouldered her bag. Erin Harris was the first to disembark. Her brother was waiting for his machine parts beside a red Dodge truck. She could see the family resemblance, since they were both ugly and both looked like men. He glanced once at Macy, recalling her from his efforts to bail his sister out, but there was no hostility in his look. After all, it was his sister whom she had maced, not him, and it didn't look like he was too fond of her anyway. She spotted the two cops,

Barker and Lockwood, and exchanged some words of greeting. They wished her luck, she thanked them, and then headed up to the Explorer.

The door of the vehicle opened and a man climbed out. Her first instinct was to wonder how he had managed to get into the Explorer to begin with. His great frame unfolded like that of some huge dark insect, until he towered almost two feet over her. His eyes were hidden behind a pair of shades and he wore no cap. He extended a hand the size of a shovel blade.

'Joe Dupree,' he said.

She allowed her own hand to be briefly engulfed in his, like a little fish being swallowed up by an eel.

'Sharon Macy.'

He released her hand. 'Put your stuff in the back. You want the tour?'

'Sure. Do we get to stop and take pictures?'

He laughed. It sounded, she thought, like tectonic plates might sound as they rubbed against one another beneath the earth.

'I think you can safely leave your camera in your bag.'

They did a U-turn, then headed up the short road that led from the jetty to the main intersection. Dupree hung a left.

'You always meet the ferry?'

'Try to. It's more important in summer than winter. We get a lot of people through here in July and August. I was only kidding about the pictures.

313

This place is beautiful in summer and there are some pretty expensive summer homes dotted around the island. Mantle, the guy who runs the Fable computer company? He has a house here. Big Time Warner executive named Sandra Morgan owns a cottage out by Beech Cove, and there are a couple of others too. They'd be real pissed if someone trashed their houses.'

He pulled in at the redbrick municipal building.

'We do it all out here. There's a doctor comes out from the mainland two afternoons a week, and Doc Bruder is still here, although he's officially retired, but we're the first point of contact. We're also the fire department, game wardens, school patrol, crossing guards, and dogcatchers.'

He left the Explorer. Macy followed. The sliding garage doors were open, revealing four vehicles parked inside. 'Medcu 14,' said Dupree, pointing at the ambulance inside the door. 'If an emergency arises we go out in this, do what we can to get the patient comfortable, then get them to the ferry landing or, in a really urgent case, out to the baseball diamond for a chopper pickup.'

He moved on to the red fire trucks, and patted the first.

'This is Engine 14. We use it mostly to pump water. Over there is Ladder 14, the primary attack vehicle. That's what we take out to fires while we're waiting for the local volunteers to get organized. That smaller truck in the corner is Tank 14. Basically, it's just a big bucket on wheels. We take it out to those places on the island that don't have hydrants.'

'Are there many of those?'

'A couple,' he said, in the tone of voice that suggested that half the island was probably without hydrants. He carried on into the station house. There was an open area with a table and two chairs, some books and magazines on the table. To the left was the communications center: a radio, a computer, a bulletin board pasted with notices, reminders, and notes. A large map of the island dominated one wall.

'We have a secretary?'

'Nope. All nine-one-one calls go through the dispatch center in Portland, but most people just call us direct. Paperwork, filing, well, we do that ourselves.'

Across the main reception area was a second room, housing an emergency generator, various pieces of equipment, and a locker containing a single shotgun.

'This is it for weapons?' said Macy.

'We don't have too much call for SWAT teams out here,' said Dupree. 'Last week I used this to kill a rabid raccoon. It had been so long since I'd fired it, I was just grateful that it didn't blow up in my face.'

Macy took the Mossberg pump-action from his hands. It had been cleaned recently, she noticed.

'Doesn't look so bad,' she said.

'I gave it a pretty good clean a day or two back,' said Dupree.

She glanced at him, alerted by his tone.

'Why, something happen?'

'No,' he said. 'But you never know.'

He wasn't smiling.

'Guess not,' she said.

Upstairs was a sofa bed, a TV, some chairs, a small kitchen area, and a bathroom with a shower stall and toilet.

'No cells,' she said.

'Nope. If we make an arrest, we call Portland. They send out a boat and take the prisoner back. Until then, there are two steel loops in the main reception area. I've had to use them a handful of times.'

'We've only got one patrol vehicle?'

'We used to have a golf cart as well, but it broke down. I live about two hundred feet from here and I've got my own jeep if we need another vehicle. Come on, I'll buy you a cup of coffee and introduce you to some people.'

As Macy followed him from the building she rubbed her fingers together, feeling the oil on her skin. She couldn't be certain, but from the smell of the shotgun it had been fired more recently than a week ago.

Somebody had been practicing.

Dupree introduced her to the folks at the market, to the Tooker sisters at the diner (Nancy Tooker half jokingly warned her to stay away from 'her' Berman), to Dale Zinner and Jeb Burris and, finally, to Larry Amerling. By then it was time for lunch, and Dupree suggested to Macy that she take the Explorer and drive around the island in the company of the postmaster while he made some calls. Amerling, the old Lothario, was quite content to spend his lunch hour in the company of an attractive woman, especially one that had read his book.

'If he tries anything,' Dupree warned her, 'shoot him.'

'What if she tries anything with me?' Larry protested.

Dupree looked hard at Macy. 'You get that desperate, shoot yourself.'

There was no road leading directly to the Site, which was surrounded on three sides by patches of bog. Instead, Dupree parked at the top of Ocean Street, which ran north from Island Avenue almost to the center of the island, and walked along the trail toward the burial ground. The forest was mainly evergreens, but there were also scattered maples and beech and hemlock. Amerling was right: the trail was obscured by the fallen branches and the last dry leaves, but tan winter maleberry had also encroached, some of its round seed capsules cracking beneath his feet, along with gray-black winterberry bushes and tattered larches. Within ten minutes, Dupree was in trouble. The trail had virtually disappeared and only his own knowledge of the island enabled him to continue in what he thought was the right direction. It came as a shock to him when he found himself approaching a stretch of road and realized that, somehow, he had walked southwest instead of southeast, and was now back on Ocean Street, except maybe half a mile below where he had started.

Frustrated, he retraced his steps and found that he had mistaken a secondary walking trail for the main path, for bushes and briers had obscured the principal artery so effectively that there was no way to distinguish it from the rest of the forest unless one knew where to look. He hacked a gap through using his Maglite and continued along the path, almost losing his way twice more when it once again began to disappear. As he drew nearer to the Site he noticed that more and more trees were dying, and that the patch of bog at the island's center appeared to be increasing in size. Still water lay like a black mirror almost level with the narrow causeway formed by the trail as it crossed the marsh. If heavy rains came in the spring, the trail would be submerged. Here the greenery was at least understandable, leaf retention being reasonably common among bog plants. Bog rosemary, bog laurel, and labrador tea grew steadily beside green tubular pitcher plants, the remains of insects still trapped in their inner pools. The trees here appeared stunted, their trunks lost beneath the encroaching bog. Others had their shallow roots layered with a dark green sphagnum moss and lush, creeping vines. The life here was hidden, visible only to those who were patient and knowledgeable enough for it to reveal itself: back swimmers and beetles, dragonfly larvae and mayfly nymphs, and smaller mammals like voles and squirrels moved busily through this world. What seemed quiet and dead was secretly alive; wary, but alive.

And yet there were no birds. Increasingly, Dupree was aware of the silence created by their absence. It was so quiet that the snapping of the twigs beneath his feet rang like small-arms fire in the forest, and his breathing sounded loud enough to be heard off-shore. He continued to walk, leaving the bog behind him and entering the deepest part of the forest. At last, he could see ahead of him the shapes of stones through the trees. Once again there appeared to be some recent growth of briers and shrubs along the trail, but these were not green. In fact, their branches broke dryly in his hand when he touched them. They seemed dead, and long dead, yet somehow they were still growing.

He was almost at the entrance to the Site when he saw movement. A patch of gray drifted between the trees perhaps fifty feet ahead of him, at the far-thest edge of the Site. It seemed to hang in the air for a moment, then was absorbed into a tree trunk. An image of Jack's painting flashed in his mind, with its gray shapes that were almost figures. It was an illusion, that was all. Still, he removed his gun from its holster, but kept it pointed toward the ground as he forced his way through the final cur-tain of briers and branches and found himself standing before the remains of the settlement. Even from this angle he could see what once were the corners of houses, the remains of chimneys, the frames of doors. In winter the patterns were more noticeable, for during the summer the rich greenery of the island obscured the man-made forms. Some unexplained growth had also occurred here, although not to the same extent as on the trail. At the very center of the Site stood the stone cross that his ancestor had raised, almost as tall as Dupree himself. The names of those who had died here were etched upon it, for most of the graves were unmarked and there were those whose remains had never been found, among them the settlers who had been cast into the marsh. Dupree thought that he had never seen this place so silent, so still.

He advanced, walking carefully around the tilted gravestones, until he reached the cross. He rested his hand upon it to draw a breath, then pulled it away as though it were a column of heated metal. He took three steps back and looked up at the cross, then slowly extended his hand again and allowed it to come to rest on the stone.

He had not been mistaken. The cross was vibrating. He could almost hear it hum.

Dupree knelt, maintaining his contact with the stone all the way down. The intensity of the vibration seemed to increase as he neared the ground. Finally, he laid a palm flat upon the earth and felt the pulse resonate through his fingers, passing along his arm and into his body until his ears rang with it and his own heart seemed to beat in time with the reverberation. It was like standing above a mine and feeling the rhythmic throbbing of the machinery far below.

From the trees at the edge of the Site, the flash of gray came again. Dupree rose and moved toward it, the gun now extended before him.

Twenty feet.

Fifteen.

Ten.

Something touched his face. He fell back a step and cried out, nearly loosing off a shot in his panic, his left hand swinging wildly and striking a glancing blow at the thing in the air. He looked down and saw the moth lying stunned upon the ground, its narrow pointed wings moving slightly. It was another hornworm. There were more of them on the tree trunk ahead of him, the yellow spots upon their abdomens like mold on the bark. Abruptly they rose, flew together, then settled again. As he drew closer, he could distinguish moths upon the branches around him, moths upon the stones, moths hidden in the tangles of the dead briers. Dupree had never encountered anything like it before. They did not belong on this island at any time, for even in the summer there were no tobacco plants, no potato plants or tomato plants, upon which they might feed. In winter, their extinction was guaranteed. They should be dead, thought Dupree.

They should be dead.

Then he turned and saw that his surroundings – the remains of the houses, the grave markers, even the great cross – were now entirely obscured by the insects, their slow movements seeming to bring the stones to life. Dupree could hear the moths brushing against one another, the sound of them like a soft whispering carried on the breeze. With the back of his hand, he touched the nearest tree and felt their wings trembling against his skin, but not a single insect fled from his touch or took to the air. Small fragments of their tissue adhered to his fingers, coating them lightly with a pale dust. He thought that he could taste them in his mouth, just as Sylvie Lauter must have tasted them in her final moments.

Dupree stood silently among them as the sun crossed the sky and the clouds lowered, until at last he left that place, the pitch of the whispering increasing in intensity as he went before abruptly ceasing entirely, as though some secret, half-heard conversation had concluded at last in unity and resolve.

9

Barron was having a very bad day.

In fact, Barron was having his second bad day in a row. The first had commenced with the phone call from Boston, advising him that his services would be required in the very near future. Barron had tried to explain to the man on the other end of the line that this wasn't a good time for him, that he was under pressure. The appearance of Parker in the bar had rattled him badly. He had no idea how much the private detective knew, or even suspected, but Barron feared his persistence. He wanted to keep his head down and behave like a model cop for a while. Still, he told the caller nothing about Parker. He was afraid that they might scent trouble and feed him to the department. They had photographs. Christ, they had a video. Barron would have to eat his gun, because there was no way he was doing jail time. No way.

Then there was Terry Scarfe. Part of Barron's deal with the Russians was that he would look out for Scarfe. Scarfe had contacts. He was a fixer. Scarfe also owed them, and he couldn't pay them back if he was stuck in jail. Barron knew that they had their hooks in Scarfe until his dying day, and that he would never be permitted to pay in full the debt that he owed. Barron understood this because he feared that he was in the same terrible position. What worried Barron was that Scarfe knew about him, and Scarfe was a screwup. The dipshit had run from him that night he was on patrol with Macy. If he had kept his head down, they might well have passed him by. Instead, Barron had been forced to chase him, to search him, and then to empty him out because the moron was carrying. If another patrol had picked him up ten minutes later and found his stash, Barron might have been compelled to explain how he had missed it during his search, assuming Scarfe didn't hand him over on a plate to save his own skin. True, he could have argued that Scarfe had been clean during the first search, and nobody would have been able to contradict him, but there was still the danger of arousing suspicion.

Then there was Macy to contend with. Barron didn't know how much Macy had seen during his search of Scarfe, but trainee cops had buckled under pressure in the past and Barron didn't know if Macy would be a stand-up girl if push came to shove. Even if she kept her mouth shut, Barron didn't like the idea of Macy having anything on him.

The Russian didn't listen to Barron's objections. He was bought and paid for. He was to wait for a call. When that call came the following morning, it marked the start of Barron's second bad day.

Because the call came from Scarfe.

Dupree made it back to town in time for the arrival of the 12:30 P.M. ferry, still shaken by his experiences at the Site. Amerling was right. Things were happening, and there was nothing that they could do except hold on tight during the ride and pray that it was over quickly.

He smelled perfume close by. He looked to his left and saw that Marianne Elliot was beside him, smiling shyly. There was a knapsack on her back, and she was sipping coffee from a steel travel mug.

'Hi,' she said.

'Hi. You going over to the mainland?'

'I've got some things to do,' she said. 'I'll get the ferry back this evening.'

'And Danny?'

'He's still with Bonnie Claessen. I dropped by to say hi. I think he's forgiven me for last night. Anyway, I promised to bring him back something from Portland and he seemed happy with that.'

She touched his sleeve.

'I had a good time with you last night,' she said quietly.

'Thank you.'

'You're supposed to say that you had a good time too,' she teased.

'I had the best time,' he said.

She leaned in the window, kissed him quickly on

the lips, then headed toward the dock. Over by the diner, Nancy Tooker, who had witnessed the exchange, raised her hand and gave him a cheerful wave.

Dupree tried to sink into his seat.

Barron met Scarfe in the parking lot behind the Levi's store in Freeport. It was relatively quiet there, and most of the cars had out-of-state tags. They sat in Barron's Plymouth, watching the lot.

'They're coming in today,' said Scarfe. 'They want to meet you.'

'No way,' said Barron.

'I don't think you're in a position to argue.'

Barron's right hand lashed out, catching Scarfe on the side of the face. Scarfe's head struck the passenger window.

'Don't you ever talk to me like that again! The fuck you think you are, talking to me that way?'

He stared straight ahead, gripping the wheel tightly in his hands, working at the plastic. Scarfe said nothing. Barron wanted to scream, to rage at the injustice of it all. He was a cop. These people had no right to put him through this. He could smell Scarfe beside him. He stank of sweat and unwashed clothes and desperation. Barron needed to get away from him.

'Give me the keys.'

Scarfe handed over the keys to an Isuzu Trooper parked out at the Maine Mall. The Trooper, sourced by Scarfe, was scanner equipped. Barron was to use

the Trooper for his part of the job, then just leave
the keys in it and walk away. Scarfe would take
care of its disposal.

'Now get out of the car,' said Barron.

Scarfe climbed silently out. There was a red mark
on his left cheek, and his left eye was tearing.

'You didn't have to hit me,' he said.

'I know,' said Barron. 'I did it because I wanted
to.'

Then he drove away.

10

They ditched the vans at a wrecking yard just outside of Brockton and prepared to pick up some replacements. Powell and Tell took care of the details, although Powell, who had grown fond of driving the Econoline, expressed his regret at seeing it go.

'Well, maybe we could hold on to it, just for you,' suggested Tell. 'We could get something written along the side, like "WE ARE THE GUYS YOU'RE LOOKING FOR!"'

They watched as the Econoline's roof collapsed inward under the pressure of the crane's jaws. Glass shattered, and the van shuddered as if in pain. It reminded Powell of the way a man's face will crumple when he's shot.

'Yeah, you're right. Still, we had some good times in that van.'

Tell tried to figure out if Powell was joking, but couldn't. 'You need to make some more friends, man,' he said.

They headed for the battered trailer that functioned as the lot's office. It smelled bad. An ancient gray filing cabinet spewed yellowed paper from an

open drawer, and the carpet was dotted with cigarette burns. Nicotine-smeared blinds obscured the
windows.

'Looks like business is booming,' said Powell.
'You guys must be planning to float on the stock
exchange pretty soon.'

There were three men waiting for them, and none
of them smiled. Two slabs of Cold War muscle
stood at either side of a third man, who sat behind
a cheap plastic desk. The seated man was wearing
a plaid jacket over a vile sports shirt. The other
men favored leather blouson jackets, the sort that
bad disc jockeys wore to public events. Even Powell,
who still missed the days when a guy could wear
the sleeves of his pastel jacket rolled up to his elbows,
thought the men were kind of badly dressed.

Tell, meanwhile, was trying to figure out where
the guys were from. Dexter had told him that the
main man was Russian, so he figured the others
were probably Russian too. They were dressed like
shit, which was kind of a giveaway. Tell didn't know
what it was about the new breed of immigrant criminals, but they had the dress sense of fucking lizards.
Everything had to shine. If these guys were making
money, they were spending it all on acrylics.

The seated man had skin like a battlefield. He'd
tried to mask the damage with a beard but it was
scraggly and untidy. His hair was thinning unevenly.
A patch of pink showed over his left ear. Tell wondered if the guy had some kind of disease, and was
relieved that he hadn't been forced to shake his

hand. He had introduced himself as Phil. Yeah, right, thought Tell: Phil, short for Vladimir.

'Dexter didn't come himself, no?' asked Phil.

'Dexter's kind of busy right now,' said Tell.

'I'm offended that he would not take the time to visit an old friend.'

'You get his Christmas card? 'Cause I know he sent it.'

'No card,' said Phil.

'Well, that's a shame,' said Tell.

'Yes,' said Phil. 'It is.'

He looked genuinely hurt.

Tell was getting antsy. Dexter had warned him to stay cool, Shepherd too, but Phil was beginning to get on his nerves and he'd been in his company for only a couple of minutes.

'We're in kind of a hurry here,' said Tell.

'Yes, always hurry,' said Phil. 'Too much rush.'

'It's the way of the world,' said Powell. 'People don't take time to stop and smell the roses.'

Tell looked at him, but Powell appeared to be genuine. The only thing Tell was smelling in here was rotting carpets and cheap aftershave.

'Your friend know,' said Phil. 'He understand.'

Tell was going to have words with Powell once they got outside. He didn't want Powell to start thinking of himself as some kind of mystic.

Phil picked up a brown envelope from the desk and tossed it to Tell. 'Two vans,' he said.

'We wanted three.'

'No three. Two only. No time.'

'Too much rush,' said Tell.

Phil smiled for the first time. 'Yes, yes, too much rush. You tell Dexter to come see me.'

Tell raised the envelope in farewell, and tried to smile back. 'Yeah, you bet.'

He and Powell turned to leave. They were at the door when Phil said: 'And, hey!'

Tell looked back. Phil was now standing, and all three men had guns in their hands.

'You tell him to bring my money when he come,' Phil said. 'And you tell him to hurry.'

Macy was enjoying Larry Amerling's company. She could tell that he was used to charming the pants off the women who came by the post office (literally, in some cases, she felt certain), but he was funny and knowledgeable and Macy was already beginning to get some sense of the geography of the island.

Amerling told her to hang a right and they followed the road uphill until they came to the main lookout tower. It had five stories, four of them with horizontal slit windows on three sides, a concrete lip overshadowing each window. There was a single chimney at the top. Five glass-strewn steps led up to the reinforced steel doorway. The door was open.

'Kids,' said Amerling. 'Joe tries to keep the towers locked up, but they just break right back in again.'

'Mind if I take a look?' asked Macy.

'Hold your nose,' said Amerling. 'I'll stay here and smoke a cigarette.'

They both got out of the Explorer. Amerling walked down to the road to light up, stealing a glance back at Macy as she climbed the steps. Fine-looking woman, thought Amerling. If I was only . . .

He tried to make the calculation, then gave it up as too depressing.

Macy pushed the door open and stepped inside. To her left, the words TOILET HERE had been spray-painted on the wall over what had once served as a fireplace. She decided not to look down. There were no windows on this level, and the floor was bare concrete. To her right, a flight of concrete steps led up to the next level. She took them and came to the second floor. The slit windows were masked with layers of Plexiglas, and dead insects were trapped inside. Macy continued to climb until the concrete steps were replaced with wooden stairs to the top floor. A ladder hung down from a square access door leading to the roof. She climbed up and slipped the bolt.

The wind hit her as she stepped onto the roof, causing her jacket to flap backward like wings. She zipped it up and walked to the edge. The tower stood high above even the tallest trees, and from her vantage point she could see the Cove, the smaller towers along the coastline, the neighboring islands, ships heading out to sea, even the mainland itself in the distance. The air smelled clean and fresh, with a faint hint of smoke, but the skies were heavy and gray and there was a bitingly cold edge to the wind. She turned to her right and saw Amerling smoking his cigarette. He looked up and waved, and she raised a hand in return until she was distracted by the sight of a blue truck rolling up the road. It was in bad shape, because gray-blue exhaust fumes not only curled from the pipe but seemed to envelop the vehicle entirely. That can't be right, Macy thought. He's moving fast, and the wind is blowing against him anyway. How can the fumes surround him in that way?

Then, as she watched, the truck slowed and the smoke appeared to peel away, forming two columns that faded into the forest to the left and right and then dispersed. Macy waited for a moment or two longer, still unsure quite what she had seen, then climbed back down the ladder and headed down to the door.

She didn't notice the crude drawings of dying men and burning houses carved into the concrete with a piece of discarded stone, or the length of white hair caught in the bottom rung of the ladder.

Or the child's cloth doll that watched her impassively from the corner of the room, its body shimmering as the moths moved upon it.

The truck had pulled up alongside Larry Amerling. The man leaning out of its window wore a dirty green windbreaker and a Sea Dogs baseball cap. His face was permanently tanned from years of working outdoors, but his nose was red and swollen and veins had broken badly across his cheeks. He

made a sucking sound with his teeth as Macy
approached and allowed his eyes to linger on her
thighs and crotch. She was relieved to note that
Amerling looked embarrassed on the man's behalf.

'This here's Carl Lubey,' said Amerling. 'He lives
up the road. Carl, this is Officer Macy.'

'Pleased to meet you,' said Lubey. He made it
sound like an invitation to his bed.

Macy contented herself with a nod and gave no
indication that the man's name meant anything to
her. So this was the brother of the man Dupree had
killed. She hated herself for agreeing with Barron's
assessment, but if his brother had been anything
like Carl, then Dupree might have done society a
favor. Carl Lubey was making her skin crawl.

'You got something wrong with your truck?' she
asked him.

'Truck's running fine,' he replied.

'Seemed to me like you were producing a lot of
fumes. You ought to get it looked at.'

'Don't need looking at. I told you: truck's fine.'

'If you say so. It happens again and you could
be looking at a citation.'

Lubey made that sucking noise through his teeth
again.

'You want to come over, maybe help me clean
out my pipes, you let me know,' he said. He winked
broadly at her, then put the truck in gear and went
on his way. This time, there was only a hint of
exhaust smoke.

'Does he live alone out there?' asked Macy.

'Does Carl look like the kind of guy who has women beating down his door? Yeah, he's alone. I don't think he ever got over—'

He stopped.

'I know about it,' said Macy.

'Yeah, well, then you understand. He always did have a lot of bitterness inside him. What happened to his brother just added a little extra piss to his vinegar, if you'll excuse the phrase. Pardon me saying it, though, it didn't look like there was anything wrong with his truck.'

Macy shook her head. 'When he was coming up the road, it seemed like he was surrounded by gray smoke. Then it just sort of . . . faded away. It was real odd.'

She turned to Amerling but he was looking away, staring at the road Carl Lubey had just taken, as if hoping to see some trace of the smoke for himself.

'I'd best be getting back,' he said. He stomped his cigarette out on the ground, then picked up the butt and put it in the pocket of his jacket. 'Mail won't sort itself.'

They drove in silence for a time, until Macy said: 'I couldn't see the Site from the top of the tower. That's what they call it, isn't it: the Site?'

Amerling took a moment to reply.

'Trees keep it hidden.'

'Even in winter?'

'Even in winter. There's a lot of evergreens out here.'

'It's over to the south, isn't it?'

'That's right, but you can't get there by car, and even on foot you need to know where you're going. At this time of year, with the light fading so early, I'm not even sure I could find it.'

'Another time, then,' said Macy.

'Sure,' Amerling lied. 'Another time.'

Moloch saw Dexter staring back at him in the rearview. Leonie and Dexter sat up front, Braun behind them, and Moloch farther back. There was a hollow panel in the floor, big enough for a man to lie in, if necessary, although if he was there for longer than a couple of minutes he'd probably suffocate. Moloch knew it was for weapons, maybe even drugs. It was a last resort for him in the event of a police search, and nothing more.

'You okay?' asked Dexter.

Moloch nodded. They had been traveling for about three hours, and his back ached. They had passed the toll booth at the New Hampshire state line shortly after nine and entered Maine. The traffic was light, most of it headed south toward Boston. They took the Kittery exit, and pulled up outside the Kittery Trading Post. Braun and Leonie went inside, leaving Moloch to rage silently alone.

As they had drawn closer and closer to Maine, Moloch had felt a pain building in his head. He found himself drifting into sleep, his eyes closing and his chin nodding to his chest, until a charge like a jolt of electricity forced him back into waking once again. But in those glancing moments of semi-rest, his body racked by exhaustion, he was tormented by visions, images of pasts both known and unknown, at once familiar and strange.

He saw himself as a small boy, hands pressed against the window of a black car as it pulled away from a suburban house, the boy's bicycle momentarily forgotten, his fingers brushing the glass as the car sped up, a man struggling in the backseat, his eyes wide with panic, two men holding him down. The man's hand reached out, as if somehow the boy could save him, but nobody could save him.

Dad?

No, not Dad, not really, but the closest he had come to finding one; a foster father and a foster mother in a street of identical houses, each with a small square of green lawn, its quiet disturbed only by the hiss of sprinklers and, now, the noise of the car as it pulled away from the curb.

Inside the house, the woman was crying. She lay slumped in a corner of the kitchen, with blood running from her nose and mouth. She had been baking a cake, and now flour and broken eggs covered the floor around her. The boy went to her, and she took him in her arms and held him to her.

The next day, more men came, and they were forced to leave the house. The boy fled with his not-mother, moving from town to town, watching her as she grew more and more desperate, descending into some terrible dark place all her own, where men came and pounded upon her body and left piles of ragged bills on the dresser when they were done. And the boy wondered, as he grew older: Who am I, and where have I come from, if I am not of this woman?

Then there were other women – mothers, sisters, daughters – flashing before him, and he heard half-familiar names spoken. He was in a house by a lake. He was on a streetcar, a man holding his hand.

He was on the island, and his voice was whispering: *Know me, wife.*

Moloch jerked into wakefulness again. Dexter was now reading a newspaper. Moloch closed his eyes again.

This is not my past. It is a past, but it is not mine. I am more than this.

The island reached out to him and he smelled the sea and the pines, and he heard a sound as of a moth tapping on glass, struggling to escape the darkness.

Or to return to it.

The others returned about a half hour later. They had bought warm clothing, waterproofs, and a selection of minor weaponry: knives, mainly; a hand-held axe; and a hunting bow for Dexter. As for guns, they already had what they needed.

Powell handed Dexter the bow case. Dexter opened it and removed the big bow contained within.

'I don't understand why you need that,' Moloch said. He still felt groggy and ill. He needed sleep, proper sleep. The tapping sound that he had heard in his dream had not gone away now that he was awake. Instead, it remained there, like water trapped in his inner ear.

'It's not about needing. I like the feel of a bow.'

'You ever kill a man with a bow?' asked Powell.

'No. Killed one with an arrow, though.' Dexter grinned.

'You really think we're going to need all this stuff up here?' Braun asked Moloch.

Moloch shook his head, as much in answer as in an effort to rid himself of the infernal noise in his head.

'We get there, find her, make her return my money, then we kill her. We don't want to make trouble for ourselves and bring them down upon us. If everything goes according to plan, we'll have her before they even know we've been there.'

'So, like I asked, why do we need all of this?'

Moloch looked at him the way he might have looked at a slow child.

'Because nothing ever goes according to plan,' he said simply.

The ferry to Portland contained just two passengers: an old man going to see his oncologist, and Marianne. She missed Danny and wished that he were with her, but she had to visit the banks and he would quickly have become bored with the waiting and the filling out of forms.

Bonnie had asked her little about her date, apart from inquiring if it had gone well. She told her that

Danny and Richie had enjoyed their evening together, and she didn't mind if he stayed with her for the best part of another day. Richie had cheered at the news. Richie was a wonderful kid – she could never think of him as anything but a kid – and the people on the island looked out for him. In some ways, Dutch was the best environment for a boy like him. No harm could come to him, and in the close-knit community he knew affection and support. To Danny, he was almost like a big brother, even though Danny, who was a smart boy, recognized that his playmate was different and that, in some ways, Danny had to look out for Richie more than Richie had to watch out for Danny.

But she had warned Danny not to follow Richie when he went exploring on the island. She knew that Richie liked to ramble through the woods and that Bonnie had given up trying to discourage him from doing so because Richie would go anyway, sneaking out of the house and sending her wild with worry. Better that he told her where he was going than to have him simply disappear without a word. While Marianne liked the older boy, she knew that he was incapable of looking after her son, and Danny had been told, on pain of eternal grounding and loss of pocket money for the rest of his life, not to go anywhere with Richie unless Bonnie went along too.

Ahead of her, she could see the boats bobbing at the docks on Commercial. Resigned now to a day without Danny, she was looking forward to getting a few things done. She planned to visit her hairdresser, browse in the stores, maybe even head out to the Maine Mall for a while to catch a movie. She would have the best part of four hours to herself.

But first, there was the money to take care of. Once that was done, she would breathe a little easier. She was wearing a money belt beneath her sweater, and while she would certainly have preferred not to have so much cash to carry around, Portland's streets didn't worry her. She would not be walking them at night.

Behind her, gray clouds gathered. There would be snow by morning, according to the Weather Channel. She had checked the forecast before leaving, and the worst of the weather would not hit until much later that night. Thorson had announced that the ferry would leave Portland at six-thirty that night, with a final sailing at ten. She would probably make the six-thirty, or else the last sailing with time to spare, and she and Danny would be locked up safe at home by the time the snows came.

In her kitchen, Bonnie Claessen was watching CNN while chopping vegetables for dinner. She thought that she might make something special, since Danny was with them: a pot roast, perhaps, and a pumpkin pie.

On the TV, she could see a vehicle being pulled from a river somewhere in the south. It looked hot down there, and the backs of the policemen's shirts were dark with sweat. She wondered if Mike, her current boyfriend, might be persuaded to chip in some cash so that they could take Richie away this summer. She'd ask him when she saw him next weekend. Mike drove trucks for a living and was kind of quiet, but he was patient with Richie and kind to her, and that was enough for Bonnie for the present.

Now the picture had changed, and a man's face filled the screen. He looked handsome, she thought, apart from his eyes. They were kind of narrow, an impression accentuated by the thin vertical lines that ran down each cheek, and the intelligence in them was marred by contempt. Maybe it was just the law he despised, she mused, but she didn't think so. She figured this guy hated just about everything.

Bonnie upped the volume in time to hear his name. Moloch. Wasn't that a biblical name? It sounded kind of biblical. Bonnie wasn't much of a one for churchgoing or Bible thumping, but the name gave her the creeps. She went back to preparing her food. The soaps would begin soon, her 'stories' as her mother used to call them.

Soon she forgot all about the man named Moloch.

But her son did not. He continued to stare at the television with rapt attention, watching the parade of faces. There was the man with the piercing eyes, and the black man, and the young man with the blond hair. Their pictures had been on TV a lot lately.

Richie sat very still and took them all in.

* * *

They arrived in Portland shortly before one. Moloch had by now moved into the front bench seat, sick of being incarcerated in the back of the van. The changes he had made to his appearance meant that only someone who took the time to examine him very closely would even begin to connect him with the face on the news reports, and if Moloch found someone examining him that closely, well, that person wouldn't live long enough to tell anyone what he or she had seen.

They pulled up on Commercial and looked out to sea. Close by was the dock for the Dutch Island ferry. There was nobody on board. Braun had gone to check the schedule.

'Last sailing is at ten,' he said when he returned. 'Ferry comes back to the mainland first thing tomorrow morning.'

Moloch considered this. 'For now, we rest up, get some motel rooms away from the center of town. We can talk about it again after we meet Scarfe.'

Dexter nodded. There was a Days Inn out by the mall. He'd seen the sign on the way into town. Dexter liked Days Inns. Once you got used to the fact that they all looked the same, they became a little like home.

Marianne had no problems at the banks. In total, she withdrew some $8,000 from three separate accounts, depositing each wad of notes carefully in the belt beneath her sweater. When she was done, she treated herself to a cab ride out to the Maine

Mall, and allowed herself to be pampered in the hairdresser's for a couple of hours. Then, feeling better than she had done in many months, she ate Chinese food at the mall's food court, then walked across the parking lot to T. J. Maxx, where she bought herself a DKNY leather jacket that had been reduced by $300, according to the tag. She bought new sneakers for Danny and added them to the Harry Potter trading card game in her bag.

She considered going to the movies. It had been so long since she'd sat in a movie theater to watch something that wasn't a cartoon or a kids' comedy. Ahead of her, she could see the Maine Mall Cinema, over by the Days Inn. She glanced at her watch, saw that it was just ten after six, and speeded up.

'What the fuck is wrong with her mouth?' said Dexter.

He and Braun were watching a pay-per-view movie in their motel room. Tom Cruise was some kind of deformed guy in love with a Spanish chick with dark hair. Tom had dumped Cameron Diaz for the dark-haired chick, which made no sense to Dexter at all, especially since the dark-haired chick seemed to have picked up the wrong mouth somewhere along the line.

'Well?' he said to Braun. 'Look at it.'

'Looks good to me,' said Braun. Dexter had run out of movies to watch on his DVD player, and had turned on the TV. Braun couldn't concentrate on his book with the movie playing so he had resigned himself to watching the screen. There was nothing else for them to do anyway, not until Scarfe contacted them.

'Nah. I ain't saying she ain't pretty or nothing. Hell, I'd fuck her for free. But her mouth . . . I don't know, it's just too big for her face. Who is she, anyway?'

'Penelope Cruz.'

'She married to him or something?'

'No, Cruz with a *z*. I hear he's dating her, though.'

'Fucking Tom Cruise. You think it's true about him?'

'What? That he's—'

'Yeah.'

'No. You think he could be going out with her if he was?'

'It might be a front.'

'Hell of a front. Hell of an ass too.'

'Yeah, but that mouth. It just looks *wrong* . . .'

Tell and Shepherd were sitting in the IHOP beside the Days Inn, eating pancakes with lots of sugar and butter and cinnamon on top. Shepherd was listening to Tell. Tell was full of shit sometimes, but it was kind of interesting shit.

Like, there they were in the IHOP, and this guy had rolled by in his wheelchair. He was wearing khakis and one of those black POW/ MIA T-shirts. His legs were gone from the knees down, and his trousers were pinned up. His arms were huge. Shepherd figured the guy must be pushing himself up the side of mountains to get arms that big. Then Tell said: 'You know, my brother was a cripple?'

'No shit?'

'Lost a leg in Vietnam, couple of months before Tet.'

'Which leg?'

'Right leg.'

'No shit?'

'Came home on crutches with one trouser leg pinned up, just like that guy, except he still had one leg. He was real upset.'

'Man had a right to be upset, he lost a leg.'

'Sure. Terrible thing, losing a limb. He stayed in his room, drinking, sleeping in his own filth. Wasn't nobody could get through to him. Then he got this phone call. Ed Sullivan – you remember Ed Sullivan?'

'Yeah, he was a strange-looking guy. Head and body didn't look like they matched.'

'He had short arms, was what it was. Anyway, Ed was a big supporter of the war, and he wanted he should do his part, so he invited some vets onto the show and my brother was one of them. He loved Ed Sullivan.'

'So he went to the show?'

'Hell, yeah, he went. He and his buddies were flown in, driven to the studio in big limousines, given front-row seats, the whole deal. They'd all lost limbs in Vietnam – arms and legs and shit. Ed insisted that all the guys should be cripples, otherwise they could be just anybody, you know?

Anyhow, during the dress rehearsal for the show, Ed calls for the lights and cameras to be pointed at them, and he starts making a big fuss, and the audience starts whooping and hollering. So Ed looks at the boys, and smiles that big smile he had, and tells them to take a bow. I mean, it's Ed Sullivan, telling them to take a bow. So my brother and his buddies, they stand up to take their bow.'

'Yeah? So they stand up . . .'

'And my brother fell over. He only had one leg. He stood up, kind of wavered for a second, then went sideways. Banged his head. Most of the other guys who'd lost legs managed to stay upright by supporting themselves on their seats, although they all looked kind of unsteady. Not my brother, though. He was gonna stand up straight and take a bow if Ed Sullivan told him to. He loved Ed Sullivan.'

'A man's got to love another man to try to stand straight on one leg just because he told him to do it. Your brother must have been kind of pissed at Ed, though.'

'No, he wasn't pissed at all. Fact was, he said he kind of appreciated someone treating him like he still had both legs. So after that my brother got himself a false leg. He wanted to be able to stand upright next time someone important told him to. He used to take it off to sleep, though. That's how he died. There was a fire in his apartment block, and when the alarms went off there was smoke and shit, and he died trying to find his false leg. He didn't want to be no cripple hobbling out. He wanted to preserve his dignity. *The Ed Sullivan Show* taught him that. He loved Ed Sullivan.'

'No shit.'

'No shit.'

Shepherd thought that was kind of interesting. That was what he meant about Tell.

'We did a bank job once, down in Pensacola,' said Shepherd, not wanting to be outdone in the storytelling stakes. 'Spent two weeks casing the bank. This was in the old days, before all them new security systems, and lasers and shit.'

'It was a different time. Man needs a degree to take down a bank now.'

'Yeah, they do make it hard for a man these days, and no mistake. Anyway, we get to the bank, morning of the job. Manager goes in, his staff after him, and we come in behind them before they got a chance to close the door.'

'And?'

'And there's two guys with masks already in there, waiting to hold up the bank. They'd come in through the roof during the night, and they were standing in there when the manager arrived.'

'No shit?'

'Well, we were kind of perturbed, you know. We must have been casing the same bank during that same two weeks, and we never saw one another.'

'Can happen.'

'Surely can. So we got this moment, right, where we're looking at them wearing their masks, and they're looking at us wearing our masks, and the manager and his people are looking at all of us. So I say, "The fuck are you doing? This is our bank." And this other guy says: "The fuck it is. We spent a month on this job."'

'Bullshit.'

'No, I don't think so. Coming in through the roof, that takes some planning.'

Tell relented. 'I guess.'

'So there's a standoff, until I say, "Well, why don't we split the take?" and the two guys look at each other and kind of shrug, and say, "Okay."'

'So you split the take?'

'Fifty-fifty, seeing as how they'd had to come in through the roof and all.'

'That was damn Christian of y'all.'

'Yep, mighty white. Like you said, it was a different time. That happened now, there'd be a blood-bath. But people had principles then. They had standards.'

'So y'all went away happy?'

'Kind of. The two guys got to their car and we held them up, took their share of the cash.'

'Survival of the fittest.'

'Absolutely. We didn't kill them, though.'

'Course not. You had standards.'

'Damn straight. It was a different time.'

'You said it. A different time. More pancakes?'

Shepherd shrugged. 'Sure, why not?'

Willard stood in the parking lot of the Days Inn,

smoking a cigarette. There was the IHOP maybe one hundred feet away, where Shepherd and Tell were eating. Willard could see them at the window. They hadn't asked him to come along with them. They were probably talking about him at this very minute, plotting how to get him out of the way. Willard wasn't too worried about Tell, but Shepherd and Dexter were real threats, maybe Braun too.

Willard hated Shepherd, Dexter, and Braun.

He pulled the baseball cap lower on his head and looked at himself in the side mirror of the van. With his blond hair covered and a thin growth of beard, he didn't look too much like the picture of him that they were showing on TV. Moloch had warned him against going out, but Willard wanted some air.

He started walking and had almost finished his cigarette by the time he reached the sidewalk. He took a last long drag on the butt and watched the woman approach. She stood at the entrance to the theater parking lot and checked the movie times. Willard registered the disappointment on her face.

'What were you going to see?' he asked.

She looked at him. She said nothing for a moment or two, then replied.

'Oh, anything really.'

'They all start round seven.'

'Yeah. Oh well.'

He smiled his best smile – 'You take care now' – and wondered what it would feel like to cut her.

Marianne smiled back and turned away. She walked quickly, but not too quickly. She didn't want

to give anything away, even as her insides churned
and she thought: Willard. It's Willard.

They're here.

It was only coincidence that had exposed her to the
man named Willard. It was during the last days,
when she was becoming more and more fearful of
Moloch and his ways. She thought that he might
in turn be growing suspicious of her, that he was
concerned at what she might know and of what
might happen if the police forced her to reveal any
knowledge of his activities, or if she chose to do so
of her own volition. One day, one week before the
date she had chosen for her escape, she had seen
Willard sitting in a car outside their house, and
knew that Moloch had told him to watch her. She
recognized the pretty young man from his photograph in the newspaper, the one linking him to the
death of the older woman, and from one previous
occasion, when she had arrived early for a rare
dinner with her husband and had seen him at the
bar, talking intently to Willard, his mouth almost
touching the younger man's ear, so that she had
thought at first that they might be lovers. She had
kept her distance, and had approached her husband
only after the young man had gone.

It was Karen Meyer who told her the young man's
name, after Marianne explained how she had seen
Willard waiting near the house. That was why she
hadn't been in touch. Karen had been angry. It was
their next-to-last meeting, arranged in advance to

clear up any remaining details or concerns. They were standing in a single stall in the ladies' room at the mall.

'You took a risk coming here, a risk to both of us.'

'No, I didn't. He followed me for two days. He didn't know I'd spotted him, and I gave him no indication that I knew. I behaved like an angel, and I know that's what he told Edward.'

Karen relaxed a little.

'Who is he?' asked Marianne.

'His name is Willard. I don't know anything more than that about him. He just looks pretty. There's something wrong with him, though, real deep down. Look in his eyes and you'll find yourself dying in a thousand different ways, with his hands on you right to the end. You see him coming for you again and you take off, you hear me? You take off and you never look back. We'll come up with another way to get the stuff to you, but you see Willard coming up your garden path and he's only going to be coming for one reason. He might drop by to check up on you again before then, so act naturally over the next few days. Don't give them any cause to suspect.'

And that was what she had done, walking calmly, ignoring the presence of the man that her husband might be planning to have kill her. On the last day, the day of Moloch's bank job, she knew she was safe. Willard would be with him, or close to him, but it was not until she was two hundred miles from the city, Danny asleep in his seat, that she began to relax even slightly. She continued to move from city to city, town to town, never staying long in any one location, before settling at last upon the island, the place to which she had decided to flee many months before after reading a feature about the Maine islands in a travel magazine, content that, for now, her trail was unlikely to be uncovered.

But she had never forgotten Willard, or the potential threat that her husband, even incarcerated, might pose to her. It could have been merely a coincidence, of course, that Willard was now up north, far from home, but she didn't think so. No, they were here, and they were coming for her, for if they were in Portland, then they knew she was on the island, and soon they would arrive upon it. As she walked away from Willard – not too fast, not too slow – she tried to retrace their steps, figuring out how they had found her. Only two people could have told.

Karen.

And her sister.

Marianne walked to Maine Mall Road and tried to hail a cab, using the opportunity to pause and glance back to where Willard still stood. He was not looking at her. Then he turned, and his eyes seemed to alight on her face. Marianne waited for him to head into the IHOP, or back toward the motel. Instead, Willard began to walk quickly along the sidewalk.

He was heading straight for her.

Willard didn't talk much. He guessed that a lot of folks considered him dumb, seeing as how he had never been much for school, and maybe they thought he was afraid to open his mouth because people might laugh at what came out. But Willard wasn't afraid of anyone, and those who might have felt the urge to laugh at him would quickly have suppressed it as soon as they looked in Willard's eyes. Sure, Willard had trouble with reading, and he wasn't so good with figures, but he had the instincts and intelligence of a natural hunter, combined with a curiosity about the nature of pain and hurt when inflicted on others.

He had sensed something from the woman when she had looked at him. It was more than the natural fear that he frequently recognized in women: the care they took not to get themselves trapped alone with a stranger; the grip with which they held onto their purses; the casual look around the smarter ones took as they prepared to open their car door in the parking lot. No, this was different, keener. Separated, thought Willard, with a husband who isn't taking it too well; or maybe trying to avoid a boyfriend who doesn't want to split from her, because then he'll have to find someone else to beat on. Willard's nostrils were almost twitching as she stood before him. He liked the scent of her. It aroused the predator in him.

He wasn't so sure about her hair, though. She'd

dyed it some dowdy color that didn't suit her, streaking it more than altering it entirely. He couldn't figure out why she'd do something like that, except he'd heard on TV that it was kind of the fashionable thing to do a few years ago. If so, this woman needed to get back on the fashion train, because it was surely leaving the station without her.

Willard watched her walk away. She had slim legs, and a nice ass beneath her coat. He could see the shape of it as she pulled the coat against herself. On another occasion he might have followed her, learned more about her, just in case he decided to visit her at some point in the future, but Moloch had warned him after the incident with the woman in the bedroom. Willard hadn't liked the way Moloch spoke to him. Neither had he appreciated the look that had passed between Moloch and Dexter afterward, like a principal and a teacher agreeing on the unspoken decision to expel him from school, once upon a time when he was young and cared about such things.

Willard saw the woman try to hail a cab. Strange, he thought. She walks to the movie theater from the mall, doesn't look in too much of a hurry, and now she suddenly has to get a cab? He rubbed his foot across the still-smoldering cigarette butt, crushing it into the sidewalk. And then there was that hair: it was shitty, almost as if it was designed to make her look more common than she was. There was a good-looking woman under there, but she seemed to be deliberately trying to hide her presence. A mental picture flashed: a woman with light brown hair, standing beside Moloch at the state fair, the woman smiling uneasily. Willard tried setting the image of the woman with the dyed hair beside Moloch's wife.

Shit.

Marianne saw the cab sign at almost the same instant that Willard began to speed up his progress. The lights were changing to amber over by Chili's restaurant, and the cabdriver seemed inclined to stop. She waved her hand frantically, causing cars to honk their horns as she ran across the road, and saw the driver glance to his right, where a competitor was exiting from the Hampden Inn with an empty cab. In that second, he made his decision and hit the accelerator, shooting through the lights as they turned to red in his rearview mirror. He pulled in alongside her and she clambered in, just as Willard started to run.

'Commercial,' said Marianne. 'Please, and quickly.'

The cab driver glanced in the rearview as he got ready to pull out, and spotted Willard.

'Hey,' he said, 'you know this guy?'

Marianne looked back. Willard was running between the traffic, dodging the oncoming hoods almost gracefully. He was maybe thirty feet from the cab.

'A guy I once dated,' she said. 'I really don't want to talk to him. There's ten bucks in it for you.'

'For an extra ten, I'll date him myself,' said the cabdriver. He swung out and shot away from the curb. Marianne heard a noise from behind, like fingers vainly dragging along the trunk of the cab, but she did not look back.

Willard stood on the curb, watching the cab head off toward Portland. Had the lights at the mall entrance gone red, then he might have caught up with them, but the cab had a free run to the main intersection. Willard took a deep breath and debated whether or not he should tell Moloch what had occurred. He might have been wrong about the woman, of course, but the look on her face as she had seen him approach through the back window of the cab told him that his suspicions were correct. It was her. She knew who he was, and if she knew that, then she must also know that they had come for her at last. The shock on her face told him one more thing: she didn't know that Moloch was free, otherwise she wouldn't have been trying to pass an idle evening with some shitty movie.

He had to tell Moloch. Already, the woman would be preparing to run again.

Willard was surprised at how calm Moloch appeared to be, at least initially. As it turned out, the calm didn't last long.

'You're certain it was her?' said Moloch.

'Pretty sure. Her hair is different, and she looked

kind of shitty, but I saw her face as that cab pulled away. She knew me.'

'How? There's no way that she could have known who you are.'

'Maybe she picked up on me when I was tailing her, back before she ran.'

'If she did, then you're the shittiest tail I ever knew.'

Willard bridled at the insult but said nothing.

'You should have caught her. Now she knows we're here.'

'Where can she go? There's no way she could have made the ferry.'

'You think that's the only boat down there? They have water taxis. She could go to another island and get someone to bring the kid to her. You think we have time to scour every island for her? Get the others. Describe her to them, and set them to looking for her in town. If nobody has found her by seven, we bring everything forward.' Willard left him. Moloch called Braun in his room. Braun listened, then hung up.

'We need to get going,' he told Dexter.

'The hell are you talking about?' asked Dexter. 'This shit is only starting to get good.'

'Willard saw the wife. He thinks she made him.'

Dexter swore, then turned off the TV. They packed up and joined Moloch and the others in his room. Shepherd and Tell had just arrived. Tell still had sugar on his sweater.

'An extra twenty-five thousand for the one that

finds her,' said Moloch. He looked at Willard. 'And I want her intact, you hear?'

Willard didn't even nod, but he could see Dexter grinning at him. Once again, he recalled the look that had passed between Dexter and Moloch. Willard decided that he was going to have to deal with Dexter, and sooner instead of later.

The cab dropped Marianne on Commercial, footsteps away from the ferry dock. The dock was empty and she could see the lights of the ferry disappearing into the evening darkness. She swore and felt the fear wash over her. It almost reduced her to tears. She tried to hold herself together.

They would be expecting her to head back to the island, if only to get Danny. Maybe if she could get someone to pick up Danny and get him off the island, then she could avoid going back to Dutch at all. Briefly, she considered calling the cops and telling them everything, but she was afraid that they would take Danny away from her, perhaps even jail her. No, the cops were not yet an option.

Except . . .

She dialed 911 and told the dispatcher that she had seen a man out by the mall who looked like the guy on TV, you know, the blond guy. She gave an accurate description of Willard's dress, right down to the baseball cap, then hung up.

That would give them something to think about.

She didn't have much time. She dropped some coins into the slot and rang Bonnie Claessen's number. The phone rang three times and then was picked up.

'Hello?' she said.

There was static on the line, but it wasn't regular static. It ebbed and flowed. It sounded like the noise of the tides converted to electrical impulses.

Then she heard her own voice, distorted now.

Hhellloooo

More voices joined it, repeating the words over and over again.

Hellohellohellohellohello

Then the line died.

She tried again, and got only a busy signal. She tried three more numbers, including Jack's, but they were all busy.

Marianne gripped her bag and ran for a water taxi, just as the first flurries of snow began to fall.

Shepherd arrived first at the pier, only to see the water taxi disappearing from sight, a tiny puff of smoke seeming to mock him as it went. He removed a pair of binoculars from his pack and found the woman in the prow of the boat. She was, as far as he could make out, the only passenger. As he stared at her, she looked back toward the pier and he was certain that she was looking at him. He thought he could read fear in her eyes.

Tell appeared beside him, and Shepherd smiled. 'She's going home.'

* * *

Willard's instincts were honed to perfection. He saw the patrol car before the cop inside could spot him, and slipped into the Starbucks in the Old Port, stripping himself of his coat and hat as he went. He didn't know who they were looking for, but he could guess. The woman had seen him, and she had called the cops to make life difficult for him.

Willard didn't care. Life had always been difficult for him.

He ordered a coffee, then slipped back out onto the streets and lost himself from view.

As soon as Willard told him of his encounter with Marianne, Moloch called Scarfe and headed for the meeting place he had suggested: the rocky outcrop by the twin lights in Cape Elizabeth. The rocks and the small beach were deserted. With the approaching blizzard, even the locals had retreated to their homes.

There were two men waiting on the beach, snow already whitening their shoulders and hair. One was Scarfe. The other was Barron.

'So this is the tame cop?'

Moloch looked at the policeman with a mixture of distaste and amusement. Barron was wearing jeans, sneakers, and a padded jacket. He looked uneasy.

'I'm not your tame cop,' he said.

'What would you prefer to be called? Pedophile cop? Child molester cop? Please, let me know. I want you to be as comfortable as possible in your dealings with me.'

Barron's face flushed, but he didn't reply.

'You should have been more careful, Officer. Your tastes have made you the bitch of anyone to whom your creditors choose to offer you.'

'Just tell me what you want,' said Barron softly.

Moloch turned to Scarfe. 'I've heard a lot about you, none of it very impressive. I advise you not to let me down. Now, tell me about the island.'

For the next ten minutes Scarfe detailed all that he had discovered from Carl Lubey, including the presence and routines of the giant cop, Joe Dupree, and the reported arrival that morning of the rookie cop, Macy. ('A rookie?' Moloch had interrupted. 'Maybe our luck is holding.')

'And the woman, Marianne Elliot?'

'She's out there. Her house is over on the south-eastern shore. There aren't too many other houses around there. The boy is with her.'

'Does she have a boyfriend?' asked Moloch.

Scarfe swallowed.

'Lubey says she's been seen around with the cop, Dupree. They had dinner together last night.'

Moloch motioned him to continue, but he looked unhappy at the development.

'There's a boat waiting for you down at the Marine Company. You go in after dark on the northern shore, some ways from the woman's house. There are no good landings over where she is, except for a little inlet that belongs to an old painter guy

who watches the bay like a hawk. You try coming
in that way and if he spots you he'll start making
calls. The sea there is threaded with rocks anyway.
Even experienced sailors steer clear of it. You need
to stay as far away as possible from the dock on
Island Avenue on your way in, and from any houses
along the shore. Like the painter, people on the
island keep a close eye on what happens there, and
who comes and goes. The northeastern shore is virtually unpopulated, though. Lubey will meet you
at the landing. He has a truck. He'll take you to
the woman's house, then bring you back to the boat
when your business is done. He doesn't want money.
He has one favor to ask.'

'Go on.'

'He wants you to kill the cop Dupree if you get
the chance.'

'No cops,' interrupted Barron. 'Nobody gets hurt,
that was the deal.'

'I don't remember making a deal with you,
Officer,' said Moloch. 'You will do as you're told,
or your superiors will receive information that will
end your career and make you the whore of every
disease-ridden rapist that your state's prison system
can put your way. Don't interrupt us again.'

He turned back to Scarfe.

'I make no promises about the cop.'

'It might be easier to get rid of him at the start.'
It was Leonie.

Moloch bit at his lip. If the cop was seeing his
wife, then the cop deserved what was coming to

him. There was nothing worse than the thought of another man inside his wife.

Scarfe unfolded papers from his pocket. 'This is a map of the island. I've made some copies. It's kind of rough, but it shows the main roads, the town, and the location of the woman's house and those of her nearest neighbors.'

Moloch took the map, examined it, then folded it and handed it, along with the copies, to Leonie.

'I couldn't help but notice that you said "you" in your detailing of the arrangements made. "You", not "us." That worries me.'

'I've done what you asked me to do.'

'You're coming with us.'

'You don't need me.'

'You know about boats, and you know this area. Some of my associates have experience of such matters, but these are unfamiliar waters and there is bad weather approaching. And if your friend Mr. Lubey lets us down, we will have someone to fall back on. Heavily.'

Scarfe nodded.

'I understand.'

Moloch turned to Barron.

'Your role in this affair is simple, Officer. You monitor the police bands. If there is even a hint of police activity that might concern us, I want you to nullify it. I understand that there is no cell phone coverage on the island?'

'There are pockets, but only close to town. The eastern shore is out of range.'

'You will take up a position on the dock. If our return is jeopardized in any way, you will signal us with your headlights as we return to land. Is that clear?'

'That's all?'

'For now. Mr. Scarfe, you'll come with us. Our departure is imminent.'

Moloch, Dexter, and Willard dropped Leonie and Braun on Commercial. The two older men sat in the van close by the Casco Bay Ferry Terminal while Willard stayed in the shadows and watched the approaches along Commercial. The plan was virtually unchanged: one group would make for the island with Scarfe, while Leonie and Braun would now follow on by water taxi and land at the Cove, as the late ferry crossing had been cancelled due to Thorson's innate caution and the early arrival of the snow. Barron would keep an eye on all new arrivals, just in case the woman managed to slip by them and make it back to Portland.

'I didn't want her to see us before we came,' Moloch said to Dexter. 'I didn't want her to know. I wanted to see the shock on the bitch's face myself.'

'You'll still see it. I reckon she has a lot of shock left in her.'

Moloch didn't look so happy, Dexter thought. He had been sleeping badly. Dexter had heard him crying out. That happened to men who had been jailed, Dexter knew. Even after their release, part of them always remained incarcerated, and that was the part that intruded on their dreams.

Dexter, meanwhile, had his own worries.

'I don't like this whole island deal,' he said. 'Too many things can go wrong. I don't like having just one escape route. I don't like having to leave the same way I came in. And we don't know shit about this Lubey guy.'

'We have a boat. One of us will stay with it the whole time. Like I told you, we can take her and be gone before anyone even knows we've been. We just need to stay out of trouble. As for Lubey, he's a driver, nothing more.'

'Do you trust the cop?'

'No, but I think he's too frightened of the consequences to cross us. Plus, our friends in Boston have promised him a little gift for his cooperation. His fear and his lust should combine to keep him in line.'

'And the policeman out on the island?'

'When they get there, Braun and Leonie will kill him, if only for having the temerity to fuck my wife.'

'And Willard?'

Something like regret flashed across Moloch's features.

'No pain,' he said. 'I want him to feel no pain.'

In the shadows, Willard was looking at a small map of the bay held behind a protective Plexiglas screen. He had changed his clothes and was now wearing a tourist's fleece with a lobster on the front. He had darkened his hair in a men's room with a kit he had bought in a drugstore, and it was now a deep, rich black. With the index finger of his right hand, he traced the route of the ferry, following each little dot as carefully as if he were tracing the route onto paper. His finger stopped on the island, then he jerked it back suddenly.

A spider was crawling across the map. Its body covered the island. Somehow, the spider had found its way inside the case and now it was trapped, vainly seeking a way out. Maybe it had been trying to shelter from the cold, but now the case would be its tomb. There would be no insects in there for it to feed upon and eventually it would grow thin and die. Willard watched it crawl, its legs occasionally slipping on the surface of the map, causing the spider to drop an inch or two before its silk arrested its slide. At last it crawled back up to the top right-hand corner of the case and huddled there, waiting for its end.

Willard's mouth was dry. He looked up from the map and stared out to sea, trying to find light in the distance, but he could not. His stomach felt bad. He was concerned about Dexter and Shepherd, but he was worried too about the island. Willard had a survivor's instincts, and now that little inner voice on which he had relied for so long was telling him to leave, to make his escape while he still could. But Willard wasn't going to run. Deep inside, he still trusted Moloch. He *wanted* to trust him. He needed him. He lived for the light of Moloch's approval. It was his weakness. Willard was crazy, crazier than even he himself knew, crazier even than Moloch suspected, but deep down, he just wanted to be loved.

11

Powell was having trouble with the boat guy. He was fat and old and dumb, with grease stains on his shirt. He didn't smell so good. Powell had to turn his face away anytime the guy spoke to him, his breath was so bad. Powell just hoped his boat didn't stink as bad as he did. Powell wasn't happy on the sea. He didn't need any encouragement to puke on boats, but he suspected that the stench from this guy's boat might be about to give him a little push in the right direction, just for good luck.

The boat was a twenty-footer, with a small enclosed cabin barely big enough for two men. Powell knelt down close to it, took a sniff, and backed off. It reeked of rotting fish and the boat guy's breath, as if it were so toxic that it had stuck to the hull and glass like gum. Powell had read somewhere that all smells are particulate, which meant that tiny little molecules of the boat guy's stench were now wending their way through his nasal passages. It made Powell even more irritated with the boat guy than he already was, and Powell had been pretty pissed at him before he even got within ten feet of his stinking boat. The guy wasn't even supposed to be here, but he had started to worry about his boat being taken out in bad weather and had come down to the dock to express his concerns. Now Powell was left to clear up the mess before Moloch and the others arrived, because if they got here first, then the boat guy was dead. The way Powell saw it, the last thing this operation needed was more dead people. They already had enough corpses to form a conga line from here to Virginia. Scarfe had assured Powell that the boat guy would keep his mouth shut, just as he had done in the past. Powell hoped that, for his sake, the boat guy started shutting up pretty soon, because Powell was starting to get seriously nauseous.

'You got paid, right?' said Powell. 'I know, 'cause Scarfe says he did it.'

'Yeah, I got paid. I got the money right here.'

'So?'

'That boat is worth more than you paid me.'

'We're renting it,' said Powell, his patience wearing thin as paper. 'We don't have to pay you what the boat is worth. That's why it's called "renting" and not "buying".'

'But suppose something happens to it. Scarfe said—'

The fat guy looked over Powell's shoulder to where Scarfe stood in the shadows. Scarfe looked away. The boat guy was on his own. Powell reached out and grabbed his shoulder in order to keep him focused, then instantly regretted touching him.

'I could give a rat's ass what Scarfe said. With

luck, you'll have your boat back tonight. Four, five hours, tops. We've been more than generous. You got insurance, right?'

'Yeah I got insurance, but insurance never pays like it should.'

'Why are you telling me? Go write your congressman. All I want is the boat.'

'It's nothing illegal is it?'

Powell looked hard at the guy. 'Are you for fucking real? Where do you get off asking a question like that? You want me to tell you?'

The boat guy started to back off. 'No, I don't want to know.'

'Then take your money and get your fat stinking ass out of my sight. This piece of shit is all fueled up, right?'

'Sure, it's ready to go.'

'Okay, then. We have any problems with this, and we're not going to be looking for a refund, you understand? We're going to want a different level of compensation.'

'I understand. You'll have no problems with her.'

For a moment, Powell looked confused.

'How do you know—,' he began, then stopped. The boat: he was talking about the boat. Shit. Powell let out a deep breath.

'No problems with her,' he echoed. 'Good. Now go buy yourself some Tic Tacs.'

Moloch, Dexter, and Willard arrived shortly after the boat guy had gone on his way, and Tell and Shepherd emerged from out of the shadows. They had wrapped up warm in preparation for the crossing, and had put on the waterproofs purchased in Kittery. The wind had picked up in the last half hour. The snow blew hard against their faces. He noted with some amusement that the snowflakes were settling neatly along Tell's cornrows, contrasting nicely with his dark skin. Powell thought that it made Tell look kind of decorative, Dexter too, come to mention it. He didn't consider sharing this observation with them.

'Storm coming in with a vengeance,' said Powell.

'Good,' said Moloch. 'So are we.'

Powell, Shepherd, and Dexter clambered down into the boat after Moloch, Scarfe following, then Willard. Scarfe started the motor. He glanced behind him, watching the four men shrug themselves into life vests, then take their seats on the plastic benches, Powell alone and holding on grimly to the side. Tell untied the boat, tossed the rope down to the deck, then clambered aboard.

Moloch stood beside Scarfe in the wheelhouse. Scarfe was looking at the sky and the thickening snow. The docks around them were already nearly lost to sight and the sea beyond was a vision in static. They were alone on the water.

'How long will it take us to get across?' asked Moloch.

'There's a head wind, and visibility sucks. We'll have to take it slow. We don't hit anything and nothing hits us, then we'll make it in two hours tops.'

'She could have been there and gone by the time we get to her.'

Scarfe shook his head. 'Uh-uh. She's facing the same difficulties as we are, plus I reckon that there's going to be no more traffic into and out of the island until morning. The ferry is bedded in for the night. Thorson is no Captain Crunch. He won't take her out if there's even a smell of danger. Unless she gets someone to take her off the island in a private boat, and I don't think that's going to happen, then she's stuck there. Problem is, we may be stuck there too.'

Moloch raised his hand, gripped Scarfe's chin, and turned the smaller man's face to his.

'That's not going to happen. You understand?'

Scarfe's reply was muffled because Moloch's grip was so tight, but it was clear that he knew where he stood. Moloch released his grip, and Scarfe pulled the boat away from the dock.

Already, Powell's face was gray. Across from him, Dexter took a package from his pocket and unwrapped it, revealing a meatball sub. As the boat moved away, Powell's cheeks bulged.

'Don't puke on my shoes,' warned Dexter.

Powell didn't.

He puked on his own shoes.

Braun and Leonie had some trouble convincing the water taxi to take them over to Sanctuary. The guy didn't want to go, but Leonie gave him a sob story about being a cousin of Sylvie Lauter, and how she had come hundreds of miles to console her mother. Leonie's tale would have broken a softer man, but the boatman looked like he was made out of teak, with a mahogany heart. Braun stayed out of it, figuring that if they both began to work on the guy they would intimidate themselves out of a ride.

Leonie gave him $100. The boatman relented. She watched him fold the bills and place them in a waterproof wallet that hung on a string around his neck, then tuck the wallet under his shirt. Satisfied, she turned away.

Leonie had none of the scruples of Powell and Braun. She did not like leaving loose ends.

She would get the money back from him when she killed him.

Marianne sat beneath the awning of her water taxi, her arms curled tightly around herself, her chin buried beneath folds of coat and scarf. She was shaking uncontrollably. The boatman, thinking her cold, offered her coffee from his flask and she thanked him and wrapped her gloved fingers around the tin cup.

But still she shook.

She had tried calling her sister before the boat left, but the phone had rung out. She had called Karen Meyer, with the same result. She knew in her heart that both were dead, that she had cost them their lives. It was her fault, all her fault.

But if she died, then Danny would also die, and it would all have been in vain. There was still a chance for them, if she could get to Danny in time. Thorson had cancelled his final sailing and appealing to his better nature was not an option. She knew his reputation and doubted if he would make even one leg of the journey and risk being stranded in Portland. Even if he was willing to go to sea, Marianne feared that someone would be watching the ferry in case she tried to escape, certainly from the mainland and possibly from the island itself.

But there were others who might be prepared to take them off the island, if not as far as the mainland, then at least to one of the larger neighboring islands. Carl Lubey had a boat and sometimes made runs if someone was in enough trouble and was prepared to pay him handsomely for it. He was an option, although the idea of being at his mercy was unappealing. Her other choice was Jack the painter. He also had a boat, and she knew that he cared for Danny. If he was sober, he was their best chance.

There were lights to her right and left: the houses on nearby islands, their windows hanging suspended in the darkness like fissures in the fabric of the night or the promise of new worlds. She fantasized about taking Danny and disappearing through one of them, sewing it closed behind her so that nobody could ever find them again. The lights disappeared as the snow thickened and the wind picked up. The little boat tossed on the waves and she held tightly to the ropes, spray drenching her face and chilling her hands. She wore the boatman's spare oilskins, but water was still finding its way through. She thought of her son, and she thought too of Joe Dupree. She could turn to him, but the risks were too great. She would be forced to reveal the truth about herself and she couldn't do that.

But there was another reason that she was unwilling to ask him for help. She had seen Willard, and knew that Moloch must be close by. There would be others too, perhaps not as bad as her husband and the pretty, dangerous boy-man, but bad enough.

Joe Dupree was not strong enough to stand against them.

If she turned to him for help, they would kill him.

They would kill them all.

Dupree stood at the station house door and watched the snow fall. Already, Island Avenue was empty. The stores had closed early and the Rudder and Good Eats would not be opening for business. The ferry would return to port any minute now and Thorson would kill the lights on the dock and hang out a Sailing Canceled sign. The snow was already sticking to the sidewalks, the shadows of the flakes made huge by the glow of the streetlights as they descended. No cars were moving anywhere on the island. The risks of ending up in a ditch or, worse, taking a tumble into the cold sea were too great.

He heard footsteps behind him. Macy was wrapped up warm. She had added an extra sweater to her uniform, and her hands were double wrapped in a pair of woolen gloves and a pair of leathers from the station locker.

'No luck,' she said. She had been trying to raise Portland on the radio for the last hour, but there was only static. The phone line, meanwhile, had exchanged a dial tone for a steady hum. Dupree had wandered over to check with Larry Amerling in his house behind the post office, but his phone was also without a proper tone. It looked like the entire island was going into communication meltdown.

'Did you get out to the Site?' Amerling asked Dupree, as the policeman prepared to leave.

'Yes, I went out there.'

'And?'

'There were moths.'

'That's all?'

Dupree debated telling him about the vibrations in the ground, or the sheer numbers of the insects that he had seen, then decided against it. The postmaster looked edgy enough as things stood.

'That's all, and after this snow I don't think we'll be seeing too many more moths on the island until the summer. Stay warm, Larry. I'll check in with you at the post office tomorrow morning.'

He left the postmaster, pulling the front door closed behind him. A moment or two later, he heard the sound of the deadbolts locking.

Now, beside him, he saw Macy trying to dial a cell phone number. The display showed a ringing phone symbol, indicating that it was attempting to make a connection, then returned to the Verizon home screen. The aerial strength indicator read virtually nil. Even the reception on the TV in the rec room was terrible.

'Guess we batten down the hatches,' she said.

'Guess so.'

He didn't even look at her.

Quiet time, she thought. I can do quiet time. I just wish you'd close the damn door.

Macy's day had been spent on largely mundane matters. There was the B&E that turned out to be nothing more than an embarrassed husband who had climbed in through the kitchen window while dead drunk the previous night, broken plates, and knocked over the portable TV in the kitchen, then fallen asleep in the spare room because he was afraid of waking his wife, unaware that she had popped enough sleeping pills to allow half of San Francisco to sleep through an earthquake. His wife had eventually come to, spotted the damage, and called the cops. The first her husband knew about it all was when Macy arrived at their door while he was throwing up in the john. The woman began hollering at her husband and calling him ten types of asshole while he just held his head in pain and shame.

Macy left them to it.

Apart from the happy couple, she had issued a warning to the owners of a scrawny mongrel dog that was trying to bite passing cars, and talked to a couple of kids who were smoking and probably drinking (they'd hidden the beer cans somewhere in the undergrowth, but Macy was damned if she was going to go beating the bushes with a stick for a couple of Miller High Lifes) out by the old gun emplacement. She'd taken their names, then told them to haul their asses back home. One girl, dressed in a black leather motorcycle jacket and combat pants, with a Korn T-shirt underneath and a spiked dog collar around her neck, hung back.

'Are you going to tell my mom and dad?' she asked Macy. The girl's name, according to her driver's license, was Mandy Papkee.

'I don't know. You got any reason why I shouldn't?'

'We weren't doing any harm. We just came out here to remember Wayne and Sylvie.'

Macy knew about the accident on the island the week before. A lot of the people she had met that day insisted on talking about it, if only to assure her that things like that didn't happen very often on Dutch. Sometimes, the older ones said 'on Sanctuary', reinforcing the seemingly dual nature of the island's existence.

'You knew them?'

'Everybody knows everyone else out here,' said Mandy. 'I mean, duh, it's an island.'

'*Duh?*' repeated Macy, pointedly.

'Sorry,' said Mandy. 'Look, we're not going to be back out here, not for a long time. I can promise that.'

'Why?'

'Because it gives us the creeps. This was, like, a stupid dare. We shouldn't have come here. It just feels wrong.'

'Because of what happened to your friends?'

'Maybe.'

Mandy clearly didn't want to say anything more, but she looked around at the trees, as if half expecting Sylvie and Wayne to emerge bloodied from the undergrowth, looking for a beer and a toke.

'Look, just give us a break, okay?'

Macy relented. 'Okay,' she said, and watched Mandy follow her friends back to the road. Something flitted across the grass toward Macy's feet. It was a moth, an ugly gray one. Macy flicked her foot at it and the moth flew away. She strolled over to the damaged tree against which the stolen car had finally come to rest and saw the little shrine that had been raised in memory of the dead teenagers. She touched nothing. By the time she got back to the Explorer, Mandy and the other kids were gone.

That was about as interesting as things got. For the most part she drove around the island, familiarizing herself with its roads and trails, talking to people as they went about their daily business. Occasionally she made contact with Dupree, but he seemed distracted. When the light began to fade she returned to the station house and stayed there.

She went upstairs to the little galley kitchen beside the rec room, poured chicken soup from a can into a plastic bowl, then placed the bowl in the microwave. She took a book from her pack, lay back on the sofa, and started to read. There was still some time to kill before the ferry arrived.

Out on Sunset Road, Doug Newton checked on his mother. Her breathing was shallow and the dark patches around her eyes were like new bruises. He touched the old woman's skin with the backs of his fingers. She felt cold, even though the radiators were turned up as high as they would go. Doug went to the hall closet and took out another comforter. He laid it on her bed, tucking it in beneath her chin, then walked to the alcove window and looked out onto his yard. The exterior lights were on and he could see the snow falling and the shapes of the trees slowly emerging as the flakes came to rest upon them. Beyond, there was only darkness.

Doug tugged at the lock on the window. It was firmly closed, as were all the windows in the house. He recalled what he believed he had seen: a little girl at his mother's half-open window, her fingers prising at the gap to widen it. When Doug had entered the room the girl had stared back at him for no more than a second or two, then retreated. By the time Doug reached the window, she was gone from sight. The little girl was five or six years of age, or so he had told Joe Dupree, but Doug had said that last part with a slight tremor of doubt in his voice, because the girl might have had the body of a child, but her eyes were much older, and her mouth was all wrong. It was very round, like it was about to give a kiss.

The funny thing about it was that Joe Dupree, old Melancholy Joe himself, hadn't laughed at him, or accused him of wasting police time the way that other cop Tuttle had. Instead, Joe had told him to do just what he was doing: keep his mother warm, and keep the doors and windows locked, just in case.

Just in case.

Doug went back downstairs, turned on the TV, and tried to watch a show through a snowstorm worse than the one outside.

On Church Road, Nancy and Linda Tooker were arguing over the dogs. They'd taken the collie and the German shepherd indoors because of the snow, but now the dogs just wouldn't stop whining. Nancy had opened the kitchen door to see if they wanted to go back out, but the dogs had instead retreated farther into the house and were now lying in the darkness at the top of the stairs, still whining.

'It was you that wanted pedigree dogs,' said Nancy. 'Damn things are too highly strung. I told you.'

'Can it!' said her sister. She was trying to connect up to AOL, but with no success. Eventually, the screen just froze and she was forced to unplug the computer from the wall. When she tried to restart it, nothing happened.

'Nancy,' she said. 'I think I broke the computer.'

But Nancy wasn't listening. Instead, she watched through the kitchen window as gray shapes danced across the snow. Her sister joined her, and together they stood in silence as the insects flew among the snowflakes, seemingly untroubled by the wind that shook the windows and caused closed doors to strike against their frames. Once or twice they banged against the glass and they got a clear look at the ugly moths.

Without consulting each other, the two sisters locked all the doors, secured the windows, and took their places with the dogs.

In his little bedroom, Carl Lubey wrapped himself up warm and pulled on a pair of steel-capped Timberlands. The wind tugged at the windows of his house, causing them to rattle furiously. What little warmth there was seeped out through count-less cracks and gaps in the woodwork. Ron was the one with the talent for houses, not Carl. Carl was the mechanic; his brother was the builder, the handyman. Now Ron was gone and Carl was left alone to deal with the wind and the rain and the snow as best he could.

He went to his bedside locker and removed the Browning. It had a shitty plastic grip plate that was supposed to look like wood but didn't, and the magazine catch jammed on occasion, but Carl wasn't fussy. He didn't think he'd have much call to use it, not if the visitors came through for him.

If things went like they were supposed to, his brother would sleep easy in his grave tonight.

At the heart of the island, close by the Site, there was movement among the trees and beneath the earth. Despite a wind that blew hard from the west, shrubs bent toward the east, and flurries of snow rose in spirals and formed shapes that almost resembled the bodies of men before they disintegrated and tumbled gently toward the ground. Seen from above, it might have appeared that gray light was seeping out from the ground, or a thin, dirty smoke that left no mark upon the snow.

And the wind sounded like voices, and the voices were joyful.

12

Macy spotted the ferry pulling into port from her vantage point on the second floor. Its arrival had been delayed by the weather, Thorson unwilling to push the ferry's speed into little more than double figures. The faint streamer of smoke was barely visible through the thickening snow, although Thorson had lit the boat itself like a Christmas tree. It almost hurt her eyes to look at it.

'Ferry's in,' she called to Dupree.

He was catching up on paperwork in the little office. The doors leading outside were now firmly closed and the heating had kicked in enough to enable him to remove his jacket.

'You don't have to go,' he said. 'I'm pretty sure it's my turn.'

'Nah, I'm dressed for it. Besides, it will give me something to do.'

'Thanks,' he said, and returned to his reports.

The wind rocked Macy on her heels when she stepped outside. It had picked up force and the snow blew directly into her face, stinging her cheeks. She removed the windshield cover from the Explorer and tossed it on the passenger seat, then started the engine and drove carefully down to the dock, parking over by the passenger shelter until the ferry came in. The chains on the wheels made a ratcheting sound on the road, and the snowplow attachment that she and Dupree had fitted earlier that evening rattled against the grille.

A handful of passengers disembarked from the ferry, all of them apparently locals who raced for their own cars or caught rides from friends or family. Macy watched them leave, then saw another, smaller vessel heading into port. The water taxi docked and a harried-looking woman was helped out by the boatman. There seemed to be some argument, and Macy was about to head over and intervene when the boatman abruptly turned away, cast off, and headed out of port. He paused briefly to exchange some words with Thorson, who leaned over from his roost to talk, then continued on his way.

The woman did a double take when she saw the Explorer, before heading straight up the hill to where her car was parked. Macy followed her, pulling in alongside her as she fumbled with her car keys.

'Everything okay, ma'am?'

The woman looked at her and tried to smile.

'Yes, thank you, everything's fine. I'm just late to pick up my son, that's all. He'll be worried.'

Macy smiled, as if she really understood what it was like to have a child waiting for her to return, but the woman was no longer looking at her. Instead, she was staring over Macy's shoulder, looking back out to sea. Macy glanced in her rearview mirror, but the ferry was the only boat in sight. The water taxi was already lost amid the snow.

'Can I ask your name, ma'am?'

The woman jerked like she'd just been hit with an electric shock.

'Marianne Elliot,' she said. 'My name is Marianne Elliot.'

'Were you having trouble with the taxi?'

'Just a disagreement about the fare, that's all. In the end, I paid a little over the odds, but it's a bad night. It was good of him to take me over after I missed the ferry.'

Macy examined the woman's face but saw no reason to doubt her story. She patted the car roof and moved back.

'Well, Miss Elliot, you take care on the road. I know you're in a hurry, but you want to get back to your son safe and sound, don't you?'

For the first time, the woman seemed to truly notice her.

'Yes,' she said. 'More than anything else in the world.'

Thorson was sipping coffee in the cabin of the ferry when Macy came on board.

The captain offered her his flask and a spare cup, but she declined.

'You're not making another crossing, right?' she asked. Dupree had told her to check, although he had been pretty certain that Thorson would not be taking the ferry out again.

Thorson stared out into the night. He even looks like a ferry captain, thought Macy: white beard, red cheeks, yellow oilskins. He was a good captain, according to Dupree; in all its long history, there had never been an accident involving Thorson's ferry. He was just more respectful of the sea than most.

'You kidding? The Casco Bay people were going to stop running at seven. There won't be a boat on the water in an hour. Soon as I finish my coffee I'm heading home, and that'll be me done until the morning.'

'Okay, just thought I'd make sure. Say, you know the captain of that water taxi that came in just now?'

'Yeah, that's Ed Oldfield. I was surprised to see him out so far on a night like this.'

'He say anything to you about the woman he brought over?'

'Marianne? No, just that she seemed to want him to wait for her and take her back to Portland. He wouldn't do it. If he waited any longer he'd be stuck here overnight, and he's got a family at home on Chebeague.'

Macy thanked him and returned to the Explorer, then headed back through town toward the station house. Dupree was still hunched over his desk, painstakingly typing details into the primitive-looking computer on his desk as he tried to avoid hitting two keys simultaneously with his big fingers. He looked up as Macy entered, brushing snow from her jacket.

'Anything unusual?'

'A few locals, and a water taxi. Just one passenger on board. She said her name was Marianne Elliot.'

Macy picked up the look on Dupree's face.

'You know her?'

'Yeah,' he said.

Was he blushing, she wondered?

'She's a friend.'

'She was in quite a hurry. Said she was late to pick up her kid. Thorson said he thought she might be trying to get back to the mainland tonight.'

Dupree frowned. 'Nobody's going back to Portland tonight. Maybe I'll take a run by her place later, make sure she's okay.'

Despite herself, Macy felt one of her eyebrows arch.

'What?' said Dupree.

'Nothing,' said Macy, trying to sound innocent. 'Nothing like a concerned, active police force.'

'Yeah.' He sounded dubious. 'Speaking of concerned and active, you mind taking a short ride out?' Dupree was worried about Marianne now. He couldn't understand why she would want to return to Portland before morning, unless there was something wrong. He'd use his own jeep to drop over to her place as soon as he had finished his paperwork.

'No problem, but that snow is falling pretty heavily and the wind is picking up some. Soon, it's going to start to drift.'

'I don't want you to make a full circuit of the island, not in this weather. Larry Amerling told me you were out by the main watchtower today. You think you can find it again?'

'It's easy enough to find: take a right on Division and straight on till morning, right?'

'That's it. Heard you ran into Carl Lubey while you were out there.'

'He was charming. Still single too. Quite a catch.'

'Yeah, like catching rabies. Could you swing by Lubey's place?' He pointed it out to her on the wall map. 'It's a shithole, so you can't miss it, even in this weather. Couple of rusted-out cars in the drive and a big screw-you satellite dish in the yard. Last night I had to roust him from the bar along with a mainland lowlife named Terry Scarfe. According to Thorson, Terry didn't come back over today, but I still don't like the fact that he and Lubey were spending time together.'

Macy zipped up her jacket and got ready to go, but Dupree stopped her.

'I guess you already know it, but Carl Lubey is the brother of a man I shot. I killed him. Carl's a sleazebag, but he's harmless alone. If I go out there, I'll only rile him up, and the next thing we know we'll have him cuffed to the chair over there, smelling the place out until morning. I hate to do this to you on your first night and all, but it will put my mind at rest if I know that Carl Lubey is tucked up safe in his bed. The tree coverage should mean that the road is still okay, but you run into any problems and you just come right back, y'hear?'

Macy told him that she would. Secretly, she was pleased to be leaving the station house. The TV wasn't working properly and she was likely to be cooped up inside for the night. One last trip out would kill some time and leave her with more of her book to read. She drove carefully up Island Avenue until she left the streetlamps behind, then put her headlights on full and followed the coast toward Division.

Carl Lubey was not tucked up safe in his bed, although he was starting to wish that he was. Curiously, he was thinking about Macy, just as Macy was now thinking about him, because he was staring into the innards of his truck, a truck that right now just would not start.

The cop had warned him. She said she'd seen it billowing fumes, but he just hadn't listened.

Son of a bitch.

It had been driving okay earlier in the day, but now, just when he needed it to run, the engine was turning over with a click. The battery was new, so it couldn't be that. Inside his garage, with the lamp hanging from the hood, Carl took a rag and wiped the oil from his hands. It could be the starter, he figured, but that would take time to repair and he didn't have that kind of time. He had people to meet, and if Scarfe was telling the truth, they were the kind of people who wouldn't take kindly to being kept waiting. He didn't want them to wait, either. The sooner they got what they wanted, the sooner he would get what he wanted, which was a big, dead policeman.

Carl was a coward. He knew he was a coward, although sometimes, when he was liquored up, he liked to tell himself that he was just smart, and that men like him, smaller and weaker than those around him, had to find other ways to fight back when people did them a bad turn. If that meant stabbing them in the back, then so be it. If they hadn't crossed him, they wouldn't have had to worry about their backs anyway.

Carl's brother was different – strong and hard and, hell, maybe even kind of mean, but a real man, one who had stood up for his little brother time and time again.

And because Ron had been a stand-up guy for Carl, when the time came Carl had been a stand-up guy for him.

Carl still remembered the call. They'd both been out drinking in Portland, and Ron had headed off with some woman he'd picked up in Three Dollar Dewey's. She looked kind of familiar to Carl. According to Ron, she was Jeanne Aiello, all grown up. Generations of Aiellos had lived out on Dutch until Jeanne's parents had grown tired of the isolation and had left for more 'civilized' surroundings. Now little Jeanne was back in Maine, working in one of those tourist stores in the Old Port, and seemed real happy to be making Ron's acquaintance once again.

Carl left them to it, and because he was still thirsty and had a beer appetite, he took a cab out to the Great Lost Bear on Forest Avenue and got himself a big basket of wings. It wasn't Carl's favorite bar, owing to the fact that the Portland cops liked to drink there, but he was hungry and the Bear served food until late. He was halfway through his wings when his cell phone started ringing and he heard his brother's voice. Ron wasn't panicked, though, or afraid. He just told Carl to get in a cab and head over to Wyndham, and Carl had done just that, leaving the cab about a half mile away from the address that his brother had given him, as he had been instructed to do. Ron was waiting at the door of the house when he got there, and waved his brother in quickly. There were cuts on his face. He looked like he might have been crying.

The woman was lying on the bathroom floor, and her face was all torn up. The mirror above the sink was shattered and there was a big shard of it in her eye. Smaller pieces were embedded in her cheeks and her forehead. Carl looked at his brother's right hand and saw that some of the woman's hair was still caught in his nails.

'I just lost it, man,' said Ron. 'I don't know what happened. She brought me back here and we was drinking, fooling around. We head for the bedroom and I try to get it on and next thing she's pushing me away, calling me an animal. We started fighting, she ran to the bathroom, and then I was just pushing her against the wall and I couldn't stop.'

He began to cry.

'I couldn't stop, Carlie. I couldn't stop.'

It was Carl's finest moment. He told his brother to go find some rubber gloves and cleaning fluids, anything that could help them clear the scene. While Ron wiped everything, Carl wrapped the woman in sheets, then double-bagged her with black plastic garbage sacks, using duct tape to bind her tight as a fly's ass. They washed down everything, until the house was cleaner than it had ever been before, then filled a suitcase with clothes, makeup, and what little jewelry they could find. There wasn't much that could be done about the broken mirror, so Carl just removed the last pieces from the frame and put a small vanity mirror from the bedroom on the bathroom sink. That way, he hoped, anyone who saw it would think that Jeanne had broken the bathroom mirror herself and was content to use the vanity until she got around to replacing it. They put the suitcase and the body in the trunk of her car and drove down to their boat. Jeanne was loaded into the cabin and covered with a tarp, and then Carl parked her car on India Street and walked back to rejoin his brother. When they were half an hour out of port, they weighted her body with Carl's old toolbox, which they kept in the boat for emergencies, and then dumped her overboard. She was never seen again by any living person, her body descending beneath the waves, lost to the eyes of the world and watched only by the ghost of a boy, for this was his place.

Jeanne Aiello was reported missing by her parents two days later, but by then her car had already been found. The cops were suspicious, maybe because Carl and Ron had gone a little overboard with their cleaning, leading the cops to wonder why a woman seemingly intent on heading off without telling anyone where she was going would clean her house so assiduously before she left. But there was no body for them to examine, and the description of the man with whom she had left the bar was so general that half the guys in Portland could have fitted the bill. It looked like Carl and Ron had managed to get away, literally, with murder.

But the relief was only temporary. It pained Carl to see the deterioration in his brother. He stopped working, started drinking more, and began talking gibberish about the woods. That was what frightened Carl most: the stuff about the forest. His brother was spending more and more time in the woods. He liked to hunt deer, and before the cull in '99, the island had been near overrun with them. Nobody objected much to folks shooting them and filling up their freezers with the meat, although there was no way that Ron and Carl had a freezer big enough for all the dead meat Ron was creating in the woods. But Ron wasn't even hunting anymore. He would just head out into the woods with a couple of six-packs or a bottle of sour mash, and when he returned he would be carrying on conversations that had clearly begun a long time before, and were the continuation of some ongoing argument.

'No, I tell you, I ain't done it. It weren't my fault. No, no, no. You got to let me be now, y'hear?'

He also stopped shaving or combing his hair, because doing those things meant looking in mirrors, and Ron didn't like looking in mirrors anymore, because Ron's reflection wasn't the only one that he saw when he looked in the glass.

On the night that Ron died, Carl had left him to go meet up with some people down at the Rudder. Ron had seemed pretty lucid, clearer at least than he had been in months.

'Hey, little brother,' he said, as Carl headed for the door. Big, old Ron was sitting slumped in an easy chair, staring at the fire. 'I been thinking. I forced you to do a bad thing that night with the woman. I shouldn't have made you get involved.'

'You're my brother,' said Carl. 'I'd do anything for you.'

'They're gonna make me pay,' said Ron. 'I have to pay for what I done. There are boundaries that you're not supposed to overstep. They won't tolerate that, so you have to pay.'

'Who? Who's going to make you pay?'

But Ron didn't seem to hear him.

'But I figure that if I pay, maybe that'll be enough. Maybe they won't want no more. Maybe they'll leave you be.'

But when Carl tried to get more out of him, Ron drifted off into a boozy sleep.

He remembered sitting at a table in the Rudder, not drinking much because he was so disturbed by his brother's words. He heard the sound of the approaching chopper, then someone came in and said that Snowman, that cop with the dumb name, had been shot, and that—

And then the guy had looked at Carl, and Carl had known.

They said later that his brother had been shooting at the houses nearby, that he was all fired up over some imaginary boundary dispute with his neighbors, but Carl never believed that was true. Ron wasn't shooting at houses when he died, and the boundaries of which he spoke had nothing to do with hedges or lawns. He was shooting at the things he imagined were speaking to him in the woods, and it was the transgression of *their* boundaries that led to his death. It was bullshit, of course. Ron's mind had just collapsed under the weight of his guilt. But since then Carl had kept well clear of the woods that surrounded his house, sticking to the roads and the main paths. Whatever had tormented his brother may have been all in his head, but Carl recalled an incident a week or two back, shortly after the fourth anniversary of Ron's death, when he was out in the yard bringing in supplies in his truck, and he looked out into the forest and saw someone watching him from among the trees. Carl didn't panic, though. Instead, he laid the brown paper bags down on the ground and, never taking his eyes off the figure in the woods, removed his shotgun from its case in the back of his truck. He loaded it up with the truck shielding him, then headed for the trees.

The figure was dressed all in gray, and seemed to shimmer.

'Who are you?' asked Carl, as he drew closer.

And then the figure had exploded, shards of it spreading in all directions, into the trees, toward the grass.

And toward Carl.

Carl turned his face away and shielded himself with one arm. He felt things striking him, felt them moving as they did so. When at last he lowered his arm there was nothing before him but darkness and trees, but something was caught in the folds of his coat. It fluttered and beat against him, until he released it and allowed it to fly free.

It was a moth, a gray moth. Somehow, Carl had managed to disturb a whole bunch of them in the trees. That was the only excuse he could find, even as he backed toward his truck and recalled the shape that they had somehow formed: the shape of a woman.

That was all by the by. Joe Dupree, the freak cop, had killed Carl's brother, and now there would be payback for what he had done. For the chance of revenge, Carl was prepared to risk a trip into the woods. After all, he would not be going in alone.

Carl looked at his watch, hissed in irritation, and returned to the engine of his truck.

The first boat, piloted by Scarfe, docked at Cray Cove shortly before nine. They could barely see the island through the wall of snow, but Scarfe knew what he was doing. Without him, they would have run aground on rocks and drowned before they even came within sight of land.

The snow, thought Moloch, was a mixed blessing: the weather would keep people indoors, and permit them to move about with greater ease, but there was now the risk of some of them getting separated and lost. And if anyone did spot them, they would have a hard time explaining why they were wandering around in a near blizzard.

Yet as soon as he set foot on the island, Moloch's fears seemed to dissipate. Images flashed through his mind, pictures from his dreams and other, less familiar thoughts. He saw trails hidden from the eyes of others. He recalled the names of trees and plants. A great wave of understanding broke upon him.

I know this place.

I know it.

Moloch gestured to Dexter, Powell, Shepherd, and Scarfe, inviting them to follow him. Tell said nothing. Willard just watched them quietly.

'You stay here for now,' Moloch told Tell and Willard. 'Watch the boat. When we get back, we'll need to leave fast.'

Then they moved away, slowly fading in the gathering whiteness.

The water taxi was within sight of the island when Leonie appeared at the boatman's shoulder. The crossing had been rough, and both she and Braun were wet and cold, their heads and shoulders sprinkled with snow.

'How do you find your way in from here?' Leonie asked.

The boatman shrugged. 'The worst is past. This is easy. A child could do it. Truth is, I could put this boat in anywhere along here. Dock is just as good a place as any.'

He smiled, and she smiled back. She was a good-looking woman. It was nice to see a mixed-race couple happy together, he thought. He looked over to the little parking lot by the shelter, expecting to see the shape of the police Explorer, but it wasn't there. No call for it, he supposed, now that Thorson's ferry was docked.

'You folks are looking for a place to stay, the motel's over there,' he said, pointing to his right. The motel had four rooms, and backed onto a slope that led down to the small, rocky cove that gave the town its name. 'If there's nobody around, call over at the bar. Jeb Burris owns both. He has his house just behind it.'

Leonie thanked him, then added: 'Looks quiet.'

'Yeah, sure doesn't look like there's anyone around.'

Leonie stepped away, raised her silenced pistol, and shot the boatman in the head.

Willard watched the group of men depart. Cray Cove was a small inlet with a jetty made of rocks that jutted out a little from the shore. It was secluded and Willard could see no lights on the shore. A pathway led up from the stony beach and he could see flashlights dancing, the only visible sign of the ascent to the road above.

During the crossing, Moloch had sat beside him and told him that he would not be joining them.

'You don't trust me,' said Willard.

Moloch touched the younger man's shoulder. 'I'm concerned about you, that's all. Maybe you've been forced to do too much this last week. I just want you to bring it down a couple of notches, take a breather. As for trust, it's Tell I don't trust, not you. We've never worked with him before. If things go wrong and he tries to leave without us, you take him apart, you hear?'

Willard nodded, and Moloch left him and returned to the wheelhouse.

Willard wanted to believe him. He wanted to believe him so badly. He might have stifled his doubts, too, had it not been for Dexter. As Dexter had disembarked, he had glanced back at Willard and Willard had understood that as far as Dexter was concerned, it was the last time that they would look upon each other.

Dexter had even smiled at him again.

The five men were making slow progress on the track, slipping on the new-fallen snow and stumbling into one another. Dexter reached the top before the others, followed closely by Powell. Moloch, Shepherd, and Scarfe were some way behind.

It was Dexter who saw the man first. He was standing at the doorway of a small, three-story tower with slit windows, one gloved hand shielding his eyes so he could better see the lights of the approaching men. Dexter's first impression was that the man was pulling a face at him, taunting him, but then Dexter spotted the heavy lids, the muted curiosity in the eyes, the slight slackness at the jaw.

'We got trouble,' said Dexter.

Richie Claessen liked snow more than just about anything else in the world. He thought about waking Danny and asking him to come out with him, but then he reconsidered. Danny was small, and didn't know the woods like he did. Instead, Richie dressed quietly, then put on his boots, his thick coat, and his hat and gloves, and headed out. He didn't tell Momma. She was asleep in front of the TV and he didn't want to wake her. Anyway, she would tell him no, and he didn't want that. He wanted to see the island in the snow, but instead of heading directly through the forest he had stuck close by the road until he found himself upon the shore.

Richie usually felt no threat from the woods, and

he was, though he would never have been able to put it in such terms, acutely sensitive to threat, a consequence of his condition that had kept him safe from harm on those occasions when he was at risk from older boys or, once, while he was in Portland with his mother and an old man had tried to entice him into an alleyway with the promise of discarded comic books. He had smelled the threat the old man posed, a stale scent of raddled discharges and unwashed clothing, and had walked away, keeping his head down, his left side to the wall, his eyes slightly to the right in case the man should choose to follow him.

The woods were different. They were safe. There was a presence in the woods, although Richie had long believed that he had no reason to be afraid of it. The woods still smelled as woods should, of pine and fallen leaves and animal spoor, but there was a stillness to them, a watchfulness, that made him feel safe, as if some stronger, older being was watching over him, just as Mrs. Arbinot in the kindergarten had tried to look out for him before they took Richie away from the other children and put him in the special school in Portland. He liked the special school. He made friends there for the first time, proper friends. He even kissed a girl, Abbie, and recalled with embarrassment the feelings that she had aroused in him, and how he had half shuffled away from her to disguise his growing discomfort.

But the woods had changed in recent times. In

the past, Richie had caught glimpses of the boy, the one who stood at the water's edge staring out at the sea, the boy who left no footprints on the wet sand. Richie had tried calling to him, and waving, but the boy never looked back, and eventually Richie had given up trying to talk to him. Sometimes he saw the boy in the woods, but mostly the boy stayed by the shore and watched the waves break. The boy didn't frighten Richie, though. The boy was dead. He just didn't want to leave the island, and Richie could understand that. Richie didn't want to leave the island either.

But the Gray Girl *did* frighten Richie. He had seen her only two or three times, hanging in the air, her feet not quite touching the ground, her eyes like the backs of black beetles that had crawled into her head and nested in her sockets, but she scared Richie bad enough to make him piss his pants. The Gray Girl was angry, angry at everyone that lived because she wanted to be alive too. The boy was waiting for something, but the little Gray Girl didn't want to wait. She wanted it *now*. So Richie had begun to stay away from the Site, where the woods were thickest, and from the tall watchtower at the center of the island. He used to like the big watchtower a lot. From the top he could see for miles and miles, and the wind would blow his hair and he could taste the sea on his tongue when he opened his mouth. But that was the Gray Girl's place now. Joe Dupree came by to check on it, and he would make sure that the door was locked, but the Gray Girl didn't like it when the door was locked so she found ways to open it again. The Gray Girl wanted the door open, because if it was open, then people might come in.

And if people came in, and they weren't too careful, then they might get to play with the Gray Girl.

She was the worst, but there were others too, and the area around the tower and the cross belonged to them. To go in there now would be like standing in front of a train. The train wouldn't mean to hit you, wouldn't have any intention of hurting you, but if you got in its way it would kill you as it hurtled toward its destination. That was what the woods now felt like to Richie: a dark tunnel, with a train rushing through it, ready to smash anything in its path.

But the shore was still safe, and there were trees beneath which to shelter. Except tonight the snow had started to fall really heavily, heavier than Richie had ever seen it fall before, and the wind had grown very strong and had blown the snow into Richie's eyes. He had sought cover in one of the old observation towers, a little one by the road, hoping to wait out the bad weather. Then the boat had come. He could barely make it out until it got close to shore, but he heard the men as they reached land.

And suddenly, he was afraid.

He wanted to go home.

He left the shelter of the tower just as the black man appeared and saw him.

* * *

Tell's voice brought Willard back. He could no longer perceive Moloch and the others, for they had now ascended the slope, but he thought that he could still catch glimpses of their flashlight beams through the snow. There was a pain in Willard's belly. It made him want to curl up in a ball like a little child. His eyes stung and he felt tears creep down his cheeks.

'I said, you want to stow these away?'

Willard wiped his face hurriedly as Tell handed him a stack of life jackets. He pointed to the storage chest at the stern of the boat.

'In there.'

Willard took the jackets in his arms, then knelt down to store them. Behind him, he heard Tell rummaging in his pack, then sensed the little man moving close behind him. He looked over his shoulder and into the barrel of the pistol. Tell's own gun, a Colt .45, was still in his belt. The gun in his hand was a one-shot .22, silenced to hell and back.

No noise, that was Moloch's instruction to Tell. No noise and no pain.

'You're a crazy bastard, you know that?' said Tell. 'You gave us all the fucking creeps.'

Willard didn't blink as the trigger was pulled.

'He's a dummy,' said Dexter.

Powell looked at him.

'What did you say?'

'The guy's a dummy,' repeated Dexter. 'He's handicapped.'

Richie stood across the road from them but didn't move. Powell squinted against the snow and saw the man's face, except now that he looked, the man seemed younger, more a kid than an adult. But Dexter was right. The kid or man, or whatever the hell he was, was handicapped.

'What are we going to do with him?' asked Powell.

'Take him back to the boat, I guess,' said Scarfe. 'Let Tell keep an eye on him until we got to go, then turn him loose.'

He heard a scrabbling sound behind him, and turned to see Moloch hauling himself up the last stretch of trail with the aid of a sapling.

Moloch looked at Richie, and Richie stared back.

'Bad men,' said Richie.

'What did he say?' asked Powell.

The handicapped man began to walk quickly away, but they could hear him muttering to himself.

'He recognized me,' said Moloch.

'The fuck could he do that? Dex said he was a dummy.'

'I don't know how. TV maybe. Stop him.'

Dexter and Powell began to move after him, but the snow was thicker up here on the exposed road, and they struggled and slipped as they tried to catch up with him.

'Hey, wait up!' called Dexter, but Richie kept his head down, his face set determinedly. It was the face he wore when other boys taunted him, or tried to show him pictures of naked ladies.

It was the face he wore when he was afraid, and trying not to cry.

'Bad men,' he whispered to himself. 'Badmenbadmenbadmen.'

Behind him, he heard the black man swear loudly as he stumbled.

Richie started to run.

Carl Lubey was beginning to panic. He had tried everything he knew and there was still no sign of life from the truck. As a last resort, he decided to change the battery. He was lifting the spare from the back of the garage when the radio in the truck exploded into life, almost deafening him with the last bars of 'Freebird'. The radio was permanently tuned to the island's amateur station, run by Dickie Norcross out of his attic, except Dickie broadcast only between the hours of two and six, and it was now well past Dickie's good-bye time.

'And that one's going out to all the folks on the island who are battening down the hatches for a hard night ahead,' said the disc jockey's voice. It sounded strangely familiar to Carl. It wasn't Dickie Norcross, not by a long distance. Dickie had a kind of high-pitched voice, and tended to limit his voiceovers to birthday greetings and obituaries. This was a woman's voice.

'Especially Carlie Lubey over there in the deep, dark forest, who's having trouble with his truck. *Ain't ya, Carlie?*'

The voice was distorted, as though the woman

had just put her mouth right over the mike.

'This one's for you, Carlie,' said the voice, and then the first bars of 'Freebird' commenced. 'Freebird': his brother's favorite song.

'It's all 'Freebird', all night,' continued the DJ, and Carl knew the voice, recalled it from that night in the Old Port as his brother leaned into little Jeanne Aiello as their voices rose in harmony over the sound of some piece of Southern rock shit playing on the jukebox.

Carl Lubey grabbed a crowbar and smashed the radio with one blow, sending the dead woman's voice back into the void from which it had issued.

'Fuck!' said Dexter. The dummy was disappearing from sight. Even in his bright orange winter clothing he would soon be lost in the snow. Already he was little more than a blur among the falling snowflakes, but for some reason he was staying away from the woods. Instead, Dexter could see him silhouetted against the cliff edge some forty feet above the water, running with a strange, awkward gait, his elbows held rigid against his sides.

Dexter drew his bow from his back and notched one of the heavy Beman Camo Hunter arrows against the string. The head was triangular, with three blades extending out from the central point.

'What are you doing?'

Dexter felt Scarfe's hand on his arm, distracting from the coldness of the arrow against his cheek.

'Get your hand off me, man.'

'He's handicapped. He's no threat to us.'

'I said get your hand off me.'

'Do as he says.' It was Moloch.

Scarfe's hand remained on Dexter's arm for a second or two longer, then fell away.

Dexter aimed, then released the arrow.

Richie could no longer hear the men behind him. Maybe he was safe. Maybe they were letting him go. He thought of his mother, and began to cry. His mother often told him that he wasn't a little kid anymore, that he was a man, and that men didn't cry, but he was frightened, and he wanted to be back at home, back in his bed. He wanted to be asleep. He wanted—

Richie felt a push at his back, as if a great hand had shoved him forward, and then a searing pain tore straight through the center of his being and erupted from his chest. He staggered, and looked down. His fingertips brushed the blades as his mind tried to register what he was seeing.

It was an arrow. In him. Through him. Hurt.

Richie did a little pirouette on the tips of his toes, then fell from the cliff into the waiting sea. The circuit was completed, and so it would begin as it had begun once before, many years ago, with the loss of a boy and the arrival of men upon the island. Sanctuary's long wait was over. It was the beginning, and the end.

And all over the island the lights went out, and

the power failed, and Sanctuary was plunged into darkness.

Carl Lubey knocked his beer from the rickety table by his easy chair and cursed the blackness. There was still a faint glow from the TV, which was always on, but it was fading rapidly. The thick drapes were drawn on all the windows, as they always were, because Carl didn't like the thought of anybody peering inside and seeing his business. He shuffled across the carpet, barking his shin painfully against the table and then catching his foot on a cable and almost sending himself sprawling on the floor, until his right hand found the switch on the wall and gave it a few futile flicks. Nothing. Not that he'd expected anything to happen, but Carl was kind of an optimist at heart and liked to think that sometimes the easiest solution was the best. To others, especially those who'd made the mistake of trusting Carl to fix their siding or pave their driveways, Carl was a lazy, corner-cutting creep. Carl preferred 'optimist' himself. It had a nicer ring to it.

Carlie had gone inside to pour himself a stiff drink, and then the lights had gone out. The incident with the radio had unnerved him, but the more he thought about it, the more he figured it was one of the island assholes jerking him around. He couldn't figure out who it might be, or how they might have done it, but it was the only explanation he could come up with. Now, lost and disoriented in his own house, he vowed revenge on whomever it was.

In the kitchen he found a flashlight, but the batteries were dead. He rummaged in the drawers until he came across a pack of candles and a box of matches. He lit a candle and jammed it into the top of an empty beer bottle to keep the wax from dripping onto his hand.

Carl heard a fluttering sound against the window, then a shadow flew above him. It was a moth, excited by the light from the candle. Carl watched it until it came to rest briefly on the kitchen sink. It was a big bastard, its long body dotted with small yellow orbs. The moth had no right to be in Carl's kitchen. Hell, it had no right to be alive at all, now that winter had come. He was so rattled that he failed to connect it with the moths he had glimpsed in the forest one week before, the moths that had briefly assumed the shape of a woman.

Instead, Carl crushed the insect with the base of the empty beer bottle.

The fuse box was in the basement, along with a bunch of spare fuses. Mind, it could be something as simple as the main switch tripping. After all, Carl had wired the place up himself and sometimes, like on the odd occasion when he decided to take a proper shower, the act of turning on the water would cause every light in the place to switch off, as well as the refrigerator.

Shit, thought Carl. He had the best part of half a cow in the freezer in his basement. As long as the weather stayed cold the carcass would be okay, but if it broke then it would be nothing more than maggot food. He raised the candle and headed toward the basement. He had almost reached the door when he heard the noises coming from below. They were soft, hardly there at all, as though someone were moving very slowly and carefully through the accumulation of garbage and stolen goods that Carl kept stored down there. There was somebody in his basement, maybe the same somebody that had caused the switches to trip, plunging Carl into darkness so he'd be easier to subdue. Carl had no idea who that someone might be, but he wasn't taking any chances.

He drew the Browning from his belt and opened the basement door.

Macy was about a ten-minute ride from Carl Lubey's house when her engine failed. She stopped the Explorer and stepped out onto the road, the snowflakes gathering on her hair. All that was visible to her was the snow and the shapes of the trees around her. She sat back into the seat and tried the radio, but there was no response. No static, no crackle, nothing. She turned the key in the ignition and received only a click in return, then banged her hands impotently against the wheel before resting her forehead against the plastic. She had three choices: she could stay here, which was hardly a choice at all; she could head back toward town and try to hook up with Dupree; or she could keep going toward Lubey's house and check him out, just as Dupree had asked her to do, and then use his phone to call for help or get him to tow her back to town with his truck. She got out of the cab again, took a flashlight and an emergency pack from the trunk, and began walking in the direction of Lubey's place.

Carl Lubey opened the basement door toward him, keeping himself away from the exposed opening. There was no other way into or out of the basement, and only two small windows in the walls, neither of which was large enough to admit anything bigger than a small child. In any case, both of those windows were firmly locked, to prevent rodents or forest mammals from making their home in Carl's basement.

There was now silence below. He wondered if it might have been his imagination, or the occasional shifting of materials that occurs in such spaces, a consequence of drafts and rot. Carl took a breath and registered, for the first time, the stink in the room. It was a dense, damp smell, like stale seawater. Something else hung behind it, something more unpleasant, a kind of stagnancy, and Carl was reminded of the time he and Ron had found a dead seal on the beach, bloated and rotten. Carl hadn't been able to eat for two days after because the stench of the dead seal seemed to cling to his skin and the insides of his nostrils.

It made no sense to Carl. It was snowing outside, and the days preceding had been fiercely cold. Nothing decayed in this cold. Even Carl's beef might survive a few more days if the weather held out. But the smell was there; he was sure of it. It trickled into the hallway now and began to adhere to his clothes, but it was definitely coming from the basement. Maybe the pipes had burst down there, soaking the stacked newspapers and cardboard boxes, even his brother's old clothes, the ones Carl hadn't had the heart to get rid of.

Carl stepped through the doorway. The candle illuminated the wooden stairs leading down into the basement and cast a faint glow into the sunken room itself. He heard the first step creak beneath his feet as he moved forward, the circle of light from the candle expanding as he advanced, catching the whitewashed walls, the shelves stacked with paints and tools, the boxes piled on top of one another, the more valuable items – a couple of portable TVs, some toasters and VCRs – off to one side, draped with a tarp.

There was movement there. Carl was sure of it.

'Hey you down there! Come out, now. I can see you. No point in hiding.'

The figure retreated back into the shadows beneath the steps.

'Come on, now,' Carl repeated. He tried to catch a glimpse of the shape through the slats of the stairs. 'I won't hurt you, but you're making me real nervous. You don't come out and I don't know what I might do.'

Carl moved down two more steps, and the basement door slammed closed behind him. He turned, and felt his feet slide out from under him. For a moment, he teetered on the very edge of the step, then his balance failed him and he tumbled down the remaining stairs.

And as he fell, his thought was: Hands.

I felt hands upon my legs.

Scarfe stared hard at Dexter but kept his mouth closed until the big man spoke to him.

'You got something to say?' asked Dexter.

'We could have taken him alive.'

'You think? I could barely see the fucking guy to take the shot. If I hadn't taken it, we'd have lost him.'

'You didn't have to kill him.'

Dexter looked to Moloch to intervene, but Moloch was already moving past them, following the road as it sloped down, the road at his right and the sound of the sea to his left.

'Listen,' said Dexter to Scarfe. 'I got six more arrows. You keep fucking with me, and one of them might just have your name on it.'

'You're forgetting something.'

'What's that?'

Scarfe was red with cold and righteous indignation. It made him forget how much Dexter frightened him. 'I'm not a dummy running away from you,' he said. 'You'll find me a little harder to kill.'

Dexter sprang for Scarfe, but the smaller man

was too fast for him. He slipped past Dexter, drawing his gun as he did so. Within seconds, Dexter was staring down the barrel of the Glock. The gun was shaking in Scarfe's hand.

'You done fucked up now,' said Dexter.

'You're the one with a gun aimed at him.'

'Then you better use it, pussy boy, or else I'm going to kill you.'

Scarfe heard movement behind him, and the sound of a hammer cocking.

'Let it go,' said Moloch. 'Both of you, let it go.'

Scarfe lowered his gun. Dexter made a move for him, but Powell reached out and held him back by extending his forearm in front of his chest.

'I won't forget that,' said Dexter.

Scarfe, his burst of adrenaline receding, backed away. Shepherd, who had stayed quiet throughout, followed Moloch to the edge of the forest.

'He should be here,' he said. 'Lubey should be here.'

'It's the weather,' said Moloch. 'It's just delayed him.'

He called to Scarfe, but Scarfe wasn't looking at him. Instead, he was staring down at the sea below.

'Hey,' he said softly, yet there was something in his tone that made Moloch and the others approach him, even causing Dexter to forget his animosity in order to follow his gaze.

'Hey,' repeated Scarfe. 'The guy. He's still alive.'

Carl Lubey lay on his back among the newspapers

and the fallen boxes, slowly coming to. His head ached. He didn't know how long he had been out, but he guessed it was no more than a minute or two. There was light coming from somewhere close by, and an acrid smell.

Burning.

He turned his head and saw the flames licking at the newspapers beneath the basement stairs. Carl tried to raise himself up, but there was a weight across his chest and he couldn't feel his legs. He reached out and encountered no obstacle, merely a coldness in the air that chilled his fingers despite the growing heat. The flames were licking against the back wall, devouring paper and clothing and old suitcases. Soon they would reach the shelves of paints and spirits.

Carl saw more flames flicker in the darkness to his left. He couldn't figure out how the fire had spread over there, because it was as far away as you could get from the conflagration down by the far wall, yet he could clearly discern flares of light close to the floor. They were moving slowly toward him, but they weren't increasing in size and he could feel no warmth. Instead, they seemed to hang in midair, like sparks carried on a breeze.

And suddenly Carl understood that what he was looking at was not fire but the reflection of fire, caught in shards of mirror that were now drawing closer and closer to him. The smell of dead fish and rotting seaweed grew stronger, filling his nostrils with the stench of decay. A woman's ruined face emerged from the shadows and Carl opened his mouth as the flames reached the paint and white spirits on the shelves, and his final agony was lost in a great roar.

13

Dupree leaned back in his chair and stretched. Chair and bones alike made cracking noises, so he stopped in mid-extension and carefully eased himself back toward the desk. If he broke the chair he would have to requisition another, and that would mean dealing with the jibes, because the wiseasses in supplies would assume – correctly, in this case – that his great bulk had taken out the item of furniture in question. In the end, it would be easier for everyone if he just bought his own damn chair.

He checked his watch and shuffled his completed paperwork to one side of the desk. None of it had been very urgent, but he had allowed untyped reports to pile up these last few weeks and the blizzard had given him an excuse to remain at the station house and catch up with the mundane details of speeding offenses, DUIs, and minor fender benders. The reports had also allowed him to forget, for a while, his worries about the island. The time spent immersed in the routines of day-to-day life had enabled him to put those concerns into perspective. When Macy returned, he would take a

drive over to Marianne's house and make sure she
was okay. He wanted to know why she had been
in such a rush to get back to Portland, and enough
time had elapsed since the arrival of the water taxi
to make it look like he wasn't checking up on her
too closely. It might have been something to do
with Danny, but if Danny was really sick, then
Marianne would have been in touch with him to
arrange emergency transportation. All in all it was
a puzzler.

He heard the main station door open and footsteps in the reception area. Dupree had asked headquarters to consider putting in a counter to section
off the office from the public area, but so far nothing
had been done. It wasn't a big deal at this time of
year, but during the summer, when the incidence
of petty thefts, lost children, and stolen bicycles
took a sudden sharp rise, there could be up to half
a dozen people crowding around the office door.

He left his desk and stepped out into reception.
To his right, a pretty black woman with an Afro
was running the fingers of her left hand along the
side of Engine 14. She wore a hooded waterproof
jacket and blue jeans tucked into shin-high boots.
The fake fur lining of her hood was spangled with
melting snow.

'Can I help you, ma'am?'

The woman looked at him, and her eyes widened.

'My, aren't you the big one?' said Leonie.

Dupree didn't react. 'Like I said, can I help you
with something, ma'am?'

'Sure, baby, you can help me,' she said. She turned away from the engine and he saw the silenced pistol in her hand. 'You can help me by taking the thumb and middle finger of your left hand and lifting that gun from your holster. You think you can do that?'

Dupree caught movement to her right as a man appeared from the shadows behind the fire trucks. He was redhaired and wrapped up tightly against the cold in a padded blue coat, but Dupree could see that he was a big man even without the padding. He too had a gun in his hand, the silencer like a swollen tumor at its muzzle, and it was also pointing in Dupree's direction.

'Now,' said Braun. 'Do it.'

Slowly, Dupree moved his hand to his holster, flipped the clasp, and drew the gun out using his thumb and middle finger, as he had been told. The two strangers didn't tense as he performed the action and he felt his heart sink. He had only read about people like this in newspapers and internal memoranda.

They were killers. Real, stone cold killers.

'Lay it down on the floor, then kick it toward me,' said the man.

Dupree did as he was told. The man stopped the gun with his foot as it reached him. Beside him, the woman closed the door to the station house and turned the lock.

'Who are you?' asked Dupree.

'Doesn't matter,' said Braun. 'Tell me where your partner is at.'

'I don't know.'

'Don't fuck with me.'

'She's out on patrol. I don't know where she is exactly.'

'Call her.'

The man and woman moved in unison, keeping the same distance from each other as they advanced on Dupree in a ten-to-two position.

'She's out of radio contact.'

Braun fired his gun, aiming to Dupree's left. The shot blew a hole in the computer screen on the desk behind him.

'Why would you think I'm fucking with you, Andre? I want you to call her and bring her in.'

Dupree shifted his glance from the woman to the man. He didn't know if the radio was still out, but he had no plans to use it even if it was functioning again. Macy would be no match for these people if he brought her back here. The way things were looking, he was no match for them himself.

'I can't do that,' said Dupree.

'You mean you won't do it.'

'Comes down to the same thing. Why are you doing this?'

Braun smiled regretfully.

'You shouldn't have fucked his wife,' he said.

He raised his gun and sighted down the barrel.

'You really shouldn't have fucked his wife.'

Then, all around them, the lights went out.

Doug Newton was sitting downstairs in his favorite

chair when the power died. His first reaction was that of most people on the island: he reached for a flashlight so he could check the fuse box. When the flashlight wouldn't work, he went scouting for candles, eventually finding a pack of tea lights behind the spare bulbs in the kitchen cabinet. He dropped a tea light in an ashtray, lit it, then took a second candle and placed it on a saucer. His mother would be frightened if she woke and found that her TV wasn't working. She liked the light from the tube, finding it comforting. Her greatest fear, Doug believed, was that she might be alone when she died, and she would rather die with Nick at Nite than nobody at all.

Doug had just begun to climb the stairs when the candles flickered slightly and he felt the blast of cold air: a window was open. At the same instant a shuffling sound came from above, then a tapping that sounded like small, bare feet running on boards.

Finally, he heard his mother cry out.

Doug knew that the cops, with the possible exception of Joe Dupree, didn't believe him when he told them about the little girl. Hell, Doug wasn't too sure that he believed it himself, but he'd seen her and he was pretty certain his mother had seen her too, although she later convinced herself that it was just a dream. Ever since then, as he had admitted to Dupree, Doug kept a pistol by his bedside and a loaded shotgun beside the hat stand in the hallway. He put the two tea lights down on the hall table and picked up the shotgun. Light filtered through

the small square window at the first landing as he
ascended the stairs, but he didn't really need it.
Doug knew this house: he'd been born here, lived
here, and would die here, if he had his way.

His mother's room was the second on the right.
The door was slightly ajar, as it always was, and
Doug thought that he could see shadows moving
against the wall. From inside came the sounds of
thrashing, and what might have been his mother
softly whimpering.

Doug hit the door at a run, the shotgun at his
shoulder.

The sheets had been thrown back from his
mother's bed and lay piled upon the floor. Snow
was blowing in through the open window, the flakes
billowing and colliding with one another before
falling gently on the carpet. The Gray Girl crouched
over Doug's mother, her mouth on the old woman's
mouth, while his mother's thin arms and skeletal
hands pushed against her, trying to force her away.
Her fingers caught in the folds of the Gray Girl's
gown, which appeared to move independently of
the limbs it concealed. It seemed to be part of the
girl, as though her body had fused with the shroud
in which she had been interred, creating a new skin
that hung over her arms like wings.

As Doug entered, the Gray Girl disengaged herself from his mother and swiveled her head in the
direction of the intruder. He saw then that she
was old, desperately old, a child in form only.
Her hair, blond from a distance, was now clearly

silver-white. Her cheeks were sunken and Doug perceived bone protruding through the parched skin below her eyes, which were entirely black. Her mouth was strangely rounded and Doug was reminded of a lamprey, a creature designed by nature to adhere to another creature and draw the life from it. Beneath the girl, he saw his mother's face, her lips trembling and tears falling from her face. Her breathing was barely audible, and as Doug moved toward the bed the light faded from her eyes and he heard the rattle in her throat as she released her last breath.

The Gray Girl hissed at Doug, and he saw the rage in her dead eyes at what Doug had done, the distraction of his presence depriving her of that which she sought. Her hand reached out, her fingers little more than bone wrapped in tattered parchment.

And Doug fired.

The force of the blast blew the Gray Girl from the bed and tossed her against the wall. She rolled when she hit the floor, then rose up again and stood before him, framed by the window. The shot had torn holes through her gown and the skin beneath, but no blood came, and there was only a smear of gray tissue where she had struck the wall. She stood and regarded Doug with a malevolence that made him want to run and hide, to curl himself up into a ball in a closet until she went away. For an instant, Doug pictured himself cocooned, listening in the darkness, then hearing the pad of those feet as they

approached and halted before his hiding place, the
door being drawn slowly open as—

Doug fired again, and the child disintegrated into
a cloud of moths.

The room was filled with snowflakes and insects
and broken glass, and the sound of Doug Newton
crying for his dead mother, and for himself.

Nancy Tooker was descending warily to the kitchen
to get some food for her sister and the dogs when
the lights went out. She was a big woman, as Officer
Berman had not failed to notice, and once she missed
her step there was no way that she could keep her
balance. She tumbled awkwardly down the stairs,
striking the slated floor hard with her head and
coming to rest with a sigh. Her sister cried out her
name, then used both the wall and the stair rail to
support herself as she descended to Nancy's side.
After a moment's hesitation, the dogs followed.

There was blood flowing from a wound in
Nancy's head. A shard of bone had broken through
the skin of her left arm and her left ankle was clearly
broken. Her breathing was very shallow and Linda
feared that her sister had done herself some internal
damage that only a hospital could ascertain. She
went to dial the station house number, but the line
was dead. She switched the phone off, powered it
up, then tried again, but there was still no tone.

Linda ran to the living room, where she removed
the cushions from the armchairs and couches, and
did her best to make her sister comfortable. She

was afraid to move her, and wasn't even sure that she could have, even if she'd wanted to, for Linda was sixty or seventy pounds lighter than her sister. Instead, she gingerly raised Nancy's head and slipped a cushion beneath it, then tried to do the same for her arm and ankle. During the whole operation, Nancy moaned softly only once, when Linda placed a pair of cushions beneath her leg. That worried Linda more than anything else, because moving that leg should have hurt Nancy like a bitch. She went to the hall closet and removed all the coats she could find, then laid them across her sister to keep her warm. Their nearest neighbors were the Newtons, just on the other side of Fern Avenue. If she could get to them she could use their phone, assuming that the problem with the phones hadn't affected the whole island. She didn't want to think about what might happen to Nancy if that were the case. Someone would just have to drive over to Joe Dupree and tell him what had happened, so he could call for assistance from the mainland.

She leaned in close to her sister, stroked her hair from her eyes, and whispered to her.

'Nancy, I'm going to go for help. I won't be gone but five minutes.'

Linda kissed her sister's brow. It was clammy and hot. She stood and shrugged on her own overcoat. At her feet, the dogs began to turn in circles, alternately barking and whining.

'No, you dumb mutts, this isn't a walk.'

But the dogs weren't following her to the door.

Instead, they were moving back from it. Max, the German shepherd, went down on his front paws, his tail between his legs, and began to growl. Something of their fear returned to Linda as she looked back at them.

'The hell is wrong with you both?' she asked.

She opened the front door, and the Gray Girl pounced.

For a moment, there was confusion in the station house. The blinds had been drawn in Dupree's office and the heavy cloud cover meant that there was no moonlight. With the loss of the streetlamps, the small station house was suddenly plunged into darkness. The silenced guns spat softly, but Dupree was already moving. Braun and Leonie heard a door opening in the far right-hand corner of the office. Both fired toward the sound.

'Go round,' said Leonie. 'Don't let him get into the woods.'

Braun ran into the street, then hung a left and made for the rear of the station. Silently, Leonie advanced toward the back room. Her night vision was already improving and she could see the shape of the doorway ahead of her. She stopped to the right of the frame and listened. There was no sound from inside. Leonie crouched down and risked a glance inside. She saw a big water tank with a small generator behind it. Oilskins were hanging from hooks on the wall. There were two lockers, one of them open. Beyond them, the back door stood ajar and snow was already beginning to cover the floor.

Leonie moved slowly into the room. To her right was a narrow gap between the tank and the wall. The open mouth of a pipe was visible in the gap. Leonie paused for a moment and the pipe belched fire. She heard the roar of the shotgun as she was lifted from the floor and hurled against the wall, and then a voice was calling her name. Braun. It was Braun. She tried to speak, but no words would form. She felt herself sliding down the wall.

'Bra—'

There was blood in her mouth.

'Br—'

And then there was only darkness.

Braun was almost at the corner when he heard the shotgun blast. Ahead of him, he could see the open back door of the station house. There were no footprints in the snow.

'Leonie,' he cried out instinctively. There was no reply.

Braun looked toward the forest. The big cop could be anywhere inside the station house. If he approached the doorway, Braun would make an easy target. He retreated instead, making his way in a wide arc into the trees at the back of the station. He moved as quietly as he could, the snow muffling his footfalls. The door was wide open, but it was dark inside and he could see no movement within. Then the reinforced steel door closed suddenly, propelled shut by the force of Dupree's shoe, and Braun swore loudly. He couldn't leave the cop alive in there. He would call for help, and next thing he knew there would be a blue army arriving on the island. Braun prepared to move just as a noise came from close by. He spun rapidly, his back to the station house. There was something big in the trees: a deer, perhaps, or maybe the rookie had come back and was already behind him.

The sound came again but this time it was far to his right. His first thought was that, whatever it was, it was moving quickly, but that was swiftly followed by the realization that nothing could move that fast through the woods. He would have heard branches rustling, twigs snapping, even in the snow. Now there was more than one and the disturbances seemed to be coming from above his head, as though some great bird were flying unseen through the trees.

Braun rose and started moving backward, trying to keep both the woods and the station house in sight, his gun panning across the trees. There were figures moving in the darkness. They were gray, seemingly iridescent, like moonlight shining on the fur of animals, and they glided across the snow or flitted through the gaps between the branches of the evergreens. Then one of the shapes seemed to halt and he caught a glimpse of gray skin and a reflection of himself in a dark pupil.

And teeth. Rotting yellow teeth.

'What the fuck?'

The gray shape curled in upon itself, like paper crumpled in a fist, then moved swiftly toward him. Braun started firing, but the thing kept on coming. Braun staggered out of the cover of the woods and turned to see Joe Dupree leaning against the wall of the station, the shotgun at his shoulder. He dived to the ground as the shotgun bucked in Dupree's hands. Bark and splinters exploded from the tree trunk above Braun's head. He heard a second shot, and felt a pull at his left arm. He looked down to see blood above his elbow and part of his forearm reduced to red meat by the blast. A searing white heat began to burn its way through his upper body.

Braun staggered into the forest, and the gray shapes followed.

Linda Tooker wasn't a particularly fast mover. Even during rush hour in the diner (which never numbered more than a dozen people, yet still put the sisters under pressure) she served at a slower pace than her sister cooked, which meant lukewarm sandwiches and cool soup for everyone. Yet in the instant after she registered the approaching figure – its tattered skin, its black eyes, its mouth like a sucking wound – she reacted faster than she had since high school. She slammed the door in the Gray Girl's face and felt the wood strike her, but the gap wouldn't close. She looked to her right and saw the child's fingers caught between the door and the frame. The nails were sharp and yellowed and there was no flesh upon the bones. They looked like twigs wrapped in burnt paper, delicate enough to be snapped off by a heavy door.

Except the fingers weren't snapping.

They were gripping.

Linda felt her feet begin to slide upon the floor as the door was pushed inward.

That's not possible, she thought. No child could be so strong. There must be someone else out there, someone helping her. Then a second hand materialized in the growing breach, this time braced against the frame, and the Gray Girl's face appeared, her black eyes focused not on Linda but on her sister.

'No!' shouted Linda. She jammed her right foot against the last stair, placed her forearm against the door, and swung her fisted right hand with all her force into the child's face. She heard bone crack as the blow struck, and the child's head rocked slightly. Then it was back in the opening again, the gray skin open across the nose to reveal the dirty bone beneath. The punch appeared only to have angered her, increasing her strength, for she pushed with renewed force, Linda's legs giving way, the gap now almost big enough to permit the child's whole body to enter. Linda heard herself sob as her strength failed and the door opened wide.

A dark blur shot by her from the hallway and she felt the dog's fur brush against her shoulder as Max leaped and struck the Gray Girl, his jaws tearing at her throat as his weight knocked her away from the doorway. Linda slammed the door shut behind them, locking and bolting it, then sliding down its length until she came to rest on the floor. The collie, Claude, began to scratch at the door, trying to reach its companion. From outside she heard scuffling noises in the snow, and Max's growls.

Then the dog howled sharply once, and all was quiet.

14

The five men stood on the edge of the shallow cliff, the stony beach some fifty feet below them, and stared at the figure that stood amid the waves. Its features could not be distinguished, but there was no mistaking the arrow that pierced its torso. It remained still, despite the force of the water rolling in from behind. To its right was a rocky outcrop, blocking the pierced man from the view of Tell and Willard on the boat.

'No way,' said Dexter. 'No fucking way. I've taken a black bear with one of those arrows. There's no way he can still be alive.'

Moloch regarded the sea in silence, then turned to Shepherd.

'Go down there and finish him.'

Shepherd shook his gray head once.

'Not me,' he said. 'No.'

'I don't think you heard me correctly. You seem to have turned an order into a request.'

Shepherd remained impassive. He had been watching Moloch carefully throughout the boat journey, growing more and more troubled by what he was seeing, and in the short time since their arrival on the island his concerns had only increased. He had seen Moloch's eyes glaze over when nobody was looking, his lips moving, forming unspoken words. During the ascent of the slope, Moloch had slipped more times than any of the others and his eyes seemed to be focused less on the climb than on the thin scrub and brush that had found purchase among the rocks. When they reached the top, it had required Dexter to alert him to the presence of the retarded man. Moloch had not been looking at the tower, or at the man in the bright orange vest. His gaze was fixed on the woods, and his lips were moving again. This time, Shepherd could distinguish words and phrases.

We move on.

Did they tell you to keep watch for me?

I told you I'd return.

The last was repeated, again and again, over and over like a mantra.

I told you I'd return. I told you I'd return. I told you . . .

'Like I just said: not me,' Shepherd said. He didn't break eye contact with Moloch, but he was aware of the gun in the other man's hand. Throughout their confrontation, Shepherd's own hand had rested lazily against the folding stock of the Mossberg Persuader that hung from a leather strap on his shoulder. He had jacked a load as soon as they landed and his finger was inches from the trigger. Shepherd did not know what would happen if he was forced to kill Moloch. He guessed that he would have to take out Dexter too. Powell could go either way, he figured. Scarfe didn't concern him. Scarfe just wanted to get out of this alive.

Moloch considered the other man carefully, then seemed to reach a decision.

'This once,' he said.

Shepherd nodded, and Moloch turned to Powell. Dexter, Shepherd noticed, had notched another arrow on his bow during the standoff. Shepherd wondered if it had been meant for him. We may yet find out, he thought.

'You do it, then follow on,' Moloch told Powell.

'Shit,' said Powell, gesturing at Dexter, 'it was this asshole couldn't kill him, and now I got to go down there?'

Dexter didn't react to the taunt. In the space of a couple of minutes, four white men had managed to get in his face, each one in a different way: Scarfe had laid a hand on him; Powell had insulted him; Shepherd had almost forced Dexter to kill him; and a retarded man with an arrow through his chest simply refused to die. Faced with so many possible targets, Dexter's wrath had simply diffused, briefly leaving him more puzzled than angry.

'Just do it,' Moloch told Powell. 'And quietly.'

Powell sighed theatrically and removed his gun from its holster. He rummaged in the pockets of his jacket until he found the silencer, then attached it to the muzzle. Moloch's insistence on silence puzzled him. There was nobody out here to hear a shot anyway, and even if someone was outside, the wind and snow would muffle any noise. Still, Powell wasn't about to argue with Moloch. Like Shepherd, he found Moloch's behavior peculiar, but he wasn't going to risk taking a bullet in order to point it out.

'How will I find you when I'm done?'

'There's a path through the forest. You'll pick it up behind the tower. Stay on it and it will lead you straight to us. For now, we move on.'

When he said the words, he looked puzzled.

We move on.

Shepherd said nothing, but his finger found the trigger guard of the Mossberg and remained there.

'We're not waiting for Carl Lubey?' asked Scarfe.

'He's not here and I want to get off the road and out of sight,' said Moloch. 'In case you didn't notice, we're on a tight schedule. We'll make for his place and take it from there.'

'There's a blizzard blowing,' said Scarfe. 'And you don't know the island.'

'You're wrong,' said Moloch. 'I know this island very well.'

Scarfe shook his head in disbelief and looked to the other men for support, but they were already preparing to follow their leader. Powell, meanwhile, shot Dexter a look of disgust, then began to descend the rocks toward the beach. Scarfe watched him go until Dexter grasped his arm.

'By my reckoning, pussy,' he said, 'you got no lives left.'

Dexter released him and spit once into the snow by Scarfe's foot. Scarfe shot one last look at the figure that stood among the waves before adjusting his pack on his shoulder and following Moloch, Shepherd, and Dexter across the white road that skirted the woods. He expected Moloch to stop and look at a map or check a compass, but instead he moved purposefully into the trees. Within minutes, the four men were on an old trail that wound its way through the forest, heading for the center of the island. While they walked, Scarfe unfolded his map from his pocket and tried to read it, hampered by darkness and snow and wind. It was a struggle, but he eventually confirmed what he had suspected from the moment that they had found the trail.

It wasn't detailed on the map.

Somehow, Moloch had found an unmarked trail.

Moloch drifted. Sometimes he was beside Dexter, moving through a white forest, the snow melting on his face and hair. At other times there was no snow, just a harsh wind and frost upon the ground, and there were other men around him, dressed in furs and hand-stitched hides. Eventually, the two worlds began to coexist, like transparencies laid one upon the other, and he was both Moloch and someone else, a man at once known and unknown. Moloch was confused but not frightened by the sensation, for what he felt more than anything else was a sense of belonging, a feeling of returning. This was not home. This was not a place of solace or comfort. There was no shelter for him here, but it was the beginning. Here Moloch, or whatever he truly was, had flamed into being. Whatever else might happen here, he would at last reach an understanding of himself, and those torn pictures that had tormented him in so many dreams would reform themselves, enabling him to see himself as he truly was.

He was coming to recognize that all this was meant to be. His wife was always going to flee here, and he was always going to follow. Men would come with him, because men had come with him before, for that was the way it had always been. It had been taken out of his hands and all that he could do was follow the path to its end, and to the final revelation that awaited him.

It took Powell only minutes to half-climb, half-slide his way down the slope to the rocky beach. When he reached the bottom he was breathing heavily, and his hands stung from the cold. His finger was almost numb as he inserted it beneath the trigger guard. He advanced to the shoreline and raised the gun, resting its barrel against his forearm.

The man with the arrow through his torso stood in the water. The sea was just below the level of his chest, but the waves that billowed against him had no effect. He remained entirely still, his orange jacket glowing luminously in the faint light that somehow contrived to penetrate the dense clouds above. Powell could even see the point of the arrow gleaming just above the water.

He's dead, thought Powell. He's dead, but he's just too dumb to realize it. He's like a dinosaur, waiting for the message to penetrate to his brain. Well, I'll help it along. I've got an express delivery for him, going straight to the head.

Powell sighted, then squeezed off two shots in quick succession, and watched in satisfaction as twin puffs of red sprang from the breast of the figure among the waves.

The man didn't fall.

Powell lowered the gun and waited. It appeared to him that the figure had drawn closer to the shore. It looked like he had moved forward a clear five feet or more, as the water was now approaching the level of his navel. Powell took aim again and emptied the clip into the injured man. He thought he saw him buck slightly at the impact of the bullets, but that was the only sign Powell got that he had struck home.

He ejected the empty clip, replaced it, then advanced into the sea. The cold was intense, but he shrugged it away. Instead he concentrated on the head of the man, moving toward him steadily despite the waves, and with every step that he took he fired a shot. The last one struck the top of the guy's head when Powell was barely five feet away. His chin lay against his chest, and no movement came from him. Powell could see the wounds left by the bullets, could even see something white glistening through a hole in the man's skull.

He's dead now, Powell told himself. There's

something holding him in place – soft sand, maybe, or rocks, or even the remains of a boat – but he's dead for sure. Whatever is anchoring him there, it sure as hell isn't free will.

At that moment Powell became aware of a presence at his back. He looked back to see a boy watching him from the shore. The boy's clothing looked dated, and the waves worshiped at his bare feet. His skin was pale and he held his hand to his throat, as if remembering some ancient hurt. Powell was about to speak to him when the dead man in the sea raised his head, a low clicking noise in his throat alerting the gunman to the movement. Powell slowly turned to face him, then rocked back on his heels, trying to steady himself against the twin impacts of shock and water. It was the dummy, but not the dummy. The distortion in his face – the drooping mouth, the too-wide eyes, the sheer strangeness of his features' composition – was now gone, and the man before him was, well, handsome, and his eyes gleamed with newfound intelligence.

Powell fumbled for a new clip, but the coldness and the damp caused his fingers to betray him and it slipped from his grasp and dropped into the sea with a soft splash. He looked down to follow its progress, then raised his eyes in time to see a huge wave rising up behind the dead man who stood before him. It lifted him off his feet and propelled him at speed toward Powell, his body riding the crest, carried forward like a piece of driftwood before it slammed into the gunman. Powell screamed as he felt the point of the arrow enter his chest, the dead man's arms enveloping him, his face pressed hard against Powell's, his mouth twisted into a smile.

And then the wave broke over them and they disappeared beneath the sea.

Carl Lubey's house was already engulfed in flames by the time Macy reached it. She had seen the smoke rising and had smelled it on the wind, which caused her to speed up her progress toward the house. She made a couple of halfhearted efforts to get close to the front door, then gave up as the heat forced her back. Her main concern was the possibility that the fire might reach the forest, but Lubey had cleared his land of trees in order to allow space for his garden, thereby creating a natural firebreak. With luck, the break, combined with the heavily falling snow, would be enough to contain the conflagration. But somebody needed to be told about it, just in case.

Macy took the radio from her belt and tried for the third time since she left her vehicle to raise someone on the system. On the first two occasions the radio had been dead, clicking emptily just like the ignition in the car. Now, as she stood within sight of Lubey's burning home, she could hear static. She brought the handset close to her mouth and spoke.

'This is Macy. Do you read me? Over.'

She tried again, using her callsign. 'This is six-nine-one. Over.'

Static, nothing more. She was about to replace the handset when its tone changed. Slowly, she raised the radio to her ear and listened.

It wasn't static now. Perhaps it had never been. It seemed to her that what she was hearing was an irregular hissing sound, like someone constantly adjusting escaping gas. She listened harder, and thought she distinguished patterns and pauses, a kind of cadence.

Not static, and not hissing.

But whispering.

At the edge of the forest, Moloch and his men watched the sky glow above the tips of trees. Their flashlights were dead and now, as they paused before the distant conflagration, Dexter took the opportunity to change the batteries, using the spares in his pack. Nothing happened. The flashlight remained dark.

'Those batteries were fresh from the store,' said Dexter. Scarfe tried changing the batteries in his own flashlight, and found that it too remained dead.

'Bad batch,' he said. 'Looks like we're shit out of luck.'

He took his Zippo from the pocket of his jacket, lit it, then held it close to the map. His finger pointed to details.

'I figure we're here. Best I can reckon it, Carl's house is over there.'

He raised his hand and pointed toward the flames.

'Since his place is the only one in that section of the island, that means—'

Dexter finished the sentence for him.

'That either we got a forest fire, which don't seem likely, or right now Lubey's house is just about the warmest place to be on this island. Explains why he didn't make it to the rendezvous. A man's likely to be distracted if his house is burning down around his ears.'

'People will come,' said Scarfe. 'The cops run the fire department. Dupree will be here soon.'

'I don't think so,' said Moloch, interrupting for the first time. He regarded Scarfe for a moment, until the smaller man's mouth gaped in understanding and he looked away.

Moloch traced his finger across the woods on the map.

'We keep going, then take a look at what's going on from cover. We need Lubey's truck if we're going to get out of here ahead of the cops. The fire will be our marker.'

Dupree was looking to the east, where a faint red glow hovered above the trees. Larry Amerling stood beside him. The old postmaster's house was nearest the station and he had heard the gunfire. Dupree had almost turned his gun on him, for Braun had headed into the forest only moments before and Dupree had been about to follow him until the postmaster had intervened. Amerling took a look at the body of the woman in the generator room. He emerged pale and gulping cold air.

'We need to get some men over to that fire,' said Dupree, 'but there's at least one armed man out there, and probably more.'

'Why do you say that?'

'Something he told me before the lights went out. I want you to go and get Steve Macomber and as many of the fire crew as you can round up. The phones are out, so you'll have to do it door to door. Make sure Steve brings a gun. Then I want you to come back here and try to contact someone on the radio. If you don't get any results within the next hour, then start sending up distress flares from the dock. We need to keep people indoors and off the streets as well.'

Already Dupree could see some of those who lived off Island Avenue approaching the station house to enquire about the power cuts. Among them was big Earl Kruhm, who had a good head on his shoulders.

'Earl can take care of that,' said Amerling. 'Nobody's going to argue with him.'

'Talk to him,' said Dupree. 'Make sure he understands that folks could be in danger if they don't stay indoors. It shouldn't be too hard to convince them, what with the blizzard and all. And Larry, tell Steve and the firemen to stay out of the forest as much as they can, you hear? Make sure they keep to the trails.'

Amerling nodded and went to get his car. He came back minutes later, just as Dupree was filling his pockets with shotgun shells.

'Joe, my car won't start.'

Dupree looked at him, almost in irritation, then took the keys to Engine 14 from a hook in his office and tried to start the truck. It turned over with a click.

'No radios, no phones, no cars, no power,' he said.

'No help,' said Amerling.

'It's begun, hasn't it?'

'I guess so.'

'Macy's out there,' said Dupree. 'She was headed for Carl Lubey's place before that fire started.'

He felt a rush of concern for the young woman. He hoped that she hadn't taken it into her head to do something stupid when she'd seen the fire. At least she didn't seem like the type for futile heroics. He put out of his mind the terrible possibility that the fire and Macy might be connected, and that she might be hurt, or worse.

'We stick to the plan,' he told Amerling. 'Go door to door. They're going to have to head for that fire on foot and do what they can once they get there.'

He hefted the shotgun onto his shoulder and started for the door.

'Where are you going?'

'I'm going after the dead woman's partner. If I'm right, he's heading for Marianne Elliot's place. I think she's in serious trouble.'

Amerling watched him go, but he didn't say what was on his mind.

I think we're all in serious trouble.

Time melted.

Scarfe felt it more acutely than the rest. They should have been at Lubey's house by now, but instead they were still walking through the woods, and the glow of the fire was no longer always visible to them. Even Moloch seemed to realize it. He paused and stared around him, momentarily confused.

'We're lost,' said Scarfe.

'No,' said Moloch. 'We're still on the trail.'

'Then the trail is going in circles.'

'Powell should have caught up by now,' said Dexter.

Moloch nodded. 'Head back down the trail, see if he's on his way.'

Dexter left at speed and Moloch drew the map from inside his jacket. Scarfe, after a moment's hesitation, joined him in examining it, while Shepherd leaned against a tree and said nothing.

'We got on the trail about here,' said Scarfe, indicating with a finger, 'and Lubey's place is here. That's fifteen minutes on a good day, twenty or more in weather like this.'

'It has to be close. Maybe we passed it.'

But when they looked up, the light from the fire was still ahead of them.

'Makes no sense,' said Scarfe. He looked to

Shepherd for support, but Shepherd was not looking at him. He was staring into the forest, his hands shielding his eyes. Moloch called his name.

'I thought I saw something,' said Shepherd. 'Out there.'

He pointed into the depths of the woods. Scarfe squinted, but could see nothing. The snow was blowing in his face, making it difficult to distinguish even the shapes of the more distant trees. He could smell smoke, though.

'It's the fire,' he said. 'Maybe you saw smoke.'

No, thought Shepherd, not smoke. He was about to say more when Dexter returned from his brief reconnaisance.

'There's no sign of him,' he told Moloch.

Moloch kicked at the newly fallen snow. 'If he's lost, he'll find his way back to the boat.'

'If he's lost,' echoed Dexter.

'You think a dummy with an arrow through him took him? Fuck him. If he got washed away, so much more money for the rest of you. We keep going.'

They shouldered their weapons and followed Moloch deeper into the forest.

15

Marianne was still shaken by her encounter with the new female cop. She had been afraid that the woman would make her follow her to the station house, that something in her face or behavior had revealed the truth of her situation. She could see it in the cop's face. Why else would she have come after her?

She knows I'm running. She knows I've been bad. She'll make me go with her and I'll break down and tell them everything and they'll take Danny away and I'll go to jail for stealing the money and—

Marianne forced herself to stay calm. She fumbled the car key a couple of times before she managed to fit it into the ignition, and watched in the mirror as the cop seemed to pause and consider her once again. Then the key clicked into place and the engine purred into life. Marianne was maybe a little too heavy on the gas as she drove away but the cop appeared content to let her go. She relaxed a little when she saw the Explorer move down toward the ferry until the enormity of the situation she was dealing with came back to her, and she gripped the wheel so tightly that the veins stood out in her hands like tree roots on shallow ground and her knuckles blanched fit to break through her skin.

She had been so distracted these last few days that she hadn't bothered to watch anything on TV except light comedies, and her absence from the market meant that she hadn't picked up a newspaper since the previous weekend, and even then only reluctantly. Something terrible had happened and now *he* was free, because he would not allow others to punish her on his behalf. No, he would want to do it himself. If they were in Maine, then he was with them. They had found her, and Moloch was probably already on his way to the island. Maybe he even had men here already, waiting for her. She would get back to Bonnie's and find Danny crying in the grip of strangers and Bonnie and Richie hurt or dead. There would be nothing for her to do but to comfort her son while they sat and waited for Moloch to come. She thought again of her sister, Patricia, and her useless husband, whom she suspected of cheating on her yet with whom she continued to stay because, despite it all, she loved him and felt that there was still something worthwhile and decent within him. Perhaps she was right, for when she had told them both of her plan to run, and reminded them that if she ran, then they would have to run too, they had accepted it with equanimity, and Bill had held his wife's hand and told his sister-in-law that they would support her in any way that they could. True, Bill had lost his job, and there was nothing to keep them where they were, but Marianne could still not disguise her surprise at his reaction. The memory of it made her ashamed, for she knew in the quiet dark places of her heart that they were both dead, and that they had died because of her. Yet part of her suspected that they were not the reason that Moloch had found her. Bill didn't know her exact location, and Patricia would never tell.

Marianne wiped away mucus and tears with the heel of her hand.

Patricia would never tell. She would die before she told.

Jesus, Pat, I'm sorry, I'm so sorry. I was so scared of him. I thought I had no other choice. He hurt me, and he was starting to hurt Danny. I should have killed him, but I'd have gone to jail and I'd never have seen Danny grow up. But now, if I could go back, I would try to take his life. I would take a knife to him in his sleep and stab him until the blood dripped through the mattress to the floor beneath. I would cut him again and again for all that he had done to us. I would tear him apart with the blade until his face was unrecognizable. I would do all of this to protect Danny, except—

Except that sometimes when she awoke in their bed during those final months, the room rich with darkness or the first dawn light seeping through the drapes, she would turn to him and find him awake, staring lazily at her, as if daring her to take him on, as though guessing the thoughts that were in her head and inviting her to test her strength against him. Then, when she did not respond, he would draw her to him and, without tenderness, work himself inside her, his hands pinning her arms to the bed. No words would be exchanged, no intimacies spoken. It was simply his way of letting her know that he could do with her as he wished, that she was alive by his grace alone, and that such grace was not without its limits.

Had she stayed with him she would have died within the year, of that she was certain. He might have let Danny live, but what life would he have had with such a man?

So they ran, and in doing so contaminated every life that they touched, and now Patricia and Bill were dead because of them.

Then there was Karen. They had stayed in touch and Marianne had recently sent her a photo of Danny on his last birthday, a smear of chocolate cake across his face and a cardboard crown on his head with his name spelled out in colored letters upon it. She had sent the photograph from Boston during a shopping trip, her first foray out of Maine since they arrived there, sunglasses permanently perched on her nose, her hair tied up tight in a bun, her face unadorned by makeup and therefore, she thought, unremarkable. She had called Karen a little later that evening from a telephone at South Station before catching her bus back north. The number that Karen had given her was a private, unlisted second line. Only a handful of people, family and friends mostly, had the number. If she was away from the phone, the call was automatically redirected to her private cell. Day or night, Karen would answer a call that came through on one of those phones.

But when Marianne had called earlier there had been no reply. Did Karen tell, she wondered? Probably, but not willingly. Marianne felt no bitterness, no anger, that Karen had revealed their location to Moloch. Instead, there was only the same terrible guilt that she felt over her sister and Bill. Her stupidity and her selfishness had exposed them to terrible harm, and they had paid the ultimate price for their affection for her. She hoped only that Karen had told all that she knew early on and had spared herself some pain at the end.

Now Bonnie's house was coming into view. Marianne braked and killed the lights, but the house was quiet as she approached, with only her friend's rust-bucket Plymouth in the drive. Through the living room window she could see Bonnie snoozing in front of the television. She pulled up hard outside the window, the gravel making a sound like the breaking of waves beneath the wheels, then ran to the door and knocked hard. It took Bonnie a couple of seconds to get to the door.

'Where's Danny?' she said, when she was facing the older woman.

Bonnie stepped back to let her in. 'He's in bed. You can leave him there if you like. Hey, hon—' She reached for Marianne, but Marianne pulled away from her and headed for the stairs. 'What's the matter?'

She took the steps two at a time, Bonnie close behind. Marianne pushed the bedroom door hard and saw one empty bed in the twin-bed room. In the other, Danny lay sleeping. She sagged back against the wall, put her hands on her knees, and lowered her head in relief.

'Aw, hell,' said Bonnie. 'Richie must have sneaked out. I don't believe that boy. I'll have to call Joe and get him to keep an eye out for him.'

Marianne laid a hand on her wrist.

'I need to get Danny out of here before you call anyone, Bonnie.'

'But Richie is out there.'

'He's always out there, Bon. I need to get Danny away from here.'

'Why? Have I done something wrong?'

'Bonnie, I can't explain it all, not now, but there are men coming and they're going to make trouble for Danny and me. I need to get us both away from the house, then find a way off the island.'

Bonnie looked distraught. 'Honey, you're making no sense. What men? If you're in trouble, we have to call the police.'

Marianne shook her head. She wanted to grab Bonnie and force her to understand. She wanted to strike out at someone and ease some of her rage and fear. Most of all, she wanted to take Danny in her arms and get him away from here. They were coming. Moloch and his men were coming. For all that she knew, they were already moving purposefully toward her home, trying to smell her out.

'No, no police. I did something bad a few years ago. I had to do it. I had to get Danny away and keep us both safe. Now I have to move again. Bonnie, please, help me get him dressed.'

Bonnie reached out and took her by the shoulders. 'Look,' she said. 'If there's one thing I know about, it's men: men gone bad or men who were bad to begin with. If these people have tracked you down once, then they can do it again. You can't run away for the rest of your life. You need to talk to Joe. You need to trust him.'

'Bonnie, I broke the law. I took money that didn't belong to me. If I can get off the island with Danny, I can make this okay.'

'Honey, you can't get off the island. It's snowing hard out there, in case you haven't noticed. They've taken all the boats off the water. It was on the news. No taxi is going to come all the way out here now, and nobody on the island is going to take a boat out in this weather. It's too risky.'

Marianne almost gave up then. It was all too much. She should stop running. She should tell Joe everything. Better still, she should just lie down in front of her house, Danny in her arms, and wait for them to find her. Then it would all be over and they could rest at last together.

'Bonnie,' she said, and this time the tone in her voice made the older woman flinch, 'I have to go.'

* * *

Tell stared down the barrel of the gun at Willard. The sound of the hammer clicking emptily still seemed to hang in the air. Tell felt it echoing through his brain. Looking into Willard's eyes, he knew that it sounded his death knell as surely as if it were he who was looking into the muzzle of the gun and the weapon was about to discharge a shot straight into his brain. He swallowed, then swiped the barrel wildly at Willard. Willard dodged it easily and something flashed in his hand. Tell experienced a fierce pain in his belly as the blade entered. Willard rose, forcing the blade up as he did so, and the tearing began. Tell could smell Willard's breath against his face. It smelled sweet, like cheap perfume.

'I could see it in your eyes,' Willard whispered. 'I could smell what you were planning to do before we ever left the dock. It was seeping through your pores with your sweat. You should never have let that gun out of your sight.'

Tell shuddered against the blade, his hands clutching tightly at Willard's shoulders.

'He told you to do this, didn't he? He told you to kill me.'

Tell tried to speak, but only blood came from his mouth.

'Good-bye,' said Willard, as Tell died against him.

Marianne had Danny, bleary-eyed and irascible at being woken from his sleep, dressed within five minutes. She left Bonnie standing at her front door, looking anxiously after her as she headed for their house. They would need clothes, toiletries. Most of all, they would need the money. She strapped Danny into his seat and glanced at her watch. There wasn't much time left. She started the car and hit the head-lights. Behind her, Danny had already dozed off to sleep again.

God, Danny, I'm sorry for this. I'm so sorry.

As soon as Marianne was gone from sight, Bonnie Claessen went straight to the liquor cabinet and poured herself a vodka. She looked at it, then on impulse walked to the kitchen and poured the drink down the sink.

She was worried about Marianne and Danny, but more than that, she was worried about Richie. He probably hadn't gone far, and nothing had ever happened to him during his wanderings on the island. He knew it well and usually stayed close to the roads and trails. But the weather was turning real bad and that was a factor her son wouldn't have taken into account on his latest nocturnal ramble. No, she had to call Joe, for all of their sakes.

She walked into the hallway, picked up the phone, and began to dial, then stopped. There was no dial tone. She replaced the receiver and tried again, but it remained silent.

No, not quite silent. She could hear faint noises. It was like holding a shell to one's ear and hearing, if only ever so faintly, the sound of the sea.

Then she heard Richie's voice.

'*Momma! Momma! Bad men. Badmenbadmen-badmenbadmenbad—*'

'Richie!' she called.

A high-pitched wailing tone, a kind of electronic scream, almost shredded her eardrum and she thrust the phone away. When it had receded, she brought the receiver back to her ear.

'Richie?' She was crying now, and felt the certainty of his loss like a great darkness that covered her, wrapping itself around her body and head, suffocating her in its depths. Then the darkness became real as the lights went out and the TV died and the buzz of the refrigerator stopped like the life of an insect suddenly cut short. And in the midst of her sorrow and pain, she heard a sound like a sudden exhalation of breath, as though a great many souls had found at last the release that they had sought for so long.

Marianne was barely on the road when the engine of her car failed.

'No!' she cried. 'Not now.'

She tried to start it again, but the car was dead. She could go back to Bonnie and ask to borrow her Plymouth, but by now Bonnie would have called the police and she would argue with her again, or insist that she needed to find Richie first, and there would be more delays, and Joe would come, and then there would be no way out.

She opened her door, then Danny's, and began pulling him from his car seat.

'No, Mommy, I'm tired.'

'I'm sorry, Danny, really I am.'

She held him in her arms and started to run.

It was Shepherd who went astray first. He was bringing up the rear, the bulk of Dexter like a great black bear before him. The shapes in the forest had unnerved him. Scarfe might have been right: it could have been smoke from the fire, or even shadows cast by it from the topmost trees. He had glimpsed them only briefly, but it had seemed to him that they were moving *against* the wind, walking in parallel to their own group. He tried to tell Dexter as they walked, but Dexter was only mildly concerned.

'Could be locals on their way to help at the fire,' he said. 'We can take care of them at the house, or avoid them. Doesn't matter.'

Shepherd didn't think it would be that simple. They *looked* almost like men, but Shepherd could have sworn that they were wearing furs, and even out here people had probably given up on furs a long time ago.

As they continued along the trail Shepherd spent more and more time looking behind him, or to either side, and less time trying to keep Dexter in sight. The snow grew thicker and the bear shape ahead grew fainter, distinguishable only from the trunks of the trees by its movement. Shepherd stumbled on a hidden stone and landed on his hands and knees in the snow. When he stood up, there was no one in front of him, and the trail was gone.

'Shit,' he said. He placed his hands to his mouth and whistled, then waited. There was no response. He whistled again, then tried calling. He didn't care about the barely glimpsed figures now. He had a gun and anybody who was out here with them would have to be crazier than—

Than Moloch, he heard himself finish. Because Moloch was crazy. They all knew it, even if none of them had the guts to say it out loud. This obsession with the woman had led them into alien territory during just about the worst snowstorm that Shepherd had ever encountered. What they had here was a full-on blizzard, with Shepherd now stuck on his lonesome in the heart of it, and he was one hundred percent pissed at this turn of events. He had come for the promise of easy money, the lure of $100,000 for a couple of days' work. That money could buy him a lot: a small house somewhere cheap and quiet, maybe a share in a business. Like Dexter and Braun, Shepherd was tired. He'd done time, and as you got older, jail time aged you faster. Even as the years inside passed slowly, infinitesimally slowly, the aging process seemed to accelerate. Dexter had seen young men come out old from a nickel stretch, and older men come out dying after a dime. Shepherd wasn't sure that he could survive another spell inside. This was to have been his final gamble, Dexter's and Braun's too, he guessed, except that Dexter had changed since last they'd met. Now he spent his spare time staring into space or watching those damn DVDs in which everybody went down in a blaze of glory at the end. Dexter had given up hope, and now Shepherd wasn't sure that he was any saner than Moloch. His was just a better organized form of insanity.

Shepherd looked at the compass on his watch. If he headed northeast, back the way they had come, he could find the road and then follow it to the boat. The way things were going, that boat was going to be a regular hot spot for lost men. He made one last effort to summon the others, then turned around and headed back toward the sea.

Dexter noticed Shepherd's absence first, but the wind had found renewed force and was now howling into their faces. When he opened his mouth to speak, snowflakes began to colonize it like bugs on a summer's day.

'Hey!' he shouted. Moloch and Scarfe paused.

'Shepherd ain't back there.'

Moloch, buffeted by the wind, the snow thick around his boots, joined Dexter. 'How long?'

'I don't know. I checked just now and he was gone.'

Scarfe joined them, placed his fingers to his lips, and whistled. The sound was loud and shrill, even allowing for the dampening effect of the falling snow. There was no reply. Dexter leaned close to Moloch's ear.

'This is turning to shit.'

'What do you suggest we do?'

'Go back.'

'No.'

'We're down to three men and we got no means of communication. I say we head back to the boat and wait this thing out.'

'Then what? You think they won't clear the roads come morning?'

'First light, man. First light and we can do this thing, be gone before the people on the island start making breakfast.'

'She knows we're here. First light, *she'll* be gone. Worse, maybe she'll figure that the best thing to do is to come clean with the cops. She does that, my friend, and we are royally fucked. We go on.'

'Listen –'

Moloch shoved him hard.

'We go on! The bitch is running now. We don't have much time.'

It didn't take Shepherd long to figure that he was lost. After all, the forest should have been thinning out by now. Instead, it seemed to him thicker than ever, even though he was still heading northeast, according to the compass. He was forced to push back low foliage from his face. His gloves were sticky with sap and his cheeks were scarred by errant branches. The only consolation was that the snow was not as heavy upon the ground, the great trees above and around him sheltering him from the worst of it.

He leaned against a tree trunk, took out his Zippo, and lit up, keeping the lighted cigarette shielded in his palm. He took a long drag, closed his eyes, then released the smoke through his nostrils.

When he opened his eyes, there were three men moving through the forest about fifty feet ahead of him. Shepherd whistled loudly but they didn't respond, so he flicked the butt into the snow and started to move after them. He had closed the gap by about twenty feet when the man bringing up the rear turned.

It wasn't Dexter.

First of all, Dex had been wearing a black jacket and green combat pants. This guy was wearing some kind of hooded arrangement made from skins and fur. His face wasn't visible beneath the hood. When he stopped, the other men paused too, and all three of them stared back at Shepherd.

Then the man bringing up the rear raised his weapon, and even through the snow Shepherd could see that it was an old, old gun, a muzzle loader.

Shepherd dived for cover as the gun flashed and smoke rose and a noise like cannon fire echoed through the forest. When Shepherd looked up, the men were spreading out. He could see the one who had fired at him reloading as he moved, his hand ascending and descending as he pressed the ball down.

Shepherd aimed his own weapon and fired two shots. He didn't give a damn about the need for silence or for concealment of their presence. Right now, his need was to survive. He saw one of the men rise and he fired again, the shot tearing through his furs, and watched with satisfaction as he went down.

And rose again.

'No way,' said Shepherd. 'No fucking way.'

They were surrounding him. He could see one of them trying to flank him, to get behind him and cut off his retreat. Shepherd retreated, firing as he went, using the trees for cover. Twice he heard the great eruptions of the muzzle loaders, and one shot came so close that he felt its heat against his cheek as it passed.

He had been backing away for about a hundred feet when he found himself in the clearing. To his rear were a number of rough-hewn houses built from tree trunks. There were six or seven in all. In the doorway of one he spied a woman's body, naked from the waist down. There was blood on her face and neck. Other bodies lay nearby, in various states of undress and mutilation. He could smell burning.

'No,' he said aloud, remembering the layout of the island from Moloch's map. 'I was going toward the boat. This is—'

The south. I could not have gone so far astray.

The image faded, and now he was surrounded only by broken rocks and old graves and a huge stone cross that cast its shadow upon him.

He registered the shot at almost the same instant as his belly exploded into pain. His dropped his shotgun and fell to his knees, clutching at his stomach. His body began to burn, as though wreathed in flame. The pain was too much. He took his hands away to examine the wound, but his jacket was intact.

But I feel pain. I feel pain.

He heard snow crunching beneath approaching footsteps and looked up to see the three figures closing on him, their heads low and hooded, their weapons held at port arms. Two of them paused while the third moved forward, so close now to Shepherd that the wounded man could smell the stink of dead animals that rose from the hunter. He tried to crawl away and felt a hand grip his leg, pulling him back. Shepherd searched inside his jacket and found the butt of his Colt. He twisted and raised the weapon, aiming it at the man who was dragging him backward, then emptied six shots into him.

The hunter released him and lowered the hood of furs from his head.

'Aw fuck,' said Shepherd, as he saw at last what had come for him. He started to cry. They should never have come here. It was a mistake, a terrible mistake.

'Aw fuck aw fuck aw fuck aw fuck . . .'

He placed the barrel of the gun against his skull.

'Aw fuck aw fuck aw—'

And fired.

Moloch and his men heard the sound of the shotgun blasts and the final shot as Shepherd turned his gun upon himself. Dexter and Moloch exchanged a glance, but said nothing.

Willard, moving along the road, skirting the outer reaches of the forest, paused as he too heard the shots, then began to run faster. He wanted answers, and dead men could tell him nothing. He also wanted to believe in Moloch, to be reassured that Tell had acted on the wishes of Dexter and Shepherd and not those of Moloch himself. If Moloch was in trouble, then he would need Willard's help. Willard would show his loyalty, and Moloch would reward it with his love.

And Sharon Macy, trying to warm herself before the flames rising from Lubey's house, heard them as well. They sounded some way off. She stared into the forest, its outer reaches now lit by the fire, and tried to discern movement within, but there was nothing. Keeping away from the flames, she circled the house and retreated into the shadows.

Moloch had grown quieter. Dexter watched him as they progressed toward the fire, but didn't say what was on his mind. They had lost two men already. Maybe Moloch was right: perhaps Powell had just given up and headed back to the boat, and Shepherd had done the same, but Dexter didn't think so. That wasn't like either man. They had been approached because Dexter knew that they would stand firm. For Shepherd it was primarily about the money, for Powell the promise of a little action. But they had also come because there were few opportunities for men like them to strike back at all that they hated: to break a prisoner loose, to hunt down a betrayer, to kill a cop. Their discipline was almost military. They were not the kind of men to turn back at the first sign of trouble.

Moloch swiped at something unseen in the air, as though swatting away a fly. No, thought Dexter, not a fly.

More like unwanted company.

There were voices in Moloch's head. They were whispering to him, saying things in a mocking, familiar tone, but he couldn't understand the words. And each time he felt his footing slip, and reached out to grasp a tree or a rock for support, he seemed to endure a kind of mental flash.

Blood.

Men among the trees.

A woman beneath him, dying even as he raped her, blade and man moving in unison.

And darkness; the sensation of being trapped in a mine, or a tunnel network, or a honeycomb.

He felt a hand on his shoulder and thought: *Gray. They're gray.*

'You okay?'

It was Dexter.

'I'm good,' he said. 'I'm—'

They're gray, and they carry lights.

'—real good.'

Braun was leaving a trail of blood on the snow. There was nothing he could do to stop it. He'd tried to stem the flow, but the cop's shot had torn up his arm badly. Despite the cold, he was sweating and feverish. He wanted to rest, to lie back against a rock and let sleep come, but Dupree was following him. He had caught a glimpse of him through the trees, and had considered waiting for him in the darkness in the hope of ambushing him, but he was afraid that if he stopped to rest he might lose consciousness and become an easy target.

And he wasn't running only from Dupree. When he paused briefly to catch his breath and examine his copy of the crude map while leaning against a big fir, the snow thick on his shoulders and bright red hair, he heard a whispering and saw the gray shapes moving along the ground, trying to get ahead of him and cut off his escape. He was delirious with pain, he told himself. His mind was playing tricks on him, forcing him to believe that gray figures were crawling along the ground, clutching at roots and stones with emaciated hands as they pulled themselves across the earth.

Braun checked the compass attachment on his watch. All he knew was that if he continued due east, he would reach the heart of the island, and from there a trail, hacked through the forest for tourists, would lead him close by Lubey's house. He broke through a bank of evergreens and found himself in a clearing filled with dead trees, most of them little more than white staves, their branches long since decayed. Some had fallen sideways, to be supported here and there by their stronger fellows, creating archways over the trail. Braun tested the black ground on either side of the causeway and felt his foot begin to sink. It was beaver bog, he figured, or something similar. He began moving, anxious to get back under the cover of the trees again. Out here, he was a sitting duck for the cop.

Braun was halfway across the bog when he realized that the gray figures were no longer shadowing him. When he looked back he thought he glimpsed a single pale shape moving across the snow, like a crazed hound chained to a post walking over and over the same ground. Braun raised his gun and fired off a shot. He didn't care about the cop now, didn't care about Moloch or the woman or the money. Braun just didn't want to die out here, among these things.

He became aware of new movement around him. The surface of the marsh rippled, the forms of what swam beneath visible briefly when they broke the surface. Braun fired down at one and something gushed darkly, then fell away. He heard a slithering sound behind him and spun just in time to see a dark body sliding back into the bog – blackened, withered feet glimpsed beneath the wetness of its shroud, its hips still round, a halo of white hair pooling briefly on the surface of the bog before sinking back into its depths.

It's a woman, thought Braun.

No, it *was* a woman.

Then a voice spoke, and he turned to see Dupree using a tree for cover, his shotgun pointing directly at Braun.

'I said, "Drop it."'

Braun started to giggle.

Dupree couldn't figure out what the gunman was doing. He had seen him pause in the middle of the trail, then begin firing wildly at the trees and the bog. Maybe he was hallucinating from the pain of his wound. If so, his unpredictability would make him even more dangerous. He made his move when the man turned quickly, seemingly distracted by something on the ground behind him. Dupree took up a position against the biggest fir he could find, then shouted a warning.

The man turned.

Dupree gave him a second warning.

The man laughed, then raised his gun and fired in the policeman's direction.

Dupree pulled the trigger and blew him into the marsh.

Braun's lower body took the force of the blast, and he fell backward, his feet slipping from beneath him. The trees tilted crazily and he was lost for a moment in snowflakes, suspended between the path and the blackness below. Then his back hit the water and his head disappeared into the murk. He tasted rot and decay, and even as the pain began to separate body from mind, life from death, he attempted to raise himself up. His face cleared the surface and he spit mud and vegetation from his mouth. He tried to open his eyes, but his vision was blurred.

He could see the shape of the cop, Dupree, the gun held to his shoulder as he approached him along the path, and he could sense movement to his right and left as the black things converged upon him.

The cop was right above him now. Braun was dying. He could feel it as a gathering darkness, punctured by slivers of red like wounds in burnt skin. It was coming slowly, too slowly. The things in the bog were faster. They would get to him first, and Braun didn't want that. He didn't want to go that way.

With a last surge of effort, Braun raised his gun from the bog and died in the shotgun's merciful embrace.

Moloch cleared the trees first and stood looking at the remains of Carl Lubey's house burning. The garage door was open and he could see the truck inside, the hood gaping, the shape of the cab behind it making it seem like the flaming skull of some great bird. Scarfe and Dexter took up positions at either side of him. Nobody spoke for a moment.

'Looks like our ride's gone,' said Dexter.

Scarfe shielded his face from the heat of the flames and thought about running. He'd take his chances with the Russians back in Boston. They were brutal, but at least they weren't crazy. It was supposed to be simple: Scarfe would do the groundwork, set them up with Carl Lubey, and take off. Then Scarfe found himself pushed into the role of boatman, and now there were cops being killed, and handicapped men shot with arrows, and his buddy Carl's place was burning like a bonfire at Halloween, with Carl, he felt sure, burning right along with it. Scarfe didn't hold out much hope for the woman they were hunting either, nor her boy. The money wasn't going to be enough for Moloch. Whatever she'd done to him, Scarfe figured it must have been pretty bad.

There was a rustle of bushes to Scarfe's right and a female cop appeared. Her gun was in her hand. Scarfe looked at her, then Moloch and Dexter followed his lead.

Scarfe recognized Macy at the same instant that she recognized him.

'Aw, this is fucking great,' said Scarfe.

Dexter didn't even wait for the cop to speak. He just started shooting.

I was too slow, thought Macy, dumb and slow, but the black man had moved so fast, forcing her to run. Then the others had joined in, and the forest around her was now alive with falling branches, shredded leaves, and the hiss of bullets melting snow. Macy hit a rock with her foot and went tumbling down the slope at the rear of Carl Lubey's property, wrenching her ankle painfully before coming at last to rest among a pile of trash and discarded metal. She was in Lubey's private dump, and it stank. Macy got to her feet, but her ankle almost instantly collapsed beneath her weight, so she leaned against a tree for support. Above her, she heard the men moving, but the trees on the slope shielded her from the light of the fire.

There was another blast of gunfire. Macy pressed her face hard into the tree and drew her body in as close as she could to the trunk. A bullet blew bark inches from her face and she closed her eyes a second too late to avoid being momentarily blinded by a spray of wood and sap. It got into her mouth and she coughed, trying desperately to mask the sound with the sleeve of her jacket.

But the men heard her.

A thrashing came from the trees above as one of them began to descend.

Macy, hurt and afraid, headed into the forest.

They sent Scarfe.

According to Moloch's map and the late Carl Lubey's directions, they were pretty close to his wife's house. Scarfe could take care of the cop while they got the woman. They would wait for Scarfe at her house, then find a car and head back to the boat.

It sounded simple.

Even Scarfe thought it sounded easy, except he had no intention of coming back to the woman's house. Scarfe wasn't really a killer. He'd never killed anybody, but he was pretty certain that he could do it if he had to. The cop knew who he was. If she got away, Scarfe would be in serious shit. Maine didn't have the death penalty, but he'd die behind bars as an accomplice to murder if the cop lived to tell what she'd seen. Scarfe was a weak man and a coward, but he was quite capable of killing a cop under those circumstances.

The ground was now rising beneath Macy's feet, the slope gradually becoming more pronounced so that she could feel the effort of the climb in her right leg. She was trying to keep her weight off her left foot, although the pain was not as intense now. It was a pretty bad sprain, but at least the ankle wasn't broken. That said, her pursuer was gaining on her. She couldn't see well enough in the snow to pick him out but she could hear him. There was only one, but uninjured and perhaps better armed than she was.

Ahead of her, a tall structure blotted out the descending snow: the island's main observation tower, the one that she had explored during her introductory tour earlier that day. Watching for rocks and stray roots, she made her way toward it.

The rusted iron door stood partially open. She had slipped the bolt earlier, she recalled, and had wrapped the chain around it. Someone had been there since then. From behind came the sounds of her pursuer. She couldn't keep running. Her ankle hurt too badly. After a moment's hesitation she entered the tower, feeling broken glass crunch beneath her feet. There was no bolt on the inside of the door. To her right, the flight of concrete steps led up to the second level. She followed them, then stopped.

A moth was bouncing against one of the windows. She looked up and in the faint light saw more of the insects fluttering around the room. One of them brushed against her face and she slapped it away, feeling it against her palm and then instinctively rubbing her hand against her leg as if she risked contamination from its touch.

A noise came from somewhere above her. It sounded like boards creaking beneath the weight of a footfall. Macy's bowels churned. She shouldn't have come in here. The realization hit her with the force of a fist. Everything about the place felt wrong. She was like a rat caught in a maze with no prize at the end of it, or an insect teetering on the edge of a jar of sugared water.

The sound came again, clearer now. She imagined that she heard someone crying. It sounded like a little girl.

'Hey?' called Macy softly. 'Hey, are you okay?'

Scarfe saw a gray shape in the shadows, moving close to the ground. He raised his gun, then pivoted swiftly to his right as he registered a second presence in the trees, then a third behind him, the shapes in a state of constant movement, circling him from the shelter of the forest.

'Who's there?' he whispered, more to himself than to anyone else. Then, louder: 'Who's there?'

The sound of the wind in the trees was almost

deafening. A mist appeared to rise before him, and he thought that he could discern figures and, for a second, even faces. Then the figures spread out, moving faster, trying to surround him.

Scarfe ran, the ground rising before him, until he came to the clearing, and the tower.

Macy walked across the floor and stood at the base of the next flight of steps. All was darkness above, but she could see, faintly, the edges of the wooden floor. She reached out a hand to steady herself against the wall, then recoiled instantly as she felt movement on her skin. There were more moths up here. As she looked closer, she saw that they entirely covered the wall beside the ascending stairs. Macy took a step back and a figure passed across the top of the steps. She had a fleeting image of something small and gray, with white-blond hair. A tattered gown seemed to hang from it like an insect shedding its skin

It was a girl, a little girl dressed in gray.

The crying came again.

'Honey, come on down,' said Macy. 'You don't have to be afraid.'

'*No, you come up.*'

But Macy didn't move. The voice was not that of a child. It was older. It sounded sick. There was desire in that voice, despite the tears, and hunger. Macy stood still, undecided, and again the image of a honey pot came to her.

Then her decision was made for her. There came

a gunshot, followed by a second. Moments later she heard the door beneath her slam closed, and then there was silence.

Willard was unusual in many ways, not least of which was his total lack of imagination. He didn't read books, didn't like movies, didn't even watch much TV. He didn't need to live in a fantasy world created by others. Instead, Willard moved through this world and carved his own reality from it.

Yet even Willard felt that there was something wrong with this island. There was a buzzing in his head, like an out-of-tune radio. He thought that he sensed movement around him, but when he looked closer there was nothing. Willard felt like he was the subject of a conversation that he couldn't quite hear, or the punch line for a joke that had not yet been told.

He considered his options. He could go back to the boat and return to the mainland, but he didn't know much about boats, and even if he could get it started, he didn't think he could even *find* the mainland in this weather. But he also had scores to settle and questions to be answered. When Willard had all the information at his disposal, he would then decide what moves to make against the others.

Macy came down the stairs as quietly as she could, carefully placing each foot so that she did not slip. She listened carefully, and once or twice she believed she heard heavy breathing, the sound of a man recovering from sudden, unaccustomed exertion. She kept her back against the wall, trying to listen to both what was below her and what was above.

She reached the second level, and the concrete steps leading down to the first floor. A shadow moved across the Plexiglas of the window and Macy, puzzled, found her attention distracted. The shadow came again, and Macy was aware of a presence hovering beyond the window, out of sight yet still capable of stealing what little light she had. She began to move down the final flight of steps, the gun in her hand making a regular arc, first pointing down toward the unknown man below, then swinging up toward the shadows above, and the child that was not a child. The darkness in the stairway was almost liquid, pouring from the walls and oozing down the stairs. She was halfway down when she heard a soft hiss and the Gray Girl's hand emerged from the shadows and pushed at her.

Macy lost her footing and stumbled down the last of the concrete steps.

The porch light was out and the house was in complete darkness as Marianne at last reached her home. Even the night-lights that came on automatically as the day faded were out.

They're here. They've cut off the power and they're here.

But then she looked to her right, where Jack's house lay, and saw that it too was dark. That never happened, for the old man stayed awake until the small hours, working in his studio. She saw him, sometimes, when she couldn't sleep during the warm summer months and sat outside on her porch, watching him working on his terrible paintings. It was a power failure, that was all, although it didn't explain her car dying. Coincidence, she decided. After all, what other reason could there be?

She found her keys, opened the door, then slammed it closed behind her with the heel of her shoe. She carried Danny upstairs and laid him on his bed, then took two bags from her closet and began thrusting clothes into them: her own first, then Danny's. She grabbed some toys and books and placed them into his bag, then zipped it closed.

Finally, she pulled down the attic stairs and headed up. Her flashlight wasn't working, and she was almost certain that she'd filled her bag with a selection of mismatched clothing, but it didn't matter. What mattered was the knapsack that lay hidden under piles of trash and junk at the rear of the attic. She stepped carefully, one hand raised ahead of her so that she would not bump her head on the eaves. Kneeling down, she began tossing bags and boxes away until she felt the canvas straps on the bag beneath her fingers. She dragged it out, hauled it to the edge of the attic door, then tipped it down into the hallway.

It landed with the kind of sound that only three quarters of a million dollars can make.

Scarfe had seen the shadows outside too. Panicked,

he held his gun in a double-handed grip and tried to catch the figures as they moved beyond the windows.

Then two noises came together: a scuffling from the staircase across from him, and a rattle as something thrust itself against the door from outside. Torn between the two threats, Scarfe retreated against the wall, just as Macy's voice called out: 'Police! Drop your weapon.'

And then the door flew open, and the man in her sights turned to stare at what lay beyond. He raised his weapon and fired. Macy, aware only of the gun and the threat that it posed, fired at the same time, and watched the man buck against the wall, then slide down, the gun falling from his hand.

Macy advanced toward Scarfe and kicked his gun away with her foot. The doorway was empty. Only snow was entering. The shot had taken him clean in the chest and he was bleeding from the mouth. She tried to open his jacket but his hand gripped hers as he tried to speak.

'Tell me,' said Macy. 'Tell me why you're here.'

'Elliot,' Scarfe whispered. '*Moloch!*'

He was staring straight at her, pulling her closer, and then his gaze shifted to a point over her shoulder and his grip tightened. She was already turning when she felt a presence close by, flitting mothlike in the shadows.

The Gray Girl hung in the air behind her, moving swiftly back and forth, trying to find some means of access to the dying man. Macy could see her eyes, jet black within her wrinkled skin, and the edges of her teeth almost hidden beneath the lips of her rounded mouth.

She raised her gun as Scarfe began to spasm beside her. His nails dug painfully into her. The Gray Girl darted forward, then retreated again as Macy shielded the dying man's body from her. Scarfe coughed once, and his fingers relaxed their grip as the life passed from him. Macy watched as the child's features contorted with rage, her head and arms trembling with the depth of her anger, and then she seemed to sink back into the shadows in the corner. Seconds later, a flight of moths burst from the darkness and disappeared into the night, forming a mist that moved against the direction of the wind, heading deeper and deeper into the forest, making for the very heart of the island.

16

Dexter and Moloch left Carl Lubey's burning house behind them, traveling southwest until they came to a road, banks of firs standing like temple columns at either side.

'You want the map?' asked Dexter.

'I know where we're going,' said Moloch. He sounded distracted, almost distant. 'We need to spread out, take them from every angle.'

Dexter stared at him.

'Spread out how? There's just you and me.'

Moloch acted like a man suddenly woken from a strange dream. Once again, the sensation of worlds overlapping came to him, but it was accompanied by an uncomfortable feeling of separation. Moments earlier, he had been surrounded by men, men willing to act at his command. He had both strength and authority. Now there was only Dexter, and Moloch himself was weakening. Increasingly, he was troubled by the sense that he was less alive here than he was in the past, that each time he flipped between worlds he left more of himself behind in an earlier life.

'They haven't come back yet?' he asked.

'Who, Shepherd and Scarfe? No, they ain't back yet.'

Moloch nodded, then pointed. 'Her house is just over that rise. Shouldn't take us more than—'

He glanced at his watch. It had stopped.

'You know what time it is?'

Dexter wore a Seiko digital. The numerals on the green face showed 88:88.

'I don't know. It's not working right.'

'It doesn't matter,' said Moloch, but again Dexter detected a wavering note in his voice. Don't fall apart on me now, man, he thought, not after all this time.

They leaped a small ditch that ran along the side of the road, now almost entirely filled with snow, and stepped out onto the trail. In doing so, they almost ran into the woman. She let out a little yelp of surprise, then saw their guns and started to back away.

'Now where are you going?' said Dexter. He advanced upon her, gripped her by the hair and dragged her back to Moloch.

Bonnie Claessen had given up on the phone, on her car, and on Joe Dupree. She had given up on everything. Something had broken inside her when she heard her son's voice echoing down a dead telephone line, and so she had retreated into a beautiful illusion. Richie, her sad, troubled, loving son, was out in the snow alone, probably tired and afraid. She had to find him and bring him home. She wore only an open coat over her sweater and jeans, and her clothing was now crusted white with flakes. Her cheap boots had not protected her feet, yet she did not feel the cold. She was lost to herself and now she wished only for her son to appear out of the darkness, his orange jacket bright against the snow, his face filled with relief and affection as his mother came for him and drew him to her.

'I'm searching for my boy,' she said. 'Have you seen him?'

She looked first at Dexter, then at Moloch, examining their faces. They seemed familiar to her. Briefly, her clouded mind was illuminated by a flash of clarity. She shook her head and moved away from the two men, never allowing her eyes to leave their faces.

They were Richie's bad men, the men from the TV. She heard her son's voice crying out its last words to her.

Momma! Momma! Bad men. Badmenbadmenbadmenbadmenbad—

Dexter saw the recognition in her eyes.

'Shit,' he said, 'now we're gonna—'

The gunshot came from so close to his head that he recoiled in shock, his ears ringing. The woman crumpled to the ground and began to bleed on the snow. Beside him, Moloch holstered his gun.

'We could have taken her with us,' said Dexter. 'She could have helped us.'

'You going soft on me, Dex?' came the reply, and Dexter was sure now that Moloch was mad. In the unspoken threat he heard the death sentence being passed on Willard, the abandonment of Powell, Shepherd, and Scarfe to their fates, and the single-minded obsession that had brought them to this place. It was no longer about money, or a woman, or a child. Moloch might once have thought that it was, but it wasn't. He had come here for some unknowable reason of his own, and those who stood alongside him were expendable.

We're going to die here, Dexter realized. I think I always knew, and just hoped that it wouldn't be true, but it will end here. I have no choice now but to follow it to its end, and to embrace it when it comes.

'No,' said Dexter. 'I ain't going soft.'

He walked over to where the woman lay and looked down upon her. She was lying very still. Her eyes blinked and he saw her chest rise and fall, blood spreading from the wound on her left breast. Her lips formed a word.

'Richie,' she whispered, for the boy was beside her now. He had always appeared wondrous to her, always kind, but now he seemed transformed, his features perfectly sculpted and his eyes alive with an intelligence that he had never known in life.

'Richie,' she repeated. He reached out his hand to her and took it in his own, and he drew her to him and carried her away so that she did not feel the bullet that Dexter fired into her.

And all pain was left behind forever.

Marianne was on her doorstep when she heard the

shots. They came from close by. Two overnight bags, crammed full of clothing, lay by her feet, and the knapsack hung over her shoulder. Danny sat on top of one of the bags, still drowsy. When he heard the shots, he looked up briefly, then resumed his previous position, his head cupped in his hands, his eyes nearly closed.

'Come on, Danny, we have to go.'

'Where?' There was that whining tone to his voice, and for the first time she lost her temper with him.

'We're going to Jack's. Now get up, Danny! I mean it! You get up or I'm going to give you such a spanking that you won't be able to sit for a week. Do you hear me? Get up!'

The boy started to cry, but at least he was on his feet. Marianne took a bag in each hand, then gave him a little swipe with one of them, propelling him toward the door. She pulled it closed behind her with her toe, then urged him on down the path to Jack's house. Once they got to Jack's, she could convince the old man to take them off Dutch. Even if they only got as far as one of the neighboring islands, it would be enough. All that mattered was that they got away from here. The weight of the gun in her coat pocket slapped painfully against her leg as she walked, but she didn't care. It had been in the knapsack with the money. She had cleaned and oiled it only twice in the years since she had fled, following instructions from a gun magazine, and had never fired it, not even on a range. She would use it, though, if she was forced to do so. This time there would be no fear. She would take his dare. She was stronger than he had ever suspected, stronger than even she had known. She would kill him, if she had to, and some secret part of her hoped that she would be given that opportunity.

From the top of the rise, Moloch and Dexter watched them leave the house, but they were not the only ones. Far to their right, almost at the edge of Jack's property, a pretty man with blond hair stood among the trees and admired once again the shape of the woman's legs, the swell of her breasts beneath her open coat, the way her jeans hugged her groin. In her way, she was to blame for all that had happened to him, for his rejection and abandonment by the man he admired so much. She had deceived him, betrayed his beloved Moloch, and he would make her pay. He vaguely recalled Moloch's warning that she was not to be harmed, but he had the hunger upon him now. He would first make her tell him where the money was, and then he would finish her.

After all, Willard had needs too.

Jack heard the banging on his kitchen door as he dozed in his armchair. He had tried to paint, but nothing came. Instead, he found himself drawn again and again to the painting with the two figures burned upon it, his fingers tracing the contours of them as he tried to understand how they had come to be. Then the lights had gone out and the heating with them. The small fire faded in the grate and he noticed only when the cold began to tell on his bones. There was no wood left by the fireplace, so he grabbed his coat and opened the door, preparing to risk the cold in order to replenish his stocks from the store of firewood in the shed.

But as he stood at the door, he became aware of a presence beyond the house.

No, not a single presence, but many presences.

'Who's there?' he called, but he expected no reply. Instead, through the thickly falling snow, he thought he saw a shadow move across the wind, gray against the flakes upon the ground, like a cobweb blown, or an old cloak. There were more shadows to his left and right. They seemed to be circling the house, waiting.

'Go away,' he said, softly. 'Please go away.'

He closed and locked the door then, and checked all the windows. He took a blanket from his bed, wrapped it around his shoulders, and sat as close as he could to the dying embers of the fire. He thought that he might have slept for a time, for he dreamed of shadows moving closer to the great picture window, and faces pressed against the glass, their skin gray and withered, the roots of their teeth exposed, their lips thin and bloodless, their eyes black and hungry. They tapped at the glass with their long nails, the tapping growing harder until at last the glass exploded inward and they descended upon him and began to devour him.

Jack's eyes flicked open. He could still hear the banging and for a moment he found himself unable to distinguish between dream and reality. Then he heard Marianne Elliot calling his name and he struggled to his feet, his joints stiff from sitting slumped against the chair. He walked to the kitchen door and saw the faces of Marianne and Danny, the woman scared and panicky, the boy drowsy and his face streaked with tears. He opened the door.

'Come in,' he said. 'What's wrong?'

She dropped the bags she was holding, then knelt down and hugged the boy close to her.

'I'm sorry for shouting at you, Danny. I'm so sorry.'

The boy began to cry again, but at least he hugged her back. Marianne, the boy's head cradled against her neck, looked imploringly at Jack.

'We need to get off the island.'

'There's no way you can get away from here until this snow storm calms down some,' he said. 'There's not enough visibility and the wind is too strong.'

'We can't wait that long.'

Jack said nothing. She understood that he wanted more from her.

'Danny,' she said, 'go inside and lie down for few minutes.'

The boy did not need to be told twice. He passed by the old man and headed for the couch, where he instantly fell asleep.

'I've told some lies,' she said, when she saw her son curl up with his eyes closed. 'My husband isn't dead. He was put in prison. I betrayed him to the police so that Danny and I could get away from him. And . . . I took money from him. A lot of money.'

She opened the knapsack and showed Jack the wads of notes. His mouth opened slightly in surprise, then closed with a snap.

'I'm not sure how he got it all, but I can guess, and so can you. Now he's here on the island and he's brought men with him. They're close. I heard shots.'

She reached out and took the painter's hand.

'My car is dead but you have a boat. I just need you to get us away from here, even just to one of the other islands. If we don't leave, they'll find us and they'll kill me and take Danny away.'

She paused.

'Or they may kill Danny too. My husband, he never had any love for Danny.'

The old man looked back at the swing door of the kitchen, beyond which the boy lay sleeping.

'You told Joe Dupree any of this?'

Marianne shook her head.

'He'll help you, you know that. He's different.'

'I was afraid, afraid that they'd put me in jail or take Danny from me.'

'I don't know enough about the law to say one way or the other, but it seems to me that they'd be a little more sympathetic than that.'

'Just take us off the island, please. I'll think about telling someone once we're away from here.'

Jack bit his lip, then nodded. 'Okay, we can try. This all your stuff?'

'It's all that I had time to pack.'

Jack took a bag in each hand, then kicked the knapsack and said, 'You'd best look after that yourself.'

They entered the living room, Jack leading. Marianne was so close behind him when the shot came that Jack's blood hit her in the face before he fell to the floor. There was a wound at his shoulder. He clutched at it with his hand, his teeth clenched as he trembled and began to go into shock. Danny awoke and started crying loudly, but she could not go to him. She could not move.

All that she could do was stare impotently at her husband, even as Dexter frisked her and took the gun from her coat. He raised it so that Moloch could see it.

Moloch grinned.

'Is that a gun in your pocket, or are you just not happy to see me?' Moloch asked.

He stepped closer to her and struck her hard with his right hand, sending her sprawling on a rug. She lay still for a moment, then crawled across the floor to Danny and gathered him in her arms.

'You'd better make that last,' said Moloch. 'You don't have much time left together.'

Moloch stared at his reflection in the painting, his

face seeming to hang suspended above the dark waves that the old man had painted, the twin arms of the outcrops like horns erupting from his head, almost touching above his hair. He moved on to the next, a watercolor filled with blues and greens, before returning to the first. The waves in this version were very dark, almost black, white peaks breaking through like the pale bodies of drowning men. A sliver of moonlight cast a weak silver glow across the skies above. There were no stars.

'I like this one,' he said.

Jack, seated on the floor, his hands bound before him with a length of clothesline, peered up at the intruder. He was deathly pale, apart from a smear of blood across his cheek. In the murk of the room, the blood appeared black against the pallor of his face, creating a strange resemblance between the artist and the work of art before which Moloch now stood.

'You go away and you can have it for free,' said Jack.

Moloch's mouth twitched, the only sign he gave that he might be enjoying the joke.

'Something I've learned,' he said. 'You get nothing for free in this life. Although I can say, with some certainty, that if you fuck with me, money is never likely to be a worry for you again.'

Dexter stood behind the couch. The appearance of the woman and the money seemed to have concentrated Moloch's mind some. He was no longer rambling. Dexter began to experience a faint hope that they might somehow get out of this alive. His hand rested on the back of Danny's neck in what might have been almost a protective way, were it not for the fact that the tips of his fingers were digging painfully into the boy's skin, almost cupping his spine.

'Make him stop,' said Marianne. 'He's your son. Make him stop hurting him.'

Moloch walked toward the boy, who attempted to shrink back but found himself anchored to the spot by the force of Dexter's hand. Moloch reached out and touched the back of his hand to the boy's cheek.

'You're cold,' he said. 'If you're not careful, you'll catch your death.'

He glanced at Marianne.

'He doesn't look much like me. You sure he's mine? Maybe he's something that you and that dyke bitch cooked up between you with a turkey baster. She's dead, by the way, but I suspect you knew that already.'

Marianne's eyes blinked closed. She bit her lip to try to keep from crying.

'Actually, I got to tell you that a lot of people are dead because of you. Your sister, her husband, fuck knows how many people on this island, all because you were a greedy bitch who screwed her own husband over. You try that out for size, see how it fits on your conscience.'

He turned to Dexter.

'How long have we been here?'

'Ten, fifteen minutes, maybe.'

'We can't afford to wait any longer for the others, but now that we have a boat a little closer to home' – Moloch kicked Jack's leg, causing the old man to flinch – 'it looks like I have some time to kill, in a manner of speaking.'

He reached out to Marianne, lifted her up by the arm, and started to guide her toward the bedroom. Danny tried to hold on to her, but Dexter's hand kept him rooted to the couch.

'I been waiting a long time to see you again,' he whispered. He grabbed her left breast and squeezed it painfully. 'Look upon this as a conjugal visit.'

Marianne tried to pull away from him. Instead he thrust her forward, sending her staggering into the hallway.

'There was a time,' said Moloch, 'when you used to beg me for what I'm about to give you.' He pushed her against the wall, the length of his body pressed hard against her, and clasped her cheeks in his hands, forcing her mouth into the shape of a kiss. He composed his own features into an expression of sadness.

'Maybe you've just forgotten the good times,' he said. 'You know, I can promise you that in all the years we've spent apart, I've never been with another woman.'

He forced his mouth over hers. She struggled, small moans of disgust coming from beneath his lips. Then her body began to relax, her mouth now working along with his. His hand relaxed its grip upon her cheeks.

And then she bit him hard in one single movement of her jaws, almost severing his bottom lip, her teeth meeting where they cut through the flesh. Moloch howled. He hit her across the side of the head with his fist and she tumbled to her right, crashing against a small table and sending a bowl of fresh cut flowers crashing to the ground.

Danny screamed.

Moloch held his hand to his wounded mouth, cupping the blood that was pouring from the cut. He stared at himself in the hall mirror, then looked down at Marianne. His words were distorted as he tried to talk without moving his ruined lip, but she understood. They all did.

'I'm going to cut you for that,' he said. 'After I've fucked you, I'm going to cut you to pieces. And then I'm going to start on the boy.'

He took his knife from his belt, flicked the blade open, then advanced on her. He caught her by the hair and began to drag her down the hallway, Danny screaming all the time, Jack struggling against his bonds.

Then the sliding doors exploded and blood shot from Dexter's chest. He tried to turn, and a second shot sent him sprawling into the fireplace. He rolled away from the red glow of the ashes. A third shot hit him in the small of the back, and he finally lay still.

Willard entered through the ruined glass, shards crunching beneath his feet.

'Y'all look surprised to see me,' he said.

* * *

Joe Dupree was almost within sight of Jack's house when he heard the shots and the shattering of glass. Marianne's house had been empty. He figured that she must have taken Danny over to Jack's. He was approaching the house from the west, so the big windows were on the opposite side from him and he could not see what was transpiring inside.

He tightened his grip on the shotgun and began to circle the house.

Moloch smiled at Willard.

'I knew you'd make it,' he said.

Willard looked confused.

'You told them to kill me.'

Moloch shook his head. 'No, that was Dexter's decision, and he didn't tell me about it until we were in trouble. I wanted to kill him for it, but by then I needed all the help I could get. There's something on this damn island, something that wants us all dead, and we need to stick together if we're going to get off it alive.'

Willard looked at the older man, and Moloch could see that he wanted to believe him. Whatever love Willard had for anything in this world, he had for Moloch.

'You hadn't killed Dexter, I'd have killed him myself once we got to land. I won't shed tears for him.'

Despite the agony of his lip, Moloch tried to seem compassionate and concerned for Willard's own pain. It appeared to work. The gun, trained on Moloch, wavered, then fell.

'Thank you, Willard,' said Moloch.

Willard nodded.

'Where we at?' he asked.

Moloch shook Marianne hard by the hair. 'My wife and I were about to make love, but now I've decided to go straight to the afterglow.'

'What happened to your mouth?'

Moloch smiled, his teeth red. 'Love bite,' he said, then looked to Jack. 'You got a first-aid kit?'

'In the kitchen, under the sink.'

Moloch inclined his head toward the kitchen. 'Go in, see what you can find for my mouth,' he told Willard.

Willard gave one last look at Dexter, lying unmoving on the floor, then headed for the kitchen, tucking his gun into his belt. The only sign of doubt he exhibited was his reluctance to turn away from Moloch. He was still looking back at him as the kitchen door swung closed on its hinges, hiding him from the view of those in the living room, and Joe Dupree's great hand closed around his throat. Willard reached for his gun, but the giant's left hand plucked it from its belt and laid it gently on the top of the refrigerator.

Willard's feet began to rise from the ground. He tried to make a sound, but Dupree's grip was too strong. He kicked out with his feet, hoping to hit the walls or the door and alert Moloch, but the giant held him in the very center of the large kitchen, away from anything that might allow Willard to give his presence away. Willard stretched for the giant's face, but his arms were too short. Instead, he dug his nails into Dupree's hand, tearing and gouging, even as he felt his eyes bulging from his face, his lungs burning. Spittle shot from his mouth, and he began to shudder.

Then the giant's grip tightened, and the small bones in Willard's neck started to snap.

Outside, Moloch's head turned sharply toward the kitchen.

'Willard?' he called. 'You okay in there?'

He discarded his knife. Keeping a grip on Marianne's hair, he drew his own gun. He pressed it hard against her temple, moving her slowly toward the living room. He saw Jack look to his right, the boy too. Moloch risked a look around the corner.

There was a female cop standing at the ruined window. Her gun was raised. She fired. The glass on the painting closest to Moloch's head shattered. At the same instant Dupree emerged from the kitchen, his great bulk filling the doorway as he crouched slightly to enter the room. Moloch instantly drew Marianne up to her full height and forced her against him, using her body as a shield, the barrel of the gun now pushed hard into the soft flesh beneath her chin. Only Dupree could see him. Macy stood uncertainly at the window. Moloch adjusted his line of sight so that he could see the hall mirror and Macy's reflection in its surface.

'Peek-a-boo,' he said. 'I see you. You stay right there, missy.'

Dupree remained still, the shotgun pointed at Moloch. The two men confronted each other for the first time, brought together by forces neither fully understood, and bound together by circumstances barely recognized: their shared knowledge of the woman who stood between them; their links to the island and its strange, bloody heritage; and finally, their own curiously similar situations, for they were both men out of place in the world and only Sanctuary could hold out to them a promise of belonging.

'Let her go,' said Dupree. 'It's over.'

'You think?' said Moloch. 'I reckon it's just beginning.'

'Your people are all dead, and you'll never be allowed to leave this place. Let her go.'

'Uh, no. I don't think that's going to happen. My wife and I have just been reunited after a long absence. We've got a lot of catching up to do.'

Moloch jerked Marianne's head back and, despite the pain that it caused him, kissed her cheek, leaving a bloody smear on her skin.

'I bet she didn't tell you about me. I'm shocked. People got to be honest right from the start, otherwise what hope is there for two lovers in this world?'

Marianne kept her eyes away from Dupree, afraid to look at his face. To her left, she could see Macy, her gun moving as she waited for Moloch to make himself a target for her.

'Yeah, I know all about you and my wife. I don't like a man who milks through another man's fence, no matter what he's been told, but I'm inclined to forgive you. After all, she used you.'

Dupree couldn't hide his confusion.

'What did you think, that she was *attracted* to you, you fucking freak? This isn't beauty and the beast. This is real life. She took us both for a ride, but hey, don't beat yourself up over it. She's smarter than I gave her credit for, and there's no denying that she's a looker. Not for too much longer, maybe, but right now most men would give a lot to split this particular piece of white oak. She used you, used you as a lookout, an early warning system so she could take off with my money when the time came.'

Marianne tried to speak, but the gun pressed so hard into her skin that she felt sure it would push through into her mouth. Now, at last, she allowed herself to stare into Dupree's face as she tried to communicate with him, to express her shame, her regret, her fear, and her feelings for him.

They're lies. He's telling lies. I never wanted to hurt anyone, least of all you.

'She'll try to deny it, but it was there in her head. I know her. Hell, I was married to her for long enough, and she still fucked me over. Maybe she even thought that you might protect her if things went wrong. Well, she was right about that much at least, because here you are.'

In the mirror, Moloch saw Macy attempt to move

off, making for the front door to cut off another line of escape. 'Missy, I said I could see you. You move another fucking inch and I'll blow my bitch wife's brains all over the ceiling.'

Macy stopped.

'Put the shotgun down,' Moloch told Dupree. 'You can get rid of the Smith on your belt as well. I won't even waste my time counting to three.'

Dupree, against all his instincts, did as he was told, laying the shotgun down gently on the floor, followed by his Smith & Wesson.

'You too, missy,' said Moloch. He kept his back to the wall so that he could see Macy clearly. She didn't move.

'You think I'm fucking with you? Do it!'

Macy began to lower the gun slowly as Moloch's attention flicked back to Dupree.

'Look at you,' he said. 'You're a freak, a giant pretending to be a knight in shining armor. But you don't read your fairy stories, Mr Giant.'

The gun moved suddenly from Marianne's face, its barrel now pointing at Dupree.

'At the end of the story, the giant always dies.'

He pulled the trigger, and the policeman's throat blossomed like a new flower.

It seemed to happen slowly for Joe Dupree. He thought that he could almost see the bullet as it moved, tearing a path through the cold air. It entered his skin in tiny increments, fractions of inches, ripping through flesh and bone, exiting just to the right of his spine. He fell backward through the kitchen door, coming to rest close to Willard's body. He tried to breathe, but his throat was quickly flooding with blood. The kitchen door was held open by his feet and he saw Marianne spin and strike at Moloch's injured mouth, then throw herself against him in an effort to dislodge his gun. He saw Macy moving through the living room, her gun extended, her face turning in horror toward him. He saw Moloch push Marianne away, then run for the door, firing as he did so, his wife scrambling for the cover of the corner as the bullets sent plaster and paint flying from the walls.

Then he was gone, Macy uncertain whether to follow him or tend to her wounded comrade. She ran to Dupree, limping slightly, favoring her right foot.

'Stay with me, Joe,' she began. 'We'll get help—'

He reached out, took her shirt in his hand, then pushed her away.

Still, she paused. He could not speak, but he pointed his hand in the direction of the fleeing man. She nodded and headed after Moloch, stopping just once to look back at the dying policeman. Already he was drowning in his own blood.

Marianne came to him. She was crying. The boy was behind her, staring at the two men on the kitchen floor.

'I'm sorry,' she said. 'I'm so sorry.'

She tried to take off her coat in order to lay it on him but he gripped her hand and brought it instead to his lips. His hand shook as he kissed her fingers.

'No,' she whispered. 'Don't. Let me help you. We need to keep you warm.'

But she registered the blood spreading behind his head, flowing from the exit wound hidden from them, and she knew.

'No,' she repeated, softer now. 'Don't do this.'

The giant coughed and began to spasm. She tried to hold him down but his great weight was too much for her. His body jerked as he clawed at the floor, an irregular clicking noise emerging from the back of his throat.

Then the spasming stopped, and Joe Dupree's eyes widened as he died, as though in sudden understanding of the nature of this world.

17

M oloch ran.
     He was conscious of movement around him
– branches whipping in the wind, dead leaves pirou-
etting, and the shapes that lingered at the limits of
his perception, not caring now whether he noticed
them or not, merely content to shadow his progress
through the forest. There was blood on his shirt
and face; he could feel it cooling upon him in the
night air. His lip ached, the pain like needles in his
mouth each time he drew a breath. He heard the
sounds of pursuit coming from behind and knew
that the female cop was coming after him. He
thought of all that he wanted to do to the woman,
all of the hurt that he desired to inflict upon her
and upon his wife. At least he'd put an end to the
big cop. That was something.

His head struck a broken branch, almost severed
by the actions of the storm, and he cried out as he
fell back against the tree. When the pain in his
mouth and head had subsided, he took a breath
and stumbled along a narrow pathway that wound
through a patch of marshland, until finally he found
himself in a clearing in the middle of the forest.

Low stones lay half buried in the ground and a simple stone cross stood at its center. He moved slowly forward until he was facing the monument. It was still possible to read the names upon it, and he found his hand reaching out to trace the letters, his bloodied finger outstretched. He touched the stone and—

Men. Forest. Shooting. Women.

Woman.

The fillings in his mouth tingled and he felt suddenly light-headed. He staggered back as the ground began to crumble under his feet. Visions of suffering and death assailed him. He felt flesh beneath his fingers, and smelled powder on the air. A noise came from below as the earth gave way under him, and Moloch tumbled into blackness.

Marianne turned Danny away from Joe Dupree's body, hiding his face in the folds of her jacket just as days – years? – before she had allowed him to shield himself from the reality of a bird's death. Willard's body lay in a corner, partly concealed by the breakfast counter. Danny wouldn't stop crying. He was holding on to her so tightly that his nails were drawing blood. Behind them, Jack had raised himself up and now stood at the kitchen door. She found a knife in a drawer and used it to cut the bindings on his hands, then gently removed Danny's fingers from her legs.

'I want you to stay here with Jack, okay?'

Danny let out a loud wail and tried to claw his

way back to her, but she kept him at arm's length and pushed him into the old man's arms. Jack held him as firmly as he could, folding his uninjured arm across Danny's chest. Marianne picked up Dupree's gun from the floor, then headed for the front door.

'I'll be back before you know it, Danny. You look after Jack for me.'

But Danny could only cry, and in the confusion and shock of the moment none of them noticed that Dexter's body was gone.

Moloch fell for what seemed like a long, long time, yet the distance could only have been twenty feet, for when he hit the bottom he could still see a ragged hole above him, loose earth spilling down from the edges, snowflakes joining it in its descent. Dim light filtered down, bathing him in a patina of gray, like one who was already fading from this world. The impact made him gag, and he lay for a moment tasting bile and blood in his mouth.

Moloch smelled damp earth and decay. He reached out a hand blindly and felt it brush against ragged hair.

Woman. A woman's hair.

He instantly drew his hand back, forcing the fear from him. The cop was coming. If he stayed here and waited to be found, he would be trapped like an animal. He needed to find a way out. He needed to know what was around him.

He advanced into the shadows, grateful now for

the improvements forced upon his vision by hours of struggling through the snowstorm without flashlights. He discovered that he had been touching tree roots, exposed by the hollow in which he now stood. Moloch released a spluttering laugh of relief, then heard it die in his mouth as he began to take in his surroundings.

He was in a semicircular hollow, about fifteen feet in diameter. At its extremities were openings, large enough for a man to crawl through on his belly. Moloch approached the biggest of the entrances and carefully reached inside, disturbing some beetles as he felt the ends of more tree roots dangling from the top of the tunnel. He listened. From beyond he could hear the sound of flowing water. He glanced back toward the hole through which he had fallen, then took another look at the earth walls that descended from it. There was no way that he could climb them. Either he stayed here and waited to be found or he took his chances in one of the tunnels. Moloch had no fear of enclosed spaces – even prison had not troubled him in that way – but he still felt uneasy about committing himself to the hole before him. He might have trouble squeezing through if it narrowed significantly farther on, and he had no idea how, or for what purpose, the tunnels had been constructed. Still, there was the sound of water, which could mean that the tunnel led to the bank of a river or stream, and he thought that he could make out a faint light ahead.

He made his decision.

He got down on his knees and entered the hole.

Twenty feet above, Macy reached the clearing. She was still feeling the shock of Dupree's death and of her own actions in the tower. Until tonight, she had never fired her gun in the line of duty, and had barely had cause to draw it from its holster. Now a man had died at her hands and another was fleeing from her, and Joe Dupree was dead because she hadn't been fast enough.

Joe Dupree was dead because of her.

Her foot struck rocks. She looked down at the monument protruding from the ground, at the others surrounding it, and at the raised stone cross at the center of the little cemetery. She was reluctant to enter the clearing. Her quarry was still armed, and she was unwilling to risk exposing herself. She crouched down low and tried to scan the forest.

There was blood upon the snow by the cross.

She swallowed, then headed toward the middle of the site. She was almost upon it when her foot trod air and she stumbled, her leg disappearing into the hole. She fell backward, then scuttled away from the gap, anticipating gunfire from below, but no sound came. She counted to five, then inched forward again. The hole was new. She could see dark earth, and the tree roots were moist when she touched her fingers to them. She risked a quick glance below, barely allowing the top of her head to appear over the rim of the hole in order to provide the smallest possible target. She could see nothing but fallen earth, broken branches, and a light dusting of snow down below.

Joe Dupree's killer was down there. He had to be.

She was about to descend when a hand gripped her shoulder. She looked up to see Marianne Elliot behind her.

'Don't,' said Marianne. 'You have to get out of here. We both have to get out of here. Now.'

Even in the falling snow, the trail left by Moloch and Macy had been easy for Marianne to discern. They were heading toward the Site. Marianne followed them carefully, checking the woods and always trying to use trees for cover, but could not see either of them. They were too far ahead.

She was almost at the clearing when something brushed by her feet. She looked down and saw a gray shape moving swiftly past her, tattered clothing hanging on mummified skin, wisps of hair protruding from beneath the folds of its shroud. It appeared to float slightly above the ground, leaving no trace of its passage, while its thin hands used rocks and tree trunks to pull itself along, like a diver exploring the seabed. Marianne shrank away from it and her legs touched another shape as it swept by her, seemingly oblivious of her presence.

She raised her head and saw that she was surrounded. Gray forms moved across the forest floor, some as big as men, others as small as children. She caught indistinct glimpses of faces lost in the folds of gowns and shrouds, flashes of torn feet, broken skin, and large, dark eyes. Rooted to the spot, she tried to scream, but no sound came.

Then a voice spoke, and it was her voice, yet it did not come from her.

'*Leave*', the voice said, and Marianne thought that she felt a hand brush against her skin and she saw—

A man descending upon her, Moloch yet not Moloch, and she felt him enter her, and the blade beginning its work, cutting and tearing at her. She was dying, and others were dying around her.

The voice came again, a soft, woman's voice.

'*Leave.*'

And the gray shapes continued to weave around her, disappearing beneath rocks and under tree trunks, descending through all the dark, hollow places into the world below.

The last to sink away was a woman. Marianne could see the swell of breasts beneath her clothing, her long hair sweeping behind her and gently brushing the snow. Before she descended, the woman stared back at her, and Marianne looked into her own face. It was a face ruined by old wounds, its nose broken and its cheekbones shattered, its eyes a deep black as though colonized by some terrible cancer, but it was still a face that closely resembled her own.

Then the woman found a gap between the roots of a great beech tree, and was gone.

Dexter had made it to the edge of the old man's yard, half stumbling, half crawling until he reached the treeline. He had jammed wads of bills, now soaked with red, into the waistband of his pants. Ahead of him he could see a narrow pathway leading from the cliff edge to the shore. The boat would be down there. If he could get to it, he would take his chances on the sea. If he stayed on the island, he would be found, or he would die.

He leaned against a tree trunk to catch his breath, but when he tried to rise again he found that he could not. His body had taken too many shots. He had lost too much blood. He was weakening.

Dexter slid down the bark until he came to rest on the ground. The blizzard was easing, he noticed. The snow was falling more gently now. He stretched his legs out before him and removed the money from his pants. The bills were smeared so thickly with his blood that he could barely read the denominations. He removed the band from one of the wads, spread the notes in his hand, and watched the wind spirit them away, some carried up into the air, others dancing across the snow.

Dexter noticed other shapes moving among the discarded bills. One came to rest on his leg. He reached down and gently touched the moth's wings. It fluttered against his fingers, then took flight. He watched it, following its progress until it came to rest upon a small girl who stood among the trees, watching him. Dexter could see her long, pale hair, but her face was lost in shadow. She looked almost like a moth herself, Dexter thought. A cloak hung over her shoulders, so that when she extended her arms they took on the appearance of wings.

'Hey,' said Dexter. 'You think you could help me?'

He swallowed.

'I want to get down to the water. I have money. You could buy yourself something nice.'

He extended one of the remaining wads of bills toward her. The girl moved forward.

'That's it,' said Dexter. 'Come on, now. You help me get out of here and I'll—'

The Gray Girl's feet were not touching the ground. She floated toward Dexter, her arms wide and her dark eyes gleaming, her skin wrinkled and decayed. Dexter opened his mouth to scream and the Gray Girl's lips closed upon his. Her hands gripped his head and her knees pinned his arms to the trunk of the tree. Blood poured from the meeting of their mouths as Dexter shook, the life slowly being drawn from him and into the Gray Girl, a life taken in return for the life stolen from her.

And then the Gray Girl drew back from the dead man, her dark eyes closing briefly in ecstasy, moths falling dead around her as she followed her companions at last into the depths.

Moloch was ten feet into the tunnel now, and rather

than narrowing, it seemed to have increased in size. He paused and listened. If the cop decided to come down after him, he would be in real trouble, but he didn't believe that she would. It was a considerable drop down. Moloch was surprised that he hadn't injured himself in the fall. No, she would wait, maybe look for a rope. She would not risk being trapped beneath the earth with him. He moved on.

He had progressed five or six feet more when he thought that he heard movement behind him. He stopped, and found only silence.

Jittery. I'm getting jittery.

Then he heard it again, clearer now. For a second he thought it was falling earth, and panic hit him as he imagined the tunnel collapsing around him, trapping him. He listened harder and realized that what he was hearing was scraping, the slow movement of earth beneath nails and hands, the same sounds that he himself had probably been making since he had begun moving through the tunnel. He tried to turn his head, but the tunnel was still too narrow to allow him to see clearly behind him.

The cop. It had to be the cop. She had come down after all. Maybe she had brought rope with her, or had found some among the detritus of the forest.

Shit.

He started to pull himself forward again, faster now. He was certain that he could hear water. Hell, he could even smell it. Cool air was coming through

the tunnel. He felt it on his face, took a deep
breath—

And then it was gone. Moloch stopped again. The
airflow had ceased. He had heard no sounds of collapse. Something had deliberately blocked the tunnel.

The sounds from behind were drawing closer,
and now another smell had taken the place of the
river and the forest, a stench like old meat left to
boil in a pot for too long, of offal and waste. He
found himself retching on it. Light filtered through
the tunnel. It was silver, almost gray. He was grateful
for it, even if he could not identify its source. He
didn't want to be trapped down here in the darkness with—

With what?

He tried to turn his head again and found that
he now had enough space to peer behind him. He
raised his right foot and looked back. The tunnel
wall curved slightly but he could still hear the sound.
It was closer now, he thought. If it was the cop,
she would give him some warning.

If it was the cop.

'Who's there?' he called.

The sound stopped, but he sensed that his pursuer was at the very edge of the tunnel wall, barely
out of sight.

'I got a gun,' he said. 'You better back out now.
I hear you following me, I'll use it.'

The light seemed to grow stronger around him.
There were gray-white worms emerging from the earth
of the tunnel wall, coiling around it, probing . . .

Then Moloch saw the nails on the ends of the pale fingers, and the wounds on the back of the hand, wounds that now would never heal.

He turned back and heard himself sobbing with fear.

And in the final seconds of life granted to him, he saw a face, its skin gray parchment, its hair a handful of strands clinging to the skull, the roots of the teeth exposed by the retreating gums and the parted lips. He could see the deep cuts on her face, the damage inflicted by fist and knife. The lamp in her hands cast a dim glow upon him, for in the darkest places even the dead need light.

He smelled her breath, fetid and rank, and he heard her voice – '*Know me, husband*' – as the light died and he was enveloped in blackness.

'He's down there,' said Macy. 'There's nowhere he can go.'

But Marianne was pulling her back.

'You don't understand,' she said. 'There's something else down there too.'

Macy looked at her. She remembered the tower, and the floating child, and the look on Scarfe's face as he stared out into the forest and saw what was pursuing him.

Macy began to run. A rumbling sound came from the ground below her, and she felt the earth begin to give way beneath her. She increased her speed, Marianne beside her, the two women racing as the ground around the Site collapsed, taking the stones and the cross and the remnants of the settlement with it, smothering Moloch's final cries in the thunder of its destruction.

18

Barron sat in the SUV over by the Portland Marine Company, an empty coffee container from the 7-Eleven on Congress in the cup holder by his right hand, the radio playing Cheap Trick for the night owls. Once or twice prowl cars had passed his way, but he'd hunched down low in his seat and the cops hadn't even slowed, the SUV just another vehicle parked in the lot. The snow was still falling, although the wind had died down some. The SUV was warm, the heating on full blast, but he had kept his gloves and coat on just the same.

Barron had spent most of his evening trying to reach a decision about the private detective nosing around. People listened when Parker spoke, and it was only a matter of time before somebody with real authority started paying attention to his noises about a sexual predator at work in the area, possibly a predator in a uniform.

The men in Boston were his only option. He was their tame cop, in so deep with them now that he could never escape. If they heard he was under threat, then they might be prepared to deal with his problem for him. The Russians didn't give a rat's ass about reputation, or influence. They were in it for the money and anything that threatened their sources of income, or their carefully cultivated contacts, would be annihilated without a moment's thought. He had once hoped that they might let him go, but it had been a faint hope. If that was the case, he might just have to resign himself to the fact and take advantage of the situation.

He glanced again at the dashboard clock: almost midnight. All was quiet. If Scarfe's buddies did come back to the port, it looked like they would be able to do so without interference. Barron had even spotted one or two ships, dense with lights, braving the bay as the snow began to ease and the wind faded from a howl to a whisper. The streets were deserted and Scarfe's battered Grand Am was parked not ten feet away from where he sat, along with two vans. They had wheels. They were free and clear once they got back to Portland. Barron had done all that he could be expected to do. He had waited, he had kept an ear to traffic on the two police bands. He had his cell phone ready, the number he had been given by the men in Boston written on a napkin and not stored in the phone's memory just in case any of this came back to bite him on the ass.

Then his scanner burst into life, and next thing Barron knew there was a chopper being readied for a run to Dutch, the coast guard was moving in, and there were enough armed police heading for the water to mount an invasion. Barron started his engine and drove.

It had all turned to shit, just as he expected.

Barron ditched the SUV at Hoyt's Pond, then retrieved his own car and headed home. He spent the next two hours pacing his apartment, wondering if he should run, fearing that his colleagues were already coming for him, sold out by Scarfe to save himself. After a while, he just had to know. He returned to Commercial and contrived to bump into one of the detectives from headquarters, who gave him the lowdown on the situation. Dupree was dead, killed by persons yet to be identified. Some, maybe all, of those responsible were also dead, but they were still searching the island. Macy had blooded herself: Terry Scarfe, who appeared to be tied in with those involved, had died at her hands. Barron was particularly happy to receive this last piece of information. If he had survived, Scarfe would have fed him to the department like fish bait.

Relieved, Barron returned to his apartment and began to feel the old urge gnawing at him, brought on in part by his relief at what he had learned about the events on Dutch. His appetites had forced him to risk his job and jail time for men whom he didn't know, yet he was still unable to control them. Lipska, the little Polack who acted as Boston's representative in Maine, had promised him some payback if he did as he was told, even as he was blackmailing him in another's name. Barron felt saliva flooding his mouth and the welcome ache building at his groin. He made the call.

'Yeah, it's me. Something went wrong, and the cops moved on the island.'

He gave Lipska a summary of what little he knew. 'Now I want what's coming to me.'

He sighed when he heard the other man's reply.

'Yeah, I know I still got to pay, but you promised me something fresh, with a little off the top for my time.'

Barron grinned.

'Man, you crack me up, you really do. I'll be waiting.'

Barron's apartment lay off Forest, close to the university. It took up the entire top floor of the building, the rooms below rented out to students, and nurses from Maine Medical. They paid their rent to Barron although they didn't know it. He used an agency. To them, he was just another tenant. Barron didn't want them bothering him with their shit.

He took a beer from the fridge, walked to the bathroom, and lit some candles, then ran a bath, testing the water with his fingers to make sure the temperature was okay. He wanted it just a little too hot, so that it would have cooled down just enough by the time the package arrived. He stripped, put on a robe, then turned some music on low. He was about to go back to the kitchen for another beer when there was a knock at his door. There had been no buzzer, no voice over his intercom. He went to his bedside locker and took out his gun, keeping it to his side and slightly behind his back as he approached the door. He looked out of the peep-hole, then relaxed and opened the door.

There was a boy standing before him, fifteen or sixteen at most, just the age Barron liked. He had dark hair and pale skin, with reddish purple smudges beneath his eyes. Truth be told, Barron thought he looked kind of ill, and for a moment he was worried that maybe the kid had the virus, but Lipska had assured him that he was clean, and that was one thing about Lipska: he didn't lie about shit like that.

'How'd you get up? I leave the door open? I must have left the door open.' Barron heard himself babbling but hell, the kid had something. He was almost otherworldly. Barron felt certain that tonight was going to be special. He stepped aside to let the kid enter, noticing his faded, crude pants, his rough cotton shirt, his bare feet. Bare feet? The hell was Lipska thinking, on a night like this?

'You leave your shoes at the front door?' Barron asked.

The boy nodded. He smelled clean, like the sea.

'Yeah, bet they got real wet. Maybe tomorrow we'll head out, buy you some sneakers.'

The boy didn't reply. Instead, he looked toward the bathroom. Steam was rising from the tub.

'You like the water?'

The boy spoke for the first time.

'Yes,' he said.

He followed the older man into the bathroom, his thumbs rubbing against his fingers, tracing the grooves that the waves had worn into his skin like an old song waiting for the touch of the Victrola needle to bring it alive.

'I like the water very much.'

Lipska arrived forty minutes later and tried the buzzer. There was no reply. He tried twice more, then tested the door with his hand. It opened at his touch. He gestured to the boy waiting in the car, and the young man stepped out. He wore jeans, a white T-shirt, and a black leather jacket. He was shivering as he followed Lipska into the house.

The door to Barron's apartment was open when they reached it. Lipska knocked once, then again, harder this time. The door unlatched beneath the pressure of his hand. Inside there was water on the floor; just a little, as if someone had left the shower or the bath without properly drying off first. To Lipska's left, the bathroom door stood half open and he heard the sound of the tap dripping. The only light came from there.

'Barron?' he called. 'Barron, man, you in there? It's Lipska.'

He walked to the bathroom door and pushed it open. He took in the naked man, his knees above the surface of the water, his head below it, eyes and mouth open, one arm dangling over the edge of the tub; registered too the faint tang of salt water that hung in the air.

He turned to the boy, who had remained standing at the door.

'Let's go,' he said.

'Don't I get my money?' said the boy.

'I'll give you your money,' said Lipska. 'Forget you were ever here. Just forget you were ever here . . .'

Epilogue

The best way to suppose what may come, is to remember what is past.

George Halifax (1633-1695)

Marianne looked out of the window to where the boy sat on the small wooden bench at the end of the garden. From that seat, it was possible to peer through the branches of the evergreens and catch glimpses of the sea beyond. She stood at the sink, her hands immersed in soapy water, and waited for him to move, but he did not.

He has not cried, she thought. He has not wept since the night Joe Dupree died. He has not asked that we leave this place, and for the present we cannot. They are still trying to work out what happened here. Men are dead, and the reporters have washed over the island like a flood, questioning anyone who will stand still long enough to talk to them. Two weeks have gone by, and still they ask questions.

So many had died because of her: Bonnie Claessen was dead, and Richie too. His body had been washed ashore the night after the blizzard, the body of another man joined with it, both impaled upon a single arrow. Joe Dupree, the man who had shared her bed, had been laid to rest the week before. She had wept by his grave, haunted by the thought that he had died believing that he had been used and that she had felt nothing at all for him. The police were unwilling to let her leave the state until they had finished their investigation, and so the bodies of Patricia and Bill remained on ice in a morgue. She had read of the discovery of Karen Meyer's body in the newspapers. Marianne had brought death upon them all, and for that she could never forgive herself.

They had found her husband's body two days before, lodged in a network of tunnels beneath the old burial ground. It appeared that he had died in the collapse. The searchers discovered dirt in his mouth; dirt, and human remains. There were finger bones lodged in his throat.

Throughout the days that followed, Sharon Macy had been her ally, her protector, the two women united by their experiences. The investigators had taken away the money, but she had been told quietly that no charges would be filed against her. The states of Maine and Virginia proved remarkably sympathetic to her plight, perhaps recognizing that a battered wife, fleeing her husband to save herself and her child, would sway even the most hard-hearted of jurors.

But Danny concerned her most of all. He had suffered through a terrible ordeal, and had seen men die in front of him. She felt that she needed to get him away from the island and the memories it held for him in the hope that time and distance might fade them. They were seated at the breakfast table, and he was merely toying with his Cheerios, when she brought the subject up for the first time.

'I don't want to leave,' Danny replied. 'I want to stay here.'

'But after all that has happened—'

'It doesn't matter. The bad men are dead.'

'We may have to leave. People here may not want us to stay after what happened.'

'They won't make us leave,' he said.

And now it was she who seemed to be the younger one, the child, and he the elder, the one offering reassurance to her.

'How do you know?'

'He told me.'

'Who told you?'

'Joe. He told me it would be okay.'

She let it rest then, not wishing to return either of them to the vision of the dying policeman on the floor, the ragged wound in his throat and his blood spilling across the tiled floor. It came to her at night, unbidden, just as she supposed that it came to Danny too. She would not allow it to torment her son's waking moments as well.

But then Larry Amerling came to her, and he and Jack sat with her in her living room. Amerling told her that nobody on the island blamed her for what had happened, at least nobody that mattered, and that she couldn't be held responsible for the actions of her husband. The deaths of Bonnie and Richie and Joe would remain with them always, and nobody who knew them would ever forget them, but they would not be brought back by forcing Marianne and Danny to leave.

'Joe cared for you, and I know Bonnie and Richie did too,' said Amerling. 'Of all people, they would want you to stay.'

She cried and told them that she would think about it, but Jack took her hand, his arm still in a sling, and hushed her and told her that there was nothing to think about. Then Larry Amerling said something very strange.

'Maybe I'm just getting fatalistic in my old age, but I think that what happened was meant to happen,' he said. 'Strange as it sounds, you and Danny were brought here for a reason, your husband too. There are things about that night that I don't understand, and that I don't want to understand. I've spoken to Officer Macy, to Linda Tooker and her sister, to old Doug Newton and others too. A lot of people on this island have tales to tell about what they saw that night. You didn't cause any of that. It was here, waiting. My guess is that it had been waiting for a long time for the chance to emerge. The island feels different now because of it. It's been purged of something that's troubled it, and it's at peace. You should stay. You're part of us. Sometimes I think you were always part of us.'

Now, as she stood watching her son, she wondered at the change that had come over him in recent days. He was quieter, more subdued, and that was to be expected. But rather than his confidence being shaken, or his becoming fearful of the world beyond the island, he seemed to have grown in assurance as a consequence of the events that had occurred. The night sounds that scared her did not trouble him, and he no longer even required his night-light to be left on, the little rocket that she had bought for him at Abacus in the Old Port for his last birthday. In truth, he now appeared happier in the darkness.

As she watched him, a shadow passed over him.

It must be clouds, she thought, straining to look up at the winter sky. Maybe it's just the play of light, but there's nothing out there, nothing that I can see. The sky is empty of clouds and the yard is clear, but for my son on his bench and the shadow that stretches across him like a sentinel.

Seated on his bench, the boy stared straight ahead. He did not look behind him, even as he saw the shadow grow and felt the presence at his shoulder.

'*Listen*', said the giant's voice. '*My father told me these things, and now I will tell you. It is important that we remember, so that the nature of the island may be understood. The first one that came was named Thomas Lunt, and he brought with him his wife Katie, and their children, Erik and Johann. That was in the spring of 1691. With them came the Leggits, Robert and Marie. Marie was pregnant at the time, and would later give birth to a boy, William. Others came in the weeks that followed.*

These are their names. You must remember them, Danny. It's very important that you remember.'

And the boy listened, and he remembered all that he was told.

Acknowledgments

W hile Sanctuary is an entirely fictitious island, elements of its history and geography are based loosely on Peaks Island, which lies close to Portland, Maine in Casco Bay. I am grateful to Officers Christopher Hawley and Bob Morton of the Portland Police Department, who carry out their duties on Peaks Island and who were kind and patient enough to answer my endless questions about the island and their work. My thanks also to Captain Russell Gauvin of the Portland Police Department, who was once again good enough to facilitate my research, and to Sarah Yeates, a font of knowledge and kindness. *Peaks Island: An Affectionate History* by John K. Moulton (1993); *Islands of Maine* by Bill Caldwell (Down East Books, 1981); *The Maine Coast Guide* by Curtis Rindlaub (Casco Bay, 2000); and *The Handbook of Acromegaly*, edited by John Wass (BioScientifica, 2001) were also useful to me. All mistakes are, as ever, my own.

On a personal note, my thanks go out, as always, to my editor, Sue Fletcher, her assistant, Swati Gamble, and all at Hodder & Stoughton for their constant faith; to my agent, Darley Anderson, and his staff, for all that they have done for me; and to the many booksellers and critics who have been generous enough to support my work.

THE
DELPHI
REVOLUTION

ALSO BY RYSA WALKER

The Delphi Trilogy

The Delphi Effect
The Delphi Resistance

Novella

The Abandoned

The CHRONOS Files

Novels

Timebound
Time's Edge
Time's Divide

Graphic Novel

Time Trial

Novellas

Time's Echo
Time's Mirror
Simon Says

Short Stories

"The Gambit" in *The Time Travel Chronicles*
"Whack Job" in *Alt.History 102*
"2092" in *Dark Beyond the Stars*
"Splinter" in *CLONES: The Anthology*
"The Circle That Whines" in *Tails of Dystopia*
"Full Circle" in *OCEANS: The Anthology*

THE
DELPHI
REVOLUTION

The Delphi Trilogy
Book Three

RYSA WALKER

SKYSCAPE

Text copyright © 2018 by Rysa Walker
All rights reserved.

Published by Skyscape, New York

www.apub.com

Amazon, the Amazon logo, and Skyscape are trademarks of Amazon.com, Inc., or its affiliates.

ISBN-13: 9781542048408
ISBN-10: 1542048400

Cover design by M. S. Corley

Printed in the United States of America

*To Courtney, editor extraordinaire, who has now moved
on to other adventures.*

Kiernan sends his love.

NEWS ITEM FROM THE *VIRGINIAN-PILOT*

April 11, 2020

Police are searching for any additional witnesses to the murder of Cameron Applebaum, 13, in Virginia Beach. The boy was struck late Wednesday night while crossing Paladin Drive on the way back from a friend's house. The killing was initially reported as a hit-and-run until images of the body posted anonymously online revealed the word *freak*, apparently written in blood, scrawled across the boy's forehead.

Four other victims have been discovered in the US with the words *freak* or *mutant* written either on or near the body since the beginning of the year. A group calling themselves The Natural Order has taken responsibility for all five killings, which they claim are not acts of murder but proactive self-defense.

Rysa Walker

A spokesperson for the Applebaum family refused to comment on whether the boy had been tested or had exhibited any sort of psychic ability, but it seems likely. Like many of the individuals who tested positive for psychic ability, Applebaum's father (deceased) was assigned to the PSYOP battalion at Fort Bragg, North Carolina, in the late 1990s.

CHAPTER ONE

Carova, North Carolina
April 23, 2020, 9:20 a.m.

The sand beneath my cheek smells of salt and fish, and of something harsh and pungent. Motor oil, or maybe gasoline.

How the hell did I get here?

I want to sit up, but my body feels too heavy to move. So I lie still, eyes closed, digging my fingers into the cool, wet sand.

Then an icy wave hits my bare legs. It jolts me awake, and I scuttle away from the tide to avoid a second dousing.

"Anna? Anna!"

I turn toward the sound as I brush the grit from my face and hands. It's Aaron, maybe a hundred yards down the beach. He's talking on his phone as he jogs toward me.

Damn it. *Damn. It.* Did he *follow* me?

Why can't I have a half hour to myself? I need space. I need room to breathe. To think. To simply be.

My heart hammers erratically in my throat as I pull my feet under me, preparing to bolt. Aaron is already winded. I'm a better runner. He'll never be able to catch me.

What? No. No, no, *no.* I draw in a deep breath through my nose and close my eyes, pushing down the panic. I love Aaron. He loves me. Why should I care if he followed me?

And then my mind starts clicking through the questions he's going to ask, and I want to run again. When did I leave? Why didn't I wake him? Why was I lying on the beach? Did I faint again?

Focus, Anna.

Aaron stashes his phone in his pocket and picks up the pace, closing the distance between us. Time to get my story straight. Employ a few selective truths detailing the things I do remember and add enough filler (*lies, you mean lies, lies, lies*) to cover the things I *don't* remember.

Out of sheer necessity, I've gotten quite good at fabricating a plausible story. These memory gaps are becoming more frequent. Longer, too. I thought my symptoms would improve steadily over time as my brain healed from the concussion. But Kelsey warned me from the beginning that progress after a traumatic brain injury isn't predictable. It comes in starts and stops, and sometimes symptoms can worsen temporarily.

I could tell Aaron the truth. That I don't remember. But that will just tighten the net around me. They won't let me out of their sight if I admit I'm blacking out.

Even worse. They'll lock you up.

Let's go with this story, then. I woke up early, just before daybreak. Couldn't sleep. Everyone else was still in bed, so I pulled on my jogging clothes and hit the beach. And I've been running for the past . . .

I glance at my watch: 9:22.

Three and a half hours? He'll never believe I've been running since dawn. I don't even believe it.

And . . . time's up.

Aaron drops onto the sand next to me, panting.

"What the hell, Anna? You know you can't leave without telling anybody."

He sounds more worried than angry, even though he has every right to be mad. This isn't the first time in the past few months, or even the second time, I've slipped away without telling anyone. It's also not the first time I've had memory lapses, but I'm getting better at disguising those.

Better at lying.

"I'm sorry. But I *did* tell someone. I told the guard I was going for a run. The night guard—the young guy with freckles?"

That part isn't a lie. I remember this. Glancing at the clock as I tied my running shoes. Thinking I needed to hurry and get downstairs before six when the guard changed. The night guard is scared to death of the Delphi adepts, especially me. He's one of the guys who received a few new memories—memories I planted in their heads—when Aaron, Taylor, Deo, and I went AWOL from Sandalford back in December. He and his buddies willingly loaded the truck with weapons, medical supplies, anything we asked for, because I made them think it had all been cleared by their boss. I even made them remember Miller ordering them to help us.

I can't mess with their heads that way anymore. That ability was courtesy of a temporary hitcher, Daniel Quinn, Aaron's half brother. When I returned Daniel's spirit to his comatose body on Christmas Eve, his powers of persuasion went too.

Or at least I assume they did. Daniel is in Maryland, no longer in the hospital but still undergoing daily rehab. Luckily, he retained a good deal of his gross motor ability. He's able to walk on his own now, and he's recovered his speech almost completely. For the first several weeks, it was just a few words, and according to his mom, the vast majority of them were impolite. That doesn't surprise me. Daniel hates being dependent on anyone. Having others take care of him has to be driving him mad.

There's no rehab for psychic abilities, however. And since his mom is still in the dark about his ability to "nudge" people, as Daniel calls it, I doubt Aaron or Taylor have had the opportunity to ask him whether his Delphi skills are back to normal.

The guards here at Sandalford seem to think I can still push them around, though. When I approached the guard at the gate this morning and said I was going for a run, he shrank back instantly. I almost expected him to make the sign of the cross to ward off evil, but he settled on a nervous nod.

"The *night* guard?" Aaron says. "But . . . that means you've been out here for over three hours! You didn't leave us a note. You didn't even sign out. We've combed the entire beach. Deo's already been down this way twice and he didn't see you."

Another wave of guilt hits me. Deo must be freaking out, the same way I would be. The same way I *was* when Graham Cregg's people nabbed him a few months back. We may not be related by blood, but he's my brother in every sense of the word, and I hate that I've made him worry. That I've made any of them worry.

"I wasn't on the beach the whole time. I ran on Sandfiddler Road for a while."

This *might* be a lie. I don't know. The truth is I have no memory of running anywhere beyond those first few steps out of the gate this morning. But you can't really hide on a wide-open beach. If Deo came down this way and didn't see me, the only logical explanation is that I was on one of the roads that run through the Currituck Wildlife Reserve.

"Look at me," Aaron says. I've been avoiding his gaze, staring out at the water or down at my knees, but now I turn toward him. He searches my eyes for a long time. Looking for the truth, I guess. Searching for some sign that I'm being honest.

Eventually he shakes his head, breaking the stare. He picks a shell out of the sand and flings it toward the water. "You're lucky Miller is with Magda. Otherwise, we'd never be able to keep this under wraps. It's almost like you *want* to end up with one of those ankle gadgets."

Magda Bell owns Sandalford—not just the big house but also the empty lot to the north and the property to the south, encompassing nearly a mile of oceanfront. She set the place up as a safe haven for Delphi adepts, most of them kids who inherited something extra from parents who were used by the military as guinea pigs. The experiment, which had its roots in the Vietnam War but reached its apex in the late 1990s, involved a serum designed to ramp up natural psychic abilities. It worked, but it also had major side effects that made many of them, especially the male subjects, violent and suicidal.

Magda's missing husband, Erik Bell, was a former TV psychic and one of the Delphi Project's civilian subjects. Both of her daughters are apparently adepts, but no one has any idea exactly what it is they can do. Magda keeps them separate from the rest of the adepts in the big yellow house on the southernmost lot, which she dubbed Bell Isle. A small team of nurses and Dr. Batra, her private physician, live there, too. Batra is the doctor who helped stabilize Deo, and he continues to monitor him to make sure that Deo doesn't have a relapse of the brain swelling that came very close to killing him after he was injected with the Delphi serum. Batra seems nice enough, but the whole thing over at Bell Isle feels off.

Concern for her daughters is the key reason Magda is bankrolling the effort to find a cure. She's made that clear from the moment she got involved. The latest addition to that effort is the small team of scientists who showed up at Sandalford three weeks ago, setting up shop in the guesthouse out back, complete with lab equipment and a half dozen caged monkeys. That bothers me. I mean, I guess they need to test whatever they're cooking up on animals before they test it on children. It feels wrong, though, and sometimes when I hear the monkeys screeching, I want to storm in and fling open their cages.

But I doubt unleashing psychic, possibly aggressive, monkeys on the beach would help either our situation or theirs.

"Do you really think I'm *trying* to make Magda angry?" I ask Aaron.

"Not exactly," he says. "But we both know it doesn't take much to set her off. And she's kind of the only ally we have against Senator Cregg right now."

Technically, Magda is overseeing the effort to expose Senator Cregg's role in the Delphi Project and his ongoing exploitation of the adepts for his own political purposes. But not much has been done on that front, as far as I can tell. The entire goal seems to be to keep the adepts in stasis. That's why she hired Miller and his company, Vigilance Security, back in November when she was still living in London. Miller is former military, and while I don't know exactly what he did during his time in the service, my guess would be drill sergeant. It's been clear from the beginning that he doesn't like children and he *really* doesn't like psychic children.

Miller would run Sandalford like a military school for juvenile delinquents if not for Kelsey. She hates him with the fire of a thousand suns, and it takes a lot to make Kelsey hate someone. I'd hoped Magda would realize Miller is a bad fit for the position once she arrived here after we rescued the other adepts in late December. But no. He remains, partly because he is the King of Suck-Ups and would lick the sand from her feet if he thought it would put more money into his pockets.

The bottom line is that Magda calls the shots. And the last time I wandered off, Magda said if it happened again, Miller would fit me with one of the ankle trackers like the ones worn by the kids who were brought in from the school on Fort Bragg. Furthermore, she'd revoke my "travel" privileges, and I'd be forced to stay "on campus" with the other adepts.

Magda doesn't have legal grounds to force anything on you, I tell myself. *You're an adult now.*

It's true. I'm eighteen. Aaron is an adult, too. And their mom refused to sign any legal agreement that would require Taylor to remain at Sandalford against her will. Kelsey did likewise for Deo, and Magda was so annoyed that I was fairly certain she was going to fire Kelsey for insubordination. In the end, Magda didn't fire her, but she made it abundantly clear that all of us would be bounced out permanently if our actions exposed the group as a whole to danger.

We can leave at any time.

But the outside world isn't exactly a safe place for adepts right now. Especially ones like me and Aaron. Our faces were plastered all over the news for a few days last fall, as *persons of interest* in the killing of six children and several adults near Fort Bragg. And even though the media has moved on to other stories now, our faces are still out there. Once something is online, it spreads like pee in a swimming pool.

"I'm sorry, Aaron," I say between clenched teeth. "I just . . . I got claustrophobic, okay? There are *so* many people in that house, and I needed to get out. I needed to run. To be *alone.*"

I emphasize the last word because I know it's the excuse most likely to resonate with Aaron, who has far more reason to feel claustrophobic at Sandalford than I do. In addition to the two of us, there are currently twenty-nine Delphi adepts between the ages of two and nineteen living there, along with three parents of those adepts, seven security guards, two nurses, and Kelsey. Every time any of those residents gets the slightest urge to smack someone, Aaron feels that anger. If anyone should be sneaking out for three-hour jogs on the beach, it's him.

"I understand the need to get away from Sandalford," he says. "You know I do. What I don't understand is your need to get away from me. From Kelsey, Deo, Taylor. The people who care about you. You can talk to us, you know."

His voice is so gentle I can barely hear it over the surf and wind. I turn away slightly, and clench my fists so hard that one of my nails breaks through the skin of my palm as I try to rein in a flood of emotions. It's partly guilt. It's also fear, because I don't know why I'm acting this way. Why I'm *feeling* this way. Why I can't talk these feelings through with the people I love.

But what terrifies me most is that behind the guilt and fear is a mass of pure white-hot rage. I'm furious at myself for playing Aaron's emotions this way, but also furious at him for turning it back around on me.

Aaron reaches up to touch my hair but stops abruptly. His fingers hover a few inches above the shorter patch, where my head was stitched up after Jasper Hawkins cracked it with the butt of his pistol, but it's not because he's worried the spot is still tender. It's been fine, at least on the surface, for several months. The reason he stops short of touching me is that his little gift from the Delphi scientists, what we jokingly call his spidey sense, is on full alert. It's telling him I'm barely holding in a feral rage—a tiger-footed rage that would love nothing more than to turn and snap, to *bite* those fingers—

He jerks his hand back.

I want to scream. I want to tell him I didn't mean it. Even though I did. Even though he *knows* I did.

And I still kind of want to hurt him. To startle him, push him away, and run, run, run.

But I don't. We both remain there, frozen in our separate thoughts, for what feels like an eternity.

Aaron finds words before I do, but his voice is shaky. "Would you just look at me, Anna? Please?"

Several deep breaths later, I turn to face him, still fuming and determined to tell him to back off. To go home and leave me the hell alone. But the instant I meet his eyes, the hard ball of anger inside me disintegrates. I can almost see it splintering, shattering, crumbling into the sand between us.

Again, I dig my nails into my palms, but this time it's to hold back tears. Crying will only make Aaron feel guilty. I'd have been perfectly okay with that a moment ago, because he might have given me some space if he felt guilty. But my anger is gone now. I just want to *fix* this. Make it right.

Except I don't know how to do that without lying. Telling him the truth—that I have no memory of the past three hours, I did indeed pass out again, and my emotions ricochet from one extreme to another— would lead to questions I can't answer. I don't want everyone, and especially not him, treating me like I'm this breakable thing that must be sheltered.

Or worse, locked away.

I've been in psychiatric hospitals before. I know beyond any shadow of doubt Kelsey wouldn't let that happen if she could prevent it. Not in the current social climate where they run tests for evidence of Delphi "contamination" in the public schools. Not when there are angry hordes who think all Delphi adepts should be eliminated.

But even if Kelsey wouldn't allow me to be sent away, there are kids at Sandalford who are on lockdown. Kids like Caleb, a toddler who has to be kept sedated and secluded because he's—well, I don't really know *what* he is, but everyone who has seen his psychic ability in action agrees he's too dangerous, too volatile, to socialize with others. Too dangerous to even be in the same house with the rest of the adepts.

Magda's own daughters, Clara and Chloe, are shut away next door. Kelsey visits them, but she's the only one, and she won't breach doctor-patient confidentiality by discussing those visits. We haven't been able to tease even the slightest hint out of her about the nature of the Bell sisters' ability.

If Magda is willing to lock her own daughters away, she'd have zero hesitation about forcing me to wear an ankle monitor and confining me to Sandalford. And would it really be all that different from a psychiatric hospital? A luxurious beachfront cage is still a cage.

Fighting another wave of panic, I rub my temples and instantly wish I hadn't because Aaron asks if my head is hurting again. And yes, it *is* hurting again, but not in the way he means. It's more that this constant emotional whiplash is exhausting.

"I'm okay. And . . . I'm sorry I didn't leave a note. I woke up early and thought a run might relax me. You were all asleep. I didn't want to wake you. And let's be honest . . . none of you really *like* to run on the beach."

"That's not true," he begins, but then stops when I arch an eyebrow at him. "Okay. I like *walking* on the beach with you."

"Exactly. Deo's even worse, and we both know Taylor wouldn't run if an army of zombies was hot on her heels. So . . . I didn't want to bother you. I ran the loop twice, walked a bit, then stopped here. I guess I lost track of time."

Aaron sighs. "In the future, if you really need to get away from everybody, at least bring your phone. And maybe Ein? He loves to run on the beach."

I don't argue the point, because it's true. But Ein's not old enough to run more than a mile or two. He weighed over sixty pounds the last time we checked, so it's easy to forget he's still a puppy and has limits.

Aaron starts to say something else, hesitates, then finally blurts out, "Did you faint again?"

I follow his gaze toward the spot in the sand where I was lying when he approached, just a few feet away from a set of tire tracks. An alert driver would have seen me in time to swerve, given that traffic is light this early in the year, but this is the main thoroughfare for Carova Beach. In fact, if I'd been lying in that spot about twenty minutes from now, it's likely that I'd have been an unexpected stop for a tour jeep carrying visitors to more remote sections of the island, in search of wild horses. Two or three of them drive past Sandalford around ten most mornings.

"No," I tell him. "I didn't pass out. That hasn't happened in weeks. I was just . . . resting. Looking out at the water."

He looks unconvinced. As he should. I'm a much better liar than I was four months ago, but I still kind of suck at it.

I reach over and take his hand between mine. To his credit, he doesn't flinch, even though he knows that, only a few minutes ago, I'd happily have bitten a chunk out of it. He can sense that the black rage has passed.

"I'm sorry." And while I feel like I've said the words so many times lately that they've begun to lose all meaning, I repeat them. With emphasis. "I'm really, *really* sorry. Everything is just so . . . scattered . . . since we got back. I'll think I've done something—left a note, or whatever—then find out later that I haven't. Kelsey tells me this sort of thing is common after a head trauma, but . . . it's been *so* long. I was really hoping that the injection Kelsey prescribed would make a difference, but . . ."

For a brief second, the rage surges again. Needles. I hate needles, but I was willing to let Kelsey poke me if there was any chance of getting my head back to normal. But she said it hadn't helped. That there was no point in continuing.

Aaron's face clouds over. It's like he's weighing what to say or do. After a few seconds, he sighs and pulls me closer. "I know it's tough, but we need to be patient. That was a bad concussion, babe. The son of a bitch whacked you twice in the exact same spot."

His voice is soft, but I can tell he's holding something back.

"It wasn't Jasper's fault," I say. "Graham Cregg was controlling him. And . . ."

I trail off, unwilling to finish the sentence. While the blunt-force trauma I suffered last December may have been the main trigger of my psychological problems, the physical and mental effort I'd expended a few days later to reconnect Daniel's spirit with his body didn't help matters. If I mention this, however, Aaron will undoubtedly add it to his list of grievances against his brother. And it couldn't be helped. Couldn't even be postponed. Daniel was only a faint presence in my mind by the time we made it to the hospital.

"Cregg was actually the bastard I meant. And he can't hurt anyone anymore," Aaron adds, thankfully interpreting my hesitance in a different way. "Well, at least *that* Cregg can't hurt anyone."

"One down, one to go. But . . . *all in good time.*" I mimic Magda's mostly British accent. Magda doesn't want us to make any moves against Senator Cregg until her science team tells her whether it's possible to reverse, or at least mitigate, the effects of the serum, both on the first generation of Delphi subjects and their offspring. She thinks having a cure in hand will give us additional bargaining power, and she could be right. But again, it doesn't really matter whether she's right, because Sandalford is not run as a democracy. Magda pays the bills, Magda makes the rules.

"She's probably right about us waiting," Aaron says.

"I'd be more likely to believe that if there was any evidence they've made progress."

None of us has a real sense of how the research is going, aside from the fact that we've all been poked for blood samples—well, all but one. Peyton Hawkins has a serious needle phobia, and given the little girl's telekinetic ability, no one has been willing to push her on this matter. As the resident psychiatrist at Sandalford, Kelsey is nominally part of the science team. She told us that they've made some progress, but I know her well enough to infer from her tone of voice that by *some* she means *very little.* Her role has been confined mostly to observer, however, and occasionally advocate for the well-being of her patients, some of whom don't really have anyone to defend their rights. Kelsey's had plenty of experience in that area. I'm not sure where Deo and I would be today if not for her tenacity.

In Deo's case, he might be better off if he'd never met me or Kelsey. It was probably inevitable that I'd get drawn into all of this insanity. Both of my parents, as I've recently discovered, were part of the Delphi Project. My dad even developed the stupid serum. But Deo? He'd still be in the foster system, but he would never have encountered Graham Cregg, never have been given the Delphi drug. He wouldn't have to avoid physical contact with me and pretty much everyone else at Sandalford, for fear of amplifying their powers. He wouldn't have to get an injection three times a week to keep his brain from swelling. To keep from *dying*.

On the one occasion that I actually got Deo to talk about all of this, he was adamant that he prefers the needles to his old life—and yes, he *does* have a family here, people who love him and accept him for who he is. But I suspect that any objective observer would say he was better off as a ward of the state.

"What's wrong?" Aaron asks.

I don't want to walk him through my convoluted train of thought, so I summarize. "Just . . . thinking that everything is complicated enough without me adding fuel to the flames. I'm sorry."

He smiles and presses a kiss to my temple. "You already said that. Just wake me up next time, okay? If you want to run on your own . . ." He shrugs. "I won't stop you, but at least someone will know where you are. You're going to give Kelsey a heart attack. She was terrified that one of the Senator's people had grabbed you. When I called the house just now to say I'd found you, she already had Taylor trying to pick up your location. But Deo was still out looking for you, and without his boost, Taylor wasn't getting anything but sand, water, and trees."

I'm not surprised. Aaron's sister has an amazing talent for remote viewing, but this is one of the more deserted sections of the island.

Beach to the left and beach to the right. The ocean is all you can see in front, and behind us, the wildlife reserve takes up the entire half-mile distance from the surf to the sound. Sand, water, and trees is pretty much all there is.

"We should go," I say, even though I'd rather get a root canal—without anesthesia—than face everyone right now.

Aaron rises and reaches down to give me a hand up. As I stand, something drops to the ground—a blank white business card. He stoops to retrieve it, and panic rises in my chest again. I don't know why, because I have no earthly idea where the card came from.

He flips it over to reveal a scrawled number. *202-555-1083.*

"Yours?" he asks.

"No," I answer, but I have to fight back the urge to snatch it out of his hand.

"Weird that it's a DC number."

"Not really. Miranda told me most of the tourists who rent these houses are from up there."

"I know," Aaron says. "I just meant it was a weird coincidence, what with me and Taylor leaving for DC this afternoon."

"Leaving?" The question is out before I can stop it, even though I'm certain this is something I should know.

"Yes," he says. "To talk to Daniel about coming down here? Magda agreed before she and Miller left the other day. That was like . . . a full-fledged negotiation. Did you forget that we—"

"No, no. I remembered you were *going.* I'd just forgotten that you were leaving today."

His skeptical look gradually fades. "Oh. Sorry." He folds the card with the phone number and sticks it into his pocket.

"Why are you keeping that?"

He gives me an odd look. "Um . . . because there's no trash can here? What do you want me to do—drop it back on the beach?"

Part of me wants him to do precisely that. But I know that's utterly ridiculous, so I force a laugh. "Guess we can't have you being a litterbug, can we?"

"Nope. That Woodsy Owl coloring book in kindergarten came with a solemn oath to give a hoot and not pollute." He brushes the sand off his jeans and then looks down the beach toward Sandalford. "Do you want to run back? Or maybe you're too tired?"

I snort at the hopeful note in his voice. "Yes, actually, I *am* too tired. I can tell you're *soooo* disappointed."

He grins. "Absolutely crushed."

Aaron and I walk back arm in arm, and the last remnants of the crazy brain fog that has been hovering at the back of my head dissipates. I actually manage to relax and enjoy the gentle rhythm of the waves lapping at the shore and the cry of the seagulls as they swoop and dive. Then I see Magda's house up ahead and Sandalford beyond, and the peaceful feeling withers into a tight ball of dread. Even if I'm good with Aaron, I've still got some major explaining to do with everyone else.

As we pass Bell Isle, I get the sensation we're being watched. No one is in the yard or out on the deck, and I'm about to chalk it up to simply being closer to Sandalford. But then I glance upward and see someone at the window. Two someones, actually—Magda's twin daughters. I can't tell if they're identical from this distance, but they could be. One stands near the middle of the picture window that spans the top floor, overlooking the ocean. Her sister is seated next to her in what appears to be a wheelchair, her head lolled to one side as though she's sleeping.

I nudge Aaron, then take a few steps toward the house.

Aaron's eyebrows go up when he sees the girls at the window. "Wow. When the mama cat's away . . ."

The girl who is awake raises her hand and waves at us. I wave back, and it's as though my movement summons a nurse, who tugs on the girl's arm, then pushes the wheelchair away from the window. One last wiggle of the fingers from the sister who is standing, and the vertical blinds snap shut, obscuring her from view.

For some reason, I'm reminded of a movie that Deo and I watched a few years back, *We Have Always Lived in the Castle*. It wasn't as good as the book, and neither of the sisters were in a wheelchair, so maybe it's just the overall mood it evoked.

"How very . . . gothic," Aaron says. "Two sisters trapped in a castle."

"Exactly." I smile and slip my hand into his. It's almost as though he plucked the idea out of my head. Not in the way that some of the kids here at Sandalford do, but in the more basic way that two people in love sometimes finish each other's sentences.

We walk on in companionable silence until we're almost to the gate of the tall wooden fence that now surrounds Sandalford. "What are we going to tell the guard?" I whisper.

"Nothing," Aaron says. "Maria already took care of it."

And sure enough, the guard opens the gate without comment. This is a new, strictly-by-the-book guy, and yet he doesn't ask where I've been and why I didn't sign out. In fact, he doesn't even meet our eyes. He just looks down at his boots, red-faced.

"O . . . kay," I say once we're out of earshot. "That was bizarre. I wonder what Maria has on him."

"She wouldn't tell me. But she did say you owe her a favor."

If there's anyone the guards like less than me, it's Maria . . . and I can't entirely blame them. She's never even tried to hide the fact that she can read their thoughts, and the scope of her ability is unnerving, to put it mildly. And while she exercises some restraint with her fellow adepts, every day is psychic open season on the guards as far as Maria is concerned. I usually don't have much sympathy for them, especially the ones who call us *freaks* and *mutants* when they think no one is within earshot, but the new guy looked mortified as we walked past. I can't help but wonder what he's so determined to keep secret that he'd risk lying to his boss.

But I guess everyone has secrets they don't want people to know. I'm one of the few in this house who doesn't have to worry about constant surveillance from Maria. Most of the time, I can block her out, but that's only because I've spent years building up mental walls to keep my hitchers and their various memories at bay. The other residents of Sandalford have a much tougher time. Kelsey has been working with Maria and the three younger telepaths—none of whom is anywhere close to as powerful as Maria—trying to make them more respectful of personal boundaries. But they slip up from time to time, and when they do, things can get nasty really quick. No one likes having their privacy violated. Fights broke out at the foster homes where I lived because some kids liked to rummage through everyone else's stuff. It's the same here, except The Peepers, as they're known by the other adepts, are rummaging through everyone else's thoughts, which is an even greater violation.

Fortunately, and sometimes *un*fortunately, all the adepts have their own abilities and they can retaliate. If a Peeper spills a secret that embarrasses one of the pyrokinetic kids—aka Zippos—the little snoop might wake up one morning to find that his or her favorite (or in the case of many of these kids, *only*) pair of sneakers is now a smoldering pile of ashes.

It took a few months, and there were several times where it seemed like the situation was escalating out of control, but the adepts seem to have arrived at a complex but relatively stable balance of power. And the fulcrum of that balance is Maria. Maybe it's because she's one of the older adepts, but I think it's more that she's got something on absolutely everyone. And given her firm conviction that this group is going to have to fight as a team against Cregg's people at some point in the future, she runs a tight ship. If someone isn't acting as a team player, she's willing to use a little psychic blackmail to coax the miscreant into line.

Aaron leads me to the service elevator, rather than the more direct route to the great room.

"Why are we going in the back way?"

"You know this place. Word gets around." He punches the button for the second floor. "There will probably be fifteen, maybe twenty, of the adepts hanging out upstairs to see if you're wearing an ankle bracelet yet. We need to give Maria some time to convince them that would be a bad thing. Anyway, Deo and Kelsey are both waiting."

"I think I'd rather run the gauntlet in the great room. How pissed is Kelsey?"

"Oh, she's pissed." I turn down the hall toward Kelsey's office once we exit the elevator, but Aaron takes my arm and pulls me toward him. He tips my face up so that I have to look him in the eye. "They're both pissed because they were both scared, Anna. And so was I."

His grip isn't tight and he's not hurting me in the slightest. Still, I feel a faint tickle of annoyance again. Some stupid tiny part of me doesn't want to be touched, and my body stiffens.

He releases my arm instantly and steps back. "Sorry. I'll just . . . I'll . . . see you later, okay?"

But I don't want him to go. Okay, yes, that stupid, tiny part of me does, but it's not going to win this time. Before he can leave, I close the distance between us and pull him in for a kiss.

There's no hesitation on his part. We haven't kissed much lately—or done anything else, for that matter—and Aaron's response is immediate. He wraps his arms around my waist, lifting me up so that my face is level with his. I miss this. I miss him. I miss us. And the fact that the disconnect between us is entirely my own fault makes the situation doubly painful.

Two girls round the corner, nearly colliding with us. One of them is Bree Bieler, whose brother was recently one of my hitchers. I can't remember the other girl's name, but she was one of the kids at The Warren. I think she's what Maria calls a Mover . . . in other words, telekinetic.

Bree herself has a smattering of different abilities, including the power to fry pretty much any electrical device simply by touching it. She burned through two PS4 controllers, apparently by accident, before the other adepts realized she hates to lose. Bree doesn't like me much. I'm pretty sure it's because she associates me with her brother's death.

Right now, though, they're just two little girls who have collapsed into giggles because they caught me wrapped around Aaron like a string of Christmas lights. I'm glad that neither of them is a Peeper like Maria, or else they'd have picked up some very R-rated thoughts just now.

Aaron says, "Begging your pardon, young ladies," in a very formal tone, then tops it off with a wink. That sends them into another peal of giggles as they retreat back down the hallway.

"Maybe we should go to our room?" I suggest before remembering it's no longer *our* room. It's now *my* room, and his room is elsewhere . . . and that was apparently my decision. I don't remember making it, and I don't particularly like it, but I haven't worked up the nerve to reverse it. My gut instinct is that it wouldn't be a good idea to reverse it right now. A lot of my memory gaps seem to come in the morning, and it's easier to hide them if I'm in my room and he's in his. I always remember waking up, brushing my teeth and so forth, but then something happens. The next thing I know, it's hours later and I have no idea why I'm on the deck or in the dining room.

He ignores my word choice, though, pressing his lips to mine again. "Mmhmm. Excellent idea. Oh. Wait . . ." My feet are now back on the carpet, and he's looking down at me with narrowed eyes. "Nice try."

"Aaron! That's not what I was doing. I swear." And it's true, although I'll admit that delaying the discussion with Kelsey would have been a nice bonus.

"Good." Aaron plants a last quick kiss on the side of my mouth. "Then we'll pick this up *after* you talk to Kelsey. And Deo." He flashes me a wicked grin, puts both hands on my shoulders, and pivots me around.

"Fine," I say. "Assuming I survive . . ."

He knows I'm joking. I'm not scared of Kelsey. She won't even yell at me. It would be *easier*, actually, if she *did* yell at me. It's the disappointment on her face that I dread.

News Item from the *Washington Post*

April 16, 2020

Sanctuary for Psychics, a nonprofit organization created earlier this year by Jerrianne Cregg, wife of presidential candidate Senator Ron Cregg (UA-PA), is urging
anyone exhibiting psychic symptoms or who knows
someone who exhibits these symptoms to call their
hotline for assistance. "The danger from these vigilan-
te groups is very real," she said. "We can offer aid and
protection. You don't need to do this alone. We still
do not understand the nature of this condition. Some
experts believe that viral transmission is possible, so if
you see something unusual, it's your civic duty to make
a report."

Mrs. Cregg's organization has been awarded a $72
million grant from the Centers for Disease Control and
Prevention to facilitate blood screenings at schools
and local clinics for all students and interested adults.
Several states are now requiring the test be conducted

along with the eye examination when granting a driver's license. Anyone who tests positive can then be tracked. The test is offered free of charge, and results are available within a week. A bill that would make this sort of screening mandatory for all US citizens and persons traveling into the country has recently passed the House of Representatives and is under consideration in the Senate.

Sanctuary for Psychics is also working in conjunction with several other organizations, including Decathlon Services Group (DSG), where Mrs. Cregg has served on the board of directors since 2014. Mrs. Cregg is currently chair of the Health, Environment, and Responsible Social Engagement committee. A DSG subsidiary, Python Diagnostics, holds the patent for an antidepressant drug that has shown promise as a psychic inhibitor.

CHAPTER TWO

Carova, North Carolina
April 23, 2020, 10:26 a.m.

Kelsey answers immediately when I tap on the door. I step inside and glance around the office, postponing the inevitable moment when I have to look her in the eye.

Even though I've been in this room dozens of times since Kelsey arrived at Sandalford, it's still a slight shock to see her behind a different desk, in a different office, instead of her old office in Wheaton. In every rational sense, this place is an upgrade—the old location overlooked a rear parking lot and a dumpster, and often smelled of stale grease wafting up from the restaurant below. This room is twice as big and it has an ocean view. But I miss the familiarity of her other office. I don't know if Kelsey misses it, but that place was one of the few constants for much of my life. Foster homes changed, foster parents changed, schools changed. Kelsey's office was the only place that felt like home, even though I was only there for an hour twice a week.

The most important thing, though, is that Kelsey is here. These past few months have aged her, but the same patient gray eyes watch me from behind rimless glasses. Her hair is the same silver-white, though a little grown out, no doubt due to the lack of nearby salons.

And it's the same blue mug—the one she gave me that first Christmas, the one with my name in white letters—waiting for me on the edge of her desk. A tiny curl of steam rises from the cup, and tears spring to my eyes as I breathe in the aroma. Black coffee, no cream or sugar, just as I requested the very first time I sat in her office chair, back when I was five and my legs were still too short to touch the floor.

It's only a cup of coffee, but it symbolizes more than twelve years of trust that I've been chipping away at over the past few months. I sink into the chair, unable to meet her eyes. Unable to say anything because I don't want to lie to her, but I'm too terrified to tell the truth. Too terrified to admit I don't know what really happened this morning.

"Oh, Anna, you look like you've been sent to the principal's office. I have no intention of scolding you. Did I scold you when you ran from the Becklers' house?"

"No."

"Did I scold you or Deo when the two of you ran from Wheelwright's house?"

"No."

"And why do you think I didn't scold you?"

I'm quiet for a moment, then say, "Because we had a reason for running. Especially that last time."

"Exactly. Scolding you would have been pointless because you were in a situation beyond your control. My concern then—and now—was keeping you out of danger. You explained the problem to me both times, and we worked together to solve it. And that's what I want you to do now. So. Try to explain why you left this morning, just two days after Magda's security team reported suspicious activity around the perimeter."

She's been using her calmest and most level therapist's voice, but worry creeps into the last few words.

"I can't," I tell her. "I can't explain. When I woke up this morning, I just . . . I wanted to run. I didn't think about whether any of Senator Cregg's people or a group of rogue vigilantes might be in the area. All I remember is putting on my shoes and telling the night guard I was going for a run."

"That's the last thing you remember?"

It *is* the last thing I remember, but I shake my head, surprised that I let that slip. "No. I just meant that's the last thing I remember *before* I left. I remember running, then sitting on the beach. Watching the waves until I dozed off. I didn't sleep well last night."

"And sitting there all alone, you didn't think at all about the reasons Magda has guards here? About how she'll want to tag you with one of those horrid trackers if she gets wind of this?"

"No . . . I didn't think about those things. It's off-season, midweek. I didn't even *see* anyone, Kelsey. I was safe."

Kelsey paces for a moment, then sits on the edge of her desk. Her voice is reflective, almost idle, when she asks, "Do you think maybe the boy in Virginia Beach felt the same way? Felt like he was safe?"

My hand tightens around the mug. Last week's murder of Cameron Applebaum, a thirteen-year-old boy with low-level telekinesis, is the fifth killing we've tracked since December. Two of those kids weren't even connected to the Delphi Project, at least not in any way we can identify. Just random kids who had a smidgen of native psychic ability. Or far more likely, they simply didn't fit into the pecking order in their communities or schools, and were singled out for removal. The current hysteria over psychic abilities gave some people a handy excuse for killing a couple of misfits.

Cameron's death came as a double blow because Magda and Kelsey—mostly Kelsey, to be honest—had finally persuaded his mother to let the boy come to Sandalford. Miller, Magda's head of security, had already dispatched a team to fetch Cameron when the boy's uncle called with the news.

The family had been receiving threats for several weeks. That's what eventually pushed them to accept Magda's offer of asylum for the boy. Cameron's mom cautioned him to stay in the house. But he decided to walk over to his best friend's house to say good-bye and, apparently, to retrieve a half dozen or so video games. Those games were found along with his body, crushed by a car on the way home. No witnesses, but just in case anyone was tempted to see this as an unfortunate accident, the perpetrator scrawled the word *freak* across Cameron's forehead with his own blood.

"He was thirteen, Kelsey. I'm an adult."

Her eyes flash, and I'm certain that she's going to say that if I want to be treated as an adult, I need to start acting like one. That's what every single one of the parents among my former hitchers would have said to an eighteen-year-old who was taking stupid risks. It's what most of the foster parents I've dealt with would have said. Part of me *wants* Kelsey to say it, to snap at me out of anger and fear. To treat me like one of her children.

She doesn't say it, though. Honestly, I'm not even sure she would have said something like that to her own two children, now adults with nearly grown kids of their own. More likely she'd do what I'm pretty sure she's about to do now—toss in a few leading questions to help me draw that conclusion on my own.

Normally, I'd play along, but I really don't have the patience for the psychiatric Socratic method today, so I jump in first.

"Yes," I say, "I've been forgetful lately. Things slip my mind. You know that and you know why. This morning, I just needed to get away. I wasn't thinking about Senator Cregg or the recent attacks or anything other than the fact that I needed to get out. Get some fresh air and exercise. I'm sorry everyone was worried. It won't happen again. I told Aaron that I'll wake him up next time, and I will. I promise. Just don't tell Magda. You know it would make me crazy to wear one of those anklets."

Kelsey remains quiet during my plea. Even after I fall silent, she doesn't speak for a moment. She just watches as I sip my coffee. Her elbows are on the desk, hands folded together, chin on her thumbs, and her forefingers steepled below her bottom lip. This is her usual pose when she's trying to think how to proceed. And after twelve years, I don't need any psychic ability at all to know the question lurking behind her expression—*what is it you're not telling me?*

Eventually, she sighs and gives me a weary smile. "Okay. You know I won't mention this to Magda, but don't be surprised if word gets back to her anyway. We have several dozen bored kids in this house. Gossip is a diversion, and there's only so much we can do to keep them in line. Hopefully they'll have forgotten by the time she gets back."

She doesn't add that some of the kids already resent the fact that I—along with Aaron, Taylor, and Deo—have been able to leave Sandalford on a few occasions, most notably back in December when we drove to Upstate New York. Magda had tentatively approved the trip, but we left ahead of schedule. The fifteen kids we rescued from the missile-silo-turned-prison where Cregg was keeping them don't generally seem to have an issue with our off-campus privileges. They know they probably wouldn't be here otherwise. And they'd much rather be here than in The Pit with Cregg's guards. The kids who were brought in from the school at Fort Bragg, however, have been at Sandalford longer. Many of them miss their families, and pretty much all of them have cabin fever. Even if you can see the ocean from the top two floors, you still know that there's now a fence and a guard.

"Thank you, Kelsey. And really, I promise it won't happen again."

Even though I was pretty sure she wouldn't rat me out to Magda, I'm amazed that she capitulated so quickly. I thought we'd spend longer thrashing it out, while she poked at my excuse, searching for holes.

She brushes off my thanks and settles herself in her chair. "We had to cut our last session short because I had that meeting with the science team. But I do have about twenty minutes before my next appointment, so . . . ?"

Ahhhh. That's the catch. We're *not* actually finished. I want to tell her that I'm too busy. That Aaron is waiting. But we both know Aaron has nowhere to be. And we both know that I've been avoiding our sessions whenever possible—something that I've never done in the past.

"Sure," I say, trying to keep my voice light. "But there's not really much that we haven't already talked about, so . . ."

"What about the nightmares?"

"I've had a few. But . . . they're just garden-variety nightmares, not the recurring ones."

As I tell Kelsey this lie, a fleeting image runs through my head. A woman's body is sprawled on a flagstone patio, one knee up and the opposite arm arched over her head near a hedge of white and pink rose-bushes. You might think she was sleeping, except for the growing red pool beneath her face and the hand on her outstretched arm, which is badly broken and bloodied. The fingers jut out in odd directions, and one—the pinky—is missing.

Sometimes, the dream starts earlier, with a sense that I'm falling through the air. I never wake up when I land. It's almost like the impact tosses me out of her body, and I walk toward her in a swirl of emotions. Grief. Guilt about an argument. *I hate you. You suck!* Terrified that she's dead. Terrified that I caused it.

The dream ends there, occasionally. Usually, however, everything around me morphs into a city scene. Downtown DC, I think, but then that's really the only city I know. The woman is still lying on the ground, but she's older now. Different face, different clothes. They're drab and ragged. Dirty. She's huddled in a doorway, sleeping next to a shopping cart full of her belongings.

In the dream, I draw back my foot and kick the woman in the stomach. I can see the shoe as it kicks again and again. It's a pink-and-white sneaker with Velcro straps and little lights. One of the lights is broken, but the others turn on when you walk—or if you kick hard enough.

The old woman pulls away from the second kick and looks up at me, shock and horror in her eyes. That's usually what wakes me up, but sometimes I keep kicking, over and over, and I don't wake up until I feel hands on my shoulders, pulling me away. I don't want them to pull me away, and it's my anger that wakes me.

This last scene has frequented my dreams for years. Kelsey and I have talked about her before. I don't know the old woman's name. I don't even think Myron knew her name. She was just there when he surfaced, a convenient target for his rage.

But the woman on the patio is new. I've never seen her before, and I've no clue why she keeps popping up in my dreams lately—at least a dozen times in the past few months. She must be symbolic. The missing pinky would seem to confirm that, actually, since I associate it with Graham Cregg's victims.

I've had symbolic dreams before, and usually Kelsey helps me sort them out. But some instinct tells me to hide this new version of the dream, even from Kelsey. Maybe even *especially* from Kelsey.

So I shift the topic slightly, hoping she didn't pick up on my lie. "But, like I said last time, I didn't have a single exit dream after Hunter Bieler left. I don't have any of his memories, either. That's odd, don't you think?"

When my hitchers move on to whatever waits beyond, I relive their last moments. I've had "exit dreams" with all of my former hitchers. I don't know if the old saying about having your life flash before your eyes when you die is accurate, but I get a wave of memories, and it's like my brain gets stuck on the last moments. And my ghosts didn't die peacefully. People who die happily in their sleep with no regrets are eager to see what's on the other side. They don't stick around with the living. There's something tethering my hitchers to this realm—something they need to know or something they need to do. And maybe I dream those last moments again and again because it takes rehashing their death multiple times for them to finally accept it as reality.

The one exception to the rule was Hunter Bieler. He was one of the six kids who were killed by Dacia Badea. She abandoned their bodies in a training area near Fort Bragg, presumably to let the military authorities know Senator Cregg wasn't impressed by their failure to keep the offspring of Delphi subjects out of the public eye. Hunter's ghost stuck around because he needed to be sure his twin sister, Bree, was safe. Once he knew that for certain, he simply vanished. No farewell, no dreams, no cabinet full of memories in the back of my head.

"It *is* odd," Kelsey agrees. "But Hunter's departure also coincided with your concussion, so . . . who knows?"

She doesn't look at me, instead she concentrates on lining up a stack of files on her desk. This is the second time I've mentioned Hunter's strange exit and the second time Kelsey has shown very little interest. Normally, she'd be all over this, asking if there were any other anomalies, hoping to make all the puzzle pieces fit. This is definitely *not* her usual pattern, although I guess it could simply be that she now has a number of other patients whose abilities fall outside of the ordinary. She may not have the mental energy to keep track of the psychic minutiae each of us is dealing with.

"You've processed all of the memories from Jaden?" she asks.

"Yes." I'm surprised she asked, since I'm pretty sure we discussed this last time. Processing Jaden's memories was fairly easy. I already knew how he died, so there were no surprises. When I heard the gunshots that day at Fort Bragg, I'd been terrified they'd shot Deo. Instead, when I entered the room, I found Deo frightened but still alive, seated next to three other adepts who were murdered as part of a twisted aptitude test devised for me by Graham Cregg. Jaden Park was one of the spirits Cregg forced me to pick up if I wanted Deo to stay alive.

"And there haven't been any more visions?"

Jaden's gift from the Delphi serum was the ability to see brief, verbatim glimpses of the future, although I think he found them more of a curse than a gift. They occurred at random, and he couldn't change anything he saw. What happened, happened. When Jaden came on board as a hitcher, I began having the visions too. Most of the time they were inconvenient as hell, but I'm not sure we'd have found the other Delphi adepts if not for the clues I got concerning their location in one of those flashes. Even though Jaden has moved on, that ability, like his memories, remains. My visions aren't as frequent, but they still hit like clockwork if I touch Deo.

"The only vision I had was the one I mentioned last session. And it was really mundane. A conversation I had with Deo about Ein needing his nails trimmed."

She nods absently. "And what about Myron?"

Her words suck the air out of my lungs. I sit there, openmouthed, hollow, unable to respond. If I live to be 120, that name will still be the auditory equivalent of a gut punch. And Kelsey knows this.

I picked up the spirit of Myron Wells when I was five. Like most of the hitchers who've taken up residence in my head, I found him at the place where he last felt safe or happy. In Myron's case, that was the back seat of a train on the DC Metro's Orange Line. He'd killed a homeless woman and her son in that seat late one night in 1996. Stabbed them repeatedly while the three other passengers, college students headed back to their dorms after a night of heavy drinking, hid at the other end of the car, terrified. When the train reached Metro Center, they ran screaming. A guard entered the car and shot Myron, who was still standing, knife in hand, smiling down at the carnage.

The gunshot wound wasn't fatal. Myron died three years later in a fight with two other inmates at the Lorton Reformatory. But eventually his spirit made it back to that Metro car, that seat . . . because it was the last place he was truly happy.

Kelsey and I have talked about Myron many times. Most of those conversations took place years ago when I was working to contain and evict his ghost, but we still discuss him on occasion. She knows when I say I'm having "garden-variety nightmares," I'm referring to dreams about Myron.

But any time Kelsey brings up Myron, she approaches the subject gently, tentatively. She asks if I *want* to talk about him. She doesn't just drop his name like a live grenade into the middle of a conversation.

"The Myron memories are behind the wall," I say, struggling to keep my voice level. "Where they *always* are."

Kelsey's eyes are sympathetic when they meet mine, but she pushes ahead. "You said there were cracks in your walls after Jasper hit you. Shattered bricks and . . ." She takes a deep breath and continues, speaking quickly, as if she's worried I'm going to interrupt. "When Myron was active, you had memory gaps. You ran off without telling anyone. You were prone to angry outbursts—"

"Myron. Is. Gone." I slam the mug onto the desk with that last word. Coffee sloshes out, pooling toward her papers. She yanks the files away, and I'm relieved to have a reason to get up so I don't feel her eyes burning into me. I grab a handful of paper towels to sop up the mess, taking my time and breathing deeply so my voice will be calm enough to finish this damned discussion.

Kelsey watches me silently as I shove the soggy towels into the trash. "You never dealt with those memories, Anna. Never unpacked them, never worked through them, so . . ."

"Fine. Yes. There were cracks in the wall around the Myron memories after Jasper hit me. Cracks and a few missing bricks. But the wall was patched the next time I checked. Good as new. And it wouldn't matter anyway, right? *They're just memories!* You're the one who told me a few years back I could tear that wall down anytime I wanted to. That I *should* tear it down. That I might be happier if I worked through those memories instead of repressing them."

"I still think that's true." Kelsey's voice is calmer than mine, but it shakes slightly on the last word. "There were things you weren't equipped to deal with at age six. You're older, and if you did it in a controlled setting, it could be beneficial. But my worry is that you're tapping into those memories in a way that's harmful, as a result of your injury."

"My recent nightmares weren't even about Myron, okay?"

It's only a partial lie. Most of the dreams have starred the mystery woman, and others featured Dacia or Grady, the guy Aaron shot when we were trying to escape from Overhills. The bodies of Hunter Bieler and the other dead children pop in from time to time. But my most frequent nightmare is still a variant of the one I began having when Molly Porter left—one minute it's Cregg holding me captive in the basement, then the face morphs into Myron. And occasionally it mutates into some creepy-looking rat-spider-thing, but that's really not as weird as it sounds. Rats and spiders seriously freak me out. Both creatures have had cameo roles in my bad dreams for as long as I can remember.

"Okay," Kelsey says. "That's what you told me at our last session, but you seemed somewhat evasive about the whole thing, so . . ."

At our last session? What the hell is she talking about? We didn't talk about Myron last time. She hasn't mentioned Myron to me in ages. I'm about to point this out, but then I remember Kelsey is sixty-seven years old. Her mind is usually razor-sharp, but she's laughed a few times about having a senior moment. Maybe she's not entirely joking when she says that?

It would be hypocritical to call her on it, given all of the things I've forgotten in the past few months. So I sidestep. "I'm *not* the only one having nightmares. Normal people tend to have bad dreams when they see horrible things, right? Aaron's had a few. Deo said he and Taylor both had bad dreams about those dead kids for weeks after we left Overhills. Have you called them in here to rehash their childhood traumas?"

"No," Kelsey admits. "But did any of them suffer a head injury? Are they having memory gaps?"

These are clearly rhetorical questions, so I don't answer. We just stare at each other silently for a moment, until she sighs and glances up at the clock.

I'm surprised to see thirty minutes has already passed. Kind of relieved, to be honest, though it felt like ten, maybe fifteen, minutes at most.

Kelsey seems surprised, too. "Oh, wow. My next appointment will be here any second. We need to wrap up. And if you still feel like you need to get out of here, like you need a break . . . let me know, okay? Maybe we could go for a walk on the beach later. Me and you and Deo. Like we did a few months ago. That was a good day."

It *was* a good day, back before the memory gaps really started. Maybe the only good day I can remember since we returned to Sandalford. It was unusually warm for early January, in the upper sixties. Bright and sunny, as though winter needed a day off before diving in to finish the job. We collected shells and chatted about nothing of consequence, which I think Kelsey needed even more than we did. After about an hour, Deo phoned Taylor and told her to grab Aaron, some matches, and a bag of marshmallows. We pulled pieces of driftwood into a circle, built a fire, ate way too many toasted marshmallows, and told silly jokes. Somewhere along the line, the pointy sticks became Harry Potter wands. Deo nearly laughed himself sick when Kelsey flicked her wand, crying *Avada Marshmahllow* in her best imitation of Professor McGonagall, and sent a flaming ball of sugar into the sand. And then we walked back to Sandalford, all agreeing we should really do that more often.

But we haven't. I think it's because Deo mentioned one of the other adepts, in passing, while we were laughing. And just that casual mention of the others brought the party to a halt. It was like that scene in *Mary Poppins* where they're having a tea party on the ceiling. The other adepts are allowed to go outside the fence in groups of no more than two, and then only if Kelsey and two of the security guards tag along. Remembering that the other kids at Sandalford lack even our limited freedoms pulled us back down to reality.

Kelsey now reaches out to touch my arm. "I'm here if you want to talk. I'm on your side. I'm *always* on your side, Anna. You know that, right?"

Her eyes, familiar and safe, fill with tears. That sight knots my stomach with so many conflicting emotions—guilt, frustration, anger, and beneath it all, a horrible smidgen of satisfaction—that I don't trust myself to speak. I simply nod, partly so this can be over, but mostly because I *do* believe Kelsey has my best interests at heart.

It's just that I believed it even more before she mentioned Myron.

News Item from the *Washington Examiner*

April 20, 2020

Two more are confirmed dead in yesterday's explosion in Colorado Springs, bringing the total to four dead and seven injured. The attack is believed to be the work of a splinter group of West Coast separatists known as WOCAN. The building that was targeted housed several military contractors, including the Decathlon Services Group, an organization linked to psychic experiments on members and former members of the US military.

Eight attacks have now been claimed by WOCAN, including one that disabled the Texas electrical grid, which left most of the state without power for nearly a week. Fourteen deaths were attributed to that outage. The group has also taken credit for two car bombs and last week's explosion on a commuter train in Northern Virginia, which killed six people and left dozens hospitalized. In addition, WOCAN claims credit for the murder of six children in North Carolina, destruction of the Tome School in Maryland, and the attack on a regional airport in Upstate New York that took the life of Graham Cregg, son of presidential candidate Senator Ron Cregg (UA-PA), and several of his associates.

Prior to this surge of violent activity, WOCAN—which stands for Washington, Oregon, California, and Nevada—was a loose-knit alliance of center-left political groups advocating economic and political independence for those four West Coast states. They blocked roads leading to several oil fields and briefly occupied one oil field in California. This resulted in a minor constitutional crisis when the president sent in the National Guard to remove the protesters, despite the fact that the governor of California opposed using military force.

Technically speaking, the original WOCAN is now defunct. Its leaders resigned last month and announced there would be no annual convention this year. Benjamin Weber, the former president of the group, claims they had nothing to do with the recent spate of attacks. "I don't know who these people are, but they didn't splinter off from WOCAN. No matter what Senator Cregg and the others claim, we've never seen a psychic supersoldier. We don't have weapons. We haven't killed anyone or engaged in an armed attack against the United States. Aside from those early efforts at the oil fields, pretty much the only thing we accomplished was adopting the WOCAN flag and the grizzly bear as our mascot."

Whether or not the current group originated with Weber and his fellow separatists is now a moot point. Each time the terrorists release video claiming credit for an attack, the footage begins with the WOCAN flag. They hide their faces behind bear masks. And they appear to be amassing an army capable of both traditional and very untraditional warfare.

CHAPTER THREE

I close the door to Kelsey's office and lean against the wall. I'm too wound up to talk to Deo or even Aaron right now. What I really want is to go directly to the beach. Do not pass go, do not sign out at the gate. Just run and clear my head. But that's what got me in trouble in the first place. Maybe I'll walk around on the deck instead.

That plan lasts all of ten seconds. As I approach the south wing, I hear Deo's voice. Talking to Taylor, most likely. They're joined at the hip these days, and I mean that both figuratively *and* literally.

But Deo's not talking to Taylor. He's in the little hallway alcove with Maria and two of the other adepts, Maggie and Stan.

Maggie is one of the little girls Cregg's guards held at gunpoint back in December until they turned the tables on him. She's very popular with the other adepts. But it's definitely not because of her conversation skills—she's painfully shy, and you're lucky if you get more than a single-word answer to any question before her nose goes right back into whatever book she's reading. I think she'd really like to spend more time alone, but you'll usually find her at the center of a group of adepts, often the most volatile ones. Maggie's a blocker, and when she's nearby, they can feel normal, without having to worry they're going to torch the place or whatever. It's probably nice to feel needed, but it can't be easy knowing people mostly seek her out because of her ability.

The guy with Maria is Stan, though Maria—with her little nicknames for everyone—calls him Fiver most of the time, after the rabbit in *Watership Down* who had visions. He's not the only "Fiver" here at Sandalford, but he must be the strongest, because he's definitely the one Maria relies on the most.

Stan, like Maria, is one of the kids Cregg held captive, first in Maryland and later in the missile silo in Upstate New York. He wears thick-rimmed black glasses that make his dark eyes look huge, but the effect is more Spike Lee than Steve Urkel. Some days he uses a cane to walk, although he seems to be pretty steady on his feet today. Stan keeps to himself for the most part, rarely taking meals with the rest of us. I don't think I've ever heard him speak. The few times I've seen him hanging out in the common areas, he's been with Maria, so Taylor's assessment that he has a crush on her could well be true.

Of course, a lot of the guys seem to have a crush on Maria. Taylor thinks it's the liberty of knowing they have no secrets from her. If she's nice to them, it's not because she's fallen for whatever suave act they've put on. She knows the person beneath the persona.

I ignore Maria and her companions and focus on Deo. Yes, I should probably thank Maria for intervening with the guard earlier, but I don't want to get sucked into a conversation with her. If she and her friends are pissed at me, I don't really care. Their opinions don't matter.

Deo's, however, does. We stick together. We don't keep secrets.

Or at least that *used* to be the case. I'm not so sure anymore. He didn't tell me about his relationship with Taylor until Aaron and I caught them in the act. And I haven't been entirely honest with him about these memory lapses. I've tried to be, but I don't want to worry him any more than he already is. And it's hard to be honest when I don't really know what's going on myself.

"Well, speak of devil . . ." Maria says as I round the corner. "We need to talk—"

"No," Deo says, "I was here first. What the hell, Anna?"

His words are a direct echo of what Aaron said on the beach earlier. And his expression is a direct echo of Kelsey's when I left her office. Worried. Hurt.

I can't delay this discussion with Deo, but I don't want to have it in front of anyone else. That's doubly true since my answers will not make Deo happy, any more than they did Aaron and Kelsey. The mere fact that I have to go through the whole process of giving my lame explanation again makes me want to punch something. Not some*one*, and definitely not Deo. Just . . . a wall or a door. Hard enough to hurt, so that I can release some of the pressure building up inside me.

Maria puts her hands on her hips. "Do not be stupid, Anna. Magda won't like if you put hole in wall, and I already cover for you once today. Go to gym and hit the bag if you are feeling punchy."

Conversations with Maria are always one-sided. It's simply quicker for her to pluck it out of your brain than to wait for the words to make it to your mouth. I think part of the reason is that English isn't Maria's first language, and mental conversations may be easier for her than actually speaking, but it's also a power trip. She swears she isn't trying to spy, and you have to be thinking something for her to pick it up, so it's not like she knows every single secret you have. But it's pretty damn close. Her one concession to life here at Sandalford is that she usually speaks to us with actual words, even though she's perfectly capable of shoving her responses to whatever you're thinking directly into your head.

Right now, Maria looks a wee bit smug that she managed to pull a thought from my mind so easily, although she could have picked up at least some of my frustration and anger simply from my expression. She doesn't get as many thoughts from me as from the others here, thanks to the tricks Kelsey taught me to help control my hitchers. I was caught off guard this time, but that's a simple fix. It only takes a few seconds to stack my mental bricks and form a privacy barrier.

Maria responds with a fake pout.

As tempted as I am to stick out my tongue, she did me a big favor earlier. So I take the high road and say in my sweetest voice, "Thank you for covering for me, Maria. I appreciate it. But I really do need to talk to Deo. Could you guys give us a few minutes alone?"

She twists her mouth to one side, considering my request.

"Okay, whatever," she says as she backs down the hallway, motioning for Stan and Maggie to follow. "I can just as easy explain to everyone at once. Meet us in rec room on top floor when you are done. But hurry. You must leave soon."

"Leave . . . to go where?" I ask Deo once they're gone. "Do you have any idea what she's talking about?"

"No. And I'm more interested in you right now. What gives? You had everyone worried."

"I needed a break, D. Some exercise. Some solitude. I *get* that it was stupid. I just . . . it was early and I wasn't thinking. And Aaron and Kelsey have already given me the third degree, so could we skip to the part where I say I'm really, really sorry and it won't happen again?"

"Sure," he says. "We can do that. *If* you tell me what's really going on. Because you might be able to convince Aaron, maybe even Kelsey, that you're into beach marathons that take three or four hours, but no one knows you better than me. Yeah, you like to run, but you rarely last more than half an hour."

"I never said I ran the entire time. Like I told Aaron—"

"You told Aaron you were on a stretch of beach I checked. Twice. There were tire tracks but no sneakers."

"Did it ever occur to you that maybe I ran along the water? That the waves erased my footprints? What exactly are you accusing me of, D?"

"Nothing! I'm just . . ." Deo looks like he wants to say something else, but he holds it back, instead running a hand through his hair. He used to do that a lot when he was a kid, especially when he was frustrated. When he started using hair putty a few years ago, he had to break that habit because his fingers kept getting stuck in his quiff. That's exactly what happens now, and it's his turn to look like he wants to punch something.

"I'm sorry," he says. "But you scared me, okay? And now we're yelling at each other, which I hate, and I can't even give you a hug to apologize without triggering one of your visions."

Neither of us has actually yelled, and this is a truly pathetic sibling squabble compared to the screaming matches Aaron and Taylor engage in on pretty much a daily basis. They don't exactly hug and make up afterward but instead act like it's no big deal. They're the same way with Daniel, and even the older members of the Quinn family. It's taken me a while to figure them out, but I've come to the conclusion they are simply so secure in their affection for each other and in their place within the family that no amount of disagreement can shake them.

But Deo and I come from a very different place. We aren't big fans of conflict, and he's right—it makes my heart ache to argue with him.

I give him a half smile. "So . . . are we at the part where I say I'm really, really sorry and it won't happen again?"

"I guess." He returns my smile, but it fades quickly. Which means he doesn't want to argue, but he doesn't believe he's gotten the full truth. "Just . . . go get Aaron and we'll go see what Maria's all worked up about."

When Aaron and I arrive, there are about a dozen adepts, mostly teens, assembled in the rec room. A few are playing table tennis, but most are seated in folding chairs pulled from the supply closet. Magda hinted a few months ago that she's planning to convert it into additional sleeping space. A bunch of adepts protested that it was the one room large enough for everyone to hang out. Eventually, Magda backed off, although that could be because the flow of new adepts arriving at Sandalford has slowed to a trickle. At this point, those who aren't with us or with Senator Cregg's crew are sufficiently hidden, hoping to ride this thing out until the world returns to normal.

Personally, I'm not holding my breath on that whole return-to-normal idea. Not with seven low-level terror attacks in the US within the past six months, all falsely attributed to WOCAN. The original leftist group's leaders have maintained from the beginning that WOCAN had nothing to do with these attacks, but their innocence is totally irrelevant in the current political environment. Their organization was a convenient scapegoat for Senator Ron Cregg, the presumptive nominee of the Unify America Party, and he's presented enough "evidence" to have them convicted in the court of public opinion.

Video released of each attack depicts a group of young people in bear masks, many of them appearing to wield strange powers—blue streaks of light that could easily be Adobe After Effects coming from their hands, a small pickup that goes flying off an embankment for no apparent reason, and security guards who fall unconscious as soon as the bear-masked brigade comes into view.

A few of the stunts might be real. We know Cregg has at least a dozen Delphi adepts working with him, maybe more. But we're pretty sure most of it is smoke and mirrors. There's no way psychically zapping a handful of power stations could have brought the entire Texas power grid to a screeching halt. That was almost certainly the work of hackers.

People are willing to believe pretty much anything, however, after the Senator's live demonstrations and actual video of Delphi kids in action. It might seem that the notion of psychics who can bring down the nation's infrastructure with a touch of the hand is a far cry from a kid predicting a tornado or propelling a dart through the air using only his mind. But it's that first leap of faith that's the tough one. Once the Senator convinced the public that telekinesis, telepathy, and other psychic abilities are real, convincing them that anyone who possesses those powers is a clear and present danger was a cinch.

In one sense, the Senator has a point. Glancing around the room, I spot several adepts who could quite easily be classified as lethal weapons. But the posts I've seen on the social media pages of anti-psychic groups make it clear they're not all that worried about the telekinetic kids (aka Movers) or even the firestarters (Zippos). They seem confident that those kids could be stopped by a bullet if necessary. No, they're worried about the ones like Maria who can read someone's thoughts if they're within her range, which can extend for around the equivalent of a city block if she's really trying. Or kids like Jeffrey, the guy sitting off by himself at the back of the room who almost everyone calls Snoop Dogg. He can do the same trick as Maria, not with the same ease or the same degree of depth, but from much farther away— he picked up stray thoughts from our crew at a distance of several hundred miles when he was with Graham Cregg. Then there's Daniel Quinn, who can sway someone's mind without them ever realizing it. The people who frequent the anti-psychic groups are terrified they could go to sleep one night as a charter member of Mothers Against Psychic Predators, convinced that psychic abilities are the work of the devil, only to wake the next morning believing psychics are prophets sent straight from God.

I'm firmly on the side of these kids. I'd like to think I would be even if I wasn't one of them. They are in a rotten situation through no fault of their own. Much of the ill will toward them is due to a steady stream of propaganda, and I suspect those screaming the loudest against the Delphi adepts would be doing the same if these were refugee kids who needed food and shelter. There are many, many good people out there, but there's also a solid chunk whose basic philosophy is: I got mine, and screw the rest of you.

Still, I can't deny that the anti-psychic brigade has some reason to be concerned.

I spot Deo and Taylor at the far side of the room, which is as close as Deo dares get to the more volatile kids. The Zippo on the other side of the room might scorch the carpet a bit if he loses control of his temper. Put Deo next to him, and that same burst of anger could set the entire room on fire.

Taylor gives me the side-eye as Aaron and I approach, but she doesn't say anything about my morning adventure. I'm tired of talking about it, so I'm perfectly happy to have her stick to nonverbal means of expressing what a total screwup I am.

Maria is perched on the edge of the pool table, next to a portable whiteboard. She taps her fingernails in a nervous rhythm against the green felt lining of the table and glances frequently at the microwave in the corner, apparently checking the time. Then she leans over and whispers something to Stan, who is standing next to her. One side of his mouth twitches upward in a bashful smile, and his eyes follow her when she turns away.

"See?" Taylor whispers to Deo. "What did I tell you? He's crushing hard on Maria."

Deo chuckles. "Can you imagine how embarrassing that must be? I mean, she has to know every little thing he's thinking. Every time he sneaks a peek at . . . her—"

Maria is staring straight at Deo, clearly annoyed. A blush creeps up his neck, confirming my suspicion that she's sending a few choice thoughts his way. She tugs up on the V-neck tee she's wearing as she sends him one last glare, then her gaze goes back to the doorway.

"What did she say to you?" Taylor asks.

"Uh . . . nothing," Deo says, although his tone is less *nothing* and more *none of your business*.

Taylor rolls her eyes.

"Do either of you know what we're waiting on?" Aaron asks.

"No clue," Taylor says. "Maria just sent out a mental blast telling us to assemble here at eleven thirty. Looks like she contacted the entire varsity squad to me. Pretty much anyone over age ten or eleven."

"Well, it can't be anything to do with the training schedule, then, right?" Deo says. "She's supposed to consult with you about that."

Taylor shrugs. "In theory, but . . ."

She trails off when the side door opens and Ashley Swinton enters. Ashley pauses and scans the room to see who else is here, giving me a brief nod when she catches my eye. I haven't seen her in weeks. Most of her time is spent as caretaker for her nephew, Caleb. At first, Magda put them in the guesthouse out back, but it was soon clear something else would have to be done. Doors would slam at random throughout Sandalford. Curtains would dance around the windows as though they were caught by the breeze, even when the windows were closed. Sometimes the walls and even the windows would seem to ripple.

About a month back when we were walking Ein on the beach, Deo and I saw something that looked like a large waterspout beyond the breakers. Except it was rising up from the water, not hanging down from a cloud. And there wasn't a cloud in the sky. The odd column of water surged maybe five feet above the surface, subsided, then rose again, ever higher as it pulsed outward, like ripples that spread when you toss a coin into the water. Only these ripples were suspended far above the water. Then it ended and the water arced downward, like a circular sheet of rain, into the waves below.

Many of the adepts also reported odd dreams, saying they kept hearing a little kid's voice in their heads. It was getting to the point where some of them couldn't sleep.

Magda had been complaining openly that Sandalford was bleeding cash, draining her financially, and she didn't have enough liquid assets to build a separate house to accommodate Caleb's needs. So her next solution was to house Maggie with Caleb, since her blocking ability makes him easier to manage. Ashley and Maria both told her it wouldn't work, that they'd tried that at The Warren but Maggie hadn't fared well. And sure enough, within a few days, Maggie began to look like the life was being sucked right out of her. Her usually pink cheeks were ghostly, and she had almost no energy. She said it wasn't anything Caleb was doing on purpose. He's a lonely kid and was delighted to have a visitor. Blocking him simply drained her, and since it takes a conscious effort for her to *avoid* blocking, her ability was working at full capacity, nonstop.

That's the most sobering indicator I've seen of Caleb's power. Maggie can be around a dozen or more Delphi adepts in the common areas, most of whom aren't psychic lightweights, and it doesn't seem to tire her out at all. But put her in a room with Caleb for a couple of days, and she comes out looking like death warmed over.

Eventually, Magda purchased the southern half of the uninhabited island in Currituck Sound where we first met Jasper Hawkins and Peyton, and a Quonset hut was set up for Caleb and Ashley. A new guard was hired, and one of the nurses goes over a few times a week to give Ashley a break. And Maggie still visits. It's partly to help Ashley, but I think she also realizes how desperately lonely Caleb is.

Ashley doesn't usually come to Sandalford, however, or if she does, she steers clear of the Quinns. Daniel doesn't blame her for pulling the plug on his life support, and yes, she *was* trying to save her sister. I can't be certain I wouldn't have made the same choice if Deo's life was in danger. But Daniel's little sister isn't exactly the forgiving type. Ashley's probably wise to keep her distance from Taylor.

When Maria spots Ashley, she heaves a dramatic sigh. "Good. You are here. Finally. We are cutting it very close now."

"Sorry," Ashley says. She doesn't seem to have any more idea why we're here than I do. "I had to wait on the nurse to arrive. It's not like I can just pick up and leave the island anytime I want. It's ten miles in the boat, and another five in the truck."

Maria nods at a girl near the back, who locks both sets of double doors and the side door. Then she taps loudly on the floor with the butt of one of the pool cues to get everyone's attention. The kids playing table tennis break off the game and take their seats, all eyes on Maria.

She leans forward, holding the pool cue in one hand like a scepter. "Okay. We must take vote today. I thought there would be more time. But Fiver says everything goes crazy a few hours ago." She gives me a look I can't quite interpret, and then continues. "We need to move fast, and so we must decide now."

One of the kids says, "Decide what?"

"If we . . . if you . . ." She huffs and lets out an annoyed string of Czech words I'm pretty sure are NSFW. "This will take too long. All of you be still and listen."

Everyone in the room jumps slightly, except for me.

She stops and turns toward me, looking injured. "Why do you block me always? You need to hear this. I won't peek at your thoughts. They are so boring anyway."

Reluctantly, I pull down a few of my bricks, and Maria's voice fills my head. Although *voice* isn't exactly right. There are some words in the mix, but it's more like she's sending her thoughts to the entire room in a massive info dump. It reminds me of this show Deo and I used to watch called *Chuck*, where the guy gets terabytes of information loaded into his brain in a matter of seconds. Except the data Chuck received from the Intersect always seemed to be relatively well organized and coherent. This is more of a jumble. The perspective shifts, going in and out of focus. Then I realize she's not just sending us her own original thoughts. She's showing us snippets from other people's thoughts at Sandalford.

We get a flash of a monkey being injected with something by one of Magda's scientists. A snippet of an argument over clinical-trial protocols with human subjects. There's a blurred image of a large white building. The street is cordoned off with construction cones and a low cement wall with *STOP* written in red near the center. A large blue box in the background. The sound of a gunshot. A scream that ends abruptly—so abruptly it feels censored, like that bit was something Maria didn't mean to let slip. Then we're back in the lab with the scientists. A fight breaking out in the monkey cage. A dead monkey. Another argument between the scientists. Frustration . . . back to the drawing board.

When the onslaught of images eventually slows, Maria pauses for a minute and then speaks aloud. "As some of you know, the doctors—scientists—who I show you just now are working on *cure*. Or what they call cure."

She lets that sink in for a moment, and I survey the expressions in the room. About half of them are excited about the prospect, but at least as many seem anxious, maybe even angry.

"Exactly," Maria says. "Is not easy question for everyone. We need to think about what this means. If we want this cure. I decide not to call in little kids—the *junior varsity*, as Taylor says—because someone else will decide for them. But all of you here are old enough to make decision for yourself."

"You didn't call in the other adults, either," Ashley points out. "Why was I invited when they were not?"

"That's a good point," I say. "Kelsey should probably be here."

To be honest, I'd rather not face Kelsey right now, but she'd be on our side. She'd be a voice for the younger kids. She'd want everyone to have a choice.

Maria shrugs. "Your doctor friend meets with the scientists. She works for Magda. One day I think maybe we can trust her, but the next day I think maybe not. She is like . . . the wind. Different directions. But Ashley—you were a helper to The Warren. Some of us would have burned up in that place if you did not help us to escape. You earn my trust, so I think you get a say, even though you have no ability for these scientists to *cure*." Maria grimaces with the last word as though it leaves a bad taste on her tongue. "Plus, you will be deciding for Caleb, and . . ."

She trails off, her face coloring slightly. As hard as it may be to imagine a toddler being part of any sort of resistance, Daniel and Jaden both believed Caleb is the strongest of all the adepts. I'm not sure if everyone in the room follows Maria's implication, but I suspect most of them do. They all know how powerful Caleb is.

Ashley doesn't respond, but her eyes narrow. She knows exactly what Maria is leaving unsaid, and she obviously doesn't like the possibility that Caleb might be pulled into the fight. I have to agree with her on that point. He's practically a baby. He should be watching *Sesame Street* and playing with Duplo blocks instead of being pulled into calculations as a potential weapon.

Taylor steps in with a question. "Okay, I get why you're concerned about this cure. But why are we rushing into action without discussing it first with *the training team*?" She raises her eyebrows on the last phrase, and I suspect even the youngest kids in the room understand that what she really means is why Maria decided to take this step without discussing it with Taylor.

Although, for all I know, the training team consists of just Taylor and Maria. I feel like I *should* know more about this. How much have I missed?

"From what you've just shown us," Taylor continues, "the scientists aren't even close to a cure. I agree this is something all of us need to begin thinking about. Maybe we even need to increase training hours." A few boos meet this comment, but others look pleased at the prospect. "But is it really so urgent we couldn't have discussed it ahead of time?"

Maria shoots a look at Stan. "It *is* urgent. Soon we will be at . . . how you say? Fork on the road? Anna will have vision tonight, and if Magda learns what Anna sees, she will send Miller and his men to get her father, this Scott Pfeifer man, and bring him here. He created this ability, so likely he can fix, no?"

No one seems surprised at the mention of my father, even though it takes me aback for a second. It's not that I was keeping the fact that my father was the brains behind the Delphi Project a secret. I just didn't think it was common knowledge. Now that Maria is at Sandalford, however, it seems like everyone knows everything.

I have no idea whether my father can undo what his Delphi serum created. But Maria's logic is sound. As the scientist behind the formula, he'd probably have a better chance than anyone else of unraveling the effects and figuring out how to mitigate them. Still, it's usually harder to restore order than it is to create chaos. Plus, the man killed my mother fifteen years ago and has been in a mental hospital ever since. I think it's safe to assume his brain is no longer in tip-top shape.

But since I really don't want to talk about any of that in a roomful of people, I focus instead on the first part of her comment. "What makes you think I'm going to have a vision tonight?"

"Fiver tells me."

"Wait," Taylor says. "Stan had a vision about Anna having a vision? It's like we wandered into one of those M. C. Escher paintings."

Stan pushes his glasses up to the bridge of his nose. "Well . . . Maria is oversimplifying things. It was a group effort." He nods toward a girl in the front row, apparently acknowledging her contribution. "The key issue is that it syncs up with minor path splinters I've been sensing for the past few weeks. But something has . . . changed."

He looks over at me. It's only a brief glance, but it almost feels like he's accusing me of something. "The entire picture is out of focus," he says, his eyes once again fixed on the floor. "So I told Maria we need to call a vote now. Because I get the feeling time is running out."

CHAPTER FOUR

Carova, North Carolina
April 23, 2020, 11:48 a.m.

Maria has divided the whiteboard behind her into two columns—*Yes* and *No*. One of the other adepts suggests adding an undecided column. Maria argues against it for a minute, then gives up and adds a narrow strip down the right margin with a big question mark at the top.

"So . . . you vote yes, that means you will take a cure if they find one. That you *want* to lose your ability." Maria tosses her dark curls over one shoulder. "Is not my choice, but I know the gift is more pain for some of you than it is for me. For others, it is *pyrrhovo vítězství* . . . a mixed-up blessing? For me, though . . . I say no. I will *not* let them take part of me."

The fact that Maria views her ability as a gift rather than a curse puzzles me. She isn't a second-generation adept like most of us. I don't know all of the details, but she was one of the kids that Cregg's company, Decathlon Services Group, "rescued" from an orphanage in the Czech Republic. Maria is nearly sixteen, which means she was brought over with the first group of girls—the same group as Dacia Badea—when she was around ten. So for most of her life, Maria wasn't fully psychic. Clearly she had some nascent ability, or she wouldn't have passed the tests that originally placed her in the Delphi program, but getting occasional psychic flashes isn't really the same as having everyone's thoughts laid out before you like an all-you-can-eat buffet.

I've spent far more time than I'd like with multiple voices in my head, and it seems to me that having so many people's thoughts buzzing around would be a distraction for Maria. But then her gift is more like Taylor's—she can shut it off at will, although she's said it's much harder to do when she's around Deo, given his ability to amplify psychic signals. Maria actually bounced one of the other adepts from a room in the north wing so she could sleep as far away from Deo as possible.

Still, Maria can remember a life without her ability, a life when the only thoughts in her head were her own. I can't. Neither can Aaron or Taylor or the vast majority of kids at Sandalford. As second-generation adepts, this is just how we're wired. We inherited the ability from our parents along with our eye color and a host of other attributes. A cure might be fairly straightforward for first-gen adepts, but what kind of side effects would it have for those of us who were *born* this way? If it simply ended my propensity to pick up stray ghosts, I might be tempted. But that's not the only aspect of my gift. I currently house the memories of at least ten hitchers. Some of those hitchers shaped who I am today—Emily, Molly, Jaden, and yes, even Bruno. Would those memories remain, or would I have massive holes in what I know and remember? Would I be able to function? Would I be *me*?

Maria draws one hash mark in the *No* column. "This is my vote. But listen to me. Those who put their mark with mine in this column—you do not just say no to taking cure. If you vote no, it means you will fight if they try to force this change on us."

One of the older kids shakes his head. "Why do you assume anyone will force us to take a cure? No one forced me to come here. My father just felt I'd be safer, given the current . . . mood . . . of some of our neighbors. Were any of you actually forced to come to Sandalford?"

A few of the kids say no, but I can tell from their expressions that most of them aren't sure how to answer the question. The kids who were housed at the special school on Fort Bragg weren't given a choice between returning home and coming here. They were drugged, then scooped up by Vigilance Security, the group Magda hired, and moved to Sandalford while they slept. I spent a few days in the Fayetteville area, and this gorgeous beach is a definite upgrade, but they didn't exactly come here voluntarily.

Many of the other kids, like those who were held by Cregg, don't have family. Or at least not family in this country, because they were trafficked in from Eastern Europe. It's not as though they have a lot of options. Like Maria, they've spent most of their lives here, with this group of people. The Warren is their family.

I expect Maria to answer the boy's question. But Aaron beats her to it. "Those of us who are adults may get a choice, but I can easily imagine Magda justifying the use of force on minors by saying it's for their own good. I doubt the authorities on Fort Bragg gave up all control when they transferred those of you who came from that school, so the decision would likely be theirs, not yours. Same goes for those of you with parents or guardians."

The kid who asked the original question says, "We have rights, though. Even if we're not adults, they'd have to give us some say if we fought it in court. My cousin was fourteen when her parents divorced. She said she wanted to live with her dad, even though her mom wanted custody. And the judge said okay."

"Maybe," Aaron says, "but your cousin didn't pose a threat to society, as they claim—with some justification—all of *us* do. So again, I think some of us might get a choice, but if they come up with a cure, I'm pretty sure the people in charge will view it as something unpleasant but necessary, like vaccinations. And I'm certain the military scientists

Magda is working with would enforce that for the sake of the good ole USA."

"Military?" I ask him in a hushed voice.

Aaron gives me a puzzled look. "Yes. You *know* that."

I don't remember any discussion about the scientists being in the military. I was under the impression this was a team Magda brought with her when she came here from London. That's apparently yet another thing I've missed during these stupid gaps. But Maria is talking again, so I make a mental note to ask Aaron about it later.

"They *will* force us," Maria says, surveying the faces in front of her. "Fiver believes this from his visions, but even if he saw nothing at all, I know they will force us. I know because I see this before. Most of you never hear how I came to be here. How I came to be orphan who was happy to get on the boat to America, happy to take these tests and play the psychic games for Graham Cregg and his Fudds."

There are a few confused looks, but most of the adepts get the reference. The adepts called themselves *wabbits* because they were stuck underground and basically treated like lab experiments. The guards were the *Fudds*, in reference to Elmer Fudd, the intrepid wabbit hunter who was always foiled by Bugs Bunny. I suspect the Fudd nickname originated with the tan uniforms they wore, and the fact that even though the guards talked tough, they usually weren't allowed to kill the wabbits. Most of the adepts were reasonably happy at The Warren until that last part began to change.

"I come to The Warren from Česko," Maria says. "The Czech Republic. But my people are the Roma. You know them maybe as gypsies. In Europe, the Roma people are thought to be bad. The Czech government force many Roma women to be sterile. Good jobs never go to Roma people. The floods happen when I was little girl, and many Roma people lose their homes and shops . . . sometimes to the flood, but more times to other people—the *gadjos*, the not-Roma—because the flood takes *their* house, *their* shop, and now they want ours. When the men come to put us onto street, they say we stole our house. That all Roma steal, that we're all just no-good *cikáni*. Before the flood, these are same men who buy food at my family restaurant. They act like friends. But when my father stand up to them, try to speak reason with them, to defend his family, they shoot him. They shoot my mother and older brother. They would shoot me too, but I am hiding under bed, quiet like mouse."

Maria's eyes grow distant for a moment, then she says, "That is how it always is. If there is problem, they blame the ones who are different. Like us. And if we say *no*, if we say *you cannot treat us like animal*, they kill us. If they can. If we let them. So this is why I vote no. And this is why I do not like having *maybe* as an option for our vote. All of you maybe people will have to make decision *very soon*."

I feel a strange shiver at her emphasis on the last two words. I know Stan had another vision, or maybe several of them, when they were being held in the silo. Maria knew all about Sandalford because Stan had seen the adepts here in one of these visions. She told me he'd seen all of us "fighting the bears" here.

A surreal image of bears lumbering down the beach flashes into my head. I doubt Dacia's people would actually wear their bear masks. And I'm certain they won't casually stroll over the sand dunes. They'll be in jeeps or Hummers. Those who aren't weapons themselves will definitely be carrying them.

Magda's security force has weapons, too. Currently they are on our side, but Magda pays their salary and she is also funding the search for a cure. I can imagine several scenarios where this group of adepts ends up fighting not just Cregg's people but Magda's as well.

Graham Cregg believed this, too. Just before Jasper shot him, Cregg warned me that Magda would turn on us if and when our interests diverged. That she would side with his father. He called her a *wolf in sheep's array*, another of his pretentious Shakespearean phrases. Normally, I'd discount anything he had to say, but on this issue, I'm inclined to believe him. As vicious and vile as Cregg was, he didn't want the adepts killed if it could be avoided, especially the young ones. And while I don't think Magda is necessarily a bad person, her main concern is finding a cure for her daughters. I have no doubt whatsoever she'd sell everyone else out if that's what it takes to accomplish her goal.

Maria is calling for the vote, but Deo holds up his hand. She sighs, and motions for him to speak.

"Two things," he says. "First, we don't even know if there's gonna be a cure, right?"

A brief shadow of . . . something . . . crosses Maria's face. I'm pretty sure she knows more than she's letting on, but she nods and Deo continues.

"Second, you left out one of the options. The most important one, actually."

Maria frowns and taps the board. "Yes. No. Maybe. What else can there be?"

"My point is, you're making it a false . . . dichotomy? At least I think that's what they call it. You're dividing us into those who will fight to avoid taking this cure that might never happen and those who will take it *without* fighting. I don't know about the rest of you, but neither of those options accurately describes me. I don't want this ability in my head, and I don't like getting shot up with medicines constantly to keep it from killing me. So, yeah . . . they offer me a cure, I'll be first in line. But people I care about might make a different choice." He glances first at me and then at Taylor. "And I would absolutely fight to keep them—to keep any of us—from being forced to take something against our will. I'm guessing a lot of you feel the same way."

There's a low murmur of consensus in the room. And while it would be easy to dismiss them as children who have no idea what they're agreeing to, these aren't exactly typical kids. Most are from military families, so they have a better understanding than many people their age of what a battle might entail. More importantly, however, they've forged friendships in the foxholes. A few of them were together at the "special school" the military set up at Fort Bragg to deal with the wave of Delphi offspring. They claim they weren't mistreated, but when they showed up here, they were all tagged with ankle bracelets, most of them a year or more behind on their academic work. They don't have fond memories of the place itself, but they're a fairly tight-knit bunch.

An even larger group was held captive by Graham Cregg, first at The Warren and later at the silo. Again, they were generally not mistreated, and some were even relieved to be somewhere their abilities didn't make them stand out as freaks. But they all felt the pressure to cooperate, to hone their abilities and show they could be useful. Older adepts who were *not* useful had a way of disappearing once they reached adulthood. The guards at The Warren told the other kids they'd been "relocated," and maybe some of them believed that. But several of these kids were reading minds before they could read Dr. Seuss. They saw straight through the euphemism and word spread through the psychic grapevine.

I don't know the kids who were at the military-run school very well, so I'm only working on conjecture there. But I have Jaden's memories of The Warren. There was a strong sense of esprit de corps, of us-against-them, along with a good deal of gallows humor. And the group from The Warren has been in battle already. I'm fuzzy on the details, since I was locked in a mental struggle with Graham Cregg at the time, but I do know Cregg would most likely still be alive and we wouldn't have escaped that airfield relatively unscathed if not for the quick action—and teamwork—of several other adepts when we fought Cregg's guards at the airfield in New York. Two of them turned Cregg's own helicopter into a weapon against him.

A stocky boy with blond hair nods toward Deo. "I agree with him. And I'd fight to get the others back, too. If they're really still alive."

Maria rubs her forehead wearily. "Your brother is alive. I tell you this before."

"So . . . we don't need to vote on anything," the boy says. "You claimed we were coming here to fight. That's the only reason I agreed to wait, instead of cutting out on my own to find Nate after we left the silo."

"We *will* fight when it's time," Maria says. "Today, we vote. We vote on whether we fight. On whether Anna tells Magda about this vision she will have."

"Wait," I say. "You're muddying the waters here. I thought the vote was whether or not to take the—"

"Is no mud in the water! This is same thing. If cure comes too soon, and if they force . . ." Maria glances again at Stan, who doesn't speak but just nods solemnly. "*When* they force some of you. Your Deo, he says he will be first in line for cure, but still fight. With what will he fight? That sock full of pennies in his bag? Or the *pepřový* spray? All of us, even if we grab gun, our best weapon is here." She jabs a finger against the side of her head. "They give us this weapon, but *we* decide how to use. So the vote on telling Magda . . . is really same thing. Stan says if your father comes here, if they do this cure too soon, we will lose."

"Then we don't have to decide today whether we'll take a cure. Everyone can decide later, if and when it becomes an issue. The only question right now is whether I wait to tell Magda about this vision I'm apparently going to have about my . . . father. Whether we delay the possibility of a cure so we'll be stronger for this fight you say is coming. But truthfully, given what you've said, I don't see why we need to vote. I don't want to tell her."

"We vote. The Warren *always* votes. Not always in person like this, but we vote. We voted on whether to try and escape on our own or wait for you guys to finally arrive and help us. And we vote now."

So we vote.

The Warren's commitment to the democratic process apparently doesn't extend to secret ballots. It also seems that their system is questionable on the issue of individual rights. What if the group decides I *should* tell Magda? That I *should* bring my father back here, even though I really don't want to? Do I have the right to say nope, sorry, not gonna do it?

I guess we'll cross that bridge if and when we come to it.

Maria has made it halfway around the room, with the result unanimous at seven to zero, when the double doors on the far side of the room fly open with enough force to shake the wall behind my chair. Judging from the noise, I'm pretty sure the lock is broken as well. One of the girls who interrupted me and Aaron in the hallway earlier stands in the doorway, along with Bree Bieler and most of the other younger adepts. Peyton is missing, along with a boy who's preschool age, and maybe one more, but otherwise it looks like everyone Maria excluded is accounted for.

"No," Maria says firmly. "Meeting is not for you, Kara. I will explain all to you later."

Kara shares a knowing look with Bree. She gives impressive side-eye for a kid still in elementary school.

"You're talking about whether we will fight. And you *need* us," Kara says with a defiant toss of her head. "That helicopter didn't spin around by itself, you know. Just because you're bigger and older doesn't mean you're the strongest."

Deo snickers softly. "Judge me by my size, do you?"

Maria, who seems flummoxed by the younger adepts' presence, turns to Stan. He just shrugs philosophically, which leaves me wondering exactly how much information he has about this confrontation they seem to believe is on the horizon. Jaden's visions only give me one snippet at a time. Stan's ability must work differently.

"You *need* us," Kara repeats, then looks over her shoulder to the back row of chairs. "And if Snoop gets a vote, so do we."

With that, she drops to the floor and folds her legs, crisscross applesauce. The rest of her crew follows suit, and we now have a pint-sized sit-in on our hands.

Judging from the shared glances between a few of the older kids, some of them are swayed by her argument—although I think many of them would like to exclude both the Lollipop Guild and Snoop.

In one sense, I agree. He combed through my brain—also Aaron's, Taylor's, and Deo's—and passed along bits of information to Graham Cregg.

But he was under Cregg's control, and the key phrase there is *bits of information*. There was a lot of information we know that he held back from Cregg, and that's no easy task. I watched as Cregg forced Deo to turn a gun to his own head. When I processed Molly's exit dreams, I *felt* him force her to snip off her own pinky finger with garden shears. The fact that Snoop was able to withhold anything if he was under Cregg's control is pretty remarkable, and if he hadn't fought as hard as he did, we might not have managed to rescue the others.

And to the best of my knowledge, Snoop hasn't been using his ability since he arrived at Sandalford—at least not on us. There's a telltale sign when he's scanning for information, a sort of feathery brush across your forehead. I haven't felt it, and I don't think any of the others have, either.

He doesn't need any kind of psychic ability to know what most of the kids think of him, though. I'm not entirely innocent in this regard—I'll admit I've gone out of my way to avoid him the few times I've seen him walking down the hall or talking with Deo out on the deck. Many of the adepts don't even bother to hide their animosity. So he keeps to himself a lot.

"Cregg tested all of us," Snoop says. "He made all of us do things we didn't want to . . . well, except maybe Maggie, since she could block him. Kinda wish you could teach me that trick, Mags."

Snoop's voice always reminds me of SpongeBob. But the effect is more eerie than comical, because it never fails to take me back to the airport. Snoop sitting on the ground, rocking back and forth, after telling Cregg that Bree and I were hiding in the shadows.

"Volunteer, then, Snoop." It's one of the older kids. "They were always looking for volunteers back at The Warren. That's how half the older wabbits died. I'm sure Magda's scientists are looking for—"

He breaks off in midsentence. Maria is staring straight at him. Wonder what she has on him to make his face turn so red.

"All I meant is that no one peeked into that man's head if they could avoid it," Snoop says. "He kept me out most of the time, but I got a few glimpses. The other Peepers can back me up on this. One minute he's thinking about lab results or some political fund-raiser or having cancer. The next it's all severed fingers, remembering his dead mom, and thinking about suicide."

Snoop pauses at this point, glancing over his shoulder directly at me. I don't know why. If he picked up my earlier thought about what happened at the airport, I would have felt the spiderweb sensation across my forehead. But I didn't.

"Suicidal thoughts can be really contagious," Snoop continues. "Took me a couple days to shake it off both times."

His tone angers me—or maybe it's the words. I can't really pinpoint why, but I want to hurl something at his head. To make him stop talking about dead mothers and suicide, because he was taken in and treated kindly and yes, it really is sharper than a serpent's tooth to have a thankless child . . .

What?

I shake my head to clear it, unsure where all that came from. My lousy night's sleep is beginning to catch up with me. Or maybe I need to fortify my walls. There are at least three adepts in this room who can broadcast their thoughts, including Maria.

I don't think it was Maria sending out that thought, however, because she's too busy arguing with Kara to look my way. And she's defending Snoop.

Deo chimes in, too. "Yeah. Not cool. If you're going to say Jeffrey shouldn't vote because he was once controlled by Graham Cregg, then I guess I shouldn't vote either." He nods toward Bree Bieler. "How about you, Bree? Anna has a tooth-shaped scar on the inside of her wrist from when Cregg took control of you, so . . ."

Bree looks hurt, and I'm not sure it's entirely fair of Deo to blame her. The kid just turned seven last week. But I guess that's kind of Deo's point. If we start blaming everyone Cregg coerced at one point or another, that's going to seriously winnow down the population with voting rights.

"Fine," Maria says, throwing up her hands. "You all can vote on if we delay the cure so we can fight. But even if your power is big, you are still little kids. Too young to make decisions on *how* we fight. You are not *velitel*, not generals. You are . . ." She pauses, trying to find the word.

"Pawns?" someone near the front suggests, and laughs when the girl seated on his right whacks him on the arm. "Okay, okay. I meant privates."

Maria frowns. At first, I think it's disapproval of the kids goofing off, but maybe it's just concentration because, after a moment, her brow smooths out. "Privates are soldiers. Yes, this is right word." She says it so confidently that I'm certain she plucked the definition right out of someone's head. "You are soldiers. Privates. You will follow orders or you will not fight."

She exchanges another look with Stan, and I'm certain she's about to add something else. But she bites back whatever she's thinking and picks up the marker again to continue tallying the vote.

When it's over, the decision is nearly unanimous in favor of delaying the cure, fighting, and me not telling Magda, or whatever the hell it was we were voting on. Not a single no vote, but we do have one abstention—Ashley. Maria doesn't comment on the result, just gives a quick nod to Stan.

Which is kind of weird. Did Stan already know how Ashley would vote? And if so, why call her here in the first place? The Sandalford grapevine is truly impressive, but it doesn't extend to the outpost on Long Point Island. Ashley would never have known we even held a meeting.

Having done their democratic duty, the adepts begin heading for the door, but Maria calls out, "Do not forget to log practice hours. If you meet objective, then try for stretch goals, yes?"

Practice hours? Stretch goals? I seem to be the only one who doesn't follow her meaning, however, because most of the others are nodding.

And with that, Maria adjourns the meeting. Ashley heads for the exit as well, but Taylor calls out for her to wait. "You're not just going to let her walk out of here, are you, Maria?"

I'm with Taylor on this one. We've seen firsthand the lengths to which Ashley will go to keep her sister and Caleb safe. Ashley was willing to pull the plug on Daniel's life support. Magda will be back tomorrow or the next day. What's to stop Ashley from simply telling her about our decision?

"I need to get back to the island," Ashley says. "I won't tell Magda or Kelsey about this meeting, if that's what's worrying you. But I'm not committing Caleb to any sort of battle. If there's even the slightest chance this Scott Pfeifer guy can help fix what's been done to these kids, I think you should bring him here immediately. Surely if there is a cure available, this battle Stan says he's foreseen won't happen. Right? I mean, I don't trust Senator Cregg at all. Not after the way he manipulated me into hurting your brother."

"Well, that's a fun little euphemism," Taylor says. "You killed him. And you don't get off the hook just because he's better now."

Ashley ignores Taylor's outburst. "My point is that once there is a cure, Cregg won't have any reason to persecute the adepts further. The public will calm down. Things can go back to normal again."

"That's really naive," Aaron says. "We're in the middle of an election year. What makes you think the Senator wants a return to normal? He's gone from being an extreme long shot to an actual contender in the past few months, something no third-party candidate has done in decades. He gets tons of free press for both himself and Unify America thanks to the panic over the Delphi program. He's also done a decent job of obscuring from the public how deeply his companies were involved in creating the very problem that caused the panic in the first place. People were killed in order to maintain that cover. He won't balk at killing more."

"We're talking about children, for God's sake!" Ashley stops and holds her hands up. I'm pretty sure she's remembered quite a few of the deaths that can be traced back to Senator Cregg were, in fact, children. "Fine. It doesn't matter. My point is still the same. Caleb is not going to be a private in your little war. The one and only concern for me is getting a cure for him—the sooner, the better."

"Do you really think it will be like flipping a switch?" I say as she retreats toward the door. "One second Caleb is a psychic anomaly in a toddler's body, and the next he's an average three-year-old, happily building LEGO castles?"

Ashley turns and glares at me. "Listen, my sister is still missing. I'm pretty damn sure she's dead, and that means Caleb is my responsibility. Right now, we're living on a freakin' island, in a tiny hut, with a portable toilet and electric generator. His only hope for a normal life—and mine, for that matter—is if they find a way to reverse this. And that's true for every single person who's been affected by the serum."

And on that note, she storms out, slamming the door behind her.

"Do not worry," Maria says. "Ashley was telling truth about keeping quiet. I peeked to be sure. And we have to let her go even if she wasn't. What else should we do? Lock her in closet for next few weeks?"

Stan clears his throat and Maria colors slightly. Another slip. Something else they didn't intend to tell us. The cloak-and-dagger secrecy between these two is beginning to grate.

Aaron also looks annoyed. "So after Anna has this vision, we just keep quiet, go about our business as usual? No trying to locate Anna's father or—"

"Oh, no," Stan says. "You still need to find him. As quickly as possible."

"And Deo must go, too," Maria says with a note of regret. "But I need him back *repede*. Pronto. Wabbits can still train while he is away, but our strategy is kaput without our amp."

"But . . ." I shake my head, totally confused. "Why? We just decided to wait on a cure, and for me not to tell Magda. I don't see the point."

"You still need to *find* Pfeifer," Stan repeats. "You just can't bring him back here. At least not until the other paths close."

I stare at him incredulously. "What other paths? This isn't making any sense!"

Stan exhales and turns to Maria. "Show them. It's easier."

Then Maria is in my head again, pushing that same scene. The image keeps flipping, flickering, like one of the old movie projectors my hitcher Emily used when she was a teacher. White office building, maybe ten stories high, with tall recessed windows. Construction cones and a barrier emblazoned with the word *STOP* block off the street.

This time, however, Maria doesn't pull back, and things get even stranger. I kind of hear the gunshot again and the scream. At the same time, I also kind of hear the sound of a horn and the squeal of brakes. It's not that I hear all of these things, one on top of each other. It's more that I hear (and also don't hear) the gunshot and the scream. And I hear (but also don't hear) the horn and the tires screeching on the pavement. Two different, mutually exclusive realities.

In addition, the video feed, if you can call it that, is split into different layers. Two men in dark suits—one of them vaguely familiar—push a third man toward shelter, but then the group splits into two separate sets of three men. Set number one pushes the man in the center toward a blue shed between the building and a parking lot across the street. My first thought is that it's a phone booth or the TARDIS. But since neither of those things currently exist in downtown DC, it must be a porta-potty. Set number two dives behind a concrete barrier, which is barely knee high. But before they can reach it, another shot rings out, and the man they're escorting crumples to the ground.

And that's not the only detail that seems to be changing. The building and scenery remain constant, but people and vehicles appear to jerk in and out of focus, or split off and go in two or more directions at once. A large, boxy shadow seems to be there but not there as well.

It's a mind-boggling effect. It makes me queasy.

"Why is everything all . . . wonky?" Deo says. "Things . . . no, it's more the people . . . are there, and then they're not. Or they've moved."

Stan nods. "What you're seeing are different paths sort of layered on top of each other. Have you seen the computer projection models they use to track hurricanes? The ones most likely to happen cluster in the same area, but then you have outliers going off in many directions."

I look at the others, and their expressions are as clueless as my own. Just as I'm about to ask Stan what hurricane predictions have to do with this, he speaks again.

"That's how my visions work. I see paths. At the beginning, they're blurred. Many different layers, many different outcomes. But the closer we get to an event, the more those paths merge. And right now, they're merging into three different groups, like bundles of wires. In one, a gunman shoots Anna's father. In another, she saves him from getting shot. And in the final group, he ends up with the Senator's people out in Nevada. But by that time, he's . . . not really Scott Pfeifer anymore."

SHARED JOURNAL

3/16/20

Dr. Kelsey:
Per our discussion yesterday, jot down all odd behaviors you've observed when interacting with Anna.

3/16/20

Taylor:
If I take those instructions literally and jot down *all* odd behaviors, this will be longer than the entire Game of Thrones series, including that one he's still writing. So I'll give some highlights and patterns I've noticed.

Most of the weird behavior happens in the morning. She's slipped by the guards twice in the early morning hours, and tried to get past on several other occasions. I'm usually up early, and I've caught her texting several times out on the deck.

She talks different most mornings, too. Has anyone else noticed that? Three times she broke into one of those Shakespeare quotes. Not the iambic pentameter stuff but just little comments I look up later, and sure enough it's another quote from Old Will himself. "There is no darkness but ignorance" is one she said while we were watching the news one morning. And this one time when we're all looking on as two of the younger kids—I think it was Kara and Bree—were engaged in an angry pushing match out on the volleyball court, Anna says, "Though she be but little, she is fierce."

Yes, one of Anna's former hitchers, that Emily woman, probably knew those quotes. But here's the thing. We all remember getting the Shakespeare text messages from Cregg last year. Anna knows how much it creeped me out. I didn't go around with tinfoil on my head because I liked the look. Those messages creeped *all* of us out, Anna included. So why would she toss out quotes like that? Anna gets on my nerves sometimes, especially when she's keeping secrets (of course, when *isn't* Anna keeping secrets?) but she doesn't go out of her way to be cruel.

And there was that one morning in mid-January when I got a close enough look at her phone to see her deleting a text conversation from her iCloud. I'm guessing you don't need a reminder of that occasion, since it's probably logged under a separate file called *Major Freak-Outs* rather than *Odd Behaviors*. I swear to God I didn't mean to set her off. I didn't even say anything about it. All I did was glance . . . I don't know, *quizzically*? . . . at the phone. Because anyone she might be texting, as far as I know, is right here at Sandalford. Anyway, next thing I know, she's threatening to do a swan dive off the deck and you're sedating her.

But you want to know the biggest tip-off, at least for me? She takes sugar in her coffee now. Not just a smidgen, but three heaping teaspoons. Mostly in the mornings, although it seems to me it's happened a few times in the afternoon lately. Any other time, she drinks her coffee black, like she always has. She still kind of wrinkles her nose in that slightly superior way when I dump sugar into mine, totally oblivious to the fact she did the same thing that morning.

So, no. You aren't going to convince me this is about some unprocessed memories. I don't know what this Myron guy did to her, but I know to my very core this isn't about him. Anna picked up Cregg in that airport hangar. He's in her head, and he's getting stronger. If the antipsychotic drug Kelsey suggested might help in any way to keep Anna in control, why not at least try it?

I don't get why all of you keep avoiding reality. Unless maybe Anna is using Cregg's ability on the rest of you, too? I'm telling you, we need to stop being alone with her, especially in the early mornings and especially when she's sitting still. When you do talk to her, keep her moving. Everyone I've talked to says Cregg can't focus unless he's still. And for God's sake, stick to the buddy system when you're around her.

CHAPTER FIVE

Southern Shores, North Carolina
April 23, 2020, 4:17 p.m.

I wipe off the thin layer of dust that accumulated on the kitchen counter in our absence, then stash the roll of paper towels back in the pantry. This storage unit was supposed to be climate controlled, but it's too hot and stuffy here in the RV for me to believe that. I'm pretty sure the AC was turned on a few seconds after we keyed our password into the security pad at the front gate.

All in all, I'd rather not be here. After we left the meeting with Maria and the other adepts, I went straight to Kelsey, hoping she would nix the idea of me leaving Sandalford. I'm not well enough to travel. As much as I hate admitting that, I know it's true. This is something that should be left to Magda's people or the police . . . okay, no, maybe not. Magda's security would bring Pfeifer straight here, and we can't involve the police.

But it should be the others without me. Aaron and Sam are detectives. What do I bring to the equation that's worth the risk of me going with them? Not a damn thing. Just because Stan *thinks* I'm somehow at the center of what's going down with my father doesn't mean he's right.

As I marched down the hallway to Kelsey's office, I had no doubt where she would stand on the issue. She probably wouldn't want any of us to go, but definitely not me or Deo. After all, we're walking into danger, and that's something Kelsey tends to oppose on general principle. Assuming Stan's vision pans out, there could be gunfire outside that building. And while Scott Pfeifer *is* my father, he shot my mom. As awful as it sounds, I'm not willing to risk our lives to save him from what feels like poetic justice.

But something went wrong before I even reached Kelsey's door. My head began to pound. The next thing I remember with crystal clarity is being in the back seat of the truck, squeezed in next to Taylor and Deo as we headed south toward Kitty Hawk where the RV is stored.

There was an argument in Kelsey's office. Even if I can't remember it, I know something is wrong simply from the way Aaron and the others keep looking at me. I don't know how much Aaron told Kelsey about what we're doing. Hell, I don't even know how much *I* told Kelsey, and I can't exactly ask without letting on that I've lost time again.

My head still hurts. But now it's more from the tension of worrying I'm going to say the wrong thing and give away the fact that I've acquired another gap in my memory. That makes two in one day, which may be a personal best. Or worst, I guess.

I shove the paper towel roll back onto the holder and look around for something else to keep me occupied until Aaron can finish checking the outside of the RV for trackers and we can hit the road. Deo and Taylor helped him for a bit, but they came back inside a few minutes ago, since we only have one of the scanning devices that checks for unusual electronic signals. The RV has been parked here for the past four months, and even though this is an enclosed unit, one of the Senator's goons could have bribed or threatened the owner and picked the lock. And I'd almost guarantee Miller, Magda's head of security, has placed a tracker somewhere on the camper—although I'm not sure why he'd bother, since Aaron located and removed it the last time we left without Magda's official sanction.

"This is beginning to feel like a pattern," Deo says as he shoves a carton of milk into the fridge. "Maybe we should put together a departure checklist for the next time we have to take off at a moment's notice."

"That's a good point," I say. "Why *did* it have to be at a moment's notice?"

"Because Stan's paths were shifting all over the place," Taylor says. "Apparently, he told Maria last week that something new was coming down the pike, but it was blurry. Then, about eight hours ago, everything started to converge."

Taylor watches me as she says these last words, like she's waiting for a reaction. I'm not sure why at first, then I remember that my morning jog on the beach was around eight hours ago. It's all I can do not to roll my eyes. As usual, Taylor has to assign blame to someone. And as usual, I'm at the top of her list. But it really feels like she's reaching this time.

"We should have brought Ein," I say, changing the subject fully so she'll know I'm not going to take the bait.

"We're only leaving him for a few days," she says. "Although I'm guessing Stan wishes we *had* taken Ein. He nearly tripped over him this morning. Right around the time he said the paths got all out of whack. When you were out on the beach."

She gives me a smug smile. Two can play the subject-changing game, and the conversation is now right back where she wanted it.

"That's why Maggie had to walk around with Stan today. Even with the cane, he was really dizzy. He told me when the paths diverge as much as they did this morning, it's like walking when you're drunk. Or at least how he *imagines* that would be, based on movies. Which makes me wonder how much of what he says is even true. I mean, he's older than I am. He has to know what's it like to walk when you're buzzed."

"Well," Deo says, "he's been at The Warren for a few years, and before that, he and his brother were in a mental hospital."

"He has a brother?" I ask.

"Yeah," Taylor says. "He didn't make it out with our group. He was in a different wing, with the other more . . . volatile kids. Stan gave me this stuffed animal so I could do a reading—a sock monkey with a Harvard T-shirt. That's the brother's name—Harvard. Apparently, his mom had Ivy League aspirations for her kids."

Her expression and tone make it abundantly clear this is another of the many things I should remember. And yeah, if Taylor did a remote viewing, I'm guessing most of Sandalford knew. She goes into full psychic-diva mode, eating enough for three and becoming annoyed at even minor distractions.

"Last time I checked," she says, "he was in Nevada with the Bear Brigade."

Aaron enters while Taylor is speaking. "I think the RV is clean, aside from Miller's stupid tracker, which I removed. Same brand as last time even. He must order the damn things in bulk."

Once we have the RV hooked up to the truck and we're out of the storage unit, I reluctantly join Aaron in the cab. Normally, I look forward to riding shotgun because we get to spend a bit of time alone. But I'm pretty sure he's going to want to talk about whatever happened in Kelsey's office before we left. And since I have no freakin' idea what happened, I'd really rather not.

But he doesn't bring it up. Maybe he's worried I'm mad at him. For the most part I'm not, although the part of me that was ready to attack on the beach this morning still seems to be hovering around. Looking for a reason to get angry.

Even once we're out on the highway, Aaron just keeps up a light banter, talking about the RV and the pros and cons of being back on the road. I pull up a Pandora station we both like and try to relax, but I remain on edge. By the time we pull through a Taco Bell near Norfolk,

I'm almost hoping he'll mention the argument just to get it over with. And by the time we reach Richmond, I'm ready to start the argument myself, even at the risk of revealing I have another memory gap.

But Aaron jumps into the breach first. "I'm sorry, okay? But I still think you shouldn't be here. And you know it's not because I don't want you with me. You're not well, Anna. If you have another of these weird . . . spells . . . you've been having, you'll be a liability, not an asset. I don't know if I'll be able to protect you, and it will make it harder to protect the others. I'm really sorry if that hurts your feelings, but . . ."

I want to argue that I'm perfectly capable of protecting myself. That's definitely what I would have argued a few months ago. The problem is, I know he's right. I *know* I should have stayed at Sandalford. I even remember walking into Kelsey's office hoping she'd veto the idea of me coming on this trip. Then . . . all of that changed, and apparently, I was arguing something else entirely. Must have been pretty persuasive, too, because here I sit.

Still, there must be a reason this angry side of my brain thinks I should be here. "Maria and Stan said I'm supposed to be with you. That he had a vision of me . . . having a vision—"

"Yeah, well, Stan's ability isn't like Jaden's, is it? Maybe the path where all of this works out was the one where you stayed back at Sandalford." He pulls his eyes from the road briefly to look at me, his eyes pleading. "But I really don't like arguing with you, so let's just drop it, okay? It doesn't matter now that you *are* here. We'll just have to make the . . ."

Aaron continues talking for a few seconds longer, but I can't hear the last bit over the blood pounding in my ears. His eyes are on the road now as he tries to shift the trailer into the other lane to avoid a slowdown on the overpass up ahead.

I'm so sick of him and the others constantly belittling me and treating me like a child. I should grab the steering wheel. That would show them. Yank it hard to the right, and we'd crash through the guardrail. Sail through the air and all of this would be over—

NO!

Bricks fly from every corner of my mind. They line themselves into rows automatically, blocking that mad impulse, cordoning it off from the rest of my mind.

But my wall comes up too late for me to hide that crazy thought from Aaron. Even as the bricks are stacking, he instinctively jerks the wheel sharply to the left to compensate for what I thought about doing but didn't. A horn blasts from the lane next to us, followed by the squeal of brakes. Our tires hit the rumble strip, but Aaron keeps the RV on the road. Two cars whizz past us on either side, both laying heavily on their horns, the driver on the right also raising an angry middle finger.

Aaron darts a glance my way, but he's too shaken to take his eyes off the road. As he opens his mouth to speak, the intercom buzzes and Taylor's anxious face appears.

"Not now," he says, and punches the button to turn off the screen.

I stare straight ahead, frozen in place. Silent, because what can I say? Aaron clearly picked up on my urge to send the RV flying over the guardrail. There's no way to sugarcoat it.

And it wasn't simply a suicidal thought. It was also *homicidal.* Three other people are currently in this vehicle. Two of them are people I actually love. No, let's be honest, three. Taylor is a pain, but she's Aaron's sister and my friend, and I would never willingly hurt her.

The blood drains from my face as I remember Kelsey's question earlier. *What about Myron?*

I *did* hurt someone when Myron was in control. I hurt her badly. In fact, I very nearly killed her . . . and I was *six* at the time.

It was a lot easier back in Kelsey's office to brush aside her fears that Myron's memories had somehow leaked out of their containment unit due to my concussion. Now, however, I'm desperately afraid she's right. The anger and the suicidal thoughts could be my way of processing those long-repressed memories. A truly stupid way of processing them, in my opinion, but still . . .

Thinking about Myron gives me a cold chill. I build a second wall, even though it feels pointless. There are no hitchers in my head to block. Memories, yes, but no hitchers. Can my walls protect me from *me*?

As soon as Aaron spots an exit, he pulls off and parks behind a McDonald's. Taylor pops up on the screen again.

"Not now," he says. "Stay in the camper. We'll be back there in a minute."

Taylor looks like she wants to argue. I guess his expression convinces her that's not a good idea, however, because she just sniffs and switches off the intercom.

"What the hell *was* that, Anna?" He's still gripping the wheel so hard his knuckles strain against his skin, and his voice shakes.

Tears burn my eyes, but I fight them. I understand Aaron well enough to know some of his anger will melt away if I cry, and I don't deserve his sympathy. "You were right. I should have stayed home."

I push the door open, shrugging off Aaron's hand when he reaches for me.

"Anna, wait. We need to—"

The rest of his sentence is cut off as I slam the truck door and hurry back to the RV. Taylor peppers me with questions about the near crash the minute I step inside. I ignore her and retreat to the bedroom I share—or at least used to share—with Aaron.

I lock the door behind me and then realize I'm not alone. Deo is stretched out on the bed with his iPad.

"What happened back there? Taylor said Aaron was pretty freaked out. And do I smell . . . fries?" He trails off, having finally looked up from the tablet to see my face. "Whoa. What's wrong?"

Shaking my head, I feel along the paneling behind me for the bathroom door. His mention of french fries was the final straw for my stomach. I barely make it inside before losing my dinner.

Deo waits outside the still-open doorway until I'm finished, then grabs a washcloth from above the sink and dampens it.

"Better?" he asks.

"A little," I say, taking the cloth from him. "Thanks."

Our hands barely even touch, but we both recoil, as if we've had a static shock. I feel myself slipping into the vision just as that odd metallic hum echoes in my head.

My foot catches on one of the bricks in the walkway, causing me to collide with the first bike. It tumbles off-balance, crashing into the second one. I grab the rail of the bike rack, partially breaking my fall, but still land on my butt.

The bus passes, headed for Union Station, according to the sign on the front.

Abbott rounds the building at the end of the block. His neck is a bright, blistered red, and he's alone. Maybe Costello bled out on the floor. One part of me says that's a good thing, and the other says I'm going straight to hell for even thinking it.

His hand slips inside his suit jacket, reaching for the gun, as he heads across Second Street. A blue banner spans the top of the building behind him, proclaiming a message the man with the gun clearly isn't following: Love Thy Neighbor.

Across the street, a black sedan is parked at the side entrance of the Hart Senate Office Building. Three men move across the courtyard toward the car. I'm pretty sure they're the ones from the flash Maria showed us. Two guys in dark suits. One looks vaguely familiar. Between them is a taller man. I only get a brief glimpse of his face, but I'm certain it's my father.

The guard at the kiosk isn't watching them. He's looking down at something. His phone, maybe.

I could yell that Abbott is armed. But the street is crowded. I doubt the guard would center in on the correct person in time. And I know Abbott is perfectly willing to shoot innocent bystanders.

But he won't shoot me. He doesn't dare shoot the vessel. Costello made that clear earlier when they were arguing.

I can't let him hurt anyone else.

And so even though every instinct says I should run away from him, I switch tactics and dash across Second Street, aiming to intercept before he can fire.

I feel a momentary pulse of rage from behind my walls, but I pull on my reserve focus to block it out. To stack the mental bricks higher so I can't hear HIM. So he can't manipulate me into doing what he wants.

My head, my body, my freakin' decision. Back off.

A horn blasts, and the guard—

NNNNNNNnnnn

My eyes open to see Deo, now sitting on the far side of the bed to maximize the distance between us. Aaron is knocking on the bedroom door, calling my name.

"She's sick," Deo says, his eyes still on me. "Give her some space. We'll be out in a minute."

I press the wet cloth to my face and close my eyes, delaying the inevitable moment when I have to tell Deo what happened out there. The thought I had in the vision keeps echoing in my mind . . . *stack the mental bricks higher so I can't hear HIM.*

"You want to talk about it?" Deo asks. "The vision? Or maybe you could start with whatever happened in the truck just now?"

I start to say no, my automatic response these days, but . . . I do want to talk about it. Not with Aaron. Not yet. Aaron loves me. I don't doubt that. But he doesn't *know* me like Deo does. That's the thing about family, even—or maybe especially—chosen family. They know you. The light and the dark. The good and the bad. The past and the present. Deo understands my demons, maybe even better than Kelsey does.

"It's him, D. Myron's thoughts keep coming through. He wanted me to grab the wheel. Yank it so we'd drive off the overpass. I fought him off, but Aaron picked up on what I was thinking and, um . . . overcorrected. So thanks to me, we nearly crashed."

"*Partly* thanks to you," Deo says. "You didn't actually grab the wheel, right?"

"No. Like I said, I fought him back."

"So it's partly on Aaron, too. He could have trusted you."

I look down at my sneakers for a moment and shake my head. "Have I given him any reason to trust me lately? Have I given any of you reason to trust me? All of this is just so damned frustrating! Myron is *gone*. I remember him leaving. These are only memories, so there's no reason for—"

Deo holds up a hand, interrupting me. "Are your walls up?" When I nod, he adds, "All the way up?"

"Yes. Double. What happened in the truck scared the hell out of me."

Something scurries spiderlike along the back of my consciousness. I'd love to put up a third layer of protection, but I'm not sure I have the focus to do that and still listen to Deo.

"Okay, then," he says. "I'm gonna try this one more time, and I want you to focus on me. Just me. You know I'd never do anything to hurt you. And I don't lie to you—okay, well, sometimes little lies to protect you, like when my fever was so high. But not about the important stuff. Not when it really counts."

I want to argue that his fever spiking to 105 *was* important stuff, but I nod for him to go on.

"So . . . yeah. One more try. Focus on me and try not to freak out like the last time."

"What *last time*?"

"The last time I told you we don't think it's just Myron memories."

"I know that. It's the concussion *combined* with the—"

"Anna." Deo stares at me intently, his dark eyes as serious, as worried, as I think I've ever seen them. "No. Not just the concussion. Not just the Myron memories. I'm talking about Graham Cregg. We're pretty sure it's Cregg *manipulating* the Myron memories. Daniel said . . ."

I don't hear what Daniel said or anything else. The spider, and it's definitely a spider of some sort, is at it again. It's not just running against the wall now but trying to scale it.

And I can see it now in my mind's eye. Big spider. *Strong* spider. Mutant wolf spider crossed with a giant rat. It chips away at the bricks in the inner wall until one leg extends through, moving back and forth to widen the crack.

The leg extends out toward the second wall. Instead of claws at the end of the leg, there are two tiny hands, pulling away pieces of the mortar.

"Anna! Stay with me, Anna."

"No." I shake my head furiously, shrinking away from Deo, back into the tiny bathroom. My shoulder crashes into the towel rack, and the linens come raining down on me, brushing against my arm and face like spiders, like giant—

"NO!"

"Stay. With. Me," Deo says. "We can work through this, but I need you here. Present. With your walls up, okay? You beat Myron when you were six. You can beat this son of a bitch, too."

He's right.

I beat Myron. I beat him. I kicked him out. Evicted him. Myron kicked and fought, but I beat him. He's nothing but memories now, and I'm working through those memories. That's all this is, just the concussion and—

Taking in a deep, deep breath, I try to force the panic into something compact. Manageable. "But Kelsey . . . Kelsey said it's Myron. It's from the concussion. From . . ."

"I know," Deo says. "And usually, I'd go with her opinion, since she's the doctor. Kelsey's had you under hypnosis, what . . . five times maybe in the past few months, so she should know. But . . ."

"Kelsey had me under hypnosis?"

He nods. "Like I said, at least five different times. And she doesn't think you've picked up another hitcher. Says all of this is just you, finally working through the Myron stuff. The concussion even gives her a handy medical explanation. That's why she's clinging to it."

"But why? If there's other evidence, why would Kelsey ignore it?"

Deo gives me a rueful smile. "Wishful thinking, maybe? She watched you walk through hell when you were six. Kelsey loves you, Anna. She doesn't want to think about the possibility of you having to go through that again. Or that it might . . . that it might be worse this time."

Worse is right. Myron was a killer. Myron was insane. But Myron didn't have Delphi powers. Myron couldn't force someone to turn a gun toward his head the way Cregg forced Deo.

That chittering noise fills my head again, scrabbling, scrambling, hairy mutant legs chiseling away at the hole. Widening it. Three legs are poking through now, extending into the mental space between my walls.

I bring a brick crashing down from above, as hard and as fast as I can. The spider-thing pulls back, but not quickly enough to save that first leg, the one that was stretched out farthest, feeling, exploring. It snaps off at one of the knees, and the truncated limb goes spinning across the floor. The fingers on those creepy, incongruous hands continue to twitch, even after it comes to a stop inches away from the cabinets that store Jaden's and Molly's memories.

Each of those twitching hands is missing the pinky finger. It's a very good thing my stomach is now empty.

"Anna? You still with me?"

Deo's voice pulls me back again, an anchor holding me to reality.

"Yes." I bite down hard on the inside of my cheek, using the discomfort to keep my mind focused here, on the outside, rather than on the nightmare within. "You think it's Cregg. You think I picked him up when . . . when we fought them at the airport."

Inexplicably, Deo smiles. It's a small, sad smile at first, but it morphs into a full grin when he sees my confused expression.

"Why are you smiling?"

"Because this makes me happy! It's *progress*. It's the first time anyone has gotten you to even admit the possibility. Every other time, you've flown into a rage. You threw a fork at Aaron so hard it stuck in the freakin' wall. But I'm guessing you don't remember that."

He's right. I don't remember that at all. What I do remember is sitting down to breakfast one morning about a month ago and finding only a spoon. Taylor saying I'd have to earn back my fork privileges. Me wondering what the hell she was babbling about as I went into the kitchen to get my own damned fork.

"Oh my God, D. What else have I done during these memory lapses?"

"Mostly you just . . . you tried to play all of us against each other. We started keeping a diary of sorts—all of us jotting down notes when you were acting extra weird. When you're ready, I'll show you."

"Did I hurt anyone?" What I really want to ask is whether I *pushed* anyone. Whether I made them do anything they didn't want to do. I'm pretty sure they'd have locked me away by now if I was going around persuading people to snip off body parts, but there are a million more subtle ways to hurt people.

"No. You didn't hurt anyone. We were worried you were going to hurt yourself a few times, and Taylor said you were a little . . . rough . . . with Ein one day. But Ein learned to steer clear when you got that weird look."

For some reason, the fact that I was mean to Ein, that I might have given him a reason to distrust me, to *fear* me, is what finally brings the tears to my eyes. I don't give in to them, though. If I allow myself to start crying, I may lose it entirely, and I know that spider-rat-thing—*him*, Cregg—is waiting to pounce the second my control slips.

It will slip eventually. He knows that. I can't keep up this level of control indefinitely. Holding my walls at full strength is exhausting. I'm not sure how long I can manage it. At some point I'll have to sleep.

"I shouldn't be here. You guys need to take me back and have Kelsey and Magda put me on lockdown."

The spider-thing doesn't like that suggestion, but its movements are more cautious now. It doesn't stick any appendages through that hole again. It hangs back, licking its wounds or whatever freaky mutant rat-spiders do.

"We sorta *did* suggest that to Kelsey earlier today." Deo gives me a sheepish look. "Only you said you were fine. And Maria was there backing you up, saying she peeked inside your head and Kelsey's right, it's not Cregg. I don't know if that's what she really thinks or if it's just because Stan and the other Fivers say you're supposed to be here. And speaking of, is it just me or does Stan's whole vision thing make your head spin?"

"Not just you."

"Yeah, well, anyway—Kelsey might have listened if it was you against me and Aaron. But being able to peek inside your head makes Maria pretty damn persuasive. She counters every argument even before you make it."

"Did you guys explain where we were going? I thought Maria wanted to keep Kelsey out of the loop on Pfeifer, at least for the time being?"

"Yeah. Maria wasn't real happy about that part. But then she consulted with her walking Ouija board and decided things were still on the right track."

"Well, either way, I've had the vision now. So I can go back . . . where I can't hurt anyone." My voice sounds totally unconvinced, even to my own ears.

Deo picks up on my hesitation. "Except the vision has something to do with your father, doesn't it? He's here . . . okay, near here. Not back in NC, at any rate. Which means *you* were here, too, because unlike Stan's weird *Sliding Doors*, alternate-paths schtick, you only see things that actually happen. Things that happen to *us*. So . . . spill. What did you see happening to us?"

I debate whether to tell him the only one of *us* in that vision was me. Truth is, I don't know why I was there on my own. Nor do I know the actual names of the men I was thinking about, although I can picture both of them clearly in my mind. The taller one really doesn't look much like Bud Abbott. He's a lot younger, for one thing. But the shorter, heavier member of the duo was a dead ringer for Lou Costello.

And I'm pretty sure he'll soon be a *dead* dead ringer. In the vision, I remembered him lying in a pool of blood on a tile floor. The floor seemed kind of familiar, then I remember the blood on the white tiles in Lab 1, back at The Warren after Lucas executed Jaden and two other adepts.

The emotion I attached to that fleeting, split-second memory of this Costello guy's body on that floor was barely even tinged with guilt. It was mostly a bizarre mix of relief and anger.

I don't know that I killed the guy. The only thing I do know with absolute certainty is that, as Deo just noted, this vision *will* happen exactly as I saw it. As I felt it. If I tell Deo or Aaron I'll be doing anything as patently stupid as intercepting an armed man, they won't let me out of their sight. And that could get one of them killed trying to protect me.

"I saw the scene outside that building," I say. "The same scene Maria pushed to us at the meeting this afternoon. Except what I was seeing was . . . maybe ten seconds earlier. It's definitely downtown DC, but we figured that out already. Two bodyguards—private, I think. They're not in any sort of uniform. And I'm certain it's Scott Pfeifer in the center."

At the sound of Pfeifer's name, that thing in my head kicks into action again. He claws at the wall frantically, but he's stuck on the other side. For now, at least.

There's a soft tap on the door, and Deo raises his eyebrows.

"Just a minute," I say, and whisper to Deo, "Can't put this off forever, I guess."

"You want me to stay?"

"No. I should talk to him alone. But I'd rather not have Taylor watch while I grovel. Could you distract her? We're parked behind a McDonald's. Maybe the two of you could go get some fries?"

He grins. "I think I can handle that. You want anything?"

My stomach churns at the thought. "No. Just . . . tell Aaron I'll be out in a minute."

I go into the bathroom. Towels are scattered all over the floor and the vanity. I don't have the energy to pick them up, so I shove them to the side and splash some water on my face. Then I brush my teeth, keeping my eyes trained resolutely on the sink.

No way am I looking in that mirror.

CHAPTER SIX

Ashland, Virginia
April 23, 2020, 8:46 p.m.

Aaron is sitting on the bed with his head in his hands when I open the door. His anger seems to have dissipated and he mostly just looks tired. Deflated.

"Are you okay? I didn't mean to—"

"Do *not* apologize. I nearly got us killed out there."

"I overreacted."

"No. You didn't." I sit down on the bed next to him, still clutching the washcloth. "I was a hair's breadth away from grabbing that wheel. We both know it. Lying to each other about it isn't going to change it."

"But . . . you *didn't* do it." I give him a look, thinking he's about to start making more excuses for me, and he shakes his head. "I'm not saying I want you riding shotgun with me again. Taylor was right. That was a really stupid call on my part. My point is, you pulled back . . . your anger."

"Not *my* anger. You mean I pulled back Graham Cregg."

An odd scraping sensation slides through my brain, almost like someone raking through it with a wire brush. The spider-thing is angry that I know he's in there. Pissed he didn't make it into the driver's seat quickly enough this time. That he didn't have a chance to make me forget.

Aaron's eyes are wary. "Deo told you?"

"Yeah." I smile weakly. "Don't worry. No forks here in the bedroom for me to throw. The only thing I could hurl at you is a washcloth."

"Last time—"

"Last time I went crazy, right? And then forgot everything?"

"Last time, Kelsey had to sedate you. You didn't speak for nearly three days. And you packed up your clothes and took a room in the other wing."

"None of which I remember."

"Yeah. I'll admit, I've gone back and forth on this. So has Deo. And Kelsey . . . she seems pretty firmly convinced this is just you working through the Myron stuff. Even Daniel isn't entirely sure it was Cregg he saw—or felt, or whatever—inside your head."

"Daniel?" I pause for a moment, confused, and then I remember. "Oh. At the hospital. He tapped out SOS, then he pointed at me. Do you think that's what he meant?"

"I do. He started asking for you as soon as he got some of his speech back. Mom and Sam didn't mention it until last month, because . . ." Aaron looks down at the floor. "Well, because of the whole competitive thing between me and Daniel. Mom thought he was trying to move in on you . . . romantically."

I snort. "Oh, we would *not* make a good couple."

Aaron's shoulders relax slightly.

"Really?" I say, both exasperated and amused.

"Okay, okay, you're right. But to be fair, Anna . . . this wasn't just me being jealous of Daniel. You began pulling away from me, acting stranger every day. You didn't want me to touch you. Kelsey said it was very common after traumatic brain injury for people to act different, to not to be interested in . . . well, sex. And—"

"Please tell me you didn't talk to Kelsey about our sex life."

I'm not sure why that bothers me. I've talked to Kelsey about sex before, even about my feelings for Aaron. And yes, I guess technically she's his therapist now, too, but she was *my* therapist first.

"Babe . . . I've talked to Kelsey about pretty much everything you've done or said in my presence. *All* of us talked to Kelsey. We've got journal entries going back more than a month, and—"

"Yeah. Deo told me." It's only a tiny dash of anger—and not even anger, really. More annoyance than anything else, annoyance that I've been so out of control that the people I love have had me under constant surveillance. But that smidgen of emotion is all it takes to set the spider-rat-thing on alert.

Cregg, damn it. It's *Cregg*. I'm completely terrified of rats and spiders individually, so it says a lot that I'm more comfortable thinking of my current resident as a giant rat-spider combo, with mutilated human hands, than I am with the notion that I've picked up Graham Cregg's spirit.

And there it goes again. *Scree-e-e-e-ch-ch-ch-ch.* The noise is like nails scraping against a chalkboard. Human nails at the end of a spider's weirdly human hands.

I clench my fists and bite down on that same spot inside my cheek, which is now sore enough to make me wince. "Never mind, Aaron. It doesn't matter." My voice is tight and too loud for the tiny room.

"No. It *does* matter. I didn't like spying on you. Neither did Deo. But the surest way to set you off was to mention anything about Cregg. Anything about Myron, even. Bottom line is we were terrified of losing you. And what bothers me most is that, in the end, all the notes we kept were for nothing. Kelsey started you on some antipsychotic meds, something she's said is good for dissociative disorders. Which you don't have, but she thought if Cregg really was in there and you were having trouble blocking him, it might trigger that section of your brain. She said it was guesswork, really, as to whether it would be effective, and to be honest, it seemed kind of odd to me. It's not like your hitchers are separate personalities, so . . ."

I shrug. "Drugs were part of the equation when I fought off Myron. And whatever is left of my hitchers is inside my head, so it's at least in the same ballpark as separate personalities. The brain isn't entirely a mystery. We know different parts have different functions. And we know which sections are most affected by the Delphi serum. So . . . it's a very educated guess. Kelsey always prescribed fewer meds than the doctors who treated me at the hospital, and she was a lot more careful about monitoring for side effects. If she thinks something will help, I'm willing to try it."

And I *am* willing to try it. What bothers me is that I have no memory of her ever discussing any of these options with *me*, and I'm certain she would have. She discussed things like this with me when I was six, explaining the advantages and disadvantages of any medication I took, doing her best to put it into terms I could actually understand. I'm an adult now. She wouldn't have discussed my treatment with anyone aside from me unless she thought I was incapable of making an informed decision. And even then, she would have also discussed it with me.

Which I'm pretty sure means she *did* discuss all of this with me, probably multiple times. I just have no memory of those conversations—so there were more gaps than I thought. Plus, it seems Cregg did some creative rewriting of my memories.

How much time have I lost in the past four months? How much of what I remember is even real? The swarm of panic butterflies fluttering inside my stomach morphs into a frenzied wave of bats. I clench my fists tight and draw in a long, steadying breath through my nose, telling myself it doesn't matter. *It doesn't matter.* The only thing that matters is I'm in control *now*. I know what's going on. I can block him out.

Only . . . how many times have I had this same exact thought? How many times has it been overwritten?

"The medication is kind of a moot point now," Aaron says. "Kelsey actually gave you an injection about three weeks ago. Rispera . . . something. I'm pretty sure Cregg was at the surface then, because it took me and Deo both to hold you down long enough for her to give you the shot. But it takes a few weeks to kick in, and you need another injection for full effect. You were supposed to be taking the oral form in the interim as well, but then Kelsey yanked the medication option off the table entirely. She seemed so enthusiastic about the possibilities at first, even discussed the pros and cons of different drugs, but then suddenly she tells us it won't help. That this is just you working through an old trauma. And Kelsey was so stubborn about it. Wouldn't listen to anything we said."

"Kelsey's not—" I break off, confused. "Kelsey didn't use to be like that. You'd have a hard time finding anyone more open-minded. Maybe it's just the stress of the past few months."

"Deo said that too, so maybe."

"Or . . ." I stop, feeling like I'm on the edge of making a mental connection, but it slips away.

"Or . . . what?"

"I don't know. Lost what I was going to say. I'm having a tough time keeping my walls up, and . . . conversation makes it even harder. I know we have a lot of things we need to work on . . . to *fix* . . . between us, but right now maybe we should just focus on what we need to do in DC. Once my father is safe, you can take me back to Kelsey so I can work on getting this monster out of my head."

"Sure," he says, squeezing my hand. "Sounds like a plan."

I give Aaron the same bare-bones account of the vision I gave Deo. And again, even though it twists my gut to do it, I leave out most of the important details. What good did it do for me to push Cregg back, to fight that impulse to hurl us off the overpass, if I'm going to put everyone in jeopardy anyway?

"That's probably the Hart Building," Aaron says. "The Senate website shows closed hearings scheduled today and tomorrow for that subcommittee. There have been rumors Pfeifer was testifying this afternoon."

"I thought they'd decided to interview him from the psychiatric hospital?"

Aaron's eyes narrow slightly, and I realize this is another one of the things I should know but don't, thanks to the memory gaps. No, not gaps. Memory *craters*.

"You've told me all of this before, haven't you?"

"Not . . . exactly. But you were there—physically there, at any rate—when Taylor told us about the article in the *Post*. They're reassessing the whole issue of Pfeifer's sanity. Most of the things that made the doctors question his competence at the time of your mom's murder have turned out to be true. So . . . they want to find out what he knows. And there's a good chance he'll be ordered to stand trial now. I guess the real question is who wants him dead. Just . . . um . . . as a heads-up, I should probably let you know Taylor thinks it's Cregg."

"I guess. Although, he's the one who started parading the Delphi adepts around like prize pigs. He's the one who's pushing for the hearings, too. So—"

"No. Not *Senator* Cregg."

"Oh." I wait, expecting a reaction from my hitcher, but he remains still. Too still. He's listening. Lurking. Waiting for a split second when my guard is down.

Aaron pulls a folded bit of paper from his pocket. I don't recognize it at first, but then I see the phone number. It's the card he picked up on the beach this morning. "I had Sam try to track down the number, but he didn't get anything. Probably a burner phone."

"Did he try calling it?"

"Well, we thought about that but decided maybe it should come from you." The panic I'm feeling must register in my eyes, because he quickly adds, "Not tonight. When you're ready."

It takes a moment for the full implication of what he's said to seep in. "Wait . . . Taylor thinks that's why I was on the beach this morning? That I was . . . arranging for someone to kill my father?"

"Yeah. Stan thinks so, too. That's when this new cluster of paths . . . spun off, I guess? Not sure what you'd call it, but he says something happened this morning that made the whole future he was seeing really blurry. Ambiguous."

"But . . . that's good, though. Right? He was predicting this huge confrontation with the Senator and Dacia before, and—"

Aaron shakes his head. "Before, Stan thought we had a reasonable chance against them. Now his Magic 8-Ball has flipped to *Outlook Not So Good*."

Some part of me—and I'm reasonably sure that part is actually *me*, and not Cregg—wants to argue against Stan's entire premise. Wants to tell Aaron I would never give away the location of Sandalford. Would never put all of them at risk. Would never hire an assassin to kill my father, no matter what he may have done.

But I don't. Taylor's right, as usual. It's the most logical explanation.

"You look beat," Aaron says. "Maybe you should rest."

"No. I mean, yes, I'm tired. I was up at dawn, and I haven't been sleeping well anyway. But Aaron . . . sleep isn't an option until we get back to Sandalford. If I fall asleep, my walls will come down, and that would be a *very bad thing*."

The realization hits him, and he pulls me into his arms. "You can't stay awake forever, babe. And you fought him off. You're getting stronger—"

"Maybe. Or maybe I just caught him off guard. And that was before . . . before I knew it was him. If he gets out again, he'll fight harder to keep control. I can *feel* it."

"So . . . no sleep. Coffee, Red Bull, and 5-hour ENERGY."

"Maybe not all at once, but yeah."

I hear the front door open, followed by Taylor's voice.

"Can you get Tay to ride up front with you? I'm not ready for the Inquisition yet."

"Sure. We've only got about another hour until we reach the campground. I'll put on a pot of coffee first, and we'll take shifts to make sure someone's with you to help keep you alert."

"Yeah, coffee's a good idea."

"You need me to send Deo in while I make it, or are you okay?"

"I'm okay."

It's a lie, and not even a good one, since it's followed by a very shaky exhale. I'm not even close to okay. Every muscle feels like it's paper-thin porcelain that will shatter if I move. I want to curl up, pull the covers over my head, have a good cathartic cry, and sleep for a week.

But I can't do that. I can't risk losing control in any way.

"Hey." He lifts my chin to meet my eyes. "We're not going to let him win, Anna. You are not alone in this."

I nod and give him the best smile I can muster. He's right. I'm not alone. There's a mass murderer disguised as a rat-spider in my head, and three other people in this RV.

Which means no tears, no anger, no sleep. I may not be able to put the last one off forever, but I can definitely delay it until I'm far, far away from anyone I can hurt.

College Park, Maryland
April 24, 2020, 1:22 a.m.

Aaron took the first shift in the Babysitting Anna Marathon. A little after one, he went to bed, tagging Deo and Taylor to take over. They sit on opposite ends of the couch, facing each other, their legs intertwined in the middle as they read. They make a cute picture, something I'm sure would have both of them rolling their eyes if they could read my mind.

Cuteness aside, their relationship still makes me uneasy. It's not really the sex part. I'm sure they're being cautious. I've talked to Deo on that front, as has Kelsey. And Aaron says Taylor is on the pill, too. So while I'm pretty confident they're physically safe, there is unfortunately nothing to prevent emotional damage if this ends badly.

At first, I was most worried about Deo—and well, to be honest, I'm still *most* worried about Deo, because he's my brother and I can't stand the idea of him being hurt. But I'm starting to worry about Taylor, too. Several times in the past few hours, I've seen her glance up from her reading and watch Deo's face, like he's a puzzle she can't quite figure out. Her eyes are so vulnerable when she looks at him—which again makes me glad she can't read my mind, because Taylor wouldn't want anyone thinking of her as vulnerable.

Taylor has been unusually solicitous, even making me an energy smoothie to help keep me awake. But she also seems on edge, maybe even more than I am. We pass the time by watching some Pixar movie and munching on microwave popcorn. It would be fun if not for the occasional movement I keep sensing behind my walls. Experimental taps at the bricks to see if they're at full strength. And when my mind isn't distracted by my unwanted lodger, it keeps straying to the question of how the hell I'm going to get out of here on my own.

Deo's head begins to droop in the middle of the second movie. I'm surprised but also very, very relieved that he conked out so easily. Now I just have to find a way to distract Taylor.

An hour later, I'm at the point where I can't help glancing over at the clock every minute or so. And then at my backpack, leaning against the kitchen bar. Then back at the clock. Luckily, she's doing something on her phone, so she's barely noticed. I'm half tempted to just snag my backpack and make a run for it. How the hell am I supposed to slip out when I'm under constant surveillance? And yes, I know I obviously *do* manage it, since I saw it in the vision, but thinking about causality loops in the wee hours of the morning is only going to worsen my current meta fog.

"You want another soda?" I ask.

Given that she's already had two, I'm not entirely surprised when she shakes her head. So much for my strategy of plying her with enough liquid that she'll be forced to take a bathroom break.

"I've had plenty," she says. "But you should probably chug that cup of coffee and get going."

My jaw drops and she waves her phone.

"Stan's been keeping me updated on the paths since we left Sandalford. He's annoyingly vague, as usual. There was some divergence earlier, but by the time Aaron went to bed, everything had gathered into two neat clusters. The largest one has me pretending to fall asleep on the sofa and you sneaking out the door. The rest of us catch up with you later."

"What happens if I don't go now?"

Her face grows grim. "According to Stan, two guys with guns show up and *take* you through that door. Aaron doesn't fare too well on that path. I'm not willing to risk it for that reason alone."

"Aaron is going to be really pissed at you. At Deo, too. I'm not sure he'll believe you both fell asleep."

"Pffft," she says. "I can handle Aaron. And the melatonin I dissolved in Deo's Dr Pepper gives him an excuse, so Aaron won't have any reason to be mad at him. Just grab your backpack and go, okay? Let me worry about the fallout."

Shared Journal

3/18/20

Deo: We were walking out by the pool with Ein this morning, and Anna gets that look. You all know the expression. Her face goes blank like she's talking to one of her hitchers, but then it gets . . . calculating, I guess. Not like Anna at all. Then she asks me if I want to cut out, just the two of us. Head back to the city. I mention that we have zero money, no place to live, and there are still people out there who think she was involved with killing those kids back at Overhills. Plus the Senator's people. Dacia and her damned Bear Army. We're safer here.

Next she says she doesn't trust Magda. Which I get. But here's the bit where she lost me. She says Kelsey's more on Magda's side than ours. That Aaron and Taylor belong here, but we don't. Says she can get her hands on a couple thousand bucks—a bank account left by one of her former hitchers. That's bullshit or she'd have mentioned it back at Bartholomew House. For that matter, she'd have mentioned it when we were talking about replacing the power cord on our laptop last month, instead of wishing she had a way to contact Joe, her old boss, to get her paycheck for the final week she worked. And it's not cash this Myron guy had and that's why she's just remembered it. He was homeless, right? I mean, he was also crazy, so I guess he could have been on the streets and still have some cash stashed away, but . . . no, not buying it.

So, anyway, I tell her I'll think about it, and she gives me this weird sneer. Again, doesn't look anything like Anna. A few minutes later, it's Anna back, clearly confused as to why we're suddenly on the other side of the deck. I wait a beat, then I mention us leaving. She looks at me like I'm out of my mind. Says it's too risky right now. And anyway, we don't have any money or anywhere to go.

I was on the fence about the whole Cregg vs Myron thing before. Now I agree with Taylor. I think Anna picked up Cregg after Jasper shot him. I'm not sure why you couldn't get him to surface when Anna was under hypnosis, but today didn't feel like Anna working through memories from a hitcher. It felt like someone else wearing Anna's skin.

CHAPTER SEVEN

College Park, Maryland
April 24, 2020, 4:27 a.m.

My foot slips on the broken pavement, and I slow my pace to a light jog. The sidewalk ended a quarter mile back, and the city of College Park seems to have skimped on streetlights along this section of road. The lack of sleep is hitting me already. Every few minutes, I get spells where I'm woozy, off-balance. It doesn't last long, but it keeps me from really getting into a good running rhythm.

A sliver of moon hangs in the sky, but the clouds have dimmed it to an insipid haze that never reaches the ground. The flashlight on my phone would be useful, but I handed it over to Aaron without argument last night. If Cregg is finding a way to break through my walls, there's no reason to make it easy for him to communicate with his allies or flunkies or whatever these people are.

Aside from the piss-poor lighting, I don't need the phone. I'm on home turf now. I spent four months in a foster home over in Eleven Cedars, not too far from here. The school bus drove down this road every day. I have thirteen dollars inside my backpack, and a Metro

SmarTrip card with five or ten bucks' credit in my pocket. I know how to get to the Greenbelt Metro station, which is about two miles from here. My pepper spray is in my hand, and my hair is tucked inside the hood of my jacket, because I also know this isn't exactly the best place for an eighteen-year-old girl to take a predawn jog.

Before I left, I scribbled out a note to Aaron and one to Deo. Mostly to apologize for what I was about to do, but also because I felt bad about leaving Taylor to face the wrath of the guys when they discover I'm gone. Hopefully that won't be for at least another hour, because I'm not the only one who is now on home turf. Aaron has connections in the DC area. Half his family are former cops. They have friends who are still on the force, including at least one who knows the claims of me being involved in killing the kids at Overhills and the attack on Daniel at the hospital are both false. I need to get some distance between me and the RV, because it wouldn't be hard for him to set up a dragnet and pull me in.

The road widens up ahead, and I jog past a small apartment complex, a Home Depot, and a smattering of other suburban stores. Just after I cross Baltimore Avenue, I spot a gray sedan that seems to be following me. I pick up the pace, aiming for a twenty-four-hour BP station just ahead. Keeping one eye on the car, I slip into the store and grab a bottle of water from the cooler. As I'm paying for the water, the car pulls up outside the door.

I get a brief flash of yellow from the license plate. Pennsylvania, I think, but my view of the rear bumper isn't clear enough to confirm. The guy on the passenger side is easily visible, short and tubby, with a doughy face. That weird feedback loop kicks in because I'm thinking he looks like Lou Costello, the old-time comedian that Abner, one of my former hitchers, used to watch when he was a kid. At the same time, I'm remembering the vision last night where I was already thinking of these two as Abbott and Costello.

My resident rat-spider kicks into motion as soon as I see Costello. He scurries back and forth along the wall, tapping each brick. There are no holes big enough for him to reach through with his spindly legs—or maybe he's simply not willing to risk losing another one. But there must be some sort of chink in the armor, because a clear thought reaches me. The voice sounds like Cregg's . . . but higher. Fainter.

> Let me handle this. We're more alike than you know. Your father killed your mother. My father killed mine. And if your father lives, we have no hope of defeating mine. You don't want that. Neither do—

"Shut up," I say aloud as I shove the door open.

The clerk, who is pushing a broom down one of the aisles, gives me a dirty look. "Shut up your own damn self."

Walking directly toward the car, I open the rear passenger-side door, as though this is the Uber I've been waiting for. Costello gets out before I can even slide into the back seat and holds out his hands. "Finally," he says. "Give me the backpack."

"What?"

"You said it might have a tracker? Here, I got it." He snatches the pack off my shoulder. My first instinct is to knock his hands away, and I fight to keep my face neutral as Costello shoves it into the trash container between the gas pumps. I've had that pack for years. It's been with me almost as long as Deo. My ID is in there. My freakin' pepper spray is in there. Even the damned bottle of water I just bought was in that bag. But all I can do is watch. Otherwise, I'll tip them off to the fact that it's me, and not Cregg, in control.

> You're in control for the moment. It won't last, Anna.

He's right. I can't keep these walls up indefinitely, and even now, with so much effort going toward blocking him, his thoughts are still getting through to me. And the reverse was definitely not true. When

Cregg was in control, he used my own walls against me, blocked me out, leaving hours-long gaps in my memory.

> Hours? Why lie to yourself? I was in control for days—
> well, a day and a half was the longest, if we're being
> technical. But I stepped back willingly in order to keep
> the others from catching on before I had everything
> planned out. I could have blocked you for longer. I'm
> stronger than you are.

Shut up!

I expect a retort similar to the one I got from the store clerk, but Cregg obediently retreats into silence. It's not a retreat based on fear, however. It's based on confidence, and that ratchets my panic up another notch.

"Thought you were going to break out last night," Abbott says. "Or at least call if you couldn't. If we hadn't spotted you back there, we were planning to storm the campground before daybreak. And that could have gotten messy."

"Couldn't call. They confiscated my phone."

Costello, who is now sliding back into the front passenger seat, says, "Why didn't you do your mind thing and make 'em give it back?"

Great. Ten seconds in, and he's already questioning me. I fight down panic and try to look disinterested.

"It wasn't worth the bother," I say. "I told you I'd get away, and I did. I'm not paying you to second-guess my actions."

"Sorry, boss." Costello's voice takes on a wheedling tone. "You're right. You pay the bills, you make the rules. And, hey, I gotta hand it to you. You ain't a tightwad like your old man. I woulda come with you in the first place, but things got so royally screwed up when The Warren caught fire that I just ran for the closest chopper, which happened to be his crew. But he's got Dacia pretty much runnin' the operation, and she's gone full soup sandwich without Lucas to . . . well . . . keep her happy, if you know what I mean."

If I didn't know what he meant simply from his tone of voice, the leer would have filled in the blanks. I don't respond, partly because I don't want to encourage him, but also because I don't think Cregg would respond either. He made it very clear he didn't like Lucas's extra-curricular activities with the girls at The Warren.

"Dacia was already halfway there, anyway," he adds. "I ain't inclined to trust nobody crazy enough to snip off her own damn pinky finger."

Abbott glances at me in the rearview mirror as he pulls onto Baltimore Avenue. I feel like I need to say something, respond in some way, but I don't really know what Cregg would say. It's clear Costello was one of the guards at The Warren, but how well does Cregg know these two men?

The Cregg-spider presses forward again, ready to argue that I should let him handle this. That we have so damn much in common. That I need to *trust him*. The enemy of my enemy . . .

Abbott's eyes keep darting from the road to the mirror, very obviously keeping tabs on me. Costello seems fairly chill, but I've obviously done something to make Abbott suspicious. So I grasp at the one sure thing I know about Cregg and toss them a line from *Hamlet*.

"Dacia is too erratic to lead. She's descended into madness, wherein she now raves."

I'm pretty sure I've mangled the quote, but I can't access my hitch-ers' memory banks without giving Cregg an opening. And I doubt either of these guys spends his Saturdays at Shakespeare in the Park.

"Man, you got that right," Costello says. "She raves."

I keep my eyes trained on the lights outside the windows, resisting the temptation to look at Abbott and see whether invoking The Bard appeased him. Aside from the fact that we appear to be headed toward I-95, I have no idea where we're going.

"Alex sent the research you ordered and some other files over to the townhouse a few days ago. Said to call once you're settled and to be ready by eight thirty so you two can take care of the bank stuff. Oh, and it turns out you were right on the whole Port Deposit thing. Your old man's got people camped out up there today right on top of the Delphi site. They're waitin' on something or somebody, and I'm guessing it's Pfeifer."

I nod, wishing I could think of something neutral to say, but apparently Costello doesn't need a conversational partner. He's perfectly capable of rambling on without any input at all from me.

"So," he says, "if Pfeifer is another one of these vessels, same as his daught—" He stops and barks out a laugh. "Now, see, that's how weird this is. I was gonna say same as his daughter, but I guess I should say same as *you*, right? We were just sayin' earlier we don't even know what gender pronoun to use for you anymore. You got a preference?"

"*She* will suffice," I say, trying to replicate the slightly prissy tone I remember Cregg using when Lucas irked him.

"Yeah," Costello says. "Prob'ly better to get used to it. But that's what I was saying before. I think I'd have waited and just jumped into Pfeifer. I mean, sure, with this one you get a few extra decades. But you have to live them as a girl, and you're gonna have to get used to all sorts of female stuff. I don't think I could live as a woman."

"A small mercy for the men of the world," Abbott says drily, and I notice he's watching me in the mirror again. "You're a lot more tolerant of his chatter than you were this morning."

"I'm not really listening."

He gives a nod of admission. "Yeah. That's the best way to deal with him."

Costello just laughs good-naturedly. "You sure you don't want us to grab Pfeifer instead of shooting him? Seems like a waste. I mean, some of those so-called gifts I saw back at The Warren were kinda pointless. I can't start a fire with my head, but, hey . . . I don't consider that much of a handicap. Five bucks'll buy me a can of charcoal lighter and a box of matches, y'know? This, though . . . I could see someone paying a whole lot of cash to buy a spare body. A lot of rich old bitches would have given top dollar for the skin you're wearing right now."

Costello ends his sales pitch by giving me a creepy head-to-toe assessment, followed by the kind of wink a guy might give a buddy he sees out on the street with a hot date. Like my body is just a thing. Like I'm nothing more than what he just called my father. A *vessel*.

"Stick to the plan." The words come out much angrier than I intended, and I'm worried for a moment that I've blown my cover. But if anything, my tone seems to put Abbott more at ease. Cregg isn't the sort to suffer fools gladly, so the anger must strike him as more genuine than my silence.

As an added bonus, the harsh tone silences Costello. He doesn't speak again until Abbott pulls up in front of a townhouse on Constitution Avenue. "You got the keys?" he asks his partner.

"Yeah." Abbott fishes out a key ring with two keys—one large, one small.

"So," Costello says, "we're obviously gonna be busy this afternoon setting up for the Pfeifer thing. You want me to get Marky or Peterson to drive you around later, or are you all set with Alex?"

"I'm set."

"And . . ." He looks uncomfortable. "You're sure you got total control? You been awake for a while now, and Alex said you were still having some trouble holding it if you were awake more than—"

"I napped this afternoon," I say, opening the car door. "I'm in control. Just do the job and let me know when it's done."

He gives me a curt nod and I exit the car. They're both watching as I unlatch the gate and approach the door. An automatic light pops on, scaring me so badly I nearly drop the stupid keys. I manage to get the larger key into the slot after a couple of tries and slip inside, closing the door behind me.

One of those weird spells of light-headedness hits me as I watch their taillights gradually disappear through the narrow windows beside the door. I lean against the wall, trying to steady my pulse, and wait for the dizzy feeling to pass.

It does, after a moment, but I'm still seriously on edge. I guess that's to be expected, though. This is a strange house, in a strange neighborhood. For all I know, this could be a trap. Someone could be lurking upstairs in the dark.

I should probably go up and check. Make sure it's safe.

On the other hand, last night's vision indicated I'm still alive and kicking later this afternoon. That thought is comforting, and I hold on to it.

"If anyone is up there," I say aloud, "bring it on. Because you either lose or I outrun your ass."

It's a pathetic taunt, given how my voice quivers, but I feel braver simply for having spoken. I flip on the interior light to reveal a nearly empty living room. Nothing but a sofa, an office chair, and a bare computer desk with a single drawer.

Inside the drawer is an iPad and a large manila envelope. When I pull them out, I notice something else near the back of the drawer. A small wooden chest. A man's jewelry chest, maybe, for cuff links.

Opening the envelope first, I dump the contents onto the desk. It's mostly legal papers. But what catches my eye first is a bundle of documents in a plastic bag. On top is a Pennsylvania driver's license with my face. The picture is from my old school ID, taken long before Taylor gave me my current neo-punk makeover. It's been altered slightly—the cheekbones are a bit more pronounced, and there's less softness around the jawline. Something about the nose is different, too. This looks more like an older sister or cousin than it looks like me, but the goal was probably to age me up so I'd match the new date of birth: April 25, 1998. That makes this version of me almost twenty-two. I guess Cregg wanted to be sure he could order his Harvey Wallbangers or whatever middle-aged body thieves are drinking these days.

The name on the license is not Anna Elizabeth Morgan. In typical Cregg fashion, he went full Shakespeare: *Ophelia Beatrice Duncan*. How fitting that he'd opt for the crazy girl's name.

Phee Duncan's Social Security card and birth certificate are also inside, along with a generic receipt for the fake IDs. I shove all three documents into my pocket along with the key ring. No point in wasting a perfectly good fake identity. Given everything I've been through in the past year, I can certainly envision scenarios where it could come in quite handy. But I don't need the receipt, so I push it out of my way in order to inspect the other papers. As I do, the date at the top catches my eye: *12/1/19*.

My first assumption had been that Cregg set all of this up recently, but from the date, it appears that Cregg was still alive when he ordered these documents. On December 1st of last year, when this receipt was written, I was at Sandalford waiting for Taylor to get a reading on the location of Bree Bieler, one of the kids Graham Cregg was holding hostage. This was weeks before Jasper shot him and I had the great misfortune of taking him on board as a hitcher.

He was still alive, but he was on chemo. And from what Maria gathered when she was bold enough to peek into his poisonous head, chemo wasn't going so well.

Cregg knew he was going to die, but he also knew a way to cheat the reaper.

All this time I've been assuming he had Lucas kill Jaden and others to test whether I could be some sort of mega-weapon, a walking toolbox of secondhand psychic abilities courtesy of my hitchers. And maybe that was *part* of the plan. But what he wanted most was to learn whether he'd still be able to play his mind games after he stole my body.

He's been planning this ever since he learned about my ability. Jasper putting two bullets into his chest just sped up the timeline.

That also explains why Abbott, Costello, and presumably this Alex person were willing to accept the possibility that their former employer was now in the body of an eighteen-year-old girl. It was something they were expecting. Something they had planned for.

I look through the rest of the papers, hoping to find cash or a credit card. No luck, although there's a lease for this apartment, registered under the new identity. Two phone numbers, as well, with names I don't recognize. Neither of them is this Alex guy Costello told me to call.

The last item in the stack of papers is a medical brochure. Pauley Plastic Surgery. Specialists in facial reconstruction.

Smiling faces stare back from the image on the front of the brochure. New body. New identity. Just tweak the facial features a bit so you can really *own* the look. So no one suspects.

The brochure makes me furious, far more so than the other documents. It feels invasive, like a violation. I wad it into a tight ball and hurl the damned thing across the room.

Scree-e-e-e-ch-ch. Tap, tap, tap, tap, TAP.

That brief burst of anger seems to have energized my new parasite, just as it did last night. The scraping sounds were frightening enough in the familiar setting of the RV, with Aaron and Deo close by. Here in this strange (hopefully) empty house, however, they have me on the very knife-edge of panic.

I force myself to focus on things here, in this room. Things that are outside my head, solid and real and not woven from the fabric of my nightmares. The sofa is blue with white stripes. The chair—black, probably fake leather. Brown desk. Hardwood floors. A small chandelier on the ceiling that casts little dots of light on the beige walls.

Take deep breaths, Anna. Focus.

I repeat all of the things Kelsey would tell me if she was here. *There are no holes in your wall. The rat-spider in your head cannot get out. It's not even a real rat-spider. Just another hitcher.*

But, of course, my walls aren't really walls, either. They're every bit as much a mental fabrication as the rat-spider. Just a handy way of blocking off the hitchers inside my head.

And yes, this *is* just another hitcher. Only he's a hitcher who can force people to mutilate themselves, even to kill themselves, using only his mind. Myron was your everyday, ordinary psychopath, and he turned me into a weapon when I was six. How much more could Cregg—

Nope. Not gonna go there.

Deep breaths. Focus. *Chill.*

My resolve sticks this time, and even though I can still hear faint scritching noises, my pulse gradually drops to a normal range.

But I know even this tiny bit of calm is unlikely to stick unless I find a distraction. Something to focus on, rather than sitting here staring at the walls.

I pull the iPad toward me. A welcome screen pops up, asking for a six-digit code. It's probably his friggin' birthday, which I might be able to find out if I had my phone. I key in *000000, 123456,* and *654321,* basically just to try something, anything. Then I stop because I have no idea how many random guesses it will take before I'm tossed into a password jail.

It's now 6:19 a.m. according to the otherwise useless iPad, and a giant yawn hits me. I need to stand up. Splash some water on my face. Find something to drink. And then I have to get out of here. If I stay put for much longer, I'm running the risk that Taylor will be able to track me via remote viewing, especially since she has Deo to amplify her ability.

The kitchen is down the hallway, just past a half bath. It's still dark outside the window over the sink, but the sky is closer to navy than black, and there are faint hints of purple around the low-lying clouds.

There are no glasses (or anything else) in the cabinets, so I cup my hands under the faucet and drink from the tap.

I rub my still-wet hands over my eyes. It helps, but it's no substitute for a large black coffee.

When I look up again, my reflection stares back from the window-pane. The face is slightly misshapen, but that's probably just distortion from the double-hung windows. There's no rational explanation for the eyes, however. Six perfectly round, jet-black eyes—two large orbs on top and a row of four smaller circles below.

My hands fly back to my face instinctively, and for one awful second, I feel the spider's face and those cold round eyes instead of my own.

Stop it! You don't scare me!

I sound like a terrified child, and Cregg calls me on it. His voice is loud and clear, piercing through my walls as though they're made of paper.

But obviously I do scare you. I scare you very badly. Otherwise, you wouldn't have me in this ridiculous horror-show getup, now would you? You can't win this battle, but if you stop this nonsense, stop blocking my thoughts, we can work together. I'm perfectly willing to share.

He's right. He scares the hell out of me. But he disgusts me even more, and that emotion allows me to get a grip on my fear.

You're willing to share? Willing to share my body?

I shove backward on those last two words, with every bit of force I can muster.

*How generous. But you know what? You are wrong. I do win
this battle, Graham Cregg. Maybe not the war, but I know
that was me in the vision. Me in control this afternoon. So
keep your body-thieving ass back behind the wall unless you
want to lose another leg.*

The words sound brave, but my knees are barely holding me
upright. I hurry back into the living room, scoop the iPad and papers
into the manila envelope, and stuff them into the lining of Aaron's
jacket.

I turn for the door, but then I remember the locked chest in the
desk drawer. It might not be jewelry. Maybe it's thumb drives, or the
password for the iPad. The chest is too big to carry easily, so despite
how badly I want to get out of here, I force myself to dig the keyring
out of my pocket.

The smaller key is dull and well-worn. It fits easily into the lock,
but I have to jiggle it a few times before the tumblers click. Black velvet
lines the inside of the case, and I'm pretty sure my original guess is
correct—it's intended to display cuff links.

Instead, it displays fingers. Pinkies, to be precise, lined up neatly
and perfectly preserved. All various shades of beige except for one—
dark brown with chipped purple nail polish. And off in the corner, one
that is nothing but bone.

Barely stifling a scream, I drop the box back into the drawer like
it's a hot coal. Two of the fingers fall out, but I can't bring myself to
put them back.

The only thing I can do is get the hell out of there.

CHAPTER EIGHT

Silver Spring, Maryland
April 24, 2020, 8:48 a.m.

By the time the train pulls into the station, my panic has subsided. Despite my desire to run, that wasn't an option with an iPad and an envelope full of documents stashed in the lining of my jacket. So I settled for walking and then collapsing onto the seat of a Metro train headed for the suburbs. Red Line. Home turf.

I'm hit by a wave of nostalgia as I exit the train at Glenmont, coupled with an awareness of how very much has changed in the six months since I last entered this station. Molly was inside my head back then, not Cregg. Deo and I were still living at Bartholomew House. I'd never met Aaron, or Taylor, or Daniel.

I'd never seen a dead body except in my dreams. Now I've seen around a dozen. The fact that *around a dozen* is the best descriptor I have for the number of bodies I've seen tells me how much *I've* changed. I seem to have lost count, and that really feels like something a person should be able to pin a specific number on.

And after this morning, I've now seen the *partial* remains of at least a dozen more. I should have counted. Again, it feels wrong—disrespectful and dehumanizing—not to know the number of fingers in that box.

But I'm not the only one who has changed. The people around me in the subway are also subtly different from the crowd back then. Six months ago, the vast majority of people pushing their way into the train for their morning commute would have largely ignored everyone else as they read, listened to music, or talked on their phones. Today, they still don't interact, but their eyes dart from one person to the next. Alert. Suspicious.

Is that man one of them?

Why is she looking at me like that? Can she hear what I'm thinking?

A year ago, most of these people would have said that psychic abilities were the stuff of fiction. They would have laughed at the notion that anyone might be reading their thoughts. Might be *feeding* them thoughts. The possibility that one of their fellow commuters might be able, with a single touch, to flick out the lights inside the train—or worse, cause it to burst into flames—would have seemed ludicrous.

I spot a few other changes scattered about the station. There have always been public service messages alternating with the paid ads, but there are a lot more of the *See Something, Say Something* variety than before.

The Sanctuary for Psychics ad is also new. In the center of the white sign is a purple drawing of an adult with arms spread wide to encircle dozens of children. The figures are rounded blobs, similar to those old toys called Weebles, and the purple is clearly meant to evoke Senator Cregg's Unify America party. A 1-800 number and web address are at the bottom, along with the words *You Don't Have to Bear This Alone.*

Deo once noted that the motto is a terrible choice, given the bear masks worn by the groups perpetrating the various terrorist acts, or at least claiming credit for them. And some Metro customer apparently agrees. A picture of the WOCAN flag, with the grizzly bear at the center, has been taped under the words *Bear This Alone*.

Oh . . . and the hats. That's definitely something new. Taylor's fashion statement from last fall seems to have caught on. It's a bit warm for hats today, but maybe a third of the people are wearing them. And if you look closely, almost all of them have a literal silver lining. There's no evidence tinfoil deters Delphi powers, but I'm sure that claim is being made on the conspiracy sites, which have spread like a virus over the past few months. And, hey, tinfoil is cheap. Why take chances?

I emerge from the escalator to the sound of traffic on Georgia Avenue. Carver's Deli is a half hour's walk from the station, a walk I can make on autopilot. I need food and, more importantly, caffeine. Every penny I had was in my backpack, and Joe still has my last paycheck. It's only for a few days' work, but it will keep me fed, hydrated, and alert until I meet up with the others. When I called back in October to tell Joe I had to quit without notice, he promised to hold the check until the next time I was in town. He usually goes to the bank around lunchtime, and since the morning rush is over, hopefully he'll have enough money in the register to cash the check for me. And if not, I know he'll give me a bagel and a cup of coffee.

I'm not entirely happy with this plan, but it's the only one I have. I switched trains three times, and I've kept a close watch since I left the station. If anyone is following me, they're damn good. My plan is to slip in, collect the money, and go. Five minutes, tops. Joe will probably want to catch up, but I'll have to cut it short. Tell him I'm in a rush and promise to get back with him later.

And I *will* get back with him later. I miss Joe.

The smell of freshly baked bagels hits my nose as I approach the door. I close my eyes for a moment and imagine myself back to this time last year. Walking through the door, slipping into my *Try Carver's Cravers!* apron, and joking around with Joe for a few hours while we prepare for the lunch crowd.

The place is fairly empty, which is the norm at nine a.m. on a weekday. Most of Joe's weekday-morning business is over by now, as people grab coffee and something portable to wolf down on their way to work. On weekends, customers linger, read the news, or just relax over their food. But during the workweek, it's strictly in and out.

Joe looks up when the bell over the door rings. He doesn't recognize me until I'm at the counter. When he realizes it's me, his face doesn't break into the smile of welcome I expected. In fact, it sort of tightens. Even though I left him shorthanded when I quit, he was sympathetic when we spoke on the phone. I thought he'd be happy to see me, and my smile fades at his uneasy expression.

"Hey, Joe."

"Anna." He casts a nervous glance around the small dining area and the one occupied table near the door. A woman is reading something on her phone while her toddler sits in his stroller, watching the cars roll by as he happily gnaws on a half bagel.

The sight of the kid eating stirs up a sympathetic growl from my very empty stomach. Joe must hear it, because he sighs and shakes his head, a tiny hint of a smile lifting the corners of his mouth. "Come on back to the office," he says, then yells into the kitchen. "Andre! Watch the front."

"But . . . you said to sauté the onions."

"Leave them. Go wipe down the condiment stand. I'll only be a minute."

Andre, who looks about Deo's age, wipes his hands on a nearby towel. Joe and I go back to his "office"—a small desk in an alcove behind the walk-in fridge, next to a waist-high filing cabinet. His computer is even older than the one Deo and I share. Joe still does a lot of his bookkeeping the old-fashioned way. I'd almost convinced him to upgrade and let me computerize everything when I had to quit.

"He's half useless," Joe mutters once Andre is out of earshot. "Third kid I've hired since you left. But hold on, let me find that check." He rifles through a file in the top drawer. "You did something different with your hair. Nearly didn't recognize you."

"It's been a . . . strange couple of months."

"Yeah. So I've heard. Ah, there it is." He pulls out the check and then turns back to me, looking me directly in the eye for the first time. There's a bit of challenge in that look, along with something very close to anger. "You do know the cops came 'round looking for you, right? You and Deo both. Also some federal investigator. Asked a whole lot of questions I didn't have answers to. I told them I couldn't picture you working with no terrorists, and no way in hell either of you would hurt any kids. So you want to tell me what you've gotten yourself mixed up in, girl? Are you really one of those . . ."

He pauses and I brace myself. He's about to say *freaks*, or maybe *mutants*.

But Joe doesn't say the words. He simply leaves the sentence unfinished and holds out the check.

I want to shove it into my pocket and just go, get out of here, before he says something else that shreds the pleasant memories I have of working with him. Before he says something that makes me cry, because until this moment I would have said Joe was a great guy. One of the best.

But I can't leave. The check has my name on it, and there's no way I'll be able to cash it with the fake ID in my pocket.

"Could you . . . cash it?" I don't want to look at him, worried I'll see fear or disgust in his expression. So I keep my eyes pinned on the floor that I mopped so many . . . times.

The *white tile floor*. The one that's almost identical to the floor in Lab 1 at The Warren. The familiar feeling I had during the vision comes rushing back. Costello. Blood on a white tile floor.

"Never mind," I tell Joe, not even bothering to take the check. I rush back to the kitchen, even though I know anything I do now is pointless. But there are plenty of places with white tile floors, right? I just have to get out of here and find another one for Costello to bleed all over.

Except . . . when I look through the order window toward the dining room, I see two men getting out of a gray car parked in front of the little Indian market across the street.

The mom and baby are still at the front table.

"Get out!" I yell through the window. The woman looks up from her phone, clearly about to protest, so I add, "Gas leak!"

That gets her moving. She spins the kid's stroller around so quickly it knocks over the chair she was in. Ramming one shoulder against the door like a linebacker, she hits the sidewalk running, just as Abbott and Costello catch a break in the traffic and start across the street.

"Get Andre and go out the back," I yell to Joe as I head for the revolving door that separates the kitchen from the dining room. If I can reach the front in time to turn the lock, it will buy them a few minutes to get out of here.

But Joe grabs my arm. "Why did you tell that customer there's a—"

I glance back to the window. They're almost across the road now. No time to lock the door.

"Joe, those men are armed. But they won't hurt me." I wrench my arm out of his grasp. "You and Andre need to get out."

Andre comes over, a rag in one hand and the metal cream pitcher in the other. "So . . . is there really a gas leak or what?"

The bell above the door rings. Damn it. Now I'm going to have to rely on my acting skills.

"I told you I had personal business to take care of," I say, moving purposefully toward the two men entering the door. "I'm not paying you to follow me around. Why aren't you dealing with the Pfeifer matter?"

Costello looks uncertain. Abbott, on the other hand, smirks. "You had an appointment at the bank almost an hour ago. Alex says you never showed up. Never even called."

"I called. He didn't answer."

There's a pause and they exchange a look.

"Oh, wow." Costello makes a pained face. "Seriously wrong answer, Anna."

He pulls a handgun from inside his jacket and points it toward me. Abbott quickly follows suit.

As soon as Andre sees the guns, the pitcher he's holding tumbles from his hand. It clangs against the floor, sending an off-white plume of half-and-half sailing into the air.

I don't know if it's the sound or the metallic glint of the pitcher as it moves in Abbott's peripheral vision, but he spins toward Andre without hesitation and fires. The bullet hits the boy in the shoulder. He cries out, and that's what finally gets Joe moving. Joe was a medic in Vietnam, so maybe it's the training from fifty years ago that kicks in. He catches Andre before the kid hits the ground and drags him back through the swinging door.

Both guns are again pointed at me. I know they won't shoot. Even though they realize Cregg is no longer in the driver's seat, there's no way they'll risk serious harm to his precious vessel. Not if they want to get paid. But they're clearly willing to hurt Joe or Andre. In fact, they may feel they *have* to eliminate the two of them as witnesses. My secondhand tae kwon do skills, inherited from Jaden, probably aren't going to cut it.

I take two quick steps backward through the swinging doors and give a hard kick in the other direction. The left door hits one of them, maybe both. There's a loud *oof*, followed by the sound of someone staggering backward.

Behind me, I hear a creak from the door that leads to the alley. It's not a loud sound, and I doubt I'd even know it was a door opening if I hadn't opened it so many times to take out the trash. Joe must have gotten the boy outside. I send up a silent prayer that Abbott and Costello don't think to circle around to the back.

That prayer is answered instantly, although not necessarily in the way I hoped, since I now have opponents on two fronts. Costello comes through the swinging door as expected, while Abbott, by far the more athletic of the two, begins climbing through the service window.

The cutting board where Andre was slicing onions is only a few feet away from the service window. As tempting as it is to go after the knife, I can't risk moving closer to Abbott.

One of those odd bits of déjà vu runs through my mind when I take my next breath. There's a hint of smoke in the air from the now-burning onions, and I remember the red mark on Abbott's face as he crossed Second Street in my vision. I can't reach the knife, but I can reach the stove.

Yanking my jacket sleeve down to protect my palm, I grab the handle of the pan and swing it in a wide sideways arc, spraying the contents in front of me. Halfway through the swing, I release the handle and the skillet goes flying.

Even though the bottom layer is burned, most of the onions are still moist. Abbott catches about half of them on his neck and face. They stick to him like scalding plaster. He falls backward into the galley between the counter and the order window as he screams, trying frantically to scrape the molten mess from his neck and hair.

The remaining onions rain down in the kitchen, along with droplets of oil from the pan. I catch a few bits on my arm, and one giant glob hits Costello in the stomach a split second before the hot skillet connects with his shoulder. He falls, landing hard on his right arm. The pistol he was holding careens across the floor until the grip lodges behind the wheel of the bagel rack.

Costello recovers quickly, though—much more quickly than Abbott, judging from the whimpering noises in the other room—and we both dive for the gun at the same instant. He's closer, but I'm less injured and about a hundred pounds lighter.

I get to the gun first, but only by a fraction of a second. No sooner has my hand closed around the grip than Costello's hand—hot, damp, and slimy from the onions—smacks down on mine.

> Let him have the gun, Anna. They won't hurt you if I'm in control.

The words in my head are accompanied by a faint buzzing noise. My walls are still up. I've been building them so long that I can do the basic level without even thinking, the same way you don't have to think to add two plus two. I can almost—but not quite—maintain a basic wall against ordinary hitchers in my sleep.

But Cregg isn't an ordinary hitcher. He's punched a hole somewhere, a hole big enough that his suggestion—his very *strong* suggestion—gets through.

I quickly reinforce the barrier, but for just an instant, my hand relaxes. It's enough to tilt the balance in Costello's favor. He pulls the gun toward him, and I'm about to lose my hold, but then his hand slips.

When I yank the gun away, I realize why. The handle is now slick with residue from the onions. I'm pretty sure that's the only reason I'm now pointing the gun at his head instead of him pointing it at mine.

Pushing with my elbows, I scoot backward on my stomach, away from Costello. I barely make it six inches, however, before my feet hit the bagel rack.

The mewling from the galley has quieted now. Abbott's voice, still shaky, says, "Give him the gun, Anna."

Even without looking, I know Abbott's pistol is aimed at me. Knowing he can't shoot me, that he *doesn't* shoot me or else I wouldn't be in DC a few hours from now, doesn't make that any less unnerving.

I roll slightly so I can watch Abbott at the same time. He's almost behind me, though, and I can't retreat any farther with the bagel rack—and for that matter, the wall—blocking my path. There's no way for me to see both of them fully from this angle, so I have to settle for shifting my eyes back and forth between the two.

"Give me the gun." Costello, who is still lying on the ground, holds out his hand, palm up. "Give it over and we won't go after your friends who ran through the back. No need for them to get hurt."

"Why should I believe that? You already shot one of them."

That faint creak comes from the back of the deli again. I wish I had Maria's ability to send a thought, so I could tell Joe to stay out. To focus on getting Andre to safety, because I know I walk out of here unharmed. All I can do, however, is hope I'm the only one who recognized that sound and that Joe has the good sense to stay out.

"Pretty sure I just winged the boy," Abbott says. "And the old guy will have called the cops. You can't afford to get caught any more than we can. So give us the gun. You won't be able to hold Cregg off forever."

Cregg's faint murmur of agreement is barely audible behind my walls, but the fact that I can hear him at all means Abbott is right. I *won't* be able to hold him off forever.

That fear must show on my face, because Abbott nods. "Yeah, you know I'm telling the truth. When you sleep, it's really easy for him to take over. He told us he could've slit your boyfriend's throat in his sleep and you wouldn't have been able to stop him."

The words are clearly meant to catch me off guard, and they do. Is that why I moved to a separate bedroom? Did I know subconsciously that Aaron was at risk and acted to protect him?

I'm so caught up in this thought that I nearly miss the blur of movement from Costello. He now has the skillet in his hand, and it's coming straight at me.

A shot rings out, and then the tiles shake as the pan smashes down, inches from my head.

For a second, I'm certain I pulled the trigger. I *should* have pulled the trigger. That would have been the smart thing to do when someone is trying to crack your head with a still-smoking skillet.

But I didn't fire. While I'm not a gun expert, I've heard several weapons fired at close range in the past few months. This sounded more like the rifle Grady fired in the woods at Overhills.

And the wound is on the opposite side of Costello's neck. Blood flows from his shoulder onto the white tile floor, a trickle that almost instantly becomes a pool, spreading beneath his head. Déjà vu all over again.

Abbott must also think I'm the one who fired. His eyes are fixed on the gun in my hand. But instead of putting the pieces together and searching for the actual source of the gunfire, his head whips around toward the front of the deli.

Now I hear it, too. A siren.

Not close. Not yet. But definitely a siren.

"You okay, Anna?" It's Joe. I can't see him, but his voice comes from back near the walk-in cooler.

Abbott turns to me, his eyes darting around as he tries to pinpoint Joe's location. He must not be able to find him, because he ducks down behind the wall. I hear footsteps, but I'm still on the floor, so I can't see which way Abbott is heading. Certain he's about to enter through the swinging door, I whip the gun in that direction. But the door remains still and the footsteps retreat.

"You can't hold him off, Anna." Judging from the sound, Abbott must be near the front of the deli. "And I know you can hear me, Cregg. Since I'm doing the Pfeifer job solo now, my price just tripled."

The little cowbell over the door jingles. I'm pretty sure Abbott's gone, but I push up onto my feet and crouch-walk toward the door, nudging it open a crack to be sure. The dining room is empty, everything in its place except the cream pitcher, which is still on its side in front of the counter. Abbott is already sprinting across the road to his car, one hand held against his scorched neck.

When I look back toward the kitchen, Joe has moved out of the shadows. A rifle hangs down at his side. It looks strange, almost alien.

That hand should be holding the large slotted spoon he uses to scoop out the bagels, not a rifle.

He crouches down and rests two fingers against Costello's neck. "Is he dead?"

"Not yet. There's a pulse, but it's weak."

"What about that kid . . . Andre? Is he okay?"

Joe nods, laying the rifle on the counter. "Cut a pretty deep groove in his shoulder. Need to get him to a hospital and get it bandaged up."

"You should have stayed out there with him, Joe. Now you're in the middle of this and the police are on their way."

"Not yet. That was a fire truck."

I didn't think about the difference in the heat of the moment, but he's right. The sound was a long, consistent wail, without the pulsing *wap-wap-wap* in the middle that marks the local police sirens.

"I'm guessing we're going to get some police attention pretty soon, though," Joe says as he pushes open the door to the dining room. I start to follow, but that wobbly sensation, almost like vertigo, is back. So I stay put, leaning back against the wall for support. I need sleep or, at the very least, coffee.

Joe comes back a moment later with a small stack of bills and a take-out bag full of bagels. "You need to get going."

I stare down at Costello. "No. This is my fault, Joe. I shouldn't have come here. I can't let you take the blame for this."

"I'm the one who shot him. And . . . it's better this way. Even if you could have pulled the trigger, I wouldn't want you to have killing someone on your conscience."

"But if he dies, you'll have it on yours."

"Yeah, well, I'm old. Less time for it to bother me, although I doubt this one will. I killed guys in 'Nam, and that haunted me because they were in the same boat I was—drafted and stuck fighting for a cause they probably didn't believe in. But I learned sometimes you have to kill to keep yourself and your friends alive. This guy, though . . . if he dies, I don't think I'll lose much sleep."

"What are you going to tell the police?"

"Asshole tried to rob me. Shot my assistant. I'll wipe your prints off that gun and I'll tell Andre not to mention you. But . . . he's pretty scared and not nearly as bright as the employee I had this time last year who *ran off on me*. He could easily let something slip. So . . . you might want to switch the hair color again or buy a new jacket."

I glance down at the bills in my hand. It's nearly two hundred bucks, way more than the three days' pay in my final check. "This is more than you owe me."

"Consider it a bonus. Given the quality of workers I've had in the past six months, I was clearly underpaying you."

"I'm really, really sorry for—"

"Just go! I need to call 911."

"Sure." I'm a few steps from the door when he calls my name, and I turn back.

"Whatever you're mixed up in, just . . . ." Joe shakes his head. There's still doubt in his eyes, but it's tempered by concern. "Just be careful, okay? And save one of those bagels for Deo."

INTERVIEW FROM THE US SENATE COMMITTEE
ON HOMELAND SECURITY AND GOVERNMENTAL
AFFAIRS WEBSITE:

Permanent Subcommittee on Investigations
Threat Assessment on The Delphi Project
Excerpt from the Testimony of Dr. Scott Pfeifer
April 23, 2020

Sen. Elena Rodriguez: How many of your subjects died as a result of these experiments?

Dr. Scott Pfeifer: There were no direct casualties. But fourteen of the roughly two hundred people who participated over the lifespan of the project committed suicide.

Rodriguez: Those suicides killed a few other people too, I believe?

Pfeifer: Yes.

Rodriguez: Were you under the effects of the Delphi drug when you shot your ex-wife?

Pfeifer: On advice of my attorney, I decline to answer.

Rodriguez: Okay. Let me ask you this, then. Is it standard for someone in your field to be a subject of his own experiment?

Pfeifer: No.

Rodriguez: During the time you've been a patient at Perkins, were you at any point contacted by your former employer or anyone else requesting your help in developing a cure for the so-called Delphi serum?

Pfeifer: No. And even if I'd had access to a lab, I doubt I'd have been much help. While I did conduct the original research, there have been a lot of advances in my field during my . . . absence. If they *had* contacted me, however, I'd have told them what I noted in my opening statement. I don't think a cure is possible, at least not in the sense of erasing the impact of the drug. You might be able to mitigate the symptoms—suppress the effects—but a *cure* would imply reversing changes to the brain structure. Based on my research, when the drug works, the changes are permanent.

Rodriguez: So you're saying this drug you created causes permanent brain damage?

Pfeifer: No. I said permanent *changes* to the structure of the brain. To the wiring, if you will. Whether that's damage or enhancement is a judgment call.

Rodriguez: And what is your view, Dr. Pfeifer? Damage or enhancement?

Pfeifer: That depends on the individual's reaction, and to some extent on the variant of the drug used.

Rodriguez: Okay, so in your view, a cure is unlikely. What about a vaccine?

Pfeifer: I . . . I beg your pardon? Could you repeat the question?

Rodriguez: A *vaccine*? To prevent further spread of—

Pfeifer: It's not a communicable disease. A person would actually have to be injected with the serum at least once for the drug to have any impact at all.

Rodriguez: Four cases of infection have been reported in Arizona. One in California.

Pfeifer: I'm sorry, but that's simply not possible.

Rodriguez: Maybe. Or maybe your earlier assessment was correct, Dr. Pfeifer. There have been a lot of advancements in your field in the past fifteen years. I yield the remainder of my time.

CHAPTER NINE

Another gust of wind whips at the umbrella anchored to the table. I'd love to move inside, but I have to watch the street. To be honest, though, I'm not sure what I'm looking for. All I know is that, at some point, something is going to make me head toward the Hart Senate Office Building, about a block away. I need to stay alert for that something.

Or not. I mean, the vision has already told me I'm going to end up there. That's one reason I'm here, drinking my third coffee of the afternoon and eating another of the bagels Joe gave me, rather than camped out across from the Hart Building, waiting.

After I left the deli, I went to the secondhand store where Deo spent most of our money over the past few years and replaced all of my clothes, right down to my shoes. D would be proud—my new red-and-black hoodie actually matches the knock-off Chuck Taylors. I also ducked into a CVS to buy a small knapsack to hold the iPad and the envelope from Cregg's townhouse. Abbott has managed to locate me twice, so they must have placed some sort of tracker on me yesterday when I was on the beach. I changed and then shoved everything I had been wearing into a trash bin outside the drugstore.

Now reasonably certain I was free of tracking devices, I took the Metro downtown and then walked around until I found my favorite place to hide when I was on the streets—a library. As long as you keep quiet and you keep reading, no one will run you out. I didn't stay long, however. It was hard to focus on reading, partly because I'm nervous and partly because I'm exhausted.

Food and coffee do seem to have warded off the dizzy spells, though. I was beginning to wonder if they were something Cregg was causing, somehow, from behind my walls. But maybe it was just the aftereffects of no sleep and losing my dinner last night.

For the past few minutes, I've been trying to guess the password on Cregg's iPad—an iPad that now has a cracked screen. I didn't even think about it being in my jacket when I dove for the gun back at Joe's place.

I wish I could call Joe and see how things went with the police. Make sure Andre is okay. But I should probably hold off for a while. Let things cool down.

When I finish the last of the coffee, I decide to start walking toward the Hart Building. I don't know exactly what time it was in the vision, but the level of light seems about right to me. And sure enough, as I'm tossing my cup into the trash, I spot Abbott's gray sedan easing into one of the metered parking spots on the other side of Massachusetts Avenue, half a block up.

At least . . . I think it's the same car. I pull the jacket hood over my hair and slouch down into a nearby chair, waiting for the driver to get out.

It's Abbott. I freeze in place, waiting for him to turn in the direction of the Hart Building. For the longest time, he stands outside the car, looking down at something on his phone. Finally, he leaves. Once I'm sure he won't spot me, I head for an alley I noticed earlier that comes out directly across from the Hart Building.

It's also right near the bike rack where I'm going to trip and bust my ass. Something to look forward to.

As I hurry through the alley toward my rendezvous with gravity, it occurs to me that the visions I inherited from Jaden are more like those that Stan gets than I'd thought at first. True, I don't actually see multiple paths the future might take. Everything I see in the vision is going to happen. But I do get this odd parallel train of thought with alternative courses of action I can't take no matter how hard I try. In some flipside universe, I could turn left and head back to the Metro. I could duck into that women's history museum next to the Hart Building and stare at memorabilia from the suffrage era while Abbott delivers long-delayed justice for my mother. Or I could keep running onto Second Street into the path of that big red bus.

That last thought is the one that brings my feet skidding to a halt and causes my sneaker to catch on the brick. My calf collides with the first bike. My hand flies out to grasp the bike rail. My ass hits the ground, and my brain enters that weird dual track where I remember having the vision as I watch myself act it out movement for movement, line for line.

The bus drives on toward Union Station, and while I'm still trying to figure out whether that brief suicidal thought came from me or from Cregg, Abbott walks into view at the corner of Second and C Streets, just as he did in the vision. His neck is a bright red, like a splotchy sunburn. And again, I experience that same feeling of relief mixed with only a tiny smidgen of guilt when I get the flash of memory where Costello is bleeding on the tile floor.

Déjà vu swings into full force as I watch Abbott reach for the gun inside his jacket. He crosses the street with the blue *Love Thy Neighbor* banner visible behind him. Three men exit from the Hart Building and move toward the black car idling at the curb—two guys in black suits flanking a third man, who is definitely Scott Pfeifer. He's maybe six two and wearing a navy jacket and tan pants. The guy on his right is muscular, but the one on the left looks like he eats Frosted Steroid Flakes for breakfast. And something about the shape of his head seems familiar.

All possible actions I could take run through my head. Even though I know I don't yell to the guard that Abbott is armed, I consider it, because in some part of my brain, this is all happening for the first time. The street is crowded. About a dozen people in all, mostly adults in business attire but also a few who look like tourists. One teenage girl walking her dogs. The guard is focused on his phone, so I have zero confidence in his ability to snap to attention and figure out which person I'm talking about in time to save my father. And I know beyond any doubt that Abbott will shoot innocent people to accomplish his goal.

But Abbott won't shoot me. If he shoots the vessel, there goes his big fat payday.

So even though I want to run away, I run toward him.

The rage building up behind my walls is also both current and remembered. I push it back and reinforce my walls, telling him it's *my* body and he has no control over me. And as much as Cregg wants to stop me, he knows he can't change anything, at least not until . . . now, when the horn I remember from the vision blasts the warning that ended my sneak preview. The guard at the kiosk is finally looking this way. I don't know if he sees the gun, but he definitely sees me tackle Abbott from behind. Abbott staggers and tumbles forward onto the asphalt. I fall on top of him, bracing myself for the sound of gunfire beneath us when his hand hits the ground.

Instead, I hear the squeal of brakes and screeching tires as a white delivery van skids to a stop mere inches in front us. It's an older van, with a dented side panel near the front tire. The woman behind the wheel is young, maybe a few years older than I am. Pink sunglasses hold back her shoulder-length brown hair. And she must have seen

Abbott's gun, because she dives at the passenger-side floorboard before the wheels even stop spinning.

Abbott pushes up abruptly, tossing me to the road as he scrambles to his feet. The gun twitches toward me, and I realize I may have made a very serious miscalculation. On the one hand, he wants the cash Cregg promised. On the other hand, I'm the reason his face and neck are a bright, blistered pink, the reason he missed his chance to complete his assignment, and the reason he was just nearly decapitated by a delivery van. His expression leaves no doubt about how badly he wants to squeeze the trigger.

He shoves the gun back inside his jacket. Either greed wins out or he simply realizes it will be easier to escape if he doesn't draw further attention to himself. I expect him to turn and run back toward his car, but instead he opens the driver's-side door and dives into the van. Great. Now he's got the driver as a hostage.

Abbott peels off, nearly taking out the guard and a woman on a bicycle. The guard runs after them at full speed, slowing slightly when the light at Constitution Avenue turns red. He probably thinks Abbott will stop, but he doesn't. The van whips through a narrow gap in traffic and hangs a sharp left.

A horn blasts, reminding me I'm still in the middle of the street. I stumble to the sidewalk and look toward the black sedan parked at the side entrance. Apparently convinced the danger has passed, the two men escorting my father are again leading him toward the car.

As they round the guard kiosk, Scott Pfeifer's eyes lock onto mine. His head tilts to the side as he stares at me. One of the bodyguards, goons, or whatever he is, opens the door, and Pfeifer starts to get in, but then he stops, wedged between the door and the body of the vehicle, still staring at me.

And yes, I'm staring back. I need to get the hell out of here, but I can't pull my eyes away. For the first time in my life—or at least the first time I can remember—I'm looking at my father.

I am ten yards away from my father.

Ten yards away from the man who killed my mother.

The two bodyguards follow his gaze. One of them says something to my father. I don't catch the words, but he finally breaks eye contact and climbs inside the vehicle. Then the larger man heads toward me.

Now that I see his face, I realize why he seemed familiar. It's the guy from The Warren. Daniel and Jaden called him Whistler, although I don't know if that's his actual name or a nickname. He was with Dacia when she questioned me at the police station last October. He was also with Dacia at the Senator's press conference. And he was with Dacia and Grady at Overhills when they killed Hunter Bieler and the other five kids.

I'm pretty sure Whistler was also the one Hunter heard say he didn't sign on for killing kids, but I can't double-check that fact because the Cregg-spider-rat is right smack between me and my memory banks. Although, on second thought, I couldn't check even if Cregg wasn't there, since Hunter's memories seen to be MIA.

The kiosk guard is back now, out of breath. His gun is still drawn, and it's pointed at me. I'm not entirely sure why. Maybe because he saw me tackle Abbott in the middle of the road, or maybe he simply needs someone to point it at now that the van is gone.

I'm not stupid. My hands go up.

In the distance, I hear a siren. Maybe Abbott won't get away after all.

"Who was that man?" the guard asks, panting heavily. "Why did you shove him into traffic?"

Whistler has paused next to the kiosk, which is about halfway between their car and the corner where I'm standing. I'm pretty sure he recognizes me, even though my hair was longer, at least five shades lighter, and far less blue when he last saw me.

"I don't know who he was. He stole my bag. I was trying to get it back."

The guard casts a skeptical eye at my knapsack, still across my shoulder.

"My *shopping* bag. From the Apple store. I just bought a new iPad, because mine has a cracked screen." At least that'll check out if necessary.

Whistler walks toward us. *Whistling*. Now I'm certain that's not his real name.

"Excuse me, Officer. Could you raise the gate?" He nods toward the barrier arm blocking the exit. "We need to get this witness back to Perkins."

"Sure thing," the guard wheezes, tapping a control attached to his belt. The parking arm slides upward.

Whistler thanks him, then says, "You need to hold that girl for questioning. She's a mutant." He gives me a smug grin and retreats back toward the car.

"He's lying! I can show you ID." I reach one hand into my windbreaker, planning to retrieve the Ophelia Duncan driver's license.

But the guard, whose name tag reads *Guffey*, is having none of it. "Keep . . . your hands . . . *up!*" he says as he reaches down to his belt to retrieve a handheld radio.

The car pulls out of the drive. Whistler grins at me as they pass, but I'm focused more on the man they shoved into the back seat. He's alive, so I guess I achieved my objective. But it's really hard to see this as a win, given that Abbott got away and I'm stuck here with the federal government equivalent of *Paul Blart: Mall Cop*.

"I have ID," I repeat. "He must have mistaken me for someone. I took the blood test and everything. I'm not a mutant. Just let me get my—"

"Save it," Guffey says. "Otherwise, you're going to have to say it all over again."

"You don't need to call this in." The voice behind me is so very familiar, I almost think it's coming from inside my head.

"Her ID checked out." Daniel's words are slurred—but not much, and I'm not even sure I'd have noticed if I hadn't heard his voice almost nonstop when he was my hitcher. "The girl didn't see anything. Go back to your booth."

Guffey looks confused for a moment, but then says, "You're clear to go. Just be more careful next time, okay?"

I nod and take a few steps toward Daniel, who is leaning against Aaron. Neither of them looks happy, but I don't know whether that's due to their close physical proximity to each other or to our current situation. Probably both.

"Nothing to see here but a dumb girl who ran into the street and nearly got herself killed," Daniel adds. Guffey doesn't hear him—he's already back inside his little hut—so that sentence was 100 percent for my benefit.

Aaron looks like he's on the brink of exploding. "We need to go," he says.

And that's *all* he says. He doesn't even look at me as he pivots Daniel back in the direction of C Street.

Once we're well past the point where the guard can hear us, Aaron stops abruptly next to one of the oak trees along the road and half leans, half shoves Daniel against it. Daniel gives him a withering look, but Aaron isn't paying attention to him. He whirls around to face me, staring directly into my eyes. He's looking for something, the same way he did at the beach yesterday. Back then, I thought he was simply trying to see if I was telling the truth. But now I'm pretty sure he's looking for Cregg. Do my eyes turn red or something when Cregg is in control?

Spider eyes. Flat black spider eyes like the ones you saw in the reflection last night.

I shove that memory away and hold Aaron's stare defiantly. "It's *me*, Aaron."

I'm fairly certain he believes me, but there's also a hefty dose of doubt. Maybe he can sense Cregg just under the surface.

"It's *me*, damn it. I've been in control since last night. The whole time."

Relief battles with hurt and anger in his hazel eyes. Eventually, anger wins out. "Which means you don't even have an excuse."

Before I can respond, Aaron stomps off toward his brother. Daniel gives me a confused but somewhat sympathetic look, and then they both start down the sidewalk again.

"Shouldn't she be in front of us?" Daniel asks. "Given her recent—"

"She wants to leave, she'll leave. Last night proved that."

I bite back my retort, since I'd really prefer to have this conversation in private. To be fair, I can't blame him for being angry. I would be, too, if he'd taken off like that, putting himself in danger without telling me.

But by the time I crawl into the Kia SUV they're driving—which is parked very illegally in an alley two blocks down—I realize swallowing my anger isn't the best idea at the moment. It seems to be strengthening Cregg, and it makes my stomach twist. Daniel and I don't have many secrets anyway. He spent enough time in my head that he probably knows exactly what I'm going to say before it's even out of my mouth.

So, once Aaron is on the road, I reach forward and touch his elbow. "I get that you're angry, okay? I'm sorry I worried you. But I did what I had to do. I did what I saw in the vision. And Stan said—"

"I don't give a damn what Stan said!" Aaron says, catching my eye briefly in the rearview mirror. "Not one single solitary damn. All I know is you didn't trust me enough to tell me what you were up to."

Daniel sighs. "Could this wait? Like, maybe, until he's not driving?"

"No. Now you know how I feel when you guys get into one of your Quinn family battles royale." I turn back to Aaron. "Do you really mean to say you'd have let me leave, knowing what I had to do? You'd have let me walk out of the camper alone knowing two of Cregg's men were going to pick me up?"

"No, because you walking out alone was stupid. You could have been killed."

"Not if they wanted to get the money Cregg promised them. I knew that. I also knew I'd get away from them unharmed in time to stop the attack on my father."

"As much as I hate to spoil your victory party," Daniel says, "your father is still in the hands of the Senator's people."

"Yes. But he's not *dead*, which is what Graham Cregg wanted. And *not dead* means we still have options."

Daniel gives me a *point-taken* nod, and I realize with a bit of surprise that I'm happy he's here. He can be annoying, and that was doubly true when we were sharing a body, but Daniel is a good guy. And the fact that he's up, reasonably mobile, and still in possession of his abilities is a big plus for our side.

"I'm glad you're better, Daniel."

"You and me both."

"Thanks for the save back there."

"No problem. I'm just glad it worked. My ability isn't back to full strength yet. It's a muscle, like anything else, and I wasn't using it in the hospital. Even so, it was a hell of a lot easier to nudge that guard using my own body than it was when I had to work through yours."

Aaron's back stiffens. I wonder whether that was a deliberate poke on Daniel's part. He knows how unhappy Aaron was about our previous living arrangements. No matter how unavoidable it may have been, having Daniel inside my head meant we had no privacy. Plus, their sibling rivalry doesn't really need extra fuel for the flames. But Daniel actually looks somewhat chagrined at his word choice.

"Well, I'm definitely happy to be spared the post-nudge headaches," I say. "Those were grueling. Are the others back at the RV park?"

The question is actually for Aaron, but he doesn't respond. Daniel gives the two of us a sideways glance and answers for him. "Yeah, they're still at the campground. Aaron picked me up this morning. Sam's out doing a surveillance job, and Mom is at the New York office until Saturday."

"Are they leaving you at the house alone when she's at work?" Aaron asks.

He's trying to keep his tone casual, but the Quinns' house was broken into last year by someone working for Cregg. And Cregg's people have killed three individuals who worked with the Delphi program back when it was connected to the government, including Jaden's mother up in Boston. All of those killed knew firsthand exactly how involved both Graham Cregg and the Senator had been in that program. They also tried to kill Beth, a friend of Aaron's dad, who handled a lot of the paperwork and contracts, but she's tough.

"Don't need a babysitter," Daniel says. "I can get by on my own now. And I'm rarely alone anyway, between Sam, Porter, the guy who does my rehab . . . seems to be someone there all the damn time. But yeah, if you're wondering about security, we've got it covered. I worry more about Mom traveling, to be honest."

Aaron gives his brother a troubled glance and then focuses on the road again. He's not even using the rearview mirror now—just the side mirrors. Worried he might catch my eye, and that wouldn't mesh with his tactic of pretending I don't exist right now. While it's beginning to bug me, I know Aaron well enough to let him stew. He has a tough time staying mad. He'll eventually step in to fill an uncomfortable silence with some comment that meets me halfway. I'll simply wait.

So I lean back in my seat and watch the panorama of buildings and people and cars. It only takes a couple of minutes, however, for me to realize this plan is flawed. My adrenaline rush is fading fast, and exhaustion is closing in. Despite multiple cups of coffee, I want nothing more than to close my eyes. Just for a few minutes.

My resident evil has been rather quiet since I foiled his plans, just hanging out in the back of my head. But that stray thought about sleep perks him right up.

Nope. Can't have that. So I rub my eyes, shake my head to clear away the cobwebs, and pick a fight. Or rather pick back up on the one Aaron and I were about to have earlier.

"Leaving by myself was the right choice, Aaron. You know it was. I understand why you're angry, and you're right. I'd be mad at you if the situation was reversed. But Stan said one of you would be hurt if I waited."

"Here's the thing, Anna. Stan's visions aren't like the ones Jaden had, that you have now. There are *always* options. Different choices that could be made. And you made the one that shut me—and everyone else—out."

"But I saw myself *here* in the vision I had last night. Alone. I saw everything exactly the way it happened."

"Including me and Aaron being there to keep that guard from carting you off to one of those Sanctuary for Psychics centers?" Daniel asks.

"No," I admit. "The vision ended before you guys showed up."

"So," Daniel says, "we could have simply dropped you there, or maybe a block away, fifteen minutes ago."

"Exactly!" Aaron says. "Rather than you running off in the middle of the night."

Fabulous. The one time Aaron and Daniel Quinn take the same side on anything, it has to be against me. When I haven't slept in about thirty-six hours.

"So, who was the man talking to the guard?" Aaron asks. "The one who was escorting your father? He knew you."

I start to correct him, since I meant Abbott, but Aaron's voice is still tight, on edge. That's when I realize the anger I sensed rolling off of him in waves wasn't just him being mad at me for leaving . . . again . . . without telling him. He was close enough to have picked up on any violent thoughts Abbott had during our struggle. Whistler may have had a few nasty impulses, too. He and Grady were colleagues. Maybe even friends. And while Whistler may not know the specifics of what happened that night in the woods at Overhills, he knows I was there and he knows Grady didn't come out of it alive. Whistler might even have been friends with Lucas, also dead, and I'm sure he knows the role I played in that.

"It was Whistler."

Daniel frowns. Aaron does too, although I think his look is more one of confusion as he tries to place the name.

"Not good," Daniel says. "Even if we had gotten here in time, I'm not sure I'd have been able to nudge Whistler long enough for us to grab Pfeifer."

"He can block you?" Aaron asks.

"Not fully. It's more that anything I tell him won't hold very long. Might not even take at full strength. He's worked at Python for . . . hell, I don't know how long he was there."

Python Diagnostic was Graham Cregg's business cover for his work on the Delphi Project. The company operated as a subsidiary of a much larger organization, Decathlon Services Group, which makes the bulk of its money from military and government outsourcing projects.

"He may even have been there from the beginning. More to the point, though, I heard Cregg put him in charge of watching Dacia a few years back because he was pretty good at keeping her out of his head. And he was also pretty good at keeping her in line. None of the other guards at The Warren wanted Dacia duty. Not even Lucas, and he was sleeping with her."

"Who was the other guy?" Aaron asks. "The guy who would have gladly dismembered you right there in the middle of the street."

As much as I hate having to tell them—or anyone—about the skirmish at Joe's, there's really no way around it. And it will keep me talking, which will help keep me awake.

So I spend the next few minutes explaining most of what happened since I left the RV in the wee hours of the morning. Amazingly, neither of them interrupt. I leave out the part about seeing rat-spiders in the mirror. And I play down exactly how close I was to getting my head bashed in at the deli.

"Oh, and I got this." I pull the envelope and cracked tablet out of the knapsack. "Mostly legal documents, from what I can tell. The tablet still works, it's just cracked . . ." I lean back into the seat as another one of those weird dizzy spells washes over me.

"You okay?" Aaron asks.

"I will be. Just . . . light-headed. Happened a few times earlier. It'll pass."

Aaron and Daniel exchange a look.

"Maybe it's lack of sleep?" Aaron says.

"Yeah, and way too much caffeine." I close my eyes and take a few more deep breaths. The two of them are mercifully silent, and the rhythm of the road is soothing. Another minute or two of this and I'll be asleep, however, so I shake my head to clear the last of the fog away and keep my eyes pinned on the floorboard as I talk.

"Like I was saying, the tablet works, but I haven't been able to figure out the password yet. Maybe Taylor can give it a go when we get back."

"I'd be a lot happier," Aaron says, "if this was information from *Senator* Cregg, rather than his son. Unless Cregg had some sort of a backup plan, in case this attempt failed, I doubt there's anything in there to help us figure out where they're taking Pfeifer. But I sent Sam the tag number to run through the system. Maybe he'll get a lead."

"Wait." I feel something starting to click into place, but it's not quite there yet. "Whistler told the guy at the kiosk that they were taking him back to Perkins. That's the hospital where he's been for the past fifteen years, right?"

"Yeah," Aaron says. "Pretty sure he was lying, though. Sam and Porter have been taking turns surveilling the entrance. Yesterday, Pfeifer came and left with the doctor and two other guys, both medical security officers from Perkins. Today, he arrives with the doctor and the same two security personnel. But he *leaves* with Whistler. I think they're headed—"

"To Port Deposit," I say.

"What?" Aaron asks.

"Yeah," Daniel says. "What makes you think they're headed back to The Warren? There's nothing of value left at the Delphi facility. It's just a burned-out husk. There have to be other, better places where they could hide your father."

"There may still be something they value inside that wreckage. They don't want to hide Pfeifer. They want him because he's a vessel. Like me. They're taking him back to The Warren to fill him up."

NEWS ITEM FROM THE *COEUR D'ALENE PRESS*

April 23, 2020

Charges will not be filed against Oscar Fray, the Kootenai County deputy who fatally shot a 17-year-old resident of Athol during a routine traffic stop on Interstate 90.

The teenager, who was identified on Friday as Isaac Eaton, was shot after the officer was hit in the head by an aluminum can. According to the officer, the can came out of nowhere, traveling at high velocity, and struck him on the temple.

"Deputy Fray remains convinced the youth hurled the can at him purposefully, using mental powers," said Kootenai County Attorney Jessica Hebert. "While we were unable to confirm the Eaton boy is infected, the officer was wearing a body camera that supports his claim that he was indeed hit by a small metal object."

There was one witness to the incident, 16-year-old Ellery Paul, also of Athol, who was a passenger in

Eaton's car. She asserts that the beer can was set into motion by a passing semitruck. The officer's body camera did pick up the noise of a vehicle at approximately the same time, but video evidence was inconclusive.

Kootenai County Sheriff Bert McAfee said the situation was traumatic for everyone involved. "Deputy Fray was reasonably convinced he was under attack. It's a tragic situation, but I'm afraid this sort of thing is going to be fairly common until we manage to round up those affected and get this problem under control."

CHAPTER TEN

Laurel, Maryland
April 24, 2020, 5:53 p.m.

The camper is near the back of the Maryland Welcome Center lot when we arrive, parked next to a Metro DC police cruiser. The sight makes me nervous, even though I know it's Detective Baker, Daniel's partner during his brief tenure on the force. Daniel called him as we fought our way through traffic, asking if some of the other officers could keep an eye out for Whistler's vehicle on the vague grounds of suspicious activity. He also mentioned the white delivery van Abbott hijacked, but I didn't see the tag, so there wasn't much for them to go on.

Baker being here shouldn't put me on edge. Daniel trusts him. But my face has been pasted all over the news as a "person of interest" since last October. Plus, this taps into old anxieties. Deo and I spent a few weeks on the streets. There may have been one occasion where I failed to pay for peanut butter and a loaf of bread when we were desperate, and we were always worried about being picked up and hauled back to the place we'd taken great pains to escape. Fear is an automatic response, even if I haven't (recently) done anything wrong. Maybe one day I'll have a nice, peaceful, law-abiding life and my heart won't start thumping like an unbalanced washing machine whenever I see a police car. But that seems like a pipe dream in the current environment where about a third of the country thinks people like me should be locked away.

Despite the fact that they're also Delphi adepts, all three Quinn siblings are outside talking to Baker. Not Deo, though. I'm guessing he had the same reaction I did. Maybe this is a good time to talk to him, since we'll actually have some privacy. For the second time in as many days, he's going to be pissed at me, and rightfully so.

Deo is in one of the recliners when I enter the RV, peeking out the window at the others. He glances up when I walk in and then ignores me, which is pretty much what I expected.

I reach inside the knapsack and pull out the last bagel. It's now cold and horribly squished. As peace offerings go, it's pathetic, but it's all I have.

"You want it as is or toasted?" I ask, holding it out to him.

"Really?" He narrows his eyes but takes the bagel. "You went to Joe's without me?"

"Believe me, you would not have wanted to be there."

By the time I finish telling Deo everything that happened, Baker has departed and the others are making their way back inside. The Quinns are arguing before they even reach the door.

"Has it ever occurred to you maybe they're doing the smart thing and waiting until morning?" Taylor says to Aaron. "You know, so they don't have to traipse around that abandoned wreckage in the dark? And for the record, Senator Cregg's house—well, one of them—is right by the golf course maybe a half mile from the Alexandria exit."

Aaron snorts. "You really think they'd be stupid enough to take Pfeifer to the Senator's house in broad daylight? Baker said the cop who reported it wasn't even sure it was the same car. He only got a glimpse of the tag as he passed the exit. By the time he backed up, it was lost in traffic. So yes, it's possible they had to make a stop first and we're ahead of them. But it's also entirely possible the officer misread the tag and they're halfway to Port Deposit by now."

"Plus, how long can the doctor hold off reporting he's lost a patient?" Daniel says. "That's assuming he's in on it, which isn't a given, so alternatively, how long before they find the doctor and those two med techs' bodies stashed in a closet somewhere? I think they'll go tonight, if they actually are taking Pfeifer to that lab."

"It'll probably be a week before they find those bodies," Taylor says disdainfully. "You heard Baker. He's too afraid of losing his job to ask questions about—"

Daniel holds up one hand to cut her off. "Baker has already stuck his neck out enough, Tay. He has three kids. There's really not much he can do anyway."

I suspect Daniel is right. Port Deposit is several counties outside Baker's jurisdiction. Plus, the human-trafficking case they were originally working on when Daniel was on the force was officially closed after The Warren burned down and they were able to neatly pin everything on Lucas and this imaginary WOCAN boogeyman.

But Taylor doesn't seem to want to let Baker off the hook. "Having three kids didn't stop Dad from doing the right thing."

"Yeah, well, Dad had a whole lot more information on Delphi than Baker does," Aaron says.

"And he was part of the damn program for five years," Daniel adds. "He felt responsible. You're just pissed Baker can't do anything about the . . . evidence . . . in the townhouse. And I get that. I really do. But Anna's prints are all over the place, including the box."

"And even if they find Cregg's prints, he's dead, so reporting that box would only risk more trouble for Anna . . . for all of us, really." Aaron shrugs. "Would you really want to upset Porter again?"

"I didn't mean we should bury it with Molly's body! Just . . . that we should bury it. Get it out of *there*." Taylor turns toward me. "I'm sorry, Anna. I don't blame you. I'm almost positive I'd have done the same thing if I'd found Cregg's box of souvenirs. That doesn't mean I'm happy leaving part of Molly behind. But fine . . . there's nothing we can do about it right now. Let's just go."

"You're not going," Daniel says. "Aaron and I will go. The rest of you wait here."

"We should take Deo," Aaron says. "I mean, I'll leave the choice up to him, but we'll have a better chance of getting Pfeifer out of there with Deo's amp ability."

"Maybe we should pull in Sam," Aaron says. "Porter, too."

"Hold on," Taylor says. "Let me get this straight. I'm staying here, when both of you know I can outshoot you?"

Daniel makes a *pfft* noise.

"When both of you *know* I can outshoot you," she repeats. "But you're going to call in two seventy-year-old men, one of whom had a heart attack last year and the other whose blood pressure puts him at serious risk of stroke?"

"She has a point," Daniel says reluctantly. "Plus, we need someone to start looking into the whereabouts of Pfeifer's doctor and the two hospital workers. Sam and Porter aren't in any shape to be hiking around in those ruins."

Even though Aaron doesn't actually say anything, his eyes move to Daniel's legs.

"I'm *fine*," Daniel says angrily. "I got a cramp this afternoon because you were moving too fast. That's it. And it's not like I can sit this one out. We don't know how many people they'll have with them, and there's no way you're going to get Pfeifer out of there by yourself with only a gun and your feminine intuition."

I'm thinking there's a really good chance Aaron will take a swing at his brother when Taylor pounds her fist on the RV wall.

"Anna and I are going."

I shake my head. "You might be an asset. I won't be. I've got enough to worry about just keeping my walls intact. Everyone will be much safer if I wait here."

"Yeah," Daniel says. "From what Aaron told me earlier, this isn't a good time for Anna to be . . . under pressure. So you and Anna stay here. I already asked Baker to tell the state police that we've got a mechanical issue with the RV, to justify parking here overnight if necessary."

Taylor sighs and takes her phone out of her pocket. "We're going. For one thing, I'm sick of your sexist attitude. Protect the women. Insult Aaron by calling his ability *feminine*. But all that aside, Anna and I have to go." She pulls up a text message and hands the phone to Aaron, giving me a look that says something—even though I have no idea what—is all my fault.

"It's from . . . Stan," Aaron says as he reads, then scrolls back a bit. I can literally see the moment when he puts the pieces together. "You just let Anna walk out of here last night? Knowing that—"

"We can argue about that later," she says quickly. "The only thing relevant right now is that Stan says there's no reason for any of us to go unless Anna goes. Otherwise, her father will end up on the other side, and he'll be crazy. Crazy *strong*, too. He'll have someone named Oksana and maybe three dozen others inside. If Anna goes, it's roughly even odds you'll get him to the mountain place, whatever the hell that means."

"Sounds like a bunch of garbage to me," Daniel says.

"He says the mountain place?" Aaron asks. When Taylor nods, he scrolls back through the messages. After a moment, he gives her back the phone and sighs, leaning against the pantry door. "I've been trying to think of a place to hide Pfeifer for a while. I just heard back from Beth. Wasn't even sure if they still owned the house. They were talking about selling it last year."

Taylor and Daniel seem to follow what Aaron is saying, but Deo and I exchange a clueless look. I do know that Beth Wilcox is the family friend who worked with Delphi. She got sideswiped when she was jogging around the same time Jaden's mother was the "accidental" victim of a drive-by shooting.

"Stan may have a point," I say reluctantly. "About my father. He seemed to recognize me, or maybe it's just that I look like my mother. And Stan's been right twice now. He knew I had to leave last night, and he saw me stopping Abbott today—"

Aaron's mouth tightens. "You said you didn't know their names."

"I don't, okay? One tall and thin, the other short and fat. Abbott and Costello. And as I was saying, one of the paths Stan saw—"

"Stan said there's not a single path where Pfeifer ends up with us unless Anna is at The Warren," Taylor interrupts impatiently. "And if Pfeifer isn't with us, we lose. If we stay here, Anna might as well have grabbed the wheel and hurled us off that overpass last night. It would have been a quicker, kinder ending for everyone."

"Okay, okay." Daniel holds up one hand. "I need you guys to explain this to me. This Stan kid was at The Warren, but I don't know what he does. What exactly is a path cluster?"

Taylor launches into the same explanation Stan gave us yesterday. Daniel's arms are crossed, with the one arched eyebrow that seems to be a Quinn family trait. You'd think, with everything he's seen, his inner skeptic would have died long ago, but he seems to be hardwired to doubt anything he hasn't experienced personally.

But he's kind of right in this case. The underlying problem is that Stan's visions aren't definitive. They're just probabilities. Likelihoods. That makes it harder for any of us to take his advice. I wish we had something more solid to latch on to . . .

Except, we do. Why didn't I think of it sooner? I motion for Deo to join me in the back of the RV where he and Taylor usually sleep.

"What's up?" he asks.

I pull the door closed. "I need a hug."

He gives me a quizzical look and then realizes what I mean. "You sure? You really want to trigger a vision on purpose?"

"Yes. We need some certainty. Stan's ability is so nebulous. So . . . fuzzy and unlike the glimpses I get from Jaden. Having that vision last night clarified what I needed to do today. I know you and Aaron didn't like it, but I knew what would happen and followed my instincts to get to that point in time. And it made me realize I'm not really using Jaden's gift at its full potential. Daniel—and even Taylor and Aaron, to some extent—question Stan's visions because he has to admit there are other possible paths. But we've all seen Jaden's visions play out in real time. Maybe I'll see something that can help us."

"Okay, but I have one question. You were saying just last night we need to take you back to Sandalford. That you don't need to be involved in this. That was . . . your smart side talking." He grins slightly at my expression. "You know I'm right. Even if this medicine is having a positive effect, I'm still right. So my question is how much of you wanting to be directly involved in this is simply because he's your dad?"

"He's not my dad. He's my father. Big difference. I don't even know him. Plus, he killed my mom . . . my mother."

Deo's expression makes it clear he caught my stumble. But he doesn't call me on it. Apparently, I do think of Leah as my mom, and I'm pretty sure it's not just because she didn't—to the best of my knowledge—kill anyone. It's also because I can conceptualize a *mom*. In my first foster family, the man wasn't around much. Most of all I remember the woman. And the little Yorkie who liked to lick my hands. Plus, there's Kelsey, who's the closest thing to a mom either of us has ever had, including Deo's still-living mother. I can't really wrap my head around the concept of a *dad*, though.

"Like I said before, I'd just as soon stay here. In fact, I'd prefer it. That's why I need to push a vision—to see if Stan is right that I have to be there. If not . . . then I'll happily back off. It's a long shot I'll even see anything relevant, but it's worth a try, right?"

"Okay," he says. "I guess you get a hug. With one condition."

"You're putting conditions on your hugs now? We're going to have to do something about that ego, kiddo."

"Not joking, Anna. The condition is that you tell me exactly what the vision is. Not just the bits and pieces that are convenient or that you think keep me safe. *Everything*. The condition is that you trust me so we're actually in this together, the way it used to be."

I give him a doubtful look. "I'm not sure you know what you're asking. If I see something that deals directly with you and I tell you about it, you can't change it. You're going to feel yourself doing things that make no sense."

He stares at me, not budging.

"Okay, fine. I'll give you the freaking play-by-play action."

"I'm actually going to need you to promise."

"I promise. But . . ."

He rolls his eyes. "Nope. No buts."

"I have a condition, too. Mine is that this is between us. I don't want everyone second-guessing themselves all the time." I glance toward the living room. They're talking over each other again to the point where it's hard to even tell what they're saying. "Can you imagine how many more arguments that would cause?"

"Yeah. You have a point. I accept your condition. Come get your hug, Short Stuff."

"Hey, watch it. I can just as easily trigger a vision by punching you. Or tickling you."

"You'd better not."

He still smells like ozone, but it's really nice to be able to hug my brother again, even if it's only for a second.

nnnnNNNNN

Black. Pitch black. The air is stale, like the townhouse last night, but worse.

155

At least I know the rungs are solid, not broken. Taylor, Abbott, and Alex have all gone down this way ahead of me. Unless, of course, there are broken rungs and there are three bodies at the bottom of the—

Which is crazy. Taylor's right below me. I would have heard her scream.

I lower one foot and wrap my arm around the next rung. If the dizzy spell hits, please, please let it be after my feet finally hit the ground.

Something brushes my hand, and I scrub it vigorously against my jeans before taking the next step. Maybe it's just as well that Taylor forgot the stupid headgear. The four senses operating right now are freaking me out enough without adding sight to the mix.

Just keep moving. Aaron could already be in trouble, and every second we waste is—

NNNNNNNnnnn

"Anna?" Deo is sitting on the floor a few feet away. He gives me a moment, then asks, "So . . . what did you see?"

"Nothing. Don't give me that look. I literally didn't *see* anything. I was going down a ladder in the pitch dark. Couldn't even hear much. I'm pretty sure I felt a spiderweb on my hand. Taylor was with me. We were . . . following Abbott and someone named Alex. They mentioned him before, some associate of Cregg's. We were trying to get to Aaron, who might have been in trouble, and . . . that's seriously all I've got."

"Might have been?"

"I was thinking he might be in trouble. That we needed to hurry. But nothing else."

"If that's all you're seeing, the two of you could be going into a trap. You could get killed."

"We could. Or we could be the ones who keep Senator Cregg from getting his hands on a very powerful weapon. Because Stan seems to think that will happen, and . . . Deo, I felt how strong the Furies were when they were inside my head. They weren't the only ones in that room, either."

"I thought you said that spirits eventually go to their last happy place?"

"That was my experience, yes. But I don't know how long it takes. What if they only end up in a happy place when they're close to moving on? Or what if they go there because it's close to the things that will help them move on? Maybe everyone killed in that lab can't move on until they're sure this is over. Jaden said he felt that to some extent, but . . . he had other things pulling him forward, not simply a need for revenge that pinned him to the past. And you know it doesn't really matter, right? Taylor and I are going to end up on that ladder one way or another."

I glance at the door. Things seem to have settled down in the other room. There's just one voice speaking now—Aaron's.

Deo follows my gaze and says, "Yeah. They're going to wonder where we are."

When we join the others, Aaron is on the phone with Sam. Daniel and Taylor are looking over some maps they've spread out on the kitchen counter.

"Aaand . . . Taylor persuaded them all on her own. I'm thinking we just wasted our time."

I nod, but I don't really think the time was wasted. I've spent the past few months avoiding contact with Deo, dreading the fact that I'll get another vision. Yes, those flash-forwards are inconvenient. It can also be really frustrating when you know things will happen and you want to change them, but you can't. Still, they've been one of the few sources of certainty we've had in the past few months, and I'm beginning to realize they're much more a gift than a curse. Maybe I need to embrace them instead of pushing them away.

LETTER TO THE EDITOR, EVANSVILLE COURIER & PRESS

April 24, 2020

If you ask most people what they want, deep down, you'll find they want security. They want their families to be safe. They want to know that when they put money in the bank, it will be there when they need to withdraw it. They want to know our police will keep hardened criminals off the streets and our military will protect our shores from invaders.

And so we lock our doors, lock our vehicles, and lock our places of business. We purchase computer security programs and jealously protect our passwords. We pay taxes to ensure that our lives, our possessions, and those we love are secure.

But what good does it do if the person who lives next to you is a psychic? He can rob you blind without you even knowing it. Your bank account numbers, passwords, and pretty much anything else of yours is his for the taking.

The president and Congress have done nothing to protect us from this threat. Our local and state officials are useless as well. It's time for a new leader who understands the only way we can be protected is by universal testing and removal of anyone infected with this plague. Senator Cregg has promised he will mandate testing on day one if elected and that all Delphi psychics will be housed in facilities where they cannot prey on law-abiding Americans.

—Dwight Witcher, Elberfeld

CHAPTER ELEVEN

Port Deposit, Maryland
April 24, 2020, 8:21 p.m.

"Up there. At the streetlight." Daniel nods toward what appears to be a small trucking company just ahead on Tome Memorial Highway. "Slow down! You're going to miss it."

Aaron cuts his headlights and whips the wheel to the left a little harder than necessary to make the turn, probably just to irk Daniel. Gravel crunches under the tires as we enter the lot and drive past one sign that reads *Portal Development* and another that reads *Private Property No Trespassing*. A small white trailer sits at the far end of the lot, near the tree line. It's dark, and aside from a couple of vehicles that look like they haven't moved in months, the place appears empty.

Of course, this is just the back entrance. And not even an *actual* entrance but a facade that kept people from wondering who was poking around the supposedly abandoned naval center. Daniel said he'd covered a couple of guard shifts in that trailer. It was a cushy assignment, aside from the boredom. If the phone rang or someone stopped by, both of which rarely happened, all they had to do was claim the company's calendar was booked and point them to another local construction firm.

"Turn the parking lights back on once we round the bend," Daniel says. "And keep to the right. There's a wicked"—the left wheel drops suddenly, tilting us slightly to the side—"pothole."

There are actually quite a few wicked potholes. The truck would have taken these bumps in stride, but we didn't want to waste any more time unhitching it from the RV. So we're back in Sam's Kia, an olive-green SUV that looks like it's seen better days. Deo and Taylor are in the third-row seat, so I think they're probably getting the worst of it.

"The gate's just ahead," Daniel says. "My passcode should still work. I doubt anyone bothered to change it since they evacuated."

We stop in front of the security gate. Daniel gets out, hobbling a bit, and punches in the code, twice. Nothing happens. He pokes around for a minute and then finally comes back to the truck. Getting into the cab seems to be even harder for him than getting out was. It's clear Aaron isn't going to do anything to help, so I start to open my door, thinking I can give him a boost or at least steady him.

"I've got it, Anna! Get back in the damn car."

Nope. Hasn't mellowed at all.

"There's no power to the gate," he says once he's back in his seat. "Battery backup is dead too, so I don't think it's a temporary outage."

"Wouldn't be much reason to restore power up here after the fire," Aaron says. "I mean, no one lives up here. Or works here. Could be good news, actually. I was worried we might end up tripping some kind of silent alarm that notifies the local police. But if the power is out, that may mean the whole security system is down."

I hear two almost identical sighs. One from Deo, in the seat behind me. The other from Daniel, in front of me. Neither of them actually says anything, but I'm pretty sure they're both thinking the same thing that I am, and it's something that might not necessarily occur to Taylor and Aaron. They've never actually been inside The

Warren, only above it. The only way the power being out is a plus is if we discover they're not already here and we actually manage to grab my dad before they get him underground. The Warren was hellish enough with the lights on.

"So what do we do now?" I ask.

Daniel grins and nods toward the gate. "I say we just back the car up and ram right through it. Unless you're too chicken?"

Aaron stares at the gate for a second. He cocks his head to the side in a way that almost looks like Ein when he's trying to puzzle something out. After a moment, Aaron's eyebrows go up and he grins back at his brother. "Challenge accepted."

"Please tell me you're joking," Deo says. "You're not really going to crash through that gate, are you?"

Aaron doesn't respond. He just pops the thing into reverse and begins backing down the road.

"Seriously?" Taylor says. "Sam just paid this thing off. He's going to flay you alive if you mess it up."

"They're right," I say. "That gate is iron. This is a truly bad idea."

"Why have a bull bar on the front bumper if you're not going to use it?" Daniel counters. "Yee-haw!"

"That's a lousy *Duck Dynasty* impression," Taylor says.

"I was actually going for *Dukes of Hazzard*, but . . ." Daniel grins even wider as Aaron accelerates. I brace for impact, but I'm actually thinking he needs to go faster if we're really going to do this. I'm not sure we'll hit the gate hard enough to take it out at this speed.

When the front of the Kia connects with the metal bar, however, there's a faint clang and that's it. The gate swings back, and we sail through without the slightest resistance. If I hadn't been watching, I probably wouldn't even have known the bar was there.

Aaron and Daniel aren't just grinning now. They're laughing.

"You can all let go of the oh-shit handles now," Daniel says.

"I'm sorry," Aaron says, flashing me a contrite look over his shoulder. "It's just . . . if the power is out and there's no battery backup, *open* is usually the default setting on most security gates."

"*Usually* the default?" Taylor says. "On *most* gates?"

"Plus . . . I have a better view from up here and—"

"And he could see I pushed the gate open a tiny bit," Daniel says. "But it was tough to shove it all the way out, so . . ."

"Should have seen your eyes, Tay," Aaron adds, making a circle with his fingers and thumb. "Like someone out of that *Sailor Moon* cartoon you used to watch."

Taylor flips him off, but she and Deo are chuckling. Even though I don't join in, it's a close call. Not because I think it was particularly funny, but because Aaron is laughing. Deo, too. When was the last time I heard them really laugh? I can't even remember.

Of course, the fact that I can't remember means nothing. They could have been laughing constantly the past few months, yukking it up on a daily basis, and Cregg just took all of the fun slots in the daily schedule.

We continue down what's left of the road. It was paved at one point, but large chunks seem to have eroded, and there's no moon to speak of, so it's hard to avoid the hazards. Daniel acts as tour guide as we drive, pointing out where to turn but also what used to exist here based on the pictures and maps he's seen. The area was originally a private boys' academy, but the school and surrounding acreage were purchased by the US government to serve as a training center during World War II. Nearly two hundred and fifty thousand recruits—both military and civilian—were processed at Bainbridge Naval Training Center. Offices, dormitories, and even small homes were located here at one point, along with a commissary, dining halls, and a movie theater. Now they're just concrete slabs.

The facility continued to be used by the government for a variety of purposes until the mid-1980s when it was finally abandoned.

Some claimed the place was contaminated by chemical-weapons testing. Those rumors seemed to be confirmed when it was designated a superfund site and scheduled for a complete environmental overhaul.

Most of the oldest buildings, the ones that were part of the Tome School for Boys, are little more than burned-out husks now, thanks to two separate fires. Local residents tend to steer clear of the place, with the exception of teens looking for a thrill or somewhere to hide out for some underage drinking and other recreational pursuits. The authorities blamed teenage mischief for the first fire, but it was really a Delphi experiment that got out of control. We're still not certain whether the second, much more extensive, blaze spread from the fire I helped set inside Lab 1 or whether Cregg's people set it to cover their escape. Or whether it was the group with Graham Cregg or the one with his father, since the camps seem to have split by the time of the fire. The blame for it was conveniently placed on the so-called WOCAN terrorist group purportedly using the facility as a sex-trafficking ring to raise money for their separatist agenda.

The place was given a clean bill of environmental health a few decades back, but it remains undeveloped, possibly because of the *other* rumors. Area residents who worked at the Bainbridge Center before it closed down said they sometimes heard noises belowground. That spurred rumors the place was haunted.

I don't know if they were right about that back in the 1980s. It's possible the noises were just from the underground tunnels that led to the secret lab a bit farther uphill, run by CIA contractors. But it's definitely haunted now. When I picked up Jaden's spirit in the lab, I sensed many others in that room. Four of them, Jaden's friend Will and three women I call the Furies, took up temporary residence in my head. They opted to stay when Deo and I ran from the lab, disgusted I wasn't able to shoot Graham Cregg as he lay on the floor, writhing in pain.

Dozens of others were killed in those rooms. A few were second-generation Delphi adepts like me. But most of them were young adults, many brought in illegally from Eastern Europe and elsewhere. If they couldn't be controlled, couldn't be shaped into some form that furthered the younger Cregg's agenda, those adepts didn't leave the labs alive.

Aaron parks in a small clutch of trees about fifty yards from the dormitory.

"We should be over the cafeteria about now," Daniel says. I nod absently, thinking he's talking about some World War II–era building, but then he adds, "The old dorm we just passed sits right on top of the testing rooms. Ashley once told me there was an old stairway going from that building down into an office near the testing center, a relic from the 1960s where there were still workers who came topside for lunch or a smoke break. But they boarded it off, along with a few other entrances, when they started using this place for the Delphi experiments."

"I think . . . I think I've been in this section before," Aaron says. "When Taylor and I were—"

"Yes," Taylor says. "Back when we were trying to find Deo. This is the building I sketched. I recognize it from those things up on the roof."

"Those castle-looking barrier . . . things?" Daniel says.

"They're called crenellations."

"Yeah," Daniel says, rolling his eyes at my comment. "Tell Emily thanks for the assist."

The last bit annoys me. He's right that I learned the word originally because of Emily and her crossword fixation. But it's stored in *my* memory now. It's not like I had to go digging through the file cabinets to find it. Daniel makes it sound like my head is empty without the memories of my hitchers. Like I'm just an empty vessel.

Aaron glances back at me in the rearview mirror. I don't know if he understands why Daniel's comment made me angry, but he seems kind of glad it did.

"Anyway," Daniel says, "during my first month undercover at Delphi, I was on grounds duty. We used that building—the one with the *crenellations*—for surveillance. From that rooftop, you can see clear down to the riverfront and the back entrance. Some of us will still need to cover the side entrance, though."

"There's also a decent chance they're already here," Aaron says. "So we split up. Who goes where?"

"You and I should head down toward the side entrance," Daniel says. "It's closer to the main road, and if I had to bet, I'd say that's the way they'll come in. We can also check the garage area while we're over there and see if there's any sign they've already come in. Deo's with us, since we'll probably need his amp power. Taylor and Anna stay here as lookout. And I do mean lookout. If you see anything at all, do not investigate. Just call us."

"No. Not on the roof," Deo says. "Anna said she was dizzy earlier."

I have a sudden flashback to the first part of that odd dream I've been having about the woman sprawled on the patio. The memory of the dream chills me, and even though I still think it's most likely symbolic, I'm relieved to know it couldn't have happened here. The house in my dream is newer, the lawn carefully manicured, not wild and overgrown like the grass in the courtyard. A smaller patio, stone, not brick.

"They don't have to go up on the roof," Daniel says. "We usually did lookout duty on the top floor. You can see almost as much from there anyway, and it's sheltered. Most of the windows are intact and the stairway is solid. Here."

He tosses something to his sister as she exits the car. A key ring.

"What's this for?" she asks.

"The lock they installed when Delphi set the place up as a guard station. Only one door . . . they bricked off the other entrances. We'd still get kids poking around up here occasionally looking for a place to get wasted. The locked door usually meant they'd head to another building . . . there are plenty to choose from. There's also a dead bolt on the inside. Use it once you get in, okay?"

"The door wasn't locked when Taylor and I were here before," Aaron says. "But it did seem to be one of the only buildings that had been maintained. No debris, just a lot of dust."

Aaron turns to face me. "Are you sure about this? You haven't slept since Wednesday night. Are you really alert enough to keep watch?"

"I've been chugging coffee nonstop since noon. I'm more wired than tired right now, but if I sit in this car by myself doing nothing, I'll fall asleep regardless of how much caffeine I've had. I need to keep moving."

He sighs.

So do Daniel and Deo.

"Taylor?" Daniel says. "What do you think?"

There's a long pause and then she looks at me. "You were feeling dizzy. *How* dizzy?"

"Just occasional light-headedness. It passes and I'm fine."

"Any other weird symptoms?"

"Well, I've got a psychopath inside my head."

She rolls her eyes. "*New* symptoms, I mean."

"No new symptoms."

"And," she continues, "is it easier or harder to keep said psychopath behind your walls today than it was this time yesterday?"

I'm wondering exactly where this game of twenty questions is leading . . . and why everyone seems to know except me.

"I'm tired, but . . . keeping my walls up definitely seems easier. His thoughts aren't intruding like they were before. And from what I've gathered over the past day, I've been in control a lot less often than I believed since Cregg came on board."

Taylor nods, then reaches into the pocket of her jacket and pulls out a small plastic bag. Inside is a syringe, a vial, and a prescription bottle. She unzips the bag and tosses me the bottle.

I'm about to ask her why she brought my sleeping meds. That's the only prescription I have, and I doubt I'd need anything to knock me out right now. But then I realize the top is a different color.

"It's still a few hours before you're supposed to take another one," she says. "I didn't give you anywhere near the maximum dose. I wanted to see how it would affect you first."

"What *is* this?"

"The oral form of the shot Kelsey gave you," Taylor says. "An antipsychotic that's often prescribed for dissociative disorders. I put one in that energy smoothie you drank last night. You were supposed to be on it until it was time for a second injection. After that, you drop the pills. That's the protocol Kelsey started, then she changed her mind. Or rather, Cregg changed her mind."

Those words trigger a reaction from the rat-spider. Legs scraping against the walls and a steady *thump-thump-thump* for a few seconds. But then it gradually fades.

"If Kelsey changed her mind, how did you get this?"

"The same meds are also used for depression and post-traumatic stress. But Jasper quit taking it. Says it made him dizzy. From what I read online, that side effect usually doesn't last, but . . ." Taylor shrugs and I nod. It's Jasper. Patience doesn't seem to be his strong suit.

"So . . . you swiped his meds and gave them to me without telling me?"

"Miranda swiped them during one of their visits with Jasper," Taylor says.

Jasper Hawkins is still living at the little fishing cabin where we first met Miranda and TJ. Over the past few months, Kelsey has gradually approved longer visits between Jasper and his family. He may not be taking his medication, but he is meeting regularly with Kelsey for anger management therapy, and to the best of our knowledge, there have been no more bruises or other indications of abuse. They began spending occasional nights and weekends together as a family at the cabin. Even if Magda and Kelsey were willing to risk him staying at Sandalford, which they're not, I doubt Jasper would agree. He still doesn't like to be around me, and that probably goes double if he realized I picked up Cregg as a hitcher.

"Although," Deo adds, "it was with his permission, so I'm not sure *swiped* is the right word. And anyway, it was a group decision. Taylor started you on a very low dose last week after we realized Kelsey might be . . . compromised. We've been sneaking it into your food and coffee, and we all watched for any reaction."

Aaron nods. "After the deal with the steering wheel last night, we agreed Taylor should increase the dosage. And eventually give you a second injection. You should have been on the oral version this entire time for full impact."

I'm pretty sure I would have taken the medicine voluntarily last night after the steering wheel incident. But probably not a week ago. And I get why they couldn't risk letting me know. Cregg would have pulled out all the stops trying to get control if he'd had any idea what they were planning.

"You're right. It was the best option. But do you really think Cregg was using me to influence Kelsey? Why didn't it work on any of you? I know Daniel wasn't there, but—"

Daniel cuts me off. "Taylor can explain all of this. We need to go."

I grab my travel mug from the side holder and slip my arms into my jacket. "Be careful. All of you."

"Yeah," Deo says. "You, too."

"Anna?" Aaron reaches out the window and takes my arm. "I'm sorry, okay? I'm sorry I've been so angry. I know this isn't your fault. I know you weren't trying to worry us, it's just . . ."

"It's just that I *did* worry you. I know. I'm sorry, too." I press a quick kiss to his lips. "And please keep an eye on D. He's new to all this."

Daniel snorts. "Don't worry. *I'll* be keeping an eye on Deo. And he definitely won't be armed."

I can tell Daniel is joking, but I don't laugh. It feels like kind of a mean joke, given the mental anguish Deo went through after accidentally shooting him. Deo and Aaron both snicker, however, proving I will never, ever understand guys. Deo, who has moved up to take my spot in the car, even prods Daniel's seat with his knee. "Better watch your back, man."

"It was my *front* last time, you jackass. And I'm—"

Whatever else Daniel says is lost as Aaron pulls away. I guess the bright side is that if Daniel is joking around with D, he must have made his peace with the fact that Deo and Taylor are together. A few months ago, I'd have been worried about *Deo's* back if Daniel was nearby, given how angry Daniel was about their relationship.

It's amazing how dark the night is now that the dim amber glow of the parking lights has vanished. I spot Taylor a few yards away, crouched next to a tree. A canvas bag and a gun are in front of her.

Taylor looks up over her shoulder as I approach. "This is mine." She slings the canvas bag over her shoulder and clips the pistol to her belt. "Meds or no meds, you won't be carrying a weapon around me until I'm convinced that son of a bitch is out of your head and on his way to whatever eternal punishment awaits him."

I don't have the slightest problem with that. Personally, I think the fact that I'm on meds is, in and of itself, an irrefutable argument against me having a gun. So is the lack of sleep.

"Understood." I pull my new can of pepper spray out of my pocket. "Do you want this too?"

Taylor looks at it for a moment, then reluctantly shakes her head. "I guess you need something on you. Just know that if you spray—"

"You'll shoot me. Yeah, yeah."

"Didn't say that," Taylor says, and stomps off through the trees toward the building with the crenellated roof.

"But you would."

"Maybe."

I pick up the pace to catch up with her. We approach the building from the rear, and it's so dark at first that it's hard to see anything as we push our way through the low-lying trees and brush. The dorm itself sits at the end of a long courtyard that stretches maybe a quarter of a mile. Once we're out in the open, my eyes identify some of the shapes in the distance that are slightly darker than the evening sky. Near the other end of the courtyard, I pick out the ruins of Memorial Hall. Two of the buildings on our end seem intact, including the one we're headed toward, but most were devoured by the fires.

We climb the steps, and Taylor inserts the key Daniel gave her. The lock opens, but the door doesn't. She tries again, even though we both heard the lock release.

Taylor curses softly. "The dead bolt. Someone must have locked it and gone out another door."

"Except Daniel told us the other entrances were boarded up. No, actually . . . he said *bricked*. Maybe a window?" The windows on this first level are barricaded, but I nod up toward the second level where about half of the glass is out.

"Maybe. I'm going to see if I can reach a window from that fire escape. Stay here."

I do stay at first, even after I hear the tinkle of breaking glass. But then something larger hits the ground, and I hurry to the side of the building, nearly tripping over a chunk of wood as I round the corner. I expect to see Taylor either on the fire escape ladder or flat on the ground. But she's gone.

"Taylor?" I say, keeping my voice low. "Taylor!"

There's a noise from above and her head emerges, framed by the window.

"Almost fell, thanks to that piece of rotted molding," she says, nodding down toward my feet. "Go back around. I'll unlock the door."

Once I'm inside, she throws the dead bolt again and inspects it with her tiny pink flashlight.

"What's wrong?"

"Nothing. That lock just . . . bugs me." Taylor takes puzzles she can't solve as a personal offense. She stares at the thing a moment longer, then shakes her head in annoyance and turns toward the interior of the building.

We continue down the foyer into a massive open space. It's empty now, except for a large pile of debris near the fireplace at the far end. Taylor gives the room a cursory sweep with the flashlight and then heads toward the staircase.

"Shouldn't we search this floor first?" I ask.

"If anyone was here, they'd have jumped out with a gun by now," Taylor says wryly. "My entry wasn't exactly silent."

I follow her up the staircase. Daniel was right about it being solid. Taylor's flashlight picks up the gleam of newer boards and nails in several places, and the banister between the third and fourth floors looks like it was replaced recently. I guess it got a safety makeover from the guards who were working with Delphi before Daniel joined.

The top floor is one long room, lined with windows on all four sides. A thin layer of dust coats the floor, rising into the air with each step we take. The pathetic little sliver of moon manages to partially illuminate the side facing the courtyard, but it's hard to even make out the edges of the windows along the sides or the back wall, which faces the woods.

Taylor drops her bag near the middle of the room and pulls out two pairs of night-vision goggles, both with *Vigilance Security* stamped on the side. As much as I detest Miller, I have to admit he has reason to be annoyed, given how often we borrow his equipment without asking.

"Maybe we should start by circling the room," Taylor says. "I'll go left and you go right, then we'll cross over. That way two sets of eyes cover each sector."

"Works for me." I'm surprised she doesn't just come out and say she needs to double-check everything I do. She's rarely tactful, and it's not like I'm going to argue the point in my present state.

"So . . . where's the headgear?" I ask, feeling a tiny bit of déjà vu. I'd forgotten that part of the vision.

Taylor frowns, confused.

"The straps that hold the goggles on your head. So your hands are free?"

"Crap. I didn't see those. We'll have to do without."

She sounds embarrassed. I have mixed feelings about that. On the one hand, Taylor doesn't make a lot of mistakes, and she's perfectly willing to gloat when normal mortals do. On the other hand, it means we're going to be stuck lugging these things around. Plus, I feel somewhat guilty, since I knew she'd forget them and forgot to tell her. Not that I could have told her, anyway, but . . .

Jaden's visions may be a gift, but they give me a headache.

I move to a window near the middle of the back wall and scan the trees for signs of movement. "To get back to what we were discussing in the car, if you think Cregg was able sway Kelsey, why didn't it work on the rest of you?"

"I think it did work on Aaron a few times. Deo, too. Not anything that stuck, but enough that they were acting . . . strange. Daniel says it could be harder for Cregg to work through you, like it was for him. Anyway, once they seemed normal again, I told them—including Kelsey—to make sure they only talked to you if you were moving. Walking. Cregg has to hold still when he uses his ability. And they did. They started noticing the same weird stuff I was seeing from you. But Kelsey wanted to try hypnosis, to get a feel for what was going on inside that overcrowded head of yours, before continuing on the antipsychotic. She said hypnosis worked well for you in the past, back with this Myron guy. It didn't occur to any of us that, in order to hypnotize you, you'd have to be—"

"Sitting still."

"Exactly," she says, moving to the next window. "And I think he turned the tables on her. After that, she was . . . different. She wouldn't even discuss the possibility of the second injection. Kept insisting it was Myron."

"Is Kelsey okay? What if he planted some sort of posthypnotic suggestion?"

Taylor's phone buzzes with an incoming text. She reads it and then says, "The guys are in place near the side gate. No vehicles or any sign Whistler beat us here. And . . . as for Kelsey, Miranda and Maria are keeping an eye on her. We're hoping whatever whammy he put on her might fade if you aren't . . . Sorry. If *he* isn't around to reinforce it."

Once we move to the next window, we're far enough apart we can no longer whisper, and talking loudly seems ill-advised. I keep scanning for anything that isn't a tree, but the only things I spot are a few abandoned houses, a raccoon, and some traffic out on the road that leads into Port Deposit.

And my face with spider eyes. It's only for a second. Just a brief glimpse of my altered reflection in the cracked window. But it rattles the hell out of me.

"Hey, Taylor?"

"Yeah?" She looks up from typing into her phone. Her face is illuminated from below by the light from the screen, and it almost looks as though her head and shoulders are floating, disembodied, in the darkness.

"When can I take another one of those pills?"

Her hand moves to the gun. "*Technically* in about an hour. But you could take it now without any problem. Is it getting harder to keep the walls up?"

"Not exactly," I say, shaking one of the tablets into my palm. "More that . . . creepy thoughts are getting through."

"Are we talking what-would-happen-if-I-grabbed-that-steering-wheel kind of thoughts? Or throw-myself-out-that-window thoughts?"

"Neither. I'm in control, Taylor."

"Okay. Take just one. Don't swallow it. Let it dissolve. And let me know if things get worse, because it doesn't kick in immediately."

"Yeah. I noticed. Things were shaky a little before dawn today, but they seemed to get better as the day went on."

Of course, around dawn I was alone in a strange house. And now I'm almost alone, in the dark, in a different strange house. There's a real possibility that circumstances are at least partly to blame for me getting spooked, but I can't afford to take any chances.

I place one of the tablets in my mouth and stash the pill bottle back in my pocket.

"We could also do the second injection. It's a day or so early, but . . ."

"Did you get that from Jasper, too?"

"Um . . . no. There may have been some minor larceny involved."

"Kelsey keeps the medications in a safe."

"And Maria . . . ?"

"Oh. She plucked the combination right out of Kelsey's head. Please tell me that's the only thing you took?"

"Why do you hear *larceny* and automatically assume it was me? It was Deo. And of course it's the only thing he took. He's not a druggie. Do you want me to give you the injection or not?"

"Here?" The word comes out as a squeak.

"Yes, *here*. It's not open-heart surgery. I have a sterile wipe, and the needle just goes in the deltoid. It's basically the same thing I did with Deo's shots before they had Magda's nurses take over. Easy peasy."

"But . . . I just took one of the pills."

"Doesn't matter. It takes time for the injected form to get into your system. We can wait if you want. I just thought . . ." She shrugs. "You're in control now. If it was me, I'd be doing everything I could to make sure I stayed that way."

I slip off the jacket and roll up my sleeve. "I'm going to have to sit down. And please don't wave that needle around."

"Jeez . . ." Taylor says, crouching down next to me. She swipes my upper arm with the alcohol pad, and I look the other way. "What a baby. This would hurt a lot less if you'd relax the muscle, you know."

I don't bother telling her that this is one of the not-so-fun side effects of being a walking ghost hotel. People leave their phobias behind along with their memories. This particular fear is a relic of the hypochondriac I hosted. She was petrified of needles, but it was her deep and abiding love for pills that eventually killed her.

"We should wait until there's someone else here."

"Too late," Taylor says as she presses the plunger.

As soon as the needle enters my arm, the clatter behind my walls escalates. I keep control, and in retrospect, it's probably a good thing we didn't try this with Aaron around. I'm pretty sure he'd have sensed Cregg raging right below the surface.

A second later, it's over. "I don't have a Band-Aid. Just hold your finger on the spot for a few."

We both go back to our lookout duties. I take extra care to keep my eyes focused for distance vision so I don't risk another encounter with my reflection. I've nearly worked my way back around to my original window when an audible gasp comes from Taylor's side of the room.

"What?"

"Come look. Hurry, before they're gone."

Something is moving through the grass below us. When I raise the night-vision goggles, I pick out a herd of deer, nine or ten at least, running together through the courtyard. It's a beautiful sight, but also eerie. Their movements are graceful, almost like a coordinated dance, and their eyes stand out stark white, while everything else about them is painted in shades of gray.

"Wonder what they're running from?" Taylor asks.

"They're not running *from* anything. I think they're just running for the sheer joy of it."

That concept is clearly a foreign one to Taylor. She sniffs dismissively and says, "They're pretty, though. I don't think I've ever seen that many deer at once." Her phone buzzes again, and she tugs it out of her pocket as she shifts over to the next window.

Once the deer have moved on, I raise the night-vision goggles and zoom in on the cluster of trees behind the spot where they were grazing. I can just make out a small house set back into the woods. It looks like it's on the other side of the road we drove in on. Daniel pointed out several of them, noting that they once housed faculty at the school and, later, the families of various naval officers who served at the Bainbridge Center.

The house isn't what catches my eye, however. It's the smaller shape behind the house, partially obscured.

"Taylor. I've got something." When she comes over, I point toward the house. "Look behind it. Is that a car?"

"Maybe," she says after a moment. "I'm not sure. I need a closer look."

She heads toward the staircase, and I follow her. "Except . . . Daniel said we were only on lookout duty. That you should text him if we see anything."

"Yeah, well . . . they're busy," she says, hurrying down the steps. "A car just entered the facility from that side entrance they were watching."

"So why even check this out, then? If they're bringing my father in the other way—"

"Aaron's text said the car they saw is a police car. Someone must have called in a report. Maybe they saw us on the way in." She draws the gun and pushes the door open with her shoulder. "You should wait here. Lock the door. I'll go check it out and—"

"Nope. Buddy system."

I don't add that I'm more worried about staying here alone than going out there with her. And maybe she's nervous about being alone, too, because she doesn't argue.

"Fine. Stick close. And stay in front where I can see you."

We work our way to the left side of the cluster of trees where Aaron dropped us off. Taylor crouches down and I follow her lead.

"Definitely a vehicle," she says. "Most likely abandoned. But we need to make sure, I guess."

She motions forward, and we both dart across the narrow road. One section of the house is entirely caved in, and vines wind in and out of what's left of the frame. The car, which turns out to be a white van, is now fully in view. And once we get closer, I see the large dent just above the left front tire.

"It's not a recent model," Taylor says. "But I don't think it has been here long."

"No. It hasn't been here long at all. In fact, the engine is probably still warm. This is the van that was hijacked by the guy who tried to kill my father."

Op-Ed from the *Hill*

April 24, 2020

Can a third party win the US presidency? Prior to 2018, the consensus among political scientists (and political junkies) was a resounding no. The two major parties have maintained a solid lock on the Oval Office since 1860, and the reason goes deeper than simply party allegiance. Unlike many representative democracies around the world, the very structure of the US political system heavily encourages only two parties, due to winner-take-all districts in most states and institutions like the electoral college.

In the wake of the 2016 election and its aftermath, however, all bets are off. Opinion polls show both major parties well below 50 percent approval. Third parties performed better than expected in the 2018 elections. Some of these were perennial also-ran parties, like the Green and the Libertarians, but the biggest gains were made by a relatively new player—Unify America. Only one senator,

Ronald T. Cregg of Pennsylvania, has switched to UA to date. Four members of the House of Representatives followed suit prior to the 2018 election—and all four retained their seats. The wave of victories was even more impressive at the state level. Three governors and over fifty candidates for state legislatures ran under the UA banner. To the surprise of many pundits and pollsters, most of them won.

But can Unify America take the White House? Senator Cregg and his opponent, Texas governor Juanita Breyer, are currently attempting to convince prospective major party voters that they can win. That is, however, pretty much the only point of commonality between the two candidates. This has caused some analysts to question whether UA is an actual political party or simply a collection of opportunistic politicians who sensed the winds of change and decided to jump before their ship went down.

Senator Cregg's current lead in the delegate count is almost, but not quite, insurmountable, due in part to his central role in the ongoing hearings on how to best address psychic terrorism. Breyer, speaking yesterday at a campaign stop in Connecticut to an audience of purple-clad UA supporters, claimed that Cregg is manipulating the Delphi situation to his political advantage and blamed the media for allowing this. "Cregg was a major player in the company that created the serum. The evidence is there if the media would investigate. But all Cregg has to do is stage another fake attack with psychic explosions, and reporters are off like kids chasing after the ice cream truck, hoping they'll be first to get a really big scoop."

CHAPTER TWELVE

Port Deposit, Maryland
April 24, 2020, 9:18 p.m.

Taylor presses her hand against the hood of the van. "I wouldn't say it's still warm. But the grass is mashed flat back there, so it was parked fairly recently. You're *sure* this is the same van?"

I nod and crouch down next to the dented area, tapping it with my fist. "I got an up-close-and-personal look at this when it nearly decapitated Abbott earlier today."

As I stand, the blood rushes to my head. I lean against the van for a moment and wait for the world to stop moving.

"You okay?"

I nod. "Just light-headed. It'll pass. Could you take a look inside the van?"

Taylor peeks through the window. "Or I could just open the door, since they didn't lock it." I brace for a body or blood, but the van is empty, aside from a hand truck and a few moving blankets.

"Good," I say. "Maybe Abbott just dropped her off somewhere."

"Dropped who off?"

"The woman who was driving the van when he hijacked it."

"Oh. Could you stop calling them Abbott and Costello? That doesn't even bring up a visual for me."

"Tall and thin. Short and fat. What should I call them? Is Laurel and Hardy better?"

"No. Bert and Ernie, maybe?"

"You okay with the fact that Ernie's probably dead?"

"Ick," she says, grimacing. "No."

"Okay, then. I'll stick with Abbott and Costello."

Taylor checks the glove compartment but only finds a stack of fast-food napkins and one of those tire-gauge thingies. So we return to the dormitory. Once we're back on the top floor, she calls to let the guys know about the van, holding the phone out from her ear as Daniel not-so-gently reminds her that we were only supposed to be on lookout.

She flips the phone to speaker mode once his outburst dies down. "It's done. We're safe. What's up on your end?"

"Police car went straight to the underground parking area. But it did *not* come out. Aaron isn't picking any vibes up, though."

"How long have they been inside the garage?" I ask.

"Yeah, that's kind of the problem," Daniel says. "It's already been more than ten minutes. We were about to text you that we're going in to check it out. But, back to the van—you sure it's the same one, Anna?"

"Positive. Same dent near the tire. You said there was an entrance to The Warren in this building?"

"No, I said there was a *rumor* of a stairway they blocked off years ago. I never saw it. It's more likely this Abbott guy used the shaft that goes down from Memorial Hall."

Deo starts talking in the background. I can't tell everything he says, but he's clearly disagreeing, and two of the words that I do pick up explains why he disagrees: *second floor.*

Aaron's voice breaks in. "Taylor. We'll call back in five." Then they're gone.

Taylor sticks the phone in her pocket and stares down at her feet before looking back up at me. "So . . . do you think Tall-and-Skinny used the entrance in Memorial Hall?"

"Not unless he's got climbing gear. That's what Deo was trying to tell Daniel just now. Without power, elevators are useless. So there'd have to be stairs . . ."

Or a ladder, I think, remembering the vision. A ladder that extends into a pitch-black hole in the ground. I don't say that, however, since my mouth and part of my mind is stuck on that other track, the one where all of this is happening for the first time.

Instead, I say, "I still think Abbott came through here, given that the van is nearby and the door was bolted from the inside when we arrived. So, now we've just got to . . . figure . . . out . . ."

"Ah, we have processor pauses," Taylor says. "Those tiny little hamster wheels in your brain are spinning, aren't they?"

I flip her off and extend my hand. "Flashlight, please."

"Nope. In case you've forgotten, this isn't just a flashlight."

"Oh, right." I'd forgotten it was a gift from Sam when Taylor went on her first date. Push one button, and it will light your way. Push the other button, and you can deliver a few million volts of electricity to an attacker.

Taylor motions toward the stairs and follows me. When we reach the ground floor, I point out the pile of junk near the fireplace.

"Aaron said earlier there was no debris in this building when you guys searched it. Do you remember seeing this pile when you were here last October?"

"I don't think so."

The junk pile turns out to be a mix of boards and drywall. When Taylor nudges one of the boards, it slips to the side, scraping a line through the layer of dust on the floor. Underneath is a crowbar and a hammer.

"Looks like someone left tools behind. But if they were uncovering a door or a passageway, where is it?"

She's right. Despite the trash all over the floor, I don't see a door. Just the walls and the fireplace. And . . . *aha*. Footprints. In the dust. Not just one set but two.

Taylor uses the flashlight to follow the prints. They lead directly to the fireplace and disappear. She runs the beam along the inside walls, and sure enough, there's a large handprint on one side of the back panel.

We both step back and look at each other. I know what she's thinking. Do we wait for the guys to call? Or do we follow Abbott and his hostage down the rabbit hole—the deep, dark rabbit hole—into The Warren?

After a long silence, Taylor says, "You know what pisses me off?"

A whole lot of things, I think. But I shake my head and wait for her to tell me what it is this time.

"This is sexist. I mean, making *you* stay here is one thing . . . there's actually a very good reason not to trust you with any responsibility right now. But Deo is younger than either of us. He's never even fired a gun—well, aside from shooting Daniel, and that isn't exactly something that should count in his favor. But he's there, with Aaron and Daniel, and I'm here."

She doesn't add the word *babysitting*, but I can tell she's thinking it.

Truthfully, I don't like that Deo is here at all. I'd far prefer that he was back at Sandalford or on his way to West Virginia with Sam, Stan, and Maggie. But he'll be an asset if Daniel or Aaron need to expand the reach of their abilities.

And Taylor knows that as well as I do. She's just trying to work up an argument for why we—or at least why *she*—should ignore Daniel's instructions to stay put.

"Aaron said they'd call back in five. And it's been at least two minutes already. So why not wait and let them know what we found? See what they're planning. Then we'll decide."

She lets out an exasperated sigh and parks herself on the floor. I join her and, for distraction, pull Cregg's tablet out of my knapsack. "Okay,

Taylor, font of all wisdom. Help me figure out what this passcode might be. I've already tried his birthday, Shakespeare's birthday, the birthday he gave my new identity, and a bunch of other possibilities. What else do we know about Graham Cregg?"

I expect to hear the scraping noise or feel some sort of movement when I speak his name aloud, but I don't. Perhaps the rat-spider is sleeping. Or maybe I have to say his name three times while staring at my reflection in order to rouse the bastard.

"Well," Taylor says, "aside from the fact that he's a mostly dead psycho who's currently hitching a ride with you . . . let's see. Rich kid, followed in daddy's footsteps working at the same companies—well, except Graham never did time in the military. Married in his thirties, two kids . . ."

"Married. That's right. You said that before—back at Kelsey's place—but I forgot. I mean, there was no wife or children with him in the silo, even though he was fighting cancer and dealing with the effects of chemo. I'd started thinking of him as a lone wolf."

"I don't think it was a happy marriage. Probably one of those merger weddings—does his estate take her estate, 'til bankruptcy do us part. That kind of thing. Anyway, his wife's face popped up in a picture with him at an event every now and then, but they seemed to go their own way a lot. And the kids are grown . . . probably early twenties."

"What about his mother?"

Oddly, it's that question that hits a nerve with Cregg. There's a faint increase in pressure along my back wall as if something slumps against it. I don't like that he can still get *any* signals through to me, but I'm not seeing spider eyes, and he's not getting full sentences through like he was yesterday. I'll count that as a win.

"I think his mother's dead," Taylor says. "Or maybe they just divorced. The Senator remarried, so the woman behind that whole Sanctuary for Psychics scam is wife number two. Graham's stepmom, and he may even have been older than she was. Actually . . ." She stops, taps something into her phone, and slides it across the floor. "Here. You want to check dates or whatever? Knock yourself out."

Senator Ron Cregg's face stares up at me from his Wikipedia page. I've read it before, but I wasn't paying attention to family details. His first wife, Penelope Arnett Cregg, was the sole heir to an auto-parts fortune. She committed suicide at age thirty-eight. I try her birthday and date of death with no result. Then I try the keypad letters for *GCregg*: *427344*. Nothing.

There's no further information in the article, so I click on the link for Graham Cregg, which is little more than a stub—wife, Marie, and two children, Alexandra (twenty-one) and Jonathan (nineteen). I hunt for their dates of birth but come up empty. Then I try the keypad code for the first six letters in his kids' names: *Jonath* and *Alexan*. Still no luck on the code, but as I'm typing in that last name, something else hits me.

"*Alex*. Damn."

"Who's Alex?" Taylor asks.

"A name that tripped me up today. I thought they were talking about a guy, but . . ."

On a whim, I check Google Images for pictures of Alexandra Cregg. There are several, most of them family shots from Ron Cregg's last Senate campaign. Her brown hair is longer, but it's definitely her.

I slide the phone across the floor to Taylor. "Cregg's daughter, Alex. Who also happens to be the girl driving the van today."

"So . . . not a hostage situation after all."

"Nope. They told me to call Alex when I was getting out of the car this morning. And they said Alex would be picking me up to take care of some financial matters. Didn't even think it might have been a woman."

"Tsk tsk. See where sexism gets us? And speaking of sexists . . . it's now been seven minutes. I'm going to call them."

"Is that a good idea? What if it rings and they're—"

"They're not total idiots, Anna. Their phones will be on vibrate."

"Hopefully they remind Deo. He's not used to keeping his phone in stealth mode."

Taylor ignores me and calls Daniel. No response. She tries Aaron next, with no result, and finally Deo, who answers but hangs up immediately without saying anything.

"So they can't or won't talk. Okay, then. That's what the tracking app is for. Locate Aaron."

After a moment, a pin appears on the map, showing Aaron less than a quarter mile to the southwest of us, near Memorial Hall. Taylor repeats the process for Deo and Daniel. They're not with Aaron but are about the same distance away to the northwest.

She pulls a copy of the print map labeled *Python Diagnostic* from her bag, the same map that she and Daniel were looking at back in the RV. "That's near the entrance to the garage," she says, tapping at the paper. We scan this section of the map, but whatever is behind the fireplace in front of us isn't listed.

Taylor rolls up the map and stashes it inside her bag. "Aaron shouldn't be going anywhere without backup."

"Right. And neither should you. I'm coming. It's *my* father down there, and I'm as worried about Aaron and the others as you are. Plus . . . I'm not staying up here alone."

Even though I know I'll soon be following Taylor down through the dark on a ladder, I half expect her to say no, maybe even to pull out duct tape and leave me here strapped to one of the support beams. But she seems to be weighing what I said. Maybe she doesn't want to be alone either.

"I can't give you a gun. You'll just be a liability."

"But I'd be a second set of eyes."

As soon as the words leave my mouth, I remember the spider face in my reflection. *Not just a second set of eyes. Also a third set, and a fourth.* I push that thought away. "More importantly, if I'm with you, you'll have a hostage. Or better yet, I can pretend to be Cregg. Plus . . . I had a vision back at the RV. I *do* go with you . . . it will be dark and—"

Taylor snorts, shaking her head. "God, Anna. You are an *unbelievably* bad liar. That's one reason I could tell when it was Cregg and not you. *He* can actually lie."

Is she saying I'm lying about the vision or saying that they won't believe me if I pretend to be Cregg? Maybe both. Either way, I'm not sure her claim makes sense. If Cregg was that good of a liar, how did Taylor know he was lying? But I don't want to piss her off by questioning her shaky logic, so I simply stick to my point.

"I won't need to convince them of anything, Taylor. Even if Cregg isn't in control, they both know that he's *in* here. Abbott won't risk losing the paycheck that he's put forth a lot of effort to get, and this . . . Alex . . ."

I stop, searching for words. It's hard for me to reconcile the Graham Cregg who tortured Molly and was the cause of countless deaths with the image of anyone's father, much less as a father who might be mourned by his offspring.

"I guess she loses what's left of her dad? I don't know. The point is, if you need leverage with them, you can threaten me because they do not want me dead. I don't even think Whistler will kill me if he can avoid it. They consider me and my father valuable commodities. Not just as weapons but as potential . . . second skins, I guess?"

Taylor wrinkles her nose. "Very glad that the Delphi gods made me a lowly sketch artist. And I wasn't actually planning on leaving you here." She pulls up a message on her phone and holds it out to me. "This came in when we were still in the car."

It's from Stan:

If you listen to your brothers, the path clusters unravel.

"I don't know about you, but I like Jaden's style of visions a whole lot better than Stan's," Taylor says, echoing my earlier thoughts. "These are way too iffy. I kind of hoped he was talking about us checking out the van. And maybe he was. There's no way to tell."

The phone buzzes in my hand, startling me to the point that I nearly drop the thing. It's Deo.

"Deo? Where are you?" I answer out of habit, not even thinking about the fact that it's Taylor's phone until she snatches it away. Which is silly, because she's right next to me and I can hear every word he says.

"Um. Not entirely sure? . . . somewhere between the gar . . ." There's about a second of silence, and then he says, "Pfeifer to the lab . . ."

"You're breaking up," Taylor says.

". . . tunnel on fire. Daniel saw something different. We're still . . . were supposed to meet Aaron"—another, longer break—"through Memor . . ."

The call drops this time. Taylor tries again, but no luck.

"So," I say. "I'm getting that they dropped Aaron off near Memorial Hall. They were going to meet at the lab—"

"And Daniel and Deo can't get through the tunnel. But why did they separate? And why didn't they grab Pfeifer before he got into the building?"

"No clue." I nod toward the fireplace. "Guess we'll have to go ask them."

"Yeah." She sighs. "Go unlock the front door. I'll text and tell them we've found a way in. They can circle around."

I start to protest that we haven't actually checked yet to determine whether this *is* a way in. But it seems kind of pointless when I'm 99 percent sure there's a pit and a ladder somewhere on the other side of that fireplace wall.

When I return, Taylor is finishing up the text. After she hits send, she says, "There. I feel better with them knowing either way. In case they can't find another route in . . . *and* in case something happens to us. I don't know if they'll even get the text if they're already underground, but . . ."

"Worth a try."

"Yeah," she says. "Before we go, here are the rules. You stay where I can see you. That means you go in first and at no time do you get behind me. Nor do you point this"—she holds up the flashlight/stun gun—"or your pepper spray toward me. Are we understood?"

I nod, then I place my palms over the current set of handprints on the fireplace wall and push. It creaks a bit as it slowly pivots inward to reveal a small room, no bigger than a broom closet. She hands me the flashlight, and I crouch down and squeeze through the opening.

Taylor comes in gun first, which I guess is logical, but it also reminds me that I need to be careful. Taylor does not want to shoot me. I'm quite certain that she will have a tough time living with herself if she does. But I don't doubt for a second that she *will* pull that trigger if she thinks my control has slipped and she's in here with Graham Cregg. And I don't blame her one bit.

I shine the light around the tiny space as Taylor slides the fireplace back into position. We're inside a plain wooden room, decorated with nothing but cobwebs. At the back, I see a door marked *Caution*. There's a metal slide bolt at eye level.

And the bolt is closed.

Taylor and I both stare at it for a moment, thoroughly confused.

"The footsteps led into this room," I say. "This is the only door. If they went through it, then how the hell is the bolt closed on this side?"

"She's a Mover," Taylor says. "Or Abbott is. Telekinetic. That's the only rational explanation."

I'm tempted to argue that it's really *not* a rational explanation, because nothing about the Delphi program feels rational to me. Taylor, on the other hand, has been around this insanity her entire life.

"It's not Abbott. If he'd had any sort of ability, I'm pretty sure he'd have used it back at the deli."

Taylor frowns, and I remember that she may not have heard all of the gory details of my day. But she just shakes her head and slides the bolt back. "Later, okay? After you."

I'm so focused on the mystery of the locked bolt that I almost forget the *Caution* sign on the door. The flashlight beam bounces off the raised rails of a metal ladder that disappears downward into the dark. Aside from the ladder's edge, there is absolutely nothing beneath the toes of my sneakers. Just a deep black pit. If I'd moved any faster, I'd have fallen straight into it.

Even though I knew there would be no staircase, it's disappointing. The loud sigh from Taylor lets me know the feeling is mutual.

"Well, then. We have a ladder." She pushes me back. "Which means I have to go first. You follow when I tell you to, okay? And give me some space. I don't want you close enough to kick if your hitcher makes a surprise appearance."

I hand over the flashlight and move back toward the center of the tiny room, still unnerved at nearly stepping into that empty chasm. Although it's completely irrational to question my decision to follow Taylor, given that I know I *do* follow her, my mind continues running along two parallel tracks, and one of those tracks is freaking out right now. Even under normal circumstances, descending a ladder into a deep, dark, possibly spider-filled hole would rank pretty high on my oh-*hell*-no list. On a day like today, however, when I've had maybe a dozen dizzy spells . . . it's borderline crazy.

But Aaron's down there without backup. And Taylor will be safer with me along.

Taylor zips up her hoodie to the very top. "We're on silent mode from here on out, since we don't know for certain where this ladder leads, and anything we say could echo. At some point, I'll have to turn off the flashlight, too. So step softly and carefully. And if you've got a hood on that jacket, you might want to use it. I'm guessing there are creepy-crawlies."

"Any idea how far down?" I ask.

"None whatsoever." She starts down the ladder, flashing me a cheerful smile that I add to my growing list of evidence that Taylor Quinn is quite insane.

CHAPTER THIRTEEN

Port Deposit, Maryland
April 24, 2020, 9:54 p.m.

I sit on the edge of the pit, waiting until she taps the rail before I turn and follow her into the abyss. For the first twenty or so steps, she leaves the flashlight on and pointed upward. The beam catches on every single strand of cobweb, but I only see one spider. Thankfully, it's a spindly, long-legged creature with a body so small I can't even tell if it *has* eyes.

Strangely enough, I'm glad when she turns the light off and also glad that she didn't pack the headgear for the goggles. In the pitch black, it's easier to forget where I am and just focus on putting one foot below the other.

The air is heavy and stale, like the place needs airing out. Like the townhouse last night but worse. As I enter the time period from my vision, one track of my mind is thinking it's nice knowing that the rungs are intact, since three other people—Abbott, Alex, and Taylor—have already used the ladder. Next comes that stupid fleeting thought that maybe they did fall, and maybe they're all lying crumpled at the bottom, even though I know I'd have heard if Taylor fell.

Even though I'm expecting the cobweb or spider or whatever the hell it is when it brushes against my hand, that doesn't stop me from nearly shrieking and frantically rubbing my hand against my jeans. I'm glad I can't see right now. I just need to keep moving, because Aaron could already be in danger, and every second I waste on this ladder will only make the situation worse.

When the vision ends, all I can think is that I wish it had been longer. I wish it had given me some idea what to expect when we finally hit the ground.

Taylor is moving quickly. I have to be cautious, looping one arm through the rungs as I travel downward, to provide me with extra stability if one of the dizzy spells hits. Soon, Taylor's footsteps and breathing are so faint that I can barely hear them at all. It's all I can do to make myself continue downward, instead of bolting back toward the surface.

Then I hear something. Not from Taylor, below. It sounds like someone above me on the ladder.

I completely forget about looping my arm through the rungs and scurry down as fast as possible. Cregg is still sluggish, but he's alert enough to sense my impending panic, and I feel him tapping away at my mental walls. It's more of an idle exploration than a full-fledged barrage, but my nerves are already stretched to the breaking point and it really isn't helping.

Something latches on to my ankle, and I barely manage to bite back a scream. It comes out as something between a squeal and a hiccup. My foot lashes out instinctively, but Taylor, I assume, blocks the kick, smacking my shin against the bottom rung.

I press my lips together yet again to keep from crying out. On the plus side, the pain in my leg makes me forget my terror a few moments ago.

"*Shhhh.*" Taylor hisses in my ear, moving back so I can take the final step down.

The noise I heard from above seems to have stopped, and the more I think about it, the more I wonder whether it was coming from the surface. Taylor was on the ladder too. Maybe I heard an echo of her footsteps. Or maybe I imagined the entire thing.

Opening my eyes slowly, I realize that even though the flashlight is off I can see, at least a tiny bit. Taylor runs her hands along the wall, moving toward the left where thin lines of light outline a closed door.

Is the power actually on down here? Or is someone simply waiting on the other side with a flashlight and a gun?

Taylor presses her ear against the gap, and I try to calm my heart down enough to listen, too. After a long moment, she nudges me and points at the doorknob.

Oh, right. We're on the ground now, so it's back to me going first. I pull the night-vision goggles out of my knapsack so that I'll have them ready and then turn the knob in tiny increments, nearly jumping when it finally clicks open. There is light, but it's off in the distance and very faint. A flashlight, or maybe a lantern. And the stale odor is now mixed with the smell of smoke.

I don't hear anything, though. Taylor nudges me, and I push the door open slowly. Goggles raised, we creep forward into what looks like a break room. There's a fridge, a coffeepot, a sink, and a round table with three cheap cafeteria chairs. Condiment packets, napkins, sporks, and other debris are scattered on the counters and the floor. Most of the cabinet doors and drawers gape open, as though someone rifled through them and couldn't be bothered to put the contents back.

After lowering the goggles, I see that the light is yellow and flickering. More like a candle or maybe multiple candles. And it seems to be concentrated in one vertical strip of light.

A shadow breaks the light pattern, and I hold my arm back to halt Taylor. The candlelight is coming from a room on the right, maybe twenty feet down the hallway. The door is partially open. I'm starting to pick up sounds now, mostly furniture scraping back and forth against the floor in a steady rhythm, but also some very heavy breathing.

I glance back at Taylor, who is staring at the door through the goggles. She motions for me to do the same. There's a metal nameplate in the center. I zoom in and read: *Graham Cregg*.

The rhythm picks up slightly. This could be our best chance to get past without attracting attention, so I move a bit faster. Taylor must agree, because she's right on my heels. We're maybe ten steps from the door when there's one last screech of wood on tile and then silence.

Taylor grabs my arm. We stop and press our backs against the wall, although I'm thinking that, if that was what it sounded like, we'd be better off running while they're getting their clothes back into place.

A giggle from inside the room is followed by a roar inside my head. The roar is muted by my walls, much the same way that the giggle is muted by the partially closed door, but there's no mistaking either sound.

"Oh, *perfect*. Light one for me, too. I'll flick the ashes all over his chair. He always got so mad when people smoked." The woman has an accent I can't quite place. New Jersey? No, I think maybe it's Philly. Her *mad* is almost *mid*, and *smoked* leans toward *smooked*. "Especially women. Pretty sure the only reason Mom took up the habit was to piss him off."

Cregg is butting his spider-rat shoulder against my walls now, a dull, frustrated thud. The sound is vaguely reminiscent of the racket the two people in that room were just making on what must be his old desk. That thought must get through to Cregg, because the thudding instantly stops.

Taylor nudges me and mouths, "Are you okay?"

When I nod, she points forward. We don't even manage a step, however, before I hear Abbott's voice. "They should have called by now. The agreement was that they'd check in every fifteen minutes unless they see activity over there. It's been nearly twenty."

"Maybe they got called out on a real police emergency," she says.

"They're off duty tonight. You think I'm an idiot? I wouldn't have hired someone who could be called away."

"Are you even sure they're bringing him here?" she asks.

"They saw two cars up here yesterday."

"So? Doesn't mean that Pfeifer is here."

"I'm going to call them. Find that map you mentioned, okay? And be quiet, unless you want them to know you're here, too."

The shadows flicker wildly as one or both of them move about. If we're going to go, we have to do it now. I half run, half tiptoe past the door toward the end of the hallway and then follow it to the right, entering a long, narrow room with several sofas. There's a television mounted on one short side of the room. A curtained window takes up most of one of the long walls. Next to it is a door.

The layout of the room seems familiar, and after a moment, I realize why. I remember sitting on that couch with Dacia Badea as she tried to access my hitchers' file. Her digging her nails into my arm, angry that Molly's files weren't available. And me discovering that it was actually Dacia who killed Molly, not Cregg. Dacia, who somehow made herself believe she was doing Molly a kindness.

I make it quick for you.

"Move," Taylor snarls under her breath. She opens the door and half shoves me back into the hallway.

We both start to run, but navigating these corridors isn't going to be as easy as it was last time I was here. Debris is everywhere. I suspect that much of this mess was the result of people who came in after the fire to investigate the mostly fictitious story that the Creggs concocted about a terrorist group and a human-trafficking ring in order to hide what was really going on here. A long strip of yellow tape cordons off the monitoring area where observers watched as researchers tested the adepts inside the neighboring rooms, and many of the computers seem to be missing.

"Hey!" a voice calls from behind us. Taylor looks back, but I don't have to. It's Abbott's voice.

A beam of light, much brighter than the one that Taylor is carrying, crisscrosses the corridor. I move closer to Taylor, trying to keep my body between her and the gun that I'm pretty sure Abbott is drawing. He won't shoot me, because that would be shooting Cregg.

Except how would he know that it's me? It's dark, and—

He fires. Misses. Fires again.

I pull Taylor to the left, and as soon as we round the corner, she turns back and fires. She doesn't even take time to aim.

"Why did you do that?" I whisper.

"Warning shot," Taylor says as she starts down the hallway. "Maybe he'll back off if he knows we're armed."

"Abbott!" a man yells. "Drop the gun!"

"Who the hell is Abbott?" Abbott says.

Two shots. Then a third shot from a different gun.

"That was Sam's voice," Taylor says. "How did he get here? I could have shot him!"

I hear the faint sound of footsteps moving our way. Taylor pulls back toward the main hallway, but I grab her arm.

"We don't know who shot who." I shine the light back behind us. "Keep your gun pointed at—"

"Or," she whispers, "I could just ask? *Sam!*" Her voice booms out the last word. "Is that you, Sam?"

There's a brief pause and then: "Yeah, it's me. Hold your fire."

A few seconds later, he turns the corner, holding up his hand to block the beam from Taylor's flashlight. He's wearing goggles that are a bit smaller and older than the pair in my hand, but at least he remembered the headgear. He looks a little surprised, and not exactly happy, to see me. It seems Aaron and Daniel have filled him in on everything that's happened.

"There were two of them back there," I say, nodding at the hallway. "Abbott—or whatever his name actually was—and a girl. Alex Cregg."

"Yeah. She was in the kitchen when I reached the bottom of the ladder. I . . . um . . . convinced her to go back into the office and then shoved a sofa and a love seat in front of the door. She's a scrawny little thing. I think it will hold her."

"Maybe," Taylor says wryly. "And maybe not. She's got muscles you can't see."

"Delphi?" Sam asks.

Taylor nods. "Cregg's daughter. She's a Mover—don't know how strong, but she locked the bolt on that door from the other side. I guess to make it look like no one went down there."

"Big difference between moving a tiny bolt and a couch, but yeah . . . we need to watch our backs. Speaking of, you want to explain that wild shot a minute ago?" Sam asks. "You could have taken my head off."

Taylor huffs indignantly. "I didn't know you were behind us. You're supposed to be driving the RV to West Virginia."

"Porter's doing it. I may be old, but the day I let my grandkids walk into danger on their own is the day you can just go ahead and roll me into my grave. And that was doubly true after I got a text from that Stan kid."

"Oh," Taylor says. "Anything new?"

"Yeah. He said all of the paths were unraveling. I don't know what the hell that means, but it sounds bad. The part that I *did* get was where he said to abort, only you were already headed down that shaft, so I followed. How confident are you that he knows what he's talking about?"

"Way less than I was ten minutes ago," Taylor says. "But Deo said Aaron is down here solo. So don't even try arguing that we should head back up."

Sam glances over at me, then back at Taylor. "I assumed you were down here with Aaron. Your brothers shouldn't have left you alone, and . . . Anna shouldn't be here at all. Both for her sake and everyone else's. No offense, Anna."

"None taken," I say. "I'd actually prefer to be elsewhere."

"I trust her, Popsy, or I would have left her aboveground. She's medicated now and she's in control. Right, Anna?" She waits for my nod and continues. "We need to get moving."

"Exactly where are we going?" he asks.

"Lab 1," I say. "I've been here before. I can take the lead."

The hallways are wide, but there's a lot of junk scattered about. We pick our way through the debris, trying to balance speed with clearing from the path as we go, just in case we need to beat a hasty retreat.

Room 81, where Caleb had been kept, is just ahead. It's nothing but an ordinary door now, half open. I peek inside as we pass and see the charred remains of furniture and, near the middle of the room, something that looks kind of like a giant white shoe with the toe cut away and propped up like a car hood. The lid is partially melted, and the entire thing is streaked with soot. I shine the flashlight through the door to get a better look and see water on the inside of the "shoe."

"What are you doing?" Taylor asks.

"This is the room where they kept Caleb. That thing in the middle— is that an isolation tank?"

"Maybe." Her tone makes it clear that identifying this object is very low on her list of priorities. And she's right, so we keep going.

A security door separates the main section of The Warren from the long tunnel leading to two labs that were kept secret from most of the guards and other workers that Cregg employed. It's the same door that Ashley opened for me and Deo on our way out last time. I'm relieved to find it unlocked, just as the gate was when we drove in.

It's colder in here, and the smoky odor seems less oppressive. The floor slopes downward for the first hundred yards or so, then flattens out. I'm also picking up a light off in the distance. When I feel the path begin to shift upward, I motion for Sam and Taylor to stop.

"We're halfway through," I whisper. "The tunnel opens into a hallway. Lab 1 is on the left, Lab 2 on the right, once we pass the cubicles. The lab walls are cement block up to about three feet and then some sort of clear glass or plastic barrier above that. The tunnel that leads up to the parking area begins just past the labs, and there's a monitoring station on the right, before we get to them."

"And you're sure they'll be in Lab 1?" Sam asks.

"No. That's just the lab that Deo and I were in. Jaden said they used the labs interchangeably. People were probably killed in both rooms. I don't know if they're aiming to have my father pick up specific talents, or if the plan is to simply fill him up with everything they've got. I don't even know if there's a limit to how many spirits he can pick up."

I don't add that I'm pretty sure there *is* a limit to how many someone can hold and keep their sanity. The ghosts I had come across made a conscious decision not to overcrowd me. Dozens could easily have rushed in, but I wound up with only five, including Jaden, Will, and the women I lumped together as the Furies. Then the other four left once they realized that I wasn't willing to shoot Cregg or Dacia unless necessary to save myself or Deo. I was very glad they left, because I'm not sure how long I'd have been me if I'd had that many hitchers in my head at once. Holding them back was nearly as difficult as holding back Cregg.

I know that one of those adepts was strongly telekinetic. Another, the girl who managed to set Cregg's phone on fire, was a Zippo. Either of those abilities seems like a pretty useful one if you're loading up a walking weapon. And from what I've seen, no two Delphi adepts have exactly the same ability. Even those who share the same talent will generally have different strengths and weaknesses, and the gift manifests in different ways.

"Fair enough. Guess that means we have to be ready for—" Sam stops and stares ahead, running one hand through his thinning gray hair. I follow his gaze, but I don't see anything, aside from the fact that there is definitely a light at the end of this tunnel. I don't hear anything either, and judging from Taylor's expression, neither does she.

"They're in . . . Lab 2." He says this tentatively, almost like it's a theory he's trying on for size. "Aaron's already there."

Sam isn't Delphi. Though he served in the military, at seventy-two, he's well past the age of the soldiers used as Delphi test subjects. But he gets hunches sometimes. Aaron says those hunches served Sam very well when he was on the police force, probably saving his life and Porter's on more than one occasion.

"I'm in front," Sam says. "Anna's in the middle, and, Taylor, keep an eye out behind us. Stay close to the wall." Sam takes off before either of us can answer, moving in a crouched run at a much faster pace than I'd have thought possible for his age. That has me worried that Aaron may be about to go in on his own.

Sam's hunch was correct. Even with the glare from what I'm now pretty sure are headlights, I can now make out a fainter light coming from the right side of the building. I raise the goggles. That . . . bothers me, because it could mean they've already been inside Lab 1 and we're too late to prevent my father from picking up those hitchers. It's not that I think they'd necessarily have taken the rooms in numerical order, but more that I know there was a lot of paranormal activity in that lab.

Of course, who knows what they did inside Lab 2? It's entirely possible that they killed even more—and even more powerful—adepts on that side of the hallway.

A dizzy spell hits just before the end of the tunnel. It's no worse than the ones I've been having all day, but I'm bone tired and I stumble, causing Taylor to trip. She lands hard on her knee and calls me several choice names under her breath when I reach down to help her up. In a perfect world, I'd have had a few more seconds for my head to stop spinning, but she marches me onward.

Something catches my eye up ahead. I raise the goggles and see that it's a vehicle parked outside Lab 1. A jeep or maybe a Hummer. It

Rysa Walker

looks weird inside the building, but the guards used to whiz around in golf carts, and I guess if two golf carts could pass each other inside the tunnels, a single vehicle could make it through as well.

Sam has already ducked through a gap between the cubicle panels in the monitoring station when we catch up to him. The fact that the cubicle walls are still there answers one question that I've wondered about since the night we left The Warren. The fire that started in Lab 1 when Cregg's phone ignited didn't spread. If it had, these fabric panels would have burned or melted and there'd be far more fire damage overall. All we've got is some smoke damage—mostly soot on the walls and ceiling. I don't know whether it was Graham Cregg's crew or the group aligned with his father, but someone set fire to the main building purposefully, in order to cover their tracks as they evacuated the kids.

Something rustles in front of us, off to the right. Taylor raises the gun automatically, but Sam holds his arm out. A moment later, Aaron comes around one of the panels. He's holding his gun, but it's not raised, so he must have gotten a vibe from one of us. He seems surprised, but definitely not unhappy, that Sam's here. He'd wanted to bring him along in the first place, and it occurs to me that Aaron, who has worked with his grandfather for several years, might have a better idea than the rest of us of how capable Sam is in this kind of situation.

"Hey, Sam." Aaron drops down between me and Taylor. "What happened with Daniel and Deo? They should have been here ten minutes ago. And you two were supposed to stay put."

"Something was blocking the tunnel," I say. "The call dropped before we could get any other details."

"Weird," Aaron says, nodding in the direction of the vehicle parked near Lab 1. "Whistler and the others drove through just fine. Daniel was supposed to follow them. We don't have time to worry about it now, though. They . . . um . . . carried Pfeifer out of the first lab just after I got here. He seemed to be unconscious."

"We need to hurry. If he's already picked up hitchers, then . . ." I trail off, my tired brain struggling to string words together.

Aaron nods. "Follow me."

The four of us wind our way through the maze of cubicles, hunched over so that our heads aren't visible above the dividing walls. When we're two rows in, Aaron turns back toward us and says, "This takes us to another exit closer to the lab door. It's just Whistler, one other guy, and a woman. The men are armed. Both are angry that Pfeifer passed out. Whistler is worried about those cops who were circling around, thinking he might have to shoot them. I don't know if the woman is armed or not. Haven't picked up any vibes from her. They've got the door pulled shut, but the power is out so it's not locked."

"So we're either three guns to two or evenly matched." Sam sighs. "This would be a whole lot easier if Daniel was here."

Taylor's mouth tightens, but I really don't think Sam is being sexist. He'd simply rather avoid a gunfight altogether, and Daniel is our only hope for doing that.

Not the *only* . . .

The thought that comes through my walls isn't fully formed, but it's clear enough for me to get Cregg's meaning. Yes, if I lowered my walls, he could persuade his father's lackeys to drop their weapons or even to turn their guns on each other. But Cregg knows there's absolutely no way I'd trust him.

None of them even suggest giving me a weapon. I'm entirely okay with that.

Someone coughs up ahead. The sound is muffled by the plexiglass, but it still echoes in the silence. We slow down, all of us walking more cautiously now. Our chance of success is heavily contingent on the element of surprise, and if any of us stumble, cough, or sneeze, that will be lost.

When we reach the other exit, we crouch around the opening. We're directly across from their Hummer and maybe five yards from the lab door.

"We go on three," Aaron says to Sam and Taylor, who both nod. "Anna—"

"I'm on lookout. I know." The words come out sharper than I intend. While I don't actually resent being sidelined, I do wish there was some way I could help.

Aaron gives me a sympathetic half smile and leans in close to my ear, whispering so softly that I feel the words more than hear them. "I love you. You know that, right?"

I nod. "I love you, too. Be careful."

He moves back to Sam. Taylor hangs back, her expression suggesting that she's trying to make a weighty decision. After a second, she shoves the stun gun toward me. "In case you need it. Turn on us, and I *will* kill you. Or haunt you."

The latter threat actually worries me more, and Taylor knows it. Having been stuck with Daniel in my head, I shudder at the thought of dealing with his younger, often less-reasonable sister.

Aaron mouths, "One. Two." On *three*, he moves into the bright glare from the headlights, bent low. The cement section of the wall isn't high enough to hide him entirely from the view of those inside the lab, but if they can avoid being detected until they bust in, we stand a better chance of getting out of here alive.

Sam and Taylor follow Aaron, guns out, and for the next few seconds, the only sound is the shuffling of their footsteps and my pounding heart. I move to the other side of the entrance so that I can keep an eye on the tunnel we came in through. Unfortunately, we're now so close to the headlights that I can't really see much at all beyond their radius.

I jump when I hear Aaron kick the door open. It bangs against the plexiglass walls, and then Sam yells, "Police! Drop your weapons!"

Excerpt from "Mind Blown" in the *Scoop*

April 24, 2020

Variants of the compound known as Delphi (street names include DS, SciPhi, and Freak) are popping up in both rural and urban centers within the United States. One of the most remarkable things about the drug is how rapidly it has spread. Sporadic reports of increased psychic activity and an uptick in violent altercations follow the drug like a malignant shadow.

But what are users actually injecting? No one is entirely sure. The chemical formula for the Delphi serum has not been made public—indeed, the US government still officially denies that such a drug even exists. And there is some evidence that the drugs being sold on the street are nothing more than LSD and a variety of hallucinogens.

Three separate confidential sources interviewed for this article claim to have worked at different times on the Delphi Project. They all stressed that the compound only enhances psychic abilities inherent in a small percentage of people. It cannot give abilities to those who lack them entirely. Nor can you pick and choose from a menu of abilities.

Those marketing the drugs on the street beg to differ, offering customers a shopping list of options such as mind reading and predicting the future. And they claim that the drug is tapping a new market of users who have not, in the past, frequented their neighborhood dealer.

"People want that edge," one source claimed. "They see stories in the paper and start to wonder whether coworkers are swiping their ideas. Maybe even putting bad ideas into their heads, you know? Most aren't worried about getting new abilities so much as blocking the abilities of others. The government isn't helping on this issue. They're gonna study it for five or six years to see who is to blame. Half of them say it's not even real. So people turn to us."

When asked whether the stuff he was marketing could actually block those with Delphi abilities, the man gave us an enigmatic smile. "Maybe. You want to find out for sure, it'll cost you three hundred bucks."

That may be a bargain compared with a drug being fast-tracked for FDA approval by a subsidiary of Decathlon Services Group. Some analysts believe the compound, known as Cerecyclo, could hit the market by late May. Demand will be high, which could dramatically increase the price (and profit margins) for the manufacturer and DSG stockholders.

CHAPTER FOURTEEN

Port Deposit, Maryland
April 24, 2020, 10:37 p.m.

Sam's right to shout *police* while kicking in a door expired a few years ago, unless he's in some sort of retired officers' reserve that I don't know about. I brace for the sound of gunfire, wishing I had a better view from here. Can't see anything but the tops of everyone's heads from this angle.

My audio is working fine, however, now that the door has been kicked open. A woman screams. Chairs or maybe a table topple over. And then I hear a totally incongruous giggle coming toward me from the other direction.

"Wow," Alexandra Cregg says as she emerges from the shadows of the tunnel. "I've never been in one this elaborate. These guys take their jobs real serious."

She's pressed up against Deo, who doesn't look too happy. His eyes drift over to Lab 1, and I'm pretty sure he's reliving everything that happened the last time we were here.

"We're going to walk closer and see if that's the exit," Daniel tells Alex. "Sit down and stay out of the way." There's a touch of extra force in his words.

Alex drops to the ground, pulling Deo down with her. "Cutie-pie can stay here with me."

"No, he can't." Daniel reaches down, grabs Deo's hand, and yanks him to his feet.

I'm still hidden behind the cubicle divider, and my mental walls are fully up, but I feel Daniel's nudge nonetheless and drop to sitting from the crouched position I was in.

From within the lab, Aaron has just finished repeating Sam's order for them to drop their weapons. Whistler, or at least I'm pretty sure it's Whistler, says something back, but I can't decipher it from out here.

"Daniel," I say, leaning out from the shadows. "You guys go. I'll watch her."

He takes one look at me, then at the lab, and curses softly. "Taylor's in there?"

"Yes, but that wasn't her screaming." I've heard Taylor scream. Her voice is a full octave higher than the woman in the lab.

"How many of them?" Daniel asks.

"Three, at least two armed."

"Pfeifer?"

"Unconscious."

Alex Cregg is staring at me. "Are you one of the actors? I haven't done this room before, but you look really familiar."

Actors? Ah . . . okay. Everything is starting to make sense now. Daniel must have persuaded her that this is one of those escape rooms where they lock you in with a group of people and you have to solve a mystery.

"No," I say. "I'm—"

"Change of plans." Daniel draws his gun and grabs Alex by the arm. "You're with me."

"Ooh. I like this better. Going right into the action! Do I get a gun, too?"

"You do not." Daniel pulls her in front of him like a shield. She tenses a bit, and he adds, "Remember, it's *all for fun.*"

"Fun!" She smiles so wide that it looks like her face will crack. I feel the corners of my mouth lift as well, even though I'm fighting it.

The spider-rat is clearly agitated now, more active than he's been since I took the pill earlier. He's still angry at Alex for defiling his desk and more than a little shocked at this glimpse of what she actually thought of him, but he definitely doesn't like the fact that Daniel might be putting his daughter in danger.

That's the height of hypocrisy coming from a man who used his own ability to force young women to mutilate themselves. Who killed them, in fact, or forced them to kill each other. But like many people born into wealth and power, Cregg doesn't seem to believe that the rules apply to him.

Unfortunately, I find myself reluctantly agreeing with Cregg on one point. It feels wrong to drag Alex into a potential gunfight when she's been made to believe that this is all an act.

"Daniel . . ." I begin.

He doesn't let me get far. "Save it, Anna! I'm not going to hurt her, and neither will they. She's the Senator's granddaughter, for God's sake."

Inside the lab, Aaron is talking again. Not as loud this time, and it's the tone he uses when he's trying to reason with someone. I can't make out the words, but it reminds me that the stakes are very high. People I love are in that room, and judging from the uneasy silence right now, I think they may be at a standoff. Alexandra Cregg came here tonight of her own accord. She seemed perfectly willing to help Abbott kill my father. I drop the argument.

"I'll go with you. In case you need a boost." Deo's voice hasn't cracked for a couple of years, but it does now. Fear this time, though, not puberty.

Daniel catches it, too. "I'll try it on my own first. I'd rather not experiment under these circumstances. But yeah, stay close."

The three of them begin walking toward the lab, and when they're a few feet from the door, he yells, "I've got your boss's granddaughter out here. Pretty sure he's not going to be too happy if you make me shoot her."

No one told me to stay put this time, and the fact that Deo is nervous tilts the balance for me. Even if we make it into our nineties, I'm pretty sure that protecting Deo will still feel like my responsibility. On the off chance that he or any of the others need me, I'm not going to do a damn bit of good all the way over here. So I shove Taylor's little stun gun into my pocket and follow them.

I'm not going into that lab, however. For that matter, I won't be touching anything that might put me at risk of picking up a hitcher. My walls are up to keep Cregg contained, and in theory, that should keep me from pulling anyone else on board. But I'm not keen on testing that theory in a lab where God only knows how many adepts were killed.

Daniel stands in the doorway with Alex in front of him and Deo right behind him. Daniel said he needed to stay close. He didn't say to make himself a target. I tug on Deo's shirt to pull him back behind the glass, being careful not to make actual contact with him. This would be a very inconvenient time for me to have a vision.

Whistler and the other man are near the back of the room, both with guns drawn. The front of the second guy's pants is wet. I'm pretty sure he peed himself.

A dark-skinned girl is crouched behind the gurney that holds my father, her hand resting on his shoulder. She's dressed in a flannel shirt that's way too large, and it looks like her face is bleeding.

"Carefully put the weapons on the floor," Daniel says. "Both of you."

Both men's knees bend slightly. Whistler recovers from Daniel's nudge first, moving the gun away from Sam and toward Daniel.

"Not going to work on me, Corben," Whistler says. "Although I guess that isn't actually your name, you duplicitous piece of shit."

"Nice seeing you again too, Whistler," Daniel says. "And Davis, how about those Orioles. Now, *put down the guns.*"

The other man, Davis, is a balding guy with pale, freckled skin. He's probably well over average height and weight, but he seems dwarfed next to Whistler. I don't remember seeing him when I was at The Warren, but he must have been one of the Fudds.

Davis is fighting Daniel's command too, but not having nearly as much luck as Whistler. He looks over at the girl. "Little help would be nice, Sophie."

The black girl looks at Davis, then at Whistler. Her free hand flies up to the cut on her left cheek and her eyes go wide. "You want me to move away from him? Are you crazy? What if he wakes up again?"

Pfeifer is strapped to the gurney by four separate restraining belts. He's not going anywhere. But if he picked up the hitchers in that other lab, I doubt that it's his physical activity that's worrying her.

"Just do it!" Whistler's hand twitches. He's gripping the gun so tightly that I'm worried he could easily pull the trigger without even intending to.

Sophie reluctantly follows his order. She takes a step forward, still keeping her hand in contact with my father's body. Daniel responds by pushing the gun into Alex Cregg's neck.

"That hurts! Let me go." Alex tries to wrench away, but Daniel doesn't let her.

"I don't think you'll actually shoot the girl," Whistler says. "And to be honest, I'm not sure the Senator much cares one way or the other."

Sophie continues to move cautiously toward the front of the lab. She tries to move the gurney along with her, but the wheels seem to be locked. Instead, she trails her hand along Pfeifer's body, keeping contact for as long as possible. Eventually, she has to move beyond the gurney, but she keeps looking back, much like a runner gauging the distance when attempting to steal a base. Like someone who's worried that each step might be the one that seals her fate because she can't return to safety in time.

The pieces fall together, and I say to Daniel, "She's a blocker. Like Maggie. Here to control Pfeifer, but she could block you, too."

Daniel takes two quick steps backward. Although, truthfully, it's more of a stagger. He's dragging Alex with him, and the extra weight seems to be more of a burden than his still-recuperating body can easily handle.

Alex frowns up at him. "Hey! I *said* let me—"

"You're having *fun!*" Daniel snaps, and the angry lines morph into the blissful expression of a five-year-old girl petting a unicorn.

Deo steps through the door and grabs Daniel's shoulder.

"Put the guns on the floor and kick them toward me." Daniel doesn't yell, but the command fills every square inch of the lab. Whistler and Davis lean down in unison, place their guns on the ground, and then kick them toward Daniel.

So does Sam. And Aaron. And Taylor. I even pull the little stun gun out of my pocket, though I manage to fight back the urge to drop it. Daniel's words even seem to have reached my father, who stirs uneasily on the cot. It the first movement I've seen from him since we entered the room. Sophie must notice it as well, because she darts back to him, grabbing his ankle.

Daniel tells Aaron to collect the guns. There's no psychic push involved this time, but Aaron still gives him an annoyed look. He picks up the guns, returns Sam's and Taylor's, and stashes the others in Taylor's backpack.

"What do you propose we do with these guys?" Sam asks Daniel in a low voice. "We can't exactly call the police, but I've got a problem with—"

"Get out!" Aaron yells. But whatever he or anyone else says next, I don't hear. My focus is on the words that flash inside my head.

TURN AWAY.

It's like a handwritten sign that hangs in my consciousness for a brief moment and flickers out. I've seen this before. It's Will, Jaden's former roommate, and one of the hitchers from Lab 1 that I housed very briefly, until they learned I wasn't quite as keen on lethal vengeance as they were.

But Will isn't in my head now. Apparently, he's in Scott Pfeifer's, sending me a message. Before I have time to respond, a second sign appears.

THEY WON'T LET THE FUDDS GO THIS TIME.

My eyes turn toward Sophie, who is clutching my father's arm even tighter now. Her eyes are squeezed almost shut, and her face reminds me of pictures I've seen of women in labor, every muscle intent on its task.

Aside from Aaron, who must have picked up what was happening with his spidey sense, no one else in the room seems to have gotten Will's message.

Scott Pfeifer remains perfectly still, except for his head, which whips toward the two former guards. His eyes are open now, and he's staring straight at Whistler.

Whistler's eyes widen. He tries to say something, but no words come out. I'm pretty sure no air is going in, either. Whistler's feet remain on the ground, but otherwise it reminds me of that scene in *Star Wars* where Vader lifts the subordinate who has displeased him by his neck.

Davis tugs at the collar of his shirt. He's not breathing either. He takes a few steps toward the gurney and then drops to his knees.

Aaron grabs Taylor's arm and begins backing toward the door, his eyes fixed on the two men. The others are frozen in place, watching as Whistler joins Davis on the floor. His mouth is opening and closing like a fish.

"I can't control him!" Sophie says. "You should get out!"

That snaps Daniel and Sam out of their stupor, and they both head for the exit. I expect Sophie to follow, but she remains in the room, still gripping my dad's arm. Her eyes are firmly closed, and her head is turned away from the two men asphyxiating in the center of the room.

"What's happening?" Alex asks in a tiny voice from her position on the floor. "Those actors . . . they *are* actors, aren't they? Actors . . ."

"Go to sleep, Alex." She curls up obediently at the sound of Daniel's voice, her hands tucked beneath her face to cushion it.

I want to join her, even though the tile looks cold and hard. Even though it reminds me of Costello on the floor at Joe's place and of Abbott back in the main ward. And now Whistler and this other guy. Lucas, Jaden, Oksana, Will. White tile. Red blood.

The others are talking, but I just stand there, staring down. Tiny motes of dust and ash dance in the air around my sneakers, illuminated by the headlights of Whistler's car. White lights. Red sneakers. White tile. Red blood. White sheets. The cool side of my pillow . . .

"Anna. Hey, hey." It's Deo's voice, and someone is tapping my cheek. I startle, expecting to hear that odd humming noise that precedes a vision, but it's Aaron's fingers on my face.

Deo stands next to him. "You were about to fall asleep standing up."

I shake my head to clear it, opening my eyes extra wide. "Yeah. I need coffee."

"You need sleep," Aaron says.

"Yeah," I repeat. "I'm running on fumes."

Daniel, Taylor, and Sam are back inside the lab now. I see the two bodies on the floor just beyond them. There's no blood this time, just bodies on the white tile. Sophie is in the same spot as before, still holding my father's arm. He seems to have lapsed into unconsciousness, and I'm again struck with jealousy for those who can sleep.

"They're dead?" I ask.

Aaron nods. "They really shouldn't be. Unconscious, yes. But it takes several minutes for someone to suffocate. It's . . . odd."

Deo gives a nervous little laugh. "The part where someone choked them without ever freakin' touching them. That was *odd*, too. It's like what happened to Lucas, when he just started sneezing and couldn't even stop long enough to catch his breath. Do you think it was the same hitchers? The—what did you call them—Furies?"

"Don't know. But I'm pretty sure Pfeifer picked up Will." I tell them about the message I got just before Whistler and Davis stopped breathing.

Taylor unlocks the brakes on the gurney, and they push my father over toward the Hummer.

I glance at Alex, who is still snoozing peacefully, then at Sophie, next to the gurney. "What are we going to do with them?" I ask in a low voice.

"That's what Sam and I were just discussing," Daniel says. "We considered taking them with us, but . . . we should probably leave them in the containment unit." He nods toward the small room near the back.

"Seems . . . harsh to just leave them like that," Aaron says.

"You have a better idea?" Daniel asks, leaning back against the soot-streaked wall of the lab.

"Taylor's got a couple of bottles of water in her backpack and a candy bar," Sam says. "We'll contact the Senator's Sanctuary hotline . . . I mean, they're both adepts, even if one is his granddaughter."

Yeah," Taylor says. "And I don't think it's too harsh at all for Alex. She may look all angelic now that you've sent her to la-la land, but she was in on the plot to kill Pfeifer."

"The lock on that containment unit isn't going to work with the power out," Aaron says. "How long do you think your nudge will last?"

Daniel shakes his head. "I don't know. Probably quite a while with Deo boosting."

"It won't work at all on me," Sophie says.

Daniel frowns. "We could move some of the equipment in front of the door. The fridge, maybe? There are also some weights in the back room that they used for testing how much the telekinetic kids could lift."

Aaron grabs Alex's shoulders, and Deo grabs her feet. They carry her into the containment area. Sophie watches but doesn't follow.

"You need to go into that cube with the other girl," Sam says. "You'll be okay. We'll leave you with water, and we'll let your employer know to come get you."

"I don't have an *employer*," Sophie says, her voice shaking. "An employer pays you a salary, right? They let you go *home* at night. All those people give me is food and shelter, and they lock me in. They point their guns or their tasers at me, just like you're doing, even though I've done nothing wrong. This isn't some battle where you're the good guys and everyone who wound up on the other side is evil. When The Warren caught fire, I ran for the nearest exit like everyone else. Those of us who went out one door were locked up in Nevada. And those who went out the other door were locked up in North Carolina."

Daniel says, "So . . . what do you want us to do?"

"I want you to take me with you. It's not safe out there. I don't have money or identification. I'm ready for a change of scenery, and you're going to need me when this guy wakes up."

"You weren't able to save Whistler and Davis," Daniel says.

Sophie cocks her head to one side. "What makes you think I was *trying*? I am glad they're dead. Do you know how many people the two of them hurt? How many deaths they were responsible for? I wasn't trying to protect Whistler and Davis. You're lucky I was able to keep them from killing all of *you*."

I'm not sure if the others notice the plural. She kept *them*, not *him*, from killing us. Does she have a sense of how many hitchers Pfeifer is hosting?

"We already have a blocker," Taylor says.

216

"Maggie, right? The Fudds tested us together a bunch of times. She's good, but she's only a kid." Sophie's hand swipes toward the cut on her cheek. "You really want to put her in harm's way? Anyhow, I don't see her with you."

"She has a point," Aaron says, and then turns to us. "Maybe she can give us some more intel. As confident as Maria is in the information from her psychic intelligence squad, I'd personally like to confirm some of their readings with people who've actually been with Dacia's Bear Brigade."

Sam still seems a little reluctant to take Sophie with us, but I caught a glimpse of Daniel's face as Aaron was speaking. The point about Sophie having information on Senator Cregg's people won him over, because she could have information on Sariah. Daniel's feelings for Sariah—Caleb's mother and Ashley's sister—are conflicted, mixed with guilt and some other emotions I was never able to pin down. And if she's still alive, she's with the other camp. I don't need to read Daniel's mind to know that he's eager to ask Sophie some questions and also terrified of the answers he may receive.

"So . . . we leave Alex"—Aaron motions toward the containment unit—"but the rest of us need to get out of here. Can we all fit in that Hummer?"

"Maybe," Daniel says, "but I don't think we can get back through the tunnel." He looks at Deo, and they both shake their heads.

"Okay," I say. "You were breaking up a lot on the phone. What exactly happened?"

"Um . . . yeah," Deo says. "We were still in the parking garage when you called. I didn't get Taylor's text until we surfaced."

He's not answering the question. Daniel doesn't look too eager to dive in, either, but he says, "I think maybe a section of the tunnel is a bit . . . flooded. We might not be able to get through."

Deo smirks. "You said there was a *wall* of water. That's not the same thing as *a bit flooded.*"

"Well," Daniel snaps, "there sure as hell wasn't—"

"Hey!" Sophie calls from across the hall. "The tunnel is fine. There's no wall of water or dragons or herds of zombie cows or whatever you think you saw. Whistler realized the cops were following us. And that *you* were following us. So he told Pfeifer to do something. To send you a suggestion. Mess with your heads."

Daniel's back is to me so I can't see his face, but Sophie can, and she laughs. "Ah. The big bad Fudd doesn't like it when the tables are turned and someone puts the whammy on him, does he?"

The spider-rat in my head doesn't like what she said either. He has stirred occasionally in the past few minutes, but he's still lethargic. Listening, and definitely still looking for any opportunities, any chinks in my armor, any chances to move to the front of my head. His reaction to what Sophie said is different, though. He retreats even more quickly than he did when I brought that brick crashing down on his leg. What Sophie said scared him. Did this ability she mentioned come from one of the hitchers in Lab 1? Someone who was particularly powerful?

The timing seems off, though. Whistler ordered my father to send out that psychic attack, or whatever you want to call it, when he realized they were being followed. So it couldn't be a hitcher who was waiting in Lab 1. They hadn't even gotten to this part of the building yet, let alone had time for Pfeifer to pick up a hitcher.

I file this away as something to discuss with the others later. Sam takes the unpleasant task of going through Whistler's and Davis's pockets to find the car keys, while Daniel tosses a few bottles of water and a Butterfinger that Taylor reluctantly parted with into the containment unit with the still-snoozing Alex Cregg.

We decide against a barricade at the last minute, mostly on my insistence. Whistler said he wasn't sure the Senator would rescue her, and I didn't get the sense he was joking. There doesn't seem to be much love lost between Senator Cregg and his son, and if Alex took her father's side against the Senator, I can't imagine her grandfather being happy about it. They might rescue her eventually, but I could easily see them leaving her here for a while as punishment. This way, when Daniel's sleep spell wears off, she'll be able to hike out. She's unarmed, so she's really not a threat.

The eight of us would probably have fit into the Hummer if not for the gurney—and none of us are eager to take the straps off Pfeifer. We load him into the rear, along with Sophie, Daniel, and Sam. The rest of us walk. I'm fine with that. It's less than a half mile to the surface, and despite being so tired that it's a major effort to put one foot in front of the other, I'd rather keep moving.

As we walk, Aaron tells us about his misadventures trying to get into the elevator shaft at Memorial Hall. This involved kicking in a lot of plaster, uncovering a host of insects, and several large rats.

"Be glad you weren't there," he says, squeezing my shoulders.

I laugh because it's a shared joke, and I definitely wouldn't have been thrilled to deal with any of that. But truthfully, I think he got the better end of the deal. I'd happily tackle an entire roomful of regular rats rather than face the spider-rat in my head.

"So," I ask Deo, "what did you see in the tunnel?"

"Fire. Well, not an actual fire, but lots of smoke. And . . . I could have sworn I heard Patrick's voice."

Patrick is his asshole stepdad. Deo has burns on his forearms, so it's not too surprising that anyone tapping into his deepest fears would dredge up smoke and Patrick. I don't ask, but I'd be willing to bet that the smoke smelled a lot like cheap cigarettes.

"Daniel backed the car out at damn near full speed," he says. "I'm amazed he didn't crash into the wall. I thought he smelled the fire, too, but then he started talking about a waterwall and . . . I could have sworn he also said something about Caleb just before he popped the SUV into reverse."

For some reason, the door of Room 81 pops into my mind. When Caleb was housed in that room, I saw the metal of the door pulse out into the hallway, almost like ripples in water. And when Daniel was in my head, it was abundantly clear that he's frightened of Caleb. Also frightened *for* Caleb. The latter seems much more reasonable. It's hard to imagine a more angelic-looking toddler. In another universe where there was no Delphi Project, Caleb could be the adorable tyke in the Huggies Pull-Ups commercial.

"Why Caleb?" Aaron asks.

I keep quiet. Daniel and I have a bargain. We learned far too much about each other during the time we were forced to share my head. He keeps my secrets and I keep his. Anyway, what I picked up about Caleb and Sariah was more emotion than fact.

What's very clear is that Deo and Daniel both thought one of their deep, dark fears was down that tunnel. Maybe not the deepest and darkest, but at least in Deo's case, I think Patrick drunk and angry with a lit cigarette comes pretty damn close.

"I don't know," Deo says. "Didn't ask him. We were too busy arguing over whether we were running from fire or water. But . . . it didn't really matter. Neither of us was eager to go back in there. Then Taylor's text came through, so we decided to take the route she and Anna found. That made me nervous. And some girl starts screaming for us to let her out. Daniel did his Jedi thing, and we found out she was Cregg's daughter. He thought she might be . . . useful . . . if we had to negotiate, but she was really freaked out when we saw that guy's body. That was Abbott?"

Aaron says, "It's a good thing Sam showed up. Otherwise Taylor might have had to take the shot. Don't tell her I said that," he adds quickly. "I'm not saying she couldn't have or wouldn't have done it. It's just . . . this isn't the first time Sam has had to shoot someone to save a life. He won't lose a lot of sleep over it."

I get a touch of déjà vu—for once, the entirely normal kind—thinking back to Joe's comment this morning at the deli about sparing me the pain of taking a life. It's not all that strange that both Abbott and

Costello died violently, given their chosen profession, but it is odd that they went down under very similar circumstances. I froze this morning, and I'm not at all sure I would have pulled the trigger in time if Joe hadn't been there.

Would Taylor have frozen, too? I doubt it. She's spent her entire life around people who have to make split-second life-and-death decisions. The gun felt natural in her hand, a tool that she'd been taught to use effectively and safely.

But all the same, I'm glad she didn't have to find out.

Winchester, Virginia
April 25, 2020, 2:33 a.m.

The waitress tops off my coffee for the second time. "Can always tell who's doin' the drivin'," she says with a wink.

I smile. No point in telling her she's wrong. She heads back to the kitchen to grab the to-go order for Sophie and Daniel, who are waiting in the Kia with my father. He hasn't stirred since we left Port Deposit two hours ago. We were all close to starving by the time we hit Winchester, especially Sophie, who seems to have Taylor's ravenous appetite when using her Delphi ability. Daniel convinced Sam to stop here at the Waffle House. It's not haute cuisine, but it's filling and at least a slight improvement over the fast food of the past few days.

Taylor mops up the last of her eggs with the crust of her raisin toast and munches reflectively as she stares out the window. The parking lot is mostly empty, just an 18-wheeler and our two vehicles.

"Wonder what they're talking about?"

I'm pretty sure I know, but I just shrug.

"Knowing Daniel, he's probably trying to nudge her," Aaron says. "He can't stand the thought that there's someone he can't push around."

"He does like a challenge," Sam says.

"Still can't believe none of you bothered to tell me." Aaron lowers his voice. "I mean, Daniel gives me all kinds of grief for my ability, which I rarely use on purpose, and he's been actively bending people to his own will all these years."

"Not *actively*," Sam says. "And not family. We had a talk about that and he stopped."

"But . . . how would you know?" Deo asks. "Maybe he used it all the time and made you forget."

Taylor shakes her head. "Doesn't make sense. Daniel pisses everyone off. Always has. He always got into more trouble than Aaron and I did. Remember that time when he was—what?—in eleventh grade, I think. The deal with the car. Mom grounded him for two solid months."

Deo shrugs. "Maybe she'd have grounded him for four months if he hadn't . . . tweaked her memory."

I catch Deo's eye halfway through the comment and give him a pleading look. I'm pretty sure it's just a logic problem to him, like the one in the movie *Labyrinth* where you have one guard who always lies and another who always tells the truth and you have to figure out which is which. Or, in this case, how do you know if someone is altering your perception of reality?

But it's not an idle question for the Quinn family. And that's why, as tempted as I am to defend Daniel on this issue, I keep quiet. They have to work this out themselves, although in some sense, I may understand Daniel better than anyone at this table. Sure, they've known him his entire life, but they've only seen the face he chooses to show them. No matter how close the friend or family, we all wear masks. They slip sometimes and reveal our inner selves, or at least the mask behind the mask. Most of the time, though, we keep our true face hidden. Protected.

It was harder for Daniel to hide his true self when he was inside my head. He could block *facts* most of the time, but he found it difficult to block his emotions. I know how deeply he feels about his family, even Aaron. He feels responsible for them, too. I'd say it goes beyond the normal older-sibling sense of responsibility, but then I'm the same way about Deo, and I didn't even know him for the first half of his life.

To my surprise, it's Aaron who comes to his brother's defense. Sort of.

"No. Daniel wouldn't do that. I'm tired and grumpy, and I'm not being fair. My ability was more visible than Daniel's or Taylor's, so, yeah . . . you were both right to tell me to keep it under wraps. And even if I don't like it, Daniel had a good reason in the few cases I know of where he *nudged* me and Taylor." He shoots me a little smile, knowing that I'm not a fan of Daniel's euphemism. It's a lot more than a nudge. "I do wish you'd trusted me with the information earlier, but I get that it wasn't your secret to tell. At some point, Daniel and I will talk it out. Clear the air."

I make a mental note to be somewhere else when that happens. Normal Quinn family discussions are explosive. This one will probably register on the Richter scale. And, as usual, ten minutes later they'll be fine.

The waitress comes over with the take-out order and starts to top off my coffee again, then raises one penciled-in eyebrow. She's looking down at my leg, twitching to the rapid beat of a nonexistent tune.

"You sure?" she asks.

A horn honks out in the parking lot. I guess this was the sign Daniel and Sam agreed upon, because Sam slides out of the booth.

"Actually," I say, "could you put it in a to-go cup?"

Sam goes to the register to pay. "Everybody hit the bathroom again. We've got over an hour before we reach the cabin, and I don't know if there are rest areas between here and there."

I've had three coffees, so I heed his warning. Taylor, however, snorts and mimics him as she heads outside. "I'm not stopping forty times on this trip, so you kids better quit drinking those sodas."

It's a pretty good imitation.

When I exit the bathroom, I collide with Daniel.

"Sorry!" I say. "I didn't . . . see you."

Daniel doesn't respond. He just keeps his head down and pushes past me.

I get a clear look at his face, though. He's crying.

News Item from the
San Angelo Standard-Times

April 25, 2020

The bodies of the two 16-year-old girls found late Wednesday in the woods near Glenmore Park have been identified as Regina Pelter and Amber Whelow, both of San Angelo. Drug overdose has been verified as the cause of death.

A third teen who was with the girls earlier that day told authorities that they were planning to purchase a packet of "freak," the street name for a synthetic drug that allegedly unleashes psychic abilities. Instead, they were sold a prescription opiate. A preliminary coroner's report revealed approximately three times the lethal dose of fentanyl in the girls' systems.

CHAPTER FIFTEEN

The room is so tiny that the gurney takes up all the space between the two twin beds. Sophie lashed her wrist to my father's with what appears to be one of Taylor's scrunchies. She doesn't look comfortable, but she's sleeping.

So is Scott Pfeifer.

Jasper Hawkins was right. I look much more like my mother, except for my nose. Hers was rounder, and it turned up a bit at the end. Mine is a smaller version of my father's—straight, narrow, slightly square at the tip.

Should I be angry at him? Probably. But what I feel is numb. Empty. So I stand in the doorway, just watching him. Almost hypnotized by his nose, which is so much like mine, flaring out with each exhale. Aside from this, the steady in and out of his breathing, Pfeifer hasn't stirred since we left The Warren.

Someone touches my shoulder, and I jump. Sam is behind me, looking very worried. How long has he been there?

"Sorry. Didn't mean to startle you. Just wanted to say there's cereal in the kitchen if you're hungry."

I'm not. I am slightly embarrassed to have been caught in stalker mode, however, so I follow him into the kitchen. Although *follow* isn't exactly right, since Sam has taken my arm and is more or less pulling me in that direction.

Deo and Taylor are at the table, looking exactly the way people who got four hours of sleep should look. Taylor is following her usual morning routine, however, iPad in hand, browsing the news as she talks.

"Can you believe this kitchen?" Deo says. "I don't know about you guys, but I'm getting a major *Brady Bunch* vibe."

"Yeah," Taylor says. "I'm pretty sure avocado-green appliances went out of style around the same time as leisure suits. You can ask Sam about those. We've got photographic evidence somewhere. I think it was baby blue, and it had bell-bottoms and a fake silk shirt and—"

"It was the seventies," Sam says. "We had style back then."

"Oh, I'm not arguing with you. I'm going to buy Deo one just like it for his birthday."

"No, you're not," Deo says and then stops, considering. "Not baby blue, at any rate."

Despite the retro color scheme, the kitchen is cozy. It's warm, too, courtesy of the woodstove in the nearby living room. Unfortunately, if I stay in here, my eyes are going to close. I pour a cup of coffee, pull on my sneakers, and step outside into a clear blue cloudless morning. There's still a hint of morning chill, and the breeze carries the scent of evergreens and smoke from the woodstove.

I walk to the far side of the property, which is easily ten times the size of the suburban backyards I'm used to. You could plop a high school football field in this clearing and still have room left over. A wooden picnic table sits near a small open shelter that houses extra firewood, a wheelbarrow, and an ancient push mower.

The table, like the shed, has seen better days. Flecks of paint, the same barn red as the cabin, cling to the sides. On top, the boards have warped and faded to a gray with pinkish-brown streaks. They look a bit like strips of raw bacon past their expiration date.

It seems sturdy enough to hold me, however, so I perch on top and take in the view. We're in the foothills, overlooking a small meadow, and you can see mountains off in the distance. It's pretty. Peaceful. A different kind of peace than I find watching the ocean near Sandalford. That's more about embracing the chaotic churn of the waves meeting the shore—rhythmic, but never quite predictable. Here, it's the sameness that's relaxing. Nothing but the faint sough of the wind and the monotonous buzz of insects in the field.

That should probably make me sleepy, but it has a bracing effect. Maybe it's the cool air on my skin, but I feel more awake now than I have since we arrived a little after four o'clock this morning.

I hear a door close and look over at the cabin. A small porch shadows the doorway, and all I can tell is that it's a tall guy in jeans, standing next to the stack of firewood. Ordinary denim, not black or purple or whatever, which rules out Deo. So, one of the Brothers Quinn. He watches me for a moment, hands in his front pockets, then finally decides to step off the porch.

Daniel. He crosses the lawn slowly, not exactly limping, but definitely favoring his right leg. When he gets closer, he looks down at my coffee. "You going for the Guinness Record?"

"It's only my second cup."

I'm not actually lying, if I count cups since sunrise. If, however, I count from the last time I woke up, then gallons would be the correct unit of measurement, and I'm probably on my third or fourth.

"I meant consecutive hours awake, not caffeine consumption. Did you even try to sleep last night?"

"No. I'm doing okay, though."

He doesn't argue the point, just sits at the other end of the table cradling his mug of tea. We're silent for several minutes. It's a comfortable silence at first, but as it stretches out, it becomes awkward.

I finally break the ice. "Do you want to talk about it?"

"Maybe. That's what I'm trying to decide. How about you go first? Tell me what's been happening since I checked out of the Hotel Anna."

"You probably know as much as I do. Apparently, you knew Graham Cregg was in here long before I did."

"I didn't know for certain. That whole scene, from the confrontation at the airport until we were back in my hospital room, is kind of a blur to me. I was in and out of consciousness on the drive to the airport. It barely registered when Jaden left. He said good-bye and I wanted to say something. To thank him for . . . I guess mostly for being a buffer between me and you, and for teaching me how to mellow out a bit."

"I miss him. Hope he found what he was looking for on the other side."

"Me, too. I wonder how much having those visions shaped his personality? It might be easier to go with the flow if you know you can't change anything."

"Maybe," I say. "Jaden wasn't a fatalist, though. It's not like he sat back and let the world roll past. He had a strong sense of right and wrong, and he acted on that. But once he saw something he knew he couldn't change, he tried to make the best of it."

"Like those *grant me serenity* posters."

"Not exactly. Jaden's world view was more like if the *grant me serenity* poster and the *when life gives you lemons, make lemonade* poster had a baby."

"That works. Anyway, I sensed he was leaving, but I couldn't . . . I don't know. Form a good-bye thought, I guess? And then the next thing I remember, everything went crazy. It was like a dark curtain—although that's not quite the right word—just enveloped the inside of your head.

I don't blame Hunter for bailing. I might have done the same thing if I'd had the opportunity."

A wave of cold washes over me. I hadn't even thought about the possibility that Hunter Bieler simply left, the same way that Will and the Furies did. That would explain why there's no file cabinet in my head marked *Hunter*. But it would also mean that there's a small, very lonely ghost in an airplane hangar in Upstate New York. I think a strong argument can be made that he's much better off there than in my head with a murderous spider-rat, but it makes me sad.

That could be why Kelsey kept changing the subject when I mentioned Hunter. Maybe she didn't think I was ready to deal with the fact that I abandoned him. Because, even though I didn't do it on purpose, and even if he chose it, she would know it still *feels* like I abandoned him.

"But even if the invitation had included me," Daniel said, "I wasn't in any shape to make that journey twice. Being stuck inside *your* head was challenging enough. I can't even imagine sharing consciousness with a little kid."

"What?"

"Bree Bieler? His sister? That's where Hunter went, right?"

I stare at him, dumbfounded. "I don't know. Maybe. At first I thought he moved on, but . . . it wasn't like the other departures. No dreams, no memories. I can't short out electrical equipment anymore. I tried, just out of curiosity, but the lamp kept right on glowing. Is Bree a . . ." I hesitate, not wanting to use the Creggs' word, but not sure what else to call my ability. Medium? Host? Ghost whisperer? "Is Bree a vessel?"

"No clue," Daniel says. "Hunter said she had a couple of talents, and they had that twin connection. She wouldn't be the only adept with more than one ability. Maria is both a Peeper and a Sender. Some of the Movers are also Zippos. And I don't even know for certain that's what happened. I'm just basing this on what I sensed from Hunter as he was leaving. For the first time since you picked him up, he was genuinely happy."

"Maybe because he was able to let go and move on? All of the hitchers feel happy when they go."

"Well, except Myron."

Yes, it's what I was thinking. I just chose not to say it.

And I guess Daniel can tell that his decision to fill in the blank annoys me, because he doesn't press. He just says, "That would have been astonishingly quick closure for Hunter, don't you think? Everyone he loved was still alive. Unlike Jaden, he didn't have anyone waiting in the Great Beyond."

I can hear Daniel's ironic caps on the phrase and smile at his skepticism. I'm not sure *what* waits on the other side of death either, but I have to believe that something does. Otherwise, all of my hitchers simply walked into nothingness on the strength of a delusion. They existed, here in my head, after death. It doesn't seem unreasonable to me that they still exist, somewhere beyond.

Daniel is right, though. Hunter was nowhere near the point of moving on. And Bree Bieler avoids me whenever possible. I'd thought it was because she was still angry about Hunter's death, somehow blamed me for it. But I didn't think much about it. After all, it's not too surprising for a seven-year-old girl to have a bit of irrational anger, especially when she's recently lost the person she loves most in all the world.

But it would make a lot more sense if she's worried that I know what really happened. If she's scared someone will try to take Hunter away from her again.

"Just a theory," Daniel says.

"A damn good one. I'll talk to Kelsey."

"Maybe you should sleep first? You're swaying back and forth like you're drunk."

"If I sleep, there's a very real risk that Cregg will be in control when I wake up. My walls—"

"Your walls remain up to some extent when you're asleep. We could see them. They're not exactly solid, but I wouldn't have wanted to cross that border."

"You never planned to steal my body." I tell him about the collection of documents that I found at Cregg's townhouse. "There were also bank accounts that Alexandra—" I stop, suddenly remembering. "Did you guys call someone? We can't just leave her there."

"Porter's taking care of it. He left a message at the local Sanctuary for Psychics office, and also with one of the Cregg campaign offices. She won't starve to death in that place, if that's what you're worried about. But . . . back to the issue. It's not humanly possible for you to stay awake indefinitely."

"I know that. I'm just trying to give the second injection a bit more time to kick in. And . . . it's getting better. He's weaker. I actually looked in the mirror when I brushed my teeth this morning and didn't see him."

Daniel looks like he wants to argue some more, but he doesn't. "You know, even without the medicine, I believe you're stronger than Graham Cregg. And I know that all of us together are stronger."

I give him a half-hearted smile. As much as I hope he's right, there's a considerable part of me that's terrified he isn't. Cregg has managed to shut me out whenever he wanted for the past month or so. He used me to set up a murder attempt on my own father. And he fooled the others on more than one occasion. Okay, maybe not Taylor, but then she shares Daniel's skeptic gene. And she's Taylor.

"I'll sleep. Just not yet."

"Okay. The reason I came out here in the first place was to ask you to hold off on mentioning Sariah to the others. Just to give me time to . . . wrap my head around it. I hate asking you to keep secrets again, but . . . none of them even know about her. I'd have to tell it all, from the beginning. I'm not ready for that yet."

"I won't say anything. But just so you're aware, Taylor was wondering what you and Sophie were talking about when we were at the Waffle House. And we both know how she feels about keeping secrets."

"You mean how Taylor feels about *other people* keeping secrets. She's perfectly happy to keep her own. But yeah . . . if Taylor gives you any crap, send her to me." He takes a sip from his mug. "And to be clear, I'm not planning on keeping them in the dark forever. I'm done with that kind of secrecy. I'm . . . I'm even going to tell Mom about my ability. She might be better off not knowing, but it isn't fair to keep her oblivious when everyone else knows. I'll tell her about Sariah and Caleb at the same time."

I'm surprised to hear him mention Caleb, let alone use his name. In the past, whenever Daniel thought about him, it was as *the kid* or *the boy*. There was a dark tinge to those thoughts, not directed at Caleb but surrounding him. Feelings of anger and of guilt. Of responsibility and of denial.

"Is Caleb . . . yours?" That question has been bugging me since I first picked up his thoughts about Sariah and her son, and it tumbles out, even as I'm thinking I shouldn't ask.

Daniel swirls the tea around in his mug for a long time before answering. "He could be. Sariah said no, but . . . she may have been lying. She did that sometimes." He laughs softly. "It's one of the things we had in common."

"How—" I stop, annoyed at myself. "I'm sorry. You say you're not ready to talk about it, and I start peppering you with questions."

"No. I said I wanted to wait to tell the others. I hadn't decided yet whether I wanted to talk to *you* about Sariah. But I answered your question about Caleb, so . . . I guess that was me deciding. You're wondering how she died?"

I nod.

His jaw tightens, and for a moment, I think he's changed his mind about answering. When he finally responds, his voice is harsh. "She trusted the wrong person."

"Senator Cregg?"

"Among others. Sariah was Delphi, too. She was first generation, though. We met when I was in the military. I joined to find out everything I could about the Delphi program. Dad was suspicious that Cregg was starting the research up again. Beth—the woman who owns this cabin? After the Delphi Project was officially shut down, she continued working with Decathlon Services Group. Beth worked with them in Afghanistan for a couple of years—nothing connected to Delphi, just general contract-management stuff. Then in early 2014, she returns stateside and finds out Graham Cregg has requested for her to be transferred to his subunit."

"That's Python, right?"

"Yeah. Only Beth didn't want the transfer. Told Cregg her current position was less stressful. That's saying something when she'd just been in Afghanistan, but I'm guessing the fatality rate was higher at Delphi."

Daniel's biological father was one of those fatalities. More than a dozen of the original subjects committed suicide during the five years after the program shifted from military to CIA funding. Even more of them suffered bouts of aggressive behavior. This included dozens of military personnel at Fort Bragg who took part in the test phases of the Delphi serum. Many second-generation adepts currently at Sandalford have a parent who died or went missing. Still others grew up in homes where abuse was common or only narrowly avoided, due at least in part to the PTSD-like symptoms the first-generation Delphi subjects experienced.

Cole Quinn, Aaron and Taylor's dad and Daniel's stepfather, was another supposed suicide. His death was much later, though, after he began poking around in Graham Cregg's efforts to relaunch Delphi. Cole struggled for more than a decade with bouts of anger and aggression. Aaron once said there were punching bags throughout the house where they grew up, so Cole would have a way to vent. It must have worked. Aaron said his dad could be irritable, but he never hit them. Never hit their mom. And it says a lot that I've never once heard Daniel refer to the man as his stepfather, or even think of him that way. He was his dad, end of story.

"But, next thing Beth knows, there's a reorg and her position is eliminated. She was pretty sure Cregg was behind it. That's when she contacted Dad, and after some soul-searching, she decided to take the job in order to pass along information to him so that he'd be in a better position to blow the whistle."

"So . . . you knew a lot more than you let on to Aaron and the rest of the family."

Daniel sighs. "You could say that. Mom and Dad kept stonewalling me anytime I asked questions. And finally I had enough of it. Dad suddenly found himself telling me absolutely everything without really understanding why. Or even remembering that he'd done it."

"You *nudged* him."

"I did. Kind of wished I hadn't afterward, since I was constantly on edge just like Mom was, worrying about what he was doing. Worrying that if he drew attention to us, Cregg would realize Taylor and Aaron were adepts. And frustrated that I couldn't do anything to help. Neither of them was happy when I joined the Army. After my brief stint at Fort Bragg, I wound up overseas, working with human trafficking—combating it, that is. Do you believe in fate?"

The question is a major non sequitur, and it catches me off guard.

"I don't know. Maybe."

"Well, I don't. I wound up stationed at a base in Italy, maybe twenty miles from the Decathlon European headquarters. And I suspect my supervisor made sure of that after I started asking around, trying to find out details on the early Delphi experiments that happened at Bragg."

I'm not following his logic. "As . . . punishment?"

"What? No, no. Because he wanted me to uncover stuff that he couldn't tell me directly. Colonel Smith is still with the unit. I gave Magda his contact info back before I wound up in the coma, although I told her it might be best to keep my name out of it. I'm pretty sure he's the reason the kids from the Fort Bragg school ended up at Sandalford when their funding got cut."

Daniel spends the next few minutes describing his assignment and how he stumbled upon a connection between the Python subgroup and a jobs program that he suspected was a cover for sex trafficking. And right in the middle of all this, he learns that the candidates—mostly girls, mostly young and pretty—were being given some unusual psychological tests.

As interesting as all of this is, I'm starting to wonder if Sariah comes into the story at some point, or if he's just spilling everything else in his head so that he doesn't have to talk about her.

"I'm getting to the part about Sariah," he says, sensing my question. It's the second time that's happened, and while it doesn't exactly surprise me, I do find it a little disconcerting. Hang out in someone's head for a few months and you get to know them pretty well, I guess.

"Sariah worked for a large international nonprofit. Her focus was the same as mine, ending human trafficking. Our paths kept crossing, although I'll admit that wasn't entirely accidental on my part. She was a few years older than me. Smart, pretty, passionate about her work. And she was seriously anti-military—not uncommon in her field, given that the military provides a huge market for sex trafficking. Sariah believed that programs like the one I was assigned to were nothing more than a microscopic Band-Aid the Army was trying to slap over a gaping wound, more to cover their ass than solve the problem."

"Was she right?"

A ghost of a smile. "Sariah was almost always right. But I wouldn't admit it. Where's the fun in that? We ran into each other in a bar one night and spent three or four hours arguing. And . . . then we wound up back at her place. When we woke up the next morning, both of us were like, major mistake. This is never happening again. But it did, two days later. And pretty much every day after that. We'd argue and then . . ."

He laughs, but it's a little tremulous, like he's close to tears. "That pretty much sums up our relationship. We'd argue, and then . . ."

I don't say anything, but I am totally and completely unsurprised to learn that Daniel finds arguing sexy. Like I told Aaron, Daniel and I would *not* make a good couple.

"Eventually Sariah and I both reached the point where we had to admit that we didn't want to stop. She had a boyfriend, a guy with her company she'd been dating on and off for a couple of years. He'd just left on a three-month field assignment—Kazakhstan, I think. She said she'd been trying to get up the nerve to end it. That she thought he was doing the same."

He clears his throat. "Anyway, long story short, Sariah had been hearing rumors since she'd arrived in Vicenza that one of the programs run by Decathlon was actually a cover for a trafficking ring. And then she's talking to her mother on the phone and discovers that one of her cousins in Bulgaria—that's where her mom was from originally—had applied for an au pair position advertised on fliers in the town square."

The cousin said the company put her through a strange battery of tests and wanted to hook her up to an EEG. Wanted to give her a series of vaccinations, even before she agreed to the job and even though she showed them proof that she was fully immunized. The girl got cold feet after the second interview, something that didn't really surprise anyone in Sariah's family. Most of the Tsvetkova women were very intuitive. Some even claimed they possessed second sight.

The local police weren't interested in investigating. Neither was the military. There was no way a big multinational with that many government contracts was involved in something as sordid as sex trafficking. And so Sariah decided to take matters into her own hands. She spoke fluent Bulgarian, along with several other languages, and even though she was twenty-three—a few years beyond the age they were seeking—she could easily pass for late teens.

Daniel didn't particularly care for the plan. It wasn't sanctioned by Sariah's employer, either. But he said they both felt they'd run into a brick wall. So the next time the employment service, which went by the name Pair Au Pair, posted one of their fliers, Sariah took a few days off and traveled to Bulgaria to visit her extended family. Daniel couldn't get clearance for travel, so he had to wait in Italy.

"She wore a wire as a precaution," he says, "and three of her male relatives—one of them local law enforcement—sat in a car a few blocks away, ready to storm the place on her signal. Nothing happened that first day, but she was convinced that it was indeed a human-trafficking setup. Told me on the phone they seemed much more interested in her appearance than in her education, even though she was told she would be tutoring kids if she was accepted. A big red flag was that they showed her a picture of the same family they'd showed her cousin, the Zimmerman family of Plano, Texas. Of course, it had only been two months. Maybe the Zimmermans were still in need of a nanny. But it seemed odd.

"Then she got a call to come back for a second set of interviews. A new battery of tests. They give her the same spiel about immunizations that they gave her cousin. She says no. They insist. And I guess they were more impressed with Sariah's test results than they were with her cousin's because they didn't take no for an answer. She gives the signal and her relatives kicked the door in. The lead tester for Pair Au Pair pulls out a fat wallet and starts handing out Euro notes. Sariah leaves with her recording, and her family is a few hundred Euros richer. Would have been a major win if not for the fact that she got a dose of mystery serum. And about three weeks later, we find out she's pregnant."

I look toward the house when I hear the screen door close again. It's Aaron. I'm a little worried that seeing me here talking to Daniel is going to trigger his jealousy, and I half expect him to turn back around. But he just watches me for a moment, hands in the front pockets of his jeans, the same way Daniel did before deciding to walk over. The Quinn brothers don't look much alike, but I'm struck by how similar their mannerisms can be sometimes.

Aaron starts across the lawn toward us.

"We'll have to finish this some other time," Daniel says. There's a faint note of relief in his voice.

"Sure," I say softly, "but can I just tell you I'm really, really sorry? I should have opened with that, but . . . it's hard to find the right words."

"There *are* no right words. But it's okay. I saw it in your eyes."

"Good morning!" Aaron gives me a smile and then looks at Daniel. "Were you guys talking about what we discussed last night?"

"Oh, no," Daniel says. "I'll let you field that one. I think she'll give you a lot more latitude on that issue than she will me."

"*She* is sitting right here," I say with a touch of annoyance.

"I know," Aaron says. "And I promise I'll fill you in, but it needs to wait. Taylor unlocked the iPad. More importantly, however, Pfeifer is awake. And he's asking to speak to his daughter."

My stomach drops. I should have been expecting this. Preparing myself for it. But I really hadn't. I stood there watching him sleep, not exactly hoping he wouldn't wake up, but completely avoiding the thought of an awake, coherent Scott Pfeifer.

"So . . . he knows who I am." It doesn't surprise me that he pieced it together. The look in his eyes yesterday—dear God, was that really only *yesterday?*—wasn't quite recognition, but it was definitely something beyond the stare you give a stranger. It held the seed of recognition, waiting to grow.

"Yeah," Aaron says. "I told him you're sleeping."

"He's got maybe a dozen hitchers in his head right now," Daniel says, "each with some sort of psychic ability. I'm guessing at least one of them picked up on the fact that you were lying."

"With Sophie blocking," Aaron says, "they may not have been able to read me. But yes. They probably also picked up on the fact that I'm worried about Anna being in the same room as him. Maybe even in the same house."

"I can't avoid him forever." I don't add that part of me would like to do precisely that.

Daniel and Aaron exchange a look, then Aaron says, "Every single one of those hitchers has a reason to hate Graham Cregg. We already know Sophie can't control him completely. If they find out killing *you* would kill *him* . . . do you think Sophie can stop them?"

I stare into my empty cup, feeling more than a little stupid. Am I the only one here who didn't even think about how my father's hitchers might react to *my* hitcher? No wonder Sam looked so alarmed when he saw me standing in the doorway, watching Pfeifer sleep.

"Do we have more of the antipsychotic?" I ask.

"We do," Aaron says. "Two more syringes and maybe a dozen pills. We weren't sure how long we'd be gone, and you'll need a shot every two weeks. Deo just grabbed what Kelsey had in stock. Which means she'll definitely know they were taken if she does any sort of regular inventory. We dissolved two of the pills in the yogurt Pfeifer is eating now. The injection would be better than constantly crushing pills, but can you imagine him—or them, to be more precise—willingly submitting to a needle?"

Daniel agrees. "I don't even think we should attempt it after what happened to Whistler and Davis last night. Plus . . . Anna was under Kelsey's care when she was started on the medication. Sam was really hesitant about us even giving him the pills, and he's got a point. What if Pfeifer has a bad reaction? Although I guess odds are he'll do okay with it since Anna did."

I start to ask why that makes a difference and then realize the answer is obvious. We share a nose. We undoubtedly share many other attributes as well. It just didn't occur to me, because having family—having anyone who is a blood relative—is an entirely foreign concept to me.

Plus, I need sleep. My mental processor seems to be snagging on obvious connections.

If the two of them weren't standing here, I'd probably give myself a good slap in order to wake up. Instead, I put my mug down and sink my face into my hands, rubbing vigorously.

"You said Taylor figured out the password? What was it?"

"2BR02B."

For the first time in several hours, I sense movement from Cregg. A long scratching sound, faint, like the screech of chalk against a blackboard in a distant room.

"Which seems pretty random," Aaron continues, "unless you think of the *zero* in the British sense as . . ."

"Naught. To be or *naught* to be. Of course it's another bloody Shakespeare reference." I pull the fake ID out of my pocket again. "You haven't seen this yet, have you? Not just one but two Shakespearean names."

"The photo looks . . . different," Aaron says. "Not just the hair, but . . ."

"Yeah. He already had a plastic surgeon picked out." I feel the tears forming, but I blink them back. There's no way I'll be able to stay awake afterward if I indulge in the nice, long, tension-releasing cry that my body really seems to want right now.

Aaron wraps his arms around me.

"I'm just . . . um . . ." Daniel clears his throat. "I'll see you guys inside, okay?"

Once Daniel is gone, Aaron steps back and tips my chin up to look at him. He doesn't say anything at first, just holds my gaze with his own. "I told you yesterday that Cregg is not going to win, Anna. I know he's not, and here's why. I've spent so much of these past few months looking into these eyes searching for you. And even when I found you, it was never *completely* you, if that makes sense? Most of the time, I'd still get this faint vibe, this faint echo of violent thought. Nothing fully formed, but . . . there. For the longest time, I didn't want to accept that it was Cregg. I tried to explain it away as the concussion, but it kept getting worse. And anytime we confronted you . . ." He squeezes his eyes tight for a moment. "My point is, I think you've got this now. How much is you finally being aware so that you can fight him and how much is the medicine, I have no idea. But when I look into your eyes right now, all I see is Anna."

He silences my protest with a gentle finger to my lips. "I *know* he's still in there. I know. But he's not hovering. I can't see him. I can't *sense* him."

"I see him as a spider, Aaron. No, not just a spider, but some sort of freaky spider-rat. It has human hands on the ends of its legs, instead of claws." The words tumble out, a torrent that I can't even begin to hold back. "And when I saw my reflection, it was my face, except with a spider's eyes, and—"

"But not now, right?"

"No. I can still feel him back there, behind the wall. Still tell when something makes him angry. So, he's . . . listening. But it's like he's drunk almost. Or drugged, I guess."

"See?" He smiles, the big smile I haven't seen much lately. The one that reaches all the way up to his hazel eyes. "Like I said, you've got this."

The tears do come then, and he wipes them away. "Here's the deal. I had Taylor run a hot bath up in Beth and Virgie's room. You're going to have a nice long soak and a nice long cry, too, if that's what you need. And when you're done, you're going to *sleep*."

"Maybe . . . maybe you could restrain me, like Pfeifer, and then if you sense—"

"I'm not going to restrain you. Unless holding you while you sleep counts. I'm perfectly willing to do that. And . . . I have a backup plan. Will you just trust me?"

I'm about to ask him what exactly this backup plan entails, but my question dissolves into a yawn. It doesn't really matter at this point. Aaron's right. I can't put this off forever.

I follow him into the house. Deo looks up from whatever he's reading and mouths "Good night." Aaron leads me upstairs and into the master bath, where one of those large claw-foot tubs is filled nearly to the brim, then tugs my shirt over my head. He undresses me quickly, in a brisk, businesslike manner. When he's done, he scoops me up like a child and carries me to the tub.

My arms slide around his neck, and I whisper, "You could join me. Pretty sure this thing is big enough for two."

He pulls in a deep, shuddering breath, and I lean forward, pressing my lips to his before he can exhale. I cling to him, needing him more than sleep, and slide one hand down to unbutton his shirt.

"No," he says, breaking the kiss and lowering me into the water, soaking the bottom half of his sleeves in the process. "And don't give me that pout. We've waited this long, we can wait a little longer until your eyes aren't drooping shut."

"You don't think you can keep me awake?" I say teasingly. "Anyway, your shirt is all wet. You might as well . . . get in." A giant yawn splits the last sentence, and he laughs. "Okay, okay. You win."

I sink down into the scented water and float weightlessly for a moment. The cabin is pretty basic, but this tub is divine. I don't even remember the last time I was in a tub, and I've never been in one like this. I can almost stretch out completely.

Aaron brings back a couple of towels and a clean pair of sweats from my overnight bag.

I float back to the surface and say, "My nightshirt is in there. Just dig around. It's probably near the bottom."

"Um . . . these are probably a better idea," he says, coloring slightly as he heads toward the bedroom.

What's up with that? Maybe the process of getting me into the bath has him more worked up than I thought and he doesn't want to test his resolve.

As wonderful as the bath is, it was probably a waste. It's hard to keep my eyes open. I only last about ten minutes before I climb out, wrap my hair in one of the towels, and pull on the clothes. My feet feel like lead as I plod into the adjoining bedroom, where Aaron is on the bed, his iPad in one hand.

And Daniel is sitting in the chair next to the window. That explains why Aaron didn't grab the nightshirt that barely covers my bottom. I rub my hair with the towel and toss it over the bedpost, then crawl under the covers next to Aaron.

"You're the backup plan?"

"Yep," Daniel says. "I don't know for certain if it will work, but if Aaron senses that Cregg is moving to the front as you wake up—something neither of us believe is going to happen, by the way—then I will tell him to get back in his corner."

"Or better yet," Aaron says, "to get the hell out of her head."

Daniel nods. "Very good idea."

"No," I say. "A very bad idea. I'm not the only vessel in this house. And I'm having some degree of success controlling Cregg, probably due to several weeks of antipsychotic meds in my bloodstream."

Judging from their expressions, this didn't occur to either of them. I feel a little better now about not considering the negative reaction that my father's hitchers might have if they discovered Graham Cregg hiding out in my head. That's something that we're going to need to reveal slowly, if at all.

"Both of you said earlier that you were confident that I've got this. So if Cregg is at the front when I wake up, please tell him to get back in his frickin' cage."

"Done," Daniel says.

I say good night and pull my pillow onto Aaron's shoulder.

The very last thing I remember before sleep is a sign flashing in my head.

THEY ALREADY KNOW.

News Item from the *Kansas City Star*

April 24, 2020

The terrorist organization known as WOCAN has claimed responsibility for yesterday's shooting at Fort Leavenworth, which killed three and wounded seven others. The incident began around 4:15 p.m. Authorities apprehended the suspected shooter on a bench outside the Frontier Army Museum.

In the statement released to the media, WOCAN said the shooter, identified as Army Lt. Col. Paul Kerry, was controlled by one of their psychics when he walked into the museum and opened fire. Col. Melanie Proust, a spokesperson for the Combined Arms Center at Fort Leavenworth, said the WOCAN claim is sheer propaganda, noting that Kerry has been under considerable stress due to the recent death of his wife.

This marks the second event for which WOCAN has taken credit in the past two days. The first was a boiler explosion at an oil refinery in Ponca City, Oklahoma, where six people were killed and over thirty hospitalized.

CHAPTER SIXTEEN

Mathias, West Virginia
April 25, 2020, 8:13 p.m.

I wake with a start, surprised to find the room dark, except for the dim glow of a lamp. Daniel's feet are propped up on the bed. He seems to be sleeping. A paperback is draped over one leg, and several discarded cups and plates lie on the floor next to his chair.

"They already know."

Aaron's arms tighten around me. "Whoa. Easy."

"God, Aaron. You sound like you're talking to a horse." Daniel leans forward and turns the lamp to a brighter setting. "Who knows what, Anna?"

"The hitchers in my father's head already know about Cregg. Will sent me another message, just before I fell asleep. He said they already know."

"Any chance that was a dream?" Daniel suggests.

I consider the possibility. "Maybe."

"You fell asleep really fast," Aaron says. "A minute later, you were snoring away."

"I don't snore. Deo would have told me."

Daniel gives me a look of fake sympathy. "Deo's probably trying to protect your feelings. Seriously, I thought someone was using a chain saw outside, but, nope, just you."

Aaron laughs and pulls me closer. "It's nothing to be—"

THEY KNOW.

The words fade, and then:

KEEP YOUR SPIDER IN ITS CAGE.

WE DON'T WANT HIM IN HERE.

"Anna?" Aaron says.

"Not a dream. The group consensus inside my father seems to be better me than them. They don't want Cregg joining their band of travelers, so I don't think we have to worry about them killing me."

"Or maybe they're just saying that so we'll let our guard down." Aaron's nose twitches on the last word. "Do you smell—"

Daniel jumps up, and the paperback that was in his lap falls to the floor and the cover begins to curl and blacken. Several of the pages have now caught fire. Daniel snatches the towel from the bedpost and drops it over the smoking book, smothering the fire, then opens the window to let the smoke out.

THEY COULD KILL ALL OF YOU RIGHT NOW IF THEY WANTED.

LIKE LUCAS. OR WHISTLER AND THE OTHER FUDD LAST NIGHT.

"Okay, okay," I say out loud. "We get it."

Opening the window apparently wasn't enough to clear the smoke. The alarm in the hallway begins beeping, but it stops suddenly a few seconds after Daniel opens the door.

"Great," Aaron says. "I'll bet they shorted the damn thing out."

Feet pound up the stairs, and Taylor and Deo appear.

"What were you guys smoking in there?" Taylor asks, wrinkling her nose.

"A book," Daniel says. "It was a good book, too. And I hadn't fin . . . ished it."

He stops, simply staring at the wall for a moment. Then he goes back into the bedroom and scoops up the charred remains of the paperback with the towel.

"Incoming transmission?" I ask.

"Yeah," he says, shooting me an odd look before handing the scorched book to Taylor. "Can you take this out to the porch? We'll be down in a minute."

Taylor narrows her eyes at him.

"I'll fill you in when I get downstairs," he says. "Just go."

Once she and Deo are out of earshot, I ask, "What was the message?"

"Be glad we didn't burn you, Fudd."

Aaron grimaces. "Maybe you shouldn't be here. These hitchers seem to have some issues with authority."

"In the case of the guards at The Warren in general," Daniel says, "it's with good reason. They have every right to be vengeful. I'd lay damned good odds that most of them were shot by someone wearing a guard uniform. But I did my best to avoid hurting anyone, and if they're peeking around in my head, they know that my goal was to get them all out of there. I only tased someone twice. One time it was the only way to keep my cover, and the other time, I was protecting two of our fellow wabbits. I don't have anything to hide from them."

He uses the nickname that The Warren adepts adopted for themselves. I suspect it's on purpose, pointing out that he's an adept, a wabbit, who was simply posing as a Fudd. And if they're plucking these thoughts from our heads—and I'm guessing Will is the one doing that—then it will be next to impossible to hide anything from them.

Daniel gets a slightly vacant look in his eyes again. "Just poking a little fun." When I raise an eyebrow, he adds, "They said they're just poking at me. That if they'd really wanted to hurt me, I'd know it. Just a friendly game of Singe the Fudd. So I guess that means they're okay with me. More or less."

We join the others downstairs, and while Aaron explains what happened with the book, I open the fridge and pull out a container of leftover mac and cheese. It's the bright-orange variety, and kind of disgusting. But I'm hungry, so I find a fork and then join the others in the living room.

"You want to heat that up?" Deo asks.

"No," I say between bites. "It actually tastes better cold. Where's Sam?"

"He went back to Maryland to pick up the RV," Aaron says. "He's going to check on Mom and be back late tonight."

"He'd better be," Deo mutters.

Taylor looks up from her iPad—although on closer inspection, it's Cregg's iPad. "He'll be back. If he's delayed for some reason, I'll drive you to Sandalford. And not just because Maria is freaking out. Magda is going to be livid that the two of you tagged along with me and Aaron without her official sanction."

No one responds. We all know she's right, but I don't really see any way around it, and I doubt the others do, either. Magda's often livid, and we're often the reason, so it's not like it's uncharted territory.

Taylor goes back to what she was doing, jotting something down in her spiral notebook.

"Have you learned anything from that?" I ask, nodding toward the iPad in her lap.

"Lots," she says vaguely. "You can see when I'm finished. Or read my notes. Your choice."

There's a faintly uncomfortable sensation at the back of my head when I look at Taylor holding the tablet. I don't exactly *feel* the urge to snatch it out of her hand. It's more indirect than that, almost like I'm watching a movie or reading a book and that's the motivation of the protagonist. Or, in this case, probably the *antagonist*.

Nonetheless, the sensation is strong enough that I look away from Taylor and shift the topic. "Have any of you talked to my father yet?"

"Not directly," Deo says. "We took some food to him and Sophie. The house didn't explode the few times she stepped out of the room, so maybe he's figuring out how to control the hitchers?"

I shrug. "Maybe. He's had this ability since before I was born, and he's been in a psychiatric hospital for years. It's possible someone taught him a few coping techniques. Was Sophie outside of the room just now when they torched Daniel's book?"

"No," Taylor says. "She was definitely in there. I don't know if she was actually touching him, though. She's been out a few times. I kept an eye on him for a couple of minutes earlier so she could grab a shower and then I stayed back to keep her company for a while. Asked her some questions about her time with the other group. I think she's had a rough couple of months. Constantly being on alert is wearing her out."

I drop the plastic container into the sink, then take a few steps down the hallway leading to the bedroom where Pfeifer is. The door is partially open, and I hear a faint burst of canned laughter. Sophie must be watching a sitcom.

It feels like the walls in the narrow hall are constricting, closing in on me.

I'm not ready to do this yet.

I say it out loud. "I'm not ready."

And then I see another sign:

HEARD YOU THE FIRST TIME.

That's creepy. Stop reading my thoughts.

SORRY. CAN'T. BUT NO ONE IN HERE WANTS TO HURT YOU.

AND EVEN IF THEY DID, I DON'T THINK SHE'D LET THEM.

Sophie?

WHO? NO. NOT SOPHIE. YOUR MOTHER.

What?

I stumble backward into the living room, bumping into Aaron.

"Anna? What's wrong?" He reaches out to steady me, but I dodge him and bolt for the door.

I need fresh air. And I need a few minutes alone before I can trust myself to speak.

Halfway across the clearing, it occurs to me that it would have been smart to put on shoes. An April evening isn't prime barefoot weather at this altitude. When I reach the picnic table, I climb on top and curl my damp, chilly toes beneath me for warmth as I try to get my head in order.

My mother? Seriously?

Will and the other hitchers don't respond. Am I outside the range where they can pick up my thoughts? Or maybe they can tell my brain is on the verge of exploding and have decided to cut me some slack.

Aaron stands just inside the open cabin door for a moment, watching me. But it's Deo who eventually crosses the lawn. In shoes, because he's not an idiot.

"What happened?" he asks, sitting on the bench below me. "Did they threaten you? Aaron said he didn't sense violent emotions, but he stayed back to make sure."

I suspect that Aaron also realized I needed some space. Deo's less savvy in that regard, but then we're not used to demanding privacy from each other. We were lucky enough if we got privacy from the rest of the kids at Bart House.

And I'm glad he's here. Aaron's life has had its share of tragedy, but he was raised in a reasonably stable home with two parents who loved him. He might understand how I'm feeling right now, but not at the same gut level that Deo will.

"There wasn't a threat." I rub my temples. "Do you have your phone on you?"

"Um. Yeah."

I go to the *Washington Post* website and search for the article about my mother's shooting. It takes a moment, but I locate it.

I'm not sure why I need to see the picture again. It seared itself into my head the first time. The image is a grainy, blurred still from a low-quality security camera. It shows a man kneeling inside an office building. A gun lies on the floor next to him. He's holding a woman against his chest. Her body is limp, one arm dangling off to the side.

It's Pfeifer. And he's definitely touching her. I knew that, but some part of me needed to see it for confirmation.

Daniel took up residence in my head because I touched his hand when he was—briefly—dead. Jaden and Hunter came on board the same way, as did Will and the Furies. As did Graham Cregg.

I knew that my ability was inherited from Pfeifer. So why did it never occur to me that he might have picked up my mother's spirit?

To be fair, it's not something I spent a lot of time thinking about. I never expected to meet him, and even if I did, I wouldn't have imagined that her spirit would still be *here*. Leah Johnson Pfeifer died in 2004. She should have moved on ages ago.

The longest I ever carried a hitcher was two years. That was Emily MacAllister, age eighty-two when she died. Emily was sweet, but I think she may have been somewhere on the obsessive-compulsive spectrum, because she couldn't leave until we tracked down the specific crossword puzzle that she'd left unfinished when she died.

All my other hitchers departed within a year. Most of them left because I was able to help them achieve closure, but a few moved on without it. It was as though the tether holding them to this realm grew thinner and thinner until they simply drifted away, like a balloon in the wind.

Deo remains quiet, but I can tell he's waiting for an explanation. I hand the phone back and point to the picture. My father's arm, clutching my mother's body to his chest.

"He's touching her. Like I touched Daniel, and Jaden, and . . ."

His eyes widen. "Oh. Oh, wow. I never even . . ."

"Yeah. Me, neither."

"You ran out pretty fast," Deo says. "You don't want to talk to her?"

"No. I do. But . . . there were just so many emotions hitting me all at once. I never thought I'd speak to her. To either of them. I put a lid on all the questions I'd never get answers to long ago, and also on the . . ."

I don't finish the thought, but Deo knows. "The anger?"

"Yes. I mean, it's not her fault that he shot her, but . . . it doesn't seem like she left me in very good hands, you know?"

Is it unfair of me to be angry? I don't know. Whoever left me in that food court clearly thought I was possessed—and they were, technically speaking, correct. There were no signs of abuse or neglect, according to the police report. They just didn't know how to help me. Maybe they hoped someone else *would* know how.

"But it's not just anger, D. My mom has been dead for fifteen and a half years. After I heard what happened to her, I've gotten used to thinking of her as being on the other side. Heaven, or wherever my hitchers move on to. And now I find out she's been stuck here all along, inside the guy who shot her. That's sad and also creepy. He must be keeping her from moving on."

"Maybe." Deo doesn't sound convinced. "But Pfeifer's been locked in a mental hospital. Think how much effort you've put into helping your hitchers. You were grounded for a whole month at the Wheelwrights' house because you ran off trying to find out what happened to that guy Abner's dog. If you'd been locked up somewhere . . ." He shrugs.

I know Deo's right, but it still makes me sad—and yes, angry—that she's been caged up all this time. Not just locked inside Scott Pfeifer's mind but locked up inside a hospital for the criminally insane. I've spent time in mental hospitals. They suck. Fifteen years in one would have to change you. And I think that's what bothers me most. This version of Leah Johnson Pfeifer could be stark raving mad, but since I can't remember her, how do I know she wasn't crazy to begin with?

On the other hand, this is the only chance I'll ever have to talk to my mother. And it's a chance I never thought I'd get.

"Kelsey helped you locate people a few times, too," Deo continues. "And, um . . . speaking of Kelsey, she called while you were asleep."

"Did you tell her—"

"That she was wrong on the whole Myron thing? Yeah. She believed me, so I guess whatever Cregg did is wearing off. I didn't get into the part about Cregg influencing her, though. She's probably pieced it together on her own, and she was already mad about me raiding her drug cabinet."

I grimace. "So you told her."

"Yeah. I figured it was better to admit it before she found out."

"What did she say?"

"There was a really, really long silence, and then she said we'll discuss it when I return to Sandalford. And that I should get back there ASAP." He stares down at his hands. "She's right on that front. Maria and Stan are getting nervous. He says some of the paths show things starting at Sandalford in a matter of days. And he's pretty insistent that our chances suck royally if I'm not there as an amp. I've already had to delay training sessions with two of the adepts."

"Okay, help me out here. This whole training thing is one of my memory gaps. I had a sense there was *some* sort of training going on to get the adepts ready to defend Sandalford if necessary, but in that meeting with Maria it was like everyone had been carrying around a Dumbledore's Army coin except me."

"Yeah . . . um . . ." Deo winces slightly. "That was intentional, once we suspected you'd picked up Cregg. We didn't know if he was passing information along to the Senator."

"He wasn't. They were obviously allies at one point, but . . . something happened. I don't understand Cregg's motivations, but I'm certain he's not working with his father."

"Well, anyway, you kept asking about the training. Insisting that you wanted to watch. It was kind of creepy, so we started keeping things more . . . discreet. Not just from you, but also from Magda and the security team. And Kelsey, too, once we realized she'd been compromised."

"Well, hopefully Kelsey's head is clear enough that she'll believe me about Cregg influencing her. And I'll make it clear that you swiping the medicine is the only reason I'm *me* right now. Maybe she'll go easy on you if I plead your case when we get back."

As I say the word *we*, I realize not all of us will be returning to Sandalford anytime soon. We can't leave Sophie and my father here on their own, and Daniel's ability may be useful in controlling him. And based on the message Will just gave me, it's entirely possible that I'm needed here, too, since my mother is helping to rein in the teeming masses inside my father because she's worried they might hurt me.

Which brings me back around to the reality that sent me running out here like a scalded cat.

"You could be right about Pfeifer, I guess. He may not have intended to pick her up."

"Even if he did, is that so bad, Anna? Would you feel better if you knew she was still wandering around that building where she was killed?"

"No, but . . ." I want to argue that she'd have eventually left that building in search of her "last happy place," like most of my hitchers. Spirits seem to gravitate toward the place where they last felt safe and happy. Or at least that was my working theory prior to the past few months. Molly was the first of my hitchers who'd been murdered, and she made it back to the homeless shelter where she'd been staying with her mom shortly before they were both killed. I doubt most people thought of the shelter as a happy place, but Molly was happy to be with her mom, happy her mom wasn't doing drugs at the moment, and happy they were, at least for the time being, away from Lucas. And she was happy to be somewhere with a piano. All it took to pull her on board was me casually running my finger along the keys when I was there to see Deo, who'd just had a disastrous visit with his mother.

But maybe my working theory needs more work. Molly was exceptionally driven. She was determined to find her way back to her family, specifically to her grandfather, Porter, so that he could solve her murder and we could stop Graham Cregg and Lucas from killing again. Her quest wasn't so much for revenge as it was for protecting others.

The Furies and the other spirits who were stuck inside The Warren, however, seem pretty hell-bent on revenge. They never moved on to their "last happy place," and I have no way of knowing whether my mother would have either. Would she have found closure on her own or would she have been stuck there, nothing more than a cold spot a few perceptive individuals felt as they walked through the building on the way to the elevator?

"You're right," I say. "She's probably better off. I was just feeling uncertain enough about talking to Pfeifer . . . and now it's *both* of them and . . ."

Deo holds out his hand, palm extended, his brows lifted in an unspoken question. "Not sure it would help, but you said we needed to stop thinking of Jaden's visions as a curse. Maybe it will give you some insight? Same rules as before, though. You tell me what you see."

I consider it for a moment and then reach for his hand.

"First, get off the table so you don't fall."

Valid point. I sit on the bench across from Deo, taking his hand across the table, like we're about to arm wrestle. There's a much longer pause than usual, enough time to feel the warmth of his palm next to mine. Enough time to wonder whether it's going to work. Then that weird metallic hum kicks in.

nnnnNNNNN

I step out into the sunshine, almost painfully bright after the dark interior of the van. That's partly due to the sun's reflection on the water, and partly due to all of the white surrounding us . . . the concrete sidewalks and the pristine tarplike covering of the amphitheater.

A shimmering veil of shattered glass covers everything around the tower—the grass, the bushes, even the rocks surrounding the railroad track. Someone seems to have swept the sidewalks, but even there, you can see tiny gold specks like glitter. A bit like the gold flecks in Aaron's eyes.

No. No. I will not go there. Aaron and Taylor are fine. They have to be. Deo is fine. Kelsey is fine. They are all completely fine, and I'll see them soon.

My father bends down to place his hand inside the area cordoned off by the police tape. He seems almost oblivious to his surroundings, completely absorbed in his task. Is this how he looked when he stared into the microscope, working on various iterations of the Delphi serum?

That thought gives me a slight shiver, or maybe it's just the sense that we're exposed, standing out here, snooping around a police barricade. And the police aren't the only ones who might have the area under surveillance. The Senator's people could be watching, as well.

Sophie opens the back door of the navy-blue van and waves for us to hurry. There's a large Coldwell Banker *magnet on the door. I see Miller behind her. He's staring straight ahead, motionless.*

"We need to go, Dad."

He looks up at me, his expression startled, as though he'd forgotten I was there. The bruise just above his left eyebrow is a deep bluish purple now.

"Come on," I say. "We have—

NNNNNNnnnn

I keep my head down for a moment after the vision ends, trying to cement the specifics in my mind. Who else was there? Sophie, my father—and Miller? A van, but it wasn't a Vigilance van. My thoughts were so focused on the scene in front of us that I wasn't thinking about much else, except for that stray thought about everyone being okay.

"So . . . ?" Deo asks when I lift my head.

"I'm . . . not exactly sure. I do know I wasn't here. Let's go in, okay? I'm cold and they'll want to hear this, too. Plus, I should apologize for freaking out."

Deo gives me a teasing grin. "You can skip the apology. We've kind of gotten used to it."

"Fair enough. Anna freaked out. Must be Tuesday."

"Actually, I believe it's Saturday. And *yes,* I got it. Have I ever missed a *Buffy* reference?"

We open the door, and Taylor slides over to make room on the couch for Deo. I sit on the edge of Aaron's chair. He flinches when I wedge my feet between his leg and the cushion to warm them up.

"Jeez, they're like ice cubes."

"It's cold out there. Sorry about running off like that. I knew my father was in there, obviously. But I just learned he's been carrying my mother around in his head for the past fifteen years."

Aaron squeezes my ankle. "No wonder you freaked."

"I don't get it," Taylor says. "That's a good thing, right? You get to talk to both of your parents. But you don't look happy."

"I am. No, *really*," I insist, in response to Taylor's skeptical look. "I'm glad. It's just complicated. Maybe I'll feel less conflicted once I talk to them."

Daniel frowns. "You're not doing that tonight. They just tried to torch the place. We need to hold off until tomorrow at the very least."

"That's Anna's decision," Aaron says. "Like I told Deo, I didn't sense any violent thoughts, at least . . . not near the surface. It's more like what I'd sometimes feel when Daniel was your hitcher and he was angry about something. Like a kettle on low boil."

"I think that's a pretty fair assessment. The message I got from Will was that, even if they wanted to hurt me, my mother would hold them back."

"How?" Daniel asks.

"Mama-bear instinct," Taylor says. "Haven't you heard those stories of a panicked mother lifting a car off her kid?"

"I don't care how protective she is," Daniel says. "You guys saw what happened to Whistler and Davis last night."

"True," Aaron says. "But remember what I just told you about sensing something under the surface? We don't know how long she'll be able to hold them all back. Maybe sooner is better."

He could be right, but I think back to the vision. Scott Pfeifer walking outside, relatively calm and at ease, even though the surroundings were in chaos.

"Maybe. But . . . I think his chill is going to last for a bit longer." I tell them about the vision, filling in as many details as I can remember.

"You don't know where this was?" Aaron asks.

"No. Like I said, there was a tall object near us, because I could see this elongated shadow. A tower of some sort, near a theater. And there were tiny gold sparkles in the bushes outside the crime-scene tape. Irregularly shaped . . . glass, maybe? My father was crouched down near a bush. I think he was inspecting them. I was worried that someone would see us. The police, or maybe the Senator's people. And . . ." I hesitate, and then look at Aaron. "I was worried about you and Taylor. Also Deo and Kelsey, but it seemed separate. Telling myself that you were fine, but still worried. So I know you weren't there. I don't think Daniel was there, either."

"Why were you worried about us?" Taylor asks.

"No clue. It was only a stray thought. I didn't want to dwell on it. It was just me, Sophie, and my dad there. And . . . Miller, but something was wrong with him."

"Miller?" Daniel asks.

"The ass Magda hired as head of security," Taylor explains. "You were there with your father willingly?"

"I *think* so. Or at least, I don't remember feeling afraid. Just a little wary, nervous that we might be exposed. I would have been looking for escape routes if I didn't trust him."

Deo looks directly at me. "You trusted him. In the vision, you trusted him."

He sounds absolutely certain on this point. Much more certain than I am, and I'm the one who had the vision.

"How do you know?"

"Think back. What did you call him a moment ago?"

I give him a puzzled look, still not following.

"Anna. You said it was you, Sophie, and your dad. You called him *dad*."

He's right. I haven't once thought of Pfeifer that way, and my discovery about my mother hasn't exactly filled me with warm fuzzies where he's concerned. Something must change between now and whenever this vision happens. And there's unfortunately no way to *tell* when it happens. The shortest amount of time between the preview and the main event has been a few hours. The longest has been around six weeks.

The bedroom door opens, and Scott Pfeifer—or *Dad*, as I will apparently think of him in the (literally) foreseeable future—crosses the hallway to the bathroom on the other side. Sophie doesn't follow. In my ongoing mental prep for talking to Pfeifer, I'd envisioned him still strapped to the gurney, like he was this morning. But that was over twelve hours ago.

He doesn't look my way. That feels intentional, as though he's giving me space. Like I'm a frightened animal who might run if he makes the wrong move. Not an unreasonable comparison, given the way I bolted across the lawn a few minutes ago.

I glance down at the bulky sweats I'm wearing and then run a hand through my messy hair. My hair and teeth are both unbrushed.

"I need to run upstairs. But yes, Daniel. I *am* doing this tonight."

My bag is next to the bed. I pull on jeans and my last clean shirt. It's crumpled from being crammed in with everything else, but I smooth most of the wrinkles away. When I'm dressed, I risk a quick glance in the mirror. No spider-rat. Just me, with bed hair that's in dire need of a brush and another dose of midnight-blue dye.

I'm almost presentable when Aaron walks in and wraps his arms around me from behind. "You look beautiful. But I also thought you looked beautiful before, so . . ."

"Baggy sweats aren't the first impression I want to make on my parents. Although I guess it's not, strictly speaking, a *first* impression. For either of us, and . . . I'm babbling. Sorry. I'm nervous."

"Do you want me to come in with you? Or . . ." He stops, shaking his head. "I was going to say Deo could, but I don't think we need anyone with amp powers that close to Pfeifer."

Like all of my other feelings right now, I'm of two minds. On the one hand, it would be really nice to have Aaron there for moral support.

But I also don't want an audience, and I don't think my father will either. And while I'm fairly confident that *I'm* safe, I'm not sure whether that safety net extends to anyone else.

"I do want you there. But . . . I have to do this alone. Well, as alone as I can be with God only knows how many other people inside my father's head."

Another message from Will floats into my head, dispelling any questions I had as to whether my father's congress of ghosts is listening.

TWELVE NEW. PLUS YOUR MOTHER.

WE WILL HEAR. CAN'T AVOID. BUT WILL NOT DISRUPT AS LONG AS HE STAYS CAGED.

Cregg is contained. But why should I even go in the room? If you can just transfer thoughts back and forth . . .

NOT YOUR SERVANT. THIS ISN'T EASY, YOU KNOW.

The tickle inside my head vanishes before I can respond.

"You okay?" Aaron asks.

"Yeah. Just . . . setting up ground rules for the meeting."

As I expected, no one is entirely happy with my decision to go in alone. Our eventual compromise is that Sophie will be in there with us, wearing earphones as she watches videos. Aaron, Daniel, and Deo will be on alert in the bedroom across the hall. I guess the hope is that Daniel and Deo together might be enough to counteract any sort of violence that Aaron picks up from the Furies and whoever else is inside my father's head, as long as Sophie is also using her blocking ability. They'd have to stay outside Sophie's blocking range to do that, but I decide not to bring that up because it would send us back to the drawing board.

I expect Taylor to protest that they're sexists for sidelining her. But she doesn't. Either she realizes that there isn't much she could do to help, since we're not in need of remote viewing, or she's simply too engrossed in what she's reading on Cregg's tablet to be bothered.

Again, I feel a wave of frustration from Cregg at the sight of his tablet in her hands. Frustration . . . or maybe *indignance* is a better word. Indignance that she's invading his privacy. Which is the height of hypocrisy, coming from a body thief.

I approach the bedroom door and knock. A man's voice says, "Come in."

The sound catches me off guard. This is the first time I've heard him speak. His voice is deeper than I expected.

I feel his eyes on me when I step inside, but I look at Sophie first. She's on the bed where she slept last night, her back against the headboard. An iPad—Taylor's, judging from the light-blue cover—is propped on her knees. I reach into my pocket and toss her a pair of earbuds. She nods, plugs them in, and goes back to her show.

The gurney is still in the room, but it's been folded flat and shoved partway under the bed. There's no chair, so I perch awkwardly on the end of Sophie's bed.

When I finally look up, Pfeifer says, "We still can't believe it's you. When we saw you outside of the Senate building, we were almost certain, but . . ."

He's using the plural pronoun. It sounds strange to me, like one of those couples who share a Facebook account. *Scott-Leah Pfeifer.*

Maybe he can tell this from my expression, because he clears his throat and says, "You look so much like Leah when we first met. Not the hair." He attempts a smile—a quick nervous uptick of one side of his mouth. "The military wouldn't have allowed that. And she was a bit older than you are now, but . . . the resemblance is uncanny."

I open my mouth, trying to think of something to say. I ran through several possible opening lines while I changed clothes, but none of them feel right. He's at a loss, too, and we both just sit there, awkward and silent.

Then his expression changes completely. The effect is transformative, like I'm looking at an entirely different person. And I'm pretty sure that's exactly what I *am* doing.

This smile is much more than a twitch. It fills the entire face, and the eyes, which were already shiny, are positively brimming now. "Anna? Oh my God."

The voice is different, too. It's still deep, but the inflections are more feminine. It reminds me of Scarlett Johansson when she plays Black Widow.

I still can't seem to find words, and after a moment, Pfeifer says, "How did you get involved in all of this? Rowena was supposed to keep you far away from anything connected to Delphi. Is she . . . she's okay, isn't she?"

"I don't know. Jasper mentioned someone by that name, but—"

"Jasper?"

I can't tell whether it's Scott or Leah asking. If I had to guess, I'd say it was both.

"Maybe we should take things in order. I didn't meet Jasper until a few months ago. And I don't remember Rowena at all."

So I begin at the food court. I don't actually remember being abandoned there, but it's the origin story in my file with the State of Maryland. It's also the first thing about my life that was documented, at least to the best of my knowledge, so it seems like a good place to start.

Sometimes it's Scott sitting across from me as I talk. Sometimes it's Leah. To be honest, the switching back and forth is creepy. I now have a much greater appreciation for Aaron, Deo, and the others who have all seen something like this on my face and didn't run shrieking.

What's weirder, though, is that feeling I had earlier, as though both of them are present at the same time. Occasionally they switch back and forth so rapidly it's like I'm talking to two people simultaneously. Him? Her? Them? I can't really tell.

When I mention the note pinned to my dress, the switch happens so fast I get mental whiplash. There's a stream of angry curses, followed by, "You should never have trusted her." Then, without missing a beat, a slightly different voice comes from the same mouth. "What choice did I have? And you're wrong. Just plain wrong."

Sophie is supposed to be watching her damn video and not listening in, but her eyes keep drifting over toward Pfeifer. I can't blame her. How could any show hold her attention with this insanity playing out five feet away? Still, I give her an annoyed look, and she reluctantly shifts her body and Taylor's tablet toward the opposite wall.

"Ro would never have abandoned her like that, Scott. Something happened. Something must have happened."

He counters, arguing that she probably just didn't want to be tied down with a kid at age seventeen. And while I really don't want to pick sides in an argument between my parents, it feels like Pfeifer is browbeating my mother. Given he's the one who pulled the trigger, that strikes me as unfair. Anyway, I'm pretty sure she's right, so I cut him off in midsentence.

"Once I found out about you from Jasper—I know, I haven't gotten to that part, but bear with me. He seemed certain you left me with your sister—Rowena, right?" A nod confirms this, and I go on. "Aaron asked his grandfather to run a background search and see if we could track anyone in your family down. Your parents died in 2012. But there's no record of your sister after 2004."

Pfeifer inhales sharply, and I quickly add, "There's no death record. No missing-persons report, even though she was a minor. She seems to have just vanished."

"Along with the insurance money and the other funds I transferred. That was plenty to disappear on, especially if you ditch the kid and only have one person to support. Leave that godforsaken town and—" Then, a split second later: "No! She *wouldn't have done that*, Scott. I know my sister." And then, "What other explanation is there?"

"Does it matter?" I snap. "It happened. I survived. Do you want me to finish or not?"

They look surprised. "Yes. Go ahead."

I continue my life story—foster care, psychiatric treatment. Kelsey. Deo. Picking up Molly and getting pulled into the Delphi fiasco. Aaron. Meeting Jasper and learning that our suspicions were true and my parents had indeed been Delphi subjects. Magda. Sandalford. Her search for a cure, and why some of the adepts aren't exactly down with that. And finally, my premonition that someone wanted to kill Pfeifer.

By necessity, it's a condensed version of *The Anna Morgan Story*, and I'll admit that I was selective in the bits that I skipped over. I left out Myron. That's not the kind of tale you roll out on first acquaintance. I also didn't mention Cregg. Will made it clear that the hitchers from The Warren already have that information, so I assume my parents do, as well. No point in stirring the pot. If anyone wants to know more about how I got stuck with this psycho, they can ask.

I also glossed over most of the problems I faced in foster care. In part, that's because I'm worried it will just reignite their earlier argument about how I *wound up* in foster care. But the biggest reason is that I don't want them to feel sorry for me.

What I said a few minutes ago is true.

It happened. I survived.

There have been some truly rotten events in my life. Many were undoubtedly set into motion when someone, probably my aunt, left me in that mall, wandering around with a teddy bear and an empty Orange Julius cup. But if I could go back in time, I wouldn't change any aspect of my life, even that one. The same action set into motion the chain of events that led me to Kelsey, to Deo, to Aaron. To all of the hitchers who combined to make me *me*.

I've always wondered what happened to that teddy bear, though.

"What are you thinking about?" Pfeifer asks. I think it's my mother this time. "Your colors changed. It was your usual indigo and pink, and then . . ."

Colors? I have blue hair and more or less pink skin, but it's an odd comment. So I answer the question. "The police report said I had a teddy bear when I was found. It must have been lost in one of those first homes where I stayed. That always makes me a little sad. It would've been nice if the bear came along for the journey."

"Not a bear. Zoe." My mother—and it's definitely her now—makes a noise somewhere between a laugh and a sob. "The orange monster from *Sesame Street.* You remember, don't you?"

I start to say no, but then realize that she's talking to Scott, not me.

"Yeah. She couldn't pronounce the name. It came out *Doughy.* She was your favorite. You took her everywhere, and they didn't even let you *keep* her." There's a dull rage in Pfeifer's voice, and his tears are pouring freely.

"No! That's not . . . I mean, I don't know that anyone took it from me." Part of me wants to go to him—to *them*—but it still feels too strange, too awkward, to make physical contact. "Maybe I lost it or it got so ratty someone had to toss it out. Really, it was just a stray thought. It's not like I've spent the past fifteen years mourning the loss of a stuffed monster."

I smile, hoping to bolster this point, but Pfeifer isn't having it.

"Maybe not now. But there was one night—probably more—when you *did* mourn for Zoe. When you couldn't sleep because that stuffed monster was gone. And I wasn't there to comfort you. *We* weren't there to comfort you, because the very *real* monster who has taken up residence in your head forced me to shoot Leah. And as soon as we figure out how to deal with the bastard without hurting you, he's going to pay for that."

News Item from the *Pensacola News Journal*

April 24, 2020

Just when we all thought flu season was over, Escambia County health officials are cautioning residents about an unusual outbreak. Six cases have been reported in the past two weeks, almost exclusively among teens and young adults, with an additional twenty-two cases and five fatalities statewide. The primary symptom is a high, often life-threatening, fever.

The CDC is tracking similar outbreaks in Alaska, California, Illinois, Michigan, and Massachusetts.

CHAPTER SEVENTEEN

Mathias, West Virginia
April 25, 2020, 9:28 p.m.

For the second time in the past few hours, I feel like whacking myself upside the head for missing something painfully obvious. Yes, it would make sense for the *average* person reading about my mother's death to assume the man whose fingerprints were on the weapon, whose hands and clothing were covered with gunpowder residue, who even acknowledged pulling the trigger, was in fact guilty. Crazy, perhaps, but still guilty.

Unlike the average person reading about my mother's murder, however, I sat in that lab at The Warren and watched as Cregg forced Deo to turn the gun to his own head. I watched Deo's hands shake as he fought for control. And I lived through the dreams where Molly was forced to sever her own finger.

I have scars, too—physical reminders of Cregg's power. One is on my arm. The tiny incisions line up perfectly with Bree Bieler's teeth. The other scar, about an inch above my temple and visible only if you push the hair aside, is from the butt of a pistol that Jasper Hawkins smashed into my head.

Graham Cregg was in the driver's seat all those times. As he was when I arranged for Abbott and Costello to kill my father. And apparently, he was in my father's driver seat fifteen years ago when he killed my mother.

"Cregg was in the doorway the night you died, wasn't he? I saw someone standing there in the newspaper photo. Two people, actually."

"The second person was the newly elected Senator from Pennsylvania. Just stopping by for a visit with his son, if anyone asked, because he gave up all interest in the business when he first ran for office back in 1998. What a joke. He may not have been interested in the other projects at Decathlon, but he followed every new development on Delphi. And his wife picked up his financial stake in the company, no matter how many times he may claim there's no link." The voice changes slightly, and then it's my mother saying, "And he was the perfect witness. They both saw Scott take the gun from my bag. Point it, pull the trigger. Open-and-shut case, even if there hadn't been security cameras."

"But why did Cregg do it?" Even as I ask, I realize this is a dumb question. We're talking about Graham Cregg. He keeps a box of his victims' fingers. The man isn't sane. Why am I searching for any kind of logic to his actions?

"I can only guess. Maybe you should ask him," Pfeifer says. And then, without even slowing down, "Really, Scott? Do you think he'd give her an honest answer?"

"Could you not do that, please? Switching back and forth constantly. It's . . . disconcerting."

"Oh. I'm sorry. I'll let Scott tell it."

I feel like I've told my mother to shut up, and that's not at all what I intended. So I roll it back a bit. "No, that's okay. I want to hear from both of you. Just . . . maybe a pause? Or a bit of warning? And I'll have to settle for your best guess on Cregg's motivations, because in order to ask him anything, I'd have to—"

"Pull down your walls. Yes. That's why the two telepaths in here struggle to read you. They can read the others in the house without a problem, but the man . . . Will? He says talking to you is like lifting a heavy weight due to all of those bricks. They couldn't read you at all a few times today. Did Dr. Kelsey teach you that trick?"

I nod but don't elaborate. It feels like they're trying to circle away from talking about the shooting, though. Like maybe they're hiding something or trying to avoid the topic. So I redirect.

"You were saying . . . your best guess on Cregg's motivations?"

He hesitates, weighing his words. Or maybe he's just trying to remember, given how long it's been.

"I'd just threatened to resign. My best guess? He was unhappy about that. There were other scientists on the team who could have picked up my notes and continued the project. In fact, I'd bet that a few of them were still on Cregg's team at this Warren facility. But I was the lead researcher. I knew the work better than anyone. Losing me was a setback, and Cregg always wanted results instantly. That was partly his father pushing, hoping for some new development they could parlay into getting government funding reinstated. I didn't want that to happen, though. It was too dangerous. My only reason for remaining with DSG after the project officially ended was to develop a treatment that might mitigate the effects for you and the other adepts."

"A cure?"

"No. A cure is something you take to get rid of a condition. There *are* some versions of the drug that don't permanently alter brain chemistry. The military was keenly interested in a drug you could switch on and off. The OA drugs were designed to temporarily boost any latent psi ability, and we used those in the lab to determine which individuals might be good long-term subjects for Delphi research. That drug reverses on its own about a month after you stop taking it. You can speed the reversal along with other medications, reduce it to a few days. All of the Delphi drugs disrupt the dopamine and serotonin balance to some degree, but the OA class causes a sharp drop in serotonin. That can have major repercussions."

"Violent outbursts," I say. "Suicide."

"Exactly. And the violence didn't simply hit those who'd already shown psychic ability. There was a control group, too, each time we tested a new formula. The project churned through people on a fairly regular basis. I ended the reversal protocol after the second suicide among the Delphi subjects. But I don't think there's any chance of a cure for subjects dosed with the permanent form. And definitely not for second-generation adepts, where the rest of the brain developed in tandem with the sections affected by the drug. Any attempt to reverse the effects would probably be futile and possibly fatal."

"That's why the second-generation adepts don't have the same problems with aggressive behavior, right? The fusiform gyrus developed in sync with the amygdala, so there's no additional pressure on that part of the brain."

"Yes. How did you know *that*?" Pfeifer asks with a surprised smile. There's a bit of pride in his smile, which is kind of amusing. Perhaps he's hoping I'm a chip off the old block, a budding neuroscientist.

"Something Dr. Kelsey mentioned a few months back. She thought the fact that the amygdala is smaller in women might also explain why male test subjects from the original group are more volatile."

"It's a little more complicated than that," he says, "at least with some of the later formulas, but that's a very good deduction. Anyway, a cure isn't possible for the second generation. My goal was to develop a *treatment* that might allow you and your fellow adepts to lead normal lives. Or, more accurately, a series of treatments, since not all of the formulas act in the same way. I stayed with the Python group at DSG because I needed lab access. No way to test the formulas without their resources. I continued to conduct the treatment research while also working to improve the on-off switch, as the temporary formulas were known in the lab, and also two new formulas that Cregg was particularly interested in. One was the amplifying serum that your friend Deo was given. The other was the suppressor serum that gives Sophie her ability to block. Flip sides of the coin."

Sophie looked up when her name was spoken, so it's obvious that she's paying almost no attention to her video. At this point, I'm tempted to tell her to go, but since that would probably worry Aaron, I opt to ignore her.

I also ignore the sick thud in my stomach when Pfeifer mentions the amp serum. It's not like he's telling me anything new. I've known for months now that his research was the genesis of the Delphi program. This man—one half of my gene pool—created the drug that nearly killed Deo. That did kill quite a few others.

"So, while I don't know for certain," Pfeifer continues, "my best guess is Cregg found out what I was doing. That I'd been stringing him along and using Delphi resources for something unrelated to his primary goal. We were already having disagreements over human testing. The blocker and amp formulas weren't stable—and the fact that there are still so few adepts with those abilities suggests to me that this hasn't changed. The only reason I was able to hide what I was doing for as long as I did is because there's a small area of overlap between the suppression formula Cregg wanted and the treatment I was working on."

A slightly dazed curtain falls over his face. "Cregg didn't have time to plan it, since he couldn't have known your mother was coming. I didn't even know. I thought the two of you were still in Colorado. Cregg simply stumbled upon a way to punish me that not only removed the possibility of me going public with the deaths caused by the Delphi Project but also guaranteed anything I said would be discredited as the ramblings of a madman. A guy who couldn't accept he'd shot his ex-wife in a fit of anger. He could sell that story, and he knew it."

"Why did you divorce?" The question isn't germane to the current discussion, but I want to know.

There's a very long pause before they answer. I suspect there's an internal debate going on about what to tell me, because my father's expression looks like the video Deo once made of me conferring with one of my hitchers—eyes vacant, mouth slightly open.

"It was . . . complicated. I think that's how people put it these days, although judging from your expression right now, maybe that term is already cliché. Our reasons were personal, and we've had fifteen years together since then to work those out. You'd be amazed how many misunderstandings disappear when you share a mind."

I'm one of the few people who *wouldn't* be amazed in the slightest. I understand Daniel—and vice versa—a hell of a lot better than I used to, and he was only in my head for a few months. But I want to hear the rest of what they're saying, so I don't comment.

"The most important reason, however, was to protect you. We started making plans even before you were born. You were a . . . surprise. Not an unwelcome one," they add hurriedly. "Definitely not."

I can tell this isn't true. I don't blame them. There is no way I would voluntarily bring a child into the mix under their circumstances at the time, even though, from a purely selfish standpoint, I'm glad for the mistake.

Pfeifer goes on to say that several former Delphi subjects had popped up at the Python offices reporting that their kids were manifesting signs of psychic abilities. Most of the parents were well past the point where reproduction violated the terms of their contract, and some threatened to sue Decathlon. The legal team pulled out their contracts, in which they'd basically signed away all rights, in perpetuity, for themselves, their heirs, and so forth. And then they pulled out a corporate checkbook, along with a nondisclosure agreement. The cash payout was a pittance that would never cover the extra expenses most of them incurred trying to care for their children. Pfeifer seems confident that at least some of those kids eventually wound up at The Warren, because the official complaint put them on Cregg's radar.

All through this discussion of Cregg and Decathlon, Pfeifer's tone is harsh and damning. I want to ask him about his own role in all this. It was *his* research, after all. He worked on the project for nearly a decade. Even if he spent the last few years working against them in some fashion, surely he must shoulder a considerable portion of the blame?

That doesn't seem like a wise topic of conversation this early in our relationship. But I know those questions will gnaw at me. I'll have to ask him eventually.

"Cole Quinn was smart about it," Pfeifer says. "Although I suspect that's because he *did* violate the terms of his contract with Decathlon. It was only three months after his contract expired when he showed up one Thursday night at a bar where he knew a group of us from the lab usually went for a drink after work. He pulled me aside and asked how my side project was coming along. I didn't even realize he knew what I was working on, but he and Beth Wilcox dealt with a lot of the paperwork. Equipment orders, lab materials, and so forth. If anyone could tell I was doing something outside my mandate, it would have been them. Anyway, Quinn asked if I'd had any luck, and I could tell from his expression that it was . . . personal for him. I ended up agreeing to take a look at his boy, even though I still didn't have anything to offer in the way of treatment."

"Aaron?"

"Yes. The kid was barely talking yet on his own, just typical toddler phrases. But he knew when someone was angry. What they were angry about, what they were thinking. He'd repeat exact words, many of them words that weren't in his vocabulary. We even did a reading with portable EEG equipment, older than the stuff in the main lab, but good enough for me to spot the signature changes in brain activity. We got a very vivid spike in the readings when the boy picked up something from one of the other hotel rooms. Right in the middle of the test, this toddler yells, 'You bastards!' at the top of his lungs."

I can't help but smile as I picture a toddler-sized Aaron in one of those EEG caps. Pfeifer doesn't need to describe it. I wore them many times back when doctors were trying to figure out what made little Anna go crazy. The worst parts were the adhesive strips that held the wires in place and that cold gel that increased conductivity but left my hair all gross and sticky.

My smile fades, however, as I think about how incredibly challenging it must have been for Michele and Cole Quinn to handle Aaron as a small child, especially when the Delphi serum left Cole with a temper that he struggled to keep under control. And how hard it must have been on Aaron, knowing every stray angry impulse that passed through the mind of his parents, his siblings, his teachers—even if they'd never act on those impulses. It's a miracle that Aaron is sane.

Pfeifer says Cole showed up about the time they learned Leah was pregnant with me. She had been part of the last test group at Fort Bragg and opted not to sign up with the civilian version of the program, partly because they were dating by then and it would have raised eyebrows. They had a long-distance relationship until her three years were up, then they married and she joined him in Maryland.

"Only a few people at work even knew. Our relationship started when we were coworkers, and . . . it seemed wise to keep our private lives private. Leah's ability wasn't exactly top priority for the military, anyway, although I suspect that Senator Cregg wouldn't mind having someone like her on the campaign trail."

"What exactly does she . . . do?"

Sophie is listening again. She's gradually pivoted back toward us as we talked, and I can almost see her ears perk up when I ask the question. While I totally get that it might be hard to ignore our conversation, it's beginning to feel very intrusive. I shoot her an annoyed look, but she doesn't turn away this time.

Pfeifer notices the silent exchange between me and Sophie. "She's been cooped up all day. All day yesterday, too, from what she told me earlier. Let her get up, stretch—"

"Don't bother," Sophie says, holding up the tablet so that I can see her ratcheting up the volume. "It will probably destroy my hearing, but whatever." Then she reaches down and tugs the quilt over her head. "Happy now?"

"We'll wrap up soon," I say. "It's late, and we aren't going to catch up on fifteen years in one sitting."

"That's true," Pfeifer says. "But to answer your question, your mother sees . . . auras, I guess?"

A laugh, and then Pfeifer's face shifts. "Always the scientist. After all this time, it still makes him crazy to talk about things he can't quantify. How do you apply the scientific method to a ring of color that shifts with a person's mood? Something a researcher can't even see? Scott has always been much more comfortable with the firestarters and telekinetic crowd, where it's easier to define variables and to measure output."

"But . . . he picks up ghosts. Which you can't measure and no one else can see."

"Yes! That's *exactly* what I told him. You'd think that would have made him less of an empiricist, but . . ." She shakes her head, smiling. "Anyway, he's right. I see auras."

"That's what you meant earlier. When you said that my colors changed. Do they look the same as they did when I was small?"

The smile fades a bit. "Mostly."

I start to press her on that, but then it occurs to me why she's being evasive. "You see Cregg, too, don't you?"

"Not completely. Your colors still predominate, but . . . your edges are murky and gray-green. And everything else is a little dim."

"Do the colors signify anything?"

"That's the part that's hard to quantify, because everyone seems to see them a little differently. What's more interesting to me than the actual color is when I notice changes. I see those when someone is happy. Or upset. Or lying. If I . . . this part is hard to explain, but if I peer closely into the aura, I can usually pick up stray thoughts and emotions. And sometimes, I can tweak those emotions to clear up the colors—to get the person into a more pleasant mood. A more cooperative mood. That last element probably *would* have made me a subject of interest to Python, even after I left the program. Someone they'd have been inclined to keep a closer eye on and maybe . . . employ. But Scott played down that side of my ability when writing up his report, because I'd made it very clear that I had serious moral reservations about using it."

"So a milder version of Daniel Quinn's ability. Like when he told Cregg's daughter to go into the containment unit at the lab last night?"

"We don't remember that." Pfeifer looks down, clearly uncomfortable. "We . . . weren't exactly in control last night. But yes, it sounds similar. It's also somewhat similar to Graham Cregg's ability. That's the side of it that bothered me, and it eventually bothered Scott, too, once we talked through the moral implications of his research. I've used the ability when I had to. A few times when you were small, I used it to convince a ghost you picked up that it was time to go. And I tried it on Cregg that night at Python labs, but . . . it backfired."

"How?"

The silence stretches out so long that I'm not sure she's going to answer. But then she shakes her head and says, "Memories can be slippery, Anna, especially the ones that are tied up with our emotions. And that's even more true of old memories. Ones that have lived in our minds for a long time, so long that they're more like a memory *of* a memory. Does that make sense?"

"Yeah. That's how it is with the memories from my hitchers. My . . . ghosts."

"Hitchers," Pfeifer says, trying out the word. "I like that. Anyway, I latched on to a memory of Cregg's that wasn't quite what I thought. It was the brightest, most vivid memory in that wretched man's head, but then it . . . *twisted* in my grasp. Have you ever watched *Snow White*?"

It's actually one of the few Disney movies that I haven't seen, or at least not all of it. Deo and I tried a couple of years ago when one of the other foster kids put it on. It was too saccharine, though, and the warbly singing made my skin crawl. But one of my hitchers watched it, and I have one of those vague memories of a memory, so I nod for her to continue.

"The apple that the witch gave Snow White was shiny, bright, and perfect on the outside, hiding the poison within. And that's what this memory of his mother was—"

The rage in the back of my head isn't as strong or as protracted as it was back at the townhouse, when I saw the spider's eyes in my reflection. But this brief flare is still more than anything I've heard from Cregg since we arrived here at the cabin. He doesn't want to hear what my mother is saying. This is a memory he doesn't want to share. That he doesn't want to relive. My walls are solid, but they don't entirely block his furious desire to *shut her up*.

Several things happen at once. The bedroom door swings open, smashing into the wall and sending one of the pictures hanging nearby crashing to the floor. Aaron rushes through the doorway, his face flushed the way it always is when he gets a vibe. Daniel is right behind him, yelling for Sophie to grab Pfeifer.

All of this is background, however. My eyes are fixed on Pfeifer's face. Seeing his expression switch between his personality and my mother's was odd, but this is terrifying. It's almost like his face is a video being played on fast-forward, or maybe one of those flip-books shifting between images at an abnormally rapid pace. He's saying something, but it's not in English. I don't think it's in any single language, but more of a multilingual word salad tossed together by the spirits hovering just below his surface.

And then, for a split second, my father turns into a giant spider-rat. He's no longer sitting on a bed. It's a stack of bodies, dozens of bodies. Some are strangers, but most are all too familiar. Deo. Aaron. Kelsey.

By the time the scream reaches my lips, the creature is gone. It's just Pfeifer, on the bed, staring at me. The only clear signal that reaches my brain is a written sign from Will.

KEEP THE SPIDER IN ITS CAGE!

CHAPTER EIGHTEEN

Mathias, West Virginia
April 25, 2020, 10:13 p.m.

Aaron takes hold of my arm and spins me around to face him. I know this look. He's trying to read my eyes, to be certain that Cregg hasn't taken over. And that tells me he didn't just pick up a vibe from Pfeifer's crew. He picked up one from my hitcher, too.

I want to hold Aaron's gaze, to reassure him. But right now, I don't want to turn my back on Pfeifer. The flip-book show on Pfeifer's face has ended, landing on my mother's expression. She looks shaken, but I can tell she's regained control.

"I'm sorry! Cregg's colors surged. It was only for a second, but I was worried your walls wouldn't hold. And as soon as that thought entered my mind, it set off a chain reaction with the others."

"A nuclear chain reaction," Aaron says, lowering the gun that I've just realized he was pointing toward my parents. That can't have made Leah's job of reining them in any easier. I shudder, remembering the shifting tide of raw emotion that washed over Pfeifer's face a moment ago. It was like the girl from *The Exorcist*. Was that how I looked to Deo when the Furies were fighting for control of me that night in Lab 1?

I'm not sure I want to know.

"You should go," Pfeifer says. "Sophie and I have things under control, but they're still really close to the surface."

Aaron backs us out the door and into the hallway. Daniel and Deo are already in the living room.

"What the hell was that?" Aaron asks.

"You saw it, too? The spider?"

"No. It was like the whole room was a mob scene. Hundreds of people, and then they vanished."

"Yeah, well, I saw Patrick, my stepdad," Deo says. "I'm guessing Daniel saw his wall of water again. What about you, Tay?"

"I didn't see anything." Her grim smile tells me she's lying. "But we need to get out of here for a while, so bundle up, kiddies."

None of us are thrilled at the prospect of tramping out to the far side of the property. But it seems unavoidable, so we pull on our shoes and jackets.

Once we're outside, Taylor tosses the keys to Sam's SUV to Aaron. "When we're finished talking, you two should clear out. Drive into Moorefield. Go to a movie or something."

"It's after ten," Aaron says.

"Then go to Walmart. Buy some food. Or you could actually follow through on what we talked about yesterday if you're feeling adventurous. Just get Anna out of here and let things calm down."

"She's right," Daniel says. "But maybe Deo and I should take her, since I seem to make them nervous, too. If anything happens, they might be less upset if Aaron was the one with the weapon."

"Could we stop thinking about shooting my father as a viable option, please?"

"I didn't mean against him," Daniel says. "I don't think anyone tracked us here by conventional means, but we're dealing with other psychics. Someone should definitely be armed if the Senator's people decide to pay us a visit. I'm not sure it will matter if there are more than a few of them, but . . ." He stops and rubs a hand through his hair. "I just totally invalidated my argument, didn't I?"

"Yes, you did," Aaron says. "The only thing I offer is an early warning system. You, and especially you combined with Deo, offer a defense. Plus, if you need actual firepower, Taylor has her gun. She's a better shot than you are, anyway."

"Then she must be twice as good as you."

I ignore their posturing and focus on Taylor. "You knew what was going to happen with my father, didn't you?"

She waves her hand dismissively. "I knew *something* was going to happen. From Stan's texts. He told me about the fire upstairs and that Aaron would . . ." She stops, pressing her lips together, but she's already said enough to pique Aaron's curiosity.

"That I would what?" he asks.

Taylor takes a seat across from us and stares at her brother for a moment. Her face softens, but she finishes the statement. "That you would overreact. Again."

The color drains from Aaron's face. I get the sense that Taylor is referring to something they've discussed privately.

Surprisingly, Daniel comes to his defense. "Aaron drew the weapon because he convinced me, ahead of time, that Pfeifer's visitors would never be able to relax as long as I was armed. They can't help seeing me as a Fudd, as one of Cregg's men. If Pfeifer hadn't managed to corral them, I'd have gotten Sophie to stop blocking so I could step in with a nudge. But that has to be a last resort. One instance of me pushing his hitchers the wrong way, and they might torch this cabin and half the valley along with it. But, Taylor—if you knew about this ahead of time, why in hell didn't you give us a heads-up *before* Anna went in? What happened to your whole we-can't-keep-secrets campaign?"

"Anna needed to talk to Pfeifer. And Stan says that all paths show Anna as stable, at least for the next few days. Otherwise, I would have told you."

"It sounds like you're giving a damned weather forecast," Daniel says. "And I'm guessing this Stan guy's predictions aren't much more accurate. You're putting a whole lot of faith in his ability, and since you're keeping secrets, you force us to do the same. That makes me very nervous. I remember Stan vaguely from The Warren, but I don't *know* him. I don't know what his motives are."

I keep quiet. This has the makings of a sibling argument, judging from the tilt of Taylor's chin. And while I really don't want to piss Taylor off, if I *had* to pick sides, I'd back Daniel on this one. I don't know Stan that well either. He strikes me as very . . . pragmatic. Plus, he claims to see dozens of different paths. There were so many ways that things could have gone horribly wrong in that room, so any claim that all of the paths Stan was monitoring were safe ones strikes me as nothing short of miraculous. He's gambling, and I'm starting to feel like we're the dice he's rolling.

"I *do* remember Maria," Daniel says. "But I remember her as a troublemaker who spent her time playing practical jokes and embarrassing people. She wasn't some Joan of Arc marshaling troops into battle."

Taylor gives him an icy look. "You remember me playing *My Little Pony* and eating fluffernutters. People *change*, Daniel. They grow up."

Deo mumbles something in defense of fluffernutters, but they both ignore him.

"This was less than a year ago," Daniel says. "Maria can't have changed that much."

"Really?" Taylor says. "Sometimes people grow up fast because their circumstances change. Maybe their dad gets killed. Or their best friend. Or both. Was I the same person a year after those things happened to me?"

Daniel doesn't respond, and I'm once again wowed by how well Taylor plays her oldest brother. It doesn't usually work as well on Aaron, although he's oddly quiet right now.

"And," Taylor adds, seizing the moment, "it's sometimes better if you *don't* know everything in these situations. Anna understands exactly what I mean."

She's referring to my own visions, and on that point, she's right. I rarely tell the others the specific details, especially if it's something that affects them. I made an exception this last time, mostly because the brief thought I had about them in the vision was vague. But it usually makes more sense to limit the number of people who have to deal with knowing what's coming down the pike, especially when it's written in stone.

Stan's visions aren't like that, however. There are variables. Things can and do change. I could bring this up, but they all know it, and what I really want is for the argument to end. My stomach is already tied in knots from the experience with my parents, and this isn't helping.

Apparently, Deo feels the same way, because he deftly changes the subject. "What did Pfeifer mean about your colors surging? That made no sense at all."

"It's kind of a long story," I say, and then give them a basic overview of my conversation with Pfeifer. They're as surprised as I was to learn that Cregg was behind my mother's murder, but not surprised in the least at my description of how his face shifted when it was my mother speaking, or during that brief moment when the Furies charged forward.

"You look nothing like Molly," Taylor says. "But that night when you let her take control at Sam's office? It was like seeing a pale, blonde version of my best friend. The facial expressions were totally Molly. That convinced me as much as anything she told us. And more recently . . ."

She doesn't finish the comment, but it's clear from her grimace that she's talking about Cregg.

"You're sure your walls are solid?" Aaron asks. "I mean, I'm not feeling anything right *now*, but I didn't charge in like that because of his gang of hitchers. That didn't hit until I threw open the door. The vibe I got was coming from Cregg. An intense split-second surge of rage directed at Pfeifer . . . and at Taylor, oddly enough."

Taylor taps the iPad next to her. "Probably doesn't like the fact that I'm digging around in his Chamber of Secrets."

Deo snickers, and I think he's about to make a joke, but then he seems to remember this is Graham Cregg we're talking about. His secrets aren't exactly a joking matter.

Cregg stirred behind the wall again when she tapped the screen just now, but it was a feeble movement. His recent burst of activity seems to have drained his energy. This is a more passive reaction—a pitiful flip of his middle finger instead of a murderous lunge at the barrier—and it doesn't even trip Aaron's radar.

Taylor's watching me, however, with same expression she wore at The Warren the other night, just before she gave me that second injection. She's measuring me, trying to gauge my limits. Despite her claims that everything is safe, that the great prophet Stan has decreed that I am stable, there's a seed of doubt. I can't fault her there, but I do wish she'd be less mercurial.

"My walls are intact, Taylor. What's up?"

"A couple of things. But maybe it would be best to wait until morning. I know you just woke up, but some of us are tired."

She's not exactly lying, but she's being evasive.

"Taylor, Cregg just stormed the castle in there, and he seems wiped. If you've got something to tell us and you're worried about Cregg's reaction triggering a response from Pfeifer's horde"—I gesture toward the cabin—"this really might be the best time."

"All right. Fine. I'm nowhere near finished, but from what I can tell, this is Cregg's . . . I don't know. Master file, I guess. Everything he'd need to hit the ground running with his sexy new body. Sorry . . ." she says, in response to my expression. "Most of the information isn't actually *on* the tablet, though. He's got links to files, probably hosted privately. I've downloaded some of those to my laptop, in case his daughter or someone else decides to scrub the server. I couldn't get them all, though—one set requires a fingerprint."

Aaron sighs. "Maybe there's a work-around? A password option?"

"And why would we need that?" Taylor asks.

"Um . . . because I don't want to find Cregg's grave and dig up his moldering . . ." Aaron stops and grins as he lifts my hand from the table. "Got it. Open sesame."

"You mean my fingerprint could have opened the thing all along? We didn't need to guess the password?"

"No. There are several fingerprints in the tablet's memory, but Cregg didn't set it up to unlock the device. It's just an extra layer of security for some of the files. Anyway, the thing is a total grab bag. Financial data—both personal financial info and also a ton of stuff dealing with Python Diagnostics and Decathlon. Some dirt on his father as well. A bunch of medical files and spreadsheets. Pages of scientific notes. Data on the adepts—information from when he had them at The Warren or down in that silo, along with more recent notes about our practice sessions at Sandalford. And also . . . personal stuff. Pictures. Some old news articles from the 1970s. A journal that goes back to his teens. I haven't had the nerve to open that one yet. Not after the box Anna found in his desk drawer."

"I'll handle it," Daniel says. "Just send me the file."

Another dim echo of protest from Cregg. More because I'm tired of his intrusions than out of a real desire to read it, I say, "Me, too."

A heated discussion follows on how to get the information to our devices. Apparently, e-mail is out, we shouldn't trust the cloud right now, they're not sure whether the wi-fi here is secure enough, and something else I'm perfectly willing to admit I don't understand. I snuggle in a little closer to Aaron for warmth while Taylor and Daniel hash it out.

"Cold?" Aaron whispers, slipping an arm around me.

I nod, sticking my hands under my thighs to warm them. "I didn't think I'd need gloves and wool socks in April."

He looks over at the shed. "I could start a fire. Except . . . I doubt any of us have a lighter."

"Plus, that would mean I'd lose your body heat while you're way over there. I'm okay."

Taylor clears her throat. "Are you two lovebirds ready to join the rest of the class?"

I stick out my tongue, and Taylor angles the cracked screen so that all of us have a semi-decent view.

"Okay, Anna, first thing—you might want to hang on to that fake ID. There's a little over half a million in a bank account registered to Ms. Ophelia Duncan. Twice that amount in stocks and bonds, plus the townhouse and two other properties. But this one file that I was just looking at puzzles me. It was created a few weeks before Cregg died."

The file in question is a spreadsheet—four unlabeled columns, with about forty entries. It's mostly numbers, although the first column is a list of names, in alphabetical order. Most of the names are foreign, so I'm not entirely sure whether they're given names or surnames. The final column is a three- or four-digit alphanumeric entry. There are at least ten different variations—AS1, OA1, OA2, B1, and so on.

Taylor points to column *C*. About half of the entries read *01/20/21*. The rest are two-letter combinations, sometimes a large number of them, separated by commas.

"Some of these are dates," she says. "Or . . . actually, a single date."

Aaron nods. "Inauguration day. Why would Cregg schedule all of these transactions on inauguration day?"

"Payoffs?" Deo suggests drily. "It's not like foreign intervention in an election is unprecedented. Maybe he's paying a bunch of teens in Macedonia to post fake stories discrediting his father's opponent."

"No," I say. "Not to help his father's campaign. If anything, it would be the opposite."

They don't look entirely convinced, but I'm certain on this point. While I have no idea what caused the split between father and son, I have a very clear sense of Graham Cregg's deep loathing for the Senator. He also feels vindicated, like he was right about something he's always suspected. His hatred for his father was suppressed for a very long time, and now he's ready for some major payback.

I'm not sure how to convince them about this, however, so I direct their attention back to the spreadsheet. "The ones that aren't dates are state abbreviations. See? That one in the middle has a bunch. AL, CA, MA, OK, VA . . ."

"Wait a minute," Taylor says. "Deo, check the primary schedule on your phone."

"Primary schedule of what?"

"The *political primary* schedule. I think those are all Super Tuesday states—they held their primaries on March 3rd. And I'm pretty sure the three states in the entry just below that one held their primaries on March 10th."

Deo pulls up something online that confirms Taylor's suspicion. All of the entries marked with state abbreviations held their Unify America party primary or caucus on the same day.

"So," Daniel says. "Foreign entries and domestic. Some sort of transaction is apparently triggered on either inauguration day or primary election day, but what?"

"Time to find out." Taylor taps one of the linked numbers. After a moment, an interface pops up indicating that a fingerprint is required. "Little help, Anna?"

The site opens when I press my thumb to the button. And equally sure enough, I hear a feeble *thump* at the back of my head.

Deo catches my reaction. "Something wrong?" he asks.

"Nope," I say with a tight smile. "Just a little confirmation that we're digging in the right spot."

The document that pops up on the screen is a contract between Franco Lucas and someone named Ambroz. In the event that Ronald T. Cregg is elected president of the United States, a transfer of two hundred thousand Czech koruna—just over nine thousand US dollars—will be initiated, on January 20, 2021, to the account number Taylor clicked.

No . . . wait. Not *to* the account. *From* the account.

Daniel notices it at the same time I do. "It looks like the funds will transfer into the account after the election . . . but only if Ron Cregg wins."

"Into *Anna's* account," Taylor says. "These are all in the name of Ophelia Duncan."

"That doesn't make it my account."

"Sure looks like you on that driver's license," Daniel says. "And the money could come in handy."

"The contract was managed by Lucas," Deo says. "That's weird. Pretty sure he wasn't a lawyer."

That's putting it mildly. Lucas was a stupid, lecherous brute, and I know from my Molly memories that he barely finished high school.

"No," Aaron says. "Definitely not a lawyer. But he had the connections to drug dealers. He spent about as much time in jail as he did on the outside until he started working as hired muscle for Graham Cregg. That's one reason he hated my dad so much. The question is, what was he helping Cregg sell? Maybe this was just drug dealing on the side, or maybe these are contracts for the women they were trafficking in?"

Taylor shakes her head. "No. Doesn't make sense. Why would deals like that be tied to election dates? More likely it's just plain old influence peddling. Paying for access once his father is elected president."

I'm about to protest, again, that I don't think Cregg and his father are working for the same team any longer. But before I can speak, Aaron says, "No. There's a product involved. This part . . ." He runs his finger back up a few lines. *"In the event that Senator Ronald Cregg is elected president of the United States, the seller grants the purchaser license to produce the specified formula or formulas within the designated country."* We all fall silent.

"He's selling versions of the Delphi serum," Taylor says after a moment. "To dozens of foreign governments."

"I don't think it's governments," Aaron says. "These are small-time buyers. And they're not all foreign."

"True." Taylor clicks the link with the Super Tuesday states, and we go through the thumbprint ritual again. Another contract pops up, this one for California. It's identical to the Czech contract we examined. We click through a few others. The amounts are all ten thousand dollars. A quick check of Ophelia's bank account shows thirteen deposits for ten thousand each during the week after Super Tuesday.

"Ten thousand is chump change," Daniel says, "given probably well over a billion dollars has now gone into research and testing for the Delphi program. And I'm no lawyer, either, but I know enough to be certain that this contract is void. Scroll down—see? No signatures. Even if it were signed, it wouldn't be enforceable, since Graham Cregg doesn't own the research. This is more . . . internal bookkeeping, maybe? A memorandum of understanding. I've seen similar pseudo-contracts between drug dealers, but they're usually even more vague. And the enforcement mechanism in those cases is somebody killing your ass if you don't hold up your end of the bargain or you spill to the cops. But I guess Cregg already knew he'd be dead, so . . ."

"Not dead. Just in a brand-new body," Aaron says. "This could explain some of the incidents we've been hearing on the news about the sudden rise in violence in some areas. They dismissed the claims of psychic activity as nonsense, but it would be really interesting to check these dates and see if there's a connection to when he transferred the formulas. I wonder how long it would take to actually get them to market? Wouldn't there be some lag time?"

"You can cook a batch of meth in like . . . a day," Deo says. "What? Nobody else watched *Breaking Bad*? This stuff could obviously be different, but we've got the number-one authority on it inside the cabin. Why not ask him? Not right this second, obviously, but later."

I second that motion, and add that my father might also be able to give us more information on whether the various codes correlate to different formulas. "I'm pretty sure he said something about OA when we were talking."

"But why," Aaron says, "would Graham Cregg sell the formulas for—as Daniel put it a minute ago—chump change? Imagine how much money he *could* have gotten. Why would he sell the formula to a few dozen people for such a meager sum when he could have made millions more from a single buyer? There are governments that would have coughed up serious cash to be the second country to have a Delphi Project."

"Unless that's the goal," Daniel says. "Think about the history of nuclear weapons. The US developed them—used them, in fact—and soon there were two countries. Then five, then nine, then ten. Being a nuclear nation gives you not just power but also a certain prestige, right? You end up with the haves and the have-nots. And the haves don't want to let new countries into the nuclear club—"

"Because they might get us blown up," Deo says.

"Yeah," Daniel admits. "That's part of it. But also because the haves lose some of their prestige and power if it's a club that anyone can join."

"Are you seriously comparing Delphi to the Manhattan Project?" I ask.

"Kind of. I don't think this research is as earth-shattering as nuclear weapons—no pun intended. But it *is* a potential game changer. And governments will actually use these. Not just for international relations, but also in terms of controlling their own populations."

Daniel has a point. Ron Cregg hasn't even been elected yet, and already he's doing a damn good job of weaponizing the program, simply by playing on the public's fears. Maybe Graham was trying to diffuse the weapon. To democratize it so that his father wouldn't be in control of the only nation with Delphi adepts.

"It's not just governments," Taylor says. "Like you were saying before, these seem to be small actors. Some of them might sell to governments. But, what if they're planning to sell it on the streets? It won't work on everyone, but . . . you could wreak a lot of havoc that way. And can you imagine how freaked out the non-psychics would be? Any government that didn't find a cure of some sort would probably be toppled."

"But Pfeifer doesn't think a cure is possible. Only a treatment, something to mitigate the symptoms for the adepts or . . ." I trail off, remembering something. "Not a cure. A block. Like Sophie, or Maggie. Can you imagine how much people would be willing to pay to ensure no one else can get inside their heads?"

"So you think he's offering them the blocker formula?" Aaron asks.

"Probably the amp formula, too. And they're both dangerous. Basically, anything he's got that will level the playing field and totally screw up his father's plans. On the one hand, that seems like a good thing, but . . ."

"On the other hand, he's a psycho with a penchant for murder and mutilation," Taylor says.

"The enemy of my enemy . . ." Daniel says with a shrug.

Taylor scoops up the iPad. "You do know that's a stupid saying, right? The enemy of my enemy is still my friggin' enemy. I can have more than one."

News Item from the *Washington Times*

April 25, 2020

The granddaughter of Senator Ronald Cregg (UA-PA) is in stable condition after two days as a captive of WOCAN terrorists. Alexandra Cregg, age 21, was locked in a holding cell at the former Bainbridge Naval Training Center in Port Deposit, Maryland. The location had been used by WOCAN earlier this year, when federal authorities, acting on a tip from Senator Cregg, raided the base, killing one of the group's leaders, Franco Lucas. Cregg's son, Graham (now deceased), was injured in that attack.

A spokesperson for the Cregg family told reporters, "Alexandra is a strong girl. She is recovering from her ordeal and is happy to be reunited with her family."

CHAPTER NINETEEN

The road is all but deserted on our way into town. We pass a few cars headed the opposite direction, but most houses along the highway are either dark or lit only by the flickering glow of televisions. Aaron seems to be stuck in his somber mood, or maybe he's annoyed that I initially crawled into the third-row seat of the Kia rather than riding up front with him.

It still seems like a safer option to me. When I pointed out that he was the one who suggested I avoid riding shotgun, he looked like I'd just punched him in the stomach. So now I'm up front in my usual role as navigator/deejay, against my better judgment. Nothing has happened. I knew nothing would happen. But I also knew that Aaron would be nervous. And he is.

"If you grip that wheel any tighter, you're going to snap it in half. And I'm riding in the back on the way home. *All* the way in the back, because there's no way you can drive safely when you're this tense."

"I'm not . . . it's not about that, okay? Yes, I'm nervous. But I'm not worried you're going to grab the wheel. I'm just thinking about what Taylor said."

"When she said you overreacted?"

"That's part of it . . ."

"You didn't overreact. You simply responded to a clear and present danger. And you didn't overreact tonight, either. I *do* think guns are a bad idea for us to have around right now, when we don't really have a good understanding of what my father's hitchers can do. But if the choice was between you coming into that room armed and Daniel coming in armed, you did the right thing."

"I love you."

"Okay, that came out of nowhere. I love you, too?"

Aaron exhales—a half laugh, half sigh—at the slight question in my voice. It's not because I'm unsure on either side of the relationship. I know that I love Aaron. And if he didn't love me, he'd have run away screaming by now.

"Sorry," he says. "You're right. It's just . . . Taylor seems to think maybe you don't fully *know* how I feel. That keeping your walls up and fighting off Cregg would be a lot easier if you—I mean, if *we*—if we were more . . ." He shrugs, a slight, almost imperceptible twitch of his shoulders. "I think the word she used was *grounded*."

"So . . . we're taking relationship advice from Taylor now?"

"I didn't say I was *taking* her advice. It's just on my mind. I don't think I'm conveying what she said very well."

The GPS chooses that instant to direct us to turn in a quarter mile. So we have to make a decision, since our dining options at this late hour appear to be Sheetz (right turn) and McDonald's (left turn). We choose the latter, and are just about to pull into the driveway when Aaron spots a restaurant down the block that isn't closed. Once we get there, we discover only the pub is still open and it's karaoke night. A woman is doing a pretty decent version of "Before He Cheats" on the small stage.

Aaron pauses a few feet inside the entrance with his eyes closed. Anyone watching him would think he's already had a few drinks, but he's gauging the mood of the place. His ability and restaurants aren't always the best mix, and that goes double for bars. Tempers flare up much more quickly after some people have had a beer or two, and any violent thoughts floating around will make it hard to have a peaceful meal.

"The drive-through would be fine with me."

"No . . . I *think* we'll be okay," he says after a moment. "Angry drunks don't usually show up for karaoke night. So what song are you going to sing?"

I laugh. "If I sing, we *will* have to leave. Every person within earshot will have violent thoughts."

The restaurant has a rustic feel, with antiques inside and out, and architecture that relies heavily on exposed beams and brick. Our food is good—the best I've had in weeks—and the smattering of people taking to the stage are still in that brief karaoke golden zone where they're drunk enough to lose their inhibitions but sober enough to stay mostly on key. And even though I'm glad to be alone with Aaron, I can't help but think that Deo would love this. He'd be itching to get up there and belt out "It's Raining Men" or "I Wanna Dance with Somebody," assuming those are on the playlist. So far, it's been a steady stream of country.

I sneak a few sips of Aaron's drink but don't order anything for myself. The ID in my pocket would definitely hold up to scrutiny, and I've had a crazy enough year that no sane person would begrudge me a margarita or five. I'm not sure how alcohol would mix with the meds, however, so I stick with ginger ale.

Whatever was bugging Aaron earlier is still weighing on him, even though he's trying really hard to pretend that it's not. So when we finish eating, I begin to work us back toward the conversation we were having in the car. I'm only a few words in when the waitress shows up to see if we want anything else. Aaron looks relieved and asks for a dessert menu.

I order coffee and we split a gooey fudge-and-cheesecake concoction. After one bite, I'm wishing we'd ordered two.

"Distracting me with chocolate. Well played, Mr. Quinn. Well played."

"I wasn't really *trying* to distract you." Aaron stops, and a grin spreads across his face. "But it's really hard to have a serious discussion when you have a glob of chocolate . . . right there." He points toward my upper lip and reaches over to wipe it away just as I'm licking the spot to remove it. My tongue grazes the tip of his finger, and a shiver runs through me on contact. Through both of us, apparently, because his eyes lock onto mine and we're frozen in place until he leans across the table to kiss me.

I pull back after a moment, very reluctantly. The bar isn't crowded, but neither of us really like attracting attention, and we're beginning to do precisely that.

When the dessert plate is empty, Aaron asks, "Do you remember that night back at Sandalford? Maybe a month before we left to rescue Bree and the others? I was worried about moving too fast for you, and we decided to put you in control of . . . this part . . . of our relationship."

"I remember."

"Okay, well . . . I'm having second thoughts. Not about us!" he adds, in response to my expression. "No. God, no. Absolutely not. It's just . . . Taylor keeps saying we should . . ."

"Just do it already? She tells me that too—on pretty much a daily basis."

It's true. If I'm snippy because I haven't had my morning coffee, Taylor will say, *Jeez, why don't you guys just do it already?* Same thing if she sees us kissing or snuggling on the couch. *You two already have a room, why don't you just do it already?* Deo joked that he's going to buy

Taylor one of those Nike shirts with the *Just Do It* motto on the front so she can point and save her breath.

"Yeah," Aaron says. "That. She's picked up the pace with me the past few days, though. And it's kind of troubling, because there's this . . . I don't know. Frantic note, I guess? I even asked her if she's learned something from Stan or one of the other Fivers. If she thinks one of us is going to be hurt or killed. And she swore she hasn't, but then she told me to think about everything that's happened in the past six months, and about what could be coming up. Any of us could be killed, she says, at any moment, so why are we wasting what we have? At least, that's her point of view."

"And what's *your* point of view?"

"I told her that the vague possibility of imminent death didn't seem like a good reason to make major relationship decisions. And that she should get off my back. Off *your* back."

I'm quiet for a moment, debating whether to share what's on my mind. It's one of the hitcher secrets I've never told anyone else, not even Deo. It kind of feels like I'm breaking a confidence, but the owner of this memory is long past the point where it could bother her. And I don't think she'd mind me sharing her secret with Aaron.

"You remember Emily? My hitcher who liked crosswords?"

"Sure. She's the reason you can kick my ass so resoundingly in Scrabble."

"Well, not the only reason, but yes, that Emily. Anyway, she was a senior in high school when her boyfriend was drafted. It was already a few years into World War II, when young men were marching off to war and never coming back. Emily was always very prim and proper, but she loved Hiram and they planned to marry when the war was over anyway, so the night before he left . . ." I shrug and give him a little smile.

"Did he die?"

"Nope. He was one of the lucky ones. They drifted apart during the war, though. Emily went to college, and in his letters to her over the next two years, she realized Hiram wanted a much more traditional marriage. The kind where he brought home the bacon and she cooked it and fed it to five or six kids. She met and married someone else, eventually. So did Hiram. But the thing is . . . Emily never regretted making love to him. Not for a moment. It was the right decision at the time, and years later, it was still a cherished memory, even after she had children and grandchildren with another man who was very much the love of her life. I'm not saying that's true for everyone, or that it would be for us, because I don't know. But it was true for Emily."

We fall silent again, and then he says, "What worries me is that you've given some really mixed signals in the past few months. Hot and cold, and not much in between. I understand why now, but a few weeks ago, you made it pretty clear that things were moving too fast for you, even though they'd actually been moving in reverse for several months. That's when we went back to separate rooms, and . . . I guess I need to know how much of that was Cregg's decision and how much was yours."

Aaron wants me to say that it was all Cregg. I can read it in his eyes as plain as day. But that would be a lie, and this is too important to lie about. "It was a mix. I wanted you with me, but it was becoming difficult to hide my memory gaps when we shared a room. And most of all, I was worried that I might . . ."

Abbott's voice fills my head. *He told us he could've slit your boyfriend's throat in his sleep and you wouldn't have been able to stop him.*

I don't finish the sentence, but I'm sure Aaron can tell from my face exactly what I was worried might happen.

"Even though I'm less worried about that now, I'd be lying if I didn't admit that it's still a concern. Before, it was Daniel and Jaden and Hunter in my head. Hunter was clearly a roadblock, given his age. But now?" I lower my voice and lean forward, tapping my temple. "Now there's a monster in here. He's locked up tight right now, but he's *still* in my head. Do you really want to make love to a monster?"

"No. I don't. I want to make love to *you*. And if that's what you want too, then Cregg shouldn't even enter into the equation, other than—" Aaron stops, and he seems to be measuring his words. "He doesn't *own* you. Now that the medicine has kicked in, you are in control. You will never be his *vessel*, you will never be this Ophelia Duncan person. Your body is yours, and yours alone. At some point, hopefully soon, we will find a way to evict him, and I'm dead certain that hell has a spot waiting with his name etched in the brimstone. But until then, maybe we should stop letting the fact that his shriveled soul is stuck in your head control our lives."

The opening bars of the next song accompany his last words. It's louder and more raucous than the previous few numbers, and we've apparently moved beyond the sober karaoke window. The guy on stage now seems to know most of the opening and the chorus, but the verses are a mix of slurred words, punctuated by long glugs from the Michelob he's holding in one hand.

"Last call," the waitress says, almost yelling to be heard over the music. "Can I get y'all anything else?"

"No!" Aaron snaps. "Just leave the check." At first, I think he's frustrated by her interruption, but his eyes dart around the room. He's picked up something, maybe from the couple near the door who seem to be arguing.

The waitress gives Aaron a foul look, and once she locates our check in the pocket of her apron, she slaps it down on the table. He hands her a credit card, his eyes still fixed on the couple. A few seconds later he breathes a sigh and his shoulders relax. Whatever their disagreement was about, they seem to have decided to hug it out rather than fight.

He glances toward the bar, where the waitress is ringing up our check. "Is it an extra ten-percent or fifteen-percent tip to apologize for being a jackass?"

"Depends. Are you paying with your money or Magda's?"

The drunk on the stage has now reached the chorus again, and he's confessing that he likes his women on the trashy side. Aaron shakes his head and sighs. "Man, I really know how to pick the romantic spots."

When the waitress returns, he apologizes profusely. He overtips. And then he apologizes to her again on our way out.

As we stand in the doorway pulling on our coats, I realize that's what I love most about this man—his inexplicable kindness. Aaron has spent his entire life bombarded by the violent and angry thoughts of others, but he steadfastly refuses to let it shape him. Sure, he gets grumpy sometimes, but if he hurts someone with a harsh word, he apologizes. He makes a concerted effort not to do it again. Rather than follow the lead of the angry parade of voices in his head, Aaron chooses to be kind, understanding that kindness is a sign of strength, not of weakness.

A cold drizzle is falling as we head out into the night. We run for the car, and he opens the door for me, but before I get in, I pull him close for a kiss. "Do you think there's a hotel in this town?"

"Probably," he says. "But . . . we need to talk. I don't want to—"

"We can *talk* at the hotel." I smile as I tug the phone out of his back pocket and slide into the car. "Okay, Google, find me a hotel room."

Ten minutes later, we step inside a jacuzzi suite at a small hotel just down from the Walmart. The décor is a decade or more past its prime, but it beats the hell out of the back seat of Sam's Kia.

When Aaron's hand, still cool from the rain, brushes the skin of my back, I arch toward him.

We have every intention of warming up in a hot bath. We have every intention of talking, of making sure this is the right time, the right place, the right decision. That this is what we both want.

But there is no question in my mind that this is right. I am no one's vessel. This is *my* body. My decision.

Our intentions wind up in the same heap as our wet clothes.

Moorefield, West Virginia
April 26, 2020, 6:10 a.m.

A door slams, followed by footsteps and the sound of luggage rolling down the hall. Someone is getting an early start to their day. Aaron stirs restlessly, his arm tightening around my waist. I watch as his breathing deepens and he slides back into sleep.

He wanted me to sleep, too, and for a few minutes there, I thought it might be possible. But I'll rest more easily back at the cabin.

Staying awake is really only a precaution at this point. I'm less worried about Cregg taking control than I was even a day ago. My thoughts about sleep no longer make him happy or eager. With the exception of that brief flare-up last night, the meds are working well. The lightheaded feeling hits me less often, and I haven't sensed Cregg lurking at all since we stepped into this hotel room, something for which I will be eternally grateful.

Of course, he could be bluffing. Playing possum for a day or so to lull me into complacency. That's certainly what I'd do in his situation. Stay back. Let me get used to falling asleep and waking up in charge of my own body for a few days. Save up enough energy for one big push to shove me out of the driver's seat.

But I don't think so. If he was alert, if he was anywhere near the front, my reading material for the past few hours would have rattled him. It wasn't picked with that intent—in fact, I ignored his personal diary for that very reason. Instead, I focused on his virtual scrapbook, filled with scanned copies of news articles, correspondence, and even a few book excerpts dealing with the early era before Delphi became Delphi. Before it was even the Stargate Project.

At the beginning, it was a research project on parapsychology at the Stanford Research Institute in Menlo Park, known only by a series of random-sounding code names, like Grill Flame. And one of the participants in that very early stage of the research was Penelope Arnett Cregg, first wife of Ronald, mother of Graham.

I'd always assumed that Graham Cregg was first-generation Delphi. Someone who, like my father, became so caught up in the potential of this new drug that he couldn't resist testing it firsthand. Cregg probably *did* test the formula, maybe even multiple formulas, on himself. In fact, I'd be shocked if he didn't, based on what I know of his personality. But he's not first-gen. His mother was a guinea pig for a forerunner of the Delphi serum, years before Graham was born.

Penelope Arnett, whose family had amassed a fortune in the auto-parts industry, was in her fifth or sixth year of art school at UC Berkeley in 1973, in no hurry and under no pressure to complete her degree.

Two of the book excerpts written in the 1980s suggested that Penelope was having far too much fun *finding herself* to focus on either studying or creating art. One picture of Pen Arnett shows a willowy girl in cutoff shorts and a halter top. Her wide eyes stare straight at the camera, and her dark hair is little more than fuzz, a remnant of her brief flirtation with a cult where all members were required to shave their heads.

Members of the cult were also required to give up all forms of narcotics. That proved to be a stumbling block for Pen Arnett. By all accounts, she managed to steer clear of heroin but freely engaged in expanding her consciousness with anything else she could lay hands on.

Penelope's quest for the ultimate high was what eventually led her to Stanford's top-secret parapsychology project, known by the inexplicable name of Gondola Wish. A photographer friend of her father's, Hella Hammid, was working with the project as a remote viewer. This task involved sketching a location sent to Hammid mentally by one of the researchers. It's very similar to what Taylor does, except Taylor picks up vibes from objects, rather than from someone mentally projecting an idea.

According to one older book on the project, Hammid and Pen shared an apartment for several months in the summer of 1973, and several sources reported they were a couple. Pen became fascinated by the description of the aftereffects of remote viewing, as described by Hammid and a mutual friend, artist Ingo Swann, who also worked on Gondola Wish. Both of them claimed that whenever they succeeded in picking up a signal sent by one of the researchers, it was like the most perfect hit of LSD. They swore it gave them absolute clarity of mind.

Hammid and Swann were eventually able to convince researchers at SRI to test Penelope for the Gondola Wish project. And Penelope was a natural, showing even greater aptitude at remote viewing than Hammid or Swann.

As an aside, the author noted that Pen also showed far more ability than a young man named Ronald Cregg, who volunteered at the end of his two-year tour of duty in Vietnam. Cregg flunked out of the program after the first round of tests, showing no natural psychic talent at all. But he did manage to land a dinner date with Penelope Arnett.

More recent books and articles barely mention Arnett. One, however, focuses specifically on Arnett's involvement with the project. There's no date, but there's a reference to Senator Cregg's presidential campaign and the Delphi Project in the first paragraph, so it must have been written within the past year.

The byline reads: *Clayton Fulmer*—San Francisco Chronicle. I suspect it's a draft version of the final article, since there are a number of author notes in parentheses, including the names of two sources who are listed as confidential in the article itself.

Sunlight now streams in through a tiny gap in the curtains, something that I know from past experience will wake Aaron up. I try to extract myself carefully so that I can close them and maybe get a drink of water before I finish reading.

But Aaron pulls me back. He's no longer sleepy. And for the next half hour, I completely forget about Penelope Arnett Cregg, her husband, her son, and the entire Delphi Project.

Later, though, as we're driving back to the cabin, my mind strays back to the odd article. "Do journalists usually reveal confidential sources to their editors?"

"Sometimes. Woodward and Bernstein didn't in Watergate. Well, at least not in the movie version. Why?"

"Hold on. Let me check something."

I hunt for a few relatively unique consecutive words from the article. *Arnett's participation in Gondola Wish* should do it. I type the phrase in quotation marks, and google it. No hits. I try Penelope Arnett's name and the author's name. Again, no hits. I search for Penelope Arnett and Penelope Cregg on the *Chronicle* website. Nothing.

So . . . it's not only a draft but an unpublished draft. Yet somehow, Cregg had a copy.

Searching for Clayton Fulmer's name on the *Chronicle* site yields a fairly long list of stories with his byline. I also find an obituary, dated December 15, 2019. A hit-and-run accident.

I fill Aaron in on what I learned while he slept and then read the rest of Fulmer's article aloud. It gives a basic overview of Pen's involvement with the experiments at SRI, many of the details the same as what I just read. But his research goes beyond Gondola Wish to a second testing protocol that Pen was part of in 1974, after she moved out of the apartment she shared with Hella Hammid and into a relationship with Ronald Cregg. Pen's success with remote viewing exceeded that of most research subjects. Her ability wasn't perfect, but that was true for everyone in the program. There were far more misses than hits, and the government was urging the researchers to move faster, wanting more bang for their buck. Since Penelope was more accurate than most of the participants, she was recruited for a side project—a drug protocol, aimed at increasing accuracy.

Apparently, the drug didn't work, and the tests were abandoned. But Fulmer claims that it had unexpected repercussions. The article includes a link to a video interview with an elderly woman who was a college friend of Arnett's. Her voice and face are digitally altered, because she wanted to remain anonymous, but a note in parentheses gives her name as Judy Hersey, followed by the words *verified AC.*

In the video, Hersey states she was aware of Pen's involvement in research at SRI, but she didn't know the details. In late 1974, however, she attended several parties where Penelope dropped acid. That was far from unusual, not just for Pen, but for her circle of friends as a whole. What made the events stick out in Hersey's mind, though, was that most of the people at those parties ended up tripping, even the few like Hersey who hadn't taken anything.

They weren't good trips, either. At first, Hersey thought that someone had slipped her a tab without her knowing or that maybe it was a flashback. But it happened again. After comparing notes with others, Hersey realized that the common denominator was their proximity to Penelope Arnett.

Hersey hadn't really thought about the whole thing in years. But then she saw Ronald Cregg—the man Penelope had been dating—talking on the TV about those Delphi kids. She was surprised to learn they married. Hersey knew that Ron was verbally abusive, maybe even physically, although people didn't talk about those things so much back then. And Penelope retaliated in her own way, taking every opportunity to tease him about his lack of culture and refinement. "She would toss quotes from Schopenhauer to Shakespeare in every conversation," Hersey recalled, "and then say, 'Oh. *Sorry, Ronald.* That's from *The Merry Wives of Windsor.*' Of course, none of us knew the reference either. I think she memorized them just to annoy him."

Fulmer's article goes on to discuss Penelope Arnett's marriage to Ron Cregg in 1975, along with her decision to appear before the Church Committee later that same year. The Church Committee was named after Senator Frank Church, who led the investigation into MK-ULTRA and other CIA programs that operated outside legal boundaries, including experimentation on US citizens. Pen Arnett Cregg swore before Congress that there was, to the best of her knowledge, no drug experimentation involved in the SRI program, and described the entire project as a "boring art exercise." A photograph of her testimony shows a woman almost unrecognizable as the waifish girl with the ultrashort hair taken only a few years prior. Her hair is longer, puffed up in a style that probably required half a can of Aqua Net, and she wears a demure high-necked blouse with a bow at the neck.

Pen Arnett didn't look at all familiar to me in that first photograph taken in 1973. In this one, however, she kind of does. But I can't put my finger on where I've seen her.

Fulmer wraps up the article with the fact that Penelope committed suicide in 1989, and then summarizes Ron Cregg's involvement with Decathlon Services Group and his entry into politics in the late 1990s. He never exactly connects the dots, never claims that the elder Cregg somehow managed to get his hands on the formula from that original project back in the 1970s. But the implication is definitely there for those willing to read between the lines.

"Maybe that's why it was never published," Aaron says. "Maybe the paper needed more before they were willing to accuse a presidential candidate and his dead wife of stealing classified material."

"Or maybe nobody wanted to touch it after the author was sideswiped and left for dead. Either way, it's definitely something that we should add to the list of things to ask my father. Because he'd know whether he started from scratch or had a sample to jump-start his research."

"What about the not-so-confidential sources who were mentioned?" Aaron asks. "If they targeted the author . . ."

I can't locate the other of Clayton Fulmer's two sources online, but I do find Judith Hersey, who graduated from UC Berkeley in 1974. She managed an art gallery in San Francisco. And she died, in an apparent suicide, two days after Fulmer.

"We need to track down the other source," Aaron says as we turn off the road and onto the driveway leading uphill to the cabin. "It may not be easy, though. Given that the article was written in California, Fulmer's sources were probably local, and I don't think Sam or Porter have many contacts on the West Coast. And speaking of Sam . . ."

The RV is parked out front now, something Taylor conveniently failed to mention when Aaron texted her last night to say that we were going to stay in Moorefield.

Taylor meets us on the porch. "Sam's back."

"No kidding," Aaron says as he tosses her a plastic grocery bag.

Taylor looks at me and then shakes her head in amazement. "I can't *believe* you're blushing, Anna. You guys slept in the same bed for months. Sam, and everyone else on the freakin' planet, assumes that ship sailed long, long ago."

"Good to know," I say drolly, and push past her.

"What is all this stuff?" she asks, looking through the bag.

"Clothes, toothbrushes, and other items that we grabbed for Sophie and Pfeifer," Aaron says. "It will probably be safer if you deliver it, though."

Inside, Deo is already up and dressed. His backpack is propped against the side of his chair, and my heart sinks into my stomach.

"When are you leaving?"

"Probably around noon. Might be later. Sam and Daniel were up talking for a while. They didn't get to bed until three."

"Are you going back with them, Tay?" Aaron asks.

She shakes her head. "I can't go yet. I'm still digging through the data from Cregg's tablet, and . . . I have a bad feeling about taking some of that information near Magda's people, especially the formulas. Stan agrees. He says the paths are more stable if I stay here. If Maria needs someone to do remote viewing, Snoop—sorry, *Jeffrey*—can handle that.

But Deo's the only amp they've got. They could use you, too," she tells Aaron. "Your spidey sense is a lot stronger than the other kid's, maybe because he's only like eight or nine. He tends to get overwhelmed. Maria says they've got enough Fivers to predict movements without Anna, though, and Stan says the paths are more stable if you both stay here. So I guess you're off the hook."

I don't argue with her, mostly because I'm pretty sure it will do absolutely no good. Taylor is smart and she's usually fairly logical, but her conviction that Stan's paths are the key to every problem is becoming something akin to religious belief. Deo seems pretty well convinced, too, but I wonder how much of this is because he feels needed.

Taylor and Aaron start making breakfast while I put away the groceries. Apparently, we bought the wrong kind of orange juice and sausage. Breakfast will now suck, according to Taylor, and she gave us a list, so how did we still get everything wrong? I shove the rest of the food into the pantry and let Aaron deal with her. It's partly because I'm tired, but also because I know she's only bitching because she's upset about Deo leaving. And so am I.

Deo pushes my phone across the table. "This was in the RV. We conferred, and you are officially off telephone restrictions."

I smile. "Thank you, Master Deo."

He snorts and then frowns as he looks closer at me. "Did you sleep?"

"A bit."

"You rotten liar," he says softly. "Aaron slept and you stayed awake."

"I couldn't, okay? And you don't have to whisper. Aaron knows I didn't sleep. We agreed to give it a few more days sleeping in shifts. Just to be safe."

That reminds me that I'll be hanging with Taylor alone on my awake shift, since Deo will be at Sandalford. This is the first time that we've been willingly separated in nearly two years. It feels wrong. And even though I know that Kelsey will be there with him, it also feels dangerous.

"Are you sure you want to do this, D?"

"Do I want to? No. But I can't just stick my head in the sand and pretend everything will go back to normal somehow. We have to do what we can to fix it. Did you guys see the latest?"

I shake my head, not liking what I'm reading in his expression. "What happened?"

"A mob torched a boarding school in Florida around midnight. About fifty miles outside Jacksonville. It was for special-needs kids, and someone got it into their heads that *special needs* meant *special abilities*. The death toll was over forty last time we checked, including several police officers who were trying to put down the riot and even a few of the rioters after one of their own turned and opened fire on them. Most of it's on video, but . . ." He grimaces, and I decide that I really do not want to see that video.

"Senator Cregg won the primary in Florida by a comfortable margin," Taylor says as she shoves the plate of eggs onto the table. "That was over a month ago. I wrote out a list of questions for Pfeifer last night and slid them under the door so he could answer them. About formula and timelines, and so forth. He said once the local dealers have the formula for OA3, one of the two that they sold to the contact in Florida, it probably only takes a few days to mix up a batch, assuming they have a decent lab. That means it could have been on the market down there for three weeks."

"So those two-letter abbreviations—" Aaron begins.

"Are codes for the formulas each state was sold," Deo says. "Just as Anna thought. Pfeifer recognized most of them, although there are apparently a few new ones in the mix. Not too surprising, since they've had other scientists working on them since he was hospitalized."

"The OA class . . ." I say. "That's the temporary serum, isn't it? The one he called the on switch. That's the one the military was interested in the most back then. He said they were working on an off switch just before my mom was killed."

"But who would be crazy enough to inject something into their body that completely alters the way their brain—" He stops. "Oh. Addicts. People already injecting other rotten stuff into their body."

People looking for a new high.

People like Penelope Cregg.

CHAPTER TWENTY

Mathias, West Virginia
April 26, 2020, 5:31 p.m.

Aaron whispers. "Would you *take your turn?*"

"I think you're bluffing."

"Not bluffing, Daniel. They're both words."

"Then define them. Use them in a sentence."

"That's not how the game works. If you don't think it's a word, then challenge it. And when I'm right, *again*, you lose fifty points."

I rub my eyes and prop myself up on the pillow. The lamp is on the floor, and the two of them have turned the nightstand into a makeshift Scrabble table.

"No," I say. "Not fifty points. That's the bonus you get for playing all seven of your tiles. He'd just lose his turn."

"Way to go, man," Aaron says. "You woke her up."

"No, *you* woke her up. And I'm adding back the fifty points you made me deduct earlier."

"Fine," Aaron says. "But then you have to skip a turn for that challenge. And you have to decide whether you're going to challenge these two words."

Daniel snorts. "No. I'm not going to challenge your stupid teeny-tiny words. But look them up because there is no way both of those are real."

I peek over Aaron's shoulder. He's played an *x* to make *xu* and *xi*. "They're real words. Xi is a Greek letter. Xu is a coin. Japanese . . . no, Vietnamese. Is that on a triple-letter tile?"

"Yes, it is," Aaron says. "Fifty-two points."

"Sweet."

Daniel glares at the two of us. "Wait a minute. Vietnamese? You said no foreign words."

"Foreign currency is allowed," I explain. "And a few other exceptions."

Aaron already has the Scrabble dictionary open on his phone. "See? It's a valid Scrabble word. Vietnamese monetary unit. One one-hundredth of a dong."

"You're one one-hundredth of a dong," Daniel mutters as he jots Aaron's points down on the envelope they're using to tally the score. "Game's not over yet."

Aaron frowns, studying his tiles. I scooch over next to him and examine the board.

"Oh, no, you do not," Daniel says. "You are *not* helping him. Get out."

I stick my tongue out at him and tap two of Aaron's tiles. "You could play—"

"Out," Aaron echoes. "Move it. I can beat him on my own."

Daniel glares at him. "Only because your eighty-two-year-old ghost girlfriend taught you a bunch of fake foreign words."

I leave them to their game and head downstairs to the kitchen. It's dark, except for the light from the open fridge, which is blocked partly by a girl's silhouette. She's crouched down in search of something on the shelves.

"Your brothers," I begin as I flip on the light, "may be the most competitive . . . Oh. Sorry. I thought you were Taylor."

Sophie tosses lunch meat and cheese onto the wooden table, then turns back to the fridge to resume her hunt. "Taylor's sleeping. Where did the bread go?"

I pull out the loaf—the *second* loaf, apparently—from the pantry next to me, and hand it to her.

"Pfeifer's asleep, too," she says, adding mustard to the collection on the table. "In case you're wondering why I'm not on duty."

I *was* wondering that, but it seems rude to admit it. Sophie can't stay cooped up in that room with him indefinitely. The whole reason she came with us was because she wanted some place where people did more than house, feed, and exploit her. Where she could have a life.

"Is he doing . . . better? More under control?"

"He was under control last night until you—" Sophie stops, shaking her head. "This is crap mustard. Crap bread, too. But I need fuel."

She spackles a thin layer of the bright-yellow stuff onto four slices of butter wheat. She piles about half of the meat and cheese to form two sandwiches and then sinks her teeth into one as if she's starving.

"I don't really like neon-yellow mustard either." I fold a slice of cheese into bread and then hunt in the pantry for chips to give it a little crunch. "Let us know what you like to eat, and we can pick up different stuff next time we're out."

Her fierce expression gradually mellows, likely because she has food in her hands. Taylor's the same way when remote viewing. It appears to be a second-generation thing, and it only seems to hit some of the adepts. Peyton Hawkins can munch her way through an entire box of cookies if she spends a few minutes moving things around with her mind.

Sophie's wearing a pair of black leggings that I picked out and a matching shirt. It would be tunic length on me, but it hits at midhip on Sophie, who is nearly as tall as Aaron. In the direct light of the kitchen, I realize that she's also older than I thought. I'd initially figured her to be about my age, but she's probably in her midtwenties.

"Are the clothes okay? I bought stretchy stuff since I didn't know your size. We can get something different, though. Someone will have to go back into town for food again eventually." And by *eventually*, I mean *tomorrow*, if she keeps eating at this rate.

"They'll do. Some color would be nice, though. I look like a damn ninja."

"Sorry. I don't . . . shop. Maybe Taylor can go with us next time. How did you end up at The Warren?"

She doesn't answer for a moment. Possibly because her mouth is full, but she might also be weighing her response. Or whether to respond at all.

"Parents couldn't handle me. Wound up in a psych ward. Must have attracted someone's attention, because next thing I know, I'm being checked out in the middle of the night."

Sophie's story is a familiar one. It's basically the same thing that Jaden told me, but it doesn't entirely ring true coming from her. It takes a minute for me to realize why. How would a blocker be hard to handle? Or, for that matter, how would they attract attention from Cregg or anyone at Delphi? Before I can ask, though, she jumps in with a question of her own.

"Why did that other guy leave today? The one with the hair." She flips her hand up from her forehead, mimicking the quiff that Deo usually wears. "And how long are we staying . . . *here*?" She looks around the cabin dismissively.

I ignore the first question. It's not that I don't trust her—okay, yes, it *is* partly that I don't trust her. Like Daniel said earlier about Stan, I don't *know* Sophie. I don't know her motivations. She seemed a lot friendlier in my vision, and apparently, I *will* trust her eventually, but we aren't there yet.

"We'll stay here until we're sure that Pfeifer is stable. We don't want to endanger the entire group at Sandalford. But we'll find a way for you to get out a bit more. Let you take some extra break time."

"I'll be *taking* that break time," she says. "Whether you *let* me or not. That room is tinier than the one I was in back in Nevada. But I'm not buying your reason. You ask me, you're the bigger danger to all those kids than Pfeifer. He has Will, Oksana, and a bunch of the other Warren people inside of him. But you? You're carrying around the son of a bitch who had them all killed."

"He's not in control."

"So you say."

Because she doesn't trust me, either.

She doesn't trust any of us. And why should she? She doesn't know me any more than I know her.

Sophie tosses her napkin in the trash. "I should get back, in case he wakes." She nods toward my phone, which is charging on the kitchen counter. "And you should check that. You had a call earlier."

Hoping for privacy from any members of my father's menagerie who might be awake and tuning in, I trek out back. It's good to have my phone again and really good to hear Kelsey's voice when she answers, even though it sounds strained and nervous.

After twelve years of talking to each other at least two hours a week, we rarely wander into awkward silences. But after she asks me how I'm handling the risperidone and how I'm sleeping, an awkward silence is exactly where we find ourselves.

"This isn't working," she says. "I need to see your face to have this conversation. Skype?"

As soon as her face appears on the screen, I know she's right. Even though I can tell she's troubled, seeing her relaxes me. Her gray eyes have helped me weather every storm I've encountered since we met. She is my anchor.

"Deo should be at Sandalford within the next hour or two," I say before she begins talking. "Don't be too mad at him, okay? Please. He was only trying to help me."

Kelsey sighs. "I'm *not* mad at him. Not really. But don't tell him that. Since I'm now his legal guardian, I have to at least pretend to be angry. He opened my safe and took a controlled substance. That's not something I can officially condone, even if I know his heart was in the right place. I need to let him reflect for a while."

"So you're sitting him down in the corner and making him think about what he's done?"

She smiles gently. "Something like that. But when he and I actually do sit down to discuss all of this, to really talk it through, I'm the one who will be apologizing. He should never have been in a position where he was forced to make that kind of choice, and the blame for that is on me."

Then Kelsey's lower lip twitches, and she begins to cry. Not just a stray tear but actual sobs. I stare at the screen, totally dumbfounded. I've seen Kelsey's eyes grow misty on a few occasions, but I have never, ever seen her lose control.

"Sorry," she says through the tears. "Maybe Skype was a mistake. It's just . . . I broke your mug."

"You . . . what?" I know exactly what she said, but I need a moment to process it.

"Your mug! The one I bought you for Christmas that first year."

I struggle to keep my face as neutral as possible, with enough sad in the mix to let her know that the cup was important to me, but not enough to let her know exactly how much it hurts. And I definitely don't want to let her see anger, because I'm not mad at her. No, the anger is all for Cregg.

He was lurking when I entered Kelsey's office the other day, knowing that the sight of that mug, filled with coffee and waiting for me on her desk, made me feel loved. Made me feel wanted. I'd bet every other possession I own that Cregg left a nice little poison-pill suggestion in Kelsey's mind, knowing that breaking the mug would be one more way of breaking me down. Of hurting both of us.

Thinking back, he even tried to get *me* to break it. That surge of fury when I slammed the mug onto her desk, spilling coffee everywhere—it came out of nowhere. And why was I even angry about her bringing up Myron? It's not like we'd never talked about him before.

"I don't remember breaking it," Kelsey says. "But the handle was still in my hand, and the pieces were scattered all over the carpet, and . . ."

"I'm sorry it's broken. But . . . it's just a *thing*, Kelsey. It can be replaced."

Kelsey snatches a few tissues from the box she keeps on her desk for patients and takes a few deep breaths before she continues. "I'm so, so sorry—not only about the mug. You're right on that. I've already ordered you a new one, although it won't be exactly the same. But how could I have misread your situation so badly? I pulled out my notes last night, the ones from our sessions over the past few months, and it's all garbage. I remember writing those things, and at the time I truly thought it made perfect sense—my diagnosis, my comments, my treatment strategy. But now I look at it, and . . ." She sighs. "I let you down."

"No, Kelsey, you didn't. You understand *why* you can't remember, right?"

There's a very, very long pause, and I don't step in to fill it. I can't help thinking how strange it feels to have our roles reversed like this. Usually Kelsey is the one coaching me, trying to help me remember or admit something I'd rather bury.

"It was him," Kelsey says. "Cregg was . . . influencing me. Probably during the hypnosis sessions."

"Yes. And you weren't the only one. He used his ability on Aaron and Deo a few times, too. Taylor was the only one he didn't manipulate."

"Perhaps she should take my job. Now I'm wondering about the advice I've given to you and the other adepts in the past few weeks. How much of what I said and did was influenced by that monster?"

"I don't know," I admit. "But I doubt he had time or energy to drop suggestions about the other adepts. I think it's like it was with Daniel. He found it harder to use his ability when he wasn't in his own body."

"Well, I hope so," Kelsey says, and I hear a tiny note of panic in her voice. "Otherwise who knows what kind of damage he might have done. I should have realized, should have been more on top of the situation."

"Don't you think you're being a little hard on yourself? Cregg convinced you to accept a perfectly reasonable explanation for my symptoms. One you probably wanted to believe, because—"

"Because I love you. And because I didn't want to think about you having yet another monster in your head. But that's *exactly* where I failed you. You and Deo both. I let my feelings blind me."

"No. First, you wouldn't even be in the middle of all this if not for me. If anything, I owe you an apology. You should be enjoying your retirement at North Beach. Spending time with your grandchildren."

"Psh. As much as I would love a few days off to curl up with a good mystery or two, retirement would bore me silly. In the past few months, I've learned things about the possibilities of the human mind that my colleagues would happily trade a limb for. Maybe two. I love my grandchildren dearly, but they are all in college now. They have lives, and so do their parents. My family loves me, but they don't *need* me. These children do. They need someone to look out for their interests. I just hate that I let my feelings get in the way of doing that job responsibly."

"Cregg *used* your feelings, Kelsey. But I totally get what you're going through. It's hard not to blame yourself for things done with your own body, even if you weren't in control. If it helps at all, you *were* the one—at least indirectly—who started me on the medication. It wouldn't even have been in the cabinet for Deo to swipe if you hadn't, and I don't think Taylor would have had the nerve to give it to me on her own if you hadn't prescribed it before Cregg started interfering."

"Well, that's something, I guess."

"When did you realize that Cregg was . . . ?"

A long pause, and then she says, "Using me? I knew *something* was wrong after you left for DC. Given your memory gaps and the episode earlier that morning, I wouldn't have approved of your travel. I might not have been able to *stop* you if you were determined, but I certainly wouldn't have advocated it. And yet . . . I sort of remember being all for it when everyone was debating the trip in my office."

"Hey, at least you have a memory of that conversation. I don't recall any of it. One second I'm walking into your office *hoping* that you'll veto me leaving Sandalford. And the next thing I know, I'm halfway to Kitty Hawk. Anyway, maybe everything was for the best. I needed to be here. It's not just Pfeifer, Kelsey. He picked up my mom when she died. And now there are about a dozen other people in his head, too, and—" I stop and shake off the tension. "Let's just say this really is *not* the way I imagined finally meeting my parents."

I spend the next fifteen minutes or so filling her in on the actual circumstances of my mother's death, my weird conversation with my parents, and everything else that's happened in the past two days.

Well, *almost* everything. I don't bring up last night with Aaron. For one thing . . . I don't really want to share it yet, even with Kelsey. But I also think Taylor may be right. Everyone we know probably assumes that it happened long ago, maybe even before I picked up Cregg.

Thinking about *why* it didn't happen months ago reminds me of Hunter and Daniel's theory about his abrupt departure. I try to come up with a subtle way to broach the subject, since Bree Bieler, like all of the adepts at Sandalford, is Kelsey's patient. But in the end, I just blurt out the question.

"Did Hunter move into Bree's head when he left? Is that why I don't have his memories?"

Kelsey doesn't respond, but I can tell.

I smile. "I'm glad. When Daniel told me he thought Hunter left, I was worried his spirit was still in that airport hangar. At least this way he had time to really tell her good-bye."

Again, she doesn't say anything, but her expression speaks volumes.

"He hasn't moved on? I thought the thing holding him here was needing closure with Bree."

Kelsey takes a deep breath, and then the words come spilling out. "Okay, fine. I was thinking about having you talk to Bree eventually anyway. To try and explain, as best you can, why it would be good for Hunter to move on. Honestly, I don't think she has any intention of him *ever* leaving. She said she won't let him die again. And I have no way of knowing whether this is what Hunter wants or not, just as I have no way of knowing whether it's what Cla . . . ra . . ."

She stops, realizing she's said too much and probably hoping I don't make the connection. But I do. That explains why one of Magda's daughters—Clara, apparently—is in a wheelchair. The twins prefer riding together in one body.

"That's in confidence, Anna. I shouldn't have let it slip. But maybe it will help you understand Magda's concern. The woman makes me crazy on a regular basis, but it must be devastating to watch your child wither away like that."

"Willingly? I mean, Clara *wants* this?"

"Chloe says she does. Just as Bree says that Hunter is happy. But . . . you can understand now why Magda is so desperate for a cure."

"There isn't going to be a cure for second-gen adepts, though. Pfeifer says it's simply impossible to do more than treat symptoms, given the way our brains developed. Magda needs to know that eventually, but . . . you can't tell her he's here, Kelsey. Not yet. I hate to ask you to keep things from her, but—"

"Oh, don't worry about *that*. I have to keep a lot of things from Magda. It's an occupational hazard. But . . . are you sure you're safe there, Anna? Even with these so-called Furies your father picked up?"

"I think so. We've reached a truce, apparently due to my mother's influence. They're not happy that Cregg is inside my head. For obvious reasons, he terrifies them. But they seem to understand he's not an invited guest, and they've assured me they'll behave as long as I can, as they put it, keep my spider in his cage."

Kelsey frowns. "Your . . . spider?"

"Cregg's . . . avatar? That's how my warped mind has decided to visualize him. And it's a spider-rat, technically. With tiny hands on the end of the legs instead of claws. Minus their pinkies, of course."

Her face grows pale and morphs into an expression that I've seen only a few times before. Grim but hesitant, like her foot is hovering above glass shards and there's no way to avoid that next step. She's about to broach a topic that she knows will upset me.

"The human hands are a new addition. But the spider-rat . . ." She pauses, waiting to see if I'll remember on my own.

My stomach clenches. I don't exactly *remember*, but I can certainly guess. "Is that how I saw Myron?"

"Not exactly," Kelsey says. "But it *is* the imagery that Myron used to control you. To keep you at the back when he wanted to take over. He would taunt you with things he knew you feared. He told you he knew a place where a giant spider lived, bigger than the rats in the downtown sewers. And he threatened to feed you to the spider if you fought him. That's a pretty effective threat against a five-year-old, especially when you already knew he had killed before."

"So you actually *were* partially right about the Myron memories. I'm finally working through them to some extent. You remember the dream I used to have, the one about the homeless woman?"

There's a long pause, and the walking-on-glass expression is back. It's almost like a flinch now, but she pushes on.

"You mean *memory* of the homeless woman, right? The memory you blocked but sometimes dreamed about." It's a gentle correction, but I can tell that she wants me to acknowledge the difference. To admit that I know it was my foot, even if I wasn't controlling it. Even though the thought that any part of me could have participated in something so evil makes me want to gnaw off that foot and fling it as far away from me as possible.

"Yes. The *memory*. I've been dreaming about it again. But there's something new. Do you know if there's anything else I may have blocked dealing with Myron? Something about a woman who died from a fall?"

There's a faint, almost imperceptible scratch along my wall, like a branch scraping at a window. Cregg. It's the first I've heard from him in about eighteen hours, and even though I barely feel it, it unnerves me. But I don't have time to harp on it, because in that instant, something finally clicks into place.

The reason the woman in the photo I saw earlier seemed vaguely familiar is because I *have* seen her before. Not in person—she died years before I was born. But I'm reasonably sure now that the recurring nightmare about the woman on the patio isn't just a dream. It's also Graham Cregg's memory of the day his mother committed suicide.

Kelsey is watching me. "I don't remember you talking about anything like that. But judging from your expression, you've just had an epiphany."

"Maybe. I need to check before I can be sure. I'll call you back later, okay? Either tonight or—"

"Okay, but wait. Before you go, there's another reason I called. Magda and Miller arrived earlier today with seven new adepts."

"Wow. That's a large group of stragglers. Aaron was saying on the drive up to DC that he thought something was going on when Magda went with Miller herself, instead of sending a team like she usually does. Taylor and Deo were even joking that it was a lovers' getaway."

Kelsey wrinkles her nose at the last comment. "I would hope even Magda has better taste. But yes, I'd wondered that too. She usually doesn't leave Chloe and Clara. But she said she went because this trip required negotiation skills, something that's not exactly Miller's strong suit. And when she got back today, I realized what she meant. These adepts weren't stragglers. They were in Nevada with Senator Cregg."

A cold chill runs down my back as I remember Graham Cregg's words just before he died. *You and I have a common goal and a common enemy. Magda Bell will turn on you in an instant if it is in her interest to do so.*

Taking in these new adepts doesn't necessarily mean that she's turned. It's definitely not a good sign, though.

"It's mostly siblings who were separated when The Warren was destroyed," Kelsey continues. "Magda said the exchange was a goodwill gesture on the part of the Senator."

"Wait. *Exchange*? And earlier, you said *negotiation*. Those words imply some sort of quid pro quo. What is Magda getting in return?"

"I have no idea."

"And why would Magda negotiate with the Senator at all? Why would she trust him?"

"According to her, we've misunderstood the Senator's motives. I'm paraphrasing here, but she claims he really has the best interests of the adepts at heart. The public comments he's made, and all the fearmongering—it's just grandstanding, the kind of thing all politicians do during a campaign. He's convinced her he had nothing to do the WOCAN terror attacks or the various murders. All of that was put into motion by Graham Cregg before his death, and the Senator is merely endeavoring to undo some of the harm his son caused. And she claims he'll be in a much better position to help the adepts if he wins . . . Anna? Are you okay?"

Cregg is raging now. I sense this, sense his anger, even though what makes it through the wall is little more than a thin wail. "I have to go," I say, hopping off the table to head back toward the cabin. "I need to tell the others so that we can figure out a plan."

"A plan for what? Anna, if Magda has decided to cooperate with the Senator, what can we do? I mean, Deo and I *could* leave Sandalford, but I'm not willing to abandon the other children like that. Yes, I know all about the training that Maria has them doing, but they're kids. They're no match for Magda's security, let alone whatever forces Senator Cregg might bring into the picture."

"Do Maria and Stan know about Magda?" As soon as the words leave my mouth, I realize that's a stupid question. Of course Maria knows.

"Maria does, at any rate. She stopped by right after I finished talking to Magda. But she's not upset. She seemed happy, and said that this is all part of the bigger picture. That the paths are aligning, whatever that means. Of course, I'm not surprised that she's happy, since her friend Pavla is part of the transfer."

Pavla. I picture her in my mind, sitting with Maria in the cafeteria at The Warren, leaning so close to Maria that their heads nearly touch. Giggling over their ongoing game of peeking at the other adepts in the shower. Pavla is telekinetic—I'm not sure what else she can do, but she's the one who left a message in the fog on my bathroom mirror. *Peekaboo. Welcome to The Warren.*

"I thought you said the exchange was sibling reunions?"

"It is, for the most part. I believe Pavla was the exception."

"What about Stan's brother? His name is Harv. Is he there, too?"

"Yes," Kelsey says. "Why?"

"I'll call you back." I pick up my pace. "I'm a little bit worried we've been played. Don't—" I stop, realizing what I was about to say is pointless.

"Don't what?"

"I was going to ask you not to tell Maria what I just said, but never mind. You can't hide anything from her. And . . . I could be wrong. I really, really hope so."

Aaron is in the kitchen pouring himself a bowl of Cheerios when I burst through the door. "You okay?"

"Not so much. Where's Daniel?"

"In his room," Taylor says.

"Go get him, okay?"

She frowns, but tosses her iPad aside and does as I asked. I take a bottle of water from the fridge and tip it back. There's no point starting until everyone is here. I'd just have to repeat myself.

As Taylor comes back into the room, her phone buzzes. "You are wrong."

Daniel follows her, yawning and a bit grumpy about being awakened. "Wrong about what?"

"No clue," Taylor says. "I'm just reading the text. 'You are wrong.'"

"Well, that was fast. It's from Maria, right? Is that all she wrote?"

Taylor gives me a quizzical look. "It's from Stan, actually. Maria doesn't have a phone, so I guess—" The phone buzzes again, and she shoves it toward me after reading. "Yeah. It's from Maria."

Yes we know about it but we do not PLAY you. So you are WRONG. This is still the paths.

"What the hell does that even mean?" Daniel asks when I read it aloud.

"Maria should have Stan translate before she hits send," Taylor says. "Please tell me she's not getting information from Jeffrey."

"You mean Snoop?" Daniel asks.

"I mean Jeffrey," Taylor says. "Deo told me he hates that name. He's the only one we know who has this kind of range without Deo there to boost the signal. Jeffrey said he was done spying on other adepts, though. He kind of . . . promised."

I hand the phone back to Taylor and sink down onto the sofa. "It wasn't Jeffrey. Maria picked up on something I told Kelsey. And if she got it that quickly, she must have been monitoring our entire conversation."

That pisses me off. Not so much that Maria listened in on our discussion about Magda and the new arrivals, or even that she overheard me questioning whether her motives and Stan's might be suspect. Any of that I'd say to her face. But the first part of that conversation was private. Kelsey was upset, and . . .

I shake it off and focus on relaying the information about the new arrivals and Magda's arrangement with Senator Cregg. "The real question," I say when I reach the end, "is exactly what the Senator is getting from Magda in return. Because I'm not buying the whole goodwill angle."

"Neither am I," Daniel says. "I've said from the beginning that, as soon as Magda's interests diverged from ours, she wouldn't hesitate to make whatever kind of deal she thought was best for her daughters. I'm not saying that makes her a horrible person, but . . . Magda has her priorities, and I don't think they necessarily sync up with ours."

"Cregg said the same thing. *Graham* Cregg," I clarify. "At the airport just before Jasper shot him. And he's emphasized it repeatedly."

"Oh, big whoop," Taylor says. "Did any of us ever really trust Magda? I know I didn't. But Maria? I trusted Maria. I trusted Stan. And . . . I still do. Even though I'll admit that all of this paths-aligning stuff is a little wack, we know where their interests lie."

Aaron agrees, although his expression suggests that he's a bit more on the fence. Daniel, the perpetual skeptic, isn't convinced. And for once, I think he's got a point.

"It's not that I *dis*trust them," I say, "but . . . just to play devil's advocate, Maria and Pavla seemed pretty happy at The Warren. I got the sense that Stan and his brother were, too. Jaden was happy, more or less—at least until the older adepts he was friends with started disappearing. Sure, he missed his parents and he wished he could let them know he was okay, but he said it was the first time he'd ever felt that he wasn't a freak. Knowing there were others like him, in a place where people believed he had visions—where they didn't assume he was crazy? That was a really big deal for him. Half of the kids at Sandalford, maybe more, don't even have families. And whatever we may think about Magda, she's no Graham Cregg. She's not killing the adepts. If they were reasonably happy at The Warren—underground and subject to Cregg's research agenda—how much happier do you think they are in an oceanfront mansion?"

"So what exactly is your point?" Taylor asks. "Maria made it clear she doesn't want a cure. Many of the others don't either. Do you think they're all lying?"

"No. But I *do* think some of them might be willing to use their abilities in exchange for living at Sandalford."

A look that I can't exactly decipher passes over her face, and I raise an eyebrow.

"Some of them already are," she says. "Well, *one* of them, at least."

"And you didn't think this was something we should all know?" Aaron asks.

She gives him a pleading look. "This was in confidence, okay? Deo wasn't even supposed to tell *me*. Jeffrey asked Deo to give him a boost for a task Magda assigned to him. He was having trouble making a connection. Deo agreed, but he had second thoughts after it was too late, wondering exactly what it was he'd helped him do. It was financial information, something to do with the stock market. But Deo said he really couldn't be mad at him, because Jeffrey was upfront about it. D has been boosting the adepts during training for months, and he can't usually tell what they're doing. Jeffrey could have lied, and . . . Deo wouldn't have known. And the only reason Jeffrey was doing it was because Magda told him she needed cash to expand, so she could help more adepts."

"Well, that does explain a few things," Aaron says. "One day Magda's bitching about how Sandalford is draining her dry and the next she's buying half an island to house Caleb without a single complaint."

"It's a pretty pathetic island," Taylor says. "I doubt it cost half as much as the beachfront lots she bought. But . . . yeah. She stopped muttering about expenses right after that."

"Do you think Jeffrey is still giving her stock tips?" I ask.

Taylor shrugs. "His gift is a bit like mine. If he doesn't have some sort of personal item from the target, he can't read them. He hasn't asked to use Deo's amp ability again, though. Deo said Jeffrey could tell that it bothered him. But sure, I guess he could still be getting tips from the same—"

A loud scream comes from down the hallway. Sophie.

Aaron and I are closest. I reach the door a split second before he does and twist the knob. It's locked, so I pound on the door. "Sophie? Open up!"

There are more sounds of scuffling, followed by a thwack and then what I'm pretty sure is the sound of a body hitting the floor.

"Sophie!"

"Step back," Aaron says. "I'll kick it open."

Before he can even try, the doorknob turns. Sophie stands there, her dark eyes wide. "He attacked me," she says, clutching Aaron's arm. "I was trying to get away, and then he just . . . passed out."

My father is sprawled facedown, his upper body draped over the collapsed gurney that's wedged between the beds. One of his legs twitches a few times, as though he wants to get up, but then stops.

I push past Aaron and Sophie, kicking aside a shattered floor lamp, and crouch down next to Pfeifer. The area above his left eyebrow is already starting to swell. It's the same spot as the bruise in my vision.

"Did he hit his head?"

Sophie nods. "On the nightstand." She's still clutching Aaron like he's a life raft. I know she's frightened, and it seems petty to be jealous. But it bothers me.

Aaron calls out for someone to get some ice while I check Pfeifer's breathing. It's even and steady, but a thin stream of blood is running down his arm toward his elbow.

"He's bleeding," I say.

"I must have scratched him. When I was trying to get away."

Something under the bed catches my eye. I stretch my arm out, trying to grab it, but it's a few inches out of reach.

I can see it now, however. It's a syringe. And that mark on my father's arm looks a lot more like a puncture than a scratch.

Sophie's not holding on to Aaron because she's frightened.

She's *blocking* him.

CHAPTER
TWENTY-ONE

Mathias, West Virginia
April 26, 2020, 7:28 p.m.

I yell out a warning to Aaron, but my words are swallowed by the sound of breaking glass. Not just a single explosion but a rapid-fire cascade. It sounds like every window in the house is shattering, except for this one. Taylor screams, and I hear a burst of gunfire as I push to my feet.

Sophie shoves Aaron straight at me, knocking both of us off-balance, and then sprints off toward the living room, slamming the bedroom door behind her. "It's me, Dacia!" Sophie yells. "Hold your fire!"

Dacia. And she's clearly not alone. There's a lot of noise outside the cabin. People moving around, and now I hear an engine. Maybe two.

Aaron draws his pistol. "Stay here. Lock the door."

Normally, I might argue about staying put. But I'm unarmed. I don't even have my pepper spray. And my father is unconscious. I can't leave him here alone.

I scan the room for something, anything, to use as a weapon. The floor lamp is the only candidate. It's pathetic, but it's better than nothing, so I grip the lamp pole and move toward the door.

They're going to be okay.

I was reasonably sure of this in the vision, and now I have a decent idea of how far into the future that vision goes. It has to be long enough for the red bump that's rising right above my father's eye to turn from red to blue. So at least a day, maybe two.

Taylor's okay and Aaron's okay. Daniel's okay. Deo and Kelsey, too. Or at least I'll believe they're all okay in the vision.

I *want* to believe all of this. Jaden's visions have never failed. But Sophie was there, in the vision. With me and my father, calling for us to hurry. And yet she has just handed us over to Dacia Badea. These two things do not mesh.

I hear voices in the distance, but I can't make out what's being said. One of the voices is Aaron's, though. I also hear crying. Not an adult. It's higher pitched, interspersed with a sound like *muhmuhmuh.* And that noise is coming closer.

Two sharp raps on the bedroom door. I jump back, nearly dropping the lamp.

"Open the door, Anna." It's Dacia. Her voice is lilting, almost like she's singing, and it still carries strong traces of her native Romanian. When I don't answer, she laughs.

The baby continues crying, calling for her mama.

"Shhshhshh," Dacia says. "You see *mami* soon. Who do I tell my people to kill first, Anna? I think maybe your little redhead *dívka,* then we watch her brothers—"

She pauses when she hears the door lock release. "I did not say unlock. *Open.* And if you have weapon when you open, someone will die. Maybe you, maybe me too if you have gun. Maybe this little one. But *definitely* your friends will die."

I drop the lamp onto one of the beds and open the door.

The Dacia Badea who occasionally visits my nightmares towers over me, but the real-life version is about my height. I glance down and realize that she's traded in the stilettos she was wearing before for a slightly more sensible heel. Her ice-blue eyes are unchanged. They stare back at me with a barely repressed fury.

Dacia is cultivating a punk dominatrix Barbie look these days—all black leather, including her trademark glove. But the baby she has gripped awkwardly against her chest totally wrecks the vibe. The little girl is about a year old, maybe a little older, wearing footie pajamas, pink with white hearts. She shares Sophie's dark skin and eyes, and it would be obvious that she was Sophie's daughter, even if she weren't crying for her mother and trying to wriggle out of Dacia's grasp.

I've been interrogated twice by Dacia. Both times she grabbed my arm and I felt a popping sensation across my forehead as she scanned my mind for information.

She doesn't grab my arm today. Maybe because she has her hands full with the crying baby, but I think she's also scared. If she scanned my mind today, she might get a response from Graham Cregg, and that's not something she's willing to risk.

Miller stands a few steps behind her in his uniform. Gray, with a red arm patch that reads *Vigilance Security*. And he's holding a very familiar-looking mask in his hand.

Well, if I had any doubt about what Magda traded, I know now. She traded *us*.

They'll be okay.

I have just enough time to wonder if it will be the vanilla-scented mask or the orange. And then the guard grabs me and forces the mask over my face.

Vanilla.

335

Bwap-bwap-bwap-bwap.

I open my eyes slowly, disoriented both by the sound and shuddering of the seat I'm strapped into. My head is heavy, too heavy to hold upright. As my eyes close again, I hear a whimper. It reminds me of the noise Ein makes when he's dreaming. My head lolls to the left, and I feel a brush of fabric beneath my cheek. A hard, unwelcoming shoulder pushes me away. I reposition toward the wall, and bump the knee of someone across from me as I slide back under the fog.

Bwap-bwap-bwap-bwap.

They'll be okay.

That thought—or really the memory of *having* that thought, with Dacia standing there in front of me at the cabin—pulls me toward consciousness again.

It's dark. Not pitch dark, though. There are tiny lights along the floor. Enough for me to make out Sophie, sitting in the center of the row of seats facing me. She's no longer gripping my father's arm, but he's unconscious and likely to stay that way, judging from the IV tube in his arm. In her lap is the baby Dacia was holding.

To Sophie's left, directly in front of me, is Daniel. He's unconscious, too. No IV, but his hands are bound with one of those plastic tie cuffs. Miller is sitting next to me.

A few stars dot the night sky, visible through the windows. I thought we were in a plane at first, but the whirring sound suggests a helicopter. Not as big as the ones we saw that night at The Warren. This sound is different, smoother. The interior is drab and functional, though. I would have expected any vehicle Ronald Cregg owned to be a bit flashier.

"Is that your daughter?" I ask Sophie.

Miller jabs his elbow into my side. "Boss said no talking."

"When you say *boss*, do you mean Magda or Dacia? And where *is* Dacia?"

"No. Talking," he repeats, tapping his sidearm. I'm oddly relieved to see that it's an actual gun, not a taser. He's not going to fire that inside a helicopter. Also, if we were expendable, we wouldn't be here. So his guidelines are the same as the Fudds' back at The Warren—he's not allowed to kill us.

I look back at Sophie. She glances down at the little girl, who's half asleep now. Then she looks back at me and gives a wordless nod.

As much as I want to blame Sophie for turning us over to the Senator's crew, I can't. Dacia was holding her child as a hostage. And Dacia is perfectly willing to kill kids, something Sophie almost certainly knew. I *am* a little curious about how Sophie managed to get word to them, however, and also where exactly she was hiding the syringe that she used on my father. Taylor and I had searched her. It wasn't a strip search—neither of us could quite bring ourselves to invade her privacy to *that* extent—but it was a serious TSA-style pat down.

I'm guessing the fact that I'm currently housing Graham Cregg, the man who no doubt pulled Sophie into all of this, may have played a role in her decision as well. Was she pregnant when she came to The Warren? I flash back to my mercifully brief encounter with Lucas, and comments that Maria made about the other girls who hadn't been lucky enough to escape him. Was Sophie one of those girls?

Sophie really isn't the one who's to blame for us being here, anyway. That distinction belongs to Magda. What I really want to know is how long Magda has been colluding with Senator Cregg. Because I don't believe for a moment that she was only interested in helping to reunify divided siblings. That's too Hallmark Movie to jibe with my knowledge of Magda. The only siblings she's *that* interested in are her daughters.

Cregg must have promised Magda the cure she's so desperate to find. Or what she thinks is a cure. Is it a drug to manage their symptoms, like the one my father was working on? Or is it pure snake oil, packaged up by Senator Cregg, who knew she'd take the bait?

"Where are we going?"

Miller backhands me, his arm jerking toward my face so quickly that I don't have time to dodge. His knuckle catches me square on the mouth, splitting my lower lip.

"What did I say, freak? No talking." He doesn't exactly smile as he speaks, but I can read in his eyes exactly how much pleasure that gave him. He's been wanting to hit me since the day he first arrived at Sandalford.

I wipe my mouth with the back of my hand. It comes away bloody, and I glare at him. At some point, he will regret that. Two can play payback.

Thankfully, the little girl is asleep, but Sophie clutches her a bit tighter, keeping her daughter's face turned away from Miller. Her mouth is set in a firm line. I don't think she likes me much, although it could just be that she hates my hitcher. But she also didn't like Miller hitting me.

The baby wakes up about twenty minutes later. Her complaints become a full-fledged cry, and Daniel begins to stir, too. Sophie looks over at Miller.

"Her dinner time is usually seven. Do you know if Dacia fed her?"

"No clue."

"That was nearly three hours ago. She's probably starving. When will we land in Knoxville?"

I send Sophie a silent *thank-you*. She managed to answer my question and also give me an approximate idea of how long I was out.

Miller realizes this, too, because he shoots her an annoyed look. *"No clue,"* he repeats and then nods toward Daniel. "Are you sure he's neutralized? Blocked or whatever you call it?"

She taps her knee against Daniel's, and I realize that her left ankle is bound to his right with one of the plastic cuffs. "As long as I'm touching him, as long as I'm anywhere close to him, he's blocked. That's how it works."

Miller curls his upper lip, and you can practically see the word *freak* written on his face. He keeps that opinion to himself, though, possibly because he considers Sophie a *useful* freak. Sophie rocks her little girl back and forth, and the crying tapers off to a few hiccupping sobs as she falls back asleep. Daniel seems to have drifted off again, too. Eventually, Miller's shoulders relax and he resumes staring out the window so that he doesn't have to look at the cabin full of freaks.

Sophie wasn't telling him the truth, though. In the lab at The Warren the other night, after the Furies killed Whistler and Davis, she told Daniel she wasn't *trying* to protect them. That they basically deserved what they got and she didn't intervene. That's the opposite of how Maggie's blocking ability works. She's an instant null-zone, blocking any psychic waves within her radius unless she turns the ability off. Maggie even blocks when she's asleep. But it takes a concerted effort for Sophie to block my father and Daniel. She has to want to block them.

Daniel's foot twitches against mine. Four small taps, then two more. And again—four twitches, then two.

Hi. Or, technically, *hi hi*, but he had to repeat it before I recognized the pattern as Morse code.

I repeat the message back and risk a quick glance at his face. His eyes are still closed, but he's making the OK sign with his right thumb and forefinger.

Is he saying he's okay? Asking if I'm okay? Or trying to tell me that the others are okay?

The tapping starts again, but I press Daniel's foot against the wall to stop him. I recognized the SOS sign he made a few months back at the hospital, and I figured out his two-letter message just now, but that was mostly a matter of deduction. Anything more complex would require me to dig around in Abner's memory files, and those are behind the wall with Cregg.

I watch his face from the corner of my eye. He mouths two words: "They're okay."

And then he "wakes up" officially, stretching, asking where the hell he is. It's a pantomime, clearly for Miller's benefit. Daniel looks at me for the first time with his eyes fully open, and his jaw tightens. "What happened to your mouth?"

"Same thing that's gonna happen to yours if you don't stop talking," Miller says.

Daniel's hands curl into fists, and Miller looks nervously at Sophie.

"Hey, I only block psychic ability. If you're worried he might get physical, you're on your own."

"I'm not worried." But Miller's hand moves toward his pistol.

In the distance, I see the lights of a city. We've passed over little pockets of light on and off since I woke up, but this is more of a widespread glow. I'm just thinking it might be Knoxville when Miller jerks suddenly, grabbing his right leg. He sucks air in through his teeth as he frantically massages his calf.

"Which one of you freaks is doing this?"

Sophie huffs. "Just *breathe*. It's a leg cramp. You've been sitting in tight quarters for nearly three hours."

Miller's eyes are squeezed shut, so he misses both the warning look she gives Daniel and the tiny quirk of a smile Daniel wears as he stares at Miller's contortions.

A man's voice comes from the cockpit. "You okay back there, Miller?"

"Yeah," he says through clenched teeth. "Just a leg cramp."

There's a privacy panel between the cockpit and the cabin, so I can't tell if the man who spoke is the pilot or a passenger.

"Speak up if you need assistance."

"10-4," Miller says.

Daniel snorts at Miller's cop code, and mutters under his breath, "10-96 says 10-4."

I'd love to ask what 10-96 means, but Daniel turns to stare out the window. And as soon as he does, Miller relaxes. He's still flexing the leg, but it's clear the pain is gone. He gives us all a threatening look, at least partly because he doesn't like that we saw him in a moment of weakness.

This city we're approaching is a lot like any other city at night. The only distinctive thing about the skyline is something that looks a bit like a giant lollipop—a butterscotch-flavored Dum Dum that towers over most of the other buildings. I'm guessing it isn't Knoxville, since we don't slow down at all.

A fine, misty rain begins to fall as the buildings thin out, and the copter veers off into the mountains. About twenty minutes later, we descend. At first, it looks like there's nowhere to land—mountains surround us on all sides. But then the lights pick up an area shaped like an arrowhead that appears to have been carved out of the mountainside.

A cluster of buildings sits at one end. Most are your typical rectangle. One is a cloverleaf shape, and the main building is shaped like an inverted cross. As we drop lower, a high wall topped with razor-wire comes into view.

The chopper lands in the clearing between the cloverleaf and the main building, and Miller turns to me. "Hands out."

I hold my wrists out in front of me, side by side. He grabs them and twists so that the insides touch, then fits me with my own plastic cuffs.

When he motions for Sophie to do the same, she glances down at the baby. "Her diaper is wet and leaking. You want to carry her?"

Miller wrinkles his nose in disgust. "Fine. Keep one arm free." Once he cuts the tie binding their ankles, Miller grabs Daniel, shoving his hands into a loop. Then he slides the other end over Sophie's hand and yanks it tight.

The rotors gradually wind down, and after a moment, someone opens the door. He's middle-aged, average height and weight, about as nondescript as they come. The only distinguishing feature is his nose, which is hawkish and looks like it's been broken. He's dressed in military camos, rather than the gray Vigilance Security uniform that I expected. In the Navy, the eagle on his collar would mean he's a captain, but I'm not sure if it's the same across all branches. The name tag reads *Smith*. As he moves aside to let me disembark, he glances at my lip, which is now swollen to at least twice its normal size, and then at Miller, but his expression doesn't change.

The exterior of the helicopter is as drab as the inside, painted a flat gray-green. Lettering on the long, thin tail reads: *US Army*. Not good. Yes, this all began as a military project, but to the best of my knowledge, the military hasn't been directly involved in any actions against the Delphi adepts. If they're now working with Cregg and Dacia, we are so screwed.

Sophie and Daniel have a harder time getting out, since their wrists are hobbled together. She also has to balance the baby, who is now screaming at waking up to the wind and rain. Miller doesn't bother to help, and Smith has disappeared around the side of the helicopter to assist a man who's trying to maneuver my father into a wheelchair.

Miller uses his pistol to herd us toward the main building. I walk a few steps behind Daniel and Sophie, holding up my cinched hands as best I can to ward off the icy needles of rain. As we approach the door, Daniel looks back over his shoulder. "Walls up, Anna. As tight as you can."

I don't think Miller was able to hear what he said, but he *did* pick up the fact that Daniel said something. That earns Daniel a shove in the back, which nearly causes all three of them—Daniel, Sophie, and the baby—to fall.

Daniel's warning wasn't really necessary. I was already quite sure that this is, or at least used to be, a prison. And the very last thing we need is for me or my father to take on any additional hitchers while we're here.

CHAPTER
TWENTY-TWO

Brushy Mountain State Penitentiary
April 26, 2020

Daniel, Sophie, and I press close to the side of the building and wait for Smith and the other man, who I presume is the pilot. It's slow going for them, since the ground is rocky and not well suited for a wheelchair. They nearly dump Pfeifer out of the chair, and I'm both relieved and worried to see they removed the IV from his arm. The good news is they didn't rip the needle out of his vein as they bounced him across the yard, but the bad news is he'll be waking up soon.

Beyond them, near the cloverleaf building, is a ray of sunshine in this otherwise dark and rainy night—a van. I can't tell for certain in the dim light, but it could be blue, and it's the same model as the one in my vision.

The wind shifts, and the baby's wails grow more frantic. "Shh, Lily Bee," Sophie croons. "Mama's here."

Daniel pivots as best as he can to shelter them from the blowing rain. But Miller isn't down with that. He shoves Daniel back against the wall, wedging the pistol into his ribs.

"Stay where I can see you, freak!"

My breath catches in my throat. I know Sophie and I make it out of here. I know my father makes it out of here. So does Miller, although I'm a bit more ambivalent in his case. But I didn't see Daniel in the vision. I didn't see the baby, either.

"I was *trying* to keep the kid from screaming," Daniel says evenly.

Miller pulls the gun away. I don't know if it's because Daniel is nudging him or if there's actually a smidgen of humanity inside the man. "Okay. If it will shut the kid up."

It doesn't entirely, but Lily does dial back to a loud whimper rather than a howl.

The pilot tosses a key ring to Miller, an exchange that could have happened back at the helicopter and kept everyone a lot drier. Miller opens the large padlock and, after a few tries, finds the key to the door itself. The door is metal, and a good six inches thick. It creaks as it opens, adding yet another horror-movie touch as Miller shoves me forward into the pitch-black building.

Smith pushes past with a flashlight. We wait in the dark for several minutes, and then a loud, whirring noise ushers in the light.

We're in what may have once been a cafeteria. Exposed ductwork runs across the ceiling. Someone endeavored to cheer the place up with a bit of color by painting the pipes red. Murals cover the upper walls between the windows, painted onto the cement by artists with varying degrees of talent. Drawings cover many of the columns, as well. Most of the artwork is outdoor scenery—a herd of deer running through the woods, a pair of raccoons peeking over a log, a large blue fish swimming lazily between the roots at the bottom of a stream.

One long cafeteria bench remains at the center of the room. Miller shoves me down on one side and tells Daniel and Sophie to take the other. The pilot parks the wheelchair next to them and slings the diaper bag over one handle of the chair. Pfeifer's head hangs to one side, and I'm reminded of Magda's daughters at the window of Bell Isle. Chloe, I guess. Or rather Chloe's shell, since she's not in there.

Smith frees Sophie's hands so that she can tend to the baby. Sophie pulls out a diaper and then tosses me a couple of wet wipes. "You've still got blood there." She taps the side of her mouth. I dab the area around the cut, wincing at the sting, until she gives me an *all-clear* nod.

"Aaron's going to kick my ass," Daniel says. "I told him I'd watch out for you."

I raise an eyebrow. "You weren't even conscious. And a split lip is the least of our worries."

Lily is rightfully indignant at having her diaper changed on a cold metal table, but the discomfort is brief. Soon she's the one person in the room who is in dry clothes, happily taking her way-past-bedtime bottle.

Miller joins the other two men, and once he's out of earshot, Daniel leans across the table and whispers to Sophie, "Our odds of getting out of here are better once Pfeifer is awake, but only if you can block him from taking on any extra hitchers. This is a bad place."

"No kidding," Sophie says. "Dacia said this is where the guy who shot Martin Luther King was held, although she didn't mention she was sending *me* with you. Hannibal Lecter was supposed to come here, too, but—"

"Lecter wasn't real," Daniel says.

"I *know* that. But in the book, this is where he was being transferred when he escaped. My point is that plenty of serial killers were housed here. Not the kind of guys you want to have in your head. But I don't know if—" She falls silent when Miller looks our way for a moment, and then continues. "I've never blocked someone from taking on ghosts. I guess it's the same principle as anything else, though."

"Is that why we're here?" I ask. "Do they want us to pick up more hitchers from this place?"

"How would I know? My only part in this was supposed to be getting you into the chopper. Lying bitch said she'd take me and Lily to Knoxville."

Sophie seems a little naive to have believed that story when they clearly need her here to block Pfeifer. And I'm guessing from her expression that she didn't believe it. Not really. She *hoped* Dacia would keep her word, but she didn't have a choice as long as Dacia had her baby.

Miller and Smith are heading over. I lean across the table quickly and tell Daniel, "The lump is gone in my vision. It's just a bruise."

"What vision?" Sophie asks, but I don't have time to answer.

They herd us into a hallway. There's a gate about ten feet down, which is closed. I assume we'll be here for a few minutes while Miller shuffles through his keys. But he just shoves the metal bars with one hand, and it slides open. I flash back on movies I've seen where all the prison doors open in unison. Maybe it was computerized back when this was an actual prison.

The corridor beyond the gate is dimly lit, and aside from the cells being stripped down to bare metal, the place resembles every cellblock I've seen in movies or on TV. As we go deeper into the facility, Sophie keeps looking back at Daniel. Her eyebrows are raised in a very clear message—*I'm not blocking you, so you know . . . anytime you're ready.*

Daniel ignores her. He may not even see her, to be honest, because he keeps looking back over his own shoulder. At first, I think he's worried that Miller is going to shove them again. But he seems to be watching Smith more than Miller.

About halfway down the long row, we reach a group of larger cells that appear to have undergone renovation. They're now double-wides— two cells combined into one. Each has four cots, where the others had two. And the cots here are topped with mattresses.

"In you go," Miller says. "The accommodations are a little less . . . posh . . . than what you're used to at Sandalford, but at least you've got a bed. Hard to believe people pay to sleep here. Gotta be an easier way to act out prison fantasies." His eyes do a perverse elevator ride, first at me and then at Sophie, which is doubly messed up since she's holding Lily.

As soon as the words leave Miller's mouth, the leg cramp comes back. He leans down, cursing and clutching his calf. Smith gives him a confused look, then steps into the cell and cuts our zip cuffs.

Blankets and clothing are piled on top of one bunk, and several crates of bottled water are stacked at the rear of the cell, along with a box of rations. The place has even been given a fresh coat of paint, and I send a silent prayer of thanks to the person who realized that tourists would be willing to give up a bit of authenticity in order to have a curtain around the toilet.

Smith loops a heavy chain through the bars to close the door. "Food, water, and a first-aid kit back there. This wouldn't have been my first choice for housing you, but it should take care of your basic needs until the others arrive and we can get you transferred over."

"Others?" I ask.

Miller limps forward and nods toward the stack of linens. There's an envelope on top. "From Magda."

The sound of Smith clicking the padlock shut sucks the air out of me. I sit on the edge of the bunk, waiting for my panic to abate. I've never been locked in a prison cell before, but I *have* been locked inside hospital rooms. It's pretty much the same thing.

I'm not the only one freaking. "Are you really going to just leave us here?" Sophie asks. "Without a guard or anything?"

"Miller will check on you tomorrow," Smith says.

"The hell I will. Not unless you're sending in some backup. I've dealt with that one"—Miller nods toward me—"for about six months. She convinced my guards to load up a truck with *my* equipment that she and her friends then drove off the premises. She convinced them to let her out of the building unsupervised on more than one occasion. We're a damn sight more likely to find all of them where we've left them if there is *no* guard nearby that she can trick into opening that lock."

"I thought your boss *solved that problem* for you?" It's clear from Smith's tone that this is code of some sort.

Miller shakes his head. "Hasn't kicked in yet. And there's no guarantee it will."

"Doesn't matter, though," Smith says. "The girl is a blocker. If she wasn't blocking them, we wouldn't have gotten them into this cell, right?"

"Hmph," Miller says. I'm not sure if he's agreeing or disagreeing.

"At least put me and the baby in a separate cell," Sophie says. "I'm the one who ratted them out. We're not safe in here. What if Pfeifer wakes up? I jabbed a needle in his arm, for God's sake!"

"Oh, he'll wake up." Miller's tone remains light, almost teasing. "I'm thinking two, maybe three, hours, now that the tube is out of his arm. Guess we'll find out how good you are at blocking, won't we?"

"What about formula for the baby? I've only got one bottle and a couple of teething biscuits."

"You've got food back there," Miller says.

"She's thirteen months old! She needs formula. And not cow's milk. She's allergic. Soy Enfamil."

Smith runs one hand across the stubble on his head and then sighs at Miller. "Go into town and get the baby's formula first thing tomorrow morning."

"There's no point!" Miller says. "We're only talking, what, thirty-six hours? They can crumble up the adult food and—"

Smith's eyes flash. "That was not a suggestion, Mr. Miller. I am in charge of these . . . prisoners. I can call your employer, if you'd like, but she instructed you to cooperate. And while you may no longer be in the military, I'm sure you remember the Geneva Conventions. There are special rules about the care and treatment of children. Those rules have already been broken once by taking that child from her mother and using her as a hostage, but that was before I was placed in charge. There will be *no* further violations. Are we understood?"

Miller nods, but he looks like he bit into something rotten. "Then you are dismissed."

After Miller sulks off, Smith tells Sophie, "I'll check in tomorrow after the conference, to make sure he actually follows orders. We'll keep your little girl healthy. You have my word on that."

She thanks him, and Smith gives the five of us in the cell one last look. Daniel, who had previously been trying to avoid the Colonel's gaze, seems to have changed his mind. He's staring straight at Smith now, and the man's frown deepens as he looks back at Daniel, like he's trying to place him but can't. He's still puzzling over it when he walks away.

As soon as we hear the loud clang of the metal gate leading out to the cafeteria, Sophie whirls around, her eyes shooting fire at Daniel.

"I wasn't blocking you!" she hisses.

"Yes," Daniel says. "I *know*. If you'd been blocking me, Miller wouldn't have been limping his way out of here. But you heard Dacia when we left the cabin. She said Taylor and Aaron wouldn't be harmed as long as Miller checked in with her by midnight."

"And you believed her?" Sophie says.

"Do I have a choice? Did you have a choice when she was holding Lily?"

Daniel's voice is raw with emotion, and I hate to pile anything else on him. But I didn't hear or see what happened in the cabin, so I have to ask.

"You weren't able to nudge her? Dacia, I mean."

"I didn't try. Miller had Taylor. Gun pressed to her temple. I couldn't risk it. If there had been even a second's delay between my suggestion and his reaction . . . Plus, *she* was in the room," he adds, jerking his head toward Sophie. "What if she was blocking me?"

"You weren't in my radius at the beginning. I've got a ten-foot span, max, and it gets weaker the farther out I am. Or if I use it too often. But yeah," Sophie says, getting right up in his face, "once I got into the living room, I was blocking the hell out of you. Because *that* was the *deal*. I get the three of you on the helicopter, and Dacia doesn't hurt Lily."

Dacia's voice runs through my memory, whispering to Hunter Bieler, *I make it quick for you.*

"You were smart not to test her, Sophie. She's killed at least six children. I doubt she'd balk at one more. Do you think Dacia will keep her end of the bargain with Daniel?"

"Don't know . . ." Judging from her tone, I'm certain she's going to add *don't care*. But she doesn't. She just stands there, rocking Lily back and forth, hovering on the brink of tears. "Dacia didn't exactly keep her end of the bargain with *me*. Sure, I got Lily back. But we're inside a prison, in a cell with a man whose head is chock-full of ghosts that aren't exactly friendly. I jabbed them with a needle a few hours ago, so I'm a little worried they're going to forget I was in The Warren with them. A little worried we might not get out of here alive. So, yeah, maybe Dacia will do as she promised. Senator Cregg told her to behave while he's still negotiating with this Magda woman and the military officials. That's why they're involved in transferring you guys over. But even if she keeps her promise about your friends on paper, she's Dacia. She'll put some kind of psycho spin on it."

We're all silent for a moment, even Lily, who's studying her mother's face with worried eyes. Sophie kisses her on the forehead and says, "Mama's okay, little one," before looking back over at me. "What were you saying before about a vision and the bump on your dad's head?"

"You don't have to worry about whether we get out," Daniel says.

"We do. It just may be a few days."

I give her a brief overview of my visions in general as we make one of the cots so that she can put the baby down to sleep, and then explain about my most recent flash-forward.

"You were inside a van in the vision. And I can't be sure, but I think it's the one parked over by that cloverleaf-shaped building."

Once Lily is down, pacifier securely in her mouth, Sophie turns back to me. "And these visions are solid? Not crystal-ball stuff that sometimes happens and sometimes doesn't?"

"Rock solid," Daniel says. "I've been in her head when she has them. The only limitation is that the vision only shows what she's seeing and thinking at that moment. And"—he turns toward me—"that's why I'm not worried about the fact that you don't remember seeing me in the vision. If you were worried about me or even if I was dead, you'd have been thinking about me."

Sophie rolls her eyes, possibly because it sounds egotistical when he puts it that way. Or, even more likely, because she can see that Daniel is very much alive, and all of the other hitchers she's heard of, either in my head or my father's, are dead.

"Daniel used to be dead. But now he's not."

I leave Daniel to explain that one while I open the note from Magda. There's no salutation—as usual, Magda is as blunt as a sledgehammer.

I regret that this is the only option, but please trust that it is. You were dishonest with me in several regards. I, on the other hand, have never hidden from anyone the fact that my chief concern is the welfare of my daughters. Most of the adepts will remain here at Sandalford at least through the end of the year. Caleb will be transferred to Senator Cregg's custody, due to his volatility. Once I have the formula for the cure in hand, Deo will be transferred as well, again due to the danger he poses to the larger community of adepts. You have been transferred to the Senator's custody because you are apparently housing his psychopathic son, and the Senator wants to ensure that he does not harm anyone else.

After the election, the Senator has assured me that he will reunite you and Deo with the other adepts if he

*is satisfied that it can be done safely. By that point, he
believes that many will be stable enough to return to the
general population. In the interim, he has promised you
will not be harmed and my daughters will have the medical treatment they need. Again, the next few months may
be unpleasant for you and indeed for the other adepts who
are averse to change. Maria will do her part to ensure
they adjust to the inevitable. I just wish you and the
Quinns were even half as cooperative. But rest assured
this is all for the best.*
    Magda Bell

I toss the note to Daniel when I'm finished, and he reads it aloud.

"What she said about Maria," Daniel says once he's finished. "You think it's true?"

I consider my answer, but in the end, I shake my head. "No. Just before we left, she was saying how easy it is for people to turn on those who are different. How easy it is to scapegoat them for everything that goes wrong in your life. Her family was killed in that sort of violence, and . . . if that was a performance, she wins the Oscar. Plus, most of the other things Magda said are bullshit. Why should that part be true?"

"So you think Pfeifer's right when he says that a cure isn't possible?" Sophie asks, confirming what I suspected—she was listening the whole time my father and I were talking the other night.

"Yes. For one thing, he's the expert, but it also syncs up with every-thing Dr. Kelsey—the psychiatrist back at Sandalford—told me about the regions of the brain the drug affects. But Pfeifer did say they were close to creating a drug that would mitigate symptoms even before he was imprisoned. And it's been fifteen years since, with others probably continuing his work. So maybe this formula the Senator is supposedly handing over will actually be helpful for some of the adepts."

"I think it's equally likely that he'll give her the formula for drain cleaner," Daniel says. "I don't get why Magda would believe him. She never struck me as naive, but suddenly she's accepting everything the Senator tells her at face . . . value."

A far more likely explanation has just occurred to me. Judging from Daniel's expression, he's reached the same conclusion.

"But if she was nudged by one of Cregg's adepts," I say, "why would she hold back on handing over Deo? If you were doing it, wouldn't you have just convinced her to hand everyone over at once?"

"Maybe. But a hard push like that would be less likely to stick. I might be able to do it, but . . ." Daniel turns to Sophie. "Does the Senator have any adepts with my ability?"

"You mean useless tricks like giving people leg cramps?" she asks. "No, I know what you mean. Pushers. Yes, they've got two, at least. Otherwise they wouldn't have been able to pull off most of their fake terrorism stuff. I know one of them. Terrance. He wound up at The Warren about two years ago, after he was arrested for holding up convenience stores. He was, like, thirteen years old, and he'd just stroll in and convince the cashier to give him a few hundred in change for that ten-dollar bill he paid for the Slim Jim or whatever. The video shows what happened, but the cashier didn't even remember the kid coming in. First two times Terrance got caught, he convinced the cops to let him go, but he has trouble sending out a group message—like when you told everyone to hand over their guns in the lab. If there's more than one person in a room, someone will know Terrance is lying. And it usually wears off after a few days, anyway. How long does it stick when you do it?"

"Depends," Daniel says. "Sometimes it's permanent. Is this Terrance the strongest . . ." He hesitates, clearly not liking the label, but it's the one that all of the adepts seem to use. "Is he the strongest *Pusher* . . . they have?"

"Maybe. But they could easily have someone more powerful or even have more than two. We had several dozen new adepts come in while I was there. Most of them within the past month, and most brought in through that Sanctuary organization Cregg's wife runs. Some were like . . . *really* new. Not second-gen and not stable yet. One died, and a bunch of them had that . . . smell. Like your boy back at the cabin. The kid with the hair."

"The ozone smell?" I ask.

"I guess? Kind of burns your nose. The girl who died had it bad. She only lasted about a week after she reached the camp in Nevada. She was like most of the newbies they brought in. None of them seemed to know what had hit them. I'm beginning to think they're right about it going viral."

"Not viral," I say. "But it's definitely spreading, at least in areas that have early political primaries."

Daniel gives me a cautionary look. "Do we want to go into that right now?"

"Sophie's telling us what *she* knows," I say. "And a few days from now, we—or at least I—will consider her an ally. There's a chance she could turn on us *after* the vision happens, but I suspect the Senator's people have already figured out what's going on with the drug sales. They probably got Cregg's iPad from Taylor, too. Plus, to be honest, if Sophie spills this information to the Senator and he somehow manages to stop the transfer of drug formulas to those dealers, would that be a bad thing? It's killing people."

So we grab food and water from the boxes at the back and exchange information. I've no clue how long we talk because we don't have phones or watches.

Sophie doesn't know as much about the Senator's operations as we'd hoped, but at least she's able to provide us with a rough estimate of the people he has working for him—or simply has captive, in some cases—and what they can do. They have a few Zippos, a half dozen or so Movers, and some low-level Peepers. A couple of Fivers, including Olivia Wu, the girl who gave us the information on where to find Hunter Bieler and the other kids at Overhills. Sophie says they have two adepts who might be able to blow the circuits on household appliances, but none who could blow out an entire electrical grid. The two Pushers she mentioned. Terrance has been traveling with the Senator, and the other one with Dacia. She doesn't believe they have an amp, which explains their interest in Deo, and as far as she knows, they don't have any vessels. But with the steady stream of new people coming into the camp, she really couldn't be certain about anything.

"As for the Senator himself," she says, "I've only seen him once, and that wasn't for long. He arrived home maybe five minutes before Whistler showed up with Pfeifer. They ran their test, which took *forever*, and then we left for The Warren. Anything else I know about the Senator is via Dacia. I know he told her not to touch you, Anna. That he had questions for you. Dacia wasn't happy about that one little bit. I think she has a score she wants to settle, but I'm not sure whether it's with you or with Graham Cregg."

"Most likely both."

We're all yawning, all fighting the inevitable, when we finally roll Pfeifer's wheelchair next to the bunk where the baby is sleeping and Sophie crawls in next to her. We debated pulling down the mattress and moving my father out of the chair but finally decided it's better to wait until he wakes up on his own.

The fact that he's still unconscious worries me. Sophie must sense my feelings, because she presses her fingers against his wrist.

"I'm not an expert. But it feels okay to me."

"Do you have anything in that diaper bag that we can use to tie your arm to him?"

"Probably," she says. "But that was mostly for show back at the cabin, and my arm hurt like hell the next day. This cell isn't large enough for him to get outside my range anyway. You should get some sleep, too."

As we're making up our bunks, Daniel mentions the other thing that's had me concerned since we entered the prison. "Are you worried about picking up other hitchers if you sleep?"

"A little. But more worried for Pfeifer than me. I was me in that vision. And . . . you were on board when I picked up Hunter. Remember how crazy those first few days were? If I had a new hitcher, it would have crossed my mind during the vision. Plus, I haven't sensed anyone in this cell."

"That's not a good sign for the paranormal tourist business," Daniel says.

"Just because I haven't sensed anyone in *this* cell doesn't mean the entire place is empty." I don't add that if I could just walk into a room and tell for certain whether there were hitchers hanging around, I'd simply avoid touching anything.

"At least the mattress is new. I don't think anyone died on it. And it even has that plastic smell, so if it was the site of someone's last happy memory, he or she got lucky at the mattress factory."

I crawl into the top bunk and look over at Sophie to be sure she's asleep. We've been really open with her, but some sixth sense told me to wait on this question because I felt that it might make Daniel a little uncomfortable.

"So . . . exactly who is Smith? You recognized him when we came into the building, and he was trying to figure you out when he left."

"Remember when I was telling you about Sariah? I mentioned a supervisor at Bragg."

"Yeah. You said I didn't think it was entirely a coincidence that you wound up with that assignment."

"Exactly. That was Colonel Smith. And . . . um . . . I may have kind of nudged him a few times back at Bragg. Not to do anything he didn't want to do. Smith wanted to find out what the hell was going on with the Delphi research, too, he just wasn't willing to push things. When I got back, I tried to tell him that Decathlon was testing new versions of the Delphi serum. But he was up for promotion, and keeping his nose clean, so he chose not to believe it. Higher-ups had assured him, blah, blah. It was clear he wasn't going to be any help in stopping them, and he might even be a hindrance if he mentioned it to anyone else. So I nudged him to forget I'd ever spoken to him about it. He probably scratched his head a few times trying to figure out why he pulled strings to get me that Italy assignment. He's a decent guy, but he puts too much faith in the chain of command. I was hoping to get him to *remember* just now, but . . . maybe I nudged him too hard the first time."

My father coughs, a dry rattling noise. It's the first sound I've heard from him since we got here.

"I really wish we had that risperidone."

"I thought Taylor gave you another shot?"

"I didn't mean for me." I nod toward Pfeifer.

He gives me a warning look, but my father still seems to be out. Plus, from what I've seen, we have very few secrets from the hitchers in his head. They must know about the medication, and they don't seem worried.

Once we're in the bunks, though, neither of us can sleep. So we play a whispered game of twenty questions. The pauses grow longer, and our words grow more slurred, but each time I'm about to drift off, another wave of panic grips me.

"I feel like this cell is Schrödinger's box."

"What?"

"Schrödinger's box. Or maybe that's a bad analogy. It's more like everything outside this cell is the box. It's past midnight, so Miller either did or did not call Dacia. And Dacia either did or did not keep her word. As long as we're in here, as long as we don't know, it's like Aaron and Taylor are both alive and . . ." I can't bring myself to even say the alternative. "Like the cat. In the . . . experiment."

"No," Daniel says. "They're okay. I'm not basing that on Dacia. She probably lied. But . . . they're smart. Both of them. And I'd know. I don't get Aaron's vibes, but I'd *know*. They're okay."

News Item from the *Washington Times*

April 26, 2020

Alexandra Cregg, the granddaughter of Senator Ronald Cregg, has been taken into custody for psychiatric evaluation. Witnesses say that Ms. Cregg, 21, attempted to stab the Senator following a campaign rally earlier this evening. The attempt was easily averted by Cregg's bodyguard, and no one was seriously injured.

A spokesman for the Cregg campaign noted that Ms. Cregg seemed to believe that the Senator was a member of the WOCAN group that held her captive for two days earlier this week. "This could simply be post-traumatic stress," the spokesman said, "although we are not ruling out the possibility that someone was manipulating Ms. Cregg's mind, hoping to use her as a weapon against her grandfather. That sort of terrorism could happen to any of us, but it's even more likely that Senator Cregg would be a target due to his strong stance against psychic terror."

CHAPTER
TWENTY-THREE

Brushy Mountain State Penitentiary
April 27, 2020

The lights on the sparkly pink sneaker flick on and off as I kick.

No, Myron, no.

I watch the lights go on and off. On, off. On, off.

Hands grip my shoulders, pulling me away from the old woman curled on her side, clutching her abdomen. She stares at me with a look of complete horror as I try to kick again.

Unexpectedly, the woman grabs my foot and twists. "She jumped to get away from you."

The woman's wrinkled face morphs into Senator Cregg, and then into Graham Cregg. I can't hear what he's saying because someone is screaming, but I can read his lips.

We're more alike than you know.

I sit up so quickly that the top of my head scrapes the ceiling. The small room is in a state of chaos—baby crying, Daniel asking if

I'm okay, and Pfeifer in the bunk below me, yelling at me in a foreign language.

And then he yells in English. "Keep the spider in its cage!"

As I'm telling them that he *is* in the cage, I get a visual from Will.

NOT A SPIDER NOT HIS FAULT

Yes, Will. It's not really a spider. It's Cregg. I know that.

JUST PASSING ON A MESSAGE.

I lie back down, rubbing my injured scalp. "Sorry. It was a dream. A nightmare."

There's a tiny bit of doubt in my mind, given the words that jolted me out of the dream. But I'm almost positive those words didn't come from behind the wall. Everything seems quiet back there. Not even the scritch of his spider legs against the brick. I was remembering Cregg's words. Only a memory.

I curl up facing the wall, in almost the same position as the old woman from my dream—*memory*—and try to block out the noises in the cell until I get my head together. No matter where this particular dream ends, I always wake feeling as though someone has kicked me in the stomach. But it also seems *right* that I should feel that way, like long-delayed justice.

"Anna?" It's Pfeifer, standing next to the bunk. "Are you okay? One of our . . . hitchers picked up on your nightmare, but Leah calmed them down."

"I'm okay."

He stands there for a moment, and then he pats my shoulder. It's such a hesitant, awkward gesture that it makes me want to cry. "It was just a nightmare. Not real."

I blink away the tears and sit up, more carefully this time. Pfeifer steps back quickly, like he's worried about invading my space now that I can see him.

"I'm okay," I repeat. "Sorry if I woke you guys up."

"What happened to your mouth?" he asks, tapping his lower lip. "It was bleeding."

I run my finger over it, and a few flakes of dried blood fall onto the bed.

"Miller happened," Daniel says, adding several choice words to illustrate his opinion of the man. "He's been wanting to do that since last December."

"It doesn't hurt much," I say. "But I'm going to make him pay for it later."

Pfeifer gives me a grim nod. "You didn't wake us, actually. We've been up for several hours." He takes a seat in the wheelchair. The bruise on his head is no longer raised and has deepened to a reddish-purple. "Daniel said you haven't slept much this past week. I guess you had some catching up to do."

The facial expression, as much as the tone, indicates that I'm talking to Scott, not Leah. I don't know if the others can tell them apart, but I'm getting good at it. It was like that for Didier, my hitcher from Rwanda. He had identical twin boys, and it was difficult to tell them apart when they were sleeping. But he could always tell Jean from Joseph when they were awake, even as infants. If pressed as to how, he could only say it was the light in their eyes.

Sophie and Daniel are sitting on the lower bunk across from me. The baby, who looks like she might start crying again at any moment, stands next to Sophie with her head against her mother's knee.

Daniel's concern is clearly etched on his face. He knows my nightmares better than anyone, since he's lived through quite a few of them. I can't remember if I had the dream about the old woman when he was inside my head, but it seems likely. And I know for certain that he was around for some rip-roaring Myron dreams.

"Who is Myron?" Sophie asks.

"Someone she doesn't want to discuss," Daniel says with a slight hint of venom.

"Hey," Sophie says. "Back off. She screamed his name. Just wondering if it's someone I need to be worried about."

"Myron's been gone a long time," I tell her. "But . . . another dream seems to have stirred those memories up a bit. And it's connected to Graham Cregg, so I think maybe that's why it caused a commotion with his hitchers."

"Yes," Leah-Pfeifer says. "I've seen that dream before. It's the memory I mentioned the other night, or at least part of it. The one I tried to latch on to right before he forced Scott to shoot me. And even if I don't actually know whether he made her kill herself, it's still sad. He loved her. That's why I latched on to that memory in the first place."

For the first time since my conversation with Kelsey, I feel movement behind the wall. Nothing that concerns me, really, but Pfeifer's expression tells me that his hitchers sense it, too.

"My walls are solid," I say, holding his gaze firmly, even though I'm pretty sure it's no longer my father or my mother behind those eyes. "He's not getting out. But he doesn't like us talking about this subject. I think it hurts him."

My words are somewhat calculated. The hitchers in my father's head certainly won't object to making Cregg feel a little pain. But the fact that I know this, the fact that it weighed into my calculations when I decided to make the comment, would be obvious to Will or any other mind reader he's housing. They'd know I mentioned it purposefully.

"It's still true," I say aloud, feeling a little sorry for Sophie and Daniel. They're only getting my verbal cues and not the mental game of chess that's going on beneath the surface.

"Is not chess for you," one of Pfeifer's hitchers says. "More like checkers."

I have no idea which one is speaking, but I ignore them and ask about the message Will telegraphed to me a few minutes back.

"You don't think Graham Cregg killed his mother?"

Leah-Pfeifer says, "I didn't send a message, but no, I don't. She's hard to read, though. Thirty years is a long time to just . . . hover. And she was unstable even before she died."

It takes a moment for me to realize who she means. "Penelope Cregg?"

"Yes. That was the Senator's test at his home in Virginia. The kind of test that his son gave you at The Warren. That's why he wanted Sophie there, too . . . so she could block his late wife's ability if she decided to give him too much of a bad trip."

"That's what happened in the cabin, isn't it? And in the tunnel with Daniel and Deo."

"I didn't try to calm her down in the tunnel. Not even sure that I could have, since Sophie wasn't blocking. Penelope had only just come on board, and she went wild when Davis pointed the gun at us. He and Whistler got a taste of what she could do as well. I don't know what they saw, but that's when Davis peed himself. She doesn't want to hurt you or anyone here . . . but she's not happy about the current situation with Graham."

"So that's why she sent that message through Will? Not a spider. Not his fault."

Pfeifer nods.

I hesitate. The last thing I want is to anger a hitcher with her ability. I definitely don't want to watch my father morph into the title character from a drive-in creature-feature again. And while Sophie might be able to block it, she said her ability gets weaker if she uses it too much. So I need to step carefully.

"I agree on the first part. I'd much rather he took a different form, too, but it's not something I know how to fix. If she's claiming he's innocent . . . well, people can change a lot in thirty years. There's solid evidence back at that townhouse to show that she's very, very wrong. My memories of Molly Porter make it crystal clear that, even if Graham Cregg is not a mutant spider-rat, he's most definitely a monster."

"I can back her up on that," Daniel says. "He ordered people killed. And he forced people to harm themselves, to harm others. Might not be easy to hear that about your child, but like Anna says, a lot changes in thirty years."

"Where did you pick up Penelope?" I ask.

"At the house in Alexandria. Like Sophie said earlier. The Senator was testing us."

"No. I mean *where* at the house. Was it on the patio?"

Sophie and Daniel both give me an odd look, and maybe they're right. It's not really important. But this is the first time I've been able to talk to someone else who picks up hitchers, and I'm curious. Was she still hanging out where she died? Or was she in her last happy place?

"Not on the patio," Pfeifer says. "But that *is* the first place he took me. I spent ten minutes there, touching the bricks, the rosebushes, the metal edging around the bushes."

Scritch. Scritch.

Pfeifer's eyes widen and he falls quiet. Someone in that head of his is definitely monitoring the activity behind my walls. After a moment, he goes on. "Then they took me to the kitchen, a couple of bedrooms, onto the balcony that overlooks that patio. I ran my hands over most of the surfaces, even though some of the stuff wasn't anywhere near three decades old. Senator Cregg was starting to get annoyed, I think, but then we stopped in this library up on the second floor. There was a piano in one corner. A few Impressionist-style paintings. All very expensive looking, and that's probably why the small sketch drew my attention. It was in a plain wooden frame on one of the shelves, next to a leather-bound edition of Shakespeare's collected works. The drawing was decent enough, although the perspective seemed—" His face goes blank for several seconds. "Okay. Guess I'll keep my art criticism to myself. Anyway, the sketch was of a boy sitting on the patio outside. I think it was drawn from the library window. I picked up the frame, and nothing happened. But my thumb brushed over the canvas briefly as I was setting it down, and then . . ."

"Then everything went crazy," Sophie says. "I saw it happening. That's how I block. It's like these little waves radiating out of a person when they use their ability. I focus on pushing the waves back."

Lily has gotten braver now and is exploring the room, keeping up a steady stream of chatter, mostly nonsense syllables mixed with an occasional emphatic *no* or *mama*. She's pulled most of the food packets out of the box and is now gnawing on the edge of a bag of freeze-dried lasagna. I don't know if she's hungry or just teething.

"So, sort of like an aura?" Leah-Pfeifer asks.

"Maybe," Sophie says. "But no colors. Just sort of a pulsing in the air around them."

Her description reminds me a bit of Caleb—how the door of Room 81 at The Warren pulsed outward, and the strange hovering waterspout offshore near Sandalford.

"I only see a small pulse for something like that leg-cramp trick Daniel did. But it's bigger—way bigger—for the stuff Oksana and the others did to Whistler and Davis." Sophie startles, and I guess she just received a mental flashcard from Will, because she says, "Yes. They *did* deserve it. I wasn't passing judgment, just stating a fact. The waves coming off his body when they killed those guys reached clear into the middle of the lab. I couldn't have pushed them back even if I'd wanted to."

The baby shoves aside the food packet and pulls herself up to standing using my leg. Maybe that means I'm forgiven for frightening her when I woke up. I tug the collar of my T-shirt up over my eyes to play a few rounds of peekaboo and finally get a smile from her. Then she toddles back over to Sophie repeating the word *boo*.

"Has she shown any abilities?" I ask.

Sophie shrugs. "Nothing I can pinpoint, but you better believe that was something both of the Creggs were interested in. Same with the other three babies who were at The Warren, except they were just second-gen adepts. Lily is third-gen. The only one, far as I know. She's not a Mover or a Zippo, or I think we'd have had a sign by now. But I was a low-level Peeper before they shot me up with this blocking serum. And Lily seems a little more intuitive than most babies. At least to me. But then she's mine, and everybody thinks their kid is special, right? I hope she's not *this* kind of special, though. Things would be a lot easier for her if she's not an adept."

I don't ask whether Lily's father was an adept, and the uncomfortable expression that Pfeifer is wearing leads me to think one of the hitchers picked up on something disturbing. If I was forced to hazard a guess, I'd say the father was one of the Fudds, and I doubt it was consensual. No point stirring up bad memories for Sophie.

"We're just lucky she's not like Anna was at that age," Leah-Pfeifer says. "Before she learned to keep her walls in place, Anna was a regular spirit vacuum, sucking up anything in her path. Not a huge deal in most places, but there's *so much* negative energy here. I can't sense the actual ghosts, but Scott says there are dozens of them. That's one reason he's . . . hanging back a bit. We're worried that he could pick someone up, and it's already rather crowded in here. The atmosphere in this place has several of our current guests on edge, as it is. Keeping them mellow is going to become a challenge if we're stuck here for much longer."

I look around the cell nervously, even though I'm still not sensing anything. But then, I've got my walls at maximum and risperidone in my system.

The faint noise of helicopter rotors causes me to automatically look toward the wall, even though there's no window in this cell. We haven't heard any noises from outside since last night when we heard the chopper take off. This sounds different, although I guess it could just be the difference between takeoff and landing.

"If that's Smith coming back to check on Miller, he's not going to be happy that his orders weren't followed," Daniel says.

Pfeifer's eyes go vacant and he stands silently for a moment, head cocked to the side like he's listening. "It's not Smith. Can you fly a helicopter?"

"Me?" Daniel asks. "No. I've jumped *out* of a few . . ."

Sophie and I both shake our heads, and Leah-Pfeifer crawls back into the bottom bunk. "It's going to be hard to control them, and this is not our best chance to get out of here. So, if she asks, Miller is keeping me drugged."

If *she* asks . . . "It's Dacia?"

"Yes," Pfeifer says, and I'm getting the sense that both my mother and my father are in the back seat right now. "Seven others. Two are kids. I can't read one of them clearly. Drugs, maybe."

Daniel's face falls. There are a number of kids at Sandalford who might need to be medicated before a flight—all of the Zippos, for example. But we already know that Caleb is one of the adepts that Magda traded, so odds are strong that two of the four additional people in the helicopter are Caleb and Ashley. I can't imagine they would risk taking Caleb without the one adult who has had at least some degree of success keeping him calm.

About ten minutes later, the gate clangs open and someone enters the corridor. Even without Pfeifer's advance warning, I'd have known it was Dacia from the telltale clack of heels on the cement floor. But there's another set of footsteps as well.

"Sophie?" Dacia calls out. "Are you in this block? We are looking all over."

I can tell that Sophie is struggling with whether to answer. She looks around at the rest of us, and Daniel nods. There's really no point in keeping silent. Maybe this is how we get out of here?

"I'm down here."

The heels head this way.

"Ugh," Dacia says as she comes into view. "This place is *oribil*. Worse than they told me. I am sorry you must stay here, Sophie, but is only a few days. Where is that man? Miller. He is supposed to be here."

The guy walking behind Dacia is dressed in one of the all-black uniforms that the WOCAN bear brigade tends to favor. He looks like a young Steven Seagal, with a face that might be tolerable if not for the sneer. One of his hands is wrapped around the arm of a frightened little girl.

Maggie. I didn't even hear her footsteps over the noise of the others. Her eyes are red and swollen from crying, and her cheeks lack their usual pink hue. I give her a small wave. She bites her lip and stares down at her shoes as the tears start again.

"Is he still unconscious?" Dacia asks, nodding toward the bunk where my father is stretched out.

"More or less," Sophie says. "Miller gave him another shot this morning."

"Maybe for the best," Dacia says. She takes one of the grocery bags the man is holding and pulls out a six-pack of Enfamil. Regular, not soy.

"I have food for the Lily Bee! Milk and baby bananas and cereal . . ." Dacia shoves a container of mashed bananas through the bars and then hands the bag back to the man. "Why do you just stand there? Break them apart! Put them through bars."

While the guy breaks the formula bottles out of the case, Dacia pulls a ball out of the other bag and holds it up for the baby to see. "And look! Just for Lily Bee." The ball is too large to fit through the bars, though. Dacia tries to flatten it a bit but finally gives up and drops it on the floor. Lily isn't interested anyway. She's clutching Sophie's shirt with both hands.

Aside from her question about Pfeifer, Dacia ignores everyone in the cell other than Sophie and Lily. I'm generally okay with being ignored by psychopaths, but this really isn't Dacia's style. She's more the kind to kick you when you're down, and it's hard to believe she's passing up a chance to taunt me about being on this side of the bars, especially when it means that Graham Cregg is locked up in here as well.

But her attention is fixed on Sophie, and when Sophie doesn't answer or respond in any way, Dacia makes an exaggerated sad face. "It is out of my way to come here, but I take trouble on a *very busy day* to make sure you and Lily are comfortable. You do not even say thank you."

"Thank you." Sophie's voice and expression are both as dry as bread crumbs, but she snatches up the baby food and formula.

Dacia sighs. "Sophie. I know this is not what I promise. But you are needed more here, so you must . . . how do they say? Take it for team. Maybe it is safer for Lily, too. The new boy . . . he may make a bigger bang at the lab than we are thinking."

I don't know if she notices Daniel's eyes narrowing, but she turns toward him. "Yes, I see you trying to push me around, Daniel Quinn. You squint your eyes up all you want. Even if Sophie and Maggie were not here to block you, I do not *push* so easy as Alexandra Cregg. Not anymore. And maybe I have my own pusher now."

On the last two words, she grips the cell bar with her gloved hand—the one with the missing pinky.

"It was you, no? You leave the little poison pill in her head to kill grandpa. It might have worked, too, if I hadn't been there to peek inside her tiny little mind." Then her eyes take on a malicious glint. "Not going to ask me about your family?"

"No point. You'd only lie. And we already know they're okay."

Dacia arches an eyebrow. "Do you, though? Are you so sure? The Senator says they are of value, so maybe I left the *soldati* behind to watch them. Or maybe because you are big pain of my ass I stay behind at cabin. Maybe I take care of them myself."

She draws out the last sentence deliberately, baiting us. Tall, Dark, and Scowling is getting impatient, though. "We need to go, babe."

Dacia gives him a *wither-and-die* look, but she turns to follow.

"Maggie wasn't part of the agreement, Dacia. Senator Cregg isn't going to be happy about this."

I'm not sure why I say it. It's likely to rile her up, and I don't even know for certain that it's true. I guess I just want Maggie to know that someone gives a damn. That she's not simply a pawn.

My words hit a nerve, apparently. Dacia stomps back toward the cell, blue eyes blazing. "Maybe I do not care what the Senator wants or about his agreements or his timeline or if he will be stupid *preşedinte*. Who is *he* to tell me what to do? If I did not tell him Alex is brainwash, he would be dead. Lucas was right. He is a nothing and a thief. Big-shot Senator can do *nothing* with his normal, boring brain, and so he thinks to tell *me* how to lead?"

"You could just leave Maggie with us. Miller could take her back to Sandalford, and . . ."

Dacia laughs and tosses a remark over her shoulder as she walks away. I don't understand Romanian, but I'm certain it wasn't a compliment.

Once the gate clanks behind her, I turn to Daniel. "You couldn't nudge her?"

"I wasn't trying. Pfeifer's right. They didn't have the key to the lock, and I had no way of knowing if Maggie was blocking. Dacia said Miller isn't here. So he must have gone into town for supplies for Lily. The smartest move is to wait until he gets back."

"Did you actually nudge Alex Cregg to attack her grandfather?"

"Yeah. Figured it was worth a try."

Pfeifer tosses the blanket back and sits up. His movements don't look . . . right to me, and he's tilting his head to the side again. Listening, but not with his ears.

"Dacia seems awfully eager to keep in your good graces," Daniel tells Sophie.

"Why wouldn't she be? I'm a blocker. We're rare . . . it's just me and Maggie, unless they've managed to make another one who survived. And Dacia's lying when she says you can't nudge her. She's built up a little resistance, but she can be pushed, her mind can be read, she can be set on fire by a Zippo. All of it. And do you have any idea how many people Dacia has pissed off? Her plan is for me to be her shadow. She'd be even happier if Lily inherited my ability, because she'd be a lot easier to brainwash."

"But if she's got Maggie now," Daniel says, "doesn't that mean she no longer needs you?"

"I think it's more likely Maggie winds up with the Senator and his wife. A politician would find it a lot easier to sell Maggie as a niece or as some poor little orphan they adopted. A twenty-three-year-old black girl with a mixed-race baby might raise a few eyebrows among the Senator's base. So if Maggie can shield the Senator, and I get Dacia, it might maintain their rather shaky balance of power. Those two have some trust issues, believe you me."

"Maggie may not last long enough to do the Senator any good if they're using her to block Caleb. Magda already tried that. It drains Maggie. When she's around Caleb for more than a few hours, she comes back looking like a zombie."

"Which means they're both in danger." Daniel pauses as we hear the helicopter take off. "Along with Ashley and anyone else in that helicopter."

It occurs to me as he's speaking that there's a very real chance Deo could be one of the passengers. Maggie wasn't mentioned in Magda's note, and yet she was just here. Who's to say Dacia didn't ignore the agreement to save herself a second trip?

Daniel paces the length of the cell. "Do you know where they're going, Sophie? Dacia mentioned a lab."

"I . . . can't remember the name. But it's outside of Knoxville. They're planning to do another one of their WOCAN attacks there. Something to give a boost to the Senator's antiterrorism speech tonight."

"They have no idea what they're dealing with," Daniel says. "Miller better get back soon because we need to get the hell out of here."

"No," Pfeifer says. "We're not waiting on Miller."

His face goes blank for a moment. Then he stands up and pulls the mattress off the bottom bunk. He's moving oddly again, the way he did earlier, and I'm not seeing Scott-Pfeifer or Leah-Pfeifer in his eyes. This is more Furies-Pfeifer.

He looks over at Sophie and says something in a different language, pointing to her and the baby. Then he holds up the thin mattress in front of him.

"Bareeyeer. Mattress bar-ee-yeer."

And then he gestures toward Daniel's mattress. "Go. Get."

I catch on before Daniel does and tug the mattress off the bed. "She wants us to get behind it. Mattress. *Barrier.*"

Daniel and Sophie exchange a glance that says they're not at all convinced this is a good idea. I agree. But I don't get the sense it's negotiable.

"I think that's . . . Oksana."

The name puts both of them in gear. I never saw her alive, but Jaden once described Oksana as *not the most stable isotope in the lab.* And in my experience with her spirit, I think that may have been an understatement.

Sophie scoops up Lily, and we hunker down behind the mattresses. I'm a little worried about Pfeifer, who is standing off to one side, totally exposed, but he's okay in my vision. And I don't think Oksana would be reckless enough to hurt the body that's carrying her around.

The sound of screeching metal is almost earsplitting, and it's joined a second later by a series of pings. I feel something—several things, actually—ricochet off the mattress.

When the barrage stops, we slowly lower the mattresses. Tiny chunks of the chain are scattered on the floor. Every single link was shattered, and the lock itself, one of the heavy-duty types, is now a twisted mess.

My father grins, a bright, maniacal expression that's more than a little unnerving, and then Oksana, or whoever that was, is gone. It's just Pfeifer now, befuddled, looking at the scraps of metal around his feet. Not a single one hit him.

"Seems a bit . . . dramatic," he says. "Could have popped a single link, and we'd have gotten the same result."

"Or simply waited until Miller arrived and let me nudge him to unlock the cell," Daniel says.

"No," Pfeifer says. "He'll have his weapon drawn, and he'll be expecting trouble. This way, we stand a better chance of taking him by surprise." He glances toward the windowless wall, and I think he's heard something outside, but maybe he's just listening to one of his inner voices. "We need to go."

We grab some of the supplies and push the door open. As we head toward the exit, I notice the ball that Dacia brought, still leaning against the bars. I check to ensure that no chain shrapnel is embedded in the plastic and then extend it to Lily.

She frowns at first. Then she takes the ball and hurls it past me with a defiant *"No!"* as it bounces down the hallway. I go after it, mentally kicking myself for not realizing she'd think it was a game, and worried that she'll start screaming for the damned thing when we're halfway to the exit.

But when I bring it back, her bottom lip juts out. "No. No baw."

She clutches her mom tighter, and her frown doesn't go away until I put the ball back on the floor. I half expect her to change her mind before we reach the gate, but she'd doesn't. Lily remembers exactly who brought that toy.

There's no sign of Miller when we reach the cafeteria, and a quick look outside confirms that the van I saw parked by the cloverleaf building last night is gone. It's possible we could just walk out the front gate, but given that someone has invested money to renovate those cells, I suspect it's locked. They'd need to keep out thrill-seeking teens wanting to snoop around a purportedly haunted prison. We also have no idea how far it is to the main road. Plus, Miller and a van (probably this van) are in my vision. So the only sensible alternative is to wait until he returns.

Daniel and my father head to the far end of the room and take up position on opposite sides of the door we came through last night. There's really not much Sophie or I can do, so we take the baby into a small guard station inside the cafeteria. Someone removed the door and, judging from the wires jutting out of the shelves, the monitoring equipment. I do a quick search for weapons, but the place is empty, aside from one battered office chair and a crumpled MoonPie wrapper.

And I'm pretty sure there's a spirit in here, too. My walls are up, so I'm probably safe, but no way am I touching that chair or anything else in this room. I crouch down on the floor near the doorway, next to Sophie.

I'm a little worried Lily will start chattering again and inadvertently tip Miller off. But for the moment, at least, she's happily gnawing on a teething biscuit and tugging items out of the diaper bag.

Luckily, we don't have to wait long. Lily has barely made a dent in the teether when I hear the metal door creak open. The noise is followed by a guttural scream and a heavy thwack as something hits the floor.

Daniel says, "Any weapons on your body are now red-hot, Miller. They're burning through your pockets . . ." Whatever else he says is drowned out by whimpering noises and the sound of weapons clanking to the floor.

Lily's interest is piqued by the action in the cafeteria, so I shift over to block the doorway. I have a clear line of sight now and see Miller currently suspended about eight inches above the floor, pinned to the wall. Blood trickles from his nose, and he's holding two fingers in his mouth. A plastic grocery bag is on the floor in front of him, along with a pistol, a taser, car keys, his wallet, a couple of spare zip cuffs, and his phone. Miller wasn't taking any chances. Apparently, everything that was in his pockets has been dumped onto the floor in front of him.

After Daniel scoops everything up, the force causing Miller to hover above the ground ends abruptly. Miller crumples to the cement, landing hard on his knees. He screams again, muffled this time by the fingers in his mouth. The burns were all in his head, but I'm pretty sure those fingers are now hurting for real, since they were between his teeth when his knees hit the floor.

Daniel shoots an annoyed look at Pfeifer. "That was risky. I mean, he deserved the punch. But why didn't you pin him to the wall first?"

"Because it was one of my guests pinning him up there, and I wanted to actually *feel* his face under my fist," Pfeifer says, and then looks back at me. "If you'd like to hit him yourself, Anna, I'd be happy to—"

"That's okay," I say quickly. To be honest, I do feel a *tiny* bit annoyed. I was fully planning on getting even with Miller for this puffy lip at a later date. And it probably would have been safer to let Daniel disarm Miller first. But there's also a part of me that's touched that my father wanted to punish Miller, too.

Miller is curled up on his side, holding his hands up to his quite-possibly-broken nose. Sophie picks up the grocery bag that's near his feet, peeks inside, and then hurls it at Miller. Daniel gives her a baffled look.

"It's not soy. And the last damn thing we need is a baby with an ear infection right now."

There's a brief argument about what to do with Miller. As much as I'd love to toss him into one of the cells, the only chain we have was just disintegrated. And even if that weren't the case, I know Miller was in the vision. Leaving him here isn't an option, so Daniel pops one of the cuffs on Miller's wrists and hauls him outside.

Something is off when I see the van. It's navy blue, and I'm certain it's the same one. But I definitely don't remember that sign on the side panel.

"Why didn't you mention the advertising?" Daniel says.

"It wasn't in the vision. I mean, there was a sign, but it can't remember what it said. Believe me, *Tennessee Ghost Tours* would have stuck in my memory."

The others are getting into the van, but Pfeifer hangs behind, just inside the doorway. His body is rigid and shaking. The red pipes along the ceiling are also shaking now. One of them quivers itself out of its support bracket and comes crashing to the floor. Along the wall, the windows rattle once, twice, then shatter outward.

The wall catches fire.

That's not quite right, though. It's more like a flame sprite dances across the cement, from one mural to the next, igniting the paint as it goes. Deer and raccoons now seem to be in a hopeless race against a raging forest fire. The fish pond ripples and blackens. A column near the middle of the room that once depicted a panther climbing a boulder is peeling away, leaving only scorched concrete below.

And then the fire stops as suddenly as it began. It's like a blowtorch is turned off, and the flames instantly extinguish.

The reek of smoke and burned chemicals hangs in the air. Few traces of the artwork remain, and most of the paint has been scorched away from the metal pipes. All of that creative effort has literally gone up in smoke.

Pfeifer's head jerks toward me, and for a second, I'm afraid that I'm next on the to-be-incinerated list. Daniel must think so, too, because he's yelling for him to stop.

But whichever Fury is in control simply says, "Is not a happy place. This is how they *feel*."

And then Leah-Pfeifer is looking back at me.

"It was building up. Too much for me to control. They needed to vent."

Daniel stands beside me, mouth open, as he takes in the smoking ruin.

"Good decision," he says. "Definitely better out than in."

News Item from the *Knoxville News Sentinel*

April 26, 2020

Presidential candidate Senator Ronald Cregg (UA-PA) and scientists from Oak Ridge National Laboratories are among the speakers scheduled at the upcoming Shield2020 Psychic Security Conference, sponsored by Decathlon Services Group.

The conference, which will take place on Monday and Tuesday at the Knoxville Convention Center, will bring together more than 400 state and local law enforcement, military, and government leaders with the nation's leading authorities on the Delphi Project and its potential impact on national security. Participants will share best practices and lessons learned in controlling and apprehending individuals with psychic abilities.

When the conference was first announced in January, government officials and members of the two major political parties derided it as a campaign stunt in support of Senator Cregg, who was once on the board of DSG. There was a push to boycott the event. The escalating crisis, however, has made it far more difficult for Congress and the White House to ignore the issue, since Senator Cregg, who is essentially assured as the Unify America nominee, has made the battle against psychic terrorism the cornerstone of his campaign. With state and local officials now demanding action and resources, Republican and Democratic leaders seem to have reached a tacit agreement to scrap the boycott. Instead, they will use this conference to demonstrate what they are doing to address the crisis, although some of the participants stress that their attendance is simply to address the panic over the issue, and not a confirmation that psychic terrorism actually exists.

CHAPTER
TWENTY-FOUR

Oliver Springs, Tennessee
April 27, 2020, 3:54 p.m.

Daniel opens the van door, peels off a fifty, and hands me the debit card along with the rest of the cash he withdrew from Miller's checking account. "I'm going to walk across to the drugstore. They should have soy formula. Hopefully burner phones, too."

The cell signal came in on Miller's phone as soon as we reached the main road leading out of the prison. Daniel was worried about Miller's communications possibly being monitored, but we decided it was worth the risk to call and check on Aaron and Taylor. We've all had to change phones several times over the past few months, and neither of us committed their new numbers to memory. The number for Sam's company, Quinn Investigative, is the same, however. Unfortunately, we got the answering machine, and Daniel didn't want to leave Miller's number, so we're still in limbo.

Rysa Walker

"Be nice if that drugstore had a car seat," Sophie mumbles, glancing down at Lily. The baby is crawling around on the floorboard now that I've stopped the van, but Sophie was holding her before that. Or trying to. The kid has a major case of the wiggles.

My father is in the seat behind Miller. He hasn't said much, and his eyes are closed most of the time. I don't think he's sleeping, it's more like meditation. Maybe he's still trying to rein in Oksana or whichever whirlwind it was that trashed the cafeteria.

"We'll find a car seat as soon as we get to Knoxville." I stuff the money and debit card back into Miller's wallet. There's a corporate credit card in there as well, along with his driver's license and a loyalty card from Harrah's casinos. That was a lucky find, because it gave Daniel the idea to tell Miller this is a paid excursion to a casino in New Jersey. He was in a chipper mood after that, despite his badly swollen nose. It's the first time I've seen Miller with a genuine smile.

Having Miller along may already have bought us some time, though. A text came in on his phone a few minutes after we turned onto the main highway. It was from Magda, letting him know that the Senator's people had taken Maggie, and cautioning him to be alert for any other deviations from the agreement.

My hands shook as I sent back a simple *10-4*, which seems to be Miller's default response to most texts. Magda knows that this is a dangerous situation for Maggie. She saw firsthand how Maggie looked after a couple of days with Caleb. But it sounds more like she's annoyed at Cregg for changing the terms of the agreement than actually concerned for Maggie's welfare. Senator Cregg's people could probably march in and take custody of all the adepts, and she'd stand aside as long as she gets what she wants.

Miller hasn't given us much information beyond what we already know, however, despite Daniel's interrogation, which was heavy on the nudge. As far as we can tell, Miller doesn't know anything beyond the basics of the agreement that Magda made with the Senator. And he doesn't seem to be especially easy for Daniel to manipulate. It took two tries to get the debit PIN, and I'm not sure how long any of Daniel's suggestions are going to hold. About ten minutes ago, Miller started to look confused and angry, more like his usual abrasive self. Daniel gave him another, slightly stronger nudge, and Miller went back to telling us how much he won at blackjack last summer. I think the plastic zip cuff he's wearing might be part of the problem. Each time he remembers his wrists are bound, it chips away at the casino cover story Daniel planted in his head.

"Yes, it's soy," Daniel says as he hands the bag back to Sophie. "No burner phones, though. We'll try the Walmart in Oak Ridge."

We're about a mile down the road when Sophie leans forward and taps Daniel's shoulder. "Where did you say we're going?"

"Walmart."

"No . . . the city. Oak Ridge. That's the part of the name I couldn't remember. The lab that Dacia is targeting."

"Oak Ridge *National* Laboratory?" There's a note of alarm in my dad's voice, and I try to place the name. Something connected to World War II, I think.

"I don't remember the *National* part," Sophie says. "But yeah. It was Oak Ridge."

My brain finally makes the connection. "The Manhattan Project."

"When are we going to be at the casino?" Miller asks.

Daniel sighs. "I'm going to put him to sleep. If his phone rings, we'll wake him up. Miller, *go to sleep*."

"I'm not . . ." But then his eyelids droop, followed by his head.

"Is it still a nuclear facility?" I ask Pfeifer.

"Yes. Although a lot of other research goes on there now as well. Security is pretty tight at those places, though. They wouldn't be able to just land a helicopter there."

"Maybe not." Daniel grabs Miller's phone and begins dialing. "But I could probably talk my way past the guard. From what Sophie said, Dacia's got at least one adept who can be persuasive."

"Are you trying Sam's again?" I ask.

"No. I'm calling Baker. Someone needs to raise the alarm."

But Baker isn't on duty, and Daniel can't remember his personal number. We debate calling the police on Miller's phone, but we're close enough now that it seems wise to wait for a burner phone that can't be traced.

Twenty minutes later, Daniel is able to place a brief, anonymous 911 call in the shopping center parking lot while my dad—or more accurately, my mother—and I try to figure out how to safely install Lily's new car seat. We're the only ones with any experience at all in that regard, but Leah's is at least fifteen years out of date and mine is a vague hitcher memory.

Sophie paces around the parking lot as we wrestle with straps and hooks. I'd expected her to tell Daniel to buy a specific type of car seat, since she was particular about the type of baby formula. But she had no idea, and she's totally clueless about installing it or getting Sophie strapped in. I can tell this really bothers her, and I realize for the first time that Sophie has never cared for Lily in the outside world. All of her experience with parenting has been at The Warren or at the Senator's facility in Nevada. All of her experience as an *adult*, for that matter, has been inside an institution of some sort. She can't drive. She's never had a job. While she's definitely smart, the educational program at The Warren wasn't exactly top notch. No wonder she was willing to cash in on her blocking ability. That's probably Sophie's only marketable skill, and she has a daughter to support.

I turn my attention back to the car seat, which now seems to be correctly secured. Sophie heads back once we have Lily situated, carrying two large blue-and-white rectangles over her arm. Her expression is a little less miserable than it was a moment ago, and when she reaches the van, she slaps a rectangle over the *Tennessee Ghost Tours* logos on either side of the van. A bit of the *T* still shows, but the rest of it is neatly covered by a navy-and-white *Coldwell Banker* sign.

"Problem solved," she says. "But we should probably get out of here. Otherwise we may have an angry realtor chasing us."

One of the new phones rings just as Daniel pulls back onto the main road. It's Porter. I put him on speaker.

"Thank God, Anna. Are the others with you?"

Daniel frowns. "*I'm* with her. We've also got Pfeifer and another adept. Have you heard from Taylor and Aaron?"

There's a long pause before Porter answers. "Last I heard, Sam had turned the truck around and was heading back up to that cabin in West Virginia. Had one of his hunches. That would've been around seven thirty last night. I left two messages already, but was hopin' maybe his phone's just got bad reception. Mine never works worth a damn in the mountains. What—"

"I'll fill you in later," Daniel says. "Right now, you need to contact someone and tell them to increase security at the Oak Ridge National Lab. Baker, if you can reach him. I don't have his home number. I made a call about twenty minutes ago to the local police, but I couldn't give them any identification. They may have thought it was a prank."

"On it." Porter ends the call.

"It's too late," Pfeifer says. "Look over there, to the right."

A massive plume of smoke is rising in the woods behind a Bojangles' and a storage facility. As we watch, it seems to get another burst of fuel, and the cloud rises higher.

"Are you sure that's the lab?" Sophie asks.

"No," Daniel says. "But it's sure as hell in that direction."

He nods toward the sign we're approaching, which directs us to turn right for Oak Ridge National Lab.

We do *not* turn right. The light ahead is yellow, and it's clearly going to change to red before we get there, but Daniel floors it.

Just as we clear the intersection, we hear another explosion. It's loud. Loud enough that we feel it. Still, it's not *nuclear* loud.

My dad echoes my thoughts. "They blew *something* up, but that wasn't a nuclear detonation. Not even close."

"Yeah, well, there are nukes in the vicinity," Daniel says. "We're not waiting around for the fire to spread."

He gets no argument. We drive in silence for the next few minutes, except for Lily, who is not used to a car seat and probably frightened by the explosion.

Once we're well clear of Oak Ridge, I lean toward Daniel and ask, "Can Caleb *do* that?"

"Caleb's not even three. I don't know what he can do. He's definitely telekinetic. And while I was at The Warren, we had one incident that . . ." He shrugs. "He *could* be a Zippo, yeah. Or there could have just been a short in the equipment that he moved, and that's what started the fire. But I don't think that was Caleb. It's much more likely that Dacia and her bears pulled a conventional attack. Not nuclear, not psychic. That sounded a lot like an IED. They may not still be around here. I just wish I knew where they were going."

"I don't know about Dacia," Sophie says, "but the Senator is at the terrorism conference. He's giving that speech tonight. Follow the Senator, and eventually you'll find Dacia and Caleb, because he's definitely going to make sure Dacia did as she was ordered. Like I said before, they've got trust issues. Oh, and can you give this guy back here another push? He's moving again."

Daniel curses softly and says, "*Go to sleep*, Miller."

Sophie doesn't know where the convention is taking place, so I google it and learn that the Shield2020 conference, hosted by Decathlon Services Group, is being held at the Knoxville Convention Center downtown.

The website declares that hundreds of officials and law enforcement officers will be there to share best practices and lessons learned for controlling and apprehending Delphi psychics. That sounds like the last place we need to be. But since we have no other ideas on how to find Dacia, I guess we'll have to stroll into the lion's den.

"Traffic's probably going to get worse," Daniel says, "once the situation at Oak Ridge hits the news. I'm guessing that, even if they don't officially evacuate the area, a whole lot of people are going to decide it's a good night to go for a long drive. Just to be on the safe side."

Porter calls back a few minutes later. By the time he reached Baker, reports of an explosion near Oak Ridge were already coming in. Daniel brings Porter up to speed on everything and asks him to forward Sam's cell number and any others he might have.

"I'm headed to West Virginia now. Your mama was ready to get into the car herself when I talked to her, but I told her it might best to . . ." He falls silent, and his unspoken words drive a stake of fear straight through me. Porter didn't want Michele Quinn to go because he's scared. He thinks he may find them dead.

"Anyway," Porter says. "Gonna take a while to get out of DC this time of day, so I don't know when I'll get there. I'll be back in touch as soon as I can."

We're about to end the call when Porter says, "Oh, one more thing. I got an odd call from someone I know over at Montgomery County Child Welfare. They remembered me asking around about Anna last year when . . . um . . . when I . . ."

"When you thought I was a scam artist. It's okay, Porter. What did they want?"

"Well, they had a call from someone who wanted to track down a girl who was abandoned at Laurel Mall in 2004. Said that she knew the girl had been adopted, but that she'd be an adult now and graduating from high school next month. Thought she might need money for college. At first, I thought it was one of Senator Cregg's people . . . only they *know* where Anna is. And then they tell me the person's name.

Leah Johnson. Seems she adopted her sister's identity. She's living in Colorado. Runs a small art gallery in a resort town."

"Manitou Springs," Pfeifer says. "I told you, Scott. I told you she wouldn't . . ."

The last part trails off, but my father's face goes blank again, so I suspect the conversation has just shifted to internal mode.

"Um . . . yeah," Porter says, obviously confused by the dialogue. "Right near Pikes Peak. I'll text the number when I stop for gas."

All of this sort of floats over me, because my mind is still on the words that Porter left unsaid. I pull up the map again and start typing in a new route.

"What are you doing?" Daniel asks.

"Finding the quickest route back to West Virginia."

"Anna." He reaches over and grabs my hand. "We're at least six hours away. Maybe more. Porter will be there in three hours, tops. There's nothing we can do. But maybe we can find a way to help Caleb and Maggie."

He's right. I know that. But it doesn't *feel* right.

It's after six thirty when we finally reach the exit for the Knoxville Convention Center. Lily quieted down, thanks to a bottle, but she's tired and cranky and wants out of the car seat. I scan the map, trying to find a place to park and maybe a hotel, because we can't risk taking a baby—or for that matter, Pfeifer, whose face has been all over the news—anywhere near that conference. Or Miller, who is still in zombie mode. Daniel and I will stand out badly enough as it is, with our jeans and sneakers in a sea of business suits.

As I zoom in on the area nearby, however, the vision begins to replay in my mind. The World's Fair Park is right next door to the convention center. Beyond it is the water, and the white tarplike building, and the odd lollipop-looking building I saw from the helicopter.

We turn the corner, and the convention center comes into view. It's a huge building constructed mostly of glass. The large golden globe atop the tower, which is called the Sunsphere according to the map, reflects the lights of the city below. From this angle, I can tell that the bottom section is the tower from my vision.

"There's going to be another attack. The glittery stuff I saw in the vision . . . it's that giant gold disco ball. There will be police tape around this entire area tomorrow. At least, I think it's tomorrow . . ."

I glance back at Pfeifer, but it's too dark to see his forehead, and I'm not even sure I remember exactly what it looked like in the vision anymore. His eyes are closed again. I don't know if the baby's cries stressed him out, or if it's something else, but he looks like he did at the prison when my mother said one of the hitchers needed to vent. What if *he's* the reason that thing explodes?

"How much destruction are we talking?" Daniel asks.

"I think it's mostly the Sunsphere, although I didn't look toward the convention center, so I'm not certain. The tower part of the Sunsphere was still standing, though. So was that white thing next to it, which is some sort of outdoor theater. And they had this road open again, so the damage can't have been too extensive, right?"

"Look over there," Sophie says. "The theater area is lit up like they've got something going on. There are a lot of people hanging around. A concert, maybe? That's not good . . ."

Daniel slows the van almost to a stop. A car behind us honks. There's no parking available, so he pulls into the bike lane. The street we're on is elevated above the amphitheater. I get out and run to the other side so that I can get a better look at the gathering.

The amphitheater sits in front of a lake, or maybe *lagoon* is a better word. It's clearly man-made, curving like a snake between the convention center and the theater. The crowd under the canopy is mostly male, mostly in business suits, with a decent representation of military uniforms. The website listed two events today, the Shield2020 conference and a high school academic awards banquet. It's pretty clear which one this is.

White-clad tables are arranged near the edges of the stage, with steamer trays and platters of food. A bar is set up at one end. According to the conference agenda, a cocktail reception and the keynote speech were supposed to be held in one of the first-floor exhibit halls, but apparently, they decided to move it all outdoors.

"Not a concert," I say as I get back into the van. "They relocated the Senator's speech."

"Great." Daniel pulls back into traffic. "And we don't have any idea when that thing is going to blow."

"Or *why* it's going to blow." I tap Daniel's arm and flip the rearview mirror down so that he can see my father, whose eyes are squeezed tight.

"Okay," Daniel says, flipping the mirror back up. "I was going to suggest a hotel room. But maybe we'll drive down to the other end of the park. Let everyone get some fresh air."

I saw the sphere in my vision, and I know it's going to blow. But maybe getting my father out of here is what limits the damage to a big gold ball rather than a big glass building with hundreds of people inside.

CHAPTER
TWENTY-FIVE

Knoxville, Tennessee
April 27, 2020, 6:33 p.m.

I locate a huge paved lot near a park about a half mile from the amphitheater. It appears to be overflow parking.

"Can you walk that far?" I ask Daniel. "If not, we can drop them off and circle back."

I'm worried he'll be defensive about it, but he nods. "As long as I take it at a moderate pace. But you need to stay here. Someone needs to keep an eye on your father and Miller. I've leave you his gun."

"We lock Miller in the van. Sophie takes Lily for a walk. And my dad has some alone time in that empty lot. I'm coming with you."

It was clear from Daniel's tone of voice that the suggestion was a trial balloon, and he doesn't seem surprised that it failed to fly. I would have argued for the buddy system regardless, but it goes double since I don't remember seeing Daniel in my vision. I know the rest of us currently in this vehicle will be fine when the sun comes up, but Daniel wasn't there. He may have promised Aaron he'd watch out for me, but I have a responsibility to look out for him, too.

There are a few cars near the end of the lot closest to the park, but the section beyond the railroad tracks is as empty as it was in the satellite photo, aside from scattered fast-food containers and a few beer bottles.

Once we're parked, Daniel gives Miller one last mental nudge to keep him sleeping while I open up the back of the van and tap my father on the shoulder. He jumps, hitting his head on the ceiling of the van. But nothing explodes, so I count myself lucky.

"We're going to leave you here, okay, Dad? We'll be back. And if anyone inside your head needs to . . . vent"—I nod toward the parking lot—"this might be a good spot. But try to keep it low-key. We're in the middle of the city."

Pfeifer gives me a shaky smile and unbuckles his seat belt. "Low-key. Sure."

I'm about to close the hatch when the umbrellas in the storage area catch my eye. I grab two.

"Do you think Miller is pretty well under?" I ask as Daniel and I begin walking back toward the Sunsphere.

"Yeah," he says. "It should hold. Even if it doesn't, he's in the cuffs. He's really . . . obstinate."

I hand one of the umbrellas to Daniel. He gives a confused glance at the cloudless sky and then says, "Oh. Got it. Not for rain."

"They may not offer much protection from flying glass, but it's better than nothing. Do you think it would do any good to call security?"

"Not really. And like you said, some protection is better than nothing. Everyone is under the amphitheater canopy, right? Even if we could convince them to evacuate, what if that thing blows right in the middle of them leaving? What I'd really like to do is find Colonel Smith. Give him a heads-up, so that maybe they can do some crowd control. Keep people seated until it's clear that there's no danger."

"Smith is here?"

"Yeah. Remember? He said he'd check back in on us after the conference. And he was overseeing the school at Bragg before they relocated those kids to Sandalford. I'd say he fits the description of someone who could share best practices for dealing with Delphi psychics."

Daniel manages to keep up a decent pace. We're a little over halfway there when I hear microphone feedback off in the distance, and a woman begins talking. As we get closer, I hear applause, and then a voice I recognize from too many TV news clips thanks the woman for the introduction.

The response from my hitcher is strong. Stronger than I expect, strong enough that I miss a step as I shore up the ramparts holding him in.

"You okay?" Daniel asks.

I nod. "Tripped on the sidewalk."

He gives me a skeptical look. "You need to let me know if there's an issue . . ."

"There's *no issue*, Daniel. I tripped."

As we approach, I see that the crowd is larger now. A little over a third of the seating beneath the canopy is occupied, looks like mostly by the people at the reception earlier. But a new crowd has formed around the edges of the auditorium. This group, three or four dozen at least, is dressed mostly in purple-and-white T-shirts. A few have their children along. Some are carrying *Unify America* or *Cregg for Our Future* signs. One sign has the Republican elephant and Democratic donkey on the right and left, respectively. They're both crossed out, and *For 2020 Vision: Unify America* is printed in the center.

That explains why the event was moved outside. Even though this kind of conference shouldn't be a political event, the Senator isn't about to miss out on a chance for extra publicity.

Daniel and I circle around back to the grassy area behind the seats. The food tables have been removed from the stage, and the podium is now decked out in purple-and-white streamers with the Unify America

393

logo in the center. It sits between two giant monitors running Senator Cregg's usual backdrop, a slightly hypnotic video clip of gently waving red-and-blue stripes that float across the screen, merging to purple when they meet.

The Senator thanks the conference attendees and also the small crowd that has gathered, calling them unintended, but very welcome, guests. That gets a snort from two men sitting in the upper seats, who seem to understand exactly why this change of venue happened.

"Given recent events at Oak Ridge, I'll keep my remarks brief . . . and yes, it *is* possible for a politician to do that if we try really hard." Cregg pauses, and several people oblige him with a half-hearted laugh.

His spider-rat son responds too, scratching again at the bricks in my wall.

Okay, fine. I get it. He's the enemy. But you're not helping.

Two more scratches and then silence.

"The attack at Oak Ridge this afternoon was far more serious than I . . ." Senator Cregg stops and clears his throat. "Than any previous attempt by the WOCAN terror group. This rapid escalation of violence is the very reason conferences like this are so vital to our national security."

He sounds like his usual bombastic self on the surface. But I've listened to his speeches a lot lately, and I can tell he's nervous. If the audience notices, they probably think it's because of the attack at Oak Ridge. But the attack wasn't a surprise to the Senator. Something else must have him on edge.

The control booth for the theater is a large concrete box at the center of the structure. We stop on one side of the box, and Daniel pulls out his phone. He zooms in and holds it up like he's recording the Senator's speech. But I can see the screen, and he's not watching the stage. He's looking out at the audience, scanning the seats for Colonel Smith.

"Strong and committed leadership at all levels of government is the only hope we have of combating this plague and those who have been afflicted by it," Cregg says from the podium. "We can show mercy to those who, through no fault of their own, are caught up in this storm. But there can be no mercy for those who would use these powers against their nation, to terrorize their own people.

"And that is the reason," the Senator continues, "that I gladly agreed to be here tonight, even though we have primaries in five states tomorrow. I have always believed that this is an issue that must transcend politics, but the horrific actions taken by . . ."

"Got him," Daniel says softly as the Senator speechifies on, and motions for me to take the phone. "Hold it there until I get back."

I have no idea what Daniel is up to, but I nod. He takes off, not toward Smith, as I expect, but over to a man in a purple *Cregg for Our Future* shirt who's standing a few yards to the left of us. The guy follows him back to where I'm standing.

"See that man?" Daniel says. "Eight rows down, three seats in. His name tag will say *Smith*. Go tell him one of his soldiers needs to speak with him behind the control booth on an urgent matter. Then say, *persuade, change, influence*. Repeat that back."

The guy does, and then Daniel nods toward the aisle. "After you tell him, take a seat. *Under the canopy*."

"What is *persuade, change, influence?*" I ask once the man leaves.

"PSYOP motto."

Two little boys are running around on the lawn near the lake. I cast a nervous glance up at the Sunsphere. "Listen, you do what you can with Smith, but I'm going to try to herd some of these folks toward the seats. That sphere could go any minute, and . . ."

He's hesitant, but then he follows my gaze toward the two boys, who have now been joined by a third. "Okay, but . . . don't be too obvious."

Smith rounds the corner as I'm walking past. He recognizes me and moves in my direction, but then Daniel steps forward. I don't hear what he says to Smith—I'm not even positive he says anything out loud—but the man immediately forgets all about me and follows Daniel back around to the side of the control booth.

Cregg is now detailing his five-point plan for dealing with the crisis. The flowing stripes on the monitor have faded into the background, behind the word *IDENTIFY* in large, bold type.

I approach a small cluster of people near the edge of the amphitheater and tap the shoulder of a woman in a *Unify America* shirt. "Excuse me. I'm a volunteer with the Senator's campaign."

She gives my definitely-not-purple and definitely-not-business attire a questioning glance, but I keep talking. "There are several reporters here, and I just saw one tweeting about all the empty seats. Could you and your friends help me spread the word to everyone standing out here on the lawn? Young, old, everybody—we need to fill in those gaps in the audience as fast as possible."

"Sure! Happy to help."

The woman talks to her friends, and they fan out into the crowd, which soon begins moving toward the shelter. I circle behind the stage to the other side and find a second volunteer to get that group of people into the seats.

Dozens of people taking seats at once isn't a quiet enterprise, and the Senator seems a little annoyed at first. But he pauses his speech and waits for everyone to get seated. "Sure. Come on in," he says with his usual snake-oiled smile. "Plenty of seats for everyone."

His comment draws in a few more of the stragglers. There are now only two people out on the lawn, down near the opposite end of the lake, on one of the curved benches near the fountain. They're much more interested in each other than in Senator Cregg's speech, and I'm just going to have to hope they're outside the blast radius.

As I head back to rejoin Daniel, the door to the control booth opens, and a young man in a purple shirt steps out. He closes the door, latches it with a padlock, and then begins walking briskly up the path that leads to the main road.

Daniel must have nudged Smith into listen-only mode. He's standing rigidly against the wall, his cell phone in one hand, looking stunned. His eyes widen slightly when he sees me, but he remains silent.

"How did you do that?" Daniel asks, nodding toward the last group of people moving into the seating area. His eyes are slightly narrowed, and I realize what he's thinking.

"It's *me*, Daniel. I'm not going to let him out of his cage for something like this. I just employed a little basic psychology. Maybe we didn't need to pull the Colonel into this after all."

"No," Daniel says. "We need him. Not for crowd control, but—"

A horn blasts twice. I look toward the road but then realize that the noise is coming from the speakers over our heads. On the stage, the Senator's bullet points have disappeared from the monitors. In their place is a video. A group of around fifteen people stand in front of a dark-gray pickup truck parked on the side of a two-lane road. Some of them wave little WOCAN flags. All of them are dressed in black, and all are wearing bear masks, except for the woman in front, the one bear who doesn't care. Dacia's mask is tipped up to the top of her head, and she's smiling gleefully at the camera.

"Hello Shield2020 people! Enough of boring speech. Let's take a trip!"

The people in the video pile back into the truck. They're mostly male and mostly adult, but I see three children. I'm pretty sure one of them is Maggie. The woman next to her is Ashley. I would have guessed it simply from her build—she's a bit more curvy than the other bears—but I also recognize the vivid abstract print on her shoes. It reminds me a bit of Van Gogh's *Starry Night*. She once told me they were nursing clogs, and said that when you wear scrubs every day, you need some outlet for individual taste.

The child she's carrying is definitely Caleb. His head rests against her shoulder, and a fringe of blond curls peeks out from his mask.

The video isn't live. It looks like it was filmed this afternoon in Oak Ridge. They pass a sign on the right that reads *Y-12 New Hope Center* a few seconds after the truck moves back onto the road. The camera pans to show the building, the other "bears" in the back of the truck, and then cuts to the truck driving down a long, two-lane road toward a checkpoint in the distance. Dacia is on the passenger side with the camera in selfie mode.

"We are humans of the future. You are humans of the past. We will no longer allow you to treat us like animals, to lock us away. You call us freaks and mutants. But we are superior. And there are more of us every day."

She pans again to show that the driver and the person sitting next to her, who is either a kid or really short, are both wearing bear masks. Up ahead, a gate blocks the road, and two armed guards, one male and one female, approach the truck.

"Drop your guns." The bear in the middle has a high voice. A girl, I think, and no more than nine or ten years old. But the guards obey her command without question.

"The ID in his hand is good," Little Bear says slowly. She's looking down, and I'm pretty sure she's reading a script. "His name is Fred, and he's the only person in this truck. You know Fred. He makes this delivery every week."

The driver holds up his hand, and the audience can see that he's holding a pack of cigarettes, not identification. The guard closest to the truck, however, gives it a cursory inspection.

A boom sounds in the distance, and the camera pivots behind the truck. All of the bears are watching the New Hope building, about a quarter mile back, when a second explosion rips the roof off. One of them pumps his fist, and a few others high five.

The guards are watching, too. "What the hell?" the female guard says, and then Little Bear glances back down at her lap and says, "That's the controlled demolish . . ." A little sigh of frustration, and then she repeats, "The controlled demolition scheduled for today. You got an e-mail about it. Open the gate now so we can go."

"We got an e-mail," the male guard says, tapping the gate control with a badge that's attached to his belt. "You can go."

Here in the auditorium, feet pound up the stairs toward the control booth. A woman grabs the door handle and yanks, apparently hoping the giant padlock in front of her is an optical illusion. When it doesn't open, she pounds on the metal door in frustration.

Senator Cregg is no longer at the podium. He's tugging on the cord to one of the monitors. It blinks out, and he runs to the other side of the stage to take care of the second monitor.

Behind him, a second fountain springs to life. At first, I think it's simply on a timer, but then the fountain grows, surging at least three times as high as the one at the far end of the lake.

Back on the remaining monitor, Little Bear is telling the guards, "Get in the booth and forget we were here." And then the monitor goes black.

But the audio, which must be run separately, continues. "See? We simply drive through the gates to where the nukes are!"

The guy who locked the control door is still visible at the very end of the path. I need to see where he's going and, more importantly, determine whether that second fountain behind the stage is what I think it is.

Dacia's voice rings out, giddy with excitement. "We have an army now, and it grows each day. Just now, you watched us control weak minds of these guards. And we could be *anywhere*. Maybe we are sitting next to you right now. This time our psychic did not blow up nukes. Only buildings, and mostly buildings with no people. That's why we wait until they close for the day. But next time? Who knows. Stop listening to the *politicieni* like Senator Cregg. Give us the WOCAN states for our homeland. Let us live in peace, and we will leave you alone."

I'm almost to the path when the burner phone rings. It's probably Daniel asking what the hell I'm doing, but I can't stop. I look behind me, planning to signal to him that I know what I'm doing, but my eyes never make it that far. They stop at the overpass, where Ashley stands at the wall, holding Caleb. She's still in the black clothes she was wearing in the video, but the bear mask is gone.

Caleb stares at the water, transfixed by the new fountain he's created. Ashley glances over her shoulder and then at the convention center, with its hundreds of glass panes. She says something to Caleb, and the fountain subsides instantly. The only hint it was ever there are the ripples in the water.

He's now looking up at the Sunsphere. There's a crackling noise. I panic, before remembering the umbrella.

I don't know if it's my panic or just a stray thought that reaches him, but Caleb is looking straight at me now.

ANNA BIG BALL GO *BOOM*.

Then the cracking sound grows louder, and tiny golden and clear crystals rain down from above, covering the sidewalk and the grass. The people in the amphitheater are screaming, but they all stay beneath the shelter.

I stand alone on the lawn, beneath my umbrella, as the gilded snow falls.

CHAPTER
TWENTY-SIX

Knoxville, Tennessee
April 27, 2020, 7:33 p.m.

The fact that I am alone in the middle of a glass blizzard, under an umbrella on a cloudless night, is going to raise eyebrows. It might be best not to wait around for questions. As soon as I'm certain the storm has ended, I toss the umbrella into the bushes and head for the park where we left the van. I'll call Daniel when I get there and we can set up a rendezvous point.

It's a little slippery at first. The glass fragments are so small that it's almost like walking on sand. But the blast radius was limited, almost unnaturally so, and I'm reminded of the space around my father's feet in the cell, which was clear of shrapnel from the chain. I suspect there's a similar fragment-free circle near the spot where Ashley and Caleb were standing.

By the time I'm across the street, I'm able to pick up the pace to a run. Just another jogger in the park. Pay no attention to the gold glitter on my shoes.

My father is on the curb when I reach the empty lot. I sit next to him, and he glances at what remains of the Sunsphere. "I didn't do it," he says with a hint of a smile.

"I know."

"But . . . you might want to avoid walking on that parking lot for a bit. The asphalt is a little spongy."

"Oh. Well, at least you picked up the trash."

"I got *rid* of the trash. I didn't pick it up."

Now that I look closer, he's right. There are several small piles of ashes scattered about, along with a few oddly misshapen mounds that appear to be melted glass.

"The little boy did it, right? The one Daniel worries about."

"Yes. Caleb. How did you know?"

He gives a small one-shoulder shrug. "There's a seer in here. She's just not very . . . reliable. Some of the things she sees never happen."

"That seems to be pretty common with adepts. Stan, the guy back at Sandalford, is like that."

"This one is also a bit unstable, though. Most of the adepts that Graham Cregg had killed were unstable."

I nod. The only exception I know of was Jaden, and he seemed to think he got pulled in because he and Will were roommates and the Fudds needed another body to test my ability.

"So, you're getting to know your hitchers," I say. "Is that why you've been meditating in the back seat?"

"Partly. I want to know what they can do. But mostly because your mother finds it easier to keep all of our guests calm if I can shut out the external world. They were a little unnerved just after you left . . . a lot of talk about spiders and cages. Is it getting harder to hold him back?"

"Generally speaking, no. It was just when he heard the Senator's voice. I . . . I used his own logic on him. Said we have a common enemy, so he needed to get the hell back. And it seems to have worked, at least for now. Tell your crew not to worry. The walls are intact."

"But . . . you won't be able to *keep* them intact." The voice has changed, and even though I can't see his eyes clearly in the dim light, I know that I'm talking to my mother now. "You can't hold him at bay forever, Anna," she says softly.

"With the injections, I could. Probably."

"But, at some point, you need to pull down the walls and deal with him. Make him leave. Right? You don't want him in your head. And we don't want that *for* you."

"I know. And when this is over, I'll talk to Kelsey, and . . ." I don't finish, because that reminds me that I don't really know how much Kelsey can help me this time. We relied heavily on hypnosis to evict Myron, and that won't work with Cregg. Usually I'm glad that I have only vague memories of those last sessions. My strongest memory is from after, when Kelsey held me while I cried. But it might be helpful to have a clear understanding of exactly *how* we made him leave.

"It's okay, Anna. I'm not trying to push you. It's just . . . you said you kept him at bay by pointing out your common goal. It seems the one driving motivation he had was finding a way to protect the adepts—at least the younger ones. Yes, he's a monster. But he had at least that as a redeeming quality. And you may have to find the humanity in him in order to evict him."

My phone rings. It's Daniel. He didn't see Caleb and Ashley, but he'd already guessed the boy was there due to the water plume behind the stage. Water effects are Caleb's calling card. No one was injured, but people are still panicked, and the second day of the conference has been cancelled.

We agree to meet outside a nearby hotel in ten minutes, and as I'm hanging up, I see the call that came in just before the explosion. It wasn't Daniel, as I'd thought. It was Porter. I freeze, scared to listen to the message. I guess my dad picks up on that, because he reaches over and squeezes my hand.

"If it helps, my seer is positive that your friends at the cabin are all okay."

That's not exactly reassuring, given what he just said about her reliability rating. But it's the thought that counts, so I give him a shaky smile and tap the phone to play the message.

The voice isn't Porter's. It's Aaron's. Tears stream down my face as I listen. "They're okay. Deo and Sam, too. Colonel Smith's men—not Dacia's—were guarding them, and he called to order them released."

"Are they going back to Sandalford?" he asks.

"He didn't say. I'll call him when we get to the hotel and let them know about Magda's deal with the Senator. I'm just so relieved that they're safe."

Pfeifer smiles, but there's something a little strained about it. Like he knows something I don't. Or maybe he's just not very experienced with the whole dad thing and doesn't really know how to handle an emotional daughter. Or he realizes that safe only means safe for now.

When we get back to the van, Sophie is waiting on a bench near the play fort. A large Subway bag is next to her, and Lily is asleep in her lap.

"Guess you were right about the gold ball," she says, standing carefully to avoid waking Lily. "I heard a splintering noise, and when I looked up, it was like fireworks with all of the pieces catching the lights from the city."

"I didn't do it," Pfeifer says. "It was that Caleb kid."

"And I think we're lucky it was just the ball," I say, remembering the way Ashley kept looking at the larger target off to her left—the very large, very fragile-looking convention center.

"Oh, FYI," Sophie says, "Miller's awake again."

I sigh, wishing I'd gone back for the gun rather than leaving it with Daniel. We walk over to the van, and I look inside. Miller's eyes are wide open, staring balefully back at me. I pause before opening the door. His hands aren't visible through the window, so I have no way of knowing if he's still restrained.

"Just slide the door open and we'll check," Pfeifer says in a voice loud enough for Miller to hear. "I'd be happy to 'vent' again if he gives us any trouble."

Miller hasn't freed himself, fortunately, although the red grooves on his wrists, which are almost as vivid as the self-inflicted bite marks on his fingers from earlier today, suggest that it's not from lack of trying.

It takes longer than ten minutes to get the hotel, even though it's only a few blocks away. We could have walked in half the time, if not for Miller. Cars are clogging the intersections, and the area around the convention center is now cordoned off and teeming with police.

Daniel is at the curb.

"Aaron called," I tell him, fighting the tears again. "They're okay."

He nods. "Yeah. I convinced Smith to have them released."

I'm not sure if Daniel means convinced or *convinced*, but I guess it doesn't really matter. He nudges Miller again and removes the restraint. I'm a little nervous about that, but we'll need a credit card and ID to check into the hotel. The only ID we have has Miller's face on it, and it would be a bit awkward to have him sign for the room with his hands bound. As it is, the clerk gives Daniel an odd look, because Miller seems to be waiting for instructions from him before doing anything. It's not like it was with Alex Cregg, where he nudged her about the general scenario, and her mind filled in the blanks on its own. Miller seems to be getting better at resisting. I think back to what Daniel once said about Whistler—nudging him didn't always stick, because he'd built up some resistance from being around Dacia and the other adepts at The Warren. Maybe Miller is building up an immunity due to his time at Sandalford.

"Where's the Colonel?" I ask once we're inside the elevator.

"He's meeting us in the bar in half an hour. I told him we needed food and a shower, although I guess we're stuck in these clothes."

Daniel grabs one of the sandwiches out of the Subway bag, rips off the wrapper, and takes a bite without even checking to see what kind it is. "Obviously, I wasn't able to follow the Senator," he says around a mouthful of sandwich. "His security team was already on alert after Dacia hacked into his presentation, and they closed ranks as soon as that thing exploded. I couldn't even get close enough to get the tag from his car."

"There's probably no point, anyway. I think it's safe to assume the Senator will follow Dacia, and we know where she's going."

Daniel raises his eyebrows. "We do?"

"In the video, she said she has an *army*. And we both know that's only partly true. Most of her bears aren't psychic at all. She's going to Sandalford, to try to get the rest of the adepts to side with her."

"Would he follow her immediately, though? You heard him tonight—there are primaries in five more states tomorrow."

The elevator opens and we file out. Except Miller, who is reaching for the operating panel when my father grabs his arm and yanks him out into the hallway.

Daniel huffs angrily. "Walk in front of me until I tell you to stop, Miller."

The two rooms are adjoining, and Sophie takes Lily into one of them, hoping for a little quiet. Once we're inside the other room, Daniel pulls out both the last zip cuff and the gun, pointing the latter at Miller.

As I put the cuffs on Miller, my dad says, "Make it as tight as you like," in a vaguely British accent. I snort out a laugh, partly because I wouldn't have pegged him as a *Princess Bride* fan, but also because I know Deo would laugh at that line, too. And after being constantly on edge all day, it's an unbelievable relief to have a thought like that enter my head without it pushing me into a worry spiral.

I duck into the adjoining room for a quick shower. Sophie and Lily are both sprawled out on one of the beds. When I get back, Daniel is on the phone with Aaron and the others, except for Porter, who is driving back to DC. They're in the truck—I can tell from the background noise—and I feel a wave of homesickness. My place is there, with them.

"But the whole WOCAN thing was a joke," Taylor is saying. "Cregg was just using them to stir up fear. Why is Dacia suddenly beating that drum? It doesn't make sense."

"She's not simply calling for separate states," Daniel says. "It sounds like she wants that area to be a . . . I don't know, a reservation, I guess? For Delphi adepts."

"Of which there are maybe a few hundred, total," Taylor says. "Okay, let's say a few thousand, with the new cases cropping up."

"And the bulk of those are most likely temporary," Pfeifer says. "Unless they've changed the formula names on the spreadsheet that Taylor showed me, the vast majority of what Graham Cregg has been selling to the dealers is the short-term variety that the military wanted."

I ask if he thinks that's why so many deaths are being reported right as Taylor says that it's still way too few people to fill up the West Coast.

"Maybe that's just her opening pitch," Deo says. "Ask for five states, and they'll give you one?"

Daniel says we need to leave if we're going to meet Colonel Smith on time, but I take the phone. "Please tell me you guys are not headed back to the Outer Banks."

"Well . . . not tonight," Deo says, in a voice that I know from long experience indicates he's just told me a partial truth, at best.

"Sam, you're a responsible adult," I say. "Dacia is heading for Sandalford. The Senator will almost certainly follow her. Please, take them back to DC."

"Um . . . Sam's not here. He rode back with Porter," Aaron says. "I'm the only responsible adult, and as much as I'd love to avoid it, the fact that Dacia and Cregg are headed toward Sandalford means we're needed there, too. Deo, especially."

"Because Maria and Stan say so? You were the one saying you didn't believe his stupid paths. That things could be changed. At least wait until we can all go together."

"Kelsey's there," Deo reminds me.

"And a bunch of other people we care about," Aaron adds. "You want us to abandon them?"

"No. Of course I don't. I just . . ."

I just want them to be safe. I want everyone I care about to be safe and for all of this to be over.

"Come on," Taylor says. "Give her a break. She's worried. We're not going directly to Sandalford, Anna. We'll stop for the night, and then we're going to meet up with Kelsey, Maria, and some of the other adepts tomorrow. We don't have a location yet, and I don't know how long we'll be able to keep what we're up to from Magda, or even how many of the adepts will be able to sneak out. But . . . we'll let you know where we are."

Taylor Quinn being the voice of calm and reason is probably a sign of the apocalypse. But I say okay and promise that we'll be leaving around daybreak.

I missed the first half of the conversation, so Daniel gives me a quick recap as we go downstairs.

"Porter arrived to find Aaron, Taylor, and Deo under military house arrest, but Smith called and instructed the guards to release them."

"Because you nudged him?"

"Yeah. Then I nudged him again to meet us here. To *listen*. To give us a chance to explain what we know about the Senator's role in all of this. If I have to do more, I will. But I'm tired. Dealing with Miller is draining. And . . . Smith thinks I started investigating all of this out of concern for Aaron and Taylor. He does *not* know my biological father was in the program or anything about my ability. We need to keep it that way, because I don't think he's the type who will appreciate knowing I pushed him around."

"You had him pinned against the concrete wall out there earlier while you were talking. What does he think happened?"

"He . . . kind of doesn't remember that bit."

Okay, so it's not just controlling Miller that's draining Daniel. He's burning the candle at both ends—nudging both Miller and Smith.

"What exactly do you think Smith can do to help us?"

"At a minimum, provide us with transport back to North Carolina in the morning. The Outer Banks isn't that far out of his way, since they'll be flying him back to Bragg. That keeps us from driving fourteen hours in what will likely be reported soon as a stolen vehicle . . . those real estate signs Sophie slapped on the side aren't going to help if they call in the tags. But ideally, I'm hoping Smith will realize he's playing for the Dark Side. He'd be one hell of an ally to have against Dacia and the Senator. And that's the key reason you're here—as a visual aid."

"What?" I glance down at my disheveled clothes, not sure whether I should be offended or amused.

"The cut on your lip," Daniel says. "I want Smith to have a visual reminder of the kind of people we're dealing with. To let him know that Senator Cregg, Dacia, Magda, Miller—none of them have the adepts' best interests at heart."

"And you think Smith does?"

"Yeah. I'd like to think that would be true even if he didn't have a son at Sandalford, but . . ."

"What? You're kidding."

"No. The boy has low-level telekinesis. They were able to hide it by homeschooling him, but I'd heard a couple of rumors when I was stationed at Bragg . . . and Smith admitted it when we spoke earlier at the amphitheater."

Again, I'm not sure whether he means Smith admitted it voluntarily or via nudge, but I don't have time to ask. Smith, who has spotted us, is seated at a two-person table. I guess he wasn't expecting me to join them. Daniel must have wanted his visual aid to be a surprise.

The place is crowded, so Smith carries his beer out to a fire-pit table on the patio. Daniel joins him, and I go to the bar to order food. The last thing I ate was before we left the prison, and that was a rock-hard atrocity that claimed to be a breakfast bar, so I'm starving. Daniel asked me to order him a burger and fries, despite scarfing down two of the subs before we left the room. This is the first time that I've seen him as ravenous as Taylor. Nudging these guys must be draining him even more than he thought.

When I join them on the patio, Smith stands up and introduces himself, which is kind of weird. Yes, he's now in civilian clothes without a name tag, but he still knows who I am, and I know who he is. It could be a memory gap due to Daniel messing around with his head, but I suspect it's more Smith's way of distancing himself from what has happened over the past few days. Or signaling that this is a fresh start. That seems a little convenient to me, as though he wasn't complicit in our being abducted and locked in an abandoned prison overnight. But Daniel seems to think he's a decent guy, so I'm willing to give him the benefit of the doubt. Plus, he went all *you will obey my orders* on Miller last night when it came to Lily's welfare. That earns him a few brownie points.

"You're sure it's safe for her to be here?" Smith asks.

At first, I think he means because my face has been in the news in connection with the murders at Fort Bragg, but this must be a follow-up to some conversation the two of them were having, because Daniel says, "She's in control. The psychiatrist at Sandalford prescribed a drug that has helped her to block her . . . unwanted guest. And we need to get her back there so that Dr. Kelsey can evict him."

I don't think it's going to be quite that simple. But I keep silent, partly because I have no idea how much Smith knows about Graham Cregg and his abilities. In the note that Magda left, it was clear that the Senator convinced her—either legitimately or through one of his own psychics—that he's simply been an innocent bystander and that the real fault for any mistreatment of Delphi adepts lies with his dead son. He may have done the same with Smith.

I'm also worried that my spider-rat managed to chip away at my walls earlier this evening. He's nowhere near full strength, but the fact that he could throw me off like that is disturbing. Granted, he was responding to the voice of someone he hates. The voice of someone I'm increasingly certain was an emotionally—and quite possibly, physically—abusive parent.

You may have to find the humanity in him in order to evict him. I can see the logic behind my mother's advice, but I don't really want to humanize that monster. With Kelsey's help, I got rid of Myron by sheer brute force. We can do the same to Graham Cregg.

A TV screen mounted at the end of the patio is tuned to CNN. Captions scroll below a reporter standing before the hollowed-out shell of a building that used to be the New Hope Visitors Center. Twenty-five people killed and more than sixty wounded. Two other buildings were damaged—an office building and the water treatment plant—although there were only minor injuries.

"Doesn't seem to be much rhyme or reason to what they hit," Smith says. "Why a water treatment facility?"

I pull out my phone to check the map I was looking at earlier. "I'm not sure about the other building. But the water treatment plant was located right near the gate. It would have been the very next building they saw after New Hope."

Smith takes the phone from me and examines the map for a moment. "So . . . a target of opportunity? Could be. Especially if it turns out that the third building they destroyed was one of the next stops on that road." He gives me back the phone. "Any particular reason why you were looking at this map?"

Daniel is about to answer for me, but I hold up a hand to tell him I can manage on my own. "We were hoping to rescue the children Dacia Badea is holding captive, since she has a record of killing kids. Sophie remembered her mentioning the lab at Oak Ridge. We might have made it there in time to stop them if someone hadn't locked us inside a prison cell last night."

Smith gives a little *point-taken* nod. "Quinn was just saying that you saw the child responsible for the destruction tonight."

"Yes. I saw Caleb with his aunt, Ashley Swinton, above me on the Clinch Avenue overpass. But I don't think the Sunsphere was their assigned target. I think their instructions were to hit the convention center, and Ashley redirected Caleb's focus in order to limit casualties. She kept glancing over at the building, and then she whispered something to Caleb about the big gold ball."

"You were close enough to hear what she said?" Smith asks.

"No, but she didn't *need* to be," Daniel says, clearly annoyed. "You know that. You've dealt with psychic phenomena for several decades now. And Caleb is . . . multitalented. He's telekinetic, but he can also push thoughts to people at a short distance, among other things."

"He pushed my name," I say. "And 'big ball go boom.' After which the big ball did indeed go boom."

"And you think Dacia Badea was targeting the convention center because of the Shield2020 event? We were all outside."

"All outside in seats pointed directly toward the convention center," Daniel says. "What better way to get Dacia's point across. Do you know when they changed the venue of the speech? And why?"

Smith shakes his head. "There was a sign inside the building directing us to the amphitheater. Most of us assumed it was just the Senator seeking out the cameras."

"If you have such a low opinion of him, why are you cooperating with him?" I ask. "For that matter, why would someone in the military be working with a presidential candidate who is trying to unseat your commander in chief? Aren't there rules about politicizing the military?"

Daniel shoots me a cautionary look. Maybe these *aren't* the best questions to ask someone whose help you're seeking. But we need answers before we even consider trusting this man.

Smith catches the look and gives a soft chuckle. "Fair enough. I'll assume Quinn shared with you my . . . family connection . . . to the program. Most of the people who were used as guinea pigs by your father and Graham Cregg were enlisted personnel, but I volunteered. Dumbass move, but I was a brand-new lieutenant who wanted to show the older enlisted I wasn't afraid. The serum didn't have any effect on me, so I thought I might have been one of the control group. A few years later, Dalton was born, and when he's about six months old, my wife watches his pacifier float across the room toward him. He's a good kid, and his ability is pretty limited. Still can't levitate anything more than a few pounds, and he's got good impulse control. But he's slipped a few times, when he was upset or nervous. Especially as a little kid. My sister-in-law lives in town, and she has a big damn mouth, so . . . yeah. There were rumors. And when things began to heat up and those kids were found dead at Overhills, well . . . Magda Bell's proposal to move the kids and shelter them until we could figure out what was happening seemed like a godsend. Eventually, we decided to send Dalton, too, although my wife still isn't fully onboard with that decision."

I don't respond, and I'm trying really hard to keep my face neutral. People who need a *family connection* in order to sympathize with those who are different or at risk seriously try my patience.

My poker face must suck, though, because Smith says, "My decision wasn't simply because I have skin in the game, Ms. Morgan. That school fell under my command. Those children are my responsibility. And even though I was a fairly green officer when this program began, I gave it my tacit approval when I volunteered as a subject."

He takes a long swig of his beer. "As for working with Senator Cregg, you're right. The military steers clear of anything even faintly political. But the White House has been under a lot of heat for not taking . . . control . . . of this situation. And my command has likewise been under a lot of heat over the past six months for not 'containing the problem' when we had the chance. The directive—to make the Delphi problem go away—came from the *current* administration."

Daniel and I exchange a look, and then Daniel says, "Wait a minute. You think Dacia Badea was taking orders from the White House when she killed those kids at Overhills?"

"I don't know," Smith says. "Probably not. What I will say is that if it spares the White House any sort of political embarrassment, I can promise you they will not bat an eye if Dacia Badea kills every single adept, as long as she cleans up the mess and that's the last they hear of her. This program has been covered up by leaders of both parties for decades, and the president doesn't like the fact he's the one in office, facing a tight three-way race, when the whole damn thing blows up. Have you seen the polls? Cregg could win this thing." He stops, shaking his head in dismay. "My new orders were simply to help facilitate this transfer, and I don't know anything for certain. But I think the administration cut some sort of deal with the Senator. Cregg solves the Delphi problem, and he's added to the ticket."

Daniel looks skeptical. "What about the current VP?"

"They'd just dump him," I say. "FDR had three different running mates. But what do you mean by *Cregg solves the problem*?"

"Cregg says they've got a cure."

"He's lying. At least concerning the second-gen Delphi. My father says it's simply not possible. Maybe a treatment to . . . curb our abilities. But it's not permanent. It might not even be safe."

"No offense, Ms. Morgan. But your father has been in a mental institution for the past fifteen years. Science has made many advances—"

"Not that many," Daniel says. "The section of your son's brain that houses his Delphi abilities is deeply connected to the rest of his brain. Are you going to let them test this so-called cure on *him*? Or is he exempt?"

Smith clearly isn't happy with Daniel using his son as the hypothetical test case, so I shift the topic. "Tell the White House this is a bad idea. Graham Cregg left behind ample evidence of his father's involvement in every aspect of the Delphi program. We have spreadsheets, diaries, bank accounts. He and his wife—his first wife—stole the formula they were testing at Stanford back in 1973, hoping they'd eventually be able to cash in on it. And they did, once they found my father."

Daniel eyebrows quirk up slightly, but his poker face is probably better than mine. He's right. I don't know for certain that what I've just said is accurate. I still haven't gotten around to having that conversation with my father, and to be honest, I'm not entirely sure he knows how Cregg obtained the original research. But even though I can't be positive that the puzzle pieces are in the right places, they seem to fit.

A loud *thump* at the back of my head comes just as the waitress arrives with our food. I'm glad for her interruption because it gives me cover. I take a bite of my pasta and send a loud message back to my hitcher.

Chill out, Cregg. If you want us to stop your father—

Another *thump*.

—then stay back.

Again, he thumps. Just a single light knock, almost a tap. Is he trying to signal? One thump for yes, two thumps for no?

Thump.

"And you have sources to back these assertions up?" Smith asks.

Thump.

"Yes," I say.

"Not *with* us," Daniel adds quickly. "We don't even have toothbrushes with us, because we were abducted at gunpoint. But yes. We can back all of that up."

There's a tiny note of hesitation in his voice, but I nod. Even if Dacia confiscated the iPad, which I doubt, Taylor said most of the information was housed on a server.

Thump.

Smith is about to ask something else but then stops, staring over my shoulder at the television. I turn to see a reporter in front of the amphitheater. The *Breaking News* chyron at the bottom reads: *Woman Found Dead at Site of Knoxville Attack.*

I give Daniel a questioning look, because I thought he said there were no serious injuries, let alone a fatality. He shakes his head.

"There was a couple on the bench at the other end of the lake," I say. "But I didn't think the explosion would carry that far. I thought they'd be safe."

But the camera isn't focused on the far side of the lake. The police are gathered around the bushes near the Sunsphere. It's the same spot, in fact, where my father stands in my vision.

I can't see the body. There are police standing all around, blocking the view. But I can see one of the shoes. A nursing clog, in a Van Gogh print.

Ashley.

News Item from the *Knoxville News Sentinel*

April 28, 2020

The firm that manages security for Oak Ridge National Laboratory issued a press release today confirming that video footage of a breach at the facility yesterday afternoon was fake. The WOCAN terror group released the footage in order to claim responsibility for a chemical explosion that began in a tank at the water treatment plant and spread to two other buildings on the Oak Ridge campus.

Authorities claim that video footage of the gate shows no breach. The two guards who were featured in the video appear to be actors, as no one matching their description is currently employed by the security firm, GuardTech International, a subsidiary of the Decathlon Services Group. The background footage has been identified by the company as identical to footage prepared for an unpublished documentary on the Manhattan Project.

A spokesman for GTI noted that it is sadly very easy for people with basic video-editing skills to create a convincing fake in a matter of hours.

When asked how the explosions could have spread to buildings located nearly a half mile apart, a GTI spokesman said the facility is connected by a number of underground tunnels. A request for additional details on the tunnels and the precise cause of the explosion at the water treatment facility was denied on the basis of national security.

CHAPTER
TWENTY-SEVEN

Knoxville, Tennessee
April 28, 2020, 6:11 a.m.

I wake screaming for the second night in a row. Or maybe the third. The days are running together at this point.

It wasn't the first bad dream of the night, just the first that jolted me completely out of sleep. My shoe, kicking the old woman. Someone grabbing me, pulling me away. And then the body morphs into Penelope Cregg, sprawled on the patio. Someone holding me by the back of my shirt, lifting upward and twisting the collar so tightly that it cuts off my air. Standing on my tiptoes, straining to pull in the tiniest bit of air.

You did this. Your fault.

Lily doesn't seem as upset by my outburst as she was yesterday. She's sitting on the other bed with her mother, her lower lip quivering as if warning me that she *will* start crying if I scream again.

"It's okay, Lily. Go back to sleep."

"No!"

Sophie laughs, sitting up. "She was already awake. Lily is a morning person. Can you watch her while I get a shower? Give her some of those banana puffs if she gets fussy."

I find something on the TV to amuse Lily, keeping the volume low so that Daniel and my dad, in the adjoining room, can get a bit more sleep.

It ends up being a moot point. Miller, who spent the night duct-taped to a chair in their room, is now awake and loudly demanding the bathroom. Daniel quiets him, either by waving the gun or giving him a mental nudge. Then I hear muted voices and furniture moving around, so Miller must have convinced them that he actually needs to pee.

Once I have Lily settled, I send a text to Aaron, telling him to call me when he wakes up. The odds of it being a private call seem slim, since he'll be in the truck with Taylor and Deo, and we've got nineteen or twenty people jammed into these two hotel rooms, if you count the ones residing inside heads. I need to let them know about Ashley, though. It's not like we were especially close—and Taylor still holds a pretty sizeable grudge about Ashley pulling her brother's life support—but I still feel awkward telling them via text.

The phone rings almost as soon as I hit send. And *he*, at least, has privacy—Deo and Taylor are apparently still asleep back in the RV. They made it as far as Chesapeake, Virginia, last night and then parked in a store lot to get a few hours of sleep. That's still a few hours out from Carova Beach, so he decided to get an early start.

"Couldn't sleep anyway," he says. "It feels weird to be in the RV without you."

"I miss you, too."

"What on earth is that music in the background?"

I laugh. "*The Mickey Mouse Club*. I'm babysitting right now. Aside from Lily, none of us has had much sleep. Daniel and I didn't get back to the room until around midnight. After we finished talking to Colonel Smith, we had to go in search of something to restrain Miller. He's pretty resistant to Daniel's influence, and you'd be surprised how hard it is to find duct tape in the middle of the night."

"What did you guys find out from Smith?"

"He thinks Cregg has brokered a deal with the White House. Cregg solves the Delphi problem, and in exchange, he's the next vice president."

"Why would Cregg take VP? He stands a decent chance of winning outright."

"Yeah, but an even better chance of winning in 2024 if he spends a term in the number-two slot. Third parties are always at a disadvantage, and you've got the whole electoral college issue to consider. Smith says he isn't certain they've struck a deal, and it's possible that even if they have reached an agreement, it's off the table after last night. The good news, though, is that Smith agreed to fly us to the closest heliport to Sandalford. And Daniel and Smith are scheduled to talk with someone from DHS before we leave, a friend of Smith's who's familiar with the Delphi Project and is somewhat sympathetic to the plight of the adepts. We leave after the meeting, so we'll be there by two at the latest."

"So . . . that's why Daniel isn't in your vision."

"Yes. One part of the mystery solved. And . . ." I sigh, really hating to deliver the next bit of news. "I also know why we'll be nosing around the site of the explosion. I'm guessing you guys haven't seen the news yet?"

"No," he says, yawning. "Did something else happen?"

"Yeah. They found a body. And unless someone swiped her shoes, it's Ashley."

"Damn," he says. "I thought . . . Daniel said she was holding Caleb when that thing blew up. Is Caleb okay?"

"She wasn't killed by the blast. I think Dacia ordered Ashley to have Caleb hit the convention center, and Ashley directed his attention to the Sunsphere instead, to protect the people inside the center. When Ashley didn't follow orders, Dacia killed her and they dumped the body there."

"How did they do that? The place had to have been swarming with police last night."

"Probably the same way they talked themselves past the security gate at a nuclear facility."

"So . . . your dad is going to try and pick up her spirit? Is that a good idea, when he's already got a dozen in his head? I mean, I'm definitely not suggesting that you do it instead, but . . ."

"Don't worry about that," I say as I divert Lily's attention away from an electrical outlet with a handful of banana puffs. "Ashley would think she's gone straight to hell if she had to cohabitate with a giant spider-rat. And I don't know if it's a good idea, but she could have information that will help us. Plus, we both know it doesn't matter. It was in the vision. It's going to happen."

I don't mention the other argument in favor of scooping her spirit up. Much like Hunter's ghost back at Overhills, we can't just leave Ashley here in Knoxville. There's no doubt in my mind that she's stuck on this plane of existence. She had too many questions about her sister, too many worries about Caleb, and too much guilt about what she did to Daniel to allow her to move on quickly. The odds seem strong that she died violently, and that will likely hold her here as well. Ashley will need closure before she can go gentle into that good night, and she stands a much better chance of getting that closure if she's not left to roam around the Sunsphere in search of answers that won't be here. Molly told me that it took months for her to make her way back to the women's shelter, and she died only a few hours away from DC. How much longer would it take Ashley to work her way toward the answers she needs if she's left here?

Of course, I could be entirely wrong on that point. Hitchers aren't physical, so maybe they don't have to walk from point A to point B. Maybe they just have to think about their last happy place really, really hard, and then they're transported back, the way Dorothy got home from Oz.

"Just . . . be careful," Aaron says. "Okay?"

"I will."

"Oh, before I forget, do you have another number for Kelsey? Deo tried the number he had in his phone last night, and we couldn't reach her. I tried again this morning, even left texts, but no response."

"You could check my phone and see if she called from a different number when we talked . . ." I have to think back to when this was. "Day before yesterday, I guess. But I don't think so."

"Okay. Maybe she'll get back with us. She's the one who's setting the place and time for all of us to meet up. I'm assuming it's not too far from Sandalford, since no one there has access to a car—"

"You may be underestimating Maria and her wabbits."

"True."

We talk a bit more about our meeting with Smith, their night under house arrest, and engage in some idle speculation about whether the current administration is really corrupt enough that it would want to simply erase the adepts for political gain.

"If so," Aaron says, "then Graham Cregg inadvertently did us a huge favor by releasing the formula to those dealers. Although not a favor to the . . . okay, I'm just going to borrow a label and call them the neurotypical population. Way too many of them are dying for a temporary thrill. But the government doesn't know it's temporary. And it's going to be a whole lot harder to hide wiping out thousands of people than it would be wiping out dozens. And five more states vote today."

"Maybe Cregg won't win the primary in those states. That can't have been good publicity for him last night. That should give the other woman . . . what's her name? The governor of Texas? It should give her a boost, right?"

Aaron laughs bitterly. "I was going to argue your point, but I think you did it for me, babe. Juanita Breyer is still *what's-her-name* to most of the public. Senator Cregg, on the other hand, just got a ton of free publicity. He's out there, trying to engage other leaders in fighting against these terrorists, and they attack him and his followers. He's going to be spinning this like crazy on the morning shows, the same way he did the attack by his granddaughter. And that will only make it more likely that this deal he's brokered goes through."

"Do you think Dacia's still working with him? Maybe they planned this. She sounded furious at him when she was at the prison, and Sophie keeps saying that she and the Senator have some major trust issues, but . . ."

"It's possible they're still working together. Or the Senator could simply be doing what all good con men do—seizing every opportunity to take advantage of people when they are scared, misinformed, and at their most vulnerable."

"Well, at least I know now why my dad needs to pick up Ashley. She'll know whether Dacia's anger at Cregg is an act or if she's really a rogue bear."

After we hang up, I check local news to see if there's any new information about the explosion or Ashley's murder. The only thing I find is an article claiming the attack at Oak Ridge was an accident and the video shown at the amphitheater last night was faked. I click on the comments, because I'm a masochist, and there are already a half dozen people saying any idiot should be able to see that it's faked. No one asks the obvious question. If this was really an accident, how could WOCAN have found relevant background footage, filmed a fake attack, edited it into the foreground, and planted it at the rally in Knoxville in a little over two hours? Hopefully reporters *will* ask that question eventually, and push until they get answers, but from what I've seen over the past few years, it seems just as likely they'll let this fade away. The press release invoked the magic words *national security*, which acts as a Cloak of Invisibility to hide all logical inconsistencies.

We leave at eight and manage to get Miller out of the hotel and into the parking garage without attracting attention to the fact that his hands are bound or that I'm hiding a gun behind the diaper bag I have clutched to my chest. Before he left for his meeting with Smith and the woman from DHS, Daniel gave Miller a strong nudge, instructing him to follow my orders. But I'm not taking any chances.

I'm not too keen on being the designated driver, either. It's not really Graham Cregg's occasional suicidal urges that have me worried. He seems, at least for the moment, to be in cooperative mode, and I think he'd much rather have revenge on his father than plunge all of us to our deaths.

Thump.

My bigger issue is that, once we pass the point in time where I have my vision, it's entirely possible that I could have another one. It's unlikely, since I've never had them that close together, but I can't rule it out, and then I'd be unconscious behind the wheel.

Sophie's nose wrinkles as she crawls into the van with Lily. "What's that smell?"

"Probably the smoke on my clothes," Pfeifer says. "Or maybe it's this guy. He's pretty ripe."

As I get into the driver's seat, I get a good whiff, and yes, Miller needs a shower. We should probably have found a way to make that happen while we were at the hotel, since we're going to be enclosed in a helicopter cabin with him for the next few hours.

There's something else underlying the body odor, however. It smells a bit like something burning . . . like *ozone* burning.

What was it that Colonel Smith said to Miller back at the prison? *I thought your boss solved that problem.* And Miller responded that something hadn't kicked in yet.

"He's had the blocker serum," I say out loud.

"You're sure?" Pfeifer doesn't wait for me to answer, just grabs the duct tape and begins securing Miller to the car seat. "That would explain a lot. Daniel was saying last night that he'd never dealt with anyone so difficult to push, and I can't say that Miller strikes me as particularly bright or strong-minded."

The fact that Miller doesn't react at all to that comment, or to the fact that he's being bound to the seat, tells me that he's still under the influence of Daniel's command. So either it hasn't kicked in fully or it only suppresses, rather than fully blocks, the impact.

My dad manages to wrap the tape around Miller twice before the roll runs out. He then presses the back of his hand against Miller's neck. "He's hot. Not dangerously so, but that's more evidence supporting your hypothesis."

As we're exiting the hotel garage, my phone rings. It's Deo. He doesn't waste time with hello but jumps to his point as soon as I answer.

"We're in Corolla, where the four-wheel-drive road begins. I still can't reach Kelsey. Can't reach Stan, either. Taylor even called the landline."

"And we had to leave the RV in a parking lot," Aaron adds. "The storage place was being watched. One of Dacia's bears . . . not in uniform, but I picked up some stray thoughts that identified him."

"We're scheduled to leave at nine, but I'll call Daniel and see if—"

"Anna," Deo says, "it's a *four-hour* helicopter ride. Taylor checked. We can't wait."

"Damn it, D," I begin, but I know I don't have an argument. If our positions were reversed, I'd be storming Sandalford without them, even though there's really not much I could do to help. Deo, on the other hand . . .

"Go. Be careful. Call me. I love you guys—wait, wait, have you tried Miranda? She and the kids may be with Jasper."

There's a long silence on the other end, and then Aaron says, "I'm still not sure I trust him in a high-pressure situation, Anna."

"I'm not saying to pull Jasper in. My point is that, unless Magda gave her the weekend off, which she never does, Miranda would have been down there twice a day to cook. So she may know if anything unusual is going on. But . . . Aaron, if Miranda and his kids *are* at Sandalford and there's a problem, then you absolutely *do* want Jasper with you when you go in. Because if they're in danger and you don't let him know, he's going to consider you as much the enemy as Magda or Dacia or Cregg."

We say our good-byes, and I toss the phone back to Sophie. "Text Daniel. Tell him what you just heard and see if they can speed things up."

As we approach the convention center, I get a good look at the shattered Sunsphere. It no longer looks like a giant lollipop. Now it reminds me of those utensils you use to dispense honey without making a mess. Each layer of the sphere is open to view. Some layers are empty, but the ones that have furnishings—tables, chairs, and so forth—are remarkably intact. It doesn't really look like it was the scene of a massive explosion, but more like someone opened the gold-colored blinds that were hiding the interior.

Clinch Avenue, the upper-level road that passes by the Sunsphere, is open. I'm not surprised to see traffic cones blocking off the entrance to the lower-level road, World's Fair Park Drive. I glance around quickly, and when I don't see any police cars, I decide to interpret those cones as a suggestion rather than an iron-clad rule and bump the passenger-side tire up onto the sidewalk in order to pass without crushing them.

The fact that the road and several walkways pass under Clinch Avenue means that there are convenient places to hide the van. I pull into one that seems to provide the best cover from the road. There are two trucks parked here as well. Maintenance vehicles, I think.

"Are you sure about this?" I ask my dad.

He gives a wry chuckle. "Not entirely. But you are." He shakes his head when I start to protest. "There's room for one more. At least this one won't have abilities that your mother has to monitor."

"But she's going to be frantic. The newly dead are different."

"In most cases, I'm sure they are. But your mother had to calm *me* down when she came on board. That is—or rather *she* is—the only reason I made it through everything with my mind mostly intact."

My dad and I exit the van and step into the scene from my vision. The morning sun is amplified by the water, the stretches of white concrete, and the bright-white of the amphitheater, but most of all by the glittering glass fragments that cover everything that couldn't be swept—the lawn, the bushes, the rocks near the railroad tracks. Even the sidewalk is only partially clear. Tiny gold specks remain, and now I'm thinking of Aaron's eyes and remembering having that thought in the vision. Worrying about the people I love, and remembering feeling that gut-wrenching dread and pushing it away.

No. No. I will not go there. Aaron and Taylor are fine. They have to be. Deo is fine. Kelsey is fine. They are all completely fine, and I'll see them soon.

Pfeifer crouches down next to bushes and runs his hand along the leaves. Then he touches the ground, the sidewalk, the police tape, taking his time to cover each surface carefully. His approach is analytical, scientific.

I shiver, looking around. Cars are driving on the road above. I doubt we'll be able to stand here much longer without someone noticing. The police. And the Senator could have someone watching, waiting.

Sophie must have spotted something that alarms her, because she opens the door and waves for us to hurry.

"We need to go, Dad."

Pfeifer looks at me, startled. As his eyebrows go up, I notice the bruise on his forehead, no longer red but now bluish purple.

"Come on," I say. "We have to go. Sophie's—"

"Ashley's here, Anna. I can feel her. She's just . . . slippery. It's like I can't quite latch on to her. Or maybe I was wrong, maybe it's just too crowded and chaotic in here . . ."

Glancing down the sidewalk, I see what alarmed Sophie. Two police officers have just turned this way. I hold one palm up toward the van in a gesture that I really hope Sophie interprets as *stay where you are.*

And then I turn my attention to my hitcher.

*We need Ashley. And we don't need her to be frightened. Stay
in the very back. Do you understand?*

I get a solitary *thump* in response. Of course, he'd thump if he was
lying, too.

And then I dismantle one of my walls. Not all of them. My trust is
exceedingly thin, and I'm not budging a single brick on the two layers at
the back. If Ashley can't exist in the cramped mental space that remains,
we'll simply have to leave her here, because this is all I have to offer.

CHAPTER
TWENTY-EIGHT

Knoxville, Tennessee
April 28, 2020, 8:21 a.m.

When the front wall is down, I brush my hand along the upper leaves of the bush. I don't expect an instant response, but then I feel Ashley whoosh in like a shopper when the doors open on Black Friday. She's frantic, just as I told my dad she would be, but she's suppressing it. Holding it back, because she knows exactly where she is and why.

My dad's arms are wrapped around me, and I lean into him until the wave of dizziness passes. He's talking to the police officers, one young and one middle-aged, explaining that we were walking on the upper sidewalk looking for this place a friend said had a really good breakfast buffet when I began feeling faint. He was trying to get me to the benches over by the restrooms. To get a wet paper towel. Thought maybe I was overheated.

I'm steady on my feet now, but I play along, still leaning against him. And then Sophie appears, holding Lily. She has the diaper bag slung over her shoulder.

"I couldn't find paper towels. But then I realized I have wipes in the bag."

One officer says we need to get back to the upper-level sidewalk. This is a crime scene. The other asks if we need an ambulance, and I decide that's my cue for an expedited recovery.

"I think I'm okay."

"Could we just get a cab back to the hotel and order room service?" Sophie says testily as she shuffles Lily to her other hip. "If I'd known we were going to walk this far, I'd have brought her stroller."

The younger officer points us to the elevator that leads to the upper level. My dad thanks him, apologizes again, and then we leave.

"That was close," I say once we're inside. "But I wonder how we're going to get the van?"

"We're not," Sophie says, handing me Miller's wallet. "I cracked a window. Left the keys inside. There's nothing in there we need. We definitely don't need Miller."

It takes a few minutes, but we manage to catch a cab in front of the hotel across the street. As we pull away, there's no sign the police have discovered a van parked between the maintenance trucks with a man duct-taped to the back seat. The temperature is in the low eighties, and he's in the shade. His mouth isn't taped, so if they don't find him by the time Daniel's nudge wears off, I'm sure he'll start screaming.

I lean back in the seat and take some deep breaths. Ashley seems to be doing the same. She's remarkably chill for a new hitcher.

Because I was waiting for you. I wanted *you* to pick me up. Not Pfeifer. I don't know him.

We didn't think you'd like being housed with Graham Cregg.

I don't. But my transportation options are limited, and . . . the enemy of my enemy.

Taylor's assessment of that aphorism runs through my mind, and Ashley says:

She's not entirely wrong. But right now, we have to prioritize. Not just for Caleb but for all of the kids at Sandalford. That's where Dacia's heading—

We know. We're on our way.

We need to hurry. Dacia believes she can manage Caleb on her own. She said she's good with kids. Right before . . .

Ashley doesn't finish the thought. I'd have been very surprised if she had, actually. Even though she's clearly accepted that she's dead, the process of *becoming* dead is not something my hitchers like to think about, especially at the beginning.

She's crazy if she thinks she can handle him. *I* can barely handle Caleb.

Dacia is crazy, period. And judging from Lily's reaction to her, she's not good with kids, either.

She'll kill him, Anna. When she realizes she can't control Caleb, she will kill him.

We're not going to let that happen. And . . . I think Caleb might have something to say about it.

Maybe. He's strong. But he's still a little kid. You can distract him. And he'll have these brief flashes of insight where it seems like he's almost an adult, but most of the time, you can't really reason with him. And I'm worried about Maggie. Caleb sucks the life right out of her. He doesn't mean to, but . . .

I know, Ashley.

How did she die?

It's such an abrupt change of topic that I think for a moment Ashley is still talking about Maggie. They I realize she means her sister.

I don't know, exactly. Daniel and I started that conversation, but we never had a chance to finish it. And I think maybe he wasn't ready to talk about the details. He just said Sariah trusted the wrong person.

Yeah. That was sort of a habit with Sariah. A family trait, I guess, since I trusted Senator Cregg to let her go. I don't think she was alive, even then. Oh, and I can promise you that Dacia and the Senator are no longer working together. Dacia was screaming into the phone yesterday. Something about money he'd stolen from joint accounts she held with Lucas. And she was pissed about the military guy ordering her around. Said she was not a *soldat*. That they were supposed to be partners, and it was time he realized that she's the one with the real power. That's why she decided to ratchet things up at Oak Ridge. The original plan was to blow up the sign at the entrance and leave. Another low-level attack to scare people. But when we got there, Dacia starts telling Caleb we're going to play the "go boom" game. I'm surrounded by assholes in bear masks, so I can't talk him out of it, although it really didn't take much encouragement. Caleb likes to use his ability. He doesn't want people to get hurt, but . . . he's a little kid. Easy to manipulate.

Daniel thought the explosions sounded like IEDs.

The one at the visitor center *was* an IED. They set that up yesterday morning, just in case Caleb didn't come through. But Caleb was responsible for the damage to the water treatment plant and the other building. The second building wasn't even something Dacia planned. It just sort of . . . happened . . . once Caleb got started.

Is that why you had him create the waterspout first? At the park last night?

Yes. Water calms him, maybe because he spent so much time in the isolation tank when he was a baby. If Caleb had fired full blast, it wouldn't just have been that sphere. Dacia would have gotten her wish for a bloodbath, either at the amphitheater or over at the convention center. That's why she . . .

And we're back to the thing Ashley can't face yet.

The airfield is located on an island in the Tennessee River. You can see the water beyond the landing strip, blocked in some places by bushes. A small airplane is on the runway, preparing for takeoff, and an Army helicopter—hopefully ours—is parked on the tarmac nearby. Once the cab drops us off, Sophie goes inside in search of a changing table for Lily, and my dad and I take a seat on one of the outdoor benches so we can watch for Daniel and Smith.

"Are you all right?" my father asks. He hasn't spoken since he finished giving our cover story to the police, and he sounds annoyed.

"It wasn't your fault, Dad. Ashley apparently has a thing about hitching rides with strangers. And Cregg has agreed to behave. To stay behind the wall. I don't think he wants to share my head with someone who's freaking out, and she definitely would be if he breaks that barrier."

He shakes his head and sighs. "I don't trust him. You shouldn't either."

"I don't."

"Well, you may *have* to trust him to some extent." The voice is my mom's now. "I'm not saying he's innocent. But some of his madness was inherited. And some was shaped by his father. When you're told that you're a killer from a young age, does it make you more likely to kill?"

"Maybe. Or maybe it makes you determined to *never, ever* do it again. Even when our choices are limited, we have to take responsibility for the decisions we make."

I don't want to back down, even though I get the sense that my mother is partly playing devil's advocate. And, to be honest, I *do* understand what she's saying. Those who grow up in abusive situations are more likely to abuse. They have a major disadvantage compared to those who grow up in loving and supportive environments. But at some point, they decide which path to follow. Maybe they deserve a less harsh judgment when they simply follow the path of least resistance, but they aren't blameless.

Leah-Pfeifer smiles softly. "You're right. But the easiest way to get Graham Cregg out of your head will be to help him find peace. And to do that, you may need to understand his perspective."

"I don't think it's peace he's looking for. I think it's vengeance."

A loud and resounding *thump* comes from behind the wall. For the first time since she came on board, Ashley screams.

It's okay, Ashley. That's just code. One thump for yes, two for no.

Maybe from your perspective. But there's *mortar* on the floor in here, so could you avoid getting him to agree so strongly next time?

Sophie and Lily rejoin us as a black car pulls up to the tiny terminal building. Three people get out—Daniel, Colonel Smith, and a very short, middle-aged woman in a gray pantsuit. She shakes hands with Daniel and Smith, and looks like she's about to get back into the vehicle, but then she changes her mind and walks briskly toward the bench where we're sitting. Her eyes are blazing and locked directly on my father.

We all stand. Sophie hands Lily to me and does a little head nod to indicate that I should step back, just in case things get nasty. Then she moves closer to my father so that her block will be stronger.

The angry little woman doesn't introduce herself but simply says, "Dr. Pfeifer, I just wanted to tell you that your research has created more problems for this nation than *anything* I've dealt with in thirty-two years of government service. Your decision to play God is killing people."

It's definitely my mother looking back at first, and her expression is angry, almost defensive. But then she moves back, and my father speaks, his voice thankfully calm and level. "Guilty as charged, Ms. . . ."

She doesn't answer for a minute and then spits out her name. "Janet Berman, DHS."

"Ms. Berman. This is my daughter, Anna. That's Sophie and her daughter, Lily. As I was saying, I'm guilty on several counts. But the Delphi serum didn't begin with me. When the US government began funding that research, I was in kindergarten and my prized possession was a *Six Million Dollar Man* lunch box."

Berman starts to interrupt, but he holds up one hand. "No. You marched over here and started indicting me, so have the decency to let me tell you my side. I've spent the past fifteen years thinking about this, and I freely admit that I didn't pause to consider the ethical issues when I accepted government funding for my research. My only concern was learning more about how the brain worked, and how we could build on hidden talents that, frankly, I would have sworn didn't exist before I joined the project. I was in it for the *science*, for the knowledge, and if you'd asked me back then, I'd have told you that my responsibility ended there. If you had complaints about the application of that research, I would have directed you to take it up with Washington. My views changed over time, mostly because my wife forced me to look up from my research occasionally and pay attention to the world outside my lab. So yes, I *am* responsible." He glances at me. "As my daughter said a moment ago, we all have to take responsibility for the decisions we make. But there are a whole lot of people in the government—the government that pays your salary and that of Colonel Smith—who share in that responsibility. One of those individuals is currently exploiting my research to further his own economic and political interests at the expense of pretty much everyone else. I'm going to do what I can to stop him, and it would be nice if others who work for the government who funded the mess actually stepped up to the plate to do the same."

Berman's narrowed eyes remain fixed on my father's face as he speaks, her mouth pursed into an angry little bow. When he finishes, she continues to stare at him for a moment and then shifts her gaze toward Smith.

"Call me once you land." Then Berman turns on her heel and returns to her car.

Smith doesn't say anything, either to her or to us. He just begins walking toward the helicopter.

Daniel follows Berman for a few steps, and I hear him thank her for the meeting. He motions for us to follow Smith to the helicopter, although I can't say I'm entirely certain whether Smith's offer of a ride still stands.

Pfeifer veers slightly to the right of where the helicopter is parked. "I'm going to go . . . vent . . . over by the river. I'll be back."

"Very good idea," I say, handing Lily back to her mother.

"Not much of a diplomat, is he?" Daniel says when he catches up to us.

I fight back a laugh at the irony of that coming from Daniel. "Maybe he just has a low tolerance for hypocrisy."

"So . . . was he able to pick up Ashley?"

"No. She decided she'd rather ride with me."

"And that's . . . safe?"

"Graham Cregg's key goal in all of this is stopping his father. He's agreed to stay behind the back wall in the interest of accomplishing that goal."

"Don't—"

"Trust him? Don't worry. I won't."

NEWS ITEM FROM CREGGFOROURFUTURE.COM

April 27, 2020

All campaign events scheduled for tomorrow have been canceled due to a family illness. Senator Cregg urges all supporters in Connecticut, Delaware, Maryland, Rhode Island, and Pennsylvania to get out and vote. The campaign will resume its regular schedule on Friday with rallies in Indianapolis and Gary, in preparation for next Tuesday's primary election.

CHAPTER
TWENTY-NINE

Carova Beach, North Carolina
April 28, 2020, 3:17 p.m.

"It's pretty, isn't it, Lily?" Sophie points down at the water. "See? That's the ocean."

"Not yet. That's just the sound." Daniel points off in the distance to the wider expanse of blue. "That's the ocean over there."

I tell the pilot to pivot to the north as we cross the sound, so that we can land at the fire-and-rescue station without flying directly over Sandalford. The station is only a few miles up the coast, however. If Magda has the guards watching in both directions, they may notice that it's a military chopper, rather than one of the rescue helicopters that more typically fly along the coast.

"That's Long Point Island," I tell Daniel. "The one shaped a bit like an arrowhead. You can see the Quonset huts that Magda had built on that side. And . . . there's a boat up on the shore."

"Do you think it's Jasper and Miranda?"

"No clue. But I'd feel a whole lot better if we knew whether Aaron managed to contact them."

The pilot curves down to the south as we approach Carova Beach and the coastline comes into view. "I've never seen the ocean from the air," I say. "The waves look like tiny little dots from up here, but they can pack a pretty big wallop down there on the shore."

"I've never seen the ocean at all," Sophie says. "Lake Michigan a few times. And Lake Erie a bunch of times, but the beach there is mostly rocks and dead fish, at least where we went. I like to swim, though. There was a pool at The Warren."

That surprises me, but Daniel is nodding, and I get internal confirmation from Ashley.

> You didn't see all of The Warren. There's a reason that many of the kids were happy there. It was a pretty good place from their point of view. Until it wasn't.

Sophie seems happy right now, looking down at the beach. Happier than I've seen her before. Lily is chattering and pointing out the window, too. I think Sophie could be right about Lily being a bit of an empath.

A twinge of worry twists my gut as I watch the two of them, and I can tell that Daniel is thinking the same thing. Maria's talk about the adepts fighting the "bears" on the beach keeps running through my mind. I have no idea what we're heading into. Stan's paths could be wrong. We could be wrong about Dacia heading here—

Thump. Thump.

And then Ashley gives Cregg's opinion a strong second.

> We're not wrong. She's here.

> *Okay. Dacia's here. But we still shouldn't be bringing a baby into this.*

So what's today's cutoff for too young to be in a war zone? Caleb's age? Peyton's? Maggie's?

Fine. We shouldn't be bringing another baby into this.

Smith clearly thought so. He'd tried to convince Sophie to stay at Fort Bragg. To be honest, I thought Smith was going to keep all of us there. I'm pretty sure he toyed with the idea, otherwise we'd have been here two hours earlier. We sat in the helicopter for nearly an hour, and then Smith sent some enlisted guy out to tell us we should come inside. By that time, we didn't argue because we were all in dire need of a bathroom.

But Sophie and Lily got back into the helicopter with the rest of us. She was adamant that she will be needed, and after her recent separation from Lily, there's no way Sophie would leave her daughter behind. As much as I hate to admit it, she's right. Dacia may think she can handle Caleb, but Maggie is doing the handling, and she can't do it alone.

Daniel's meeting with Berman apparently consisted of him talking and her listening. He spoke to Smith a few times on the flight from Knoxville to Fort Bragg, but he got only monosyllabic responses, and Smith offered no guarantees on whether he'll be supporting us. He simply told Daniel he has to make some calls and that he'll be in touch. You'd think he could have made those calls during the two hours we were stuck at Fort Bragg or, better yet, let us leave and *then* make them.

Leaning forward, I ask Daniel, "How much *influence* were you able to exert over Berman and Smith?"

"Some." He rubs his forehead. "I gave Berman an extra nudge as she went back to her car. But here's the deal. They're both operating within a bureaucracy. Nothing gets done on the say-so of any one person. And if a political deal has been reached . . . do you really think this administration will *care* if Cregg is dirty? Or if his family profits from the drug sale?"

Sadly, I know he's right. And that means this lift to Carova may be the only bit of help Smith gives us. Maybe all he can give us. And when the time comes to fight, we could be facing not just Magda's private security and Dacia's bears but also Smith and whatever military force he's been ordered to use against us.

Could the government simply wipe out the adepts without anyone knowing? It's possible. Carova Beach is still relatively empty this time of year, although a few cars and brightly colored beach umbrellas are out. There will be even more a week from now. This stretch of the island is less densely populated than most areas, but warm weather is on the horizon, and soon, most of these houses will be occupied. People would definitely notice then. They wouldn't be happy about having their vacation disrupted.

But given the recent mob violence against adepts like Cameron Applebaum and against those simply perceived as *possible* psychics, like all of those kids in Florida, I can't help but wonder whether the rest of the nation would even care?

If the public was magically granted an eyewitness view of our battle against Cregg and, quite likely, US soldiers, would they cast us as the heroes or as the villains of this tale? Would it matter to them that we are fighting to protect children? That most of the people who will be fighting on our side *are* children?

Maybe I've spent too much time reading the comments sections lately, but I suspect that it will not matter to most "neurotypical" people. They will view us as a mistake of science to be purged from the face of the earth. A select few will be sincerely troubled. A larger group will tsk and say it's a pity, but hey, that's what happens when you tamper with nature. Others—a far larger group than I would have believed even a year ago—will cheer our demise, and the fact that most of the victims are children will not matter to them at all.

It will not matter because these children are not like *their* children. It will not matter to them that the adepts never asked for the powers they have or that the vast majority of these kids worked hard to avoid trouble. They struggled to keep their light hidden, because they understood the consequences of being different. Most of them were even willing to live belowground, like rabbits in their warren, to avoid those consequences.

And then Senator Cregg came along and decided a little fear might help him win the presidency—or at the very least be a nice fat windfall for his bank account. Time to pull these kids out of the shadows. Time to put them on display and reap the full payoff for Penelope's theft of the Delphi formula all those years ago.

If Colonel Smith is right, if the current administration simply wants the Delphi problem managed and doesn't care how, then there will be no better time for them to manage that problem than the present. Each day brings us closer to vacation season, and armed troops rolling down the beach scares away the tourists.

I check my messages again to see if there is anything from Deo or Aaron, but Daniel's text telling me they were on the way to the airfield is the last thing on my list. Should I try calling them or wait? I'm about to ask Daniel when I feel something brush lightly across my forehead, like a spiderweb or a strand of hair. My hand goes up automatically to check, even though I'm certain nothing is there. It's Snoop—and if he's peeking into my head right now, he knows I'm using the nickname he hates. So I lamely add an apology. And then I think that he could be colluding with Magda. Or even Dacia . . . and add another apology, because I don't really believe that. Deo and Taylor both seem to think Snoop—*Jeffrey, his name is Jeffrey*—is a good guy. I trust their instincts.

A moment later, Daniel's phone buzzes. He stares at it, confused, and hands me the phone. "Do you know what this means?"

No big deal. Getting used to Snoop.

"Yes. I was looking at my messages just now, and your number was the last thing I saw. Snoop must have snagged that thought." The phone buzzes again.

Do NOT come to Sandalford. 202 Crane Rd. Code is 15*234439. Leave lights OFF.

Keep to back road. Be careful. Bears on patrol.

Another message from Snoop comes in as I'm texting back to ask if he's heard from Deo.

And that formula thing you were thinking about. His mother regretted stealing it. She wanted the Senator to destroy it after she saw what it did to Graham. That's why the Senator pushed her out that window. I picked that little gem out of the Senator's head just before they burned down The Warren last October. I hate Graham Cregg as much as anybody, but he didn't kill her.

Thump.

Still no response to my question about Deo. I scan back through Snoop's final text again. It explains a lot, and I find myself fighting a tiny bit of sympathy for Cregg. It would be awful to have a parent who committed suicide, but how much worse to think that you had something to do with it? And then to learn that your father—the person who had been fanning the flames of guilt all those years—was actually the responsible party? No wonder Graham turned on his father when he learned the truth.

We touch down next to the fire station. Our heads have barely cleared the rotors when the pilot takes off again. Apparently, he was told to dump his human cargo and get back to Bragg. Sophie holds one hand up to shield Lily's face from dust and sand. The station, mostly staffed by volunteers, is either empty right now or we're not enough of a curiosity to generate interest, because no one steps outside during our brief landing and takeoff.

It's a little over a mile to the address on Crane Road. We stay two blocks back from the shore, where there's tree cover we can duck under if we hear or see a vehicle. Sophie and Lily would both be much happier about the trek if we were able to walk along the beach. They seem to have warmed up a bit to Daniel, however. When I look back at one point, Lily has a bird's-eye view from her perch on his shoulders, and Sophie seems happy to have a break from carrying twenty-five pounds of wriggle.

The warning about bear patrols has me jumping at the slightest sound, however. I wish Aaron were here, not only for the usual reasons, but also as an early warning system. I feel exposed.

"We're okay," my dad says.

"Is that based on something you know or simply to keep me from worrying?"

He smiles. "A little from column A and a little from column B. My seer seems to think the worst thing that will happen between here and that address is we pick up some sandspurs on our jeans. You want to explain why she thinks of herself as a Fiver and not a seer?"

I spend the next few minutes explaining The Warren and its slang, with Daniel and Sophie chiming in.

"Sandalford was Aaron's contribution," I say. "An in-joke. The name is a pun on a warren in *Watership Down* that isn't quite the happy place it seems to be on the surface. Magda seems to love the name, so she must not have read the book."

"Or," Daniel says, "maybe Magda *did* read the book and knew exactly what Aaron was implying."

That hadn't occurred to me. But he may be right.

The house on Crane Road sits one row back from the ocean. It's fairly new construction and considerably smaller than the mansions along the beach. A *Carova Realty* sign is nailed to one of the beams on the porch. That's the company Miranda Hawkins works for on occasion as a house cleaner. Either Miranda gave them the code voluntarily, or Maria plucked it out of her head last time she was at Sandalford.

We brush the sand from our feet and enter the house. The blinds are closed, so it's dark. I make out a sofa and a large table—a pool table, maybe. When we close the door, a scuffling noise comes from up ahead. Daniel hands Lily back to her mother and draws Miller's gun, pointing it toward the sound as we move forward. And then, from the other direction, I hear footsteps hurrying down the stairway. Not thundering down, though. Someone relatively small. Female.

Daniel pivots around, pointing the gun at Kelsey.

She gasps. "Dear God! Put that thing away!"

I rush forward and wrap her in a hug. "We've been trying to reach you. I thought you were in the lockdown at Sandalford. Why didn't Snoop tell us you'd be here?"

"I *was* at Sandalford until a few hours ago. I'm not entirely sure he *knows* I'm here. Maria is running the operation in cells, telling people only what they need to know. That will go double now that Dacia is there, although secrets never last long at Sandalford."

"Is Deo—"

"No. He's still there. I'll explain later. We have an emergency. Is this Sophie?"

Sophie nods, looking confused.

"Good. We need you to take over."

"Take over what?" Daniel asks.

"Caleb." I say the name at the same instant that Kelsey does. The same instant that Ashley thinks the name. "Maggie and Caleb are here, too," I add.

Daniel intercepts Lily and puts her back on his shoulders. She happily grabs a handful of his hair while he laces his fingers together to form a baby backrest behind his head.

"You should probably stay down here with them," I tell my dad, nodding at Daniel and the now-laughing Lily.

"As should you, Anna," Kelsey says. "He's medicated, but—"

"No. I have to see him. I'm not sure if it will make things better or worse, but Ashley is in here." I tap the side of my head.

"Oh. We thought your father . . ." Kelsey glances over at my dad and gives him a nod. I feel like I should make introductions, but then she turns and heads back up the stairs. Sophie and I follow.

"He's had as much sedative as I can safely allow. It should have kicked in by now, but it hasn't. Dr. Batra gave me several vials of morphine, too, but Caleb's so small . . . I wanted to hold off until there was no other option. If he doesn't calm down, though, he's going to hurt himself. Maybe others, too. He blew out that entire wall of windows in the great room at Sandalford this afternoon."

She turns down the hallway toward a bedroom on the second floor. "This suite has the largest tub. Taylor mentioned there was an isolation tank back at The Warren. I have the lights dimmed, the water warm, and soft music playing, but . . ."

Kelsey's comments raise about a half dozen questions for me, chief among them how Caleb wound up at Sandalford and now here. But I push these aside and focus inward, because I need Ashley's advice on what to say to Caleb.

> If he blew out of a wall of windows, he already *knows*, Anna. Dacia had me put him on an IV sedative before . . . so he wouldn't see what she did to me. But you can't keep secrets from Caleb. He doesn't read people automatically like Maria. His ability is more like Dacia's, I guess. If Caleb thinks you aren't telling him something, he'll go hunting around in your head until he finds it. As soon as I knew Maria wanted to pull him in to fight, Caleb knew, too.

And he was frightened.

No. He was *excited*. Ready to fight. As I said, he likes using his ability. And he knows how much I hate the Creggs and Dacia. But we can't allow him to follow that instinct. He's still just a little boy, and . . .

Will he know that you're . . .

That I'm in here? Probably. Depends on how much Maggie and Sophie are blocking him.

If he doesn't know, should I tell him? Will that make things better or worse?

I don't know. But Caleb feels very alone right now. Daniel Quinn is paying attention to the wrong child.

I don't think that's entirely fair to Daniel. Sophie is nervous enough leaving Lily in the same room with my father, given what she's seen him do. There's no way she would have handed her child over to him. And if Caleb had read Ashley's thoughts, he would have picked up a whole lot of ambivalence about Daniel.

But Kelsey is standing with the bathroom door open. There is a hurt, angry, and extremely powerful child waiting, so I don't have time for any more internal dialogue.

The first thing I notice when I step inside is the wall of water rising straight up from the edge of the large garden tub in one corner of the room. It doesn't quite touch the ceiling but hangs in midair, a bit like a shower curtain, just translucent enough for me to see a tiny huddled figure at one end.

Maggie is propped against the outside of the tub, near where Caleb sits. Even in the dim light, it's obvious she's not well. A small mountain of empty granola-bar wrappers is next to her feet, but she looks like she's lost weight since yesterday. Her cheeks are almost sunken.

"Get her *out* of here," Sophie says to Kelsey. "Downstairs or outside. And if you can, find some more food . . . for both of us."

Kelsey's already on it.

The curtain of water ripples, thickens, as we move closer, surrounding Caleb like a cocoon. He's watching me, although I sense this more than see it.

ANNA. *GO. AWAY.*

The words are clearly a command, accompanied by a gentle push that slides my feet across the marble tile toward the door. He's pushing Sophie toward the door as well. He's straining to do it. I can tell because the water curtain drops about a foot. But Sophie is straining, too, her jaw clenched tight as she braces herself against the wall.

Caleb's tone reminds me of Peyton Hawkins last fall, when I first told her about Kelsey. As soon as she heard the word *doctor*, Peyton said her monkey—her name for the force inside her head—didn't like needles. Fine. Neither do I. So it was easy to back off and give her space.

But Peyton wasn't alone. She had—and still has—her mother, her brother, and her father, all of whom love her and will do their best to protect her. And her talent is aptly called a *monkey*. I was worried that she might break a few glasses if she didn't get her way. Caleb's ability is King Kong. He can level buildings.

Making him angry is a bad idea. But the instincts of every parent I've ever hosted tell me that Caleb doesn't really want me to go. Or at least, he doesn't really want *Ashley* to go.

"I'm sorry, Caleb. I'm sorry you're hurting. But I won't go."

The wall of water forms a giant hand that reaches out and pushes me toward the door again. It's not as forceful a push this time, but I'm now drenched. Sophie is still dry. It's almost like he splashed me in anger.

But . . . he only *splashed* me. Even with Sophie blocking, Caleb could have done worse than splash. That hand he sent to push me could as easily have been two streams of water up my nostrils. Into my lungs. But instead of drowning, I'm wet, like him. It might not be an invitation to join him, but I'm going to take it that way.

I kick my shoes into the corner, peel off my jeans, and step through the wall of water. It doesn't part easily. Caleb seems to be reinforcing it the same way I reinforce my own walls inside my head. But I persist and eventually step into the other end of the tub, giving Caleb as much space as I can while still being here with him.

The water is warm. Some guest must have left behind bath salts, because I catch a hint of lavender in the steam surrounding us. Kelsey was clearly desperate, resorting to every trick she knew to try to calm Caleb down.

I lower myself into the half-full tub and meet the red-rimmed eyes of a toddler in superhero underwear. Aquaman. I don't know if that reflects Caleb's sense of humor or Ashley's, but it fits.

Ashley is in there. In there with Spider Cregg.

Yes. But not in the same room, okay? He can't hurt her.

I want to add that Cregg doesn't want to hurt her, but I don't know that for certain. And absolute honesty is probably the best bet with Caleb. If he senses that I'm misleading him, that I'm lying in any way, things could go very bad, very quickly.

Do you understand why she's in here, Caleb? Why Ashley's in my head?

451

He stares back at me, and the expression is so familiar that I have no doubt Daniel is his father. It's the same look Daniel wore when he sat on the picnic table the other day, trying to decide whether he was ready to talk about Sariah.

Maybe Caleb doesn't trust himself to talk, either, because when he answers my question, it's with a flood of images and sensations rather than words. I see Ashley's face close up, under the streetlight, and then I watch as the Sunsphere cracks and the fragments take flight like seeds from a dandelion puff. Dacia's angry face and Ashley telling him, *sleep, baby, it will be okay in the morning.* Waking up at Sandalford with no Ashley, no Maggie. Dacia telling him Ashley will be back soon. That he will stay with her and Maggie for a bit. Staring into Dacia's ice-blue eyes and extracting her memory of shooting Ashley. Her memory of shooting the children at Overhills. Of shooting a string of other people. He pauses for a moment longer on one face, a woman with curly light-brown hair. Then I see a baseball bat, long before Dacia had a gun, coming down to hit Molly.

I make it quick for you.

The next memory isn't Dacia's. It must be from Caleb's perspective. The glass wall behind Dacia explodes out toward the ocean and Dacia flies backward, clutching Maggie to her body. The picture freezes with Dacia inches from the window.

The bear lady made Ashley dead because Ashley told me to only explode the big gold ball. I wanted to explode the whole house when I found out. Not just the window. But Maggie was there. Other wabbits, too. It would be bad to hurt them.

Yes, Caleb. You were a very good boy.

Tears spill over, streaming down his little face. "Don' wanna be good boy *any . . . more.*"

It's the first time I've heard Caleb speak aloud. He sounds younger than the voice in my head, and the quiver in that last word absolutely breaks my heart. I pull him into my arms without thinking, and I don't hesitate when Ashley moves to the front, even though it's a risk, even though it pushes me to the back of my head and closer to Graham Cregg. Ashley knows how to soothe Caleb better than I do. And as for Cregg, I am so angry right now, so livid in the face of this child's pain, that I will rip into that mutated spider-rat with my bare hands if he so much as touches the wall between us.

I haven't been inside my mind office in a while. At least I don't *remember* being back here, although I guess Cregg must have stashed me somewhere when he was cruising around in my body. Once I find the two file cabinets marked *Jaden* and *Molly*, I huddle down next to them. I could use Jaden's calm right now. I could use Molly's determination.

Even back here, I feel Caleb's small body shaking against my chest, his hands clutching my shirt just as they clutched Ashley's coat yesterday. I can only imagine his pain at seeing Ashley killed. And that one image, the woman with the light-brown hair. He lingered on that one face, like it's someone he knew. Someone he remembered.

I've never seen a picture of Caleb's mother. I don't even know how old Caleb was when Sariah was killed. I don't know how much he remembers about her. But that was her. I'm certain. He pulled out Dacia's memory of killing not just the aunt who has taken care of him but also his mother. It's a miracle that the kid was able to pull back his anger when he saw Maggie.

The thought that enters my brain next isn't one I want to entertain. In fact, I spend several minutes trying to convince myself that it's being planted by Graham Cregg. I visualize myself standing up, moving around to escape him, to escape the thought, but I know that it's pointless. What I'm thinking, what I'm remembering from the nightmares I've had lately, isn't something that Cregg is pushing on me. If anything, I can blame my mother's comment about needing to hunt for the human side of the monster.

All I can think about is the dream this morning. Standing on the patio, staring down at the broken body of Penelope Cregg, her pinky neatly severed by the metal edging strip around the rosebushes. A hand gripping my collar, twisting, lifting me off my feet. *Your fault.*

I don't want to feel sympathy for the monster. But I do. Sitting here in this tub, one step removed from my body that clutches a sobbing boy that much of the world would call a monster, too.

Graham Cregg had choices. Most of the ones he made were horribly wrong. But would any of that have been changed if he'd had someone to hold him that day as he stared at the broken body of the person he loved most?

CHAPTER THIRTY

Carova Beach, North Carolina
April 28, 2020, 5:42 p.m.

When Caleb is cried out, the waterwall surrounding us rolls down, refilling the tub almost to overflowing. I feel Ashley stand and carry Caleb out of the bathroom. Kelsey is waiting with towels and blankets to replace our wet clothes. Caleb curls up into a small, still-damp ball in the middle of the large bed, his eyes drooping with exhaustion, as my hand gently rubs his back.

Then, without a word, Ashley swaps places with me. The filmy barrier between my brain and my body slips away. I feel the fuzz of the blanket beneath my fingers and hear Caleb's soft, ragged breaths as he drifts into sleep.

I'm surprised at how late it is. I wouldn't have thought we were in there more than ten or fifteen minutes, but the clock says it was more than an hour. I'm also surprised to see that the dry clothes Kelsey is holding are actually *my* clothes.

"Taylor grabbed the things you left behind at the cabin. I can stay here with Caleb if you want to go up and talk to her."

"Maybe we could talk in here? I don't think I should leave him yet."

Kelsey goes to get Taylor, and Sophie, who has been sitting in a chair on the other side of the bed, says, "You think it's okay for me to step out? Lily's hungry and tired . . ."

"She's had a rough couple of days and she needs her mom. I think we're fine, at least for now. And thanks for your help, Sophie. I wouldn't have been able to get through to Caleb without you holding him back."

She nods and gives me a nervous smile. "I'm glad I could help. But I'll be honest. He makes me nervous. When I block the others, even your father, I see clear waves. Actual patterns that I can push back against. But I was having to shift constantly with Caleb. I don't know if he was purposefully trying to get around my block or if it's because he's dealing with so much emotion right now, but it was like fighting a hurricane."

Once she's gone, I discard the blanket I'm wearing and change into the jeans and sweater on the dresser. Caleb tosses a bit, but by the time Taylor comes in, I'm next to him again and he settles back down.

Taylor hands me the drawstring bag I bought in DC. "Your phone and some other stuff."

"Why aren't Aaron and Deo here?"

"Why hello, Anna. Happy to see you too." She grins. "Don't look so guilty. If you showed up here without Daniel, I'd have asked you the same thing. Aaron will be back soon. And coming here without Deo wasn't my idea, okay? Kelsey needed someone to help her with Caleb and Maggie. No one was really in need of a remote viewing, so I was the obviously expendable member of the Scooby Gang."

"Okay, I've got a lot of questions, but maybe we should get Daniel and my dad in here so you can catch us up all at once?"

"I already filled them in, and . . . they're . . . sort of not here anymore."

"What?"

Caleb stirs uneasily, and Taylor says, "Okay, you need to listen and not get upset. They just left with Aaron and Jasper Hawkins."

I'm stunned into silence. All I can think of is Jasper standing on the beach at Long Point Island last autumn, gun in hand, clearly fighting the urge to shoot me for simply being Scott Pfeifer's daughter.

"That's . . . not good. Jasper *hates* my dad. He'll kill him."

"Maybe he would, except Dacia has his wife and children at Sandalford. Your father wants to help rescue them. I can't guarantee the truce will last beyond that rescue, but Jasper has a nice little cache of weapons—some at their fishing cabin and others stashed over at Long Point Island. Weapons are something we're seriously lacking, so that's where they've gone now. And from what Daniel was saying about this Colonel Smith, Jasper may be the only armed ally we have."

"Did Daniel hear back from Smith already?"

"Not yet. Against my better judgment, I just e-mailed the Colonel links to most of what we have on Senator Cregg. But Daniel doesn't seem hopeful. Do you think he's wrong?"

I just shake my head. Daniel knows Smith better than I do. If he isn't hopeful, neither am I.

"They're stopping here on the way back to pick us up. Well, *us* if you think you can leave Caleb."

"We'll see how well he's sleeping. I'm not sure how much I can—"

"He's Daniel's kid, isn't he?" Taylor interrupts, nodding toward Caleb.

Her question surprises me. And the fact that I didn't respond with a quick *how the hell would I know* seems to be all the answer Taylor needs.

"I should have noticed the resemblance before. I've seen family photos from when Daniel was only a little older than that. His hair darkened, and he keeps it short now, but he had those same curls back then. And that same little dimple in his chin."

I'm worried she's going to ask more questions. But luckily, Kelsey arrives, bearing a tray with three mugs. I'm hoping it's coffee, but as she comes closer, I catch the scent of chocolate.

It will do.

"There *is* no coffee," Kelsey says with a knowing smile. "And I'm afraid this cocoa is from a packet. We had to jimmy the lock on the owner's closet, and there's not a lot to choose from. Mostly granola bars and beef jerky."

She puts the tray on the bedside table and sits down next to me.

"When did Dacia arrive at Sandalford?" I ask.

"A little after three this morning," Kelsey says. "It was Dacia, seven additional guards, an unconscious Caleb, Maggie, and another child. The helicopter landed right in front of the house, so there's no way they could have taken Magda's security by surprise . . . the noise woke the entire house. I think Magda was expecting something of this nature. Maybe Senator Cregg offered Miller more than Magda was paying him."

"According to Ashley," I say, "the Senator and Dacia have definitely parted ways."

"But that's a fairly recent development, right?" Taylor asks. "And since Miller was . . . indisposed, shall we say . . . the news may not have filtered down to his team. They probably got their marching orders back when Miller left with Dacia."

Kelsey sniffs. "Miller has always thought Magda is too lenient with the adepts, so whoever paid him probably didn't need to sweeten the pot much. Whatever the reason, they walked right past Miller's men and into the house. Into Bell Isle, as well. Magda knew something was going to happen. Even before she got back to Sandalford, the military scientists had packed up and moved out. The three parents who were there as well, along with their kids, because they refused to leave them. Magda called a meeting last night to inform me and the nurses that we'd be receiving medication—a *cure*, to use her words—for the adepts within the next few days and would need to monitor them closely for at least a week. And then she went back to her house and we went to bed. I think she was expecting the Senator. If she'd thought Dacia was the one who'd be showing up, and that Dacia's guards would be holding her captive in her own house, she'd have grabbed her girls and left without giving anyone else a second thought. The adepts knew, though. There was this sense of . . . anticipation . . . all day. The only thing I have to compare it to is how kids act right before Christmas, but it wasn't as positive. When the helicopter landed, the children were awake. Maria greeted Dacia like a long-lost friend."

"But . . . that doesn't make sense. Snoop sent me this address, saying Maria gave it to him."

"She did," Taylor says. "Snoop has also been sending messages from Maria to someone in Dacia's camp for the past month now. Offering to help them fight the Senator if she'll help protect the adepts. I suspect Dacia fully intends to renege on that deal, but it doesn't matter. Maria is playing Dacia."

"You don't *play* Dacia Badea!" I lower my voice to keep from waking Caleb. "She reaches out and combs through your mind to see if you're lying, Taylor. To see what you're hiding. And that other kid Kelsey mentioned? She's probably the little bear in the video they played at the Senator's speech last night. If she could talk her way through the gates at a nuclear facility, the kid can convince Maria or Stan or any of the others to tell the truth. This plan can't possibly work."

"Do you remember the way Maria sent you the information about your dad?" Taylor says. "In the meeting. How she kind of pushed it out to us?"

I nod. It's pretty much the same thing Caleb did a few minutes ago. Only a few of the Peepers can both send and receive. None do it quite as well as Maria, but Caleb could give her some real competition in a few years.

"Okay," Taylor says. "That's the rest of the plan. Maria will be sending a message when Dacia scans her thoughts."

"More likely she's already sent it," Kelsey says. "Dacia hugged Maria for a very long time when she first saw her last night. It was long enough that some of the older boys were exchanging glances. Normally they'd have been snickering or telling them to get a room. But none of them said a word."

"What message was Maria sending?"

"The script Stan and I helped write," Taylor says. "Training the adepts, but only the stuff we *want* Dacia to know about. How much Maria hates the Creggs. Why she doesn't trust Magda. A few fake personal details that Maria wouldn't want revealed so Dacia will think she has leverage. Maria shoved all of that out while Dacia was scanning, and hopefully Dacia thinks she *pulled* the truth out of her. Oh, and as for that kid in the video . . . she was one of the wabbits. She only wound up with Cregg because she was on the wrong side of The Warren that night. Maria doesn't think she'll take Dacia's side."

"You may be underestimating Stockholm syndrome. Most of the adepts at The Warren seem to have had a rather healthy case of it. They may think of Dacia as their friend."

But Ashley disagrees.

No. Not Dacia or Lucas. They considered them worse than Graham Cregg. I was there for nearly a year, and I can tell you those two were universally hated. Even the teenage guys who I'm certain thought Dacia was hot steered clear of her.

Couldn't that have been because they were afraid of Lucas, though?

Maybe. But don't forget, Dacia could read Lucas's mind. Which means she *knew* what he was into and tolerated it. Or more likely, enjoyed it. There were no secrets

in The Warren. They knew which Fudds were the bad
ones.

Kelsey is watching me closely when I return to the world outside
my head. So is Taylor.

"That was Ashley. Not Cregg. She doesn't think any of the adepts
would side with Dacia over Maria. But . . . even if we grant that, which
I think is a very dangerous assumption, what's to stop Dacia from scanning someone who can't send her a false script?"

"Absolutely nothing," Taylor says. "The other adepts will steer clear
of her as much as possible. And Maria will stick by Dacia's side like glue.
She'll try to send a message to block their actual thoughts if Dacia reaches
out and grabs one of the other adepts. But we couldn't write a script for
everyone. Maria will have to improvise, based on what she knows about
the person. And then there are language issues . . . Maria's English may trip
her up. Also, Dacia's ability is probably a little different from the Peeper we
used during our practice sessions. It might not work exactly the same . . ."

Taylor trails off, probably because I'm staring at her, openmouthed.

"Yes, okay? We're well aware that there are several dozen ways this
could go horribly wrong. That's one reason Maria needed Deo there to
boost her ability. And that's also why this has to end tonight. According
to Stan, every path on which we survive ends in a fight with the Senator
tonight. The longer we drag things out, the more danger for everyone,
but I'm guessing especially for Maria."

Kelsey nods. "Maria's the one who convinced Dacia to let me take
Caleb and Maggie from Sandalford, although . . . Dacia believes we're
back in the hut on Long Point Island."

"Dacia trusted you to go back there on your own?" I ask. "That
doesn't sound like her."

"No." Kelsey looks down at her lap, and even in the very dim
light, I can see that she's uncomfortable. "She assigned two guards to
transport us."

"Which is about the time we entered the picture," Taylor says. "Aaron followed your advice about calling Miranda, but we couldn't reach her. So . . . he called the construction company where Jasper has been working and left a message. Jasper called back almost immediately. He hasn't been able to touch base with Miranda since yesterday morning. She has the kids call him every night before bedtime, but there was no call last night. He tried to call again early this morning, and it kept going through to voice mail."

Taylor says that Jasper decided to give it until his lunch break and then drive over to see what was going on. But he left early when he got Aaron's call. They agreed to meet at the halfway point, a few miles north of Sandalford.

"Which meant we had to drive right past Sandalford on the beach," Taylor says. "This was a little after nine, so we decided to wait until the wild-horse tour showed up and join them. We drove past quickly, but even from down on the beach, we could see there was an extra guard at the gate and guards on the deck over at Bell Isle, which was new."

Once they met up with Jasper, he'd agreed to drive Deo to Sandalford. They worked up a cover story claiming Deo had been over on Long Point Island, hoping it wouldn't clash with anything Maria might have concocted if Dacia was already asking why the resident amp was missing. The guards let Deo in, but not Jasper.

"It's a miracle Jasper kept his cool," Taylor says. "But he knew he couldn't take on all those guards on his own. So he meets us back at the rendezvous point. Once Deo was inside, we started getting a much clearer picture of the situation. That's why Snoop was finally able to get the message to you, even with your walls up. And I suspect that's also why there's no window in the great room at Sandalford now."

Kelsey nods. "Dacia seemed to think Caleb was a one-trick pony, possibly because she was relying on the records from The Warren. They show him as strongly psychokinetic. That's something they'd have trouble hiding with an infant. But the other things we've seen him do—planting thoughts, clairvoyance, precognition—none of that's mentioned in the records. I suspect Ashley did that?"

I check and report back. "Yes. Ashley hid his abilities from them as much as possible. Also, Caleb's mom before she was out of the picture. Daniel, too. They were worried that Cregg might decide Caleb was a . . . liability. Or maybe just too much of an asset. The more they could hide, the better."

"Well, Dacia seriously underestimated him," Kelsey says. "It's a miracle no one was hurt. When he woke up asking for Ashley, Dacia thought she could lie. Or maybe she just thought Maggie could block him sufficiently if he was upset. Apparently, she told Caleb he'd see Ashley soon. But first, they were going to go outside and play the "go boom" game again. I guess she wanted to test him further, to see what he could do. Caleb must have picked up on her lie about Ashley. A few seconds later, the window shattered and Dacia was flying backward along with the glass. And Maggie."

"Caleb showed me that part. He said he didn't want to hurt Maggie or the other adepts. I just don't get why Dacia wants to use Caleb. She's got hired guns. People who can blow things up the old-fashioned way. And now she's got other adepts, although a lot may be the temporary kind."

"It's probably for show," Taylor says. "Or poetic justice. I mean, I'd settle for simply taking down Ronald Cregg. But wouldn't it be sweet if he was taken out by a force he's tried to twist for his own personal and political gain for the past four decades?"

Thump.

Ashley doesn't startle at Cregg's nonverbal communication this time.

I'll second that *thump.*

"Anyway," Kelsey says, "Maria convinced Dacia to keep Caleb away from the other adepts for the time being. Away from Deo, too. She tried to get Dacia to let the other little ones go as well. Dacia almost agreed, but then one of her bodyguards said the little kids would be useful as hostages, if nothing else. And so it was just me and Maggie and Caleb in the van."

"What happened to the guards?"

"Jasper shot the one who was driving. Caleb disarmed the other one," Kelsey says. "Jasper would probably have killed the second guard, too, but we convinced him that one shot might be mistaken for a car backfiring. Two shots might make someone come investigate. We have the guard locked up downstairs, but he should have already been back at Sandalford with Maggie. Dacia is nervous without a blocker. Before Daniel left, I had him nudge the man into calling his supervisor to say there was trouble with the boat, but—"

Kelsey stops, listening, and for a moment, I think she's worried that the guard has gotten free. But the noise is outside. The glow from outside is a little brighter, too.

Taylor goes to the window. "The guys are back. We should have disabled the stupid motion sensor, though. What good is sitting in the dark if it flicks on every time someone comes to the door?"

Kelsey heads down to open the door and caution them to be quiet. Assuming Sophie had any luck with Lily, there are two sleeping babies in the house. I put a small pillow against Caleb's back and tuck another blanket around him. When I look up, Aaron is in the doorway.

"And . . . that's my cue to leave," Taylor says.

I'm glad. Not because I have any qualms about kissing Aaron in front of his sister. But tears are stinging my eyes, and I actually do have qualms about crying in front of Taylor.

The past few days have been a rollercoaster of worry, and it's unbelievably wonderful just to have Aaron's arms around me. I breathe him in, and the stress drifts away. I'm sure it will be back, but I want to savor this moment.

"Taylor said you picked up Ashley. Does Caleb know?"

I nod. "She's the reason he finally calmed down."

"Do you think you can leave him?"

"Maybe? Kelsey has him pretty heavily sedated, and now that he's under, he'll probably sleep. And Sophie is here. But . . . I might be better off staying here, just in case. There's not much I can do to help."

Thump. Thump.

Ashley doesn't second these *thumps*, though.

> You should stay here. If Caleb wakes up, and I'm not around . . . I mean, if you're not around.

> *It's okay. I know what you mean.*

But Aaron is shaking his head. "We can always bring you back here if necessary. But Deo wants to see you. And don't give me that worried frown," he says, kissing the crease between my brows. "If one of Stan's paths shows something happening to Deo, he hasn't told any of us. Deo just suggested that it might be useful to trigger one of your visions. Maria has several Fivers, but most of them fall toward the *probabilities* side of the spectrum rather than the *certainties* side."

"I can try. But there's no guarantee that I'll see anything that's relevant. You know that. It's . . . random."

"Is it, though?" Daniel asks. I'm not sure how long he's been standing in the doorway. It's almost like he's afraid to step over the threshold, and I know why. His eyes travel toward Caleb, as though he can read my thoughts, and then he clears his throat.

"Is it really random, I mean? I know that's how Jaden said it works, and I know that a lot of the things you've seen have been pretty inconsequential. But when you've triggered a vision with Deo, it's always seemed to be something you needed to know. Like it was a guided vision."

"Guided by whom?" Aaron says.

By Jaden, I think.

But Daniel says, "By Anna, obviously."

He's right about the boosted visions, though. Each time that I've chosen to trigger a vision, it has given me some bit of knowledge I needed. As though being open to the gift changed it.

And maybe I *am* the one guiding the gift toward that spot, but I'm not entirely willing to discount where my mind went first. In one sense, I really do hope that wherever Jaden is now, he's totally unconcerned with what is happening in this realm. I'd like to think that he and his mother are sitting in a park on a summer day, with their favorite books in hand. But I know that if he can see us in this world, he'd do whatever he could to push me in the right direction.

Jaden Park would be a damn good guardian angel. He'd laugh at that, but it's true.

I'm about to tell Daniel he could be right, but something in Aaron's expression stops me cold. He freezes, and then tears out of the room just before a gunshot rings out. Engine noise. Someone's yelling, and there's a thud and two more gunshots.

"Please tell me you didn't leave Jasper alone with my father," I say to Daniel as we run down the stairs after Aaron.

"No. Taylor's with them."

I reach the ground floor, taking the last few steps on a skid. But we're too late. Through the open door, I can see Jasper. His gun is drawn, and my father is sprawled on the other side of the dirt road.

CHAPTER
THIRTY-ONE

Carova Beach, North Carolina
April 28, 2020, 7:28 p.m.

I charge toward Jasper, screaming. He fires again, not even glancing at me, or at Daniel, who is holding me back.

But Jasper isn't aiming at my father. He's shooting at a vehicle, now nothing but taillights that are barely visible in the cloud of dirt churned up by the tires as it drives south.

"A Vigilance van," Jasper says. "It shot once, then swerved off the road. I don't know if he was aiming at Pfeifer specifically, or at all of us."

Taylor and Aaron are bending over my dad. He's conscious, but his head is bleeding, and his left leg is very clearly broken.

"I'm sorry," Aaron says. "Miller was driving, so I didn't pick anything up until he entered my range. By then it was too late."

"Miller?" Taylor says. "You left him in Knoxville. How did he get here so soon?"

"Probably the same way we did," I say. "And he wasn't stuck at Fort Bragg for two hours."

My dad is mumbling something. I pick up the words *not ideal* and *risperidone*.

"We're going to get help," I tell him. "We'll call an ambulance."

"Dacia was expecting the helicopter to return with more people this evening," Kelsey says as she drops down onto the sand next to me and begins examining Pfeifer's leg. "Mostly adepts. They may have stopped to pick up Miller."

"Let's get inside," Daniel says. "He could circle back around."

"Okay," Kelsey says. "It may not be just his leg that's broken, though. We need to find something flat so that . . ."

The rest of what she's saying fades away as Pfeifer grips my arm. Even with his face twisted in pain, I can tell it's my mom at the front. "Anna. I need you to lower your walls. You'll be in charge, I promise. I'll control them."

My mind flits to my bigger fear. Not the hitchers inside of Team Pfeifer, but the one inside of me.

"She will control *him.* I need you to trust me."

"I do."

"Anna? No!" Aaron tries to pull me away, but my father's hand is like a vise on my arm. I'm thinking, *Ow, that's going to bruise,* when a wave of energy surges through me.

I don't have time to pull down a single brick. The entire horde tears through my walls like they're made of wet paper.

I'm not sure how long I'm out. Long enough for them to get me and my father into the house. Dad is lying on what appears to be half of a Ping-Pong table. Jasper is at the window, watching in case the vehicle returns for a second pass.

These aren't things I see. My eyes aren't even open. I simply know.

For several minutes, I lie perfectly still, finding my equilibrium. I'm at the front of my head, but the front feels narrow. Constricted.

I slip back a bit to survey the rest of my mind office. The wall is still in place, but it doesn't look anything like my usual neatly stacked bricks. This reminds me of the waterwall Caleb built. It's *not* water, but it has that same rippling quality. More like a force field.

There's a crowd behind that barrier. Some appear more solid than others. I scan quickly, locating a few faces I recognize. My mother and Ashley are near the front. Will and Oksana are a bit farther back. I assume the other two women I lumped together with Oksana as the Furies are there, too, but they weren't in my head long enough for me to give them faces.

Near the back, I see Penelope Cregg. Next to her is a boy of around twelve. I don't recognize him at first, but something about his features is familiar. When I make the logical assumption that this is a younger Graham Cregg, my mind promptly substitutes the spider-rat avatar I've been using. Penelope turns toward me, snarling, and he morphs back into a boy. Except for the eyes. He has spider eyes, like the ones I saw in my reflection. And then those vanish, too. Just a boy now.

> Having him appear as you think of him won't help hold this coalition together.

I don't argue my mother's point, even though I suspect quite a few of her fellow hitchers would agree with me that there's a lot to be said for truth in advertising.

Outside my head, my father is cursing, loudly and fluently. I want to open my eyes, but my mother isn't finished.

> Scott told them no ambulance, and you need to back him up on that. He'll be okay until—

A vision flashes through my mind. There's no humming sound preceding it, so I don't think it's one of Jaden's visions. I'm inside a house. Not this one and not Sandalford, but still on the beach. Through the windows, I see the night sky over the ocean. And vehicles on the beach. Two jeeps, parked facing north. It looks like there's something between them—traffic cones, maybe?—but it's too dark to tell anything else.

I'm not even sure *vision* is the right word. This is only an image. A still shot, frozen in time. I can't even pan around. It's worthless, a stupid stock photo dropped into my mind without context. But then I see the reflection in the windows and realize where I am—Bell Isle, the house where Magda lives. She's standing next to the girl in the wheelchair. Clara or Chloe? I can't remember. Miller is there, too, on the sofa. They don't look happy.

NOT YET. BUT SOON.

Will's message appears as the image fades.

"We have to go," I say.

Everyone in the rec room falls silent. And then they all start asking questions at once.

I hear them, but I don't answer. Aaron seems to think it's because I'm still disoriented. He tells them to back off. To give me space. I feel strangely buoyant as I get to my feet. Even though I'm in the driver's seat, in control, I'm somewhat disconnected from my body. Not in a bad way, though. It's more like the body is irrelevant.

Like it's a vessel.

"We have to go," I repeat. "Miller is back at Sandalford. The Senator, too. Or . . . he will be soon."

"Anna," Kelsey says, "before you go anywhere, please talk some sense into your father. We need to call—"

"No," Pfeifer says. His face is pale, and he's clearly in pain. But he's shaking his head adamantly.

"He'll be okay." And I do think that's true. I don't know for certain, though. There's only one thing I'm certain about. "We have to go. *Now.*"

"Okay," Daniel says. "But . . . what's the plan?"

I'm about to tell him I haven't had time to think up a plan yet. That I've just taken on more than a dozen new boarders, and maybe someone else could brainstorm that problem? But my hitchers have apparently been giving this a great deal of thought. My mouth opens and words roll out.

"Nudge the guard again. Hard enough for him to forget Jasper shot his partner. He's supposed to take Maggie back to Sandalford. We go along for the ride."

I reach up and touch my face as I speak. My hands are under my control. And it's me talking. But it's also *more* than me.

"A Trojan horse strategy," Taylor says. "And once we're inside?"

"We wait until Maggie is safe. And then we fight."

Again, the words are out before I know what I'm going to say. It's as though there's a conference going on inside my head, but I can't hear it. I only get the action memo.

That frightens me. It's not like in the visions where every step, every word, is foreordained. And unlike the memory gaps when Cregg was in charge, I know what I'm saying.

You're in control, Anna. But if I let you hear everything going on back here, I don't think you'll be able to function. It's a bit—

Chaotic. Yes. I remember from when I picked up the Furies that night in the lab.

They like that name, by the way. They say they are all Furies now. United. One goal. But . . . we have to go.

"Getting through the gate isn't going to be easy," Taylor says. "There are *five* of us. Against fifteen guards, at least. Even with Jasper's weapons, we're seriously underpowered. Our best bet is to simply go in and tell Dacia we're joining her. Maria told Dacia that she trusts us. That we will fight with them against Cregg."

"Dacia won't believe that," I say, this time not drawing on whatever psychic consultations are going on at the back of my head. I know this because I know Dacia. The Furies know her too, and none of them disagrees. "Dacia's not stupid. She knows we'll turn on her. If we wait, we'll be fighting her people and Senator Cregg's people at the same time. Maybe even the damn military."

Taylor shrugs nervously. "Fighting her first *is* one of the main paths. But Stan said the odds . . . You know what, never mind. Let's just go."

Daniel and Aaron fetch the guard and move my father to one of the beds on the ground floor while Kelsey goes up to get Maggie. I thought Maggie might be hesitant to leave, but she seems eager. Caleb still exhausts her, even when she's not in the same room. She crawls into the passenger seat and buckles up as soon as Jasper brings the van around from behind the house.

Kelsey pulls me aside. "I gave your father the morphine intended for Caleb, over his protests. His leg is badly broken, and I don't want him moving around. Are your walls still up?"

"Sort of. There's *something* there, but it's not my usual barrier. I'm in control, or maybe I should say we're in control. My mother is doing some of the . . . management tasks."

Kelsey still looks worried. "And Graham Cregg?"

"He's behind the wall with the rest of them."

"Is your mother managing him, too?" There's a question in Kelsey's voice, and I understand why. She knows how easy it is for Cregg to turn the tables.

"He's under control," I say, trying to remember how much, if anything, I've told Kelsey about Penelope Cregg. "We have to go."

"I know." She hugs me tightly. "Promise me you'll be careful. Remember what happened when you tried to use Hunter Bieler's ability? Don't take any unnecessary chances."

"I'll be careful."

Taylor is next to me. Kelsey reaches out to hug her too, but then sees the gun Taylor's extending toward her.

"I don't want that," Kelsey says. "I don't know how to use it. Give it to Sophie."

"Already gave her one," Taylor says. "Safety is here. Trigger is here. Turn safety off. Point. Pull trigger."

Sophie stands on the steps, arms crossed, a small silver pistol in one hand. She looks annoyed, but I don't think it's about the gun. "I'm not certain I can block that kid if he's as wound up as he was today."

"It shouldn't be as bad," Kelsey tells her. "Even if he wakes up, he released a lot of the pain earlier. We'll manage."

Sophie looks less convinced, but she nods. "Be careful."

We crawl into the back of the van for the short ride to Sandalford. Whatever Daniel said to nudge the guard seems to be working. The guy slides behind the wheel without the slightest hesitation and seems relaxed, no doubt relieved that the "freak" he's transporting now isn't one of the dangerous kind. He's totally oblivious to both his injured trigger finger and his five extra passengers.

Daniel and Jasper take up position at the back of the van, rifles in hand. I sit closer to the front, next to Aaron. Taylor offers me one of the guns from the stack, and everyone looks a little nervous when I laugh. To be fair, the laugh didn't really sound like me, maybe because it was both my laugh and a reaction from the steering committee. But if Taylor had seen what the Furies did to that cafeteria at the prison, she'd understand that I do *not* need that rifle.

Something occurs to me then. One of the words my dad mumbled when Kelsey was examining his leg. *Risperidone.* Yes, he was on the drug, too, and at a much higher dosage. But it probably hadn't had time to kick in. I've been on it for weeks. So yes, me taking on the Furies is probably *not ideal*—which is the other thing he mumbled.

> Your father had to hold back. He struggled to control their abilities, especially for those first few days. That's why he had to keep venting, but . . . think of the damage at the prison and in that parking lot as a tiny valve letting off just enough steam to keep him stable. The risperidone isn't going to stop the Furies from getting the job done. If we have to, we'll crank it up to eleven.

I think of Kelsey's comment about Hunter Bieler. I'll be perfectly happy to get out of this with a blistered hand. But Hunter's ability is a tiny match. The firebug inside me now is a blowtorch. Nothing happened to my dad, but who knows? As Jaden often noted, different brain, different rules.

> I'm *not* suggesting we put you in danger. Kelsey's right. I said, if we *have* to, we crank it to eleven. We won't start there.

> *Do what you have to do. I've been singed before.*

Aaron moves closer. "Talk to me, Anna. Let me know what's going on. It's still . . . you, right?"

"Cregg's not in control."

"Yes. I can see that. But it doesn't answer my question."

"I think I'm a group project now. *Anna to the Infinite Power.*"

"I don't know what that means."

"Neither do I, actually. But someone back there must." He raises his eyebrows, and I go on. "It's like . . . I'm in control for the most part, but some preliminary negotiations for what I do happen behind the force field. My mother is . . ." I stop, trying to think of a way to explain it. "She's the conductor. There are different instruments, and she's controls when they play and how loud. But I can pull the plug if . . . Never mind, it's a crappy analogy."

Aaron smiles. "Now *that* comment sounded like you."

I hold his gaze for a long moment. "This *is* me. But Kelsey was right to be nervous. Everyone needs to remember that Cregg is still in here. So is his mother, and she seems to be holding him at bay, but . . . keeping an eye on me might not be a bad idea."

"Always happy to do that." He leans in and kisses me before the van rounds the curve onto the shore road, jostling us apart.

Another van passes, heading in the opposite direction, as we turn onto the shore. The driver flashes his headlights in greeting. Snoop's warning that Dacia has bears combing the beach was dead on.

I exchange a nervous glance with the others as we approach the gate, wishing that Daniel would tell the driver to hold our course and keep going down the beach, even though I know we can't do that. Judging from the expression on Aaron's face, he's feeling the same way, but then he's always on edge when we're at Sandalford.

The man at the gate isn't with Vigilance Security. Must be one of Dacia's men. He waves us through without question, though, and the driver heads down the path toward the guesthouse where they park the company vehicles. The fist clenching my stomach loosens a tiny bit.

Maggie looks back at me, a question in her eyes. I nod, and Maria's voice immediately fills my head. Taylor, Aaron, and Daniel look up too. A conference call, apparently.

> Finally you are here. We could not reach you even by the text. Miller is back. And Dacia knows Caleb is not on the island.

The driver pulls up next to one of the other vans and is about to turn the engine off when Daniel yells, "Turn the van around!" Our driver obeys and heads back toward the gate, but Maggie is struggling to keep her blocker off. She can normally hold it longer than this, but she's exhausted.

Maria continues broadcasting while Daniel issues commands. Apparently, Dacia left several minutes ago with one of the adepts and someone Maria calls Dacia's *ugly sex bear*.

Two guards, one male and one female, are near the guesthouse. The female guard waves for our driver to stop.

"Keep driving!" Daniel says, but Maggie's shaking her head. She can't hold back the block any longer.

My mind is veering into panic mode. The van we passed must have been Dacia. And that was three, maybe four, minutes ago.

Our driver lowers the window, and the woman says, "Hey. Thought you got the suck assignment of staying on the island with the superfreak? How'd you talk Weaver into swapping duty?"

The guard's weapon isn't out, so she must think it's just the driver and Maggie. I motion for Maggie to get out of the van. She looks frightened but opens the door. "I want to go inside. I'm tired." The other guard mashes out his half-finished cigarette, clearly annoyed that his break was cut short, and follows Maggie.

Our driver is still pondering the woman's question. "I . . . I don't know . . ."

"They're coming," Aaron whispers. "Get ready."

I'm puzzled for a second, thinking he means the driver's uncertain response has blown our cover. But he's also picked up a vibe from four guards rushing toward us. One of them is holding Maggie, who's struggling to get out of his grasp.

The female guard leans forward. "Who the hell have you got back—"

"DROP YOUR WEAPONS. HIT THE GROUND."

All but two of them comply with Daniel's order. The guard holding Maggie and the guy next to him, who must also be within her blocking radius, aren't affected. Then one of the two still standing begins firing at the van.

"Go!" Daniel yells. "Get us out of here." The driver accelerates, but the guard at the fence is advancing on us and reaching for his weapon.

There's no conscious thought in my next action, no consideration of how to respond. I simply *push* the guard running toward us. A piercing wail fills my head, metal on metal, like the sound that I get when a vision hits, but louder. Then the guard flies back toward the wooden slat fence, maybe fifteen yards behind him. He smacks it hard, and the fence splinters, instantly dumping him onto the dunes beyond.

But the guard isn't all that gets pushed. The windshield of the van shatters outward, along with both of the front windows. The driver, too, along with the headrest from his seat and the rearview mirror. Daniel and Aaron slam into the front seats. Only Jasper and Taylor, who are behind me, escape the impact.

The metallic screech inside my head fades. I slide closer to the driver's seat as the van decelerates, and look out the now-shattered window. The only guards now standing are the two within Maggie's radius.

"If you don't want the kid hurt, get out of the van, hands behind your heads. Now."

Maggie screams something. It sounds like *no*, but it could be . . . *go*.

Daniel begins yelling commands again, and I feel Maria trying to send a message, but it's drowned out by the *NNNNN* sound again, painfully loud, as I pin my focus on the guard holding Maggie. Again, there's no conscious questioning, no debating what course of action to take. Something inside me merely reaches out in the direction of the two men and *squeezes*. The only physical action is my hand clenching.

Maggie wrenches free of the guy holding her, who's now only worried about getting air through his constricted windpipe. As soon as she's under the raised deck, four metal chairs fly off the upper level and crash into the backs of the guards still on their feet, both of whom are clawing frantically at their throats. They two men face-plant into the sand.

The noise in my head stops as soon as I release the guards.

"The chairs weren't mine," I say.

"Good," Aaron says. "That means Maria's wabbits are giving us some help."

Taylor shoves past me, grabs the wheel, and floors it, swerving toward the deck and very nearly hitting our former driver. "Get ready to bail, guys."

She brakes inches from the columns that support the upper deck, and Daniel throws the door open. The guys pile out. I expect Taylor to follow suit, but she yells, "Be careful!"

"You, too!" Aaron reaches forward and gives my hand a quick squeeze. And then he's gone.

"I thought you were staying with them," I say to Taylor.

"Buddy system. Strap in."

The guard at the gate is struggling to his feet, but he shuttles out of the way like a crab when he sees the van barreling toward the cracked section of fence. Taylor plows through, taking the van over the slight incline and onto the shore.

I say a silent prayer that the tires didn't hit any nails or sharp edges. If they did, we're going to be hoofing it.

"They've only got a few minutes' head start," Taylor asks. "Dacia may not even know which house—"

"She knows. Maybe not the specific address, but Miller will remember where he hit my dad."

"Miller's not with her, though. He's at Bell Isle. You didn't hear what Maria said?"

"Not the last bit. There's a really loud noise when they take over. It drowns out everything. My head is still ringing. And . . . I'm starving. Like, I-could-eat-the-dashboard starving."

"Not surprised. Welcome to my world. I'd usually have something on me, but I gave my last Snickers to Maggie."

"I'll be okay."

"No," she says. "You'll be useless."

I dig around in the glove box and find an economy-sized bag of gummy bears. They've clearly been in the van for a while because it's more like a solid lump of gummy. I pry the mess out of the wrapper and take an experimental bite. And then a bigger bite.

"That's gross," Taylor says.

"Tastes *good*."

"Hopefully there's something more substantive in the storage closet when we get there. You need fuel. Maria seems to think you play a central role once the Senator and Smith arrive . . . which is soon. She didn't want you to leave Sandalford, but I knew that wasn't negotiable."

Taylor turns off the lights and parks the van two houses down.

I don't see headlights or a vehicle in the drive. Only the light by the front door, the one Taylor said is on a motion sensor. The air around the house is thick with dust, just like it was after Miller's hit-and-run. I abandon stealth mode, taking off at full speed.

Even before I see the body in the doorway, I know.

Hunter Bieler's face flashes in front of me, and I know there will be one bullet wound to Kelsey's temple. *I make it quick for you.*

She's slumped forward, half in the doorway and half out. I drop to the ground and pull her into my arms, screaming her name.

And searching.

I knew Kelsey was dead before I rounded the corner. I knew it.

But I can't believe she's also *gone*.

CHAPTER
THIRTY-TWO

Carova Beach, North Carolina
April 28, 2020, 8:42 p.m.

I shove another handful of stale Wheat Thins into my mouth and wash them down with flat, sickly-sweet cola. My stomach churns, and for a moment, I think I'm going to have to tell Taylor to stop the van. But I fight the nausea. She says I need carbs in order to end this. I want to end this.

And I have to focus on that. Otherwise, I will curl into a ball of anger and misery.

A small part of me also wants to go back to the house and unleash that anger at the one person Dacia left there alive. But it would be pointless. Pfeifer is unconscious, plus I don't think my mother would let me. And my anger at him isn't entirely fair. Aside from his larger role in creating this insanity, he's not responsible for Kelsey's death. He's so drugged he probably never heard them come in. The fact that he was drugged and silent is probably the only reason he's alive. If they'd checked the place thoroughly, he'd be dead, too.

Also, as Taylor pointed out, Sophie knew my father was in the house. She didn't tell them. The fact that he isn't dead tells us that she didn't go with Dacia willingly.

Taylor got a brief text from Deo as we were walking to the van. Sandalford is secured. A few of the guards retreated to Bell Isle, and one of the Vigilance vans is parked over there, so he's pretty sure that's where Dacia has gone.

She responded simply that we were on our way back. Nothing more. I won't let Deo learn about Kelsey from a text.

I see the lights of Sandalford ahead, but something's different. "What happened to the fence?"

The slat fence surrounding Sandalford has vanished. Well, not entirely. Boards, some of them charred and smoking, lie scattered along the beach, in the dunes, and even a few in the water. One sticks up from the sand, pointing out to sea. Farther down the beach, the identical fence around Bell Isle remains standing.

"Wow," Taylor shakes her head in amazement. "The wabbits just blasted the holy hell out of their cage. And look . . ."

Pieces of board are arranged on the wide expanse of sand in front of the house to form two words: *WABBITS ONLY.*

I wish Kelsey could see it. She hated that fence. Hated that the children at Sandalford, even those who could control their abilities, looked out at that beach every day but were rarely allowed on it.

Grief washes over me again. How do I tell Deo?

But Deo is sitting on the deck stairs when we pull up. His face leaves no doubt that he knows. He's in a house full of psychics. Of *course* he knows. Stan was probably monitoring six or seven paths in which Kelsey died, and the son of a bitch never bothered to tell us.

Maggie is next to Deo. While I appreciate the thought, I really don't care if we trigger a vision.

> Not a good idea, sweetie. We've got a lot more going
> on inside here than just the visions right now, and I'm
> not sure . . .

My mother doesn't finish the thought. Several times on the ride over, I've felt her hovering. Trying to decide what to say. How to console me. Scanning my colors or whatever to manipulate me into feeling better about this.

I'm angry at her, too. I know that's not fair. It's not like my mom is to blame. Yes, she's here and Kelsey isn't, but they're both dead, and I'm about to make sure that the Senator, the person responsible for setting this entire fiasco in motion, pays for it.

> *Then I guess it's a good thing we're outside, because I'm going*
> *to hug my brother.*

I open the door and go to the one person in the world who I know shares the pain I'm feeling right now. Over the past eight years, I've held Deo many times as he cried. Many times, I felt like crying, too, but I drew my strength from the knowledge that Deo was counting on me. That he needed me to be strong.

And now he's the strong one. His jaw is clenched tight as he pulls me to him and my tears spill against his chest. He doesn't say anything. He doesn't need to. My pain and his are the same.

A voice says we need to get inside. Rifles and scopes or something, but the other words are drowned out by the humming sound of an approaching vision. It's faint enough that I think I could move down a step and maybe the vision wouldn't happen, probably because Maggie is here. But if I can get any information that will help us—

nnnNNNnnn

Deo and Aaron alone. Walking down the beach toward me. I watch and wait.

nnnNNNnnn
*Most of the ashes are gone by the time they reach me. Deo scatters some
into the water. Some more along the beach.*
nnnNNNnnn
*It rained all morning, but now there's sun. The beach is empty. Peaceful.
I'm glad they both—*
NNNnnn

The vision was different. It kept fading in and out. Maybe interference from Maggie? And it was so short.

When I open my eyes, Aaron is carrying me toward the service elevator. Deo must have gone up the other way. I lean my head against Aaron's shoulder, glad that at least the vision pulled me out of a grief spiral. There will be time for grief later.

Aaron presses his lips to my forehead and holds me tighter, but doesn't speak. He lost his dad. Maybe he understands that words, no matter how well-intentioned, do more to soothe the person speaking than they do for the person in pain. I struggled to find the right words to say to Daniel when he told me about Sariah, but what he said then is true. There are no right words.

The only thing that will help is time. And in this case, maybe some justice. Not revenge, not lashing out in anger, but ensuring that these kids aren't treated as a means to an end.

Aaron sets me on my feet. "I got a vibe from the woods out back. One of Dacia's men must have come over from Bell Isle. That's why we were getting everyone inside. Are you ready? Because if you need some time . . ."

"No. I'll have time later. What happened here after we left? Were any of the adepts injured?"

"Two, but not seriously. One was grazed by a bullet. Another was just a stupid accident—one of the Zippos got carried away blasting down the fence and burned the arm of the kid next to him. Two guards are dead, and two ran down the beach to Bell Isle. The rest are barricaded inside the walk-in freezer. Did you get anything from the vision?"

"No. It was weird. Everything was fuzzy, and it was really short. You and Deo are walking toward me on the beach, scattering Kelsey's ashes—"

I stop, realizing that the vision *did* give me something I needed. Nothing that will help with tactics or strategies. Nothing that says when the Senator will arrive and whether we'll be facing another set of security guards or actual military personnel and equipment. All of those things remain unknown.

But no matter how blurry and choppy it was, the vision gave me the one bit of knowledge I needed desperately after having a chunk of my heart ripped out tonight. The two remaining pieces of my heart were there, on that beach with me.

Losing Aaron or Deo after losing Kelsey would absolutely end me. I don't know what else happens tonight, but I know that they will be on this beach sometime in the near future. That's the most powerful weapon the vision could have given me. It gives me hope. It gives me the freedom to protect these kids in a way that would make Kelsey proud.

It makes me fearless.

"I got *something*," I tell Aaron. "It won't make sense to anyone except me, but . . . let's go."

My initial reaction when we enter the great room is that it looks basically the same as before. Fewer knickknacks on the shelves, and one of the couches is now out on the deck. It's only when you feel the cool ocean breeze coming in that you realize this room is now a large, open-air patio.

The entire Warren seems to be gathered in the adjoining dining room, seated at the tables arranged in four long rows. Mostly empty platters of sandwiches and crumpled chip and cookie bags are scattered in front of them. They're quiet. Subdued. It's not just that they've worn themselves out fighting the guards and wrecking the fence. It's Kelsey. She wasn't a wabbit, but she was part of The Warren nevertheless. They're mourning her, too.

Behind the wall in my head, I feel the hitchers move forward, scanning the tables, looking for people they know. The Furies were also part of this family.

"Where is Ein?" I ask Aaron. Normally, he'd be hanging out near one of the tables, begging for crusts. But I don't see him.

"He's in the rec room with the two injured kids. Miranda has Peyton and TJ back there, plus a couple others who are still a little young to be . . . useful."

The older adepts cluster at one table—Maria and her friend Pavla, Stan with a guy who must be his brother, Harv. Taylor, Daniel, and Deo are there, too, seated a little away from the others.

They all look up when we enter. In this house with no secrets, they must know I have an entire chorus in my head right now. Not only their former friends but also Graham Cregg. At least a few of them have known that for months. Certainly Maria did. Any shred of doubt I had on that point is erased when Maria's eyes dart toward me, then quickly back down to the table, as soon as the thought enters my head.

Maria and Stan probably knew there was a good chance Ashley and Kelsey would die. It just didn't serve the greater purpose of The Paths to tell me. A hot coal of anger builds inside me, but I fight it back. Not the time.

"Do we know when the Senator arrives?" I ask. "And how many people are at Bell Isle, total?"

Stan says, "Our best guess is that Cregg will arrive in about twenty minutes. The paths—" He jumps, and looks toward Maria. I think she kicked him. She knows I don't want to hear about his damn paths right now.

"Four guards," Maria says, "including Miller. He plays like he is not working for Senator, but Dacia knows. Her guys took his weapons.

Dacia is also there now. Sophie, Lily, Caleb, and one other adept. The girl Dacia brought who can push minds like sexy Fudd over there. Magda and her daughters. The nurses, Dr. Batra. So . . . fewer than we fought here, and not so many guns."

"For now." I start to tell her about the picture vision I got earlier, but she holds up one hand.

"I already tell them. Your walls are flimsy now. I pick this bit up from earlier, before you and Taylor go . . ." Maria stops, looking like she's about to cry. "Our two Fivers see them, too. Jeeps. Soldiers."

A couple of boys at the table across from us exchange a look. One of them is the kid who asked the question at Maria's meeting last week about whether any of the adepts were forced to come here. "Okay, I get that this Senator is crazy. But I don't believe soldiers are actually going to hurt us. Most of our parents served in the Army."

"Maybe they got orders," one of the girls says. "They have to follow orders."

"Not illegal orders. And killing a bunch of civilians, even ones like us who are different, is an illegal order. Most soldiers won't do it. My father wouldn't do it. He wouldn't give that order to his men, either."

I look over at Daniel with a question in my eyes. *Is that Smith's son?* But it's clear he doesn't know.

"Can you read the people at Magda's house?" I ask Maria. "Maybe with a boost from Deo?"

"Very little. Sophie is blocking. Or . . . maybe not Sophie. Maybe there is other blocker. Maybe the ugly sex bear. Maybe Miller. They both stink like the new kids at The Warren. The smell that burns . . . the . . . nose."

Aaron's arm tightens around my waist, and he glances toward the deck. Maria looks in that direction, too. The dunes make it hard to see from this angle, but headlights are illuminating that section of beach. And they're stopped in front of Bell Isle.

Stan's paths seem to be off by about eighteen minutes. I turn to Taylor. "Get your best people and let's go."

"No," Maria says softly. "You can be mad at me later, Anna. But I am second-in-command, not Taylor. I am never the general as you joke to others. Stan tells me since before you rescue us from the silo place that every path where we win, *you* are general. But almost every path where we *lose*, you are general, too . . . so don't think you are so big shot." She gives me a sad smile, then calls out, "Teams Alpha, Beta, and Psi. Go. Everyone else, to defense stations. Jasper and Pavla, take the other vans. Sexy Fudd, you are my driver."

"I have a *name*," Daniel says.

Four of the older kids, including Taylor, head to the far end of the room and pick up weapons. Others grab protective gear, most of which is too large for them and all of which is stamped *Vigilance Security*, from another pile. A few take up positions here in the great room. The majority of them, however, head down to the second floor. Every room on that floor has a view of the beach, and most have a glass door leading to the deck.

"I'm reading seven people," Maria says. "Senator is in one jeep. Other jeep is Dalton's father. The Army man who came here before. Five more people I don't know."

Daniel, Maria, Taylor, and I head toward the elevator. I expect Aaron to follow, but he holds back. "I'm on defense, babe. I know my limits. Here, I may be able to pick up something in time for us to act. But put me in the middle of a conflict between Dacia and the Senator, with everyone wanting to murder everyone else, and I'll be useless. I love you. Please be careful."

"I love you, too."

One much-too-short kiss later, I hurry to the stairs.

"So," I ask as we pile into the van, "am I the only one who didn't know Maria thinks I'm leading this show?"

Taylor snorts. "God no. If they'd told me that part, do you really think I'd have agreed?"

Daniel doesn't answer, but he wasn't here during their training sessions and is therefore in the dark about everything. Deo also doesn't answer, but he *was* here. So I ask again.

He sighs. "They never gave me details. But she did say a few times that you and I were central to the plan. I didn't know you'd be turning into a psychic version of Ben 10, though. I thought it was about the visions, since yours are the only ones with any clarity or certainty. Did you get anything?"

I don't have time to respond, because Maria gets in the front passenger seat and yells, "Go, go! Follow the others to back road, then turn around and drive along Magda's fence toward shore. It will hide us." Then she turns to those of us in the back. "Okay. Intelligence brief. Two men are already sneaking around behind Sandalford. But we have people waiting. So if you hear a crashing noise, maybe a fire alarm, just ignore. Anyway, Senator is bringing the money Dacia is so angry about. He is very worried right now because on verge of big political deal. He gives Dacia the money so she goes away, but . . . he won't let her keep it because he is *kokot*. And he won't let her keep Sophie as blocker. Dacia does not trust. There will be fight."

Daniel turns toward the shore when we reach the edge of the fence, but the other two vans keep driving down the rough path that runs behind Sandalford and Bell Isle. Taylor tells him this is her stop. She grabs a rifle, then leans forward to kiss Deo.

"Stay safe. See you guys soon." Then she disappears around the fence with one of the older adepts.

"Where's she going?" I ask.

"Sniper duty, apparently," Daniel says. "Although it's the first I'm hearing of it."

"Because you are not in chain of command," Maria says. "We could not practice with guns before. So we only have six who say they can already shoot. Taylor's psychic stuff is no help here, and she tells me she is damn good with gun. So Taylor is sniper."

"She *is* damn good," Daniel says. "I taught her. Doesn't mean I want her out there. And where are the other vans going?"

"They'll unload most of the adepts into the woods," Deo says, "and then keep driving as decoys. Hopefully if Smith brought backup, they'll see the vans, think wabbits are escaping, and give chase."

Maria rolls down the passenger-side window and is still for a moment. "Our lookout says Dacia is getting in van with Caleb, Sophie and baby, Miller, and two of her bears. We will hear van start."

Right on cue, an engine cranks.

"Go," she says. "But stop before end of the fence."

"And then?" Daniel asks.

I field this question. "Then I get out so Graham Cregg can have a little chat with his father. None of them knows I've picked up the Furies or Penelope Cregg. I stand the best chance of getting close enough to grab Caleb when the opportunity arises. And he'll come with me because of Ashley."

"I thought we had to get inside Magda's house," Deo says. "You had that vision from inside Bell Isle."

"That's what I thought, too. But it's more like remote viewing—a glimpse of the future through someone else's eyes."

"We're coming with you, though. Right?" Daniel says.

"No. This is just me and Deo. He's the other one they want, and . . . too many of us will spook them. And I think you're right that it would be better if Smith doesn't know you've been influencing him. You need to be our last resort."

"She is right. Stan says . . ." Maria stops, catching my expression and says, "I am sorry, Anna, but Stan has helped us too. He did not hurt anyone, and I will not let you blame him. His paths helped bring us here. And he says in the only path where we make it to the happy place, Daniel stays quiet until the battle ends. If you step in and shove the soldier man around, Daniel, we may live, but we will be in cages. I don't like cages."

I exchange a look with Daniel. When he was my hitcher, the close space tormented him. That was part of his frustration during rehab from the coma, too. Deo has never been caged in a hospital like I have, but he and I both have lived in too many houses with bars on the windows. So, *no cages* is one point on which all of us can agree.

My plan is to stay back far enough that Sophie or Miller or whoever is blocking shouldn't keep us from communicating with Maria. I know Sophie's range, but not knowing for sure who's the blocker has me worried. You'd think the temporary serum Miller and maybe this other guy were given would be weaker. But I suppose it could also be one of those things where you burn bright until your flame dies.

As we move toward the beach, Deo asks again what I saw in the vision. I debate for a moment, then decide it might help him, too.

"It was blurry and short. Maybe because of Maggie. The vision kept cutting in and out, but the whole thing was you and Aaron. Walking toward me. When you get closer, I saw that you were sprinkling Kelsey's ashes. So the three of us, at least, are safe. I don't know about Taylor or Daniel or anyone else. I wish I did. But you, me, and Aaron will be on this beach together soon."

"Why weren't you sprinkling Kelsey's ashes, too?"

"I was. I mean, I was *there*. Maybe it was your turn?"

He nods and gives me a shaky smile. "Okay, Short Stuff. Let's do this."

As we approach the shore, I hear the other engines idling on the beach. And I hear Dacia. Her voice is higher, carrying over the roar of the surf. Plus, I'm pretty sure she's yelling.

One of the men standing near the jeeps yanks his gun toward us as soon as we round the corner of the fence that surrounds Bell Isle. Deo curses softly. I echo the sentiment in my head, and we both raise our hands.

"No weapons," Deo says. "We're here to talk."

Another of the Senator's guards keeps his gun trained on Dacia. Ugly Bear has his gun pointed at the Senator. What a fun little standoff we've strolled into. It occurs to me that all of this could be solved if Daniel could just get a suggestion through to the two bodyguards. *Are they really worth it? Let's both shoot on the count of three, and go grab a beer.*

Dacia stands a step away from the van door, clearly trying to stay within Sophie's range. She holds Caleb clumsily in front of her. His head lolls against her chest, but he's moving fitfully and rubbing at his eyes. Maybe she intends him as a shield, but her head seems the more likely target for the Senator's guard.

Sophie sits in the van a few feet away from Dacia, holding Lily. Another girl is in the row of seats behind them. I don't recognize her face, but she's about the same height as the little bear who manipulated the guards at Oak Ridge.

"Oh, man," Deo whispers. "Get a load of Miller."

Miller stands on the other side of the vehicle, although *stands* is far too generous a word, given how heavily he's leaning against the frame. The glow of the headlights makes everyone look sickly, but Miller looks like death on toast.

Once again, I have the odd sense of being only mostly in control of my body as I walk a few steps forward. "The boy is right. We're unarmed and we're not looking for a fight, *Ronald*. Just the little talk we didn't get around to before I *shuffled off this mortal coil.*"

Senator Cregg, who is standing behind the open door of one of the jeeps, bristles at the sneering use of his first name, and bristles again at the quote. But when he notices Colonel Smith watching him, his smooth politician's face slides back into place.

"Anna. I've been looking forward to—"

"Oh, shut up, you fat fraud." Dacia gives me a death stare over her shoulder before looking back at Cregg. "Give me the money you stole so I can go. Then you can do family reunioning with your psycho son and go back to your politics."

"What a terrible era in which idiots govern the blind." I speak the quote so softly that I doubt anyone hears it aside from Deo. But Dacia and the Senator would probably have ignored the comment anyway. They're totally locked on to their dispute.

"The money is here," Senator Cregg says. "But the terms we agreed upon are that you leave all of the adepts here, including that blocker in your van."

"This man can block, too," Dacia says, pointing at Miller. "I did not say *which* blocker I was leaving."

"Him? He's half dead!"

Miller looks up but apparently lacks the energy to contradict the point.

"Blame your stupid drug. And if he dies, you have other blocker anyway—the girl at the big house. Sophie goes with me. Send with me one of your men, and I will leave them Caleb, but he is with me until we are safe away from here. My insurance. This boy blew the windows from that house today when someone threatened me."

"What a liar," Deo says under his breath.

I don't think she could have heard his words, but she nods toward Deo. "And there is your amp. So you collect all the toys you want for your army. You can give the others your cure, and everybody has happy ending. Well, unless they have reaction like this one." She nods her head toward Miller.

The Senator is watching me now, instead of Dacia. I'm not sure why until he yells for me to start walking. "That one needs to be moving at all times," he tells the guard who is covering us. "If she stops, shoot."

The other jeep opens and Smith gets out. "Belay that order. The adepts are to be placed in my custody. So is Pfeifer. That's the agreement. And I think we're going to have to track most of them down. I've just gotten a report that two of your security vans are headed south toward Corolla. I have a car in pursuit, but you need to resolve this standoff. Give her half now and wire the rest when we get the kid back."

"Not half," Dacia says. "Three-quarters now."

Cregg considers the offer and huffs. "Give it to me," he says to someone still inside the jeep. He unzips a small duffel and shows Dacia the contents. Then he removes about a dozen stacks of bills from the case and tosses them into the jeep while Dacia keeps a careful eye on the process. Caleb squirms again, and she huffs, tightening her grip on the boy.

Miller has been in my line of sight each time I looked toward Dacia, but he's no longer slouching against the van. He must have gotten back into the vehicle. Either that or he's passed out on the ground.

"Happy?" Cregg asks Dacia. "It might even be eighty percent." He hands the case to one of the guards. "Go with her. Call to let us know where to pick you up."

"No weapons. And turn out your pockets." This comment is from Ugly Bear, the first time he's spoken. The guard with the duffel reluctantly removes his gun belt and empties his pockets.

"She'll kill *both* of them," I say, not looking at Dacia or the Senator but directly at Smith. "Or sell the kid to the highest bidder." I hate saying the words when Caleb is half awake, but I can't let her get him into that van.

Dacia spins toward me, yelling something in Romanian.

I don't see the pistol she's pointing at me until she fires.

CHAPTER
THIRTY-THREE

Carova Beach, North Carolina
April 28, 2020, 9:31 p.m.

The bullet goes wide, missing me. Missing Deo. It was aimed right at me, so I don't know why the shot was so off. Then Caleb slips from Dacia's grasp, and she crumples face-first into the sand, revealing Sophie holding the small silver pistol Taylor gave her earlier tonight. Dacia's guards would have checked her for weapons, so Sophie must have hidden it in the diaper bag.

Ugly Bear has vanished, too, so I rush forward to Caleb, veering away from Dacia out of instinct. One look at the back of her head, though, and I know she's dead. As I bend down to grab Caleb, I see two dark lumps on the other side of the van. Miller and Ugly Bear. I'm not sure if it was Taylor or the other sniper wabbit, but someone is damn good with a rifle.

I give Sophie a silent look of thanks and lay Caleb on the floorboard next to Lily, who is wailing. A gun blast in that close space had to have been terrifyingly loud.

Deo hasn't moved. He looks a little stunned, and I walk toward him.

"Well," the Senator says. "That was . . . intense, wasn't it? Mrs. Bell has some excellent snipers on her security team. Colonel Smith, perhaps your men can handle this now?"

"No," I say. "This isn't over. That guy you called half dead a minute ago was having a reaction to the blocker serum. My brother had a similar reaction to the amp serum. This flu that has been spreading around the country—coincidentally in states where you won the Unify America primary—is also due to the drug. The primary researcher for the program is convinced that it could cause permanent damage to second-generation adepts like me. Some of the adepts would love a cure, but not one that could kill them. And we won't let you force it on the ones who don't want it. The ones who just want to be left alone."

Smith glances over my shoulder, a look of grim recognition on his face. Probably Daniel. I'm about to turn and confirm this, but then movement along the dunes beyond the jeeps catches my attention. Now that the standoff has ended, all eyes, all guns, are pointed this way.

And one by one, the wabbits are creeping out of the woods.

"We're not planning to force anyone," Smith says. "I'll be taking all of you to a secure facility where we will administer the cure, but only once it has passed all safety protocols. Surely you know that the adepts can't remain here. This was *always* a temporary solution. Magda Bell wants her daughters to be given the treatment. Other parents have . . . also . . ."

He sniffs. I smell it too. Burning rubber. One of the guards moves away from the jeep and drops into the sand, patting his pants leg, which isn't quite on fire but is definitely smoking. And then all eight jeep tires burst into flames.

A wet plank, no doubt a remnant from the hated fence around the Sandalford warren, whirls across the sand like a propeller blade, clipping the Senator in the ankle. Shells, sand, and assorted debris rise up from the beach, hover, and then dart like a swarm of bees toward Smith and the guards, who raise their arms to cover their faces.

Two shots ring out, and then a command booms through the night so loud that I cover my ears. It's an automatic reaction, and pointless, since the sound is in my mind.

DROP YOUR GUNS! HANDS BEHIND YOUR HEADS AND FREEZE.

The voice is high, reedy, and frightened. Familiar but definitely *not* Daniel Quinn.

My hands, already raised to cover my ears, quickly slide into place and clasp behind my head. So do Colonel Smith's. The guard who was ordered to go with Dacia now has not just his hands, but also the duffel bag, behind his head. Every guard but one complies.

Every wabbit on the beach is also standing stock-still, hands behind their heads. Senator Cregg must be unarmed, because like me and the duffel guard, he only follows the last half of the order.

The guard standing next to the Senator seems unaffected, however. He's still pointing his gun at me, or maybe behind me, as he speaks into a cell phone.

Someone behind me sighs. Then she sends a second mind blast.

EXCEPT WABBITS. YOU CAN . . . MOVE. AND PICK UP YOUR GUNS IF YOU HAVE THEM.

Oddly, it's the girl's sigh that I recognize more than the voice, the same little huff she gave in Dacia's video when she mispronounced a word in the note to the guards. I didn't even hear her moving toward us. Maria was right. The girl *is* more wabbit than bear, and she moved next to Deo to be sure her words were properly amplified.

"These are parlor tricks, Anna." The Senator flashes me a malicious smile. "And we can play, too. You're outgunned, outmanned, and definitely outmaneuvered. Do you think this is *all* the force that we can bring to bear against you? If you've been listening to my son, remember that he's been insane since birth. I let him keep his pets and run his little science experiments to humor him, hoping we'd find something the military could use. And we did. I think they'll find you and a few of your friends *very* useful. Those who can't be employed will take the cure we're offering and have a chance at normal lives. The only alternative you offer them is a life cut tragically short."

Maria's voice fills my head, at a volume much lower than Little Bear. The volume is even low for Maria, and there's an underlying note of panic.

More weapons. Five more jeeps coming. Go back to home base!

Many of the kids obey instantly, clambering back into the woods or across the dunes toward Sandalford. Others, mostly the older adepts, hold their position at both edges of the fence. Colonel Smith's eyes keep moving in that direction. When I glance back, I see his son, Dalton, standing with the others.

And then, just as Maria said, headlights appear down the shore. I'm angry at myself for standing here, listening to the Senator ramble on when we were facing just the one guard who was resistant to Little Bear's nudge. Maybe Daniel could have stepped in, pushed him harder.

But I know that would only have delayed the inevitable. It's five jeeps now, but it could be fifty within a few hours. At some point, we have to show them we will not be bullied.

The only person on this beach I have any desire to hurt is the Senator. And maybe that resistant guard just a little bit, because his smirk is pissing me off. I don't want to hurt the people in those approaching vehicles. But I can't let them hurt these kids. If they will not deal fairly with us out of compassion, then I will make them deal fairly with us out of respect.

"Why didn't that one drop his gun?" Little Bear asks. "Is Maria okay?"

That second question alarms me, because I'm unsure why she's asking. My answer is the same for both, however.

"I don't know. But he's going to drop it in just a minute. And when he does, I want you to run back to the van, okay? Deo, stay close."

"Right behind you."

The guard may be resistant to psychic force, but he is not immune to physics. I send a chunk of wood toward his temple, but before it connects, a second object—a shell, maybe?—knocks the gun from his hands with such force that it flies out over the ocean. I don't know what the second object is because I didn't throw it. The gun splashes into the water at almost the same instant that the man topples over onto the sand.

That gets the Senator's attention. Smith is looking beyond me, however, toward the line of adepts standing with his son.

I'm not done. Let's see how they like *these* parlor tricks.

One small shove, and the jeep closest to the shoreline flips twice, landing upside down. The money the Senator tossed onto the seat drops to the sand, and waves begin lapping at the stacks of bills. A second flick of my hand, and the other jeep rolls backward like some invisible driver has shifted into reverse and floored the pedal. The back end lodges into a sand dune about fifty yards away, and the vehicle pops an extreme wheelie and lands on its back, the still-smoking tires spinning in the air.

A waterspout is now approaching the shore. Caleb is sitting up, his legs hanging over the edge of the van. His funnel rises out of the ocean and spins lazily for a few seconds before traveling toward the toppled jeep. The wind picks up, sending drops of seawater toward us like horizontal rain, as the water churns and spins, taking the jeep and the money out to sea.

But the headlights are still rolling this way, close enough now that I can tell there are indeed five sets. I focus on the sand in front of the jeeps' lights and shove downward. The sand buckles and rises into a sand berm high enough that I can no longer see the headlights, and seawater rushes in to fill the gully. If they come at us now, it will be on foot and through water.

Colonel Smith surveys the damage and says, "Anna, you're only making this more difficult. I don't like the situation either. But I have orders, and if I don't follow them, they'll just send someone else. Someone who might not be averse to mistreating these kids. This is not a battle you can win."

From behind me, Dalton Smith screams, "You're talking about putting us in a cage! Locking us up. How is that not mistreating us?"

He says *us* each time, even though I'm sure he knows that his father can find a way to remove this cup from his own son. Dalton was sent here for his protection, after all, and rank has its privileges. But the fact that Dalton has chosen to cast his lot with his fellow adepts is not lost on the Colonel. I can't tell if he's angry or proud. Maybe both.

"You are being dangerously naive," Senator Cregg says. "Those men you just blockaded have already called for support. Helicopters will arrive within the hour. Even if you're willing to risk your own life, do you want these other lives on your conscience? Because if you fight us, many of these children will die, Anna. And it will be *your fault*."

Those last two words are a tripwire.

"NOT MY FAULT!" My mouth screams the words, but they're not mine. "I didn't make her do anything. *You* shoved her out that window. You!"

In the part of my brain occupied by Graham Cregg, a young boy who once stood on a patio with his mother's broken body at his feet panics as his collar tightens around his throat and he's lifted off the ground. And the part of my brain occupied by Penelope Cregg, whose spirit could only watch helplessly while her son was manipulated and abused, dissolves into a wall of white-hot rage.

Her anger combines with the rest of my hitchers—all Furies now—and launches like an arrow with pinpoint accuracy toward Ronald Cregg, who seems to realize he's made a grave miscalculation. Perhaps he notices a slightly different light in my eyes, a light that reminds him of his late wife. Whatever the reason, Cregg starts screaming several seconds before the others. Several seconds before almost everyone on that beach, including me, receives an up-close-and-personal visit of their own worst nightmare.

I don't know what Ronald Cregg's imagination conjured up in that moment. His heart was sixty-eight years old and not in the best of shape, so he will never tell us. I like to think, however, that he saw the same thing I did the first time Penelope Cregg took me on a bad trip. I like to think he saw a giant spider-rat with human hands. And I like to think that's what he still sees in his nightmares, wherever in hell he may be.

Carova Beach, North Carolina
April 29, 2020, 11:16 a.m.

Two emotions are at war in my head today. One is an emptiness that extends to my very core. The part of my heart that connected me to Kelsey is a raw, gaping wound utterly at odds with another emotion—an almost overwhelming sense of relief.

Aaron lies beside me, still sleeping. Deo and Taylor are somewhere in this vast house, unharmed, probably with Ein stretched out between them, happy that his mom and dad are home. Not a single wabbit was killed on the shore last night, and none are in cages. No fence surrounds Sandalford now. We're even down a few glass walls.

The relief is also because I have only *one* hitcher inside my head this morning. The Furies are gone. If any remained on that beach last night, I could not sense them. Their desire for justice or maybe even vengeance must have been the one thread that tethered them here. I don't know what that says about their final destination, but I will not judge them.

A part of me continues to judge Graham Cregg, however. If hell exists, I suspect he's there. But perhaps it's only a minor hell, because I don't think he's there alone. Whether or not Penelope Cregg earned that fireside seat, I believe she's there with him, gladly enduring fire and brimstone to be with her child, as many parents do.

The one hitcher who remains already feels faint. I know Ashley is mostly here to help ease the transition for Caleb, but I think there's a little something else holding her back, too. Something she needs before she can move on.

My mom is right back where she wants to be—with my dad, enduring the shared pain of a shattered leg and probably making plans for a trip to Colorado to visit my aunt when all of this is over and my father is, hopefully, free to travel. When I asked her what she needed in order to move on, she said she has everything she needs and she'll move on when my father does. 'Til death do us part. Or not, I guess. It isn't exactly a traditional marriage, but hey, it's lasted fifteen years.

I'm a little nervous about the four new file cabinets inside my mind office, though. *Graham. Penelope.* One marked simply *The Furies.* They shared a name, and apparently, they're willing to share a filing system. But the one that looms largest is marked *Myron.* None of the cabinets are behind a wall, or under lock and key, but Myron's is still wrapped in several layers of duct tape. Baby steps.

I don't know if I'll inherit all of my former hitchers' abilities. Part of me hopes I don't, and it's not something I'm going to test today. But

I'll handle all of their exit dreams gladly. They're not real. And none of them will hurt as much as the nightmare I faced on the beach last night.

If I'd known what was happening, I might have tried to rein it in. Not to spare Senator Cregg. Not even to spare Colonel Smith or the guards, because they needed a wake-up call. But there were still dozens of kids on the beach. Deo, too. Taylor says there was a moment of sheer, unbridled panic at Bell Isle, where she and the rest of Team Beta had secured Magda and her few remaining guards.

Even at Sandalford, Aaron said he was convinced for a split second that the entire beach was engulfed in flames and he couldn't get there to save us. It's not the same nightmare he faced last time, but your worst fears can change. I know, because mine changed, too.

There was no spider-rat this time. Instead, I'm holding Kelsey's body in the doorway of the house on Crane Road. Her spirit is somewhere. I can hear her, sobbing. But I can't find her. I can't help.

Only four people escaped Penelope Cregg's Magical Misery Tour—Sophie, Lily, Caleb, and Little Bear, whose actual name is Abby. Maria and Daniel escaped the worst of it, since they were in the back of Bell Isle with Dr. Batra and one of the nurses. Daniel says Maria wouldn't have been alive if the medical team hadn't been there to stabilize her.

And Maria is the only reason that Abby left the van. Maria couldn't get a message through the block, so she crept around the fence, over the bodies of Miller and Ugly Bear, and told Abby that no one blamed her. That the wabbits all knew someone who wound up with the Senator and Dacia through no choice of their own. Most of all, Maria convinced Abby that she was needed, and like Dalton Smith, she chose to lend us her voice.

The bullet caught Maria in the side on her way back to the van, seconds before Abby disarmed all but that one stubborn guard.

Senator Cregg spoke one true thing just before his final words. Helicopters arrived within the hour—one of them to medevac Maria, my father, and three wounded guards to the nearest military hospital and one to carry away the bodies.

Not Kelsey's, though. I strongly suspect most of the people who died last night in front of Bell Isle will be disposed of without ceremony. But Kelsey has a family who loved her. In fact, she has *two* families. One by blood, and one by choice.

Aaron's mom called this morning to say she'll contact Kelsey's family. I protested that it wasn't fair for her to take on such a sad task, but she wanted to help. She said it was one thing that she could do, one thing that her overprotective children would *let* her do, and so I agreed. Deo and I have never spoken to Kelsey's family, and I don't know how much Kelsey told them about us. But she must have told them something, because Deo will eventually be holding the blue velvet pouch of ashes that I saw in my vision.

When Aaron wakes, we pull on semi-clean clothes and go to the rec room. Taylor is already there. We're supposed to have a video conference with Colonel Smith at noon to iron out the details of the tentative agreement we reached last night on the beach, after everyone recovered from their waking nightmare.

"Is Deo still asleep?" I ask.

"No. He said he needed some time alone. And maybe he does, but . . . I think it's more he just didn't want to deal with this meeting. I would have put it off, but there's a lot that has to be decided."

I'm of a similar mind to Deo, so I tell her I'll go look for him. Not that I actually have to *look*. I know where he'll be.

When I get to Kelsey's office, I tap on the door and then push it open.

Deo is sitting on the carpet, with Ein next to him. His eyes are dry, but yesterday's purple eyeliner is even more streaked than it was last night.

"Can I come in?"

He gives me a *duh* look, and I join him on the floor. Ein gives me a feeble tail thump in greeting. Does he sense what happened? Or is he miserable only because we are?

"I didn't want to be around anyone else yet," Deo says. "So I thought I'd come in here and sit where I usually sit and it would be like talking to her, you know? And then when I got here, I couldn't sit in my chair. It just felt wrong without her here."

"I know."

"Taylor wanted me to go to the meeting. Thought it might help . . . distract me. But I've heard all about it from her anyway. She gets into this stuff, all of the politics and the strategies, but I don't really want to look at how the sausage is made. At least not right now. Does that make sense? I want someone to fix it. To make things right, but . . . this part? Kelsey? That can't be fixed."

We sit there silently, each scratching behind one of Ein's long brown ears.

"Kelsey wasn't still . . . there . . . when you found her body. Did your dad pick her up?"

"No. I asked. And I couldn't find her. So . . . I guess she moved on. At least, I hope she did."

"She was murdered and she didn't know we were okay. Didn't know her other patients were okay. Does that sound like someone who could instantly move on? I mean, I hope she did, but it doesn't fit to me."

It doesn't fit to me, either. All I can think of is my nightmare on the beach, but sharing that won't help Deo right now.

"I checked the house on Crane Road, D. Before I went to bed last night, I also checked in here and in her room. I'll keep checking, but maybe she was able to let go without answers."

We sit there for few minutes longer, and then he gets up. "Taylor was right. I need a distraction."

So we join the meeting, already in progress.

"It's not like we're asking for the West Coast," Daniel says. "We're not even asking for a state or a city. And don't pretend the government is giving us anything out of generosity, because you're getting a lot out of this bargain. There may be minor stuff we haven't thought of, so don't hold me to this until it's in writing, but we have three major requirements. First, no adept will be forced to work without his or her consent. If it's physically dangerous or violates their moral code or they just don't want to do it, they can opt out. Second, no adept will be forcibly medicated, unless it's for his or her own safety. That includes this so-called cure. Third, we need a safe space that isn't a damned prison. The adepts aren't criminals, and we're not going to allow them to be treated that way. Those who want to live in the larger society will be allowed to do so as long as they do not draw attention or use their abilities in an illegal or unethical way."

"That last bit will be hard as hell to enforce." Smith's face is tired and drawn. "One option for the safe space would be the Brushy Mountain facili—"

Taylor says, "Which is a *prison*. We tell you no prison, and the first option you mention is a prison."

"My point," Smith says, "was that we could renovate it. It's isolated and secure."

"It's the secure part that's troubling," Daniel says. "Secure for whom? But here's one option. There's a huge expanse of public land to the north of us, just across the Virginia line. It's definitely isolated. It gets a handful of hikers, but that's it, because there are no roads."

"And it would require more paperwork than you can imagine."

Taylor smiles sweetly. "So . . . how much public land has been sold to private buyers by this administration? They'll find a way."

I'm not sure whether the sound that Smith makes is a huff or a laugh. "Listen, we don't have to work everything out today. As long as Daniel and Pfeifer are both willing to testify on the agreed points, the administration seems to think they can make this fly. Their key concern is whether all the formulas that were distributed illegally really were the temporary variety. Because if they weren't, and if we have a whole new crop of adepts out there, no agreement is going to last."

"They were all either temporary formulas or the blocker," I say. "My guess is that Dacia and Lucas were planning to wait and sell the permanent variety to governments. But that takes longer to set up, and they'd have been much more credible once they'd stirred up a solid panic."

Colonel Smith seems a little unnerved by my presence, which is both totally understandable after what he saw me do on the beach last night and also amusing, since we're on Skype. Although I guess the fact that his son is under the same roof as me, at Dalton's insistence, might make him a bit nervous, too.

My mind keeps straying back into my grief each time something reminds me of Kelsey. When Smith mentions sending in new staff, including a counselor. When he mentions that Magda Bell is returning to London today, with her girls and a very questionable "cure." There's nothing Smith could do aside from warning her that it could harm the girls. They're her daughters, and not even US citizens. Even though I know Smith is right, it still makes me uneasy. It would make Kelsey uneasy, too.

The topic has changed when I tune back in, and I realize with something close to amazement that the administration is seriously planning to spin the past few months as a massive hoax perpetrated by Senator Cregg. And yes, it *was*, in one sense, but . . .

"They think they can sell it," Smith says. "With some cut-and-paste work, and your testimony. They've fed three major news outlets pieces of information from the documents you sent over last night, so we've already got evidence of a conspiracy. All they have to do now is piece together a confession to match the evidence. The Senator was a publicity whore, we all know that. There are hundreds of hours of that man talking into a camera. And they'll have a body—"

"Which died of natural causes," Deo says. "Okay, not *natural* natural, but not suicide."

"Pfft." Taylor waves her hand dismissively. "That part will be a piece of cake. I think the bigger issue is going to be convincing people they didn't see what they think they saw. Not the taped stuff, but the ones who actually saw their neighbor set something on fire without striking a match."

"There weren't that many, though," Smith says. "The serum only worked on those who had underlying abilities. It made more people angry than psychic, and more people sick than angry. We don't have to convince them all, anyway. Just most. And . . . we've got people pushing the LSD-in-the-water-supply angle on social media."

"Could that really work?" Aaron asks.

"They're saying it's a new variety of LSD, several thousand times as potent, and that the government is trying to cover it up because . . . some reason." Smith gives him a grim smile. "Depends on how many idiots out there retweet it or send it to their cousin on Facebook. So . . . yeah, I think it will work."

"PSYOP," Daniel says. *"Persuade, Change, Influence."*

"And retweet," Taylor says. "Don't forget that one."

News Item from the *Washington Examiner*

May 2, 2020

A source close to the investigation reports that the death of Senator Ronald Cregg last week was due to an intentional overdose of fentanyl. This follows the release yesterday of a videotaped confession by Senator Cregg in which he confirmed leaked documents showing that the Delphi Project and the WOCAN terrorist threat was a hoax designed to help win his party's nomination and, ultimately, the presidency.

Cregg's family and sources within the campaign initially disputed the video, claiming it was faked. Jerrianne Cregg held a press conference earlier today, however, to confirm that her husband was under considerable stress and may have exaggerated some aspects of the program. She does not, however, believe allegations that Cregg or anyone connected to him was involved in drugging the water supply in cities visited during the campaign.

Federal authorities stress that there is no evidence to support the claim that any terrorist group has contaminated water supplies within the United States.

EPILOGUE

Aaron slows the truck as we pass the two beach houses, both with large *For Sale* signs out front. The sign at Sandalford is in almost the same spot as when I first saw the place last November. The windows have been repaired, along with the assorted scorch marks on the walls. Magda is, of course, determined to make a profit on the place, so the price is several hundred thousand dollars above what she paid.

I don't walk, or even run, along this stretch of beach. There *are* ghosts here, just not the one I'm seeking. And so we've picked a spot a bit farther up to do this, a spot where Kelsey used to walk with some of the younger adepts to collect shells.

We're not expecting to find her there. I checked the location long ago. But Deo decided earlier this week that it's time. He needs the closure. Maybe we both do. I still have the dream where I'm searching for her spirit. It's my one recurring *actual* dream mixed in with a regular rotation of exit dreams from my recently departed hitchers.

It's now been over two months since Kelsey's daughter placed the dark-blue pouch in my hand at the memorial service and asked if we would sprinkle the ashes near the pier at North Beach where Kelsey and her sister used to go fishing. She asked us in part because they were flying back to Indianapolis that night, but also because Deo and I now *own* Kelsey's house at North Beach.

When we learned Kelsey had left the place to us in her will, we felt like thieves. It should go to her family. But her children and grandchildren all assured us that Kelsey had told them she was changing her will when she petitioned the state for legal guardianship of Deo. It was only a small part of her estate, and they supported her decision. Other people might have been suspicious, but Kelsey's children seem to have inherited her generous nature. If they resented her bequest to us in any way, they hid it remarkably well.

And so Kelsey's last gift to us was the one thing I've never really had—a place to call home. Deo and I both thought perhaps we'd find her spirit there on that fishing pier. I ran my hand over the boards at the end of that pier over and over, but the only thing I picked up was splinters. Kelsey wasn't on the fishing pier. Not at the beach house either. Those are places she was happy, but none of them was her last happy place.

We saved the last of her ashes to sprinkle here. Sandalford wasn't Kelsey's last happy place either, but it was her last helpful place. A place where she felt needed, and that's a kind of happiness all its own.

There are also some ashes mixed with the sand about eight miles up the coast, where construction has begun on the new Warren. I wanted Kelsey to be part of that. The adepts have been there for the past two months, in temporary buildings. Roughly twenty acres are now classified top secret. Satellite photos of the area will not show the buildings under construction, which are designed to blend into the terrain. We've flown into the area on several occasions, and the location is hard to spot.

A narrow strip of beach remains open to anyone who wants to make the trek into North Carolina on foot, but large red-and-white signs are posted along the tree line: *Warning No Trespassing Restricted Area.* Some who've made the hike recently may have noticed that odd things tend to happen along that stretch of beach. Waterspouts have been known to emerge out of nowhere. You might feel a faint brush across your forehead, like a feather or a spiderweb. And in the midst of the quiet sounds of nature, you may hear a giggle and someone saying you have a nice *zadek*.

Maria held a meeting just before the private groundbreaking ceremony to vote on a new name for the place. There were three finalists, and I don't even remember which was chosen, because everyone just calls it The Warren. That name will never have warm and fuzzy connotations for me, but to the adepts who lived there, it was never about the building. It was certainly never about the Fudds or Graham Cregg or the endless tests. The Warren was their community, their sense of belonging. And if calling it The Warren will help the wabbits hold on to that, it doesn't matter what it's named on paper.

Taylor and Daniel should be here with us today. It only seems right. But Deo didn't want to put this off any longer, and they're both really busy. They spent weeks preparing for Daniel's testimony where he acknowledged leaking the files that he found while working at Python Diagnostic, all of which incriminated Senator Cregg in the Delphi hoax. My father's testimony was even trickier because he had to admit to lying in his previous appearance before Congress. That's technically a felony, and there was a lot of legal wrangling prior to his being guaranteed immunity in exchange for his help in exposing the conspiracy. He's in DC for a few more weeks, but then he's planning to spend a few months out in Colorado where his sister(-in-law) runs a small art gallery.

Pfeifer has been coming to North Beach on the weekends, and I'm gradually getting to know my parents. It's hard, though. Like most abandoned kids, I spent the first part of my life wanting to find my family. That was my wish on each falling star and every birthday candle, and I grew a little more disillusioned each time it didn't come true.

At some point, though, I realized that wish *had* come true. Deo and Kelsey were my family. And even though it's not rational, even though I don't really blame my parents for what's happened, I can't help but feel that some evil twist of fate made me trade Kelsey for them.

I'm hoping to join them in Colorado, at least for a short visit. My parents—both of them—are now convinced that Ro couldn't help what happened. I get the feeling that there's a lot they aren't telling me, but the gist is that Rowena was seventeen and the decision was taken out of her hands. When she tried to find me later that year, she was told I was being adopted. A happy ending for me, or so she thought. She set aside the money my parents had left me and resolved to find me when I reached eighteen.

I think—I *hope*—that I'll grow close to my new family in time. But they don't feel like family yet. It's not comfortable, like being with Deo and Aaron. Or, for that matter, with Daniel and Taylor.

Daniel began his new job with Homeland Security two weeks ago. He has an official title, which is pretty much meaningless, but his real job is liaison between the government and The Warren. I think he's feeling a bit overwhelmed with the paperwork and the research, and he's been relying on Taylor to help behind the scenes. Taylor is the detail person. Daniel is the salesman. He's *good* at persuading people to see things his way.

The best thing about the job is that it allows him more time with Caleb, who shares one of the larger temporary huts with Sophie and Lily. Daniel isn't willing to let the doctors at The Warren test the new treatment, Cerecyclo, on Caleb just yet. But they're having some success with a moderate dose of risperidone. It's easier for him to be around the other adepts now.

When we visited in early June, the first thing we saw was Caleb and Daniel sitting in one of those little kiddie pools together, laughing as Caleb levitated a big ball of water over Daniel's head. That sight dissolved the last tether holding Ashley to this realm, and the next day she was gone.

Since then, Aaron and I have been happily, blissfully alone. And we've made exceptionally good use of our privacy.

Despite the diligent efforts of the government, I wasn't sure that the hoax story would work. It was a huge scandal, and there were major holes in the story. Holes big enough to drive a tank through. The press prodded at those holes for a few weeks, and then they moved on to the next scandal. Because there's *always* a next scandal.

As usual, the conspiracy sites protested that the public had been fooled. For once, they were right. And the little part of Bruno in me was thrilled to belong to the small select crowd who knows that *it was all true*.

The one thing that keeps suspicion about the Delphi Project just the tiniest bit alive is the occasional odd story that defies any quick or rational explanation. A carnival psychic who is a little too good. Reports of a five-foot-nothing woman shoving the moving van that is blocking her parking space into a streetlight. An eighteen-year-old stockbroker who's having way too much success to be legit. That sort of stuff. And since it sometimes takes a psychic to catch a psychic, Taylor thinks it might be time to borrow the RV that Porter bought back from Magda and hit the road. Maybe paint some 1970s-style flowers on the side and call ourselves the New Scooby Gang.

I think she could be right.

But for now, we need to say good-bye. Deo is the last out when Aaron parks the truck. He's in navy blue from hair to toe, even his eyeliner matching the velvet bag he's holding. As usual, he makes me feel underdressed, but I'm used to it.

"Are you really ready to do this, D? Because we can wait. We'll be visiting The Warren again at some point, and we can come back."

"No. It's time."

And looking around, I think he's correct. The beach looks right, the way I remember it from the vision. We've triggered that vision again, four times, and it's always the same odd, choppy version. I don't even think it's sequential. Maybe Jaden's visions are starting to fritz out. Or maybe Maggie's blocking interfered with the signal initially and it's like a recording—all you'll ever see is what was captured the first go-around.

I hope it's the latter. It would be nice to keep something of Jaden. I haven't been willing to test whether I have any gifts from Penelope or Graham Cregg. Those aren't abilities that I want. Daniel may be able to toe that line, and only nudge for truth, justice, and the American way, but I don't need that sort of temptation. I do know, however, that the Furies left behind a little something extra. Just a tickle, really. I can't rip up a coastline or flip a jeep over with a wave of my hand. But I could move the ball and the cup if I were to retake that original test back at The Warren. And if we wanted to toast marshmallows like we did that time with Kel . . . sey—

I stop and stare at the beach up ahead. It's a good half mile away, and I'm almost certain that's the spot. But I won't get Deo's hopes up. Not until I know for sure.

"Guys, I've got too many pent-up nerves. I need to run a bit. Meet you up ahead." And I take off before they can tell me I'm crazy or that this really isn't appropriately sober behavior for the occasion.

The three logs are still pushed together in a triangle, right where we left them, and one of the sticks we used to roast marshmallows is wedged beneath the log where Kelsey sat. The rain washed away the remnants of sticky white goo long ago, but the tip of the stick is still charred and black.

Have others built a fire here this summer? Could they tell that this was someone's last happy place? Because she's here. Not screaming like in my dream. No longer in pain. But more like the beach after the rain. Quiet. Peaceful. Not quite happy. Not quite where we were when she sat around this pit hamming it up just to make Deo laugh.

When I look back up, Deo has stopped walking and is staring at me. Aaron must recognize the place at the same moment, because the two guys I love most in the world, who both hate to run on principle, are sprinting toward me.

"Is she there?" Deo is smiling, but it's tinged with worry.

"She's here. But, D . . . I think she'd find her way on her own soon. Maybe just from us being here. I wanted to see if you're sure. If *both* of you are sure."

Aaron knows what I'm asking. It's not just the loss of privacy. It's the loss of peace and serenity as the nightmares, which have gradually faded away in the past few weeks, come roaring back. Reliving Kelsey's last moments will be brutal, and if it's brutal for me, it'll be brutal for Aaron. But he pulls me toward him and says, "You never need to ask me that question. *Never.* If Kelsey's here, and she can't move on yet, you'll help her. It's who you are, Anna. It's what you do. It's part of you."

Deo seems torn. "I don't want to hold her back, but . . . the only thing to do is let Kelsey decide. She knows we love her. If she's at peace, then I say we're good."

So I kneel next to the makeshift fire pit and pick up the pointy stick. The one Kelsey waved through the air, shouting *Avada Marshmahllow,* while Deo laughed so hard he fell into the sand.

Then I break down the wall that Kelsey taught me to build when I was small and alone. When I needed someone to protect me.

And I let Kelsey decide.

Because Deo's right. Either way, we're good.

ACKNOWLEDGMENTS

Writing the final book in a trilogy is truly bittersweet. If I count the time that Anna and her friends had to wait patiently for me to finish writing the CHRONOS books, I've spent the past six years with these characters in my head. I'm going to miss them. Even when real life occasionally mirrored fiction a bit too closely, these characters kept me eager to uncover what came next in their story. I occasionally had to lure them back with a glass of merlot and chunk of extra-dark chocolate, but I owe them a huge debt of gratitude for not running out on me when things got tough.

If you've made it to the end of this series, you probably know that I like to add a brief discussion of settings and circumstances that are based on real life.

The Delphi Project is fictional, but predecessor programs like Stargate and Project MK-Ultra are based on actual history. Two of the individuals mentioned, Hella Hammid and Ingo Swann, were participants in the early research on remote viewing that took place at Stanford Research Institute in Menlo Park, California. The Church Committee Reports (1975 to 1976) are a treasure trove of information on this period in American history.

When last I checked, the Tome School and Bainbridge Naval Training Center in Port Deposit, Maryland, remain abandoned and undeveloped. There are a number of locals who continue to believe the area is haunted, but there's no evidence that psychic "Zippos" started the fire that destroyed Memorial Hall.

If you google *Brushy Mountain State Penitentiary*, you'll find that it is an abandoned prison where you can book a tour with paranormal investigators. They also hold concerts and other events on the site. My descriptions of the location were greatly enriched by a number of online photographs by John K. Clark. You can see them on his blog: http://johnkclark.com/blog/2015/5.

Oak Ridge National Laboratory was actually the site of a break-in back in 2012—by an eighty-four-year-old nun and two middle-aged companions. Their goal wasn't psychic terror or destruction but rather an antinuclear protest.

The Sunsphere was built as part of the 1982 World's Fair in Knoxville. It was still standing when I drove past this week and does remind me a bit of a giant butterscotch Dum Dum lollipop.

The Outer Banks of North Carolina are obviously real, and gorgeous, and you should go if you get the chance. There is even a long strip just north of the North Carolina line that is accessible only by foot, but to the best of my knowledge, it is a sanctuary for birds and wild horses, not psychic children.

My team at Skyscape is always a joy to work with. This book is dedicated to Courtney Miller, who has been my editor since *Timebound*. She has moved onward and upward, and I will miss her wise counsel tremendously. Paul Morrissey and Adrienne Procaccini have done an incredible job since Courtney's departure, and I was delighted to have the opportunity to work with both of them again. Amara Holstein, my developmental editor for the entire Delphi Trilogy, has consistently given me sage advice and helped trim away the deadweight to keep the narrative on track. I'm also grateful to the wonderful crew behind the scenes at Skyscape who copyedit, proofread, and keep things running smoothly.

Special thanks to Mike Corley for creating vibrant, eye-catching artwork for the Delphi series. I'm perfectly happy for people to judge these books by their covers.

Kate Rudd—you are, as always, a rock star. I could not ask for a more gifted storyteller to help bring my characters to life.

If you're among my friends on Facebook or Twitter, or in one of my online author groups, thanks for keeping me informed and entertained when I needed a brain break . . . and for being an island of sanity in a world where that is increasingly rare. My beta readers deserve a special mention for their detailed feedback: Cale Madewell, Karen Benson, Chris Fried, Karen Stansbury, Hailey Mulconrey Theile, Billy Thomas, Meg Griffin, Kristin Ashenfelter, Shell Bryce, Fred Douglis, Jen Gonzales, Donna Harrison Green, Dori Gray, Susan Helliesen, Stephanie Johns-Bragg, Cody Jones, Christina Kmetz, Jenny MacRunnel, Trisha Davis Perry, John Scafidi, Antigone Trowbridge, Meg Watt, Jen Wesner, Dan Wilson, Jessica Wolfsohn, Tracy Denison Johnson, Becca Porter, and Sarah Kate Fisher. (And, as always, apologies to the person—or more likely, persons—I forgot.)

Thanks to Pete for his patience and support, to Ian for keeping the Griffin-beast entertained in the morning so that I could sleep after writing into the wee hours, and to Ryan for tapping on my door at two a.m. to see if I needed another cup of tea (Earl Grey, hot).

Finally, special thanks go to you, the reader, for coming with me on this journey. It was a pleasure to write, and I hope you enjoyed the mind trip.

ABOUT THE AUTHOR

Rysa Walker is the bestselling author of The Delphi Trilogy (*The Delphi Effect*, *The Delphi Resistance*, and *The Delphi Revolution*). *Timebound*, the first book in her CHRONOS Files series, won the Grand Prize in the 2013 Amazon Breakthrough Novel Awards. Her career had its beginnings in a childhood on a cattle ranch, where she read every book she could find, watched *Star Trek* and *The Twilight Zone*, and let her imagination soar into the future and to distant worlds. Her diverse path has spanned roles such as lifeguard, waitress, actress, digital developer, and professor—and through it all, she has pursued her passion for writing the sorts of stories she imagined in her youth. She lives in North Carolina with her husband, two youngest sons, and a hyperactive golden retriever. Discover more about Rysa and her work at www.rysa.com.